The Word We Celebrate
Commentary on the Sunday Lectionary, Years A, B and C

Patricia Datchuck Sánchez

A SHEED & WARD BOOK

ROWMAN & LITTLEFIELD PUBLISHERS, INC.
Lanham • Boulder • New York • Toronto • Oxford

A SHEED & WARD BOOK

ROWMAN & LITTLEFIELD PUBLISHERS, INC.

Published in the United States of America
by Rowman & Littlefield Publishers, Inc.
A wholly owned subsidiary of The Rowman & Littlefield Publishing Group, Inc.
4501 Forbes Boulevard, Suite 200, Lanham, Maryland 20706
www.rowmanlittlefield.com

PO Box 317
Oxford
OX2 9RU, UK

Copyright © 1989 by Patricia Datchuck Sánchez

All rights reserved. No part of this publication may be reproduced, stored in a retrieval system, or transmitted in any form or by any means, electronic, mechanical, photocopying, recording, or otherwise, without the prior permission of the publisher.

British Library Cataloguing in Publication Information Available

Library of Congress Card Number: 89-61926

ISBN 1-55612-302-7

Printed in the United States of America

⊖™ The paper used in this publication meets the minimum requirements of American National Standard for Information Sciences—Permanence of Paper for Printed Library Materials, ANSI/NISO Z39.48-1992.

Introduction

Almost two thousand years ago, on the desert road that stretched from Israel to Gaza, a well-to-do businessman commuting home from Jerusalem was puzzling over a difficult passage from the prophet Isaiah. For all his adeptness in the world of high finance, the commuter was at a loss as to what the prophet's message meant for his life and times . . . "How can I grasp it," he complained, "unless someone explains it to me?" Fortunately, Philip came to the rescue and, as Luke explained it, he "launched out with the Isaian scripture text as his starting point and told him the good news of Jesus!" (Acts 8:31, 35).

In two thousand years, the situation has changed little. All of us are still commuters in this life (the second Vatican Council called us *pilgrims*), searching for meaning and purpose. Like the ancient Ethiopian on the road to Gaza, we have discovered that the source of all meaning and our purpose for being lies in the mystery we name as God and in the word through which he communicates himself to us. But—and in this we are also like the Ethiopian—most of us need help in discerning that word . . . in understanding what it meant when the author wrote it and what it means for us and our own world today. For this help, we rely on those whose special vocation it is to celebrate the mysteries of our salvation and to elucidate those mysteries for us.

Recognizing both the need and desire of the faithful to become more attuned to the Word of God, the participants at the Second Vatican Council initiated a liturgical reform which accented the importance of the Word *incarnate* (Jesus), and *inscribed* (Scripture).

In their first document, promulgated 4 December 1963, the Council members declared, "The treasures of the Bible are to be opened up more lavishly so that richer fare may be provided for the faithful at the table of God's Word. In this way, a more representative portion of the Holy Scriptures will be read to the people over a set cycle of years." Then, in order to make the Word more easily accessible to the believing community, the importance of the homily was underscored: "By means of the homily, the mysteries of the faith and the guiding principles of the Christian life are expounded from the sacred text during the course of the liturgical year. The homily, therefore, is to be highly esteemed as part of the liturgy itself . . ." (*Constitution on the Sacred Liturgy*, #51, 52).

Following the Council's directives, the Sacred Congregation for Divine Worship, exactly twenty years ago, published the order of readings for the liturgy as we know it today. Previous to 30 November 1969 the lectionary followed a one year cycle of readings with two texts being featured at each celebration. Now the Sunday celebrations present the praying congregation with three biblical selections from both the Jewish and Christian Scriptures and the cycle for the Sunday texts has been extended over a three year period.

This book, *The Word We Celebrate,* has been written in an effort to aid all who are involved in the sacred liturgy, from the pulpit to the pew. By *no means a substitute* for personal study, prayer and reflection on the Sacred word, this work nevertheless acknowledges the exigencies of busy schedules and offers itself as a quick and ready reference. While this work will provide commentary on the scriptural texts, it does not in any way purport to be a ready-made collection of homilies. Only the homilist, sympathetic to the needs of his/her congregation and in full awareness of their pastoral situation can use this material to shape an appropriate message for his/her community.

Perhaps those who prepare to elucidate the sacred Word for the sake of the community would also do well to remember young Eutychus. Though Paul was, no doubt, enthusiastic and eloquent, nevertheless by midnight, Eutychus grew weary and fell asleep; then he suffered a fatal fall from a third-floor height. Although Paul raised the boy to life, few of us share the apostle's talents or powers. Suffice it to say, the Eutychus incident in Acts 20 makes a clear case for homilies that are succinct and challenging.

If the Word of God becomes more tangible, better understood and more central to the lives of those who read it . . ., if more people are challenged through the Word of God to live according to the values of the gospel, then this work will have accomplished its purpose.

Most of the pages that follow were first published in the monthly issues of *Celebration,* beginning in 1984. At the suggestion of William Freburger, editor of *Celebration*, and due in no small part to his efforts and insight, this work has been updated and completed. I am indebted to Bill for his collaboration and will always be grateful for the opportunities in ministry this work has afforded me.

Contents
Year A

The Advent Season

First Sunday of Advent 1
Second Sunday of Advent 3
Third Sunday of Advent 6
Fourth Sunday of Advent 8

The Christmas Season

Christmas 11
Holy Family 13
New Year's Day 15
Epiphany 16
Lord's Baptism 19

The Lenten Season

First Sunday of Lent 21
Second Sunday of Lent 23
Third Sunday of Lent 24
Fourth Sunday of Lent 26
Fifth Sunday of Lent 27
Passion (Palm) Sunday 29

The Easter Season

Easter Sunday 31
Second Sunday of Easter 33
Third Sunday of Easter 35
Fourth Sunday of Easter 37
Fifth Sunday of Easter 39
Sixth Sunday of Easter 41
Seventh Sunday of Easter 43
Pentecost Sunday 45

Ordinary Time

Second Sunday in Ordinary Time 48
Third Sunday in Ordinary Time 50
Fourth Sunday in Ordinary Time 52
Fifth Sunday in Ordinary Time 53
Sixth Sunday in Ordinary Time 54
Seventh Sunday in Ordinary Time 56
Eighth Sunday in Ordinary Time 58

Ninth Sunday in Ordinary Time 60
10th Sunday in Ordinary Time 62
11th Sunday in Ordinary Time 64
12th Sunday in Ordinary Time 65
13th Sunday in Ordinary Time 67
14th Sunday in Ordinary Time 69
15th Sunday in Ordinary Time 71
16th Sunday in Ordinary Time 73
17th Sunday in Ordinary Time 74
18th Sunday in Ordinary Time 76
19th Sunday in Ordinary Time 78
20th Sunday in Ordinary Time 80
21st Sunday in Ordinary Time 82
22nd Sunday in Ordinary Time 83
23rd Sunday in Ordinary Time 85
24th Sunday in Ordinary Time 87
25th Sunday in Ordinary Time 89
26th Sunday in Ordinary Time 91
27th Sunday in Ordinary Time 93
28th Sunday in Ordinary Time 95
29th Sunday in Ordinary Time 97
30th Sunday in Ordinary Time 99
31st Sunday in Ordinary Time 101
32nd Sunday in Ordinary Time 103
33rd Sunday in Ordinary Time 105
34th Sunday in Ordinary Time 108

Movable Feasts

Trinity Sunday 110
Corpus Christi 112
Feast of the Lord's Presentation 114
Birth of John the Baptist 117
Transfiguration 119
Solemnity of Sts. Peter and Paul 120
Feast of the Triumph of the Cross 123
Solemnity of all Saints 125
All Souls 127
Dedication of the Lateran Basilica 129

Contents
Year B

The Advent Season

First Sunday of Advent	133
Second Sunday of Advent	135
Third Sunday of Advent	137
Fourth Sunday of Advent	139

The Christmas Season

Christmas	142
Holy Family	144
New Year's Day	146
Epiphany	148
Lord's Baptism	150

The Lenten Season

First Sunday of Lent	152
Second Sunday of Lent	155
Third Sunday of Lent	157
Fourth Sunday of Lent	159
Fifth Sunday of Lent	161
Passion (Palm) Sunday	163

The Easter Season

Easter Sunday	165
Second Sunday of Easter	167
Third Sunday of Easter	169
Fourth Sunday of Easter	172
Fifth Sunday of Easter	174
Sixth Sunday of Easter	176
Seventh Sunday of Easter	179
Pentecost Sunday	181

Ordinary Time

Second Sunday in Ordinary Time	184
Third Sunday in Ordinary Time	186
Fourth Sunday in Ordinary Time	188
Fifth Sunday in Ordinary Time	190
Sixth Sunday in Ordinary Time	193
Seventh Sunday in Ordinary Time	195
Eighth Sunday in Ordinary Time	197
Ninth Sunday in Ordinary Time	199
10th Sunday in Ordinary Time	201
11th Sunday in Ordinary Time	203
12th Sunday in Ordinary Time	205
13th Sunday in Ordinary Time	208
14th Sunday in Ordinary Time	210
15th Sunday in Ordinary Time	212
16th Sunday in Ordinary Time	214
17th Sunday in Ordinary Time	217
18th Sunday in Ordinary Time	219
19th Sunday in Ordinary Time	221
20th Sunday in Ordinary Time	223
21st Sunday in Ordinary Time	225
22nd Sunday in Ordinary Time	227
23rd Sunday in Ordinary Time	230
24th Sunday in Ordinary Time	232
25th Sunday in Ordinary Time	234
26th Sunday in Ordinary Time	237
27th Sunday in Ordinary Time	239
28th Sunday in Ordinary Time	241
29th Sunday in Ordinary Time	243
30th Sunday in Ordinary Time	246
31st Sunday in Ordinary Time	248
32nd Sunday in Ordinary Time	251
33rd Sunday in Ordinary Time	253
34th Sunday in Ordinary Time	255

Movable Feasts

Trinity Sunday	258
Corpus Christi	260

Contents
Year C

The Advent Season

First Sunday of Advent	263
Second Sunday of Advent	265
Third Sunday of Advent	267
Fourth Sunday of Advent	270

The Christmas Season

Christmas	272
Holy Family	274
New Year's Day	277
Epiphany	277
Lord's Baptism	279

The Lenten Season

First Sunday of Lent	282
Second Sunday of Lent	284
Third Sunday of Lent	287
Fourth Sunday of Lent	289
Fifth Sunday of Lent	291
Passion (Palm) Sunday	293

The Easter Season

Easter Sunday	296
Second Sunday of Easter	298
Third Sunday of Easter	301
Fourth Sunday of Easter	303
Fifth Sunday of Easter	305
Sixth Sunday of Easter	308
Seventh Sunday of Easter	310
Pentecost Sunday	313

Ordinary Time

Second Sunday in Ordinary Time	315
Third Sunday in Ordinary Time	317
Fourth Sunday in Ordinary Time	320
Fifth Sunday in Ordinary Time	322
Sixth Sunday in Ordinary Time	324
Seventh Sunday in Ordinary Time	326
Eighth Sunday in Ordinary Time	328
Ninth Sunday in Ordinary Time	331
10th Sunday in Ordinary Time	333
11th Sunday in Ordinary Time	335
12th Sunday in Ordinary Time	338
13th Sunday in Ordinary Time	340
14th Sunday in Ordinary Time	342
15th Sunday in Ordinary Time	345
16th Sunday in Ordinary Time	347
17th Sunday in Ordinary Time	349
18th Sunday in Ordinary Time	351
19th Sunday in Ordinary Time	354
20th Sunday in Ordinary Time	356
21st Sunday in Ordinary Time	359
22nd Sunday in Ordinary Time	361
23rd Sunday in Ordinary Time	363
24th Sunday in Ordinary Time	366
25th Sunday in Ordinary Time	368
26th Sunday in Ordinary Time	370
27th Sunday in Ordinary Time	373
28th Sunday in Ordinary Time	375
29th Sunday in Ordinary Time	377
30th Sunday in Ordinary Time	380
31st Sunday in Ordinary Time	382
32nd Sunday in Ordinary Time	384
33rd Sunday in Ordinary Time	386
34th Sunday in Ordinary Time	389

Movable Feasts

Trinity Sunday	391
Corpus Christi	394

Year A

The Advent Season
First Sunday of Advent

When the day that will never end finally dawns, humanity will be called to render an accounting of its stewardship (Romans). How will we explain war? How will we account for the death by starvation of entire populations? What will the prince of peace and justice say when he finds portions of the world he redeemed made uninhabitable by nuclear mistakes (Isaiah)? In that moment, pride and ambition will be cast aside and those who survive the test of his love will enjoy his presence forever (Matthew).

Isaiah 2:1-5. As the new liturgical year begins, it is not without a remembrance of the passing year. On this, the first Sunday of Advent, the lectionary selections bring to a climax the themes featured in the last weeks of the old year. Concerned with the *eschata* or last things—the end of time, the final judgment, the reward for the just and retribution for the evil—the passing year left in its wake the theme of the second, definitive coming of the Son of Man. On the second Sunday of Advent, the focus shifts to the *first* coming of the Son of Man and the themes of incarnation, messianism, etc. Because of these revised selections in the new lectionary, liturgy has become the church's teacher, theologian, catechist. With these revisions, the faithful are drawn to focus on Advent's *true* concerns, the *comings* of Jesus, incarnate *and* risen. During Advent the realities of the first coming and of the final coming dovetail; Advent hope anticipates and prepares, *not* for a baby, earthly Jesus but for a risen and exalted Christ who will judge all peoples. These themes of judgment and justice are featured in today's three readings.

Isaiah of Jerusalem, the prophet and author of Isaiah 1-39, lived in Judah during a turbulent period of political and religious decay. Isaiah was witness to at least part of the reigns of four of Judah's kings (Uzziah, Jotham, Ahaz, Hezekiah) whose combined rule spanned almost 100 years. Active as God's prophet for about 40 years beginning with his call in the year Uzziah died (ca. 742 B.C.E., Isaiah 6:1), the prophet watched as Israel fell to Assyria (722 B.C.E.) and warned his fellow countrymen that a similar fate awaited Judah if faithfulness in God was not restored.

While his contemporaries experienced a loss of confidence in Yahweh and sought to forge political alliances with foreign nations against Assyria, Isaiah pointed to what he considered an even greater crisis, the spiritual disintegration of the nation due to covenant infidelities. Because their God was Yahweh, the holy one, *sin* (taught the prophet) had no place in the lives of those who belonged to Yahweh. Therefore if they would be truly fortified against their enemies, Judah could make alliances only with the Lord. Their only sure defense would be the eradication from their midst of all injustice, greed, dishonesty and idolatry. In an effort to convert his people to God, Isaiah shared with them his oracles and visions.

Today's first reading is one of several visions (2:1—12:6) the prophet shared concerning Judah and Jerusalem. Most scholars believe that this vision and those that follow it belong to the first period of Isaiah's prophetic career, ca. 740-730 B.C.E. During these years, Isaiah foresaw the Assyrian invasion of the north and its possible repercussions for his own countrymen. To bolster his people's hopes and to rekindle their attentiveness to the Lord, Isaiah offered them a vision of peace and unity that encompassed all the nations of the earth. Because the same text (2:2-5) also appears in the work of Isaiah's contemporary Micah (Micah 4:1-3), the actual source of these verses is not easy to establish. A few scholars are of the opinion that Isaiah borrowed from Micah or vice versa, but the majority agree that both prophets were quoting a third and earlier source.

In the vision, at once eschatological and messianic, Jerusalem plays a central role in the history of *all*, even the gentile nations (v. 2). Because it is eschatological, the vision is concerned with the *ultimate* events, not necessarily a time *during* history but that era after the end. Notice that Isaiah did not envision any *human* program or effort as being capable of achieving peace. Rather, peace would come only after Judah and all the nations had learned the ways of the Lord. Jerusalem would become the center of instruction (v. 3), the place where all would gather to be taught the Torah or the law of the Lord. Torah, or the law, was that way of living God himself had revealed to his people; it was a *divine* program of peace. With the training in the Torah would come *judgment*. In this sense the text reflects the spirit of messianism associated with the Day of the Lord.

Only when all the peoples of the earth had gathered in a peaceful assembly, had learned the truth of the law and had been judged by the Lord himself, would *true* saving peace prevail. As a symbol of that messianic era, the tools that had once made war and brought death (swords, spears) would be refashioned into instruments to build and plant and bring life. Similar symbols and visions can be found among the works of classical literature (Virgil, *Georgics* I, 509; Ovid, *Fasti* I, 699; etc.), revealing that Isaiah's aspirations are shared by peoples of all creeds and backgrounds. If the prophet wrote today, he may have envisioned nuclear silos emptied of their implements of death so as to be filled with grain to feed the world's hungry . . . or of the glut of oil hoarded by a few shared so as to warm the millions of the world's homeless.

Romans 13:11-14. Since Jesus Christ is the light that pierces the darkness and brings the dawn of salvation to a waiting world, Christian behavior and attitudes must be consonant with that fact. This is the basic premise behind the metaphors that comprise today's second reading. The traditional epistle for the First Sunday of Advent (retained by the new lectionary only in year A), this excerpt from Paul's letter to the church at Rome identifies the effect Christ's presence should have in the world. Because of Christ's first appearance, the new age of salvation has dawned upon humankind. But even with the dawn, there still linger vestiges of the dark night of a needful, sinful world. These shadows will be fully illumined only with the climatic *second* advent of the Lord.

By means of the eschatological comparisons and metaphors (day-night, light-darkness, wake-sleep, etc.), Paul interpreted redeemed Christian existence as a life lived in tension. Christians live because of Christ in the *new* era but are still a part of the *present* age. For that reason, Christian existence before the second advent is characterized by a struggle to keep sin's darkness at bay and to glory in the light of holiness. In this struggle, a daily renewed effort, the believer is not alone. Indeed, victory could never be achieved solely by human resources. By "putting on" (v. 14) the Lord Jesus Christ, Christians are strengthened to live with the tension of daily conversion. In his earlier letter to the church of Galatia, Paul used the same term, "to put on Christ," to refer to baptism: "As many of you as were baptized into Christ, have *put on Christ*" (Galatians 3:27).

Through the sacramental grace of baptism, Christians have already begun to live in the new age or the eschaton. In v. 11, Paul exhorted the Roman believers to recall the "time in which we are living." Time in this sense referred, not to a chronological or measurable moment but to the *kairos*, the critical period of Christian existence that transcends the convention of hours, minutes, years, etc. *Kairos* began with the death, resurrection and glorification of Jesus. By their faith in Jesus and by their moral response to his saving death, believers can appropriate the effect of what Jesus has achieved once and for all.

Integral to that process of appropriation would be the waking from sleep and casting off deeds of darkness (vv. 11-12). *Night* or darkness lent itself (especially in Rome, a city notorious for its "nightlife") to deeds of evil of which one would be ashamed when exposed to the light of day. Darkness was considered in Jewish apocalyptic and in the writings of Qumran as the realm of Satan (Belial). With the saving activity of Jesus Christ, the power of darkness has been defeated. With nothing to bring them down, therefore, Paul challenged the Roman Christians and all believers to live according to the victory Christ had achieved, to live as people of the light.

Matthew 24:37-44. With the new liturgical year, we turn our attention to another of the four evangelists. In year A, Matthew is our host in the ever new unfolding of the good news of salvation. For centuries, readers of the gospel supposed that the author of the Matthean gospel was the tax collector named Matthew who was called by Jesus to be a disciple (Matthew 9). Due, however, to the efforts of critical biblical research, especially within the last century, the authorship of the gospels as well as many other scriptural works has been reassessed. What is known of the author of Matthew today has been deduced from internal evidence within the gospel and a knowledge of the history of his times. The author, whom we shall for the sake of convenience call Matthew, was a learned Christian who may have been active in founding the community in which the gospel originated, and may in that way have been an inspirational influence on the gospel. The author exhibits a theological outlook, a command of Greek and a world view that suggests he was a *second*-generation Christian (J. Kingsbury, J. Meier, D. Senior).

Antioch in Syria seems to have been the most likely context for the origin of the gospel because the social conditions reflected in the gospel correspond most readily with circumstances that existed there in the late first century C.E. A large, prosperous city, home to a large population of both Jews and gentiles, Antioch was introduced to Christianity ca. 40 C.E. There Hellenist Christians (from Cyprus and Cyrene) first made the radical decision to accept gentiles into the community without requiring that they be circumcised. In Antioch, believers in Jesus were first called Christians (Acts 11:26). As the new Christian community grew, it became more and more distinct from its Jewish origins and from those elements that continued to reject Jesus as messiah. In the late 80s C.E., the trauma of separation from their Jewish roots received the ultimate blow: Jewish Christians were ousted from the synagogue. No longer accepted as part of

Judaism, a licit religion according to Roman law, Christians were then subjected to increased persecution.

In order to accommodate the shift in the religious and ethnic complexion of his church while retaining and respecting both its Jewish and gentile members, the author of the Matthean gospel undertook the task of reinterpreting older, treasured traditions according to the new outlook necessitated by faith in Jesus. His was a task of creating new wineskins (or a vehicle of expression for the faith) for a precious new wine (i.e., faith in Jesus as the flower of Judaism and hope for the world). That Matthew understood and accepted this challenge is beautifully underscored in the self-styled signature that appears in chapter 13 of his work: "Every scribe who is learned in the reign of God is like the head of a household who can bring from his storeroom both the new and the old" (13:52). Matthew *was* this Christian scribe who tried to give to each member of his community, Jews as well as gentiles, a new way of looking at old traditions, at their scriptures (Old Testament), at morality and at their cult, so as to accept Jesus Christ and the salvation he offered to all of humanity.

Today's gospel pericope, in particular, was intended to give his contemporaries a more enlightened view of eschatology and of the final judgment that would accompany it. Using three short parables colored with details borrowed from Jewish apocalyptic tradition, Matthew exhorted his church to the vigilance that would prepare them for Jesus' second appearance. Because of this emphasis on the suddenness and unpredictability of the "end," many of today's foremost scripture scholars believe these were authentic sayings of Jesus preserved in a collection called Q or *quelle* (German: source).

Matthew couched his first call to vigilance in the parable about the legendary Noah story. Notice that those who lived during the time of Noah were not necessarily cited for their wickedness, but for their preoccupation with the affairs of everyday living. Caught up in these preoccupations, they were surprised by the flood and perished. Evidently, some of Matthew's contemporaries in the 80s C.E. had allowed themselves to become so immersed in the daily pursuits of earning a living, raising a family, etc., that their sense of eschatological expectation had become dulled. The parable's message is clear: Be alert! Raise your eyes above the morass of routine existence and remember the purpose of all of living—to put on Christ, to live Christ and to await his return!

In the second exhortation to vigilance, Matthew described two pairs of workers. At a distance, two men working in a field look alike and for all practical purposed are indistinguishable. So too, the two women grinding meal would be difficult to distinguish. But, as the parable states, at the coming of the Son of Man, one man will be taken and one left; one woman will be taken and the other left. The final judgment will bring to the light of day differences and distinctions between persons heretofore hidden. Moreover, the division or judgment between persons will be made according to divine, not human perception. While the parable does not give the basis for the distinction between persons, it underscores again the need for preparedness.

In the final exhortation of today's gospel, Matthew drew upon the figure of the night burglar, a recurrent theme in Christian eschatological literature (1 Thessalonians 5:2-4, 2 Peter 3:10, Revelation 3:3). Prudent homeowners were always prepared for the most unwelcome "guest" of all, the thief. Based on this wisdom, Christians who await Jesus' final coming and his judgment should be in a constant state of alertness. Thieves do not telephone ahead to announce their "visit," nor will the Son of Man give warning. His visitation will be sudden and unexpected. Therefore, the only protection is an attitude of preparedness at all times. As this new season of Advent begins, believers are reminded of the *certainty* of Jesus' return and warned to be prepared for the uncertainties as to the time and/or means of his arrival.

1. Peace will grow when military maneuvers are replaced by mutual respect and meaningful negotiations (Isaiah).

2. The most eloquent profession of faith is a life lived in accord with Jesus' teaching and example (Romans).

3. No one is ever prepared for a surprise unless the preparation has become a matter of daily routine (Matthew).

Second Sunday of Advent

Remorse is one aspect of conversion; the other is positive growth and deepening commitment manifested in deeds of love and justice (Matthew). For those who long for a world in which peace and harmony prevail (Isaiah), the daily work of conversion never ends. With patience, faith and mutual support, all our hopes and dreams can become tangible, enjoyable realities (Romans).

Isaiah 11:1-10. One of the most familiar texts of the Jewish scriptures quoted even by those whose interests in it are purely secular, this pericope from Isaiah is part of the so-named "Book of Emmanuel" (7:1—12:6). Closely related to similar oracles in 9:1-6 and 7:14, today's first reading represents the prophet's description of an ideal king. Sprung from David's line, this king was thought to embody in his person and reign those qualities that would underscore Israel's importance and reaffirm her position as a force to be reckoned with.

Although late dates have been suggested, the more probable origin and background of the reading were the years of the Syro-Ephraimite War (ca. 735-732 B.C.E.). During this stormy period, Ahaz was the king of Judah. While Ahaz favored foreign alliances to shore up his defenses against foreign invaders, Isaiah counseled a more sublime strategy. Reliance on and alliance with the Lord alone was the only sure path of survival according to Isaiah. Even in the wake of the Assyrian invasion, the prophet tried to reassure Ahaz that Yahweh's intervention on behalf of his people would bring about the demise of their enemies.

Closely linked to the prophet's promise of divine intervention was the figure of a future king, a messianic personage in whom all of Israel's (and Judah's) hopes would be realized. As king of Israel, his reign would be coextensive with and representative of the sovereign domain of Yahweh, Israel's only true king and God. When Isaiah spoke this oracle in the latter half of the eighth century B.C.E., his hopes were rooted, no doubt, in Hezekiah, the son of Ahaz. In and through Hezekiah (Isaiah hoped), salvation would come to his people; therefore he would truly be for Israel their messiah, i.e., God's anointed one, the savior.

Later, when Hezekiah and his successors proved unworthy of and unequal to the task, Isaiah's oracles were remembered and his words gave voice to the continued messianic aspirations of his people. With the prophet's promises, the people painted for themselves visions of a glorious future, presided over by a royal messianic figure. Christians, of course, understand that all these aspirations have become an actuality in the person and mission of Jesus.

Throughout biblical and extrabiblical literature the image of a tree customarily represented the royal dynasty. Drawing upon that imagery, Isaiah compared the Davidic dynasty (of his day) to a "stump" (v. 1), that seemingly lifeless vestige of what had once been a flourishing tree. But he encouraged his contemporaries not to lose heart, because even from the stump of "Jesse" (David's father) the Lord could bring forth a new shoot.

As a result of the establishment of divine justice among all peoples, the world of nature would correspond in kind and reflect a harmony reminiscent of Eden. The picture of the universal and idyllic peace (vv. 6-10) has corollaries in several classical works, e.g., Virgil's *Georgics* (IV 22, V 60, 61) and Horace's *Odes* (XVI 32, 33). As A. Penne has pointed out, a strictly literal interpretation of Isaiah's idyllic description would reduce the text to absurdity. Rather than focus on the feasibility of a child playing near the cobra's den (v. 6), the pericope was meant to convey the harmony that would exist within the *human* family during the messianic era. Evildoers and their wicked deeds would be dissolved in order to make way for those who acknowledge and follow God's will.

Romans 15:4-9. While Isaiah envisioned a future harmony among all peoples, made possible by the reign of an ideal Davidic king, Paul told the Romans that, because of their commitment to Christ, that harmony was to be a reality in their everyday lives. Like many of the larger communities of Christians in the early church, Rome was beset by factions, certain groups whom Paul labeled simply the "strong" and the "weak." Today's second reading is from a longer section of his letter (14:1—15:6) in which Paul addressed these two groups, set forth their points of disagreement and resolved their differences, at least theologically, invoking among them the unifying reality of Jesus Christ.

Within the Roman church, those whom Paul called the "strong," and with whom he personally identified, were those who embraced Christ and his salvation without reserve. These "strong" did not regard any other rites, traditions or laws to hold any meaning for them; in Christ they had found everything and because of Christ nothing else mattered. The "weak," on the other hand, had been steeped in the traditions of their ancestors and brought many of these ways with them when they became Christians.

Many different solutions have been offered as to the actual identity of the "weak" element within the Roman church. Some have proposed that the "weak" were converts from Judaism who still lived according to the Mosaic law and its custom. Others have suggested that the "weak" were former Essenes who kept strict laws of abstinence concerning wine and meat. Still others think that the more conservative among Rome's Christians were former adherents to the Orphic-Pythagorean cult or perhaps they were simply those whose scrupulous consciences would not permit them to eat idol meat or to drink wine that may have been first offered to the gods.

Whatever their identity, Paul was truly concerned for those whom he called the "weak." To that end, he called upon the "strong" to bear the burden of their scruples and baggage from the past. Paul challenged the "strong" as well as the "weak" to that degree of mutual acceptance with which each of them had been accepted by Christ (v. 7). Rather than engage in mutual criticism that would only engender hostility, Paul encouraged the Roman Christians to search the scriptures (v. 5) and to learn there the lessons of patience that would lead to communal accord.

Obviously, the scriptures to which Paul referred were the Jewish scriptures or the Old Testament. The New Testament, as such, was still in process and was not at that time recognized as a written work. No doubt, the apostle had in mind texts such as today's first reading from Isaiah (especially 11:10) as well as Psalm 18:50, Psalm 117:1 and Deuteronomy 32:43, when he summoned the Roman Christians to that unity that would worthily reflect their adherence to Christ. During Advent, as Christians anticipate the culmination of their commitment to Christ, all are reminded to look to their right and to their left and to embrace in mutual respect, patience and love those who share a similar expectation.

Matthew 3:1-12. In Matthew's revised scheme of salvation history, John the Baptizer represented the end of the first era that encompassed the age of Israel from the patriarchs through the prophets. As the last chapter in Israel's history and as her final prophet, the Baptizer reminded his contemporaries of what they had been and called them to what they could be. John signaled the inauguration of a new era whose central focus would be Jesus and his earthly ministry.

John's appearance and the radical nature of his message, "Reform your lives: the reign of God is at hand," precluded a return to the past and obliged his contemporaries to engage in that process of positive conversion that would assure their future in the kingdom. When Matthew wrote his gospel for the Syrian community of Antioch in the 80s C.E., he called his readers to the same spirit and practice of conversion as John had done half a century before. Matthew's call and John's program of reform remain a constant challenge to all who would be worthy of the name "Christian."

John's call to conversion was based on an earlier summons made by the prophet, Deutero-Isaiah (40:3). In its sixth century context, the prophet's invitation, "Prepare the way of the Lord," evoked a new exodus whereby God would bring home to Israel those who had survived the exile in Babylonia. But the synoptics altered the Isaiah text which originally read, "A herald's voice that cries: *in the desert prepare* the way," to read "a herald's voice that *cries in the desert:* prepare the way." Thus, John appears to be the voice of God and friend of the bridegroom, calling his bride into the desert.

Christian tradition unites the Isaian theme of the new exodus, objective and historical, to that of an espousal more intimate and subjective. It converts the unilateral intervention of God in Isaiah 40:3 into a dialogue and a loving encounter of two freedoms (T. Maertens). In Hebrew, the word for conversion (*shubh*) indicates that one has taken a wrong path, and once he/she has become aware of his/her detour, the individual returns to God (Jeremiah 7:5-11, Isaiah 2:6-22, Jeremiah 31:16-22). So too in Greek, *metanoia* involves not just a static remorse but a dynamic and determined about-face, a positive commitment to a new way of life. Significantly, conversion is not a purely *human* decision or endeavor. Rather, conversion is a human response to the prior initiative of God.

In the New Testament, conversion or repentance is a response to Jesus in whose person and mission God's kingdom becomes an emerging reality. Thus, as J. Meier has observed, "the concept of the kingdom is a dynamic one; it is the New Testament equivalent of the psalmist's cry: Yahweh is king! For Matthew, the coming of the kingdom is a 'process-event.' To a degree it was present in the Old Testament; it comes in the person of Jesus. It impinges even more forcefully during his ministry and breaks in definitively in the death-resurrection of Jesus. In the interim between the two advents of Jesus, the reality of the kingdom matures until its full flowering in the parousia."

That John's mission was a prophetic one was illustrated in his apparel and diet as well as in his words. Dressed in the mantle of camel's hair like Elijah (2 Kings 1:16) and feeding on honey and grasshoppers, John in demeanor and appearance recalled the desert days and he thus poignantly underscored his message of expectation and hope for deliverance. Members of the Essene community at Qumran believed that the messiah would make his appearance in the desert; hence they withdrew from society to await his coming in the desolate region of the Dead Sea. Many believed that John had lived with or at least associated closely with the Essene sectarians and shared their expectations.

Similarly, John (like the Essenes and the Jews) practiced a ritual baptism. But while the Jews and the Essenes repeated the practice daily and regarded it as a self-administered means of ritual purification, John's baptism went beyond legal and ritual purity to signify *personal conversion*. Still, John acknowledged that his baptism was merely preparatory. One more powerful would come, he promised, bringing a baptism of the Holy Spirit and fire. Claiming complete inferiority to the one who would come, John understood—or more correctly the evangelists had come to understand—his role as preliminary, temporary and subordinate to that of Jesus. While John called God's people to conversion, Jesus would be the one who would judge whether or not their conversion was authentic.

The unquenchable fire, the wrath, the ax, the winnowing fan and the Holy Spirit (vv. 10-12) all point to the sifting and separation of peoples that would accompany the appearance of the Lord himself. But John's message (and that of Jesus after him) was not received by all. At those whose external acts of piety were not supported by an internal spirit of humility and repentance, John hurled a powerful epithet: "Brood of vipers!" (v. 7)

Like Jesus, John was aware that neither perfect lineage (Abraham is our father, v. 9) nor any amount of purely external behavior, however laudatory, could simulate conversion or manipulate the kingdom. Only the truthful heart, responsive to God's grace in sincere repentance, will be blessed with salvation. John's warnings and his exhortations to repentance are still valid and while the winnowing fan has not yet dealt its final blow, the wise would do well to return to the Lord, to straighten his paths and watch for his appearance in the "desert."

1. Peace does not just happen; it is the result of continual human effort and cooperation with divine ideas (Isaiah).

2. Those who learn the lessons of the past will probably build a better future (Romans).

3. Repentance is not a purely intellectual decision; returning to the Lord requires the totality of our energies (Matthew).

Third Sunday of Advent

When preconceptions cloud our vision of the future and render us incapable of recognizing God's ways in our world, disappointment results (Matthew). But when our hearts are open to God's surprises and when we are eager to discover his ideas, there is great joy (Isaiah). Only the one who is willing to wait patiently for God will know the happiness of finding him and the joy of being fulfilled by him (James).

Isaiah 35:1-6, 10. While it appears in the section of the book (chapters 1-39) attributed to Isaiah, the eighth century prophet from Jerusalem, this pericope is believed by most scholars to be the product of a later hand at a later time. The tone of unbridled exuberance and the theme of restoration seem to suggest the period near the end of the Babylonian exile; therefore, the date would probably be the sixth century B.C.E. and the prophet would be the anonymous Deutero-Isaiah.

In an idealized and lyrical song, the prophet who had shared his people's shame and suffering in Babylonia held out to them the hope of returning home. As in their first exodus from Egypt, their route would take them through the desert. But, as the refugees from Babylon made their way home, trekking southward along the vast stretches of barren land, they would not be overcome by the ominous threats of the wilderness.

Indeed, because of Yahweh's intervention on their behalf and by his power, the path before them would be transformed. Oases would spring up to refresh and comfort those who journeyed homeward to Jerusalem. Where once brambles and thorns had made travel difficult, now flowers and rich foliage would speed them on their way. This notion of the cosmos reflecting the joy of a redeemed people appeared frequently in ancient literature where humanity and its environment were considered as integral parts of a harmonious whole. In the same way, the shortcomings and failures of humankind were thought to be translated into cosmic upheavals and natural disasters (Genesis 3:16-19).

When the prophets adopted this theme, they associated nature's rejoicing with the appearance of an ideal king (Isaiah 41:17-20, 43:20, 48:21). Lebanon, Sharon and Carmel were three geographical areas synonymous with lush and verdant vegetation. For the returning pilgrims, these rich blessings were waiting.

Corresponding to the transformation of nature, the exiles themselves were to be the recipients of God's miraculous action. Feeble hands, weak knees and frightened hearts would become strong; because of God's saving power even the blind would be able to see, the lame would walk, the deaf would hear and the dumb would sing. In their renewed state, all those beneficiaries of God's goodness would throng together and Zion itself would come alive with their boisterous joy.

A very important passage, these verses with their theme of Eden renewed or paradise regained came to be associated with the era of the messiah. In the New Testament times, these same healing activities were applied to the ministry of Jesus. In the gospel of Luke, Jesus is portrayed as delivering these verses as part of his inaugural homily (4:18). When Mark told of Jesus' healing the deaf mute, he used the same very unusual word *mogilalos* ("dumb") as did the prophet in Isaiah 35:5. In today's gospel, Matthew has presented Jesus as offering to the disciples of John the Baptist these healing deeds as a sign that the messianic era had indeed begun.

James 5:7-10. Few ways of life are more dependent upon providence or more subject to the caprices of nature than that of the farmer. Susceptible to both drought and deluge, vulnerable to the ravages of insects and disease, the farmer ekes a living from the land, supported from harvest to harvest by his patient endurance and indomitable love of the land. When the author of the letter called James wrote to his first century contemporaries, the figure of the farmer offered a ready example of trust and hope in the Lord.

The first of the so-called catholic or general letters, James has traditionally been ascribed to James, brother of the Lord and leader of the Jerusalem church. Both early (40-62 C.E.) and late (late first or early second century C.E.) dates have been assigned to the letter, dependent upon the supposed author. Most believe the letter to have originated in the Syro-Palestine area. Addressed to the 12 tribes of the diaspora (James 1:1), the letter was actually intended as a response to the problems of the church at large. Comprised of a series of self-contained and independent sections, loosely "stitched" together by catchwords (German *stichtwort*), the document is less like a letter and resembles more the Old Testament works of Proverbs and/or Ecclesiasticus.

Immediately preceding today's pericope, James had castigated the rich (5:1-6) for their lack of concern for those less fortunate. Attending solely to their wealth and to the efforts needed to acquire even more of this earth's goods, the rich (warned James) would be sadly surprised at the harvest of salvation. Nothing they had worked so diligently to possess could be carried across the threshold of eternity; in their final accounting by the just judge, their coveted inventory would be totally worthless.

After these words of admonition, James turned his attention to the poor who thought themselves to be forgotten by God. As the interim between Jesus' first and second advents grew longer, many had grown diffident. Christian hope in the rewards promised to the poor and faithful was wracked with perplexity and weakened by doubt. To this growing apathy and discouragement James addressed the words of today's second reading: "Be patient, steady your hearts, don't grumble." Like the Palestinian farmer who waited with confidence for the winter (October-November) and spring (March-April) rains, believers were to wait with courage for the appearance of the Lord, their vindicator.

As a second model of patience and endurance, James offered the example of the prophets (v. 10). Patiently, like farmers, they had sown the seeds of God's word among their fellow Israelites and confidently they had awaited its fruition. They were undaunted by the blight of human failure and the seeming slowness of God's action; they trusted fully in the power of God to save his people. Patience, an almost obsolete virtue in today's instantaneous society, must be cultivated by believers. Patience is not resignation but it is the fruit of a loving faith that is content to discover God's gifts in the manner and in the moment he reveals them.

Matthew 11:2-11. In today's gospel, the reader is presented with a classic case of disappointed expectations. John had begun his preaching in the desert, calling people to repentance and reformation. He warned of the coming one, a just judge who would lay the ax to the foot of fruitless trees. At his appearance, promised John, the messiah would sift through the peoples of the earth with the winnowing fan of his judgment. As a result, the worthy would be gathered into the barn of his righteousness while the useless would be subjugated to an unquenchable fire (Matthew 3:1-12 = last Sunday's gospel). John's expectations were similar to those shared by many of his contemporaries. A people who had been subjected to the power struggles of larger empires (Egypt, Babylon, Persia, Greece, Rome) during most of their history, the Israelites yearned for a vindicator. They conceived of the promised messiah as a conqueror with armies whose appearance would reestablish God's people as a worldly power. By his word, their enemies would be halted and vanquished; the people who had proven faithful would be rewarded with prestige and prosperity.

But Jesus appeared without an entourage save for a band of followers who were unlikely leaders let alone conquering generals. He came in meekness and humility, preaching peace and not revolution. While John looked for judgment and the violent end of the wicked, Jesus preached of endless forgiveness and of the second chances the loving Father offered to his children. It is not surprising then that the Baptizer sent a deputation to Jesus to inquire as to his messianic intentions and purpose: "Are you he who is to come, or do we look for another?" (v. 3). At this time, John was in prison, having been arrested by Herod (Matthew 4:12). According to Josephus, John had been detained in the palace fortress of Machaerus, built by Herod the Great on the desolate heights of Moab near the Dead Sea. There he was held until his death.

Jesus' answer to John represented an entirely different aspect of messianic expectation that served to correct those held by John. Not an actual claim to messiahship, Jesus' response alluded to those phenomena associated (in the Old Testament) with the messianic era. Not a messiah of worldly proportions, nor one who promised the annihilation of the enemies of the elect, Jesus embodied in his words and works a messiahship of peace and healing. The message with which John's disciples were to return to him spoke of the blind seeing, the deaf hearing, cripples walking and dead people rising.

Constructed out of familiar phrases from the prophets (Isaiah 35:1-6, today's first reading; Isaiah 29:18-19; Isaiah 25:8), Jesus' reply indicated that the climax of his works and therefore the greatest of his messianic activities was his preaching of the good news to the poor (Isaiah 61:1-2). As R. Fuller has pointed out, this recitation of miracles was traditionally used by apologists to prove Jesus' divinity. But this apologetic assertion is not scripturally sound. If, indeed, such deeds of Jesus *were* proofs, then all rational peoples who witnessed them should have believed. But, of course, this was not the case. Deeds such as those performed by Jesus, however miraculous, were not proofs but *signs* of God present and at work in Jesus. As signs, Jesus' actions were invitations or challenges to believe.

Like those who had *experienced* Jesus' healings and preaching and like those who had *witnessed* them, John (and his disciples and the readers of Matthew's gospel) was called upon to heed the challenge they proffered and to believe in God's presence in Jesus. This fact is underscored in Jesus' statement, "Blest is the man who finds no stumbling block in me (v. 6). In this beatitude, Jesus invited John (et al.) not to be scandalized (Greek *skandalon* = stumbling block) by his methods, but to believe; this alternative of faith or scandal will continue throughout the rest of Matthew's gospel. Some have proposed that the contrast presented in today's gospel between the messianic ideas of John and those of Jesus represents the essential contrast between the law and the gospel.

In the second half of today's gospel pericope, Jesus' witness to John's role and importance in the economy of salvation again contains a message about the nature of the messianic era. Jesus acknowledged John's greatness; he was a prophet, indeed the greatest of prophets. In John, the role of Elijah as herald and messenger of the Lord's Day (Malachi 3:1) had been realized. As the last of the prophets, John stood as a "sentinel at the frontier between the aeons" (G. Bornkamm), as the link between the age of promise and the era of fulfillment. "No one born of woman was greater than John the Baptizer" (v. 11). The implication here is that John was greater even than Abraham or Moses or David.

But for all his greatness and importance, John and his mission were merely preparatory. With Jesus and the era he inaugurated by his messianic deeds and presence, a new standard would be maintained and judged not by human criteria or expectations but by God alone. This new way would be learned, not through the law or in the achievements of history but in the person of Jesus Christ. For this reason, Jesus proclaimed that even the least born into the kingdom of God is greater than John (v. 11). Advent is an annual opportunity for letting go of human preconceptions in order to let God reveal to us his wonderful surprises concerning his purpose and his methods for our salvation.

1. When humanity learns to harmonize its aspirations with God's graces, even nature will benefit (Isaiah).

2. Waiting for circumstances to change is like waiting for seeds to grow. All of a sudden, without our controlling it, something happens and anxiety is transformed into joy (James).

3. Those who focus their vision on the heights to look for greatness may miss the wonderful things happening all around them (Matthew).

Fourth Sunday of Advent

As part of his redeeming plan for humanity, God promised not merely to visit but to be with us (Isaiah). That promise, fulfilled in the incarnation of Jesus, has forever dispelled the sadness and separation born of sin (Romans). All who rejoice in the fact of God-with-us are called to translate their joy into tangible service and concrete acts of love (Matthew).

Isaiah 7:10-14. Although this text from Isaiah has lent itself beautifully to the annual telling of the Christmas story, the prophet did not have Jesus or Mary in mind when he wrote it. Occasioned by the political difficulties of his own times, Isaiah's words were directed to Ahaz, king of Judah (736-716 B.C.E.). During Ahaz' reign, Rezin, king of Syria (Aram), and Pekah, king of Israel, formed an alliance in order to resist the imperial expansion of the superpower Assyria, led by Tiglath Pileser III. Both Rezin and Pekah pressured Ahaz to join them in their efforts against Assyria. When Ahaz refused, the armies of the Syro-Israelite alliance attacked Judah and laid siege to Jerusalem in hopes of dethroning Ahaz and replacing him with a puppet vassal who would prove sympathetic to their cause. With his kingdom thrown into a state of emergency by these developments, Ahaz was about to resort to the desperate measure of allying Judah with Assyria against Syria and Israel.

At this point, Isaiah paid a visit to Ahaz (2 Kings 16:5-9) and exhorted the weak king that his only chance for survival lay in faithful reliance upon Yahweh alone. Political alliances, counseled the prophet, were a direct affront to the covenantal alliance by which God protected and provided for his people. Isaiah wished Ahaz to share his confidence in the Lord's sovereignty over all the events of history.

When Ahaz rejected the prophet's advice outright, Isaiah encouraged the king to ask for a sign from God that the Davidic dynasty would be preserved if only the people remained faithful to God. When Ahaz refused to ask for a sign, offering the shallow excuse that he would not tempt the Lord, Isaiah offered a sign anyway. Sign in both the Old and New Testaments referred to some event that would assure humanity of divine intervention. A form of revelation, the sign represented God's action among his people. Many think that Ahaz refused to request a sign because his former sinful acts made him fearful of its consequences. Nevertheless, the sign was given, a sign that served to confirm and to actualize the oracle of God spoken to David through Nathan (2 Samuel 7:11-16).

According to the Hebrew or Masoretic text, Isaiah promised Ahaz that an *'almah* or young woman of marriageable age would bring forth a child. Isaiah spoke of an event not far off in the future but of some *imminent* happening that would ease the problems of Ahaz. As T. Maertens has noted, Jewish hopes for salvation or Jewish messianism always expressed an ideal, that until the time of the exile was attached to a concrete individual.

Probably the woman was Ahaz' own wife or one of the women in his harem who was or would soon be pregnant. From her would be born Hezekiah, Ahaz' own son and heir. With the birth of Hezekiah, the Davidic dynasty would continue, despite the threats of Assyria, Syria and Israel, just as God had promised (2 Samuel 7:14) and just as Isaiah's sign had indicated (7:13). The child's birth, i.e., Hezekiah's ascendency, would prove to his people that God was with them, hence the symbolic name, Immanuel, "God-with-us." Immanuel, the future king, would be the antithesis of Ahaz whose infidelities had made God seem very distant and even absent from his people.

Only later, when Hezekiah's reign did not bring the security in which the people had hoped, the words of Isaiah and the sign of Immanuel came to be applied to some *future* figure or event. Only later (ca. 150 B.C.E.) and with the Greek translation (LXX) of the Hebrew scriptures was the *'almah* (young woman) of which Isaiah spoke transformed into a *parthenos* or virgin. In his Latin translation (Vulgate) Jerome followed the Greek and translated the word as *virgo*, virgin.

Romans 1:1-7. The opening verses of Paul's letter to the church at Rome, today's second reading represents the apostle's attempt to acquaint the Roman Christians with his version of the gospel and to justify its orthodoxy. Following the literary customs of his contemporaries, Paul included in his introduction: (1) his name (sender), (2) the church at Rome (addressee), and (3) his greetings. Moreover, he gathered into these seven verses nearly all the articles of the early Christian faith, viz., (a) the fact that the gospel of Jesus Christ realized the hopes and prophecies of the Old Testament (v. 2), (b) that Jesus was of Davidic lineage, Son of David (v. 3), (c) that Jesus was also Son of God in glory (v. 4), (d) that the good news of salvation is universal in scope (v. 5).

Because Paul's methods and preaching were at times held in question (Galatians 2, Acts 15) by the existing church authorities of his day, it was important that he present himself to the Romans as an authentic teacher. In defense of himself and his work, Paul recommended himself under the titles of "servant" and "apostle" (v. 1). *Doulos*, servant, was an honorific title applied to the great figures of Jewish tradition: Moses, Joshua, Abraham, Isaac, etc. (2 Kings 18:22, Judges 2:8, Psalm 105:42, Exodus 24:31, Numbers 12:7, Genesis 26:24). In claiming the title servant, Paul did not refer to his position of honor but to his *mission*. As the servant (or slave) of Jesus Christ, he had been set apart for the preaching of the gospel.

The second title of "apostle" was not an undisputed one. Many challenged Paul's right to apostleship since he had not known the earthly Jesus or been in the company of the Twelve (1 Corinthians 9; 2 Corinthians 11:13, 23). But Paul based his claim to apostleship on his personal call from the risen Lord (Galatians 1:1) and on the fact that Jesus himself had commissioned him for his work (1 Thessalonians 1:4, Philippians 4:15, 2 Corinthians 8:18).

Far more important than the titles he claimed for himself were the titles Paul ascribed to Jesus: Son of David and Son of God. During his own ministry, Jesus shied away from those who stressed his Davidic lineage because his politically-minded contemporaries had an entirely different conception about the implications of his messiahship. The post-resurrection community, however, took pains to establish Jesus' Davidic origins (through Joseph) in order to represent him as the promised messiah and fulfillment of the ancient oracle to David (2 Samuel 7:14). At a very early date, the title Son of David was woven into the fabric of christological titles. As it appears in Paul's letter to the Romans, "Son of David" stressed the earthly or historical aspect of Jesus. "Son of God," on the other hand, established Jesus' exalted status, achieved by his resurrection from the dead. Also a messianic title, "Son of God" underscored the universal aspect of Jesus' role.

Paul explained that his *own* service to the nations was the full realization of the universal messianism promised to the Son of God in Psalm 2:7-8. For that reason, he was proud of bringing the good news of salvation to the citizens of the world capital. Whereas the economy of redemption had first been rooted in the Davidic dynasty for the sake of Israel, it was then replaced by a new economy, a new order that included all nations. "A belief in the Son of David proclaimed Son of God, nowadays amounts to a belief that civilization and history play a part in the building of the church and of the Mystical Body of Christ" (T. Maertens, J. Fisque). During Advent, then, we celebrate and remember, not just *one* people, not just *our* people, but *all* peoples in Christ.

Matthew 1:18-24. Jesus' nativity was not the result of purely human evolution but due to the loving intervention of God in human history. Represented by the evangelists Matthew and Luke in such a way as to emphasize Jesus' messianic identity, the infancy narratives and in particular the birth announcements are highly theological affirmations of the faith of the early church. Today's gospel is Matthew's version of the annunciation of Jesus's birth. Immediately preceding this gospel pericope is the genealogy with which Matthew's gospel begins, in which Jesus' ancestry was traced to David through Joseph. Where the genealogy was intended to confirm that Jesus was truly a Son of David, the announcement of his birth expressed the early church's belief in Jesus as Son of God.

A specific literary form in the Bible, birth announcements usually were (1) made by an angel (or other messenger of God), (2) indicated the name the person would have, and (3) signified the special role the person would play in the economy of salvation. As in the cases of Isaac, Samuel, John the Baptizer, etc., the announcement of Jesus' birth contained all these elements.

All too often, the chapters concerning Jesus' birth and early days have been undervalued by the majority of Christians. Matthew 1 and 2 (like Luke 1 and 2) are much more than a medley of sweet and touching stories about the baby Jesus. As J. Meier has noted, these chapters contain deep theological insights and should be understood as an overture to the gospel. A sort of gospel in miniature, Matthew 1 and 2 introduce a number of significant themes, all of which will be expanded within the gospel proper. Like the highly christological prologue of John's gospel, Matthew 1 and 2 define Jesus' significance by: (1) applying to him a series of titles (Immanuel, Son of David, Son of God, Christ, Nazarene); (2) defining his origin and goal; (3) noting the presence and guidance of the Holy Spirit; (4) connecting the reality of Jesus with the prophetic anticipation of the Old Testament.

Through a series of Old Testament citations (11 or 12 in the entire gospel), Matthew firmly established that in Jesus' person and in his mission God was carefully ordering history toward the fulfillment of his prophetic word. Today's gospel contains the first in this series of quotations. By citing Isaiah 7:14, Matthew wished to bring his readers to the awareness that in Jesus their eschatological and messianic aspirations were realized. Some have understood these "fulfillment formula" citations as serving an *apologetic* purpose. In the light of the developments at Jamia (ca. 85 C.E.) and the church's definitive separation from the synagogue, perhaps the citations were aimed at those Jews who still rejected Jesus. Others have probably been more correct in attaching a didactic significance to the citations.

As R.E. Brown observed, this series of Old Testament quotes were employed by the evangelist in an effort to further inform his Christian readers and to give support to their growing faith. Matthew wished his readers to recognize, through his narrative of Jesus' birth, that the Immanuel prophecy of Isaiah had been fulfilled. In so doing, Matthew compared Isaiah's *'almah* (young maid, in the Hebrew text), or *parthenos* (virgin, in Greek text) to Mary. The evangelist also underlined the extraordinary nature of Jesus' birth by means of the exchanges between Joseph and the angel.

According to Jewish customs, the matrimonial procedure had two stages. First, there was a formal exchange of consent between the groom (or his parents) and the bride's parents in the presence of witnesses. This first stage of consent or betrothal occurred when the bride-to-be was 12 or 13 years old. Legally, the groom-to-be had rights over the girl who for all practical purposes was considered his wife (*gyne*). Therefore, any infraction upon his marital rights could be legally prosecuted as adultery.

Nevertheless, the girl usually continued to live at her parents' home until the second stage, the formal transfer, took place. Once the girl was taken into her husband's home and he had assumed all responsibility for her welfare, the marriage procedure was completed. While it was permissible in some areas of Judah for the future groom to have sexual relations with his bride-to-be before the formal transfer to his home, this practice was not tolerated in Galilee. From the gospel narrative, it is clear that Mary and Joseph were in the interim stage *before* the formal transfer. This explains Joseph's dismay at Mary's pregnancy.

Because of his uprightness, i.e., his obedience to the law, Joseph saw no alternative but to divorce Mary. However, he was also merciful and instead of exposing her to the death penalty (as the law prescribed) he chose to divorce her privately. At this point in the narrative Matthew introduced the divine intent and involvement by means of the angel's explanation. The first of three angelic appearances to Joseph, the heavenly messenger represented special revelation and highlighted the true importance of the narrative. Joseph was not to hesitate because by God's power, i.e., by the Holy Spirit, the Immanuel-event would be actualized.

When Matthew wrote, he did not intend to defend Mary's virginity or to lay the theological foundations for the virgin birth. Only in the fourth century C.E. were these factors fully explored and only then were official pronouncements made. Rather, Matthew's major focus was upon the *name* and *vocation* of the child to be born. He would be called Jesus, a later form of the name Joshua, originally meaning "Yahweh helps." By the first Christian century the popular meaning was "Yahweh saves." Therefore the angelic messenger's explanation, "because he will *save* his people from their sins," can be enjoyed as a heavenly "pun" or paranomasia. As savior and liberator from sin, Jesus would be the very presence of the forgiving God among his people. By removing the walls of sin and the abyss of evil that alienate God and his people, by becoming God's incarnate loving goodness in time and space, Jesus is and will ever be God-with-us.

1. There is no greater or deeper or higher sign of God's concern for us than his presence with us in Jesus (Isaiah).

2. Through his Davidic ancestry, Jesus was royal; but by virtue of his divine origins, he became redeemer and Lord (Romans).

3. The "why" of Jesus' birth, i.e., to be God-with-us, is far more important than the "how" (Matthew).

The Christmas Season
Christmas

For the celebration of Christmas, the lectionary supplies several sets of texts (vigil, midnight, dawn, day). The ones treated here are for proclamation at the day mass.

Eternity enfleshed in time is the gift of grace we call Immanuel, God-with-us. Infinity is made finite in a daring act of loving and giving (John). He is good news and salvation (Isaiah). He is Father and brother and Lord; he is the message of glory we celebrate today (Hebrews)!

Isaiah 52:7-10. On occasion in the ancient world, the bearer of bad news was put to death, but there would be no danger of that happening to the messenger portrayed in today's first reading. Part of a longer enthronement hymn in honor of the devastated city of Zion (Jerusalem), today's pericope envisages the joy and hope of the people on hearing of their release from exile and their imminent homecoming. Written in the sixth century B.C.E. by a prophet known arbitrarily as Deutero-Isaiah, these verses give us a glimpse of the "phoenix quality" of Israel's hope, a quality she owed entirely to Yahweh's sustaining love and provident care.

During exile for over a generation, Israel's beloved capital city of Jerusalem had remained in its demolished condition, the ruins a bleak witness to the political and military might of its Babylonian conquerors. For over a generation, the elite of Israel's populace had been degraded, displaced in a strange land where they had no rights of proprietorship or freedom to pray and worship as was their custom. During that time of imprisonment and curtailed freedom, a liberating enlightenment gradually took place among the exiles, due in no small part to the prophets who shared the exile. As mediator to his people of God's revealing word, the prophet helped his people to interpret all that had happened to them, both good and bad, as a part of God's message of salvation and justice. Each event in their history could be read, as it were, like a word through which God was speaking his mind, his will, his ways for his people In joyous times, that word could be one of blessing. The darker periods, the failures and defeats, the prophets interpreted as God's word of redress and deserved punishment. In the *events* of history the prophets read for their people the creative, redeeming, purifying, loving, blessing word of God.

Hence the *event* of Israel's return from exile was truly a gospel—glad tidings, good news. Not only what God had *said* to his people, in spoken or in written words, but what he had *been* and how he had *acted* within the realm of their history enabled his people to know him as redeemer, saving God. In creation and in history God's plan is accomplished and clarified. As T. Maertens has pointed out, the *event* is central; all else, the spoken, written and prophesied words, are in service and in ministry to the event.

Today's feast celebrates the Christ-*event*. In fact, the glad tidings of the Deutero-Isaian messenger were only fully actualized, only fully heard and made comprehensible in the event of Jesus Christ. In the event of the incarnation Yahweh truly returns and restores Jerusalem; in the event of the nativity Yahweh draws near to comfort and console his people. In the event of Christ-made-flesh God's message of salvation achieves its utmost clarity. What we celebrate as gospel, as good news is not mere words but persons and events.

Hebrews 1:1-6. In a sort of "before-and-after" or "then-and-now" comparison, the author of the document addressed to the Hebrews enunciated the differences between the revelation of the old and new covenants. Our reading today comprises the introduction of his work which can readily be compared to the prologue of the fourth gospel. In both texts, the image is one of Christ's divinity and equality with God.

In vv. 1 to 4, the first paragraph of our text today, the author of Hebrews speaks of the *superior* revelation which God has spoken in Jesus Christ. Unlike the piecemeal and fragmentary revelation of the Old Testament which had to be interpreted by the prophets, the revelation in Jesus is whole and entire, living and absolute. J. Moffatt has said, "Christ is God's last word to the world; revelation in him is final and homogeneous." Jesus Christ is a living being. The word of God he has spoken in the event of his ministry, death, resurrection and exaltation does not cease to be heard. The word of God in Jesus is "living and active" (4:12), ever new, ever in the process of communicating to believers the love and care of God. That living, speaking word-become-flesh is the basis for our celebration today.

Besides asserting Christ's superiority to the prophets and Old Testament revelation, Hebrews also underscores the Lord's predominance over the angels. As refulgence or reflection (v. 3: *apaugasma*) of the Father and as the exact representation (*charakter* or *eikon*) of the Father's being, Christ is placed on a par with wisdom (Wisdom 7:26). In the old dispensation, wisdom was regarded as sharing with God both a cosmological and soteriological role (Proverbs 8:22-36, Wisdom 9:9-18). This equating with wisdom in such an operative role placed Jesus Christ on a level far above the angelic hosts whom late Judaism believed were present at creation and who were granted by God a role in its government. Jewish tradition called these angelic beings "sons of God," and Alexandrian Jewish theologians called them *logos,* word. Because of these prevalent notions, the Hebrews' author was adamant in establish Christ's transcendence and divinity. In New Testament times, popular Jewish belief regarded the angels as mediators of the law for humankind. In a medley of texts from the Jewish scriptures, Hebrews leaves no doubt as to Christ's superior and unequalled position. The first two texts from Psalms 2:7 and 2 Samuel 7:14 were thought messianic by late Judaism and by the Qumran community. In both quotations the unique sonship of Christ is established as well as the divinity of his messiahship. The third text (v. 6), a combination of several Old Testament citations (Deuteronomy 32:43; Psalms 97:7, 104:4), forms a compelling invitation to those angelic beings to worship the Lord Jesus Christ. With them, we the faithful join our voices in praise and honor.

John 1:1-18. John Paul Sartre in an essay on literature once wrote, "The word is a commitment, an enterprise by means of which the author embraces his age." Although unintentionally and probably inadvertently, Sartre has provided believers with an apt description of the scenario of the incarnation, the central thought of the gospel today. In the speaking into flesh of his word, in the person and event of Jesus Christ, God has committed himself to humankind and to the world in an eternal embrace.

Up until Vatican II, today's gospel text was proclaimed at the end of every Eucharist, thereby earning for itself the misnomer "last gospel." Though this practice has been discontinued, it did serve the purpose of climaxing every celebration with the compelling and beautiful truth of the incarnation. Though most situations do not warrant reading the *shortened* form of the gospel, today may be the unique instance in which the short form would be preferable for the sake of clarity. Verses 6-8 and 15 are prose comments concerning John the Baptizer which were probably inserted into the poetic prologue at a later time by the evangelist or by a disciple-redactor of the fourth gospel. To omit these comments is to allow the hymn to flow more freely with the continuity originally intended.

This hymn that introduces the gospel serves a dual function. First, it provides for the words and works of the incarnate word an eternal background or origin and proclaims as false the theories against Jesus' divinity prevalent at the turn of the first century C.E. Secondly, the prologue serves as an overture to the gospel, containing a summary of its major themes as well as a means of interpreting Jesus' message and person. Many believe the hymn to be an adaptation from a Jewish or gnostic wisdom hymn, or a preexisting Christian hymn, adapted by the evangelist for the purpose of expounding his christology. Because the hymn exhibits similarities to semitic, Greek and gnostic ideas, a clear solution as to its origins is almost impossible.

In true semitic style, the prologue begins with a genealogy; however, unlike most Jewish genealogies, it traces Jesus' origins to the eternal divinity. "In the beginning" is, of course, a deliberate reference to Genesis 1:1 and the creation by God's word of the universe. In John 1:1 that creative word is speaking again, but no longer as subject to object, as creator to created. In John 1:1 the word who speaks a new creation has become a part of creation itself by that very utterance. That word continues to speak within human history (vv. 4, 9-10) and especially through Israel (v. 11). Those who hear and truly listen to that word can become sons and daughters with the Son. Verse 14, "the word became flesh and made his dwelling among us," draws together all the Old Testament references to God's presence with his people, in the cloud, in fire, through the prophets, in his glory, by his law (Exodus 24; Exodus 33:18; Isaiah 6:1). The same root (S-K-N) lends itself to the verbs for God's presence in nature (*shekinah*) and his dwelling among us (literally: "pitched his tent") in his word (*eskenosen*).

It is difficult to ascertain whether John wanted his readers to understand word or logos in a Greek or in a semitic sense. To those of a *Hellenistic* background, the logos-word was regarded as an intermediary between God and the created universe. That logos gave the world its order, thus making it intelligible and comprehensible. Humankind, in turning to the logos, could find a key for unlocking the mysteries of the cosmos. Understood in this sense, Christ as logos-word would be the key to knowing about created things and about God. To the *semitic* mind, the logos or word is a challenge which a believer can accept or reject. A word or a call from God, the logos confronts or encounters the believer and compellingly invites a response. In this sense, Christ as logos-word would be a challenger or initiator of faith, a living epiphany of a loving, saving creator. Probably, the evangelist has combined the best of both cultures in his concept of the logos or word. As T. Maertens has said, Jesus is not only bearer of the word; he is also its content.

The figure of Moses (v. 18) brings to the fore another important semitic idea. For the Jews, Moses was *the* mediator, through whom the law or light of truth was mediated from God to his people. In the prologue, the evangelist enunciates Christ's superiority not only as mediator between God and humanity but also to the law. Rabbinical Judaism in the last centuries B.C.E. and the first centuries C.E. glorified the

Torah and identified it with wisdom, source of light and life for all (Sirach 24:22-27). In his treatment of Jesus Christ-logos as superior to Old Testament wisdom and law, John's purpose is in one sense polemical. Over and against the Jewish idea of an eternal and nearly divine law, John posited Christ the word as existing from all eternity, through whom *alone* would come truth and light, life and grace.

For us who believe and who celebrate the enfleshment of the word of God as the source of life and light and truth, today is a renewal of our faith and of our commitment to the challenge of that word. Let us remember that because of the *incarnation*, we respond, not to a concept or an ideology or a philosophy, but to a living and loving *person*.

1. The good news of Christ proclaimed by the church in the pulpit must resound more loudly and more joyfully in the marketplace (Isaiah).

2. No longer through a glass darkly, but in the light of Christ, we behold the fullness of the Father's love (Hebrews).

3. In the word enfleshed, God speaks the language of our flesh and blood, in the pulsing of our needs and aspirations and even in the shadows of our sinful darker side (John).

Holy Family

Familial bonds are the first relationships to be experienced and those that bear the most influence in human development (Sirach). For the Christian, the love learned within the family is extended and deepened through mutual care for the entire human community (Colossians). Family love is brought to its ultimate fullness in the sonship that Jesus shares with all who believe (Matthew).

Sirach 3:2-6, 12-14. From the internal and indirect references in his book, it appears that Jesus Ben Sirach belonged to a prosperous Jewish family and may even have been a member of the scribal class during the second century B.C.E. Originally written in Hebrew ca. 180 B.C.E., the work of Ben Sirach was an amalgamation of a wise person's insights on the Torah, other sacred writings on wisdom and maxims for sensible living. About two generations later (ca. 130 B.C.E.), Ben Sirach's grandson translated these writings into Greek, the lingua franca of his day, in order to make available to *all* his grandfather's wisdom.

Todays' first reading, excerpted from a longer section of commentary on family life, offers a practical application of the fourth commandment: "Honor your mother and your father" (Exodus 20:12). Numbered among the precepts of the decalogue, the care for one's parents was considered a sacred duty the breach of which was regarded as a breach of the covenant itself. Significantly, the author of Sirach did not recognize the oral tradition of the law through which the Pharisees had multiplied the various prescriptions of the law and had complicated them with a maze of loopholes for avoiding the burdens of the law's restrictions. Ben Sirach would have had no respect for the Pharisaic custom of "corban," viz., the consecrating of one's property and goods to the temple, thereby avoiding the obligation of supporting one's parents from one's property.

Rather than pervert, dilute or multiply the law, Ben Sirach respected the sacred precepts as immutable, God-given truth. Exhibiting the thought of later Judaism, Ben Sirach attached certain benefits to the correct attitude and respect for parents. For example, he cited the traditional blessings of long life and riches as rewards for faithful offspring. Ben Sirach understood the honoring of one's parents as an external activity born of an interior conviction. Fear of the Lord, or the piety learned by the living of the law (of which the fourth commandment was part), was an activity that developed a sensitive awareness to wrongdoing. For that reason, Ben Sirach could assert that the love of one's parents would atone for sin.

As R. Fuller has explained, this statement should be understood as an *incentive* for obeying the commandment and *not* as a theological *guarantee* of forgiveness. That forgiveness, of course, was achieved by the saving sacrifice of Jesus, loving Son of the divine parent. Because of Christ's atoning activity, all the disparate peoples of the earth have been adopted as children, related to God and to one another in familial love.

Colossians 3:12-21. Whenever Paul labored within a community to lay the foundations for a new center of Christianity, he tried to foster there an atmosphere of familial care and concern. When that atmosphere was disrupted by dissension, the apostle made every effort to restore peace and accord. When he could not visit the community to attend to the difficulties in person, Paul either sent an emissary or wrote a letter to the troubled church. This was the case in Paul's letter to Colossae.

Ancient Colossae was a small city in comparison to the more prominent and populated neighboring cities of Laodicea and Hierapolis. Located in the valley of the Lycus river in Asia Minor, about 110 miles east of Ephesus, Colossae was a center for textiles and dyed woolen goods. Paul did not personally bring the message of Christ to Colossae's mixed gentile and Jewish population. It is generally believed that Epaphras, one of Paul's converts in Ephesus, brought the good news to the Colossians and perhaps to the people of Laodicea and Hierapolis as well (1:6-7, 2:1, 4:12-13).

While in prison, probably in Rome (61-63 C.E.), Paul received a disturbing report from Epaphras that occasioned his letter to Colossae. The exact basis of Paul's concern is difficult to determine because we have only his response to the conflict; it seems, however, that some local teachers were confusing the Christians with false doctrines (2:8, 15-23). Introduced from both religious and philosophical spheres, these questionable doctrines were probably both Jewish and pagan in origin. From Paul's rebuttal, we can determine two major areas of concern: (1) the existence and importance of spiritual beings, (2) dietary practices, feast days, circumcision, etc.

At the root of the controversy concerning spiritual beings was the pagan belief that the universe was controlled by certain elements or angelic beings (2:8, 20). These angels were thought to act as mediators between God and humanity and contained in themselves a part of God's *pleroma* or fullness. Believed to be responsible for creation, the angels were also thought to control human affairs. Humanity for its part had to gain as much special knowledge (*gnosis*) as it could about these beings in order to propitiate them. In late Judaism, too, there existed a notion of the mediating power of angelic beings (Daniel 10:21, 12:1). To ward off the dangers inherent in these ideas, Paul expounded to the Colossians the supremacy and uniqueness of Jesus, sole mediator with the Father. All sufficient in himself, Christ possessed the very *pleroma* (fullness) of God and did not dilute his sufficiency with a need for angelic intermediaries.

The second major concern, that of the dietary customs, etc., was due no doubt to the large and powerful Jewish community at Colossae. Over and against those who would "Judaize" every Christian, Paul asserted the freedom Christians enjoy as he denied the relevance of such practices for the faith.

After dealing with the controversies, Paul devoted the remainder of his letter to a catechesis on the Christian life. Some believe this catechesis to have been part of a baptismal instruction (3:5—4:1). Exhorting his readers to "put on love" (v. 12), Paul recalled the sacramental rite of dressing the newly baptized in white garments as a symbol of their new life and of their victory over sin. Calling them to thankfulness (*eucharistoi*), Paul urged the Colossians to allow their baptismal dedication to guide their routine interactions and to inspire their public worship.

In the last paragraph of today's second reading, Paul accented the harmony that should characterize the Christian family. Nagging and bitterness have no place in the lives of those who profess faith in Jesus (v. 18). Those who belong to one another "in the Lord" should bring to that union the grace of redemption and the joyful love of those who have known true forgiveness. Today, when so many factors threaten to fracture familial bonds, Paul's call to grace and love should be remembered.

Matthew 2:13-15, 19-23. Many parents keep an account of their children's growth and development in what is popularly known as a baby book. There, the child's first steps, first tooth, weight and height, school adventures, etc., are documented with loving care and illustrated with pictures so as to afford both parent and child many fond memories in the future. Though the facts in the baby book may become confused or exaggerated with the passage of time, they are nevertheless historical and provide a verifiable account of the child's early years.

When reading the infancy narratives that purport to be an account of Jesus' early years, it is necessary to put aside all the modern notions about baby books. In commenting on today's gospel, R. Fuller explained, "Only by a questionable extrapolation from the text, involving an illegitimate historicization, would it be possible to relate this gospel to the theme of the Holy Family." Rather, the reader must learn to appreciate Matthew's intention, i.e., to present Jesus as recapitulating in his life the *history of Israel*.

Matthew has accomplished his purpose by means of a carefully constructed series of three midrashic stories. Each of the three stories—(1) escape of Jesus and his parents to Egypt, (2) the massacre of the children on Herod's order, (3) the return from Egypt and settling in Nazareth—is characterized as a fulfillment of some prophetic citation and is supported by the appropriate quotation. In the first of the three, the family of Jesus was guided by divine revelation (the intended literary function of the dream and the angel) to escape Herod's murderous intentions by fleeing to Egypt. Careful always to keep the adult Jesus in focus even in the narratives of his infancy, Matthew used the same word *apollynai* ("to destroy him") in v. 13 as he would later use in the story of the passion (Matthew 27:20). Herod had no authority in Egypt which, at the time of Jesus' birth, had been under Roman rule for over a generation (from 30 B.C.E.)

Egypt was the traditional place of refuge for those fleeing tyranny or danger in Palestine. For example, Jeroboam fled to Egypt when Solomon tried to kill him (1 Kings 11:40). When Jehoiakim tried to murder him, Uriah also fled to Egypt (Jeremiah 26:21). Even the high priest Onias IV escaped to Egypt to flee the wrath of Antiochus Epiphanes in 172 B.C.E.

Jesus' escape to Egypt with his parents and the circumstances that surrounded it (Herod, astrologers, scribes) recalled for Matthew's readers the birth of Moses. Like Jesus, Moses had been threatened by a jealous tyrant (Pharaoh). Astrologers also figured in the narrative of Moses' early life (Exodus 1:15, 22), as did a miraculous escape (Exodus 2:1-

10). By comparing the circumstances between Jesus' and Moses' birth, Matthew's concern was not so much historical as it was theological. As the new Moses, Jesus would be the legislator of a new covenant between Israel and God.

Jesus' escape to Egypt alluded also to another event in Israel's history, viz. the flight into Egypt of Jacob-Israel. As he fled to avoid Laban's persecution, Jacob was told, "Don't be afraid to go to Egypt for I will make you a great nation there. I will bring you back again" (Genesis 46:2). Reminding his readers of both Moses and Jacob and recalling the exodus whereby the entire nation was led out of Egypt by God, Matthew concluded his first story with a quotation from Hosea: "Out of Egypt I have called my son" (Hosea 11:1). By means of this citation, Matthew underscored Jesus' significance as the new Moses, the new Israel, but also and more importantly as God's own Son.

By combining these different roles of Jesus, the author illustrated the two perspectives in which Jesus' life was viewed: (1) that of his immediate dependence on God's direction and control (Son of God), (2) that of his deep immersion in the circumstances of human experience (new Moses, new Israel). This double perspective is evident throughout the stories of Jesus' childhood. Recall the Lucan Jesus telling his earthly father, Joseph, "I must be about my Father's business." As J. Gaffney has noted, that interpenetration of divine and human dimensions, that later theology expressed in philosophical terms of a "hypostatic union," is here expressed in the more universally accessible terms of simple narratives in which the divine and human dimensions are seen to interact.

The second half of today's gospel (vv. 19-23) is the conclusion of the Matthean infancy narrative and serves to explain the manner through which Jesus came to be raised in Nazareth. With Herod dead ("those who had designs on the life of the child are dead," v. 20 = Exodus 4:19), the path was cleared for Jesus to return home.

While the third fulfillment citation, "He shall be called a Nazorean," cannot be found specifically in the Old Testament, it may be an allusion to one of the following. (1) In Isaiah 11:1, the messiah was described as a *neser* or branch of Jesse. Some believe that Nazorean or Nazarite may be derived from *neser*. (2) In Judges 13:5,7, when Samson's birth was announced, he was designated as *nazir*, i.e., one *set apart* to lead a holy life and *to save* Israel. In some Greek translations *nazir* is rendered *naziraion*, hence it may have evolved into Nazorean. Certainly the descriptions of both Isaiah 11:1 and Judges 13:5,7 were applicable to Jesus who was both messiah of the line of David and the holy one who saved his people.

In conclusion, it should be noted that the historicity of these stories—the flight to Egypt, the death of the innocent children, the dreams, etc.—is impossible to document. But, as we stated at the beginning of this commentary, Matthew's intention was not to write history. Theologically, the evangelist has skillfully woven together a symbiotic presentation of Jesus' early days to portray him as a new Moses and a new Israel. Supported by references to the Old Testament, Matthew has shown that Jesus' messiahship was met from the outset by opposition that grew and culminated in his passion. There is, however, no hint of failure or defeat in Jesus' mission. Rather, all he did and all he was agreed perfectly with God's plan as expressed through the prophets.

1. To be a parent, to love a child is to share in the divine activity that resulted in the incarnation (Sirach).

2. Through baptism, believers enter into the extended family of the church that comprises all the people of God (Colossians).

3. The child who is nurtured and protected with loving care will learn through that experience of the goodness and generosity of God (Matthew).

New Year's Day

The texts pronounce a blessing on this year (Numbers) and repeat the season's basic theme, the coming of Jesus the God-man (Galatians) into our world—the first act in God's unfolding plan for our salvation (Luke).

Numbers 6:22-27. Called *Be midbar* ("In the wilderness") in the Masoretic text of the Hebrew, this fourth book of the Pentateuch purports to depict the wilderness wanderings in the Sinai and the westward infiltration from the Transjordan area into Canaanite territory. In actual fact, the book is a complex melange of various traditions, religious history, liturgical rites and legal codes which grew out of the developing faith and culture of the Hebrew tribes. These traditions "percolated" through the life and mores of the people for about ten centuries before they were concentrated in the not too orderly book we call Numbers.

While much of the material in Numbers comes from a later period, many scholars believe that the blessing, which comprises the heart of today's pericope, may be quite ancient. This formula, used by priests in blessing the people at the end of their prayer together, is very familiar to us, because it is still used in both Jewish and Christian liturgies. It is a perfect example of Hebrew parallelism in triplicate, that is, the same prayer or petition is expressed in three different ways. Because biblical Hebrew knows no superlative, the triple statement is a means of showing emphasis. The phrases (The Lord bless you, the Lord let his face shine, the Lord look upon you kindly) are but three variants for understanding the Lord's favor. The word for the Lord's face (*panim*) is always plural, a collective noun, signifying all the qualities behind a face: attitudes, sentiments, personality. In a word, God's very self or presence is invoked. The threefold prayer for prosperity, presence and peace is an excellent expression of our hope in God who alone can make ours a happy new year.

Galatians 4:4-7. While the Pauline authorship of Galatians is rarely questioned today, we still do not know to which part of Galatia Paul addressed his letter, the northern or southern region. Created a province of Rome about 25 B.C.E. by Augustus, Galatia was a cosmopolitan area and the situation there caused Paul to pen one of his most important documents.

Writing in Ephesus in the mid-fifties C.E. on his third missionary trek, Paul used the letter to attack one of his major pastoral obstacles, the Judaizers. These were a group of early Christians (probably Pharisaic, perhaps even Essene in tradition) who believed that the way to Jesus Christ had to pass through Moses. They denied Paul's claim to apostleship and accused him of diluting the power of the gospel for the sake of gentile converts. The Judaizers plagued Paul's gentile converts by their insistence on circumcision for all, as well as the observance of certain Jewish feasts and dietary laws.

Galatians is a polemic against the Judaizers, with its underscoring of the freedom in Christ and its rejection of the old law and circumcision. Today's text follows Paul's story about Abraham wherein he asserts that the promises made to Abraham can be enjoyed by all Christians because it is Christ Jesus and not the law which makes us heirs. Indeed, because of Jesus Christ and his Spirit, we are children of God, intimate enough to call him "Abba" (Daddy).

Most scholars believe that the key phrase of the text, "God sent forth his son . . . so that we might receive adoption as sons," is an ancient Christian credal text expanded by Paul. The phrases, "when the designated time had come," "born of a woman" and "born under the law," proclaim Christ's incarnation and true solidarity with the human situation to those who would deny it.

Luke 2:16-21. Today's pericope from Luke's infancy narrative, depicting the shepherds' visit to the newly formed holy family, parallels the magi story in Matthew's gospel (see gospel text for next Sunday). Both groups, shepherds and magi, come to Jesus due to an extraordinary revelation, in one case an angel, in the other a star. Both groups represent believers in the early church who accepted Jesus as the Christ, as opposed to other groups who rejected and even persecuted him (Herod, scribes, chief priests). Both groups, shepherds and magi, come to adore Jesus as savior and go away from the event believing. Both groups, however, were considered somewhat beyond the ordinary, acceptable pale of existence. The magi were foreigners and astronomers. The shepherds were regarded outside the law in that their livelihood at times required that they graze their flocks on the lands of others.

The author of Luke 1 and 2 executes a creative transition from the story of Israel (Old Testament) to the story of Jesus (gospel) and the church (Acts), depicting Elizabeth, Zechariah, Anna, Simeon and especially Mary as the personification of messianic hope. Mary in particular, as both believer and later disciple, bridges the gap between Israel and the new Israel, the church. She keeps or treasures (ponders, interprets) these events in her heart and as such becomes the model for believers (cf. 2:16, 51). Jesus referred to faith like hers later in the gospel (see 8:15, 21; 11:28). A sentimental and pietistic regard for Mary has no root in the gospel, which presents her rather as one to admired for her faith.

The last verse (2:21) of today's text gives fleeting attention to Jesus' circumcision before focusing on his naming. Contrary to custom, Joseph does not name the child. Rather, he is given the name which had been announced by the angel (1:31). In this way, the author attests to the extraordinary circumstances of Jesus' birth as well as the faith of her who had kept the angel's words in her heart and acted on them.

1. Do our lives reflect the blessings of the faith we enjoy (Numbers)?

2. Preconceived notions can blind us to the surprises of God's continuing revelation (Galatians).

3. The Christ of our faith is no longer an infant; he is the glorious, risen Lord of all creation (Luke).

Epiphany

A feast of divine manifestation and human discovery, Epiphany celebrates the dawn of salvation in a world shrouded by shadows of sin and death (Isaiah). When the Sun of Justice appeared, some refused to open their hearts to the light and life. While the disbelieving stumble in the dark, the hungry and the humble have discovered his warmth, and he has fanned into a flame the spark of their faith (Matthew). For all who have come to the light of truth, there are no longer any barriers of separation or tombs of alienation, but only light and life and joy (Ephesians).

Isaiah 60:1-6. At once eschatological and liturgical in character, today's pericope may have been the fruit of the prophet's early morning meditation. Looking out over his beloved city of Jerusalem, he saw her hills and valleys gradually transformed by the rising sun from dark shadows into light and lively places. As the city woke to a new day, caravans from far-off places carried their exotic goods through the city gates. Farmers and fishermen came also to sell their wares. Perhaps this vision of Jerusalem bathed in light prompted the prophet's oracle of the new and eschatological Jerusalem robed in God's shining glory (vv. 1-2). Similarly, the gathering of peoples in the holy city was a liturgical symbol of those promised days when not only all the tribes of Jerusalem (Deuteronomy 4:9-13) would gather for the feasting, but all the nations and kings of the earth as well (v. 3; Zechariah 14:16; Psalm 72). In this way, the holy city would become the manifestation or epiphany of God's glory and light for all peoples, for all times.

At the time of his writing (near the end or immediately after the Babylonian exile, ca. 538 B.C.E.), the prophet's vision was far from a reality. Freed from their Babylonian oppressors, the exiles returned home to a devastated Jerusalem still in ruins. In an effort to rebuild the hopes and spirits of his people, the sixth century B.C.E. Trito-Isaiah painted for them a series of verbal portraits (chapters 60-62) of what Jerusalem could be and would be once again. Spurring his contemporaries to reconstruct the spiritual and liturgical as well as the physical aspects of the holy city, Trito-Isaiah kept before their eyes the ideal city of light. What had been promised to Abraham (that all nations would, by faith, become children of Abraham, Genesis 25) and what Deutero-Isaiah has prophesied in his book of consolation (Isaiah 40-55), Trito-Isaiah would see fulfilled (Isaiah 56-66). In the metaphorical language that had become standard in theophanic narratives, the prophet assured his people that the thick clouds and darkness (v. 2) would be dispelled. For Israel, these were symbolic of its shame and alienation from God due to infidelity to the covenant. For the nations, the dark clouds were a sign of the pall of ignorance that hung over those who had not yet been enlightened by the truth of revelation. But, because of its Lord, through Jerusalem the darkness and clouds would be dispelled. Trito-Isaiah's oracular vision was one of *universal* glory and light because from within the holy and renewed city the one true God would be manifested in light and life to *his* people and to *all* peoples.

Unlike his predecessors, whose prophecies had often been directed *against* the nations, Trito-Isaiah's *universalist* vision was representative of a prophetic spirit that emerged only after the exile. Believing that Israel's restoration to its own land and its renewed dignity as God's chosen people would have repercussions on the rest of humanity, Trito-Isaiah's prophecies took on a messianic and eschatological character. Because of the saving manifestation of the Lord within it, the redeemed Israel would become the manifestation of God's forgiving goodness for all other peoples of the earth. What God had done for Israel through his anointed, Cyrus (Isaiah 45:1), he would also do for the peoples of Midian, Ephah and Sheba.

Obviously, the vision of universal salvation that Trito-Isaiah kept before the eyes of his sixth century contemporaries was completely fulfilled only centuries later in the ultimate epiphany of God's glory: Jesus Christ. Only in and through the person and mission of Jesus have the dark clouds of sin and death been forever banished. Through Christ, and through the continued epiphany of his love which is the church, the alienation and aggression that threaten the unity of all peoples can be overcome.

The new Israel of God, brought into being by the incarnate Sun of Justice, is not merely a *reflection* of God's light. By reason of our incorporation into Christ through baptism, we *become one* with the very light and life. The light and glory that once gave hope and solace to the returning exiles should continue to characterize those who by their words and works would create of the disparate peoples of the earth a family of believers in the one saving God.

Ephesians 3:2-3, 5-6. What Trito-Isaiah's vision (first reading) had anticipated regarding the universal scope of God's saving plan, the author of Ephesians had already begun to witness as an evolving reality. Through the ministry of the holy apostles and Christian prophets, the epiphany of God's glory and light begun in Jesus was continuing to be manifested. As proof of this fact, the Ephesian's author cited the union that both Jews and gentiles shared in the body of Christ. As believers in the good news, both Jews and gentiles were partners, coheirs of all the promises of life and posterity which had punctuated the long history of Israel.

Because of the general nature of the letter and because the inscription "*to the Ephesians*" was not included in the earliest manuscripts, many scholars believe the missive was originally a circular letter or encyclical written for the churches in Asia Minor. As such, it brought its insights on universalism not just to one but to many different communities of the ancient world. Traditionally, the authorship of the letter was credited to Paul, though many today dispute that attribution. If the apostle from Tarsus was indeed the author, then the letter would have been composed during his last imprisonment in Rome, ca. 63 C.E.

Resembling a discourse more than a personal letter, the document is a composite of prayers (1:3—3:22) and paranesis (4:1—6:20) intended to edify and instruct. In the latter half of the first Christian century, the second and third generation Christians were in danger of losing sight of the mystery of God's secret plan (v. 2). With the delay of Jesus' second coming and the ultimate epiphany, believers had to be reminded of God's purpose. From prison, Paul shouldered the burden of keeping before the eyes of all believers the reality and inevitability of the kingdom. In that kingdom, already established by the mission of Jesus, all peoples would enjoy solidarity in Christ. That solidarity had already begun to grow through the ministry of the church and of Paul who regarded his work among the gentiles as mandated by God, part of the "secret plan" (v. 2). Despite the efforts of the Judaizers who followed Paul from mission to mission in order to thwart his work, the apostle was undaunted in his affirmation that the gentiles were "*coheirs*" with the Jews, *members* of the same body and *sharers* of the promise (v. 6). All three words in Greek begin with the prefix *syn* which signifies oneness and/or sameness. All three words dismissed forever the rigid distinctions and barriers that the chosen Israel of the old dispensation had erected between herself and all the non-chosen (gentiles). Because of the manifestation of God's love and goodness in Christ, *all* have become privileged and chosen to share in the grace and dignity of the kingdom. The darkness of human prejudice and the thick clouds of racism and bigotry must yield to the light of God's truth.

Matthew 2:1-12. In his excellent studies of the infancy narratives, R.E. Brown has referred to the first two chapters of Matthew's (and Luke's) gospel as a gospel in miniature. In a sort of digest of his work, the evangelist has masterfully included in his first two chapters all the main features of his gospel proper: (1) the universal scope of God's revealed plan of salvation, (2) an affirmation of Jesus' divine origins and messiahship, (3) the implications of God's plan and of Jesus' messiahship for believers, namely, a missiology of worldwide proportions.

Traditionally, believers have become accustomed to associating the stories of Matthew 1 and 2 with the *baby* Jesus; but the infancy narratives are really concerned with an adult Christ. Powerful and theologically profound, the narratives' true worth and importance has only begun to be understood and appreciated in this century.

Literally similar to Jewish legends and folk tales, the infancy narratives have been classified by some as midrash or a reflective interpretation of the scriptures. From the verb *darash*, to search, midrash contained: (a) *halakah* (literally, "how to walk"): guidelines for right living, and/or (b) *haggadah*: stories that featured certain important persons or events. In composing his narrative on Jesus' birth and first years, the Matthean evangelist had obviously *searched* the Jewish scriptures and had therefrom drawn many texts, persons and events in order to construct his stories about Jesus. Still, Matthew 1 and 2 represent *more* than a midrash or a reflective *commentary* on the scriptures. In their own right, Matthew 1 and 2 *are* scriptures and inspired *revelation* of the good news about Jesus, challenging believers to faith.

Structurally, the Matthean infancy narrative can be reduced to five major episodes of Jesus' life, each of which has been juxtaposed with five texts from the Old Testament. By so doing, the evangelist variously described Jesus in terms of (1) a new Moses, (2) a new David, (3) a new Solomon, (4) a new Elijah, and (5) founder of an everlasting royal dynasty. At the heart of today's episode is the refusal of the Jews (Herod, chief priests, scribes) to accept the new king and his royal dynasty as contrasted with the gentiles (astrologers) who did accept and reverence the Lord as king. Although the Jews had been steeped for centuries in scriptural prophecies and divine promises of the messiah, they did not recognize him when he appeared. Ironically, the evangelist portrayed the Jewish leaders (chief priests and scribes) as quoting to Herod some of the treasured texts that should have prepared them to accept Jesus (v. 6 = 2 Samuel 5:2, Micah 5:1). The astrologers, on the other hand, had not the advantage of the scriptures or messianic traditions, yet through the stars or the lesser witness of nature, they came to see the truth of Jesus' appearance. Matthew has included an apologetic concern as well. By accenting in the infancy narrative the refusal of the Jews and the faith of the gentiles, Matthew was reflecting the situation that characterized not only the appearance of Jesus, but also the ministry of the adult Jesus as well as the ministry of the Matthean church of the 80s C.E. Just as the chief priests and scribes had rejected the earthly Jesus, the Jewish authorities of Matthew's day were banning Jesus' followers from the synagogue and exposing them to persecution. Just as the Sanhedrin had delivered Jesus to Pilate and thereby to death, so too in Matthew's church, the Christians were being subjected to Jewish and to Roman persecution (Matthew 10:17-18).

A variety of explanations have been suggested for *the star* that led the astrologers to Christ. By way of natural or scientific explanations, the "star" could have been: (1) A supernova or a "new star" in which an explosion had occurred that emitted light even by daylight for weeks or months (Kepler). (2) A comet with a luminous tail of gasses and dust particles. Halley's comet did appear ca. 12 B.C.E.; but then, a comet is not a star. (3) A planetary conjunction of Jupiter and Saturn. According to Kepler's calculations, such a conjunction occurred ca. 7-6 B.C.E. which would concur with the birth of Jesus.

However interesting and plausible these natural and scientific explanations may be, it is more probable that the "star" in the Matthean narrative was more important for its *theological* and christological significance. In popular tradition and folklore, stars heralded the birth of a great person. For example, when Abraham was born, the appearance of a star was said to have struck fear into the heart of king Nimrud because the star signified that Abraham and his descendants would one day rule the earth. A star was rumored to have announced Nero's birth, though many of his comtemporaries believed the rumor to have been autobiographical! Surely, Matthew and his intended audience recalled the story of Balaam (Numbers 24:17) where in a visionary from the East saw the Davidic star rise and proclaim the greatness of Israel's god. So too in the Matthean narrative, the evangelist employed an astral herald to proclaim the appearance of Jesus and to beckon the gentiles to salvation. In the persons of the astrologers, Matthew has included all of the gentile community and thus widened the scope of the message of salvation to the universal proportions envisioned in today's first reading from Isaiah. For this reason, Epiphany has been known in some places as "Christmas of the gentiles" or simply "little Christmas."

1. *The glorious future for which we hope is a reality we have already begun to enjoy (Isaiah).*

2. *Clouds of prejudice and segregation have no place in the community whose leader has defined himself as light and life (Ephesians).*

3. *Converts who have searched long and traveled far often treasure the faith more than those who have grown up in its heritage (Matthew).*

Lord's Baptism

In baptism seeds are planted, the seeds of faith, communion and service. In the furrows of darkness and doubt, faith will be tried and deepened (Isaiah). When all the world's peoples are recognized as God's own, relationships will grow and communion will be cultivated (Acts). When every human activity is motivated by altruism and love, then the seed of service will flourish (Matthew). Baptism is but a planting of seeds, not the last but the first step in a lifelong commitment to the Lord.

Isaiah 42:1-4, 6-7. Various scholarly opinions have been put forth as to the correct identity of the servant described by Deutero-Isaiah. Some believe that the prophet conceived of his own vocation or that of another prophet (e.g., Jeremiah) in terms of the servant's mission. Other scholars have proposed that the entire nation of Israel was meant to embrace the mission of the servant. Saved by the Lord with whom she had been covenanted, Israel was responsible for being light for the nations and the agent of liberation for those held captive. There is yet another group of scholars who have proposed that a certain group within the nation (i.e., the poor ones or *anawim*) was to fulfill the vocation of the servant for its own people Israel and for the nations. As one set apart by God, the servant(s) was divinely empowered to extend the light and justice with which Israel would be blessed to the rest of the nations. When later generations sang the servant songs of Deutero-Isaiah (42:1-4, 6-7; 49:1-6; 50:4-9; 52:13—53:12), they attached their hopes to some future messianic figure through whom God would act on behalf of his people.

All these varying opinions concerning the servant's mission and identity were drawn together by the authors of the Christian scriptures who understood that these ancient songs of hope had been fulfilled in the person and ministry of Jesus of Nazareth. Obviously, Matthew had these songs in mind when he wrote of Jesus' baptism and of the confirmation of Jesus by the heavenly voice, "This is my beloved Son. My favor rests on him" (3:17). Compare this heavenly affirmation with the Isaian text: "Here is my servant whom I uphold, my chosen one with whom I am pleased" (42:1). Most believe that "son" (Matthew) is an ambiguous translation of the original Aramaic word for "servant" (Isaiah). So too, "beloved" (Matthew) is an alternative word for the term "chosen one" (Isaiah). In view of the servant's mission of suffering and death (see especially Isaiah 50:4-9, 52:13—53:12), the association of Deutero-Isaiah's songs with Jesus becomes even more obvious.

When the songs were first written in the sixth century B.C.E, the liberation described in vv. 6-7 was understood by Deutero-Isaiah and his contemporaries in exile as God's pledge that they would be once more established in their homeland, Israel. For Christians who believe in Jesus as the agent of their redemption, victory and liberation are understood as freedom from sin and death. Even in its original context, the mission of the servant also had an objective of a moral and religious nature. Israel had not just failed politically; she has also fallen short of the ethical, social and moral standards demanded by the covenant. For that reason, *salvation* was not conceived of simply as a *political* victory, i.e., a return to and a reestablishment in the land of Israel. On the contrary, the return home of the exiles was an external sign of a more profound salvation—the return to and reconciliation of Israel with the Lord. Only in the mission of Jesus Christ was this saving mission truly and definitively accomplished for all peoples, for all times.

Acts 10:34-38. By today's standards, the interaction between Peter and Cornelius and the policy regarding gentiles that issued forth from those proceedings would be called a "landmark case" or "landmark decision." What happened at Caesarea marked a turning point in the missionary efforts of the early church. The groundwork for the unqualified acceptance of gentiles into the community had, of course, begun in the missionary efforts of Philip, Stephen, etc., and was later officially confirmed by the statement of James at the Jerusalem council: "From the beginning, God has taken care to draw from the pagans a people for his name" (Acts 15:14). But what happened between Peter and Cornelius was so extraordinary that some biblical scholars have called the episode a "second" or the "gentile Pentecost."

Cornelius was a Roman soldier, a centurion stationed at the garrison in Caesarea. Like many gentiles, he was attracted to Judaism's monotheistic beliefs and strict code of ethics. Known by the Jews as a God-fearer, Cornelius belonged to that group of gentiles who attended synagogue services and observed the decalogue but did not submit to circumcision or to the dietary restrictions. By accepting Cornelius and his household, and in conceding that "God shows no partiality" (v. 34), Peter was moving beyond the boundaries that he as a good Jew would have regarded as sacred and inviolable. For the Jews, holiness had been outwardly signified by keeping the law, by circumcision and by the observance of certain dietary customs and feasts. Those who faithfully adhered to these regulations were considered clean and holy; those who did not observe these rules were thought to be unclean and therefore outside the pale of God's favor and saving graces. In accepting Cornelius without reserve and in declaring him to be upright (i.e., just, righteous; v. 35), Luke was teaching by means of Peter's speech that Christianity had obviated all former boundaries or barriers of acceptability. Because of Jesus' universal saving activity, and through his Holy Spirit, Cornelius (and all gentiles) was to be considered capable of being holy and just.

Apologetically and theologically, Luke, the author of Acts, utilized the Cornelius event to put to rest two difficulties that threatened the unity of the early church:

(1) Gentiles were free to come to Jesus and to share in the blessings of the messianic era without first becoming Jews. This insight resulted in the eventual independence of Christianity from its Jewish roots and matrix.

(2) Contact with gentiles did not result in ritual defilement of Jewish Christians. No longer an issue for modern believers, the question of ritual purity was a major obstacle for early Jewish Christians. For them to celebrate the sacraments, especially the eucharist, as one body united with one head, the Lord Jesus Christ, centuries of Jewish traditions had to give way to Christian universality. Through baptism into Christ Jesus, all persons become members of the greater human family and members also of the household of salvation Jesus died to establish.

Matthew 3:13-17. By the time Matthew wrote his gospel in the eighties C.E., the fact of Jesus' baptism by John had become a christological and theological issue to be reckoned with. Why would Jesus, who was sinless, participate in a rite for sinners? So too, why would Jesus, who as messiah was clearly superior to John, submit to the authority of a subordinate? Moreover, there still survived some of the Baptizer's disciples who clung to the idea that John had indeed been the messiah. For these loyal followers of John, Jesus' baptism provided fuel to fire their claims concerning their leader's authenticity and superiority. When Matthew (Luke and John also!) wrote of Jesus' baptism, therefore, he took into account these issues. It is probably for this reason that the evangelist glossed over the actual rite of the baptism with only a simple participle phrase, "after Jesus was baptized" (v. 16). Instead, Matthew chose to use the incident to emphasize (1) Jesus' messiahship, (2) the inauguration of his mission, and, with it, (3) the messianic era.

For the most part Matthew followed Mark in his account of Jesus' baptism, but by interpolating vv. 14-15 into his Marcan source, Matthew succeeded in dealing with the partiuclar concerns of his community. Notice that, unlike Mark, Matthew has shown John as realizing *before* the baptism that Jesus is the promised one of whom he has been prophesying. Despite John's objections ("I should be baptized by you," v. 14) Jesus participated in the rite of conversion at the Jordan. Some, especially G. Barth, were convinced that Jesus did so in order to express his humility and/or to give example to sinners, that they should do likewise. Others have suggested that Jesus' baptism was, rather, a symbolic sign of his association *with* sinners. By embracing sinners aby by taking upon himself the burden of their sin, Jesus was able to redeem them from it. Certainly, this aspect of Jesus' saving activity was indicated in the event of his baptism. This meaning has been affirmed as well be the heavenly voice whose message clearly associated the mission of Jesus with that of the Isain suffering servant (Isaiah 50:4-9, 52:13—53:12).

There is yet a further messianic nuance to be explored in the episode of Jesus' baptism by John. John's preaching indicated that those who submitted to the rite at the Jordan became thereby members of a community who lived in a state of eager anticipation of the messiah's advent. By being baptized, Jesus present within that community made it *properly* messianic and inaugurated the messianic era. Jesus' statement (only in Matthew), "We must do this if we would *'fulfill'* all of God's demands," underscored the messianic character of his actions. "Fulfill" (*pleroo*) meant more than "to do" or "to obey"; in Matthew's gospel the term usually referred to the fulfillment of prophecy. Matthew portrayed

Jesus as fulfilling the scriptures, i.e., the law and prophets. By his statement about fulfilling God's demands, Matthew indicated that Jesus' messianic mission, inaugurated at his baptism, would bring to full realization all prophetic hopes and complete every aspect of God's will as enunciated in the law.

As if to affirm Jesus' identity and his mission, the voice from heaven spoke. Literally *bath gol*, "daughter of a voice," the term was often used in rabbinical literature to refer to that means by which God revealed his purposes after prophecy had ceased. An "opened sky" (v. 17) no doubt reminded Matthew's readers of the text from Trito-Isaiah (64:1) concerning the advent of the messiah. The presence of the Spirit of God certainly implied that an anointing was taking place. Just as Israel's kings, priests and prophets were anointed by God for their respective tasks, just as the suffering servant (Isaiah 42:1-2 44:2, 62:4; Psalm 2:7) was anointed for his redeeming work, so too Jesus was endowed with and empowered by God's own Spirit. Besides signifying the Spirit, the dove was also seen as a figure for Israel as God's chosen people (Song of Songs 1:15, 2:14, 4:1, 5:2, 6:9). Perhaps we could understand the presence of the dove at Jesus' baptism as the symbol of the new Israel, the new people of God for whom Jesus' saving ministry will be exercised.

Finally, Matthew has altered the words of the voice from "you are" (as in Mark and Luke) to "*this is* my beloved Son." An obvious reference to Isaiah 42:1, this declaration and the reference to God's favor resting upon Jesus (v. 17) served to enthrone Jesus as messiah and to reveal him as Son and as savior of all peoples.

1. One of the most important responsibilities of the baptized is the maintenance of God's brand of justice among all the peoples of the earth (Isaiah).

2. Baptism initiates the believer into a worldwide community where those who were once thought of as foreign and strange are accepted as friends and family (Acts).

3. Baptism precludes singularity and selfishness; those who by faith are immersed into Christ enter with him into the service of all other peoples (Matthew).

The Lenten Season
First Sunday of Lent

Temptation is very much a part of human existence (Genesis). The mystery of Christ's victory over sin and death (Matthew) gives the believer a special strength and dignity in the daily struggle to enjoy the gifts of redemption—justice, grace, life (Romans).

Genesis 2:7-9, 3:1-7. An awareness of sin and its effects pervades each of the readings of today's liturgy. Today originally marked the beginning of Lent and set a penitential tone for the period of preparation for Easter. Throughout the season the first (Old Testament) readings will focus on salvation history as the prelude to God's redemptive act in Christ. The second readings serve to advise the believer as to his/her place in that saving act, and the gospels of Lent, year A (Third Sunday and following), will treat the Johannine signs of salvation.

To the author of today's first reading from Genesis, the existence of sin in the world was a painful reality. The fact that humanity was affected by sin was an all too obvious fact. Against this grim backdrop, the beauty and poetic genius of the author stand in sharp contrast. In this attempt to uncover the root or origin of sin and in these efforts to expose the evil effects of sin in the world, the author has produced a masterpiece which has since rarely been equalled in the field of literature.

Although the creation account in Genesis 2 follows that of Genesis 1, it is by far the more primitive version and is attributed to J or the Yahwistic strand of the Pentateuch. As the earliest written account (around tenth century B.C.E.), the J source exhibits an awareness of similar stories or myths in the literature and traditions of other peoples of the ancient Near Eastern world. While retaining unique and authentic revelation in his account, the author nevertheless made use of imagery and symbols from these popular legends. One can detect vestiges of the Babylonian creation myth (Enuma Elish) as well as the Saga of Eden, a popular Canaanite and Akkadian tale. Similarities to the Epic of Gilgamesh and the myth of Ea and Adapa can also be detected. Indeed, references to the serpent and the forbidden fruit may be aimed at the fertility cults practiced in Canaan at the time of the author's writing. Regardless of such similarities, the authors of Genesis, inspired by God, have woven for the benefit of our faith a tapestry of poetic answers to all of life's most important questions. That there is obvious scientific ignorance in the text should not deter us, because the point of view is not a scientific but a theological one.

Within the pages of Genesis, the heroes of our faith are portrayed warts and all, the first of these being *Adam*. Whether we are to understand by Adam one man or the possibility of polygenism does not weaken the point of the narrative in any way. Adam's story is the story of each of us. Adam's role and therefore our own roles are depicted as unique in creation, in that all the rest of creation is *for* Adam. The integral nature of Hebrew anthropology (as opposed to

Greek) is illustrated in the breath of God infusing life into the clay. It is obvious that the Hebrews, at this point in their theological and anthropological development, did not conceive of an abiding, eternal soul. Were God to withdraw his breath, the person would revert to the dead matter from whence he came.

In the story of the fall, fragments of ancient myths abound. Adam and Eve allow themselves to be duped by a distorted truth, "You will be like gods." In disobeying God's orders, they are alienated, not only from God but from one another. Their consciousness of nakedness is more than an awareness of sex. It is a stark reminder of their shame—that God put before them life but they freely and willingly chose death. Therein we find the point of the author's poetry—that the source of sin and evil in the world is none other than the human heart.

Romans 5:12-19. While the logic of Paul's thoughts is better preserved without his digression about Adam (short form), his unique contribution to theology that compares Christ and Adam is far too important to omit. In comparing Adam's deeds and their effect on history to Christ's work and its effect, Paul works out an antithetical parallelism with Adam as type and Christ as antitype. The point of the passage is that sin and its tangled web of evil are finally overcome and that human beings are free because of the liberating act of Jesus' death and rising.

The sin which entered the world is not a crime for which Adam alone is to be blamed, because all men (and women) have also sinned. The gap between God and humanity created by Adam is widened with each one's sin. That all have inherited sin (original) was the understanding given to this text by the Council of Trent. But the Greek fathers understood that inheritance as more by way of environment than by genetics. With Adam, a chain reaction of evil was introduced into the world and no one is unaffected by it. This does not negate our personal culpability and responsibility for our own sin. Just as sin is freely chosen, so too the sins of each confirm and reiterate Adam's rebellion. Sin can be understood (v. 12, *hemarton*) in its literal sense as missing the mark: Each sin is an act by which the goal for which we were intended (union with God) is denied.

The Christian, taught Paul, should have an even keener sense of sin because of our greater awareness of the extent and magnanimity of God's love as revealed in the person and mission of Jesus Christ. An excellent reprise of the first reading, this text from Romans tells again the consequences of Adam's fall (viz. death). With Christ comes life. Just as the effects of sin were universal, a burden felt by all peoples, so too the salvation of Christ will universally free all from those burdens. Notice too the reference to "offense" and "gift." Paul emphasizes the fact of Christ's grace, the gift of love and life, as far more powerful than sin. This knowledge (that with Christ goodness will never be overcome by evil) points ahead to the gospel message.

Matthew 4:1-11. Those Christians of the 80s for whom Matthew's gospel was intended must have drawn encouragement in their trials and tribulations from today's verses. Jesus' life, totally centered on God, was to be their (and our) model in the struggle of Christian living.

Most scholars, citing the similarity between Matthew's and Luke's accounts of the temptation of Jesus, posit a common source for both versions. Other scholars, basing themselves on the fact that there were no eyewitnesses to the event (though is isn't inconceivable that Jesus may have related the happening to them), posit an origin in the early church's teaching about dealing with temptation.

Still others regard the temptation narrative as a midrash, explaining particular issues in Jesus' life and ministry in terms of Old Testament events. The comparison of Jesus and Moses has already been made in Matthew's gospel. In this pericope, Jesus is depicted as the new Israel. Israel was tested "40" days in the desert. Unlike Israel, however, Jesus emerged victorious from that which tempted him in his resolve to do God's will. The first temptation is reminiscent of the manna of the wilderness and Jesus' answer to the tempter is a direct quotation of Deuteronomy 8:3. The lesson of the manna went unlearned by Israel but is epitomized in Jesus: trust in God and in his daily sustaining care. In the second test as well as in the third, Jesus' answers are drawn from Deuteronomy (6:16 and 6:13). There is of course no mountain from which all the earth's kingdoms can be seen. Perhaps Matthew is drawing on the rabbinic legend based on Deuteronomy 34:1, that from Mount Nebo Moses could see all the kingdom of Israel. Legend has it too that Moses was tempted there by the devil. In either case the point is made that Jesus was undaunted in his resolve to do the Father's will.

The temptations described were, because of Jesus' nature and capacities, messianic. Although they are presented as a unique circumstance, these same trials probably haunted Jesus throughout his ministry. Probably too, the temptation narrative was aimed at those who refused to accept the idea of a humble, serving, saving messiah. Jesus' resistance to the fame, power and wealth offered him could be seen as a prod for those who saw these as characteristics of the messiah they awaited.

1. That God believes us worthy of a second chance is evident in the way he deals with his people throughout the ages (Genesis).

2. That one person can do so much for so many is evident in the life and death of Jesus Christ (Romans).

3. Being tempted is part of being human; overcoming temptation is part of belonging to Christ (Matthew).

Second Sunday of Lent

God's call and response in faith (Genesis) is the rhythm that has marked the seasons in the epic saga of our salvation history. In the glory of Christ Jesus (Matthew), the crescendo of the perfect response is sustained that we might have life and grace in him (2 Timothy).

Genesis 12:1-4. Throughout the centuries, the patriarchal sagas have inspired and sustained the faith of Jews, Christians and the adherents of Islam. Like any epic hero story, there is an essential truth around which has been woven a magnificent tapestry of fiction, legend, tradition and myth. Because of this element of embellishment, some scholars in the past regarded the patriarchs (as well as other key figures in Old Testament) as symbolic, eponymous ancestors. However, because of the witness of archaeology and scientific investigation, it is the more widely held conviction today that Abraham did at one point in human history respond to God's call, and as such became the father of the people of God.

In looking at human history, the believer sees God acting in time and space through men and women, such as the patriarchs, whose response to God in faith makes the will of God a reality in human existence. God's call and the human response culminated in the life and mission of Christ and through Christ in his church.

This reading is the beginning of the Abraham cycle (chapters 12-50), an introduction to the story of Israel. Abraham's faith response to God's call began a new era of salvation, punctuated by God's intervention and colored vividly by God's loving providence. When the saga was actually written down, it was infused with the faith of those believers for whom Abraham represented the first in a long line of heroes. As such, Abraham is depicted as taller than life but it is still quite clear that in his dealings with God, God was always the initiator, giver, guide and Lord. By no merits of his own did he become the recipient of God's special election. Nevertheless, though his was a posture of subordination, Abraham's response is the work of a great heart. His wholehearted answer to God's call required what Kierkegaard called so accurately a "leap of faith." His was a challenge to metanoia, a conversion. Abraham was to turn from a pagan, idolatrous past and from his homeland, to chart out a new existence in relationship with one true living God.

As reward for his response, Abraham was promised progeny, prosperity and land which may be called the ancient equivalent of life, liberty and the pursuit of happiness. Even the promised reward was a test for his faith. In Genesis 11:30, Sarah's sterility was affirmed, yet in the face of human limitation, God acts.

In direct contrast to what happened in the Babel story, i.e., that God confused and scattered those who were trying "to make a name" for themselves (Genesis 11:4), God made the name of Abraham great, so great that it became a blessing.

The verb $w^e ribr^e ku$ in v. 3 has been translated to mean that the patriarch's name would itself be a blessing. An interesting tradition has it that, in the ancient Near Eastern world, the name of Abraham uttered at the boundaries of one's land was considered as legal as a surveyor's document, as real as a fence. Then the verb is repeated in the passive sense, "all communities... shall find blessing in you" or "shall be blest in you." The promises to Abraham made him a futuristic figure—pointing ahead to the exodus of Israel, to Sinai and to Canaan. His faith Israel had to make her own.

2 Timothy 1:8-10. The letters to Timothy and Titus are generally grouped together due to a similarity in content, style and theology. Since the early 18th century, they have been called the pastoral epistles. Addressed to Timothy, a convert from Lystra (Acts 16:1) and frequent companion of Paul, the letters were intended to be an aid to the spiritual leader of the church of Ephesus. Reiterating the thought of the first reading concerning God's call, the author acknowledges the sufferings that are concomitant with one's response to that call. Besides the internal persecution caused by heresy and false teachings, the letter reflects a situation of political persecution as well. It seems too that Timothy had his own personal sufferings to deal with: lack of self-confidence in his ability to lead, health concerns and so on. To all these problems, the author posits one answer. In Jesus Christ and through him comes *grace*, and by that grace, the Christian can with Christ be victorious over all hardships, over sin and over death.

Matthew 7:1-9. Some scholars believe the transfiguration to be an anachronism, a post-resurrection appearance projected back into Jesus' ministry. Others see it as a theological effort of the early church to explain Jesus' mission as the fulfillment of the law and the prophets. While the event is probably grounded in some very real experience on the part of the disciples, it has been reconstructed and embellished so as to be a useful kerygmatic and didactic tool for evangelization in the first century C.E.

Placed (in Matthew) immediately after the confession of Peter and prediction of the passion, the transfiguration presents Jesus in a foretaste of the future glory of Jesus-messiah. It is not a coincidence that the same apostles (Peter, James and John) were singled out to witness both the transfiguration and Jesus' agony (chapter 26). Both incidents reveal the double aspect of the mystery of our salvation: Jesus' suffering (agony) and his ultimate glorification. With a myriad of Old Testament themes and ideas, Matthew has related the theophany. Although the location is rather vague, "a high mountain," the fathers in the fourth century C.E. decided that Tabor was the site. Later scholars have found this to be unlikely since Tabor is little more that a hill (1850 ft.) Perhaps a more likely spot would have been majestic Hermon (9000 ft.). In truth, the locale of the high mountain was probably of more theological significance than its geographical location. By it, the gospel writer wished to jog the memories of his hearers, to recall Sinai. Matthew intends to depict Jesus as the new Moses, with a new law for a new Israel. Several elements in today's text are also found in Deuteronomy 10:5-11 and Exodus 24:12-16. The cloud (*shekinah*) signalling God's presence is reminiscent of the guiding cloud in the desert and the cloud over the tent of meeting (Exodus 40:34). The message of the voice from the cloud is, as it was at the baptism, a designation of Jesus as the servant foretold by Deutero-Isaiah. "Listen to him" sounds very much like the invitations given in the sapiential literature, to listen to wisdom (Proverbs 5:7, 8:33; Sirach 6:35, 21:15). Christ, the embodiment of all wisdom, is to be the teacher of God's mysteries. Moses and Elijah, who represent law and the prophets respectively, teach by their presence that Jesus is the conclusion toward which both law and prophets were to move the people.

Peter's desire to extend the encounter by erecting tents has a deeper significance as well. Immediately, one is reminded of the Old Testament feast of tents (booths, tabernacles: Deuteronomy 16:13-15) which recalled Israel's wilderness days. In commemoration of that period in history, the people celebrated by dwelling in tents for seven days. In later Jewish tradition, the feast was marked by a display of lights (his face shone!) and eventually the feast of tents came to be connected with the triumphal and final epiphany of God's kingship of the world (Zechariah 14).

Even though Matthew softens Mark's version by omitting Peter's ignorance and downplaying the fearfulness of the apostles, a certain amount of fear (the Greek has "awe") was an understandable and perhaps necessary reaction. In Rudolf Otto's concept of the numinous experience, the other side of fascination is fear: *mysterium tremendum et fascinans*. By his incarnation, Jesus Christ brought into human existence the radiance of divinity. Transfigured for his disciples, Jesus pointed beyond the cross to his sovereignty over all peoples.

1. All who believe in one God are children of Abraham, and proof of God's power to keep his promises (Genesis).

2. The Christian knows that life may be difficult at times, but the Christian is confident that he/she is well-equipped for any exigency (Romans).

3. There is no greater power of personal transformation than love (Matthew).

Third Sunday of Lent

Thirst in the scriptures usually means more than the physical need for water (Exodus). So too, the quenching or slaking of that thirst has a far deeper significance (John). Complete satisfaction of all our thirsts and desires is found in the salvation effected by Jesus Christ (Romans).

Exodus 17:3-7. Water figured importantly in Palestine, historically, theologically and geographically. Creation was conceived as the spirit (God's breath) hovering over the primordial waters. Symbolic of God's power, the deluge was understood as the purification of sinful humanity. Basic to Israel's formation as a people was an historical event called the exodus, portrayed as a watery passage to freedom. Water was an absolute necessity in a land where sustenance and growth had to be wrested from a parched earth. An abundance of water was valued as God's blessing.

With water so precious a commodity, and with thirst a constant companion, these metaphors readily lent themselves to an understanding of Israel's need for God (responsorial psalm). In today's first reading, although the people were grumbling for water in the desert, their needs were spiritual as well as physical. Following immediately upon the narratives about the manna and the quail, the incident at Rephidim underscores the constant and providential care of God for his people. Bereft of human resources, their relationship to God stood out in bold relief against the threats of the desert. Without God to guide and care for them, the wilderness would have become their tomb. But with God and because of him, the desert "flowered" and "showered" for their welfare.

There are other incidents of thirst in the wilderness (Exodus 15:22-27, Numbers 20:2-13). These and the incident in today's text may be variants of the same event. The names given to the spot, Massah and Meribah, flow from Israel's attitude and posture toward the Lord and his representative, Moses. True to form, God's loving response is completely unmerited. In providing water for the people from the rock, the wondrous power of God is made manifest and the people are satisfied. In later tradition, the rabbis taught that this water-giving rock actually followed the people through the wilderness. Later, Paul perceived in this legend a type of Christ (1 Corinthians 10:4).

Romans 5:1-2, 5-8. The spirit of celebration in the psalm response is carried over into Paul's words from Romans. In 3:21-4 Paul established the fact that justification has come through the redeeming power of God in Jesus Christ. In today's pericope, based on the premise of that justification, Paul sets forth its consequences, viz., we are at peace with God, we have access to grace; we can boast in joyful hope of sharing God's glory. Paul speaks in terms of the Holy Spirit and the incomprehensible love of God. It is obvious that the apostle wishes us to understand God's love as a living reality within the believer. Naming the Holy Spirit (also a gift) as a witness to that love, Paul herein plants the seeds for the doctrine of the trinity ("peace with God, through our Lord Jesus Christ . . . through the Holy Spirit"). Today's text, taken in conjuction with Romans 8:15 and Galatians 4:6, lends itself to an understanding of the life of the Christian with regard to the trinitarian God.

Paul's joy is contagious as he describes these blessings of justification in terms of *present* realities: "now," "we are at peace," "in which we now stand." Liberated from sin and death, the Christian enjoys that freedom here and now in time and space, yet constantly moving toward the total freedom and complete perfection which will come with Christ in eternity. Because he enjoys the gifts of salvation here and now, the Christian is consequently responsible for those same gifts here and now. This world, its exigencies and problems form the training ground wherein those gifts are received and enjoyed. Hence, to wait for "pie in the sky when we die" would be completely opposed to the call to Christian living.

John 4:4-42. In this fourth chapter, the author's particular literary style is evident. John's use of replacement theology portrays Jesus as the water of life, replacing the water which quenched the thirst of Judaism throughout the ages, i.e., the Torah. In both the rabbinical writings and those at Qumran, the Torah (law) is described as water which purifies, slakes thirst and sustains life. In vv. 13-14, Jesus offers the thirsty believer the water of eternal life. By our baptism, we bathe in and drink of that source of life. Another Johannine technique was to contrast the various levels of (mis)understanding. Our text today has several such examples. Not only did the woman not understand what water Jesus offered her, she did not even understand why Jesus spoke to her at all. Rabbis did not ordinarily socialize publicly with women. Moreover, Jews traditionally disassociated themselves from Samaritans whom they considered an impure race. (Samaritans were the descendants of the northern kingdom, conquered in 722 B.C.E., who had intermarried with foreigners and worshipped on Gerizim.) That the woman came to faith (and with her many of the Samaritans) underscores another favorite Johannine theme: the Jews and their refusal to believe as contrasted with those outside the Jewish tradition who do come to faith in Jesus as the Christ. Upon returning to him, the apostles also misunderstand Jesus' reference to "food" (v. 32). John has Jesus explain that his daily bread is the Father's will. One is reminded of Jesus' answer to the tempter (Matthew 4:4; Deuteronomy 8:3).

The reference to the woman's husband(s) is obviously a display of Jesus' supernatural power, though some scholars would attach further symbolism to the *five* husbands. Origen saw it as reference to the fact that the Samaritans regarded only the Pentateuch as revealed by God. Others see it as a paranomasia i.e., husband is *ba'al* in Hebrew which is also the name for the Canaanite deity. Perhaps there is an indication of the five gods (*baalim*) which Samaria had worshipped. In any case, the woman's attempt to change the subject is a deft manuever in that she turned Jesus' attention to the main bone of contention between Jews and Samaritans: where to worship, Jerusalem or Gerizim? Jesus' answer is bound up with the concept of the "hour," his hour. Used 26 times in the fourth gospel, the word meant for the evangelist far more than a marking of chronological time. "Hour" referred to that moment for which Jesus had come, the moment or event of salvation accomplished through his death, resurrection and return to the Father. Because of that "hour" and the new relationship with God which it effects, all former approaches to God and places of worship are transcended and rendered obsolete. Because of Jesus Christ, henceforth, all would worship in his spirit and in his truth.

Samaritans eagerly awaited a messiah (*ta'eb*, returning one) as did the Jews, but Samaritan messianism was not so nationalistic, nor did they anticipate a kingly figure. Rather, the Samaritan concept was more that of a teacher and a lawgiver. Perhaps for this reason, the fourth gospel shows Jesus ready to accept the woman's identification of him. The divine "I am" was surely not lost on the woman since it recalled Exodus 3:14, the revelation of the sacred name.

In the dialogue with the disciples at the end of the discourse, the concerns of the evangelist and his church emerge between the lines of the narrative. By the time the author wrote, Samaria had been converted to Christ (Acts 8) and the harvest, which for the synoptics was to take place at the end of time, was already happening in John's church at the turn of the century.

1. At times, though hungry or thirsty, we grumble. Could it be that we are too satisfied (Exodus)?

2. The joy, which the death of Jesus has bestowed upon us, should be seen on our faces and in our lives (Romans).

3. In the wellspring of eternal life, our hope and faith in Jesus Chist will find rest and fulfillment (John).

Fourth Sunday of Lent

The blindness of disbelief is a self-inflicted wound (John) whereas the insight and illumination which the believer enjoys (Ephesians) are the gratuitous gift of a loving God (1 Samuel).

1 Samuel 16:1, 6-7, 10-13. The Bible makes quite clear the total and complete freedom of divine election. Not only did they whom the Lord chose not merit his choice, but those chosen seemed to be the least likely candidates. Moses, for example, was a murderer and had some difficulty with public speaking. Jonah hated those to whom he was sent to preach. Jeremiah was so young. In New Testament times, Peter was rash and impetuous; James and John were ambitious; and Paul started out on the wrong side of the fence! Even in his choice of Israel, God's action was not compelled by any human merits (Deuteronomy 7:7).

Today's text underscores God's method and his "madness." The least likely son of Jesse, the youngest, left at home to tend sheep, is the one whom the Lord chose to be king of his people. Samuel, in anointing David, performed the customary ritual of consecration in the ancient Near Eastern world. Not unique to Israel, anointing set one apart for a special task. Priest, prophets and even furniture and vessels were anointed (Exodus 31:25ff). In the Jewish tradition, the anointing signified the presence of the Lord's Spirit with the anointed. There are two other instances of David being anointed at Hebron, once by the men of Judah (2 Samuel 2:4) and again by the elders of Israel (2 Samuel 5:4). In these later anointings, the purpose was to affirm loyalty by pact and the anointing was a sign of veneration and allegiance.

The connection between this and the other readings may be in the anointing as a sign of consecration. By baptism's anointing, the Christian is empowered by God's spirit for the special task of reflecting the light of Jesus Christ in a world darkened by sin.

Ephesians 5:8-14. Scholars believe that the letter to the Ephesians was probably addressed to that ancient community about a century after it was written. Because it lacks personal and local references and because none of the early manuscripts contains 1:1 (title and address), it may have been a circular letter addressed to the churches of Asia Minor. Because of the reference in Colossians 4:16, Marcion entitled it "To the Laodiceans."

Up until the late 18th century, Pauline authorship remained undisputed. Since that time, however, those who reject an authentic Pauline authoring base their objections on differences in language, style, content and doctrinal emphases. Regardless of its intended designation or its author, the letter remains a magnificent and edifying compilation of prayers and paranetic preaching. If a Pauline authorship is presumed, the references in the letter to prison would probably indicate a Roman origin, in the 60s C.E. Indeed the nature of some of the metaphors betrays a gnostic influence which would fit in with a first century setting.

While the entire letter is studded with jewels of ancient prayers and hymns, chapters one through three proclaim God's plan to create a new community, comprised of all peoples, admitting of no barriers. Chapters four through six are paranetic or hortatory in style and serve to contrast the pagan way of life (or death) with the life held out to the believer by Jesus Christ.

Today's pericope deals with the subject of conversion to Jesus Christ. Conversion has been expressed in many vivid metaphors in the New Testament, viz., changing of clothes, putting on new person (man) (Galatians 3:27), putting on armor (Romans 13:14) and, in the example of today's text, moving from darkness to light. Each of the metaphors communicates a similar message. Conversion to Christ involved turning away, putting off, divestiture, rejection of all that is not Christ and a turning toward, a putting on, an investiture, an acceptance of all that is Jesus Christ.

Our text today may well have formed part of a baptismal liturgy, especially the fragment in v. 14 of an ancient hymn. One can detect the strains of hymns from the Old Testament, especially Isaiah, who envisioned the glorious age of the Lord as one of light (Isaiah 60:1; 26:10; 9:2). In baptism, which the early church called "enlightening" or "illumination" (*photismos*), the Christian shares in the radiant light of Christ's glory and truth. That same light penetrated the darkness of our earth, in its sin and death, when the word became flesh. In that same light the blind man rejoiced and found his sight (today's gospel).

John 9:1-41. The cure of the man born blind was the sixth of the seven signs in the fourth gospel. Unlike the synoptics, for whom the miracles of Jesus were primarily acts of power and for whom the wonders Jesus performed were many, John is much more selective in his telling. Relating only seven wonders, he calls them *signs* rather than miracles, and he plays down the wondrous nature of the events in favor of a symbolic intention. For the evangelist of the late 90s C.E., Jesus' wondrous deeds on earth were signs pointing to a greater, deeper reality. Within the material deed and temporal circumstance, one was to perceive a glimpse of what would actually take place when Jesus' "hour" had come at last. For those with faith, the sign is a window to eternity. For the willful disbelieving, the sign is an enigma which dies in its material circumstances. In today's wonderful story, woven through with Johannine irony, misunderstanding and replacement theology, the man born blind truly sees the sign of Jesus as light of the world and the Pharisees remain in the darkness of their stubborn refusal of faith.

John 8:12 contained the announcement, "I am the light of the world; anyone who follows me will not be walking in the dark; he will have the light of life," which served to introduce the sign in chapter 9. Besides the obvious fact of the healing of the man born blind, there are literally layers of lessons to be "peeled" from this sign. The first and most obvious is that, in the words and works of Jesus Christ, light is made manifest in the darkness. That sight came to one who had never seen was wonderful indeed. But even more wonderful was the faith of which that sight was the sign. The fact that the man was *born* blind and had never seen, is repeated in vv. 1, 2, 13, 18, 19, 20, 24, 32. Significantly the man, in the process of receiving physical sight, also becomes a believer. The gradual development of his faith in response to Jesus appears in vv. 12, 17, 33 and the culmination comes in vv. 34-36 wherein he calls Jesus by the messianic and divine titles of "Son of Man" and "Lord." The man's sight and faith are ironically contrasted to the lack of sight and faith of the Pharisees (vv. 17, 19, 24-30). They had eyes but would not see; they had the law, the prophets and the writings, but could not hear the word; they were the holy ones, but they did not believe!

Another set of lessons are apologetic ones. First, Jesus himself clears up the debate over the reason for the man's blindness. Jewish thought held that all sickness was a punishment for sin, even another's sin: "The fathers have eaten sour grapes and their children's teeth are set on edge" (Jeremiah 31:29, Ezekiel 18:2). The error persisted though the Lord, through the prophets, had corrected this idea by teaching personal responsibility for personal sin. In the Pharisees' two interrogations of the man (vv. 13-17, 28-33), the problems Jesus encountered in his ministry and the problems his church encountered after his death are evident. In the first case, the Jewish officials faulted Jesus for his attitude with regard to the Sabbath and its laws (vv. 13-17). In the second case (vv. 28-33), the strain between the Jewish Christians and the Jews was at the breaking point if in fact the breach had not already occurred at the time of John's writing. Notice the parents' fearfulness to answer and the man's bodily ejection from the synagogue. These problems arose in the last two decades of the first century and culminated in the edict of Jamnia which ousted Christians once and for all from the synagogue.

A further lesson is a baptismal one. One can readily see why this story was a favorite choice for baptismal liturgies in the early church. The healing gestures of Jesus, the anointing and the use of spittle, became part of the early baptismal ritual. That the man received his sight after *washing* in the pool of Siloam has obvious baptismal significance. John's interpretation of the word Siloam is not coincidental. His translation draws the connection between the pool and Jesus, the "one sent by God" (John 3:17) that all may have life. Significant too is the fact that water from the pool of Siloam was used in the feast of tabernacles at which (7:37-38) Jesus proclaimed himself to be the source of water for the thirsty believer.

1. By our baptism, we are anointed, consecrated and set apart for a great mission (1 Samuel).

2. Dark, secret sinful deeds have no place in the life of an enlightened believer (Ephesians).

3. There is no greater blindness than self-deception (John).

Fifth Sunday of Lent

A new life is a wondrous miracle on the purely physical level. How much more wondrous is the restoration of life to that which is parched in death (Ezekiel)? Resurrection to eternal life (John) goes beyond "wondrous" to glorious. In the very spirit of God (Romans) we are able to share divine life.

Ezekiel 37:12-14. If Ezekiel's media had been the artist's oils and canvas, he may have been named the father of surrealistic art. His unusual visions and symbolic stories, his unique allegories and bizarre ideas have earned him the dubious distinction of being thought fanatic, abnormal, even catatonically schizophrenic. But his genius and spiritual greatness belie these critical categories and he stands out, not only in biblical but in world literature, as an extraordinary giant of a man.

Identified as son of Buzi, Ezekiel (*God is strong* or *God strengthens*) was a priest of the Zadokite line and probably exercised a double ministry among his people. Preaching to those in Palestine before 587, his prophesying brought sinful Judah a message of doom. In the wake of Josiah's reform, with the religious fervor of the people at a low ebb, Ezekiel foretold the deserved demise of the kingdom. He saw his words become reality as a result of Babylon's conquering might. When he was deported, along with the elite of his people, Ezekiel's ministry was transformed from prophet of unmitigated doom to prophet of irrepressible hope. Truly he was a man for all seasons, interpreting the hand of God in human history, in good times and in bad. Our pericope for today is excerpted from a longer vision (37:1-14) and was spoken in Babylon to hearten the exiles.

Ezekiel's vision of the field of dry bones gave visual expression to the feelings of hopelessness and desperation his people felt. Without their land, they were not a people, they had no sense of purpose and no future. They were "dry bones" parched by their sins of pride and infidelity. But the exiles were not well disposed to understand their situation as justly deserved punishment and they complained against the Lord. Ezekiel tempered their arrogance by his teaching of personal and individual responsibility for sin (chapter 18). To the discouraged and the displaced, the prophet's vision of the bones taking flesh and coming to life held out new hope.

In v. 12. where our text begins, the metaphor shifts from *bones* to *graves*. Ezekiel saw the return to the land as a resurrection from the grave, as a new exodus from death to life. The rising from the graves, as described by Ezekiel, signifies Israel's corporate rising from captivity. The reference is not specifically concerned with the resurrection from the dead of individuals, but that eschatological concept cannot be ruled out.

Just as at creation God's spirit called forth life, in Ezekiel's vision that same spirit enables the people to rise from their graves of despair to a new hope. The prophet saw himself as mediator of that spirit by his ministry among his fellow exiles. In a very real sense, Ezekiel, who summoned his people from their graves to life, is a type of the Christ depicted in today's gospel ("Lazarus, come out!").

Romans 8:8-11. Basic to our understanding of Paul's words today is a knowledge of what exactly the apostle means by "flesh." Taken out of the context of the entirety of Paul's thought, it may seem he thought flesh was evil. On the contrary, he regarded all created things as good. Flesh (*sarx*) as Paul saw it was that material and natural aspect of humanity which of itself was morally indifferent, but had become for many an instrument for sinning. Because by sinning one accrued for himself the wages of death (Romans 6:23), the three concepts—flesh, sin and death—were very much interrelated for Paul. Speaking analogously, the apostle may have said: flesh is to sin is to death as spirit is to goodness is to life.

In chapter 8, Paul developed the theme of the Christian life which, when lived in the spirit, is destined for glory. The Spirit of God as the principle of Christian vitality is that same Spirit which God manifested in his plan of salvation (Old Testament) and in the ultimate bringer of our salvation, Jesus Christ. Whereas sin once found its home in human beings, those who open their hearts to the word (Christ) become homes (temples!) for his Spirit. To belong to Christ means more than grateful acknowledgment of what Christ has effected for humanity. It is more than external identification or nominal relationship with Christ. To belong to Jesus Christ is to open our hearts and minds and wills to his Spirit living in us. Such a "spirited" life anticipates in time and space the eternal realities of resurrected life. Such a life tastes eternity as it hints at the absolute and complete renewal which will take place in the end time.

Paul understood the conundrum that is the human being, possessor of a deserved mortality and an undeserved gift of immortality, in terms of the Greek anthropology. Body and spirit (*sarx* and *pneuma*) are held in tension by the call of God's Spirit dwelling in us and our response in faith to God's inspiration within us. The accomplishment of Jesus Christ, in his death and resurrection, is a force which impels us to strive toward the life his Spirit affords us.

John 11:1-45. As the last and therefore the greatest of the seven signs in the fourth gospel, the raising of Lazarus is the threshold to the Passover event which it introduces. The point of the narrative is in Jesus' words to Martha, "I am the resurrection and the life: whoever believes in me, though he should die, will come to life; and whoever is alive and believes in me will never die" (v. 25-26). Jesus' raising of Lazarus to life is in effect a visual presentation of Paul's theology in the second reading. The Bethany event holds the sum total of Jesus' words and works. He is life; he is the resurrection for all believers!

The synoptics make the cleansing of the temple the turning point of their gospels. For the author of the fourth gospel, the Lazarus event is the turning point. From then onward the plot to dispose of Jesus thickens. Ironically (Johannine irony), the act of raising his friend to life set in motion the events that led Jesus to his death. John, with his characteristic high christology, portrays Jesus as Lord of life, as life itself going to his death.

Although the synoptics do not mention Lazarus, John may have been privy to an early authentic tradition concerning the miracle. However, even with historic roots, the person of Lazarus, referred to as "the one whom you loved," is a paradigm of the Christian believer in Jesus. We too, like Lazarus, will by Jesus' power pass from death to life. As believers, eternal life is already ours. Because of this realized eschatology (baptism, eucharist) our physical death will truly be a passover, an exodus.

Several details in the narrative underscore the miraculous nature of the event. Lazarus had been dead for four days; this meant that he was most assuredly and irretrievably gone.

Rabbinical tradition taught that the life breath hovered around the body for three days. After that, all hopes for resuscitation were pointless. Recall that, in the synoptics, Jesus had raised to life people (widow's son, daughter of Jairus) who had been dead for less than 24 hours. This difference emphasizes that, for the Johannine Jesus, the impossible is merely a matter of routine. Notice, too, the reasons why Jesus delayed going to the ailing Lazarus: "so that you may come to believe" and so that "if you believed you would see the glory of God." As in the cure of the man born blind, Jesus' acts glorify God and challenge faith. In both signs, God is glorified and revealed to the believer.

The two cures (the blind man and Lazarus) revealed Jesus as light and life, putting into action the words of the prologue (1:4): "that life was the light of men." Jesus the incarnate word is also the incarnate light and life of God who by his ministry and in his hour poured forth light and life upon all believers.

Thomas' words, "Let us go along, to die with him," strike another chord of Johannine irony. Surely, in his fervor and love for Jesus, Thomas expressed his willingness to die with the master. But there is more than fervor in these words; Johannine soteriology is the hidden, deeper meaning. In Christ's death, all of us can die to sin, and by our baptism we not only die but rise with him too. Thomas' words describe what happens to all who "go along" with Jesus. All go to death and through death to life.

Jesus' emotion (v. 33: "troubled in spirit") as he approached the tomb has long been the subject of debate. Some scholars point to his sorrow at Lazarus' death. But sadness would be out of place if one knew he was about to raise his friend to life. The Greek *embrimasthai* certainly connotes intense emotion, but as some scholars suggest it is an emotion borne of indignation, a healthy and justified anger at the powers of darkness and evil with whom Jesus is about to do battle. In this emotion and the act which followed it, Jesus' victory over illness, darkness, sin, death and evil is complete and absolute. The words of Martha, "Yes Lord, I have come to believe," give expression to the faith of every follower and inspire us, as we follow the Lord in the last weeks of Lent, to look beyond the cross to life.

1. Have we become too technological, too scientific, too psychological to perceive the hand of God at work in human history (Ezekiel)?

2. Because of the incarnation of Jesus, flesh has become a sacred place (Romans).

3. The seed of eternal life has already been planted in our hearts. Has it faith enough to grow (John)?

Passion (Palm) Sunday

When he appeared most defeated, he was truly triumphant. The servant Son who suffered for the sake of us all won victory through his innocence (Isaiah). Without a thought for himself, he gave all he had and all he was for others (Philippians). By virtue of his innocence and his loving selflessness, all who believe are made holy and whole (Matthew).

Isaiah 50:4-7. Suffering in and of itself has no genuine value. No one seeks out suffering for its own sake.

In ancient Israel, for example, the prophets, for the sake of God's word and the integrity of the covenant, were persecuted and rejected by their contemporaries. Ostracized because of the message they proclaimed, many prophets suffered physical abuse; some were even put to death. When he included the four servant songs in his prophecy to an exiled Israel, Duetero-Isaiah described therein a prophetic figure who would suffer for the sake of God's word and for the benefit of his people. He would suffer at the hands of his own people in order to bring about their salvation.

Some have suggested that Deutero-Isaiah based his doctrine about the suffering servant on Jeremiah's prophetic career. Others have suggested that the prophet had his *own* mission in mind as he proclaimed the servant's expiatory ministry. Still others have suggested that Israel was to understand its own experience of persecution and exile as having salvific value for the sake of other peoples.

That Jesus consciously identified with the servant's role is evident from the way in which he directed and exercised his ministry. That early Christians associated Jesus with the Isaian servant is obvious from the way in which the gospels and especially the passion narratives were written. A just man, Jesus suffered for the sake of sinners that by his death, all others may have life.

Philippians 2:6-11. With Ephesians, Colossians and Philemon, Philippians has been classified as a "captivity" letter. Most believe that Paul wrote to the church at Philippi while he was imprisoned in Rome, ca. 61-63 C.E.

In calling the believers at Philippi to strengthen their common bond, Paul urged them to imitate Jesus. Quoting an earlier Christian hymn (not his own creation), Paul exhorted the Philippians to make their own the attitude (mind) of Christ Jesus.

Besides its value as a liturgical expression of praise, the ancient hymn is a profound theological and christological statement: Christ, in becoming flesh, emptied himself (*kenosis*) in purposeful, deliberate renunciation.

A remarkable feature of the hymn is the fact that its theology and soteriology are spelled out by the arrangement of the strophes or stanzas.

This downward thrust and upward ascent recall the divine promise recorded by Deutero-Isaiah: "The word that goes forth from my mouth does not return to me empty without carrying out my will and succeeding in what it was meant to do" (Isaiah 55:11). Christ is that word, spoken by the Father, into time and space.

In returning to the Father, Christ draws all of us with him because his saving sacrifice embraces us all. By baptism, believers enter with Christ into the "parabola" of salvation. With Christ, we descend into the waters of life where we die to sin, and with Christ we emerge from the waters to live a new and higher life in his Spirit.

Matthew 26:14—27:66. Each year of the three year lectionary cycle (A, B, C), the church puts before us on this Sunday one of the synoptic versions of Jesus' passion and death. While the rest of the gospel material is composed of a variety of literary genres from a variety of sources, arranged and rearranged by several authors and redactors, the passion narratives represent single units of literature and were the earliest, fixed gospel material.

Because each of the gospel authors wrote for his own community and had his own particular sources (besides the shared common sources) and theological concerns, each of the passion narratives communicates a unique message about the salvific death of Jesus.

For today's gospel, the community, the sources, the concerns and the message are those of Matthew. Written in the 80s for an urban, cosmopolitan community (probably Syrian Antioch), Matthew's gospel has been called a "Christian response to Jamnia." The evangelist (not the apostle Matthew but a Greek-speaking Christian) wrote in an effort to consolidate his community in the wake of Jamnia, where Jewish Christians were definitively ousted from the synagogue and officially denounced by Judaism.

In helping his church to define its identity with regard to its Jewish roots and its increasingly gentile complexion, Matthew presented Jesus as the messiah foretold in the Jewish scriptures and as the redeeming savior of *all* peoples. In an effort to associate Jesus with Judaism, Matthew has skillfully informed his gospel with a series of formula citations or reflection quotations.

Besides apologetically relating Jesus to Judaism as its long-awaited savior, the citations served a didactic purpose in helping believers to understand that *everything* in Jesus' life and *every* moment of ministry, his passion and death were part of God's foreordained plan for the salvation of all peoples. Nothing happened accidentally, nor was Jesus a victim of circumstances or inevitabilities; he was in all his words and works fulfilling God's will. With this understanding of Matthew's methods, the various Old Testament allusions in the passion narrative can become meaningful learning experiences for *modern* believers.

In telling of Jesus' *betrayal* by Judas (26:14-16), Matthew alluded to Zechariah 11:12 where the measly sum of 30 pieces of silver was the amount paid for the rejected shepherd, and to Exodus 21:32 where 30 silver pieces were prescribed as damages for a slave or servant's life. This same sum, the price of his betrayal, serves to portray Jesus as the shepherd and servant (Isaiah) who has been rejected by his people. By means of these Old Testament allusions, Matthew explained this "apparent tragedy as proceeding from a subtle interaction of God's will as foretold in prophecy and man's sinful heart" (J. Meier).

In the institution of the eucharist (26:26-29), the statement "blood of the covenant" recalled for Matthew's readers the covenant sacrifice of Exodus 24:8, whereby God forged with his people a common bond, which demanded a new quality of life from the people. The phrase may also refer to Zechariah where the prophet quoted God as promising, "Because of the blood of my covenant with you, I will set your captives free" (Zechariah 9:11). In the eucharist, the Matthean Jesus explained that his life's blood would soon be poured out. Because of his sacrifice, all who were captives of sin and death would be freed to enjoy a new relationship with the Father. As J. Meier has pointed out, for Matthew the Christian experiences forgiveness of sins neither through baptism (which aggregates one to the life of the trinity) nor through the "binding and loosing" of the church (which refers to excommunication and readmittance) but rather through the *eucharist*.

In Gethsemane, Jesus' attitude of sorrow recalled Psalm 42:6 and Jonah 4:9 and the reference to the cup (vv. 39, 42) was a familiar Old Testament symbol of one's lot in life as foreknown by God (Psalm 11:6, Lamentations 4:21, Isaiah 51:17, 22) At the time of his arrest, Jesus is portrayed as interpreting the events; it had to be this way in order for the scriptures to be fulfilled (*pleroo*). This is not a statement of defeat in face of the inevitable but rather Matthew's way of teaching his community that Jesus freely and obediently accepted the plan of his Father as it unfolded through people and events.

During the trial, the silence of the Matthean Jesus (compare to Mark, Luke, John) recalled the Deutero-Isaian servant who did not protest the evil done him (Isaiah 53:7). So too, the mistreatment of Jesus (spitting, mockery, brutality, etc.) evoked the injustice done to the innocent one (Isaiah 50:4-7, see first reading).

On the cross, at the time of his death, Jesus is represented by the evangelist as the truly innocent and just one. Jesus' prayer, "My God, my God, why have you forsaken me" (27:46), has often been misunderstood as a cry of discouragement. Some have even suggested that Jesus had momentarily despaired of his Father's presence. But Matthew and his readers recognized Jesus' cry as the opening lines of Psalm 22, a song that begins as a lament and concludes on a note of triumphant joy and confidence in God! A comparison of Jesus' time on the cross with Psalm 22 will reveal several elements of similarity (mocking, garments divided, etc.).

Finally, the apocalyptic events that Matthew included (earthquake, darkness, saints rising, etc.) underscored the fact that the death of Jesus was a theophanic moment, the long-awaited Day of the Lord (Amos 8:9). The tearing of the curtain of the sanctuary enunciated the fact that a *new* way had come to experience God's reign; all peoples would henceforth be brought near to God, not through temple rites or sacrifices but through the saving death of Jesus Christ.

1. In God's eyes, the disadvantaged and the persecuted possess a far greater dignity than those who abuse them (Isaiah).

2. To give completely, to hold nothing back is to live fully the life of the Lord (Philippians).

3. Through Jesus' sorrow and suffering, joy and healing have become blessings for all (Matthew).

The Easter Season
Easter Sunday

The feast of life, Easter, is not simply the celebration of one man's victory, but a universal triumph in and because of that one man (Acts). Those who share in Jesus' victory are to live like winners, no longer losing the battle to sin and evil (Colossians, Corinthians). Because of Jesus, death has lost its finality and has become a passageway to a new and lasting life (John).

Acts 10:34-37-43. Closely connected with belief in the resurrection of Jesus was the conviction that such faith should issue forth in a *universal* mission. While both Matthew and John portray the gentile mission as a *secondary* shift of emphasis after the Jewish rejection of the gospel, Luke consistently presented the mission to the gentiles as an *integral* aspect of God's foreordained plan for salvation. This conviction is reflected in both the gospel according to Luke as well as in his second volume (Acts) from which our first reading for today has been excerpted.

Peter's kerygmatic discourse at Cornelius' home as well as other discourses in Acts were not just sermons delivered on one specific occasion. Rather, these discourses are highly stylized, theological vehicles through which Luke responded to the pastoral needs of the growing church community An extremely effective tool, the speeches of Acts were intended to reach beyond their historical and literary context in order to inform the reader of Luke/Acts of the meaning of a particular issue or event.

With the baptismal initiation of Cornelius and his household, the early community took according to Luke its first official step toward realizing the universal scope of Jesus' mission. Of course, the gentile mission had been begun *before* the Cornelius event and was for the most part due to the missionary efforts of the Hellenistic Christians, e.g., Philip, Stephen, etc. But Luke's theological concerns led him to relate *all* significant expansion and development in the early church to the Jerusalem church. Therefore Luke has featured Peter, the leader of the Twelve, as welcoming Cornelius to the faith.

A comparison of this speech of Peter, addressed to *gentiles*, with those speeches intended for Jews reveals the method developed by the early disciples for proselytizing gentiles. Unlike those sermons geared toward Jewish audiences, there is in Peter's discourse at Cornelius' home no indictment for Jesus' death. Similarly, those discourses intended for Jews began with Jesus' rejection and death, whereas the sermon to Cornelius et al. made mention of Jesus' life and ministry of healing and good works. Instead of supporting his claims with references to the prophets, which would have been significant for Jewish hearers and readers, Luke portrayed Peter as offering the testimony of *eyewitnesses* to substantiate his statement.

With the Cornelius episode, the early church aligned itself with Jesus' universal concerns and opened itself to accept "everyone who believes" (v. 43). That this open-hearted and open-minded policy was not to be wholly credited to human insight or initiatives was made quite clear by Luke who throughout this narrative and his entire work credited the Holy Spirit for the growth and continued development of the church.

Colossians 3:1-4. Founded by Epaphras, a disciple of Paul who had been converted when the apostle preached the good news in Ephesus, the community of Christians at Colossae had fallen prey to an incipient strain of gnosticism that threatened to dilute and/or distort the integrity of the faith. When he wrote to the community, Paul addressed this issue and restated the centrality of the resurrection of Jesus.

While the proponents of gnosticism in Colossae entertained a dualistic philosophy that regarded matter as evil and therefore the resurrection of the body as utter nonsense, Paul emphasized the fact that without the resurrection, life "in Christ" would be an absurd impossibility. But it is precisely *because* of the resurrection that Jesus' victory over sin and death was afforded to all believers. Heirs of that victory or, as Paul said, raised up in company with Christ (v. 1), all believers are called to bear witness by living worthy lives in justice, peace and truth.

Redemption, as Paul explained to the gnostics, was not an exercise of freeing oneself from the body or of transcending one's lesser self by the attainment of secret knowledge (gnosis). Redemption, taught Paul, was God's gracious gift to a sinful and needy humanity. Therefore, all the believer's energies and attentions are to be focused, not on his/her own personal achievements but "on things above." This focus on Christ and on the gift of salvation is the first step toward life and glory.

1 Corinthians 5:6-8. In ancient times leaven or yeast was used as it is today to cause dough to rise and thus to produce a lighter bread. But because it was a fermenting agent (known today to be caused by bacteria), the use of leaven was prohibited in those foods that were to be sacrificed. As J. Porter has explained (*Harper's Bible Dictionary*), leaven seemed to have a life of its own (it moved! grew! expanded!) and therefore should not be destroyed. Leaven was considered the life force of the vegetable world, as blood was of the animal; neither could be burnt.

Precisely because of its mysterious effect on dough, leaven became a symbol for sin and corruption. *Unleavened* bread, on the other hand, became a figurative sign of purity and holiness. Jesus reflected this idea in his teachings (Mark 8:15 and parallels) and Paul used this symbolism to call the Corinthian believers to live the life demanded by their allegiance to Christ.

Because of Christ's passing over from death to life, Christians are called to a new wholeness and holiness in him. When Paul exhorted the Corinthians to "get rid of the old yeast" (v. 7), he was referring to the Palestinian custom of cleaning the entire house on the eve of Passover to rid it of all traces of old leaven. Paul thus reminded the Corinthians that Christ's sacrifice had "swept the house clean" of sin and evil. Therefore, the Passover purity Jesus achieved on the cross became a permanent requirement for the redeemed. Easter people are to celebrate their new life in Christ with the unleavened bread of sincerity and truth.

John 20:1-9. If anyone *truly* anticipated Jesus' resurrection from the dead, the scriptures are silent about their expectations. Instead, each of the resurrection narratives contains evidence that Jesus' followers did *not* expect him; indeed they seemed to have despaired of him as the long-awaited savior. For example, the women wept at his passing, his friends fled and hid for fear that they might suffer a similar fate for having associated with him. When the empty tomb was discovered, it was assumed that the gardener had removed the body or that the authorities had done so as an act of hostility. Even when the risen Lord *did* appear to his own, they appeared *incredulous* with joy.

However, in the wake of the resurrection event, with the faith that developed because of Jesus' glorification, the early church took an entirely different view of Jesus' death and subsequently of his life. Written in the aftermath of the resurrection, the gospels (and the entire New Testament) reflect this enlightened perspective. As P. Perkins has pointed out, resurrection is present in the scriptures as the "culmination of the biblical story of human captivity and God's deliverance." It is not merely an assertion of the creed but a factor that pervades all of human existence.

In his book *On Becoming Christian*, H. Kung explains that "Jesus' resurrection cannot be described as an historical event in the ordinary sense of the word." There were no human witnesses. No press passes were distributed; no cameras recorded the scene for all posterity. Rather, as the New Testament consistently attests, the resurrection of Jesus was an eschatological act of God, an integral part of the final transformation of the world.

Kung goes on to explain that this perspective implies that the resurrection event is more than the divine vindication of a *particular* person, Jesus of Nazareth. God's saving plan is involved in Jesus in such a way that after Easter, Jesus becomes the *norm* for the relationship between humanity and God. When the evangelists wrote of Jesus' resurrection, they informed their narratives with the joy and hope spawned by this realization.

Today's text from John's gospel represents the empty tomb tradition. In this Johannine version, the beloved disciple believed in Jesus' resurrection simply by seeing the burial cloths left in the tomb. Here the beloved disciple functions as did the angel interpreters in the synoptic accounts, i.e., to explain the significance of the empty tomb and to make the Easter proclamation. Although the account of the empty tomb appears in all four gospels and was an *early* tradition, it was not included in the *earliest* testimonies to Jesus' resurrection (1 Corinthians 15:5).

An empty tomb is not *proof* of Jesus' rising from the dead. Rather, Christian faith in Jesus' victory over death is rooted in the *appearances* of the risen Lord to his followers. For those who came to faith in Jesus-as-risen by virtue of his appearances to them, the ambiguous witness of the empty tomb contributed to an understanding of the mysterious reality of Jesus' *bodily* resurrection, i.e., the same person who had walked and talked and had eaten with his followers, who had died and was buried, was by God's power the same Christ who was raised and now lives forever.

Sceptics have suggested that the resurrection narratives were fabricated by a group of loyal disciples made desperate by the death of their leader. In answer to these sceptics, Paul stated unequivocally, "If Christ is not risen from the dead, our preaching is empty, your faith is worthless and we are the most wretched of people!" (1 Corinthians 15:19). Therefore, when we read the resurrection narratives, we are reading, as it were, not the last but the first chapter in the story of our lives as Christians.

In Jesus' resurrection, all believers are afforded a new and lasting relationship with the Father, a relationship that will culminate in our own particular salvation and on the "last day" in universal glory. To celebrate Easter is not merely to remember that Jesus lives but that, because of him, we live and shall live forever.

1. Jesus' resurrection victory is not a selective blessing for a few but a grace that gathers all peoples to life (Acts).

2a. Those who have heavenly ideals can bear patiently with the reality of everyday life (Colossians).

2b. Christians are to rise above pettiness and deceit because of the new life they enjoy in the Lord (Corinthians).

3. Jesus lives. The mystery of his rising gives meaning to his sufferings and sustains the hope of all who believe (John).

Second Sunday of Easter

Before Jesus' death and exaltation, those who followed him were frightened and confused by his failure to meet their expectations. After Easter, because of his victory, those same people gathered together and zealously continued the mission Jesus had begun (Acts). Born anew in his death and healed by his sufferings (1 Peter), Jesus' disciples launched a worldwide mission of peace and forgiveness. All who live in him, made whole and holy by him, are called to the same missionary effort (John).

Acts 2:42-47. On this Sunday in each year of the three year cycle, one of the summaries from the Acts of the Apostles is read as the first reading (Year A: 2:42-47; Year B: 4:32-35; Year C: 5:12-16). A Lucan literary technique, the summaries functioned in a descriptive manner to allow the reader a glimpse into the daily life of the early Christian community. Granted, the summaries represent an idyllic and schematized picture of the growing body of believers, but they nevertheless feature the principles upon which the life of faith was founded and upon which it grew and developed.

In each summary, the community has been portrayed as closely knit, sharing goods and talents in common and gathering around the Twelve for liturgical celebrations and catechetical nourishment. Because of the summaries, the modern reader can appreciate the formation of these structures and institutions whereby the early believers actualized the reality of the resurrection in their daily lives. The miracles of healing and conversion as well as the increasing size of the community were understood, as they were in Jesus' ministry, as due to the Father's power and as signals of the eschatological age of salvation.

In the earliest stages of its development the growing church relied upon the knowledgeable and experiential witness of the disciples who had known the earthly Jesus. Their kerygmatic preaching challenged people to believe in Jesus while their continuing catechesis of those already initiated assured their steady growth in faith. Gradually, a fixed method and set content for preaching were developed, based on remembered sayings of Jesus, his words and works and especially the passion event.

By the time Luke wrote Acts, the second volume of his two volume work, the authoritative eyewitnesses to Jesus and to the major events of his life had *virtually* disappeared. Luke's contemporaries were those second and third generation Christians of the 80s who needed to experience the continuous character of the faith apart from Judaism and to deal with a delayed parousia in an oftentimes hostile environment. For these reasons, Luke sought to teach through his gospel and through Acts how to survive, how to grow and flourish as a vital and vibrant faith community.

The unique two volume structure of the Lucan opus can be compared to the ancient literary genre called the cultic biography. Usually these cultic biographical works were produced and used within religious communities or philosophical schools. In part one of the work, the life and career of the group's founder would be recounted as a norm and inspiration for the devotees. Part two was comprised of a narrative in which the life and careers of the founder's successors and other selected disciples were retold.

The main purpose of the two volume work was *legitimation*, i.e., the cultic biography would *legitimate* the founder's successors at the time of the document's writing by tracing the unbroken line of tradition from the founder to his successors and by illustrating the continuities between the disciples' words and works and those of their founder. By means of this literary genre, Luke showed that the work begun by Jesus was being maintained by the Twelve and by those whom the Twelve taught and to whom they witnessed.

The major factor of continuity between Jesus and the church, operative in both the age of Jesus and the continuing age of the church, is the Holy Spirit. The Spirit that empowered Jesus to live for others was also with the burgeoning community of believers in the first (and 20th) Christian century, enabling them (and us) to believe, to share all things, to break bread together, to praise God and to grow day by day in sincerity and truth.

1 Peter 1:3-9. Those who received this letter, purported to have been written by the apostle Peter, were the genuine heirs of the blessing the Lord spoke to Thomas: "Blessed are they who have not seen and have believed" (see gospel for today, John 20:30). As the author, probably a disciple of Peter who wrote ca. 80 or 90 C.E., has noted, "Although you have never seen him, you loved him and without seeing you believe in him" (1 Peter 1:8). Addressing himself to the persecuted Christians, mostly gentile converts from the churches in Asia Minor, the author's words resemble more a homily than a letter in the usual scriptural sense. Some scholars consider the homily to be liturgical in character, containing some sizeable fragments of ritual material (1:3—2:10) probably intended for use at baptismal celebrations.

Using the major moments of salvation history as recorded in the Jewish scriptures, e.g., exodus, desert wandering, promised land, etc., the author sought to reapply these moments to the conversion of the gentiles to Jesus. For gentiles, for all believers in Jesus, the Jewish exodus could be considered as a type of Christian baptism; the desert wandering could be thought of as the struggles of daily life and conversion to the Lord. So too the promised land could be thought of as a preview, albeit a dim one, of eschatological glory.

The first three verses of today's pericope were probably quoted from an earlier hymn of thanksgiving that praises God for the wonderful gift of baptism. Here the author refers to the sacrament as a new birth unto hope and unto an imperishable inheritance to be revealed in the last days. At the time of his writing, the author knew that his fellow believers were being subjected to persecution for their faith. In a sense one might say that their *birth* into the life of Christ had become a "life-threatening" endeavor. For many that faith made death an inevitable reality and suffering a common occurrence.

In order to encourage those who were persecuted for Christ, the author of 1 Peter urged them to regard their sufferings as a temporary and passing purification (vv. 6-7). Just as the desert wanderings had been a prelude to Israel's glory in her own land, just as Jesus' passion had been a brief passage to his exaltation, so would the believer who remained faithful survive the "moment" of persecution to enjoy a "forever" of glory.

John 20:19-31. If this resurrection appearance narrative were the only one included in the New Testament, nevertheless we would still have the *entire* legacy of Easter. Here the Johannine author has told the story of Jesus' triumph and the effects of that triumph for all generations: peace, the universal mission, the ever present dynamic Spirit, forgiveness and faith.

Proclaimed on this Sunday in each year of the three year cycle, today's gospel is comprised of two resurrection appearances, one on Easter evening and the second a week later. For pedagogical and theological reasons Luke separated the moments of the salvation event (Jesus' resurrection, ascension-exaltation, gift of the Spirit). But the Johannine author's coalescence of these moments into one event is a more accurate and true presentation of the fact.

In the Johannine account, the risen Lord is portrayed as bestowing the Spirit and mandating his disciples on the same day. Implied in these actions is the fact that Jesus had *already* "ascended" to the Father, been glorified and was therefore empowered to give the Spirit.

With the conventional Jewish salutation, *shalom*-peace, Jesus greeted his disciples. But, in the context of the resurrection, this greeting took on added significance. Peace and exultant joy were signals of the messianic era (Isaiah 11) inaugurated in Jesus. With the gift of the Spirit, Jesus fulfilled the messianic prophecies of Joel (3:1) and Ezekiel (36:27) and his Easter legacy became one of realized eschatology.

With the wounds of his passion in evidence, the risen Jesus proclaimed the continuity between the risen cross and his exaltation; the risen Lord was one and the same person as the earthly Jesus. No doubt, John accented the physical details of Jesus' passion as a polemic against a late first century gnostic movement that preferred to overlook the passion and death of Jesus in favor of a wonderworking divine-man christology.

In addition to the concern for continuity between the earthly and risen Jesus, the resurrection appearance narratives were also geared toward the survival of the eschatological community until the second advent. Jesus' mandating of his disciples for their mission of mercy and forgiveness assured that the ministry he had begun would continue to give life to his community.

The sending forth of the disciples to forgive sins has become a source text for understanding the sacrament of reconciliation. Some theologians interpreted the forgiving or binding of sins (v. 23) as a reference to the church's responsibility of withholding baptism depending upon the initiate's acceptance or rejection of the kerygma. Others, drawing on the rabbinic terms *asar* and *sera'* (bind, loose), have interpreted v. 23 in the context of church discipline i.e., the right of the church to grant or to revoke membership in the community for reasons of sinfulness.

Although these later ecclesiastical and juridical developments may find support in today's gospel, its primary message of peace and forgiveness should not be diminished. Jesus conquered sin and death on the cross; as the exultant risen Lord, he shared the fruits of his victory with all who believe.

Following the commissioning of the disciples, the story of Thomas provides an excellent lesson in faith and makes a case for the value of doubt in the life of the believer. As one who hesitated and questioned the Lord, and then moved from scepticism to a firm and committed faith, Thomas is a source of encouragement for all who struggle to believe. Moreover, the Thomas episode helped to answer a problem that troubled the early church and that became more and more acute with the deaths of the authoritative eyewitnesses to Jesus, i.e., how could a person believe in the risen Jesus without having *seen* him? For a time, those who had not seen the risen Lord relied on the testimony of those who had. But, as the Thomas episode illustrated, even *seeing firsthand* was no guarantee of faith.

By means of Thomas' doubting, the evangelist put forth several apologetic and theological points: (1) Jesus' body was not an illusion or vision; it was real and, as the wounds attested, was the same Jesus who died on the cross. (2) Believers are to move beyond the sensational aspects of the resurrection to a committed faith. Note that Thomas did not actually *touch* Jesus but came to faith when Jesus challenged him: "Believe!" (3) "My Lord" (*Kyrios*), "My God" (*Theos*) on Thomas' lips reflected the church's ever deepening understanding of Jesus as equal to the creator God and powerful Lord of all.

1. Every believer is called to answer daily the challenge of communal living and to enjoy forever its rewards (Acts).

2. The wonderful paradox of baptism is that it is a birth into the death of Jesus that gives life (1 Peter).

3. When sceptics become believers and warriors make peace, the legacy of Easter will be known (John).

Third Sunday of Easter

Jesus who died is now risen! God has vindicated his words and works and given him a place of glory (Acts). Although now exalted, Jesus is not gone away from those who believe in him. Each time the bread of his word and of his body is broken and shared, he is here (Luke). Each time we meet him in the sacrament, we celebrate his victory and make it our own (1 Peter).

Acts 2:14, 22-28. Compare the conduct of Peter as presented in today's first reading with his behavior during Jesus' passion and one cannot help but wonder how to account for the radical difference. When Jesus was being interrogated by the high priest, Peter was recognized by three different people as one of Jesus' companions. Peter emphatically denied any connection with Jesus and in the course of his triple denial, he even cursed the thought of being associated with the Lord (Luke 22:54-61). However, after the passion and death and in the wake of Jesus' resurrection, Peter not only claimed association with Jesus but boldly and publicly acclaimed him as Lord and savior!

What had happened to Peter? The radical change in Peter's attitude and behavior (as well as that of the other disciples) can be accounted for only in terms of Jesus' resurrection. That reality and the faith of the early church in Jesus as risen transformed "wimps" into "warriors."

But Peter and the other followers of Jesus did not simply *decide* to believe. Rather, as the author of Luke-Acts has made quite clear in his writings, it was by the power of the promised Spirit that Jesus' frightened followers became his fearless proclaimers. In his gospel, Luke portrayed Jesus as endowed by the Spirit (4:16-30) to preach and to perform the messianic deeds of salvation. In Acts, the sequel to his gospel, Luke portrayed the disciples of Jesus as endowed with that same Spirit and empowered to perform in the same saving manner as did Jesus.

Today's pericope is an excerpted text that represents only a part of Peter's Pentecost sermon (Acts 2:24-36). Although there is probably a genuine historical basis for the content of the sermon, nevertheless, the modern consensus would attribute most of this sermon as well as the other speeches in Acts to the author, Luke. All the speeches and/or sermons in Acts, regardless of whom is speaking, are structured similarly.

All reflect the same basic formula or pattern for preaching the kerygma (fundamental message) of Christianity to would-be believers. Considering the fact that Luke composed Acts in the latter decades of the first Christian century, the fixity in the structure and content of the speeches may represent the tendency of the church toward a set of fixed credal formulae—a tendency Ernst Kasemann has called "early Catholicism."

Indeed, the essential elements of faith are present in every kerygmatic declaration, viz., (1) Jesus was sent by God; (2) he was empowered by God to do the great works of salvation; (3) he was betrayed, put to death; (4) he was raised to life and vindicated by God. All that happened to Jesus was (as the author of Acts will stress repeatedly) according to "the set purpose and plan of God" (v. 23). In so emphasizing the plan of God in Jesus' death, the early church sought to lessen the sting of the scandal of the cross.

Notice the extensive Old Testament quotation in today's text. Quoting Psalm 16:8-11, the author of Acts cited the first "scriptural proof" and prophetic foundation for the resurrection. As the Lord's holy one, Jesus was not subjected to the corruption of death or of the nether world. Rather, Jesus was freed from death and raised up by God (v. 24).

H. Conzelmann has labeled this manner of expressing Jesus' resurrection as "subordinationism." By making God the subject of the verb (to raise) and Jesus as the object (he was raised *by God*), Luke reflected the terminology in the earliest Easter proclamations (1 Corinthians 15:12-34). Those ancient formulations should not be taken out of context but should be seen as part of a whole progression of thought and deepening understanding of the nature of Jesus as Christ and of his power over death in his resurrection.

1 Peter 1:17-21. Writing from Rome in the 80s and 90s C.E. the author of 1 Peter (obviously not Peter the apostle who had died in the mid-60s) was concerned that the gentile converts to Christ recognize themselves as *belonging* to the church, the people of God: "Once you were no people, but now you are the people of God" (1 Peter 2:10). Because of Christ, the gentiles had become heirs to the Jewish privileges of being "a chosen race, a royal priesthood, a holy nation" (1 Peter 2:9).

As R.E. Brown has noted in his book, *The Churches the Apostles Left Behind*, the author of 1 Peter believed that "if people feel that they get something worthwhile from being members of a church, that church will survive." To that end, the Petrine author sought to inculcate in his intended readers (the gentile Christians of Asia Minor) a sense of belonging by relating the aspects of their new life in Christ to the rich heritage of the Old Testament.

For example, just as the Hebrews who left Egypt were told to gird up their loins for a rapid departure (Exodus 12:11), so the gentile Christians were told to gird up the loins of their mind (1 Peter 1:13). Similarly, the Israelites who murmured against the Lord and wanted to regress to the fleshpots of Egypt (Exodus 16:2-3) were compared to the recipients of 1 Peter who longed for their former ways of ignorance (1:14). Just as Moses had charged the people, "Be holy, for I, the Lord your God am holy" (Leviticus 19:2), the author of 1 Peter made a similar challenge (1 Peter 1:15-16).

Today's text picks up the comparison by likening Israel's desert trek to the sojourn of the Christian life (1 Peter 1:17). Strangers in an alien (pagan) environment, Christians hope for heaven just as the Jews yearned for the promised land. Positing the primacy of Christ and Christianity over Judaism, the author compared the golden calf the Israelites made and worshiped as the god who had delivered them from Egypt (Exodus 32:1-4) to the deliverance wrought by Jesus. While the Israelites had been spared from the tenth plague of death by the blood of the lamb (Exodus 11:2), the blood of Christ, the unblemished and spotless lamb, has saved all peoples (1 Peter 1:18-19).

Having supplied them with these "roots" as the basis for their belonging to God's people, the author of 1 Peter challenged the Christians of the churches in Asia Minor to live lives centered on God. So too, he called all believers to be full of hope and trust that our baptism into Christ is the first step of a lifelong sojourn that will one day know the glory of eternity.

Luke 24:13-35. A superb story even from a merely literary viewpoint, the Emmaus episode represents a magnificent treasury of theological and christological insights at several different levels of development. At the very basis of the story (on the whole a Lucan composition) is the authentic experience of the church in Syrian Antioch in the 80s C.E. In the almost two generations following Jesus' death, the Antiochene Christians had been encountering the risen Lord in the breaking of the bread. In fact, the observant reader will notice that the narrative follows the pattern of ideal liturgy: in both word (v. 27) and sacrament (v. 30), the risen Lord is manifested and communicated to the believing community.

As in most of the resurrection appearances, delayed recognition played an important part in shaping the Emmaus narrative. The initial lack of recognition on the part of the two travellers was a popular folkloric motif in both biblical and extra-biblical literature. Recall the Genesis narratives wherein Abraham and Lot, though unaware, extended hospitality to the Lord and his messengers (Genesis, 18:1-8, 19:1-3). In his *Metamorphoses,* Ovid told a similar story about Philemon and Baucis. Attesting to the popularity of this belief is the advice given by the author of Hebrews, "Do not neglect to show hospitality, for by that means some have entertained angels without knowing it" (13:2).

No doubt, Luke had an apologetic motive for including the delayed recognition motif in his narrative: The disciples did not recognize Jesus because he was totally transformed by the glory of his resurrection. Still, Luke was careful to illustrate the fact of continuity between the earthly Jesus and the risen Lord by portraying him as performing the same ministries—he taught them, ate with them, opened their eyes to the truth, etc.

In the simple statement, "We were hoping" (v. 21), the evangelist summed up the attitudes of despondency and disillusionment that had overwhelmed Jesus' followers at his death. It is significant that at this point in his narrative (v. 19) the followers of Jesus had not come to believe in him as Lord but as a powerful prophet like Moses. Faith in Jesus as Lord and savior and as the one who vanquished death would come later, at the moment of revelation in the breaking of bread. By means of this progressive development, Luke taught a valuable lesson to those who depend on word and sacrament for the nurturing of faith.

At that point in the narrative when the still unrecognized Jesus "acted as if he were going farther" (v. 28), Luke heightens the pathos of his story and hints at the loss Jesus' disciples felt at his death. "Stay with us" could have been understood as a plea made out of curiosity or out of a desire to diminish misery by sharing it ("misery loves company").

But Luke clearly intends his readers to understand that the invitation to "stay" was a necessary factor for further revelation. "Stay with us" represents that response to revelation (however confused and feeble) that opens the heart of the believer to further truth. "Stay with us" also draws attention to the sacrament of the Eucharist, the means by which the Lord *did* and *does* stay with us.

By referring to the approach of evening, the evangelist conjured up for his readers the powers of darkness, doom, alienation and evil dispelled by Jesus, savior and light of the world. In the darkness of persecution that threatened the Lucan church of the 80s, the Emmaus episode offered the encouragement needed to persevere in a life of faith nourished and strengthened by the Eucharist. As in the narratives of the institution of the Eucharist, the still unrecognized guest "took," "blessed," "broke" and "gave" the bread to his disciples. Only at this point in their encounter are the disciple's eyes opened (v. 31) and they recognized their visitor as their Lord.

"Opened eyes" (a phrase that occurs eight times in the N.T., six of which are in Luke-Acts) always referred to a deepened understanding of revelation. The fact that Jesus vanished at this point did not deter or lessen their faith but pointed to the means by which all disciples of the Lord Jesus would thenceforth encounter him. In the breaking of the bread and in the sharing of his word, the Lord would abide forever with his followers.

For us, who have been born on *this* side of the resurrection event, the Emmaus story is a source of encouragement. Like the two on the road, in our journeys through life we will be visited by unrecognized guests who will reveal the truth to us. Like the two on the road, we will be able to meet the Lord in the breaking of the bread of his body and his word.

1. To live full of faith and joy, to bring hope to the downcast are ways of preaching the message of Easter (Acts).

2. Through baptism, we become heirs to all the mysteries of salvation (1 Peter).

3. Whenever bread is broken, whenever words are shared, there is an opportunity to meet the Lord (Luke).

Fourth Sunday of Easter

Every great leader is also a great follower of Jesus who recognizes the Lord's voice in the circumstances of daily life and responds to him in faith (John). In following the Lord, the great leader becomes familiar with suffering and learns through the mystery of the cross the lessons of compassion and caring (1 Peter). When great leaders call for repentance, they move the hearts of their followers to reform because they have been the first to admit guilt and to beg forgiveness (Acts).

Acts 2:14, 36-41. Peter and the Eleven were not the only ones who experienced the power of the Holy Spirit on the day of Pentecost. It seems obvious that those who responded so whole heartedly to Peter's sermon were also moved by the Spirit. When Peter concluded his kerygmatic message (begun last week) with the profound christological statement, "God has made both Lord and messiah this Jesus whom you crucified" (v. 36), those who heard him responded, "What are we to do?" (v. 39).

This sincere question recalls the preaching of John the Baptizer and the reactions of the people to it. The crowds asked, "What ought we to do?"; the tax collectors also inquired, "Teacher, what are we to do?"; and the soldiers wanted to know "What about us?" (Luke 3:10ff). As did John the Baptizer and Jesus, the apostles advocated a program of repentance and reform. Contrition for sin was the first step in the process of turning to the Lord.

For the Jews in his audience, Peter's preaching would also have evoked a call to reform that involved a radical openness to and reevaluation of the identity of the person of Jesus and of his significance for them. For the idolaters among his hearers, Peter's challenge would necessitate a turning *away* from false gods and turning *toward* the one true God and to Jesus in whom God was made manifest.

For those today who hear the same kerygmatic message, the call to reform is just as challenging and urgent. Like those who heard Peter and the Eleven and were baptized into Christ Jesus, all baptized believers are thereby initiated into a *lifelong process* of reform. It is important to realize that *true* reform is not merely a program of character study or personality evaluation. Nor is it merely a regimen of self-help or self-improvement techniques.

According to the ancient Christian hymn (Philippians 2:6-11) true reform is conformity to Christ in mind and heart; it is a daily turning toward and transformation into the one who died to sin and rose in freedom to life. True reform involves the appropriation of these rich gifts of salvation; it requires the strength to live in the Spirit as forgiven and forgiving people.

In keeping with his theological concerns, Luke emphasized the universal nature of God's promises and saving gifts "to all those still far off" (v. 39). Significant also is the reference to the *growth* of the community ("some three thousand were added that day," v. 41). Luke made other similar references (2:47, 5:14, 6:1, 9:31, 11:21, 16:5) and in each instance the credit for the increasing number of members in the church was owed to God himself working through the Holy Spirit.

Luke envisioned a *universal mission* that would form a *universal community* wherein Jesus would be proclaimed as both Lord (*Kyrios*) and Christ (messiah).

1 Peter 2:20-25. As the author mentioned in the salutation of his letter, 1 Peter was addressed to Christians in the Roman provinces in Asia Minor, viz., Pontus, Galatia, Cappadocia, Asia and Bithynia. At the time of the author's writing (ca. 80s-90s C.E.), Domitian was emperor (81-96 C.E.) and the persecution of Christians had evolved from a local purge (centered mostly in Rome, as during Nero's reign) to an empire-wide campaign. Knowing that Rome's rage at Jesus' followers had extended into the far reaches of the empire (even to Asia Minor), the exhortation to patience in today's pericope becomes all the more remarkable.

But persecution from the Roman authorities was not the only suffering to which the recipients of 1 Peter were subjected. Many of those who had been converted to Christ were slaves (1 Peter 2:18, Colossians 3:22—4:1, Ephesians 6:5-9). Slavery was an ancient and generally accepted institution the existence of which went virtually unchallenged by Peter or Paul. Like the other new Testament writers, the author of 1 Peter recommended a sort of "grin and bear it" attitude toward slavery.

Some have suggested that vv. 21-25 of today's reading were originally an early Christian hymn patterned on Isaiah 53:4-12. In quoting the early hymn, the author of 1 Peter proposed that slaves take Jesus Christ as their model. In so doing, slaves would be better able to endure their lot in life, even under harsh masters and even in persecution from Rome.

There is also an indication in today's reading of the developing concepts of church leadership toward the end of the first Christian century. The Petrine author described the gentiles' conversion to Christ in terms of straying sheep returning to their shepherd and guardian (v. 25). The Greek word *episcopos* (overseer or guardian) eventually designated the heads of the Christian communities.

These ministerial designations (Acts 20:28)—shepherd = pastor and guardian (overseer)—were based on the divine christological functions of shepherd and guardian. In the exercising of these ministries by his earthly followers, the risen Christ himself was thought to be both shepherding and guarding his flock. Therefore, both sheep and shepherd are called by 1 Peter to model their attitudes and their behavior on the Lord Jesus Christ.

John 10:1-10. For this Fourth Sunday of Easter in each year of the three year lectionary cycle, the gospel is from John 10.

Verses 1-5 of today's gospel represent a fusion of two parables, followed in vv. 6-10 by an allegorical interpretation. Most scholars agree that the two short parables are based on authentic sayings of Jesus fused together in the process of oral transmission by the church and then later interpreted by the evangelist and/or redactor. Therefore, in a few short verses the modern reader has been gifted with almost 60 years' worth of theological and christological developments.

Aware of the various stages or levels of development (Jesus, church, evangelist, redactor) within and behind the gospels, it would be naive and even unjust to interpret the texts from a one dimensional (fundamentalist) vantage point. So, when the evangelist painted his portrait of the true shepherd, he probably had in mind the situation that existed during Jesus' earthly ministry as well as that which his contemporaries (in the 90s C.E.) experienced. Just as the Pharisees posed a problem for Jesus of Nazareth, the Jewish leaders of the evangelist's day were no less a problem to the followers of Jesus. The first parable then (vv. 1-3) and its teaching can be seen as a challenge to religious leaders of the 30s, 90s and 1990s.

In these verses, Jesus is portrayed as both the *gate* through which all sheep must enter the sheepfold *and* as the *shepherd* who knows and is known by the sheep. As the *gate*, Jesus is the *way* through which all who would be saved must pass. As the *shepherd* who knows his own intimately, he is also the *leader* behind whom all who recognize his voice (i.e., who see him as Son and savior) will follow. All others (all who do not accept Jesus as gate and as leader, e.g., the Pharisees and later the anti-Christs) are labeled in the parable as thieves and marauders. No doubt the evangelist had in mind the powerful prophecy of Ezekiel on true and false shepherds (Ezekiel 34:1-16).

A clearer idea of the symbolism of the parable is possible when the reader has an understanding of ancient Palestinian sheepfolds and shepherding techniques. Sheepfolds were enclosures walled in by stones and/or briars, located inside or on the immediate outskirts of the village. At night all the sheep of the village were corralled into the sheepfold and the shepherds took turns acting as guard and gatekeeper. Often the gatekeeper would lie down to rest at the opening of the sheepfold, becoming as it were the "*gate*."

In the morning, in order to take their sheep to the hills for pasturing, the shepherds had an unusual method of separating their sheep from the general flock. Each sheep had a name and, with his own particular method of calling or whistling, the shepherd would round up his flock. Each sheep would respond *only* to its own shepherd; even if another shepherd called the sheep by name, it would not respond. Rather than *follow* his herd as modern sheep-owners do or send out trained dogs to gather strays back to the fold, the ancient Palestinian shepherd went *before* his sheep (v. 4) as their leader. Given this background, John's parables are all the more powerful and challenging to those who read them. Just as the true shepherds of the sheep acted as the "gate" of the sheepfold, guarding it with their very lives, so Jesus is the true gate who gave his life for his sheep and through which the true sheep will pass unto salvation, light and life.

It is in Jesus and through baptism into him that the Christian finds the way to the Father. In Jesus' example of leading the way, being the gate and knowing his followers personally and intimately, all leaders gave an ideal on which to model their own particular styles and methods of leadership.

1. To move the hearts of one's hearers to the Lord is a talent to be attributed to the Holy Spirit (Acts).

2. Suffering is an inevitable part of life; suffering endured out of love for others in the name of Jesus is the path to inevitable glory (1 Peter).

3. Recognizing the voice of the Lord requires an openness to all media of communication (John).

Fifth Sunday of Easter

Called together in one hope by their faith in the one Lord, believers have the responsibility of respecting the variety of opinions, life styles and theologies that constitute the church (Acts). An institution of living, growing stones welded together in visible union by the Holy Spirit (2 Peter), the church is home to all who believe and to all who work for the present and coming kingdom (John).

Acts 6:1-7. From the very beginning, the community of believers in Jesus was heterogeneous; the pluralism and diversity that exist today among believers existed from the outset. For this reason, the unity that grew among the early followers of Christ was union born of tension—a balancing act, as it were, of various ideals, motives and visions.

It would be naive to attribute the differences among the early Christians to the fact that some were Jewish and some Greek. Just as within Judaism there were various schools of thought (Pharisees, Sadducees, etc.) and degrees of liberalness and/or conservatism, so too there were varying philosophies and theologies among the gentiles. Both groups and all their sub-groups brought their ideals with them to Christianity.

One must also take care not to dichotomize Jewish and Hellenistic cultures as though each stood at opposite ends of the spectrum. Beginning in the fourth century B.C.E. during Alexander's reign, the process known as Hellenization had begun to spread throughout the empire. While some groups staunchly resisted this acculturation to Greek ways, others assimilated it entirely and others were affected in varying degrees.

Members coming from each of those groups were drawn to Christ but baptism did not automatically eradicate their differences. R.E. Brown has made an excellent job of identifying at least four major types of Jewish/gentile Christianity in the early church (see *Antioch and Rome* by Brown and J. Meier).

Two of these types of Christianity are in evidence in today's first reading. The problem of inequities in the daily distribution to the poor was symptomatic of deeper differences. The recognition and appointment of the seven by the community and the Twelve represent a foreshadowing of the emancipation of the early church from Palestinian Judaism. In Acts 8:1 and 11:19-26, we learn that these Hellenists were expelled from Jerusalem and the outward missionary thrust of the early church was inaugurated first in Samaria, then in the diaspora.

Though the seven men, all of whom had Greco-Roman names, had seemingly been appointed to oversee the distribution to the needy, nowhere in Acts are we told that they actually did so. Luke described their word as service, *diakonia*, a word from which our word deacon was later derived. From what can be ascertained from Acts, Philip, Stephen et al. preached, evangelized, baptized and ministered much in the same way as did the apostles.

The very fact that they were commissioned for their service *by the community* and recognized *by the apostles* in the gesture of the laying on of hands bears witness to the importance of their roles. Although the laying on of hands took on the significance of ordination to "orders" only at a *later* date (1 Timothy 4:14, 2 Timothy 1:16), nevertheless the gesture in Acts 6 conveyed the traditional sense of special designation for a task and the expression of solidarity between the person and the community (Numbers 27:23, Deuteronomy 34:9).

Many scholars believe that the seven had already been active in the service of the word and that the gesture of laying on of hands by the Twelve was a sign of acceptance of the Hellenistic Jewish Christians by the more conservative Jewish Christians. As such, the event is a source of encouragement for all believers who strain for union within a pluralistic and diverse community.

1 Peter 2:4-9. Any one of the ecclesial metaphors in today's second reading could be the basis of an excellent homily. In its original setting (which most scholars believe to have been a sacramental one), this text was part of a longer homily intended as a catechesis for baptismal candidates. Some have suggested that the homily was delivered at the Easter celebration, after the reading of Exodus 12:21-28.

Divided into three sections, the homily first gave a Christian interpretation of the Exodus text (1 Peter 1:13-21), applying the elements of Israel's history to the Christian life. In its second section the homily treated of the joys of being Easter people (1 Peter 1:22--2:2), and in the third section (from which today's pericope has been excerpted) the author considered the repercussions of the Easter mysteries upon community life (1 Peter 2:3-10).

With a medley of Old Testament quotations (Isaiah 28:16, Psalm 118:22, Isaiah 8:14-15, Exodus 19:6), the author constructed a vision of the *new* Israel (church) and of the *new* temple of living stones (believers in Jesus). For the readers of 1 Peter who lived in Asia Minor in the last quarter of the first century C.E., the metaphors were intended to impart a sense of belonging to a new people of God. As such, this new "chosen race" and "consecrated nation" (v. 9) had inherited the promises made to Israel and was to enjoy the fulfillment of all of Israel's potentialities.

In quoting Psalm 118:22 (v. 7), "a stone the builders rejected that became a cornerstone," the author drew upon a motif very popular among early Christian writers. By means of this "no-yes" motif, the author contrasted the rejection ("no") of Jesus by disbelievers with the vindication and exaltation ("yes") of Jesus by God.

Unlike the rock of Sinai that could not be approached under pain of death (Exodus 19:2-3), Jesus the living stone *invites* nearness. Indeed, he gathers unto himself the living stones of the new covenant to form an entirely new system of religion. Instead of an elitist priesthood, the entire new people of God is a royal priesthood (v. 9). Instead of animal and grain offerings, the new liturgy of God's people will be celebrated with "spiritual sacrifices" (v. 5).

Unlike the offerings of the old Israel that were not pleasing to the Lord, those of the new people of God would be acceptable to him because they are one with the sacrifice of Jesus. On the other hand, those who do not believe will find in Jesus the rock and in his church of living stones "an obstacle and a stumbling stone" (v. 8).

As T. Maertens has observed, the church still continues to define herself in terms of the holy nation, priestly nation, etc., to avoid any overly clerical concept of the church.

John 14:1-12. Unlike the synoptic evangelists whose narratives of Jesus' last meal with his followers were quite brief, the Johannine author elaborated in great detail on those last moments with the earthly Jesus. One of the major concerns of Jesus' disciples was the course their future would take. When his death seemed inevitably near and when disillusionment with what they had hoped might happen (i.e., the establishment of an earthly kingdom with Jesus as head and the Twelve as his heirs) threatened to overwhelm his disciples, Jesus offered them a double assurance: (1) of success and (2) of a future in eternity. When the Johannine author wrote his gospel, he geared it toward the disciples of Jesus in the church of the 90s and held out for them the same double assurance.

Jesus' "formula for success" did not involve material gain or fame. Instead, he promised "who has faith in me will do the works I do and greater far than these" (v. 12). In this legacy the community of those who follow Jesus are reminded that *faith* is the "oil that greases the machine" and without it even the most extensive and organized programs are doomed to a creaking failure.

As for their future in eternity, Jesus assured his disciples, "In my Father's house, there are many dwelling places" (v. 2). A Greek word of disputed meaning, *mone* can more properly be translated as resting places or rest stops. By *mone* we are to understand not a palatial dwelling as the English translation "mansion" (from the Latin *mansio*) would seem to indicate. Nor were Jesus' disciples to understand "my Father's house" to be the temple in Jerusalem.

Earlier in his gospel, the evangelist had distinguished between the temple that had become locus of crass commercialism and formalistic worship (John 2:17-20) and the true temple or house of God who is Jesus (John 2:20-22). Now, as T. Maertens has pointed out, Jesus is revealing that the true house of the Father is the *glory* into which he is about to enter and that he will one day share with his faithful followers. "My Father's house" could be thought of as the experience of living with the Father and with Jesus for ever.

Thomas serves as the fourth gospel's representation of doubt-that-grows-into-faith, of misunderstanding-that-is-transformed-into-true-insight. His question (v. 4), occasioned by Jesus' announcement of his departure, served to introduce one of the profound "I am" (*ego eimi*) revelations of this gospel: "I am the way . . . truth. . . life" (v. 5). As the full and true revelation of the Father, Jesus is the way or path through whom and in whom the Father is known to humanity and vice-versa. Philip's eager but obtuse "Show us" could perhaps be a Johannine slur on the Jews who, even in the wake of Jesus' resurrection, still clamored for signs.

The word "way" recalled for John's readers the many Old Testament references to the law; conformity to the precepts of the law was considered the way (*ha derek*) of truth and life (Psalm 119, Wisdom 5:6, Tobit 1:3, etc.). Later, the sectarian community at Qumran thought of *itself* in terms of the "way." Taking literally the exhortation of Deutero-Isaiah to prepare in the wilderness a *way* for Yahweh (Isaiah 40:3), the Essenes regarded their life of strict observance of the law in the desert as a pathway to God. John the Baptizer understood his mission as herald and preparer for the way in similar terms. Early believers in Jesus also described themselves and were known as followers of "the way" (Acts 9:2, 19:9, 22:4, 24:14, etc.).

"I am the way . . . truth . . . life" was a christological statement about Jesus but it was and is also a challenge to his followers. Functioning in the fourth gospel as did the kingdom of God ("heaven" in Matthew) sayings in the synoptics, the "I am" (*ego eimi*) proclamations are multi-dimensional. Drawing on the words and works of the earthly Jesus, and relating these to the risen Christ, the "I am" statements should also be predicated of each believer.

Because Jesus has returned to "his Father's house," i.e., because he is one with the Father and because of the Spirit he has bestowed, each believer is called to proclaim in both deed and word, "I am the way . . . truth . . . life." To be the way and not a detour or a dead end street, to be the truth and not a lie, to give life and not to take it—this is to do the works that Jesus did.

1. Appointed to serve its many members, the ministers of the community are deserving of respect and support (Acts).

2. Without the Spirit of Jesus within us, binding us to one another and to God, the church of living stones would be a mere pile of pebbles (2 Peter).

3. Those who believe in Jesus as way, truth and life are called by that faith to be way, truth and life for others (John).

Sixth Sunday of Easter

Healing miracles and acts of power were integral to the ministry of the early church (Acts). These signs and wonders cannot be relegated to the distant past, as if they are impossible or anachronistic in today's world. As he promised, the Lord Jesus has given his Spirit to empower his followers to continue his work and do similar deeds (John). All who love him, all who have been saved by his suffering and death are called to glorify him in great and small miracles of service (1 Peter).

Acts 8:5-8, 14-17. Whereas the fourth evangelist included in his gospel a missionary venture of Jesus into Samaritan territory (John 4), Luke reserved the campaign into Samaria for his second volume, Acts, and credits the Hellenist Christians for the effort. Relating this missionary thrust to the death of Stephen and the ensuing hostilities against the church, Luke showed that persecution, far from hindering the work of the gospel, served as an impetus and a catalyst for its promulgation (8:1). Actually, it seems that, initially, the persecution was limited to Hellenist Christians (Acts 6; 11:19) and for a time Jewish Christians went unmolested.

Philip, one of the seven appointed for service by the community (Acts 6:5), carried the good news to Samaria and met with considerable success—in sharp contrast to the generally poor reception given to the good news by most of official Judaism. Remember that the Samaritans were Jews by ancestry who worshipped Yahweh and practiced circumcision. At the time of the demise of the northern kingdom (eighth century B.C.E.), some of the conquered Israelites intermarried with their foreign oppressors and were thenceforth regarded as deviant, unacceptable to their Judean brethren.

Samaritans awaited a messiah, whom they called *Ta'eb*, "the Returning One," and rejected Jerusalem in favor of Mt. Gerizim as their official religious center. During Jesus' day, Judeans would go out of their way to avoid Samaritan territory.

As is indicated in the gospel, Jesus' attitude toward the Samaritans was one of acceptance and love (Luke 10:25-37, John 4). That this same tolerance and openness was shared by Jesus' followers *after* his resurrection attests to the power of his Spirit within them, helping them to bridge the gaps of human limitations and to overcome centuries-old prejudices.

As is our understanding today, the early believers knew that the reception of the Spirit was a consequence of baptism (Acts 1:5, 2:38, 9:17-19), but v. 16 seems to imply an inferiority or a lack in the baptism of the Samaritans by Philip. This text does, however, hint at the later liturgical distinctions between baptism and confirmation.

1 Peter 3:15-18. When the author of 1 Peter wrote to the Christians in Asia Minor, he described himself as a "witness of the sufferings of Christ" (1 Peter 5:1). Though he was not an eyewitness to Jesus' passion and death on the cross, he was however one who had experienced the passion of Christ in his life's struggle and who looked forward to a share in the glory yet to be revealed (1 Peter 8:1). In the same way, the author called his persecuted readers to understand their sufferings in a similar light and thereby to bear powerful, eloquent witness to Christ.

The author of 1 Peter viewed these sufferings as a natural consequence of faith; in other words, those who "took up their cross daily" to follow Jesus were experiencing its burden. Therefore, he counseled that their attitude in the daily struggle should be modeled on Jesus. By responding gently and respectfully to those who wronged them, they would disappoint and shame their persecutors.

One is reminded of the Isaian suffering servant whose silent innocence spoke volumes about injustice and about the power of self-effacing love. There is also a similarity in this idea to the proverb Paul quoted to the Romans: "If your enemy is hungry, feed him . . . by doing this you will heap burning coals upon his head and the Lord will reward you" (Proverbs 25:21, Romans 12:20).

John 14:15-21. During the Easter season it may seem strange to modern readers that the lectionary returns so quickly to that period in Jesus' life immediately *before* his passion and death. In these weeks after Easter, why not choose gospels that treat of the appearances of the *risen* Lord, we might be inclined to ask.

Today's gospel, continued from last Sunday, is from the lengthy last discourse of the fourth gospel (John 14-17). Most scholars agree that it was mainly the work of the evangelist who gathered together the meditations and reflections of his community upon the authentic sayings and teachings of Jesus, all this in an effort to live as Easter people in the decades after Jesus' resurrection. So, in effect, the deep theological and christological insights expressed in the "last" discourse could be regarded as an "Easter program" for living out the implications of Jesus' victory over sin and death.

Today's pericope begins and ends with an appeal to love the Lord and to manifest that love in obedience to his commands (vv. 14, 21). Usually the gospels exhort the followers of Jesus to *believe* in him. But here in the fourth gospel, faith and obedience to Jesus' commands have been deepened and raised to the level of love. Recall that at the institution of the Mosaic law, observance of its statutes was based on Israel's covenant relationship with God.

Other peoples also had laws by which they were governed (e.g. Code of Hammurabi, etc.) but the motivating factor did not derive from a relationship with their deity. Rather, (1) the proper ordering of society, (2) justice or (3) even fear of reprisal assured these other nations of the observance of their laws. Breach of the law was punished but remained on the level of civil disobedience. Moral, ethical imperatives and/or breach of communion with God did not figure at all.

With Israel, however, ideal observance of the law was raised to a transcendent, supra-political level. Breach of the law, therefore, was regarded as a breach of the union between God and humanity. Those who would call themselves God's people were required to infuse their actions with an attitude of love: "You shall love the Lord your God with all your heart" (Deuteronomy 6:5).

In today's gospel, the Johannine Jesus' words, "If you love me," reveal an identification with the God of the Old Testament, the Father, and an affirmation of the right attitude toward law and life. By virtue of the incarnation, the Father was made manifest. Through their experience of the paraclete, the Spirit of truth whom Jesus would send (vv. 16-17), believers of every age could know and love both Jesus and the Father.

Meaning "helper," "comforter," "advocate," etc., paraclete is a distinctively Johannine term, further explained in 14:26 as well as in 15:26 and 16:7-14. In 1 John 2:1, the term is applied to Jesus himself. The fact that Jesus designated "*another* paraclete" (v. 16) indicated that he understood his *own* role as helper, mediator, advocate between God and his people. Just as Jesus revealed the Father (14:10), so would the paraclete reveal Jesus (16:13-15).

As today's gospel indicates, the Johannine community of the 90s C.E. recognized that the Spirit (paraclete) was for them what the historical Jesus had been for his disciples during his ministry. Just as Jesus had been the "way to the Father" (see last week's gospel), so too in the "post-resurrection pre-parousia era" the Holy Spirit is the way by which and through which the believer knows the way to the Father.

In addition to revealing the "way" of Jesus and the "way" to the Father, the Spirit-paraclete will be a source of truth (v. 17) for the community (just as Jesus is, John 14:5). *Always* with us, as Jesus promised (v. 16), the Spirit enables the church to search sincerely for what is right. This, of course does not preclude the fact that mistakes can be made.

As T. Maertens and J. Frisque have explained, "The real marvel of assistance from the Spirit of truth is not that no error has been committed by the church, but that, over and above all errors, the church has never been deserted by the truth of God. The fact is that the truth in the church is not the result of reflection but a gift!"

Having bequeathed to his followers the gift of the Spirit who would continue to show the way to reveal the truth and to impart life, the mission of the earthly Jesus was not ended but entered upon a new phase. That new phase, in which the Johannine church of the 90s once participated and in which we now participate, is the interim between Jesus' resurrection and the resurrection to glory of all who believe in him.

During this interim it is the privilege of the church to be "another paraclete." In that capacity, believers in Jesus, motivated by love (vv. 14, 21), are responsible for keeping his commands (v. 21), for recognizing the Lord and for making his truth known (v. 17).

1. Cooperation between the charismatic and administrative elements within the church is an unbeatable combination (Acts).

2. Just as we unite our struggles to the suffering of the Lord, so we will share in his glory (1 Peter).

3. Keeping the law can be raised from the level of mere legality when a heart is motivated by love (John).

Seventh Sunday of Easter

In Jesus' sacred, saving hour, a great liturgy of love began upon the earth. Through his word and in the sacred bread of his body, all are drawn toward the Father to receive life and glory (John). Because of Jesus, all who suffer are privileged to share in his redemptive power (1 Peter); all who pray and wait in hope will know the fullness of his Spirit (Acts).

Acts 1:12-14. Movie buffs will recall the delightful old westerns in which certain scenes would be separated by a message, flashed upon the screen, that read, "Meanwhile, back at the ranch . . ." This transitional message served to change gears, as it were, by heightening the suspense and alerting the viewer to a new wrinkle in the plot.

In a sense, today's first reading from Acts could be thought of as a "meanwhile-back-at-the-ranch" literary signal to Luke's readers. In this seemingly insignificant bit of narrative, the author has made several important points.

First of all, the text established the centrality of the apostles in the nascent church. With the historical Jesus gone from their midst, Luke has shown that contact with the Lord would not be lost but would still be possible in and through the apostolic eyewitnesses.

Another function of today's pericope was to provide a dramatic interlude between two great moments of our salvation, ascension and Pentecost. For theological and pedagogical reasons, Luke chose to separate the mighty deeds God performed in Jesus. Tradition has followed the Lucan schematization; certainly, it is more easily adapted for celebrating these saving realities liturgically. But it should be understood that these events (passion, resurrection, ascension, Pentecost) are various facets or moments of *one event* and should not be thought of as segmented entities.

One of Luke's intentions in separating the great event of salvation into its various moments was to illustrate the fundamental Christian posture, viz., waiting in hope for the Lord. Karl Barth called the artificial Lucan interim between ascension and Pentecost "a significant pause" between the actions of God.

Waiting and praying (v. 14) together, the believers could better perceive the God-who-acts and assimilate the consequences of his revelation. This first official gathering of the post-resurrection church to pray, to wait and to hope together was intended by Luke as a model for all believers living in the interim between Jesus' advents.

In addition to the apostles, Luke mentioned Mary, Jesus' mother, other women and Jesus' brothers. "Brothers" did not necessarily indicate a sibling relationship to Jesus; according to Jewish custom, all male relatives (whom we would call cousins) were termed "brothers." This concept of the extended family, common throughout the ancient Near Eastern world, is still known and applied today.

Of greater importance than their physical relationship to Jesus was the *attitude* of those who gathered in his name in Jerusalem. During his ministry, Jesus' "brothers" often misunderstood him and on occasion feared that he had gone quite mad (Mark 3:16). When he was arrested, he was deserted by those who were closest to him all during his ministry (Matthew 26:56). At his trial, there were none to speak in his defense.

As he hung on the cross, only a few ventured back to him (John 19:25-26). In sharp contrast was their change of heart in the wake of Jesus' resurrection. The apostles' (et al.) waiting in prayer together bears witness to their faith and new awareness of all Jesus was and had become for them.

Mary, of course, as elsewhere in the Christian scriptures, represents the believer par excellence. As such, she was present at each significant moment of Jesus' life: at the beginning of his earthly existence (Matthew 1—2, Luke 1—2), at the beginning and end of his ministry (John 2, 19), at the emergence of the church (Acts 1—2), and at the eschatological fulfillment (Revelation 12). In both volumes of his work Luke paralleled the story of Jesus' beginnings (Luke 1—2) with the beginnings of his church (Acts 1—2). In both accounts, the Spirit was manifested (Luke 1:35, Acts 2:4) and in both instances Mary was represented as a model of faith for all believers.

1 Peter 4:13-16. At the time when the author of 1 Peter wrote the exhortation that comprises today's second reading, it was becoming increasingly difficult to be a follower of Jesus. No longer accepted as sectarians of Judaism (a licit religion, tolerated by Rome) because of the Jamnia edict in the mid-80s C.E., Christians were deemed a dangerous and illicit group of troublemakers. *Persona non grata* throughout the empire, every Christian was thereby subjected to persecution and suffering.

To those who were experiencing the imperial wrath, the author of 1 Peter offered the consolation of seeing their suffering *as one* with the sufferings of Jesus. Today's text, with its great similarity to the counsels of the beatitudes (Matthew 5:3-12; Luke 6:20-26), is a locus classicus in the New Testament for the interpretation of Jesus' death in terms of redemptive suffering.

It is also an excellent example of the manner in which the existential situation can be the impetus for deeper theological and ethical insights. Honed to a fine sharpness by the pain of persecution, the perception of the author and his readers penetrated deep into the mystery of Christ's passion and enabled them to find positive redemptive value in their personal passions as well.

To lift the hopes of his readers beyond their present difficulties, the author reminded them that, just as Christ's passion had been a prelude to glory, so too would theirs. For this reason the call to "rejoice insofar as you share Christ's sufferings" (v. 13) is not a sadistic statement but an expression of holy acceptance of the extremely dear cost of discipleship.

Present also in the text is the underlying theme of the "last days." Christians had come to associate adversity and suffering with the final times; indeed, as other New Testament writers had pointed out (Matthew 24:2, Thessalonians 2:1-8), the eschatological climax could *not* be realized *without* prior suffering. But just as Jesus had assured his followers that they would not be left alone, so too the author of 1 Peter reminded his readers of the presence of the Spirit (v. 14).

The theme of tribulation and the presence of the Spirit was frequent in first century Christian literature (John 15:18—16:15; Romans 8:18-23). In fact, it was believed that persecution, tribulations, etc., were a *means* of manifesting the presence of the Spirit; consequently, both trials and the Spirit-comforter were signals of the inauguration of the end and the beginning of glory.

Finally, this pericope from 1 Peter is one of the few New Testament texts to use the designation "Christian" (see also Acts 11:26). The author's statement, "If anyone suffers for being a Christian" (v. 16), may remind modern readers of a similar saying that decorated many a banner over the past several years: "If you were charged with being a Christian, would there be enough evidence to convict you?"

John 17:1-11. No less than six times in today's reading (and eight times in the entire prayer: John 17:1-26) did the fourth evangelist place on Jesus' lips the word "glory." A major biblical motif, "glory" (*kabod*) was used by the Old Testament authors to illustrate God's goodness in providing for his people in the wilderness (Exodus 16:7-10). God's presence in the fire and in the cloud was called "glory" (Exodus 24:17, 16:10) and God's saving intervention was described in terms of his manifesting his "glory" (Ezekiel 29:46, Isaiah 66:18-19). God's presence made manifest in connection with the tent of meeting (Exodus 25:8, 40:34) and the temple (1 Kings 8:11) was also referred to as "glory."

Undoubtedly, the evangelist drew upon this Old Testament background when he described Jesus' incarnation: "He dwelled among us (literally: he pitched his tent among us) and we saw his *glory*" (John 1:14). Throughout his gospel, the Johannine author portrayed Jesus and his ministry as a progressive process of glorification. Through Jesus' words and works, the Father was visibly manifested and glorified (John 2:11, 11:4, 40, 12:28).

Here, therefore, at the high point of Jesus' "hour," his prayer to his Father could be called the apotheosis of glory. For it was through Jesus' "hour," i.e., through his passion, death, resurrection and exaltation, that the Father's loving intervention would reach its climax.

Already in the fifth century C.E., Cyril of Alexandria referred to John 17:1-26 as Christ's "priestly prayer" and in the 16th century Lutheran theologian David Chrytraus called it the *high* priestly prayer. Both Cyril and Chrytraus recognized that the priestly character of Jesus' prayer was similar to the prayer of Aaron (Leviticus 9:16). As high priest, Aaron was to offer prayer: for himself, for his household and for all the assembly of Israel.

So too in John 17:1-26 Jesus is portrayed as praying: for himself (vv. 1-5), for his followers (vv. 6-19) and for all who would come after him (vv. 20-26). Our gospel pericope for today is comprised of Jesus' prayer for himself and an excerpt from his prayer for his disciples.

Forming as it does the conclusion of the farewell discourse to his disciples, John 17 may be compared to the book of Deuteronomy, purported to be Moses' farewell address to his people. Integral to the genre of the farewell address was an air of poignancy because it was placed on the lips of one soon to die. Therefore, the message and its impact were very intense and moving.

As he had taught during his ministry, Jesus' "hour," i.e., his reason for coming among them, would culminate in gifts of salvation for those who believe in him. In his prayer, Jesus explained those gifts in terms of "eternal life." By means of the parenthetical comment in v. 3, the Johannine Jesus equated eternal life with knowing God. Some have suggested that this reference to "knowledge" reflects a gnostic tendency or influence in the fourth gospel.

But such an observation reads too shallow a meaning into John's use of the word knowledge. The evangelist was drawing upon the Hebrew sense of the verb which involved more than an intellectual type of knowing. "To know" connoted the intimacy of immediate experience. In Genesis, Adam was said to have "known" his wife Eve and from that "knowing" a child was born. "To know" God, therefore, in the sense of John 17:43 meant to be called into an intimate relationship with the Father, like the one that Jesus the Son "knew" and enjoyed.

Knowledge of God was also one of the characteristics of the eschatological age when the whole earth would be filled with God's glory (Habakkuk 2:14). Paul had referred to the enjoyment of this sort of knowledge as a *future* blessing: "I know now in part, but then I shall know even as I am known" (1 Corinthians 13:12).

However, for the author of the fourth gospel, future eschatological realities and the joy of knowing God have penetrated human existence in the hour of Jesus. The Johannine Jesus did not speak only in terms of a *future* glory or a *future* knowing or an hour yet to come. On the contrary, knowledge of and intimate participation with Jesus in his hour, in his glory, is to taste eternal life *here and now*.

Some have suggested that because of its context in the gospel, John 17 could be regarded as a sort of eucharistic prayer. Spoken at the end of his teaching mission (liturgy of the word) and before his sacrifice (breaking of the bread of his body, liturgy of the Eucharist), Jesus in John 17 is celebrating a liturgy of life. In this prayer, Jesus blessed and consecrated *in himself* all who would enter with him into his hour and through that hour pass with him into the glory of eternal life.

1. Life is a process of waiting for the Lord and of finding him in prayer together (Acts).

2. All who suffer for belonging to Jesus will also know the joy of his glory (1 Peter).

3. Eternity begins in every moment when Jesus is recognized as the life and hope of the world (John).

Pentecost Sunday

Ushering in the new age of salvation and giving new meaning to human existence, the Holy Spirit bolstered the fearful and made them bold in their preaching of the Lord (Acts). Endowing each with a specific and necessary talent, the presence of the Spirit made the community of believers cohesive and charismatic (1 Corinthians). Filled with Jesus' Spirit, his followers go forth to a universal mission of peace and forgiveness (John).

Acts 2:1-11. Pentecost is a term Christians have come to associate with the outpouring of the Spirit upon the apostles of Jesus, but originally the feast had its roots in Jewish tradition. Pentecost (Greek: 50 days) or Shevuoth (Hebrew: Weeks) was an ancient agricultural feast that celebrated the grain harvest. Called the Feast of Weeks or Firstfruits, Shevuoth or Pentecost was historicized in later Judaism and, in addition to its agricultural associations, became a commemoration of the gift of the law at Sinai.

According to Jewish tradition, Moses and the escapees from Egypt traveled for seven weeks from Egypt to Sinai. During that period, the people were morally formed by Moses, and the gift of the law was purported to be God's approbation of their efforts. Similarly, contemporary reformed Judaism dedicates the seven week period between Passover and Pentecost to the intense religious education of young people who on the feast of Shevuoth or Pentecost affirm as a group their willingness to live according to the law and its divine principles. In Jesus' day, the Essenes of Qumran admitted new members to their community on the feast of Shevuoth-Pentecost. Probably Luke had in mind all these ideas (moral formation, the law, affirmation, new membership and harvest) when he associated the gift of the Spirit with the Jewish feast of Pentecost. Indeed, all these elements are featured to a greater or lesser degree in the celebration of the Spirit in the church.

With regard to the aspect of moral formation, there was no doubt that a transformation had occurred among Jesus' followers. The very people who had been frightened by both Jewish and Roman authorities at Passover, the very ones who had been disappointed at what they had hoped might have been accomplished by Jesus, the very people who had deserted Jesus in his final hours—these were the *same* ones who affirmed their faith in him at Pentecost and were able to appropriate for themselves and for others the realities of Jesus' cross, his rising, exaltation and glory. What had been for the Jews a celebration of the ingathering of grain and of the law had become for Jesus' followers a feast of the new law of Christ's love and of the ingathering of all peoples to the Father in Jesus.

Always careful to illustrate the continuity between the disciples and Jesus, and thereby to legitimize and authenticate the work of the church, Luke posited the Spirit as the chief source of that continuity. A comparison of Luke's first volume (gospel) with his second volume (Acts) will reveal a deliberate correlation of the major events of Jesus' life with those of the developing church. For example, in both Jesus' birth and in the birth of the church, the overshadowing presence of the Spirit figured very importantly (Luke 1:35, Acts 2:2). Just as the Spirit had empowered Jesus (Luke 4:18) for his mission of healing and preaching, so that same Spirit would make his disciples bold and strong to continue his mission.

Although in his schema of salvation Luke has separated the great moments of our redemption (resurrection; then 40 days later, ascension; then ten days later, Pentecost), the reader must bear in mind the fact that Pentecost or the outpouring of the Spirit is inextricably bound to the reality of the resurrection. Moreover, the gift of the Spirit was not a *unique* incident that could be relegated to *one* particular date, place or time. Rather, the risen Jesus unleashed the Spirit, as it were, a continuous, powerful and empowering gift. In an effort to do justice to the unquantifiable and limitless qualities of the Spirit, Luke described Pentecost in terms of wind and fire. Standard props for the Old Testament theophanies, the literary signals of wind and fire announced a new theophany: the Spirit-filled manifestation of Jesus in his followers for the sake of the world.

1 Corinthians 12:3-7, 12-13. Some have suggested that Paul derived his analogy of the body (v. 12) from a similar metaphor used by the philosopher Zeno (Stoicism). If this suggestion is true, the concept would have been well known in Corinth, a center for the ancient Stoic philosophers. Others have proposed that Paul had in mind the gnostic myth of the cosmic redeemer whose body was thought to be comprised of the saved. More recently, some have suggested that Paul's ideas were influenced by the Corinthian god Asklepios. Archaeological excavations have unearthed numerous terra cotta heads, arms, feet, hands and eyes at the site of the ancient sanctuary to Asklepios, god of healing. But Paul's ideas and theology are far superior to Stoic, gnostic and Greek mythical thought; in fact, Leander Keck has proposed that the analogy of the body of Christ is Paul's *unique* and *distinctive* contribution to ecclesiology and community self-understanding.

Paul had labored for 18 months in Corinth and had succeeded in drawing together into a viable community people from a variety of backgrounds. Some had come to Christ from the background of the mystery (Orphic) cults where they had been engaged in bizarre and fanatical orgies masquerading under the guise of religion. In an effort to initiate these former cult members into the faith, Paul endeavored to temper their emotionalism and to channel their energies into a sincere and powerful force for Christ. When the Spirit of Jesus impelled a believer, the result would not be individualistic, frenzied or uncontrolled behavior (as in the cults). Rather, the one who acted in and by the Spirit of Jesus contributed in a charismatic but ordered way toward the benefit of the entire community (v. 7).

Paul's remarks that comprise today's second reading were probably occasioned by a dispute concerning those who claimed to possess the *true* Spirit. For Paul, the union of the Lord with the faithful and of the faithful with one another was possible *only because of the Spirit*. Not only did the Spirit make one capable of authentic faith (v. 3) but the Spirit was also the impetus of the graces that built up and enhanced the quality of communal life.

John 20:19-23. When the New Testament authors composed the resurrection appearance narratives, it was not their intention merely to sensationalize the fact that one who had died had been seen alive by some of those who loved him. On the contrary, the resurrection appearance stories represent a deliberate theological effort on the part of the early believers in Jesus to explain: (1) how the absent Jesus remained present to the community, (2) how the community should conduct itself in light of the reality of Jesus' resurrection, and (3) how the Old Testament promises and prophecies had been fulfilled in the risen Jesus. As P. Perkins has noted in her excellent study, *Resurrection* (1984), the appearance narratives enabled the church to "extend the presence of Jesus back to the promises of salvation as well as forward to the experiences of the community." In today's gospel, a Johannine appearance narrative, all the above concerns can be identified.

With regard to the concern about how the absent Jesus remained present to the community (number 1 above), the Johannine evangelist has portrayed the risen Lord as bestowing the Spirit upon his followers. As promised in the gospel (14:16-17, 26), the Spirit-paraclete would be for them a source of peace and joy (14:27, 16:20, 22) as well as an impetus and strength to enable the disciples to do the same works as Jesus "and even greater" (14:12).

Notice that the Johannine author (as distinct from the Lucan evangelist) has made a deliberate association of Jesus' resurrection with the gift of the Spirit, presenting both as occurring on the *same day*, the first day of the week. He also takes care to establish a continuity between the cross and the resurrection, between the Jesus of history and the Jesus of faith. Displaying the character of his risen, transformed state (the doors were locked, but suddenly Jesus was there) as well as the physical qualities of Jesus' wounds (he showed then his hands and his side), the author thus explained that the risen Jesus and the Jesus of Nazareth are one and the same reality.

In an effort to illustrate the manner in which believers should conduct their lives in the post-resurrection era (number 2 above), the evangelist has depicted Jesus' commissioning of his followers to a ministry of mercy and of forgiveness. In later centuries, this mandate of Jesus was cited as a source text for understanding the sacrament of penance or reconciliation. Some have proposed that the reference to forgiving and binding (v. 13) should be understood as the prerogative to confer or to withhold baptism, depending upon the catechumen's acceptance or rejection of the kerygma. Others, citing the rabbinical equivalents, *asar* and *sera'* (bind, loose), and referring to Matthew 18:18, would have us understand Jesus' mandate in the context of church discipline--the granting or refusing of admission to the community based on reasons of worthiness or sinfulness.

While these later anachronisms may find *some* support in today's gospel, there is a more primary meaning intended by the evangelist. Combined with the gift of peace, the mission of forgiveness to which the risen Lord commended his followers is an indication that, by virtue of Jesus' passion and death, he can share with all believers his victory over sin and death. The message of the cross was not failure but forgiveness; that message makes the day of Pentecost a celebration of power and peace.

Finally, today's gospel underscored the aspect of fulfillment (see number 3 above) in Jesus' death and resurrection. Jesus' double salutation, "Peace be with you" (vv. 19, 21) and his breathing on his followers (v. 22) were a sign that a new era was dawning upon the human community. As promised by the prophets (Joel 3:1, Ezekiel 36:27), the new age of God's saving intervention was associated with an outpouring of the Spirit. This new age of salvation, a new creation, as it were, was realized in and through the mission of Jesus who suffered, died and rose to glory in complete acceptance of and obedience to the Father's will. Because of his saving deeds, all who believe would be freed from the shackles of sin to experience the new freedom of mercy and forgiveness in his Spirit.

In the same manner in which the creator God breathed into his creatures (Genesis 1 and 2) and sustained them, so would the redeemer God, Jesus, breathe into his followers the saving breath of life. In its mission of mercy and forgiveness, the church must continue to breathe life into all peoples.

1. Because of the Spirit, all languages can sing the same song of victory and joy (Acts).

2. When the gifts of each are put at the service of all, the result is charismatic; when the gifts of each are used for selfish purposes, there is chaos (1 Corinthians).

3. Peace, mercy and forgiveness are the fruits of the true Spirit (John).

Ordinary Time
Second Sunday in Ordinary Time

Christianity is a continual process of survival and celebration. Those who recognize the salvation effected by Jesus are graced with his victory and light (Matthew). Survivors of the darkness of sin and death are called to celebrate their blessings in Christ (1 Corinthians) and to extend a saving, helping hand to a still struggling humanity (Isaiah).

Isaiah 49:3, 5-6. Traditionally, this week has been set aside by the church and dedicated to a special period of prayer for church unity (January 18-25; Church Unity Octave). Politically, this week is also important for citizens of the U.S. because the president will appear before Congress to deliver his State of the Union address. In a very real sense, both of these ideas (that of unity of all peoples in God, and a program for the just and equitable government of these same people) are encompassed by today's first reading.

Second of the four servant songs included in the work of Deutero-Isaiah (Isaiah 40-55), today's pericope was originally intended to encourage those Israelites who were exiled in Babylon (587-538 B.C.E.). In this second song, it seems that the author intended Israel to think of itself as a nation in terms of the servant. "You are my servant, Israel" (v. 3) reflects that special election that began in Egypt, was solidified by the covenant at Sinai and for which Israel was to be responsible in all its undertakings. Because the nation proved itself unworthy of God's call and of his special covenantal care, the prophets warned that Israel would suffer divine retribution. When Babylon overpowered Judah and deported the elite of the people, the prophets believed that God had acted to chastise his erring people. But, the prophets assumed, God would not completely desert his people. Faithful forever to his covenant alliance (2 Samuel 7:14) with Israel, God would act to bring about their restoration. Deutero-Isaiah recognized in the person of Cyrus, the king of Persia, the saving power of God. When Cyrus and his troops defeated the Babylonians and allowed all the displaced peoples in Babylon to return to their own lands, Deutero-Isaiah interpreted this political act as a religious reconciliation. Returning home to Israel and the political reinstatement of its government was symptomatic for Isaiah of Israel's religious and moral return to the Lord.

Later, when the early Christians looked to the Old Testament scriptures for texts with which to substantiate their faith in Jesus, the servant songs proved to be most worthy vehicles apologetically and theologically. Israel's return from Babylon was seen as a mere prefigurement of the return to God that would be accomplished by Jesus. By his words and works and by the saving act of the cross, Jesus effected a moral return or conversion to the God not only of Israel but of all the nations of the earth. By dispelling the spiritual darkness that had become a part of human existence due to sin, and by bringing the light of God's own justice to *all* the nations, Jesus extended the blessings of salvation to the ends of the earth (v. 6). His sacrifice on the cross effected redemption once and for all. Nevertheless, the daily challenge of returning to the Lord remains the responsibility of the church that claims him as its head.

1 Corinthians 1:1-3. Paul's greeting to the church at Corinth that comprises today's second reading serves to introduce us to that community and to the wise counsel the apostle shared with his converts there. For about 18 months, Paul had labored (Acts 18:1-17) in Corinth (ca. 50-51 C.E.), the largest city of Greece at that time and the capital of the Roman province of Achaia. A seaport city located on the trade route that connected east to west, Corinth was home to a vast and varied array of cultures and peoples. It was these very features which attracted Paul to the city; if he could establish a firm foundation of the faith in Corinth, it would spread easily from there to other areas of the province. While it was an ideal geographical location for a foundation, Corinth was by no means an easy mission. Infamous for its many taverns and loose living, Corinth's patron deity was Aphrodite, goddess of love. Throughout the city there were numerous temples where devotees of the goddess could offer homage and exercise her "virtues." For all its cosmopolitan attractions and shortcomings, Corinth was surprisingly receptive to Paul's efforts and proved to be one of the apostle's most enthusiastic communities.

About six years later while in Ephesus, Paul received news of problems in Corinth that threatened the unity of the community and the integrity of the gospel. Paul's response to those difficulties probably took the form of several letters, only two of which have survived. Some have called the 16 chapters of 1 Corinthians a grand overview of Christian theology and morality because, within these chapters, Paul had considered the meaning and nature of salvation, the source and bond of community, morality, marriage, Jewish-gentile relations, conscience, discipline, the sacraments (especially the Eucharist), spiritual charisms and the resurrection.

In his greeting, Paul addressed his converts as "the church of God that is in Corinth" (v. 2). By placing Corinth in the context of the universal church, he called the community there to an awareness of itself not as autonomous (for this was a tendency of the Corinthians) but as a local representation of the greater cosmic reality of church. Unfortunately, some in Corinth has lost sight of the larger picture and regarded *themselves* and their particular gifts as central. Throughout his preaching to the Corinthian Christians, Paul never ceased to remind them of their union in and mutual dependence on Christ and one another. "In Christ" (v. 2), a favorite phrase of Paul's occurring some 165 times in his correspondence, meant having a personal relationship with Christ so intimate and so all encompassing as to empower the believer to become *like* Christ.

Quoting the customary literary salutation, Paul informed the words with soteriological significance. Grace (*charis*), God's saving gifts, and peace (*eirene*), the joy of forgiveness and reconciliation, were to be valued as blessings from the Father bestowed on all believers because of and *in Christ*.

John 1:29-34. By the time the Johannine author wrote his gospel, the "problem" of Jesus' being baptized by John had become even more acute than in Matthew's day (see commentary on last Sunday's gospel). Similarly, as is readily seen in a comparison of the gospels, the christology of the fourth gospel reveals a marked development over that of the synoptics. Both of these issues, Jesus' baptism and John's high christology, are treated in today's gospel pericope.

In the Johannine gospel, there is no doubt as to the superiority of Jesus over John the Baptizer. Always deflecting the crowd's attention away from himself and toward Jesus, the Baptizer (in the fourth gospel) declared again and again his subordinate position. "*After me* is to come a man who ranks *ahead of me,* because he was *before me*" (v. 30), proclaimed the Baptizer to his followers. In this statement the Johannine author has answered those among his contemporaries who erroneously revered John the Baptizer as messiah. In age, John was older than Jesus; how could he speak of Jesus being before him? Obviously, the point in question was not simply one of chronology. Rather, the issue was both a theological and christological one. As is reflected in Mark's gospel, the Christians of the 60s C.E. and/or early 70s C.E. believed that the christological moment (i.e., that moment when Jesus became messiah) occurred at Jesus' baptism. As knowledge about Jesus deepened, as reflected in the later gospels of Matthew and Luke (80s C.E.), the church began to realize that Jesus was Lord and savior from the moment of his conception. Hence, the authors of Matthew and Luke included in their gospels a section (Matthew 1 and 2, Luke 1 and 2) known today as the infancy narratives. In these stories of Jesus' conception and birth, he is already portrayed as Son of God and savior. But in the church of the 90s C.E., as reflected in the Johannine prologue, as well as in today's text, there was a realization that Christ existed (preexisted) before John and *indeed* that he was *with* God and *was* God from all eternity (John 1:1-14).

By having John bear witness to the higher christology of the late first century church, the Johannine author has also made the Baptizer the enunciator of several messianic titles: "Lamb of God," "God's chosen one" and "he who is to baptize with the Holy Spirit." "Lamb of God" (v. 29) was a title that recalled for John's readers several different images. Perhaps the one that springs to mind most quickly is that of the paschal lamb. According to the tradition recorded in Exodus (12:22), the Israelites were saved from death by smearing the blood from a lamb on the lintels and doorposts of their homes. That the Johannine author understood Jesus' mission in terms of the paschal lamb symbolism has been borne out by further references in the gospel. For example, in John 19:14, the evangelist made a point of mentioning that Jesus was condemned to death at noon on the eve of Passover; this was the very time when the priests began to sacrifice the passover lambs in the temple. Another association is made between Jesus and the paschal lamb when the evangelist noted that none of Jesus' bones was broken on the cross (see Exodus 12:46 and John 19:36). Another image evoked by the title lamb of God can be traced to the book of Revelation (5:6ff). There the slain but victorious lamb *does away with* the sins of the world (John 1:29). Yet another lamb image can be found in the fourth servant song (Isaiah 52:13--53:12) where the suffering lamb *bears* the sins of others, thereby affording salvation to those who would otherwise not receive it. The title "God's chosen one" (v. 34) may also be drawn from the servant songs (Isaiah 42:1, 49:3) and the reference to Jesus' baptism with the Holy Spirit (v. 33) served to underscore the *preparatory* nature of John's work as compared to the *salvific* nature of Jesus' mission. Where John's had been a baptism of repentance, Jesus offered to the world a sacrament where those who believed entered with him into death and emerged with him, victorious over sin, to live forever.

1. The mission of the Lord's servant, i.e., the responsibility of bringing light and life to the nations, has been delegated to all who call themselves followers of Jesus (Isaiah).

2. Whether it be the church of God which is in Corinth or Chicago or Cincinnati or Chattanooga, all churches and all citizens of the earth are made one by and in Christ (1 Corinthians).

3. Though he did not fully understand or recognize the man or his mission, John was nevertheless a true and faithful witness to Jesus (John).

Third Sunday in Ordinary Time

If we had the power to save humanity, where, with whom and how would we begin? There is a valuable, albeit paradoxical, lesson to be learned in the divine "modus operandi." To preach the most eloquent news the world would ever know, God chose simple Galilean fishermen (Matthew). He drew together into a community people who had lost sight of that good news and became instead enamored of its various messengers (1 Corinthians). He taught the lessons of freedom through slavery's chains and let his people discover light through the lessons of darkness (Isaiah).

Isaiah 8:23--9:3. Light and darkness, harvest and famine as naturally occurring phenomena have readily lent themselves to the scriptural authors as symbols for goodness and evil, life and death, salvation and perdition, etc. When Isaiah of Jerusalem, the eighth century prophet, proclaimed the oracle that comprises today's first reading, he perceived as darkness and gloom the fact that the northern kingdom was tottering under the blows of foreign oppression. As indicated in today's pericope, the northern territorial provinces of Zebulun and Naphtali had already fallen to the Assyrian troops led by Tiglath Pileser III. For those who regarded this political crisis in the north as the death knell for the southern kingdom, Isaiah held out the hope of a new harvest, the hope of a light in the darkness, i.e., the hope for the salvation that the Lord alone could effect for his faithful ones. Just as he attributed the dark shadows of defeat in Napthtali and Zebulun to God's just chastisement of an unfaithful people, so too, Isaiah promised that spiritual and ethical fidelity would be blessed with the light of victory and political stability. Some scholars have proposed that in its original context, Isaiah spoke this oracle to celebrate the accession to the throne of one of the Judean kings. All of Israel's hopes for a sure and glorious future could be hung on such a king who would by God's power realize for all the people the promises of 2 Samuel 7:14. With an allusion to Gideon's victory over the Midianites (Judges 7:16-25), Isaiah gave voice to the desires of his people to leave behind the signs of their oppression, i.e., the burdening yoke, the pole and the taskmaster's rod (Isaiah 9:3).

When those who came to believe in Jesus as the saving light of the world remembered Isaiah's oracle, they understood it in reference to their Lord. For example, this same Isaian text overlaps with the first reading chosen for the Christmas liturgy at midnight. Read in the context of the Christmas feast, the Isaian oracle forms an apt description of what the birth of Jesus meant for the world. As the light who shines in the darkness of human need and suffering, Jesus' advent could be described as a saving dawn, as a penetrating ray of truth and justice.

Today, on the Third Sunday in ordinary time, this same text has been applied by the Matthean evangelist to the beginning of Jesus' public ministry in Galilee. In both instances, i.e., in Jesus' nativity and in his mission, the light of God's goodness, acting in and through Jesus, dispelled the darkness of sin. As R. Fuller has pointed out, the two moments, Jesus' nativity and his mission, cannot really be separated. Both are integral aspects of the single Christ event. For those who have been incorporated into the totality of the Christ event through baptism, there remains the responsibility of *being* and *bringing* light to all the Zebuluns and Naphtalis of our world.

1 Corinthians 1:10-13, 17. Prior to coming to preach the good news in Corinth, Paul had been in Athens (Acts 17). There, despite valiant efforts on his part, Paul had made no headway and was unable to establish a community of Christians. Only later did the seeds Paul had planted in Athens begin to grow through the continued apostolic efforts of other witnesses to Jesus. Paul had met the Athenians on their own terms. He had taken a heady and philosophical approach, speaking only in general terms of humanity's search for the divine. After hearing him, the people of Athens, who prided themselves on their intellectual appetite and acumen, told Paul that *maybe* they might hear him again on another occasion. This was hardly the response desired by the apostle whose goal was to convert *all* peoples to the Lord. Perhaps the disappointment he experienced in Athens made Paul all the more adamant when he came to Corinth. Wisdom, he insisted, was not a matter of human philosophy or mental gymnastics but the gift of God made flesh in the person of Jesus. The only true wisdom, Paul claimed, consisted in learning the mind and heart of the God who chose to express his love in the contradiction of the cross.

When worldly and/or philosophical preferences threatened the unity of the church in Corinth, Paul was quick to act. News had reached Paul in Ephesus, via messengers from Chloe, that human preferences were creating factions in Corinth. Four competing groups each claimed that its own leader was superior to other leaders and therefore that its version of the gospel was superior to that of other groups. Some claimed: "I belong to Paul." Paul had probably been the first to bring the gospel to Corinth. Paul's style of preaching the gospel appealed largely to the poor and uneducated members of society. Probably the Pauline faction was composed of such people. Apollos, who came to Corinth after Paul's departure, had attracted a more educated audience. He was a native of Alexandria, the most notable intellectual center of its day, famous for its allegorical method of scriptural interpretation. P. Wrightman has suggested that Apollos' esoteric style probably appealed to those who were already tempted by gnosticism, a philosophic fad of the day that maintained secret knowledge was the key to heaven. Another faction whose members attached themselves to Cephas (Peter) was probably comprised mainly of Jewish Christians who clung to the law as central and claimed it to be essential for Christian faith. Still another group of Christians prided themselves as belonging exclusively to Christ from whom they claimed to receive direct special revelation and extraordinary charisms.

Directly confronting each of these factional groups, Paul reminded the Christians of Corinth of their basic unity in Christ. That unity, challenged Paul, was to supersede every human preference and was superior to every human wisdom, however attractive.

Matthew 4:12-23. Matthew's gospel is the outgrowth of a deeply theological mind (or "school" of minds: Stendahl) and as such it reflects the abilities of its author(s) whose faith in Jesus was matched by an ardent desire to *share* that faith with others. A complexity of pastoral concerns has shaped the gospel, not the least the intention of proclaiming Jesus as the fulfillment of all of Israel's centuries-old expectation. To accomplish his purpose, the Matthean evangelist has created for his gospel an infrastructure of fulfillment quotations. Drawn from both the Hebrew and Septuagint versions of the scriptures, these quotations (totalling 11 or 12) have each been introduced by a stereotyped formula that underscored the idea of fulfillment and applied the quotation to a specific event in the life of Jesus. Because these fulfillment quotations are a unique feature of Matthew's gospel, scholars believe that this series of scriptural references provides us with a clue to the origin and purpose of the evangelist's work. Scattered throughout the gospel, the quotations touch upon all the major features of Jesus' life: his birth (1:23; 2:6,15,18,23), his entry into Galilee and the inauguration of his mission (4:15-16), his healings (8:17), his love and compassion (12:18-21), his teachings (13:35), his triumphal entry into Jerusalem (21:5), climaxing with his passion and death (26:56, 27:9-10).

Some have proposed that Matthew utilized the fulfillment quotations for *apologetic* reasons, i.e., to *prove* that Jesus was the messiah. Others have discerned a more *polemical* motivation, believing the evangelist used the quotations to *contradict* and *counteract* a growing rejection of Jesus and of Christians. But Stendahl, a leading Matthean expert, proposed that Matthew used the quotes to interpret the life of Jesus for his followers. Gundry (et al.) claimed that Matthew's Old Testament quotations outlined a whole kaleidoscope of Israel's hopes for salvation. Because Matthew used a mixture of sources (Hebrew, Septuagintal and Aramaic), his structure of quotations accurately reflected the trilingual and tricultural matrix of late first century C.E. Palestine. Therefore, Matthew's series of quotes served to answer the hopes of these different cultures and to portray Jesus as royal messiah, Isaian servant, Danielic son of man, shepherd of Israel, savior from sin, giver of rest, a new Moses, son of David and true Israel.

In today's gospel, the universal character of Jesus' saving mission has been highlighted. By quoting the Isaian text concerning Zebulun and Naphtali, the Galilee of the gentiles, and by placing the beginning of Jesus' ministry in that region, Matthew has also outlined the universal scope of the mission of Jesus' followers. Matthew's version of Mark's "Day in Capernaum" (Mark 2), today's pericope contains in a nutshell the essentials of Jesus' ministry. He proclaimed the kingdom, he called disciples to follow him and to share in his work. He worked great signs of healing for all peoples. By interpolating the quotation from Isaiah (8:23—9:1) into his Marcan source, and by expanding upon a minor point of geography, Matthew succeeded in making a major theological statement about salvation, viz., it is *for all*, it is *universal*. In order to accomplish his theological purpose, Matthew had to deal inaccurately with some geographical details (4:13). For example, in Isaiah's oracle, the "sea" referred to the Mediterranean Sea or the Great Sea as it was called, not to the Sea of Galilee. Also the Isaian text called "heathen Galilee" that area of the northern kingdom that had been overrun by Assyrians. Matthew used the same text to refer to the religiously impoverished hinterland of humanity in need of salvation.

When recounting the calling of Jesus' first disciples (v. 18-22), Matthew underscored the fact that the initiative came from the Lord. Meeting the would-be followers within the milieu and circumstances of their daily lives, Jesus' call challenged them to reach into the depths of their faith and to grow beyond it, to change (reform) their hearts and their minds so as to follow him into an unknown and greater mission.

Matthew concluded his typical "day" in the life of Jesus with a summary statement (4:23) concerning Jesus' continuing activities. As J. Meier has observed, this summary serves a double function: (1) it concludes the narrative portion of book one of the gospel; (2) it acts as a bracket for the "diptych" of Jesus as messiah of the word and Jesus as messiah of the deed. In 9:35, the evangelist repeated the summary statement of 4:23, thus forming an inclusion around that section of the gospel that portrayed Jesus as teacher of salvation and healing savior (5:3—7:27, sermon on the mount; 8:1—9:34, miracle stories). As teacher and healer, Jesus still calls disciples to his service; as his church, we must recognize our mission and respond to his mandate.

1. Greater joy comes after sadness and a deeper appreciation of God is found in his "absence" (Isaiah).

2. Although the medium is not the message, it is helpful if those who mediate the good news to others are faithful to and worthy of it (1 Corinthians).

3. With the least likely helpers in the least likely locale, Jesus began his saving mission; his church is also called to discover the hidden values in the world's "least likely" (Matthew).

Fourth Sunday in Ordinary Time

Those who humbly and trustfully follow only the Lord (Zephaniah) will be out of step with the worldly wise (1 Corinthians). They will fall prey to the inevitable persecutions and hardships that lead to happiness of the kingdom (Matthew).

Zephaniah 2:3; 3:12-13. Zephaniah (*God protects* or *God treasures*) is a little known prophet, cited but once in the New Testament (Matthew 13:41). His contribution, however, to biblical spirituality is quite substantial. Active during the reign of the religious reformer Josiah (about 640-609 B.C.E.), Zephaniah urged his fellow Judahites to learn from Israel's downfall to Assyria, 100 years before, and to recognize that those circumstances that had brought the northern kingdom to its knees were rampant in Judah as well.

In the few chapters attributed to him, Zephaniah described the aberrations in morality, religious pride, lack of faith in Yahweh's power to save and the false sense of security brought about by prosperity. These factors had turned his people from their need for God. Following his predecessor Amos (see Amos 5:18ff), Zephaniah foresaw a "day of the Lord" which would bring retribution for *all* the nations, *including* Judah. Before Amos, Israel had yearned for the day of the Lord as the dawn of her own triumph and the sunset of destruction for the gentiles.

Today's verses are a promise (2:3) and fulfillment (3:12-13) sandwiched around the prophecies against the nations and Judah as well. Only "the humble of the earth," "those who take refuge in the name of the Lord" would survive the "day." These poor ones (*anawim*) are those who find their riches in the Lord alone and their power in doing his will. This source text for our understanding of the concept of the poor ones obviously implies more than material poverty although the material aspect cannot be downplayed. The poor ones, or humble of the earth, are the "remnant" from which the new Israel will grow.

1 Corinthians 1:26-31. Paul had a difficult time trying to convince the Corinthians of the value of poverty of spirit and meekness. Bustling with their own importance, some of the Corinthian Christian tended to a pretentiousness born of a self-centered rather than a christocentric spirituality. Because of the dualistic nature of their philosophical systems, the Greek Christians in Corinth brought to their following of Christ a somewhat unenlightened view of material creation, seeing it as something to be overcome. To think of a God incarnate in flesh was unthinkable. Paul had to convince them of the goodness of the body (1 Corinthians 6:19-20, 15:35-44).

The Corinthians regarded salvation as "pulling oneself up by the bootstraps," rather than as the gratuitous gift of a loving God. They thought their intellectual pursuit of wisdom would justify them. Believers in a spiritual, intellectual elitism because of their initiation into Christ, they felt themselves privy to a special wisdom and therefore superior to others.

Within this atmosphere of self-sufficiency, Paul preached the all sufficient Christ, wisdom of God, in whom alone is salvation and justice. Reminding them of their rather ordinary origins, much in the same vein as Deuteronomy 7:7, the apostle tried to show the Christians at Corinth that God's wisdom, exemplified in the person of Jesus, was not to be limited to human norms or expectations. In fact, God's ways seem foolish to those who do not accept the mysterious wisdom of Jesus Christ crucified.

In the last verse of today's pericope, Paul echoes Jeremiah 9:23-24, "If anyone wants to boast, let him boast of this: of understanding and knowing me." Those who knew that absolutely everything came from the Lord and that all depended upon him could boast of nothing else but his wondrous goodness.

Matthew 5:1-12. Just as the law of the Old Testament was the guide according to which all should conduct themselves, so too the "beatitudes" in the gospels of Matthew and Luke may be seen as the "bill of rights" of the new Israel. The beatitudes not only delineate membership in the kingdom (poor in spirit, sorrowing, lowly and so on) but they also describe the ethic whereby such membership can be attained (peacemaking, showing mercy, enduring persecution and so on).

Unlike Luke, who sets the scene for this teaching of Jesus in a plain, Matthew puts the setting on a mountain, wishing to portray Jesus as the new Moses, giver of a new law. Just as

Moses on Sinai received God's law for the people of Israel, so Jesus on the mountain delivers the teaching of the new people of God. The very formal "He opened his mouth and taught them" signifies magisterial (rabbinical) authority. The first four beatitudes pertain to the unfortunate ones, the humble and lowly of the earth who are without influence, dignity and means of support. These resemble the poor ones (*anawim*) of Zephaniah and Isaiah who rely totally on the Lord for everything. They are therefore the survivors.

The second four groups actively seek to effect goodness and justice on the earth. They are the architects of the kingdom. The attitudes described in the first four beatitudes make possible the activities of the last four. Matthew's gospel was written in the 80s C.E. The temple had been razed in 70 C.E. and Christians had been barred by edict from the synagogues. They were persecuted by Jews and Romans alike. They were like a people without a nation, a nation without a land. To them, the beatitudes were words of comfort.

Lest it be understood in too narrow a sense, the "poor" certainly referred to the economically disadvantaged. But to leave it at that would be to limit the concept. On the other hand, to spiritualize totally the concept would fall short of the mark also. To be poor in the gospel sense is to be one totally in need before God and for God. The poor ones are not an easily recognizable and fixed group. They live in castles and caves, in temples and in tents. The gospel poor are those who find their home in Christ's word and their treasure in his kingdom.

1. In the scriptures, survival is measured by one's total dependence on God (Zephaniah).

2. To understand God's ways and wisdom, we must often reach into the realms of the incredible and the impractical (1 Corinthians).

3. We cannot take "by storm" a kingdom that grows only in the hearts of the poor and humble (Matthew).

Fifth Sunday in Ordinary Time

Ours is a faith which bids us discover God's ways and wisdom (1 Corinthians) in all things and impels us to share our discoveries with the hungry and thirsty (Isaiah), thereby bringing the taste of glory and the brilliance of salvation to all (Matthew).

Isaiah 58:7-10. Never concerned with self-denial or negation for its own sake, the spirituality of the Hebrew prophets is highly positive and altruistic in concept and in praxis. Today's text from Trito-Isaiah or Third Isaiah (chapters 56-66) speaks to the veterans of the exile (late sixth century B.C.E.) about the importance of that sincere spirituality or true religion which finds expression in the triple dimension of prayer, fasting and almsgiving. True prayer gains energy from fasting which frees the spirit, thus making one more sensitive to God's ways as well as the needs of others ("sharing one's bread, sheltering the homeless, clothing the naked"). Prayer and fasting can never be purely personal or private: Both impel the believer to that third and social dimension of almsgiving, self-giving.

Excerpted from a longer section of post-exilic poems (57:4—59:21), today's pericope reveals the discouraging times experienced by the returnees from Babylon. Before the exile, there had been one official prescribed day of fast annually, the Day of Atonement or Yom Kippur (Leviticus 16:29-30). But after the exile, as hardships, sadness and disappointments weighed upon the people's hearts, the practice of fasting became quite commonplace. By Jesus' time in the 30s C.E., it was the custom for pious people to fast twice a week.

Evidently though, in Isaiah's day (as in Jesus' also), some tended to regard fasting as mere physical abstinence. For these, the prophet advocates an interiorization of the practice which would involve the curbing of one's pride and the refraining from malicious talk. Others looked upon fasting as a *do ut des* mechanism to piously extort favors from God. To these, as did Amos, Jeremiah and Micah before him, Isaiah held out the needs of the hungry, the homeless, the naked and the afflicted as a challenge to the self-satisfied and egotistical fasting ones.

Only an interiorized fast of self-forgetfulness and humble self-awareness gives meaning to outward abstinence. This comprehensive fast, which involves both body and will, can lead one to true prayer, true religion. True fasting can be a prayer, like the prayer of the "poor ones" (see last Sunday) who hope for the satisfaction of all their hungers and thirsts from God alone. True fasting makes the rich poor and the poor ones can then share their spirit of trust with the wealthy. In this way all are led to the Lord.

As a result of this holistic or integral approach to spirituality, Isaiah prophesied light dawning in the darkness, the healing of wounds, the coming of glory and vindication. To one whose fast or self-imposed restraint can lead to the care of another, the Lord would answer, "Here I am."

Today's text contains elements of discipline or sacrifice and light or salvation and serves as a liaison between the seasons of Lent which it heralds and of Christmas which it remembers. Both seasons, culminate in the act of Jesus Christ, whose sacrifice brings to the world the light of salvation.

1 Corinthians 2:1-5. Many scholars are of the opinion that Paul adopted a new, simpler and more direct approach in his preaching to the Corinthians after his apparent failure with the Athenians at the Areopagus (see Acts 17). In debating with the Epicurean and Stoic philosophers, Paul waxed eloquent, matching them wit for wit, premise for premise, pithy saying for pithy saying. It seems, however, that for all his mental gymnastics, Paul was relatively unsuccessful in Athens and some think that is why he took the hard line of the cross with the Corinthians. This "new approach" is rather unlikely since the speeches of both Peter and Paul in Acts are difficult to authenticate. In fact, many of them are the product of Christian apologetic and may be attributed to the author of the Acts of the Apostles. Moreover, a closer look at Paul's experience in Athens reveals that he lost his audience when he began to talk about the *resurrection* of Jesus after his philosophical debates.

Today's text is a continuation of Paul's teaching about the wisdom of God which was perceived as folly by the unbeliever (see 1 Corinthians 1). To the Greeks who devoted themselves and their energies to the search for wisdom (*sophia*) and who considered themselves to be lovers (*philo*) of wisdom, viz., philosophers, the very idea of the crucifixion as a source of saving value was absurd. In the same way, they scoffed at the resurrection of the body, because they considered matter as evil, a deterrent to be overcome.

Never one to mince words, Paul realized that the "wisdom" of Jesus Christ, crucified and risen from the dead, could not be achieved by argumentation or any amount of mental reaching. Rather, the Spirit by whose power Paul preached would enable his hearers to come to faith.

Matthew 5:11-13. "Salt of the earth" has always been a complimentary statement. A precious commodity in the ancient world, salt was at one time meted out for pay, hence the word salary (*salarium*). It was used to preserve food and give it a more pleasing taste. Newborn babies were rubbed with salt for what was thought medicinal purposes. Covenants of friendship were sealed by taking salt together (Numbers 18:19, 2 Chronicles 13:5). All these thoughts and more must have come to mind when Jesus said, "You are the salt of the earth, . . . the light of the world." Following upon the statement that the disciples would be persecuted in the same way as the prophets (Matthew 5:12), Jesus' words indicate that henceforth they would, by their words and works, be light and salt for the earth. Matthew, in whose gospel Jesus is portrayed as the new Moses and the answer to all the Old Testament questions, saw the disciples and followers of Jesus as the new Israel.

In today's first reading, as in Isaiah 60:3-5, the keepers of the old law are described as the light of the world by which all nations could stream to Yahweh. Jesus' charges (you are salt, you are light, let your light shine before all) reveal a transformation through a new Moses and a new law to a new Israel. All that Israel should have been for God and for all peoples is now assumed by Jesus Christ and those who would belong to his new and eternal kingdom. The verbs are not in the future tense, i.e., you *will be* light or salt, but rather you *are*. The follower of Jesus was not to wait for a kingdom to come but was to recognize *in Jesus* and *in his words and works* the establishment of the reign of God. Granted, it was a kingdom proleptically present—begun and growing but not yet in full bloom. By their good works and their witness in faith to the Lord, the disciples were to convey to all people the same properties as salt: seasoning, preservative, cleanser, sign of friendship. In the same way, a failure to believe and to live a life worthy of their calling would make them tasteless and therefore useless.

Some scholars see the tasteless salt as a reference to the obsolescence of the old law. The light for all and the city set on a hill remind us of the Christmas season. As Christ was the epiphany of God, manifestation of the light of salvation for all, so too the lives of his followers manifest the light, love and saving action of Jesus Christ.

1. Fasting **from** *renders one free* **for** *doing, giving, being for others (Isaiah).*

2. The temptation to want to appear wise often springs from foolishness (1 Corinthians).

3. A little salt, like a little leaven, goes a long way in making things better (Matthew).

Sixth Sunday in Ordinary Time

Jesus came into the world, incarnating in time and space God's wisdom (1 Corinthians). At that moment, the law which supplied the norm for freedom (Sirach) became a concern of the heart (Matthew).

Sirach 15:15-20. The book of Sirach was a family endeavor. It was written in Hebrew about 190 B.C.E. by Sira or Ben Sira, a cultured man, possibly a diplomat to foreign courts. Widely travelled, he later used his talents and vast experience to hand on to his interested students in Jerusalem the long cultivated practical wisdom and love of the scriptures he had acquired through the years. About two generations later, in the wake of the Maccabean revolt, Jesus (Joshua or Yeshua, son of Eleazar, son of Sira) translated his grandfather's work into Greek in an effort to defend and preserve the precious heritage of Hebrew faith and culture from the all pervasive and conforming influence of Hellenism. To the Jews in Palestine and to those in the diaspora, the book illustrates the author's conviction that the seeker of true wisdom could only be satisfied in Israel, in its God, in his ways.

Considered outside the pale of acceptable theology by Pharisaic Judaism, Sirach was not accepted into the Jewish canon. Today, Protestant churches consider Sirach an apocryphal work whereas Catholics regard it as deuterocanonical. Among early Christians the book was quite popular. Called *Ecclesiasticus* in Latin, meaning *the church book* or *book of the church*, the writings of the wise Jewish grandfather served as an excellent guide for the moral and religious training of catechumens. Chapters 1-43 consist of pithy sayings about life and living, while chapters 44-50 treat of God's wisdom as it is revealed in the care he providently bestows on his people.

Today's selection is part of a witty commentary on the world and its people. Like Deuteronomy 30:15, it treats the issue of the freedom of will to choose between right and wrong. So adamant is the author concerning the utter freedom to choose that, if this statement were taken out of context, it would smack of Pelagianism. In fact, the heresy which surfaced about 400 C.E. may well have drawn scriptural support for its erroneous ideas from today's pericope. Pelagius, a monk of the fifth century C.E., rejected the doctrine of original sin and emphasized natural over supernatural qualities to the extent that he believed salvation possible without grace. Condemned by Augustine and the councils of Carthage in 411, Miletis in 416 and Ephesus in 431, this heresy gradually died out.

This was not, however, the vision of Ben Sira. The Greeks saw themselves as pawns of an olympiad of fickle gods who wrought upon the earth evil as well as good. Sirach juxtaposed his theology of a good, loving and caring God who allowed the human person freedom to be and to exercise his/her will. His purpose was to place the responsibility for evil in the world on human shoulders and to exonerate God from all blame (see also Sirach 17:1-14). In creating the human person God endowed him with *yeser*, an inclination or free will to choose. Moreover, the commandments were given as aids to guide human freedom. Fire and water can be understood as sanctions or consequences of one's free choice, the rewards of life being symbolized by water and the requital of death by fire. As the author of Genesis saw the problem of evil in the world and sought to explain its origin, so the author of Sirach faced the problem of that existing evil and sought a solution for it in the proper use of free will.

1 Corinthians 2:6-10. Appearing to contradict previous statements that wisdom has no place in explaining the mysteries of Christ (see last week's commentary), Paul now relegates that wisdom to its proper perspective. The only true wisdom, the apostle argues, the only wisdom that has any value is not of this world but has its origin in God and its location in the cross of Jesus Christ. For the Corinthians, the cross was an ignominious and shameful symbol, a reminder of an event they would rather forget, the death of the Christ. Impossible! Illogical! But Paul would have them recognize in the crucified one the Lord of glory.

Chiding them for their refusal to believe and accept the wisdom of God revealed in the cross, Paul made use of some terminology familiar to his audience. His talk about the spiritually mature (*teleios*) as being possessors of a certain ("special") wisdom appealed to the Greeks with their background of mystery cults and gnostic tendencies. They latched onto this idea, thought of themselves as an elitist group of mature sages initiated into a secret revelation at baptism. Paul pulled the reins on their egotism and accused them of being immature and in alignment with the "rulers of this age," the earthly agents of the powers of evil who had perpetrated the travesty of the cross. By not accepting the cross and its wisdom, they were showing their immaturity.

Paul's reference ("it is written") to the ensuing quotation is difficult to place exactly. It may be a paraphrase of Isaiah 64:4 and Isaiah 65:17. Some commentators suggest it may be from the Apocalypse of Elijah. At any rate, the expression "eye has not seen, ear has not heard, nor has it so much as dawned on us" underscores Paul's assertions that sophism or human wisdom cannot of itself achieve that which God, through the Holy Spirit, freely reveals to the faithful lovers of the cross of Jesus Christ.

Matthew 5:17-37. When Jesus said, "I have not come to abolish the law and prophets but to fulfill them," he set into motion a series of challenges and demands which were to lead his disciples far beyond even the perfect outward observance of the law. Part of the sermon on the mount, in which Jesus enunciates the law of the new and eternal kingdom, today's pericope consists of four out of a group of six (see fifth and sixth ones next week) antitheses which contrast the old law with the new interpretation and wider application which Jesus gave.

The structure of the antitheses is probably Matthean: (1) juxtaposition of old law and Jesus' demands, (2) practical example or illustration of Jesus' interpretation, (3) positive command.

In each of the four cases that follow, Jesus sets for his followers higher, almost impossible standards. The Pharisees who prided themselves on their strict observance of the 613 precepts of the law must have been appalled at the idea of a further challenge. So too must Jesus' disciples have been shocked, because the Pharisees were considered by all to be righteous. Yet, Jesus' interpretation of the law called for a far greater righteousness which included outward behavior *and* inner motive. Pharisaic Judaism considered the law as perfect (see Psalm 119) and complete. Jesus' statement implies an imperfection and an incompleteness.

Each of the four antitheses is introduced by the formal "You have heard the commandment" and followed by a verbatim quotation of the law. With his "But I say to you," Jesus pushed for a broader interpretation and wider application. The prohibition of murder (vv. 21-26) from Exodus 20:15 is enlarged to forbid even anger. In the event that one did become angry and use abusive language, the responsibility for reconciliation is imposed on *both* parties. The angry person as well as the one who bore the brunt of the anger are required to make reconciliation before any participation in worship. Jesus emphasizes, as did the prophets, the interdependence of brotherly love and true worship.

The prohibition of adultery (vv. 27-30, see Exodus 20:13) is expanded to include lust. Again it is evident that Jesus aims at the motivating force behind one's actions. Divorce (31-32) was a sticky problem in Matthew's church. There were two prevalent views, that of Rabbi Shammai who permitted divorce in the case of adultery and that of Rabbi Hillel who permitted divorce for reasons as minute as too much salt in the stew. Jesus in Mark and Luke allows of no exception to the prohibition of divorce, and it is thought that the exception "lewd conduct" is a Matthean addition. The term is an attempt to define the difficult word *porneia* which could possibly mean concubinage or premarital sexual intercourse with one's betrothed or, as some suggest, incest.

1. Freedom to choose entails freedom to be responsible and freedom to be culpable as well (Sirach).

2. The Christian who finds wisdom in Christ crucified has to accept that he may be regarded as a fool (1 Corinthians).

3. Jesus believed in our infinite capacity for God's grace and in our potential for goodness (Matthew).

Seventh Sunday in Ordinary Time

Be holy (perfect) as the Lord is holy (perfect): This exhortation forms an inclusion around our liturgical texts today (Leviticus, Matthew). Within the inclusion we can trace the development of Judaism's ethical standard (Leviticus) and its subsequent reinterpretation by Jesus (Matthew) as well as its implications for the early Christian community (1 Corinthians).

Leviticus 19:1-2, 17-18. Liturgy or the public worship of a community is, at its best, supposed to give expression to the life of the people. The book of Leviticus, for all its rubrics, rituals and "legalese," does reflect for us the life of worship of the Jewish community as it had evolved by the sixth century B.C.E. Our name for the book is derived from the Vulgate or Latin translation of the title in the Septuagint whereas the Hebrew name *Wayyiqra* ("and he called") is from the first few words of the scroll.

While the book is truly informed by the spirit of Moses and as such is regarded as part of the Torah or Pentateuch, the detailed and elaborate system of sacrifice, as well as the evidence of a highly developed priesthood, cannot be traced to the wilderness time of the 13th century B.C.E. Indeed, the obvious sedentary life of the people as well as the existence of the temple with all the surrounding cultic activities reflect a much later period.

Though some of the material (viz., chapters 17-26) may be regarded as quite ancient, the book of Leviticus is more properly appreciated as the effort of many hands, throughout the centuries, adapting Israel's worship to changing times according to principles given in the Mosaic era. Most probably, chapters 17-26 were the heart or kernel around which the rest of the book was built. A priestly editing is evident and probably took place in post-exilic times (sixth century B.C.E.) when the system of worship was undergoing reorganization. It should be noted that all the laws and regulations concerning the cult, whether early or late in origin, were determined by the principle that holiness should be a distinguishing characteristic of Israel, derived from and based on the holiness of its creator and Lord.

Our text for today is part of the longer, primitive "holiness code" (chapters 17-26) and more specifically, it is from chapter 19, a miscellaneous collection of statutes regarding social justice, charity and chaste behavior. While chapter 19 is certainly dependent on and inspired by the decalogue, the repercussions of its prescriptions can be detected in post-exilic legislation as well. Verse two of chapter 19, with its injunction "to be holy for I am holy," is adapted slightly by Matthew in the gospel (be perfect). However, the fact remains that God's holiness was considered the basis for the human response to God in ethical, moral behavior. In v. 18 the reference to loving one's neighbor comes at the end of a list of social offenses which should be avoided: theft, deceit, cruelty to handicapped, and so on. "Neighbor" was a term limited to that category of persons to whom one was related by familial or political bonds, e.g., same nation or tribe, fellow villager, and so on. Besides expanding this law to the love of one's enemies, Jesus in the New Testament moved the parameters of neighborhood to include all the world and all humankind as well (Matthew 5:43; Luke 10:36-37).

1 Corinthians 3:16-23. Desecration of a temple was considered a criminal and hateful offense by believers of all persuasion, Jews, Christians and those who subscribed to the Greek mystery cults. Paul's use of the temple metaphor grew out of a longer pericope wherein the apostle compared the work of the servants or ministers of God to that of a builder and he likened the Christian community itself to a building (see 1 Corinthians 3:9-15). Describing himself and his efforts as those of a master builder, Paul saw Jesus Christ as the only firm and suitable foundation for the edifice of the church.

Elaborating on the temple metaphor, Paul's query to the Corinthians ("Are you not aware that *you* are the temple of God?") narrows the comparison to the Christian community at Corinth. Later, in 6:19, Paul applies this idea to the individual Christian as well. The word Paul uses for temple is *naos,* the sanctuary or innermost part of the building. In Judaism, this would correspond to the holy of holies, that sacred place wherein no one entered (except once a year) because the Lord Yahweh was thought to dwell there. In pagan temples, *naos* designated the small building within the temple which housed the statue of the god.

To his Christians of Corinth, Paul taught that the presence of God's Holy Spirit dwelling in them made of their community at Corinth a holy temple, the *naos* of God. In warning them of possible desecration or destruction, Paul assumes once again his comparison of worldly and divine wisdom. Describing that worldly wisdom which favored one preacher (or builder) over another as folly and a threat to the sacredness and unity of the temple, Paul counselled the Corinthians to focus on Christ. With a rather liberal translation of Job 5:13 and Psalm 94:11 respectively, Paul concludes his preaching with the exhortation to seek wisdom in the foundation of Jesus Christ to whom all builders and preachers are subordinate and in whom the believer can find a life and a future in God.

Matthew 5:38-48. Incredible as it may seem, the law of retaliation (*lex talionis,* "an eye for an eye, a tooth for a tooth") was instituted in the ancient Near Eastern world as a safeguard. More often than not, the person, who had sustained some injury or insult at the hand of another, would undertake to avenge himself with such fury that the guilty party often died as a result. The Mosaic law which Jesus cites here (Exodus 21:24, Leviticus 24:20, Deuteronomy 19:21) is an adaptation from the Code of Hammurabi and was seen as just legislation in that it limited the injury one could inflict so as to be proportionate to that inflicted by the aggressor. In referring to this long standing principle of acceptable self-defense, Jesus proceeded to replace it with his principle of non-resistance.

Lest anyone misunderstand, Jesus illustrated his principle ("Offer no resistance to injury") with some concrete examples. That physical violence was not to be parried in kind was simple enough. But the next illustration concerning one's shirt (tunic) and coat (cloak) moved on to the kind of conduct Jesus advocated in the case of a legal suit (no pun intended). Not only should one not contest the legal action but one should yield what is contested and yield even more. The garments in question, the tunic (shirt) and coat (cloak), were the only garments owned and worn by the poor. Mosaic law permitted the cloak of a borrower to be held by a creditor as a pledge, but since this garment served as blanket, bed, raincoat and so on, it was to be returned at sundown, lest the borrower suffer the cold of the night (Exodus 22:25-26).

Jesus does not advocate loaning. Rather, he says, "give" to the one who begs. It seems to be implicit in his examples that Jesus would have his followers exact no pledge, even though it had been permitted by law for centuries. No amount of rationalization and/or accommodation can dilute the powerful challenge of Jesus' interpretation.

With the command to love enemies and to pray for persecutors we have Matthew's sixth in the series of six antitheses (begun in last week's gospel). As the last in the series, it is the greatest and it sums up the other five antitheses by providing the rationale for Jesus' reinterpretations of the law. Neither the law nor the rabbinical writings contained any citation about hating enemies. In adding this to his command to love one's neighbor or countryman (Leviticus 19:18), Jesus was probably verbalizing a popular attitude of his day. Indeed, it seems that hatred of those outside the community was considered normal. Jesus extended the narrow concept of neighbor to include even enemies. The injunction to pray for persecutors could certainly have been Jesus' advice but the fact that the same word is translated "as those who treat you badly" by Luke in his 6:28 may reflect the situation in Matthew's church in the 80s. Persecution was directed at the Christians not only from the Jews who had recently expelled them by edict from the synagogues, but also by the Romans who subsequently regarded the Christians as an illegal sect.

The followers of Jesus were to interpret the law of love of neighbor in a magnanimous way, not judging between people or bestowing charity selectively. Just as God allowed his sun to shine on all, so must Christians let their love shine like a city on a hill and a lamp on a stand (see Matthew 5:14-16) for all. Called beyond the mere ethical humanism which even pagans and tax collectors practiced, the disciples of Christ were vowed to divine perfection. The norm for living was no longer the decalog carved in stone, but the holiness of the Lord himself. To be true sons and daughters of their Father, Christians had to sublimate their human capacities for revenge, favoritism and prejudice in order to embrace the Father's holiness of loving, giving and forgiving.

1. *The whole of the Israel was called. Holiness is not just for a few (Leviticus).*

2. *The Christian is a sacred place where love is free to happen (1 Corinthians).*

3. *How does today's Christian answer Jesus' call for non-resistance and non-violence (Matthew)?*

Eighth Sunday in Ordinary Time

Personal and parental, God's love creates, redeems, forgives and renews all peoples (Isaiah). Provident and caring, God's concern for all our needs enables us to focus our energies on lasting realities (Matthew). Made confident by God's love and freed by God's attentiveness, we can serve wholeheartedly in a manner worthy of the blessings we have received (1 Corinthians).

Isaiah 49:14-15. For the first nine months of human life, in the intimacy of an intrauterine environment, a bond is forged between mother and child—a bond that grows and deepens at birth, a bond that will be tried and tested as the years pass, a bond that *ideally* is never weakened or broken. When Deutero-Isaiah undertook his mission of bringing comfort to an exiled Israel, he relied on that universal human experience of a mother's love in order to illustrate God's fidelity and care for his people.

Companion to his people during their exile in Babylonia, the sixth century B.C.E. prophet was also aware of Israel's sense of loss and frustration when the people were finally free to return home. As the exiles were reunited with a now decimated and powerless population, as they beheld their ruined lands, they no doubt remembered the comparatively comfortable existence they had built for themselves in Babylon; naturally, the temptation to despair was great.

Cyrus, the victorious Persian king, had released the captives held by Babylon and had beneficently provided leadership and materials for the rebuilding of Israel's land and temple. But the process of physical renovation did not automatically rebuild the broken spirit of the exiles; this was the task of the prophet, one he readily embraced.

In Isaiah 49, the chapter from which today's pericope has been excerpted, Deutero-Isaiah has reprised many of the themes he introduced in his opening chapter (Isaiah 40). Because of the several points of similarity between the two chapters, some scholars have compared them as "before and after" texts, e.g., chapter 40:1-11 depicted the people *before* their return home and compared their situation to that of their enslavement in Egypt. Chapter 49:8-13 seems to pertain to the time *after* the people had returned home and had experienced God's saving plan. Understood in this sense, the "after" texts perfectly complement the "before" texts and the prophetic process of "promise-and-fulfillment" is accomplished.

Today's first reading with the prophet's rhetorical question "Can a mother forget her infant?" and its solemn pledge "I will never forget you!" is one of the most eloquent and touching expressions of love contained in the scriptures. But Deutero-Isaiah was not *unique* in his portrayal of God's "motherly" love for his people. Nor was he the *first* to attribute feminine characteristics to God. In the eighth century B.C.E., Hosea had spoken of the transcendent God, creator of heaven and earth, holding Israel to his cheek and teaching Ephraim to walk (Hosea 11:3-4).

When Israel cried out in despair, believing themselves to be forgotten by God, Deutero-Isaiah pointed to the most altruistic and selfless love of which humans are capable, the love of a parent for a child. But even the best of human love is only a shadow of God's eternal, life-giving love for his people.

1 Corinthians 4:1-5. Wherever he went, Paul seemed to attract controversy like a magnet. Having been "born out of time," he came late to Christianity. He had not walked with the earthly Jesus through the hills of Galilee; nor had he heard Jesus preach or seen him die. In fact he had done his best to eradicate the Christian movement in its early stages of development. For this reason, many questioned his right to call himself an apostle and criticized his claim to teach authoritatively in Jesus' name. In order to substantiate his claim to apostleship, Paul recounted on several occasions the circumstances of his vocation and conversion to Christ.

First and foremost, Paul claimed to be a *servant* of Christ. The Greek word *hyperetes* was originally used to designate the oarsman on the lower level of the galleys of a ship. According to this metaphor, Paul envisioned Christ as the captain of the ship, and himself as one who received and carried out Christ's orders.

Paul also referred to himself as an *administrator* or steward (*oikonomos*) of the mysteries of God. In that capacity, Paul was entrusted with his master's plans and the responsibility for executing them. Nevertheless, Paul understood his administrative role as entirely dependent on and subordinate to Christ. As Christ's servant and administrator, he was accountable to Christ alone. For that reason, Paul shrugged off the criticisms of the Corinthians (et al.) as insignificant. Only his trustworthiness and Jesus' assessment of him were of value.

Paul also had his share of legal battles. On several occasions he was brought up on charges. But he did not give much importance to human courts or human judgment (v. 3). Instead, he looked ahead to the *one* judgment and to the *only* judge who mattered, the Lord Jesus Christ. The children of the old covenant looked ahead to the Day of the Lord and the judgment that would accompany it; those of the new covenant looked ahead to Jesus' return. On that occasion, *all* peoples would be judged according to the *only* standards worthy of note, those set by God.

With hope, Paul looked forward to Jesus' second appearance, confident that his performance as Christ's servant and administrator would be judged worthy by God. Paul's willingness to forego human praise and his patience in waiting for God's praise (v. 5) remain an excellent example for those in public and/or religious service.

Matthew 6:24-34. At first glance, Jesus' advice to his followers—look at the birds and flowers and cease worrying about food, clothing and shelter—may sound very naive and simplistic. Indeed, how much meaning would such advice have for the victims of famine in Africa or the homeless millions in our large American cities? How can a hungry person *not* think of food? What *else* occupies the thoughts of a freezing, homeless person *except* warmth and shelter? How then are Christians to interpret this gospel?

The point of the entire pericope (which actually began at v. 19) is contained in v. 24. Believers must choose either to worship God or to be caught up in the idolatry of worldly possessions. Choices or options are of paramount concern because the right choices lead to life and the wrong choices will lead to perdition. "Money" (v. 24) is a limited translation of the Aramaic *mammon* that actually meant "property."

Another suggested definition links the word "mammon" to the Hebrew root *'emen* which means "that in which one puts one's trust." In either case, the point is clear: the believer chooses and serves God and from that principal option will flow all other choices in life.

Notice the radical quality of the statement: "No one can serve two masters. He will either *hate* one and *love* the other or be *attentive* to one and *despise* the other." The hate-love antithesis indicates that the basic choice in life is unavoidable and naturally exclusive (J. Meier).

Once the *basic* life choice has been made (for God or not), then the rest of life's ethical questions and choices fall into place. Not a once-in-a-lifetime event but a daily process of evaluation and of ordering one's values and priorities, the task of living *for* God requires a lifelong and total commitment. Only when God is valued above every other value will the subordinate values of food, clothing, livelihood, etc., fall into their proper perspective.

When during his earthly ministry Jesus taught this lesson about life's priorities, his audience probably consisted mainly of poor people, whose poverty may have predisposed them to look for God's provident hand in their lives. Later, when Matthew recast Jesus' teaching and directed it toward his own community, Jesus' message reached quite a different audience.

The evangelist's community, probably Antioch in Syria during the decade of the 80s C.E., was a prosperous and urban one. Rather than be deterred from life's basic and lasting values by a preoccupation with riches, the Antiochene Christians were called to examine their world and their lives. True disciples of Jesus could not be encumbered by worries; anxiety about life's daily needs is an exercise in futility.

It is noteworthy that Matthew included this pericope about proper values and correctly ordered priorities shortly after his account of Jesus' teaching his followers how to pray. Some scholars understand this entire passage as a commentary on the fourth petition of the Our Father: "Give us this day our daily bread" (Matthew 6:11). Jesus' disciples who pray this prayer in faith are not dispensed from life's worries. But they are granted a higher security even in the midst of trials.

In addition to their freedom from worry over the goods of this world, Jesus' disciples *were* and *are still* summoned to direct their energies into seeking the Father's kingship over them (v. 33). As J. Meier has pointed out, the seeking and commitment that define us must not be a pagan one. We must seek (not create or build!) the kingdom God is bringing into the world. Likewise, we are to seek out his saving action in our midst. Notice, Matthew has specified, "Seek *first*...," indicating that other needs are subordinate to the kingdom, not negated by it. To put the kingdom first requires faith (v. 30) and a constant commitment to God's way of holiness.

That faith and commitment enable the disciple to turn life's pages one by one, to live each day to the ultimate, to set aside yesterday's regrets and to deal with tomorrow's troubles *only* when tomorrow becomes today.

1. From our mother's arms, we begin to learn of the extravagant love of God (Isaiah).

2. In the last analysis, public opinion will remain just that, public opinion, but God's evaluation of our service will result in a final and lasting judgment (1 Corinthians).

3. Undue concern with unnecessary things results in blindness toward the absolute and lasting values in life (Matthew).

Ninth Sunday in Ordinary Time

The law was supposed to free the believer for loving service (Deuteronomy) but instead it became a shackling limitation. Faith in Jesus Christ, the rock and foundation of salvation (Matthew), leads one to transcend the desire for self-righteousness and self-justification (Romans).

Deuteronomy 11:18, 26-28. While the origin of the book of Deuteronomy remains a subject of debate, there can be no doubt as to the work's value and influence on subsequent Old Testament thought. Erroneously named due to a mistranslation of its 17:18, it is in fact not a *second* law (*deuteronomos*) but rather a copy of the law. Granted, the law at Moab (Deuteronomy) is not identical to that of Sinai (Exodus); it is an adaptation that nonetheless finds its roots in the principles of Mosaic law. Written as if it were Moses' farewell address to his people before they entered Canaan from Moab, Deuteronomy pulls together all of Israel's traditions with its own particular concerns.

Since the early 19th century, some scholars have thought that the "scroll of the law" found in the temple during the reign of Josiah (640-609) was probably Deuteronomy (2 Kings 23:8ff) or at least some part of the book (chapters 12-26?). These scholars based their supposition on the fact that the principles of Josiah's reform greatly resembled the central concerns of Deuteronomy (viz., central sanctuary, avoidance of all foreign influences, emphasis on covenant life according to law, and so on). Some scholars regarded the "finding" of the book as a pious fraud, a ploy to lend authority and authenticity to Josiah's reform. Therefore, a seventh century B.C.E. date was assigned to the book. Other scholars attest that Deuteronomy was rather a guidebook for an earlier reform and would date it as early as Hezekiah. Still others, attesting to the archaic character of some parts of the book, push the date back to the Shechem covenant (Joshua 24). The variety of dates and origins conjectured for the text points to the fact that Deuteronomy is not a homogeneous work. It is rather an assimilation of information and traditions dating from the 13th up to the seventh century at which time it received its final touches from a Judean editor.

The central focus of Deuteronomy is an understanding of law (i.e., the terms of the covenant) as the human response to God's special election. From this pivotal point, the author explained the successes and failures of Israel's checkered history in terms of fidelity to or disregard for the law. With this principle as a premise, Deuteronomy serves as an introduction to the historical books which follow it

In the Shema (6:5ff), the importance of the law is stated in a beautifully worded challenge requiring the response of one's whole being, interior motivation as well as external actualization. Verse 18 of today's pericope is a repetition of part of the Shema (6:8, see also Exodus 13:9, 16). It is not certain as to when this exhortation was actually taken literally (some say after the exile) but these words gave birth to the use of phylacteries or prayer boxes. Some texts of the Torah (Exodus 13:1-10, 11-16; Deuteronomy 6:4-9, 11; 13-21 are suggested) were inscribed on parchment and enclosed in small boxes worn on the arm (hand?) and the head by Jewish men at prayer. Whether or not these phylacteries were in use in the seventh century B.C.E., their existence underscores the danger against which the prophets warned continually, that of mere lip service or external behavior as a substitute for interior dedication. The outward observance of the law as signalled by the phylacteries was to be a true reflection of an interior attitude an motivation.

The blessings and curses described in vv. 26-28 were dependent upon Israel's performance of her covenant responsibilities. Such sanctions (as in Hittite suzerainty treaties) were deemed necessary to assure fidelity to the terms set (in Israel's case, the law). That the author(s) of Deuteronomy saw the hardships which befell the people as consonant with their behavior toward the law is evident throughout the book. Deuteronomy presents the correct attitude toward law as a love response, involving one's whole being, relating one to God and to others.

Romans 3:21-25, 28. Rome was to be for Paul a stepping-stone to the rest of the then known world. Although the apostle did not continue on to Spain after Rome, he made his influence felt far beyond the borders of Rome, and far beyond the first century, in his treatise to this city. Writing from Corinth around 57-58 (see Romans 15:25, Acts 20:3) in order to announce his coming visit, Paul's words to the church of Rome reflect his missiology, namely, that God who revealed himself in human history has offered salvation to all the peoples of the earth in the good news of Jesus Christ. Paul saw himself as God's messenger in making known that good news and hence offering salvation to all.

Paul's experience among the gentiles in the East and his conflict with the Judaizers made him adamant in his preaching that human beings depend (for salvation) not on the "deeds of the law" but on faith in Jesus Christ. By that faith, the believer is enabled by God to appropriate the effects of the saving act (death-resurrection) of Christ. Using the Greek literary style of the Stoic diatribe, Paul juxtaposed his main ideas about faith and justification over and against the law and the righteousness it afforded.

In Romans 3:21-4:25, from which our pericope today is excerpted, Paul set out the means (faith) by which salvation is to be obtained. Citing Abraham (Romans 4) as the example par excellence of salvation by faith, Paul would have his readers understand faith as a total commitment in trust to God which expresses itself in obedience. The uprightness, like that of Abraham, which the Jews thought they could achieve by observing the law, was to be achieved not by works according to any law (Torah, moral philosophy or conscience) but by faith. Moreover, that faith, like the salvation to which it led, was to be accepted as God's gratuitous gift. A glance backward at the failures in Israel's history should be proof enough, taught Paul, of the inadequacy of the law. By sin (see v. 23) one was deprived of God's glory, but by faith in the redemptive value of Christ's work, one could forever enjoy that glory.

Perhaps more than any other New Testament book, Romans has affected the development of later Christian theology. Echoes of these same ideas are seen in 1 Peter, Hebrews and James. Clement, Ignatius, Polycarp and Justin were obviously influenced by Romans. Controversy as to the correct interpretation of today's text played a major part in heating up the Reformation debates. Luther's addition of *"alone"* was probably an attempt at clarification, but it led others to the false conclusion that works (of the law, etc.) are of no account whatever. Origen foresaw this danger and warned against it. It should be noted that although Paul denied the power of works to *merit* salvation, he did not negate the value of works done after justification (being put right with God). Indeed, one's faith would naturally overflow in deeds of goodness.

Matthew 7:21-27. With the words of today's text, the great sermon on the mount draws to an end in Matthew's gospel. Over against Pharisaic Judaism with its over-emphasis on law, Matthew posits Jesus, a new lawgiver and bringer of a new kingdom. Besides the problem of Pharisaic rejection, Matthew's church of the 80s was also afflicted by a plethora of charismatics whose sensational displays of prophecy and healing belied the simple truth of Jesus' message. Paul encountered the same problem in Corinth, as is evident in his letters to that Greek community. Like Paul, Matthew regarded these gifts as suspect and valueless without the proper underpinnings. For Paul, the basis for authentic use of charismata was love (1 Corinthians 13:2) and reliance on the Holy Spirit of Jesus. Likewise, Matthew saw that the basis for all gifts was a firm foundation built on Jesus Christ.

In describing the true disciple, Matthew presented an understanding of Christianity as lived out in the works of love and mercy which Jesus expounded throughout the great sermon. In these works and in the attitudes expressed in the beatitudes, Jesus saw the accomplishment of the will of the Father.

To merely call out, "Lord, Lord," seems to be a criticism of nominal Christians whose faith remains a matter of talk or thought alone. Perhaps too, these words were leveled at the Pharisees who wore the letter of the law on their heads and arms (phylacteries) but did not let its spirit penetrate their hearts. That faith in Christ should move one to action is illustrated in the metaphor of the houses. Using the Palestinian environs of his community, Matthew envisages a house built on rock withstanding the early and the late rains which would wash away the sandy foundation. To be a hearer as well as a doer of the word is a favorite teaching of Jesus which is reminiscent of Deuteronomy as well as the prophets who constantly railed against mere lip service. Some see this gospel as radically opposed to the teaching of Romans. In truth, the contrast of the two texts underscores the tension between faith and works. But it is part of the task of Christian discipleship to survive that tension by finding the proper time and season for each manifestation of dedication to Christ.

1. The law as a guide and norm was not to be stagnant and external but an interior act of love, lived in community (Deuteronomy).

2. All of us are sinners, eligible for redemption because of God's great love (Romans).

3. The faith we speak must also be the faith we live (Matthew).

10th Sunday in Ordinary Time

Despite what seemed to be insuperable human circumstances, Abraham hoped and believed in God's power. The same power that made Abraham great (Romans), was extended, in the form of healing forgiveness to Israel (Hosea). That same power reaches out to lift up and renew every repentant sinner (Matthew).

Hosea 6:3-6. Active among his contemporaries during the death throes of the northern kingdom (i.e., 750-732 B.C.E.), Hosea structured his prophetic oracles in a *rîb* or trial-judgment pattern. Interpreting Israel's frequent political dalliance with foreign powers and its perennial attraction to the Canaanite fertility cults as the causes for its downfall, Hosea called his people to return to Yahweh and to covenantal integrity.

Himself the cuckolded husband of a repeatedly unfaithful wife, the prophet used his personal circumstances as a vehicle for his prophetic message; he compared Israel to an adulterous woman as he likened Yahweh to an ever-loving, patient and forgiving husband. Acting as prosecuting attorney, citing indictment after indictment against his people, Hosea built an airtight case. But his was not a message of unrelenting doom. Indeed Hosea's touching prophecies include some of the most moving assurances of divine love and forgiveness in all of scripture (Hosea 2:18-25, 11:1-11).

Today's first reading is part of a longer passage (5:15 to 7:2) in which the prophet described the inadequacy of Israel's repentance. So numerous had been their transgressions that it seemed as if the people had almost forgotten how to repent. Even their best efforts, viz., a multiplicity of sacrificial offerings, fell short of the mark because the people were lacking in the one thing basic to any sincere repentance—true knowledge of God. True knowledge of God, taught Hosea, would have resulted in a sincere love of God, in humble recognition of personal sin, in renewed dedication to the covenant and, last but not least, in social justice and compassion for the disadvantaged.

Intended to be understood as a dialogue with Israel speaking the first verse (v. 3) and Yahweh responding in the remaining verses (4-6), this short pericope is actually a sarcastic prophetic parody on Israel's futile attempts to gain divine favor. Some have suggested that Hosea was quoting part of a liturgical rite, perhaps an expiatory ceremony. Even as the people prayed, "Let us *know*, let us strive to *know* the Lord . . ." (v. 3), their thoughts were still influenced by pagan cult. "He shall come to us like the rain . . . like spring rain" reflects a preoccupation with Baal, the Canaanite god believed to bring forth rain upon the earth. As elsewhere in his prophecies, the prophet decried the people for approaching Yahweh as they would Baal ("no longer will she call me, 'My Baal,'" 2:16).

Yahweh's response, which comprises the remainder of this reading, underscores the fickleness of the people and the shallowness of their worship. Their sacrifices, however many and often they were offered, were empty without a steadfast and sincere commitment to Yahweh and to his will as it was revealed in the covenantal law. The value of love over animal sacrifices and knowledge of God over holocausts is borne out in today's gospel wherein Jesus cites Hosea 6:6 in defense of his ministry among the tax collectors and sinners.

Romans 4:18-25. All of chapter four of Paul's letter to the church in Rome represents a digression into the Jewish scriptures to illustrate his point that justification by faith was already operative before the law. Indeed, Paul wished his readers to understand that justification by faith not only predated the law but confirmed it. Justification by faith (R. Fuller calls this shorthand for "justification by the grace of God manifested in Jesus and apprehended by faith") finds an eloquent expression in the person and life of Abraham. Pronounced just or upright by God because of his faith (4:1-8) and not because of his circumcision (4:9-12) or the law (4:13-17), Abraham represents the epitome of the true believer.

Despite the fact that his human circumstances seemed to militate against God's promises to him, Abraham believed in God's power to effect the impossible. An elderly, sterile wife and an aged husband hardly seemed suitable candidates for the progeny God had promised. Yet, as Paul stated, "Abraham believed, hoping against hope." Literally translated, v. 18 reads, "Contrary to all expectation, he believed in God . . . ." Abraham's faith trusted that God could suspend all determinism in nature, that God could bring about a new and unexpected future from what seemed a dismal and unlikely past.

While he did not question or doubt the validity of God's promises and his power to effect them in his life, Abraham was not naïve, his was not an unthinking blind faith. Appreciative and entirely cognizant of his own situation, he fell on his face and laughed when he heard he was to become a father at such a ripe old age (Genesis 17:1ff). But his laughter was not born of cynicism; nor did it stem from a lack of trust in God. Because of his faith and his hope against hope, Abraham was credited as just.

Using a *midrashic* technique popularly employed in rabbinical teaching, Paul intended for his readers in Rome to apply the lesson of Abraham to themselves and to their faith in Jesus' resurrection from the dead. As A. Theissen and P.

Byrne have noted, Abraham's faith has become the pattern or model of Christian faith because its object is the same, viz., belief in God who makes the dead live. Just as Abraham and Sarah's "dead" bodies (v. 19) yielded to God's power to bring forth life, so too did this same God raise his crucified Son from the tomb to life eternal. Our faith in the totality of the Christ event, i.e., in Jesus' passion, death, resurrection and exaltation as it has been effected by God, "will be credited to us" as our justification (v. 25).

Matthew 9:9-13. In vivid contrast to Abraham (second reading), whose righteousness was the fruit of his belief in God, stand the Pharisees in today's gospel, whose self-righteousness hindered their ability to believe in Jesus. Following immediately upon the cure of the paralytic (9:1-8) whose faith and the faith of his friends elicited a physical healing from Jesus as well as a spiritual healing (the forgiveness of his sins), the narrative of Matthew's call and the reaction to it by the Pharisees illustrates another sort of paralysis, viz., the rigidity which comes from second-guessing God. Whereas the self-righteous Pharisees believed themselves to be justified by their impeccable observance of the law and subsequently judged those who did not do likewise to be outcasts and accursed by God, Jesus habitually exhibited a distinct predilection for sinners. In this way, he manifested God's special care for those whom the self-righteous deemed as unclean and outside the pale of acceptable, saveable society.

Painted with the same brush as sinners, tax collectors were considered by the Pharisees to be among those who disrespected the law. Hired by Rome to collect the variety of tolls the empire exacted, tax collectors were actually local people (in this case, Jews) who had bid for and had won the option of collecting taxes from their neighbors. Since Rome required its tolls to be paid in advance, the collectors did so; then they hired agents to assist them in recouping their initial outlay and in making a handsome profit besides. Extortion was rampant and, because of their reputation for dishonesty as well as their cooperation with the occupying forces of Rome, tax collectors were feared and hated.

Matthew's gospel is unique among the synoptics in that it alone identifies the tax collector as Matthew; Mark and Luke call him Levi in parallel narratives. While there is no historical evidence of a person named both Levi and Matthew, the fact that this evangelist changed Levi to Matthew may be an autobiographical signal. Or, more probably, it may be that the evangelist named the tax collector Matthew because he was listed among the Twelve and because that apostle was the source of special traditions in the evangelist's community (J. Meier).

In any event, the tax collector called Matthew responded enthusiastically to Jesus' challenge to discipleship. During the table fellowship which followed in Matthew's home, Jesus grievously offended the moral sensibilities of the Pharisees. His free and willing association with those whom the Pharisees deemed unclean served as a double affront. Not only did they disapprove of Jesus' actions in themselves but they were equally peeved that, after associating with sinners and thereby rendering *himself* unclean, he then proceeded to converse with the Pharisees, thereby making *them* unclean as well. In order to avoid any ritual impurity, the Pharisees in this instance asked Jesus' disciples for an explanation of his actions: "What reason can the teacher have for eating with tax collectors and those who disregard the law?" (v. 11).

Hearing their remarks, Jesus responded directly to their criticism. His response included three distinct points. Jesus' first statement (v. 12) was based on a proverb, undoubtedly familiar to his contemporaries: "People who are in good health do not need a doctor; sick people do." Instead of despising sinners as the Pharisees did, Jesus saw them in need of healing and he reached out to bring them to wholeness and holiness once again. The Pharisees, on the other hand, were so self-righteous as not to recognize their own need for healing; for them, there would be no cure because integral to the healing process is the admission of guilt and the recognition of Jesus as the healer.

Jesus' second statement (v. 13a) in which he quoted Hosea 6:6 illustrated what should have been the Pharisees' attitude toward their fellows. Mercy, over and above ritual sacrifice, even perfectly performed ritual cult, is of greater value in God's eyes. Those who set themselves up in opposition to God's mercy as it was manifested in the mission of Jesus would one day find themselves as outsiders looking in at the eternal messianic banquet. With the quotation from Hosea, Jesus challenged his critics to recognize God's truth and wisdom at work in his own person.

In the final verse of the pericope, the Matthean Jesus underscored the purpose of his ministry among humankind, viz., to extend to sinners the call of God's salvation. As J. Gaffney has commented, Jesus' actions taught us that God does not passively await the sinner's conversion. Rather, he actively seeks, assists and precipitates it. God is not a dispassionate critic of our moral life. He is the active inspirer and reformer of it; he is a healer, not a connoisseur of health.

1. Sincere conversion begins with a commitment to love and to know God (Hosea).

2. Because of grace and by faith, even that which seems impossible can happen (Romans).

3. To be aware of personal guilt and to acknowledge our sin is the first step in the process of spiritual recuperation (Matthew).

11th Sunday in Ordinary Time

With a great and gracious love, our God has loved us and called us out of sin (Romans) to be his special people, to be his ministers and witnesses of his reign (Exodus). His love and the power of his forgiveness impel us to spread the good news to others (Matthew).

Exodus 19:2-6. For centuries, both Jewish and Christian scholars have studied and debated over the precise location of the mountain where Moses met God (v. 3). Relying on a variety of theories concerning the actual route of the exodus, the mountain has been alternately placed in Kadesh, Petra or even somewhere east of the vast Sinai Peninsula. Today, however, most critical scholars concur that the mountain of God may be identified as Jebel Musa, a peak in the Sinai which rises to a height of 7,500 feet. While it may be interesting to speculate on specific geographical sites, the theological importance of the encounter between Moses and God is far more significant and worthy of consideration.

Recalling the exodus, that pivotal event from which all of Israel's subsequent history evolved and by which it was interpreted, the Lord offered those he had chosen and saved the chance to enter into covenant with him. A unique pact, albeit expressed in terms similar to the Hittite suzerainty treaties, the covenant relationship which God made with Israel became the matrix from which the people drew all their theological awareness and national identity. Long after the Sinai event, Christians regarded Yahweh's covenant with Israel as the type and prefiguration of the relationship afforded to humanity in the person and saving mission of Jesus Christ.

Upon the conditions set by Yahweh, viz., that they would listen to his voice and remain faithful to the covenant, Israel was to enjoy special blessings. They would be for God a kingdom of priests, a holy nation (v. 6). Not in the clerical sense of the Levitical literature but in the prophetic sense of Isaiah 61:1-6, Israel's priesthood was to be exercised as a testimony to the Lord before all the nations. Because of their nearness or easy access to God by virtue of their covenant relationship, Israel would represent God's will to humanity. So too, Israel's holiness was to serve as a call or a challenge to the nations to come to God.

As the consecrated priestly people (1 Peter 2:1-10) of God of the *new* covenant, the church is to fulfill a similar vocation. Whereas Israel passed over from slavery in Egypt to freedom with the Lord in the Sinai, Christians pass over from death to life through baptism into Christ Jesus. Baptized believers are thereby empowered to live their entire lives as witnesses of the saving sacrifice and rising of Jesus for the rest of humanity. As J. H. Elliot, an eminent Lutheran scholar, has pointed out, the priesthood of the church is *sacrificial*, not in a cultic but in an *ethical* sense; the supreme sacrifice of the royal Christian priesthood is to live fully the life of the gospels in the midst of its contemporary culture.

Romans 5:6-11. On one particular occasion when speaking of the South he so dearly loved, the great Mississippian William Faulkner said, "You don't love because, you love *despite,* not for virtues but despite the faults." Paul had a similar notion in mind when he expounded to the church at Rome on the undeserved grace which is salvation. Paul's enthusiasm and joy almost leap from the page as we read his description of God's gratuitous love. The love which God has for humanity despite its sinfulness is *agape* love.

A Greek term, *agape* refers to that love which is *uncaused* by the attractiveness or worthiness of the object; in a word, it is selfless. *Eros,* on the other hand, is a lesser love which is evoked by some attractiveness in the object loved. Most human love needs some basis in objective reality; as Paul pointed out, "it is barely possible that for a good man, someone may have the courage to die" (v. 7). But God's love does not require this causality. As E. Maly has noted, "God doesn't love us because we are good; rather, we are good because God loves us."

In his commentary on this pericope, R. Bultmann observed that Paul emphasized the *event* character of God's love. Our justification by the blood of Christ is not just a vague idea or a benevolent sentiment. It is not simply a vague conviction that God will keep us from harm. Rather, our justification is a reality which happened quite concretely in the event of the cross. Therefore, it is in the cross that we learn most fully and experience most deeply God's love.

Previously in chapter five, Paul had referred to "boasting." First, he declared that believers *should boast* in their hope for glory (v. 2). Then he added that we should also *boast* ("rejoice" in some translations) in our sufferings because these prepared us for glory (v. 3). In v. 11, Paul made a third mention of boasting when he called his readers to boast in God himself (v. 11). God, who is the reason for our joy, the source of all hope and glory, has reconciled sinful humanity to himself by the blood of Jesus. As E. Maly explains, in the scriptures, reconciliation is never the movement of the person back to God. Rather, reconciliation is the action of *God* drawing the sinner back to himself. For this reason, the verb usually appears in the passive voice. In Paul's words, "We have now received reconciliation." Surely, the implication of this term was not lost on the Judaizers. Their emphasis on drawing near to God through the works of the law was in direct contradiction to the Pauline teaching of salvation as a gratuitous gift of a loving God to sinners.

Matthew 9:36-10:8. Today's gospel pericope is an excerpt from the missionary discourse wherein Matthew has portrayed Jesus as opening his ministry to his disciples and mandating them to proclaim the nearness of the reign of God to their fellow Israelites. Jesus was moved with compassion for the plight of the people; whereas the NAB has described the crowds as "lying prostrate from exhaustion," the actual Greek term is somewhat more vivid. As J. L. McKenzie has explained, the crowds were actually depicted as being "harassed" or "bothered" with the thousand petty persecutions and annoyances to which the poor are routinely subjected.

Not least among their persecutions was the fact that the people had no true leaders; they were "like sheep without a shepherd" (v. 36). Although the Pharisees considered themselves to be leaders among the people in the sense that they set the example for keeping the law, they scorned the general population. "People of the land" was the epithet applied by the Pharisees to those whom they regarded as outside the law. But Jesus, who understood himself to be Israel's shepherd, had concern for the people. That Matthew looked upon Jesus' ministry as the gathering of his scattered people back to God is borne out in the harvest imagery of v. 37.

With their many pressing needs, the people were like a field fully ripe for the harvest. A frequent symbol for the messianic era, the harvest imagery indicates that the mission of Jesus and that of his apostles should be understood as part of the eschatological event. While the demands upon the apostles will be great, viz., much work, few laborers, etc., nevertheless it is their shared mission with Jesus which sets in motion the eschatological ingathering.

Up to this point in his gospel, the Matthean author had named only five of the apostles and, unlike the other synoptics, he included no formal account of the special election of the Twelve. It is quite significant, therefore, that at this point he names the Twelve and in 10:2 identifies the twelve *disciples* with the twelve *apostles*. As E. Maly has pointed out, in the early church of Paul's day (ca. 40-60 C.E.), "apostle" was a term with a variety of applications. For Paul, being an apostle meant that one had experienced the risen Lord and been commissioned by him to preach the gospel.

Matthew's gospel reflects the later situation of the church of the 80s C.E. and a need to legitimate the authentic teaching of the community over and against the false teachers. This need for legitimation and authenticity led the later Christian authors to emphasize the position of the original guardians of the tradition and their official successors. By equating the twelve disciples with the apostles, Matthew showed them both as the original followers of Jesus and as the church's first leaders. They were also the paradigm for all later disciples and all future leaders in the church.

Matthew's list of the Twelve varies slightly from his Marcan source (Mark 3:13-19), but it is clear that Matthew, like the other evangelists, regarded the Twelve as the foundation of the new Israel. Charged by Jesus with a share in Jesus' healing work, they were also empowered by his authority over sickness and evil. Although by the time Matthew wrote his gospel the mission to the gentiles had been well established, he nevertheless preserved the fact that Jesus' earthly ministry was confined to Israel. No doubt Matthew emphasized this fact to illustrate the privilege which the Jews had indeed had and which they had rejected.

Finally, Jesus sent forth his emissaries of the reign of God with the exhortation to give freely what had freely been given to them. Besides underscoring the eschatological urgency of their mission, the injunction against getting rich in the name of religion reminded Jesus' disciples of God's provident care for them. Given this stringent advice, one wonders about the authenticity of contemporary media-evangelists and the financial ultimatums they place upon the people they are meant to serve.

1. It is the call of God to every believer which imparts dignity and identity; by virtue of that call we become ministers of his reign (Exodus).

2. There is no logic to be found in God's love, but precisely because of that "divine foolishness," sinners can draw near and be saved (Romans).

3. Those who are commissioned for the gospel mission are also given a share in the power and authority of Jesus (Matthew).

12th Sunday in Ordinary Time

Though his/her life be fraught with persecution, the true and faithful disciple is nevertheless glory-bound (Jeremiah). Because Jesus has broken the grip of sin and death (Romans), his followers may serve the cause of the good news enthusiastically and be unafraid (Matthew).

Jeremiah 20:10-13. Active as a prophet among his people during the reigns of Josiah, Jehoiakim and Zedekiah, Jeremiah witnessed the demise of Judah and the subsequent deportation of his people to Babylon. Called while still a young man (ca. 627 B.C.E.), he was reluctant to accept the unpopular and thankless task of interpreting God's will for his contemporaries. His reluctance appears in the book which bears his name. Indeed, the mournful, complaining style in which he couched much of his message has survived in the English figure of speech called a jeremiad.

Because of the frank nature of Jeremiah's harangues regarding his vocation, his mission and the people among whom he worked, more is known of this prophet's personality than any other. As he wrestled with the burden of God's word and with a people unwilling to hear it, Jeremiah developed a special literary genre called the confession. By means of this literary tool, the prophet gave vent to the tension he experienced because of God's involvement in his life.

But the confessions were not simply the ravings of a depressed paranoiac. Rather, it was as if the prophet were leading a liturgy of lamentation. Recall the many psalms of lament. These compare favorably to the prophet's confessions. In both the lament psalm and the confession there is an underlying positive aspect of hope. Never is there any doubt that God will act—only a question of *when!* Never is there a notion of, "*Will* you save us God?"—only, "*How long*, O Lord!"

In today's first reading the deep commitment of the prophet is evident as he recognizes the forces that militate against him but never doubts in the abiding presence of a caring, saving God. "Terror on every side" was an expression of warning frequently used by Jeremiah (6:25, 20:3, 46:5, 49:29). Annoyed with his browbeating, the people of Jerusalem eventually tagged the prophet with this derogatory nickname (see 20:10).

Occasioned by the prophet's altercation with Pashur (20:1ff), this pericope represents one of his most resounding complaints. His request to witness God's vengeance (v. 12) is a repetition of 11:20 and reflects a religious matrix in which justice meant retaliation (*lex talionis*) and earthly retribution. Obviously, this line of thinking was far from the notion of forgiveness which Jesus was to teach and practice six centuries later.

The final verse of this reading is styled as a doxology, praising God who will rescue the poor. Poor or *'ebyôn* in Hebrew did not refer to a sociological or economic condition; rather, the prophets used "poor" in a religious sense to describe those who depended fully and faithfully on Yahweh for their well-being. In today's gospel, the Matthean Jesus challenges his disciples to develop a similar spiritual posture.

Romans 5:12-15. One of the most controversial and significant texts in all of Paul's writings, the pericope which comprises today's second reading has exerted an enormous influence on the Christian understanding of sin and salvation. But while Augustine in the fourth century and the Council of Trent in the 16th century interpreted Paul as propounding a dogma of original sin (committed by Adam) and of the hereditary nature of that sin, great care should be taken not to anachronize later dogmatic developments into Pauline thought.

To correctly appreciate what Paul meant when he said, "Through one man sin entered the world," the reader should be aware of the semitic sense of corporate personality of or solidarity among the people. As P. Wrightman has so succinctly explained, "The biblical idea of 'corporate personality' is somewhat analogous to the modern idea of an ecosystem in which everything in that system is perceived in terms of interdependence. Just as human choices affect our environment, Adam's choice affected all of us." Without attending to the argument for or against polygenism or monogenism, this understanding of the social effect evil has, once it has been introduced into the environment, is superior to the notion that sin is inherited.

Paul's intent in mentioning Adam was to make a comparison between Adam, the first man, and the head of the new humanity, Christ. But, as several experts on Pauline style have noted, Paul digressed from his original intent; rather than pursue the Adam-Christ analogy (v. 12) with continuity, he launched into a discussion on death, to return to his original intention only in v. 15.

Within his digression on death (vv. 13-14), Paul alluded to the rabbinical teachings concerning the ages of humanity. Dividing history into three periods, the rabbis numbered the years from Adam to Moses as 2000. So also they counted the period from Moses to the messiah as 2000 years of law, and the period from the messiah onward as 2000 years of blessing. Paul recast the traditional divisions of time in light of the Christ-event. In the first double millennia, sin was a reality in the world but without impunity since there was no law. Nevertheless, humanity was subject to death as a result of its solidarity with Adam, whose sin brought death into the world (Genesis 1-3). In the second period, transgressions versus the law increased the effects of sin but in the third period, with Jesus Christ as messiah, believers enjoyed freedom from sin and death as well as from the law.

Returning to his original analogy, Paul called the freedom which Christ has wrought a *gift*, a *grace of God* of far greater significance than the offense of Adam. In the Christ-event, taught Paul, God has offered humanity the wonderful and comforting lesson that divine grace is more powerful than sin, that goodness will never be overcome by evil!

Matthew 10:26-33. When Jesus sent his disciples forth to share in his mission, he described them as "sheep among wolves" (10:16). With this graphic simile, Jesus attested to the cost of discipleship and the tension inherent in living according to the gospel. Christianity, viz., the way of life and commitment to God that developed in the wake of Jesus' resurrection and by virtue of his teaching, is of its very nature and by its very posture counter-culture. Just as the radical ethic Jesus lived and preached placed him in opposition to the religious and political establishment of his day, so does the follower of Jesus (if his/her discipleship is true and authentic) find himself/herself at odds with the status quo. But Jesus, the true and good shepherd, did not send forth his own defenseless. As today's gospel pericope reveals, the disciples of the Lord are protected and cared for by the Father himself.

An excerpt from the missionary discourse, these verses represent a collection of sayings from the Q (*Quelle*) source and are structured upon a triple injunction not to be afraid. The first "fear not" in vv. 26-27 assures the disciples that what is secret will be revealed. Matthew has departed from his fellow synoptics in giving a different context and meaning to this saying.

In Mark the thing hidden referred to the reign of God which seemed obscured but which would one day be visible to all (Mark 4:22). Luke applied this saying as a warning by Jesus against the hypocrisy of the Pharisees (Luke 12:2-3). In Matthew, however, the thing now hidden refers to Jesus' teaching. Limited at first to a few, it would later be spread through the mission of the disciples. By the time Matthew's gospel appeared, the teachings of Jesus were indeed being proclaimed from Jewish as well as gentile housetops.

In the second injunction against fear (v. 28), Jesus acknowledged the sure presence of persecution in the lives of his disciples. There would be those who will harm and even kill the followers of Jesus but they were to fear only the one who could administer the truly fatal blow, viz., God. Persecution could be understood as a sure sign that the disciples were producing the friction necessary to bring the message of Jesus to an unwilling world.

Conversely, can the general dearth of persecution in today's society indicate that Christians are not regarded as a serious factor? In his commentary, W. Barclay recalled the words J. P. Mahaffey, a scholar from Trinity College in Dublin. Asked if he were a Christian, Mahaffey replied, "Yes, but not offensively so!" His interpretation of the Christian life-style made no waves, rocked no boats. In conforming to the society within which it finds itself, this version of Christianity can be described as lukewarm at best. And we all remember what the faithful Witness told the Christians in Laodicea (Revelation 3:16)!!

While Jesus acknowledged the fact that a share in his mission would bring persecution, he reminded his disciples of the Father's care for each of them. His assurance constituted the third injunction against fear (in vv. 29-31). Fully aware of their needs and the dangers which beset them, the same God who created the universe would provide for Jesus' followers. The comparison of the sparrows becomes more poignant when the reader realizes that "*falls* to the ground" (v. 29) is more accurately rendered, "not a single sparrow *lights* upon the ground without your Father's consent!" The innumerable times that birds light and then take wing again attest to the careful and constant love of God for his faithful. So also the very idea of counting the hairs on one's head!

In the final verses of today's gospel, the Matthean author made a case for witnessing to Christ. By the time this gospel tradition was committed to writing, many had already lost their lives for acknowledging their faith in the Christ-event. As "sheep among wolves" the early Christians struggled to bear witness to the good news of Jesus within a culture that rejected its values. Because of loyalty to Christ, the church survives and flourishes. To encourage their fellow Christians to a similar loyalty, the Anglican Bishops at the 1948 Lambeth Conference, prayed: "Almighty God, give us grace to be not only hearers but doers of your holy word, not only to admire but to obey your doctrine, not only to profess but to practice religion, not only to love but to live the gospel."

1. Those who live in fidelity to the word of God are often by their very being a reproach to the unfaithful (Jeremiah).

2. In the saving acts of his Son Jesus, God has declared, "Goodness will never be overcome by evil" (Romans).

3. Fear cripples the ability of the minister to serve; trust in the Father sets him/her free (Matthew).

13th Sunday in Ordinary Time

A hand held out in welcome, a cup of water shared in love—these are the signs of a heart open to the Lord's words and ways (Matthew). In this atmosphere of receptivity the good news of Christ's death and rising will find a home (Romans). Through the sacrament of hospitality the wonders of salvation can be experienced by all who believe (2 Kings).

2 Kings 4:8-11, 14-16. Like his predecessor Elijah, Elisha involved himself in both the personal and political affairs of his fellow Israelites. Active in the northern kingdom for a period of about 50 years during the reigns of Joram, Jehu, Jehoahaz and Jehoash (ca. 850-800 B.C.E.), the prophet left no written records of his exploits for the Lord. Nevertheless, the Elisha (and Elijah) narratives were preserved orally, widely circulated and later committed to writing (ca. 700 B.C.E.), thus providing Judaism with a lively illustration of how God cared for his people in times of personal need and political crisis.

Today's first reading represents just one episode in the prophet's vast repertoire of wonders performed for individuals in need. The woman from Shunem, in a truly Semitic gesture of hospitality, offered Elisha a furnished room in her home. Her motivation for doing so, as stated in v. 9, was that she believed him to be a "man of God." An honorific title that recognized Elisha as a genuine prophet whose authority (1 Kings 17:24) came from God, "man of God" also reflected the theological concerns of the Deuteronomic historian and author of the book of Kings.

In recounting the wonderful works of Elisha, the Deuteronomist intended not to write a biography but to establish the divinely given authority of the prophets and to illustrate the effective power of their prophecies to come to fulfillment. In every instance, in every wonderful work, either on a personal or political level, Elisha's deeds underscored *God's* word as effective in human history.

No doubt it was because of the woman's attitude toward Elisha, her receptivity and faith in the word he spoke, that this pericope was chosen to introduce today's gospel. In the story of the woman of Shunem, the gospel text finds vivid expression: "he who welcomes a prophet because he bears the name of a prophet receives a prophet's reward . . . he who welcomes you, welcomes me" (Matthew 10:41, 40).

Romans 6:3-4, 8-11. Up to this point in his treatise-like letter to the Roman Christians, Paul had expounded upon the nature of justification by God's grace and through faith. In chapter six of Romans, the apostle introduced the matter of sanctification. In other words, what sort of behavior, what quality of moral response is demanded by the fact of the believer's being justified by God?

For the first and only time in his letter, Paul brought up the subject of baptism, explaining that it was *in* the sacrament of baptism that God's justification encountered human faith. As a result of that encounter, the believer has been visibly and spiritually identified with Christ's death and resurrection. That solidarity with Christ must result in a new and transformed way of life.

Paul's query in v. 3, "Are you not aware," reminded the Roman Christians and all who would subsequently read this letter of the instructions they had received as catechumens. As in today's initiation programs, the Roman converts to Christ had received catechesis concerning baptism and its effects. Recalling their shared commitment to Christ in baptism, Paul exhorted the Roman Christians to live up to what they had become.

Paul understood the insertion into Christ at baptism as the first step in a lifelong process of becoming *like* Christ. "Ontologically united with Christ, the Christian must deepen his faith continually to make himself aware psychologically of that basic union. Once thus consciously oriented to Christ, he would never again consider sin without bringing about a rupture of that basic union" (J. Fitzmeyer).

Paul's graphic theological expressions about being *buried* with Christ and *being dead to sin* in Christ (vv. 4, 11) were borne out in the symbolism of the ancient baptismal ritual. Generally, baptism by total immersion was the norm; as the catechumen entered into the baptismal waters, her/his descent signified the death to his/her former life of sin. As the believer emerged from the pool, his/her ascent was symbolic of the risen life in Jesus that is begun in baptism.

But, as any baptized Christians can attest, the sacrament of initiation into Christ does not automatically make one *immune* to sin. Ours is a world that exists in the tension between what is and what will be, between promise and fulfillment. The promise of freedom from sin and death has been made but, as P. Wrightman has stated, just as life is developmental, so is salvation.

Our fulfillment as Christians is not magically bestowed in the moment we accept Christ as savior. Rather, our salvation, our fulfillment is worked out gradually in relation with the Lord. Each day brings possibilities of dying to sin and an opportunity for a fuller life in grace. Each day, the promise of baptism draws us nearer to its fulfillment in the eschaton.

Matthew 10:37-42. By the time the gospel according to Matthew was written, in mid-80s C.E., believers in Jesus were quite familiar with both the rigors and the joys of being Christian. Those who had been initiated into Jesus' death and resurrection (see second reading) were experiencing firsthand the consequences of their baptism as they daily learned the demands of discipleship. Ostracized from the synagogue by the edict of Jamnia, *Jewish* Christians searched for an identity distinct from their traditional Jewish matrix. *Gentile* Christians sought to maintain their freedom from the Torah, ascribing to as authentic a commitment to Christ as their Jewish Christian brethren. *All* Christians, regarded as political enemies by the Roman state, were subjected to persecution and even death.

In an effort to help the members of his community (probably Syrian Antioch) to assert their identity as Christians in the midst of an often hostile and rapidly evolving environment, the Matthean author proclaimed his version of the good news about Jesus. At the very root of their identity as believers in Jesus, the Matthean evangelist posited the cross. Christians were to define themselves, their way of life, their response to their world in the same terms as did Jesus.

That Jesus' commitment to the Father's will resulted in suffering and death set the course for those who would follow after him. That Jesus' presence on earth caused a radical disruption of the status quo and breaches in even the closest of relationships (father, mother, son, daughter: v. 37) indicated that Christianity demanded an absolute and unique commitment. The radical and absolute nature of Christian commitment is the subject of today's gospel.

As the conclusion of the missionary discourse (10:1—11:1) and the end of book two (8:1—11:1) in Matthew's gospel, today's pericope is part of a longer section of instructions for disciples. Because the evangelist has reflected the concerns and circumstances of his own church into the text, the reader may detect elements proper to Jesus' ministry as well as elements from the second and third generations of the post-resurrection church. Regardless of whether the reflected concerns are those of the ministry or those of the Matthean community (or those of the 20th century church), the same principle prevailed: The way of Jesus becomes the way of those who would be his disciples. Those who in faith and service continue Jesus' work will also share his death and ultimately his glory.

Three points are made in today's short gospel: (a) that discipleship is a bond that supersedes all other bonds, (b) that true discipleship will lead inevitably to the cross, (c) that discipleship also has its rewards. While the first two points deal with the proper attitude of disciples, the third deals with the proper attitude *toward* those who are disciples.

By his words and works, by the very fact of his *presence*, Jesus created a crisis. One had to choose the way of discipleship or one had to reject it. The choice to follow Jesus in love and service often created factions between believers and non-believers, even between family members. But the challenge of the gospel is explicit and firm. The ties that bind believers to the Lord are more precious than any other relationship.

A post-resurrection anachronism, the reference to the cross (v. 38), recalled for Matthew's readers that cruel form of execution reserved by Rome for rebels and slaves. A familiar portent of the imperial power, the cross was an all too frequent symbol on the Judean hillside. When Varus, the Roman general, quelled the revolt led by Judas of Galilee, he crucified 2,000 Jews and placed their crosses by the wayside along the roads to Galilee.

Because the cross was the physical means whereby Jesus effected the salvation of all peoples, that ignominious sign of disgrace became a symbol of life for believers. Just as Jesus embraced the inevitable suffering that his way of life precipitated from Rome and from the Jewish authorities, so believers must accept the suffering integral to discipleship. Finally, in vv. 40-42, Matthew appealed to the church to recognize in every disciple a representative of Jesus and to pay the same respect to disciples as one would offer to the Lord himself. As J. Meier has pointed out, these verses reflect the dynamic relationship of the apostles to Jesus himself; to receive Jesus is to receive the Father.

This idea has been aptly expressed in the rabbinic statements: "The *shaliah* (messenger) of a man is as the man himself" and "He who welcomes his fellow man is considered as though he had welcomed the *shekinah*" (visible presence of God in cloud). Like the woman in the first reading, those who receive the Lord's disciples and care for them simply because they *are* disciples will receive a disciple's reward.

1. Hospitality, freely and generously offered, never goes unanswered (2 Kings).

2. To be truly vibrant, life in Christ demands a daily dying (Romans).

3. Belonging to Christ does not negate all other relationships; rather, Christian commitment makes all other relationships holier and happier (Matthew).

14th Sunday in Ordinary Time

Because he came in peace, he was unrecognized; because he did not pillage and plunder, his voice went unheard (Zechariah). But to those who had grown weary and disillusioned with the technicians of the law (Matthew), the Spirit of Jesus gave rest and freedom and a share in his eternal kingship (Romans).

Zechariah 9:9-10. Zechariah brought a new meaning and gave a new dimension to the concept of messianism in the post-exilic era. Unlike his contemporaries, and unlike the prophets before him, who centered hopes on a future Davidic messiah whose military and political prowess would regain Israel her tribal solidarity and national superiority, Zechariah's visions were more universal and eschatological in character. Perhaps because Judah had been without a king for almost 300 years, perhaps because the reconstruction of the temple had not succeeded in rebuilding the broken spirit of the people, perhaps because Alexander the Great's conquering armies made the future seem tenuous—whatever the reason, Zechariah's hopes seemed directed not toward a *new* era for his people, but to a *final* era of judgment for *all* peoples, ushered in by the messiah.

Calling his contemporaries to rejoice (v. 9), the prophet intended more than a word of good cheer to the desolate. Indeed, such rejoicing heralded the advent of the king (1 Samuel 10:24) and, more importantly, the epiphany of Yahweh as king (Psalms 97:1, 149:2; Numbers 23:21; Psalm 81:2) and of his saving help (Isaiah 34:1-4; Joel 2:21, 23). Even though the boots of Alexander's armies could be heard in nearby Syria, Phoenicia and Philistia (Zechariah 9:1-8), still the prophet would have his people *rejoice* in the figure of their messianic king (9:10). Riding on an ass or the colt of an ass, he came in peace. The donkey, as opposed to the horse which was an instrument of war (see v. 10), was not a sign of humiliation but of triumph. From ancient times (so unlike our "Hee Haw" concept of a mule), the rider of a donkey was singled out as distinct and distinguished (Genesis 49:11, Judges 5:10) and even as majestic (2 Samuel 13:29, 18:9; 1 Kings 1:33, 38). It is interesting that nowhere in the canonical New Testament is there a reference to Joseph obtaining a donkey for his wife and the child to ride (see Matthew 1-2, Luke 1-2) and yet legend down the centuries has preserved that image. Significant, too, is the message Jesus gave by entering Jerusalem astride a donkey's colt. Indeed, all four evangelists noted the messianic overtones of the act (Matthew 21:1-11; Mark 11:1-11; Luke 19:28-38; John 12:12-16).

Romans 8:9, 11-13. Up to this point in his treatise to the church of Christ in Rome, Paul's description of the effects of justification had been negative in presentation. In chapter five, the apostle depicted justification as deliverance from the wrath of God, in chapter six as redemption from the reign of sin and in chapter seven as deliverance from the burden of the law. In each case the saving activity freed the believer *from* sin, death, law; but in chapter eight, in a more positive mode of expression, Paul speaks of what the Christian is freed *for*, viz., a life in God.

Because of Christ's saving sacrifice, the believer is "in the Spirit," i.e., his life is home to the activity of Christ's own Spirit. In more graphic terms, the prophet Ezekiel had described the new life given by God's Spirit as a heart transplant of sorts whereby God removed the heart of stone or principle of death from his people and replaced it with his own spirit or principle of life (Ezekiel 36:26-28). Elsewhere in the Old Testament, the Spirit of God "came upon" certain individuals, enabling them to perform the works of the Lord for his people (Judges 3:10, 13:25; Isaiah 42:1). Surely, Paul with his rich background of rabbinical studies knew and included these aspects in his description.

In 8:1-8, Paul had described the power of the indwelling Spirit in the *living* body of the Christian. Christian existence, no longer prey to the flesh but dominated by the Spirit, is possible because of the sonship and daughtership afforded us in the sacrifice of our brother, Jesus. Then, in v. 9 and following, with what critics have termed a seeming abandon of all logical principles, Paul applied to the *dead* body of the individual believer the same privileges the risen Jesus enjoyed. Ignoring the barrier of death and mortality, Paul reasoned that God will do for each Christian what he has done for Jesus Christ. Just as in the natural order the believer is privileged to share in the life of God in the Spirit, this privilege carries over into the supernatural order. The future tense of the verb "will give life to your mortal bodies" indicates the eschatological character of the individual believer's resurrection. Rules of temporal, finite logic are far too inadequate and inapplicable when, by the grace of God and by the Holy Spirit, the believer and member of Christ's body is borne into the transcendent reality of eternal life.

Matthew 11:25-30. Following immediately upon Jesus' castigation of the scribes, Pharisees and the lake towns' inhabitants who had rejected his teaching, Jesus' words in today's gospel pericope expand his instruction on discipleship and membership in the kingdom of heaven. Consonant with Matthew's untiring indictment of the Jewish leaders, the prayer of Jesus to his Father (vv. 25-27) must have fallen hard on the hearts of those who prided themselves on their cleverness and mastery of the law.

Viewed as a whole, today's chosen text is rich in Old Testament imagery with roots in the sapiential, apocalyptic and prophetic literature of ancient Israel. By calling upon the Father in an intimate way (*Abba*) and claiming a unique relationship with the Father ("No one knows the Father but the Son"), Jesus echoes in his own person the personification of wisdom, the reflection of eternal light and image of God's goodness (Wisdom 7:22-30). Moreover, the yoke of wisdom, i.e., the law, was considered a "source of joy" and a "golden ornament." Indeed the "yoke of her instruction" satisfied the "thirsty soul" and was "worth more than gold" (Ecclesiastes 6:25, 51:27). Obviously, the Matthean text reveals that Jesus has transferred this wisdom and its fruits to himself.

However, there is a novel twist in the gospel text. Unlike the sapiential traditions of old, Jesus declared that the wisdom of God's revelation was hidden from the "learned and clever" and revealed to "merest children."

Indeed, this text implies that traditional wisdom, learning and the law may be obstacles to grasping the wisdom of Christ's message. Moreover, it is clear in v. 25 that the wisdom of Christ's message was not to be attained by human understanding but only by the revelation of the Father. The more Christ's listeners were steeped in the traditions of the law, the harder it seemed to be for them to open themselves to his words. So letter-perfect was their observance of the law that they could not see the freedom of Spirit with which Jesus interpreted and reinterpreted it.

In direct contradiction to the traditional claim that God's revelation is fully contained in the law and the prophets is the statement of Jesus, "Everything has been given over to me by my Father." "Everything" refers to revelation and that knowledge of the Father which only Jesus can give. Clearly, this revelation and this knowledge provide the believer with a release from the law, hence a lighter load. In sharp contrast to the Pharisees who "tie up heavy burdens and lay them on men's shoulders," and then offered "not a finger to move them" (Matthew 28:4), Jesus could say, "Come to me." Rather than the yoke of the law, Jesus offered his yoke, that of acceptance and submission to the reign of his Father. Such acceptance would impose no further burden. Moreover, the knowledge of God and the loving relationship which sprang from that acceptance served to lighten one's loads.

1. To banish bows and chariots, MiGs and missiles, bombs and battalions . . . is this not the legacy which the rider of the donkey left to his followers (Zechariah)?

2. In the incarnation, God spoke his opinion of humanity. In the resurrection, he sang a song of eternal love (Romans).

3. The good news finds a home in those seeking true revelation, rest and peace (Matthew).

15th Sunday in Ordinary Time

God's word of self-revelation is continually spoken (Isaiah). It is at once good news about God's love and a challenge to humanity to answer that love (Matthew). Formulating an adequate and an authentic response is the task of a lifetime and is not without pain and doubt. And we, the crown of creation, are the only beings who can give voice to the universal and cosmic yearning for our maker (Romans).

Isaiah 55:10-11. No more positive missiology has ever been propounded than Deutero-Isaiah's description here of the efficacious word of God. Part of a poem with which he concludes his prophecy of consolation, our text today reflects the prophet's conception of the divine purpose. Going forth into the world, summoning into existence the events of our salvation, echoing unto cosmic and universal dimensions, the word of God becomes comprehensible in the language and accents of human life.

Forming an analogy drawn from natural phenomena, vv. 10-11 may be regarded as a divine pledge concerning the longer passage (vv. 1-13) from which it is excerpted. Never failing in his posture of consolation and encouragement to his people in exile, the prophet concludes his poem with a veritable symphony of hope, a reprise in which he orchestrates all his earlier themes. Inviting the thirsty and hungry poor (*anawim*) to the eschatological banquet prepared for them by the Lord himself, the prophet recalled the Davidic covenant and pledged that the partakers of the banquet would enjoy in the present and in the future those promises made long ago (2 Samuel 7:14). Moreover, those who would "bend their ear and listen" (v. 3) would receive not only bread and water but milk and wine as well. Marks of an eschatological or messianic era, these commodities were regarded as precious signs of divine favor and the security of prosperity (Genesis 49:11-12, Song of Songs 4:10). Jerome tells us these verses led the early church to give some wine and milk during the rite of baptism as a sign of the divine blessing which the newly initiated were to enjoy.

In addition to the privileges of the eternal covenant and the enjoyment of peace and plenty, the invitation contained a number of imperatives to "seek the Lord," "turn to him." In return, the revelers at the divine feast would become his witnesses, guides and masters of all peoples. Then in a dramatic climax, lest there be any doubt or despair in the veracity of his promises, the prophet portrays the Lord as saying, "I give you my word" (vv. 10-11).

Rain in the ancient near eastern world was thought to be the most treasured gift of the gods. Deutero-Isaiah regarded it as a sign of a far greater reality: the loving, creative, redeeming, forgiving word of a personal God. Just as the waters from the sky brought the possibility of growth and abundance to the barren desert land, so too the word of God had called forth life from the clay (Genesis 2:7), called Israel out of Egypt (Hosea 11:1), called the prophets to guide and chide, and called Cyrus to be his anointed for the sake of his own people (Isaiah 44:27-28). With utmost certainty, the prophet could speak of the fulfillment of all he had promised, because he based all on the fructifying and creative word of God.

Romans 8:18-23. Entirely biblical in his affirmation of human solidarity with the material universe (*ktisis*), Paul, like his ancestors in the faith, regarded human destiny and nature's destiny as contingent realities. From the beginning, the primeval historians understood that the material universe was made by God and subordinate to humanity (Genesis 2:19). The harmony the first humans enjoyed in God's companionship was reflected in the natural order as well. When humanity sinned and broke relationship with God, this breach was felt in the created order. The author of Genesis observed, "Accursed be the soil because of you" (3:17). Paul regarded this "curse" as the reason for nature's "futility" and "slavery to corruption." Like the prophets before him, Paul too believed that nature would participate in the benediction of the messianic age. Isaiah's imagery of the future age (Isaiah 65:17-25) was not without its parallels in the New Testament (Revelation 21:1, 2 Peter 3:13). But nowhere else in the scriptures do we find the striving of humanity and the yearnings of nature for fulfillment so interwoven as in Paul's words today. Indeed, his understanding of the social and environmental consequences of human sin give a much better basis for understanding the sin called original, and all subsequent sin, than do statements about "inherited sin."

Suffering, groaning and agony are not only the consequences and by-products of sin but also a natural result of the believer's commitment to Christ. Just as suffering was for Jesus the path to glory, so too it will be for the follower of Jesus the means to exaltation. However, the apostle to the gentiles is adamant in making clear to the Christians of Rome the wonderful disproportion between present suffering and future glory. Temporal suffering, he taught, would pale into insignificance in the light of the eternal joy to come. This tremendous imbalance should orient Christian hopes forward and with them the yearnings of nature as well. The age to come, then, would not be an era of "future shock" but one of glorious freedom and joy. Not without substance, the hopes of the Christian and of all the material universe are already in the process of being fulfilled; here and now, the believer shares in the firstfruits of the Spirit due to Christ's redemptive activity.

Matthew 13:1-23. Besides the excellent lesson provided the believer in today's parable of the sower (v. 1-9, short form), the evangelist has also given the reader an exercise in redaction criticism. While the parable itself may be understood as a product of Jesus' ministry, the second (vv. 13-17) and third (vv. 18-23) sections are later additions and represent the use made of Jesus' parable by the Matthean church of the 80s. Therein, a new situation and new ramifications dictated an adapted interpretation of the original teaching. C.H. Dodd and J. Jeremias would have us find this double setting in all Jesus' parables, i.e., their original historic context in the life of Jesus and their subsequent setting in the preaching ministry of his church.

All the synoptics relate the parable of the sower (Mark 4:1-9, Luke 8:4-8) and set the scene in Galilee. Only Matthew refers to "the house" indicating that the city of Capernaum, Jesus' "home away from home," was the probable setting. Notice Jesus' posture: He is seated, the customary posture of the rabbi imparting wisdom to his own. Notice too the fact that the crowd stood on the shore separated from Jesus by the lake water. This nuance may represent the baptisimal waters through which the believer, moved by Jesus' teaching, would come to him. To the farmers within his hearing the circumstances of Jesus' story were all too familiar: Palestine's rocky soil, the scorching sun, the thorns. The farming technique of sowing and then plowing the seed under was peculiar to Palestine. But the familiar aspects of the parable end when the yield of the harvest is described in terms of 100, 60 and 30 fold. Ideally, the Palestinian farmer was satisfied with a yield of seven and a half and he would have been ecstatic if he reaped ten fold. The yield described in Jesus' parable was miraculous indeed. Notice the fact that Matthew has reversed Mark's 30-60-100 fold and has attached an exhortation to hear.

What was Jesus' point in telling this agrarian story? The general purpose of the parables was to proclaim the kingdom or, more precisely, the *reign* of God. In describing the obstacles to growth (thorns, bad soil, birds, etc.), Jesus recognized there would be certain difficulties and even resistance to his preaching and thus to the establishment of the reign. In spite of the hindrances, the reign would come as surely and as richly as the harvest he described. Such certainty of success should inspire the preachers of the good news to withstand the rocks and birds and thorns of the Pharisees, Romans, Judaizers, etc. In Jesus' own ministry, many had rejected his words and works but, in those who received him ("good soil"), the success was like the abundant harvest associated with the messianic era.

In the third section, vv. 18-21, the parable receives an allegorical interpretation, the circumstances of which were proper to the Matthean community of the late 80s C.E. "*Seed*," the operative word of the interpretation, has a rather fluid meaning, referring at one point to the apostolic preaching of the good news and at another point to the respondents to that word. While this interpretation of the parable is certainly based on the first meaning given by Jesus, it nevertheless illustrates how his Spirit helped his followers accommodate the principles of his teaching to their changing times and circumstances.

In identifying the particular reactions to the preaching of the good news, the Matthean community could formulate an appropriate missiology and plan of evangelization. First, there were those who did not *understand*. Elsewhere in Matthew, *understanding* would more precisely mean acceptance. Second, there were the fair-weather Christians, who rejoiced at the positive elements of the message but rejected the cross and persecution. Third, there were those whose good intentions were detoured by worldly interests. Finally, there were of course those who heard, kept and lived the word, thus yielding a rich harvest. With this profound insight into their own community and its responses to the good news, the early preachers of the good news were better equipped for their apostolate. Encouraged by Jesus' teaching of the inevitability of the reign of God, they became invincible, even in the face of their expulsion from the synagogue and the persecution from Rome.

1. Though it be subtle as the dew or overwhelming as a torrent, the word of God is never ineffective (Isaiah).

2. The created universe is given over in trust to the stewardship of the believer (Romans).

3. Preachers of the word can learn much from the patient, trusting farmer, who every season devotes all his energies and fortunes in hopes of a harvest (Matthew).

16th Sunday in Ordinary Time

Salvation history attests to the fact that our wise and patient God is a believer in second chances (Wisdom). He alone understands the combined potential of the resilient human spirit and the indomitable Holy Spirit (Romans). With him alone rests the power to decide between "weeds" and "wheat" (Matthew).

Wisdom 12:13, 16-19. Purported to be pearls of wisdom from Solomon, the book of Wisdom as we have it today was written some eight centuries after the great king, about the first century B.C.E. Moreover, it was probably written in Greek in Alexandria, Egypt, educational and scientific center of the Mediterranean world.

Doctrinally, the author's thoughts reached profound depths as he urged his readers to seek wisdom (Hebrew: *hokmah;* Greek: *sophia*) so as to gain eternal life. Although in some instances his personification of wisdom is quite extreme, it must be remembered that this technique of personification was a literary device quite popular in Greek literature. In no way did the author intend to present wisdom as an hypostasis. Our pericope today is from a longer section (11:2-19:4) in which the author recapitulates the major aspects of Israel's salvation history while informing them with his own theological insights so as to edify and instruct his contemporaries. The particular literary form, called a midrash, was a popular oral and literary technique, especially in rabbinical literature. While the entire section 11:2-19:4 is a midrash on the exodus event, our text belongs to a subsection (11:17-12:22) in which the author digresses to speak of God's merciful castigation of sinners.

With a strong affirmation of the strictly monotheistic belief held by Jews (v. 12), the author attests to the omnipotence of God over all. Although the punitive aspects of the following verses may seem negative, the author intends to underscore the divine attributes of benevolent mercy and just clemency.

This accent on God's forbearance and compassion while guiding the destiny of his people links this Old Testament selection to the gospel parable of the weeds and the wheat.

Romans 8:26-27. Though justified by faith and privileged to share the life of God by the indwelling of the Spirit, humankind is, according to Paul, still weak. Caught in the tension of being finite creatures with infinite desires and eternal potentialities, believers need the Spirit to voice the hopes and prayers which are beyond human capacity even to imagine. Although this weakness is part of the human condition, redeemed humanity is aided by a divine advocate or paraclete (John) who not only gives expression to human prayer but provides its inspiration as well.

Not only does this Spirit prompt the believer to call upon God as Abba-Daddy-Papa (Romans 8:15), but the Spirit can even make intelligible the "groaning" of the believer for sharing in the life of God and for the fulfillment that derives from such participation. This Spirit is the Spirit of Jesus himself, and the aid afforded believers is a natural consequence of our adoption as sons and as daughters of the Father.

Utilizing a familiar Old Testament expression, "he who searches the heart" (Proverbs 20:27, Psalm 139:1), the apostle to the gentiles assured the believers in Rome that God himself, the giver of the old covenant and the initiator of the new covenant, willed that the Spirit should be so dynamically involved in the faith odyssey of the Christian. In prayer, the Spirit enables the believer to bridge the gap between his finitude and the infinite greatness of God. In prayer, the believer experiences, because of the Spirit, both the immanence and the transcendence of God.

Matthew 13:24-43. In a series of three parables and amid three levels of tradition (Jesus, church and evangelist), the believer's knowledge about the nature of the kingdom is further enhanced by today's gospel text. With an agrarian motif and a rather unusual method of farming, the first parable (vv. 24-30) is unique to Matthew's gospel, though some scholars consider it Matthew's version of Mark's "seed growing in secret" parable (Mark 4:26-29).

The weed in question (darnel or tares in other translations), more specifically *lolium temulentum,* was a common growth in Palestine. When just a new sprout, it was remarkably similar to wheat. With prudence, the farmer advised his slaves to allow it the grow with the wheat until reaping time. In fact, at the harvest the wheat would have grown considerably higher than the weed and would be easily distinguished. If we are to understand the point of this parable in the context of Jesus' ministry, we should keep in mind that the goal of Jesus' preaching, as per the Matthean gospel, was to proclaim the reign. It would seem, then, in this story Jesus was teaching that various elements, i.e., all types of people, were to be included in the kingdom. Moreover, it is very likely that this particular parable was Jesus' response to the Pharisees who criticized him for eating with sinners and associating with people of ill repute. Unlike the worldly caste system that pigeonholed people into neat though underserved categories, the kingdom would admit of no judgmental processes. All persons of any station, nationality or background were allowed the chance to grow and to thrive together until the time of reaping. Harvest was a popular symbol for the era of the eschatological manifestation of the messiah. Then and only then, the Lord of the harvest, and he alone, would decide between wheat and weeds. For the wheat or faithful ones as judged by God, there would be a gathering unto him. On the other hand, the weeds would meet the reaper.

In the allegorical interpretation (vv. 36-43) of Jesus' parable, the early church's understanding of its role is clarified. Like Jesus during his ministry, its mission was to be *for all others*, patiently leaving the task of judging to the Son of Man. The Matthean church of the 80s was not without its weeds, viz., the disbelieving, the scandalous, the persecutors, the heretics, etc. But just as in Jesus' parable, time had to be allowed for conversion, repentance and renewal. In an atmosphere of tolerance and patience, given the power of God's Spirit helping the weak (Romans), perhaps some of the "weeds" could have turned over a new leaf. Then too, those who at first glance may have been mistaken for weeds might have the qualities of wheat after all. This valuable lesson from the church of the first century also applies in the church of the 20th century. While here on earth we live in the era of the *second chance*. Since harvest time has not yet come, judgmental attitudes and behavior have no place among us.

Considerably shorter than the sower parable, the other parables of the mustard seed (vv. 31-32) and the leaven (vvs. 33) both made the same point: From small and even insignificant beginnings come forth great and astounding results. In truth, the mustard seed was not the *smallest* seed, and it was not the first nesting choice of birds, being a shrub about 10-12 feet tall. Nevertheless, the point of the story lay in the contrast and in the remarkable growth. Moreover, for the Jewish audience in the Matthean community, the reference to the birds making nests in a great tree was reminiscent of one of Ezekiel's visions (Ezekiel 17:22-23) and was a symbol of the last times wherein all people (birds) would find a home in the kingdom. The leaven parable has obvious eschatological dimensions also. According to the specified measurements, (about 50 lbs. of flour), the woman was preparing a meal for some 100 people or more. But as with the mustard seed, a small amount of leaven accomplished a mighty task. In Jesus' day, as in the Matthean church of the 80s, the response to the preaching of the good news was unimpressively small, marked by frustration and failure, But the parables of the mustard seed and the leaven promised great eventualities from a seemingly insignificant start. Reassurance such as this was encouraging for the early believers and should be so for us as well.

1. Greater wisdom is found in forgiveness than in revenge (Wisdom).

2. A prayer which rolls too glibly off the tongue may not be true to the ineffable longing of the heart for God (Romans).

3. Any attempt here and now to label "weed" or "wheat" is an attempt at playing God (Matthew).

17th Sunday in Ordinary Time

For the believer in Jesus Christ, life is a continual ordering of values and a centering of energies on the kingdom (Matthew). Discipleship requires a wisdom which only God can give (1 Kings), a wisdom which can perceive God's good and provident plan in the contradiction of the cross (Romans), a wisdom willing to search for the pearl of great price inside the crustiest oyster.

1 Kings 3:5, 7-12. Given a sufficient lapse of time and the distance of perspective, heroes of past historical epochs tend to be "writ larger then life." Such is the case with the sagacious king Solomon. His was certainly a prosperous reign, perhaps even a golden age, in the stormy history of the people of Israel. But he was not without his failings and shortcomings with regard to the covenant standard. Perhaps, because the author of Kings wrote at a time (during the exile) when his contemporaries were desperately in need of heroes and a reminder that better days lay ahead . . . or perhaps, because Solomon had built the temple which was so central to the author's religious concerns . . . whatever the reason, Solomon for all his faults and foibles is portrayed in the book of Kings as a human wonder, a repository of God's wisdom.

Using history as a vehicle for their theological purpose, the authors of Samuel and Kings idealized certain aspects and individuals of their people's past. The four books (1 and 2 Samuel, 1 and 2 Kings) cover a period of about 400 years, from the reign of David to Judah's last king and the subsequent exile. As part of the entire chronicle called the Deuteronomic history, these four volumes bear the distinctive mark of the Deuteronomic editor. Shaped by his two principal tenets, viz., (1) the central sanctuary and temple of Jerusalem and (2) fidelity or infidelity to the covenant as a gauge of success or failure in Israel's endeavors, the author's work passed judgment in turn on each of the kings of his people. Though his moral evaluation of most of them was quite negative, nevertheless, the author was adamant in keeping before the minds of his people the promise of Yahweh to David (2 Samuel 7:14).

While the crisis of exile militated against all their hopes for deliverance, the author of Kings recounted for his people the legendary stories of better times. His extensive and colorful description of the reign of Solomon (1 Kings 3-11) illustrated the success that could be enjoyed by king and by people if fidelity to the covenant were upheld.

Besides offering a fine tribute to Solomon, today's pericope shows a significant development in Israel's understanding of wisdom. Unlike the Hellenistic mind, which perceived wisdom as the object of philosophical speculation, the earlier Hebrew writings saw wisdom as more a matter of practical knowledge. For this reason much of that early wisdom literature reads like a "Poor Richard's Almanac" of wise and pithy sayings based on human experience. Later, of course, and not without the influence of Hellenistic thought, the Hebrew concept of wisdom developed to the point of being a personified divine attribute. Today's text represents later Hebrew thought concerning wisdom as a gift from God, a charism thought to be of supreme value.

Romans 8:28-30. Many scholars believe that v. 28 was a popular and well-known religious maxim which Paul brought to Christianity from his Jewish background. While there are a variety of translations for this verse, due to discrepancies among several manuscripts with regard to the subject of the sentence, Paul's point is clear nevertheless. Whether one assigns God (*ho Theos*) or "all things" (*panta*) as the subject of the verb (*synergei*), God's invincible plan and purpose for humankind and for all creation is perceived as good, as based on love and as glory-bound!

Life for the Christian, taught Paul, was no longer defined by the flesh or by the law. Nor was it spelled out in sin according to the way of the old Adam. Because of Christ and the Spirit, a revolution had taken place, and humanity along with all of creation (see last Sunday's second reading comments) is now geared to a far greater destiny. No longer slaves to sin but adopted children and heirs to the privileges of the risen Lord, "those who love God" could look to a positive and wonderful future.

Foreknown, predestined, called, justified and glorified ... each term communicates a further step in the wonderful process of salvation, all of which are signs of God's provident care. God had willed, taught Paul, that the believer would reproduce the image of Christ by a progressive share in the life of Christ through the Spirit.

Paul's anthropomorphisms should be understood as the apostle's attempt to communicate the graciousness and the bountifulness of God's love. Augustine and Calvin were pushing Paul's ideas to the limits of rigidity by concluding systematic predestinarianism from his assertions. In no way did the apostle to the gentiles imply that only certain believers were predestined. This would, in fact, be contradictory to Paul's conviction that God's plan of salvation encompassed all of creation throughout all of history. Not only did Paul refrain from placing limitations on those who enjoyed the fruits of Christ's sacrifice, but his use of the word "predestined" should be understood along with "foreknew" as indications of the eternal divine plan. God's purpose *from* all eternity was to unite the destiny of humankind with the destiny of Christ himself.

Matthew 13:44-52. Anyone with a head for business knows that to sink all one's capital and collateral into a single investment is far from wise. But the principles of the business world do not apply when the *investment* in question is the kingdom of heaven and the *transaction* has eternal consequences. Indeed, there is a far greater and a more transcendent wisdom which governs the acquisition of divine realities. The first two parables of today's text are peculiar to Matthew's gospel (as is the third parable) and both have similar structures and significance. However, as J. Jeremias points out, though the parables may be thought of as twins in that (1) both have the element of a surprising and joyous discovery, and (2) both indicate that the person sold *all* to obtain the discovered treasure, there is one distinctive difference. In the parable of the treasure hidden in a field, the discovery was made by a (literally) *laborer,* and in the parable of the pearl a wealthy or rich person (merchant) is in quest of the kingdom. But both give all! The reign of God is beyond price and requires of each person who seeks it, whether rich or poor, the gift of all he is and all he has.

In the perilous conditions which existed in Palestine under Roman occupation, hiding one's treasures (jewels, money, etc.) in a field was a common practice. Even today, archaeologists are unearthing the precious belongings of those who were unable to return to dig them up. Notice that Jesus makes no reference to the avarice of the finder of the treasure or to the dubious morality. In fact, Jesus uses that unattractive behavior to make his point: Even drastic and perhaps over-zealous actions are necessary in the quest for the reign of God.

Pearls were a valued and precious gem in the ancient world and merchants from the orient were often dispatched by royalty to search out these treasured items. Caesar is said to have purchased a pearl (for the mother of Brutus) at a price of over 16 tons of gold. Cleopatra was thought to possess a pearl worth over ten times that amount! Indeed one can understand the merchant's willingness to sell all in order to possess the cherished pearl.

Recalling that these parables were addressed to Jesus' would-be disciples, we may find a further clue to their meaning. Discipleship, like the discovery of the treasure and the search for the pearl, was not without great joy because the disciple (like the laborer and the merchant) found in Jesus, in his words and in his works, a treasure beyond all price. However, like the laborer and the merchant, the disciple's discovery of the truth of Jesus and of the kingdom was not without sacrifice. However joyous, the discovery and acceptance of the way of Jesus was a value that cost not less than everything. Surely, the disciples of Jesus in the persecuted Matthean community of the 80s had learned by personal experience and sacrifice the infinite worth of the kingdom.

In the third parable, that of the dragnet, the message is similar to that of the weeds and wheat (last Sunday's gospel), viz., various elements will thrive together until divine judgment separates the valuable from the worthless at the end of time. There is however an additional point. Palestinian fishermen used a dragnet some 500 yards in length and about one yard wide with large pieces of cork sewn into it to keep it afloat. With one group of fishermen on shore paying out the net, another group in a boat would carry the end of the net out in the lake, forming a huge circle. Then, the net was pulled into the shore while its bottom was drawn tight to keep its contents from being lost. In using this particular fishing technique to teach about the kingdom, Jesus reminded his followers of their role as fishers of men. Indeed, as emissaries of the reign of God, they would go out and embrace (encircle) all, bringing good news to rich and poor, valuable and valueless alike, allowing none to slip through the all encompassing message (net) of God's love and redemption.

In concluding this parabolic discourse on the kingdom Matthew's statement about the scribe may be thought of as a mini-parable about evangelization. The scribe in question would be a Christian scribe, i.e., one learned in the law and the prophets as well as the gospel. Responsible for his household (his community), he would bring forth for their benefit from his store old things (law and prophets) and new things (good news). Surely, Matthew understood his role as an evangelist in these terms. Is not this also the responsibility of every modern evangelist: to bring together the "old," i.e., the teachings of Jesus, and the "new," i.e., the contemporary situation of his community, harmoniously blending the two in perfect fidelity to the reign of God.

1. The ability to govern wisely and well is a rare and precious gift, professed by many, possessed by few (1 Kings).

2. The belief that all will turn out well is not childish naivete but the secure hope of those who love God (Romans).

3. Before one sells all to purchase the "pearl of great price," one must pray for the insight to recognize that "pearl" when he/she finds it (Matthew).

18th Sunday in Ordinary Time

Christianity's mission consists in more than providing a "free lunch" to proselytes. Each believer must by his/her way of life challenge those he serves to a love and a generosity far greater than what they deem themselves capable of (Matthew). At the basis of this challenge is God's irresistible invitation to a faithful relationship with him (Isaiah) and the pledge that his love will ever be with us in the person of Jesus Christ (Romans).

Isaiah 55:1-3. In concluding his message of consolation to his fellow exiles in Babylon, Deutero-Isaiah issued in Yahweh's name an offer only a fool would have refused. How wonderful his invitation to the divine feast must have seemed to his fellows in suffering. A sumptuous menu, not merely of subsistence foods (water and bread) but of wine and milk as well, was spread for the people. Moreover, in contrast to the sentence passed on Adam's progeny ("With sweat on your brow shall you eat your bread"), no toil was exacted from the guests at the table Yahweh would set. Thirst was the only requisite for admittance to this marvelous feast. But this thirst implied not merely a physical need for bodily satisfaction but a spiritual desire for a renewed relationship with the God from whom the people's hard hearts had long been absent. At the root of the return to their own land, and their enjoyment once again of God's provident care, was Israel's need to renew its moral and religious commitment to the Lord by accepting once again its covenant responsibilities (v. 3). Israel's breach of the covenant had, according to the prophet's interpretation of history, resulted in the forfeiture of the covenantal blessing, namely its land and status as an independent people. Restoration to its own land, due to Cyrus' policy toward prisoners (Cyrus was the conquering Persian general), would consequently involve a renewal of the covenant celebrated, promised Deutero-Isaiah, by a banquet of eschatological proportions.

Not a unique invention of the sixth century B.C.E. prophet, the banquet and banquet imagery figured very importantly in Israel's past traditions. From the beginning of its history as a people, Israel had celebrated the Lord's love for his people in the context of a banquet. Israel's passage from slavery as a motley band of rebels in Egypt to freedom as an identifiable people was marked by a feast. In Exodus 12, the prescriptions for the Passover feast and the feast of unleavened bread transformed these ancient pastoral and agrarian feasts into a banquet of national pride and religious thanksgiving. To celebrate the ratification of the covenant with the Lord at Sinai, a great feast was prepared and enjoyed by all in the presence of Yahweh (Exodus 24:5-11). In the Isaian and Trito-Isaian apocalypses, whose verses burst with messianic and eschatological hope, the era to be ushered in by the messiah is depicted in terms of a rich and lavish banquet laid out for all peoples to enjoy (Isaiah 25:6ff, 65:11-15).

Romans 8:35, 37-39. Paul may have intended to remain for an extended period in Rome before proceeding on to his mission to evangelize Spain. Indeed, the itinerant apostle seemed determined to include the entire burden of the good news in his letter to the church at Rome. More like a treatise than a letter, his missive to the Romans has been called the "Pauline gospel," albeit without Jesus' miracles and sayings.

Today's pericope is from Paul's erudite theological argument concerning the benedictions of a life lived in Christ. Humankind—called, redeemed, justified and destined for glory—has been the object of divine predilection. In today's verses Paul's ideas form a triumphal hymn of hope and confidence concerning that divine favor. Up to this point, Paul has argued that humanity's election by God and the justification by Christ's redeeming action are but a prelude to glory. That hope of glory affords justified humanity the perseverance to endure life's troubles. But Paul has also painted a very realistic verbal portrait of human weakness and suceptibility to sin. However, as he pointed out in Romans 5:8, "Christ died for us while we were still sinners!" This immense love of God assures us of our final victory. If sin cannot separate us from God and Christ and their love, then nothing can. At this point, and with poetic rhetoric, our text resumes today. Sin is the ultimate barrier, yet even sin crumbles into insignificance before God's forgiving, redeeming, justifying, glorifying love.

Various translations have interpreted "the love of Christ" (v. 35) as either an object genitive ("our love for Christ") or as a subject genitive ("the love Christ bears for us"). The context would suggest the use of the subject genitive as does v. 39, "the love of God that comes to us in Christ Jesus our Lord." In either case, Paul's enumeration of the seven troubles and sufferings of human living (v. 35) and his list of the ten possible obstacles between God and humanity (vv. 38-39) posit nothing as superior in any way to God's all powerful love. Surely the believers at Rome were familiar with Paul's first series of difficulties. Indeed, authorities from both the civil (Rome) and the religious sphere (Judaism) were intent on causing the followers of Jesus to suffer trials, persecution, want and so on.

In his second series of obstacles, however, Paul has gone beyond the temporal sphere of existence. His reference to the angels and principalities was a sure indication of his Jewish background. In the second half of the first century C.E., the rabbis had a highly developed angelology, and popular belief held that every created thing was guarded by an angel. In ranking these spiritual beings, the rabbis taught that there were three levels of angels: (1) thrones, cherubim, seraphim; (2) powers, lordships, mights; (3) angels, archangels, principalities. On several occasions, Paul too referred to these angelic beings (Ephesians 1:21; Colossians 2:10, 15; 1 Corinthians 15:24). But the attitude of these beings toward humanity remained uncertain. Indeed, the rabbis taught that, although they were to care for humanity, the angel hosts were somehow resentful of God's involvement with humankind and were somehow hostile toward these lower creatures. Although based on legends (Lucifer) from intertestamental literature, this negative attitude of the angels does fit with Paul's reference in Romans 8:30-39.

Matthew 14:13-21. Withdrawing to a deserted place must have been a difficult feat in populous Galilee in the early first century C.E. A small territory measuring some 50 miles north to south and 25 miles east to west, Galilee was comprised of 204 towns and villages. Josephus tells us that each of the 204 numbered no fewer than 15,000 inhabitants! If the Jewish historian's statistics are accurate, then during Jesus' ministry there were 3,060,000 people in Galilee, an area of 1,250 square miles—2,448 people per square mile. Compare that figure to the 64 inhabitants per square mile in the U.S. (World Almanac Statistics for 1984) and it becomes obvious that Matthew may have had another motive for alluding to a "deserted place." Indeed this allusion and others that permeate the narrative of the loaves and fish would certainly have reminded the believers of the Matthean community of the 80s of their rich biblical heritage concerning God's care for his people in the wilderness. This, as well as other messianic and eucharistic concerns, have influenced the evangelist's portrayal of this wondrous event.

Related a total of six times among the four gospels, the miraculous feeding of the multitudes has been shaped in various ways and given different contexts by the four gospel authors, but the essential point of the event remains the same.

Jesus, like the God of the fathers of the Old Testament, was capable of satisfying the deepest needs of his people.

Drawing on the richness of biblical tradition, the miraculous event in Matthew recalls God's feeding of his people in the wilderness (Exodus 16:13-14). In a deserted place, with no resources of their own, the wilderness wanderers looked to their Lord and he fed them. There are remarkable similarities as well to the instance when Elisha (2 Kings 4:42-44) fed 100 men with 20 loaves. Indeed, it seems that the Matthean evangelist shaped his account after the Elisha story. In both accounts, servants indicate the impossible nature of the situation, yet are told to feed the crowd. In both accounts, the servants distribute the food, and in both accounts the people eat, are filled and the leftovers are collected. Of course, the fact that the numbers in the gospel are greater (100 and 5000) and the ratio of bread to people is far more unequal (20/100 and 5/1000) indicated that Jesus is far greater than the prophets (Elisha), a favorite Matthean theme.

Besides the exodus and early prophetic traditions, the Matthean account conjures up a host of messianic allusions as well. Notice that, even in that deserted place, the people were made to sit on the grass. Those who hoped for a new shepherd-king of the line of David were surely reminded of that psalm (23): "in meadows of green grass, he lets me lie" and "you prepare a table before me." From the Qumran writings we learn of the popular belief that the messiah at his advent would repeat some of the greatest events of Israel's salvation history, especially the miraculous feeding of God's people.

Then too, there are the obvious eucharistic allusions and concerns. It is generally accepted that the eucharistic terminology, viz., "took, looked up to heaven, blessed, broke, gave," is probably a redactional feature; nevertheless, it cannot be denied that the early Christians regarded the event as eucharistic, if not in character, at least in sign. Contemporary Christians tend to associate the Eucharist only with the Lord's last supper with his disciples. However, it has become increasingly clear that the evangelists read eucharistic significance into Jesus' eating with his own in Galilee, his miraculous feeding of the crowds and especially in those meals he shared in his post-resurrection appearances. Perhaps the Johannine omission of a last supper Eucharist account and his extensively eucharistic chapter six are our best attestations to this suggestion.

Various interpretations of this wondrous event have been proposed for the edification of 20th century believers. However many meanings may be proposed for today's gospel, one fact remains clear: Those who were privileged to share in the bread and in the gift of Jesus were satisfied and an abundance remained. Jesus' presence, his words and works, heralded a new era wherein past traditions, messianic hopes, eucharistic concerns and community caring were manifest in his very person. These same concerns, hopes, traditions and caring must be kept alive by those who follow his lead.

1. Thirst is the only protocol for the banquet feast hosted by the Lord (Isaiah).

2. If no natural or supernatural power can come between us and Christ's love, how then can we explain the discrepancies that exist between Lord and his followers (Romans)?

3. Though the time was inconvenient and inopportune (he had just lost his cousin and friend), though resources seemed wanting, Jesus could satisfy completely the needs of the crowds (Matthew).

19th Sunday in Ordinary Time

In soft and whispering silence the Lord can reveal himself and his ways (1 Kings). Amid fearful cataclysms of nature and tempests of human discord he can speak with power and reassurance (Matthew). Yet, even though his voice speaks and his words reveal his love, there are those who may choose not to listen (Romans).

1 Kings 19:9, 11-13. Elijah's spiritual encounter on Horeb marked a development in the perception of God's revealing presence and ushered in the prophetic era in Israel. The author of Kings obviously wished to compare Elijah to his great ancestoral hero, Moses, and has modeled the Elijah experiences on Horeb to that of Moses on Sinai. Horeb and Sinai are two variant names for the same mountain; depending on the source (J or E), the name changes. While Moses had been called by God to Sinai to receive the law and to mediate the covenant with his people (Exodus 19), Elijah fled to Horeb to bemoan the fact that his people had shamelessly violated that Mosaic law and had broken that sacred covenant. Both Moses' and Elijah's experiences contained a time factor of 40 days, a crevice in the rock and the standard properties for a theophany, viz., thunder, earthquake, wind and so on. We may even draw a comparison between Elijah and Moses on the basis of lack of "popularity" among their people. Moses, in his attempt to guide his people in the ways of the Lord, met with criticism, rebellion and antagonism. Elijah, too, had become "persona non grata" in his northern kingdom homeland. Openly defiant of Ahab and his Sidonian queen, Jezebel, Elijah railed against the importation of the foreign queen's gods (Baal and Astarte) and the idolatrous behavior of both king and people. Fearless of their evil intentions against him, Elijah challenged Jezebel's hired prophets and in a unique and entertaining confrontation (1 Kings 18:20-40), bested them at their own craft. Not only did the bogus prophets appear ridiculous and powerless (Elijah slaughtered them!), but Jezebel was humiliated as well. From the fury of that woman's scorn, Elijah fled to Horeb, but only after he had lifted the curse of the drought he had ordered (1 Kings 17:1; 18:41-46).

Given the similarities between the Moses story and that of Elijah, it seems that the author of Kings wished to portray Elijah as a new Moses or perhaps as the "prophet like Moses" (Deuteronomy 18:18). If that be the case, then it is here that the similarities come to an end. Indeed, the revelation of God to Elijah assumed a new mode of communication altogether. Hitherto, cataclysms of nature such as thunder, lightning and earthquakes had embodied the message of the Lord. But with Elijah, the Lord was doing something new. Our pericope points out that there was a heavy, rock-crushing wind, an earthquake and fire, but in each case the Lord was not there. Rather, only in the "tiny whispering sound" was the Lord truly present, revealing himself to Elijah. The Hebrew text defies translation; what the NAB has rendered "tiny whispering sound" might more literally and more accurately though enigmatically be translated as "a still small silence." In this unusual encounter with Elijah, the Lord was indicating that henceforth his voice would be heard and his will made known through a new medium. No longer would the cries of nature speak for the Lord. But with Elijah and through those who would, like him, be his prophets (mouthpieces, Greek *prophetes*), the Lord would speak in the small, still silence of private inspiration. Those so inspired by him would be impelled to speak and even to shout aloud the message they had learned in the silence to all who would listen. Elijah would be the forerunner of a long line of prophets who would perceive the Lord's ways after the storm had been calmed.

Romans 9:1-5. Though Paul had been thrown from his horse of prejudice and blinded for a time, once he had received the sight of faith and the richness of the good news of salvation, he did not forget his Jewish heritage or his brothers and sisters in the covenant of old. In Romans 9-11, Paul seems to depart from his subject to deal with the problem of the Jewish rejection of Jesus as messiah. His personal concern is obvious as one reads these chapters full of pathos and regret. Paul strikes a middle position toward the Jews, neither condemning them outright (anti-semitism) nor fully condoning their refusal to accept Christ. Of course, the apostle is speaking of the Jews in general as a corporate body, and not of individuals. Like Moses (Exodus 32:32) and Elijah (Kings 19:14-19) before him, Paul desired to assume the burden of blame for his offending people. His willingness to endure being "separated from Christ" is a New Testament corollary to the appeal of Moses: "Then blot me out from the book (of life) you have written" (Exodus 32:32). In addition to his admission of sadness, Paul assembled in chapters 9-11 a sound presentation of the Christian position, challenging the Jewish "hardness of heart." These chapters comprise the first organized theological defense of the Christian sect over against the theology of the synagogue.

In recounting all the privileges Israel had enjoyed throughout salvation history, Paul seems to underscore more and more the Jewish culpability. It is Israel whom God had called "my son" (Exodus 4:22; Isaiah 1:2; Hosea 11:1) and toward whom he had behaved as an indulgent parent. It was Israel who had been privy to resplendent epiphanies, secure in the presence of the God whose glory had guided them (Exodus 40:34) and assured them of his nearness (1 Kings 8:10-11). It was Israel with whom God had entered into a covenant relationship of love and caring (Genesis 15:8; Exodus 24:7-8). It was Israel who was privileged to receive the revelation of the divine will in the law (Exodus 20:1-17). It was his people, Israel, whom he had inspired in the exercise of true worship and to that end had sent the prophets to correct and to guide them (Amos 5:21-17). God made and kept his promises to his chosen people (Romans 4:13-20, 9:6). And finally, it was the lineage of these very people that God chose for his Son Jesus, who was in fact their messiah!

Matthew 14:22-23. True to his ecclesiastical concern to instruct the Christians of the 80s C.E. in the responsibilities of discipleship, the author of the Matthean gospel adapted the Marcan account of this pericope and shaped it according to his purposes. A comparison of the two accounts reveals the fact that Matthew, writing almost a generation after Mark and after the deaths of most of the apostles, has softened the apostles' apparent lack of comprehension concerning Jesus' mission and identity. Mark had repeatedly pointed out the apostles' inability to understand in keeping with his literary technique of the "messianic secret" and had indicated that full understanding came only after the cross and Jesus' resurrection. Mark's somewhat harsh treatment of the Twelve was not a deliberate attempt to degrade. When he wrote his gospel, popular belief held that the messiah's return was imminent. Delayed eschatology, however, soon altered the tone and theme of subsequent New Testament literature. In his pastoral concern for his community, Matthew drew on a special Petrine tradition to portray the deceased apostles as heroes in the faith for the persecuted church. Whereas the Marcan account of today's pericope had ended with the apostles "utterly and completely dumbfounded . . . their minds were closed" (Mark 6:51-52), the Matthean account climaxes in a profound act of faith, "Beyond doubt, you are the Son of God!" (Matthew 14:33).

Moreover, only Matthew related the account of Peter's "faith-adventure" on the water. Some scholars considered the entire episode with Peter to be a reworked post-resurrection appearance. The fact that the evangelist had placed the event *before* the resurrection is indicative of his efforts to illustrate the growing faith of the apostles and to use that growth to instruct his own community in the challenges of discipleship. Given that purpose and the tenuous circumstances of the Matthean church, the entire story becomes a lesson in the faithful following of the Lord.

Immediately following the eucharistic event of the miraculous feeding, the disciples departed in the boat at Jesus' bidding. Symbolically, that boat and its "eucharistically-sustained sailors" represent the church. Because it was evening (realm of fearful evil and sin), the storm with its threatening winds could certainly have compared to the strife and travail which beset the believers of the late first century C.E. Though Jesus seemed absent from his own whom he had left to pray, he was present and powerful nevertheless. This is a lesson for those who, in service, would follow his way. When Jesus did at last manifest himself, fear was dispelled. Once the apostles acknowledged his abiding presence, the storm lost its power to terrify. Peter, representative par excellence of the apostles as well as of the community of believers, illustrated by his impulsive act that even seemingly impossible situations can be dealt with when one is *in Christ* and *with Christ* in faith.

1. A very necessary and important part of prayer is the silent listening that waits for the Lord to speak (1 Kings).

2. One can pray for another, instruct and teach the other, but faith, like the growth of a seed, must come freely and from within (Romans).

3. Why is it that, when the tempestuousness of life has abated, so does our awareness of our need for the Lord (Matthew)?

20th Sunday in Ordinary Time

Christ did not come to found a church limited in membership and purpose (Matthew). He came to call to faith the faithless and to hope the hopeless. He came to restore love and life to the sinful and the hateful (Isaiah). He came to teach the world that God is an unpredictable master of surprise (Romans).

Isaiah 56:1, 6-7. Because of its special and undeniable election as God's chosen, Israel as a people had developed an aura of uniqueness and distinction. At the same time, however, Israel suffered from a certain, self-inflicted syndrome which was a side effect of its supposed greatness. Whether we facetiously call it "chosen people-itis" or a "holier-than-thou complex," Israel's sense of self-importance did not go unnoticed by the inspired authors of its scriptures. Indeed, Israel was consistently counselled (and, at times, castigated) to maintain a proper perspective concerning its role in God's plan of salvation history.

Moreover, the experience of the exile seemed to harden Israel's generalized distrust and disdain for those who were not of the progeny of Abraham. While Deutero-Isaiah had preached to his fellow exiles concerning the universal dimensions of God's plan, his message was for the most part poorly received and untried. During the exile, the Israelites made great sacrifices to preserve the deposit of their faith, the wealth of God's revelation, their liturgical rites and rituals, the compendium of their hymns and prayers, as well as their sacred history as a people. As a result of this attempt to survive, much of the Old Testament as we know it today was written, ordered, edited, transcribed and preserved. In this situation, where Israel's identity and continued existence as a people was threatened, foreign influences were held suspect and ultimately rejected.

Trito-Isaiah probably wrote in the period of repatriation after 515 B.C.E. (completion of second temple). Following the lead of his mentor and master Duetero-Isaiah, he continued to put before his people the reality of God's universal scheme. However, that which Deutero-Isaiah had formerly described as Yahweh's divine attributes, viz., justice, righteousness and universal compassion, became in Trito-Isaiah moral imperatives for the people. That which they as a people had previously regarded as prerogatives of God alone became demands upon their own conduct as godly people. It must be admitted, however, that the scope of universalism which Trito-Isaiah advocated for his people was qualified and offered only a hint of that largeness of heart and mission to which the gospel would challenge it hearers.

Romans 11:13-15, 29-32. Delayed eschatology moved Paul, like the other New Testament authors, to make adjustments in his understanding of the schema of salvation history. Eventually, the plan he had envisioned concerning Israel, as reflected in Romans 9-11, had to be rethought. With almost simplistic idealism, Paul had hoped that Israel's first rejection of the gospel would be transformed into a wholehearted acceptance of Jesus as its messiah. He regarded himself as the human instrument of Israel's conversion. By his preaching to the gentiles of the good news of salvation, he had hoped to provoke his fellow Israelites to jealousy and ultimately to acceptance of the gospel and of Jesus Christ. In his mind, all this would precede the second coming of Jesus. Then Israel, along with the all the others who had come to the truth of Jesus, would sit at his right hand in glory. But, as with the "best laid plans of mice and men," Jesus' second coming did *not* occur as imminently as was expected, *nor* did Israel become envious of the treasure of the gospel.

Our pericope today consists of two excerpts from a long, complex and at times unharmonious discussion of Israel's place in God's overall design. Paul could not accept that Israel's rejection of Christ would result in its permanent forfeiture of salvation; as he posited so accurately, "God's gifts and call are irrevocable" (v. 29). Just as a mother could not forget her own child (Isaiah), God would not forget Israel, his chosen people.

Reminding the gentiles of their own former state of disbelief and sin (Paul calls it disobedience), Paul exhorted them not to bask in pride or to harbor ill will against the Israelites. He warned that Israel's rejection had paved the way for the reconciliation of the gentiles to the Lord. In the same vein, if Israel's rejection had wrought such a wondrous result, how much more stupendous would be its coming to faith. Indeed, Paul described Israel's acceptance of Jesus as *zoe ek nekron*: life from the dead (v. 15). From earliest times, Origen and Cyril of Alexandria took this expression to refer to the general resurrection at the end of time. Others interpreted "life from the dead" in a figurative sense and envisioned the general conversion of Israel to be an event of such joy that all peoples would be revitalized by it. Still others, applying the term "life from the dead" to all of Israel, understood it as a reference to their coming to life. By turning to Christ, by their acceptance of him in faith, Israel would pass through the baptismal waters from death to life, just as once it had passed from slavery to freedom in the Sea of Reeds.

Regardless of the interpretation, Paul's point is clear. As an apostle of Jesus and a son of Abraham, he could not deny his heritage. One day, because of God's mercy and unending love, Israel too would share in the life-saving news of the gospel and participate in the reconciliation accomplished by Jesus for all of humankind. Israel who had relinquished its birthright by its disbelief would once again return to the Father as adopted sons and daughters in Christ Jesus (Romans 8:14ff).

Matthew 15:21-28. Following immediately upon the castigation of the shallow Pharisaic interpretation of the law (Matthew 15:1-20), the story of the Canaanite woman's faith shines out like a beacon in contrast to the darkness of the "blind guides, leading the blind into a pit" (15:14). Although the woman was a gentile who came to Jesus from the gentile territory of Tyre and Sidon (present day southern Lebanon), and although she had not any of the advantages of tradition or heritage or privileges of the Israelites, nevertheless, she called upon Jesus by the messianic title "Son of David." Without the law and the prophets to guide her, she became a living example of the faith which alone was necessary to come to Christ.

Interesting too are the variations Matthew made when adapting the original Marcan text (Mark 7:24-30) for use in his situation. Mark had said that the woman was Syro-Phoenician, which for his gentile audience was not an unusual fact. But Matthew changed her origin and called the woman a Canaanite. From their first infiltrations into the promised land (Canaan), the Israelites had been immersed in that foreign culture, the source of much of Israel's waywardness and infidelity both to the covenant and the law. How shocking, then, for Matthew's Jewish Christian believers to find a Canaantite revered as a heroine of faith!

Notice that Matthew has omitted the Marcan Jesus' statement: "The children (viz., Israel) should be fed first" (Mark 7:27). By the time Matthew wrote, the general Jewish rejection of Jesus was a known fact and the mission to the gentiles was well underway. Unlike Mark, Matthew tells us that Jesus praised the woman for her faith (v. 28) and pointed to her belief as the reason for his granting her request. Such a statement signaled the end of the old era of the law and the inauguration of the new era of the kingdom of the faithful. The disciples' reaction to the woman and even Jesus' initial reluctance were representative of the anti-pagan sentiment that prevailed not only in Jesus' day but in the church of the first century C.E. as well. Jesus' compliance with the woman's request, therefore, was made in total contradiction to popular opinion. But then, so was the faith of the woman contrary to all expectation. Such is the unpredictability of the ways of the Lord. Defying the norms and conventions by which humanity can predict and subsequently limit the outcome of things, the grace of God and his gifts can override all prejudices, surpass all expectations and bring harmony to the most discordant factions.

This grace and faith allowed the woman to see the truth of Jesus without the light of the law to guide her. Her faith moved Jesus to act. Following Jesus' leadership, Matthew instructed his community of the first century C.E. to be willing to seek for listeners to the good news in the most unlikely places and among the least likely candidates. His message remains pertinent in the 20th century as well: Expect the unexpected; never predict the unpredictable. In matters of the faith, statistics are irrelevant, for our God is full of surprises!

1. Among brothers and sisters in the "house of prayer," the distinguishing qualities are loving concern and mutual service (Isaiah).

2. Once spoken, God's call is never silent, gently but persistently seeking an answer in faith and commitment (Romans).

3. *The success of missionary activity is an unquantifiable reality: Faith cannot be predicted, measured or limited by human statistics (Matthew).*

21st Sunday in Ordinary Time

Authority is a precious, fragile gift from God. If used too often, vigorously or selfishly, it tends to become rigid and purposeless (Isaiah). Authority must be wielded with a spirit of service and respect, with the knowledge that one's charges are a sacred trust (Matthew). Worthy stewards of the kingdom and worthy keepers of the keys realize that all true authority is a share in the inscrutably wise and unfathomable plan of God (Romans).

Isaiah 22:15, 19-23. Rarely in the prophetic works of ancient Israel was time given or energy spent in castigating one particular individual. With the exception of today's Isaian pericope and a few other isolated instances (Amos 7:16-17, Jeremiah 20:1-6), the prophets directed their oracular fury at the nation(s) in general or at groups within their nation. However, even in the case of the personalized oracle against Shebna, there was a lesson for the community at large.

Shebna was a high official in the royal court of king Hezekiah of Judah at the end of the eighth century B.C.E. Identified in various translations as royal steward, major domo, treasurer or prime minister, Shebna enjoyed great prestige and exercised considerable influence in the court: He granted or denied admission to the royal presence. As bearer of the key, Shebna's authority was virtually unequalled. Worn on the shoulder, the key was a symbol of his share in the royal power. Ancient keys, unlike their modern corollaries, were unusually large and cumbersome. Measuring up to two feet long, the key was fitted at the end with wire iron pins which would fall into corresponding holes and loosen the fastening of the lock. But far more significant was the *power* wielded by the keeper of the key.

That Shebna enjoyed the full exercise of his power is evidenced in the fact that he was one of the small group of advisors who had the ear of the king. Indeed, he was among those who had tried to convince Hezekiah to ally his forces with Egypt and revolt against their Assyrian oppressors. This, of course, was completely contrary to the prophet Isaiah's counsel of single-hearted faithfulness to the divine covenant alliance and noninvolvement with other nations (Isaiah 7:4). Probably this infidelity was the real reason for Isaiah's antagonism and condemnation, although it is not explicitly stated as such.

Rather, Isaiah prophesied the deposition and degradation of Shebna, blaming his penchant for roving about the kingdom in a chariot (v. 18) and the fact that he had designed and ordered the construction of an ostentatious sepulcher for himself on some high place (v. 16). Not only was the style of the tomb a break with the Jewish custom of subterranean burial, but the mention of the "high place" hints at the possibility that Shebna had designs upon the throne. Customarily, the kings (not those of Israel and Judah) of the ancient world were buried in prominent places where their remains would forever memorialize their reign.

Although Isaiah's oracle did effect the dismissal of Shebna as steward, we learn from Isaiah 36:3, 22 and 37:2 that he was demoted to serve as a royal secretary. In designating Eliakim as Shebna's successor, Isaiah hoped to safeguard the integrity of the dynastic authority and the well-being of the kingdom. Shebna had proven an unworthy steward of the mysteries which were far greater even than his ambitions and more enduring than the reputation he had tried to build.

Today, those of us who ascribe to a more democratic form of government may still find a lesson in the power struggles of the ancient world. Stewardship, i.e., the care and responsibility for others in one's charge, is a sacred trust. Whether the authority so delegated is political (Isaiah) or religious in character (Matthew 16:13-20, today's gospel), it devolves upon the wielder of that authority to be true to the divine source whence it came.

Romans 11:33-36. In concluding his complex discussion of Israel's place in the schema of redemption (Romans 9-11), Paul sounds much like Job after God's speeches to him (Job 38-42:6). Like Job, Paul had attempted to understand a situation that defied human comprehension. In Paul's case, he had struggled to find a clue to understanding the evolution of God's plan of salvation as it involved Israel. More disconcerting and probably more disappointing than any of the issues he had to wrestle with was the Jewish rejection of Jesus as messiah. In the end, he was forced to conclude that Israel itself, though called and chosen and specially blessed as the people to whom the messiah had come and through whom he wished to work his wonders . . . Israel itself, Paul was compelled to admit, was responsible for its repudiation of Jesus. Paul was not bereft of all hope, however, because he envisioned a future wherein Israel too would be gathered to the Lord in acceptance and salvation. Throughout chapters 9-10, Paul had been theologizing in an attempt to wrap his finite mind, with its limited logic and comprehensibility, around the infinite mystery of God's ways. Valiantly he had tried to perceive and elucidate God's purpose. He made great efforts to understand the perversity of Israel and of historical events and to harmonize these with God's inscrutable and omnipotent plans.

But like Job, Paul had reached that point in his rationalizing where theology failed him and, like Job, he resorted to prayer. Theology can approach but not encompass the mind of God. A finite science at best, it can only glimpse the absolute. Theology must always include within its exercise the mechanisms for growth and the openness to change and development. But there must always come a point in the study of the divine when one must pause, to admit not defeat but limitations . . . not to wallow in frustration but to wait in awe, thirst and confidence for light. Because revelation is a continuing process, the light will never be extinguished and because our God is infinite, there will always be moments in which the theologian must stop and admire and, as does Paul in today's text, render praise!

Theology is best accomplished in the context of liturgy and as such it must be doxological. Some scholars attribute Paul's doxology in vv. 33-36 to the influence of Hellenistic philosophical thought, and more particularly to that of Marcus Aurelius (*Meditations*, 4:23). But we may more precisely attribute the spontaneous acts of praise of both Paul and M. Aurelius to the God who inspired both.

Matthew 16:13-20. While Shebna may have proven an unworthy steward of the Davidic dynasty under King Hezekiah, Simon showed himself worthy of his new name, Peter-Rock, and his new mission of stewardship in the eternal dynasty of Jesus, the kingdom of heaven. Under the leadership of Peter, and others who shared his stewardship, the first generation of believers survived the aftermath of Jesus' death, the subsequent persecution of Judaism and then of Rome, delayed eschatology and the internal turmoil of conflicting cultures, theologies, missiologies and pastoral policies. The scene at Caesarea Philippi, as told by Matthew, enunciated the importance of Peter's position in the early community. As leader of the Twelve, he was charged, not only with the burden of authority but with the welfare of those who would come to believe through the words and works of those apostles. Like Shebna of old who had borne the keys of his office upon his shoulder, Peter was charged by Jesus with loving stewardship.

Besides the obvious significance of Jesus' words and of Peter's confession, there are certain geographical aspects which contribute to the momentousness of the occasion as well. Caesarea Philippi, formerly the ancient sanctuary of Pan, had been rebuilt and renamed by Philip when he was tetrarch of Galilee. An unusually pleasant spot in hot and humid Galilee, Caesarea Phillipi was located near the main source of the river Jordan in the rich, verdant foothills of Mt. Hermon. A traditional site for encounters between God and people, Mt. Hermon provided a fitting backdrop for this scene of Jesus' revelation, Peter's recognition in faith and the stewardship mandate. In popular Jewish legend, the source of the Jordan river was thought to be the opening to hell. Hence, Jesus' reference to "the jaws of hell not prevailing against his church" was all the more poignant.

Peter's confession at Caesarea Philippi, although it is thought to belong more properly to a post-resurrection period, is placed by the Matthean evangelist at the end of a section (Matthew 14:13—16:20) on the special instruction of the disciples. As the climactic moment of the apostolic training, Peter's confession illustrates the goal of the apostolate, viz., to lead others in faith by the witness of one's own belief. As bearer of the keys, Peter became steward of the faith and of the faithful. With the 12, the 72 and the 144,000 who would follow, he was to help the faithful and the weak in faith to be alert to further revelation, so as to recognize and confess the Lord in times of joy as well as doubt. His burden of the keys and his responsibility of stewardship passes to all who, like him, lead others to Christ.

1. Responsibility poorly borne creates a heavy burden for the leader and the led (Isaiah).

2. There comes a time in the pursuit of divine knowledge when the mind fails to grasp what only the heart can love and accept (Romans).

3. Authority is not a license to "throw one's weight around" but a responsibility to bear the burden of stewardship and service (Matthew).

22nd Sunday in Ordinary Time

Even with the shadow of the cross looming dark upon his horizon, the Lord was able to speak of eternal life and glory (Matthew). For our part, we who follow him cannot turn back when treachery or disappointment threaten (Jeremiah). In the end, ours, like his, will be a life which speaks a perfect prayer of praise to the Father (Romans).

Jeremiah 20:7-9. In the unlikely event that the guild of prophets would have ever had a membership campaign, it is even more unlikely that Jeremiah would have been designated to recruit new members. No other prophet has portrayed his vocation with its perils and pitfalls as vividly and as pessimistically as did that seventh century prophet. Nevertheless, Jeremiah's description of his ministry was quite realistic and accurate. Centuries before the word became incarnate in the person of Jesus, Jeremiah was called to be a disciple of that word, preaching the message in season and out of season. For Jeremiah and his tragic times, it was mostly an "out of season" experience.

Born about 80 years (around 640 B.C.E.) after Assyria had conquered the northern kingdom and had annexed it as a province, Jeremiah lived to see the demise of the southern kingdom of Judah as well. Amid the capricious cresting and ebbing of the waves of political energies, Jeremiah prophesied to a people who were too often deaf to the very word which impelled him.

A contemporary of the reformer king Josiah, Jeremiah began his public career in earnest about 609 B.C.E., the same year that Josiah died in battle at Megiddo. Then, under the political suzerainty of Egypt (Pharaoh Neco), Judah soon regressed to her pre-reformation ways. A syncretism of astral cults (Mesopotamia) and of fertility cults (Canaan) enjoyed a revival.

Jeremiah, not one to exaggerate in the niceties of etiquette and tact, earned the hostility of Josiah's kingly successors. He publicly denounced the corruption of the temple liturgy and boldly predicted the destruction of Jerusalem (Jeremiah 19). For these actions, during the reign of Jehoiakim, the prophet was beaten and put into stocks at the gate of Benjamin, the upper gate of the temple. Familiar with adversity and persecution, Jeremiah was undaunted in his attacks against the religious and political leaders of his day.

Nevertheless, from the biographical material in his writings, of which our text is a part, it is evident that Jeremiah's discipleship to the word of God took its toll on the prophet personally and spiritually. Our text today, inserted in its position by a redactor, is excerpted from part of his "confessions" and reveals the pain and suffering his vocation brought to him. Jeremiah's boldness in proclaiming the unpopular message to his people was matched by the audacity with which he complained to God.

In terms ordinarily applied only to sexual seduction, Jeremiah described his commitment to God and his message in shocking terms. *Pata*, rendered "duped" in the NAB translation, is more accurately and literally translated as "seduced" (JB). "You were too strong" is more literally rendered, "You seized me and you prevailed." Perhaps it was because his idealistic concept of his role as prophet was shattered . . . perhaps it was because his preconception of what the people's response to him should be was met with disillusionment . . . or perhaps it was simply because the task seemed too great for him . . . whatever Jeremiah's reasons were, it is obvious that his was not a coveted profession.

More important, however, than Jeremiah's complaints is the information he gives concerning the phenomenon of prophetic inspiration. He described the irresistible nature of his mandate in terms of a fire within (v. 9). Even if he tried, he could not suppress the power welling up within him; he could not silence the word that demanded utterance. Dungeons, stocks, floggings, derision, persecution and even the threat of death could not quell the message that had to be given expression by Jeremiah.

What would be the reaction today to a 20th century Jeremiah? Would his boldness be labelled fanatical? Would he be censured today because of a so-called blasphemous approach to God, his unconventional pastoral style . . . or his blatant disregard of position and protocol?

Then, on the other hand, in the face of such opposition, what would prompt someone to undertake such a mission of unpopular preaching in today's church? Our answer to this second issue is the eternal living word of God. That same word which stirred and impelled Jeremiah is active today, lighting its fire in the hearts of would-be prophets.

Romans 12:1-2. Wise teacher that he was, knowledgeable in the realm of human psychology, Paul did not begin to make an ethical challenge to his listeners until he had first established, at length and in detail, the redemptive gift of God as it evolved in the context of their salvation history. For 11 chapters, Paul had poured forth the good news of the wondrous and magnanimous gifts of God. Then he waited until the question should form within their own hearts, "What can we do in the face of such love . . . how must we be?" Then, and only then, did Paul propound what Fuller has described as his "therefore ethics," as the only fitting response to all that God had done in Christ. The moral response of believers to God is not to be dictated from without in terms of a codified observance of legal prescriptions. This, unfortunately, is what the Mosaic law had become. As such, a program of behavior dictated from without is in danger of effecting only an outward conformity. Moreover, a fixed system of codified regulations can actually place a *limitation* upon the human capacity to respond. Once the fixed system had been fulfilled, once the prescriptions have been completed, there is a tendency to say, "There, I've done it . . . I've performed all that has been legislated," and to remain self-satisfied.

Paul, however, would have believers in Christ find the basis and impetus for their ethical response to God, *not* from without but from *within* themselves. In other words, the believer, by his transformation from within and by interior conversion to Christ in heart and mind and will, can offer his outward self, his body and all his actions to Christ in moral response as well. Any valid conversion, any sincere transformation must necessarily begin from within the person and is effected by the presence of God's own Spirit in Christ. Then and only then, taught Paul, can a person offer the self as a living sacrifice. In this way, true worship is achieved. In truth, Paul's exhortation here is not so different from that of Micah of Moresheth when he advised his fellow believers: "What is good has been explained to you, man; only this, to act justly, to love tenderly and to walk humbly with your God" (Micah 6:8).

In this same paranetic vein, the apostle to the gentiles continues through chapter 15. However, he is careful to keep his exhortations general in scope as he avoids the tendency to specify. In this way Paul disallowed the Christians in Rome the possibility of curtailing their response to God in ethical behavior. Never could they say they had done enough or been enough, because the Spirit of Christ and the love of Christ urged them to do and be more. Moreover, Paul was careful to counsel them that, besides its liturgical character, their ethical behavior was destined not for the limited goal of self-perfection but for the general good of the community.

Matthew 16:21-27. With the adjustments Matthew has made in the Marcan text of today's gospel, it is evident that delayed eschatology and the persecutions of Judaism and of Rome were having their effect upon the believing community of the 80s C.E. Following immediately upon Peter's confession of faith, which served to climax the section on apostolic instruction, Jesus' first prediction of his passion and the series of sayings concerning the cost of discipleship were not without their modern counterparts in Matthew's community.

In the heated conversation between Jesus and Peter, several important issues are clarified. (1) Although Peter (we may presume that he spoke for the others as well) had come to accept the fact of Jesus' messiahship, he had not yet comprehended that Jesus' role would not be exercised as the political, triumphant liberator of Jewish tradition, but as the suffering servant of the Deutero-Isaian prophecies. (2) Jerusalem and the events which were soon to transpire there would be central and necessary to Jesus' mission. (3) Those who believe in him and would follow him should expect to share in the cross of Jesus. (4) The manner in which Jesus chose to accomplish the redemption of humankind was according to the will and the ways ("standards," v. 23) of God.

By human standards (Roman, Judaism), the Matthean church of the 80s had been declared an illicit religion but the words of Jesus to Peter advise that the only judgment worth fearing and preparing for was that which God would mete out. And that judgment, promised Jesus, would come under the aegis of the Son of Man who would appear in his Father's glory, accompanied by angels (vv. 27-28). Notice the alteration Matthew made in his Marcan source (Mark 8:38). The evangelist of the 60s C.E. preached the coming of the Son of Man as the vindication of the believing community and the condemnation of the disbelieving world. Matthew, on the other hand, warned that the Son of Man would come to judge *his own*, viz., his church of disciples. This idea, Jesus' judging his followers in the end time, is a recurring theme in the Matthean gospel and culminates in the separation of the sheep and goats in chapter 25.

For the Matthean community of Christians who were being brought before earthly tribunals and subjected to unsympathetic systems of justice, there must have been some comfort and strength in the fact that only the eternal judge warranted their respect and acquiescence. Moreover, only his verdict upon their lives would have any significance.

1. The conviction that one is doing the right thing is sometimes a lonely feeling (Jeremiah).

2. Sincere prayer involves the entire person: mind and heart, deeds and doubts, hopes and fears (Romans).

3. Though familiar with suffering, the Christian is a realist—always . . . a pessimist—never (Matthew).

23rd Sunday in Ordinary Time

From the time Cain asked his evasive question, "Am I my brother's keeper?" the answer has been an unequivocal and indisputable yes! Through the prophets (Ezekiel), God made known his care and guidance; in the presence of his Son Jesus he revealed the fullness of his compassionate love (Romans). As members of his body we must translate those qualities into our human words and illustrate them in our human actions. We are indeed "keepers" of one another in the Lord (Matthew).

Ezekiel 33:7-9. Far from George Orwell's "Big Brother is watching you!" Ezekiel's perception of his vocation as a prophet is more aptly described as that of a concerned brother *watching out for* his brothers and sisters in the faith. Ezekiel compared his role to that of a sentinel or watchman who searches the moral horizon for impending disaster and then sounds the warning so that others may take heed. In a land without radar or even the simplest telegraph, the alert sentinel was the only early warning system available. A familiar figure in Palestine, the loyal sentry was an invaluable resource (1 Samuel 14:16, 2 Kings 9:17, Isaiah 21:16) to whom other people entrusted their safety and ultimately their lives.

Probably the entire oracle (33:1-20) of which our text today is an excerpt was inspired by the invasion of Nebuchadnezzar's forces and the impending destruction of Jerusalem. Ezekiel was one of those Judahites who had been deported to Babylon (about 597 B.C.E.) about ten years before the final onslaught and subsequent razing of Jerusalem. In that capacity, he prophesied warning to those left in the besieged kingdom and consolation to his fellow displaced Jews. It was not the ravages of war and the powerful forces of the enemy which presented the gravest danger. Rather, these threats, taught Ezekiel, were merely symptomatic of a far more destructive menace which would eventually obliterate his people *"from within."* Sin, wicked ways, infidelity to the covenant were more powerful than battalions of Babylonians, because these eroded the relationship which Israel enjoyed with its God and decayed the justice of God which his people were to reflect.

Notice: Ezekiel at this juncture in his career directed his message not to the corporate entity of the nation but those individuals who comprise it. Due to the fact that Israel had lost the first campaign and was obviously doomed to imminent defeat, the prophet no longer addressed a corporate personality. Nor for that matter did he entertain the traditional concept of corporate responsibility. Rather, with Ezekiel (18:1-4), culpability and accountability were laid squarely on the shoulders of the individual. In the same way, our selection today indicates that Ezekiel saw his prophetic responsibility as distinct from those to whom he was mandated to prophesy. He, as prophet, was responsible to warn his fellow Jews, and, if he did not do so, he would be remiss and therefore guilty of not performing his duties. But, once he had executed his duty as the Lord's watchman and had warned his people, counselling them to repent and reform their ways, then his obligation was fulfilled. Whether or not the individuals, to whom Ezekiel prophesied, acted upon his word, no guilt could be imputed to the prophet who had performed faithfully.

One wonders how Ezekiel even gained a hearing as the bearer of such unpopular and unpleasant news. But, as we learn later (33:30-33), Ezekiel was described as a singer of love songs. As communicator for the Lord he also had the happy task of assuring people of God's goodness. Regardless of his personal feelings for the people (remember how Jonah disdained the people of Nineveh?!), the prophet was to put himself and his preferences aside in favor of the Lord's work and the ultimate good of those whom he served.

Romans 13:8-10. Continuing his exhortation concerning the sincere ethical response to God's great gifts of salvation, Paul sounds very much like a Christian scribe or rabbi. It was customary for avid students of the law to poll the various scribes and rabbis in their vicinity, asking of each the same question: "What is the greatest commandment of the law?" Priding themselves in their profession of interpreting the law, the scribes would wax eloquently on this favorite topic. In rabbinical schools too, much verbal energy was devoted to the matter of deciding upon which law all the other laws hung. Tradition had it that Rabbi Hillel once said: "What you hate for yourself, do not do to your neighbor. This is the whole law; the rest is commentary. Go and learn." Rabbi Akiba is quoted as saying, "You shall love your neighbor as yourself—this is the greatest general principle in the law."

In keeping then with these notables from his Jewish heritage, as well as the good news of Jesus, Paul too claimed that love was the basic principle on which hinged all the precepts of the law. Unlike his Jewish kinsmen who restricted their neighborly concern and duties to their fellow countrymen, Paul of course followed the unlimited concept of "neighbor" which Jesus had taught (Luke 10:29-37). In this vein he counselled the Christians of Rome on their behavior toward all others. Following immediately upon his exhortation concerning the believers' duties toward civil authority (13:1-7), Paul emphasizes his basic idea that right living in all spheres of one's life should be motivated by a higher imperative, viz., all that one is and does should translate into a worthy response to God's gifts. Even imperial Rome could be utilized by the Christian in the formulation of a worthy answer to all that God had done in Jesus.

Notice the interesting terminology with which Paul has introduced our selection today, "Owe no debt to anyone except . . . ." In the realm of mutual love the very idea of owing falls away in favor of a more sublime attitude. That attitude should flow from an inner principle based on the conviction that love is the basis of all the commands of the law. In citing the decalog, Paul has referred to the version found in the Septuagint translation of the book of Deuteronomy (5:17-18). Even then, he has inverted the order of the precepts (7, 6, 8, 10) following the traditional Hellenistic Jewish numeration followed today by the Reformed and Anglican churches.

Matthew 18:15-20. By the last third of the first century C.E. the debt of mutual love about which Paul had written to Rome about 58 C.E. had become a sometimes burdensome reality. As the community of believers grew, the ordinary frictions of interpersonal and at times interracial relationships taxed heavily their patience and commitment to communal living. In chapters 14-17 of his gospel, Matthew has assembled the instructions of Jesus concerning discipleship. If we accept the traditional view that these three chapters represent one of Matthew's five narrative sections, then chapter 18 is the corresponding discourse, in this instance, on the subject of the church. Herein (chapter 18) the evangelist has compiled, edited, ordered and given his personal touch to the various sayings of Jesus concerning community life.

As a community which had formerly enjoyed the organizational roots of Judaism with its institutional structures and solid system of authority, the Matthean community after 70 C.E. (destruction of temple) and especially after 85 C.E. (ousted from synagogues) had to redefine itself and to reassert its own identity according to its Christian roots and concerns. In this endeavor, therefore, Matthew sought to formulate his ecclesiology and his morality, based not on the law or principles of Judaism but on his christology, i.e., on the person of Jesus Christ. Indeed, as our text points out at its conclusion today, the presence of Christ is what constitutes the church, the *ekklesia*: "Where two or three are gathered *in my name, there I am* . . ." (v. 20). This abiding presence of God in Christ, this Immanuel principle (1:23; 28:20), constitutes the basis of Matthean ecclesiology and dictates the ethical response of that community to God and to one another.

On this basic Immanuel principle, the evangelist has laid out the procedure for the correction of one's counterparts in the family of the faith. In the verses immediately preceding our text for today, Matthew spoke of searching for the one lost sheep. In a sense, brotherly and sisterly correction should follow the same idea. One who has sinned has, according to the Hebrew (*hattat*) or the Greek (*hamartia*) etymology of the word, "missed the mark." Therefore, correction's goal is not retaliation but reconciliation, i.e., to bring the one who has "missed the mark" or gone astray back to Christ.

Some scholars believe that Matthew may have borrowed his formula for the stages in leading a sinner aright from the Qumran community since a similar procedure was followed there. However, this same measure already existed in mainstream Judaism (Leviticus 19:17, Deuteronomy 19:15) and it may be from that source that both Matthew and Paul (1 Corinthians 5:9-11) based their formulae. In the progression from the private "between the two of you" to "two or three witnesses" to "the church," the same atmosphere of reconciliation and forgiveness was to prevail and to color all the proceedings. However, in the face of obstinate recalcitrance, the church was permitted the right of sanction. "To treat him as a gentile or a tax collector" sounds quite contrary to the mind and heart of Jesus who during his ministry went out of his way to seek out these very people. Probably this statement (v. 17) comes not from Jesus but from the early Christian community. "Gentile" and "tax collector" were stock Jewish terms used to refer to anyone considered unacceptable.

Significantly, the power to bind and to loose which had been conferred by Jesus upon Peter (16:19) is in chapter 18 applied to the assembly of believers in general. While the original version (Mark 16) of this text probably has a post-resurrection setting and referred to the power to admit or to exclude persons from the community based on their acceptance or rejection of the apostolic preaching, here the power has become a function of the community and probably refers to an administrative discipline.

Concluding with the reference to the power of united prayer, Matthew implies that this spiritual force can be a powerful influence in unifying and reconciling the members of the community to Christ and to one another. By prayer, the believers acknowledge the presence of the Lord, who is the basis for their *being church* and the reason for their fellowship in the faith. Indeed, sincere prayer should be the first step in any procedure of correction or confrontation in truth. In that way the believers are assured of the presence of the Lord in whom they believe and of the light of his Spirit which he had promised.

1. Are the sentinels among us afraid to speak for fear of our violent reaction or have they wearied of speaking to deaf ears (Ezekiel)?

2. Mutual love is a debt which is unquantifiable, yet more valuable than any other aspect of the Christian life (Romans).

3. Prayer together in Christ is a more formidable force than any disagreement, estrangement or schism (Matthew).

24th Sunday in Ordinary Time

The embrace of the Lord's forgiveness ensures the continuity of our happiness and well-being (Romans). At the least inkling of repentance, he runs out to meet us with open arms (Sirach). If he be our norm and our model in the faith, then surely our days together as his followers will be filled with celebrations of reconciliation and peace (Matthew).

Sirach 27:30—28:7. In an age when the powerful and pervasive influence of the Hellenic culture threatened to dilute and even eradicate the traditions of Judaism, Jesus Ben Sirach wrote an apologia to defend the cultural, sapiential and religious heritage of his people. Addressing his work to his fellow Jews in Palestine, as well as to those in the diaspora, the author wrote in Hebrew around 180 B.C.E., giving it the title *The Wisdom of Jesus Ben Sirach*. *Ecclesiasticus* (book of the church), the second title for the text, signals the popularity of the work among believers in the early church. Considered a deutero-canonical book by Roman

Catholics, Sirach has been evaluated by Jews and Protestants as an apocryphal work.

While he maintains that the law must be followed as one's God-given guide in all aspects of life, nevertheless, in certain passages, the author of Sirach seems to reach beyond the second century B.C.E. and beyond pre-messianic Judaism to the mind of Jesus himself. Indeed, the selected pericope for today may be thought of as a commentary, albeit an anticipatory one, on the sixth petition of the Lord's prayer, "Forgive us our trespasses as we forgive those who trespass against us." With its doctrine on forgiveness of others as a condition disposing one to divine forgiveness, Sirach is a far cry from the law of retaliation ("an eye for an eye") of Leviticus. In imitation of the God with whom they were covenanted in love and peace, Israel was to practice toward its fellows in the faith those very virtues which their God epitomized. In mercy and compassion he had taken Israel back after its many sins; so too Israel must remember and do likewise in its dealings with others. As an added incentive beyond the ideal of being like the Lord, Sirach urged his readers to remember that one day they would inevitably face death. In that moment, they would be most in need of divine forgiveness and mercy. How could they possibly expect to drink from the font of everlasting life and to know the healing of the Lord's pardon, unless they too had made an effort to reflect his goodness in life on earth?

While the Pharisees excluded Sirach from their canon of the scriptures, the Essene community did not. Not only did they accept the work as canonical, they ascribed to the teachings within it and many are reflected in their rule of life. If, as many propose, Jesus had contact with the Essenes before he began his public ministry, then perhaps it was his presence among them that caused them to be accepting of Sirach's wisdom. Or perhaps Jesus, in Qumran, learned with the Essenes the wisdom of such teaching and integrated it into his own understanding of living according to God's ways and God's will. In either case, his teachings on forgiveness find an excellent herald in Jesus Ben Sirach.

Romans 14:7-9. Although the brief pericope selected for today's liturgy seems to be hymnic in style and may be perhaps a short baptismal song, it is part of a longer exhortatory section in Romans within which Paul tackles the problem of unity and diversity within the community of believers. Rome was a bustling metropolis, which even in ancient times was a melting pot of cultures, languages and religions. As such, it had the problems common to any large city. In this particular instance, the conflict seemed to stem from a difference of opinion and praxis concerning matters of diet and the observation of special days (feast days? fast days? or both?). It is not known whether news of this problem had come to Paul's awareness via a messenger or letter or whether he just presumed that in a mixed populace such as Rome such difficulties would inevitably arise. He had counselled the Colossians (Colossians 2:16-21) and the Corinthians (1 Corinthians 8, 10:14-33) similarly.

In any case, the difficulty was obviously a common one and Paul's exhortations were general in nature, in keeping with the nature of all the paranetic material of chapters 12-15. Paul's bias is obvious as he designates the two conflicting factions as "weak" and "strong." Nevertheless his advice is valuable and can be aptly applied by believing communities everywhere. Several possibilities have been proposed for those so-called "weak" members of the Roman church: (1) Were they Jewish Christians who continued to observe the Jewish feast days, fast days and dietary prescriptions? (2) Were they former Essenes who continued the strict abstinence they had followed in Qumran? (3) Were they Christians whose conscience forbade them to eat meat or to drink wine for fear it had been first sacrificed to idols? (4) Were they converts from a mystery religion (Orphic-Pythagorean cult) who had, as cult members, abstained from meat and wine? (5) Were these "weak" ones Christian ascetics who imposed the rigors of fast and abstinence on themselves for purposes of mortification? (6) Or were they merely overly scrupulous Christians? Since Paul does not specify, neither can we. Suffice it to say, the issue was not a simple one and Paul's general principles were to be applied in whatever particular circumstances warranted it.

To all factions he proposed the same principles: (1) avoid criticising one another (14:1-12), (2) refrain from giving scandal (14:13-23) and (3) relinquish selfish preferences or wonts in deference to others. To both weak and strong, he advised following one's conscience without offending those whose consciences were convinced otherwise. It is significant that Paul did not demand *uniformity* of opinion and/or practice, realizing that conformity does not create unity. Rather, he advised mutual respect and tolerance so that a plurality of opinions and a diversity of practices might find their union in the one faith and the one dogma of the church.

Matthew 18:21-35. When Peter asked Jesus, "Shall we forgive *seven* times," he thought he was being magnaminous in offering to forgive an erring brother *repeatedly*. Seven is a perfect number, implying a completeness, a fullness, but is still a definite number with a definite limit. Jesus' answer and the parable, with which Matthew elaborated upon that answer, indicated that among believers, forgiveness was to be an indefinite quality, with no possibility of limitation. This exchange between Jesus and Peter recalls the statement of Lamech to his wives (Genesis 4:24). That descendant of Cain vowed to place no limit on the degree of blood revenge he would seek for a wrong done to him. Jesus in the gospel transforms this limitless revenge in blood to unlimited forgiveness in love.

In the parable which follows (vv. 23-35), one unique to Matthew's gospel, the obligation of forgiveness is strengthened by an appeal to believers to remember the lavishness and frequency with which God has forgiven each of them. As the conclusion of the Matthean discourse on the church, it provides a fitting moral exhortation on the forbearance and understanding necessary to sustain the frictions of life in common.

While the particulars and circumstances of the parable are of a pagan origin, there is no reason to minimize its applicability or to doubt its authenticity. Evidently, the king so named is an oriental shiek or chieftain and the official is, in actuality, a high officer of the court with the funds at his disposal. Having absconded with an enormously exaggerated sum of money (some $9,000,000), he is to be punished by being sold with his entire family and household (not a Jewish practice). When this fantastic amount of money is compared to that owed to the court official, viz., about $15, the callousness and mercilessness of the king's servant becomes all the more poignant. He who was completely forgiven of his dishonesty and whose debt had been eradicated was himself devoid of compassion for another whose debt was insignificant and in whose case there is no mention of dishonest behavior.

We must remember that our message for today is couched in the literary vehicle of a parable and the details of the parable should not be allegorized. Therefore Matthew's redactional moral conclusion at the end of the parable (v. 35) should not lead us to believe that the conduct of the king is illustrative of God's conduct. As in any parable, there is one basic point which carries the burden of the message. In this case, our clue is in the fact that the debt owed by the wicked servant was impossible for him to repay. Yet he was forgiven totally and completely exonerated. He was undeserving and yet the kindness of his master was heaped upon him without limit, without measure.

In this aspect of the parable we find our message. We who have been undeserving have been forgiven totally. "While we were *still sinners*, Christ died for us" (Romans 5:8). A debt which was beyond our power to repay has been written off and with Christ we are allowed the glories and joys of eternal life and the blessings of the Father. What, then, must our behavior be toward others? With our hearts filled with gifts of freedom and forgiveness, must not that same quality of generosity by which God has redeemed us color and influence our dealings with one another?

When the treasures of heaven, viz., election, justification and redemption, have been showered upon us, can we be miserly with our brothers and sisters in faith? To do so, to be so, would be irresponsible and disloyal to the giver of graces, the source of life. If God's generosity to each of us were the norm by which we measured our dedication and commitment to the community, then there would be no request too great, no fault too large, no affront too grave to forgive.

Matthew, in counselling believers in the sacrifices necessary to successful communal living, reminded them (and us) of the cross. Their sins, the "national debt" as it were that none of them could "repay," the breach with God that none of them could heal, had been removed in the mysterious contradiction of Jesus' cross. "Look at the gift of the cross," we can hear Matthew saying, "and then look upon one another with a similar love and a limitless forgiveness."

1. Revenge strangles goodness and blinds the heart to truth but pardon, freely given for the sake of the Lord, is a balm that soothes and a healing power that restores life (Sirach).

2. Neither peer pressure nor human respect may guide or shape our behavior. There is only one person's opinion that matters and his is an eternal one (Romans).

3. Forgiveness is as vital a part of community living as is love (Matthew).

25th Sunday in Ordinary Time

There is a comfort in knowing that ours is a God who defies out abilities to conceive him and who is greater than our wildest dreams can imagine (Isaiah). Even more astounding is the fact that he loves us (Matthew) and has involved himself in our existence to the point of becoming one of us in Christ and showing us how to live as worthy reflections of his love in our world (Philippians).

Isaiah 55:6-9. All that had transpired within Israel during that sixth century B.C.E. was a perfect illustration of the truth which the first reading exclaims, "God's ways are not humanity's ways!" Had history run its logical course and the inevitable conclusions been drawn, the people conquered by the Babylonians would have remained so . . . their city razed, their wealth pillaged, their elite in exile, their hopes dashed!

But the ways and thoughts of God are far beyond our capacity to predict or to deduce. Hence by God's design and according to his inscrutable plan for his people, Israel was to be restored. Jerusalem, a city ravaged by the powers of paganism with which she had toyed for centuries, was to rise again. Like the mythical phoenix rising from the ashes, she was to live once more in splendor and in glory. Her miraculous restoration described by Deutero-Isaiah in eschatological terms was to be effected, in part, by the hand of Cyrus the Persian, who had rousted the Babylonians. Because of his conquest and his lenient policy toward the people he vanquished, all the displaced peoples in Babylon were permitted to return home.

Our chosen text is an excerpt from a longer pericope, 55:1-11, in which the exiles' return home is described in terms of a banquet lavishly laid out on the tables of the ideal city. The optimism with which the invitation is extended to the hungry and the thirsty reflects the confidence of the prophet and the comfort he wished to communicate to his people. Our verses explain that the only prerequisite for attendance at the glorious feast is a desire to turn from evil ways to the Lord, to hunger for righteousness and to abstain forever from wickedness.

Philippians 1:20-24, 27. Incarceration may limit the physical freedom of an individual but, as history has proven, the bars of the jail cell and the dank walls of the dungeon need not in any way tether the human spirit. Dietrich Bonhoeffer's *Letters From Prison*, Viktor Frankl's *Meaning of Life* and Anne Frank's *Diary* are but a few examples of the power of the imprisoned personality to soar beyond its shackles. Paul's letters from prison are no exception. Indeed, like his letters to the Galatians and to the Corinthians, Paul's letter to the Christians at Philippi reveals the freedom he had found in Christ and the fact that imprisonment in no way affected his ability to preach the good news and to witness to the love and goodness of his Lord.

While the actual site of Paul's imprisonment is still the subject of debate, recent evidence seems to point to an Ephesus location. From there, Paul wrote several letters to his beloved Christians at Philippi and it seems that what we have today is a conflation of two or three shorter letters, written over a period of several months. A consensus of scholars divides Philippians in this way: (1) 4:10-23, a thank you note for their package to him; (2) 1:1—3:1, 4:4-7, news of his own welfare and his situation in prison, news that Epaphroditus had recovered from his illness, a message that Paul wished to send Timothy to Philippi to aid them in combatting the false teachers; (3) 3:2-4:3, 8-9, Paul's rebuttal of the false teachers.

Following this proposed division, our text today is taken from a second letter of Paul to Philippi. Besides his special love for the Philippians, Paul had an added incentive in assuring their fidelity and uprightness in the Lord. Philippi was a strategic city in Paul's plan of apostolic preaching and teaching. His first European foundation, Philippi was situated on the Roman Via Egnatia linking Byzantium in the East to Dyrrhachirem in the West and Apollonia on the Adriatic. The city had gained fame as the site of Anthony's defeat of Brutus and Cassius in 42 B.C.E. Later, in 30 B.C.E., Octavius renamed it Colonia Augusta Julia Philippensis and designated it a Roman colony with the privilege of *ius italicum*. As such, the citizens of Philippi, mainly veterans from the Roman army, were granted the right of proprietorship according to Roman law and were freed from paying land and poll taxes.

In Acts 16 (vv. 11-40) we learn from Luke of the ministry which Paul had exercised in Philippi around 50 C.E. While staying at the home of Lydia, a woman who bought and sold fine fabric, Paul preached outside the city at a prayerful place near a river bank. One day, he had exorcised a clairvoyant slave girl but her masters, who had used her "gift" to make a living, accused Paul and Silas of disturbing the peace. They were arrested, beaten and imprisoned but were miraculously freed during an earthquake. Paul, not satisfied to have escaped, demanded to be exonerated on the basis of his Roman citizenship. His concern, however, was not a purely personal one; rather he wished to win some respect and dignity for the community of believers he had established in Philippi.

Our pericope today reveals a similar concern. Though he was aware that his term in jail in Ephesus might end in death, Paul knew the work he had begun would live on and the good news would be proclaimed whether by his life or even in his death. His ambiguity is obvious; he sees an advantage in living and continuing his preaching and yet he would also desire death so as to be with Christ. By saying "life is Christ," Paul does not merely indicate that he is united with Christ but that all the energies and each life's breath was to be spent in doing Christ's work. He knew that "life" in Christ would also mean a share in Christ's passion and death.

In v. 23, Paul's desire to "be freed from this life and to be with Christ" indicates his awareness that, although he may not live to see the day of the Lord, nevertheless he would somehow be with Christ after death and before the resurrection of the last day. His exhortation in v. 27 to "conduct yourselves . . ." makes use of a Greek verb *politeuesthe* ordinarily meant to describe the proper and patriotic behavior of a good citizen. In addressing citizens of a colony of the great Roman empire, Paul used that same word and applied it to the fact that, for believers, their citizenship is of the kingdom and their "constitution" is that of the gospel of Christ.

Matthew 20:1-17. Union organizers would have a fine time with the situation described in today's gospel, a parable uniquely Matthean. Surely the estate owner would have been charged with unfair labor practices at least and, at most, burdened with a strike which would have crippled any hope he had of productivity. But this is precisely Matthew's point. The manner in which the owner conducted himself is "objectionable" and even shocking because it reflects a mode of behavior which is, unfortunately, foreign to us, one to which few of us would ascribe, viz., the manner of the heart and mind of God.

An examination of the parable reveals several layers of meaning. Originally, that is, during the ministry of Jesus, it was probably an illustration of Jesus' response to the objection that he squandered his time and talents among the pariahs of society. Addressed to those who resembled the disgruntled laborers, viz. the Pharisees and scribes, Jesus probably told the parable to defend God's ways against human conceptions of how God should act. Just as God, the good and eternal shepherd (Psalm 23), would seek out the stray and come to the aid of the poor and downtrodden, so too would Jesus, his regent incarnate, devote himself to those most in need. The parable does not defend Jesus' actions but merely puts them on a par with those of his Father and thus in sharp contrast to the leaders of his day.

With the passage of time and given a different audience, the parable was applied in a variety of ways. For example, at the second level of meaning, that of the church (oral tradition), the parable may have provided a solution to the Jewish-gentile problem. Jewish Christians may have questioned whether the gentiles who came "late" to Christ were equal in the kingdom. Indeed, the parable is quite clear in pointing out that, whether one came early or late, the share was equal. Hence the church of the first decades concluded, not without conflict and debate (Galatians), that gentile Christians were equal sharers with Jewish Christians in the economy of salvation.

It is thought that v. 16 was added during the phase of oral tradition and was not an intrinsic part of the parable. Probably circulated as an independent saying, v. 16 was utilized at will and in a variety of applications by the evangelists or their redactors (Mark 10:31, Luke 13:30). As such, it makes the message of the parable very similar to a problem posed in IV Ezra. Nonplussed as to whether those who survived to see the day of the Lord would have an advantage over those who died before, the seer Ezra received this answer: "I will make my judgment like a circular dance; the last therein shall not be behind, nor the first in front."

If we examine a third level of meaning, that of the evangelist, then the parable and the general conclusion in v. 16 point to another possible interpretation. Matthew, true to his style and concerns, consistently refers to the kingdom in the eschatological sense. Hence the "pay" or reward and retribution of the last days would be, taught Matthew, totally devoid of earthly norms and priorities. Notice that Matthew has addressed the parable to the *disciples*. Just as in the preceding chapters 14-18 the disciples had been advised about their conduct as leaders in the faith, so too, this parable counsels them in their role as pastors. Just as they were to seek the stray and to reconcile the errant, so too should the "latecomers" and the "lazy" be their particular concern.

1. The God we worship is not a figment of our imagination or an object of wish-fulfillment. He is far beyond us, yet nearer than we are to ourselves (Isaiah).

2. If "life is Christ," then there is no room in such a life for pettiness or mean concerns (Philippians).

3. Indignation at God's goodness to others indicates that we are very far from the kingdom (Matthew).

26th Sunday in Ordinary Time

Who has never rejoiced in a new beginning or exulted in the joy of being given a second chance?! Our gracious God holds no grudges and does not allow our clouded past to dim his gifts of grace (Ezekiel). He waits patiently while we balk and even rebel against his will (Matthew). For he understands us as we are; he, who emptied himself to be our brother, has first hand experience of our weakness and of our need for him (Philippians).

Ezekiel 18:25-28. Commiserating with one another in Babylon, the exiles from Jerusalem might have remembered the words of Exodus 20:5 and blamed their present hardships on their fathers and grandfathers. "I punish the father's fault in the sons, the grandsons, and the great-grandsons" reflects a philosophy of corporate personality and corporate responsibility widespread in the ancient Near Eastern world. Like its neighbors, Israel did not regard the individual as distinct from the community or the nation. As a result, there existed the mythological idea of the "family or tribal curse" and the hereditary vendetta. Although historians have termed these phenomena "uncivilized" and "primitive," the vendetta and the tribal curse are remarkably similar to the clan feuds which existed in this country in the not so distant past (Hatfields and McCoys?!). Reflected in the conversation between Job and his three friends, as well as in the literature of Proverbs, the idea of hereditary blame and punishment was deeply engraved in the Hebrew consciousness. Therefore it was only after a struggle of centuries that the idea was eradicated. Vestiges of this concept are evident, centuries after Ezekiel, in the gospel of John. Recall the sign of the man born blind and the questions the disciples asked of Jesus, "Who sinned, this man or his parents, for him to have been born blind?" Besides the persistent belief in inherited punishment, this query also reflects the prevalent idea that physical ailments were a punishment for sin.

But with Ezekiel in the sixth century B.C.E., the Lord was teaching his people something new about himself and about their relationship to him as individuals. Our text is from an entire chapter devoted to the concept of *individual* responsibility and *individual* sin. Besides the revelation of God made known in the prophecy of Ezekiel, external circumstances contributed as well to Israel's change in emphasis from the idea of absolute solidarity to one of individuality within a corporate entity. The loss of its national identity due to the Babylonian conquest, coupled with the demise of its cherished institutions, provided added impetus for increased emphasis upon the individual.

Moreover, as today's pericope asserts, not only would the individual not be culpable for ancestral or national guilt but neither would his own past be held as witness against him, should he repent. This tabula rasa idea is comforting when viewed from the aspect of the repentant sinner but is quite disconcerting when Ezekiel states that the same principle applies should the just person turn to evil. However, the prophet's intention in this text is to stress the importance of repentance. Because of divine "amnesia" and God's merciful goodness, the contrite sinner can enjoy a bright future with a new life, not conditioned or predetermined in any way.

Even from a purely human and psychological point of view, this is an encouraging thought. To proceed with life, unhampered by the baggage of past guilt, allows the believer the joyous freedom of a new beginning. This was the comfort Ezekiel wished to offer his fellow exiles in Babylon as he promised them a new start and a new life. The same beginning is ours at baptism, renewed again and again by our sincere repentance and reconciliation.

Philippians 2:1-11. Swinging the pendulum from one extreme to the other, we move from Ezekiel's concentration on the individual to Paul's accent on the community. Of course, the believer's life is a tension of balancing the two emphases and finding the union of the two in Christ. Following the style of his other moral exhortations, Paul was reluctant in his advice to the church at Philippi to impose purely external moral restraints or to legislate, from without, a code of ethical behavior. Rather, he wished to awaken in thought and in deed a response which originated within his hearers, based on interiorized principle and conviction. In our text, Paul asked his friends at Philippi to allow the fact that they were "in Christ" to permeate all their actions, especially their interaction with one another in community.

Several translations have been proposed for v. 5 which NAB renders, "Your attitude must be Christ's." It is difficult to know Paul's thought on this statement, because the Greek text simply reads, "which in Christ Jesus," omitting the verbs. Karl Barth suggests "which you have in Christ" as the most suitable translation since it is consonant with the Pauline doctrine of living "in Christ," being "in Christ." This rendering illustrates the fact of the believer's being part of the mind, mission and message of Christ, not merely by a conformity of life style but by incorporation into Christ. Because of the incorporation, being of one body with Christ, Christian ethics may be seen as an overflow of that gradual process of transformation into the body of Christ. In the same way, the excellent virtues of communal life to which Paul called the Philippians in vv. 1-4 would be the fruits, a logical result of being in Christ.

Paul regarded disunity as a blight which could destroy the foundation in Christ which he had worked so hard to build in Philippi. Though enthusiastic and fervent, none of his beloved communities were immune to this fatal cancer. Knowing this, Paul warned the Philippians to guard against selfish ambition which put one's own interests above those of others. He counselled the believers at Philippi to ward off the danger of self-seeking, *eritheia* (v. 3), and to inform their dealings with one another with humility. In so doing, he taught that they would be translating into the reality of routine communal life the union they share "in Christ."

For a model and an example, he held out to them the mystery of Christ. Citing an earlier popular hymn (vv. 6-11), Paul recommended that his believing community enter *with* Christ and *in* Christ into the mystery of his *kenosis* or self-emptying. He, in whom they found their unity and identity, had divested himself of the privileges of his divinity, and had embraced finite existence to the point of suffering and death. As a community of believers *in this Christ*, they should do likewise.

Matthew 21:28-32. Although this parable is peculiar to Matthew's gospel and bears several earmarks of his particular Matthean style, one need not doubt the authenticity of the parable as one which originated with Jesus. Besides being consonant with Jesus' special concern for the strays and the outcast (tax collectors, prostitutes), the parable also reiterates the theme which colored all of Jesus' ministry, that of the poor and the sinful as more cognizant of eternal values than the self-acclaimed righteous. In its original context, that is, at its basic level of meaning, this parable was addressed to the chief priests and elders and probably consisted only of vv. 28-31 in which the responses and subsequent behavior of the two sons are compared. Judging by his audience and the previous exchange concerning the origin of his authority (vv. 23-27), it seems clear that Jesus is directing his words squarely at those who regarded themselves as authoritative exemplars of the law of Yahweh. Jesus pointed to the lacuna that existed between the lip service they paid in public and the actions which should have followed their verbal avowals of goodness. Jesus seems to be saying, "Good intentions do not a good son (daughter) make." Indeed the full fury of his invective against such hypocrisy is unleashed in chapter 23.

In sharp contrast to the son who said well but did nothing is the initial rebellion of the second son who eventually obeyed. But Jesus' conclusion concerning the tax collector and prostitutes deals the shocking blow. Those whose lives had been in open conflict with the law and with righteousness were the very ones who in the end found salvation. To those in authority who should have understood Jesus' tactics and his ministerial methods, the parable defended the mission of Jesus and the mercy of God for sinners which it made manifest. To those elite members of the Sanhedrin who had the light of the law to guide them, the parable underscored the blindness of their ways and their delusions of self-grandeur while it lauded the vision of those sinners whose humility and need had allowed them to perceive God's ways in Jesus. The Jewish authorities had come to regard the salvation of tax collectors and prostitutes to be impossible. According to the Torah, repentance had to be accompanied by retribution. Since the sinful situations of tax gatherers, etc., made retribution nigh unto impossible, they were regarded as lost by the Jews. But with the gospel of Jesus and the truth which it embodied, the message of God's mercy was preached. All that was required was repentance; into the contrite heart, the Lord would pour his healing and restoring mercy. None who would sincerely repent would be lost to the Lord of all goodness.

In adapting this parable to the concerns and situation of his own community, Matthew has positioned it as the first of three in a series (wicked husbandmen, great banquet) which illustrates his soteriological ideas. In this context the parable becomes Matthew's commentary for the redirection of the mission away from the Jews and toward the gentiles. Matthew's message to the Jews is clear. They whom the Jews had regarded "least likely to suceed" would forge ahead of them into the kingdom. In a similar vein, the point about John the Baptist recalls the Jewish rejection and the acceptance on the part of sinners.

The other point made in the parable links it to the Ezekiel reading. Just as Ezekiel proposed the possibility of a wicked person turning from evil to good and vice versa, so the two sons in the parable are not irrevocably tethered by their past. Indeed, the son who said yes but did not go seems to represent the Jewish attitude. As the chosen people, whose heritage had been one of revelation, Torah, prophets and God's caring providence, they should have been predisposed to Jesus. On the other hand, the son who rebelled but then acquiesced was representative of the sinners and/or gentiles whose checkered past would seem to have left them closed to change and to accepting Jesus. It would seem that preconditioning and past habits are not decisive in charting a course for the future.

What does seem vital however is personal need, truth and the openness to the grace and mercy of God. With such powerful help, even the most tawdry past can be forgotten. For those of us who look back at countless failures in our own lives, this parable gives hope and encouragement.

1. If by God's grace we are afforded chance after chance, must we not, at least, grant to one another the benefit of the doubt (Ezekiel)?

2. The enemy of community is not conflict but conceit (Philippians).

3. Tax collectors, prostitutes, sinners . . . those who find this roll call of the kingdom shocking may not feel at home there (Matthew).

27th Sunday in Ordinary Time

Creation, election, exodus, covenant, monarchy, prophecy, incarnation, cross, eternal life—what more could our God have done that he did not do (Isaiah)? What response can worthily match such love and care? Grateful prayer, communal solidarity, familial peace (Philippians). Also, fidelity and a rich harvest, borne of the fruitful stewardship of his gifts (Matthew).

Isaiah 5:1-7. Imagine a gathering in the fertile terraced foothills on the outskirts of Jerusalem. It is the time of the vintage harvest and the workers have gathered along with the owners of the vineyard to celebrate the harvest. With the sound of the shophar, the feast begins. It is evening and spirits are mellow because the harvest has been a particularly fine one. In the gathering darkness by the light of torches, some have already begun to press the grapes. As the crushing sound is heard, a singer begins to entertain; his ballad is as sweet as the ripe grapes. But then his words turn sour as he makes manifest his metaphor: He is singing of the bitter strain which exists between Israel and her God.

The scene described here was possibly a very real one and provided the context for our pericope today. Those gathered were the people of Judah; the time was probably the feast of tabernacles. The balladeer was the prophet Isaiah at some early period of his ministry and his song was at once a reproach and a warning bound up in a melodic parable.

In the familiar imagery of vines and vineyard, Isaiah described his people Israel; and in the figure of the grape farmer he portrayed the loving care that Yahweh had lavished upon his people. In a style typical of Palestinian cultivation, Isaiah sang of the tower and the wine press and the clearing of stones. Towers were erected by vineyard owners as a vantage point from which to oversee and to guard their fields, especially as harvest time grew near, because then the grapes were most susceptible to thieves—both the two-legged as well as the four-legged and winged types. Many owners may have actually "camped out" in the tower for the duration of the harvest. Besides this careful preparation and constant watchfulness, the "friend" of Isaiah was not remiss in his choice of seedlings. Only the finest, choicest vines from Sorek (a valley west of Jerusalem) were suitable for his vineyard. Reputed for their ruby red color and sweet taste, these grapes were considered the best in all of Palestine.

When the "friend" asks, "What more was there to do for my vineyard?" the answer is of course a resounding one! Nothing better could have been provided by the vineyard owner for his vines or by Yahweh for his people. Indeed, because of the great care lavished upon the vineyard and the paltry results his labors wrought, his wrath and disappointment are all the more understandable. The figure of a vine or vineyard as a symbol for Israel was a familiar one to Isaiah's listeners (Psalm 80), and so, of course, was the meticulous care of their Lord. In reminding them of that care through the person of the grape farmer, Isaiah recalled for his people the cavalcade of their past blessings, the exodus, the covenant, the conquest, the provident protection, etc. With several characteristically Hebrew word plays, he described Israel's disappointing and unworthy responses to that great care and love. Not only did she yield *wild* grapes (*soreq*) rather than *choice* grapes (*sorek*), but her grapes according to the literal translation were "sour" and "stinking rotten" (v. 2). Moreover, in the concluding rejoinder of the parable, the Lord claims to have looked for judgment (*mispat*) and instead found bloodshed (*mispah*), for justice (*sedaqa*) but he was confronted with outcry (*se'aqa*). Granted, these paranomasias do not carry the same weight after translation because the similarity in assonance is lost. (Thanks to the efforts of G.H. Box a satisfactory equivalent in English could be: "For *measures* he looked, but lo *massacres*! For *right*, but lo *riot*!")

Philippians 4:6-9. Certainly Philippi was a city fraught with the worries and troubles of routine living. The fact of Christianity probably made those difficulties more acute because it is hardly likely that, among the varied population of that Roman colony, believers in a crucified and resurrected Lord were well accepted. Moreover, besides the conflicts which the Christians encountered because of unsympathetic neighbors, there were internal struggles as well. Paul alluded to this fact earlier in chapter four as he called upon Evodia and Syntyche to settle their differences. To aid them in arriving at some mutual understanding, he enlisted the aid of his comrade (Luke? Silas? Clement?) to act as arbiter. Evidently the squabble that separated these two women was somehow a threat to the unity of the community as a whole. For that reason, as our text today indicates, Paul recommended the power and the peace of prayer to the entire assembly of believers.

Sounding very much like his ancestor Qoheleth of Hebrew wisdom tradition (Ecclesiastes 11:10), Paul advocated a philosophy of prayer that led one to shed anxiety and to enjoy the peace of God himself (vv. 6-7). Then, sounding very much like the wisdom of Greek philosophy, he cited several ideals for right living, all of which are classical categories of Stoic ethics (vv. 8-9). Today's text is actually comprised of two conclusions, the first (vv. 6-7) being the end of letter no. 2 and the second (vv. 8-9) being that of letter no. 3.

Difficulties arise even in the most virtuous of assemblies and prayer is the one foolproof means of settling such disputes. *By* prayer and *in* prayer, the God of peace becomes present and his peace provides a serenity that human power cannot achieve. In addition to the harmony of communal solidarity, it becomes possible for those so united to produce together the excellent fruits of charity, mutual care and respect, so unlike the bitter fruit of the disappointing community of the Isaian ballad.

In concluding, Paul affirmed the witness he had provided by his preaching and teaching in Philippi and called the believers to imitate his lead. Possibly, the apostle was anticipating the danger to the community posed by the presence of false teachers (3:2-21). These overly zealous advocates of perfection, the Judaizers, minimized the value of Jesus' cross while requiring gentile converts to Christ to follow first the way of Moses, the Torah and circumcision. In opposition to their misplaced piety, Paul advised prayer, peace and a life conformed to gospel values. In any community, in any circumstance, in any culture, such advice is timely and true.

Matthew 21:33-43. By the time Matthew wrote his gospel, the mission to the gentiles was well underway, spurred by the Jewish rejection of Jesus as messiah. For this reason, Matthew's adaptation of the Marcan parable is a highly allegorized polemic against that rejection as well as an ecclesiological message concerning membership in the new and eternal "vineyard" of the church (v. 43). Although a shorter, less allegorized and perhaps earlier version of the parable is found in Luke (20:9-17) and in the apocryphal gospel of Thomas, nevertheless the interpretations given by both Mark and Matthew provide us with valuable information concerning the growing sense of identity of the early church as distinct and unique from Judaism.

By quoting almost verbatim part of Isaiah's ballad of the vineyard (Matthew 21:33), Matthew makes the point that Jesus is not merely musing about grapes and vines but that he is speaking specifically of God's own people, for whom the vine (or vineyard) was a favored Old Testament metaphor. Given the fact that the vineyard symbolized the people, surely the figure of the tenants was not lost on the chief priests and elders to whom the parable was directed (v. 33). In fact, these prided themselves as custodians of the Torah. The mere mention of vintage time automatically conjured up the coming of the messiah, whose advent was traditionally regarded as a time of reaping of the harvest of humanity.

The point of the ensuing drama is as obvious to the 20th century audience as it must have been for its original first century hearers. Those appointed to care for the welfare of the people (the vineyard) had not only proven unworthy of their charge but disloyal to the property owner, their Lord, as well.

Matthew's alterations of the Marcan parable, however, serve to make the meaning of the parable even more poignant. The addition of the season as vintage time is a Matthean touch, as is the fact that Matthew changed the single servant in Mark (12:2-3) to several servants. While Mark's narrative tells of the servant being beaten and sent off, Matthew leaves no doubt as to whom he is describing when he inserts the fact that one servant was beaten, another killed and a third stoned. Indeed, stoning was traditionally regarded as the classical death of a prophet. Matthew's point is a clear and accurate commentary on Israel's past treatment of those who came in the name of the "owner of the vineyard" to assess matters and to set his affairs aright, viz., the prophets.

Following this train of thought, it is logical therefore and correct to assume that the "son" in question is indeed Jesus. As Jeremias has pointed out, the plot to kill the son is not altogether preposterous and unrealistic: When a person died intestate, his estate became unclaimed land which would thereafter belong by right to the first claimant. In the parable, the tenants would be the automatic first claimants by reason of their occupation of the land. Matthew makes an obvious reference to Jesus' crucifixion by altering the Marcan version. While Mark related the son's being killed and then dragged out of the vineyard, Matthew reverses that order and tells us that the son was thrown out of the vineyard and then killed. Although a minor detail, this allusion recalls Jesus' crucifixion outside the city and drives home Matthew's polemic versus the Jewish rejection.

A further clarification comes in the reference to Psalm 118 (vv. 22-23). The image of the stone rejected by the builders may have also caused the priests and Pharisees to remember a reference in Daniel (2:34, 44-45). In that apocalyptic work, a stone symbolized the indestructible kingdom set up by God himself; that kingdom was supposed to shatter and absorb all previous kingdoms and to last forever. Lest there be any lingering doubt as to his point, Matthew added v. 43 as his conclusion to the parable. That vineyard, or kingdom, and the fruits and privileges thereof which had once belonged to the Jews would be henceforth the proper inheritance of those who accepted Jesus as messiah, viz., the church. But the evangelist adds an implicit challenge to his good news by exacting of Christians the necessary yield of "a rich harvest" (v. 43).

1. More bitter than hatred is apathy in response to a generous outpouring of love (Isaiah).

2. Military deterrents to war do not build peace; true serenity grows within the hearts and minds of praying believers (Philippians).

3. As tenant farmers of the earth and its treasures, of the gospel and its truth, we must give an accounting at harvest time; how shall we answer for pollution, for war, for racism and for poverty (Matthew)?

28th Sunday in Ordinary Time

You are cordially invited to a cosmic celebration of life (Isaiah). Place: here and hereafter. Time: now and evermore. Attire: Breastplate of justice, helmet of truth, and over all put on love. Kindly bring with you the poor, the outcast, the sinner and the strayed (Matthew). Prepare for the feasting by learning to hunger and thirst for the one who fulfills all needs (Philippians). R.S.V.P.

Isaiah 25:6-9. Today's liturgical selection is part of a longer distinctive unit of literature, chapters 24-27, which has traditionally been called the Isaian Apocalypse. Although these chapters do exhibit certain eschatological motifs, viz., universal judgment, monsters, signs in the heavens, etc., nevertheless, most serious scholars today deny their apocalyptic character because of the absence of pseudonymity, bizarre symbolism, dualistic cosmology and numerology. Still it must be admitted that both the apocalyptic and prophetic authors dipped into a common tradition of eschatology and therefore similarities in their literatures would be inevitable.

Because these four chapters are comprised of a collection of distinct eschatological prophecies interspersed by a variety of psalms (work of an editor), Lindblom has opted to title them "Isaian Cantata." Written probably in post-exilic times, during the era of Persian dominance, Isaiah 24-27 was appended to the earlier edition of Isaiah 1-23 and for that reason is rather out of place contextually. A more appropriate context, both thematically and stylistically, would be in the work of Deutero-Isaiah (chapters 40-55).

Just as the vine-vineyard metaphor (see last Sunday, first reading) became a standard symbol of the people of Israel, so too the divine or eschatological banquet became an apt sign of God's limitless love, care and self-gift to humankind within the parameters of time and space, as well as a pledge of the eternal kingdom. This meal shared by friends in a totally ideal state became the type for the messianic banquet and a favored image for God's intimate communion with the entirety of humankind. Clearly, Jesus ascribed to this ideal as illustrated by his preaching and preference of table guests. Dining with the poor, the pariah, the unacceptable, as was his habit, Jesus' actions made a clear statement concerning membership in the everlasting kingdom and the prerequisites for sharing in the eschatological blessings. Indeed the ultimate and lasting gift of himself was initiated in the context of a banquet meal (Passover-Eucharist). Moreover, many of his parables (e.g., today's gospel) concerned feasting and banquets, and the figure of the heavenly banquet signalled the new era of peace and salvation which by his redeeming action Jesus would inaugurate.

Finally, one cannot overlook the special locus of this excellent eschatological feast . . . the mountain. While the idea of climbing a height to be nearer to the deity may seem the product of a primitive mind, it is nevertheless a convention of thought common to most ancient cultures. Most of the significant encounters with Yahweh in the Old Testament occurred on a mountain.

Philippians 4:1-14, 19-20. Truly, in all seasons Paul was first and foremost a man for Christ. As he indicates to his friends in Philippi, his life and all his energies had become so centered upon Christ that all else took second place in his system of values.

Probably the occasion that prompted these words was the gift sent to him from Philippi while he was in prison. Usually, Paul refused to accept any support from those among whom he preached and taught. A tentmaker by profession, Paul would, when entering a new city, attach himself to the local guild of tentmakers and ply this trade industriously, thus earning his keep and paying his way. Perhaps it was because he did not want to be associated with others who grew fat from doing God's work, or perhaps it was his "sturdy bourgeois independence" (C.H. Dodd), whatever Paul's motivations, it was clear he regarded his mission as marked by the cross of Christ and was determined to be faithful to that reality in every aspect of his existence. In this particular instance, however, Paul set aside his personal preference and accepted the material kindness proffered him by the Philippian church.

Unfortunately our text omits v. 18 in which Paul described their gift as a sacrifice that would prove pleasing and acceptable to God. Nevertheless, in v. 19, Paul alludes to that fact by calling their gift "a share in his hardships." Describing hardships as *thlipsis,* Paul has reached into apocalyptic terminology in order to relate his sufferings for the gospel (in prison at present) to the trials and struggles of the "last days" which were believed to immediately precede the parousia.

Matthew 22:1-14. Although the banquet described in the first reading from Isaiah exuded an air of peace and joy, the tone is decidedly different in the gospel. Matthew has injected an atmosphere of conflict and divisiveness. As a metaphor for the reign of God, the banquet is a reality that challenges those invited to a worthy response. Matthew, in contrast to his predecessor Isaiah, believed that the reign of God was a *present* reality, as did Jesus with whom the parable originated.

When Jesus told the parable within the context of his ministry, his message was most probably aimed at those who criticized his motives and methods. In answer to those critics of his good news, the parable (like those of the laborers in the vineyard, lost sheep, etc.) vindicated Jesus' actions and pastoral manner. Indeed the parable, addressed to the chief priests and elders (v. 1), explains that because these have chosen to resist the revelation of Jesus, and therefore of God himself, attention now turns toward the poor, sinners, outcasts, etc.

In adapting the parable to his own situation and apostolic purposes, Matthew has greatly allegorized several features of the story.

Concerning the Jewish rejection, it is obvious that those guests first invited to the feast represent the chosen people. Matthew has adapted his source, changing a *man's private dinner party* to a wedding *banquet* given by a *king* for his *son.* This adaptation in itself deepens the eschatological implications of the story. Jewish tradition had come to look upon the day of the Lord in terms of a great feast (Isaiah). Hence, according to Matthew's parable, those first invited (the Jews) have turned their backs, not merely on a great dinner but on the treasure of salvation itself, as revealed in the person of Jesus Christ. Following this allegorization, then, the first servants (v. 3) sent to the invited guests represent the prophets. When these were ignored, a second group was sent. According to the Matthean frame of thought, this second group of servants (v. 4) would represent the apostles and their mission first directed to Israel. The maltreatment of the servants could well have corresponded to that endured by the prophets of the old dispensation as well as that heaped upon the missionaries of the new dispensation. Although an unlikely reaction to the refusal of a dinner invitation, the destruction of the city may correspond to the 70 C.E. razing of Jerusalem. Perhaps the allegorized parable was the church's interpretation for what had transpired just 10 to 15 years previously. For its rejection of the gospel, for persecuting its messengers, for killing its ministers, Israel had received its just desserts. Granted, this is a rather primitive idea, but nevertheless it was a prevalent concept in the early decades of the church. As a final point in his message directed toward the Jews, Matthew has interpreted the sending out of the servants to the byroads "to invite anyone you come upon" as the shift in energy and direction from the Jews to the gentiles. Considering Matthew's allegorical adaptations and interpretations in their entirety, he has so constructed his message as to form a commentary on the history of salvation from the prophets to the apostles, including the fall of Jerusalem and the outreach of Christianity to the gentiles.

With regard to his own community and the other edge of his two-edged message, Matthew has added a second parable (vv. 11-13) to the first, as well as his customary moralizing conclusions (v. 14). Indeed there were some in the Matthean community, a mixed group of believers, who fit the description of the guests in the first parable. Some ignored the message, caught up in worldly concerns. Others not only resisted the message but also tried to hamper its proclamation (Judaizers?). Then, there were those (second parable) who carelessly appeared at the feast without their appropriate attire, the white festal garment! Added here to the first parable, the second concerning the garment probably circulated independently at first. This explains the lack of continuity with the first. . . how could a person just called in from the byroads be expected to come properly attired in festal dress? Some have tried to answer this problem by citing the Old Testament custom of giving garments to invited guests. But there is no evidence of the survival of this custom in New Testament times. Matthew, ignoring the unrealistic result, saw fit to join the two parables, as befit his pastoral concerns.

Perhaps the wedding garment was intended as a baptismal allusion. The guest without the garment could have represented those who had put on the Lord Jesus at baptism but had not lived up to their commitment. The harsh treatment of the ill-clothed guest serves as a warning to lax and/or merely nominal Christians in every age.

1. The same eagerness with which we anticipate a party or a celebration must be ours as we set our hearts upon the kingdom (Isaiah).

2. The believer should be able to cope as gracefully with plenty as with poverty (Philippians).

3. Invitations to the kingdom have already been issued. By our words and works here and now, we formulate our R.S.V.P. (Matthew).

29th Sunday in Ordinary Time

"Everybody that is, is holy for him who knows how to see," said Thomas Merton. There are no limits to God's providence and the faithful believer finds peace and joy in this reality (Matthew). To those whom God had called and blessed (Thessalonians), the search for his hand and his power leads to every heart, to every corner of the universe; and the discoveries are never a shock but always a pleasing surprise (Isaiah).

Isaiah 45:1, 4-6. In the throes of those crises which shaped its history as a people, Israel also deepened in its awareness and understanding of its God. For example, the motley band of escaped slaves who followed Moses from Egypt to the desert learned of the God who was at once liberator, provider, guardian and lawgiver. During the process of settlement, whereby the wandering desert shepherds were gradually transformed into settled agriculturists, Israel learned the very difficult lesson that the God of their desert days was also their God in Canaan, their promised land. The modern believer may be inclined to say, "Well, of course!" But the ancient Near Eastern believer understood that gods enjoyed a somewhat localized power, e.g., Marduk was powerful in Babylon but not in Egypt where Ra was supreme. When Israel settled in Canaan, the temptation to leave Yahweh in the desert and to go to worship Baal, god of Canaan, was ever present. Indeed, one need only read the prophetic oracles from the eight century B.C.E. to realize that vestiges of this idea remained for centuries after the conquest. During the crisis of the exile in Babylon, Israel made even more progress in understanding the nature and being of its God. Not only did Israel perceive that Yahweh was their God *wherever* they were, but that this power, far from being localized, was supreme and universal. Moreover, not only was he more powerful than other gods; *there were no other gods* but Yahweh!

Our pericope for today is an excellent example of Israel's developing concept of the Lord and his power. Not only was he present to his displaced people in Babylon but he was instrumental in the unfolding of history, not merely Jewish history but all the world's events! Extending his providence to include even Cyrus the Persian, a pagan king, Yahweh accomplished his purpose for his people. From localization, Israel had grown to comprehend the universality and uniqueness of its Lord.

Cyrus receives more respectful treatment in the scriptures than did many of Israel's native kings. Though he considered Cyrus a pagan enemy, Isaiah dares to call him God's anointed, messiah (in Hebrew) and Christ (in Greek), a title reserved for Israel's own kings (1 Samuel 16:6), for some prophets (Psalm 105:15), and for priests (Leviticus 4:3, Daniel 9:25-26). A Persian of Indo-European blood, Cyrus rose to power meteorically. In two decades he went from being a vassal king of the Medes in Anshan to benevolent despot conqueror of Babylon. With his accession to the throne in Babylon, the Semitic era of world dominance came to a halt, never again to gain prominence. Israel saw in Cyrus' lenient policy (allowing all exiles the freedom to return home and to practice again their religious beliefs) the hand of Yahweh at work, "for the sake of Israel my chosen one." The prophet looked upon these events not merely as Cyrus' foreign policy but as the Lord's fidelity to the covenant, shaping the course of world events.

Written in the style of a decree, heralding the royal enthronement of Cyrus, Isaiah 45:1-8 (of which our text is an excerpt) assigns to the foreign king credit for carrying out the will of Yahweh, though in terms borrowed from pagan literature. Using language he may have learned as an exile, Isaiah describes (v. 1) the Lord grasping Cyrus' right hand. At the coronation of the king of Babylon, it was proclaimed that thenceforth the king would act under the aegis of Bel-Marduk, because that god "had taken the king by his right hand." In applying this action and power to Yahweh, Isaiah gives yet more evidence of Israel's awareness of the universality of their God.

Besides revealing Israel's developing awareness of God, this text points also to a unique aspect regarding that nation's concept of government. Theocracy, a government of, by and for God, was the unique politico-religious system by which Israel was ordered. For this reason, there were no distinctions drawn between synagogue and state, between religious and civil law. As Isaiah's words reveal (v. 1), such a theocratic system was to be applied to all powers of the earth based on the universality of the one Lord. In the gospel for today's liturgy it is obvious that Isaiah's ideal has not been realized and the dichotomy between church and state remains a challenge for believers.

1 Thessalonians 1:1-5. Little wonder that Paul saw populous Thessalonica as a strategic locale for the spread of the faith in Macedonia. Regarded as the most important city in that Roman province, it was the residence of the proconsul and, for all practical purposes, the capital.

The greeting that comprises our reading today underscores some of Paul's most strongly held convictions as it reveals the warmth he felt for his converts in Thessalonica. Grace and peace (*charis kai eirene*), his customary salutation, as well as his reference to "how you were chosen" (by the power of the Holy Spirit), indicate that in all his endeavors, Paul attributed his success, not to his own efforts and skills (which were outstanding!) but to God's grace and power. Praising the young community for its excellent response to the good news, Paul singled out their faith, hope and love, later to be termed the theological virtues. By their laboring in love (literally, Greek *kopos*: hard, strenuous work) and their steadfast hope (*hypomone*: patient endurance of all suffering in a spirit of anticipation of God's saving work), Paul assured his friends that they were proving their faith (*ergon*: total assent expressed in complete commitment). As always, in what became a hallmark of his teaching in the face of skeptics, Paul asserted the full divinity and equality of Jesus Christ with God the Father (v. 1). Words and wishes such as these surely bolstered the newly formed community in their faith, in the practice of gospel values and in their endurance of the growing persecution by their Jewish neighbors.

Matthew 22:15-21. Never a popular issue, the question of taxes raised the hackles of Jesus' contemporaries just as it would arouse a negative reaction today. In actual fact, taxes were at the heart of the discussion presented in today's gospel. Rome imposed several taxes upon those nations and territories over which it had dominion, e.g., (1) income tax: one per cent of one's income was to be given to Rome, (2) ground tax: one tenth of all grain and one fifth of all oil and wine were to be paid in kind or in coinage to Rome, (3) poll tax: a denarius or a day's wage was to be paid to Rome by all men ages 14-65 and all women ages 12-65. Other taxes were imposed as well; one in particular was most distasteful to the Jews. While the temple stood in Jerusalem, each male Jew was required to pay a half sheckel tax for its support and maintenance.

On this particular occasion in Jesus' ministry, however, the Pharisees and Herodians, ordinarily archenemies, rallied together to try to foil Jesus on the issue of the poll tax, or tribute coin as it was called. The Herodians, who supported the dynasty of Herod (at that time, Herod Antipas), were loyal to Rome because it served their purposes and such loyalty gained them favor, wealth and relative independence. A rejection by Jesus of the poll tax would have been reported as treason to Rome by the Herodians. Pharisaic opinion, on the other hand, was against the Roman occupation and taxes but these had contented themselves to tolerate the tax for the moment.

Jesus' response to the Pharisees and the Herodians cut through their hypocrisy and political differences to the very heart of the matter. Refraining from taking one side or the other, his answer indicated that each party was erroneously bound up in irrelevancies to the extent that each had missed the one essential point. In asking for the coin, the very fact that they so readily produced it indicated that they were already involved in the Roman political system. Without justifying or attacking the imperial occupation, Jesus pointed out their implicit acceptance in the fact that they dealt in the currency. Granted, they probably had no choice but Jesus did not defend Rome. He merely underscored the status quo. Probably the inscription on the coin was that of Tiberius Caesar. Minting coinage in one's likeness was an act of sovereignty, a right jealously safeguarded by the Romans, to the extent that a newly crowned emperor often destroyed all currency minted by his predecessor. Jesus' simple answer in no way defended or detracted from the Roman right to mint coins or to exact taxes from its constituents. Rather it pointed to the fact that concern for God and what was due him should have been as important a concern as taxes! Instead of legislating on the matter proposed to him, Jesus refrained from giving pat answers and provided his listeners with a principle, whose application he left to their responsible consciences.

For that reason, it would be an error to seek in this teaching of Jesus justification for any particular theory of church-state relations. Still, "Give to Caesar what is Caesar's and to God what is God's" has been applied as rationale in various and sundry political contexts throughout the centuries: the medieval two-sword theory, the throne-and-altar theology of Lutheran orthodoxy, the separation of church and state in the North American constitution. Yet, in all these applications, there has been an injustice done the original principle given by Jesus. "Give to Caesar," difficult though it may be, represents the loyalty one owes to temporal authority. But "Give to God" is a challenge which taps not merely our financial resources or political allegiances. "Give to God what is God's" is a demand with no limitations.

1. To see and accept the hand of God at work in the "least likely" people is a part of responsible believing (Isaiah).

2. One does not join the church as one would a club; one is called to respond to God in faith within a faithful community (Thessalonians).

3. Within the heart of the one totally committed, there are no compartments labelled secular, sacred, church, state. There can be no dichotomy, therefore, in one's activities (Matthew).

30th Sunday in Ordinary Time

Responsiveness to the call of God implies responsibility for one another as well (Exodus). Before cult, ritual or creeds, the Lord has required that we love (Matthew). Our love for one another becomes a prayer, worthy of celebration, a truthful witness to his goodness (Thessalonians).

Exodus 22:20-26. Legislation like the decalog was not unique to or original with Israel. Centuries before Moses' Sinai encounter, legal codes were imposed upon the peoples of the ancient world. The code of Hammurabi (Babylon) and the Assyrian law code are just two examples. What was unique, however, to Israel and to its concept of law was the fact that by reason of the covenant even civil legislation was raised to the level of religion. Observance of the law was considered an ethical, religious response in faith to the one whose will the law was believed to reveal. Keeping the law was not merely a means of maintaining an ordered society but a way of communing with and manifesting one's union with the Lord himself.

In today's pericope, which treats of social legislation, this principle lies at the basis of the formulation and the observance of the prescriptions. Because the revealed nature of the God with whom Israel was covenanted was compassionate, the law that flowed from that relationship automatically ruled out exploitation of others. Moreover, because of Yahweh's particular concern for the poor and the bereft, those covenanted to him must necessarily share those same concerns. At issue were three very prevalent problems in the ancient world: the treatment of aliens or strangers, the welfare of widows and their children, the making of loans and the charging of interest.

Strangers or aliens were susceptible to maltreatment because they did not have the protection of their tribe or clan. There were many such displaced persons in Israel who, because of wars, famines, plague or in some cases bloodguilt (remember Moses, Exodus 2:15), were forced to seek hospitality elsewhere. As a foreigner in a strange land, the newcomer did not enjoy the same rights as the local citizenry. Hence the prescription concerning the alien provided for their welfare. To motivate them in their concern and treatment of these aliens, the people were to recall their days as outsiders in Egypt and to exercise the compassion learned from Yahweh toward the less fortunate.

Widows and their children, termed "orphans" even though their mother lived, were to be the object of special predilection because with the loss of the head of their family, they were considered to have no rights at all. According to the law of *go'el* or redeemer, the widow's eldest brother was to provide for her, but this was not possible in every circumstance. Therefore, these widows and their children were to be the special care of the community. With the shift from the imperative to the first person in our text, it is obvious that Yahweh himself has assumed the role of *go'el* for widows and orphans. Notice the swift and severe punishment promised to those who would harm these disadvantaged ones.

Evidently, the ancient world was not immune to loan sharks and their heartless methods as the prescription concerning loans and interest indicates. Although it was forbidden to extort interest from a fellow Israelite, a pledge could be required. In the case of a very poor person, whose only possession was his cloak, the law required that this be returned by nightfall so that the poor person would not have to sleep unsheltered in the cold Palestinian night. Requiring the creditor to keep no pledge (of clothing) overnight proved such an inconvenience to the creditor as to discourage the practice. Interest could, however, be required of foreigners (Deuteronomy 23:20-21), and at times the amount exacted bordered on viciousness! Said Rashi, an 11th century C.E. Jewish scholar, said in his commentary on the Pentateuch, "Interest in Hebrew shares the same root (NSK) as the word to bite; interest resembles the bite of a snake which inflicts a small wound. At first the victim may not feel it, but soon it saps the victim of all his strength . . . so it is with interest!"

In light of the inherent danger of loans and interest as well as the plight of strangers, widows and orphans, the Old Testament characteristically urged its people to a motivation that went far beyond legality to compassion. In the gospel, we can see this compassion of God made incarnate in Jesus. Paul, who modeled his own life after Christ, called the Thessalonians to do the same.

1 Thessalonians 1:5-10. Formerly known as Thermai due to the many hot springs located there, present day Salonika is home to approximately a third of the inhabitants (70,000) as in Paul's day, midway through the first Christian century. Then named Thessalonica, the city was like most of Paul's mission choices: strategically located and, as such, an advantage in the growth and spread of Christianity. For this reason the apostle encouraged the believers in Thessalonica to be models for all of Macedonia and Achaia to emulate and to imitate.

In all his efforts and in the efforts of those who learned of the Lord Jesus from him, Paul credited the Holy Spirit. Indeed, the very fact that Paul came to Macedonia at all was due, he believed, to the Spirit of Jesus guiding and inspiring him. Having passed through Phrygia and Galatia with the Hellespont immediately ahead of him, Paul had to choose to go either to Asia or to Bithynia. Allowed by the Spirit to turn neither to the left or to the right, he forged ahead, and, impelled by a nocturnal vision, sailed on straight ahead, bringing the good news to Europe and to Thessalonica for the first time. Undoubtedly, Paul's conviction in his vocation, his faith in Jesus and his trust in the Spirit were contagious: In a short time he had established a viable, model community in that city. Moreover, it is evident from the text (vv. 9-10) that the vast majority were gentiles from pagan, polytheistic backgrounds.

In the last two verses of our pericope, Paul gives a concise description of the type of kerygmatic preaching directed toward pagans. The good news of salvation, or the kerygma, challenged pagans and idolaters to (1) a strict monotheism which required the forsaking of all former idols (*eidola*, idols of false gods) and an embracing in faith of the one true God. Those who would open themselves to the Spirit of truth were called to accept (2) a christology which recognized Jesus as one with and equal to the Father. Converts to the gospel were called to hope in an (3) eschatology, a glory in heaven which believers would share because of the saving acts of Jesus. This glory, however, would be preceded by "great trials" (v. 7). Again, as in last week's text, Paul uses here the special word *thlipsis* borrowed from Jewish apocalyptic. *Thlipsis*, or the oppression of the just in the last times, was considered the birth pangs of glory. *Thlipsis*, Jesus' passion and death, had been his prelude to glory. So too the persecution endured by the Christians at Thessalonica was the sure sign they would soon be with their exalted Lord.

Matthew 22:34-40. Politicking and the antics which accompany it have not changed much over the centuries. In Jesus' day the major Jewish parties vying for influence and power were the Pharisees and Sadducees. As the gospels reveal, their political and religious conflicts often brought them into the presence of Jesus. Occasionally they even banded together in a tenuous partnership against their common enemy from Nazareth.

The Pharisees were spiritual descendants of the *hasidim* or pious ones, whose fierce allegiance to the law and whose national pride had spawned the Maccabean revolt in the second century B.C.E. For the most part, the Pharisees were a middle class lay movement, men who believed themselves to be "separated" (meaning of Pharisee) or set apart by God for full observance of the law. Josephus (*The Jewish War* II, 162) tells us that they were the leading sect and the most accurate interpreters of the law. More liberal and progressive in their thinking than the Sadducees, the Pharisees regarded the law, the prophets and tradition, both oral and written, as God's revealed truth and thus a normative guide for life.

Claiming to be descendents of Zadok, the high priest appointed by Solomon, the Sadducees were of the wealthy aristocracy and regarded themselves as the custodians of written and oral tradition and accepted as normative only the Pentateuch. Hence, all later doctrines concerning the resurrection, eschatology, angels, etc., were rejected by them. Because of their belief that one could worship only in the Jerusalem temple, the Sadducee party lost prominence and fell into oblivion after the temple was razed to the ground in the Jewish war of 66-70 C.E.

At issue in today's pericope is a question of the law, a subject which, despite all their differences, was a favorite topic of debate for both parties. As one in a series of controversy stories, the encounter between the Pharisees and Jesus served to underscore their basic differences. Matthew's version is decidedly less cordial than either Mark's or Luke's and may reflect the widening gap of misunderstanding and animosity between Jews and Christians in the 80s C.E. The question asked of Jesus, concerning the greatest command of the law, was asked of all reputable rabbis and Jesus' answer was not entirely original. Quoting two well known prescriptions (Deuteronomy 6:5 and Leviticus 19:18) from the Pentateuch, Jesus said nothing that his audience had not already heard. In fact, Jesus was not even the first to combine these two laws concerning the love of God and the love of one's neighbor. But, and this was original to Jesus, no one had ever before made the two laws *parallel* to one another and of *equal* importance. Of the 613 precepts which the Pharisees prided themselves on observing, 248 were positive and 365 were prohibitive. Moreover, the 613 were classified into "light" and "heavy" categories according to the gravity of their concerns. Jesus had placed a "heavy" or serious precept, that of loving God, with a "light" precept, that of loving one's neighbor. This was a *new*, a revolutionary thought! Combined with Jesus' radical concept about the identity of one's neighbor (even a Sadducee!), these ideas were all the more astounding to Jesus' hearers!

For centuries the Pharisees had kept the two laws cited by Jesus. In fact, the precept concerning the love of God (Deuteronomy 6:5) had become an invocation, inviting faithful Jews to morning and to evening prayer. It was also one of the texts worn in the phylacteries or prayer boxes by devout believers. Known as the "Shema Israel," the prayer was the first uttered each sabbath and each new moon when the shophar (ram's horn) sounded the beginning of the feasts. When Jesus placed the law of loving one's neighbor in the same category as the great "Shema," it was clearly an original interpretation of the law. Jesus was not making the law of loving God a less serious demand or a lighter law. Rather, he was raising to the level of God, to the level of covenant fidelity, the social demands of community living.

1. Among all who call God "Father," there can be no alien, no poor, no widow, no orphan, because these have become brother and sister and mother to the believer (Exodus).

2. Though they are called by other names, today idols still exist (Thessalonians).

3. To know the law requires wisdom; to keep it requires love (Matthew).

31st Sunday in Ordinary Time

Leadership is not only a privilege to be enjoyed but a fragile gift to be exercised for the well-being of others (Malachi). It requires a continual integration of faith and life on the part of him/her who leads (Matthew). One who would have others follow him/her must be, first and foremost, faithful to the gospel of Jesus (Thessalonians).

Malachi 1:14—2:2, 8-10. Traditionally, the Roman Catholic ritual for priestly ordination has contained the words, *Agnoscite quod agitis; imitamini quod tractatis*—"Understand what you do; imitate what you handle." These words form an echo of the demands placed upon the priesthood of the old covenant. In fact, it would not be difficult to imagine them as a part of our pericope for today.

The anonymous author of the work called Malachi exercised his ministry in the difficult period after the exile. Although the Jerusalem temple had been rebuilt, the spiritual renewal of both clergy and laity had not kept pace with the architects and fervor was at an all-time low. Malachi's author blamed the disorder in society, the chaos in politics (Judah was governed by a Persian) and the decadence of family life on the lack of quality of faith life of the people. Probably written in the mid-fifth century B.C.E., the anonymous work named Malachi ("my messenger," 3:1) attacked the very issues targeted by the subsequent reformers, Ezra and Nehemiah.

Structurally, the prophet's work is quite simple and its question-answer style is not unlike catechetical books of the late 19th and early 20th century. It consists of six sections. Each part (called oracles in some translations) is based on a statement made by Yahweh or the prophet. Following the statement, the audience or hearers pose a question, to which the prophet responds in a short discourse. Our pericope for today is from a volley concerning priests. Malachi makes no distinction between priests and Levites since he follows the Deuteronomic tradition (Deuteronomy 18:1-18; 33:8-11). This fact alone probably made him an unpopular personage in Judah, where the Jerusalem clergy presumed a special role and status for themselves, regarding themselves as priests and relegating all other clergy to the rank of Levites.

Ordinary Time —Year A **101**

Fierce defender of the religious traditions of his people, the author of Malachi unleashed his harshest invective against those self-fashioned holy men whose lives should have set the tone for the spiritual welfare of the nation.

Another factor, a major one, was the fact that, although the people had returned from exile in Babylon, they had not totally divested themselves of the ways of that land. Nor were they immune to the enticements of foreign culture and religion present in their own land because of their Persian overlords. Malachi was adamant in warning against perversions of cult and culture and admonished his people to purity of religion devoid of foreign influences. Should the priests fail in leading the people in purity of worship, they would, he promised (2:1-3), suffer the consequences. Their blessings, probably their levitical privileges and revenues, their special portion (Deuteronomy 18:3), would be transformed into a curse.

In the final verse of today's text (2:10), we have what is actually the first verse of another issue, that of mixed marriage and divorce. Malachi was entirely against the marrying of foreigners, not necessarily due to a prejudice against them, but rather because of the foreign influence such marriages inevitably brought to Judaism's religion. Marrying outside one's own people was regarded by Malachi's author as a breach of the covenant. His reasoning went like this: Since Yahweh was God and Father of all Jews, they were therefore bound to one another as members of one family. To marry a foreigner was to disrupt familial unity and thus to desecrate the "home" (temple) of the one Father. Although this reasoning is contrary to the universality of Deutero-Isaiah, it was motivated by a good intentioned desire to preserve the integrity of Judah's faith.

1 Thessalonians 2:7-9, 13. A glimpse of the great apostle's gentler side, this excerpt from his first letter to the Thessalonians is illustrative of his apostolic conviction. In this work of preaching the gospel to those who had already come to believe, Paul gave not only his gifts as a disciple but the gift of himself as well (v. 7). Excellent teacher that he was, Paul knew that the pedagogy involved in apostolic preaching was unlike any other. One might impart the principles of mathematics, astronomy, physics or even philosophy without ever involving one's ideologies or personal commitments.

But the gospel and the ministry accorded it were different. Before one could preach the Lord Jesus, one had first to believe, to be fully given in faith and to live according to that profession. Only then by the total witness of one's words *and works*, could one be an effective preacher and teacher of the good news. It is a travesty when the words of the minister are not consonant with his deeds. Paul knew this and could truthfully compare his relationship to the believers at Thessalonica to that of a mother, nursing her child. By completely involving himself like a parent, by sharing his own beliefs and experiences as well as the news about Christ, Paul could say that he was totally given to the Thessalonian community.

Some scholars propose that Paul's mention of his "efforts and toil . . . so as not to impose" refers to his independence at earning his livelihood as a tentmaker. It would seem, however, in the given context, that Paul is rather referring to his diligent and untiring efforts for the sake of the gospel. How could he expect (impose?) the rigors of gospel values and Christian life-style from his hearers if they had not witnessed those same qualities in their teacher?

In his final point concerning their receiving the gospel, Paul used a very technical term (*paralambano*) which implied an official or public acceptance of New Testament preaching. Such acceptance meant more than hearing and acquiescing; *paralambano* implied a *living* and a *doing* as well. We are reminded of Jesus' "Blessed are those who hear the word of God and put it into practice."

Matthew 23:1-12. Although they were probably not his favorite people, it is difficult to imagine Jesus' launching into such a fierce and lengthy tirade against the scribes and Pharisees. Chapter 23 of Matthew's gospel, though purported to be the words of Jesus, is the product of a later age, that of the struggling Matthean community of the 80s C.E. While this chapter of invective was probably based on a statement made by Jesus (Mark 12:30-40?) during his ministry, and although the evangelist has drawn on traditional material, the conflict which underlies the words is more complex than that which existed between the Pharisees and Jesus of Nazareth in the 30s C.E. Because of the Jewish War (70 C.E.) and the destruction of the temple, because of the reinforced Roman occupation and the splintering threat of Christianity, Judaism experienced a great spiritual and political upheaval. Gathered at Jamnia outside Jerusalem, the rabbis pooled their efforts in consolidating Judaism's authority and verifying her orthodoxy. Meanwhile, the relations between Jews (especially Jewish authorities) and Christians deteriorated. The condemnation of the hypocrisy of the scribes and Pharisees in chapter 23 of Matthew's gospel must be seen in that light.

Another salient point to keep in mind as we read chapter 23 is this comparison: "We are the Pharisees!" In other words, *we* are those lay, middle-class, basically good-intentioned people, concerned for their nation, upholders of the law, open to new ideas while rooted in precious traditions of the past. Realizing that, we may not stand on the *outside* like spectators, looking *in* at the gospel. Rather, we must find ourselves *within* it and let the living word speak to us, cleanse us, strengthen and impel us as it did centuries ago, as it does today and as it will for always.

Our pericope for today (vv. 1-12) serves as an introduction to the "seven woes" or seven-fold indictment which follows it (vv. 13-31). It should be noted that the valid authority of the scribes and Pharisees is not attacked or rejected. As successors of Moses, they were said to occupy his "chair," a metaphor for his teaching authority. But, there may be reason to interpret this text in a more literal fashion as well. Archaeologists have recently discovered a special chair, believed used by rabbis in the first century C.E. While Moses probably did not use such a chair, he did assume a sitting position when rendering judgment (Exodus 18:13). Sitting was also the official posture for imparting rabbinical knowledge (Matthew 5:1). Hence it is easy to see how the metaphor may have been a reality and to draw the connection to the "chair of Peter" (*ex cathedra*).

Jesus in today's gospel accepts the right of the scribes and Pharisees to teach but he attacks their hypocrisy because their behavior was inconsistent with their preaching. Learned as they were in the law and in the tradition of their people, it had become the task of the scribes to advise the ordinary people on the observance of the law. Citing precedents and quoting commentaries to support their judgments, their insight was revered and at times even feared.

Jesus condemned them for the fact that they had ceased to be guides and had become rigid taskmasters for the people. For themselves, however, their adroitness at finding loopholes and exceptions was unsurpassed! Moreover, their acts of piety were performed, not in a spirit of adoration but in a desire for adulation. Adhering to the letter of the law when it suited their purposes, they substituted for an interiorization of the law's tenets an external wearing of the law (Exodus 13:1-16, Deuteronomy 6:4-9, Deuteronomy 11:13-21) in prayer boxes or phylacteries on their foreheads and arms. But this practice was symptomatic of a far greater aberration . . . the fact that their "good deeds" were dramatized for others to see rather than for the "Father who sees what no one sees" (Matthew 6:6). Tassels on the hem of garments (as per Numbers 15:38) were a common practice, one which it seems Jesus also kept (Matthew 9:20) but, as in their other displays, the scribes and the Pharisees enlarged these as a sign of their importance and sanctity.

Concluding his introduction (vv. 1-12) to chapter 23 with his characteristic tagline (v. 12, "Whoever exalts himself..."), Matthew provides a clue to the nature and purpose of his scathing attack on the Jewish authorities of the day. For the Jewish Christians within his community, the forces of Judaism and its persecuting energies remained a power to contend with. In his desire to help his church to be secure in the following of Jesus apart from Judaism, Matthew pointed to the hypocrisy that grew in the hearts of some of its leaders. At the same time, he was admonishing his own listeners about the importance of truthfulness. Though negative in its presentation, all of chapter 23 points to the positive necessity of the integration of faith and life for all believers.

1. From those to whom much has been given, much will be expected (Malachi).

2. Gospel pedagogy involves not merely an imparting of knowledge but the gift of oneself in the process (Thessalonians).

3. An artist can turn a mental picture into reality in oils or clay; the Christian must translate an inner faith into words and deeds (Matthew).

32nd Sunday in Ordinary Time

Time and space and the experience of the seasons of our life are the gifts of a gracious God that allow us to prepare for the unexpectedness of his appearance (Matthew). Yet, even now we can recognize him in the order and wonder of creation, in one another and in the wisdom of his ways among us (Wisdom). For our part, we must hold ourselves in readiness and live in joyous anticipation of the wonderful reunion to come (Thessalonians).

Wisdom 6:12-16. Traditionally acclaimed as Israel's most famous native sage, Solomon was purported to be the author of the book of Wisdom, but the work actually belongs to an era centuries later than the great king. Although the book supports the literary fiction of its psuedonymity by direct quotes from Solomon, nevertheless the concept of wisdom which it conveys belies a backdrop of Hellenistic culture of the first century B.C.E. Probably written in Alexandria in Egypt, home to a large community of diaspora Jews, the work was probably written in Greek, although there is some evidence that chapters 1-10 may have first been written in Hebrew in Palestine and then translated into Greek in Alexandria. The author was a Greek-speaking Jew, well versed in the traditions of his people and the Hebrew scriptures. At the same time, the anonymous author was proficient in the Greek language and knowledgeable about Greek philosophy and literature.

Our pericope for today is from the conclusion of the first part of the book, the theme of which is, "Seek wisdom and live"—wisdom is the path to immortality. While our text today does not allude to the fact, its context is an eschatological one and as such makes this reading complementary to the second reading and the gospel. In Hebrew, wisdom (*hokmah*) is in the feminine gender and thus lends itself readily to personification as a woman. Although distinct from God, she is like God—intelligent, all powerful, unchanging (7:22-27). She was at his side at creation as his counselor and accomplice (8:4). It is obvious that this first century B.C.E. portrayal of wisdom lent itself to John's high christological concept of Jesus as God's wisdom or word (*logos*). Moreover, this late Old Testament Judaeo-Hellenistic idea provides a fitting background for the later trinitarian understanding of God. Wisdom is compatible with many New Testament ideas; indeed the earliest mention of the book is in the Muratorian fragment of the third century C.E. which includes it as part of the New Testament canon!

Contextually, today's text is presented as advice given by Solomon to fellow monarchs. Exhorting them to seek wisdom wholeheartedly and untiringly, the author makes it clear that, because wisdom is a divine gift, she does not elude the sincere searcher, but places herself in his way. Attesting to this quality of divine graciousness, the author indicates that even to begin the search is to discover wisdom. Finding her "sitting at the gate" would be a source of strength and joy for any ruler (Solomon's audience). The gate of the city was the site of commerce and the seat of justice. It was there that the elders sat to hear cases, large and small, which were brought before them. If wisdom were the overseer and guide of his city's commerce and jurisprudence, then well equipped would be that ruler!

Searching for wisdom as she makes herself known requires vigilance and keen perception. These same qualities are underscored in the other readings for Christians who would live worthily and thus be prepared for the ultimate manifestation of God's wisdom when he comes again.

1 Thessalonians 4:13-18. Perhaps it was Theocritus the Greek who best expressed the popular opinion among unbelievers concerning life after death: "There is hope for those who are alive but those who have died are without hope." Although the Thessalonians had come to believe through Paul's preaching, nevertheless it is quite possible that they were not entirely immune to their former hopelessness concerning the dead. Indeed, as today's pericope reveals, their concern about the welfare of those "who had fallen asleep" caused great unrest in the community. This issue was one of the two questions which troubled the community at Thessalonica and which Timothy, acting as Paul's emissary, brought back to the apostle who was then in Corinth. Beneath their expressed concern for the "holy dead," one can detect the deep and sincere love which the believers had for one another. Looking forward as they did with joy to the day of the Lord's coming again in glory, they desired that all should rejoice with them in the glory he would bestow.

Paul must have preached with great vigor and conviction as to the imminence of that "Day," because the Thessalonians were certain (as was Paul in his early ministry) that all their contemporaries would be witnesses to the parousia within that generation. With the passage of time and the realization that God's imminence was not ascertainable, this sense of urgency became less acute. But during the 50s C.E. it remained a burning question . . . not whether *there would be* life after death, but *how* would those already gone enjoy the second advent? In seeking to dispel the fears of his converts and probably to rethink and articulate more clearly his own ideas on the matter, Paul stressed his theology of the believer being *in Christ* (*en Christo*). Those who had, while here on earth, lived *in Christ* and through baptism *into Christ* had come to share his life, his death and his rising, would also share in the Lord when he comes again. Though the Lord's day would come suddenly and unexpectedly, there would be one glorious celebration for the holy dead as well as the faithful still bound by time and space.

Then, as if to give a preview of the glory to come, Paul with imagery borrowed from Jewish apocalyptic tradition (vv. 16-18), endeavored to describe the indescribable. The details of Paul's vision are unimportant. They are a poetic, mythological attempt to define the undefinable, to approach with finite words and images an infinite reality. Trumpets, angels and clouds conjured up for Paul's hearers a theophanic experience. Aside from that fact, any attempt to demythologize the details of the vision would be to miss the point the great apostle intended: "We shall be with the Lord unceasingly" (v. 18).

Matthew 25:1-13. Times have changed and, with the times, so have wedding customs! Today, we sometimes hear of a groom left waiting at the altar. In Jesus' day, it was the bride who waited, at home, for the coming of the groom. What may seem like a bizarre and highly unlikely story was probably quite true to reality in Jesus' day. When Jesus first used the example of the wedding feast, to tell a parable within the context of his earthly ministry, its original meaning was probably very simple and forthright. But, as the parable passed from generation to generation, from oral to written form and from one audience to another, it became embellished, embroidered and allegorized, first by the community within which it circulated, and then by the evangelist-redactor. To understand the parable at its basic level, we must desist for the moment in applying the later allegorical interpretations. Like many other parables Jesus told, the point of the story was to teach about the kingdom (v. 1). With Jesus' appearance among humankind and with his revelation of the Father in his words and works, the kingdom had begun to dawn in the world. Some heard the message and thus welcomed the kingdom; others rejected it for one reason or another and by the same token rejected the kingdom as well.

In couching this simple point within the framework of the wedding parable, Jesus may certainly have drawn his example from the Palestinian world he lived in. While the parable is peculiar to Matthew, nevertheless, its authenticity need not be questioned, nor should its circumstances. Weddings were a grand occasion, to which all in the village were invited. "Everyone from 6 to 60 will follow the marriage drum" goes an ancient Jewish saying. An evening or even a midnight wedding would not have been a rarity because the bartering which preceded the nuptials often went on for hours and even days . . . not necessarily because the groom was reluctant to pay the dowry, but out of respect for the bride. Bartering at great length was considered a compliment and a sign that the bride was indeed treasured and priceless.

While the men were bargaining, the bride and her retinue waited in full wedding garb, ready to begin the feasting at a moment's notice. When the groom's party was sighted, all would process out to meet him . . . hence the need for oil, lamps and vigilance. Honeymoons were spent at home and, once begun, the feasting lasted for at least one week. During that time, the newlyweds' home was open to all who would come to congratulate them and to celebrate their union.

As the parable was transmitted orally by the first generations of believers, the details of the wedding story readily lent themselves to allegory. In the post-Easter community of Christians, the groom, of course, was Christ; his coming suddenly and by night, the parousia. The wedding feast was a common figure for the messianic banquet and the foolish and wise virgins may have been compared to either fervent and lax Christians or believers and unbelievers. Later, the wise virgins were thought of as Christians and the foolish as those Jews who should have been prepared to accept Jesus and the kingdom but did not do so.

References to the parousia were not included in the original parable as told by Jesus but were added later by the church and the evangelist. Like other parables (the thief who came by night in Matthew 24:43, and the return of the master in Matthew 24:45-50), this parable of the wise and foolish virgins centered on the element of suddenness and unexpectedness (of the groom's arrival) and hence were adapted pedagogically as "second coming" parables. One can easily understand the mind of the early believers in shaping Jesus' message to their existential needs. Delayed eschatology gave rise to disappointment, discouragement and, at times, even doubt. These negative attitudes and emotions had to be channelled into positive and worthwhile behavior. Therefore the parables were reshaped to stress vigilance, preparedness, watchfulness and, above all, a convinced hopefulness in Jesus' return.

In its third level of evolution, that of the evangelist-redactor, this parable and others like it (talents in Matthew 25:14-30, sheep-goats in Matthew 25:31-46) became lessons for the believing community. Matthew himself linked chapter 25 to chapter 24 by use of the word "then" (omitted in most manuscripts from v. 1), thereby connecting what has been called his synoptic apocalypse to his parousia material. The independent logion which Matthew tagged onto his parable (v. 13) gears the parable toward the last judgment which would occur at Jesus' second advent. For Matthew's community of the 80s C.E., the parable thus became a lesson on preparing for that divine reckoning by doing the will of God here and now. Throughout the reworked parable, Matthew interspersed clues, subtly indicating his intent. For example, in v. 1, the verb for "delay" was customarily used of the delayed parousia. Then again, v. 11's "Lord, Lord" (translated "Master" in NAB) recalls Matthew 7:21 and is obviously a reference to the fact that merely crying "Lord, Lord" is not preparation enough to enter the feast (kingdom). Following this line of thinking then, the oil may be thought of as the doing of the will of the Father (7:21) which is the best means of preparing for the judgment the Son will bring. Others have compared the oil to the relationship to the Lord which must be cultivated over the years of one's life, through experiences both good and bad. Such an "oil," such a relationship must be truly one's own and may not be borrowed at the last moment when the bridegroom has been sighted on the horizon.

1. True wisdom may elude the intelligent but never the faithful (Wisdom).

2. Our hope in immortality gives joy and purpose to this mortal life (Thessalonians).

3. Preparedness is not just a "waiting for" something to happen, but participation in making it come to pass (Matthew).

33rd Sunday in Ordinary Time

We who live between the appearances of the Christ are stewards of the earth and of the treasures made present by the Holy Spirit. As keepers of these charisms we must allow them to transform us as persons so that we become all that we might be (Proverbs) for the sake of all others. While there are risks involved and failure is a possibility (Matthew), we are, nevertheless, children of the light, and the Lord of endless day is our helper and guide (Thessalonians).

Proverbs 31:10-13, 19-29, 30-31. Each of us has known the relief that comes when a speaker punctuates his endless rambling with a "peppery" witticism, a pithy statement or even a proverb. Oftentime, more can be said in a brief well-turned phrase than by a deluge of monotonous verbosity. J.T.

Forestall once wrote concerning the existence of proverbs: "Wherever men are governed, there is bound to grow up a body of acute observations, based on experience, which will serve subsequent generations of administrators in the difficult art of dealing with men and affairs." Such is the beauty and usefulness of the biblical book we call Proverbs.

Originally known as *Mishle Shelemoh* ("Parables of Solomon"), some sections of the book do date as far back as Solomon (e.g. 10:1—22:16, 25:1—29:27) but most of the work as we know it was compiled in the fifth (some say third) century B.C.E. in post-exilic Judah. *Mashal*, usually rendered "parable" in English, is literally "likeness," "resemblance" or "a short comparison." But, and this is the sense in which it applies to the biblical book, *Mishle Shelemoh* is an anthology of moral injunctions geared toward the successful ruling of one's life and conduct according to the wisdom of God.

Popular throughout all the ancient Near Eastern world, the wisdom movement was first fostered in Israel by its patron and mentor Solomon. That king's openness to other cultures (especially Egyptian and Phoenician) caused the movement in Israel to expand beyond its Hebrew traditions, culture and mentality. Much of the Hebrew book bears striking similarities to the wisdom literature of those other nations. For example, our text today finds its parallel in the Egyptian wisdom text on women, *Instruction of Ani*.

With the exile and its radical reshaping of Israel's treasured institutions, the recognized teaching authority in Israel became centered, not in the priesthood or in the prophets, but in its wise men. These sages became the principal educators and were instrumental in helping to adapt Israel's religious beliefs to its evolving mentality and the changing times. Rooted firmly in Israel's past traditions and relying heavily on the groundwork laid by his predecessors (the priests and prophets, especially Isaiah, Jeremiah, Deuteronomy), the wise man was also open to the new ideas and systems of philosophy emerging in the world of which Israel was a part. This openness led to the concept of a personification of wisdom which ultimately laid the foundation for recognizing the incarnate wisdom when he appeared.

Although Proverbs contains much material from sources outside Israel, nevertheless, as W.F. Albright has pointed out, that material has been "saturated with Israelite theism and morality." For this reason the work was considered canonical by the Jewish synagogue and has been accepted as such by Christians. Indeed, the New Testament contains 14 specific citations and many allusions to Proverbs. Jesus himself was obviously familiar with its wisdom and at times manifested this fact in his teaching (Matthew 7:24-27, Luke 14:7-11).

Our text for today is from the final chapter of Proverbs and, though it is a portrait of an ideal wife, the virtues and good qualities therein enunciated should and can be emulated by all who would be wise with the wisdom of God. One may wonder why the author chose to extol the praises of a woman when, in his society, women were less than second class citizens, considered subordinate to their husbands in every way. Perhaps his choice of a feminine ideal may lie partially in the fact that chapter 31 forms a perfect inclusion with the author's description of wisdom, personified as a woman in chapter one. Written in acrostic or alphabetic form, Proverbs 31:10-31 has been called the ABC's of an ideal or worthy wife. This truly beautiful verbal picture "painted" by the author reveals a woman of strength, industrious, given to her family, hardworking, generous and altruistic. These qualities must be found not only in the faithful wife and mother, but in all who would espouse wisdom and the way of the Lord.

1 Thessalonians 5:1-6. The end *is* coming, but *no one* knows the specific time or moment. This fact which comprises the subject of our text today was Paul's answer to the second question Timothy brought him from the Thessalonians. Paul's preaching in Thessalonica had filled the newly converted believers with fervor and eager anticipation to meet the Lord whom they had come to know in faith. Many were so convinced of the immediacy of Jesus' second advent that they had retired from their jobs, had put on their "glory robes" and waited for the great day to dawn. As time passed these retirees became a burden on the working members of the community and their style of waiting for the Lord was a source of conflict.

In light of these well-intentioned aberrations, Paul had to rethink his own ideas about the imminence of the parousia and consequently to revise his teaching concerning it. Drawing on Jesus' own ideas and teaching (Mark 13:32ff), the apostle assured the Christians at Thessalonica that Jesus would certainly come again but that no one, not even he, knew the exact time of his arrival. From oral tradition, the Thessalonians probably knew the parable of the thief in the night (v. 2), therefore Paul's reference to it was not novel or unexpected. But Paul's subsequent exhortations did give a new twist to that familiar idea. Rather than curious speculation as to the *future* time of the Lord's coming, the elements of suddenness and unpredictability should inspire the Christian to assume a responsible and sensible posture toward existence *here and now*. As children of light, believers *are* (notice Paul's use of the present tense) to live, not as pawns of fanaticism or idle curiosity but as persons inspired with the dynamism of future realities. Jesus will come again, yes, BUT he has already come, and by his very existence in this world, the kingdom *is* begun. We who are baptized into him are members of that kingdom which is here now and yet to come in its fullness at his return. We have already begun to participate in the everlasting wonders of the parousia and hence must live accordingly. Our words and deeds, thoughts and motivations must be so transparent as to emit the light of eternal goodness in which we have already begun to share.

Paul's reference to those people preaching "peace and security" (v. 3) may be veiled criticism of the *pax romana* or imposed peace and false security which the imperial Roman empire prided itself in maintaining throughout its conquered lands. On the other hand, the apostle may have been referring to those false prophets who tried to placate the people with promises of continued peace and prosperity (Matthew 24:24, Luke 17:26-30).

Matthew 25:14-30. In the three decades that elapsed between Paul's writing to the Thessalonians and Matthew's gospel, the developing Christian community had begun to learn the lesson of today's parable, viz., how to wait wisely for the Lord. The last of Matthew's series of three parables on the reckoning to come, today's pericope, like most of Jesus' teaching, underwent a marked evolution and adaptation in the years between the earthly Jesus' ministry and that of his church of the 80s C.E.

As its basic level, the parable was probably addressed by Jesus to the religious leaders of his day who were entrusted with the responsibility of guiding the people in their traditions and in the light of the law. But like the third servant of the parable, who lacked courage and resourcefulness, the scribes and Pharisees had succeeded in burying the truth in their misguided efforts to preserve its purity. Not open to risk their comfortable positions by "investing" in new ideas, viz., Jesus' teachings, they were not productive but were destructive of the treasure entrusted to them. Jeremias has labeled this type of parable at the Jesus' level a "crisis parable," whose purpose was to alert a deluded and/or confused populace (confused and deluded by irresponsible leaders) to the urgency of the moment. Indeed, Jesus' appearance and the opportunity for truth and fulfillment his presence afforded created a crisis of choice. Either one risked, chose Jesus and grew, or one chose safety, negated Jesus and stagnated. There was no middle path.

As the community of Jesus' followers grew and developed, the parable was adapted to meet their changing needs. At its second level, that of the oral tradition of the church, the parable became allegorized, taking on a christological and eschatological flavor. Allegorically, the master in the story was a figure for Jesus, and his departure on a journey was thought of as the ascension. His long absence was compared to the delay of the parousia and his return was compared to the second advent. Understandably, the settling of accounts with his servants was seen as the judgment which would occur at the coming of the Son of Man, and the servants' reward was their share in the eschatological glory. The lesson was a clear one. Certain gifts or *charisms*, some great, some less great, were entrusted by the Lord to be developed and used to their fullest extent for the benefit of the community. Of course, there were risks involved, i.e., persecution, rejection, ostracization, even death. Some (like the third servant) feared these negative possibilities and allowed their charisms to die of misuse. Swift and severe reprisal would meet those unproductive and irresponsive Christians at the time of the second coming.

At this point, one must face the paradox of Christianity which Matthew's third level of interpretation underscores. To those who have been responsive to God's grace and have used their gifts and talents well and wisely, the reward is even greater responsibility ("Give his to the man with 10,000!"). Experience bears proof of this fact. All of us know people who are and who do much for the good of others. As a result, these industrious people are never given a rest but are inevitably asked to do and to be even more, for even more people! On the other hand, those who refuse to use the talents they have, for whatever reason, are left to "grind their teeth," as in the parable. This grinding is a typical Old Testament expression describing the reaction of the wicked person to the just person. At times it signals fury (Job 16:9); at other times derision (Psalm 35:16) or annoyance (Psalm 112:10). In other cases, grinding of teeth is evidence of plotting against a just one (Psalm 37:12). Whatever their motivations, those left grinding their teeth are in no sense happy or fulfilled in contrast to those who share in the joy of the Lord.

Like the proverbial ideal wife of the first reading, this parable of Matthew's gospel encourages a responsible and altruistic use of one's time and God-given talents within one's situation. Not all have the same gifts or abilities, as is evident in the parable: "to one he disbursed 5,000, to a second 2,000 and to a third 1,000." However the burden of responsibility is the same . . . to utilize, to the best of one's potential, those gifts and abilities within the time allotted. Notice that the third servant was not told to go out and try again. Once the master had returned, an accounting was required, a decision was made, its finality was irrevocable. Rather than frighten us, the severity of the parable's ending should forewarn us.

1. The family is the ground for friendship, citizenship and Christianity (Proverbs).

2. Worry about the "end" stifles creativity in the present (Thessalonians).

3. Who does not dare does not grow (Matthew).

34th Sunday in Ordinary Time

Not a scepter but a shepherd's rod, not a crown but a staff, not a commander of armies but a seeker of strays (Ezekiel), not on a throne but on a cross, not with acts of war but with simple deeds of kindness (Matthew), our king comes among us. Without edict or royal decrees he reigns, not imposing his authority from without, but moving us from within. By the power of his love he has overcome sin and death, and so shall all who believe in him and in his reign (1 Corinthians).

Ezekiel 34:11-12, 15-17. From the time of David in the tenth century B.C.E., the institution of the monarchy in Israel was, at least ideally and theoretically, intrinsically bound to the pastoral concept of shepherding. Recall the narrative concerning Yahweh's designation of a successor to Saul. Samuel (1 Samuel 16), driven by the Spirit of Yahweh, mustered each of Jesse's eight sons and settled on the least likely candidate, the youngest who had been tending the family's sheep. Anointed on the spot, David, then seized by the Spirit of Yahweh, led his people from their abject status under the Philistines to the highest pinnacle of power and prosperity the nation ever had. Like a shepherd, he gathered all his subjects around his capital city Jerusalem and made it the religious and political center of his kingdom. In all his actions, David was representative par excellence of the true shepherd of Israel, the Lord himself (Psalms 80, 74, 23), and as such was to protect and nurture, guide and secure, for Yahweh's people, plentiful and safe pasture. So strong and so prosperous was the kingdom of Israel under David's leadership that his mistakes and blunders were overlooked and his reign was called, in retrospect, the golden age. As each of his successors disappointed the people and fell short of the ideal David had established, the Israelites looked for a "David redivivus," a messiah-shepherd who would once more lead the people to rich pastures.

By the time of Ezekiel and the Babylonian exile, and with the long line of failures who had been hailed as king both in the northern and southern kingdoms, hope in the monarchy diminished. Indeed, with the capture of Zedekiah in the summer of 587, it seemed that there would be no earthly representative to lead, unite and protect Yahweh's flock. In view of the abysmal failure of the monarchy, Ezekiel sought to restore hope in the hearts of his fellow countrymen and women by hearkening back to the form of government Israel was meant to have from the outset, a theocracy. In 34:1-10, which immediately precedes our pericope for today, Ezekiel unleashed a harsh indictment against those false shepherds who had failed their people. The prophet blamed these unworthy shepherds, viz., Israel's kings, priests and false prophets, for the demise of his people and their present disgrace as displaced persons in Babylon. Restoration, Ezekiel predicted, would be accomplished by the rod and staff of Yahweh himself, true shepherd and only king of Israel. Yahweh himself would do for his people all that the former, false shepherds had failed to do. As in the days of old (exodus event, desert wandering, etc.), he would gather them and tend them. Quite beautiful and comforting to the exiles must have been the words about their shepherd's being "among his scattered sheep" in the "cloudy, dark" days of their exile, for they had begun to think the Lord had deserted them. In the references to bringing back, giving rest and healing, Ezekiel's listeners found hope in a return to their own land and a new beginning. Where earthly, human leadership had failed them, the eternal shepherd would succeed.

In v. 16, the parenthetical phrase, "but the sleek and strong I will destroy," is a gloss and should be omitted as a later interpolation. It is, in fact, totally out of context with the sense of care and love communicated in the rest of the passage. An element of judgment enters in v. 17 and gives an eschatological character to the text. Only the Lord has power to separate and to judge among those he shepherds. This same power is attributed to Jesus Christ in the gospel reading.

When we examine the gospels, it becomes clear that Jesus drew upon this Ezekiel text in the formulation of his mission and purpose among humankind (John 10:1-8, Matthew 18:12-14, Luke 15:4-7). It is also obvious from these references and today's gospel, in particular, that the early church looked upon Jesus as the shepherding presence of their God among them. Therein lay the power of his kingship and the authenticity of his reign.

1 Corinthians 15:20-26, 28. Chiliasts or millenarians have found fuel to feed the fire of their ideas in this text from Paul's letter to the Christians in Corinth, but have unfortunately read into the apostle's words a too literal, incorrect and faulty interpretation of the last days. Combining this text with the scriptural symbols of Revelation 20 as well as those of Jewish apocalypticism, proponents of this thought believe that with Christ's second coming, the just will reign for a period of 1000 years. Before that, however, a fierce war will be fought (between Gog and Magog). From its beginning in Asia Minor in the first centuries C.E., this movement has grown and finds it adherents today among some fundamentalists who erroneously draw a very literal and therefore limited meaning from certain eschatological and apocalyptic texts of scripture.

Misguided though they be, millenarians are correct in one important fact: the reality of the reign of Christ in hearts of all who are on the way to salvation. Unlike the millenarians, Paul taught that Christ's glorious reign began in the event of his resurrection-ascension (glorification) and continues until the second coming (vv. 23-24a). As Oscar Cullmann has pointed out, Christ's reign is coterminous with the era of the church and both will, at the time of the parousia, become consummated in its eternal glory (v. 28).

1 and 2 Corinthians represent theological advances in Paul's thoughts concerning the eschaton in the years since his letters to Thessalonica (see previous week's readings). An important aspect of his developing theology was the Adam-Christ typology (see also 1 Corinthians 15:44-49, Romans 8:12-21) whereby the apostle paralleled the "first man's misdeeds to the new Adam's redeeming works. This comparison lent itself to Paul's teaching of the primacy and centrality of Jesus' resurrection for Christian faith. With Adam, sin and death, he taught, but with Jesus, victory and life! Resurrected life and freedom from sin are not triumphs to be enjoyed only at the end of time, but can be enjoyed here and now by the believer who, in faith and by baptism, participates in the saving mystery of Christ.

But there is even greater joy and even more wondrous glory yet to come and as a pledge of this future fulfillment we have Jesus Christ himself as "firstfruits." A Jewish cultic term, "firstfruits" (*aparche*), were a sign of the consecration of the entire harvest to the Lord. In the same way, the exaltation in glory of Jesus is our surety! Jesus' resurrection is our firstfruits, a sign that promises the same glory, the same life in abundance to all who are incorporated in him by faith.

For the present, we who believe live in that dynamic evolving process of prolepsis . . . the "here and now but not yet complete" time of the kingdom. It is the era of the reign of Jesus . . . it is the era of his body, the church. In the sacraments, in his word, in the witness of one another's faith, we taste eternity but, impelled by the Spirit, we are moving toward a "time" beyond time and a "space" beyond space wherein this present taste of glory shall be fulfilled eternally. In that moment, which will be forever, the reign of our Father will have come, his will shall have been done on earth and in heaven.

Matthew 25:31-46. In this era of the church, in this period of Christ's reign, how is his power being manifest, in what way are his subjects witnessing to his authority? Matthew's gospel for today answers these and other questions concerning the presence of Christ's kingdom in the world today. Wherever one recognizes the light of Christ in the eyes of the hungry . . . wherever the stranger is taken by the hand of friendship, in these places and in these hearts is the kingship of Christ established and perpetuated.

Unique to the Matthean version of the good news, the scene depicted in today's pericope is actually a compilation of several different literary genre at various levels of interpretation. A dramatic conclusion to the liturgical or church year, the central points of the text are the short simile about the sheep and the goats (vv. 32-33) and the series of sayings of Jesus (vv. 35-39, 40b, 41-45). To the early church we owe the combination of the simile and sayings as well as the implied allegorization, and the evangelist has provided the introduction, conclusion and contextual framework. Following his three judgment parables, today's gospel provides the criteria by which Matthew believes the eschatological judge will formulate his verdict. Similar judgment scenes can be found in Jewish literature popular at the time of Jesus, in the rabbinical midrash to Psalm 118 and in the Egyptian Book of the Dead. But, while there are definite corollaries in these other literatures, the gospel retains the unique feature that the criterion for judgment will be *love*, active love, overflowing into simple deeds of goodness and charity. In the loving acts of giving water to the thirsty and clothes to the naked, the believer can discover the presence of Christ reigning within the hearts of his people and by those same deeds can profess his faith in that presence. These small, routine and seemingly insignificant deeds have ramifications of eternal proportions for the believer and upon these shall we be separated, like wheat from chaff, sheep from goats.

When Jesus used the simile of the sheep and goats in his preaching, he borrowed his metaphor directly from Palestinian life. By day, sheep and goats were pastured and tended together. Toward evening, however, the animals were separated from one another by their shepherd. Sheep are hardier animals and can endure the cold Palestinian night but goats need shelter. The point of the metaphor is not the comparison of sheep and goats but the *separation* of the two by the royal judge. Like the parable of the wheat and weeds and of the dragnet, separation (i.e., judgment) is left until the harvest time or end time and is to be accomplished *only* by the eternal shepherd-king.

At its basic level (during Jesus' ministry), the criterion for separation was the acceptance or rejection of Jesus' message, and that separation anticipated the ultimate judgment. It should be noted that the simile was addressed to Jesus' *disciples* (v. 31) and hence what is said of Jesus and his message would apply as well to his disciples and their preaching. Those who accept or reject the good news as preached by Jesus' disciples in the 80s or even in the 1990s are thereby separated and judged.

One may not overlook the fact that only here in all the gospels is the role of king actively accepted by Jesus. While this identification of the Son of Man (v. 31) with the shepherd-king (v. 40) may be evidence of a later level of interpretation (church and evangelist), it does, nevertheless, underscore Jesus' royal dignity and equality as Son at the right hand of the Father.

In concluding, we come full circle to our first question: How is the power of the Son of Man-shepherd-king manifest within his kingdom today? How does his church translate the reality of his reign into significant acts of power? From the gospel, we learn that it is *not* by earth-shaking deeds or headline-making activities. Simple acts of love, of which anyone, at anytime, is capable, are the deeds which wield his power in time and space. Care and acceptance of one another as emissaries of our king—such are the actions whereby his authority is established. A frightening and yet challenging thought remains with us from today's gospel: Those who were condemned to eternal punishment were separated from the just, not for dastardly deeds or heinous crimes, but for the little acts of love they had *neglected* to do. In failing to feed the hungry, visit the imprisoned, etc., they had summarily rejected not only their king and his reign but their own inheritance of salvation as well. While we still enjoy the mercy of time, we can awaken ourselves to the presence of Christ's reign and seek out the message of need in the faces of the poor and the downtrodden. In so doing, we shall discover the power of our king and establish his reign of peace and love.

1. The peripheral of society, the weak, the uncommitted and the poor are the special concern of those who believe in the shepherd-king (Ezekiel).

2. As sign and sacrament of the risen Christ, believers are to be hopeful, joyful life-givers for the world (1 Corinthians).

3. We will be judged, not for the wondrous and difficult feats we have performed, but according to the quality of life we have provided for those in need (Matthew).

Movable Feasts
Trinity Sunday

With infinite love, God provides for those who believe an infinite number of ways of experiencing him/her. As Father and as Mother, God is love that creates, nurtures, protects and guides (Exodus). As Brother, Friend and Confidant, he shares the burden of our sins and makes us sharers in eternal life (John). As Sister, Companion and Helper, she inspires us to build up the human family in harmony and peace (2 Corinthians).

Exodus 34:4-6, 8-9. Tertullian, the early church father (145- 220 C.E.), is generally acknowledged to the first to use the term "trinity" and to apply it to God. Formulated only in the post-biblical period and not officially defined until the great church councils of the fourth and fifth centuries, the doctrine of the trinity can nevertheless be found in seed in several New Testament texts.

For the purpose of analysis, T. Longstaff has identified three categories of scriptural texts, representing a gradual development in theological understanding on the part of early believers. At the first level, there are a number of passages that refer to the incarnation and describe the close relationship of Jesus to God. While some of these texts suggest a subordination of Jesus to the Father (Romans 8:31-34; 1 Corinthians 11:3, 15:20-28; 2 Corinthians 4:4-6), others clearly emphasize the unity and equality between Jesus and the Father (Matthew 11:27; John 10:30, 14:9-11, 20:28; Colossians 2:9; 1 John 5:20).

A second set of passages can be identified as stressing Jesus' close relationship to and identity with the Holy Spirit (Luke 3:22; Acts 2:33; Romans 8:26-27, 34; John 14; Galatians 4:6). Finally, a third set of texts (while not necessarily written at a later date) mention all three persons of the trinity in the same context. The most important of these passages is the very *early* text included in today's second reading (2 Corinthians 13:14). The apostolic benediction of Matthew 28:19 is also included in this third category of texts but was written almost 40 years later than the Pauline text.

While the trinitarian doctrine was not present in the Old Testament, some scholars have suggested that there was a "triadic" character in the manner in which humanity experienced God. At the heart of the scriptures is the fact that God is always in the process of revealing himself. This outward flow of self-communication from God is received and responded to by the believer. Revelation-response is the dual action that creates the rhythm of the scriptures, whose third aspect is the fact that the very God who communicates himself/herself to the human heart is the same God who creates in us the capacity to respond in faith. This triadic quality characterized the Mosaic covenant and became more obvious in the new covenant in Jesus.

Today's first reading from Exodus represents the fulfillment of God's earlier promise (Exodus 33:18-23). In a wonderful anthropomorphic narrative, the Pentateuchal author portrayed the almighty and infinite God as tenderly caring for the finitude of Moses by placing him in a cleft of a rock and allowing him to glimpse a revelation too great for him. Moses was then instructed to meet God on Sinai with two stone tablets.

Present to Moses and symbolized by the cloud (v. 5), the Lord renewed with his people the relationship they had broken by their infidelity (Exodus 34:1) and revealed himself as compassionate, kind and faithful (vv. 6-7). Symbolic of God's presence in the wilderness and on Sinai, the cloud also figured in apocalyptic literature wherein "one like a Son of

Man would come on the clouds" to judge all peoples (Daniel 7:13).

In the Christian scriptures, the cloud was a symbol of Jesus' divine aspect (Luke 9:34-35, Acts 1:9) and was a signal of the last days as well (Mark 13:26). Early church fathers understood the cloud and the cleft in the rock as symbols of the incarnation in which God did not only "pass by" (Exodus 33:22) but involved himself physically and personally in human existence. On this feast of the trinity we celebrate that personal involvement of God with us as Father, as Son and brother, as Spirit and life.

2 Corinthians 13:11-13. Helmut Koester, in the second volume of his award-winning (Biblical Archaeology Review: New Testament Book of the Year 1984) work, *Introduction to the New Testament*, has distinguished between the opponents Paul addressed in 1 Corinthians and those in 2 Corinthians. While those with whom Paul did battle in his first letter were the Judaizers, those he confronted in 2 Corinthians were Jewish Christian missionaries who boasted that they were "Hebrews," "Israelites," "seed of Abraham" (2 Corinthians 11:22). These missionaries did not stress the necessity of the law of circumcision (as did the Judaizers); they nevertheless placed great emphasis on Jewish tradition.

Believing that the Christian proclamation was merely the renewal of the true Jewish religion, these opponents of Paul concentrated on powerful deeds, miracles and mystical experiences (2 Corinthians 12:1-9, 2 Corinthians 3:4-18), as manifested in Moses. Because they accented only the "divine man" and "wonderworker" aspects of Jesus' ministry, while downplaying the passion and cross, Paul called them "false apostles" (2 Corinthians 11:13) and warned the Corinthian Christians against them.

Today's second reading is actually the *conclusion* of Paul's second letter to Corinth in which he promised that he would visit the Christian community there a third time in order to rectify the situation created by the "false apostles." Paul's concern for the cohesion within the community is obvious throughout the letter and reaches a high point in his closing words. Calling for reform and social harmony, the apostle advised the Corinthian believers in Jesus to offer to one another a holy kiss.

Scholars agree that this is probably a reference to the greeting of peace customarily exchanged at the breaking of the bread, i.e., the Eucharist. Indeed, the table of the Lord provided the perfect context for repairing relationships, for mutual encouragement and for community growth. Those who would in sincerity and truth share together the meal of the new covenant were challenged by the very fact of the body of Christ to put aside all petty and even great differences in order to become one body in him.

Striking because of its very early date (ca. 54 C.E.), the triadic benediction with which he closed his letter represents a departure from Paul's customary valediction. In most of his other greetings, Paul's wishes were purely christological. The addition of the Father (God) and the Spirit in this pericope probably flowed from the basic Christian experience. For example, in Jesus, the incarnate God, one can experience the immense and incredible love of the Father. Belief in Jesus and encounters with Jesus are automatically understood to be belief in and a means of encountering the Father (John 14:23-24). In Jesus and his saving work, all who believe can share in the life of the Spirit. Later theologians would look to this Pauline valediction and similar texts (1 Corinthians 12:4-6, John 14, Matthew 28:19) for evidence of the church's gradual and growing understanding of the nature of God.

John 3:16-18. No greater love story has ever been written than that which Jesus told Nicodemus that night so many generations ago: "God so loved the world that he gave his only Son" (John 3:16). Martin Luther called this verse a "gospel in miniature" because it proclaims in but a few words the incredible dimensions of Gods' love as well as the salvific effect of that love on the course of human history. In its original context, today's short gospel pericope was part of the conclusion of the conversation between Jesus and Nicodemus concerning rebirth unto eternal life through water and the Spirit.

The Johannine community of the late first century C.E. had come to understand that the believer was able to appropriate *through baptism* into Christ Jesus the gifts of salvation Jesus had effected. Today's gospel identifies salvation with *eternal life* and underscores the fact that the believer can experience eternal life, not only *after* death but *here* and *now*. This notion of eternity impinging upon time and space in the flesh and blood reality of the incarnate word and in the sacraments has been called "realized eschatology" by Johannine scholars.

Asserting that the divine motivation for involvement with humanity is love ("God so *loved*")—inexplicable, unmerited, immeasurable and unrequited love—the Johannine author reminded his readers that *love* was the hallmark of *all* God's dealings with his people. Recall that in the election of Israel, love was the only reason for God's choice, as explained by the Deuteronomic author: "If God set his heart on you, and chose you, it was not because you outnumbered other peoples: you were the least of all peoples! It was for love of you!" (Deuteronomy 7:7-8). The Johannine community referred to this love (*agape*) of God (a love that is uncontainable and must burst into activity) some 37 times and concluded that in fact God *is* love (1 John 4:16).

Since love was the motivating force behind the gift of the Son, it would follow that Jesus as Son is the preeminent revelation and most eloquent expression of God's love. It is significant that the Johannine evangelist placed such stress on the *love* and *eternal life* aspects of salvation. In many of the New Testament references, the sending of the Son by the Father was for the purposes of *judgment* (see Matthew 25:31ff). For the Johannine author, the presence of Jesus as light (John 3:19) and as love "provokes *self-judgment* as men line up for him or against him; truly his coming is a *crisis* in the root sense of that word, where it reflects the Greek: *krisis* or judgment" (R. Brown).

As recipients of God's gratuitous love, humanity therefore cannot remain passive in the face of such a gift. To do so would result in a self-judgment and condemnation (v. 18). God's love made present in the person of Jesus presents a challenge, the response to which can result in life or in death. *Faith* is the only suitable and worthy response—a faith that translates conscious, deliberate choice into loving, committed service. To *believe* is to *know* Jesus, is to have *eternal life*.

The antithesis of faith is not doubt, as one may suppose, because doubt is an integral and necessary aspect of the process of believing and a catalyst to deeper, firmer faith. Faith's antithesis is *disbelief* that expresses itself in *disobedience*. The one who refuses to believe refuses life and thereby choses death (v. 18).

Like so many words in the fourth gospel, "gave" (v. 16) carries a wealth of meanings and implications. That God *gave* his Son referred primarily to the incarnation but this statement includes a portent of the cross as well. Foreshadowed in the narrative of Abraham and Isaac (Genesis 22:1-18) by the references to the "only son, whom you love," God's gift of his Son recalled Abraham's faithful willingness to *give up* his only son to death. Indeed, as Abraham's obedient faith found its beneficiaries in all the nations of the world (Genesis 22:18), so too God's gift of his only Son is for the *world* (John 3:16).

There is also a reflection here of the Deutero-Isaian suffering servant who was "*given* up to death" (Isaiah 53:12). No doubt, John had this in mind when he portrayed Jesus on the cross as saying, "Now it is finished," as he *gave* up his spirit (John 19:30). That God *gave* up his only Son out of love is the total and absolute expression of the incarnation, and the challenge of the cross calls all who believe in Jesus to that same measure of great and giving love (John 13:34-35, 15:12-13).

1. Since we are sinners, our survival is dependent upon the gracious kindness and mercy of our forgiving Father (Exodus).

2. Community harmony is possible if the Spirit of Jesus inspires every diverse voice of its membership (2 Corinthians).

3. Great love is shown in that selfless magnanimity that places no limits or barriers to its giving (John).

Corpus Christi

A new alliance between God and humankind grew out of the gift of Jesus' flesh and blood (John). Promised in the testament of our ancestors (Deuteronomy), this bond was personalized in the incarnation and immortalized on the cross. We who come together at the table of the Lord draw our strength from that union and bear witness to it in our lives (1 Corinthians).

Deuteronomy 8:2-3, 14-16. Nostalgia can prove pleasant even if the subject of one's reminiscing was not quite so pleasant at the time. Deuteronomy as we know it today probably received its final form in the seventh century B.C.E. Glancing back as it did to the exodus period, the book idealized the major aspects of Israel's early days and held these up for the emulation and edification of the seventh century Israelites. In this way, the desert period which was probably a horrendous experience for Moses and company became a romantic symbol of simple, true religion. The desert hardships, the grumbling, rebellions, factions, deaths and failures faded into the background as the prophets, reformers (Josiah) and scribal authors sought to restore Israel to the zeal of first love, to the fire and fidelity of her first covenanted response and responsibilities. In a sort of divine rendition of "Give me that ole time religion," Hosea actually portrayed the desert as a type of honeymoon hideaway (Hosea 2).

Just as the desert period had become a symbol of first love and fidelity, so too the events of the desert became immortal symbols of God's constant care. Manna and water from the rock were precious gifts of sustenance in the wilderness and pointed to humanity's complete dependence on God. Later the manna and water would hauntingly remind a wayward people of God's care even when they were undeserving and ungrateful. Still later, in New Testament times, Paul (1 Corinthians 10:1-4) and the Johannine Jesus (John 6) would see the manna as a type of the eucharistic bread of life and the water from the rock as a sign of Christian baptism.

All of Deuteronomy 8 may be understood as an anamnesis of the wilderness wandering with its central focus on God as giver, guide and guarantor of his people's well-being. Our text recalls the fact that not only did the desert pilgrims miss the message of the trials, viz., the hunger, the thirst, the serpents, scorpions, etc., but they also overlooked the true meaning of the manna and the water. In all the desert happenings, in the dark days as well as in the good times, they tended to lose sight of the point and purpose of it all—namely, their growing relationship with the Lord. Their hunger and thirst, the manna and water and even their satiety were signs to draw attention to the one for whom and because of whom they lived.

The Lord was trying to raise the consciousness of his people concerning himself, "not by bread alone, but on every word that comes from the mouth of God." Verse 3 recalls not only God's creative word (Genesis 1) but also his revealing word and ultimately the incarnate word of God (John 1:14). These expressions of God's words give life and sustain it.

Filled with the manna, the desert wanderers were to look beyond the gift to the giver, beyond the expression of love to the one who spoke it. Various possibilities have been proposed to explain the wilderness food. Regardless of its scientific origin, the Israelites looked on the manna as an act of God, a gift of bread from heaven. The fact that the people were to gather it only once a day and were forbidden to store it points to the attitude of reliance upon the Lord which they were to have. On the other hand, they were to preserve a portion of manna in a jar and place it beside the tablets of the law (Exodus 16:32-34) as a sign of God's sustaining mercy. Torah and manna became a sign and a taste of a far greater care and a far more loving act of providence. Bread in the wilderness and water from the rock previewed the greatest feast of all—that to which the God of creation would call all humankind. In Jesus the incarnate word, the bread of life come down from heaven, the perfect revelation of the Father, we discover the food which forever puts an end to hunger, thirst and the wilderness of sin and death.

1 Corinthians 10:16-17. Part of a longer section (vv. 14-22) concerning Christian participation in meals sacrificed to idols, our verses today must be understood in their proper context. Paul was counseling the believers at Corinth with regard to their social activities. Their every action had to be consonant with their commitment to Christ. To partake in a sacrificial meal in the temple of an idol, even though one's motive was social and not religious, would constitute acceptance of that idol. Presence in the idol's temple could not be considered an indifferent or neutral act, because attendance at the rite was tantamount to full participation. Eating and drinking in the idol's presence forged a unity between idol and worshipper. Pouring a libation out on the earth (a cup of wine) to honor the idol was an act of worship which no Christian should perform, whatever the social custom or pressure to do so.

On the contrary, the cup and the bread, the only meal of unity with which the believer *should* associate, is that of the Lord. With language borrowed from the Passover meal, Paul described the cup of blessing of the Christian Eucharist as a participation or fellowship in Christ. In like manner, the breaking of the bread unites the believer to the Lord. In both acts (cup and bread, blood and body), the believer partakes and celebrates not merely the things in themselves but the saving events of Jesus in his redeeming death as well. In comparing the Christian Eucharist to Jewish and pagan sacrifices, Paul wants us to understand the truly sacrificial aspect of the Eucharist. Because of the sacrifice of Jesus, redeemed humanity can once again participate in God's life.

Paul's shift of meaning, from a sacramental and christological understanding of the body of Christ (v. 16) to a communitarian or ecclesiological understanding (v. 17) of that body (viz., the body of the believing community), underscores the unifying power of the eucharistic Lord. The idea of the body and blood of Christ (Eucharist) creating the body of Christ (church) also sent a message to the individualistic Corinthians of the middle first century C.E. Participation in the sacramental body (and blood) of Christ meant incorporation into, participation in, and responsibility for the body of Christ (the church). To answer "Amen" to the sacramental *Corpus Christi* meant an "Amen" to the assembly gathered to celebrate. Full participation in the Christian Eucharist must override any tendency toward a "Jesus and me" spirituality. To say "yes" to Jesus in the sacrament necessitates a living of that same "yes" to Jesus in his body the church. In this way the union which Jesus died to achieve, and of which his body is the symbol, will be a reality.

John 6:51-58. Our pericope today comprises the heart of the bread of life discourse (John 6:1-58). It is one of Jesus' most challenging teachings, borne out in the reaction of his disciples, then and now. These responses (6:60, 66) characterized many of Jesus' contemporaries. Ironically, even today this very special revelation of Jesus, which was to be a source of unity for his church, is also at times a source of contention. But if we examine the gospels carefully, we find that *every* revelation of Jesus, and especially the *person* of Jesus himself, presents the reader (listener) with a challenge to faith and an invitation to live according to that faith.

Coming at the climax of Jesus' teaching of the bread of life, our pericope today should be considered in relation to the rest of the discourse. In 6:59 the Johannine author designates the synagogue at Capernaum as the site of Jesus' instruction. Some have suggested that, since the season was near Passover (see 6:4), Jesus could have been leading the synagogue service on that particular occasion and, consequently, his discourse on the bread of life may have been prompted by the readings of the season. Scholars of ancient ritual believe that, at Passover time, the Jewish lectionary proposed reading from the scrolls on the exodus experience and the manna passages would have been included (Exodus 16; Numbers 11; Deuteronomy 8, etc.). Discoursing of the bread of life, and his own flesh and blood, the Johannine author portrays Jesus and his sacrificial death as the divine replacement for the Passover lamb (John 19:33).

Other scholars propose that all of John 6 represents a Christian Passover feast, characteristic of the Johannine community of the 90s, a celebration which would have begun with the retelling of the exodus event and culminated in the Christian seder, the last supper. It is significant that the eucharistic material in the Johannine account has been gathered into chapter six and that there is no account of the institution of the Eucharist on the eve of Jesus' passion. In vv. 26-51, the bread come down from heaven is described in terms of the activity of Jesus the incarnate word of God. Verse 51, "the bread I give is my flesh for the life of the world," describes the supreme gift of Jesus—his death in sacrifice for all. Then the following text (vv. 52-56) explains the way in which believers may appropriate and share in the salvation wrought by Jesus, bread of life. Clearly, John would have us understand this sign of Jesus, this sacrament of his flesh and blood, as the means by which his saving action is offered for the believing participation of his followers.

Notice the three dimensions of this saving sign. Not only is the past made present to us who believe (the Calvary event and the reconciliation it reaped) but a taste of the future and the eternal is also ours to savor: "If anyone *eats* (now) he shall live *forever*" (vv. 51, 54, 58). In Jesus' holy and eternal "manna" we meet the Jesus of the cross, the risen Lord, the exalted Lord of eternity and we also meet one another. Besides the dimensions of time (past, present, future), there are horizontal and vertical aspects to the Eucharist as well. In the bread of life, we encounter Jesus and the body of believers as well.

With regard to the correct interpretation of vv. 51-58, two main schools of thought stand out. Some scholars, following the lead of Clement of Alexandria, Origen and Augustine, regard the entire discourse as sapiential and believe that the references to *bread* refer to Jesus' *teaching*, his *revelation* of God's wisdom as in Ecclesiasticus 24:20. According to this interpretation, since Jesus metaphorically referred to himself as bread (as in "I am the door, vine, living water," etc.), then to *eat* this "bread" would be to *believe* in Jesus' teaching. To feed on Jesus' words, his works, his ways, his mind—this is the meaning of the bread of life.

Other scholars recognize the sapiential character of the discourse but insist on a eucharistic and nonmetaphorical interpretation of vv. 51-58. Whether or not vv. 51-58 are a later interpolation by the evangelist or other redactor, the forceful and stark vocabulary shows that the understanding of bread and eating it was to be realistic and in no way symbolic. Unlike the synoptics who speak of "my body," the Johannine Jesus speaks of my "flesh" and "blood." Brown suggests that, to have any positive meaning whatsoever, these terms must refer to the Eucharist. To eat another's flesh was a semitic figure of speech for slanderous, hostile action (Psalm 27:2). To drink blood was totally repugnant and forbidden by law (Genesis 9:4; Leviticus 3:17). Moreover, it was a semitism for brutal slaughter (Jeremiah 46:10). Flesh and blood should be understood as in the Old Testament, a designation for human life, flesh and blood meaning the living person. In the flesh and blood, that is, the life of Jesus as the Son of Man, believers can meet God. In that flesh and blood, eschatology is realized and the *giving* of that flesh and blood is the sharing of eternal life here and now with believers. That Jesus actually challenged his disciples to "feed on," "eat" (*trogein*—literally "munch," "gnaw") indicates in stark boldness the participation to which he called his own.

1. Remembering the good things God had done in our lives will whet our "faith appetite" for him in times of mediocrity or doubt (Deuteronomy).

2. Shared bread, shared talents, shared joys and sorrows bear witness to Christ's presence among us (1 Corinthians).

3. With the bread of his word, with the bread of his works, with the bread of his life, Jesus feeds the hungry believer (John).

Feast of the Lord's Presentation

Israel had waited for generations for the Lord of glory to appear. When at last he graced the temple with his presence, the proud and self-righteous lost sight of him in the smoke of their burnt offerings, while the apathetic failed to hear him above the droning of their empty prayers (Malachi). Welcomed by the humble, poor ones, Jesus revealed his saving light to all who hoped in him (Luke) and blessed with life and forgiveness those who believed in his victory over death (Hebrews).

Malachi 3:1-4. Structurally, this book can be divided into six sections, each of which has been constructed around a question and the prophet's reply to it. Remarkably well preserved, the prophet's work was originally anonymous and, as such, was appended (along with Zechariah 9-11, 12-14) to the larger collection of major prophetic works. An editor who later composed and added the superscription (1:1) understood the messenger referred to in 3:1 (my messenger: *mal'akhi*) to be the prophet, hence the name of the book, Malachi. As R. Dentan has observed (*Interpreter's Bible*), the work may have been better named "A Message for an Age of Discouragement" because of the unknown prophet's attempt to lift his contemporaries from their depression.

Although his thrust and parry technique of question-and-answer catechesis was mainly a literary device, it may also have reflected the life-situation of the prophet. As one who defended the faith and as one who desired to preserve intact the religious and liturgical traditions of his people at a time when these values seemed worthless or at least disadvantageous, the prophet was probably often pelted with questions (and more!). Laboring for the Lord in post-exilic Judah, the author was confronted with a frustrated people whose return home had not measured up to their expectations.

Governed by a foreigner (Persian governor, 1:8), they had struggled to rebuild the temple and the work was completed by 515 B.C.E. (Ezra 6:15). But the newly constructed house of worship did not, ipso facto, re-create the prayerful assembly; at the time of the prophet's oracles (ca. 460-450 B.C.E.) the liturgical and communal life of the people had greatly deteriorated. In an effort to rekindle the fervor of his people for their faith, the prophet railed against the laxity of the priests, slovenly ritual (1:6—2:9), social injustice (3:5), withholding of tithes (3:8, 10-14), mixed marriages and the foreign ways these unions introduced into Judaism (2:10-16).

For the pious Israelites who had hoped their return home would be the inauguration of the messianic age and whose disappointment threatened to weaken their fidelity, the prophet discoursed on Yahweh's inscrutable justice and unwavering loyalty (1:2, 2:17, 3:14). When post-exilic Judah looked at her shrunken domain (as a Persian province, Judah's territory was a small 500 square mile area) and doubted God's love (1:2), the prophet promised retribution and reward.

Today's pericope is from the fourth section of the book concerned with the Day of the Lord.

Pointing ahead to an eschatological future, the prophet described God's sure intervention as a two stage event. First, the *messenger* would appear to prepare the Lord's way by purifying the clergy and reforming the cult. Then the *Lord himself* would come, bringing with him justice and judgment.

Although the editor of Malachi believed the "messenger" to be the author of the oracles (1:1), later tradition assigned the preparatory task of "messenger" to Elijah (4:5-6). Jerome believed Ezra the Scribe had functioned as "messenger-purifier" by means of the sweeping religious reform he initiated.

Christians, in retrospect, understand that John the Baptizer served as the Lord's messenger, as the precursor of Jesus and herald of the good news. In both Jesus' presentation in the temple (see today's gospel) and in the action of his cleansing of the temple, believers recognized the promised visitation of the Lord to his temple (Malachi 3:1).

By virtue of his appearance, the corrupt ways of false and empty worship were made to yield to the light of his truth. Whereas animal sacrifices had once served to express the worship of the people, with the advent of Jesus and his messenger and because of the perfect sacrifice of the cross, a new liturgy of spirit and truth was initiated. Celebrated and renewed at each Eucharist, the liturgy of the Lord continues to purify and to refine as it nourishes and heals.

Hebrews 2:14-18. Part of the basic premise of the letter to the Hebrews was the author's assertion that Christ was the perfect high priest. As representative of his brothers and sisters before God and as their mediator, Christ perfected his service by virtue of his being one with those he served. In today's second reading, the oneness of Christ with human nature (people of blood and flesh: v. 14) was described by the author in terms of the abasement that necessarily preceded Christ's exaltation (2:5-18). Sharing fully in human nature, even to the point of dying, Christ was able to undo (rob the devil: v. 14) the bonds of death and sin, thus overcoming the power of Satan.

Hellenistic Judaism (Wisdom 1:13, 2:23-24) associated death with the devil and contended that death was not originally part of God's plan for humankind. Because of the supposed connection between sin and death, Christ's victory over sin (2:17) was regarded as a victory over Satan and therefore over his evil handiwork, death. In two parallel series of antitheses (vv. 14-15) the Hebrews' author juxtaposed "devil-sin-death" with "Christ-salvation-life" to explain the saving mystery of the incarnate Son and eternal high priest.

Verse 16, "He did not come to help angels," is better translated, "He did not take an interest in (or take note of) angels." Jesus' attention to the children of Abraham (v. 16) recalls the ancient promises made to the patriarch and underscores the author's contention that believers in Christ are indeed Abraham's true descendants.

Human in every way, Christ was tested and tried as humans are (vv. 17-18) but he did not err and through his strength has earned the title of "pioneer of salvation, pioneer of glory" (2:10). "Pioneer" (*archegos*) has a wealth of meanings, all of which add to our understanding of Christ's union with believers. In its simplest sense, it means head or chief, and could refer to Christ's role as leader. *Archegos* can also mean founder or originator, source or origin.

As W. Barclay has explained, "An *archegos* is one who begins something in order that others may enter into it; an *archegos* is one who blazes a trail for others to follow . . . . Suppose a ship is on the rocks and the only means of rescue depends on someone to swim ashore with a line. Once that line has been secured, others can follow it to safety. The one who is first to swim ashore will be the *archegos* of the safety of others." As one who immersed himself in our human existence, and as one who led to victory over sin, death and Satan, Christ can most correctly be called the *archegos* of the triumph that is salvation.

Luke 2:22-40. Several decades ago, some areas of the world and this country practiced the custom of "churching" women after childbirth. Their months of "confinement" ended, the new mothers appeared at the church to be blessed in a simple rite of thanksgiving that found its origin in the episode narrated in Luke's infancy stories and ultimately in the Old Testament legislation (Leviticus 12:2-8). According to the law, a mother was required to be purified 40 days after the birth of a son and 80 days after the birth of daughter. As a holocaust or burnt offering, the woman was to offer a lamb and, as a sin offering, a pigeon or a dove. For those who could not afford a lamb, another dove could be substituted for the holocaust. The purification rite was performed strictly for legal purposes to restore ritual purity and did not imply or assume a moral fault. While the purification of Mary *does* form a part of today's gospel, it was by no means Luke's main consideration, which was to show Jesus as the fulfillment of both the law and the prophets.

From the outset of the presentation narrative and all through the infancy stories (2:22, 1:11, 57, 2:6, 21), the evangelist used the word *eplesthesan* (when the day came) to indicate the passing of time. A special word, *eplesthesan* suggested the inauguration of the age of the messiah. So too, the several references to the Spirit underscored the eschatological significance of the event. Recall the association made by the prophets (especially Joel 3) concerning the outpouring of the Spirit that would accompany the appearance of the messiah. Coupled with the fact that Jesus' presentation recalled the prophecy in Malachi (3:1) of the Lord coming to his temple, the Lucan narrative can be understood as a messianic statement. This idea is reinforced in the interchange between Jesus' parents, and Simeon and Anna.

Simeon, described as a just and pious man who awaited Israel's consolation (Isaiah 40:1), and Anna the prophetess who devoted her life to prayer and fasting were representative of those faithful Israelites who could recognize in Jesus the promised messiah. Simeon's double pronouncement (vv. 29-32, 34-35) casts him in the role of an aged sentinel whose long watch has ended. With the appearance of Jesus, his vigilance was rewarded: The object of his hopes had appeared at last. In Simeon's first pronouncement, traditionally called the *Nunc Dimittis*, the universal scope of Jesus' mission was emphasized in Isaian terms: "for all the peoples to see . . . a light to the gentiles" (Isaiah 52:9-10, 49:6, 46:13, 42:6, 40:5).

Simeon's second pronouncement addressed to Mary was more ominous in tone (vv. 34-35). Describing her son as a sign that would be rejected (a stumbling block), Simeon's oracle pointed ahead to the way in which the saving deed (v. 30) would be accomplished. Notice that Luke spoke of a "downfall" before the "rise" (v. 34). Some have seen in this a reference to the cross and death of Jesus (fall) that preceded the resurrection and glorification (rise). Indeed, "rise" (*anastasis*) is used elsewhere in the gospel to describe the action of rising from the dead.

J. Fitzmeyer understands the reference (downfall and rise) in terms of the goals and goodness preached by Jesus which would force all people to face up to their great sinfulness (fall). This knowledge can completely destroy, as it would, the proud; or it can prompt the humble to turn to the messiah and through him *rise* to new life.

A variety of unsatisfactory explanations have been proffered for the "sword" that would pierce Mary. Origen thought it to be the sword of doubt and scandal Mary experienced when she saw her son suffer on the cross. Others have said it was the pain Mary suffered from gossips who scorned Jesus as illegitimate!

More correctly, the sword should be understood in terms of the context in which it appears. Like the sword of discriminating judgment in Ezekiel (14:17), Jesus' presence would bring division among people and even within families (Luke 12:51-53). Like a sword (Luke 8:19-21) cleaving father from son and daughter from mother, the presence of Jesus would demand a choice. For those who recognized him and believed in him, thereby doing God's will, a new bond would be forged, one even more binding than that of familial love. R. Brown understands the "sword" as Mary's (and every Christian's) realization that the claims of God on Jesus (on each Christian) are greater than any human attachment. As mother of Jesus, she was united with him by her caring mother's love; as a believer, she was even closer to Christ in her fidelity to the will of the Father.

Anna's reaction to Jesus reinforced Simeon's pronouncements, and her spontaneous sharing of her realization about the child can be understood as evangelization, the preaching of the good news of salvation (vv. 36-38). The Lord had indeed come to his temple. In him was revealed the saving light of God's justice challenging peoples to believe.

1. Many come to the temple to meet the Lord who comforts, only to be confronted by the Lord who challenges and chastises (Malachi).

2. The ideas we have about death dictate to a great extent the attitudes we have about life (Hebrews).

3. The Presentation feast celebrates in grateful awareness the fact that all we are and all we have is the Lord's (Luke).

Birth of John the Baptist

He was the herald of the Christ-event (Acts); the quality of his faith and the radical ethic by which he lived still witness to the good news (Isaiah). In the person and mission of John the Baptizer, we are challenged to prepare a straight path for the one who is coming again (Luke).

Isaiah 49:1-6. Ordinarily, this servant song (the second of the four compositions included in Deutero-Isaiah) was understood by the early church as referring prophetically to Jesus and to his mission. But here, on the feast of Jesus' herald, the sixth century prophet's words apply aptly to John the Baptizer. Depicted in all four gospels and in Acts, John was cast as a prophetic figure (like Elijah) who came out of the desert to preach repentance and thereby to prepare his contemporaries for the coming of the messiah. As a comparison with his birth announcement will reveal (Luke 1:5-25), John was called from birth and given a name while still in his mother's womb (Isaiah 49:1). His challenging and often harsh message was a sharp-edged sword (Isaiah 49:2) that cut to the quick of the hypocritical and the mediocre; his was indeed a mission of gathering Israel to the Lord (Isaiah 49:3).

Because John had such an impact upon his contemporaries, each of the evangelists labored carefully to distinguish John and his role from that of Jesus. Often, the words clarifying John's subordinate position were placed on the lips of the baptizer himself (John 1:19-23, 29-34). Many scholars believe that John's impact upon Palestine was so great as to outlive him; some of his followers even revered *him* as the messiah. His fiery message and fierce delivery seemed to be more in keeping with the general tone of messianic expectation. Quite frankly, Jesus, with his "turn the other cheek" policy and call to humble service, proved disappointing to many.

That John may have had some association with the Essene community at Qumran near the Dead Sea has been widely accepted today. His desert mission, his preaching on conversion, his choice of wardrobe and diet and especially his practice of ritual ablution (baptism) could all reflect an Essene influence.

Perhaps the one aspect of today's Isaian text that would *not* apply to John is the reference in v. 6, "I will make you a light to the nations." This role was applied to Jesus before his birth (John 1:4-9), at his infancy (Luke 2:32) and during his ministry (John 8:12). In fact, the very day on which John's birth is celebrated attests to Jesus as the light. Falling at the time of year when the sunlight begins to diminish, the June 24 feast underscores the baptizer's claim, "He must increase but I must decrease" (John 3:30). In this, John becomes a model for every believer. A witness to the light, John humbled himself before the light, allowing it to shine forth unencumbered, leading others to its radiance.

Acts 13:22-26. An excerpt from Paul's kerygmatic discourse (13:13-52) in the synagogue of Antioch in Pisidia, today's second reading (like all the other discourses in Acts) was largely a Lucan composition. Stereotypical in structure and content, the discourses attributed by Luke to Stephen, Peter, Paul, etc., comprise approximately one third of the book of Acts. Aimed primarily at the reader, the discourses serve as teaching tools whereby Luke interpreted for his different audiences (gentile, Jewish, pagan) the message intended for their salvation.

In Antioch of Pisidia, Paul and Barnabas would have encountered an audience which included Jews and gentiles sympathetic to Judaism, God-fearers as they were called. Intent upon appealing to every member of this mixed audience, Luke placed on Paul's lips a survey of history which showed Jesus as springing from the David kingly line and as the fulfillment of all the Jewish prophecies. This lengthy discourse climaxes in a challenge to Paul's present audience not to repeat the mistakes of the past, i.e., not to reject Jesus as the Jews in Jerusalem had done. I.H. Marshall suggests that this particular discourse may be understood as a *midrash* on 2 Samuel 7:6-16, i.e., "as an exposition of the passage (concerning the promises to David) in order to bring out its continuing significance by applying it to a contemporary event, the resurrection of Jesus."

Today's pericope includes what seems to be a digression within the discourse. But Paul's reference to John and to his ministry was a deliberate decision on Luke's part and reflects his view of salvation history. In looking at Luke's historical perspective, three distinct periods can be distinguished: the period of Israel, which extended from creation to John the Baptizer; the period of Jesus, which extended from the time of his ministry to his ascension; the period of the church (J. Fitzmeyer calls this segment the period of the church *under stress*), which extends from the ascension to the parousia. By his mention of John in v. 24, Luke was signalling the end of the period of Israel and the emergence of the period of Jesus.

Moreover, he clarified John's status of herald and witness to Jesus but also as subordinate to him. To those who supposed him to be (v. 25) and perhaps still clung to the hope that he might indeed have been the messiah, John is depicted as declaring, "Look for one who comes after me." This pericope concludes with a citation from Luke's first volume (Luke 3:16) and a call to all people of faith (children of Abraham and you others) to accept the message by which we are saved.

Luke 1:57-66, 80. In recent decades, erudite scholars of the Christian scriptures, e.g., R. Brown and J. Fitzmeyer, have suggested that the infancy narratives, viz., the first two chapters of Matthew and of Luke, are like gospels in miniature. These same scholars agree that, even if these initial chapters were all that survived of the Matthean and Lucan versions of the good news, modern readers would nevertheless have a complete christological and soteriological presentation of Jesus.

Indeed, a thorough investigation of the infancy narratives will reveal an ingenious blend of literary technique and theological expertise, the result of which is not just a nostalgic or imaginative journey into a beloved hero's origins but a profound and persuasive call to faith! "Written to make Jesus' origins intelligible against the background of the fulfillment of Old Testament expectations . . . the infancy narrative was to supply a transition from the Old Testament to the Gospel—the Christological preaching of the Church presented in the imagery of Israel" (R. Brown).

An excerpt from Luke's infancy account, today's gospel concerns the birth, circumcision and naming of John the Baptizer. Because it was Luke's intention to parallel Jesus and John, he arranged his first two chapters in a diptych comprised of seven episodes: (1) John's birth announcement, (2) Jesus' birth announcement, (3) Mary's visit to Elizabeth, (4) birth, circumcision and naming of John, (5) birth, circumcision and naming of Jesus, (6) presentation of Jesus in the temple, (7) finding of Jesus in temple.

The verses recounting John's birth (vv. 57-58) recall the numerous instances of surprising and/or wondrous births recorded in the Jewish scriptures. Like Abraham and Sarah before them, Zechariah and Elizabeth were elderly; both wives were considered sterile. The *joy* surrounding John's birth recalls the joy of Rebecca upon giving birth to Jacob and Esau (Genesis 25:24), as well as Sarah's happiness in becoming the mother of Isaac (Genesis 21:6).

As J. Fitzmeyer has noted, John's birth was recounted by Luke as an event that manifested the mercy of Yahweh for his people. This mercy was shown in removing from Elizabeth the stigma of sterility. This manifestation of mercy is borne out in the name of John; *Yôhanan* means "Yahweh has shown favor." As the rest of the gospel would thereafter attest, the mercy of God shown to Elizabeth would be experienced by *all* the people of Israel.

John's circumcision underscored his membership in the covenant between Yahweh and Israel (Genesis 17:11) and showed him to be a true Israelite and a righteous heir to the blessing promised by God to his chosen ones (Joshua 5:6-7). Because of this, John functioned in the gospel as the bridge between the testaments, the last of the line of Jewish prophets and the first in a long line of Christian witnesses to Jesus. With John, the period of Israel came to an end and the period of Jesus began. By so portraying John in the infancy narrative, Luke was in effect answering the question in v. 66, "What will this child be?" He would be as Jesus would later say of him: a prophet and something more, the messenger to prepare the way, the greatest man born of woman (Luke 7:26-28).

Omitting the canticle of Zechariah, today's gospel concludes with v. 80 wherein Luke assured his readers that the Holy Spirit which filled John in his mother's womb would be the impetus for his growth and future mission. By referring to John in this manner, Luke cast him in the same light as other famous sons from Jewish tradition. The Genesis' author had described Isaac in similar terms: "The child grew up" (Genesis 21:8). Samson was depicted in this way: "The child matured; the Lord blessed him and the Spirit of the Lord was upon him" (Judges 13:24-25). Samuel also was described as "waxing mightily before the Lord" (1 Samuel 2:21). Like the heroes of his Jewish heritage, John was to be the hero and herald of a new heritage wherein the root of Judaism would come to full flower in the person and mission of Jesus Christ.

1. In John and in Jesus, the Lord revealed the light of his salvation (Isaiah).

2. Preaching repentance, John prepared the way for the one who was to bring forgiveness (Acts).

3. Those who are called by the Lord for great service are also empowered by him with the Holy Spirit (Luke).

Transfiguration

Transformed and radiant, Jesus affords his disciples a glimpse of his risen glory (Matthew). Our experience of him as the victorious Son of Man (Daniel) becomes a pledge of the future glory we shall share with him and the source of our hope in present trials (2 Peter).

Daniel 7:9-10, 13-14. Written in the mid-second century B.C.E., the book of Daniel is a composite of haggadic (chapters 1-6, 13-14) and apocalyptic (chapters 7-12) literature set artificially by the author in the sixth century B.C.E. By means of the six edifying stories (haggadic literature) and the four apocalyptic visions, the author of Daniel intended to encourage his contemporaries to remain faithful to their Jewish faith and ancestral traditions despite a growing persecution from their Hellenistic overlords on the one hand and a tempting attraction to Hellenistic culture on the other. Through the book's protagonist, Daniel, the anonymous second century author sought to illustrate the superiority of Israelite wisdom over all other philosophies. To that end, he portrayed the God of Israel as the Lord of *all* human history, who is at once the source, guide and goal of every human destiny.

Today's first reading, a pericope excerpted from the apocalyptic section of the book, is part of a longer vision (7:1-28) in which Daniel saw a series of four beasts, each in turn overpowering its predecessor. Representing the four successive empires of the Babylonians, Medes, Persians and Greeks, the beasts were all condemned in a heavenly court scene, part of which is included in today's reading. As a witness to all these events, Daniel shared his heavenly vision of the Ancient One and of one like a Son of Man.

Whereas the beasts had emerged from the abyss, i.e., from the domain of evil, the Son of Man was of celestial origin, "coming on the clouds of heaven," i.e., from God, the "Ancient One." So too, while the beasts were representative of pagan kingdoms, the Son of Man, receiving universal dominion, glory and kingship, became the figure par excellence for the kingdom of the holy ones of God most high (7:18). In later Jewish literature (2 Esdras, Enoch), the Son of Man was represented as an *individual* and came to be understood as a heavenly being now concealed but who would appear at the end of time.

In the gospels, Son of Man was a self-descriptive favored by Jesus but he united the notion of humble suffering (Mark 8:31, 9:31, 10:33, etc.) to the eschatological motifs of Daniel 7. Consequently, when the early Christians searched the Jewish scriptures for a foundation and a means of explaining the Christ-event, they had to couple the glorious Son of Man figure in Daniel with the suffering servant of Deutero-Isaiah.

2 Peter 1:16-19. From the beginning, the Jesus-movement was beset by nay-sayers who accused the Christian community of fabricating like a well-woven tapestry of deceit the entire story of humanity's redemption. When confronted by sceptics, Paul had argued, "none of this, i.e., the Christ-event, was done in a dark corner!" (Acts 26:26). Similarly, when the author of 2 Peter was challenged as to the veracity of the kerygma and the so-called delay of eschatology, he countered with witnesses of his own.

Writing pseudonymously near the end of the first or in the early second Christian century, the author of 2 Peter purports to be the apostle Peter himself. Near death and wishing to leave a reminder of his teaching so as to preserve and hand on intact the "deposit of the faith" (2 Peter 1:12), "Peter" is represented in this letter as warning the community against false teachers as well as heretical and apostate Christians. Evidently some of the author's contemporaries, basing themselves on the ever lengthening *delay* before Jesus' return, began to argue that the parousia would never come. Moreover, the same false teachers denied that what they had been taught with regard to these matters had been nothing more than "cleverly concocted myths," invented to frighten and or manipulate believers!

In order to illustrate his point that the Christian good news was not fabricated on myths but on an historic event, viz., the Christ-event which included the incarnation, mission, death, rising and exaltation of Jesus, the author cloaked himself in pseudonymity. As R. Fuller has explained, pseudonymity was a device which enabled an authoritative eyewitness, who had died, to speak to the changing circumstances of the church after his death. By means of this literary tool, "Peter" who had witnessed Jesus' transfiguration was able to remind the second century church of what he had experienced!

In defense of the parousia and to assure his contemporaries of Jesus' glorious return, the author recalled Jesus' power and majesty as it had been glimpsed decades earlier by Peter, James and John. These apostolic eyewitnesses and their testimony concerning Jesus' transfiguration in glory should, thought the author of 2 Peter, dispel the falsehoods and doubts concerning the parousia. Just as Peter and the others had seen Jesus in glory, so would the faithful who awaited his return. Similarly, just as the prophetic word which had foretold his first appearance was fulfilled in Jesus, so too the apostolic teaching which foretold his return was reliable.

As an encouragement to those with whom he endured the dark times of persecution and false teaching, the author of 2 Peter advised that they regard the prophetic teaching and apostolic tradition as a shining lamp. The light from that lamp, i.e., their sacred traditions, would sustain them in faith until the morning star (Revelation 2:18, 22:16) made his final appearance in glory.

Matthew 17:1-9. Also featured as the gospel for the Second Sunday of Lent (Year A), Matthew's version of Jesus' transfiguration in glory underscored several of the evangelist's theological and pastoral concerns. Intent on presenting Jesus as a *new* Moses bringing a *new* law for a *new* Israel (chapters 5-6), Matthew—like his Marcan source—placed the mysterious event on a *high* mountain. From as early as the fourth century C.E., the church fathers identified Tabor as the location specified in 17:1, but Tabor hardly rates classification as a mountain, rising just 1,850 feet above sea level. Perhaps, as many contemporary scholars believe, Mt. Hermon which towers 7,000 feet above Tabor was a more likely site for such an event. Nevertheless, the theological significance of the "high mountain" environment was probably more important than its exact geographical locale.

By placing the experience which his disciples had of Jesus' glory on a high mountain, the evangelist wished to remind his readers of *other* important theophanic events in similar locations. On Sinai's mountain, Moses had experienced the glory of Yahweh; the Exodus' author had described Moses' face as shining with light. It was also on Sinai that Moses became the mediator of the covenantal law for his people. No doubt, Matthew had Moses and Sinai in mind as he portrayed a radiant Jesus with a new law for God's people.

Several other features in this gospel pericope are evocative of Old Testament elements. The cloud (*shekinah*) which overshadowed Jesus signified the divine presence as had the guiding cloud in the wilderness and the cloud over the tent of meeting (Exodus 40:3-4). The message which came from the cloud identified Jesus (as it had done at his baptism) with the servant, prophetically acclaimed by Deutero-Isaiah (42:1). The instruction, "Listen to him" (v. 5), recalled for Matthew's readers similar invitations, issued in the sapiential literature to "listen to wisdom" (Proverbs 5:7, 8:33; Sirach 6:35, 21:15).

In the event of his transfiguration, Jesus, the wisdom of God, was revealed as the teacher and elucidator par excellence of God's plans for his people. Moses and Elijah were representative of the law and the prophets; their presence with Jesus and then their absence ("Jesus was there alone," v. 8) taught early believers that Jesus was the theological conclusion *toward which* both the law and the prophets had pointed and *in whom* both law and prophets found fulfillment.

Many scholars believe Jesus' transfiguration to have been a post-resurrection appearance projected back by the evangelist into the period of Jesus' ministry; others believe the event may have been grounded in some historic experience, reconstructed and theologically enhanced so as to be a powerful kerygmatic tool in the first Christian century. In its given literary context, i.e., immediately after Peter's confession and the prediction of Jesus' passion, the transfiguration event offered a glimpse of Jesus' future glory. But this was not to occur until after the cross.

Certainly, there is significance in the fact that the disciples who were given a glimpse of Jesus' glory were also present to witness his profound suffering in the garden (Matthew 26:36-37). The presence of the same witnesses, Peter, James and John, threads together both ends of the spectrum of our salvation, viz., the *suffering* that leads to *glory*.

Peter's expressed intention to erect tents was more than an enthusiastic desire to prolong the moment of joy. No doubt the evangelist wished his readers to associate the event on the mountain with the Jewish feast of tabernacles (Deuteronomy 16:13-15). In annual commemoration of Israel's wilderness days, the people erected tents or booths in which they lived for the eight days of the feast. In later Jewish tradition, the feast was celebrated with a display of lights ("His face became as dazzling as the sun, his clothes as radiant as light," v. 3). Eventually, based on the prophecy in Zechariah 14, the feast of tabernacles came to be associated with the triumphal appearance of the messiah. When Matthew constructed this glimpse of Jesus' glory, he intended that his readers recognize Jesus as their messiah and the fulfillment of all their hopes for deliverance.

1. The dominion of the Son of Man who suffered and died on the cross is forever; the kingship of the humble servant of the Lord shall never end (Daniel).

2. Cleverly concocted myths do not survive; faith in the reality of Jesus creates and sustains his church (2 Peter).

3. Every experience of grace is an opportunity to become transformed by the power and wisdom of Jesus Christ (Matthew).

Solemnity of Sts. Peter and Paul

Heroes lend honor and pride to a society by their courageous and exemplary lives. So too in the church, heroes such as Peter and Paul continue to inspire by their faith and motivate by their zeal. Ordinary people made extraordinary by grace, the heroes and heroines of the church were undaunted by the censure of a fearful, irresponsible authority (Acts). They did not flinch even at the prospect of imminent death (2 Timothy) but lived by their faith in the person and power of Jesus, Son of God and savior of all peoples (Matthew).

Acts 12:1-11. At numerous times and in a variety of ways, during the course of his compelling and highly theological narrative, the author of Acts has succeeded in bringing home to his readers the burden of his message: Despite difficulties from within and from without, the Jesus movement survived and would continue to develop and flourish because of the presence of the Holy Spirit.

According to the narrative, James, the brother of John (one of Zebedee's sons, one of the Twelve), had been beheaded and Peter had been incarcerated. The Herod featured here was Herod Agrippa I, son of Aristobolus and Bernice and grandson of Herod the Great. Agrippa I had been sent to Rome at age six and was schooled in the company of Drusus (son of emperor Tiberius) and Claudius. In Rome, Agrippa I (who later called himself Julius Agrippa) met and formed a lifelong friendship with Gaius (later emperor Caligula). Because of his relationships with influential Romans, due in no small part to his own political ambition, by 41 C.E. Agrippa I had achieved control of the vast territory over which his father had reigned.

When in Judea, Agrippa I adhered strictly to Jewish customs and rituals, thereby cultivating the admiration of the Pharisees. It is said that his behavior was not so orthodox when he was outside Jerusalem and away from the close scrutiny of the legal experts. When Herod escalated the persecution against the followers of Jesus, this probably ingratiated him even further with the Pharisees who were eager to squelch the "heretical sectarians."

Since it was the holy season of Passover (somewhere ca. 43 C.E.), Herod delayed punitive action against Peter but detained him in prison. Four squads of soldiers (four men in each squad) seemed a ridiculous show of force against a chained man, but the sheer impossibility of Peter's situation underscored the wondrousness of the event. Meanwhile, the believing community had gathered to pray. Luke's use of imperfect tenses throughout vv. 6-11 made it clear that Peter's imprisonment and the community's prayer for him continued for several days. On the night of his rescue, Peter was asleep, exhibiting the confidence and resignation of one who trusted in God's power and purpose.

Peter's passivity, the presence of the angel of the Lord, as well as the extraordinary nature of the rescue (shining light, chains dropping from his wrists, gates opening of themselves, and guards seemingly oblivious to it all) served to illustrate that the sparing of Peter was understood by the early community as due to God's intervention. Moreover the entire episode, told against the background of the "church praying fervently to God" (v. 5), underscored the importance and effectiveness of united prayer. A belief existed among the first generation of Christians that the risen Lord would return again at Passover time. This tradition may have added to the anticipation of divine intervention on Peter's behalf.

2 Timothy 4:6-8, 17-18. Biblical scholars are divided over the Pauline authorship of the pastoral letters (1 and 2 Timothy, Titus). In either case, whether one accepts Pauline authorship or not, the debate will continue. Nevertheless, the essential purpose and message of the pastoral letters will stand and continue to speak to the church. N. Perrin had called them a "manifesto" written to respond to the threat of heresy within the church and to the growing need for an organized front against false teaching.

In today's pericope, the author has employed three metaphors adapted from his Hellenistic environment to describe the rigors of Christian commitment. A libation of wine or oil often accompanied Jewish sacrifices (Numbers 18:7). Both Greeks and Romans ended their meals with a libation (v. 6: *spendesthai*), the sacrifice of a cup of wine poured out upon the ground in reverence to the gods. That the author understood the end of his life in this way meant that he viewed his death as a sacrifice. Not merely the consequence of hostility against him, the author's death was to be the "amen" to a long life of fervent praise and service that had brought honor to Jesus and to the Father.

Referring to his death or dissolution (v. 6), the author used the picturesque word *analusis*, usually applied to the unyoking of an animal from its harness to the plow or cart. *Analusis* was also used for loosening the mooring ropes of a ship. The author, therefore, understood death as an untethering experience that freed him for eternity's joys. The fight and the race were used metaphorically in the Hellenistic world to describe the course of a person's life. Obviously, the author was confident that his life had been a fight well fought and a race well run. He looked ahead for a merited crown (v. 8). Besides being the prize awarded the victor in an athletic contest, the crown often appeared in Greek or Roman funeral art as a symbol of immortality (Wisdom 4:2).

A caring pastor even at the very end of his life (when his concerns might have been purely personal), the author assured all the believing community that those who were brave in the fight and persevering in the race would one day share the joy and crown of victory with him.

Matthew 16:13-19. Not one of the four canonical gospels actually bears a signature identifying its authors, but Matthew's gospel does contain a "signature" of sorts. In chapter 13 of his gospel, the evangelist wrote, "Every scribe who is learned in the reign of God is like the head of a household who can bring from his storeroom both the new and the old" (13:52). In a sense, the author understood his role as that of the scribe; therefore, his description can be appreciated as a self-portrait. Throughout his wonderfully structured gospel, the Christian scribe whom we call Matthew drew upon the *old* heritage of Judaism's law, prophets, messianic expectation, etc., and held these treasures up to the light of the *new* revelation of truth and salvation that had come into the world in the person and mission of Jesus Christ.

Writing during the 80s C.E. for an urban church, probably that of Syrian Antioch, Matthew dealt carefully and effectively with the problems of his sub-apostolic church as it struggled with finding its identity. Rooted in but also distinct from its Jewish matrix, the Christian community was with Matthew's help to understand itself as the new and eschatological Israel, viz., the expression in the present of the coming and eternal kingdom of God. Intrinsically bound to the community's evolving understanding of itself or its ecclesiology was its evolving understanding of Jesus or christology. As J. Meier has observed, today's gospel pericope manifests perfectly Matthew's desire to join together christology and ecclesiology. To that end, Peter's confession of Jesus (christological statement) has been coupled with a "confession" of Jesus (unique to Matthew's gospel) concerning his future followers, the church (ecclesiological statement).

Jesus' question, addressed first to his disciples, "Who do people say that the Son of Man is?" served to introduce the various popular conceptions of him. Matthew has altered his Marcan source by replacing "I" with "Son of Man." In the longer passage from which our gospel has been excerpted, the title Son of Man would be explained (1) as applicable to Jesus in his earthly ministry (v. 13), (2) as the suffering savior (v. 21), and (3) as the judge who would come in glory at the end of time (vv. 27-28). With regard to the popular opinion as to his identity, some thought Jesus was John the Baptist redivivus, believing that John had been the messiah. Indeed, in the sub-apostolic community, some still clung to that belief. Those who thought of Jesus as Elijah based themselves on Malachi's prophecy (3:23-24) and the tradition that Elijah had not died and would return as a messianic herald in the last days.

Only Matthew had included Jeremiah in the popular poll about Jesus. In first century Judaism, the long-suffering Jeremiah had become a popular figure. Regarded as a protector of God's people, it was believed that he would put into the messiah's hands the sword that would free Israel from her oppressors (2 Maccabees 15:14, 2:1). Because Jesus' activities and character had not satisfied the popular messianic hopes for a political liberator, some thought he was probably only a herald of the messiah to come. Each of the conceptions was corrected by the special revelation given to Peter.

Because Peter acclaimed Jesus as messiah and as Son of the living God, most scholars believe the original context of his confession was a post-resurrectional one. This was a correct christology, not one born of false political expectations, as explained in Jesus' response to Peter. The heavenly Father who alone can reveal the Son revealed to Peter the true understanding of Jesus. From that point onward, Peter would become the leader of those who acclaimed Jesus as savior and Lord.

Conferring upon Simon a new title and a new mandate, Jesus assumed the role that had been God's alone throughout the Old Testament. Abram's name had been changed and his faith had been blessed by God with promises of land and posterity; so too Simon was to receive the promise of an eschatological community and an important role in its development. Rock (*kepha*: Aramaic; *petros*: Greek) was not at that time a known personal name. As Simon's new title, it signified the stability and reliability he would need as leader of the new foundation. In the Old Testament, Abraham was referred to as the rock from which Israel had been hewn (Isaiah 51:1-2). In Daniel, the rock was the symbol for the new kingdom that would supersede all others (2:34-35, 44-45). In Jesus' designation of Peter as rock, it is clear he was establishing the everlasting community of the last days.

The giving of the keys was a symbolic ritual (that survives even today) whereby authority was conferred. Recall the episode in Isaiah (22:15-25) wherein Shebna who had been majordomo of the palace was replaced by Eliakim. In giving Eliakim the keys, King Hezekiah said, "I will commit your authority to his hand." O. Cullmann referred to Peter as the one who would "lead the people of God into kingdom" and contrasted Peter's leadership with that of the scribes and Pharisees who "shut the doors of the kingdom in men's faces!" (Matthew 23:13).

Peter's (and the disciples'?) authority was further clarified by means of the semitic expression "binding and loosing." According to the rabbis, "to bind" was to render a decision that imposed an obligation; "to loose" was to render a decision that removed an obligation. Binding and loosing could also refer to the admitting or excluding of a member from the community. J. Meier points out that, given the context of chapter 16 wherein Jesus criticized the magisterium of the Jewish leaders (16:1-12), the terms "binding/loosing" probably refer to the teaching authority conferred by Jesus upon Peter. Today the ecclesial community, founded on faith in Jesus as messiah and Son of the living God, hewn from the rock of apostolic teaching, still survives to answer the ultimate question: "Who do you say I am?"

1. Even when physical freedoms are curtailed, the believer's awareness of spiritual and psychological freedoms ensures survival (Acts).

2. If life is to be compared to an athletic race, then real living does not end at the finish line, but begins there in a new and wonderful way (2 Timothy).

3. The church that calls itself Christian must be constantly redefining itself and its mission according to its evolving awareness of who Christ is (Matthew).

Feast of the Triumph of the Cross

Sign of contradiction, sign of victory—the portent of the cross speaks volumes about the mysterious plan of our salvation (John). To listen to the cross is to hear the loving goodness of the Father spoken in the words and works of Jesus (Philippians). To look upon the cross and to respond in faith to its message of life brings healing and reconciliation (Numbers).

Numbers 21:4-9. As a symbol, the serpent has figured in a variety of ways in the myths and legends of the ancient world. Regarded as a positive as well as a negative symbol, the serpent alternately portrayed both the powers of life and death. For example, in the myths of Mesopotamia, Egypt, Greece and Rome, the serpent was a demonic or totem emblem with beneficent and maleficent powers. As a cosmic figure, the serpent was associated with the monster of chaos vanquished by the creator deity (see cosmic myths of Ugarit). As a divine symbol, the serpent was closely identified with the fertility deities and those concerned with health and life. Those who observed the snake shedding its skin to renew itself associated it with the power of healing. According to the ancient Greek myth, a serpent was said to have brought to Aesclepius (god of healing) herbs with healing powers. For this reason, the emblem of modern medicine, the caduceus, features a serpent entwined on a staff.

In both the Jewish and Christian scriptures, the serpent figure communicated a mixed symbolism. In some instances it signified healing and life; in other instances it was a portent of evil and death. Therefore, the precise meaning of the serpent symbol must be deduced from the context in which it appears. The Numbers text that is our first reading for today includes both the positive and negative aspects of the serpent symbol.

As is clear from its Hebrew title, "In the wilderness," the book of Numbers was primarily concerned with the wanderings of the Israelites from the region of Sinai to the plains of Moab. Moses and the people had camped near Sinai where they remained for an extended period, during which they developed a relative degree of social and religious organization. Eventually, they traveled northward to Canaan, and from Kadesh they tried to infiltrate the land but were thwarted in their attempt and returned to Kadesh where they remained for several years. From the geographical references in today's text, scholars have concluded that the incident, if historical, took place in the vicinity of Punion in the 'Arabah, one of the great copper sources in the 13th century B.C.E. Recent excavations in the region of the Punion mines have unearthed a small shrine that featured a bronze serpent. Similar discoveries have been made in the Lachish region whose serpentine artifacts date from the Late Bronze Age, approximately the same period as the exodus. These similarities have caused some to dismiss the incident depicted in Numbers as an example of the vestiges of sympathetic magic. However, as is evident in the text derived from both Yahwist and Eloist sources, the serpent was not a magical or mythical figure with powers of its own but a sign of the Lord's power to heal and care for his people. The God who could punish his people for their ungrateful complaints with the sting of the seraph (*sarap* = fiery) serpents has also the power to heal and to restore them.

Many scholars also recognize an apologetic feature in the incident. As R. de Vaux observed, the Numbers pericope was clearly connected to the circumstances of 2 Kings 18:4 where Hezekiah smashed the bronze serpent Moses had made because the Israelites had begun to worship it under the name of Nehushtan. There can be no doubt, said R. de Vaux, that this serpent to which the Israelites offered sacrifices in Jerusalem was a Canaanite cultic object which Israel had borrowed but which they claimed could be traced originally to Moses. H.H. Rowley agreed with R. de Vaux that the story in Numbers 21:4-9 may have been invented to substantiate the fact that the serpent was correctly ascribed to Moses. This is a real possibility since the final editing of the book of Numbers was done by the priestly authors in the sixth century B.C.E.

Whatever the derivations and original significance of the serpent story in Numbers, the key to its primary importance lay, not necessarily in the ancient tradition but in the type that the figure of the serpent became. An ambivalent symbol with evil and good connotations, the raised serpent and the healing effect of God's power upon his people became the type of the cross. Also an ambivalent sign, the cross embraced the contradiction of a suffering that healed and a death that brought life.

Philippians 2:6-11. Paul quoted this early Christian hymn to the community at Philippi in an effort to illustrate the ideal of charity that should characterize the followers of Jesus. In the example of Jesus' self-emptying, the Christians were to find their model for that selfless love and faith that would bind them to one another as a community.

Paul founded the church at Philippi during his second missionary journey. Along with Silas, Paul traveled to Philippi in response to a dream (special revelation) and was the first to bring Christ to the European continent (Acts 16:9-12). Philippians, is one of the captivity letters, but recent scholarship has put forth a reasonable case for an Ephesus incarceration and origin for the letter to Philippi. Though the letter is one of the least doctrinal of the Pauline compositions, nevertheless, a wealth of theology is contained in the hymn that comprises today's second reading. J.L. McKenzie describes it as a monument of primitive Christian faith. The six strophes contain the following theological elements: (1) the divine preexistence of Christ, (2) the incarnation, (3) the saving death of Jesus, (4) the exaltation of Christ, (5) the praise of the cosmos for Christ, (6) the new name of the risen glorified Lord.

Besides being a magnificent theological composition, the hymn illustrates its soteriology by the very arrangement of the strophes. Characteristically structured by its pre-Pauline author, the hymn's downward thrust is perfectly balanced by an upward elan. In a movement of descent the divine, preexistent Lord, who shared the same *morphe* (substantive form) as the Father, emptied himself. Forgoing the rights and dignity of divinity, he became man. *Kenosis* or self-emptying implied a purposeful, positive and voluntary renunciation. Paul understood the incarnation and its culmination on the cross as the most eloquent expression of Jesus' *kenosis*, a divine selflessness to be emulated by all believers.

Having accepted and endured the ignominy of the cross, Jesus was then exalted. The upward movement of Jesus' victory and his adoration by the entire cosmos resulted in his being given a name above all others, i.e., being acknowledged as the almighty God (Exodus 3:14). If the motions of the hymn were to be graphed geometrically, the downward and upward movements would form a perfect parabola. At the point of convergence is the cross, sign of contradiction, emblem of our salvation.

In the motion of the hymn, the reader is also reminded of the Isaian text: "The word, that goes forth from my mouth, does not return to me empty without carrying out my will and succeeding in what it is meant to do" (Isaiah 55:11). Christ is the word of our salvation, spoken into time and space; Christ is the word whose message reached into the depths of human sin on the cross and returned to the Father after his sacrifice had spoken the fullness of salvation for all peoples. This excellent hymn of the ancient church proclaims the mission of Christ and the contradiction of the cross.

John 3:14-21. Given the task of mapping out a plan for salvation and given free rein concerning the strategy we might choose, it is unlikely that many (or any) of us would opt for the cross as the means of accomplishing our purpose. Nevertheless, the cross with its inherent mystery and contradictions was the means by which Jesus effected the redemption and reconciliation of all peoples. As they grappled with the seeming scandal of the cross and the fact that Jesus received a criminal's sentence, the early believers looked to their traditions and drew upon the scriptures for support and understanding. By citing texts like the one from Numbers 21 (first reading), Christian authors were able to explain the difficult events that preceded Jesus' resurrection (his passion and death) as an integral and necessary part of God's foreordained plan of salvation.

In order to illustrate the mystery of God's saving action in Jesus, the fourth evangelist referred to the wilderness period in Israel's history. Stricken by fiery serpents for their impatient grumbling against Moses and against God, the Israelites begged Moses to act as their intercessor. As a result of his mediation, the people were instructed to look upon the bronze serpent Moses was to lift up. As a result of this action, the people were healed (Numbers 21:6-9). Centuries later, the author of the book of Wisdom (16:6-7) referred to the bronze serpent Moses had made as *symbolon soterias*, a symbol of salvation. When the Johannine author sought to explain the mystery of Jesus' saving action, he drew upon the actions of "lifting up" and "looking upon" (the bronze serpent) as having soteriological and typical (type) significance.

An excerpt from the discourse following the Nicodemus episode, today's gospel pericope is concerned with the necessity of being born again in water and the Spirit as a prerequisite for eternal life. In this discourse, the evangelist explained that rebirth in water and the Spirit, as well as the joys of eternal life, are possible only because of the "lifting up" of Jesus. *Hyposothenai* (lifted up), like so many of the words in the Johannine vocabulary, has a double meaning. Besides referring to the "lifting up" of Jesus on the cross (8:28; 12:32), it also pertains to the resurrection and exalted "lifting up" of Jesus in glory. Undoubtedly, the evangelist wished his readers to recall the Isaian suffering servant: "Behold my servant shall prosper; he shall be lifted up (*hypsoun*) and glorified exceedingly" (Isaiah 53:13). As a consequence of the servant's suffering, many were healed by "looking upon," i.e., by believing in God's power as symbolized in the bronze serpent. So also would believers in Jesus be healed and saved by the "lifting up" of the crucified, risen Lord. As a result of their looking upon, i.e., their belief in the crucified-exalted one, the faithful would be granted life in him, i.e., a share in the same process of death-to-life exaltation (v. 15).

As the motivating factor for the suffering and exaltation of Jesus, the evangelist cited the overwhelming love of God: "For God so loved the world that he gave his only Son" (3:16). In describing God's giving (*didonai*) of the Son, the Johannine author once again employed a word with double significance. That God "gave" his only Son referred not only to the incarnation but also to the sacrifice of the cross. With echoes of the Isaac story (in Genesis 22:2, 16) as well as the Isaian servant song (Isaiah 53:12), the evangelist plumbed the depths of the Father's love. "Sent" (v. 17) is to be understood as parallel to "gave" (v. 16) and implies the missionary aspect of Jesus' saving activities that began with the incarnation and culminated on the cross. The loving gesture whereby God sent his Son among human beings was a word of redemption but also a word of judgment. The one who believed in the Son and accepted the Father's love would be saved. But those who chose to reject the Son and, with him, the Father's love thereby wrought their own condemnation (vv. 17, 18).

Nicodemus had come to Jesus by night (John 3:2). A Pharisee and a member of the Sanhedrin, he may have been reluctant to approach Jesus in the light of day when his actions would be known by all. He had come to Jesus also in a condition of darkness as regards the truth of salvation. As a result of his encounter with the Lord, Nicodemus learned the lessons of light and life. From the darkness and obscurity of ignorance and sin, Nicodemus was challenged to "look up" and see the light of salvation in the mystery of the cross. For Nicodemus and for all who will embrace the conundrum of the cross in faith and hope, the promise of rebirth and triumph will be fulfilled.

1. Chastisement and healing are integral to the process of reconciliation (Numbers).

2. Jesus' total gift of himself in the incarnation and on the cross is the ideal of that altruistic love that creates and builds community (Philippians).

3. By virtue of the unlikely strategem of Jesus' ignominious death on the cross, all peoples are blessed with life (John).

Solemnity of All Saints

Saints are ordinary people who have an uncommon talent for doing ordinary things extraordinarily well. Saints come in all colors, shapes and sizes; they speak different languages but all their voices blend into one song as they join to praise the one from whom their greatness comes (Revelation). Saints have an uncanny ability for recognizing the Lord even in the darkest night (1 John) because they have learned the secrets of the kingdom, viz., that true riches are found only by the poor, that only the lowly will achieve lasting honor, and that there is no persecution greater than heaven's reward (Matthew).

Revelation 7:2-4, 9-14. Immediately following the vision of the Day of Wrath (6:12-17) and interpolated between the breaking of the sixth and seventh seals, the prophet John recounted two (7:1-8, 9-11) visions, both of which portrayed the salvation of the just. Our first reading for today is a composite of two excerpts, one from each of the two visions. According to J.L. D'Aragon, the purpose of these two visions was to contrast the church, glorious and protected by God, with the inhabitants of the earth who are seized with panic at the approaching judgment (6:15-17).

In the first vision, John saw the people of God on earth (or the church militant) placed under divine protection against coming adversity. The second vision was intended to encourage the faithful to persevere even unto death. Entrusted by God with his seal (v. 2), an angel came to God's people from the east. Traditionally, the east was thought to be the direction from which the messiah would come; it was also considered to be the birthplace of the sun and the location of Eden (Genesis 2:8).

In the ancient world, seals were used as a means of identifying property. An item affixed with the seal of the king was regarded as an extension of his person and authority; therefore, the seal afforded the ruler's protection to what was sealed. In John's vision, the seal belonged to the living God; those sealed belonged to God and were under his protection (see also 2 Corinthians 1:22, Galatians 6:17, Ephesians 1:13).

For those who endured the tribulation (persecution under Domitian, 81-96 C.E.), the seer painted a hopeful future, rich in Old Testament imagery. The 144,000 from every nation signified the fullness and universality of God's salvation. Twelve, a perfect number multiplied by 12 and by a thousand, did not indicate a *specific* and/or a *limited* number but a vast multitude whose ethnic diversity included *all* the faithful.

Dressed in white robes, the faithful celebrated the victory they enjoyed because of the lamb. Their garments symbolized their inner attitude and moral disposition; repentant and forgiven, the exultant throng had shed the scarlet robes of sinfulness (Isaiah 1:18), had been washed in Jesus' blood (v. 14) through baptism and had been clothed in his forgiveness and victory.

It should be noted that the white robes and their moral significance were not a *consequence* of eschatological glory but a *condition* of entering into it. A symbol of baptismal initiation as well as the daily process of conversion to Christ, the white robe could be thought of as the survivor's work uniform.

1 John 3:1-3. In his excellent commentary on the epistles of John (Anchor Bible, volume 30), R.E. Brown proposes that this literature presents the modern reader with "the life-and-death struggle" experienced by the late first century Christian community. At the heart of this struggle were two conflicting interpretations of the Johannine community's tradition, known to us as the gospel of John.

Evidently, two groups formed within the community, one of which eventually seceded from the church (1 John 2:19). The two groups disagreed about the importance and role of Jesus, about the ethical demands of Christian living, about the Spirit and eschatology. Those who seceded did not acknowledge the incarnation and, although they claimed to enjoy a union with God, they did not reflect this union in deeds of love for one another (2:9-11, 3:10-24, 4:7-21). In an effort to combat the secessionists (whom he called "Antichrists"), the author of 1 John repeatedly offered his contemporaries criteria for recognizing and refuting their errors.

In today's pericope, the author called his readers to an awareness of the gifts God had already lavished on them and to a hope in even greater gifts yet to come.

The reference to the "world" that did not recognize the believers (or the Son) was, no doubt, directed at the secessionists who considered themselves *above* the demands of ethical living. According to the secessionists, their *initial* contact with Christ made them pure and perfect, hence there was no need for daily striving or hope in a better future.

Unlike the secessionists who distorted the Johannine tradition of realized eschatology, the author of 1 John understood eschatology as a process that has begun but is not yet completed. He expressed this in terms of sonship as a present reality ("children of God . . . that in fact is what *we are*," v. 1) that will continue to grow toward an eschatological fulfillment ("what we shall later be has *not yet* come to light," v. 2).

With Paul, the author of 1 John shared the conviction that believers who enjoy a present status as God's children are growing in Christ into that perfect union that Christ shares with the Father: "We shall be like him" (v. 2).

Possessing this vision, the Christian will then be truly like Christ, sharing in his unique relation to the Father (see also 1 Corinthians 13:12, 2 Corinthians 3:18). Later Jewish tradition shared a similar hope in a glorious future: "In this world Israelites cleave to the Holy One, but in the time to come, they will become like him" and "When the children of Israel see God in the world to come, they will become saints" (Pesiqta Rabbati 11.7, Midrash on Psalm 149). Today, on this Feast of All Saints, we celebrate the present process and the future realization of our sainthood.

Matthew 5:1-12. "Some have found in it a pernicious document which has wrought incalculable harm by presenting an utterly impossible ethic. Others have found in it the finest statement of the highest morality that mankind has known." In this comment, W.D. Davies attested to the wide range of conflicting opinions stirred up by the profoundly Christian statement that has come to be known as the sermon on the mount (Matthew 5-7).

Today's gospel comprises the beginning of the great sermon, a catalog of those ideals which could be called the "bill of rights" of the new Israel. Traditionally called the beatitudes, those ideals not only *delineate membership* in the kingdom (poor in spirit, sorrowing, lowly, hungry, thirsty, persecuted, etc.) but they also describe the *ethic* whereby such membership can be attained (showing mercy, peacemaking, persecution for holiness' sake, etc.). Unlike Luke, who set the scene for this teaching of Jesus on a plain (Luke 6:17-26), Matthew drew upon Old Testament symbolism and portrayed Jesus on a mountain. Just as Moses on Sinai received the law for Israel, so Jesus put forth the normative guide for the new Israel. But, where Moses functioned as a *mediator* of the law and functioned with an authority derived from God, Jesus taught and interpreted the law from the basis of his *own* authority ("You have heard the commandment. . .but *I* say to you"). The formal expression, "He opened his mouth and taught them" (literal translation of v. 2) as well as Jesus' seated position (v. 1), were literary indicators of Jesus' magisterial authority.

The first four beatitudes pertained to the unfortunate ones, viz., the lowly and humble of the earth who are without influence or means. These were the spiritual descendants of Israel's poor ones or the *anawim* praised by the prophets, Isaiah and Zephaniah. These poor ones who relied completely and trustingly upon Yahweh constituted the surviving remnant of the people of the old covenant. Similarly, the poor ones who would place all their faith and trust in Jesus would be the inheritors of the new covenant.

The final four beatitudes described those who dedicate themselves to the causes of justice and peace on the earth; these are the architects of the kingdom. The attitudes and spiritual postures of the first four beatitudes make possible the activities of the last four. During his ministry, Jesus epitomized in his person and in his message each and all of the ideals put forth in the beatitudes.

By the time Matthew wrote his gospel in the 80s C.E. and formulated the beatitudes from the sources available to him (Mark, Quelle, Matthew), Jesus' followers were experiencing firsthand the challenge of those same ideals. Barred from the synagogues, persecuted by Rome and official Judaism, Christians had become like a people without a nation, a nation without a land.

To these hungry and thirsty architects of Jesus' eternal kingdom, the beatitudes offered comfort and encouragement. Though poor, they had found the lasting treasure of salvation; though sorrowful and lowly, they looked forward to a share in glory; though persecuted, they knew they shared in a victory over sin and death that could never be taken away from them. Today on this Feast of All Saints, the church celebrates all those who, by faith, make the "impossible" challenge of the beatitudes a lived reality.

1. In the eternal kingdom, there are no nationalities, no distinctions among races or ideologies or religions . . . imagine that! (Revelation)

2. Just as children begin to discover who they are by looking at their parents, so must believers find themselves in Jesus (1 John).

3. Those who have discovered the "value" in lowliness, in hunger, thirst and persecution will recognize the Lord when he appears again (Matthew).

All Souls

Salvation is not an end-of-the-world or an out-of-the-body experience. To be saved is to grasp the grace-filled gift of life held out to us by the Father in Jesus (John). Salvation consists in living here and now the joyful communion with God and with one another that will be consummated in heaven (Isaiah). Once initiated into the process of salvation by faith, the believer grows, suffers, serves, dies and lives with the Lord Jesus Christ (Romans).

Isaiah 25:6, 7-9. Visions of a glorious and joyful future were often incorporated into the religious literature of ancient Israel. At those moments in its development when the future seemed most bleak, those visions provided the hope and encouragement necessary for continued survival. An example of such a vision, today's first reading is from a longer section (chapters 24-27) in the book of Isaiah that has been labeled by some scholars as the "little" or the "Isaian Apocalypse" (Duhm, Procksch, Marti, Gray). Other scholars (R. Scott, etc.) reject an *apocalyptic* designation and regard chapters 24-27 of Isaiah as an example of eschatological prophecy interspersed with psalms and prayers. Dating from the post- exilic period in Israel and later appended to the rest of the prophet's work, these four chapters *do* nevertheless contain certain motifs similar to those found in apocalyptic literature, viz., universal judgment, portents in the heavens, messianic banquet, the resurrection of the dead at the end of time, etc. Missing, however, are the typically apocalyptic numerical symbols, beasts, cataclysms of nature, etc.

One of the classic symbols of eschatological prophecy, a motif that became closely associated with messianic expectation, was that of the *great banquet*. A consummate celebration of God's blessing for his people and the climax of his saving purpose, the great feast was universal in scope, bringing together all nations. Banished forever would be the enemies of God's people. At the feast, a new era of peace and salvation would be inaugurated to last for all eternity. Because of the many similarities between the Israelite motif of the great feast and the mythology of northern Canaan, it is probable that the Jewish literature represents an adaptation of the pagan myths.

As R. Scott has pointed out, it is hardly accidental that the destroying of death (literally: swallowing up of death; Hebrew: *maweth, moth,* v. 8) is paralleled in the Canaanite myth of Baal's victory over Mot, the god of death and the underworld. Likewise, the destruction of the veil and the wiping away of all tears (v. 7) correspond to similar ideas in the Canaanite poem of Baal. However, the discovery of antecedents in mythological language and ideas to this (or other) biblical texts does not in any way diminish their value as expressions of Hebrew faith. In the Isaian adaptation of the text, the prophet reflected the deep conviction that the Lord Yahweh, not Baal or any other god, was the all powerful and unequaled savior of his people.

Notice the special locus of the eschatological feast, viz., the mountain (v. 6). A very important geographical site throughout the ancient world, the mountain also figured very *prominently* in the religious development of Israel. It was on the mountain called Sinai (or Horeb) that God initiated the covenant-relationship with his people (Exodus 19:24); on the mountain, God communed with Moses (Exodus 19:3, 10; 24:9). On the heights of a mountain, God showed himself a creator and redeemer (Exodus 19:16, 18) and as one who desired the truthful sacrifice of the heart, not human sacrifice

(Genesis 22). The Jewish scriptures are replete with references to the mountain as the sacred abode of God (Exodus 3:1; Deuteronomy 11:29; Joshua 8:30; 2 Kings 4:25; Isaiah 2:2, 8:18; Ezekiel 28:14; Psalms 68:16, 84:5).

In the Christian scriptures as well, mountains played a significant role. While Jesus made it clear that God was not to be relegated to any *particular* mountain (John 4:2-24), mountains were the locus of special revelation (Matthew 5:1—7:29), of prayer (Matthew 14:23, 6:46; Luke 6:12, 9:28; John 6:15). On a mountain, Jesus experienced the struggles of temptation (Matthew 4:8) and allowed his followers to glimpse his glory (Mark 9:2, Acts 1:9-12). Given these historical references and religious associations, it is not surprising that the eschatological feast for all peoples was to be celebrated on a *mountain*.

Besides the obvious joy that would come from being in God's presence, the great feast also marked the end of all suffering and the reproach (v. 7) of God's people. In its original context, the "reproach" that the author and his contemporaries experienced may have referred to Babylon or Moab. But when these same verses were repeated by the first century Christian author of Revelation (21:4), they were understood in a new light. Through his death and by his rising, Christ had made good on all of God's promises. From the moment of redemption, the real joy of the banquet would endure and the special symbolism of the mountain become a reality for all peoples forever.

Romans 6:3-9. When Martin Luther was tempted to leave the challenges of faith and the Christian life unanswered, he reminded himself, *Baptizatus sum*. When Paul wrote to the Christians at Rome he reminded them of the same fact, that they had each been baptized into Christ Jesus. By virtue of their baptism, therefore, believers were called to live differently than they had before receiving the sacrament. Baptism, because it effected a solidarity with Christ and with the Father in whom all holiness abounds, requires that the baptized believer break with sin (v. 6). However, as anyone can attest, the mere fact of being baptized does not ipso facto eradicate sin as an entity from the world. Sinlessness is not an effect of justification; rather, sinlessness becomes an *attainable goal* when a person has been justified by God. Through baptism, and by virtue of the gift of grace it imparts (sanctifying grace), the task of becoming holy and of sanctifying daily life becomes a possibility. Since this is a task that requires constant effort and in which the believer can and does fail, the believer must cultivate a deep faith and responsiveness to God's grace-filled gifts.

When Paul exhorted the Roman church toward that deeper faith and responsiveness, he drew upon the symbolic meaning of the ceremonies performed in baptism. In the early church, those to be initiated into the life of Christ through baptism were immersed in the baptismal waters. Paul referred to this *descent* into the waters when he reminded the Roman Christians that they had been *buried* with Christ; they had been baptized into his death (v. 4). Because of incorporation into Christ's death, the attitude of believers must be that of Christ, i.e., dead to sin and to its effects. The Greek verb *baptizein* means to plunge into; hence, the catechumens were plunged into or incorporated into the total saving mystery of Christ. As they emerged from the baptismal waters, Christians rose with Christ to a new life. Through Christ's redeeming work, the transition from death to life and slavery to freedom had been accomplished. For the baptized believer, the maintenance of this transition is part of the constant struggle of life in Christ.

As R. Fuller has pointed out, all the verbs in today's pericope that speak of dying with Christ are in the past tense, whereas those that speak of rising with Christ are in the conditional future tense and depend upon moral choices. But these choices are made attainable by the solidarity with Christ that baptism effects. Five times (vv. 3-6) in today's text, Paul affirms the union of the believer *with Christ*. Being with Christ, the believer lives together with Christ. *Symphytoi* (vv. 5-7, lives or grows together, v. 8) refers to a young branch grafted onto a tree and nourished by the main stock. With this vivid image Paul reminded the Romans, and all who believe, of the new life *in Christ* that begins at baptism and that will be enjoyed for all eternity.

John 6:37-40. When John wrote his gospel in the last decade of the first Christian century, he reflected in it the developing awareness of the community with regards to eschatological fulfillment. In general, the biblical authors (including the authors of the synoptic gospels) had a "linear" or "horizontal" perception of salvation. Throughout the pages of the scriptures, the reader can trace God's interventions into human history; through history God guided the course of humanity to a salvific climax. But in the fourth gospel, there is *another* view or perception of God's salvific action as well. According to R.E. Brown, the Johannine "vertical" view conceives of two coexistent worlds, one heavenly, the other earthly. The earthly world is but a shadow of the heavenly. Earthly existence is a fallen existence; therefore, human history is a prolongation of meaninglessness. Salvation comes through entrance into the heavenly world but this is made possible only when someone or something comes down out of the heavenly world to free humanity from earthly existence. In John's gospel, the Son of God came down from heaven (John 3:13) and became incarnate, a part of human, earthly existence (John 1:14). Because of this loving intervention and the redemption of humanity in which it culminated, Jesus brought into this world an experience of the heavenly or eternal world.

While the other evangelists portrayed a Jesus who preached a *final,* apocalyptic eschatology (Mark 13, Luke 23, Matthew 25), the Johannine Jesus proclaimed the presence of the kingdom and its fullness (*basileia tou theou*) in his very person, by virtue of his words and works. C.H. Dodd (et al.) described this presence of the reign of God in the ministry of Jesus as *realized eschatology.* The synoptics stressed a *final* intervention and judgment wherein the good would be separated from the bad (weeds from wheat, goats from sheep, etc.) but the fourth gospel understood Jesus' presence in the world as *already* provoking a judgment. As the light of the world separated children of the light from children of the darkness, Jesus' very existence created a "crisis" situation. Crisis, from the Greek *krisis,* in its root sense, means "judgment." Those who accepted Jesus in faith were saved but those who refused to believe wrought judgment upon themselves (John 3:18) and thereby forfeited the joy of eternal life.

As R.E. Brown has pointed out, the synoptics saw eternal life as something one receives at the final judgment or in a future age (Mark 10:30, Matthew 28:8-9), but for John it is a present possibility: "The one who hears my words and has faith in him who sent me *possesses* eternal life . . . that one *has passed* from death to life!" (John 5:24). For Luke (6:35, 20:36) divine sonship is a reward of the future life. For John (1:12) it is a gift granted here on earth. An awareness of the Johannine concept of realized eschatology helps us to understand the words of Jesus in today's gospel.

Set within the context of the lengthy "bread of life" discourse (John 6:25-59), today's gospel pericope stresses the necessity of believing in Jesus in order to have eternal life. According to the discourse, those who believe in Jesus accept to be fed by the revelation of his teaching and by his sacramental presence in the eucharistic bread. By so doing, believers have life in this world *and* on the last day (v. 40). In v. 37, Jesus promised that he would not reject anyone given to him by the Father. This is the same expression the synoptics used in the context of final judgment when people will be rejected or driven out of the kingdom (Matthew 8:8-12, 22:13). Although the context in John 6:37 is initially one of *realized* eschatology, there *is* also in the pericope (*and* in the Johannine gospel) an appreciation of final eschatology. Notice that v. 40 combines both elements: everyone who looks upon the Son and believes in him shall *have* eternal life; I *will* raise them up on the *last day.*

Some have suggested that this gospel text ("all that the Father gives me shall come to me," v. 37) reflects an element of predestination and as such has lent fuel to those who believe salvation is limited in its scope. Actually, it is an anachronism to draw such a psychological (and erroneous) reasoning from the gospel in order to explain why people do or do not believe. Again, as R.E. Brown has explained, the New Testament gives its explanation for this on a very simplified level. *All* happenings in the New Testament (and Old Testament) were attributed to divine causality without any sharp distinction between primary and secondary causality. Therefore, these verses do not support *or* resolve the disputes about predestination that have been the subject of theological debate since the Reformation. With all John's insistence on humanity's choosing between light and darkness, it would be nonsense to ask if the evangelist believed in human responsibility. Obviously he did. It would be just as nonsensical to *doubt* that John (like the other biblical authors) saw God's sovereign choice worked out in those who came to Jesus. Obviously, he did.

What, therefore, do John's insights into eschatology as a *realized* and *final* experience say to those who pray today for the faithful departed? Eternity with all its joys does not begin only at death. Rather, eternal life is a cumulative experience, afforded to humanity by virtue of the incarnation and begun when the life of faith in Jesus is initiated. In the word of God, through the sacraments, by indwelling presence in every believer, eternal life is tasted and enjoyed. Not "pie-in-the-sky-when-you-die," eternity is also an existential joy *and* responsibility.

1. Those who feed the hungry as well as those who are fed anticipate the joy and fulfillment of the coming kingdom (Isaiah).

2. Baptism is the first step of a lifelong journey toward the Lord (Romans).

3. For those who belong to Christ, the promise of eternal life is already being experienced (John).

Dedication of the Lateran Basilica

Massive pillars, golden altars and ornate windows may constitute a beautiful meeting place but only the faithful, whenever and wherever they gather, are church (1 Kings). In Jesus' name they are united, and in his Spirit and truth they can offer true praise to God (John). Within that holy gathering, all peoples become a family of faith—one holy, living, dwelling place for the Lord (Ephesians).

Oldest and first-ranked among the four great patriarchal basilicas of Rome, Saint John's was surnamed "Lateran" because it stands on the site occupied in ancient times by the palace of the family of the Laterani. During Constantine's reign as emperor, he gave the palace and its lands to the church, 311 C.E. A church council was first held at the Lateran in 313 C.E. Formerly a papal residence, Saint John is considered the cathedral of Rome and the mother church of Christendom. From the 12th century, November 9 has been observed as the anniversary of its dedication.

1 Kings 8:22-23, 27-30. Part of a much longer section in the first book of Kings concerned with the building and furnishing of the Solomonic temple, today's first reading is from the section of the temple's dedication. While there is an historical basis for the account, the text has been extensively expanded by the Deuteronomic author and other editors after the exile.

During a two-week period of dedication at which Israel's leaders hosted an enormous group of guests including foreign dignitaries, the ark of the covenant was ceremoniously carried to the temple. Acknowledging God's abiding presence with his people, Solomon stressed the continued presence of the Lord now symbolized by the temple. In v. 23, the Deuteronomic teaching on reciprocity was invoked; Solomon acknowledged that God would keep in covenant and bless his people as long as they continued to walk in his ways. It is significant that, even at this very early stage in her relationship with Yahweh, Israel had an awareness of his transcendence and omnipresence. On the lips of Solomon, in vv. 27-30, the Deuteronomic author acknowledged the fact that God did not need, nor was he to be thought of as *contained* within, the temple precincts. God could not be limited even by the highest heavens; yet he, of his own loving volition, had deigned to draw near to his people. Therefore, when they gathered for prayer, they could petition God in complete confidence.

Beginning during the monarchy in the tenth century B.C.E. and until 70 C.E., the temple was the major site of Israel's sacrificial worship and the center of socio-political life of the people. In actual fact, there were *three* temples during this millennium; the first was built during the reign of David's son, Solomon. The decision to build the temple coincided with the formation of the monarchy and the emergence of Israel, for the only time in its political career, as a power that was not only independent but *the* dominant force in the area. For almost a century, the dominance continued and this period (10th century—9th century) could well be labeled Israel's golden age. The construction of the temple, as the visible symbol of God's presence among his people, was a most effective way for the leaders of the country to communicate (in the days before mass literacy and broadcast media) the fact that God blessed and favored the political organization that was being established. It may be said that the temple added an essential note of absolute legitimacy to the monarchy (*Harper's Bible Dictionary*, C. Meyers).

After the Babylonians devastated the land and decimated the population (586 B.C.E.), Israel's temple lay in ruins for about 70 years. Work on the second temple, also called the Zerubbabel temple (because Zerubbabel was the chief political officer in what became the Persian subprovince of Judah at the time of its reconstruction), began in 520 B.C.E. Although the restored temple was a crucial aspect of Israel's continuity, radical changes had taken place since the Babylonian conquest. Without a king to sit on David's throne (the Persians appointed governors), the legitimizing role of the temple in national life had shifted to the priests and the Torah became the central focus and guide of religious and social life.

After the Greeks (ca. 325 B.C.E.) and Romans (ca. 63 B.C.E.) desecrated and robbed the temple, another reconstruction and enlargement of the temple was begun by Herod the Great who reigned from 37 B.C.E. to 4 C.E. More is known with certainty about this temple than any of the others because Herod's efforts were documented by extra-biblical historians (e.g., Josephus in the first century C.E.). Because Herod was descended of an Idumean and was not a full-blooded Jew, he was regarded as a usurper to the throne. For that reason he hoped that his work on the temple would win over the dissidents among his people and cement his authority. When the Roman legions led by Titus destroyed Herod's temple in 70 C.E., Israel saw the end of that period in her history. Today, upon the ancient temple site, the proponents of Islam worship Allah in the Mosque of Omar, also called the "Dome of the Rock."

Ephesians 2:19-22. Without a specific meeting place like a temple but with the awareness that Jesus Christ had in his person replaced the temple and its significance, Christians developed new analogies for identifying and understanding their cohesiveness. The term "church" was not an architectural concept evocative of a certain building; rather, for the early Christians church meant the body of believers called together in Jesus and bound together in faith.

Many of the early analogies for describing the community of the faithful have been attributed to Paul. Two of those symbols of unity, the household of God and the building, are included in today's second reading, an excerpt from the letter to the Ephesians. The letter rejoiced in the graciousness of God's plan of salvation that *included* all peoples. Unlike the former tradition that rejected gentiles as less than human and outside the scope of God's concern, Christians were called to look upon all peoples of every status as members of the same family or household. Also, unlike the situation in the Jewish temple where gentiles were separated from the chosen people, there would be no segregation of peoples in the new religion constituted in Jesus. In the verses (17-18) immediately preceding today's pericope, the Ephesians' author declared that the good news had been announced to those who were far off (gentiles) as well as to those who were near (Jews) and that in Christ all had been granted access to the Father.

With former alienation and inequity resolved in Christ, those who believed formed, as it were, a living building (v. 20). Because of this term, building (*oikodome*), some exegetes have proposed that the author referred specifically to the local church. But as J. Grassi has noted, *oikodome* also designates the *action* of building and can refer not only to a local church but to every work of edification. Moreover, the *living* nature of the "building" of the church has been expressed in the fact that it has been founded on the apostles and prophets. Probably, this foundation referred to the preaching and teaching of the good news (Ephesians 3:5, 4:11; Romans 12:6; 1 Corinthians 12:28).

The nature of the community as a living, growing organism is further stressed in the reference to Jesus Christ as the capstone. A better English rendering than the usual "cornerstone," capstone communicates a more accurate picture. Ancient architects who followed the Romanesque style of arch-building set the capstone (or foundation stone) in place *last* and at the center of the overhead arch. In that position the capstone crowned and completed their effort as it functioned to hold the entire edifice together. In this light, the statement in v. 21 is better understood: "Through him the whole structure is fitted together and takes shape." With Christ as the source of cohesiveness and viability, the community of believers becomes the dwelling place of God.

John 4:19-24. An excerpt from Jesus' conversation with the woman at the well and another aspect of John's developing theme of replacement theology, the teaching in today's gospel pericope was occasioned by a centuries-old disagreement. Although Jews and Samaritans had originally shared the same heritage, a rift between the two groups developed when the Jews of the conquered northern kingdom of Samaria intermarried with their Assyrian overlords (ca. 722 B.C.E.). Thereafter, the northern Jews, called Samaritans, were regarded as unclean outcasts by their southern brethren. Calling themselves Shamerim, i.e., observers of the Torah, the Samaritans regarded only the Pentateuch as valid and rejected the prophets and later writings. Samaritans claimed that *they* were the true descendants of the Joseph tribes of Israel and believed that Judaism was spawned by a heresy that could be traced to Eli at Shiloh. Rejecting the Jerusalem temple, its cult and priesthood, Samaritans worshiped on Mount Gerizim in a region known today as Nablus. Since the Jews believed that valid and true sacrificial worship could be offered only in their central sanctuary of Jerusalem, the dispute between the two groups remained unsettled.

When the Samaritan woman brought up the subject of which sanctuary was the valid one, she did so in order to shift the conversation away from herself. Jesus had displayed what the woman perceived as an uncanny insight into her personal life and, in particular, on the subject of her several marriages. Because of his perception, the woman acknowledged Jesus as a prophet, probably in the tradition of Deuteronomy 18:15-18. Like the Jews, the Samaritans anticipated the advent of a prophet like Moses. The Samaritans also expected their messiah, whom they called Ta'eb (the returning one), to restore proper worship and to vindicate Gerizim as the true sanctuary. When the woman referred to "our ancestors" (v. 20) worshiping on Gerizim, she referred to the altars set up by Abraham and Jacob (Genesis 12:7, 33:20) and particularly to that set up by Joshua on Mt. Ebal (Deuteronomy 27:4), transformed into Mt. *Gerizim* in the Samaritan Pentateuch.

Instead of engaging her in debate, Jesus made the woman aware that there was a far greater issue that deserved her attention. Indeed, the sanctuary dispute was soon to be totally irrelevant because it would be superceded by Jesus' revelation. "An hour is coming," Jesus told the woman, "when you will worship the Father neither on this mountain nor in Jerusalem" (v. 21). "Hour," without the article or a possessive did not *necessarily* mean Jesus' hour, but R.E. Brown says that this may well be the intended meaning here. "Hour," i.e., Jesus' hour, referred to his glorification and to his death on the cross and resurrection that comprised it. By virtue of Jesus' hour, God's salvation was extended to all peoples and the era of messianic liberation from sin and death was inaugurated.

Because of Jesus' hour of salvation and glorification, a new form of worship would be instituted, worship the Johannine Jesus described as worship in Spirit and truth. This worship in the Spirit and truth would be determined not by human means or geographical localization but by God himself who is Spirit (v. 24). To say that God is Spirit does not define God's immaterial essence, but is rather an expression of the *way* God deals with humanity. As lifegiver, God sends his Spirit into the hearts of the faithful, creating and re-creating them (John 3:5-8, 6:63, 7:38). Two other similar identifications in the Johannine literature (God is light: 1 John 1:5; God is love: 1 John 4:8) refer as well to the manner in which God acts among his people. The point the Johannine author wished to make was that the place of worship (vv. 20-21) was no longer important; but the *manner* of worship had to be consistent with the God who inspired it.

As R. Fuller has pointed out, this dialogue as well as the other dialogues and discourses in the Johannine gospel should not be regarded as actual transcripts of what the earthly Jesus said. While there was, no doubt, an original historical nucleus to the story (probably a pronouncement as to the imminence of the kingdom), the story as it has come down to us had been expanded to include various concerns of interest to the Johannine church. In general, the dialogue may be understood as an early Christian meditation on the meaning of Jesus for faith. In effect, Jesus is the one by whose hour salvation was effected. He is the one who knows and exposes sin yet he is also the one who forgives and liberates from sin. In Jesus, that true worship of God that transcends every other human approach was inaugurated. It is at once a worship in the Spirit and a way of praying that bursts the limitations of mortar and concrete to stand in truth before God himself.

1. Holy places are made holy by holy people (1 Kings).

2. A living edifice, the church is cemented together not by mortar and cement, but by the continuing and faithful witness of its prophets and apostles (Ephesians).

3. When ecumenical efforts finally reap their fruit, then, not one place but every place will be a holy sanctuary in which we will worship the Lord together (John).

Year B

The Advent Season
First Sunday of Advent

We keep careful vigil for the Lord who shall come again in glory. Our recognition of him will depend, in part, on our expectations. Shall he be judge? Vindicator? Shall he be Father? Redeemer? Creative potter (Isaiah)? Attentiveness to Jesus' advent requires, not a last minute rush to get ready but a progressive, grace-filled preparedness (1 Corinthians), marked by hope and celebrated by the joy with which we share in his mission (Mark).

Isaiah 63:16-17, 19; 64:1, 3-8. On this, the first Sunday of Advent and the beginning of a new liturgical year, the readings serve as a climax to the eschatological themes which have been growing in the last Sundays of the passing old year. In the subsequent Sundays of Advent, our attention will be turned to the incarnation. Hence Advent is a season wherein eschatology or the second advent dovetails with the incarnation or first advent of Jesus Christ.

Described as a jewel of Old Testament poetry, the pericope from Isaiah chosen for today's liturgy is from a longer psalm which sketches for us the morale of the exiles soon after their return from Babylon. Trito-Isaiah wrote in the period of sadness and disillusionment (536-520 B.C.E.) before the reformers Ezra and Nehemiah had begun to fan into flame the flickering hopes of their people.

Most scholars accept the work of Trito-Isaiah (chapters 56-66) as distinct from that of his predecessor Deutero-Isaiah, who wrote his "Book of Consolation" (chapters 40-55) during the exile in Babylon in order to sustain his fellow countrymen and women. Believed to be a disciple (or *disciples*) of Deutero-Isaiah, the author(s) of Trito-Isaiah echoes some of his master's optimism and doctrine (universalism, imminence of salvation, etc.) but for the most part the reader is aware that a curtain of somber frustration and desperation has fallen upon the scene. In Trito-Isaiah's emphasis on temple, fasting, law and Sabbath, there is evidence of a new and different spirituality emerging. Staggered by a sense of guilt and sin, post-exilic Israel was subject to ambivalent emotions. Happy to be home and relatively free (a Persian governor ruled Israel) yet frustrated in beginning the enormous process of reconstruction and reestablishment, many gave in to despair, thinking themselves deserted by God.

Confessing the sinfulness of his people, to which Trito-Isaiah attributed God's absence, he led his people in a community lament (63:7-64:11), hoping to move the God from whom they felt so distant. Comparing themselves and their sinful state to "polluted rags" and "withered leaves," the prophet underscored the helplessness of his people without God, as well as the futility and uselessness of even their good deeds. Calling upon God as their Father and redeemer, Trito-Isaiah begged for the Lord to exercise his *hesed*, the caring love he showered upon his people, because of the bloodbonds of their everlasting covenant. As their Father (63:16, 14:7) and redeemer, he had imparted to them life and, more importantly, his saving love which had sustained them in the desert. During the conquest, that love had guarded them from the onslaught of enemies and had assured their survival of the exile. In pleading for God's involvement and intervention on their behalf, the prophet begged that the Lord *return* and *remember* (*zakar*) his past deeds for his people. "Remembrance" here signifies, not merely a recalling to mind or to memory but a *making-present-once-again* of his redemptive fatherhood on behalf of his people.

The rigors and sufferings of the exile had taught Israel the lesson of the clay and the potter (v. 7) which Jeremiah had tried to impart almost a century before (Jeremiah 18). No longer brittle and unyielding, Israel had learned through the docility and suppleness needed to respond to the creativity of the redeeming potter. Israel's independence and self-sufficiency had mellowed into a healthy dependence and acknowledged need for God. For this reason, the experience of his "absence" and Israel's sense of his uninvolvement was all the more poignant.

1 Corinthians 1:3-9. In ancient times, before Rome's rise to power, Corinth had been an elegant and wealthy city. Cicero called it the "light of all Greece." Corinth's location, at the southern end of the isthmus that joined the Peloponnesus to the mainland, made it a center of commerce both by land and by sea. Accessible to merchant vessels via the Adriatic Sea on the west and the Aegean Sea on the east, Corinth played host to sailing ships from all over the then known world. Every other year during the spring, athletes from all over assembled there for the Isthmian games which were more important and more prestigious than even the Olympic games.

Amid the multiplicity of temples and schools, archaeologists have also unearthed more than 30 taverns and Corinth's reputation as a city of libertinism was well deserved. Indeed the city lent its name to a verb in Koine Greek, *korinthianzein*, which meant "to live like a Corinthian" or, more precisely, "to live a life of debauchery and flagrant excess." To be called a *kore korinthe* or Corinthian girl was equivalent to being labeled a prostitute. Aphrodite was the patron goddess of the city and the temple in her honor was purported to house over 1000 sacred prostitutes, called euphemistically priestesses of love.

Such were the circumstances Paul encountered when he arrived in Corinth on his second missionary journey. For 18 months he labored there, between 50 and 52 (Acts 18: 1-18) and, when he departed, he left behind an exuberant community whose heterogeneous nature reflected the city in which it flourished. Some of the factors that had contributed to Corinth's loose style of living (viz., being a port city and center of trade routes) also proved advantageous in the spread of Christianity and its good news. Knowing this, Paul made great efforts to firmly establish in Corinth a viable and strong community of believers. It is not surprising then that, when news of factions and internal strife within the community at Corinth reached Paul's ears, he wrote quickly and at length so as to correct the course of the straying members.

On the whole, 1 Corinthians provides us with a window through which to view the life of the early Christian community, less than a generation after the resurrection. In general, the letter can be divided into two major parts: (1) chapters 1-6, Paul's reaction to the news of the community and (2) chapters 7-15, Paul's projected solutions to the problems of the community.

Our text for today is part of the customary salutation that introduced all the New Testament letters. In it the apostle wishes for the recipients grace and peace from God the Father and from Jesus. Both grace and peace (*charis* and *eirene*) are used in the New Testament in a soteriological sense. Grace is the goodness and favor shown by God in bestowing upon humankind the gift of salvation in Jesus Christ. Peace is the wonderful fruit of that salvation, manifested in the forgiveness of sins, in reconciliation with God and in the harmonious solidarity among believers. Grace and peace were gifts which the Corinthian Christians as believers already enjoyed, hence Paul's greeting was simply an acknowledgment and a reminder of that fact. It is significant that Paul did not (as was his custom in his letters) commend the Corinthians for their love and charitable ways: It was these virtues which the community was lacking. In referring to their "waiting for the revelation of Jesus," i.e., the parousia, Paul's words belie the spirit of eager anticipation which characterized the early believers. The same avid longing and hope must be the hallmark of those who, like the Corinthians, still wait in hope for the second coming of the Lord of peace and grace.

Mark 13:33-37. Couched in the genre of the farewell discourse and shaped by apocalyptic images and symbols, chapter 13 of Mark's gospel is quite different in content, tone and presentation from the rest of his gospel. Within this chapter, two major themes are interwoven, that of the destruction of Jerusalem and that of the glorious and definitive return of Jesus as Son of Man. At times it is difficult to extricate one theme from the other, for the simple reason that, in Mark's day, it was believed the two events would occur simultaneously as part of the whole eschatological process of the advent of the parousia.

As is the case in all three of the synoptic apocalypses, the evangelist has gathered together independent parables and sayings of Jesus concerning eschatological realities and given these sayings a futuristic framework. In the parable which constitutes the gospel reading for today, the point of the entire apocalyptic composition (chapter 13) is made, viz., the importance of vigilance and preparedness. Vigilance was a posture of paramount importance to the early church whose members believed themselves living in the last days, on the precipice of eternity.

Although the parable of the gatekeeper has a simple and straightforward message (vigilance), nevertheless it is the product of a long and complex history. Even though Mark's is believed to be the earliest gospel, the parable shows evidence of secondary features, probably acquired in the process of oral transmission. At the basic level, that of Jesus' ministry, it was a crisis or challenging parable concerning the reaction of the people to Jesus, to his words and his works. Watchfulness and vigilance were necessary in order to recognize Jesus as master of the house, inaugurator of the kingdom and revelation of the Father.

To the disciples (v. 33), the parable's message was similar to Jesus' admonition in the garden of Gethsemane (14:38): "Watch, therefore, lest you fall into temptation." Jesus' warning explained that his very presence had set in motion the final *peirasmos* (eschatological tribulation) during which it was thought that Satan's forces would be on the prowl, seeking to overcome the saints (disciples) of God. To the crowds within Jesus' hearing, his words served to warn the wise against the coming calamities. To the scribes who were proud to be considered the "gatekeepers of heaven" (Matthew 23:13, Luke 11:52), the parable signalled their special responsibility for the rest of the community. Their "sharp eyes" should have been the first to recognize the truth in Jesus and to lead others to its light.

As the parable was filtered through the pastoral concerns of the early Christian community, secondary features were added to adapt it more readily to the needs of the growing body of believers. The additional feature about the master's being on a journey (Luke 12:35-38) may indicate the temporary absence of the ascended Jesus. Likewise, the master's return indicated the coming back of Jesus to his own at the parousia. By adding, "Putting the servants in charge, each with his own task" (v. 34) and "What I say to you I say to *all*" (v. 37), the evangelist enlarged the scope of the parable to apply to the entire community of believers. In joining these two elements of waiting wisely and watching vigilantly, Mark made of the original parable a lesson in how and what to do in the interim between Jesus' comings. Essentially the Marcan admonitions were the same as Paul's advice to the eager Thessalonians, viz., continue to work calmly (2 Thessalonians 3:6-15) while living in a spirit of expectation (1 Thessalonians 5:1-11).

1. Our God's involvement with his people is not a "deus ex machina" but the personal relationship of a loving Father (Isaiah).

2. Grace and peace are afforded us here and now that we might experience the joys of everlasting life and labor toward its advent (Corinthians).

3. Watchfulness, tempered, not with anxiety but with serenity, is the mark of a true believer (Mark).

Second Sunday of Advent

When humanity reaches its lowest ebb and hope seems impossible, the Lord of life and new beginnings reaches out to cradle the sinner in his loving forgiveness (Isaiah). With God's merciful gift of time, crooked ways can be mended and straightened (2 Peter). Hollow hearts can be filled with joyful welcome for the one who brings to the world God's own Spirit (Mark).

Isaiah 40:1-5, 9-11. Israel's exodus from Egypt—its wondrous liberation from its oppressors and its trek in the desert wherein they became a people, bonded in love and by law to Yahweh—became for the Jews a central experience through which all the other events of their history were filtered and understood. No wonder, then, that the prophet whom we call Deutero-Isaiah chose to describe the momentous occasion of Israel's restoration to its own land after years of bondage in Babylon, in terms of that first exodus event. Envisioning the return of his people as a *second* exodus, the prophet consoled his people with the knowledge that the miracles of God's power that marked their first exodus were to be repeated, viz., "the desert would become their highway," "the high mountains would witness their glad tidings," "God, their shepherd king would carry and lead them."

Aside from his contribution to typology, the prophet Deutero-Isaiah gave his contemporaries in exile in Babylon a means to interpret the events which had contributed to their downfall and a perspective of hope from which to view their future. After about a generation's time in exile, when it is believed the prophet's ministry was exercised, a faint glimmer of hope began to stir in the saddened hearts of the exiles. At first, their hope had its basis in political realities, i.e., Cyrus the Persian was rising rapidly to power and posed a threat to the continued dominance of Babylon. True to his mission as prophet-interpreter and mouthpiece of God, Deutero-Isaiah saw in this political event God's rescuing hand at work on behalf of his people. To this end he helped Israel interpret its history, not from a political but from a religious perspective, attributing its fall and subsequent disgrace in exile to its sinful and unfaithful ways. In the same way, he viewed Cyrus' rise to power as God's hand, using history to teach the lesson of his involvement and abiding concern for his people. While the prophet never consciously conceived of the figure of Jesus Christ and of his mission, Deutero-Isaiah's prophecies concerning restoration, new beginnings and imminent salvation provided the literary and spiritual framework within which the New Testament authors explained the reality of Jesus.

Our pericope for today is from the prologue (40:1-11) to Deutero-Isaiah's work (chapters 40-55) which announces to Israel its imminent homecoming. These verses represent the prophet's call and commissioning (as in Isaiah 6). Because of the plural verbs in the mandate (vv. 1-2), some scholars believe that God's decree was addressed to the company of heavenly angels, whom he sent to care for his people (Psalm 91:11). Others posit Deutero-Isaiah's selection from a group of prophets. Probably the better interpretation would be one which coincides with the biblical tradition of a heavenly court which witnessed and approved of the divine decrees (1 Kings 22:19-23, Job 1-2) as reflected in the earthly sphere.

Once mandated, the prophet's message was one of a new age for God's people, an era of restoration, reestablishment and reconciliation, inaugurated by the power of God's word. The same word whose creative power had accomplished the universe and all its wonders by a majestic "Let there be..." was now speaking to the heart of his people of a new beginning, a new life. Once reinstated in their own land, the people would see God's glory (v. 5).

2 Peter 3:8-14. As the interlude between promise and fulfillment yawned wider and wider, some of the early believers began to lose heart and to doubt that there would ever be a second advent of the Lord Jesus. To exacerbate the situation, there were a number of false teachers within the primitive communities who pointed to the extended delay as proof of their teaching that the parousia would never be realized. This situation prompted the author of 2 Peter to write the words that comprise our second reading today.

A pseudonymous work ascribed to Peter, the second letter of Peter reflects the circumstances and difficulties of a more developed organization of believers and, for this reason, most scholars assign it a date in the early or middle second century C.E. Probably the last written of the canonical New Testament documents, 2 Peter shows a marked correspondence to the letter of Jude (also a late document) and contains several clues regarding its post-apostolic setting, viz., (1) reference to the apostles in the past tense (3:2, 4), (2) reference to the letters of Paul as "scripture," a late development, (3:16), (3) evidence of gnosticism, a second century problem.

Addressed to the churches in Asia Minor, 2 Peter was written to support believers in the true faith and to counteract the work of the heretical and the unorthodox. In asserting the certainty of Christ's return, the author of 2 Peter sought to raise the level of expectation of his readers by explaining that time and waiting for divine realities cannot be measured by human conventions. "A thousand years are as a day in the Lord's eyes," he explained, and hence what humans perceive as delay and perhaps divine procrastination is in all truth an act of mercy. Second Peter interprets the interval between Jesus' appearances as time given for conversion, repentance and reconciliation. Therefore, he counsels, one must use the time wisely and well. In that way, when the Day *does* appear, we all shall be ready. Moreover, good deeds and holiness can hasten the advent of that glorious day. This advice was in direct contrast to that of the gnostic false teachers who saw no hope of judgment in the future and thus implicitly condoned immorality and hedonism.

With regard to 2 Peter's description of the end, one can detect therein the images and symbols that have traditionally lent themselves to popular opinion concerning the last days. Today's pericope is unique in all of scripture in its account of a final conflagration (v. 10), but this idea is not unique to Christianity. From Persia, the belief in total destruction by fire at the end of time had spread to the Greco-Roman world where it was a favorite topic of philosophers. Similar ideas are also found in Jewish apocalyptic. Such opinions are not scientific assertions but mythopoeic images. Some scholars suggest that *heurethesetai* (v. 10) should be rendered "will be laid bare" rather than "will be burned up." In any event, the author's point is clear, regardless of its mythic presentation, i.e., there will be a transformation of all creation at the Lord's second advent. To that end, Christians must become part of the process of transformation by moral and spiritual conversion, by living according to God's holiness as revealed in the words and mission of Jesus Christ.

Mark 1:1-8. Traditionally the Marcan gospel was thought to be an abbreviated version of Matthew's gospel, written in Rome by a Mark who functioned as Peter's secretary. Today, scholarly opinion is less stringent because it has been discovered that, not only did Mark's version antedate Matthew's, but the author of Mark was in his own way an eminent craftsman who developed the genre we today call "gospel." The most recent evidence reveals that Mark wrote his gospel before the fall of Jerusalem, probably in 63 or 64 C.E. for a gentile community in the Roman empire outside of Palestine. Moreover, Peter did not merely dictate the gospel to Mark, but may be regarded as its guarantor.

Because of Mark's emphasis on the suffering aspects of Jesus' mission and of those who would call themselves Jesus' disciples (8:34-36; 9:42-47; 10:35-45; 10:17-31), his gospel has been called an extended passion narrative with an introduction and a conclusion. One of Mark's most noted features is the concept of the messianic secret, a literary device the evangelist employed to explain why Jesus was not hailed as messiah until after the resurrection.

Concerned with revealing the person of Jesus Christ, Son of God, his authority, power and mission, Mark states his purpose in his first line (1:1) and unfolds the meaning of that declaration for the rest of the gospel. As herald of Jesus' person and power, John the Baptist is featured in our text today and in next Sunday's gospel as well. Leaving no doubt as to the differences between John and Jesus, Mark, like the other evangelists, portrays John as secondary and subordinate, with an introductory and temporary role. Mark's statement of the theme of John's preaching (v. 7) is drawn from an ancient Egyptian court hieroglyph wherein a slave is portrayed as the bearer of Pharaoh's sandal. John's humble profession not only enunciates the enormous distinction between Jesus and himself but serves also to quell a problem that existed in Christianity's early decades. Some misguided believers thought that John the Baptizer had been the messiah and sought to gain proselytes from among Jesus' followers. All four gospels are adamant in clarifying the truth in this matter.

What Mark quotes as an Isaian text is in fact a melange of three Old Testament texts (Exodus 23:20, Malachi 3:1, Isaiah 40:3) which had in their respective contexts referred to the exodus, the exile and the return. By drawing all three of these momentous events together to herald the advent of Jesus and his mission, Mark succeeds in portraying Jesus as the fulfillment of all these Jewish hopes. As messenger, the "way" which John has been mandated to prepare is not to be understood in the geographical, topographical sense but in the *moral* sense of a new way of life. John's preaching of judgment, repentance and forgiveness of sin challenged his listeners to turn to the Lord and to rethink their way of life. Later, during his ministry, Jesus would declare himself to be *the way* (John 14:6, Hebrews 10:20), i.e., the path of life that leads to the Father. Still later, those who had answered Jesus' call and had modeled their lives on his, would be called *the way* (Acts 9:2; 19:9, 23).

As an external sign of their interior moral cleansing, John baptized his followers but even this act is placed in a subordinate position to the baptism of the Holy Spirit Jesus would bring. Just as the first Israel had learned of God by her passing through the waters of the Reed Sea and in the desert, so too the new Israel, the new people of God, were first to learn of him in John's baptism and in his wilderness preaching. It is difficult to determine whence John derived his practice of baptizing. Dead Sea scroll findings reveal that in the Qumran community baptism as a ritual purification was practiced daily and in private, but this baptism was nor considered a sign of conversion, not was it a part of initiation into the community. Perhaps John's baptism was more similar to the Jewish practices of baptizing proselytes or baptizing as a sign of renewal (2 Kings 5:14).

Mark's description of John's clothing and food (v. 6) are reminiscent of those of Elijah and may indicate the evangelist's desire to cast John in the role of prophet. But Mark was probably also attempting to serve the legend, popular in his day, that Elijah would return to announce the day of the messiah. The Baptizer's diet of locusts (grasshoppers) and wild honey may not seem delectable to modern palates but to Mark's listeners these foods were the traditional symbols of judgment and comfort. Locusts in the Old Testament were regarded as the Lord's instruments of judgment since they were agents of bitter and punishing destruction (Exodus 10:4, Psalm 105:34, Isaiah 33:4). Honey, on the other hand, signified peace and plenty and was a symbol of God's comfort and reward (Exodus 3:8, Deuteronomy 6:3). Locusts and honey were mentioned by the evangelist, not merely to describe John's menu but to announce the double nature of the gospel, to which the Baptizer acted as forerunner. Like the locusts, the gospel would judge between people; and like the honey, Jesus' words and works would bring peace and comfort to the just.

1. When the burden of sin crushes the spirit, comfort, not scorn, will bring new hope (Isaiah).

2. Waiting time is not wasted time if each day is regarded as a gift of God's patience and is used to turn more fully to his goodness (2 Peter).

3. Those who would prepare others to recognize the Lord must first become a clear and straightened path (Mark).

Third Sunday of Advent

When all the spirited have prophesied, when the healers have soothed all the pain, when all the chained are unfettered, when all the naked and shamed are clothed with justice and dignity (Isaiah), one will come in whom hope and healing, freedom and salvation will find their true and full meaning (John). He is the one for whom we wait in joy (Thessalonians).

Isaiah 61:1-2, 10-11. When the prophet exclaimed this message to his people, he was probably standing in the midst of the ruins that had once been Jerusalem. So joyful and exuberant is his proclamation that it is hard to imagine the sad and desperate context in which it was uttered. Our pericope is comprised of the introductory and concluding verses of the prophet's poem, while the intervening verses (3-9) actually reveal its historical situation.

One of the most beautiful and well known passages from Trito-Isaiah, today's verses describe for us the prophet's call and inaugural mission in terms very similar to the servant songs of Deutero-Isaiah. In fact, some scholars regard this as a *fifth* servant song. Excerpted from a longer poem or series of poems (chapters 60-62) which describe the new Jerusalem in eschatological terms, today's text was written in the period immediately after the exiles had returned home to Israel from Babylon. With the enormous task of reconstruction and restoration facing them, and with doubt in their hearts as to their status with their Lord, their spirits faltered in frustration.

Convinced that his mission was God-given ("the spirit of the Lord is upon me, . . . he has anointed me"), the prophet described himself in terms of an evangelist, a bringer of glad tidings (v. 1) to the poor. The same Spirit of God whose hovering power (Genesis 1:2) had created Eden, would through the mission of the prophet re-create in the hearts and minds of his people a vision of a new and glorious Jerusalem and so encourage them to rebuild it. This same Spirit would endow the messianic king (Isaiah 11:2) and, in the era of the messiah, all the people (Joel 3:1, Zechariah 12:10). "Lowly and brokenhearted" are terms which aptly describe the newly released captives and prisoners from Babylon. These same terms were used by Deutero-Isaiah to portray the "poor ones" of the Lord. It may be said that Trito-Isaiah attempted in his mission to his people to help them interiorize or spiritualize their external poverty and find in it a new dependence and complete trust in their Lord.

By proclaiming a "year of favor," the prophet drew upon his people's tradition of the 50th year or year of jubilee. As legislated in the book of Leviticus (25:9-19, 23- 55), the jubilee year was a social and economic institution founded upon religious principles. In the year of favor, the land was free to lie fallow; property once seized or borrowed or rented was to be returned to its rightful owners. Slaves were freed and debts were either remitted or suspended. Such was the freedom granted Israel by its liberator and redeemer. The fallow land and the property seized by the Babylonians would once more be their promised heritage. Israel's debt of sin had been repaid and slavery was at an end. In this manner, Isaiah the Old Testament evangelist proclaimed the gospel of salvation to his people.

In the Targum, vv. 10-11 of today's text are introduced by the words, "Thus says Jerusalem," and are purported to be the people's answer to Isaiah's jubilant proclamation. Images of the bride and bridegroom express Israel's joy in the renewed covenant with Yahweh and its hopes for a spiritual and moral fertility. In the festal garment of salvation and in the robe of righteousness, the unfaithful bride is called to celebrate the forgiveness of the bridegroom. In the last verse, the prophet draws together the physical and spiritual universe: Just as the earth (*adamah,* Hebrew) can bring forth life and reflect the creative power of God, so too will humankind (*adam*) bring forth, in justice and praise, God's redemptive power.

1 Thessalonians 5:16-24. Paul's imperative "Rejoice" and the entrance antiphon for this Sunday's liturgy gave it the name "Gaudete" or "Rejoice Sunday." This quality of joy was one of the most attractive and distinguishing characteristics of the early communities of believers. In an effort to temper excitement in regard to Jesus' second advent, Paul took great care to preserve the enthusiasm of the Christians at Thessalonica. The verses which comprise our reading today are part of the conclusion of Paul's first letter to the Thessalonians, written in 50 or 51 C.E. and are believed to be the first written of all the Christian scriptures. During the middle of the first Christian century, when not even a generation had passed since Jesus' resurrection, expectation of his return was unbounded. As first pastor of several of the new foundations, Paul utilized that expectation to its fullest extent, teaching those who waited together of their responsibility for one another. The hope they shared in the one in whom they had come to believe must be enunciated in love and in works of love for one another.

Like the Corinthians (1 Corinthians 12,14), the Thessalonians were counselled in the proper attitude toward the Spirit. Gifts of the Spirit or charismata were to be valued and accepted but not without valid evaluation. Prophecies were also to be tried and tested. Paul knew that healthy, truthful skepticism would be necessary in an atmosphere so ripe with expectation and anticipation.

In his final invocation that the God of peace grant not only *holiness* but *wholeness* to his church, Paul reveals a sound knowledge of human psychology. A modern psychologist, Joseph Goldbrunner, has repeated the Pauline idea in his statement, "Holiness is wholeness." Like his 20th century counterpart, Paul knew the necessity of balancing the spiritual and physical sides of a person's nature. *All* aspects of the Christian's life—his prayer, his response to the Spirit, his job or chosen occupation, his social life—must be gathered up into preparing for the Lord's coming. In this way, whether at work or at play or at prayer, the Christian becomes a living sign of the joy of the parousia to come. This same joy should characterize 20th century believers. We who wait for the Lord to return must be no less enthusiastic, no less holy, no less whole than our ancestors in the faith.

John 1:6-8, 19-28. When Jesus of Nazareth as the incarnation of the word and power and love of God for humankind intervened in history, the atmosphere was ripe with messianic anticipation. While the majority of the Jewish people awaited eagerly the manifestation of their Lord in time and space, there was not *one uniform* expectation of a *single* eschatological figure. Many, of course, basing their hopes on Yahweh's promise to David via Nathan the prophet (2 Samuel 7:14), were looking for the appearance of a messianic Davidic king. But others, either disillusioned or frustrated with the monarchy, looked in other directions for the intervening activity of God. In the intertestamental apocryphal book of Enoch (ca. second century B.C.E.), there was a saving figure called the Son of Man, the Elect One, whom it was believed would act as savior for God's people. In the same book, there is an allegory concerning the appearance of Elijah as herald of the apocalyptic lamb (Enoch 90:31, 89:52). Indeed, so popular was this tradition that the expectation of Elijah in Palestine survived until the second century C.E.

In the first paragraph of today's gospel, whose verses (6-8) are a prose insertion in the logos hymn or prologue of the fourth gospel, the evangelist sought to clarify for his late first century contemporaries both the role of John who baptized and of Jesus who saved. As the last in the long succession of prophets who pointed toward a messianic future, John the Baptizer was *witness* (v. 6) par excellence to the one who would come after him. *Witness* is one of the several important concepts in the fourth gospel. Throughout his work, the evangelist brings forth as if in a legal action witnesses who testify to Jesus. Beginning with the Baptizer (1:6-8), the steady stream of testimony issues forth from the Samaritan woman (4:39), Jesus' own works (5:36), the record of the Jewish scriptures (5:39), the Father (15:27), and finally from the evangelist himself (21:24). In each of these instances, the witness of the believer causes others to see the light of truth and faith and so to believe as well. Later in the gospel, John has Jesus describing John, not as the light but as the lamp (5:35), a *bearer* of the light who is Jesus (8:12, 9:5). There can be no doubt that John considered the Baptizer in an important but secondary and subordinate position to Jesus. In the second passage of the gospel (vv. 19-28), the evangelist repeats his clarification in a narrative context.

As guardians of orthodoxy and of ritual, the priests and Levites were probably sent to conduct an official inquiry with regard to the person of John, the son of Zachary, and his strange activity in the desert. Usually, when John the evangelist uses the term "the Jews" (v. 19), he is referring to the representatives or leaders of Judaism who were distrustful of and hostile toward Jesus. Ordinarily, the term is a selectively pejorative one in the fourth gospel and as such does not apply to the people in general. The Pharisees (v. 25) were a group of laymen who acted as self-appointed guardians of Jewish law and practice. Their coming to question the Baptizer, together with the priests (who were Sadducees), is unlikely because the two groups were rivals. It may be that the evangelist has melded two inquiries (or more) into one. To the pointblank question "Who are you?" the Baptizer answered in a series of negatives. His "I am not" statements can readily be contrasted with Jesus' "I am" (*ego eimi*) statements (bread, life, way, good shepherd, vine, etc.) which punctuate the rest of the gospel with high christological assertions. In repudiating the titles of messiah and prophet (as per Deuteronomy 18:15-18), the fourth gospel is consonant with the synoptics. But, in the case of Elijah, the synoptics and John differ. Because of his clothes (2 Kings 1:8, Zechariah 13:4), his manner and his mission, the synoptic evangelists (Matthew 11:14, 17:12) looked upon the Baptizer as an Elijah figure. But, by the 90s C.E., when the fourth evangelist wrote his good news, he made every effort to disassociate the Baptist from the Elijah role, because it had become a popular belief at the turn of the first Christian century that Elijah was to return as the messianic inaugurator of God's reign. Knowing this and the fact that there were some in the 90s C.E. who regarded John the Baptizer as the Elijah-like messiah, the gospel author was careful to cast the Baptizer's role in its proper light.

After denying the messianic titles, the one identity John the Baptizer claimed for himself was one which had validity only in reference to Jesus—that of the "voice in the desert" (Isaiah 40:3). Saint Augustine, in his Sermons (293:3), referred to John as "a voice who cried out for a time, but Jesus is the eternal word from the beginning." John saw his role as preparatory and understood his baptism in the same way. He was a voice crying out that the way or the road of the Lord should be readied. It is a documented fact, that at the visit of a political official or on occasions such as religious processions with statues of gods, the roads of the ancient Near Eastern world were repaired. Bumps were flattened; holes were filled in and flowers decorated the roadsides in honor of the visiting dignitary. When John preached about a "straight way," he did not expect the Roman civil engineers to set to work on Palestine's roads. Rather, he sought by his preaching of repentance and by his baptismal washing to make straight, in a moral and religious sense, the hearts of his listeners. Then, when the word of God, whose voice he was, and the light of the world, to whom he bore witness, came, he might be recognized and confessed as Lord and savior.

Today, the Baptizer exercises for all who would hear him the same role. He points not to himself but to Christ. He prepares us, not only to acknowledge the Lord who has come, but also to recognize that same Lord and Christ when he comes again in glory.

1. The wounded healer best proclaims the freedom and favor of the good news (Isaiah).

2. "Rejoice always" does not mean continual laughter or a perpetual smile but looking ahead with hope to the future (Thessalonians).

3. Bearing witness to the light may mean resisting the temptation to shine (John).

Fourth Sunday of Advent

In ancient times, our ancestors in the faith were led by the power of God in the desert. Then there came a time when they thought they might better meet their God in a temple of cedar and juniper (Samuel). But only when that creative and caring God came near in human flesh and spoke in time and space the language of our humanity did true meeting occur (Luke). For this mystery of his mercy and the intimacy of his love, praise him (Romans)!

2 Samuel 7:1-5, 8-11, 16. Among his many achievements as king of his people, David was the architect of Israel's greatest successes and, as such, ruler of his people at the height of their political career and religious fervor. After a series of skirmishes and battles from which he had emerged victorious, David was acknowledged as liege by the various factions among his people and he established Jerusalem as his capital city. This he had accomplished in part by bringing the ark of the covenant from Shiloh to rest in Jerusalem. A small (3'9"x2'3") portable chest made of acacia wood, the ark purportedly was carried at the head of the people as Moses and the escapees from Egypt made their way through the desert (Numbers 10:33). Like a standard or flag, it was also carried before the troops into battle to give them courage and purpose (Numbers 14:44).

While 2 Samuel 7 has been reworked by later theologians and contains evidence of a Deuteronomic editor (7th century B.C.E.), the scene in today's first reading is presented as a "typical day at the palace" (10th century B.C.E.). Seeming to chat nonchalantly with Nathan, his court prophet, David is suddenly appalled at the discrepancy between his fine cedar house and the tent wherein the ark was reserved. At first Nathan is in full agreement with David and declares (v. 3) the "Lord is with him." This is an obvious reference to the Emmanuel prophecy (Isaiah 7:14) and an indication of later editing. In a private revelation (dream? vision?) Nathan is, however, convinced otherwise by Yahweh and communicates this fact to David in the oracle which begins at v. 4 and continues to the end of the reading.

Essentially, God's answer to David's idea about a temple is based on the temple-desert conflict. Verse 5 contains a pejorative note and a hostile view of the temple due, we may assume, to the emptiness of the degenerate cult. Of course, this dissatisfaction with formal ritual and the sacrificial system is an anachronism from a later age (eighth-sixth century B.C.E.) when the desert days and the simplicity and intimacy of Israel's worship were preferred to the empty cult of the temple.

In Yahweh's declaration that he would build a house (dynasty) for David, a house of rest and a kingdom of everlasting proportions, there is a recapitulation of all the promises to the patriarchs. A "fixed place" with "rest from enemies" and "fame like the great ones" were the divine covenantal pledges that had bolstered Israel to surge ahead through the desert to the infiltration and then the conquest of Canaan. In the promise of the perpetuity of David's throne and his house, future generations found hope and consolation. Even when the political succession and continuity of the Davidic line were broken (587 B.C.E.), Israel remembered this promise. Indeed, in the generations after David, in the most dismal of situations, the promise in today's reading became the root of a strong and vibrant messianic tradition that looked for God to raise up for his people one of David's line. The Essenes of the Qumran community looked for "a shoot of David who would stand with the Interpreter of the Torah in the end of days" (Cave 4 Midrash on 2 Samuel 7). Christians see in Jesus, Son of David, the fulfillment of the ancient promise, "Your house and your kingdom shall endure forever."

Romans 16:25-27. With these verses and their doxology, the canonical letter to the Romans is concluded, though most would argue that Paul actually completed his letter at 15:33. Chapter 16:1-24 was probably a separate letter, written by the apostle to recommend Phoebe as minister and deaconess to the church of Ephesus. Because vv. 25-27 depart from the customary Pauline style and manner of concluding his missives, it is generally agreed that these verses were composed by a later redactor when the Pauline corpus was being formed. In fact, in several old manuscripts, this same doxology appears in a variety of positions within the letter to the Romans.

Regardless of its source or original position, the short doxology that comprises our second reading today puts before us an idea that became quite popular in later New Testament writings. Revelation of the *mystery* is the essential message of these lines of praise. Within this doxology we find the seed of an entirely new and different approach to the Jewish scriptures, developed by the authors and believers of the Christian scriptures. Paul, or his editor, believed that the great mystery or hidden plan of God, gradually unveiled in the course of human history, was only truly and fully understood in the light of Jesus' advent. The author of Romans 16:25-27 regarded Christian faith, enlightened by Jesus Christ, as the key to the correct judgment and interpretation of all the prophetic utterances of the Old Testament, because all these prophecies found their ultimate meaning and actualization in the Christian epiphanies. Moreover, in keeping with the later universalism of the sixth century prophets, the author considered the mystery's revelation to be open to all who would believe, not only Jewish Christians, but gentiles as well. With the advent of Jesus, this mystery, as well as the law and the prophets which announced it, was no longer the special possession of a particular people, born of a certain tribe or amphyctionic union. With the advent of Jesus, not only was the mystery revealed, but God came nearer and more knowable to humankind than he had ever been before. With the wonder and glory of God made incarnate in Christ, a new type of union became possible, a union with God which eradicated among believers their differences of race, class, language and background. For those of us who live, as did Paul, his editor and the first Roman Christians, in the age of the unfolding of God's great saving mystery, we look forward as one people to the final chapter, the second advent of Jesus, wherein the revelation shall be complete.

Luke 1:26-38. Unlike contemporary birth announcements which detail only the newborn's weight, length, hour and date of arrival, ancient annunciations of birth served as a literary device to acquaint the reader with news of the mission and purpose in life of the one who had been or who would soon be born. In reading Luke's account of Jesus' birth announcement, the believer should keep in mind the author's purpose, and refrain from treating the pericope as strict historical narrative. Though an excellent and quite original author in his own right, Luke did not invent this particular literary genre but followed the lead of biblical authors before him (birth announcements of Isaac, Samson, Samuel) and secular authors as well (Plutarch's treatment of Coriolanus etc.). With regard to these illustrious persons, their births were unusual in that they were born to elderly and/or barren couples, but the annunciation of Jesus' birth contains elements that make it far superior and more remarkable than other stories of its genre.

Couched within the infancy narrative of Luke's gospel, the annunciation of Jesus' birth must be understood and evaluated as part of the whole framework to which it belongs. Only Matthew and Luke, both of whom wrote probably in the 80s C.E., prefaced their gospels with a sort of gospel in miniature, the infancy narrative, which served to clarify the divine origin and purpose of Jesus against the background of Old Testament prophecies and expectations. Far from mere midrash or commentary, the infancy narratives are jewels of imaginative and creative theology. No less creative than the narrative of which it is a vital part, is the birth announcement of Jesus, our gospel for today.

Writing in excellent Greek for a gentile audience, Luke composed the birth announcements of Jesus and John the Baptizer in a similar fashion. The two announcements are of equal length and contain the same elements. Though arranged in an almost perfect diptych, it is clear that the birth of Jesus is more wondrous (he is not to be born in the usual fashion) and John the Baptizer's role remains a secondary one.

Many scholars cite this text of Luke as support in their argument against a virginal conception, e.g., J.A. Fitzmeyer, following the thought of Lyonnet, has said, "When this account is read, in and for itself, without the overtones of the Matthean annunciation to Joseph, every detail of it could be understood of a child to be born to Mary in the usual human way." Jesus' birth, says Fitzmeyer, could still be regarded as the work of the Holy Spirit even if Mary and Joseph had had relations, because the birth had been so foretold and the child was to possess a unique role as God's son. Other scholars, however, argue for a virginal conception from the text itself (1:27, 1:34) wherein the evangelist states unequivocally and without question, that Mary was a virgin. It seems, says R.E. Brown, that the evangelist found no point for argument in the tradition of Mary's virginity and accepted it as factual.

More important, however, than Mary's biological condition was the spirit of faith she exhibited in her vital role in the course of salvation history. This faith and Mary's position are attested in the greeting paid her by the angel-messenger. "Rejoice, O highly favored daughter!" (*Chaire kercharitomene!*) is a far more accurate and descriptive translation of the Greek than the Vulgate's "Hail, full of grace!" These words communicate not only a very wonderful acknowledgment of Mary's special role but they serve to herald the messianic age as well. This same manner of greeting was addressed by the prophet Zephaniah (3:14-17) to the daughter of Zion (Israel) when he declared: "Yahweh, king of Israel is in your midst." The believers of the old covenant applied these words to the age and advent of the messiah. Addressed to Mary and combined with the declaration, "The Lord is with you," they proclaim the long-awaited era of Emmanuel—God with us (as per Isaiah 7:14). Further explaining the reason for rejoicing and the purpose of Mary's special election, the messenger announces the birth of the Son of the most high and son of David. These were Jewish messianic titles which did not automatically or necessarily imply divinity. Luke, however, makes certain that his readers comprehend his purpose in the ensuing verses where he speaks of the Holy Spirit, the power of the most high and the newborn Son of God. In v. 35, the Holy Spirit coming upon Mary and the power of the most high overshadowing her are to be understood in synonymous parallelism. We are reminded of the hovering spirit of Genesis (1:2) which effected the first creation. Luke would have us understand that this same Spirit is present once again, effecting a *new* creation in Mary. We are also reminded of the several Old Testament references to God's overshadowing presence (*episkiazein*) of the tabernacle (Exodus 40:35), of his people (Exodus 25:20).

When Mary consented to become a part of God's creative, redemptive and incarnate purpose for his people, Mary made a true act of faith. She probably did not fully understand all the implications of her assent. In fact, Luke tells us that she was troubled and wondered (1:29), that she did not understand (2:50) but that she pondered (*dielogizeto*, 2:52) all these things in her heart. This wondering and pondering were a profound and prolonged reflection, a prayer which moved her to vital and sustaining faith. Because she did not fully comprehend and yet believed, Mary is an attractive and realistic figure, a true heroine for all Advent Christians. In this capacity, in her unique role in the mystery of salvation, we can revere and acclaim her.

1. It is more important to be than to build a temple for the Lord (2 Samuel).

2. Making mysteries manifest is part of the joy of Advent (Romans).

3. To demand fullness and clarity of understanding before assent is not faith (Luke).

The Christmas Season
Christmas

For the celebration of Christmas, the lectionary supplies several sets of texts (vigil, midnight, dawn, day). The ones treated here are for proclamation at the day mass.

Eternity enfleshed in time is the gift of grace we call Emmanuel, God-with-us. Infinity is made finite in a daring act of loving and giving (John). He is good news and salvation (Isaiah). He is Father and brother and Lord; he is the message of glory we celebrate today (Hebrews)!

Isaiah 52:7-10. On occasion in the ancient world, the bearer of bad news was put to death, but there would be no danger of that happening to the messenger portrayed in today's first reading. Part of a longer enthronement hymn in honor of the devastated city of Zion (Jerusalem), today's pericope envisages the joy and hope of the people on hearing of their release from exile and their imminent homecoming. Written in the sixth century B.C.E. by a prophet known arbitrarily as Deutero-Isaiah, these verses give us a glimpse of the "phoenix quality" of Israel's hope, a quality she owed entirely to Yahweh's sustaining love and provident care.

During the exile, for over a generation, Israel's beloved capital city of Jerusalem had remained in its demolished condition, the ruins a bleak witness to the political and military might of her Babylonian conquerors. For over a generation, the elite of Israel's populace had been degraded, displaced in a strange land where they had no rights of proprietorship or freedom to pray and worship as was their custom. During that time of imprisonment and curtailed freedom, a liberating enlightenment gradually took place among the exiles, due in no small part to the prophets who shared the exile. As mediator to his people of God's revealing word, the prophet helped his people to interpret all that had happened to them, both good and bad, as a part of God's message of salvation and justice. Each event in their history could be read, as it were, like a word through which God was speaking his mind, his will, his ways for his people. In joyous times, that word could be one of blessing. The darker periods, the failure and defeats, the prophets interpreted as God's word of redress and deserved punishment. In the *events* of history the prophets read for their people the creative, redeeming, purifying, loving, blessing word of God.

Hence the *event* of Israel's return from exile was truly a gospel—glad tidings, good news. Not only what God had *said* to his people, in spoken or in written words, but what he had *been* and how he had *acted* within the realm of their history enabled his people to know him as redeemer, saving God. In creation and in history God's plan is accomplished and clarified. As T. Maertens has pointed out, the *event* is central; all else, the spoken, written and prophesied words, are in service and in ministry to the event.

Today's feast celebrates the Christ-*event*. In fact, the glad tidings of the Deutero-Isaian messenger were only fully actualized, only fully heard and made comprehensible in the event of Jesus Christ. In the event of the incarnation, Yahweh truly returns and restores Jerusalem; in the event of the nativity, Yahweh draws near to comfort and console his people. In the event of Christ-made-flesh, God's message of salvation achieves its utmost clarity. What we celebrate as gospel, as good news is not mere words but persons and events.

Hebrews 1:1-6. In a sort of "before-and-after" or "then-and-now" comparison, the author of the document addressed to the Hebrews enunciated the differences between the revelation of the old and new covenants. Our reading today comprises the introduction of his work which can readily be compared to the prologue of the fourth gospel. In both texts, the image is one of Christ's divinity and equality with God.

In vv. 1 to 4, the first paragraph of our text today, the author of Hebrews speaks of the *superior* revelation which God has spoken in Jesus Christ. Unlike the piecemeal and fragmentary revelation of the Old Testament which had to be interpreted by the prophets, the revelation in Jesus is whole and entire, living and absolute. J. Moffatt has said, "Christ is God's last word to the world; revelation in him is final and homogeneous." Jesus Christ is a living being. The word of God he has spoken in the event of his ministry, death, resurrection and exaltation does not cease to be heard. The word of God in Jesus in "living and active" (4:12), ever new, ever in the process of communicating to believers the love and care of God. That living, speaking word-become-flesh is the basis for our celebration today.

Besides asserting Christ's superiority to the prophets and Old Testament revelation, Hebrews also underscores the Lord's predominance over the angels. As refulgence or reflection (v. 3, *apaugasma*) of the Father and as the exact representation (*charakter* or *eikon*) of the Father's being, Christ is placed on a par with wisdom (Wisdom 7:26). In the old dispensation, wisdom was regarded as sharing with God both a cosmological and soteriological role (Proverbs 8:22-36, Wisdom 9:9-18). This equating with wisdom in such an operative role placed Jesus Christ on a level far above the angelic hosts whom late Judaism believed were present at creation and who were granted by God a role in its government. Jewish tradition called these angelic beings "sons of God," and Alexandrian Jewish theologians called them logos, word. Because of these prevalent notions, the Hebrews' author was adamant in establishing Christ's transcendence and divinity. In New Testament times, popular Jewish belief regarded the angels as mediators of the law for humankind. In a medley of texts from the Jewish scriptures, Hebrews leaves no doubt as to Christ's superior and unequalled position. The first two texts from Psalm 2:7 and 2 Samuel 7:14 were thought messianic by late Judaism and by the Qumran community. In both quotations the unique sonship of Christ is established as well as the divinity of his messiahship. The third text (v. 6), a combination of several Old Testament citations (Deuteronomy 32:43; Psalms 97:7, 104:4). forms a compelling invitation to those angelic beings to worship the Lord Jesus Christ. With them, we the faithful join our voices in praise and honor.

John 1:1-18. John Paul Sartre in an essay on literature once wrote, "The word is a commitment, an enterprise by means of which the author embraces his age." Although unintentionally and probably inadvertently, Sartre has provided believers with an apt description of the scenario of the incarnation, the central thought of the gospel today. In the speaking into flesh of his word, in the person and event of Jesus Christ, God has committed himself to humankind and to the world in an eternal embrace.

Up until Vatican II, today's gospel text was proclaimed at the end of every Eucharist, thereby earning for itself the misnomer "last gospel." Though this practice has been discontinued, it did serve the purpose of climaxing every celebration with the compelling and beautiful truth of the incarnation. Though most situations do not warrant reading the *shortened* form of the gospel, today may be the unique instance in which the short form would be preferable for the sake of clarity. Verses 6-8 and 15 are prose comments concerning John the Baptizer which were probably inserted into the poetic prologue at a later time by the evangelist or by a disciple-redactor of the fourth gospel. To omit these comments is to allow the hymn to flow more freely with the continuity originally intended.

This hymn that introduces the gospel serves a dual function. First, it provides for the words and works of the incarnate word an eternal background or origin and proclaims as false the theories against Jesus' divinity prevalent at the turn of the first century C.E. Secondly, the prologue serves as an overture to the gospel, containing a summary of its major themes as well as a means of interpreting Jesus' message and person. Many believe the hymn to be an adaptation from a Jewish or gnostic wisdom hymn, or a preexisting Christian hymn, adapted by the evangelist for the purpose of expounding his christology. Because the hymn exhibits similarities to Semitic, Greek and gnostic ideas, a clear solution to its origins is almost impossible.

In true Semitic style, the prologue begins with a genealogy; however, unlike most Jewish genealogies, it traces Jesus' origins to the eternal divinity. "In the beginning" is, of course, a deliberate reference to Genesis 1:1 and the creation by God's word of the universe. In John 1:1 that creative word is speaking again, but no longer as subject to object, as creator to created. In John 1:1 the word who speaks a new creation has become a part of creation itself by that very utterance. That word continues to speak within human history (vv. 4, 9-10) and especially through Israel (v. 11). Those who hear and truly listen to that word can become sons and daughters with the Son. Verse 14, "the word became flesh and made his dwelling among us," draws together all the Old Testament references to God's presence with his people, in the cloud, in fire, through the prophets, in his glory, by his law (Exodus 24; Exodus 33:18; Isaiah 6:1). The same root (S-K-N) lends itself to the verbs for God's presence in nature (*shekinah*) and his dwelling among us (literally: "pitched his tent") in his word (*eskenosen*).

It is difficult to ascertain whether John wanted his readers to understand word or logos in a Greek or in a Semitic sense. To those of a *Hellenistic* background, the logos-word was regarded as an intermediary between God and the created universe. That logos gave the world its order, thus making it intelligible and comprehensible. Humankind, in turning to the logos, could find a key for unlocking the mysteries of the cosmos. Understood in this sense, Christ as logos-word would be the key to knowing about created things and about God. To the *Semitic* mind, the logos or word is a challenge which a believer can accept or reject. A word or a call from God, the logos confronts or encounters the believer and compellingly invites a response. In this sense, Christ as logos-word would be a challenger or initiator of faith, a living epiphany of a loving, saving creator. Probably, the evangelist has combined the best of both cultures in his concept of the logos or word. As T. Maertens has said, Jesus is not only bearer of the word; he is also its content.

The figure of Moses (v. 18) brings to the fore another important Semitic idea. For the Jews, Moses was *the* mediator, through whom the law or light of truth was mediated from God to his people. In the prologue, the evangelist enunciates Christ's superiority not only as mediator between God and humanity but also to the law. Rabbinical Judaism in the last centuries B.C.E. and the first centuries C.E. glorified the Torah and identified it with wisdom, source of light and life for all (Sirach 24:22-27). In his treatment of Jesus Christ-logos as superior to Old Testament wisdom and law, John's purpose is in one sense polemical. Over and against the Jewish idea of an eternal and nearly divine law, John posited Christ the word as existing from all eternity, through whom *alone* would come truth and light, life and grace.

For us who believe and who celebrate the enfleshment of the word of God as the source of life and light and truth, today is a renewal of our faith and of our commitment to the challenge of that word. Let us remember that because of the incarnation, we respond, not to a concept or an ideology or a philosophy, but to a living and loving *person*.

1. The good news of Christ proclaimed by the church in the pulpit must resound more loudly and more joyfully in the marketplace (Isaiah).

2. No longer through a glass darkly, but in the light of Christ, we behold the fullness of the Father's love (Hebrews).

3. In the word enfleshed, God speaks the language of our flesh and blood, in the pulsing of our needs and aspirations and even in the shadows of our sinful darker side (John).

Holy Family Sunday

Bonds of love that grow stronger in moments of shared pain and joy—this is family (Sirach). Fostered by a forgiving-and-forgetting love, these bonds become sacred when the family celebrates in prayer their union in the Lord (Colossians). From within a human family, the incarnate word first began to speak and to reveal to all the peoples of the earth the eternal familial bonds of Father, Son and Spirit (Luke).

Sirach 3:2-6, 12-14. Joshua Ben Sira was a faithful Jew of the second century B.C.E. steeped in the traditional values of his people. Besides fidelity to the Lord and his covenant, one of the preeminent values in his life (in the life of any Jew) was the family, essential and nuclear cell of the clan, of the tribe, of their beloved nation. Within the family the future generations were nourished spiritually, physically, morally and culturally to carry on with dignity and with purpose the faith and traditions of the holy nation of Israel. An inhabitant of Jerusalem and possibly a member of the scribal class, Ben Sira was fortunate to have been born into prosperity and to have maintained the wealth necessary to devote his time and efforts to study and travel, thus gaining the experience that comes from these endeavors. Recall the wish of Tevya in *The Fiddler on the Roof*, "If I were a rich man," as he yearned to devote his time to the holy book and to conversation with the rabbis.

Ben Sira had had the good fortune of being both educated and educator. Indeed, his book, written in Hebrew ca. 180 B.C.E. and translated into Greek by his grandson in ca. 132 B.C.E., is a gathering of his insights on the law, other scriptures, on wisdom as God's gift and on life in general. Sirach, or Ecclesiasticus (book of the church) as it has been called in Greek, is a synthesis of Ben Sira's response to revealed truth and his advice concerning the application of this truth to the various circumstances of human life. Written for post-exilic Jews whose infatuation with Hellenism threatened to dilute and alter their traditional practices and beliefs, Sirach was greatly valued by Judaism even though it was not accepted as a canonical work. In the following centuries, the book was also highly regarded by Christians. In fact, no other Old Testament book except the psalms was used as extensively in the Christian liturgy.

Today's pericope, quite fitting for the feast of the Holy Family, was part of a longer commentary on family life and on the fourth commandment in particular (Exodus 20:12). Caring for and honoring one's parents was regarded as a sacred duty which admitted of no dispensation or violation. Indeed, Ben Sira would have probably reacted like Jesus in confronting those Pharisees who had declared their possessions *corban*, i.e., consecrated to God (Matthew 15:6). By so doing, they shirked their responsibilities toward their parents and nullified the divine law of parental honor. Not one to pervert the law, Ben Sira would rather channel all behavior according to its sacred principles.

Exhibiting the thought of later Judaism, Ben Sira attached certain benefits to the correct attitude and respect for parents. For example, he cites the traditional blessings of long life and riches as rewards for faithful offspring. Moreover, he proposes that the honoring of one's parents may even atone for sin. Christians, of course, accept this exhortation in the general sense in which it is made, as an incentive to obedience, and not as a blanket guarantee of forgiveness. Ben Sira understood the honoring of one's parents as the external activity born of an interior conviction. Fear of the Lord or the piety learned by the living of the law (of which the fourth commandment was a part) was the activity that made proper atonement for sin. This atonement was of course brought to perfection only in the sacrifice of Christ, loving, faithful Son of the Father. Because of that atonement, we of the human family are privileged to belong also to the family of God.

Colossians 3:12-21. Ancient Colossae was a small city whose importance as a center for textiles and dyed woolen goods was overshadowed by its more prominent neighbors, Laodicea and Hierapolis. Nestled in the valley of the Lycus river in Asia Minor about 110 miles east of Ephesus, Colossae's lack of prominence is evidenced in the fact that it has never been excavated but still lies buried in the silent ruins of centuries of earthquakes. Paul did not personally bring the message of Christ to Colossae's mixed gentile and Jewish population. It is generally believed that Epaphras, one of Paul's converts in Ephesus, brought the good news to Colossae and perhaps to Laodicea and Hierapolis as well (1:6-7; 2:1; 4:12-13).

While in prison, probably in Rome (61-63 C.E.), Paul received a disturbing report from Epaphras which occasioned his letter to the Christians of Colossae. The exact basis of Paul's concern is hard to determine because we have only his response to the conflict; however, it seems that some local teachers were confusing the Christians with false doctrines (2:8, 16-23). Introduced from both religious and philosophical spheres, these questionable doctrines were probably both Jewish and pagan in origin. From Paul's rebuttal, we can determine two major concerns: (1) spiritual beings, (2) dietary practices, the observance of certain feasts, circumcision, etc.

At the root of the controversy concerning spiritual beings was the pagan belief that the universe was controlled by certain elements or angelic beings (2:8, 20). These angels acted as mediators between God and humans and contained in themselves a part of God's *pleroma* or fullness. Believed to be responsible for creation, these angels were also thought to control human affairs. Humanity, for its part, had to gain as much special knowledge (*gnosis*) as it could about these beings so as to be able to propitiate them. In late Judaism, too, there was a notion of the mediating power of angelic beings (Daniel 10:21; 12:1). The community at Qumran entertained a fascination with the names of these heavenly beings and the roles each of them played. To ward off the dangers inherent in those controversial ideas, Paul expounded to the Colossians the supremacy and uniqueness of Jesus, *sole* mediator with the Father. All-sufficient in himself, Christ possessed the *pleroma* of God and did not dilute his sufficiency with a plethora of angelic intermediaries.

The second major concern, that of dietary practices, circumcision, etc. was due, no doubt, to the strong Jewish community at Colossae. Over and against these practices, Paul asserted the freedom Christians have, and denied the relevance of such practices for Christian belief.

Having addressed the controversies and their proponents in Colossae, Paul then devoted the remainder of his letter to a catechesis on the Christian life. Our reading forms a part of this catechesis which some believe to have been an early baptismal instruction (3:5-4:1). After a litany of virtues, mercy, kindness, forgiveness, etc., Paul exhorted the believers to "put on love" (v. 12). "Putting on" recalled the rite of vesting the newly baptized in a white garment as a symbol of the new life of goodness and grace into which they had been initiated. Calling them to thankfulness (*eucharistoi*), Paul urged the Colossians to allow their baptismal dedication to guide their routine interactions and to inspire their public worship. As such, in Christ, their liturgies would be as they should be, the crowning expression and celebration of their daily lives as believers (v. 16).

In the last paragraph of today's reading, Paul's catechesis touches upon the harmony which should characterize the Christian family. Nagging and bitterness have no place in those whose lives are lived "in the name of Jesus" (v. 18). In contrast to being "in Adam" (1 Corinthians 15:21-22, Romans 5:21), those who belong to one another "in the Lord" bring to their relationships the added grace of redemption and the powerful love of those who have known true forgiveness. That grace and love are no less powerful and effective today, for the 20th century family of believers "in the Lord."

Luke 2:22-40. Every society observes certain rituals that accompany the birth of a child and Israel was no exception. Although Luke in his infancy narrative has amalgamated two of these birth rituals and speaks of purifying "*them*" (v. 22), the rites of the presentation or consecration of the firstborn and the purification of the mother were distinct and separate. The evangelist's intention, however, was not merely to describe the birth mores of the Hebrew people, but to underscore from the very beginnng of Jesus' life his messianic character and purpose. In the action of Mary and Joseph, in the canticle of Simeon and in the witness of Anna, Luke's purpose is achieved and clearly enunciated.

According to the law (Leviticus 12:2-8), a mother was to be purified after childbirth—in the case of a son, 40 days after giving birth. Such purification was required, not because of any moral uncleanness but simply for legal or ceremonial purposes. The law designated two offerings, a lamb for a holocaust of praise and a turtledove or pigeon for a sin offering. Mercifully, the law permitted the offering of two birds, should the couple not be able to afford a lamb. Like Jesus, Mary conformed to the law and was thus restored to ritual purity. With regard to the other ritual, that of the presentation or offering of the firstborn, this act, too, was done in obedience to the law. According to Exodus 13:2, 12, all firstborn sons belonged to the Lord, but once presented, could be redeemed by an offering of five shekels to the temple treasury (Numbers 18:15). Ordinarily, it was not required that the child be brought to the temple, but it served Luke's purposes that Mary and Joseph do so, because the evangelist wished to cast Jesus in the light of his ancestor Samuel (1 Samuel 1:11, 22-28). Both children were presented and consecrated to the Lord and both children remained in the Lord's service. Notice that Luke makes no mention of the offering of the five shekels; moreover, in a later episode, he shows Jesus "busy with his Father's affairs" in the temple (2:49). His implication, though indirect, is clear: Jesus belonged to the Lord and was always in his service.

In the back of Luke's mind, implicit in his narrative, were three other messianic references. By introducing the scene of the presentation with the phrase, "when the day came" (v. 22), Luke employed a special term which meant more than the chronological completion of a specific time. *Eplesthesan* referred to the arrival of the messianic age and the evangelist used this term to communicate that fact at several different points in his infancy narrative (2:22, 57; 2:6, 21). Moreover, Luke (unlike John) regarded John the Baptist as an Elijah figure, and hence as the legendary messenger (1:16) of the messiah. Surely Luke had Elijah and Malachi 3:1 in mind when narrating Jesus' presentation in the temple: "Behold, I send my messenger to prepare the way before me and the Lord whom you seek will suddenly come to his temple." In a third messianic text (Daniel 9:21-24), reference was made to the angel Gabriel (Luke 1:26), and to the fulfillment of the 70 weeks of years, at which time the holy one of Israel (Luke 1:35) would be consecrated to the Lord. In Jesus' consecration in the temple, Luke saw the fulfillment of all these prophetic hopes.

With the introduction into the narrative of the persons of Simeon and Anna, Luke's narrative draws even more heavily upon the wealth of Hebrew prophecy concerning the messiah. In the Deutero-Isaian tradition of messianic hope, Simeon is presented as one who awaited Israel's consolation (Isaiah 40:1; 49:13; 51:12; 61:2). The rabbis taught that this "consolation" was the subject of the final conversation between Elijah and Elisha (2 Kings 2:11) and would be manifest when Elijah returned. According to Luke's evaluation of the Baptizer, Elijah *had* returned, hence Jesus *was* the promised messianic *consolation* awaited for centuries. Notice too that Luke has referred to the Holy Spirit three times in just two verses. The pouring out of the Spirit on all humankind (Joel 3) was a portent of messianic times, as was the prophesying of Israel's sons and daughters (Simeon and Anna?!).

Simeon's canticle (vv. 28-32), the *Nunc Dimittis*, serves the same function in Luke's narrative as do the other canticles, the *Magnificat* (1:46-55), the *Benedictus* (1:67-79) and the *Gloria* (2:13-14). In each instance, the canticle gives expression to the vibrant faith of the speaker and also proclaims the saving action of God. With R.E. Brown, we agree that the canticles were probably pre-Lucan prayers, not composed by the evangelist but inserted by him into his infancy narrative. Each canticle is greatly imbued with Old Testament as well as intertestamental ideas and theology. A faithful sentinel, whose life had been spent in watching and waiting for the consolation of the messianic age, Simeon's prayer revealed that his long wait was over; his prayers had been answered in the person of Jesus. Peace, fulfillment, saving deeds, all peoples, light and glory were all hallmarks of the age of the messiah (Isaiah 40:5, 42:6, 46:13, 49:6, 52:9-10; Psalm 72:7; Zechariah 8:12). In his prayer, Simeon declared that all these long awaited realities had become present joys. But Simeon's proclamation had a double edge (vv. 34-35) and his words to Mary revealed the conflict and division which the presence of the messiah would bring into the world. Jesus himself was to later (Luke 12:51-53) acknowledge the challenge which faith in him would entail. Indeed, like a sword of judgment (Ezekiel 14:17), Jesus' involvement with humankind would demand of each person a choice, to accept or to reject him. Notice the Isaian universality in the prayer (v. 32) of Simeon, conveying the fact that the challenge of Jesus would be presented to *gentiles* as well as to the people of Israel.

In the manner of Simeon, Anna, too, as a prophetess recognized and proclaimed the advent of God's consolation in Jesus. Together, these two figures represent the culmination of the age of prophecy as they witness to the fulfillment of the hopes of their people in the person and mission of Mary's firstborn son.

In the conclusion of today's pericope, Luke alludes to Jesus' growth in spirit, in mind and in body. This development took place in virtual anonymity within his human family at Nazareth. Light of the world and savior of humankind, his maturation was a *gradual* process. Such is the beauty of the incarnation . . . God-made-man, God-with-us, in each stage of human development, blessing and gracing every level of growth. As providers of a family environment for our loved ones, and as members of the greater family of humankind, we too are graced by the presence of the incarnate Lord among us. *From* that presence we draw our strength and *to* that presence we must witness.

1. In parenting, catechesis or faith-sharing is as important as being a generous provider (Sirach).

2. In a healthy, happy family, "I'm sorry" and "I forgive you" are heard as often as "I love you" (Colossians).

3. Because of the incarnation, every aspect of human development can be a manifestation of God's goodness and wisdom (Luke).

New Year's Day

The texts pronounce a blessing on this year (Numbers) and repeat the season's basic theme, the coming of Jesus the God-man (Galatians) into our world—the first act in God's unfolding plan for our salvation (Luke).

Numbers 6:22-27. Called B^emidbar ("In the wilderness") in the Masoretic text of the Hebrew, this fourth book of the Pentateuch purports to depict the wilderness wanderings in the Sinai and the westward infiltration from the Transjordan area into Canaanite territory. In actual fact, the book is a complex melange of various traditions, religious history, liturgical rites and legal codes which grew out of the developing faith and culture of the Hebrew tribes. These traditions "percolated" through the life and mores of the people for about ten centuries before they were concentrated in the not too orderly book we call Numbers.

While much of the material in Numbers comes from a later period, many scholars believe that the blessing, which comprises the heart of today's pericope, may be quite ancient. This formula, used by priests in blessing the people at the end of their prayer together, is very familiar to us, because it is still used in both Jewish and Christian liturgies. It is a perfect example of Hebrew parallelism in triplicate, that is, the same prayer or petition is expressed in three different ways. Because biblical Hebrew knows no superlative, the triple statement is a means of showing emphasis. The phrases (The Lord bless you, the Lord let his face shine, the Lord look upon you kindly) are but three variants for understanding the Lord's favor. The word for the Lord's face (*panim*) is always plural, a collective noun, signifying all the qualities behind a face: attitudes, sentiments, personality. In a word, God's very self or presence is invoked. The threefold prayer for prosperity, presence and peace is an excellent expression of our hope in God who alone can make ours a happy new year.

Galatians 4:4-7. While the Pauline authorship of Galatians is rarely questioned today, we still do not know to which part of Galatia Paul addressed his letter, the northern or southern region. Created a province of Rome about 25 B.C.E. by Augustus, Galatia was a cosmopolitan area and the situation there caused Paul to pen one of his most important documents.

Writing in Ephesus in the mid-fifties C.E. on his third missionary trek, Paul used the letter to attack one of his major pastoral obstacles, the Judaizers. These were a group of early Christians (probably Pharisaic, perhaps even Essene in tradition) who believed that the way to Jesus Christ had to pass through Moses. They denied Paul's claim to apostleship and accused him of diluting the power of the gospel for the sake of gentile converts. The Judaizers plagued Paul's gentile converts by their insistence on circumcision for all, as well as the observance of certain Jewish feasts and dietary laws.

Galatians is a polemic against the Judaizers, with its underscoring of the freedom in Christ and its rejection of the old law and circumcision. Today's text follows Paul's story about Abraham wherein he asserts that the promises made to Abraham can be enjoyed by all Christians because it is Christ Jesus and not the law which makes us heirs. Indeed, because of Jesus Christ and his Spirit, we are children of God, intimate enough to call him "Abba" (Daddy).

Most scholars believe that the key phrase of the text, "God sent forth his son . . . so that we might receive adoption as sons," is an ancient Christian credal text expanded by Paul. The phrases, "when the designated time had come," "born of a woman" and "born under the law," proclaim Christ's incarnation and true solidarity with the human situation to those who would deny it.

Luke 2:16-21. Today's pericope from Luke's infancy narrative, depicting the shepherds' visit to the newly formed holy family, parallels the magi story in Matthew's gospel (see gospel text for next Sunday). Both groups, shepherds and magi, come to Jesus due to an extraordinary revelation, in one case an angel, in the other a star. Both groups represent believers in the early church who accepted Jesus as the Christ, as opposed to other groups who rejected and even persecuted him (Herod, scribes, chief priests). Both groups, shepherds and magi, come to adore Jesus as savior and go away from the event believing. Both groups, however, were considered somewhat beyond the ordinary, acceptable pale of existence. The magi were foreigners and astronomers. The shepherds were regarded outside the law in that their livelihood at times required that they graze their flocks on the lands of others.

The author of Luke 1 and 2 executes a creative transition from the story of Israel (Old Testament) to the story of Jesus (gospel) and the church (Acts), depicting Elizabeth, Zechariah, Anna, Simeon and especially Mary as the personification of messianic hope. Mary in particular, as both believer and later disciple, bridges the gap between Israel and the new Israel, the church. She keeps or treasures (ponders, interprets) these events in her heart and as such becomes the model for believers (cf. 2:16, 51). Jesus referred to faith like hers later in the gospel (see 8:15, 21; 11:28). A sentimental and pietistic regard for Mary has no root in the gospel, which presents her rather as one to be admired for her faith.

The last verse (2:21) of today's text gives fleeting attention to Jesus' circumcision before focusing on his naming. Contrary to custom, Joseph does not name the child. Rather, he is given the name which had been announced by the angel (1:31). In this way, the author attests to the extraordinary circumstances of Jesus' birth as well as the faith of her who had kept the angel's words in her heart and acted on them.

1. Do our lives reflect the blessings of the faith we enjoy (Numbers)?

2. Preconceived notions can blind us to the surprises of God's continuing revelation (Galatians).

3. The Christ of our faith is no longer an infant; he is the glorious, risen Lord of all creation (Luke).

Epiphany

When the radiance of salvation and peace began to dispel the darkness of sin, the saving light came, not from a faraway star or from the distant horizon (Isaiah). In the word made incarnate and from within the heart of hopeful humankind, the light began to warm, enliven and transform (Matthew). Now revealed, the splendor of this saving word does not cease to speak the good news of love and forgiveness (Ephesians).

Isaiah 60:1-6. At times, the relationship between Yahweh and Israel sounded very much like a weather report. Thick clouds and darkness, glorious light and shining radiance were metaphors used to describe God's presence as well as his absence, his favor and his disfavor, etc. Today's first reading is one of many examples wherein the concrete phenomena of nature communicate deeper, intangible and transcendent realities.

Writing either near the end of the Babylonian exile (ca. 540 B.C.E.) or immediately after the exiles had returned to their beloved but devastated Jerusalem, Trito-Isaiah (chapters 60-62) painted for his people, in a series of poems, verbal portraits of what Jerusalem would and could be, once the process of reconstruction had been completed. In an effort to revive Israel's hope and to allay the pessimism that threatened to overwhelm it, the prophet portrayed a city full of light, made so by the consoling and healing presence of Yahweh. What Deutero-Isaiah had prophesied (chapter 40), Trito-Isaiah saw fulfilled (chapter 60). Once there had been darkness and thick clouds over the earth. For Israel these would have been symbols of its shame and disgrace due to its infidelity; for the pagans or gentiles the darkness and clouds would have been signs of their ignorance and lack of enlightenment concerning the true God. But Trito-Isaiah's song was one of light and glory, because within the restored city God would once more manifest himself to his people. Just as the darkness and clouds had been signals of disgrace, the light and radiance signalled for Israel the good news of salvation.

Moreover, in the spirit typical of the exilic and post-exilic prophets, Trito-Isaiah believed that Israel's good fortune, i.e., the restoration to its own land and its reinstatement in dignity as God's people, would have repercussions on the rest of humankind as well. Because of the epiphany of the Lord within it, Israel would itself become the manifestation of God's presence and goodness for the nations. Trito-Isaiah's vision of the peoples from far off lands coming to Israel bearing gifts had been prophesied by Deutero-Isaiah during the exile (49:18,22). Inhabitants of Midian, Ephah and Shebah who lived in the coastal regions (Gulf of Elam) were originally descendants of Abraham (Genesis 25:1-4). Therefore, the prophet's consoling picture of peoples from afar streaming to Israel was consonant with the promises God had made to Abraham: "All the tribes of the earth shall bless themselves by you" (Genesis 12:3).

Trito-Isaiah considered his the messianic era, the eschatological era of salvation wrought by God's hand in history through Cyrus the Persian. For his people, the prophet believed his age would be one of dominance not only in the political sphere but in the religious sphere as well. Because of Yahweh's sovereignty, Israel's sovereignty would be secure and everlasting. Because Yahweh had once again become "epiphany," because their invisible God had become visible in the events of her history, Israel had become radiant.

For those of us who live in the era of God's ultimate epiphany, we understand that Trito-Isaiah's vision was fulfilled, not only in the return of Israel to its own land and in its reconciliation with Yahweh but in the person and the event of Jesus Christ and of his church. What God did for the Israel of the old covenant, he has done for all of humankind, the new Israel, in Jesus. With Christ and through him, darkness and clouds, sin and separation have been dispelled. With Christ and with his church, light illumines and warms an alienated world, so that all peoples can walk in the freedom and healing of that light. Trito-Isaiah thought Israel reflected the epiphanic light of Yahweh. Because of Christ and his incarnation, we do not merely *reflect* the light of God but, by our incorporation into Christ, we have *become* light.

Ephesians 3:2-3, 5-6. By the time the letter to the Ephesians was written, the sharing by the gentiles in the manifestation or epiphany of God's plan of salvation had become an accepted fact. In other words, the visions of Trito-Isaiah (first reading) had begun to be realized. The author of the missive to the Ephesians firmly believed that the fullness of God's epiphany in Jesus Christ continued to be manifest in the apostles because of the work of the Holy Spirit. Although very little is known for certain about the author and destination of the document we call Ephesians, it remains nevertheless a valuable collection of prayers (1:3-3:22) and paranetic preaching (4:1-6:20) concerning the Christian life.

More in the style of a sermon or a discourse than a letter, the document's destined audience remains a mystery. Ephesians 1:1, the title of the text, is a non-canonical and non-authoritative addition, probably added to the body of the document in the second century C.E. Because of the lack of personal references and general tone of the text, some believe it was a circular letter intended for the churches in Asia Minor. Marcion, basing his claims on Colossians 4:16, entitled the letter "To the Laodiceans." If Paul wrote the letter, which many doubt, he did so around 63 C.E. during his incarceration in Rome. If he did not actually write the "letter," it may be credited to one of Paul's followers who wrote in the first decade of the second century from Asia Minor. Such disparity about authorship, date and destination does not in any way detract from the valuable lessons of theology and christology contained in Ephesians.

In the second half of the first Christian century, when the eager anticipation of an imminent parousia had been mellowed by its delay, the hearts and minds of believers needed to be refocused on their present situation. To this end the author of Ephesians propounded his ideas about the kingdom of God here and now as a foretaste and a preparation for the eternal kingdom to come. With the memorable, vivid analogies of head-body and stone-temple, the author regarded Christian living as the only appropriate response to all that God has done and given in Christ.

Today's second reading reveals the author's understanding of the kingdom as universal, comprised of both Jews and gentiles, not as strangers or enemies but as heirs of the same gift of good news, members or the one body of Christ. The three Greek words (v. 6) for "coheirs" (*sygkleronoma*), "members," (*sysoma*) and "sharers" (*symmetocha*) dismiss once and for all the ideas of the old dispensation concerning Israel's "special" or "chosen" status. The author of Ephesians teaches that in the light of Christ's manifestation or epiphany, former barriers and distinctions have melted away. In the light of Christ and by faith, all have become privileged to share in the dignity and grace of the kingdom. Race and nationality, darkness and thick clouds have no place in the kingdom of light begun in Christ Jesus.

Matthew 2:1-12. Even if Matthew had never written chapters 3-28 of his gospel, he would nevertheless have earned the title evangelist because chapters 1-2 of his work contain the burden of the good news of our salvation and the proclamation of Jesus as savior. For this reason some scholars have called the first two chapters of Matthew and Luke (the infancy narratives) a "gospel in miniature." Within the context of the wonderful stories of Jesus' birth and early days, Matthew has posited (1) the universal scope of Christian revelation, (2) an apologetic concerning Jesus' divine origin and messianic authenticity, (3) the necessity for the worldwide missiology of Jesus' church. Far from being sentimental stories of "sweet baby Jesus," the infancy narratives are a powerful, paranetic teaching tool whose implications have begun to be discovered only in this century.

As a literary form, the infancy narratives are markedly similar to Jewish legends and folk stories prevalent in the last century B.C.E. and the first century C.E. Some have compared the narratives in Matthew and Luke to Jewish midrash (from the verb *daras*, to search), a reflective interpretation of scripture. Divided into two categories, midrash contains (1) rules of conduct or guides for living (*halakah*) as well as (2) narratives (*haggadah*) or stories that declared the importance and significance of persons and events. It is obvious that the New Testament authors were aware of this Jewish literary form and accepted it as a legitimate method of scriptural interpretation. Matthew may have had this midrashic method in mind and may have used it when formulating his narratives. But chapters 1-2 of Matthew are *more* than stories and *more* than an interpretation of known scriptures. Matthew 1-2 is good news in its own right, revelation in its fullest sense and kerygmatic teaching, demanding a response in faith.

Various motifs in today's gospel were reminiscent of traditional stories known to Matthew's audience. For example, before Moses was born, his birth had been foretold; according to legend, this news filled Pharaoh with fear and dread, causing him to consult his sages to determine a course of action. Similarly, the star figured very largely in traditional folk stories about the births of great men. A star is said to have appeared when Abraham was born, striking fear into the heart of king Nimrud because of its message that Abraham and his descendants would one day rule the earth. So too, a star is said to have proclaimed the birth of Nero. Popular also was the motif of a reigning monarch plotting to kill a child whom he feared would supplant him (Romulus and Remus).

Regardless of the similarities of motifs, the reader must maintain focus on Matthew's theological and christological intentions. The evangelist was concerned to portray Jesus as messiah of David's line. For this reason, he left no doubt as to Jesus' birth in Bethlehem and supported this fact with the scriptural references from both Micah 5:1 and 2 Samuel 5:2 (v. 6). Bethlehem had been David's ancestral hometown, the site of his anointing as king (1 Samuel 16:1-13; 17;12, 15;20:6, 28). It was fitting then that Jesus, as messiah and son of David, should be born there and receive the homage (v. 11, *proskynesis*) due him as everlasting king.

With regard to the star, Matthew may have had in mind the Balaam story (Numbers 24:17) wherein the greatness of Israel's ruler was witnessed by a star. Through the star or natural phenomena, the astrologers (magi) or gentiles were led to Jesus. But notice (vv. 5-6) that the natural phenomena were explained clearly and interpreted for them only by the scriptures. Herein is another of Matthew's points, an apologetic one: Gentiles who did *not* have the scriptures, but only the lesser witness of nature, were open to the truth and came to believe in Jesus. But the Jews, on the other hand, who were steeped in centuries of scriptural prophecies and attestations to the messiah did not believe in or accept Jesus. This was true not only in Jesus' day during his earthly ministry but also in Matthew's church of the 80s C.E. Just as the chief priest and scribes had rejected the earthly Jesus, the authorities in Matthew's day were ousting Jesus' followers from the synagogue. Just as the Sanhedrin delivered Jesus to

Pilate, so too in Matthew's church the Christians were subjected to both Jewish and Roman persecution (Matthew 10:17-18).

In the person of the astrologers from the east, Matthew has embodied all of the gentile community and thus widened the scope of the message of salvation beyond Judaism unto its intended universal proportions. Some scholars regard the gifts presented to Jesus (v. 12) as attestations to Jesus' kingliness and divinity. Gold and frankincense were gifts usually offered to God alone (Isaiah 60:6, Jeremiah 6:20). These same scholars regard the myrrh as an omen of Jesus' passion (Matthew 15:23), a portent similar to Simeon's prediction of the piercing sword (Luke 2:35).

1. As the new Jerusalem, believers in Jesus are to radiate joy and light so that the dark clouds of doubt and alienation may be dispelled (Isaiah).

2. In the kingdom Jesus came to preach, there were no distinctions as to class or race, nor can there be in the church that preaches Jesus (Ephesians).

3. Every gift we have to offer the king he has already bestowed upon us (Matthew).

Lord's Baptism

At his inauguration, there was no fanfare. . .no parade. . . no speeches. . .only the testimony of the Father who loved him (Mark). Once his campaign was inaugurated, Jesus fulfilled the promises of justice, enlightenment and freedom that had sustained the faithful and the hopeful for centuries (Isaiah). When his term of mission had ended, his death and his rising assured that the grace with which he had served would be a legacy for all who, in faith, would become part of his constituency (Acts).

Isaiah 42:1-4, 6-7. Called "servant" (but in no way subordinate), the figure outlined in today's first reading had a mission that left no doubt as to his very special position in the saga of Israel's salvation. As one set apart or consecrated, he was empowered by God to extend the light and justice with which Israel would be blessed to the rest of the nations. His words and works would join the destiny of Israel to that of the gentiles. Today's text comprises the first of four songs or poems whose subject is the mysterious servant. Because of the similarity of style and literary quality among the four pericopes, and the artificial and awkward placement of these songs in the context of Deutero-Isaiah's work (chapters 40-55), it is thought that the "servant songs" were an independent collection, composed by a disciple of Deutero-Isaiah and later inserted into the text. Indeed, if the four poems were to be read consecutively (42:1-4, 6-7; 49:1-6; 50:4-9; 52:1-13 53:12), they may be more properly appreciated and the portrait of the servant perceived more clearly. Like the context into which they have been interjected, the servant songs are pieces of prophetic comfort and assurance. Written probably during Israel's years of disgrace and exile in Babylon, the songs offer to a desperate people hope in the person of the servant, the chosen one who pleases Yahweh.

Various attempts have been made to identify the servant whom the author had in mind. Some believe that the author-prophet conceived of his own vocation or that of another prophet (Jeremiah?) in terms of the servant's mission. Others think the role of the servant is more in keeping with the task of the entire nation of Israel. Saved by the Lord, Israel was to be light for the nations and the agent of liberation for captives. Still others, drawing on the remnant motif in Deutero-Isaiah, contend that a certain group, the poor ones (*anawim*) within the nation, were to fulfill the vocation of the servant for the rest of Israel and for the nations. Still others regard the servant songs as referring to some future messianic or eschatological figure through whom God would work his wonders for his people.

While the author's intentions remain uncertain, there can be no doubt that the authors of the Christian scriptures (and Jesus himself) understood that these four songs of hope had been fulfilled in the person and ministry of Jesus of Nazareth. Clearly, Mark had these songs in mind when he wrote of Jesus' baptism (today's gospel) and of Jesus' transfiguration as well (Mark 9:7). The heavenly voice at the scenes of Jesus' baptism and transfiguration declared, "Here is my son." It is probable that "son" is an ambiguous translation of the original Aramaic word for "servant." Moreover, "beloved," (Mark 1:11) is an alternative word for "chosen one" (Isaiah 42:1). In view of the servant's mission of suffering, humiliation and death in the third and fourth songs, the association of the Isaian songs with Jesus becomes even more obvious.

When the songs were first written in the sixth century B.C.E, the liberation described (vv. 6-7) was understood by the exiles as God's pledge that they would be reinstated in their own land. In the light of Christian faith in Jesus and his redemptive efforts, the victory and liberation are understood as freedom from sin and from death. Even in its original context, the mission of the servant was more than a political effort. As bringer of justice, freedom and light, his objective was a moral and religious one. Israel had not been a political failure as much as it had fallen short of the ethical, social and moral standards of the covenant. For that reason, salvation was not simply a return to their homeland of Israel, but more a return to and reconciliation with God.

In addition to being empowered by God's own Spirit to liberate and to establish justice, the servant would bring light to Israel and the nations by his teaching (v. 4). A task usually performed by prophets (Isaiah 8:16, Zechariah 7:12) or priests (Jeremiah 2:8, Ezekiel 7:26), the teaching of truth and fidelity imparted by the servant would prove mightier than any weapon for war. It is significant that, when the evangelist Mark identified Jesus as the long-awaited servant at his baptism, Jesus' mission as a teacher was also inaugurated. By his teaching the servant Jesus would bring about what John's baptism signified, a transformation from within. By this same teaching, in word and in work, we too are transformed and made just and free.

Acts 10:34-38. The book of the Acts of the Apostles is a masterful piece of theology, yet it reads like an adventure tale. In his pictorial and dramatic approach, Luke presents for the reader scene after scene in which he skillfully imparts his message, a tapestry of historical theology and theologized history, woven together by his own perception of Jesus and the church. In the numerous speeches or discourses in Acts, we find the Lucan hand most evident. Comprising approximately a third of the whole of Acts, the speeches are for the most part Luke's in composition and serve the purpose of explaining the significance and importance of the particular event in question. Modeled after the literary style of the Greco-Roman histories and Hellenistic romance literature, the speeches were placed on the lips of the stars or heroes of the story and were often occasioned by turning points in the history of the church. For example, the speech attributed to Peter, from which today's reading is excerpted, marked the beginning of the acceptance of gentile Christians by Jewish believers in Christ. Notice that, while most of the efforts in this regard were probably made by Paul and others, Luke considered Peter's authority as providing an official approbation or guarantee and thus depicts it as a Petrine act. In addition to the explanatory nature of the speeches, Luke has included several apologetic motifs within his writings. One such motif figures in today's pericope, i.e., Luke's intention to illustrate the works and words of the Christian missionaries as "acts of God."

In accepting Cornelius, in conceding and then declaring forthrightly that God shows no partiality and has no favorites (v. 34), Peter was moving beyond the boundaries which he as a good Jew had always regarded as sacred. For the Jew, holiness and/or wholeness had been outwardly signified by the law, circumcision and the keeping of certain dietary practices and feasts. Those who observed such practices were considered clean, holy, covenantal people; those who did not so observe were unclean and outside the pale of God's partiality and favor. In accepting Cornelius without reserve and in declaring him to be upright (v. 35), Luke was teaching by means of Peter's speech that Christianity placed no boundaries or barriers of acceptability. In Christ Jesus, all such exclusiveness had been obliterated. In Christ Jesus, Cornelius the God-fearer was capable of that righteousness and uprightness which hitherto had been expected only from those who had inherited by blood or by faith the traditions of Judaism.

Peter's message to Cornelius and his household was his last major speech in the Acts of the Apostles and consisted of kerygmatic preaching. A sort of gospel in a nutshell or a distillation of Christian belief, Peter's words contained the fundamentals of faith, viz., (1) that God's plan of salvation first announced to Israel was fulfilled in Jesus, (2) that Jesus' words and works were of God and had ended in a redemptive death, (3) that Jesus had been raised to life by God, was revealed as risen to the apostles and was being preached by them, (4) that belief in the Jesus who died and who rose was necessary to salvation.

Mark 1:7-11. For the early church, Jesus' baptism by John posed a problem in that (1) there was an implied subordination of Jesus to John and (2) John's baptism was for sinners and Jesus was sinless! Mark, however, did not gloss over the event as did the subsequent evangelists. Matthew (3:13) had Jesus only presenting himself to John and said nothing of the actual baptism. Luke spoke of Jesus' baptism in the past tense (3:21) but did not describe it, while John omitted the event altogether and included in his gospel only John's witness to Jesus' greatness and superiority. But Mark, who opened his gospel with a text from Isaiah (and Malachi) which explained John's mission as herald and preparer, utilized the moment of Jesus' baptism to elucidate another set of texts from Isaiah (servant songs), one of which comprised our first reading today.

Rather than dwell on the problem of Jesus' being baptized by John, Mark chose to emphasize the significance of the event as the inauguration of Jesus' mission as suffering, redeeming servant-Son of God. By calling forth three witnesses—John, the voice and the dove—Mark leaves no doubt in the reader's mind as to the person, the purpose and the significance of the event. But, it should be noted that, in keeping with the Marcan technique of the messianic secret, the *divine* witness (dove and voice) was perceived only by Jesus (v. 10, "*he* saw"). Hence, Jesus' baptism was the first in a sequence of secret manifestations of divinity or epiphanies, known to the believing reader but not to Jesus' contemporaries. Only at Jesus' death is the mystery proclaimed (Mark 15:39) and only then does the series of secret epiphanies become clear to Jesus' followers.

With the "rending of the sky," Mark alluded to the Isaian prayer (Isaiah 64:1) that God inaugurate for his people a new existence. Clearly the evangelist wished to show that the new life for which Israel had yearned was to become possible in Jesus Christ. The presence of the Spirit descending recalled for Mark's readers the promise of the outpouring of the Spirit as a sign of the messianic or eschatological era (Isaiah 44:3, Joel 3:1). In the ensuing chapters of his gospel, the evangelist portrayed Jesus as empowered by God's Spirit, doing battle with the spirit of evil and in each instance emerging victorious. It is this same Holy Spirit with which Jesus will baptize (v. 8) those who believe in him. In the Bible (Hosea 11:11; Psalms 68:13, 74:19, 56:1) and in some rabbinical commentaries, the dove was regarded as the symbol of Israel, just as is the eagle for the United States. With the Spirit descending on Jesus like a dove, the implication is that he has become a new Israel, a new people of God, and that all is summed up in him.

Lest there be any doubt as to the significance of the event and its theophanic characteristics, the *voice* from heaven uttered the last word. Its message is christological in that it unites, in two succinct phrases, the messianic themes of Jesus as Son of God a Jesus as suffering servant. Obviously, Mark understood the baptism of Jesus and the inauguration of his ministry as the fulfillment of the first reading (Isaiah 42:1-4, 6-7). Linguists assert that the Greek words for "my son" (Mark 1:11) may be understood as equivalent to the Hebrew for "my servant" (Isaiah 42:1). God's favor or love is upon Jesus as he begins to accomplish the divine will of salvation for all of humankind.

Filled with God's own Spirit, the servant-Son Jesus began in his baptism to form unto himself a new people, a new Israel, of which we are all a part. Announced by John and testified by both the Spirit and the voice, Jesus and his mission are the cause for our celebration. In all who are baptized in water and in the Spirit and who believe in his name, that mission is inaugurated a new today.

1. The mission of the servant remains a present challenge to service for all who believe in the servant-Son par excellence (Isaiah).

2. Partiality, prejudice and discrimination threaten the magnanimous grace which baptism imparts (Acts).

3. With the favor and the Spirit of baptism come the responsibility and the power to live by the words and works of Jesus (Mark).

The Lenten Season
First Sunday of Lent

God's giving and forgiving are beautifully tangible in the multicolored arc he splashes across the sky to remind us of another ark and the saving love it signified (Genesis). Because of the strength and power of his living, redeeming word (Mark), that forgiveness and loving kindness have become accessible to believers in the sacramental flood waters of baptism (1 Peter).

Genesis 9:8-15. During the annual period of preparation for the celebration of the Easter event, the readings of the lectionary have been chosen for their instructive value. Selections from the Old Testament highlight significant events in Israel's history while the choice of the gospels relates these events to the saving activity of God in Jesus Christ. Pericopes selected for the second reading ordinarily elucidate the meaning of Christ's passion and death and/or refer to baptism, the means whereby believers are initiated into all that Christ is and does. More perhaps than during any other liturgical season, the Lenten readings exhibit the care taken to correlate both the texts and themes of the selected passages.

Like the other stories of the primeval history, the story of the flood and the covenant with which the author climaxed his narrative is at once theological and etiological. Just as the story of Adam and Eve was an attempt to explain the origin of evil in the world, the story of the great deluge and its aftermath attests to the author's belief in the divine preservation of humankind as well as a mythical explanation of the origin of the rainbow. The ark or *tebah* which sheltered Noah's group and preserved them from the flood became known in subsequent Israelite history and literature as an instrument of salvation. In fact, the same term, *tebah,* was used to designate the basket in which little Moses was said to have sailed safely away from threatening danger (Exodus 2:3). It is significant that the ark (or box) in which Israel later carried the tables of the law was also a source of salvation and for that reason became a symbol of preservation and unity for the people. In the New Testament, the ark (as well as the flood waters) was seen as a type of Christian baptism (1 Peter 20-22). Later, the church fathers further developed the ark typology so that it became symbolic of the church itself, "the bark of Peter," and a popular symbol in Christian art, as a visit to the catacombs will reveal.

A rather ambiguous symbol, the flood water spelled destruction for the wicked but became the vehicle of salvation for the just who sailed upon them by God's provident care to safety. In describing the deluge, the priestly author to whom we owe today's text used the same word, *tehom,* first employed in the creation account to describe the primordial chaos. Therefore, the covenant which followed the deluge (*tehom*) may be understood as a *new* creation, a *new* beginning, wrought by God's mercy and power. Moreover it should be noted that the covenant made with Noah (unlike the subsequent covenants with Abraham, Moses, Israel, etc.) was made with *all creation*.

Standing as a memorial and a sign of that cosmic covenant, the rainbow was to be forever a witness to God's fidelity. Among other ancient peoples, the rainbow was thought to be a divine "bow" or weapon utilized by capricious gods to inflict harm and punishment on humankind. With the biblical story of Noah, the rainbow became a sign of God's eternal providence. Perhaps it might also be a reminder of *our* obligations with regard to the cosmic covenant and a colorful witness against improper care of the earth. As stewards of the new creation, we breach the covenant of divine preservation by pollution, waste and misuse of the riches of the earth just as we do by infidelity to the God who has created them. As we begin the preparatory season of Lent, let the flood, the ark and the rainbow remind every believer, not only of God's covenant loyalty but also the Christian's baptismal responsibilities for all of creation.

1 Peter 3:18-22. This first letter is purported to be the work of the apostle Peter written during the mid 60s C.E. but the bulk of scholarly findings and opinions would assign a later date to the letter (90s?) and ascribe it to the hand of a pseudepigraphical writer, e.g., Silvanus (1 Peter 5:12). Written in a more masterful Greek than would be expected from a Galilean fisherman, with its Old Testament citations taken from the Septuagint, the letter was addressed from Rome to the Christians in Asia Minor, north and west of the Taurus Mountains. In essence, the missive is an exhortation sent to strengthen those believers whose faith in Jesus had become the cause of their persecution and suffering. Because of its emphasis on baptism as the basis for Christian hope and confidence, the letter has been called by some a baptismal liturgy wherein the sacrament would have been conferred at 1:21. Because of the lack of convincing evidence in this regard, it is more prudent to accept the internal evidence (1:1, 5:12) and to regard the work as a *letter* infused with baptismal theology and allusions.

In the pericope chosen for today's second reading, many recognize the vestiges of an early christological hymn which expressed the doctrine of Christ's atoning death and vicarious suffering for the sake of sinners. Early Christian theologians and New Testament authors interpreted the victory of Christ *over sin* and death as a triumph *over Satan* and the powers of evil. This victory and the manner in which it has been explained ("he went to preach to the spirits in prison," v. 19) has made this passage a difficult one to which *many* varied solutions have been offered throughout the ages:

(1) Following the lead of Clement of Alexandria (*Stromateis* 6:6) and Origen, the majority of Protestant scholars understand the text to refer to the descent of Christ's soul to Hades during the *triduum mortis* to preach conversion to the sinners of Noah's day who had not repented before the flood came.

(2) Augustine believed the statement to say that Christ in his preexistent and divine nature preached through the person of Noah to sinners of the era of the great deluge.

(3) The work of Robert Bellarmine (*De Controversiis* 2, 4, 13) abandoned Augustine's idea in favor of the opinion that Christ's *soul* had "descended into hell" or some limbo-like place during the *triduum mortis* and proclaimed freedom and salvation to those wicked ones of Noah's day who had repented before succumbing to the flood's devastation. This interpretation of 1 Peter 3:19 was prevalent among Catholic scholarship until this century.

(4) J. Harris amended the text by introducing Enoch and interpreted the verse to mean that *Enoch* preached to the spirits in prison. Harris substantiated his proposal by relying on Genesis 5:21-24 and on Jewish apocryphal literature. Therein (1 Enoch 12-16), Enoch, father of Methuselah, was believed to have been mandated by God to proclaim the destruction of those evil spirits which had caused humanity to sin, thereby precipitating the flood. In the letter of Peter, the disobedience of these same spirits (1 Peter 3:20) may have been associated with the sin of the "sons of God and the daughters of men" (Genesis 6:1-4). Traditional Jewish beliefs charged these "sons and daughters" with the subsequent moral chaos from which Noah and his family were delivered. It obvious that the author of 1 Peter regarded the salvation of Noah as a foreshadowing of the salvation of all humanity by Jesus, and Noah's victorious emergence from the flood as a type of the victory afforded to all believers by immersion in the *baptismal* waters.

While all these proposals are interesting, each has misinterpreted the basic distinction which the New Testament author had made with regard to "spirit," the "realm of the spirit," and "fleshy existence." As R. Fuller has pointed out, the scriptural author has made use here of the Hellenistic concept of the two spheres of existence, *not* body and soul, but the earthly sphere (fleshly existence) and the spiritual or heavenly or resurrected sphere (realm of the spirit). Therefore, the popular medieval idea of Christ's "harrowing of hell" as well as the aforementioned opinions fall short of a correct understanding of the text. It was not the dead or those in hell or limbo to whom Christ preached. Rather, in his glorious and exalted existence as the risen Lord, Christ proclaimed the triumph of his victory over sin and death as he passed through the heavens to his Father's right hand. To put it rather simply, it was in going "up to heaven," not "down to hell," that Christ preached victory to the cosmic forces of evil, believed by early Christians to dwell in the second heaven (2 Enoch 7:1-5). At God's right hand, i.e., in the seventh heaven, Christ enjoyed both the dignity and the power which were his. This same victory and power over sin and evil belonged to those who follow him. At the beginning of this Lenten season, because of the resurrection, we who are baptized into him can be sure of triumph in our continuing conflict with the powers of evil.

Mark 1:12-15. No one could ever accuse Mark of being verbose. On the contrary, in the briefest of narratives he has described not only Jesus' inaugural victory over the powers of evil (vv. 12-13) but also the summary of all of Jesus' teaching! Unlike his fellow synoptic evangelists, Matthew and Luke, Mark's account of Jesus' temptation is devoid of detail and references to the Old Testament and dialogue. Nevertheless, in his abbreviated account, Mark has not omitted the elemental features of the event or the theological import of the moment. Without any allusion to the psychological effects of the ordeal upon Jesus, Mark has made it clear that he considered Jesus' conflict with Satan as the beginning of the messianic or eschatological turmoil during which Jesus would be revealed as the new Israel, a new Moses and a new Adam through whom the powers of evil would be forever destroyed and in whose words and works the reign of God's peaceable kingdom would be established. One might look upon the temptation scene in Mark as the "declaration of war" between good and evil which would continue to be waged throughout the rest of the gospel, with Jesus emerging victorious in exorcisms, healings, authoritative teaching and ultimately in his triumph on the cross.

The wilderness was known as the habitat of evil spirits. Moreover, the desert was reminiscent of the wilderness of Sinai, through which the refugees from Egypt had trekked with Moses. Through many trials, they had learned of Yahweh, had become his people and were covenanted to him in love and by law. In the wilderness, Satan (Hebrew name for tempter) was thought to be on his own turf, as the ruler of a vast evil kingdom with subjects (demons, evil spirits) at his beck and call, whose special function it was to tempt, to test and to solicit to evil. Therefore, Jesus' victory was all the more impressive, because he vanquished the perpetrator of evil in the midst of his own empire. It should be noted that Mark did not clearly pronounce Jesus as the victor in the desert but chose to illustrate Jesus' triumph and superiority in the power he exercised over evil in the subsequent public ministry.

In the Judean desert, wild beasts were commonplace and in the wilderness Jesus may have been in contact with leopards, bears, wild boars and jackals. But the biblical significance of these creatures is more important than the physical threat they may have posed. Wild beasts were commonly thought to house demons and were therefore an added threat of evil to Jesus' power (Psalm 22:13-22, Isaiah 13:21-22). But notice that Mark does not indicate any conflict or struggle with the beasts. Therefore, their presence with Jesus in the wilderness could signify the beginning of the era of peace brought by the messiah. Isaiah (11:6) and Hosea (2:11, 11:6) had described the harmony of the kingdom in terms of a restored Eden. In the same way Mark's mention of Satan, the wild beasts and the ministration of the angels is an echo of the psalms (91:11-13) and of Jewish apocryphal literature (Testament of Naphthali 8:4) wherein the man of God is portrayed as protected by angels, victorious over the devil and at peace with the fierce beasts of the wilderness. Perhaps the evangelist also had in mind the psalmist's (78:25) reference to God feeding Moses and his people in the Sinai, as well as Elijah's being sustained (1 Kings 19:5-8) by angels during his journey to Horeb. In all these references and echoes of the Old Testament, the evangelist's point is clear: Jesus, empowered with God's Spirit and authority, inaugurated his mission of overthrowing the reign of sin, evil and death in order to establish the reign of God.

In the second half of today's gospel (vv. 14-15), the evangelist has summarized the means by which the reign of God would be secured, viz., through the good news of the teaching of Jesus Christ. Like all of Jesus' subsequent teachings, his inaugural message challenged those who heard it to action. Reformation of life and faith in the good news were demanded by the presence of God's reign. It is significant that Mark chose to invert the order (reign—reform and believe) of this initial message (Matthew 4:17), thereby underscoring the eschatological nature of Jesus' inaugural appearance and the immediacy of the nature of the kingdom. In all of Jesus' words and works, this same immediacy would be obvious as each act and each word of his challenged to decision and commitment. Today, no less than the first time it was proclaimed, Jesus' message speaks to us: The reign of God is at hand! Reform your lives, believe the good news!

1. A rainbow can be either the refraction of light through the moisture droplets in the sky or a pledge of God's abiding love ... like so many things, it all depends on one's perspective (Genesis).

2. Baptism is at once a washing of sin and a flood of life and grace (1 Peter).

3. Temptation passes, but the consequences of our choices and decisions remain (Mark).

Second Sunday of Lent

With sighs of relief, all rejoice that Isaac was spared and, in his place, a ram was offered by Abraham to God (Genesis). But in the case of another Father and another Son, there was no ram (Romans) but still we rejoice with sighs of relief and gratitude. In the loving sacrifice of Jesus, the sinful world is transformed from sin unto freedom, from dark death unto the transfigured glory of salvation and resurrected joy (Mark).

Genesis 22:1-2, 9, 10-13, 15-18. From the very outset, those who first heard this portion of the patriarchal saga had the psychological advantage of knowing that Abraham, their father in faith, was being "put to the test" (v. 1). Even that fore-knowledge, however, cannot immunize the reader from being swept up into the profound pathos of the episode. As B. Skinner has pointed out, "It cannot be read without tears." Devoid of any exact chronological or geographical references, the story is obviously one in which the theological implications are far more important than its historical significance. Although the land of Moriah (v. 2) is specified, this land has yet to be correctly identified (the Syriac has land of the Amorites), nor for that matter has the mountain (height) to which Abraham journeyed at God's behest. Clearly the Eloistic tradition, to whom the story is for the most part attributed, did not intend a chronicle of Abraham's undertakings. On the contrary, it is the spirit of Abraham's obedience, the endurance of his faith and the correct manner of sacrificial worship which the author wished to convey.

Besides the central motif of Abraham's faith and obedience, one cannot overlook the subordinate, but very important, motif of sacrifice. There existed among the peoples of the ancient Near Eastern world the custom of sacrificing children by fire to the god called Molech by the Canaanites, Milcom among the Ammonites, Muluk in the Mari texts, etc. During the prophetic ministry of Elisha (ca. 800 B.C.E.), the Moabite king whose power was threatened by war burned his firstborn son on the city walls (2 Kings 3:27). This act of desperation and the gravity of the sacrifice were thought to have propitiatory value and would thus prompt the god Molech to turn the tide of the war. Considered an abomination among the Israelites, child sacrifice was strictly forbidden (Leviticus 20:2-5). Nevertheless, there were certain low ebbs in Israel's history during which some of its kings resorted to the crude practice of immolating their sons (2 Kings 16:3, 17:17, 21:6).

In sharp contrast to such an aberration of Israel's sacrificial worship, the story of Abraham and Isaac was told as a polemic. As an answer to the question, "With what gift shall I come before the Lord? . . . Must I give my firstborn son?" (Micah 6:6,7), the answer illustrated in the story of Abraham is a resounding "No!!" In Abraham, Israel was to learn that the true spirit of sacrifice consists not so much in what is offered but in the manner, spirit and motivation with which that gift is offered. The *value* of Abraham's sacrifice was not in any way diminished by the fact that he did not take Isaac's life. Indeed, his willingness to offer back to the giver the most precious gift he had received was more powerful than any blood offering. With the substitution of the ram for Isaac, Israel was to learn that their Lord did not require human sacrifice.

Romans 8:31-34. Paul did not found the Christian community of believers in Rome, nor had he ever visited the capital of the empire. He did, however, intend to go to Rome to set up there a base of operations for the expansion of his apostolic endeavors (to Spain, etc.). In writing to the community of Rome, the apostle wished to introduce himself and to give a summary of his ideas and teachings which some have called his "confessions." Although it is difficult to ascertain from Paul's letter the exact situation of the church in Rome, there are some extrabiblical facts which can help the modern reader to better understand the conditions that existed there.

Claudius was emperor in Rome (41-54 C.E.) when the Christian foundation was first established. He was thought to be retarded and his own mother had described him as "a monster whom Mother Nature had begun to work upon and then flung aside." Claudius had *few* likeable qualities. A drunkard and a gambler, he married five times, had little respect from the Senate or the Guard, and frequently satisfied his insatiable lust for bloodshed by the execution and torture of prisoners. Mad for power and suspicious of any threat to his sovereignty, Claudius acted quickly when unrest broke out among the Jews in Rome.

In fact, it was the conversion of Jews to Jesus which caused the conflict within the Jewish community. Writing the biography of Claudius (ca. 120 C.E.), Seutonius described the situation in this way: "Because the Jews at Rome caused continuous disturbances at the instigation of a certain Chrestos, Claudius expelled them from the city" (*Vita Claudii*). "Chrestos," of course referred to Christ, or more properly the gospel of Jesus Christ and the year of the edict of expulsion was 49 or 50 C.E. Incidentally, Priscilla and Aquila were among those who were forced to leave Rome. They went on to Corinth and then to Ephesus, carrying with them the message of Christ and one might say that, in a sense, Claudius was *helpful* in the spread of Christianity! After Claudius' death in 54 C.E. the edict was relaxed, due in part to the sympathy of Nero's wife for the Jews.

Once returned to Rome, the Jewish Christians found that the gentile Christians who had not been subject to the edict had developed without them and without the influence of the synagogue and its authority. The divergence in the two groups of Christians (Jewish and gentile) was a source of disagreement and disunity and serves to explain the conflict reflected in Paul's letter to the Romans written during this period. It is against this background and in the spirit of reconciliation in which it was written that we may best understand Paul's words in today's reading.

In a series of rhetorical questions, the apostle expressed his belief that the sacrificial and redeeming power of Jesus' death has expressed God's love in a manner unsurpassed. Because of that love and its consequences, all human problems and differences pale into insignificance. Moreover, all charges (v. 33) and condemnations (v. 34), whether from *within* the community (Jew vs. gentile Christians) or from *without* (Romans, Jews) are meaningless. Because of the justification won by Jesus, human accusations carry no weight and therefore should not be a source of fear or anxiety for the believer. Paul sought to lay to rest the differences within the community of Rome by moving the attention of the church to the one difference that truly mattered. They had once been in sin and subject to death's finality, alienated from God's love and devoid of purpose. But *with* Jesus Christ and *in* him, they were freed of sin's bondage, they were heirs of heaven and sons and daughters of the Father. What more cogent proof of God's love could there be than the sacrifice of Jesus?

Mark 9:2-10. By the use of certain literary signals, Mark has indicated to the reader from the outset that what follows is a special revelatory event. Whenever the evangelist explains that Jesus took the apostles "off by themselves" (*kat'idian*), he is designating by use of that particular caveat the theophanic and christological importance of the moment. In the case of today's gospel, that revelatory moment is the transfiguration of Jesus. Similar signals (*kat'idian*) were used by the evangelist in several other moments of special revelation or teaching (4:34; 6:31-32; 7:33; 9:2, 28; 13:3) throughout his gospel.

While the special revelatory character of the transfiguration of Jesus is a foregone fact, it is difficult to be sure of the actual historical situation and character of the event. Was it a symbolic vision, a spiritual encounter, a deep religious experience? And when did it occur? It would seem that the transfiguration of Jesus is a post-resurrection appearance which the evangelist has projected back into the ministry. This would account for the eschatological character of the event as well as the fact that after the transfiguration the apostles did not seem any more sure of Jesus' messianic identity than before it! The fact that Mark inserted the event into his account of Jesus' ministry would indicate that he intended to give his hearers and readers an anticipated glimpse of the risen Lord and to point to the resurrection (v. 9) as the decisive moment of Jesus' full manifestation.

Elijah and Moses represent the law and the prophets and witness to the fact that, in this glimpse of the risen Jesus, both law and prophets are fulfilled. That only Jesus was left (v. 8) is a further indication of his superiority as well as a Marcan correction of false christologies in his community. There were some who, basing their hopes on ideas from later Judaism, looked for Elijah to return as messiah. Moreover the heavenly voice (v. 7) served to clarify and to ratify Jesus' role. Just as at Jesus' baptism (1:11) the testimony of the voice identified Jesus with the prophet-suffering-servant as foretold by Isaiah (42:1), so too, the mandate to "listen to him" would suggest that Jesus was *the prophet*, promised long ago (Deuteronomy 18:15-18) whose teaching should be heeded.

Many have interpreted the reaction of Peter, "Let's build three tents (booths)," as a naive joy and desire to make the moment last. Actually, Peter's joy is better understood in terms of the eschatological significance of his statement. Every autumn, the Israelites celebrated *Sukkoth* or the Feast of Tabernacles (tents, booths) to give thanks for the harvest and to commemorate the desert sojourn en route to the promised land. In late Judaism, the feast acquired a messianic character and it was believed that during the feast, the messianic savior would appear and make his glorious power known (Zechariah 14:16-19). That Peter wished to erect tents for Moses, Elijah and Jesus would seem to indicate that he believed the time for eschatological feasting had arrived. But the evangelist was swift to point out that the feasting would come only at the resurrection and after the harvest of sinful humankind by the divine reaper on the cross.

Mark's use of the messianic secret technique is more understandable in this transfiguration (v. 9) narrative than in any other instance. Full revelation and full comprehension of Jesus' glory and identity would come only after he had risen from the dead. During the ministry, however, the transfiguring power of Jesus would be manifested in the transforming and healing power of his words and works in those who believed. As he worked his metamorphoses, changing sinners to believers and the alienated into friends, transforming the sick and maimed into whole and healthy people, expanding provincial, nationalistic horizons into cosmic ones, the transfiguring power of Jesus anticipated the life of the world to come and established the reign of his Father.

Though already risen and glorified, the transfiguring activity of the Lord is still present among us. Through the sacraments of his word, his church and his abiding presence in the eucharist, he is still transforming unto wholeness, holiness, faith and grace all who would go "off by themselves with him."

1. As with any gift-giving, so too in the case of sacrificing, it is the thought that matters (Genesis).

2. Human respect and public opinion can cripple and thwart good intentions but in the end only the divine evaluation matters (Romans).

3. The transformation of sinful people into faithful disciples is a share in the transfiguration of Jesus (Mark).

Third Sunday of Lent

Precepts of the law can protect, guide and provide the freedom with which to live a life of virtue and value (Exodus). But Jesus called his followers to move beyond legality to love, to forsake empty ritual for relationships (John). Those who would become disciples must be ready to risk absurdity and foolishness in order to be, with Jesus, signs of power and wisdom (1 Corinthians).

Exodus 20:1-17. Many modern believers, when thinking of Moses and the giving of the law on Sinai, have engraved upon their memories the scene from Cecil B. De Mille's *Ten Commandments*.

With a fiery flourish, figures were carved on the tablets for Moses, who then enunciated the law to the people who waited at the foot of the mountain. While the entrepreneur of Hollywood may have greatly embroidered the event, one thing is accurate in the De Mille dramatization. Israel believed the law by which she strove to live represented the will of God with whom she was covenanted.

Other ancient Near Eastern peoples governed their lives by similar legislation, the formulations of which antedated the decalog or ten words by several centuries, e.g., the Code of Lipit-Ishtar, the Code of Hammurabi, Hittite codes, etc. In all these law codes, however, the basis for adherence to the law was for the sake of civil order, societal harmony, etc. Only in Israel was the keeping of the law raised from a civil level to the level of religion and ethics. Israel had adapted the *structure* of the Hittite suzerainty treaty to express the covenant relationship she shared with Yahweh, and her law coincided with the treaty stipulations or terms of that covenant.

In addition to the difference in motivation for keeping the law, the manner of expression of Israel's law also differed from that of her neighbors. Other codes of law were based on casuistry and were conditional in their expression, e.g., if you do *"such and such,"* then *"such and such"* will be operative. Notice the apodictic or unconditional character of Israel's decalogue: "You shall . . . You shall not." When the prescriptions or terms of the Sinai covenant were first formulated, the list was probably shorter and was expanded to 10 only over the course of time. Some of the commands are terse and succinct, "You shall not kill," whereas others are more elaborate, including motivational and explanatory aspects (sabbath law). It is believed that these expansions, too, were the product of later interpretations and applications of the simple basic precepts to changing times and circumstances.

Commandments one through three concern the proper attitude and conduct with regard to one's relationship with God. While the first statute is clearly monotheistic, it should be noted that strict monotheism did not prevail among the Israelites until almost the end of the period of the classical prophets. Other gods were not necessarily worshiped but their existence and power were recognized, as passages like the following would indicate: "Who is like unto you among the gods, O Lord" (Exodus 15:11). Only several centuries later did Israel profess: "Thus says Israel's redeemer, Yahweh, 'There is no other God besides me'" (Isaiah 44:6). Evidently the prohibition against images of Yahweh was taken very seriously because, in all the archaeological excavations of the ancient Israelite civilization, not one image, statue or likeness of Yahweh has been discovered. Taking the Lord's name "in vain" referred to the evil use of the name to support perjury, magical formulae and incantations. Later Judaism, in an extreme interpretation of the law, avoided pronouncing the divine name at all and instead substituted *Adonai* (Lord) or simply *Ha Shem* (the Name). Many ancient cultures observed a rest day and Israel attached to its observance of the day of rest or seventh day (sabbath) a religious motivation. To the priestly tradition is owed the idea of resting in imitation of God who rested after six days of creative work.

Commandments four through 10 have been called the natural law and are similar to prescriptions in other ancient cultures which legislated proper conduct in interpersonal relationship. In each precept, those values upon which a sound and sane society is built, are safeguarded, e.g. family (4th), life (5th), marriage and fidelity (6th), property rights (7th), truthfulness (8th), home and hearth (9th and 10th). Significantly these commandments were on a par with the first three concerning God and all were thought to be an expression of the divine will. Centuries later, the prophets, in calling their people back to a faithful living of that will, would correlate Israel's respect for God with social justice (Amos 5:21-24, Hosea 6:4-6). Still later, Jesus would berate those who had so twisted the law as to find in it an excuse for the neglect of social responsibilities (Mark 7:10-12). A similar aberration of basic values of true religion and justice prompted the action of Jesus as portrayed in today's gospel.

1 Corinthians 1:22-25. If Paul had lived to minister in the 20th century, the style and content of his preaching would have been labeled controversial just as it was in the first century. But many of the Jews and Greeks who heard his message on the subject of Christ and the cross were in agreement on one thing at least: They thought the very idea was ridiculous and nonsensical! Today's second reading is a pericope from a longer section of Paul's letter to Corinth wherein he contrasts worldly wisdom with the wisdom of God as manifested in the crucifixion and death of Jesus. Without diluting the import of his preaching, Paul made it clear that he understood the reservations which both Jews and Greeks had with regard to a crucified Christ (messiah).

For the Jews, the idea of a suffering messiah was a contradiction in terms. The messiah, God's anointed one, was thought to be highly favored, endowed with the Spirit of Yahweh and blessed in every way with the ability to lead Israel to its former might and honor and dignity. As a proof of his legitimacy, the messiah would, they believed, perform signs, viz., sensational acts of power which illustrated his participation in the divine plan for Israel. Jesus himself during his ministry had to contend with the Jews' unslakable thirst for signs (Matthew 16:4, John 4:48, 6:30, etc.). In Paul's day too, messianic pretenders were present everywhere, promising signs to validate their claims.

Over and against the preconceptions and prejudices of both Jews and gentiles, Paul offered the crucified Christ as an expression of God's power and wisdom. God's wisdom was a mystery which could only be penetrated by faith. To both Jews and Greeks, Paul offered the challenge of overcoming their seemingly insuperable notions of salvation in order to accept the "foolishness" of God. Only faith could pierce the folly and find wisdom. Only faith could see the sign of the cross and not be scandalized. Paul's words are also a challenge to the 20th century philosophers and sign-seekers. To be a Christian is to risk being thought foolish and absurd in a world whose values are often at odds with the message of Jesus. As adherents of the crucified and risen Jesus Christ, we have the paradox of the cross as our heritage and our glory.

John 2:13-25. It is difficult to imagine that Jesus behaved in the manner described in today's gospel and then proceeded, unaccosted by Jewish or Roman authorities, to exercise his ministry for three more years! Unlike the synoptics, who place the temple cleansing episode at the *end* of Jesus' public activity, the Johannine author chose to place the event at the *beginning* of Jesus' ministry. But the author's reasons and purpose were more theological than chronological; he saw in the authoritative actions of Jesus in the temple a dramatic announcement of the fulfillment of Israel's messianic expectations. Both Malachi (3:14) and Zechariah (14:1-21) had envisioned the inauguration of the messianic era in terms of the Lord "suddenly coming to his temple, to purify and to cleanse." On that day, they had prophesied, "no trader would be seen in the house of the Lord." Jesus' bold actions in entering the temple and throwing out the merchants and animals made it clear from the outset of the fourth gospel that the goal of his ministry, of all his words and works, would be to overthrow the "tables" of the Jewish law and to cast out the "merchants" of hypocrisy and legalism. He would replace the old dispensation and old system of worship with the new and living temple of his body. In the place of the alienating minutiae of the law he would offer to all who believe a share in his own relationship with his Father.

In the 18th year of his reign, Herod had begun to build the temple in question (20-19 B.C.E.) and it was not completed until 63 or 64 C.E. Only a few years later, it was totally demolished by the troops of the Roman general Titus during the Jewish War. At the time of Jesus' activity there, the gospel tells us the temple was about 46 years old; hence the year would have been ca. 27 or 28 C.E. As depicted in the gospel, the foray took place in the temple precincts or the outer court of the gentiles. There it was customary to offer for sale a variety of animals which had been procured for the Passover feast. Pilgrims who had traveled great distances to Jerusalem for the feast could then easily purchase an animal without having to bring it with them from home. As R. Brown has pointed out, Jesus' attitude toward the dove-sellers was a bit milder than his behavior toward the oxen and sheep sellers. Perhaps this is because doves were the prescribed offering of the *poor* (Leviticus 5:7). Money changers performed the service of exchanging foreign currency for the Tyrian half sheckel, the only coinage accepted for the temple tax. In the transaction, these merchants made a profit and some have suggested that Jesus' anger was vented at their dishonesty in swindling the people.

In narrating the fury with which Jesus acted, the evangelist may have had in mind the prophet Jeremiah's words (7:11-14) which spoke of the people's evildoing as destroying the temple. In the same line of thought, both Tobit (14:7-10) and Zechariah (14:20ff) had prophesied about an ideal temple in which no commerce would be tolerated. Jesus' reference to the temple as "my Father's house" and the quotation from Psalm 69 ("Zeal for your house . . .") underscored the special relationship with the Father which Jesus' presence on earth made available to all believers. Used a total of 27 times in the fourth gospel, "my Father's house" took on added significance when Jesus used the same term in speaking of the kingdom of eternal life (14:2) which was opened to all by his saving work.

"The sign" of the temple cleansing (though the evangelist does not include it as one of his seven signs) can be understood by way of comparison with the sign at the wedding feast at Cana. Just as Jesus had replaced the water with wine, so too would he replace the temple and its liturgy with himself. It is noteworthy that while the synoptics separated the two episodes of the temple cleansing and Jesus' prophecy of the temple's destruction, the fourth evangelist has related the two incidents very closely. A favorite Johannine literary technique of double entendre is well illustrated in the Jewish misunderstanding of Jesus' statement, "Destroy this temple" (v. 21). To further clarify his point that it was Jesus *himself*, and not the earthly temple, which was referred to, the evangelist changed the synoptic reference "and I will *build* it up" to "I will *raise* it up," using the same technical term as that which described Jesus' resurrection.

1. Legislation does not create values but upholds those which already exist (Exodus).

2. Christians, as living signs of the crucified-risen Lord, must risk being thought absurd (1 Corinthians).

3. Integrity in liturgy flows from right relationships and not from ritual (John).

Fourth Sunday of Lent

In weaving the tapestry of human events, there are many hands at work, nimbly plying multicolored threads to create the beauty, the lights and shadows and even the flaws. But only the artist who has conceived the work knows the overall plan and the expected result (Chronicles). Unlike any ordinary weaver, the great artist has shared his insight, his abilities and his purpose (Ephesians). When at long last, time fades and unravels the tapestry, the vision created by both artist and multicolored threads will live forever (John).

2 Chronicles 36:14-17, 19-23. To Saint Jerome we owe the more easily pronounced title (Chronicles) of the two volumes which were once called by the Greek name, Paralipomenon. A merciful change, which benefitted lectors and preachers alike, the adaptation of the title to 1 and 2 Chronicles was not only less tongue twisting, but more in keeping with the contents of the works. Most scholars today would group 1 and 2 Chronicles with Ezra and Nehemiah and view these four books as the annals of the people of Israel from their origins to the period of reconstruction after the exile. Compiled between 400 and 200 B.C.E., all four volumes (1) share similar vocabulary and syntax, (2) favor lists and genealogies, (3) describe in detail and in similar fashion the functions of the levites, (4) concentrate on Jerusalem and its temple as the liturgical center of Israel, (5) exhibit a high regard for the Torah, (6) stress the superiority of the Davidic covenant over the Sinai pact, (7) encourage a messianism based on the promise of 2 Samuel 7:14, (8) provide the modern believer with an insight into Israel's unique method of interpreting history. This last point is illustrated in today's pericope.

When the Chronicler set out to record the history of his people, he did so according to his understanding and perception of that history. Of course, all history recording is in some sense subjective, as a comparison of the winners' and losers' accounts of the same war would prove. But in Israel, the events and circumstances through which the nation evolved were considered in a religious and theological sense. Israel, as Wolfhart Pannenberg has pointed out, perceived its nation's history as revelation, i.e., the self-disclosure of God. In history, "Yahweh himself becomes visible in his powerful acts of salvation. He becomes known through these acts; whoever sees and experiences them can know God in them." To an historian with this conviction, specific dates, meticulous accuracy in reporting and compiling data from the past would be subordinate to his definitive analyses in faith of God's workings and his ways. In fact, in ancient Hebrew, there is no specific word for history per se. Modern Hebrew's *toledot,* rendered "acts of generating," comes nearest to defining the Old Testament concept of history. Therefore, the literary vehicle or genre for this concept might be more correctly called "edifying narrative" or "juridico-theological theses" (R. North).

With little regard for political or socio-economic explanations, the Chronicler, as the prophets before him, interpreted the prosperity, successes and victories which Israel enjoyed as God's reward for fidelity to the law and the covenant. Consequently, the tragedies, failures in war and natural calamities through which Israel suffered were attributed to its infidelity to God's desires as manifested in the law. Our reading for today cites these failures as the cause of the Babylonian exile and the disasters that accompanied it. For not listening to the prophets who were the interpreters of Gods' revelation in time and space, Israel lost lives, power, prestige, homeland, as well as political and religious freedom. Yahweh's righteous anger would be expressed in terms of a 70 year exile (v. 22). Evidently the Chronicler numbered the years from 586 B.C.E., when the temple was destroyed and Jerusalem burned, to the time when the temple was rebuilt under the supervision of the Persian king Darius, 520-515 B.C.E. Because of its neglect of the sabbath, viz., the practice in truth and justice of sincere liturgy, Israel would be forced to let the land lie fallow, at rest (Leviticus 25:4, Exodus 23:10) for 70 years.

In the opinion of the Chronicler, *all* were guilty, *priests, people and princes.* Due to this and other slurs (v. 14) against the priests as well as his emphasis on the role and importance of the levites, it is believed that the author of 1 and 2 Chronicles was himself a levite, probably of the class of cantors. Because he was a temple functionary, his interest in its welfare and integrity was a subjective but a sincere one. An underlying theme throughout the two volume work is a polemic against those survivors of the northern kingdom who posited their own Samaritan temple as the true center of cult for God's people. Against the Samaritan claim, the levitical author of Chronicles defended Jerusalem, its temple and the line of David, as the only means whereby divine worship and authentic authority would be restored when at last God had relented from punishing his sinful people.

Just as he had interpreted the Babylonian conquest of Israel as a revelation of divine indignation, the Chronicler understood the *end* of the exile as the restorative and forgiving hand of God at work. His citation of the edict of Cyrus is repeated in Ezra (1:1-3). As the conclusion of 2 Chronicles and the last words of the canonical Hebrew Old Testament, it lends a note of optimism to an otherwise sobering account.

Ephesians 2:4-10. A commercially active seaport city on the western coast of Asia Minor (modern day Turkey), Ephesus was made the capital of the Roman empire's Asian province and as such enjoyed the status of a "free city." For a total of three years during his second and third missionary campaigns, Paul had either ministered there or used Ephesus as his base of operations. Because of the length of time he had spent there, one would expect to find more personal references in the letter to the church at Ephesus. However, aside from a reference to Tychicus (6:21) at the end, the letter is quite impersonal and bears no identifying internal evidence to link it to Ephesus. Some have proposed therefore that it was intended as a circular letter destined for all the churches in Asia Minor.

Since the 18th century C.E. the letter has been considered by many to be of the Pauline corpus. It is not impossible that the apostle Paul actually wrote it and, if he did so, the date would have been ca. 63 C.E. However, a great number of eminent scholars today doubt a Pauline authorship due to the late first and early second century influences which the letter exhibits. In Ephesians, the church is considered not as the local community of believers, but as the transcendent and universal assembly of all the faithful. In Ephesians (in contrast to Romans 6 and Colossians 2:12), the Christian believer is presented as *already* participating in the resurrected life by baptism. The missive concentrates on realized eschatology and concerns itself more with the church developing here and now than with the second advent of Jesus. Whereas other letters attributed to Paul greatly emphasize the cross and the saving passion of Jesus, Ephesians is centered primarily on the risen and exalted Christ. There is an extensive relationship between the letters to the Colossians and to the Ephesians, with the two sharing over one third of their verses in exact form and content. But, as Willi Marxen has pointed out, Colossians is primarily a polemic against heresies and Ephesians is an exhortation to unity in faith.

Compared with the work of the Chronicler, Ephesians evidences a marked development in soteriology. The Chronicler, with his interpretation of history's ups and downs, successes and failures, intimated that these were understood as a type of divine teaching method based on a Skinner-like system of rewards and punishments. The author of Ephesians, on the other hand, understood the "rewards" of grace and salvation, resurrection and exaltation as totally undeserved by sinful humanity and due solely to the gratuitousness of God. This concept is beautifully expressed in our reading for today.

Contrary to the growing gnostic influence of his day, which thought of the initiation into the Christian life as an "illumination of one's own inner self," the author understood and emphasized the free gift of grace (v. 5, "favor") as the basis of moral responsibility to which the faithful were called by God. As opposed to the gnostics, Christians were to appreciate grace, or God's favor, not as a *consequence* of one's own efforts or good deeds, but to consider good works and salvation as a consequence of God's grace.

John 3:14-21. What the Ephesians' author had begun to unravel concerning God's gratuitous gifts and the appropriate response to them, the Johannine author continued to elaborate and in so doing reached sublime literary and theological heights! To illustrate the mystery of God's saving action in Jesus, the fourth evangelist referred to the period of Israel's wilderness wanderings. Stricken by fiery serpents for their impatient grumbling against Moses and against God, the Israelites begged Moses to act as their intercessor. As a result of Moses' mediation, the people were instructed to *look upon* the bronze (brazen) serpent, which Moses was to lift up, and they would live (Numbers 21:6-9). Significantly the image of the serpent on a pole has become the emblem of the healing profession. Centuries later, the author of the Wisdom of Solomon (16:6-7) referred to Moses' bronze serpent as *symbolon soterias,* a symbol or sign of salvation. But the Johannine author understood the *actions* of "lifting up" and "looking upon" (the serpent) as having soteriological significance.

Today's gospel pericope is from the discourse following the Nicodemus episode wherein being born again in water and the Spirit was cited as the prerequisite for eternal life. In this discourse the evangelist went on to explain that the rebirth in water and Spirit as well as the joys of eternal life are possible only because of the "lifting up" of Jesus. *Hypsothenai* ("lifted up"), like so many words in the Johannine vocabulary, has a double meaning. Besides referring to Jesus' being "lifted up" on the cross (8:28, 12:32), it also pertains to the resurrection and exalted *lifting up* of Jesus in glory. Undoubtedly, the evangelist had in mind the Isaian description of the suffering servant: "Behold my servant shall prosper: he shall be lifted up (*hypsoun*) and glorified exceedingly" (53:13). In addition, healing was accomplished for many by the servant's suffering. Just as Moses' followers in the desert were healed by looking upon, i.e., believing in God's power as manifested in the brazen serpent, so also would believers in the *lifted up*, crucified and risen Lord be saved. As a consequence of belief in the crucified-exalted one, the faithful would be granted life in him, i.e., a share in the same process of death-to-life exaltation (v. 15). Moreover, the quality of this life would be eternal (v. 15).

What logical explanation could possibly account for the gifts of rebirth, the Spirit, life in union with God and exalted glory? While gnostic influences proposed that such riches might be attained by intellectual or even ascetic endeavors, the evangelist's discourse makes it perfectly clear that no amount of effort on the part of humankind could "earn" or merit or even deserve such generosity. The only *credible* explanation is the *incredible* love of God. The Johannine statement, "God so loved the world that he gave his only Son" (v. 16), leaps off the page and defies human logic in its simplicity and incomprehensibility. In describing God's *giving* (*didonai*), the evangelist once again employed one of his words with double significance. That God *gave* his only Son referred not only to the incarnation but also to the sacrifice of the cross. With echoes of the Abraham-Isaac story (Genesis 22:2, 16) as well as the suffering servant figure (Isaiah 53:12), the evangelist explained the depths of the Father's love. *Sent* (v. 17) is to be understood as parallel to *gave* (v. 16) and implies the missionary aspect of the mystery of Jesus which began with the incarnation and ended with the cross and exaltation.

1. To admit of God's involvement in human history does not lessen personal responsibility for human affairs (2 Chronicles).

2. God's rich mercy and lavish love cannot be explained, only appreciated (Ephesians).

3. To see Jesus cruciform against the sun and to believe is to open ourselves to healing and to life (John).

Fifth Sunday of Lent

When the sower throws his seeds to the earth, he knows that the silent death and the waiting in hope are prerequisites for the harvest of abundant life that will follow (John). So it is with the eternal sower and the seed of everlasting life: In suffering and in docility, the seed of the word was plowed under the furrows of sin and infidelity (Hebrews) in order to reestablish the cycle of life and love (Jeremiah).

Jeremiah 31:31-34. In an era when political fortunes ebbed and flowed at an alarming rate and when religious fervor vacillated between reform and ruination, Jeremiah served as God's prophet to his people. During the 40 years of his active ministry, Jeremiah of Anathoth witnessed the weakening of the Assyrian empire under Ashurbanipal (669-633 B.C.E.) and the daring seizure of power by the Aramean Nabupolassar in 626 B.C.E. In that same year, Jeremiah received his prophetic call and, though still quite a young man, he was supportive of his king's (Josiah) reform. Enlivened by the "finding" of the book of the law in the temple, the reform effectively reduced the influence of Mesopotamian astral cults and Canaanite fertility rites on Judah's Yahwistic religion and succeeded in centralizing the cult in Jerusalem. When Josiah fell in battle at Megiddo (609) trying to prevent Egypt from coming to Assyria's aid, Jehoiakim proved a weak successor. Not only did the reform instituted by Josiah fail but the political strength of Judah had been so weakened that she became easy prey for the conquering Babylonians.

At Sinai, a covenant had been forged, whose terms were engraved upon stone tablets (Exodus 31:18, 34:27). A bilateral contract initiated by Yahweh, the Sinai covenant was conditional in nature, so that Israel's successes and/or failures were contingent upon her loyalty and/or disloyalty to the covenant prescriptions. The bulk of prophetic literature had concerned itself with interpreting historical events according to the climate and quality of covenant fidelity which existed. Having observed his people and the working of their Lord among them for almost a generation, Jeremiah had correctly concluded that all observable breaches of the covenant and therefore the plight of his people stemmed from unresponsive hearts (5:23, 13:10, 23:17). The prophet was also aware that only God, who had created the human heart, knew it intimately and completely (11:20, 12:3, 17:10, 20:12). Any genuine fidelity to law, therefore, had to spring from within the heart of the person.

To that end, Jeremiah envisioned a new covenant which would be defined, not on stone tablets in an exterior manner, but engraved on the very hearts of God's own people by God himself. This interiorization of law, Jeremiah called a *new covenant*. Inspiration from God would move the covenanted person to act in conviction and in faith. External forms of obedience and loyalty were not precluded by this new covenant but were considered the consequence and not the cause of an interior commitment. Ezekiel also expressed this idea of the interiorization of law and cult in his concepts of the "heart of flesh" and the "new spirit" (Ezekiel 11:20, 18:31, 36:26).

Unlike the former or the old covenant which was to be *taught* (Deuteronomy 6:7) to the next generation, the new covenant envisioned by Jeremiah (v. 34) would have one teacher only, Yahweh himself. From within, his divine pedagogy would so transform the hearts of his people that they would "know" him. "Knowing" in the scriptures connotes an intimate relationship, personal recognition and deep communion. From the biographical material in his writings and from his "confessions," it is evident that the prophet himself *knew* and lived according to this interiorization and personalization of covenantal values.

Hebrews 5:7-9. In the old covenant formulated at Sinai, Moses' role as mediator and agent of God earned for him the respect due his priestly functions. Writing in the first century of the Christian era (ca. 80-96 C.E.), the anonymous author of the letter to the Hebrews wished to portray Jesus as minister and priest par excellence of the new and eternal covenant, formulated at the Passover-eucharistic supper and sealed on the cross. Gathering the tools of ethical exhortation (13:22) and theological exposition under his pen, the Hebrews' author could more properly be called a composer because his exquisite work exhibits the technical and artistic skill of a musician rendering a symphony. Due to the similarities which exist between the Hebrews letter and the literary efforts of the Alexandrian Jew, Philo, it is generally believed today that the Christian author was a Jewish Christian of Hellenistic background. Many possible authors have been proposed, e.g., Barnabas, Apollos, Prisca, Luke; but Origen and Jerome were probably correct in their respective conclusions: "In truth, God alone knows who wrote the epistle" and "It matters not who wrote it, for he is a man of the church."

Regardless of the author's true identity, there is no doubt as to the main theme of his missive, viz., "We have a high priest, one who is seated at God's right hand" (8:1). With that major point in mind, the author wrote to exhort his fellow Christians to a firm faith in Jesus the high priest and mediator who has won once and for all God's merciful forgiveness for sinners.

Our second reading for today is from a longer section (4:15—5:10) within which Jesus' high priestly qualities are enunciated. Though not of the tribe of Levi, and therefore not heir to the Aaronic priesthood, Jesus nevertheless shares the priestly qualification of Melchisedek, the ideal high priest of tradition. As high priest, Jesus has satisfied all the requirements of his office in that: (1) he has acted as mediator, (2) he has offered sacrifice, indeed, the sacrifice of himself, which has rendered meaningless and obsolete all other sacrifices, (3) he has offered supplication to God for sin. The definitive result of Christ's high priestly activity has been the new and eternal covenant.

Today's text, while establishing Christ's superior requisites for his office as high priest, sounds like a description of Christ's anguish in the Gethsemane garden. Through his obedience to the Father and the suffering which that obedience entailed, Christ became "*perfected*" (v. 10). "To make perfect" or *teleioun* is a technical term employed in the Septuagint (LXX) to refer to the conferring of priestly power. Because of his obedient suffering and the soteriological quality of his sacrificial death, Jesus received the crown of exaltation and became the eternal high priest of the new covenant. To all who believe and accept this good news, Christ is the forerunner and pledge, mediator and manifestation of the fruits of salvation.

John 12:20-33. Any farmer who heard Jesus speaking about the grain of wheat falling to the earth and dying (v. 24) knew from experience that those words were true. But as in so many instances in the fourth gospel, the Johannine Jesus was communicating on an entirely different level. The grain, the dying and the fruitful harvest of which Jesus spoke were not merely agricultural phenomena but were vital aspects of his own soteriological mission for the world. In today's gospel pericope, Jesus makes it clear that his hour, i.e., the time of salvation's harvest, has arrived (vv. 23, 27-28).

It was the season of Passover and some Greeks, viz., gentiles, had come requesting to see Jesus. In sharp contrast to the doubting cynicism of the Pharisees (preceding episode, 12:19), the sincerity of the Greeks was evidenced by their presence among the worshipers (v. 20) at the gathering. Godfearers or proselytes who were attracted to the monotheistic beliefs of Judaism, the Greeks did not observe *all* the Mosaic precepts or customs with regard to diet, circumcision, etc. Nevertheless, their presence and their desire to "see" Jesus is of great moment at this point in the fourth gospel, when Jesus was about to embark upon his passion. Mere curiosity had not drawn the Greeks to Jesus, but a sincere desire to believe.

Recall that in the unique Johannine usage of vocabulary, "to see" was but another way of saying to perceive with the insight or the eyes of faith. When Andrew and the other disciple of John the Baptist first encountered Jesus, they were invited to "Come and *see*!" (1:39), i.e., to come and believe! That the Greeks had come seeking Jesus at this point of his ministry was sure indication that his hour, his time of being "lifted up" and of "drawing all men to himself" (v. 31), was at hand. Significantly, the narrative never states that the

Greeks actually saw Jesus. Such seeing, such faith would be saved for the hour of the cross and exaltation.

Throughout the account of Jesus' ministry in the fourth gospel, references (26) were made to Jesus' hour (2:4, 4:21, 5:25, etc.). In most cases, the word used was not *chronos*, indicating the time of day or chronological time. Instead, the evangelist used the terms *hora* or *kairos* to refer to the special and momentous period in Jesus' life wherein he would return to his Father. The process of return would be enunciated in the mystery of his passion, death and resurrection. Hence, when Jesus announced in v. 23, "the hour has come," the mysterious process of his return and therefore of our salvation was begun.

The imminence of Jesus' hour filled him with ambivalent feelings which were "troublesome" to his spirit (v. 27) but did not in any way lessen his resolve. Obediently he would live out the hour of his dying, and thereby reap a rich and saving harvest. Although the fourth evangelist has omitted a Gethsemane episode from his gospel, today's pericope contains all the elements of the traditional synoptic accounts, viz., the acknowledgment of the hour having come, the anguish, the prayerful appeal to the Father, the acceptance of the ordeal and the affirming consolation from heaven. The voice from the sky (v. 28) is reminiscent, not only of the traditional accounts of the divine approval of Jesus' baptism and transfiguration, but also (as R. Brown has pointed out) of the apocryphal Testament of Levi. Therein it is stated "the skies shall be opened and sanctification shall come upon him from the temple of glory with the Father's voice, as from Abraham to Isaac; and the glory of the most high shall be uttered over him" (18:6-7). Though the voice was dismissed or misunderstood by the crowd, the evangelist's point is not to be mistaken. Just as the Father's glory had been manifest in Jesus' words and works, so too would the cross and resurrection be an epiphany of that same glory: "I *have* glorified it... and *will* glorify it *again*."

To those who would *see* Jesus and thereby become by faith participants in his *hour*, Jesus promised the honor of the Father (v. 26) and eternal life (v. 25). The losing or hating of one's life implies a dying with Jesus—as the grain of wheat dies to produce even greater life. Ignatius of Antioch understood well the consequences of "losing" and "hating" life so as to a part of Jesus' hour. As he was being taken to a martyr's death, he prayed, "I'm God's grain . . . May I be ground by the teeth of wild beasts" (*Letter to Romans*, 4:1).

Finally, the paradox of Jesus' being lifted up from the earth (vv. 32-33) in ignominy and in glory will result in the judgment of this world. Those who have rejected the life of the dying "grain of wheat" have brought upon themselves the judgment of darkness and have shown themselves akin to the prince of this world. But those who, like the Greeks (at the beginning of today's gospel), would *see* Jesus, his lifting up upon the throne of the cross and his exaltation in glory will be a sign and a pledge of eternal life.

1. Commitment based on inner conviction can sustain the ravages of time and temptation (Jeremiah).

2. Firsthand experience of suffering and weakness can make the minister more sympathetic and supportive (Hebrews).

3. Dying to give life is an observable wonder of nature and a necessary aspect of redemption (John).

Passion (Palm) Sunday

They began the week by hailing him with branches from trees; but by week's end it was upon the tree that he hung in seeming failure, in utter loneliness and disgrace. What had turned the tide of human emotions? What had completely transformed the cries of adulation into shouts of defamation? Not a human plan or purpose but an eternal, divine hand had guided the events that led, not to defeat but victory on the cross (Mark). For those who by faith can pierce the paradox, the cross is a sign and a pledge of life and glory (Philippians), a daily reminder of the love which inspired it (Isaiah).

Isaiah 50:4-7. In those instances when the people of Israel looked to the scriptures to lend definition and substance to their messianic hopes, it is doubtful that they turned to the suffering servant songs of Deutero-Isaiah. Written during the Babylonian captivity (ca. 597-538 B.C.E.), these four songs (42:1-4, 49:1-7, 50:4-9, 52:13—53:12) described as their central figure a servant whose characteristics did not in any way resemble the kingly, powerful, militaristic messiah for whom the people of Israel prayed and yearned. Companion to his people in the shame and pain of their exile in Babylonia, the author of the servant songs sought to find sense, meaning and purpose in the suffering which threatened to overwhelm them. For this reason, many scholars agree that in their original context the songs were composed in order that Israel might identify *itself* as the servant. Through humiliation and suffering, Israel was to become for the rest of humanity God's message of salvation and deliverance.

Our first reading for Passion Sunday is excerpted from the third of the four songs. Herein the servant is portrayed as specially equipped by God himself for his work of teaching and exhorting the weary (v. 4). Although the song is not specific, it may be that the people were weary, not only of the exile but of the servant's message as well. This would explain the maltreatment of the servant described in the subsequent verses. But like the great prophets who had preceded him (Isaiah, Jeremiah, Amos, Hosea, etc.), the lack of public acclaim and acceptance did not in any way deter the servant from his task. It is entirely possible that the prophet, Deutero-Isaiah, experienced the abuse of which he has spoken in the third servant song. If so, it is obvious from the song that he found strength to persevere in the Lord's help (v. 7). His message and his purpose were to liberate, i.e., to proclaim the inevitable end of the exile to his people as well as to announce the end of their bondage to sin. Both freedoms, in the physical and moral senses, were gifts from the God with whom they had broken faith. For the sake of that faith and the relationship (covenant) with God which alone could sustain his people, the servant was willing to endure the brunt of their anger and scorn (beatings, buffets, etc.). Undaunted ("face like flint"), the servant exhibited great confidence, not in his *own* stamina or courage, but only in the power of the Lord who commissioned him. In the fourth servant song (52:13—53:12), the servant's faith is proven in the ultimate test of a shameful and humiliating death.

Philippians 2:6-11. Often called the "fifth" or the "New Testament servant song," the hymn Paul quoted in his letter to the Philippians, our second reading for today, was probably composed by a pre-Pauline author for use at early Christian liturgies. The beautiful song blends the insights of prophetic messianism with the christological mysteries of Jesus' saving death and resurrection. It weaves the depths of humiliating degradation with the heights of honor and glorification, both of which are integrated in the paradox of Jesus' passion. As a summary of Jesus' mission the hymn forms a parabola in which the "downward" movement of Jesus, from his rightful status at God's right hand, plunges to the nadir of the cross. From the cross, or Jesus' being lifted up, proceeds the "upward" movement of his going back to the Father through the glorious processes of his resurrection and exaltation. Drawn together and upward with Jesus to the Father are all those who, because of Jesus' incarnation, passion and death, have been redeemed from sin and death.

Acquisition of goods whether in a material, spiritual or psychological sense, or the "grasping" (*harpagmon*, v. 6) of which the hymn speaks was a just right of which Jesus was totally divested in his self-emptying *Kenosis* or emptying implies a purposeful, positive and voluntary renunciation. Paul understood the incarnation and ultimately the cross as the most eloquent expression of this kenosis, that divine "poverty" which must be emulated by all believers. Theodosius in his spiritual writings placed great emphasis on this self-emptying aspect of Christian commitment.

Mark 14:1—15:47. Because Mark's was the first written gospel of which we may be certain, many scholars have regarded it as the simplest, most factual and the least theological. This, however, is far short of the truth and a misrepresentation of the Marcan genius! Like the other evangelists, Mark gleaned facts from his particular sources and existing traditions and shaped these according to his own unique faith, interests and insights into a christological statement no less masterful than those of Matthew or Luke or even John. Central to his concerns and interests were the passion, death and resurrection of Jesus Christ. For this reason, Mark, as did the other evangelists, formulated the passion narrative first. Secondary and supplemental to the passion accounts was the material concerning Jesus' ministry and early life (Matthew, Luke). R. Fuller believes the passion narratives were constructed in the style of a Passover Haggadah or cult narrative and were intended for recital at liturgical celebrations. Whatever their ritual setting, each passion narrative exhibits a particular style and theological emphasis. In the case of the Marcan passion narrative, two particular emphases can be discerned: (1) an apologetical motif, (2) a christological, theological motif.

The plot (14:1-11). Throughout his gospel and in the passion narrative as well, Mark has employed what might be termed a "sandwiching technique" wherein he begins a theme, interrupts it with another idea and then returns to his first theme. By so doing, he contrasts the two ideas, relates them to one another and clarifies both. In this particular passage, the plot to kill Jesus is interrupted by the episode of his anointing. By interpolating the anointing (vv. 3-9), with its messianic significance and foreboding of Jesus' burial, between the passages of the plot against him (vv. 1- 2, 10-11), the evangelist has dramatically contrasted the faithful acceptance of Jesus by the woman with the rejection of the chief priests and scribes and the betrayal of Judas. The extravagance of the woman's act in pouring the expensive oil upon Jesus' head (John has "feet") recalls the practice of the anointing of Israel's kings (1 Kings 1:39, 2 Kings 9:3). Moreover, it underscored Jesus' true identity as the anointed one of God or messiah. But, without rejecting the woman's act or its significance, Jesus referred the anointing to his burial (15:46, 16:1), indicating that his messianism would not be one of earthly kingship but one of eternal dominion accomplished through suffering.

The meal (14:12-25). In this section of the narrative, during the context of the annual feast of the Passover, Jesus revealed in the gift of his body and blood that he was beginning his own Passover. In the context of the Passover meal, the head of the household would bless, break and explain the symbolism of the bread of affliction (Deuteronomy 16:3) before sharing it among his family members. In that atmosphere of remembering the first Passover and the Sinai covenant, Jesus blessed, broke and gave the food of the new Passover and of the new, eternal covenant.

Gethsemane (14:26-42). Jesus' initial encounter with evil at the beginning of his ministry took place in the solitude of the desert. Near the end of his earthly service, he was again alone in the small garden on the hill to the east of Jerusalem beyond the Kidron. The reference to the shepherd and his scattered sheep (Zechariah 13:7) indicated the fact that, though *one* would betray him, *all* would indeed desert him. The loneliness and anguish of the moment were heightened by the disciples' continued misunderstanding. So uncomprehending were they that they fell asleep at the hour of Jesus' greatest need.

Arrest, trial, denial (14:43—15:15). Many have assumed that the young man who fled naked (v. 51) was the evangelist himself, as none of the other passion narratives included this incident. Though this may be so, the significance of the young man's presence here (v. 51) and at the empty tomb (16:5) is of much more importance than his identity. During the arrest, the young man (*neaniskos*) was *seized,* as was Jesus (vv. 44, 46), yet he escaped, leaving only his cloth (*sindon*) behind. The same word *sindon* was used (15:46) to describe Jesus' burial cloth. Could it be that Mark intended for us to regard the young man, not as the evangelist's signature of his work, but as an "angel messenger" whose presence explains and connects the arrest and the empty tomb? By his presence at the two events, by the special words used (seized, *neaniskos, sindon*), the young man serves as a sign that, although arrested and condemned, Jesus could not be "seized" by death, but would leave his "burial cloths" behind and rise from the dead. At the empty tomb, the young man reappeared to announce, "He has been raised up, he is not here."

Sandwiched in between the trials of Jesus, both the Jewish and Roman proceedings, the evangelist has related the denial by Peter. By juxtaposing these events, Mark has compared Jesus' loyalty to the Father with Peter's infidelity to Jesus. Moreover, Jesus' affirmation of his messianic titles (14:62) and tacit acceptance of his authoritative status as king (15:2) stand out in poignant contrast to Peter's unwillingness to be recognized as a disciple or even an associate of his Lord.

Cross and death (15:16-47). The irony of the torture and execution of Jesus was overwhelming. Mocked by the soldiers, crowds and dressed in royal garments, hailed in jest as king, Jesus was the butt of their jokes. But in very fact he *was* king and deserved their homage! Throughout this section of the passion narrative, the evangelist substantiated his portrayal of Jesus with references to Psalm 22, Isaiah 53, Lamentations 2:15, while marking regularly the passage of time in order to show that none of the proceedings was haphazard. On the contrary, all was according to the plan of God. In stark simplicity, "they crucified him," (15:25), Mark announced the brutality of human revenge and prejudice, but also the enthronement of the Lord of life. With the loud cry (*phone megale,* v. 34), the victory over evil was proclaimed once and for all. Four times in his gospel, the evangelist used the term "loud voice" or "cry," twice to refer to the scream of a conquered demon (1:26, 5:7) and twice in reference to Jesus himself crying out against evil (15:34, 37). Though misunderstood by the onlookers who thought he was calling for Elijah, the cry of Jesus signaled the end of the reign of sin, death and the old order (the curtain was torn in half, v. 38), the irruption of God's reign and a new order of peace and forgiveness. In the triumphal moment of Jesus' dying, the "messianic secret" was finally and dramatically disclosed . . . not by a Jew, but by the centurion: "Clearly this man was the Son of God" (15:39).

1. Discipleship requires daily resolve and resiliency (Isaiah).

2. "To give and not to count the cost, to fight and not to heed the wounds" . . . requires an attitude which can only be borne of faith (Philippians).

3. In the paradox of the cross, we have Jesus' own pledge that goodness will never be overcome by evil (Mark).

The Easter Season
Easter Sunday

That Jesus' public career ended in humiliation on the cross seemed to be a logical consequence for one whose life had been lived in radical contradiction of traditional values and official norms (Acts). But the fact that he rose in glory to triumph over sin and death vindicated who he was and what he had done (John). In the illogical mystery of Christ's dying and rising, we have been set free. His vindication has become our victory, his triumph our salvation (Colossians, 1 Corinthians).

Acts 10:34, 37-43. When early believers in Jesus assumed the task of preaching the good news of salvation, they offered themselves as *witnesses,* not simply to Jesus' words and works or to his death but also to the fact of his resurrection. Without his rising, the cross of Jesus would have been no more than a grim reminder of his defeat, the emblem of a victim. But by virtue of the resurrection, his cross became a symbol of victory, a sign of salvation.

With the Cornelius episode, the church proclaimed itself open to accept "everyone who believes in Jesus" (v. 43). Luke made it quite clear that this ecumenical posture was not entirely a human achievement by repeatedly crediting such developments to the Holy Spirit. That this step was not *easily* made was attested in the proceedings of the Jerusalem council (Acts 15) and in the conflict that existed between Peter and Paul (Galatians).

Had this openness not been attained, Christianity could have withered as a sect on the vine of Judaism. Instead, due to the efforts of believers in cooperation with the Spirit of Jesus, Christianity has become the flower, the fruit and the harvest of all humanity.

Colossians 3:1-4. Because of the influence of gnostic thought upon the Greek world, some Hellenistic Christians like those in Colossae were unwilling to accept the reality of the resurrection. Gnosticism (from *gnosis,* knowledge) was an esoteric philosophical system whose proponents ascribed to the dualistic principle that matter was inherently evil while the spirit was essentially good.

When Paul wrote to the Christians in Colossae, a community probably founded by Epaphras (Paul's convert in Ephesus), he was aware of these gnostic tendencies that threatened to dilute and distort the integrity of their faith. As he addressed this issue, Paul reiterated the necessity and centrality of Jesus' resurrection. As a result of Jesus' redemptive death and through baptism into that saving mystery, Christians have "been raised up in company with Christ" (3:1).

As P. Wrightman has noted, the term "raised up" is more correctly rendered "co-raised" and underscores the believers' solidarity with Christ. Because of that solidarity, even here and now, while in the *body*, Christians are called to a quality of life consonant with their status as redeemed persons. While others searched for *hidden knowledge,* Paul exhorted the Colossians to "hide" themselves in the life of Christ (3:3).

Reminding his readers that they had died with Christ, Paul urged them to put off the old ways of death and to participate in the life and grace of Easter glory. The fact of Jesus' triumph *in the body* over sin and death is a moral imperative for all believers to reflect here and now, *in the body,* the victory of the risen Lord.

1 Corinthians 5:6-8. An excerpt from a longer section of Paul's letter to Corinth (5:1-13) in which he dealt with a case of incest, today's short pericope underscores the effect that sin, even private sin, has upon the community as a whole. Referring to the recalcitrant sinner as "leaven," Paul chastised the Corinthians for not taking care of the matter themselves (see 5:1-5). In the ancient world, leaven was generally regarded as an impurity. Because of its mysterious and misunderstood effect on dough, leaven was prohibited in those foods that were to be sacrificed, and became a figurative sign of sin and corruption. Jesus warned his disciples to "watch out for the leaven of the Pharisees," referring to their hypocritical teaching and obsequious behavior (Matthew 16:6, 11, 12; Luke 12:1). Unleavened bread, on the other hand, had become a metaphor for purity and holiness.

Warning the Corinthians to guard against the "bad apple syndrome" or the leaven in their midst (viz., the incestuous sinner), Paul urged the community to deal with the matter by sweeping out or getting "rid of the old 'yeast'" (v. 7). Perhaps Paul was alluding to the Palestinian custom of sweeping clean the entire house on Passover eve to rid it of all traces of old leaven. Only then was the unleavened bread baked for the Passover feast.

In a sense, Paul was reminding the Corinthians that "Passover purity" had become a permanent requisite for all those redeemed by Christ. Since Jesus' death on the cross had "swept humanity clean" of sin and evil, the leaven of corruption no longer had any place among them. Only the unleavened qualities of sincerity and truth would constitute a worthy response to the saving sacrifice of Christ.

John 20:1-9. Few of us relate in truly personal manner to the fact of the resurrection, except perhaps as a *past* event whereby Jesus' death on the cross was vindicated and/or as a *future* blessing we hope to enjoy. But the *centrality* of the resurrection calls believers to a continuing and ever more profound recognition of that reality as an integral aspect of *daily* life.

As the gospels reveal, even Jesus' contemporaries did not anticipate his resurrection; each of the resurrection narratives contains evidence that his disciples had despaired of him as the long-awaited messiah. Even when the empty tomb was discovered, no one concluded that Jesus had risen. Indeed, had the empty tomb been the *only* phenomenon surrounding Jesus' death, it certainly could not have become the basis for Christian faith in the resurrection.

When Mary discovered the tomb empty, she ran off to report what she thought to be foul play: "The Lord has been taken from the tomb! We don't know where they have put him" (v. 2). The Talmud dismissed the empty tomb by explaining that Jesus' body was stolen. Although the account of the empty tomb was recorded in all four gospels and *was* an early tradition, it was not included in the *earliest* testimony to Jesus' resurrection (1 Corinthians 15:5). Christian faith in Jesus' victory over death is rooted in the *appearances* of the risen Lord to his followers.

For those who believed in Jesus as risen by virtue of his appearances to them, the ambiguity of the empty tomb was resolved. Moreover, the narratives of the empty tomb helped to explain the reality of Jesus' bodily resurrection, viz., that the same Jesus who had walked and talked and had broken bread with them and had died and was buried, was the same Christ who was alive and ever present to them. Even from the early centuries of Christianity, sceptics, even Christian sceptics, have suggested that the resurrection appearances were fabricated by the disciples, disappointed at the death of their leader. In the face of such scepticism, Paul stated unequivocally: "If Christ is not risen from the dead, our preaching is empty; your faith is worthless and we are the most wretched of people" (1 Corinthians 15:19).

In more contemporary terms, J.L. McKenzie has reiterated Paul's proclamation: "The resurrection is a fundamental component of Christian faith which collapses without it. Faith is not a doctrine which survives its teacher; it is an experience of a reality, and that reality is the risen Christ, without whom it is an experience of nothing."

In the Johannine version of the empty tomb tradition, the beloved disciple ("the one Jesus loved," v. 2) functioned as did the angel messengers in the synoptic narratives, viz., to *explain* and to *interpret* the empty tomb, burial cloths, etc. The beloved disciple had run ahead and arrived at the tomb first but then he waited to allow Peter to enter first. By means of this small detail the Johannine author coordinated his narrative with the earliest tradition that stated, "He appeared *first* to *Cephas* and then to the Twelve" (1 Corinthians 15:5).

Perhaps the most significant statement in today's entire gospel pericope is the evangelist's editorial comment that "as yet they did not understand . . . about Jesus rising from the dead" (v. 9). As yet, it had not become clear that Jesus' rising was not simply the last act of one single life but the first moment of a new and eschatological dimension in which all peoples would share.

As H. Kung has explained, by virtue of his resurrection, Jesus became the *norm* for the relationship that will culminate in our own resurrection. To celebrate Easter is to remember that Jesus *lives*; we rejoice in the fact that because of him we also live today and for an eternity of tomorrows.

1. Jesus has risen. In him is realized every past hope; because of him every future hope will be fulfilled (Acts).

2. (a) Those who belong to the risen Lord are to reflect that relationship in their daily lives (Colossians).

2. (b) There is no such thing as a private sin. Every evil act threatens the welfare of the community; so too, every good deed can be a source of edification (Corinthians).

3. Our faith in the risen Lord enables us to interpret the contradiction of the cross and the crucified Jesus (John).

Second Sunday of Easter

In the wake of Jesus' death and rising, those who believed in him gathered together; sharing their time, their talents and their treasure, they became church (Acts). Inspired by faith in Jesus as Christ and motivated by love (1 John), this church continues his mission of peace and forgiveness for the sake of all peoples (John).

Acts 4:32-35. In the second volume of his two volume opus, Luke has traced the process whereby the *proclaimer* of the kingdom became the *proclaimed*. In the wake of Jesus' saving mission, those who believed in him and in his proclamation became a community, a church. More than any other piece of New Testament literature, the Acts of the Apostles provides the modern believer with insight into the growth of that early church as it extended beyond Jerusalem.

Today's first reading is one of three similar summary texts in Acts (see also 2:42-47, 5:12-16) through which Luke provided his readers with a glimpse of life in the early Jerusalem church. These summaries serve as literary signals, to remind and to encourage the reader that the Jesus movement was making sure progress. Highly idealized and idyllic presentations, the summaries featured the community as a closely knit group that shared goods and talents in common, gathered around the Twelve for liturgical and catechetical nourishment, and steadily increased in number.

In its earliest stages of development, the church relied solely on the knowledge and experience of the apostles. Their kerygmatic preaching made converts for Christ while their continuing catechesis assured the growth in faith of those already initiated. Gradually, a set or fixed method of preaching was developed, based on remembered sayings of Jesus, his parables, his works of healing and especially the passion event.

Communal living (*koinonia*) or fellowship was centered on and flowed from the believers' relationship to the risen Christ and, with him, to the Father. The sharing of goods was a natural consequence of their unity of heart and purpose. As J. Crowe has noted, the early Christians fulfilled the noblest human aspirations of the Hellenistic world, the ideal of friendship enshrined in slogans older than Plato and Aristotle: "Friends are one heart and one soul," "The possessions of friends are common property." But Luke was quick to assert that the communion of believers in Jesus goes deeper than pagan aspirations; the sharing of goods is a sign of the deeper life they share in their faith.

From Paul's letters we learn that the early community's sense of mutual responsibility extended beyond the local church. Collections were taken up and sent to needier groups. That this ideal of mutual sharing and caring was not always fully realized can be seen in the next chapter of Acts. The selfishness and duplicity of Ananias and Sapphira (5:1-11) indicated that the growing church was sill an imperfect and struggling community—much like our own.

Nevertheless, today's pericope puts before us the goal toward which we must aspire.

1 John 5:1-6. Raymond E. Brown, in his unequalled commentary on the epistles of John, explained that these letters give the modern reader a sense of the "life-and-death-struggle" experienced by the late first century C.E. community. At the heart of the struggle were two conflicting interpretations of the Johannine community's tradition, known to us as John's gospel. Evidently, two groups formed within the community, one of which eventually seceded from the church (1 John 2:19).

The two groups disagreed about the importance and unique role of Jesus, about the ethical demands of Christian living, about the Holy Spirit and eschatology. Those who seceded refused to acknowledge the fact of the incarnation and, while they claimed to enjoy a close relationship with God, they did not reflect this union in deeds of love for one another (2:9-11, 3:10-24, 4:7-21). In an effort to combat the secessionists (whom he referred to as "Antichrists"), the author of 1 John repeatedly offered his contemporaries criteria for recognizing and refuting their errors.

In today's pericope, the author called his readers to exercise their professed faith in Jesus as Christ and their love of God by keeping his commandments and loving one another. Previously (1 John 2:22, 4:20) John had described as a "liar" the person who says he loves God but hates his brother. Here, the point is the same. Those who *believe* in Jesus are *begotten* by God and love all others so begotten.

As Brown has pointed out, "it has been fashionable to affirm that what is demanded is not belief in an intellectual truth about Jesus but belief in a person with whom one enters a relationship." Brown does not deny this but also insists that there *is* an intellectual aspect in the Johannine challenge to believe: One must *know* and *understand* Jesus correctly in order to have a salvific relationship with him.

According to the author of 1 John the secessionists did not acknowledge or accept Jesus for who he was, viz., the incarnate word and Christ; therefore, their profession of faith was a sham and their unethical behavior was further proof of their heretical ideas. But the true believer knows Christ and has been begotten by God, taught John; therefore, certain Christian behaviors must follow. Since the secessionists withdrew from the community and showed hostility rather than love, the author of John concluded that they were not true believers and therefore not begotten by God.

Sounding very much like John the seer and author of Revelation, the author of 1 John described the believer begotten by God as a *conqueror* of the world (v. 5). By faith in Jesus as Son of God, who came in water and in blood, i.e., as a true man who *truly* suffered and died for sin, those begotten by God can overcome any adversity. Today, all who believe and are baptized into the life and death of Jesus may experience a daily share in his conquest of sin and look forward to an eternal enjoyment of his victory.

John 20:19-31. All the promises Jesus had made to his disciples—concerning his abiding presence, the gift of the Paraclete, forgiveness, peace and eternal life—find their fulfillment in today's gospel. The traditional gospel for the Second Sunday of Easter proclaimed in each year of the three-year cycle, this Johannine narrative is comprised of two resurrection appearances—one on Easter evening, the second a week later. Where the Lucan narrative presented the various moments of Jesus' saving work (resurrection, ascension, gift of Spirit) as separate entities, the fourth evangelist has coalesced these moments into one event. Therefore, in the Johannine account, Jesus is portrayed as risen, as bestowing the Spirit and mandating his apostles, all on the *same* day.

Shalom, peace, was the conventional Hebrew salutation, but in the context of Jesus' resurrection triumph, his double greeting of peace took on added importance. Peace and joy were signals of the messianic era (Isaiah 11) that had been inaugurated by Jesus' saving deeds. In bestowing the gift of the Spirit, the Johannine Jesus was portrayed as the fulfiller of the messianic prophecies (Joel 3:1, Ezekiel 36:27). With the same Spirit of God that had brought forth order and life (Genesis 1), with the same Spirit that breathed life into clay and created humanity (Genesis 2), with the same Spirit that had anointed kings, priests, prophets and the Lord's own servant (Isaiah 42), Jesus empowered, inspired and anointed his followers.

Following his first salutation Jesus showed his wounds. Notice the reference to hands and *side*, rather than hands and *feet* as in the synoptics. Recall that in John 19:34 the evangelist made a point of mentioning the blood and water flowing from Jesus' pierced side. Besides the sacramental allusions (eucharist, baptism), there is also the idea of the Spirit being poured forth on humanity by virtue of Jesus' death. With the wounds of his passion in evidence, the risen Lord proclaimed the continuity between the cross and his exaltation; he was one and the same Lord as the joyful recognition of his disciples attested.

With the second salutation, "Peace," Jesus mandated his followers, sending them forth as he had been sent by the Father, to heal and forgive sinners. Some scholars have interpreted the forgiving or binding of sins (v. 23) as a reference to the church's responsibility of withholding baptism depending on the initiate's acceptance or rejection of the kerygma. Others, basing themselves on the rabbinic terms *asar* and *sera* (bind, loose), have understood this verse (23) in the context of church discipline, i.e., the right to grant or to refuse membership in the community for reasons of sinfulness.

While these *later* ecclesiastical and juridical developments may indeed find some support in today's gospel, its primary message of *peace* and *forgiveness* should not be diminished or overshadowed by legalism. Jesus conquered the power of sin and death on the cross; as the risen Lord, he shared the fruits of his victory, viz., peace and forgiveness, with all who believe.

Following the commissioning of the disciples, the story of Thomas makes a case for the place of doubt in the life of the believer. As one who hesitated, questioned and then moved from scepticism to a firmer, more committed faith, Thomas is a source of encouragement for struggling believers of *all* ages.

Moreover, the Thomas episode helped the late first century church to come to grips with a problem that became more urgent with the deaths of the authoritative eyewitnesses to the risen Lord, viz., how to believe in Jesus as risen without the benefit of an appearance of him. For a time, those who had not seen the risen Jesus relied on the eyewitness testimony of those who had. But as is clear in the Thomas episode, faith was not an automatic result of hearing eyewitness testimony ("I'll never believe it").

Nor was *seeing* firsthand a guarantee of faith. Even when he *saw* the Lord, Thomas still had to come to faith. In the story of Thomas' doubting, the evangelist made several apologetic and theological points:

(1) Jesus' invitation to touch him underscored the *reality* of his body and contradicted those theories that attributed the resurrection appearances to the wishful imaginations of Jesus' apostles.

(2) Thomas was called (and with him are called all who believe) to move beyond the sensational aspects of the resurrection to a committed faith in Jesus as ever present to his followers. Notice that Thomas was moved to faith not by actually *touching* Jesus but by the risen Jesus' challenge, "Believe!"

(3) Thomas' "My Lord (*Kyrios*) and my God (*Theos*)" united in one profession of faith the church's growing christological awareness of Jesus as equal to and one with the eternal creator and Father of all peoples.

Finally, Jesus' beatitude of the unseeing believer, "Blest are they who have not seen and have believed," encourages all of us who do not see or touch Jesus but still hope and believe in his abiding presence and future appearance.

1. The needy and the homeless in our society are living and painful proof that the preached gospel has not yet become the practiced gospel (Acts).

2. All those who belong to God by faith must necessarily unite with one another in love (1 John).

3. While we may not see Jesus, we can experience him in the sacraments, hear him in his word and touch him in one another (John).

Third Sunday of Easter

Standing at the center of human history, the incarnate word summed up in his person every best hope of humanity (Acts). Because of his saving mission and his victory over sin and death, believers are gifted with a knowledge of the God (1 John) whose power to forgive has healed every believing heart (Luke).

Acts 3:13-15, 17-19. According to Luke's account in Acts, when Peter made the speech that comprises today's first reading, he did so with the healed lame man still clinging to him (Acts 3:11). Although the crowds were attracted to Peter and John because of the sensational nature of the cure, Peter grasped the opportunity to turn their attention to the God by whose power he had acted. Like the other speeches in Acts, this one attributed to Peter is largely a Lucan composition; nevertheless, it is well suited to the occasion and is comparable to other speeches made in Acts to Jewish audiences.

As I.H. Marshall and J. Crowe have noted in their commentaries, Luke has adhered to the same pattern he observed throughout Acts, viz., an act of power or a miracle (in this case, the cure of the lame man) was followed by a discourse (speech). In the discourse, the event was interpreted as a fulfillment of God's foreordained plan of salvation as revealed in the scriptures. While the miraculous nature of the cure attested to the power of the gospel and was a demonstration of its authenticity, nevertheless, Luke regarded the discourse or speech as more important. It was as if he was saying to his readers: "The lame walked . . . now that I have your attention, let me preach to you the kerygmatic message of salvation."

Similar in structure to Peter's speech on the occasion of Pentecost, this discourse is, however, more harsh in its indictment of the disbelieving and more urgent in its call to conversion. Attributing his own power to Jesus, Peter proclaimed Jesus as the glorified servant. As J. Crowe has observed, the power to save is the way God has vindicated Jesus as the servant who suffered in accordance with his will (Isaiah 52:13). The servant's glorification is a total reversal of the sinful action of the inhabitants of Jerusalem in delivering Jesus to Pilate and in denying Jesus even after Pilate decided to release him. While the crowds chose Barabbas, a murderer, God vindicated his righteous one, the author of life. The fact of Jesus' resurrection is the divine declaration of Jesus as savior, a salvation manifested in the acts of power worked by the apostles.

In v. 17, Luke has softened the indictment against those who rejected Jesus and against Peter's audience, excusing them on the grounds of ignorance. However, with the preaching of the good news by the disciples, those who heard Peter et al. could no longer plead ignorance. Indeed, as Peter extended the invitation to repentance and conversion, his hearers were forced to choose for themselves.

This notion of the awesome responsibility that knowledge brings can be found throughout the Christian scriptures. In the Johannine gospel, we are reminded, "If you were blind, you would have no guilt; but you say, 'We see,' therefore your guilt remains," "If I had not come and spoken to them, they would not have sin; but now they have no excuse for their sin" (John 9:41, 15:22). If those who heard the kerygma that day acknowledged their sins, turned to God and accepted Jesus, they would live and sins would be forgiven. If they did not, then, of their own volition, they condemned themselves.

In today's world, it is virtually impossible to hide behind a cloak of ignorance, because we have seen him, we know what he has done for us; we encounter him in the sacraments and in his word. Therefore, we are entirely responsible for the gift of our salvation and we will be held accountable for it when the author of life returns.

1 John 2:1-5. (For an explanation of the "secessionists" and of the conflicting views within the Johannine community, see the commentary on 1 John 5 for last Sunday).

In an effort to correct the false claims made by the secessionists, the author of 1 John composed a critique of their views. This critique began at 1 John 1:5 and continued through 1 John 2:11; today's second reading should therefore be understood within this context. Influenced by a Greek culture that virtually deified human reason, some in the Johannine community claimed to possess so superior a knowledge of God that they were excused from the demands of ethical behavior. As R. Brown has pointed out, these secessionists were not "libertines notorious for scandalous behavior"; rather, they "were indifferentists who attributed no salvific importance to moral behavior."

Basing themselves on the tradition later recorded in John's gospel, viz., that eternal life consists in *knowing* God, these proto-gnostics believed they *already* enjoyed an intimate union with God, a union that obviated the commandments. Some scholars find an excuse for the secessionists' misconceptions in the fact that the Johannine gospel tradition placed *little* emphasis on ethics. Compared with the Matthean criteria as expressed in the great sermon, the Johannine tradition is remarkably silent. Nevertheless, the author of 1 John was adamant in upholding the integrity of the Johannine tradition and in maintaining it as a guide for believers.

To refute the misconception that knowing God places the believer above the demands of morality, the epistolary writer argued that one cannot know God without keeping his commandments. Moreover, those who claim to do so are liars (v. 3)! As R. Brown has explained, John understood that one gains a knowledge of God through behavior, when that behavior is governed by God's commandments. Keeping the commandments is not merely a way of verifying a claim to know God; rather, it is a criterion that has an essential relationship to the claim made.

For the Semite, knowledge is more than an intellectual matter; it involves an experience of the whole person. To know God is to share his life; sharing God's life means living in accord with his will. Therefore, Brown concludes it is by keeping the commandments that one comes to know God intimately. Bultmann preferred to call keeping the commandments "not a condition but the *characteristic* of the knowledge of God."

Finally, although the secessionists claimed that their knowledge placed them above sin, the author of 1 John reminded the community that sin and its consequences were an ever present threat (vv. 1-2). While the ideal would be to avoid sin, nevertheless, those who sin should have confidence in a forgiving Father and in a brother whose intercession has empowered those who believe him to be victorious over sin and death.

The author of 1 John called Jesus an "offering" (v. 2) for our sin and that of all the world. The Greek term for *offering* is *hilasmos* and is more properly translated as *expiation* or, as C.H. Dodd has preferred, "disinfection." Even those who *know* God can sin; and knowledge, even absolute knowledge, cannot atone for sin. For that reason, sinners need Christ to disinfect them from the taint of sin; by his sacrifice the union between God and those who would know him is restored and strengthened.

Today the dangers of gnosticism that divided the Johannine community still persist. There is a tendency to substitute the intellectual advances of technology for the only knowledge worth acquiring, viz., the knowledge of God in Christ, which is life.

Luke 24:35-48. As the aftermath of the Emmaus episode, this narrative of the appearance of the risen Lord to his disciples in Jerusalem parallels the Emmaus event in that: (1) in both accounts, the risen Lord was not immediately recognized; (2) both narratives tell of an instruction based on scripture that led to recognition; (3) in both accounts Jesus and the disciples shared a meal. However, this latter appearance story differs from that of Emmaus because it includes a commissioning or mandating of the disciples by Jesus.

As in all of the New Testament appearance narratives, the primary intention of the Lucan evangelist was to show the continuity between the risen Christ and the earthly Jesus. Obviously, the risen Lord was somehow different because, when he appeared in the midst of his followers, they thought he was a ghost. Literally translated, v. 37 should read "they seemed to gaze at a spirit." Luke heightened the intensity of the disciples' reaction by his multiple description of their emotions, e.g., "panic, fright," "incredulous for sheer joy and wonder."

Luke probably had an underlying apologetic motive for so enhancing the scene. Many of his contemporaries accused believers in Jesus of fabricating the notion of his resurrection. By telling of the disciples' initial incredulity, the evangelist sought to dispel the idea that the risen Jesus was a figment of wishful imaginations. Luke's narrative combats these false notions with physical proof of two types: (1) the disciples were invited to touch Jesus—the reference to the hands and feet recalled the wounds of Jesus' passion; (2) Jesus asked for food and ate in their presence.

As C. Talbert has noted, the significance of this action for the Jewish mind is clear: "angels do not eat," nor do ghosts or phantasms. R.J. Dillon believes that the Lucan church was already being confronted with a naive docetism that denied the bodily character of the resurrection. Luke has certified the bodily reality of the risen Lord by portraying him as touchable and as capable of eating.

Dillon has also emphasized the fact that, unlike the Jesus of the Johannine appearances or of the Emmaus account or of the last supper narratives who gave food to his disciples, the risen Lord in this account *receives* hospitality and food *from* his disciples. Perhaps this narrative has been colored by the missionary traditions of the Lucan community; herein, Jesus represents the missionary who receives hospitality. Those who offered such hospitality were promised blessings; in this account the blessings are enunciated as a share in the life of the risen Jesus.

Talbert understands Luke's narrative as an explanation about Jesus' victory over death: "It is not to be understood as an escape from this perishable frame but as a transformation of it. It is not to be understood as a transformation into a purely spiritual angelic being because Jesus remained flesh and bones, though immortal and not limited by time and space." Luke understood the risen Christ as a prototype of Christian existence. His triumph in the body over sin and death is a pledge of victory for all who believe in him.

Having established the bodily reality of the Lord, the evangelist then focused on the mission of the disciples (vv. 44-49). As Fitzmeyer has observed, each of the synoptics has included a commissioning scene. In each case the mandate has reprised a major theme in the theology of that particular gospel. For example, in the *Marcan* account (though not part of the original gospel, Mark 16:15ff), the evangelist emphasized preaching the gospel, thus recalling the same theme from Mark 8:35, 10:29, 13:10, 14:29. In the *Matthean* commissioning account, the distinctive element was that of making disciples by teaching (Matthew 28:19, 20). This element recalled Jesus' five great teaching discourses as well as the 73 references to discipleship in Matthew's gospel. The *Lucan* mandate stressed repentance or conversion, forgiveness of sins and witness, all elements featured prominently in the Lucan gospel.

A unique feature included in this and the Emmaus account is the instruction from scripture by which the risen Lord showed his life and death as the fulfillment of scripture. Although there is no known pre-Christian Jewish text concerning a suffering messiah who would rise from the dead (Fitzmeyer calls v. 46 a "christologoumenon"), nevertheless, Luke—like the other evangelists—filtered the Jewish scriptures through the apologetic prism of Christian kerygma. By gathering all the texts concerning salvation, kingship, the vindicated servant and the suffering just one (Psalms 118:2, 16:8-11, 110:1, 2:1, 7; Isaiah 52:13—53:12; Deuteronomy 18:15-19; 2 Samuel 7:14, etc.) and applying them to Jesus, Luke wished to offer his readers assurance that their faith was well-founded.

Just as the Jewish scriptures provided prophetic roots for understanding Jesus' mission and saving death, so did the resurrection offer legitimation to the mission of his followers. In his name and by virtue of his saving death and glorious resurrection, we are his witnesses. His mission of forgiveness and reconciliation has become our own.

1. Ignorance of the Lord can be offered as an excuse only once; after that, those who reject Jesus become responsible for their actions (Acts).

2. True knowledge of God spills forth in good deeds; similarly, good deeds lead to deeper knowledge (1 John).

3. All that went before Jesus anticipated his coming; all that has happened after his appearance witnesses to his victory (Luke).

Fourth Sunday of Easter

The God in whom we believe has many names and faces. He is the model shepherd who snatches strays from the jaws of sin by laying down his own life; he is also the lamb victorious whose risen glory is a pledge of our own (John). He is father, he is son and he is brother to all who recognize and accept his love (1 John). He is the cornerstone of the living church and the healer of cripples. He is spirit and power, he is word and light. He is the Lord in whose name alone we find salvation (Acts).

Acts 4:8-12. In Excursus B of his commentary called "Reading Luke," C.H. Talbert has explored the various attitudes toward miracles that existed in the first Christian century. In order to properly appreciate Luke's use and treatment of miracles (like the healing of the cripple that is the basis of today's first reading), it is helpful to have an understanding of the postures taken toward miracles in his milieu.

While the pagans either accepted miracles as a proof of divinity or discredited them as mere magical displays, the Jews believed that miracles: (1) legitimated the word or position of a person or of God himself; (2) proved one's innocence (as with Daniel in the lion's den); (3) were effective in gaining acknowledgment of the superiority of Israel's God (as in the case of Naaman the Syrian, 2 Kings 5:15-19; or the pharaoh during the plagues, Exodus 10:16-17). Against this background Luke presented the healing of the cripple (3:1-9) and its aftermath.

Today's pericope is from Peter's speech before the Sanhedrin. Because of the attention the cure had gained for Peter and for the Jesus movement, and because they wished to rid themselves of any last vestiges of their problems with Jesus, the Jewish leaders had Peter and John put in jail for the night (4:1-7). The next day, Peter and John were brought before Annas the high priest, Caiaphas, John and Alexander.

It is significant that Luke made specific mention of Annas and Caiaphus; by doing so he indicated that the disciples were sharing in the trials Jesus had endured. Moreover, the fact that the disciples were "brought before the synagogue and put into prison" and that they "had words and a wisdom to which none of their adversaries could take exception or contradict" (Luke 21:12, 15) was a fulfillment of Jesus' own words in the gospel.

As with the other speeches or discourses in Acts, Peter's sermon was largely a Lucan composition and functioned to explain and interpret the circumstances that occasioned it. As the speech reveals, Luke regarded the healing of the cripple as a challenge to faith. It provided legitimation for the apostles' position and preaching, and established as the source of the apostles' power Jesus Christ the Nazorean. While not a *proof* that compelled one to believe and be converted, nevertheless, the miracle was a *sign* of the salvation wrought by Jesus and preached by his followers.

As R. Fuller has noted, the affinity between the sign and its significance is more obvious in Greek than in English. In v. 9, the word used to describe the man "healed" (R.S.V.) or "restored to health" (N.A.B.) is the same word used to define the "salvation" effected by Jesus. Both words come from the same verb *sosthenai* which means to be saved *and* to be healed or made whole. The healing of the cripple, therefore, can be thought of as a signature of the saving power of Jesus.

Luke concluded Peter's speech with a reference to Jesus' own words in the gospel (Luke 20:17), a quotation from Psalm 118:22 concerning the stone rejected by the builders. Believed to be one of the earliest pieces of Christian apologetic, this psalm celebrated Jesus' vindication. Rejected by those who would not accept his brand of messiahship, Jesus has been raised by God and given a name above all other names (Philippians 2:9, Acts 4:12). He is the cornerstone of the new creation. In him and by him cripples are healed, and sinners saved.

1 John 3:1-2. Not even Shakespeare at his most articulate or the Brownings at their most eloquent could compare to the magnificent expressions of love found in the Johannine tradition. "See what love the Father has bestowed," exclaimed the author of 1 John. He referred primarily of course to the Father's gift of his Son as savior (John 3:16). By virtue of the incarnation, God's infinite love became flesh and blood and expressed itself in the finite language of human existence.

But John was speaking to his contemporaries in the late first Christian century. How, then, could he say "See" as if the incarnate Jesus were still present to his disciples? Obviously, he was referring *also* to the gift of sonship that the only Son by his saving mission had made possible for every believer. Because of the love of the Father made visible and tangible in the Son, all who believe have the privilege of being *children of God*. However, the relationship believers enjoy as children, here and now, has also an eschatological dimension that has yet to be brought to light (v. 2).

As B. Vawter explained, one proof of sonship can be found in the mistreatment believers experience in the world. Recall the Johannine double usage of the term world. In one sense "world" referred to the entire cosmos redeemed by Jesus. On the other hand, "world" referred to the disbelieving element that chose to reject the living word of God spoken in Christ Jesus. It is this latter, pejorative notion to which John refers in v. 1. Those who would follow Christ and share the inheritance of being children of God should expect the same treatment he received.

As Maertens and Frisque have noted, there were other organizations in the first century that conferred the title children or sons and daughters of God. For example, the title "children of the Lord" was a frequent appellation for the Israelites and, as such, was a reference to their dignity and sacred vocation from among all the peoples of the earth (Deuteronomy 14:1). Proponents of the Greek mystery religions and orphic cults also conferred the title on their initiates.

But as the author of 1 John has made clear, for Christians, "children of God" is not a mere title; it is a present reality and a future fulfillment: "That is what *we are* . . . we are God's children now . . . what we shall be has not come to light." R.E. Brown believes that the author of 1 John related the present status of God's children, viz., realized eschatology, to the revelation of Christ yet to come (future eschatology) in order to give his contemporaries an incentive for persevering in the faith. For those who remain faithful, the epistolary author promised, "we shall be like him, we shall see him as he is."

Throughout the centuries, the precise meaning of this promise has been debated. Athanasius saw no problem speaking of a future deification (*theopoiesisthai*) of the believer, but Thomas Aquinas preferred to emphasize the aspect of the beatific vision, i.e., seeing God in his essence. For the author's first century contemporaries and for his 20th century readers, his words offer hope for an eternal future with the Father and the Son who had made us heirs of light and life.

John 10:11-18. On this Sunday in each year of the three year lectionary cycle, the gospel texts are chosen from John 10, the good shepherd discourse. Unique to the Johannine tradition, the discourse is based upon two short parables or sayings of Jesus (vv. 1-5) that were fused together in the process of oral tradition and then later interpreted (vv. 6-20) by the evangelist and/or redactor of the gospel. Today's excerpt is comprised of an interpretation of the second short parable (vv. 3-5) concerning the sheep who are called by name and follow the shepherd because they recognize his voice.

An appreciation of ancient Palestinian shepherding techniques makes the implications of the parable all the more vivid. Sheepfolds were enclosures, walled in by stones and/or briars, located either inside or on the immediate outskirts of the village. At night, all the village sheep were corralled together in the common sheepfold, and the various shepherds took their turn acting as guard and gatekeeper. When all the sheep were accounted for, the gatekeeper would lie down to rest at the opening of the sheepfold, assuring their safety with his very life.

In the morning, in order to take them to pasture, each shepherd would separate his herd from the common flock. Each sheep had a particular name and, when it heard the familiar call or whistle of its own shepherd, would respond to him but to no other. Rather than follow his flock as modern sheep ranchers do, or send out trained dogs to gather strays, the Palestinian shepherd went *before* his sheep. He led and they followed, because they knew his voice (v. 16). Given this background, John's parables and their interpretation present a powerful image of God's love to those who read them.

Just as the woolly Palestinian sheep recognized the voice of their shepherd and followed him, those who recognize Jesus as Lord and messiah and *know* him (i.e., share with him an intimate relationship based on faith and commitment) will follow him. But as R.E. Brown has noted, the Johannine shepherd exhibits a unique feature in that he was willing to die for his "sheep." This, of course, is what Jesus did for the sake of sinful humanity. But John has also given special expression to the way Jesus died.

In vv. 17-18, the evangelist described the model shepherd, i.e., Jesus as laying down his life freely. Recall the practice of the guardian shepherd who lay down across the opening of the sheepfold. Jesus' laying down of his life secured the safety, the salvation of all his sheep believers. It is significant that Jesus lay down his life *to take it up again.* Brown refuses to weaken the telic force of v. 17 and translates it "*in order to*" take it up again, explaining that, although many feel uneasy about the idea of Jesus laying down his life with such *calculated* purpose, that was precisely the meaning the evangelist intended.

As Brown stated, "The resurrection is not a circumstance that follows the death of Jesus but an essential completion of the death of Jesus. In Johannine thought the passion, death, resurrection and ascension constitute the one indissoluble salvific action of return to the Father." Notice also the high christology of the fourth gospel that portrays Jesus himself as having power to take up his life (v. 18). Whereas earlier credal formulae stated, "God raised up Jesus" (Acts 2:24), John understood the Father and the Son as equal sharers of the same power.

Finally, it should be noted that the good shepherd discourse followed immediately upon John 9 wherein Jesus had castigated the Pharisees for being willfully blind and unwilling to recognize the revelation of God made manifest in him. Unlike the faithful sheep who recognized their true shepherd and followed him, the Pharisees refused to accept Jesus' leadership.

Moreover, they were looked upon as revered leaders among the people because of their scrupulous observance of the law but they were no better than "hired hands who had no concern for the sheep." There is also an echo here of the Ezekiel text concerning false shepherds. In Ezekiel 34, Yahweh himself denounced those who called themselves shepherds (kings, rulers) but cared nothing for the flock (Israel). God's promise in Ezekiel—to take his flock away from the false shepherds, gather his flock from wherever they have been scattered and give them good pasture—has been fulfilled in Jesus.

As both shepherd and paschal lamb, he has shown his care for all God's people. He has laid down his life and taken it up again; in the process he has brought home with him to the Father all who hear his voice and know him as shepherd, Lord and Christ.

1. The saving name of Jesus still has the power to heal cripples and to make whole and holy all who believe (Acts).

2. Those who call the one God Father must also accept and love one another as brothers and sisters (1 John).

3. True leadership is a rare phenomenon because it requires that the leader place the welfare of every one of his/her followers before his/her own (John).

Fifth Sunday of Easter

The church of Jesus is a living and growing reality and therefore vulnerable to decay and deprivation. Vitality and fruitfulness are contingent upon and directly proportionate to the union of all members with Jesus, their source of life (John). Because of the Spirit of Jesus, diversity and plurality can thrive (Acts) and committed consciences can rejoice in his peace and love (1 John).

Acts 9:26-31. In ancient times, the title *Praxeis* (Acts) was affixed to the second volume of Luke's writings, thus classifying it with similar works in Greek literature which related the historical deeds and adventures of Hellenistic heroes, e.g. Hannibal, Alexander the Great, etc. A thorough reading of the Lucan work, however, reveals that in spite of its title, Acts of the Apostles (viz., Peter and Paul), it is not primarily an historical endeavor. On the contrary, Luke's purpose in writing was *theological* and, although the characters of Peter and Paul seem to be the central figures, the true "star" of his writing is the Holy Spirit as *guide, shaper* and *growth-giver* of the Christian community. Of course, history and historical data are present in Acts but they are subordinate to Luke's theological interests. In describing the evolution of issues that concerned the early community, Luke constructed an ingenious theological essay in which (as today's text will show) Jerusalem was central as mother church and base of apostolic operations. In his first volume, the gospel according to Luke, the author traced Jesus' mission to its climax in Jerusalem; correspondingly in his second volume, Luke traced the missionary efforts of Jesus' church *from* Jerusalem *to* the gentile world. By means of the summaries (e.g., 2:42-47, 4:32-35, 5:11-16) and the discourses (which constitute about one third of the book), Luke succeeded in shaping, interpreting, analyzing and communicating that data about the early Christian community which witnessed to its growth and divine provenance.

Luke's version of Paul's first contact with the apostles is thoroughly colored with the evangelist's concern for the centrality of Jerusalem and the pervading authority and guidance of the Holy Spirit (v. 31). After the disciples' initial distrust of Paul's sudden change of heart was dispelled through Barnabas' mediation, Paul was able to "move freely about Jerusalem" (v. 28). Literally translated, "went in and out with them," the phrase Luke used, conveys the idea of intimate companionship. Moreover, the impression given by Luke is that Paul's stay in Jerusalem was longer than the two weeks indicated in the Galatians letter. Note also that Luke recounted no Pauline mission to Arabia (as in Galatians), nor did he indicate that Paul began any ministry among the gentiles before meeting with the Jerusalem college. All of Paul's efforts seemed subordinate to the authority of the apostles to the extent that they were instrumental in saving his life and in *sending* him to Tarsus (v. 30).

1 John 3:18-24. Some of the difficulty in interpreting today's second reading can be lessened by a greater appreciation of the life situation of the author and his community. Although the letter had from ancient times (Irenaeus) been attributed to John the beloved disciple, many modern scholars now concur that the author of 1 John and the evangelist (gospel of John) were not the apostle John. Moreover, and in agreement with R.E. Brown, it is very probable that the author of 1 John and the author of the gospel were one and the same person, viz., a member of the Johannine school.

More a treatise than a letter, 1 John shares many of the same ideas as the Johannine gospel, viz., (1) Christ as *incarnate logos*, (2) *eternal life* gained by *faith* and by *knowing God*, (3) the *paraclete*, (4) *realized* eschatology, (5) emphasis on *love* as paramount virtue. In addition to these shared theological and christological emphases, 1 John and the Johannine gospel exhibit a similar vocabulary and style. One difference between them concerns the "opponents" or "adversaries" of the proclaimed word. Whereas the gospel exhibited a struggle with those who rejected the faith and preferred a position of unbelief *outside* the community of believers, the first letter of John evidences a struggle *among* believers *within* the community. Both groups in the Johannine church were believers, but each had arrived at a different interpretation of the gospel message. Obviously, the author of 1 John considered *his* evaluation of the gospel kerygma to be normative and thus regarded those who disagreed to be in error. Some have labeled those who did not agree with the Johannine author as gnostics or docetics. Although they may have exhibited some gnostic or docetic tendencies, true gnosticism as such did not emerge until the second Christian century. Therefore, it would be more appropriate to follow R. Brown's brilliant thought and refer to the adverse faction in the Johannine community as "secessionists."

Throughout the short work of 1 John, the modern reader should recognize the author's many attempts to set right those ideas of the secessionists which he regarded as heretical, especially with regard to christology, ethics, eschatology, and pneumatology. Admittedly, because we do not possess any written material representing the thought of the secessionists, we must deduce their ideas from the argument of the author of 1 John against them. Evidently, the secessionists denied that Jesus was the Christ and incarnate Son of God. Many held the idea (e.g., Cerinthus) that the spiritual Christ adopted the body of Jesus at his baptism and departed at his death. Over and against this erroneous christology, the author of 1 John reiterated the facts of Jesus' divine sonship, full humanity and messiahship (3:23; 3:22; 4:3; 5:5). With regard to ethics, that behavior which should flow from faith in Jesus as Christ and Son of God, the Johannine author castigated the secessionists for their disregard of the commandments (3:22-24; 2:3-4; 5:2-3) and their failure to translate their faith in God into love of neighbor (3:11-18; 4:20; 2:9-11). To the detriment of community relationships, the secessionists claimed a personal and private relationship with God which obviated fraternal responsibilities. In the third area of dispute, that of eschatology, the Johannine author adhered to the realized eschatology as propounded in the fourth gospel, understanding that the privileges of the Christian (mutual indwelling of the Spirit, etc.) were not without their demands. From what we can ascertain from the text of 1 John, the secessionists understood realized eschatology and its blessings as a freedom from responsibilities and lawful obligations. In the final area of disagreement (pneumatology), the secessionists had evidently withdrawn from the community and had claimed to be possessors of the Spirit, capable of teaching and prophesying. Johannine thought, on the other hand, regarded the Spirit, the paraclete, as Jesus' abiding presence *with his church*. In today's pericope, all of these disputed issues are present.

In addition to these issues, the author's reference to conscience (*kardia*) is a valuable insight for believers of any century. Commitment to God, in deed and in truth, i.e., knowing God in faith and living according to that faith in love, assures the Christian of Jesus' own abiding presence in his Spirit and the peace of a clear heart or conscience.

John 15:1-8. Anyone who has visited an area that produces wine may remember the gnarled, fiercely intertwined vines, not so much for their beauty but for their rugged strength and endurance. Staked on poles or small wooden gibbets, the pruned vines look cut to the quick; but in several weeks, their verdant foliage is laden with sweet, succulent fruit. Once the grapes are harvested, the cycle begins again . . . from seeming death to abundant life. To those who follow Jesus, his metaphorical use of the vine and branches provided familiar images from which to understand the deeper reality of Jesus' sharing his life with his disciples.

Peculiar to the fourth gospel, the vine and branches metaphor was not however uniquely Johannine. Indeed, a wealth of Old Testament support can be found in which Israel is portrayed as the vine or vineyard (Hosea 10:1, Isaiah 5:1-7, Jeremiah 2:21, Ezekiel 15, Psalm 80:9-16). The prophets had often compared Israel's infidelity and unproductiveness to a barren, fruitless vine (Isaiah 22:2-6; Jeremiah 5:10, 12:10-11). Relying on his Old Testament sources as well as the influences of wisdom literature, apocryphal literature and Qumran, the fourth evangelist communicated his theology of grace and indwelling in the Hebrew genre of *mashal*. *Mashal* includes the characteristics of parable, allegory, metaphor, simile, proverb, maxim, etc.

In its original setting, if one accepts a special Johannine *source* rather than a Johannine *construction*, the vine and branches motif could have been used to describe the special life-giving relationship the faithful shared with Jesus. Following this line of thought, the fruitless branches which were cut away from the vine (Jesus) by the vinedresser (Father) would be those who chose sterile unbelief rather than fruitful faith. Fuller suggests that the branch cut away and intended for the fire may have, in its original context, referred to Judas. In its secondary or applied setting, that of the Johannine community of the late 90s C.E., the *mashal* of the vine and the branches took on added meanings. As a possible apologetic against the synagogue, the vine and branches *mashal* could have sent a signal to those Jews who rejected Jesus, his life and his followers, and believed themselves to be the only true vine. Josephus in his *Antiquities* (XV, 11:3) described the Jerusalem temple as decorated with a vine and branches motif. Archaeologists and numismologists have dated the special coinage of the Jewish war (66-70 C.E.), minted with a vine and branches design. After the destruction of the temple, those who assembled in Jamnia to preserve Judaism from further destruction, called themselves the "vineyard." Over and against the synagogue that rejected Jesus, the Johannine *mashal* underscored Jesus (not Judaism) as the *true vine* (v. 1). In his person, Jesus had replaced the old Israel, the temple, the law and any prerogative of special relationship to God that Judaism had formerly considered its unique privilege.

The vine and branches also had eucharistic symbolism. Set as it was within the context of the last supper discourse, the vine and branches *mashal* served as an illustration of the unity with Jesus the eucharist afforded his disciples. As O. Cullmann has pointed out, "The relation between the branch and the vine is, therefore, above all the eucharistic communion of believers with Christ." Pruned away (*airein*) would, of course, be those who rejected Christ, and the communion of the eucharistic assembly. But even the fruitful ones would be "trimmed clean so as to increase their yield" (v. 2). Many see in this a reference to the episode (13:10) wherein Jesus washed his disciples' feet and declared them clean. Associated with Jesus in faith and in service, the disciples would be cleansed by means of his word (v. 3) of life, light and love, and by means of his hour which had already begun to transpire (12:23). By that hour, *all* of humanity would be trimmed clean of sin and death and made capable of fruitfulness in union with the true vine. The persecution Jesus' followers endured for the sake of their union with the vine was also a way of being "trimmed clean." Furthermore, one cannot overlook the sacramental symbolism of baptism as a way of being cleansed and prepared for the fruitfulness of fidelity and service.

As stated in the vine-branches pericope, the goal of trimming clean the fruitful ones was to enable them to remain, abide, live on (*menein*) in Jesus (v. 4). Such union with Jesus enabled the believer to share the same principle of vitality and life that united Jesus with the Father. For this purpose Jesus came into the world and for it he died (John 17). Not to "remain" or to "live on" in Jesus the true vine is to forego that share in the divine life of grace or, in other words, to die. Moreover, in agreement with the second reading (1 John 3:24), good works do not *create* or *merit* the indwelling of Jesus' life in the believer. On the contrary (v. 5), good works, fruitfulness and faithful deeds flow *from* that union of life and grace.

1. Submission to a higher authority does not require the relinquishment of initiative or of a diverse opinion (Acts).

2. The only voice worthy of more attention than our conscience is the voice of the one who created it (1 John).

3. In Christianity, yield and productivity are contingent upon unity and loyalty (John).

Sixth Sunday of Easter

Christ's association with those who came to him in faith developed into a vital bond, the strength of which could support even the ultimate self-sacrifice (John). A living link of love, the union of the faithful admits no prejudice or partiality (Acts) but thrives on the love begotten from the source of all love (1 John).

Acts 10:25-26, 34-35, 44-48. One of the most decisive events in the growth process of the early church, the conversion of Cornelius and his household is analogous to the transformation of the apostles on Pentecost. Luke regarded it that way because he took great care to include precisely the same elements in both the Jewish Pentecost (Jerusalem) and the gentile Pentecost (Cornelius' home). The landmark nature of the Cornelius event is further underscored by the length and detail of the narrative, by the fact that the event was repeated in its entirety in Acts 11 and by the reference to the event at the Jerusalem council in Acts 15.

Although historically the gentile mission was begun *before* the conversion of Cornelius and was probably due to the efforts of Hellenist Jewish Christians (Acts 11:10-20), Luke's theological concerns led him to relate all significant progress and development in the early community to the auspices of the Jerusalem church. Therefore it is Peter, and not one of the Greek-speaking Christians, whom Luke has featured as an effective instrument in the story of Cornelius' coming to faith.

Today's first reading is from a longer narrative and contains two distinct and significant statements by Peter but omits the apostle's sermon (see Easter Sunday liturgy), thereby giving the erroneous impression that Peter's words precipitated the coming of the Spirit (v. 44). While Peter's two statements are disjointed, they are, nevertheless, in perfect conformity to another Lucan concern, viz., the universality of the church and the equality of all members in Christ. In his first statement, Peter's claim to be "only a man" enunciated the human element of the church and the lack of superiority of one aspect (Jewish) over another (gentile). Peter's reluctance to accept Cornelius' homage for himself remains a lesson for all servants of the Lord who may at times be tempted by pomp and purple.

Peter's second statement, concerning God's utter lack of partiality, underscored the universality that inspired both volumes of the Lucan opus. Recall that Peter's awareness of God's impartial nature had been developed by means of a visionary experience (Acts 10:9ff.) The task of translating that awareness into reality proved arduous, because the walls of prejudice and separation were not easily toppled. The heated debate between Peter and Paul and the Judaizers at the council of Jerusalem proved that Peter's enlightenment concerning the universality of the church was not easily communicated. In fact, this very issue of Jews vs. gentiles would continue to plague the church and threaten its unity for some time.

Significantly, and much to the surprise of those present, but in keeping with still another Lucan theological concern, the Holy Spirit was poured out upon Cornelius' household *before* they were baptized. Throughout the Acts of the Apostles, the evangelist clarified, time after time, the fact that the Holy Spirit was leader and motivator, inspiration and guide of the Jesus movement. In the Pentecost at Cornelius' home, it was clear that the Holy Spirit was forging a union between gentiles and Jewish Christians in spite of human hesitation and reservations. With such an overwhelming attestation of God's presence and approval, Peter did the only logical thing. He acquiesced to divine persuasion, overcame a centuries' old prejudice and initiated the new believers into the mainstream of the faith-life of the church.

With the action of Peter and the Holy Spirit, the third stage or level of missionary endeavor was formally inaugurated. According to the Lucan version of Jesus' exaltation, the ascending Jesus (Acts 1:8) commissioned his followers to witness to him first in Jerusalem (Acts 1-7), then in Judea and Samaria (Acts 1:8) and finally "to the ends of the earth" (Acts 10-28). Beginning with chapter 10 of Acts, and the gentile Pentecost, the missionary activity of the early believers began in earnest the harvesting of the gentile vinyards or the "ends of the earth." With the inauguration of the gentile mission, represented today by Cornelius and his household, the universal scope of Jesus' saving activity became normative for his church. Guided and supported by Jesus' own Spirit, his church would not be limited by human prejudices or even by ritual signs (circumcision). The messiah had come in the person of Jesus and the Spirit had been poured out (Joel 2) *indiscriminately* and lovingly upon all of humankind. From that moment on, the old order with its separations and distinctions had passed away. From that point on, the question of Peter, "What can stop these people . . .?" (v. 47), would describe the nature, scope and power of the Christian mission.

1 John 4:7-10. One of the key texts in the New Testament scriptures concerning the distinctively Christian concept of love, today's second reading also provides us with the continuation of the author's argument against the secessionists in his community (see commentary for Fifth Sunday of Easter). In contrast to those progressive, philosophical thinkers, the author of the Johannine letters understood knowledge of God in a strictly biblical or Hebrew sense, viz., in a practical, realistic and tangible way. "To know" in the scriptural sense is to have intimate interaction with. Christians can claim *knowledge* of God and can *know* God as *love* only because of the fact of the incarnation (John 3:16) and not because of any mental gymnastics (gnosticism) on their part or due to an intellectual "pulling up of oneself by one's own bootstraps." According to the author of 1 John, "God is love" is a confessional statement made possible only by coming into contact with God in the person and reality of his Son, Jesus Christ.

Against the secessionist Christians who downplayed the reality of the incarnation and its ethical implications for the believer by arguing instead for a philosophical framework, the author of the Johannine letters understood that love originated with God and was in fact the very essence of God. Therefore, those who would seek to attain knowledge of God must be begotten of God. To be so begotten is to recognize oneself as loved *first* by God and to accept the inherent responsibility of being loving persons.

Evidently the secessionists claimed a special knowledge of God. By way of refutation the Johannine author put to them a challenge. Only those who *love* God *and* neighbor can rightfully claim knowledge of God. Without such love their profession of knowledge is but emptiness and lies. In no way would the Johannine author permit theology or christology in particular to be separated from its correlative ethical response.

It is remarkable but true that the practical, ethical response of love to which the author exhorted his congregation was one he considered limited to the community of the faithful of the "brethren." The Jews and the secessionists, etc., were considered as outsiders, albeit by their own choice, and therefore not within the realm of communal, responsible love. But a wider interpretation is more consonant with the teachings and the life style of Jesus, whose *love* was limitless and whose responsibility for others was boundless. Of that limitless and boundless love all believers have been made aware in the redemptive mission of the incarnate God of love, which are all called to emulate.

John 15:9-17. In 1648 George Fox became the founder of a small group of Christians who called themselves the

"Society of Friends." Intent upon returning to a primitive Christianity, the little foundation adhered closely to gospel principles and dedicated themselves to a simple style of living. The concept or model of church which Fox envisioned, viz., a society of friends, was in principle quite similar to the ecclesiology presented in today's gospel. In the *mashal* of the vine and branches, the relationship between Jesus and his followers had been expressed in terms of a living, vital and fruitful organism. In the discourse following the *mashal*, whose verses (9-17) comprise our reading for today, that ecclesiology is explained, not in terms of hierarchical structures or staid institutionalism but in terms of responsible friendship and sacrificial love. Today, the Society of Friends is better known by the name Quakers, which unfortunately does not reveal their founder's ecclesiological insights.

Set within the context of Jesus' lengthy farewell address in the fourth gospel, today's reading clarifies for Jesus' disciples and all would-be believers both the privileges and responsibilities of being branches on the vine who is Jesus. The benefits of joy, love and friendship must be answered by a return of love, as well as fruitfulness and fidelity. All this is made possible because of the indwelling of Jesus in the Father and in the believer. This indwelling is made evident in the love of the Father for the Son and in the Son's obedience (keeping the commandment of love) to the Father. In the same way, Jesus' followers can enjoy the continued indwelling presence and love of the Father and of Jesus by their faithful keeping of the Lord's commands. Not only does love effect communion with God, it also transforms the one who loves (vv. 9-10), and the fruit of that transforming indwelling is joy (v. 11).

As an example of the love to which he called his own, the Johannine Jesus spoke of the sacrificial gift of one's own life (v. 13). R. Brown, citing Jacobs, has pointed out that most of Jewish teaching has been fairly unanimous in rejecting such an absolute demand of self-sacrifice. But such a challenge is intrinsic to Christianity and constitutes one of the major distinctions between Judaism and Christianity. In the period before his passion, Jesus was able to speak firsthand of the quality of such love because he himself would soon be the primary expression of it. The act of self-giving love which was his passion and death established the group who would forever be called his friends (v. 14). Contrary to Jewish thought (*chosen* people) and to the gnostic ideal of an *elitist* group with special secret revelation, the friends (*philai*) of Jesus would become so by *faith* in him. In the Old Testament, Abraham was called the "friend of God" (Isaiah 41:8) and Moses too was said to be a friend of God (Exodus 33:11) with whom God spoke in an intimate manner. By making of his followers friends, first of himself and then of the Father, Jesus performed in the same manner as did divine wisdom: "In each generation, she passes into holy souls and makes of them the beloved (*philai*, friends) of God" (Wisdom 7:27). Later in the gospel (John 20:17) Jesus would bestow an even greater title upon his followers—that of being called his brothers (sisters). The progressive intimacy from slaves or servants (13:13-16) to friends (9:14) and then to brothers (20:17) seemed to keep pace with the gradual unfolding of the Father's love gift in the person of Jesus.

At the turn of the first Christian century, when the fourth gospel received its final and present form, and when the persecution of Domitian was most acute, the message of today's gospel must have proven a source of moral and spiritual support for the persecuted Christians. Because of the Johannine insight into the value of self-sacrificing love, the Christian martyrs could understand their personal suffering or the "laying down of one's life" (v. 14) in terms of their love for Jesus and one another. Moreover, they were strengthened by the knowledge that their sufferings and even their death would not separate them from the vine who was their source of faith and life. On the contrary, suffering could be considered a "pruning" which in effect increased the fruitfulness and yield of the vine and branches.

Like the Pauline doctrine of the mystical body, the Johannine model of the vine and branches provided the followers of Jesus with a personal, living and vital figure through which to understand their relationship to the Father, to Jesus and to one another. In the interest of maintaining the vitality, intimacy and fruitfulness Jesus intended, great efforts must be made to guard against rigid, impersonal structures. E. Kasemann has contributed greatly to a correct understanding of ecclesiology in the New Testament. Warning against the danger of absolutizing the church, he understands the church not as an end in itself or the focal point of salvation, but only as a means to Christ. For that reason, the church or those who would follow Jesus as a community must preach *not* the church, but the person, words and works of the Easter Lord. He is the vine and we who believe are the branches.

1. The impartiality and magnanimity which characterize the Spirit of God should be reflected in the lives of those who have experienced Pentecost (Acts)

2. Love is a divine prerogative, not a human invention (1 John).

3. Only the bonds of intimate friendship can support the ultimate sacrifice of self (John).

Seventh Sunday of Easter

Christ's mission among us did not end on Calvary or even upon his return to the Father. So great was his impact upon the world that humanity will remain forever changed. For those of us left behind (Acts), the challenge is to appropriate that change and to understand it in terms of the gift of salvation which transforms us (1 John)! We have not been left alone or unequipped. Consecrated by the Lord (John) and infused with the Spirit of the God who is love, we shall know no defeat!

Acts 1:15-17, 20-26. In the first volume of his literary contribution to the Christian scriptures, Luke portrayed Jesus (Luke 4) spending in the desert the interlude between his baptism and the beginning of his public ministry. During that period, Jesus was filled with the Holy Spirit and, though tempted, did not fall prey to the wiles of the evil one. In no way was his resolve to complete the mission entrusted to him by the Father averted or lessened. Like Israel's desert wandering, Jesus' time in the wilderness may be understood as a period of preparation for what would follow. In the second volume of his work, the Acts of the Apostles, Luke depicted a similar preparatory interlude, shared by Peter and the others between the ascension of Jesus and the Pentecost experience. Unlike the Johannine author, Luke, for purposes of simplicity and ease of comprehension, has separated and schematized the "hour" of Jesus into its various moments, viz., the passion and death, the resurrection, the ascension and glorification, and the sending of the Spirit. Therefore the interlude between these moments should be understood as a Lucan contrivance suitable to his pedagogical and theological concerns.

The maintenance of the company of Jesus (v. 20) at 12 was important for the unity and well-being of the church. Called personally by Jesus, the Twelve provided continuity between the earthly Jesus and the Jesus of faith in the era of his church. Symbolically, the Twelve were representative of the patriarchal leaders of the new Israel. Like the 12 tribes of the old Israel, the Twelve were unique leaders of the eschatological kingdom of the new Israel, and the founding fathers of the heavenly Jerusalem (Revelation 21:14). On the lips of Peter, Luke stated the qualifications necessary for being numbered among the Twelve, viz., to have been a witness to a resurrection appearance (see 1 Corinthians 15:7-9) and to have been in Jesus' company all during the earthly ministry, i.e., from the days of John the Baptizer until the glorification of Jesus.

It should, however, be admitted that the identification of the Twelve with the apostles *was* due to the church. In today's text, Luke has proven to be especially instrumental in underscoring the coextensiveness of the two. Originally a wider term, applicable to a greater number than only the Twelve, the term apostle could have been inspired either from its usage in the gentile world or from Jewish influence. Among the gentiles, the word apostle (from *apostellein:* to send) referred to a naval fleet or army on an expedition or to a colonist sent to settle an area. From Jewish rabbinical sources, the correlative term in Hebrew (*shaluah, sheluhim*) referred to a commissioned emissary. In the first Christian century, the *sheluhim* had become a legal institution and as such functioned under the aegis of the Palestinian authorities.

Sent out by the rabbis, the *sheluhim* preached with full power and shared the same authority as those who sent them (note John 20:21, Luke 9:48). Commissioned or ordained with the laying on of hands, the *sheluhim* were considered as perfect representatives of those who had mandated them. In the Old Testament, Moses, Elijah and Ezekiel were considered God's *sheluhim* and it is not unlikely that Paul understood himself as such, and brought this missionary aspect to his understanding of himself as God's emissary and Jesus' witness. As later tradition equated the Twelve with the concept of apostle, and limited the number of apostles therefore to an even dozen, the church looked to the Twelve as the unique transmitters and guarantors of the word, the Spirit and the authority of Jesus. The limiting of the title "apostle" to the Twelve alone would explain Paul's repeated insistence on his apostleship and the community's initial resistance to his claims (Galatians 1:1, 1 Corinthians 9:1, 15:8).

As the central body of the post-resurrectional church, the college of the apostles received the Spirit (Acts 1:13, 2:1), set policy in the church (Acts 6:2), conferred authority on others (Acts 8:15) and guarded the authenticity of the magisterium (Acts 9:27).

In order to afford apologetic support from scripture for the action undertaken in today's reading, Luke has Peter citing Psalm 69:26 and Psalm 109:8. By so doing, Luke, who understood all the events of Jesus' life as willed (*dei*) and foreordained by God, applied that same principle of the divine will to the events and circumstances of Jesus' *church*.

The casting of lots, far from being a superstitious act or a chance happening, was again a further indication that the divine initiative was given free rein in the choice between Joseph and Matthias. Remarkably, neither man is mentioned again in the entire text of the book of Acts. Moreover, Peter's prayer (vv. 24-26) underscored the fact that the apostolic leadership within the community of believers was due to God's action and initiative and not to human preference alone.

1 John 4:11-16. No one could rightly accuse the author of the Johannine letters of ascribing to a philosophy of ethical humanism, viz., loving and humanitarian behavior for its own sake and for the sole benefit of a well-ordered society. Of course, the Johannine author had no objection to humane behavior or to an orderly societal setting, but, contrary to the ethical humanists, he understood that the source, center, cause and motivation of love and truly ethical behavior are found only in God himself. Today's second reading is from a longer section of the letter (4:7-5:4) which comprises the longest discourse on love in 1 John. Within the discourse, little distinction is made between the love the believer professes to have for God and the very real and tangible love the believer should have for his fellow believers. Indeed, the author has asserted that one love without the other is impossible. Later in his writings, he would call such a discrepancy a "*lie*"and he would declare those who would engage in such disparate behavior "liars" (1 John 4:20).

Because love is *of* God and because Jesus, incarnate and crucified, is the most eloquent expression of the love of God (John 3:16), those who profess faith in God must likewise profess faith in the one whom he sent in love. The secessionist Christians within the Johannine community denied the importance of Jesus' incarnate presence and redemptive activity and presumed a relationship to God without Jesus' mediation. Impossible, taught the author of the Johannine letters. Moreover, he counseled those whom he shepherded that fellowship with, or a vital relationship to, God was based on two criteria, one of which was faith in Jesus Christ. Such faith could not be selective, picking and choosing those aspects of Jesus that appealed to the intellect, while rejecting others. On the contrary, the entire mystery of Jesus, flesh and blood, dying and crucified, risen and glorified, preexistent and eternal, was to be accepted not merely intellectually but in faith. To those who desired and claimed an elitist and visionary knowledge of God (pre-gnostics), the Johannine author's teaching was a direct challenge.

Secondly, the author declared that another criterion, one correlative to the first, for discerning true communion with God, was love of one's fellow believers (v. 11). Just as scripture has illustrated who God is, viz., love, by the works of God in human history, so must the believer who would be one with the Lord of history exhibit that union and faith in a love made tangible and real within the community. As Aquinas has pointed out, "In this life, we come closer to God through love than through knowledge." Neither the Johannine author nor Aquinas were anti-intellectual or adverse to the pursuit of knowledge. However, both understood knowledge and knowing in the biblical sense of intimate interchange and loving interaction. Such knowledge involved not only the cerebral aspect of the believer but the heart, will, mind and strength as well (Deuteronomy 6:5).

Just as Jesus set on a par love of God and love of neighbor, the author of 1 John understood loving the unseen God as conditioned by and given perfect expression in loving others. Theologically, his point has not been improved upon in the past 20 centuries. Morally and ethically, his challenge to believers is as poignant as when it was first made.

John 17:11-19. In the Johannine version of the good news of Jesus Christ, there is no account of the eucharist within the last supper discourse. Scholars are in agreement, though, that chapter six is comprised of a compilation of eucharistic material and theology and represents the Johannine viewpoint on the sacrament. Fuller has pointed out, however, that, while the actual words of eucharistic institution are not to be found in the fourth gospel, the prayer of consecration from which today's gospel is excerpted constitutes the Johannine equivalent thereof. Within the prayer, called the "high priestly prayer" or "sacredotal prayer," a term ascribed to the Lutheran theologian David Chytaeus (died 1600 C.E.), Christ consecrated himself as a messianic and saving sacrifice. By so doing, he offered the total gift of himself in fulfillment of the Father's will for him. Besides offering himself, the prayer also represents Jesus as consecrating those who have come to believe in and follow him.

Set within the context of the lengthy discourse at the last supper, the prayer (and the discourse in general) are purported to be Jesus' last will and testament or final words to his disciples. Having completed his earthly mission, his parting words to his friends expressed the intensity of his hopes and aspirations. Within both extra-biblical literature and the scriptures we find other such farewell discourses or testaments, whose message has been made more significant by the fact of their literary genre. For example, all of the seventh century book of Deuteronomy has been assigned the historical setting of Moses' farewell address to his people, before leaving them in death prior to their infiltration of Canaan. That historical setting and orientation lent importance and significance to the entire book. So too, the Johannine author's use of the farewell testament genre has contributed to the poignancy of the teaching it contains.

Throughout the fourth gospel, numerous references were made to the "hour" of Jesus, a term used by the evangelist to refer to the saving event of Jesus' passion, death, resurrection and exaltation. Most of the references indicate that the "hour" had not yet come but, within the context of the farewell address and with Jesus' death an imminent inevitability, his statement is a declarative: "The hour has come!" (17:1). Once arrived, the hour represents the climax and culmination of Jesus' mission. For that reason, Jesus' consecratory prayer provides the believer with an understanding of his hour and of Jesus' motivation in fulfilling it.

Divided into three major sections, the high priestly prayer is offered first for Jesus himself (vv. 1-3). It was the custom for Jewish high priests to pray for themselves before rendering their ministerial services for the community. So too, Jesus prayed for himself before offering the ultimate sacrifice of himself which effectively rendered all other sacrifices obsolete. The second section of the prayer (vv. 6-19) was offered for Jesus' disciples and the third portion was dedicated to those future believers who would come to faith because of the disciples' work (vv. 20-26). Because of this structure and similarity to the eucharistic canon of the mass, some scholars propose that the Johannine author reflected in this prayer the structure of the eucharistic liturgy of his community of the 90s C.E. Others, citing the great similarity of spirit and content of several of the prayers' petitions, view it as a Johannine version of the Lord's Prayer.

Today's gospel is a portion of the second major section, the prayer of Jesus for his disciples. Comprised of four petitions, the prayer was (as were all of Jesus' prayers) addressed to the Father. Qualifying the Father and his name as "holy" (v. 11), the author underscored the distinction that separated Jesus' followers from the world. As children of the Father, begotten of water and of the Spirit (John 3), the friends (John 15) of Jesus were to be made holy by means of the sacrifice he was soon to make. In the first petition for his followers, Jesus' prayer was offered for their protection, i.e., for their continued union with Jesus, the Father and one another. That union had been protected by the presence of the earthly Jesus, but with the expiration of his hour, their faith in his risen presence would have to sustain them. The explanation of Judas' defection and the apologetic support for it (vv. 12-14) are surely a product of the Johannine community (cf. Psalms 41:9, 109:5-8).

The second petition of Jesus' prayer for his disciples was for their *joy* (v. 14). A share in the deep and vital joy of Jesus himself would serve to bolster his flock against the hatred of the world. Thirdly, the Father was requested to guard the disciples against the evil one (vv. 15-16). Lastly, Jesus prayed that those who had believed in him and followed him in life would be consecrated by the Father, so as to continue to believe in him and follow him after his death. As followers of Jesus, his disciples would inherit his mission (v. 18). The divine missiology which had dispatched the incarnate word to the world on a mission of light and life-giving would also equip the disciples of Jesus for a similar mandate. Consecrated in the truth which is the word of God (Psalm 118:142, John 17:17), those who believed would be consecrated along with their master and made holy by the sacrifice of his blood.

1. Ministry, like any precious gift, must be handled with care and exercised with respect (Acts).

2. Authentic loving can only come from God (1 John).

3. Christians are not conscripted but consecrated for service (John).

Pentecost Sunday

Greater than any political or social reform, the transforming power of the Spirit of Jesus effectively changed the course of human events. For those who accepted and believed, the Spirit provided the enthusiasm and inspiration to announce the good news of Jesus' victory over sin and death (Acts). Those who have accepted and believed were able, because of the Spirit, to appropriate that victory and to share it with others by continuing Jesus' mission of forgiveness and mercy (John). Because of the Spirit, the many and diverse individual followers of Jesus became one in a formidable and powerful union (1 Corinthians).

Acts 2:1-11. Many scholars dispute the accuracy of the title of the second volume of Luke's work and suggest that Acts of the Apostles might be more correctly entitled Acts of the *Spirit*. Indeed, it is the Holy Spirit, not the apostles (Peter and Paul), who is the key figure in Acts. The Spirit guides forms, creates, renews and inspires the church. Peter and Paul and their importance cannot be overlooked, but these great apostles appear as subordinate to the Spirit. The secondary role of the apostles is underscored by the fact that each, in turn, fades out of the picture without even a mention of their deaths!

Careful to illustrate the continuity between his gospel and Acts, Luke posits the presence of the Spirit as one of the chief sources of that continuity. In fact, a comparison of the birth of Jesus (gospel) and the birth of the church (Acts) reveals the overshadowing presence of the Spirit, powerful in both nativities. Just as the Spirit of God led Jesus, so too, in all the significant events of the life and development of the church, the Spirit would be operative. For example, the Spirit gave the impetus that thrust the followers of Jesus into the mission fields for the first time (Acts 1:8, 2:33). That same Spirit enlightened and enlarged the parochial attitude of the Jews toward the gentiles (Acts 10; 13:2,4). Once gentiles had been admitted to church membership, it was the Spirit who helped to relieve them of the added burdens of Jewish cult and customs (Acts 15:28). When the body of believers grew beyond the borders of Judea and Samaria and when leadership for the expanding church was needed, it was the Spirit who guided the choosing of competent, worthy leaders (Acts 20:28).

In today's first reading, the importance of the Spirit to the church is featured in the Jewish Feast of Weeks. An ancient agricultural feast which originally celebrated the abundance of the grain harvest, Shevuoth (Hebrew: Weeks) or Pentecost (Greek: 50 days), was also called the Feast of Firstfruits. In later Judaism, the feast was associated with and became a commemoration of the gift of the law at Sinai. Tradition taught that Moses and the refugees from Egypt had travelled for seven weeks from Egypt to Sinai. During that period, the people were morally formed by Moses, and the gift of the law was regarded as God's approbation of their efforts. Similarly, reformed Judaism today uses the seven week period between Passover and Pentecost for intense religious education of young people who on the feast of Shevuoth or Pentecost affirm as a group their willingness to live according to the law and its divine principles. In Jesus' day, the Essenes of Qumran admitted new members to their community on the feast of Shevuoth-Pentecost. Perhaps Luke had all these ideas, viz., the moral formation, the law, affirmation, new membership and harvest, in mind when he associated the gift of the Spirit with the Jewish feast of Pentecost. Indeed, all of these elements are included in the celebration of the Spirit in the church.

With regard to the aspect of moral formation, there was no doubt that a transformation had occurred among the followers of Jesus. The very same people who had deserted him at Passover were confessing their faith in him at Pentecost. Frightened and terrorized by both Roman and Jewish authorities, the disciples had hidden at Passover, disappointed that the one in whom they had hoped had failed. But by the feast of Pentecost, these same people had become so bold and enthusiastic in their witness to Jesus that some thought them to be intoxicated!

What had happened? What had made the difference? Jesus Christ, risen and transformed in glory had effected in his followers a moral transformation as well. The resurrection of the Lord had been the key factor in the disciple's transition from fear to faith. At Pentecost, with the power of the Holy Spirit, Jesus' followers were able to appropriate the realities of his cross, his rising, his exaltation and glory.

1 Corinthians 12:3-7, 12-13. In all likelihood, there were many metaphors in Paul's mind when he began to describe the unity and diversity that characterized the followers of Jesus Christ. Literary genius that he was, the apostle could have drawn upon any one of several comparisons to make his point clear. For example, he could have likened the community of believers in Corinth to a precious gem, whose many and varied facets lent themselves to a common beauty and preciousness. Or he could have compared the assembly of the faithful to a rainbow with its several different colors. But, Paul chose to describe the relationship of believers to Christ in terms of a *living* body. No static entity, no matter how precious or magnificent, could sufficiently or adequately communicate the mystery of Christ *with* his Christians or of those Christians *in* Christ. Leander Keck has suggested that the analogy of the body of Christ (v. 12) is Paul's unique and distinctive contribution to community self-understanding. Others have suggested that Paul was relying upon a metaphor popular among the Stoic thinkers of his day. If so, the analogy would have been well known in Corinth which was a center for the ancient Stoic philosophers. Still others have suggested that Paul drew upon the gnostic myth of the cosmic redeemer, whose body was thought to have been comprised of the saved. Recent archaeological excavations of the sanctuary of the god Asclepius of Corinth have unearthed numerous terracota heads, hands, feet, arms, eyes, etc., and some have suggested that these figures had shaped Paul's concept of community. But Paul's ideas and theology for surpassed both Stoic and gnostic thought, and the Asclepion artifacts were a mere shadow of his insight.

For Paul the union of the Lord with the faithful and of the faithful with one another was a transcendent and living entity, held together and vitalized by the Spirit. Not only did the Spirit make one capable of authentic faith (v. 3: "No one can say Jesus is Lord except . . .") but the Spirit was also the impetus of the graces which built and enhanced the quality of community life. In the 18 months he had spent in Corinth, Paul had succeeded in establishing a community of believers in Jesus. Many had come to Christ from a background of mystery (Orphic) cults and had previously engaged in frenzied, bizarre and fanatical orgies masquerading under the guise of religion. In an effort to educate the newcomers to the faith and to temper their emotionalism into a sincere and powerful force for Christ, Paul taught them of the dynamism of the Spirit. When the Spirit of truth, i.e., the Spirit of Jesus, impelled a believer, the result would not be frenzied fanaticism or uncontrollable behavior. Rather, the one who acted in and by the Spirit of Jesus contributed toward the common good for the benefit of the community (v. 7).

The remarks of Paul which comprise today's second reading were probably occasioned by a dispute concerning those who claimed to possess the true Spirit. The apostle offered the community the following norms for discerning the truth of the spirits: (1) Does the spirit profess faith, not only in a spiritual Christ but in the reality of the earthly Jesus as well (v. 33)? This would have applied directly to the gnostic influence in the group which chose to ignore the value and impact of the earthly, *bodily* Jesus. (2) Does the spirit enhance and edify the community? This would have applied to those who tended merely to emote and excite. (3) Finally, does the spirit make, of the disparate members, *one* body?

Today, no less than in Paul's Corinth of the 50s C.E., these criteria are invaluable to the community of believers in Jesus. Discernment of spirits remains a challenging community task just as fidelity to the Spirit of Jesus is a community responsibility.

John 20:19-23. While the Lucan schematization of the saving mystery of Jesus' passion and death, resurrection, ascension and his gift of the Spirit may prove easier to understand and to explain by reason of their presentation in Luke/Acts, it is probable that the Johannine author is more accurate in coalescing the various moments of Jesus' hour into one. Whereas Luke in his accounts separated the resurrection of Jesus from the bestowal of the Spirit by some 50 days, the Johannine Jesus is portrayed as giving the gift of the Spirit on the same day as his resurrection. Moreover, in a deliberate effort to assert the continuity between the earthly Jesus and the risen Jesus or the Jesus of faith, the Lord as giver of the Spirit is presented in today's gospel with the wounds of his passion in evidence. Lest the gnostic influence within his community convince the body of the faithful of the irrelevance of the earthly Jesus, the Johannine author established a sure link between the cross, the resurrection and the advent of the paraclete. Indeed, it is significant that the disciples recognized Jesus and rejoiced in his presence upon being shown his hands and side (v. 20).

As in all the resurrection appearances, there was an obvious concern on the part of the evangelist for the believers left behind by the risen Lord. In the case of today's gospel, that concern was channeled into a mission of mercy and forgiveness. The sending forth of the disciples in the Spirit to forgive sins has been cited as a source text for understanding the sacrament of penance or reconciliation. Others have understood the forgiving or binding (v. 23) of sins as referring to a withholding of baptism depending on acceptance or rejection of the kerygmatic preaching. Still others, citing the rabbinical equivalents *asar* and *sera'* (bind, loose) and referring to Matthew 18:8, would have us understand v. 23 in the context of church discipline, i.e., to grant or refuse admission to the community for reason of sinfulness. While these later anachronisms may certainly find some support in today's gospel pericope, there is a more primary meaning to be gleaned from the text. Combined with the gift of peace, the mission of forgiveness to which the risen Lord dispatched his disciples is an indication that, because of his passion and death, he can share with all believers his victory over sin and death. The message of the cross was not failure but forgiveness, and that message made of Pentecost a day of power and peace.

More than an ordinary greeting, Jesus' double salutation (*shalom*) was a sign that, because of the fulfillment of Jesus' hour, a new era was dawning upon all of humanity. Because of the rising of the Sun-Son of Justice, the eschatological age of utopian bliss and harmonious solidarity had begun. The outpouring of the Spirit upon all of humanity promised by the prophets (Joel 3:1, Ezekiel 36:27) was realized in the person and mission of the risen Lord Jesus. It is significant that the fourth gospel is not specific in stating exactly who were present. Luke had indicated that Peter and the Eleven (Acts 2:14) were recipients of the Spirit but, by the turn of the first Christian century (90s C.E.) when the Johannine author wrote, the Twelve were dead and the community understood that the Spirit of Jesus abided with each of them by means of baptism. Hence the fourth evangelist refers simply to "the disciples" (vv. 19, 20). The Christians of the first century C.E. knew themselves to be infused and mandated by the same Spirit as had been their ancestors in the faith.

Because of its less dramatic presentation, the Johannine Pentecost may perhaps convey a more accurate idea of the gift of the Spirit than the Lucan account with its winds, fiery tongues, great noise, etc. Although it was certainly not the intention, Luke's Pentecost narrative in Acts may give the false impression that the Spirit was bestowed on one particular occasion. In the fourth gospel, the Spirit was closely connected with the risen Lord and was presented as an act of creation or re-creation. Jesus' breathing on his disciples recalled the creative breath of God in Genesis. Just as God's breath sustained life and supported each member of humanity in a continuous act of life-giving, so too the Spirit of Jesus would sustain and enliven his disciples in an act of continuous love. Pentecost, or the gift of the Spirit, is not a one-time event but a never ending fruit of the dying-rising Lord.

Finally, the appearance of the risen Lord and his gift of the Spirit served to fulfill the promises Jesus had made to his disciples during his earthly ministry. That they would know great joy and peace (John 14:27, 16:20), that they would be able to do the same and even greater works than he (John 14:12), that he would send to them a helper and an advocate (John 14:16-17, 26), and that he would always be with them . . . all these promises were fulfilled in the gift of the Spirit. Today, those same promises are fulfilled and the same mandate and mission are shared by all who have become, by reason of Jesus' hour, recipients of his powerful, peaceful Spirit.

1. Which was more astounding . . . the driving wind and fiery tongues or the transformation of cowards into champions (Acts)?

2. The harmonious blending of the many and the diverse into one can only be achieved with the divine effort of the Spirit (1 Corinthians).

3. Forgiveness is the mission entrusted to those who share the victory of Jesus over sin (John).

Ordinary Time
Second Sunday in Ordinary Time

Like an echo that resounds in hearts of kindred spirits, the Lord's call touches the community through the individual and the individual in the community. Mercifully, he calls again and again until we learn to recognize his voice (Samuel). He does not call disembodied spirits, but the whole person—body, heart, mind and memories (Corinthians). He calls to us, one by one, and in our response we find union and companionship with one another in him (John).

1 Samuel 3:3-10, 19. Along with Ezekiel and Hosea, the books called 1 and 2 Samuel enjoy the dubious reputation of being regarded as the most corrupt books in the Bible. Corruptness, as it is used of scriptural texts, has nothing to do with an ethical judgment or moral evaluation but with the measure of accuracy with which the text can be reconstructed. In the cases of the aforementioned books, reconstruction has been made exceedingly difficult and accuracy a debatable matter due to poorly preserved texts, a multiplicity of versions and translations, etc.

In the Hebrew canon, 1 and 2 Samuel were considered one book and part of the former prophets or historical collection of Joshua through Kings. When the Hebrew Bible was translated into Greek (LXX) and subsequently vocalized for easier reading, the lengthier text took up two scrolls. The Septuagint paired these with the books of Kings and named these the four books of the Kingdoms (*Basileiai*). Catholics may remember the time when their Bibles, following the Vulgate (which followed the LXX), listed these books as 1, 2, 3, 4 Kings. Today the more facile Douai designation of 1 and 2 Samuel, 1 and 2 Kings is utilized by both Protestants and Catholics.

Although the Talmud regards Samuel as the author, basing itself on 1 Chronicles 29:29-30, the books reveal the work of many hands at many different periods in Israel's history. Perhaps the attribution to Samuel was due to the fact that he as a prophetic and priestly figure dominates the story. Some of the material in 1 and 2 Samuel is as ancient as the monarchy itself (2 Samuel 9-20), but the entire work was probably given final shape by a Deuteronomic hand shortly before or during the exile, some 400 years after Saul was first acclaimed as king. In spite of its poorly preserved state, and the numerous hands and eras through which the text called Samuel has passed, the work is useful nevertheless because it provides us with valuable insights into: (1) the transition from a relatively loose tribal amphictyony to a monarchy, (2) Israel's early religious practices, (3) the beginnings of prophetism as an institution.

Today's text provides us with a glimpse into the vocational experience of Samuel who was to become a key figure in Israel's history. Coming as it does immediately after Jesus' baptismal experience (last week), one cannot help but connect the two figures. Samuel's call, like that of Jesus, resulted in his becoming the servant of the Lord. As such, Samuel and Jesus were instrumental in bringing their people to a greater and a deeper understanding of their God and his ways. An examination of Samuel's life, the circumstances of his birth, his mother's song of joy at conceiving him, his call and his mission, have led scholars to think of Samuel as a type of Jesus Christ.

Samuel's call may be compared to that of the classical prophets who came after him. Each of these calls contains the elements of readiness, recognition and response (the three R's?) and each resulted in a prophetic mission for the benefit of the nation of Israel. Notice that Samuel was *already* in the service of the Lord when he received the call to even greater service. Dedicated by his mother at this birth, Samuel functioned in the temple under Eli's tutelage. Some scholars regard Samuel's slumber in the temple as a type of "sacred sleep" from which the dreamer hoped to obtain a special revelation. Such a practice was common among many ancient tribes. But Samuel's sleeping in the temple was probably due to his being assigned to tend the sacred flame (Exodus 27:20) or perhaps to guard the ark. Priestly rubrics required the lamp to be kept alight from dusk to daybreak as a sign that the Lord was present. It is significant that another (Eli) helped Samuel to evaluate, *recognize* his call as authentic and to *respond* to it.

1 Corinthians 6:13-15, 17-20. Corinth's notorious reputation as a seaport of sexual delights had been cultivated through centuries of self-indulgence and wanton nonchalance with regard to moral norms. Long before Paul's mission in that city, Aristophanes (450-385 B.C.E.) had coined the verb *korinthiazesthai* which meant "to act like a Corinthian" or to engage in lewd conduct. Plato in his *Republic* (404 D) had used the term *korinthia kore*, "a Corinthian girl," to refer to a prostitute.

Paul's response to this attitude and his affirmation of morality or "body" ethics is found in chapters 5-7 of his first letter to the church at Corinth. Our text for today is a brief except from that longer piece, and contains within it the basis of Paul's theological position: "The body is for the Lord!" Some in Corinth who argued, "All things are lawful for me" (6:12), may have been basing their claim on a twisted interpretation of Paul's statement that all things are lawful and pure (Romans 14:14) for the Christian. Paul, however, had been referring to the liberty which Christians enjoyed with regard to dietary practices, etc.

The apostle's answer to those who had misinterpreted his thought, as well as to those who had no regard for the body as a moral entity, was the same: "Your bodies are members of Christ!" To support and elucidate his teaching Paul drew upon the fact of Jesus' resurrection. Raised up by God in his *body*, Jesus in his resurrection is a pledge that all believers will enjoy the same resurrected dignity and glory. As Lord of both heaven and earth, of *matter* and spirit, Jesus has a claim on the bodily aspect of the person as well as the spiritual counterpart. Indeed, by fact of the incarnation, matter (and therefore the body) cannot be thought of as evil. Jesus by his involvement with humanity, even to the point of becoming flesh and blood, has redeemed *all* of the human person. Moreover, Jesus imparted his own Holy Spirit to remain as helper, guide and sanctifier. While the gnostics believed that the body as matter inhibited the spirit, Paul taught that Jesus' Spirit made the body of the Christian a temple. The Spirit's sanctifying power is a moral process with which the believer must cooperate. To regard the body as evil and as useless would be to deter this moral process of becoming. In a final point, Paul appealed to the fact of Jesus' passion and death, calling it a purchase price or a ransom paid (v. 20). While the metaphor he chose may have been borrowed from the slave market and seems to place a "price tag" on redemption, his point nevertheless is clear.

John 1:35-42. Each of the three readings for today deals with the subject of vocation. In the Samuel text, the vocation is to greater service; in the letter to the Corinthians, Paul reminded the Christians of their baptismal call to holiness and union with Christ. In the gospel according to John, the subject is the call to discipleship and to a way of life which would by its very quality *be* a vocation, calling others to union with the Lord.

Typical of the more developed theology and high christology of the fourth gospel, today's pericope is in truth a distillation into one scene of several important events and ideas which were historically spread out over a much longer period of time. For example, (1) the confession of John the Baptizer (v. 36), (2) the changing of loyalties of the disciples from John to Jesus (v. 37), (3) the recognition of Jesus as messiah (v. 41), (4) the change of Peter's name indicating his changed mission in life . . . all these developments were far more gradual that the fourth gospel indicates. A comparison of John with the parallel synoptic accounts will illustrate the fact that John has amalgamated several processes into one event. Suffice it to say that the evangelist of the fourth gospel is not merely a chronicler of historical events but a theologian, interpreting those events of history according to his own purposes.

John's purpose in this particular instance is to elucidate the mystery of revelation and response which is intregal to discipleship. While only the fourth evangelist tells us that Jesus' first disciples had first been disciples of John, it is nevertheless a quite understandable and feasible idea. As followers of the Baptizer's preaching of repentance and preparedness for the "coming one," they would have been well disposed to accept the testimony of John concerning Jesus and subsequently to begin to follow him. But the evangelist's purpose is also polemical. In the years after John's death, a sect professing faith in the Baptizer as messiah sprang up. Besides suppressing the embarrassing fact of Jesus' baptism by John, the author of the fourth gospel made John's subordinate position abundantly clear by implying that the Baptizer himself directed his disciples to follow Jesus.

As a title, "lamb of God" contained many facets of meaning, three of which have been identified by R.E. Brown as among the most important: (1) evocative of the apocalyptic lamb, the title "lamb of God" applied to Jesus would emphasize his mission as the crusher of evil in the world (Testament of Joseph 19:8) and as conquering leader of all peoples (Revelation 7:17); (2) in the suffering servant songs of Deutero-Isaiah, the servant is compared in the fourth song (Isaiah 53) to a *lamb* led to the slaughter and his vicarious suffering is proclaimed as redemptive and salvific; (3) to call Jesus lamb of God may have been an attempt to identify him with the paschal lamb whose blood had saved Israel from destruction (Exodus 12).

In the fourth gospel the entire episode of the calling of the first disciples is replete with theological terminology. What may appear at first glance to be simple verbs, viz., "follow" (vv. 37, 38, 40), "stay" (vv. 38, 39) and "see" (v. 39) are in reality profound theological ideas when used by the Johannine author. For example, "following" or "to follow" means much more than travelling behind another person. When John refers to someone as following another, he wants the reader to understand by that word the dedication and commitment of discipleship. Jesus' question, his first words as recorded in the fourth gospel ("What are you looking for?"), is by no means a nonchalant query. It is, rather, a challenge to discipleship addressed, not merely to a few men in Bethany in the first Christian century, but to all who would become disciples of the truth and the light. As R.E. Brown has pointed out, the initiative or the vocation to discipleship lies with Jesus and is reiterated later in the gospel, "You have not chosen me; no, I have chosen you" (15:16).

Jesus' invitation to those who sought after him to "come and see" was more than oriental hospitality. Coming to Jesus and seeing Jesus are terms used throughout the fourth gospel to mean that one has *come* in faith and that one *sees* or perceives with the insight of faith (3:21, 6:35, 7:37). Moreover, there is contained in this simple invitation, "come and see," an echo from the Old Testament wisdom literature, wherein wisdom invites humanity to "come and see" (Proverbs 1:20-28). John's motif of identifying Jesus with wisdom is further clarified by the text: wisdom is *seen* by those who love her and found by those who *seek* after her (Wisdom 7:12).

When Andrew and the unnamed follower (John?) bring Simon to Jesus-wisdom, Jesus looks at him and changes his name. Unlike Matthew, the fourth gospel writer places this change of name at the beginning of the ministry. Certainty as to the exact point at which Simon was renamed is not possible but putting it at the beginning of the gospel and of Peter's discipleship serves the author's purpose well. Having opened themselves in faith to the revelation of Jesus and having responded in faith, the disciples are thereby transformed by the person and power of Jesus. Andrew's transformation was manifested in enthusiastic service; he sought to bring others to faith. Simon's transformation was manifested in a new name, Peter (Rock), symbolic of the role he would be asked to play. Today, Jesus continues to ask, "What are you looking for?" and to challenge, "Come and see!" For those who would "follow" and "see" and "stay," the transforming power of his grace is still present and his Spirit is still creating disciples.

1. Willingness to serve is a predisposition necessary to recognizing God's call to greater service (1 Samuel).

2. Morality is not based on law or precepts but on the dignity each person enjoys because of Jesus and his redemptive mission (1 Corinthians).

3. Bringing others to recognize and to follow Jesus is a vital aspect of discipleship (John).

Third Sunday in Ordinary Time

Discipleship as a way of life is a premium value, costing not less than everything (Mark). Who would become a disciple of Jesus Christ must undertake daily to answer the call to conversion and repentance (Jonah). Besides reordering heart and affection, purposes and goals, the disciple must reorient all his/her activities, ideas, loves and loyalties to God's present, future and eternal reign (Corinthians).

Jonah 3:1-5, 10. For those who would interpret the scriptures literally or fundamentally, the story of Jonah is probably one of the greatest and mind-boggling challenges, both to common sense and to faith. The author of the book of Jonah seemed to have no care for the improbability of several aspects of his story and he certainly did not expect his audience to limit his message to a merely literal interpretation. Rather, the true meaning of the story of Jonah is far more important and far-reaching than the great fish or Nineveh. Although classified among the prophetic works, Jonah is quite different from the bulk of prophetic literature and should more accurately be designated as a didactic fiction, told in narrative form with satirical overtones. The author of Jonah had a profound theological purpose in mind as he wove his tale of adventure. Purported to be the work of Jonah (2 Kings 14:25), a prophet who lived and ministered during the reign of Jeroboam II (783-743 B.C.E.), the book is actually the product of a much later time after the exile, probably between 400 and 200 B.C.E. During this period of their reconstruction and reestablishment as a people, Israel's efforts to rebuild the nation's spirit resulted in an extreme of nationalism. The anonymous author of Jonah, in an effort to combat the narrow-minded parochialism of his people and to uphold more universalist values, created the person of Jonah, bigot par excellence.

Through the caricature of Jonah, Israel was chided into an awareness of itself and its shortcomings. Jonah's unwillingness to go to the foreigners in Nineveh to preach to them of God's purposes, his efforts to escape his mission, his annoyance and resentment at the Assyrians' repentance and at God's forgiveness, even the great fish . . . all these aspects of the author's story served to communicate his message: God's merciful forgiveness and caring involvement were to be enjoyed by all peoples and were not the exclusive prerogatives of Israel. With this as its essential message, the book of Jonah, or at least the mentality it promoted, served as an impetus in the developing notion of universalism only fully realized in the Christian era.

Nineveh *was* a great city, the capital of Assyria, but was in fact only about 3 miles in diameter and 8 miles in circumference. Though his purpose in exaggerating the size of the city was probably to accentuate the greatness of its conversion, it may be that the author was alluding to the entire territory around Nineveh (from Khorsabad to Nimrud) which extended for about 26 miles. In either case, the essential point is the fact that a Jew was being sent with God's message to a *gentile* territory. In eight short words, Jonah delivered the entire burden of his message as God's prophet, "Forty days more and Nineveh shall be destroyed." That alone bears witness to the fact that it was *God's power* at work in Nineveh. Surely the spontaneous reaction of the Ninevites could not be attributed to Jonah's silvery eloquence or persuasive preaching. Although the Septuagint renders the time as *three* days, forty days is more in keeping with the traditional period of repentance. Tradition taught that Israel had spent 40 years in the wilderness, about 40 years in exile and that the flood waters had cleansed the sinful earth for 40 days (Genesis 7:17).

In sharp contrast to Israel's intransigence to the prophetic word was Nineveh's complete docility. Verse 5 tells us they *believed* God, using the same word as that which described the belief of Abraham, great father of the faithful (Genesis 15:6). In Nineveh, that belief was translated into repentance, signified by fasting and sackcloth. This same spirit of repentance was preached by John the Baptist, herald of the kingdom and the two imperatives, *repent* and *believe*, are paired and placed on the lips of Jesus by Mark (1:15) as part of his summary of Jesus' ministry.

1 Corinthians 7:29-31. Without an adequate understanding of Paul's situation and his frame of reference when writing to the Corinthians, his advice in today's second reading could easily be misinterpreted and misconstrued. Much of 1 Corinthians is devoted to answering a number of ethical issues and problems which had been sent to Paul from Corinth. In chapter seven, from which today's second reading is excerpted, the apostle answered questions which had arisen concerning circumcision (vv. 18-20), slavery (vv. 21-24), marriage and celibacy (vv. 25-40). Paul's responses must be considered in light of his statement, "Let everyone lead the life which the Lord has assigned him and in which God called him" (v. 17), as well as his idea concerning the parousia. For Paul, at the time of his writing to the Christians at Corinth (57 C.E.), the parousia was an imminent reality. As he has put it in our reading today, "the time is short" (v. 29) and "the world as we know it is passing away" (v. 31). In order to be prepared for Jesus' advent, Paul advocated that Christians here and now anticipate by their actions and life the world to come. To that end he advised detachment from this world, its cares and concerns, so as to be attached to the one person and the one reality that would endure forever, Jesus and his kingdom.

Because of the vigor with which Paul preached, many were perplexed and confused and some even thought to detach themselves from spouses and marital responsibilities so as to concentrate on eschatological realities. To these, Paul counselled, "Live in a spirit of *hos me*, i.e., *as if* not of this world." Urging the Corinthians to maintain their present states and callings in life, Paul taught that all states in life were brought under Christ's redeeming power. However, the Christian should be aware that present structures and institutions, whether physical, social or economic, would yield to eternity and therefore the believer should not be unduly attached to passing entities. During his ministry Jesus preached the same idea in a more positive way when he said, "Seek first the kingdom!"

The modern believer may be tempted to dismiss Paul's ideas as time-bound and irrelevant in light of the delayed eschatology. But it remains true, nevertheless, that this world *is* passing away and the parousia *is* coming. But we may not use that fact as an excuse to shirk our existential responsibilities nor may we become so time-bound as to forget the absolute and ultimate values of life. Such a perspective should serve to make the believer more accountable here and now, as well as to prevent an unhealthy and unholy obsession with matters of no consequence. Though he may not have expressed it in precisely this way, Paul regarded baptism as an initiation into the future. Because of that initiation, the believer has to adjust his values, his time, his energies and his loyalties so as to be consonant with and consequent to the privileges and responsibilities of being redeemed.

Today, in an effort to help people to discern their values, psychologists might ask the question: "If the house were about to burn down, what would you grab before you ran out to safety?" Paul, eminent psychologist-theologian of the first century C.E., told the Corinthians in effect: "The house (this world) is already burning. Jesus is at the door; the only thing you can take with you is yourself . . . how well-prepared are you to meet him?"

Mark 1:14-20. What Jonah, grudging and unconvinced, had preached to Nineveh Jesus preached with power and immediacy. In his person, in his words and works the reign of God had become present. The only worthy response to that reality was repentance and faith. Verses 14-15 of the first chapter of Mark's gospel are actually the evangelist's summary of Jesus' ministry, expressed in the confessional language of the post-resurrectional church. Placed at the head of the gospel, these verses form a sort of precis of what will follow.

Like John the Baptizer and the prophets before him, Jesus preached repentance, which involved not merely a regret or sorrow for sins and failures but a positive determination to begin a new life. While Jesus probably used the Aramaic term *shubh* which meant to return (to God) or to turn around, the Greek word *meta-noiein* is more graphic. *Meta-noiein* or *metanoia* involves a radical change of heart, a complete about face, a resolve to reorient one's entire being, energies etc. In the sense in which this word was used in the gospels, *metanoia* or *shubh* involves a turning completely to God, a renunciation of all that would deter from total commitment and a personal attachment to Jesus who makes present God's reign or the kingdom. But in addition to the prophets and to John the Baptizer's teaching on repentance, Jesus added the imperative to *believe*. Guilt for its own sake is not enough; regret and repentance had to be translated into a positive faith commitment.

One may not overlook the eschatological nature of these verses (14-15) either. Notice that Mark does not declare that the kingdom is *coming soon,* or that it was *not far off.* Rather, the appearance of Jesus in Galilee marked the *beginning* of the kingdom or reign of God and therefore of the eschatological era which would be consummated or brought to fulfillment at the time of Jesus' second appearance. Moreover, Mark's eschatological announcement of the reign of God is introduced with an ominous portent, which signalled the manner by which Jesus would effect his wondrous work of redemption. "After John's arrest," or literally, "after John was *handed over*" (v. 14), alerts the reader that this reign will not be accomplished without sacrifice. The same terminology used to describe John's demise will be used of Jesus, in reference to his passion and death (9:31; 10:33; 14:10, 11, 44). In the same way, those who would follow Jesus in discipleship should expect to experience similar treatment (13:9) for the sake of God's reign. In the second part of today's pericope this subject of discipleship is introduced (vv. 16-20).

Once the reign of God and its prerequisites, repentance and belief, have been announced, the duties of active membership in the kingdom are enunciated. The call of Jesus to his first followers may seem to be a casual or chance encounter, but it is in truth an epiphanic experience. "As Jesus made his way" (v. 16) is literally translated "as Jesus passed by" and the verb *paragein* (*parerchesthai*) is the same word used to describe the "manifestations" of God's glory and "showing forth" of his goodness in the Old Testament (1 Kings 19:11, 2 Samuel 23:4, Exodus 33:19, 22). When the word is used in the gospels in reference to Jesus, the indication is that of an epiphany or revelation of power and divine glory. Hence the meeting of Jesus with his first disciples was one in which his glory and power were made manifest to them.

Both calls, that of Andrew and Simon and that of James and John, are an echo of the call of Elisha by Elijah in the Old Testament book of Kings (1 Kings 19:19-21) and are a model of the call and response of every disciple. Elisha, and the followers of Jesus of the first as well as of the 20th centuries, received a call which was at once a revelation of who God was and a challenge to respond in service to that revelation. Promptness or immediacy of response and the totality of one's dedication must be sustained through periods of growth and conflict. Moreover, the prerequisites of the kingdom, viz., repentance and belief, remain a constant and daily challenge for every disciple. In this way, the disciple becomes with Jesus not merely a *member* of the kingdom, but one who, by his words and works, by his service and witness in faith, can effectively *establish* the reign of God. In other words, the disciple, like Jesus, can become for the world not only the *proclaimer* of the gospel but with Jesus can *be* the good news.

1. Even the least likely messenger can deliver God's powerful, saving word (Jonah).

2. Attachments to unchanging structures and time-bound institutions can dim one's eschatological perspective (1 Corinthians).

3. Repentance and belief are contingent realities; who feels no need for repentance probably does not truly believe (Mark).

Fourth Sunday in Ordinary Time

Our God who became a word enfleshed never ceases to speak. In every age and season, there are those who hear his message and make it heard (Deuteronomy). There are those who by their life prophesy here and now of the possibilities to come (Corinthians). And there are others who by their words and works make present the reign of that word whose power silences evil forever (Mark).

Deuteronomy 18:15-20. The Hebrew title of Deuteronomy, *Debarim,* i.e., "these are the words" or simply "the words" is nondescript, in that it does not reveal anything of the nature or contents of the book, but that title is in no way confusing. On the other hand the Greek title, *deutero nomos,* or *second* law, is a misleading misinterpretation of Deuteronomy 17:18, wherein the work is actually called a *copy* of the law. As a matter of fact, neither title does justice to the fifth book of the Pentateuch which is an original theological compendium. Like the New Testament scribe who "brings from his storehouse treasures old and new," the authors of Deuteronomy have compiled both archaic and contemporary (to their times) materials concerning the major events in Israel's salvation history (desert, settlement, etc.), its sacred traditions, cult and institutions and have gathered this collection of data and commentary under the umbrella of a theology of renewal and reform.

Today's pericope is from a longer section (12:2—18:22) concerned with the centralization of Israel's cult, its theocratic government and the officials thereof. Having treated of the offices of judges, king and priest, the Deuteronomic theologians then turned their attention to the prophet and the institution of prophecy as an authoritative interpreter of the law for Israel. As a mediator between God and humankind, the prophet, according to Deuteronomy, exercises his role as a successor of Moses. Today's reading places on the lips of Moses the assurance that the sequence of prophetic utterance would not be interrupted (v. 15) as well as the security of knowing how to discern between true and false prophets (vv. 19-20).

In Israel, the institution of prophecy underwent a marked development from its earliest emergence as the prophetic guild whose ecstatic, frenzied utterances were often questionable at best (10th century) to the upright and authentic holy men whose messages were truly from God (Elijah, Elisha, Isaiah, etc.). Moses, as the first mediator of God with his people, was considered the prototype of the true prophet and for that reason the author of Deuteronomy cited Moses as the criterion, viz., "a prophet like me" (v. 15).

When the exile threatened the foundations upon which Israel was built and seemed to silence as well the voice of the prophets, the promise of today's text, "the Lord will raise up a prophet" (like Moses), was remembered and interpreted eschatologically. Indeed, among the Essenes at Qumran, there grew a hope in one last prophet sent by God whose mission would be to announce the end of time. That this same hope prevailed in Jesus' day is obvious from questions asked of him and comments made in reference to him, e.g., "Are you the prophet" (John 1:14), "This is really the prophet who is come into the world" (John 6:14), "Surely, he must be the prophet" (John 7:40). Jesus' understanding of himself and his role reveals that he considered his mission as the eschatological, prophetic proclaimer of God's reign and mediator par excellence between the Father and all of humankind. After the resurrection and with the light of Easter faith, the early believers preached about Jesus in terms of this Deuteronomy reading (Acts 2:22ff) and explained that all prophetic expectations were consummated in Jesus and his ministry.

1 Corinthians 7:32-35. Marriage as an institution received mixed reviews in the ancient Near Eastern world. Among the Jews, marriage was considered a necessity and regarded as a sacred duty. Not only did it assure the continuity of the chosen people, but the survival of one's name as well. Orthodox Judaism taught that, if a man were not to marry and to have children, he could be guilty of "slaying his posterity and lessening the image of God in the world." At the top of the list of those whom the Jews regarded as cursed forever was "a Jew who has no wife or who has a wife but no children." Membership in the Sanhedrin required that one be married, because it was believed that married men were more compassionate and merciful.

Remaining single and therefore celibate was rare and held suspect except for the sole reason of studying the law. Rabbi Ben Azai is quoted as saying, "Why should I marry? My love is the Torah! I shall leave it to others to prolong the human race." Among the Greeks, there were some who regarded celibacy as superior to marriage, because it allowed them more freedom for intellectual pursuits.

Lest anyone be tempted to absolutize Paul's remarks concerning marriage and celibacy, it is necessary to put the apostle's advice in relation to his statement in the verses preceding today's text: "About remaining celibate, I have *no* directions from the Lord, but give my *opinion* as one who, by the Lord's mercy, has stayed faithful" (7:25). In addition to this disclaimer of Paul's, the modern reader should also remember that the letter to the believers in Corinth was written at a time when the expectation of an imminent parousia was heightened and Paul's advice was, therefore, colored by that anticipation. Because the apostle believed he and his converts lived in the throes of the last times, his words to them could be characterized as "crisis advice." Such advice would necessarily be drastic, and would deal only with eternal realities. What purpose could be served, reasoned Paul, by entering into a temporal union with its duties and obligations, when one could make better use of one's time and energies in making preparations for a lasting union with Christ? Essentially, the apostle's comments on marriage and celibacy are best considered as a sharing of common sense, rather than the imparting of binding spiritual principles. It should also be noted that, in later writings traditionally attributed to Paul (Ephesians), he lauded the marriage bond as an example of the relationship between Christ and the church.

Mark 1:21-28. If a group of people were asked what Jesus' *first* miracle was, nine out of ten would probably answer, "the changing of water into wine at the wedding feast of Cana." While the answer is correct in reference to the Johannine gospel, it would not be for the synoptics, or Mark in particular, as today's gospel illustrates. Many are surprised at this fact because they regard the gospels as chronological accounts of Jesus' activities. Needless to say, this is not the case, as hermeneutical studies have illustrated. Not only are the gospels, and all of inspired scripture, for that matter, filtered through the perspective of the author and his community, but his language, his situation and later editing have also helped to shape the text as it has come to us. As Sigmund Mowinckel pointed out so accurately, "The Bible is God's word in *human* words." With this in mind, then, we are compelled to ask why does Mark portray Jesus' initial act of power as one of teaching and exorcising?

Today's gospel is part of what has been called "a typical day in Jesus' ministry." In it, Mark is faithful to his prime purpose of proclaiming the reign of God as present and active in the person and in the ministry of Jesus Christ. To that end he portrays Jesus as teacher and elucidator as well as agent provocateur of that reign. Moreover, in establishing the reign of the Father, Jesus is depicted as actively combative with the forces of evil but, because he is endowed at his baptism with God's own Spirit, the Spirit of goodness and truth, he shall emerge victorious. All these various motifs have been ingeniously women by Mark into Jesus' "typical day." Today's gospel text and next week's comprise the events of that "day."

By "authority" we are not to understand that Jesus merely had a compelling or riveting style. Surely there were many such orators in his day. Rather, his "authority" was due to the effective power his words had, making things happen in the people who heard them, changing their lives forever. One might regard the exorcism of the demon as an audio-visual aid, illustrating dramatically the authoritative and powerful effectiveness of Jesus' teaching. In each of the exorcisms in Mark's gospel (and there are several), the hostile forces of evil are met and overcome by Jesus and his authoritative goodness.

Ironically, it is the demon or evil spirit itself who recognizes and acclaims Jesus' superior nature. Rebuked (*epitaniao*) by Jesus, i.e., given a formal command which permits no disobedience, the evil spirit shouted out the truth, albeit in a hostile manner. Calling Jesus of Nazareth the "holy one of God," the demon gave voice to the faith of the Marcan community in Jesus' power. "Holy one of God" was a divine and eschatological title; to apply it to Jesus was to classify him as the charismatic prophet, long awaited by God's people. Mark signaled the demon's defeat by the convulsions and loud shriek. In the ancient world, demons or evil spirits were considered the cause of all maladies, physical, psychological, emotional and spiritual. That Mark named Jesus' expulsion of such evil as Jesus' first miracle or act of power (*dynameis*) signified that the reign of evil which for so long had tormented humankind was being supplanted by the reign of God.

After such a display of superior power and authority, *why*, we might ask, did not *everyone* who witnessed these events come to believe in Jesus? Throughout the gospel, Mark will record many diverse reactions to Jesus' acts of power. (1) Some regarded these acts of power as magic or sorcery because they had seen the same deeds done by other wonderworkers such as Rabbi Hanina Ben Dosa or Rabbi Honi. (2) Others, such as the Pharisees and scribes, dismissed Jesus' powers as demonic. (3) Still others thought Jesus to be crazy or demented. Even his family harbored this fear (Mark 3:21). (4) Jesus' own disciples were confused, did not comprehend or fully believe until after the resurrection.

All these reactions indicate that acts of power or miracles *do not* coerce or *cause* one to believe by presenting undeniable proof. Rather, each of Jesus' acts of power or signs or miracles, when combined with the authority of his teaching, presented those who witnessed them with a *challenge* to believe. Jesus' words and works were mutually clarifying prophetic phenomena which *announced* God's reign, *effected* its presence and then *called* for a response in faithful commitment.

Like those who heard Jesus' teaching and witnessed his power over evil on that day in Capernaum, we must ask, "What does this mean?" (v. 26). Jesus continues to teach, to compel with his power and to overcome evil through the church that preaches him and teaches him to the world today. That teaching and those acts of power do not *prove* anything empirically but remain a constant call to faith for all of humankind. The response to Christ of the believing community becomes in itself an authoritative teaching and act of power that further establishes the reign of God initiated by Jesus Christ.

1. The voice of the prophets has not been stilled but their accents may have changed from Hebrew to Polish (Walesa), to Spanish (Chavez), or to English (Tutu), etc. (Deuteronomy).

2. Marriage is not a shackle but an aid, enabling two hearts together to come to the Lord (1 Corinthians).

3. Those who would teach as Jesus did should be prepared to meet the demons of ignorance, poverty, apathy and greed (Mark).

Fifth Sunday in Ordinary Time

Suffering faces the one afflicted with two alternatives. One can either dwell on the pain and thus despair of any hope for a better tomorrow (Job) . . . or one can allow that suffering to hone the spirit and enlarge the heart to accept the gracious, life-giving, healing power of Christ (Mark). Once restored, the former sufferer is called to minister with sympathy and strength (1 Corinthians) to all those in need. Like the wounded and risen healer, the sufferer can impart hope, joy and purpose to even the darkest days.

Job 7:1-4, 6-7. A perennial problem which has both plagued and intrigued humankind from time immemorial is the meaning of human suffering and, in particular, the issue of *innocent* suffering. Because of his exquisite literary and theological treatment of the subject, the author of the biblical book called Job has earned for himself such a reputation that the name "Job" has become synonymous with the entire phenomenon of suffering and retributive justice, good and evil. A legendary hero known in several cultures of the ancient Near Eastern world, the figure of the "suffering innocent" was featured in similar stories in Egypt (1800 B.C.E.) and in Babylonia (1500-1200 B.C.E.) While echoing to some extent these more ancient traditions, the author of Job has far surpassed these earlier stories by sheer dint of his poetic genius as well as his superior monotheistic theology.

Classified among the writings (*kethibh*), the third section (first = Torah; second = prophets) of the Hebrew scriptures, nevertheless, the book of Job is a unique piece of literature. Within the context of sublime poetry and didactic prose, the author has waged war on the traditional and conventional moral code of his day, which attributed suffering to iniquity. As T.H. Robinson has said, "Seldom if ever has a great poet ventured in so ruthless an exposure of the futility inherent in beliefs which rest on too shallow foundations."

In the story, Job is presented as a patriarchal sheik, a holy and good man, blessed with an abundance of wealth, family and good fortune. In a heavenly court scene, Satan dares God to allow him to attack Job and thereby cause him to lose both his integrity and faith. Permitted by God, Satan afflicted the good man with every kind of calamity; he lost family, possessions, respect, honor, health, but never his stalwart faith in God.

In the persons and speeches of Job's "friends" (with friends like that, who needs enemies?!), Eliphaz, Bildad and Zophar and later Elihu, the author presents the traditional case for retributive justice as his contemporaries understood it. In essence, their ideas could be summed up as follows. Suffering is caused by sin. Either the suffering one or one of his kin must have sinned. God does not punish the innocent, but only the evil. Hence Job must have sinned. In answer to the glib advice and pious platitudes of each of the friends, the author presents in the words of Job the profound realization that certain puzzles in life have *no* answers. Job was aware he had not sinned; moreover, he stated unequivocally, as did the prophets Jeremiah and Ezekiel, that someone else's sin was not at the root of his problems.

Today's text is part of Job's answer to Eliphaz, wherein the just man detailed his misery, comparing himself to a slave or a hired man. The futility he experienced and his ignorance of a future life of happiness are obvious in the tone of desperation with which he described his plight. Countering the facile and shallow solution Eliphaz offered, Job underscored the fact that the good and the innocent do *indeed* suffer and not necessarily as a punishment due to sin.

As the story progresses, and as more well-meaning but useless advice is offered, the author's point becomes clear: Human suffering is a far deeper mystery than mere retributive justice for sin. Facile and glib explanations fall far short of the truth. There is no satisfactory human solution to the inscrutable will of God. In the end, after being enlightened by a dialogue with God himself, Job witnessed to that fact by his statement addressed to God, "I know you are all-powerful: what you conceive, you can perform . . . I have been holding forth on matters I cannot understand, on marvels beyond me and my knowledge . . . I retract all I have said, and in dust and ashes, I repent" (Job 42:2, 3b, 6).

When compared with today's gospel, Job's litany of misery stands in sharp contrast to the healing power over suffering and sin which God manifested in Jesus. Moreover, Jesus by his own innocent suffering and death brought to the subject an entirely new meaning. Suffering for the sake of *others*, death endured by a just one for the purpose of *redeeming* the unjust—therein we find an even more profound and inscrutable mystery. But it is a mystery into which those who would follow Jesus must allow themselves to be led. Moreover, it is a process in which believers must be willing to actively participate. With the ancient Job, the 20th century believer in Jesus Christ must confess, "I know that my redeemer lives" (Job 19:25). And to the friends who would offer glib answers and pious, empty platitudes, we must declare, "My footsteps have followed close in his, I have walked in his way without swerving" (Job 23:11). Thereby shall the suffering which shapes our lives find meaning and purpose in the healing and redemptive mystery of Jesus himself.

1 Corinthians 9:16-19, 22-23. Bonhoeffer in this century described Jesus Christ as a "man for others." To his credit, Paul in the first Christian century had already understood his vocation to discipleship in these same terms. Like Jeremiah (Jeremiah 20:9), Paul regarded his vocation to be an apostle as a *compulsion* (v. 16) to preach the good news, regardless of the hardships such work might bring to him. Like Jesus, Paul understood his vocation to *be* that gospel, that good news of salvation for whomever and in whatever media it might be best understood and accepted. For Paul, therefore, it was necessary that he be accepted as an apostle, a title previously assigned only to those who had been personally called by the Lord Jesus, had walked and talked with him and witnessed his saving ministry. But Paul claimed the title apostle because he knew his vocation to be as valid as those first called. Indeed Paul was perhaps one of the first to equate the Jesus of faith with the earthly Jesus and to help the church of his day to bridge, by faith, whatever gap may have been imagined between the two.

Today's second reading is from the Pauline defense of his apostleship and therefore of his right and authority to preach the gospel in Jesus' name, to enjoy the rights accorded such a ministry. Among these rights were the (1) freedom to live as a married man and (2) the right of recompense or economic support from his apostolate (1 Corinthians 9:4-5ff). Although he stated his absolute right to these privileges because of his apostleship, Paul nevertheless chose, for reasons of his own, to forego the right to marry (again?) and the right to recompense. Serious doubts have been raised as to Paul's single state. Some scholars say that, as a good Jew, he was probably married as a young man. It is not known whether his wife died or left him but it is certain that the vigor with which he exercised his service for Christ and his constant travels would have militated against a stable married life. Others propose that Paul chose a celibate life so as to dedicate himself to the law. Whatever the case, it is obvious from today's text that Paul considered himself as celibate and regarded that state as an aid to his work. Still, he defended his right as an apostle to have a wife or the services of a maidservant so as to facilitate his service as God's preacher.

Paul's refusal (in most cases) to accept recompense is easier to explain. He regarded his work as preacher of the good news as a *vocation* from God and not as an *occupation* which he himself had chosen and for which he had acquired the appropriate training. His call and qualifications, he contended, were God-given. Moreover, he refused payment for his services so as not be bound (v. 22) or beholding to anyone. A share in the blessings of the gospel would be his reward (v. 23). It is a known fact that Paul was by trade a tentmaker and, upon arriving in a new locality, would join those of the same profession and thus pay his own way while bringing to the people the good news of salvation.

In addition, Paul had an abhorrence for those who became comfortable and even wealthy by piously parasitizing the people. It may be that Paul did not wish to be associated with these false teachers in any way! Paul preached a crucified, not a comfortable Christ. As a faithful witness to the Lord, his life style had to be consonant with his preaching. For all who regard themselves as apostles and ministers of the gospel, the purity of Paul's motivation remains an inspiration and an ideal.

Mark 1:29-39. As a continuation of a "typical day" in Jesus' ministry, today's gospel should be understood as the conclusion, a second part of last week's gospel text (Mark 1:21-28). Viewed as a whole, the "typical day" and the activities Jesus performed during it reflect the popular Old Testament conceptions of what the "day of the messiah" would be like. For example, in the eighth century B.C.E., Isaiah (35:5-6) and his sixth century follower, Trito-Isaiah (61:1-2), painted for their contemporaries images of hope and healing, of feasts and freedom, all of which would be realized on the messiah's day. Steeped in this tradition of anticipation, the first believers in Jesus were quick to associate his healings and exorcisms with their centuries-old political and messianic hopes. In today's gospel, however, Mark makes it clear that, while Jesus' works and words may have indeed been regarded as messianic, nevertheless, Jesus was bringing to the concept of messiah an entirely new and astonishing dimension. For this reason, we will detect in this gospel a muting of Jesus' wondrous powers and contrived "secrecy" concerning his true identity. For Mark, the greatest wonder Jesus ever performed (as well as Jesus' true identity as messiah) appeared only in the mystery of his suffering and death on the cross (15:39). Until that moment, readers will meet in the first gospel what has been termed the "messianic secret."

As in last week's gospel, the demons (v. 34) exorcised by Jesus "knew him" and hence were not permitted to speak. A variety of explanations have been proposed to explain the puzzle of this "secrecy" in Mark's gospel. Wrede and, after him, R. Bultmann explained the secret as a literary technique invented by the evangelist himself to explain the fact that Jesus was not recognized and acclaimed as messiah during his ministry. Others have proposed that Jesus himself imposed such secrecy in order to prevent a misunderstanding of his role as messiah. As stated previously, the general population, fired by Old Testament hopes and images, looked for a wonder-working messiah by whose political might Israel might be reestablished in power and honor. This misconception of Jesus' person and mission is evidenced in today's gospel selection. Simon and the others were searching for Jesus (v. 37), saying that everyone was "looking" for him. By using a particular verb *"zetein,"* which means a misguided and even hostile sort of seeking, the evangelist conveyed the idea that the crowds and even the apostles misunderstood and misconstrued Jesus' purpose. On the cross and in his resurrection, all misguided seeking was put to rest once and for all. There, Jesus' true mission and identity had been made known. His was a messiahship of service, suffering and salvation.

With regard to the cure of Simon's mother-in-law, it should be noted that this healing was performed, not in public but in the privacy of the home. Again, this detail is an attestation either (1) to Jesus' retreat from the uncomprehending adulation of the crowds, or (2) to Mark's intention of toning down the wonder-working aspect of Jesus' mission so as to give more stress to the meaning of the passion. Besides being a healing story, albeit one told in the starkest simplicity, the episode with the mother-in-law of Simon (Peter) reveals a very important aspect of discipleship. Once healed by Jesus, the woman began immediately to serve him and his followers. While our text tells us that Jesus "helped her up," the actual verb the evangelist used was *egeiro*, literally, "raised her up." This same verb will be used later in the gospel and is employed by other New Testament authors in describing Jesus' resurrection (Mark 14:28, 1

Corinthians 15:4, Acts 3:15). Given these allusions to the resurrection, this simple cure becomes a foreshadowing of the mission of Jesus for all of humankind. By his power over sin and death, he heals; raised up himself, he raises up to new life all who believe. Like Simon's mother-in-law, the only adequate and worthy response of those redeemed by Christ is faithful service to Jesus and his church.

After the evening cures and the acknowledgment of Jesus by the demons, Jesus retreated to pray (v. 35) only to be sought out by those who would pervert his purpose (v. 37). It is significant that the evangelist has revealed this aspect of Jesus at prayer, here and in 6:46 and 14:35, 39. Each of these instances were periods of stress for Jesus because his messiahship was being misunderstood. Following Jesus' lead, disciples of the 20th century would do well to afford themselves such time in quiet prayer, away from the exigencies of the apostolate, in order to reevaluate, reassess and refocus on their central direction and goals. From that prayerful moment alone in the desert, Jesus emerged, despite the insistence of his followers to the contrary, with a firm resolve to direct his mission to all of Galilee. The "man for others," he had not come to bask in the fond admiration of a few, but to give himself in word and work to all peoples. And so he went, "preaching the good news and expelling demons" (v. 39), teaching and healing until he would teach the ultimate lesson upon the cross.

1. Were it not for the resurrected Jesus and the reign of God present in him, life would be a meaningless cycle of misery (Job).

2. Even though the gospel ministry is its own reward, the laborer may not be cheated of his just recompense (1 Corinthians).

3. Once healed and made whole, the true disciple is compelled to minister that same healing and wholeness to others (Mark).

Sixth Sunday in Ordinary Time

Insidious disease frightens and we seek cures at all cost (Leviticus). But there is something more dread and subtle than any physical illness, against which we win immunity only by conversion to the healing power of Jesus Christ (Mark). Against the scourge of sin with its threatening to alienate, the community of believers must stand in strength as one (1 Corinthians).

Leviticus 13:1-2, 44-46. Considering the fact that Leviticus was Israel's liturgy sourcebook and guide, it may seem very surprising to find in it material such as our first reading for today. But conditions therein described (scabs, pustules, etc.) did indirectly affect Israel's liturgy because such maladies were thought to render the person unclean and therefore ritually unfit to participate with the rest of the community in worship. While the concept of "uncleanness" with regard to ritual may appear rather unattractive and even strange to the modern believer, it was nevertheless an intrinsic part of Israel's legislation. Separated into four categories, the distinctions of clean and unclean pertained to (1) food, (2) death or contact with corpses, (3) sexual functions and (4) leprosy. When uncleanness was incurred due to, for example, contact with a dead body, or the eating of some "unclean" food such as pork, then the person affected had to submit to a priestly regulated time of quarantine, abstain from community functions, undergo ritual purifications, etc. It is significant that morality was not necessarily a consideration in determining what was clean or unclean.

Leprosy (Hebrew: *sara'at*, LXX and Vulgate: *lepra*) was a term indiscriminantly applied to many types of skin problems, from acne, dandruff, eczema, ulcers to the "heartbreak of psoriasis!" Even baldness of some types was labeled leprosy! Of course, in some cases, the term did actually pertain to leprosy or Hansen's disease, a dread affliction in the ancient world. In all cases of dermatologic disorders, the sufferer was referred to the priest who would decide whether such a condition required purification and excommunication. As today's reading indicates, those afflicted had to make known their condition by wearing torn garments, by displaying loose, long, uncovered hair and by announcing their wretched state as "unclean." Notably, the torn garments and unkempt hair were also signs of mourning. Given these added miseries, it is not surprising that leprosy became a symbol for sin. Like the disease, sin isolated and alienated the sinner from community life. Just as leprosy rendered one ritually unclean, sin was a defilement of the spirit from which the sinner must turn. Today, the quarantine which sin creates is no less real even though this isolation may be purely subjective and unobservable by others. Reconciliation can, therefore, be compared to a "cure" which restores the sinner to healthy relationship with God and with others in the community of humankind.

1 Corinthians 10:31—11:1. While the Jews bickered over the intricate categories of clean and unclean and the effect such concepts had upon individuals and upon the life of the community, the Christians in Corinth had other problems to contend with. In fact, in most areas of the gentile world, the issue discussed in today's letter to the Corinthians was a problem with which Christians had to wrestle. To eat or not to eat food which had first been offered to gods in pagan rituals had become a burning question for many and a source of division among believers. Christians, of course, socialized with non-Christians and were often included as guests at feasts, dinner parties, etc. Meat was not a customary item on the menu since it was expensive and difficult to store. Corinth was a port city and, hence, seafood was more regular fare. However, on the occasion of sacrifices, meat was readily available in the marketplace.

Within the Christian group, there were different opinions on and solutions to the problem. One group, whom Paul referred to as the "strong" (thereby showing his personal preference and bias), based their decision on the fact that the gods to whom such meat was offered did not exist. Therefore any sacrifice in their honor was meaningless. Because their conscience offered no objection, these Christians did not hesitate to eat the so called "idol meat." Another group among the believers, whom Paul referred to as the "weak," could not reconcile the eating of such meat with their tender consciences.

Conscience or *syneidesis* was a term employed by the "knowledgeable (gnostic?) ones" of Corinth. Originally a term used by the Stoics in their moral philosophy, conscience was defined as that inner guide by which the wise person regulated his/her activities regardless of and in spite of the opinions of others. Although Paul had probably borrowed the term from the gnostic and Stoic elements of Corinth, nevertheless, he did not agree that conscience guaranteed free autonomy. Rather he argued for a surrendering of the autonomy of conscience to the higher good of fraternal charity. For that reason Paul counselled the strong and knowledgeable ones of the community to relinquish their freedom to eat "idol meat." Should their choice to partake be a cause of scandal for the weak, then, for the sake of community edification and love, even rightful freedoms must be foregone. In this way, Paul was helping to form in his converts consciences which guided not only personal actions but which were sensitive and responsible to the needs of others. In a word, Paul advocated Christian consciousness and conscientious Christianity.

As a model for the believers at Corinth, Paul offered himself: "Imitate me as I imitate Christ (v. 1). On several occasions, Paul claimed to preach a *crucified* Christ, one who had emptied himself in becoming human, in suffering, in humiliation and ultimately in death (Phillippians 2:6-11). It was this aspect of the self-sacrificing "man for others" which Paul tried to emulate by his life choices, in his words and in his works. It was this principle of self-emptying by which problems such as "idol meat" had to be judged and peacefully settled.

Mark 1:40-45. The fact that the man in today's gospel pericope suffered from leprosy and was cured by Jesus was, in itself, an amazing event. But the *daring* with which the leper approached Jesus and the utter abandon with which Jesus spoke to him and touched him were equally astounding. As has been established in the commentary on the first reading from Leviticus, leprosy (and those conditions which fell under the same sentence) was a dread disease, considered a scourge from God and called by the rabbis "the living death." Leprosy debilitated not only the body but the spirit as well. Cut off from the life of the community, labeled unclean, the leper had to live outside the city. Virtually nothing was prescribed in the law for his cure but severe measures were taken to protect the community. Jesus, however, made it a practice to disregard the traditional categories of clean and unclean, the ritual taboos and imposed quarantines. He not only allowed the outcast and forsaken to approach him but he made it a point to seek them out. On this issue he was severely criticized by the Pharisees and Jewish officials. "See, this man talks with sinners and eats with them," they accused. As part of his prerogative as messiah, Jesus set about redrawing and redefining the traditional barriers which separated persons from one another and from God. Indeed, because of Jesus' messianic activities, manifest in his words and works, an entirely new set of standards was established, based not on race or tradition but on faith and forgiveness.

Besides being a dread disease, leprosy was also equated with sin, and release from its defilement required a conversion on the part of the sufferer as well. Jesus' curative powers, therefore, were remarkable not only for the physical restoration which they effected, but also for their reflection of the uniquely divine prerogative of healing and forgiving sin. Moreover, leprosy, as were all illnesses, was thought to be caused by a demon and this fact is underscored by the evangelist Mark. Although the N.A.B. translates v. 41 as "moved with pity," the literal meaning of the verb employed by Mark is "moved with *anger*."

It should be noted here that, as a child of his times, Jesus accepted the notion that illnesses were caused by demons and hence his cures reveal that aspect. Throughout the gospel of Mark, the popular belief of demon-caused maladies is evident and Jesus' ministry is thus portrayed as a battle with the forces of evil. This would explain the rather strange statement in v. 43: "Jesus gave him a stern warning and sent him on his way." "Stern warning" is the translation of a technical Semitic term for the exorcising of demons. That Jesus was so addressing the powers of evil with such a severe statement is readily understood whereas it is hard to imagine Jesus speaking in such a manner to the leper. Moreover, the evangelist's statement about the cure, "the leprosy *left him*" (v. 42), underscores the aspect of healing as exorcism. Once the "demon" had left, the leprosy too was gone. Recall the similar incident with Simon's mother-in-law where her cure was described as "the fever *left her*" (1:31).

Once cured, the man was ordered by Jesus to tell no one of the great things that had been done for him. Such a command would have been virtually impossible to obey: Even if the man *said* nothing, his condition had been common knowledge and his reappearance in the community would speak for itself! Furthermore, how could anyone be expected to maintain their silence in such an overwhelmingly joyful moment? These facts illustrate the artificiality of the so-called messianic secret in Mark's gospel. Although the full burden of the "secret" of Jesus would be revealed only on the cross, the gospel is full of "windows of light" through which the secret penetrates little by little. Today's cure is one of those little windows.

Many have interpreted Jesus' sending of the cured man to the priests as an indication of his acceptance of the authority of the law and its representatives. The law prescribed that, before a cured or recovered person could be readmitted to the community, he had first to present himself to the priests (Leviticus 14:2-32). But the statement, "That should be proof for them" (v. 44), whether it was made by Jesus or his evangelist Mark, indicates that something more than acquiescence to the law was intended. As W. Harrington has pointed out and as Paul has so succinctly expressed: "God has done what the law, weakened by the flesh, could not do" (Romans 8:3). Jesus shared God's power to save which exceeded that of the law and this power was evident in the authoritative manner with which he effected the cure of the leper. Moreover, the fact that Jesus sent the healed and whole former leper to the priests was a sort of living challenge to them to accept Jesus as being, not from Beelzebul but from God (3:22).

As one might expect, the cured man was anything but secretive with regard to what had transpired. On the contrary, he freely proclaimed the matter, making the story (literally: the word, *logos*) public. To proclaim (*keryssein*) carries with it catechetical overtones as this term became the technical word (*kerygma*) for the preaching of the gospel in the early church. Given this terminology, it is obvious that Mark and the Christian community of the 60s C.E. looked upon the leper as a symbol of the believer. Baptized into Christ and thus cleansed of sin and the defilement of death, the Christian is restored to the communion with God and to the community of humankind. Once integrated into life and wholeness by Jesus, the believer is then compelled by joy to preach and to teach the good news he has so personally experienced. May we also be drawn like the leper to make public freely and joyfully the "secret" of our salvation.

1. To ostracize the sick or the sinner is to lay a double burden upon their shoulders (Leviticus).

2. Mountainous problems can shrink to molehill size in communities motivated by mutual love (1 Corinthians).

3. Daring is an elemental aspect of Christianity: Dare to approach the unapproachable, dare to confess the Lord, dare to hope for healing and forgiveness, dare to spread the irrepressible secret of salvation's good news (Mark).

Seventh Sunday in Ordinary Time

When Jesus walked the earth, healing bodies and forgiving sins, they questioned his credentials (Mark). Those who thought they had a monopoly on predicting how and when and through whom God would act were surprised by something new (Isaiah). In Jesus, God kept his word to humanity, making good on every past promise and holding out a future full of blessed surprises (2 Corinthians).

Isaiah 43:18-19, 21-22, 24-25. In her book, *Passages in Adult Life*, Gail Sheehey studied the variety of changes and the processes of development through which humans pass on their way to maturity. When Israel reflected on its own development as a people, it could also recount numerous passages throughout its history. First and foremost among those passages was the exodus from Egypt under the leadership of Moses. The nation's founding moment, the passage from Egypt was regarded as a pivotal event in Israelite history; thereafter it became a *type* for understanding other events and other passages.

As today's first reading illustrates, the author whom we call Deutero-Isaiah understood the primal passage of his people or their exodus from Egypt as a *type* of their release from exile in Babylon. For that reason, he described the return home across the Syrian desert in terms and images borrowed from the pentateuchal narrative of the Exodus.

Writing during the latter part of the sixth century B.C.E. as one who shared the pain of his people's shameful detainment in Babylon, the author of Deutero-Isaiah (Isaiah 40-55) labored to lend hope and encouragement to his fellow exiles. The prophet exhorted his countrymen and women to look to the past and to remember the wondrous acts of their God all through the various passages of their development as a people. But, while reminding his contemporaries of their history, he challenged them not to *dwell* in the past for its own sake but to take *hope from* the past and to look for similar but *new* acts of mercy and power in the *future*: "The things of long ago consider not; see I am doing something new!" (v. 18).

By means of this statement, Deutero-Isaiah called his people to prepare themselves, not for a *repetition* of an ancient happening (exodus) but for the *continuation* of the process of redemption initiated by that event. Rather than look upon what happened to them as a merely historic occurrence, the prophet presented the facts to his people in terms of a *relationship*—a relationship that had been endangered by their infidelity and subsequent alienation from Yahweh but that was in the process of being renewed and reconciled by the suffering and penance of the exile.

By describing the return of the exiles to Israel in Eden-like images and by his use of the exodus motifs, the prophet dovetailed all the decisive passages in Israel's history, from the primeval creation and its birth as a nation to its reinstatement as a free people. God's forgiveness of Israel's past sins (vv. 24-25) and the new life which that forgiveness afforded to his people forms a fitting backdrop for understanding Jesus' healing of the paralytic's body and spirit in today's gospel.

2 Corinthians 1:18-22. When Paul was accused of some fault or wrong-doing, he invariably reacted in a vehement manner. Some of his reactions have been preserved in his letters to the various churches he established, e.g., 1 Corinthians 9, Galatians 1-2, etc. In today's second reading, a pericope from Paul's second letter to the church at Corinth, the apostle reacted to those who accused him of breaking his promise to revisit Corinth. Evidently, Paul had announced that he would be paying a visit to the city on his way back from Macedonia (1 Corinthians 16:5-6).

Then, something occurred in Corinth. A conflict within the community precipitated a short sudden visit by Paul. On that occasion, he promised the Corinthians that he would visit them twice more, on his way *to* and then *from* Macedonia. Later, however, Paul reconsidered and decided against a *double* visitation. Angry at what they regarded as a slight by the apostle, some in Corinth accused Paul of a certain capriciousness and inconsistency. Paul's reaction to this accusation was swift and severe, not simply because he had been personally insulted but because he saw such criticism as detrimental to his credibility as an authentic preacher of the good news.

In verses immediately preceding today's text, Paul argued that he had a clear conscience in all he said and did (2 Corinthians 1:12ff) because he was motivated in all things by his relationship with Christ. This, declared Paul, gave him the right not merely to *defend* himself against an unfounded accusation but to *boast* of his actions. As Paul Wrightman has noted in his commentary, timid Paul definitely was not. Indeed, he openly and energetically celebrated God's gifts to him.

After boasting of the veracity of his word, thereby denying any notion of inconsistency ("My word to you is not 'yes' one minute and 'no' the next), Paul then shifted from a posture of self-justification into a theological reflection. Jesus, he claimed, was never insincere. His *yes* was always yes; his *no* was always no. Believers, taught Paul, should think of Jesus, the incarnate *word* of God, as the "yes" of the Father to a world waiting for salvation. Jesus is the "Amen" of God to all the promises made to the patriarchs and remembered by the prophets.

As James Gaffney has remarked, Jesus Christ confirms the impeachable sincerity of God; because of this, he is the foundation of Christian prayer. As Paul noted, when we say our Amen to God, we are affirming our faith and trust in his promises, in his word, in his "yes." In this world, when so many decisions and commitments become befuddled in the mediocrity of "maybe," Paul's words excite us as they challenge us to be true to our own word and to the word who is God's "yes" to us.

Mark 2:1-12. When the 1938 movie "Boys Town" was released, an entire population became aware of the wonderful work of Father Edward J. Flanagan, who founded a home for boys in 1917 in Omaha, Nebraska. Chances are that, even today as soon as the movie is mentioned, most of us think of the touching scene of an older boy struggling to carry another child on his back. "He ain't heavy," declared the boy, "he's my brother." The love that motivated that declaration is reflected in today's gospel. Imagine how deeply the four people who carried the paralytic man must have cared for him; imagine the hope and trust they had in Jesus as they struggled to make their way into his presence.

Experts in ancient architecture have determined that Palestinian homes of Jesus' day had a flat beamed roof held together by clay, reeds and straw. The task of dismantling such a roof was relatively simple. Nevertheless, Jesus acknowledged the ingeniousness of those who did so and accredited their actions to faith (v. 6).

At the heart of today's gospel is a miracle story: Jesus cured the paralytic. But, before healing the man's physical malady, Jesus healed the man of an even greater malady: his sins. This fact provoked the controversy that surrounds the miracle. In the hidden thoughts (v. 7) of the scribes (albeit thoughts that were perceived by Jesus), Mark expressed the problem the Jews had with Jesus' actions. Basing themselves on their traditions as preserved in their scriptures (Exodus 34:6-7, 2 Samuel 12:3, Isaiah 43:25, Psalm 51), the scribes believed that forgiveness of human sin was a divine prerogative and one that would be exercised only in the hereafter. The fact that Jesus presumed this prerogative for himself was, in the eyes of his detractors, blasphemous!

As Wilfred Harrington has pointed out, the accusation of blasphemy here, at the outset of Jesus' public career, serves as a foreshadowing of the same accusation brought against Jesus at his trial (Mark 14:60-64). In both instances, those present refused to recognize Jesus as the messiah and initiator of the era of salvation. Because of their rejection of him, his accusers failed to participate in the forgiveness and healing mercy that were available to all by virtue of Jesus' words and works.

As W. Harrington has also noted, this gospel serves as an apologia for Mark's church of the 60s. Claiming to share in the authority of the Son of Man (v. 10) to declare the forgiveness of sins by baptism in Jesus' name, the church set itself up in *opposition* to Judaism. This opposition eventually erupted into a final breach between the church and the synagogue in the 80s C.E.

Although in his teachings (e.g., John 9) Jesus worked to correct the centuries-old notion that physical illness was caused by sin, his contemporaries clung to their ancient beliefs. *Without* associating the man's paralysis with sin, Jesus offered the physical healing of the man as an *illustration* of his authority to forgive sin. As W. Barclay has observed, "the experts in the law were hoist with their own petard." It was their understanding that the man could not be cured *unless* he was *first* forgiven. Since he *was* cured by Jesus, they were confronted with the fact that Jesus *did* have the power to forgive sins.

Silent about the reaction of the scribes to Jesus' actions, Mark has however recorded the amazement of the other onlookers. Here, as elsewhere in his gospel (1:27-28, 3:10, 4:41, 5:51), the evangelist underscored the unique power and authority of Jesus. His was not a derived authority: When he taught, Jesus did not refer to the prophets or any other tradition. Rather than say, "Thus it says in the law" or "Thus it says in the prophets" or "Thus said Rabbi 'so-and-so,' " Jesus spoke in the first person: "*I say to you.*"

In his acts of power (*dynamis*) and by virtue of his own authoritative teaching (*exousia*), Jesus revealed the reign of God. Those with the insight of faith recognized Jesus' deeds as genuine and his teaching as truth; these experienced the reign of God in their lives. Others remained in their self-imposed blindness and isolation.

1. Those who have faith look to the past for inspiration and to the future with hope (Isaiah).

2. Mediocrity has no place in the life of the committed believer (2 Corinthians).

3. Sin is a spiritual paralysis that isolates and kills; forgiveness is a power that bestows healing, life and freedom (Mark).

Eighth Sunday in Ordinary Time

Jesus has come among us to call us home to the Father (Hosea). He has challenged us to be open to a new way of looking at God, at life, and at salvation (Mark). Those who believe and accept his forgiveness, those who serve him and all others in spirit and in truth become his credentials, recommending him and his love to a needy world (2 Corinthians).

Hosea 2:16-17, 21-22. According to the figures tabulated by the U.S. Bureau of Vital Statistics and recorded in the Encyclopedia Britannica (1988), one out of every two marriages in the U.S. ends in divorce. With facts as dismal as these, one wonders whether the marriage metaphor is still an apt one for describing the relationship between God and his people. Statistically speaking, Hosea, the prophet who favored the marital analogy, did not fare very successfully either.

Indeed, in his stormy marriage to Gomer, the prophet has more than sufficient grounds to file for divorce. On any number of occasions the Mosaic law would have supported him if he had decided to dismiss her, or even to have her stoned (the prescribed penalty for adultery). The fact that Hosea did not do so earned him the ridicule of his contemporaries. But, unlike his contemporaries and many of his modern readers, Hosea did not consider divorce as an option. Because of this, *his* marriage remains a suitable vehicle for expressing the constant love Yahweh had for his unfaithful people, Israel.

Ministering to his people in the northern kingdom of Israel (ca. 745-722 B.C.E.), Hosea labored to warn his people of their impending ruin. Employing the *rîb* or lawsuit pattern for his oracles, Hosea called his contemporaries to a renewed covenantal fidelity. He urged them to turn away from their wickedness and return to the Lord with whom they had entered, centuries before, into a special relationship in the Sinai desert (v. 16).

Using his personal experiences with an adulterous wife as a background for his message, Hosea compared Israel's time in the desert to a sort of "honeymoon intimacy" to which they must return. Rather than dally with the Canaanite fertility cults and the temple priestesses of the god Baal, Hosea called

Israel to renew its monogamous and monotheistic relationship with its true Lord, Yahweh.

If Israel would not turn away from its infidelity, Hosea warned that is would suffer divine retribution. In 722 B.C.E., the prophet's warnings were realized when Samaria, the capital of the northern kingdom, fell to the Assyrian troops led by Sargan II. But Hosea had not prophesied that this retribution would spell the end of his people. Indeed, he did not equate *retribution* with *rejection* by God. He saw it rather as a deserved chastisement.

All through his work and especially in chapter 14, Hosea portrayed Yahweh as a loving personal God who *desired* his people to become *reconciled* with him. As L. Boadt has pointed out, Hosea did not succeed in changing the fate of Israel; but his words captured so powerfully the enduring meaning of the covenant and the tension between human sin and the search for God's love that they continue to be a source of reflection and hope for both Jewish and Christian believers.

2 Corinthians 3:1-6. It is impossible to read Paul's letters and to be unimpressed with the zeal and energy with which he ministered for the sake of the good news. An ardent preacher, an untiring traveler, it seems that nothing could deter him in his commitment. Still, as dedicated as Paul was for the cause of Christ, there were others who worked almost as tirelessly to thwart his efforts. Some of those who worked against him in Corinth Paul labelled as false teachers who "traded in the word of God" (2 Corinthians 2:17).

A variety of proposals have been put forth regarding the identity of Paul's opponents: Some say they were Judaizers, others call them Jewish allegorizing pneumatics, still others say they were gnostics. From Paul's own words, we can deduce that the false teachers were quite selective in their appreciation of the gospel. They accepted the idea of Christ as a heavenly man but rejected altogether the reality of his humanity. In this way, they were able to ignore the suffering and sacrificial aspects of Christ's saving work which they, with their gnostic tendencies, found repulsive.

These Hellenistic teachers travelled from city to city to preach their diluted and distorted message. As they went, they acquired letter upon letter of recommendation from the communities they had visited. Recorded in these letters were the miracles they had effected, the ecstasies, visions and instances of glossolalia they had exhibited. Brandishing their letters, these false teachers followed in Paul's wake, criticizing his efforts, denying his apostleship and striving to undo the work he had accomplished.

As he wrote to Corinth to defend himself against these false teachers, Paul was vehement in his claim to be a true apostle who needed no letters of recommendation. If anything or anyone could recommend him, declared Paul, it would be the Corinthian Christians themselves. *Their faith* and *their exemplary lives* bore witness to the authenticity of the gospel that had been preached to them by Paul; it was their own commitment to Christ that underscored him as a true apostle.

Switching metaphors (v. 3), Paul then told the Corinthians that they were a letter authored by Christ himself through the power of his Spirit. By this statement, Paul affirmed the fact that the work he did was Christ's and the power that enabled him to do so was the very Spirit of God. Unlike the false teachers who seemed to have been motivated by a certain superior egotism and/or ambition, Paul was uniquely qualified for his ministry by the Spirit.

In v. 4, Paul begins his comparison of the old and new covenants (which continued until v. 18) and the effects of the Mosaic law as contrasted to the salvation wrought by Jesus. Whereas the letter of the law was incapable of giving life, the Spirit of Jesus Christ will give to those who believe life and grace and every good blessing. The contrast between the old and the new dispensations will be continued in today's double gospel parables of the cloth and the wineskin.

Mark 2:18-22. Fasting, the issue under discussion in today's gospel, is an ancient practice that predated both the Jewish and the Christian traditions. Soldiers frequently abstained from food, drink and even sexual relations, believing that the deprivation would enhance their powers of concentration and battle skills. Others fasted to prepare for the rites of passage or for marriage. Still others fasted in an effort to gain control over what was regarded as the lesser aspects of their humanity.

In the Jewish scriptures there are several different occasions that warranted fasting: (1) As a sign of their grief, mourners fasted (1 Samuel 31:13, 2 Samuel 1:12, 3:35). (2) Those repenting from sin also fasted (1 Samuel 7:6, Nehemiah 9:1 ff, Jeremiah 14:12, Jonah 3:8). (3) In times of crisis or when petitioning the Lord for his favor, people also fasted (2 Samuel 12:16, Judges 20:26, 1 Kings 21:9, Ezra 8:21-23. (4) Some fasted to prepare themselves for receiving divine revelation (Exodus 34:28, Deuteronomy 9:9, Daniel 9:3, 10:2). The only fast actually prescribed by law was that of Yom Kippur or the Day of Atonement (Leviticus 16:29, 23:17; Numbers 29:7). The prophets criticized the sort of fasting that was a purely *external* observance (Isaiah 58:1, Jeremiah 14:12, Zechariah 7:5ff, Amos 5:21) but, as the New Testament reveals, for some, fasting had deteriorated into an ostentatious display of piety (Matthew 6:16).

According to William Barclay, the Pharisees were accustomed to fasting two days a week, on Mondays and

Thursdays. There is evidence too that John the Baptizer fasted and fostered this discipline among his adherents. What is at issue in today's gospel is not whether fasting is a worthy practice but whether it is an appropriate one in the presence of Jesus.

As was illustrated in last week's gospel, the presence of Jesus meant that the reign of God had erupted among humankind; with that reign came forgiveness of sins, healing of bodies and the authoritative preaching of the good news of salvation. In the face of salvation, forgiveness and healing, fasting is inappropriate.

Using the analogy of the wedding feast, Jesus compared himself to the bridegroom. One of the most joyous events in one's life, the marriage feast is not an occasion for fasting! Most scholars agree that the ominous statement in v. 20 concerning the bridegroom's absence as a time for fasting is a post-Easter reflection inserted here by the Marcan community.

In order to illustrate the character of the new era of salvation that he had ushered in, Jesus followed his pronouncement on fasting with two short sayings. Both were drawn from every day occurrences in Palestinian life. As W. Harrington has noted, the two appended sayings are designed to teach that "the new movement which Jesus inaugurated cannot be confined within the limits of the old religion." These two sayings may be compared to the sign at Cana in John's gospel. There the fourth evangelist has Jesus replacing the water used for ablutions prescribed by the old law with the wine of the new messianic era.

Mark used other images but the implication is the same. An old piece of cloth cannot be repaired by a patch of new cloth. In an age before sanforization, any housewife knew that the cloth would shrink in the first washing, thereby ruining the garment. Jesus' listeners also knew that the new wine still in the process of fermenting would emit gasses, thus expanding and taxing the old skin to the bursting point. The lesson taught by Jesus in both Mark's and John's gospels is clear.

Paul also stressed a similar point: Jesus' message of salvation must be perceived with a new spirit, with a new vision or new spectacles as it were. The new way of Christianity was not simply a bandage applied to an ancient tradition (Judaism), nor was it a tonic added to "beef up" the old ways. The way of Jesus, the way of salvation is a new spirit that entirely re-creates and transforms the former ways of looking at God and at salvation. Those who would not open themselves to the new spirit at work in Jesus were in effect choosing to be torn into tatters and/or to stretch and burst. Today, the new age of salvation is still at work among us. The gospel challenges us to remain supple and open to the new discoveries afforded us in Jesus.

1. Knowing that God is always ready to receive us makes it easy to turn to him for forgiveness (Hosea).

2. Credentials may impress but faithful commitment and service last (2 Corinthians).

3. Those who look forward to the eternal wedding feast are fasting now—fasting from selfishness, from injustice, from duplicity and from sin (Mark).

Ninth Sunday in Ordinary Time

Shielding themselves in a tangled web of legalism, Jesus' contemporaries failed to see that by his very presence he had brought to bear upon the earth the Sabbath rest (Deuteronomy). In his words and in his works, Jesus enabled humankind to participate in the eschatological blessings of the eternal kingdom (Mark). Those who profess him are, likewise, to make present for a needy humanity the very treasure of heaven (2 Corinthians).

Deuteronomy 5:12-15. Sabbath, from the Hebrew "*Shabbat*" which means "to cease, to desist," is that sacred period observed by Jews from Friday at sundown until Saturday at sundown. During this special time of the week, *rest* is enjoyed by all. Rest, more than just leisure time, is a concept rooted in the ancient tradition of the covenant. Rest was regarded as a gift from God to those in fellowship with him. Considered one of the fruits of covenantal fidelity (Exodus 33:12-14), the rest of the Sabbath was legislated in the decalog.

While it appears in both versions of the decalog, each version presents a different rationale for the Sabbath observance. For example, in the earlier tradition preserved in Exodus 20:11, the rationale is more theological. Etiologically, the Sabbath rest was associated with the Genesis depiction of creation. Since God rested after the work of creation, and since he blessed the seventh day and made it holy (Genesis 2:1-3), those who observed the Sabbath rest were to do so since it was, in effect, divinely ordained.

The later Deuteronomic recension of the decalog, of which today's first reading is an excerpt, invested the Sabbath with a more humanitarian rationale. According to the seventh century B.C.E. author of Deuteronomy, the Sabbath rest was to be observed as a remembrance of the deliverance from Egypt. Just as Yahweh had liberated his people from Egypt's slavery and given them the rest and security of their own national identity, so should Israel thereafter observe the Sabbath as a memorial to the pivotal event in its history.

Notice that the rest and all those who should enjoy it was stipulated in detail, as everyone from the head of the household to the alien dwelling in the land was mentioned. Maertens and Frisque understand this detailed specification as a reflection of the social evolution that had taken place in the centuries between this and the earlier Exodus version of the law. As small property owners were ousted from their lands by larger land-owners, those dispossessed people found themselves obliged to hire themselves out or even sell themselves into slavery in order to survive. Here, the law calls for compassion to assure these poor ones of at least one day's rest.

R. Fuller has called the Deuteronomic motivation for keeping the Sabbath an "*anamnesis*" of sorts: a time for remembering and for formulating anew a grateful response for God's blessings. In a similar vein, J. Gaffney compares the Sabbath rest to a "eucharistic interlude," a pause for recalling with thanksgiving the mighty deeds of God. As today's gospel illustrates, Sabbath legislation had become so complex by the time of Jesus that there was a tendency to concentrate on what people could *not* do on that day (work, etc.) than on what God had done for his people.

2 Corinthians 4:6-11. A continuation of Paul's defense of his ministry, today's second reading puts before us the marvelous conundrum which is the Christian minister. Like an exquisite and flawless diamond in cheap setting, those who minister in the service of the good news bear and communicate an infinite treasure in the finite vehicle of an imperfect humanity. As a minister of the good news, Paul was well aware that the power through which God enabled him to serve coexisted with the foibles of his own humanity. That Paul recognized his shortcomings in the same breath that he boasted of his apostleship is a credit to his insight, to his humanity and faith.

Whereas those opponents, whom Paul sarcastically referred to as "superapostles" (2 Corinthians 11:5), flaunted glowing resumés and letters of recommendation, Paul refused to do so. While his adversaries prided themselves on the numbers of miracles they had worked, on the ecstasies and on the eloquence of their scriptural exegesis, thereby demanding for themselves special privileges and an exalted status, Paul saw his vocation as the gratuitous gift of a merciful God to a sinner. As P. Wrightman explains, Paul remained in a state of wonderment at God's choice of him to be an apostle; so awesome was his conversion experience that he compared it to God's action of creating the universe (v. 6). Indeed, Paul's whole ministry could be thought of as his personal "thank you" to God for his boundless grace in calling him to service.

Let others boast of their accomplishments; Paul chose to boast of his sufferings because he saw his afflictions as a means of identifying with the saving work of Jesus Christ. Because of his union with Christ as the head of the body (1 Corinthians 12), Paul understood that his trials and tribulations witnessed to the redeeming love of Christ for a sinful humanity. So too, Paul understood, that because of his union with Christ, his sufferings were not a mere exercise in futility but did, in fact, have redemptive value. As he suffered for the sake of the gospel and witnessed to the dying of Jesus, Paul believed that the resurrected power of Jesus was also being revealed in him. He proclaimed the *suffering servant*, Jesus Christ; for Paul, this meant not just a proclamation of *words* but the proclamation of a life lived in *suffering* and in *service* as well.

Mark 2:23-3:6. Today, Jews who observe the Sabbath usher it in with *kiddoush* or blessing: "With loving favor you have given us the heritage of the Holy Sabbath, a memorial of your work of creation. This day is the first of the Holy Convocation, recalling our going forth from Egypt." Still celebrated as a day of rest, the institution of the Sabbath as a day devoted to God has been regarded by some as one of Judaism's greatest contributions to civilization (Lionel Koppman).

In Jesus' day, the centuries-old tradition of the observance of the Sabbath had taken on an added significance. In an era rife with messianic expectation, the Sabbath rest was regarded as a sign of the eschatological and saving rest with which God would reward his faithful people. Conflict arose between Jesus and his contemporaries when they refused to recognize that the eschatological salvation for which they yearned had become present in Jesus; therefore, *signs* that had pointed toward it, e.g., the Sabbath, the law, etc., had to give way to the reality, viz., Jesus.

Bogged down in the ritual of Sabbath observance and blinded to the true spirit of the day, the Pharisees called Jesus and his disciples to task on two legalities. Picking ears of corn while walking through a corn field was permissible on any other day of the week (Deuteronomy 23:25) but, on the Sabbath, picking an ear of corn was defined as work. In fact, the disciples would have been thought guilty of breaking four Sabbath rules in that they picked the corn, husked it, cleaned away the corn silk and removed the kernels from the ear. According to the *Mishnah* (Sabbath 7:2), the disciples had reaped, winnowed, threshed and prepared a meal—four of the 39 categories of work forbidden on the Sabbath.

In response to their objections, Jesus drew the Pharisees into a discussion which ordinarily would have delighted them a discussion of legal precedence. Recalling the incident in 1 Samuel 21:1-6 when David and his men ate the showbread (12 loaves of bread on a golden table in front of the Holy of Holies; this bread was considered an offering to God and was replaced once a week; then, only the priests were permitted to eat it: Exodus 25:23-30, Leviticus 24:9), Jesus not only illustrated his point that human need superseded the Sabbath law but he also (and *this* is Mark's point) compared himself to David. As W. Harrington has noted, Mark's interest (unlike Matthew or Luke's) in this incident is christological: Jesus as God's anointed, as messiah, has the same freedom (and even greater) as David with regard to the law.

The second issue of legality arose when Jesus healed the man with the shriveled hand. The lost apocryphal gospel according to the Hebrews described the man as a stone mason, whose injury had cost him his livelihood. Jesus made the issue one of good deeds and of preserving life (3:4). Who could argue against such values? Outclassed, the Pharisees were left to glower in silence at Jesus' actions. Mark has interpreted the Pharisees' silence as due to their closed minds (v. 5). This condition was frequently attributed to Israel in the Jewish scriptures as the prophets railed against their people's hardness of heart (*sklerokardia!*). Not a physical condition, hardness of heart is the end result of countless refusals to see the light of truth. Jesus, by whose presence the light and truth of God was afforded to humanity, had compassion of heart and healed the man. His presence and his actions gave the man an experience of true Sabbath rest.

But the Pharisees refused to see and began to plot against Jesus. As Maertens and Frisque have explained, they insisted on being the architects of their own salvation; they absolutized and sacralized what they considered to be the means toward salvation, e.g., the Sabbath. They harassed and excluded those (Jesus) who threatened their security by making the means relative. They refused to recognize Jesus as lord of the Sabbath.

Today, Christians celebrate not the Sabbath but Sunday. It should be stressed that Sunday is not simply the Christian Sabbath; Sunday is the *fulfillment* of the Sabbath because it celebrates as a present *reality* what the Sabbath *remembered* as a *past event* and hoped for as a *future blessing*.

1. The Sabbath rest gives the believer time to remember and be grateful for God's blessings (Deuteronomy).

2. Those who minister in the name of Jesus have been entrusted with a sacred and awesome responsibility (2 Corinthians).

3. Compassion for the needy and a willingness to find the Lord whenever he calls—these are the qualities that make the Lord's day holy (Mark).

10th Sunday in Ordinary Time

Accused of doing malicious deeds and of emanating from an evil origin (Mark), Jesus had by virtue of his words and works redeemed humankind from evil (Genesis) and has made eternity an attainable joy for those who believe (2 Corinthians).

Genesis 3:9-15. "The devil made me do it!" With this disarmingly simple statement, many of us have denied our free will as well as our intelligence and attempted to lay the culpability for our actions at another's feet. Though it may seem that this is precisely what Adam and Eve were doing when Adam blamed Eve and then Eve blamed the serpent for their actions, it is actually much more complex. Part of the so-called primeval history (Genesis 1-11), today's text is an excerpt from a very special literary treasure.

When the ancient Israelites reflected on the meaning of life and of the cosmos, they asked those basic questions which every thinking human being asks at one point or another: *Who* am I? *Why* am I here? *How* did I get here? *Where* am I going? How did things get to be this way or that way?

At the heart of today's first reading is the question, "Why is there evil in the world and how did it get here?" A masterpiece of Yahwistic literature, today's text represents ancient Israel's (10th century B.C.E.) etiological reflection on the issue of evil and sin and the effects evil has upon the human environment.

It should be noted that, while the serpent has figured in the *occasion* for human sin, Adam and Eve were not simply the unwitting pawns of a superior evil force. Their choice was a free and knowledgeable one; the fact that each cast blame upon the other and then on the serpent illustrates their guilt and their shame at what they had done. Similar to the Mesopotamian myth, the Legend of Adapu, and the Babylonian Epic of Gilgamesh, the Genesis story focuses on a breach of harmony between God and humanity. But in the Yahwist's presentation, the breach was due to a sin of disobedience.

Having eaten of the tree of the knowledge of good and evil, the first humans were in effect choosing to follow their own desires rather than the will of God. As Lawrence Boadt has pointed out, "to know good and evil" often referred to sexual maturity in Hebrew. Taken together with the serpent, a pagan symbol of fertility and the fact of their shame at being naked, it seems clear that the Genesis author was connecting the fundamental sin of prideful disobedience with the sexual excesses of pagan cults and the lustful aspect of human nature. But the main thrust of the story is not sexual even though this has been a favored and trendy interpretation of late.

Called by the early church fathers the "protoevangelium," the final verse of today's pericope is in effect a mythical malediction. In other words, it underscores the disharmony and conflict sin introduces into the world, "I will put enmity between you and the woman, between your offspring and hers." But it also represents the earliest promise that evil will, in the end, be defeated, . . . that goodness and those who choose goodness will never be overcome by evil. While the early fathers compared Eve's role to that of Mary, Paul drew a comparison between Adam and Christ. Those statues of Mary represented as crushing a serpent's head may be better understood as an illustration of the Yahwist's optimism—that despite human sin and its consequences, goodness and immortality shall prevail for those who believe.

2 Corinthians 4:13-5:1. In his commentary on *Paul and His Letters*, Leander Keck described Paul as a "problem" for the church. Distrusted by some Christians who hold him responsible for replacing the religion *of* Jesus with a religion *about* Jesus, blamed by the Jews for apostasy, resented by women who blame Paul for their second-class status in the church and their inferior role in a culture shaped by it—Paul is not so much a problem, claims Keck, as he is a victim of misunderstanding and misinterpretation. A figure to be reckoned with, Paul is responsible for almost one fourth of the Christian scriptures, yet he did not relate one parable, one miracle story, one discourse of Jesus. Indeed, he seldom even quoted a saying of the Lord.

What, then, has recommended him to the hearts of believers for almost 2000 years? The answer to this question is contained in the beautiful confession of Paul in today's second reading. More than any other quality, it is Paul's *faith* and power of that faith to sustain him through every trial that recommends him and will continue to recommend him to sincere disciples for all time.

Quoting the Septuagint version of Psalm 116:10, Paul declared to the church in Corinth, "Because I believed, I spoke out." Not only was he *sustained* by his faith, Paul was absolutely *impelled* by it; like Jeremiah (Jeremiah 20:9) before him, Paul could not contain himself from proclaiming the one in whom he had found salvation. Even when his proclamation placed his life in jeopardy, as was frequently the case, Paul was not silent. His faith in the resurrection of Jesus and in his own resurrection filled his message with irrepressible joy and hope (vv. 14-15).

Unlike most of his Greek contemporaries, Paul did not believe in the dualism of matter and spirit and, therefore, that the body was an evil entity imprisoning the soul. Preaching the incarnation and the resurrection of Jesus, Paul exhorted his contemporaries to recognize the goodness of the body as created by God and as raised by him. For this reason, he viewed the suffering he daily endured in his body for the sake of the gospel as having redemptive value. Whereas others purged their bodies as inferior things deserving of abuse (Stoics, etc.), Paul realized that even in his earthly body he carried the seeds of eternity. Therefore, his sufferings were not seen as a deserved punishment but as a source of glory in that they identified him with Jesus and the cross.

Finally, Paul believed that he would one day enjoy the resurrection in a body made for him by God, in an eternal and glorious dwelling place. For this reason, he was able to look at life in the perspective of eternity and see his present suffering as a prelude to immortality.

Mark 3:20-35. Wherever Jesus went, he provided a variety of responses. Many were amazed (Mark 1:27); others could not contain their reactions and proclaimed him publicly (Mark 1:45). Some believed in Jesus (Mark 2:5), while others questioned his methods (Mark 2:7,18). At one point, even his family thought he had lost his mind (Mark 3:21). In today's gospel, Mark teaches his readers a lesson in the proper response toward Jesus and he does so by means of an interesting literary technique.

Frequently employed by the evangelists, the chiastic structuring method drew together and related as a unit two or more topics. At the outset of this pericope, Mark introduced the subject of family and familial ties (vv. 20-21); the same topic comprises the conclusion of this gospel (vv. 31-35). In between the two discussions on family, the evangelist has sandwiched the discussions with the scribes concerning the source of Jesus' authority. By means of this sandwiching technique, Mark illustrated what it meant to receive Jesus and to relate to him in faith.

In v. 21, the Greek term (*hoi par' autou*) translated "family," could also mean "neighbors," "friends" and/or "relatives." In any event, those who came to take Jesus home did not understand him any better than did the scribes. Indeed, as the text indicates, they too thought Jesus was somehow in collusion with evil spirits, viz., as one possessed. Perhaps it was the fact that Jesus seemed to have chosen for himself a course bent on destruction. After all, he had left the secure life of a village carpenter to preach an unpopular message to audiences who were frequently hostile and unreceptive. He challenged the respected religious leaders of his day; he spoke and acted in a manner considered suspect by many. It was this that provoked the scribes of Jerusalem.

Leaving the subject of Jesus' family for a moment, Mark presents his readers with a more official reaction to Jesus.

Accused by the scribes of being possessed by Beelzebul and of acting on power so derived, Jesus responded to the accusations with a spate of logic that rendered their case against him groundless. Although the NAB refers to Jesus' defense as "examples," the actual term used was "parables" (v. 23). As W. Harrington has noted, it was Mark's theological position that all of Jesus' discourses directed to non-believers or non-disciples were in parables (4:33-34, 7:17, 12:1). The gist of the argument is clear. If Jesus' power were truly from Satan, then why would he work against Satan by casting out demons? This would only weaken the control Satan wished to command upon earth. But, in fact, Jesus *had* entered the strong man's house, i.e., he *had* encroached upon Satan's domain and had proven himself and his power to be stronger than Satan's (v. 27).

As a final word to those who accused him of an evil origin (v. 30), Jesus spoke the word concerning the sin against the Holy Spirit (vv. 28-29). Given a different context and interpretation by Matthew (12:31-32) and by Luke (12:10), the sin that will never be forgiven according to the Marcan Jesus is precisely that which has been perpetrated against him by the Jerusalem scribes. By attributing his ministry to Satan thereby refusing to accept the reign of God as present in Jesus, the scribes were in effect negating the power of salvation held out to them in Jesus. But blasphemy against the Holy Spirit is not merely a one-time act. Rather, it is a habitual refusal to accept the light, a refusal so frequent that the mind becomes perverted and no longer even recognizes light and/or truth.

Coming full circle to the subject of family ties, Mark concludes his third chapter with a word about acceptance of Jesus. Without detracting from the special care and love that binds family members to one another, Jesus called his would-be disciples to a relationship with him that superseded the familial relationship. Those who would be close to him, and thereby close to the reign of God that he made present, would have to open their eyes in faith to the will of God as it was made manifest in Jesus. Today, the risen Lord continues to call would-be disciples to experience the reign of God in him, to be—by faith—brother and mother and sister to him.

1. Those guilty of sin are often the first to cast blame on others (Genesis).

2. Faith that impels the believer to witness to Christ is the faith that will move mountains (2 Corinthians).

3. Good deeds and good words are the fruits of a good heart (Mark).

11th Sunday in Ordinary Time

To observe the miracle of a small, insignificant seed evolving from its death-like hardness into a leafy plant or fragrant flower is to understand the power of God's word (Mark). Through human hearts, hands and voices, the truth of his loving care is told in a multitude of saving ways (2 Corinthians). All that lives and grows and flowers and gives fruit and falls to the earth to die and then to grow again bears silent, solemn testimony to God's perennial involvement with his creation (Ezekiel).

Ezekiel 17:22-24. Ezekiel, son of Buzi, was priest and prophet, mystic and poet and great "imaginator" of the reality of God's involvement with his people. At times he spoke in an "abnormal" manner and on occasion he did "abnormal" things so as to shock "normal" people out of the rut of their complacency and mediocrity. Because of his exotic style and eccentric behavior, armchair diagnosticians have proposed that Ezekiel suffered from a variety of ailments, e.g., aphasia, catatonic seizures, hallucinations, etc. Perhaps it would be more accurate to attribute Ezekiel's seemingly drastic manner to the drastic times during which he lived. True to his name, Ezekiel—"God strengthens"—the prophet sought to help and encourage his people during one of the most tragic periods in all of Jewish history, the exile in Babylon. From the time of his call and for the subsequent years, Ezekiel labored first to make his people aware of their failings and then to shore up their hopes when that awareness caused some to despair.

In the concluding verses (22-24) of the chapter, which comprise today's first reading, Ezekiel's vision for Judah's future should be understood on two levels. First the prophet foresaw the *proximate restoration* of his people to their homeland and then he envisioned the *future establishment* of the messianic kingdom. Both these dimensions and levels of hope should be considered when studying the text. Ezekiel portrayed Yahweh as a divine forester, lopping off the top of a tree (v. 22) in order to transplant it on Mount Zion or Jerusalem. Because of God's care and fidelity, the shoot planted on the mountain grew into a mighty cedar (v. 23), full of branches and fruit. Though great trees ordinarily do not sprout from the *tip* of a tree, nevertheless, Ezekiel's concern was not botanical but theological. Like the "couple of legs or bit of an ear rescued from the lion's mouth" (Amos 3:12), Ezekiel understood the lopped off tip of the cedar to be the remnant from which God would re-create his people.

In today's vision from Ezekiel, the majestic tree which Judah would once again become by God's power recalls the promise of posterity to David (2 Samuel 7:13-14) and the shoot of Jesse (Isaiah 11:1) which was to sprout forth unto messianic proportions. As host to all birds of every kind (v. 23), the great tree of Ezekiel's imaginings becomes a symbol par excellence of the messianic kingdom wherein all peoples woudl find shelter and shade. In the final verse of his vision (24), the prophet made it unmistakably clear that whatever befell the tree of Judah was due to the Lord himself. So, too, the heights to which the tree of his people would grow was the Lord's prerogative. In this way, Ezekiel sought to make his people aware that the exile as well as their restoration to their own land was not a mere happenstance of nature of history but part of the divine plan of their salvation. Jesus will refer in the gospel to this same inscrutable plan.

2 Corinthians 5:6-11. In the 18 months that elapsed between the writing of 1 and 2 Corinthians, apparently much had happened in Corinth. This would account for the great differences between the two letters. Writing to Corinth from Macedonia (Philippi?) in the fall of 57 C.E. on the last leg of his third missionary campaign (see Acts 20), Paul wrote primarily to combat the evil influences that threatened the community of believers. Though it is difficult to reconstruct the actual situation in Corinth because we only have Paul's reaction to it, it seems that there as an "enemy force" at work, trying to undermine the church Paul had labored so arduously to establish.

Today's pericope is a prime example of Paul's evolving thoughts and theologizing with regard to eschatology. Part of a longer section on the appropriate attitude of the Christian toward death (4:16-5:10), our reading is part of a very speculative discussion on what happens in the interim between the believer's death and the return of Christ. In his earlier writings (1 and 2 Thessalonians, etc.), Paul reflected the popular opinion that Jesus' second advent was imminent; hence, anxiety about this interim had little value. With the delay of Jesus' return, and out of concern for the faithful dead, Paul and his contemporaries were developing an appropriate theology of alert preparedness and waiting in hope.

From the text it appears that the apostle was addressing the worries of those who feared the loss of personal identity and alienation of death. Rather than waste their time and energies in fruitless speculations, Paul exhorted the Corinthians to take heart and make the most of their lives while "in the body" (v. 6). Paul understood life on earth and in the body as a period of faith (*dia pisteos*) and of hope which, after the passover of Christian death, will be blessed by full revelation. Maertens has compared the Christian's sense of separation from Christ here on earth to the feeling of the diaspora Jews longing for the Jerusalem temple. But that feeling of exile in the Christian is not well founded, as Maertens points out: On earth the Christian's own body is the terrestrial temple of the Lord because of the Holy Spirit. For this reason, Paul could urge the Corinthians to be full of confidence (v. 8). The apostle's paranomasia (v. 8) of being "at home" (*endemountes*) and "being away from the body" (*ekdemountes*) cannot be appreciated because it has been sacrificed in the translation. Nevertheless it is clear that Paul chose not to concentrate on the fearsomeness of death but on its value as a passage to glorious union with God. Concluding with the reference to the general judgment (v. 10), the apostle reminded the Christians of Corinth that the outcome of their appearance before Christ at the parousia would depend upon the quality of their lives in the body. For all who agonize over an unknown future, Paul seems to be saying, "Live one day at a time in fullness of faith and hope."

Mark 4:26-34. When reproached about the seeming ineffectiveness of his methods and the apparent lack of success of his preaching, Jesus answered the impatience of his compatriots with a lesson of trust and hope. It is very possible that his message about the slow but inevitable growth of the kingdom was couched in the vehicles of the parables which comprise today's gospel. Of the parables, both of which are botanical metaphors, the first is peculiar to Mark (vv. 26-29). Coupled with the wisdom sayings (vv. 21-25) and other parables (vv. 3-9) of Mark's fourth chapter, all seek to clarify a poignant issue: Why was he not more forceful in bringing about the kingdom? In Mark's day the question was: Why is there so little progress being made in establishing the reign of God which irrupted in Jesus? While the parables in their simple form can be ascribed to Jesus during his earthly ministry (e.g., vv. 26-29 and 30-32), their allegorical interpretations and the explanations as to why Jesus taught in parables reflect the second (church) and third (evangelist and/or redactor) levels of tradition (e.g., vv. 10-12, 13-20, 33-34). The very manner in which chapter four (et al.) of Mark's gospel has been constructed, with its explanation and interpretations and applications to the contemporary situation of the author, editor, etc, provides an excellent example of methodology for the modern homilist who would be accurate both in his/her reading of scriptures and of the needs of his/her community.

In the first parable, that of the seed growing to harvest (vv. 26-29), several elements concerning the reign of God are clarified. First, there is no hint of doubt that the seed *will* grow. Moreover, even though the growth proceeds slowly, the harvest will surely come. Second, there is a distinct contrast between the routine, seeming inactivity of the sower and the certainty of the harvest. "Without his knowing," the seed grows imperceptibly and irrepressibly to ripeness for the harvest. As with all of his parables, Jesus taught in this manner to provoke thought and to challenge to moral and decisive action. Those who heard *and* listened to this parable of the "seed growing to harvest" were reminded that moral growth and ethical maturity were also imperceptible at first but would become evident in the harvest of faithful words and works. Patience and hope were necessary qualities for those who would become involved with the reign of God. Moreover, the growth of the believer, like the growth of the seed, was due to the one who created and sustained the believer in life. Paul had apparently learned the lessons of sowing and discipleship as indicated in his words to the Corinthians, "One plants, another waters but God gives the growth" (1 Corinthians 3:6). In spite of the imperceptible nature of spiritual growth and in spite of the thorns of discouragement and apathy, the growth of the seed (i.e., of God's reign) was assured.

Harvest in the Jewish and then later in the Christian scriptures was a symbol of God's definitive intervention (Joel 3:13, Revelation 14:14-20). In the farmer's intervention, the believer can identify God himself who will act as judge, wielding the sickle at the end of the growing season of life. For Jesus and for Mark's readers, the harvest would signify the second advent of Jesus and, with him, the parousia. The growth of the seed of the kingdom was God's special domain; so, too, would be the ingathering of all peoples.

In the second and sister parable, that of the mustard seed, the smallness of the seed is contrasted with its end result, a mighty shrub. Actually there were in the Palestine of Jesus' day smaller seeds than the mustard (e.g., the poppy) but, as Jesus knew, the details of the parable were unimportant and may even have been fictitious. Rather, the simple lesson the parable taught was of paramount importance. The mustard seed growing into a great shrub provided an apt metaphor for illustrating the great results that could occur from insignificant beginnings. A modern maxim similar to Jesus' parable might be: "Even mighty oaks from little acorns grow!" What could have been more insignificant than one gentle man without crown or armies or title or fame? What could have been less significant than a small group of unsure, unfunded and unknown disciples preaching an unpopular message to an unhearing populace? Like the "lopped off tip of the tree" of the Ezekiel reading and the "remnant" of the Old Testament prophecy, the seeds of the reign of God planted by Jesus and nourished by his disciples would grow to immeasureable proportions.

Given adequate care and a conducive climate, the mustard shrub could grow as high as eight to ten feet and may have provided a home for some small birds. In the Jewish prophetic and apocalyptic literature, the great sheltering tree was a symbol of a great empire or kingdom offering protection and security to all peoples (Daniel 4:7-21; Ezekiel 17:23, 31:1-9). Jesus understood his mission in those universal terms and Mark's church of the 60s had begun to realize that the nesting places in the kingdom were for gentiles as well as for Jews.

1. Even the person thought least likely to succeed can, with God's help, bloom and flourish (Ezekiel).

2. To live today to the best of one's ability is the best provision one can make for the future (2 Corinthians).

3. If you can believe that a hard and dormant seed can become a soft and fragrant flower, you can believe in the establishment of God's reign upon the earth (Mark).

12th Sunday in Ordinary Time

When the sufferer cries out to God that life has become a chaos of evil and a sea of torment threatening to overwhelm both hope and faith, that sufferer must listen to the voice that, out of the whirlwind, speaks power and peace (Job). In the person of Jesus, God spoke into the world the word of love that gave meaning to the torment and overcame the evil (Mark). Those who believe in him continue to share that victorious love with all others (Corinthians).

Job 38:1, 8-11. In his book, *Naming the Whirlwind: the Renewal of God Language*, Langdon Gilkey addressed the issue of speaking about God and retaining faith as an integral part of life in a society whose secularity militates against all traditional religious symbols. In a sense, the author of Job faced a similar problem in attempting to illustrate the inadequacy of the conventional moral attitudes of his day to explain the mysterious, unfathomable workings of God. Writing in post-exilic Israel in the late fifth or early fourth century B.C.E. and incorporating into his work the much more ancient and popular legend of Job, the author sought to explain what in the end he admitted was inexplicable: Why does the good person suffer? Popular throughout the ancient Near Eastern world, the story of Job had it corollaries in Egypt (*Dialogue of the Despairing One*, 1800 B.C.E.) and in Babylon (*Ludlul bel Nemezi*, 1500-1200 B.C.E.) as well as in Sumeria, among the Akkadians, etc. Although the Hebrew author probably knew of these earlier tales and borrowed from them, he demythologized them to a great extent and informed his writing with the strict monotheism of post-exilic Judaism.

Job, the chief character of the book, was a wealthy sheikh with a large family, a man of integrity whose blessings were popularly regarded as evidence of God's approval of him and his actions. Hence, when God allowed Satan (Job 1) to tempt Job by divesting him of his wealth, lands, possessions, friends and health, Job was believed cursed by God. Conventional morality, represented in the persons and advice offered by Job's friends, interpreted Job's misfortune as punishment for sin. The causal relationship of sin and suffering was generally accepted, as the dialogues between Job and his friends reveal.

Today's pericope occurs at the point in Job's story when each of his friends has offered advice to Job, cajoling, accusing, arguing and finally deserting him in their frustrated attempts to explain his situation. Job in return replied to each, protesting his innocence and becoming gradually more exasperated until at last he poured out his complaint to God in a beautiful, bittersweet torrent. Then, in the distinctly theophanic style, out of the whirlwind (or tempest), God answered Job (Job 38:1ff) with one of the most magnificent pieces of literature ever written. In words that leap off the page to paint the pictures they describe, the author of Job ascribes to God a litany of questions which assert his utter transcendence in contrast to the earthly finitude of Job. Asserting the absolute sovereignty of God, the author drives home his point in verse after verse that human standards (traditional morals, etc.) are totally inapplicable to God.

Our passage for today is from a longer section on creation as God's handiwork, in particular, the power of God over the sea. The text relies on Hebrew cosmogony which viewed the sea as having been born, although its origin was not directly attributed to God until later (2 Maccabees 7:28). Israel's primitive worldview was greatly influenced by ancient Near Eastern mythology which understood the sea as the domain of Tiamat, source of chaos and evil. In fact the Hebrew *tehom* which means "the deep" or "the watery abyss" is the philological equivalent of Tiamat, the personification of chaos and the principle nemesis in the Enuma Elish (Babylon creation myth). Hence, for God to exercise control over the deep, as in today's first reading, was a clear indication of his power over all of the created universe *and* over evil as well. Therefore, Job, who was ignorant of the mysterious and at times paradoxical workings of nature, had no right to demand explanations about evil and innocent suffering. Though vindicated by God, Job never did arrive at a solution to his personal trials and his name has remained throughout the centuries for believers and for non-believers a synonym of patience, endurance and faith. As for God's authority over the vast power of the sea, the first reading provides an excellent background and preparation for Jesus' mastery of the elements in the gospel.

2 Corinthians 5:14-17. Part of a longer section in which Paul defends his right to the title apostle, today's selection is aimed in part at the "super-apostles" or counterfeit apostles as Paul called them (2 Corinthians 11:14). Those whom Paul criticized for being "dishonest workmen disguised as apostles for Christ" had evidently launched a personal attack on Paul, accusing him of weakness, ambition, fanaticism and pretentiousness. In answer to their false accusations and in order to defend himself and his work in Corinth, Paul explained that his motivation in all his efforts was the love of Christ (v. 14). Impelled by that love, Paul admitted that his behavior and outlook on life were radically different. Indeed, he no longer judged by human criteria (v. 16). Formerly he had viewed Christ as a messianic pretender, a condemned and accursed failure who had disappointed the hopes of the people and died a criminal's death. Jesus of Nazareth had been, in *Saul's* eyes, a blight upon the purity of Judaism. As an honest son of Abraham, Saul had wholeheartedly devoted himself to the eradication of the followers of the fool who died on the cross. But the Damascus encounter and the gift of faith he received had changed Saul's life so completely that *Paul* emerged to proclaim the very one whom Saul had so adamantly tried to silence. While defending his own mandate to serve Christ, Paul helped the Corinthians to see their own lives and missions in the same light.

As new creatures (v. 17) by baptism and the power of the Holy Spirit, the believers at Corinth were to live on a different plane than they had formerly. Because of the incarnation and the redemptive passion of Jesus, the old order of sin, immorality and its slavery was at an end; because of the incarnation and redemption wrought by Jesus, a new order is begun. *Kaine* or "new" (v. 17) designates an entirely *new* manner of being. For Paul the difference between old and new, between immorality and integrity, between sin and life is the person of Jesus Christ, crucified and risen.

The itinerant super-apostles criticized Paul's ideas and preached Christ as an earthly wonder-worker or divine man. Paul castigated their limited vision of Christ as "mere human judgment" (v. 16) and emphasized the transforming power of the *risen* Lord (v. 15). The great apostle's insight into the paschal mystery is evident in his statement, "Since one died for all, all died." Not a Greek mystery cult in which secret ceremonies initiated one into a dubious union with an idol, the paschal mystery is that great act of selfless love whereby all of humanity enjoys union with and life in the one true God. Because of that realization, Paul, like Jeremiah who felt seduced by God (Jeremiah 20:7), allowed the power of the paschal mystery, i.e., the love of Christ, to inform his actions (v. 14). He encouraged the believers of Corinth to do the same.

Mark 4:35-41. Sudden squalls were not an unusual occurrence on Lake Galilee. Very rapidly and with little warning, the fierce winds from the plateau of Trachonitis and from the heights of Hauran and Hermon could stir up a storm that would earn the respect of even the most rugged and experienced sailor. The situation described in today's gospel, therefore, was probably not contrived, and the disciples were certainly relieved and grateful at Jesus' manifestation of power over the watery elements. But to stop at the literal aspect of this episode, however wonderful it may be, is to overlook a deeper and even *more* wonderful meaning the story communicates.

The story of Jesus' calming the sea is a miracle story. Miracle as defined by Webster is "an occurrence contrary to known scientific laws." Aquinas designated as miraculous those "actions which surpass the power of all nature." Our English word miracle is derived from the Latin *miraculum* which means "something to be wondered at." Perhaps this last meaning is truer to the idea of the biblical authors who wrote at a time in which there was no *commonly* accepted concept of known scientific laws. Significant, too, is the fact that the word *miracle* does not actually appear in the New Testament. It is a modern term applied to those actions or events that were a sign of God's presence and power. Therefore to gain a biblical understanding of the episodes in the gospels subsequently called miracles, we must look beyond the marvelous and sensational medium in which the author's message is couched. It is important to remember when reading (or preaching or teaching) the "miracle stories" that for Mark (et al) the miracles were of secondary importance to their didactic or catechetical purpose, viz., to proclaim the eschatological reign of God irrupting in the person and mission of Jesus. Rather than an end in themselves, the miracle stories were told to support the message of Jesus by serving as "visual aids." Students of the gospels have discerned four types of miracle stories: healings, exorcisms, resuscitations and nature miracles.

A rich Old Testament tradition forms a fitting background against which the scene on Lake Galilee can be understood. For example, throughout the Jewish scriptures, control of the sea and storms was a uniquely divine characteristic (Job 7:12, 38:8-11; Jonah 1:4-15; Psalm 74:13, 89:8-9, 93:3-4). Not only had God stilled the primeval chaotic waters at creation (Genesis 1:2), but he also had the power to part the waters of the sea in order to effect the deliverance of his people (Exodus 15:8, Psalm 74:12-14, etc.). In several of the psalms, salvation is described as a rescue by God from deep turbulent waters (Psalm 18:4, 69:1-2, etc.). The calm, untroubled sleep Jesus enjoyed in the helm of the boat was a sign drawn from the Old Testament wherein peaceful nights were indicative of perfect trust in God (Proverbs 3:23-24; Psalm 3:5, 4:8). Given this background, the question of the disciples, "Who can this be that the wind and the sea obey him?" (v. 41), literally answers itself. Only God could control the powerful deep; therefore Jesus' display of authority spoke volumes about his identity.

Characteristically, the Marcan version of the story is boldly, almost bluntly written. The command of Jesus, "Quiet, be still!," has been softened by translators. Literally rendered, Jesus' words according to Mark were, "Shut up! Be muzzled!" Also, Mark is the least sympathetic when reporting the attitude of the disciples. What the NAB has portrayed as being overcome with a great awe (v. 40), others have rendered "they feared with a great fear." *Deiloi*, the descriptive modifier applied to the disciples, is a very strong word, expressing the idea of terror or hysteria.

While the event on the lake was important in its original setting, revealing who and what Jesus was all about, the interpretation of that event by the evangelist is also valuable. Just as the disciples on the stormy lake felt abandoned and afraid, so the first century believers may have felt alone and threatened by the storms of persecution, inner strife, etc. Those who expected Jesus' return imminently may have felt that they had been left adrift on an unfriendly sea. To those Christians of the 60s, Mark interpreted the parable as a lesson in discipleship under stress. Jesus' challenge to the fearful sailors, "Why are you lacking in faith?" became Mark's challenge to his community. Faith in the one who could calm the sea would sustain them in the trials of daily Christian living and through the rigors of persecution.

Mark reminded his community (and ours) that Jesus is *awake*, i.e., risen and attentive to the needs of his own. That fact and the promise of his abiding presence should inspire confidence. P. Achtemeier draws our attention to the final statement of the gospel pericope: The wind and the sea *obey* him. By employing the present tense of the verb, the evangelist indicated that the storm at sea episode was not merely a unique event of the past, but the sign of Christ's abiding power to preserve his church from tribulation. Job had learned the lesson that he could not dissect the mysteries of the sea's creator. Jesus' disciples of every age must learn the lesson that faith and trust in the sea's master will help weather any storm.

1. Though tidal waves of human suffering threaten to overwhelm, the believer knows there is one greater than the storm and the flood and the fear (Job).

2. Love is the sincerest motivation, the purest conviction and its own reward (2 Corinthians).

3. Much can be learned from the simple fact that Jesus slept through the tempest (Mark).

13th Sunday in Ordinary Time

Death's fearsome evil should not threaten those created in goodness and graced with immortality (Wisdom). There is one who became like us to vanquish death and its offspring, sickness and sin (Mark). Faith and trust in him will bring healing, health and the ability to care for all others in grateful love (2 Corinthians).

Wisdom 1:13-15, 2:23-24. First mentioned in the Muratorian Fragment during the third century C.E. and entitled *Wisdom, written by the friends of Solomon, in his honor*, the book of Wisdom was initially included in the New Testament canon. Though dating the work precisely has proven difficult, it is probably the product of the first century B.C.E. (ca. 60 B.C.E.) and as such is the latest of the Old Testament works. Considered apocryphal by both Jews and Protestants, nevertheless Wisdom's influence is quite evident in the New Testament canon, especially in the Pauline and Johannine theologies. Written in Greek (although some propose an original Hebrew version of chapters 1-10) by a Greek-speaking Jew, probably living in Alexandria, Wisdom proved helpful to Jews and gentiles alike. For the Jews, the sapiential work offered consolation and support in times of persecution. For its gentile readers, the book called Wisdom provided a presentation of Jewish religion, history and thought in their own language. Couched in the form of a Cynic-Stoic diatribe, Wisdom can be understood as a type of midrash, i.e., a reinterpretation of the events of the past (exodus, exile, etc.) for the purpose of instruction and edification of one's contemporaries. A substantial discourse, punctuated by historical summaries, prayers and poems, Wisdom's basic premise can be summarized in the imperative: "Seek wisdom—so shall you gain life eternal!"

Today's first reading is from the first section of the book (chapter 1-6), sometimes referred to as the Book of Eschatology. In this section, the author has put forth his ideas on immortality, death and the problem of retribution for good and for evil. In the context of an exhortation to justice, Wisdom's author staunchly defended God as the source of life and goodness. As such, he is capable of bestowing immortality upon humanity whom he has created "in the image of his own *idiotetos*, nature" (v. 23: LXX). Significantly, some manuscripts (especially Syro-Hexaplar) have *aidiotetos* which would read, "in the image of his own *eternity*." Popular Mestopotamian myths portrayed the human being as a hapless creature with a directionless future who had been cheated of an immortal end by selfish gods. The Epic of Gilgamesh expressed this plight in a speech to the hero: "O Gilgamesh, why wander so everywhere? You will never attain the life you are searching for; when the gods created man, they put mortality on man and kept immortality for themselves."

As the eternal and good author of life, God cannot, taught the ancient sage, be blamed for death (v. 13). In an optimistic evaluation of life (which may have been aimed at the Epicureans or even his fellow philosopher Qoheleth), the author of Wisdom understood that all creation was good and theologically bound for goodness. The responsibility for death was, therefore, to be laid at the feet of: (1) those who of their own free will chose to alienate themselves from God by deeds of moral evil and (2) the devil himself. The devil or the Satan was thought of as the accuser (Zechariah 3:1-2), a member of the heavenly court, free to roam the earth in order to report the activities of humanity to God. If he found no sin, the Satan would goad or tempt the mortals until they succumbed, thereby reaping for themselves the bitter harvest of judgment and death. Many early Christian ideas of temptation, personified evil and retribution find their scriptural basis in this text.

Logically speaking, the thoughts of the author as expressed in today's pericope seem to overlook the obvious reality of death as an integral and biological fact of life. But, because of the author's equation of immortality with righteousness (1:15, 2:24), it would seem he was referring to spiritual death, viz., the definitive alienation from God, or the second death (Revelation 2:11, 21:8).

2 Corinthians 8:7, 9, 13-15. Karl Marx once said, "If you make a mean demand, you'll get a mean response." Paul employed the same sort of psychology in speaking to the Corinthian Christians. By appealing to their generosity, he hoped to receive for the sake of the Jerusalem church a collection adequate to meet the many needs of the poor. Paul had made a similar appeal for Jerusalem's poor in all the churches he had founded (Galatians 2) and he implored the Corinthians to be as giving as the Macedonians had been. In the verses immediately preceding today's text, the apostle had praised the Macedonian believers, who had given even what they could not afford, voluntarily and joyfully (2 Corinthians 8:1-5; also 1 Thessalonians 4:9ff, 2 Thessalonians 3:13).

As an added incentive to motivate the charitable spirit of the Corinthians, Paul cited the wealth of blessings and charisms with which they were endowed, e.g., faith and discourse, knowledge, etc. (v. 7). With so many treasures to their credit, how could they not be charitable as well? To that end, he encouraged them to "abound in their work of charity," (*chariti*), i.e., not just a one time gift or donation but the sustained activity of giving to others. Such an effort would not be "tax deductible," but it would prove an *immeasurable* and *endless* sharing of self, possessions, talents, hopes, faith and love. As an even further motivation for their charity, Paul recalled the great gift of salvation Christ had bestowed upon all, gratuitously and graciously. The favor (*charis*, v. 9) shown by Jesus Christ in becoming poor to enrich all (Philippians 2:5-11) is the example par excellence of selfless giving, pure motivation and perfect altruism.

Then, perhaps in an effort to temper the sometimes unbridled and exaggerated enthusiasm for which the Corinthians were known, Paul advised them to take care in their giving, so as not to impoverish themselves (vv. 12-13). A proportionate equality was the ideal to which they should aspire. In the desert, the manna was given to provide for all in the measure that each needed (v. 15: Exodus 16:18). It is significant that neither the Exodus text (quoted here by Paul) nor Paul himself advocated that identical amounts be given to all. In a spirit of love, each should receive according to their *needs*. For some, at certain times, the need would be greater; for others, less. In the words of R. Lauretin, "Love is not a leveler." True charity understands the depth of need and answers it generously, even if one requires more than another. Jesus, during his ministry adhered to this same standard; the *lost* sheep needed the shepherd, the *sick* needed the healer and the *sinner* received the bulk of his attention.

Mark 5:21-43. A common feature of Mark's literary style is evident in today's gospel pericope. The evangelist was adept at dovetailing two stories together by sandwiching one event in the midst of another. By so interpolating the two events, Mark allowed one story or moment in Jesus' mission to interpret the other. A small minority of scripture scholars still adhere to the possibility that Mark was merely being true to an earlier oral tradition which coupled certain stories. Others ascribe it to the often unappreciated Marcan genius. In today's gospel selection, the evangelist's skill is evident as he set the story of the hemorrhaging woman within the episode of the healing of Jairus' daughter. As the conclusion of a larger collection of wondrous deeds (4:35-5:43), today's gospel reiterates Jesus' power and authority over the elements, over evil, over sickness and, ultimately, over even death!

Jairus was an *archisynagogos* or a director of synagogue worship. The confidence and hopefulness with which he approached Jesus stood out in sharp contrast to the hostility with which other Jewish officials usually met Jesus (Mark 3:2, 22, etc.). Though the curing of the official's daughter probably had its basis in history, nevertheless, the early church in retelling the event thoroughly informed it with the overtones of resurrection faith. Even Jairus' request, "so that she may get well (*sozo*) and live (*zao*)," is a statement characteristic of Christian catechesis in the first century C.E. On the catechetical level, the words were understood to mean: that she might be saved (*sozo!*) and have eternal life (*zao!*). Raising the girl would put Jesus on the plane of the great Old Testament prophets, Elijah and Elisha, who had performed similar feats. Such an act also would define Jesus as the eschatological prophet who would bring light and life to a waiting people.

Upon arriving at the official's house, the presence of the people wailing (v. 39) would indicate that the girl had already died. According to custom, the services of professional mourners were sometimes engaged to play flutes and chant lamentations so as to signal to all that death had struck the household. Torn hair, rent garments, the beating of breasts were external signs of the interior grief and all were specifically legislated. The ridicule and derisive laughter (*kategelan*, v. 40) which met Jesus' enigmatic statement, "The girl is not dead but asleep," would indicate that those present believed the girl to be dead. The same phrase *kategelan* ("they laughed") was used to describe the scornful reaction Paul met when preaching the resurrection. Jesus' statement did not contradict the biological fact of the girl's death but explained physical death as a sort of "sleep" from which the risen Lord of life would awaken her and all believers. Jesus' words "*Talitha koum*" have been preserved in Aramaic by the evangelist and the added translation points to a non-Jewish audience. In the imperative "get up" (vv. 41-42), and in the girl's reaction (she stood up or literally "arose"), Mark made use of terms specifically applied to the resurrection of Jesus, i.e., *egeirein, anistemi* (Mark 14:28, 16:6, 8:31, 9:9, 31). In effect, the raising of Jairus' daughter was more than a loving act of a kind person; it was also the confession of faith of the early church in Jesus' power to give life and to save from death. The key to understanding the wonderful event at Jairus' home will be found, however, in the second episode of the bleeding woman.

Mark did not polish any apples with the doctors of his day; his blunt statement about their failure to heal the woman made it clear that her problem was far beyond the pale of human capacity and expertise. By use of special terms, Mark indicated that the healing of the woman, like that of the little girl, was to be understood not only in a physical manner but in an eschatological way. For example, the evangelist stated (v. 23) that the woman "had heard about Jesus" (*ta peri tou Iesou*), using the same term used to describe the paschal proclamation (Luke 24:19, 27, 44; Acts 13:29, 18:25, etc.). So great was her need that she risked breaking the laws of ritual purity to touch Jesus. A person with a flow of blood was ceremonially defiled and not fit to participate in community or public affairs. It was a characteristic of Jesus' mission that traditional barriers which had hitherto separated persons from God and from the community should yield to his new way of love and concern.

Lest anyone misinterpret the power which went forth from Jesus as a magical emanation over which he had no control, Mark made it clear that Jesus was cognizant of his status and activities at all times. Among Hellenistic Christians, there was a tendency to regard Christ as *theios aner* or divine man and to emphasize his spectacular and sensational deeds while overlooking their basis in faith. Jesus' words to the woman correct these erroneous notions and provide the catechetical point of the entire double episode: "It is your faith that has cured (*sozo*) you." In other words, it was her faith that brought her salvation (*sozo*). By means of the "messianic secret," a literary and theological device with which he concluded his series of miracle stories (5:43), Mark explained why these two wondrous events and their saving significance were not comprehended until after Jesus' resurrection. In both cures, personal encounter with Jesus brought healing or salvation. For Mark's church of the 60s C.E., contact with the earthly Jesus was no longer possible, but the risen Lord was ever present as were his good news and the sacramental signs. Through these kerygmatic and sacramental encounters and through his disciples, the processes of healing and salvation and life giving continue.

1. The source of life and goodness cannot be blamed for death or for evil (Wisdom).

2. Wealth is not necessarily the sign of a successful church (2 Corinthians).

3. Great need can eradicate the barriers of class distinction, prejudice and traditional sanctions (Mark).

14th Sunday in Ordinary Time

As in the great dramas of antiquity, God could have manifested his concern for the world in a spectacular event. But he chose to become a part of the human situation through his inspired prophets (Ezekiel) and to work wonders even through the weaknesses of human nature (2 Corinthians). He became a neighbor, a friend, a prophet and a savior in the simple man from Nazareth (Mark).

Ezekiel 2:2-5. The ordinary man or woman on the street would probably hesitate if asked to name the kings of Israel or Judah ... a good question for Trivial Pursuit. But, if asked to name the *prophets*, they would find the task easier. This fact in itself tells us volumes about the importance of prophecy as an institution in ancient Israel and of the lasting influence that small group has had on the believing world ever since. So vital was the prophetic movement to ancient Israel, said C.H. Dodd, that it answers the question of how and why the Jewish nation survived at all.

Moreover, the prophets of ancient Israel assured the continuance of the religious tradition they had inherited, viz., the ethical monotheism of the Mosaic era. This they nurtured and they thereby bequeathed to their people a rich legacy which still supports and guides and inspires.

In its embryonic stages, however, the prophetic ministry in Israel did not differ radically from that practiced in other cultures of the area. Indeed, the early prophetic guilds or sons of prophets (1 Samuel 10:6-8, 1 Kings 20:35, etc.) were groups of ecstatics who lived together, often outside the cities and villages; their frenzied antics induced similar results in their colleagues by mutual contagion. These guilds of prophets wore haircloth, and were sometimes scarred by gashes made during their ecstatic experiences (1 Kings 20:38, 41). So bizarre and exotic were these individuals and their ministry that Amos, when called by God to prophesy, refused the title prophet lest he be associated with the ecstatics (Amos 2:11). As the institution grew, developed and became informed by God's revealing word, the figure of the prophet and his mission became integral to the development of Israel as a people.

Today's text is one of four different versions of Ezekiel's call to prophesy which some regard as four distinct calls (1:28-3:9, 3:10-11, 3:17-21, 3:22-27). Each version of the call contained a commission for Ezekiel, the first being the subject of today's reading. Immediately following the initial vision or theophany (1:28) in which Ezekiel came to understand the omnipotence and omnipresence of God, the prophet was mandated to preach repentance to his rebellious countrymen. It is a significant novelty in the traditional order of prophecy that Ezekiel spoke of being filled with the Spirit (*ruah*, v. 2). From the ministry of Amos, the prophets had avoided the concept of the Spirit, perhaps because it smacked of the frenzied ecstatic type of prophetism of previous centuries as well as the prophetic style of the prophets of Baal. With Ezekiel and the period of the exile, however, the concept of the Spirit-endowed prophet would become characteristic of the prophets of Israel. Recall the servant of Deutero-Isaiah (Isaiah 42:1) which prefigured the Spirit-filled scene of Jesus' baptism (Mark 1:10-11).

2 Corinthians 12:7-10. Although there is no way of knowing what particular personal suffering Paul referred to as his "thorn in the flesh," that has not deterred the multitude of speculators from offering a multitude of solutions. Like Ezekiel, Paul had been granted some sort of visionary revelations from the Lord. Fourteen years previous to his writing to the Corinthians (2 Corinthians 12:1-6) the apostle had been "caught up." Paul's difficulty in describing that inner mystical experience was evident as he employed the language of Jewish apocalyptic to name his nameless experience of God. Not to be outdone by the "super-apostles" who claimed to be visionaries of the first order, Paul engaged in a bout of boasting for the sake of the Lord and the Corinthians themselves. He would not have his apostolate in Corinth undermined by the false preachers. But unlike his accusers, Paul gloried, not in the ecstatic moments of his service but in the agonies, for therein he was more closely aligned with the cross of Jesus Christ. Hence he resigned himself, even gratefully, to the "thorn in the flesh."

As Lietzmann has pointed out, diagnosis is difficult when the patient has been dead over 1900 years, yet the diagnoses have not ceased. Of all the interpretations that have been suggested for Paul's malady, three major categories emerged: (1) persecution, (2) disease, (3) concupiscence. Most scholars believe the great apostle suffered from some physical ailment. Some have thought he was the victim of epileptic convulsions; others think he endured a chronic debilitating disease, like marsh fever or an eye ailment (Galatians 4:14-15). Still others say it was a speech impediment or even an embarrassing lack of height! Karl Bonhoeffer, father of Dietrich and an eminent medical authority, believed Paul suffered from chronic depression.

It is significant that Paul himself chose *not* to detail the nature of his difficulties except as an opportunity for an epiphany of God. Obviously the "thorn" was a source of grave suffering for Paul; he prayed three times to be free of it. Perhaps the apostle understood hs triple pleading in light of Jesus' Gethsemane experience (Mark 14:32-42). In answer to his prayer, Paul received, not the alleviation of his pain or the removal of the "thorn" but the grace and courage to endure it. Paul had learned well the lesson of the good news that God's power is manifested in human weakness and incapacity (John 9:3, 11:4). He had made this conviction the theme of his many endeavors for the Lord and the church.

Mark 6:1-6. "Prophet" was one of the few titles Jesus readily accepted from those who acclaimed him during his public ministry. Prophetic in both word and deed, be bore the burden of God's truth to a hostile world deafened by the lies of sin and hatred. In the face of adversity he did not desist and, as with his Old Testament predecessors, Jesus' unpopular message eventually brought about his demise. For Mark, the episode of Jesus' rejection as prophet by his hometown of Nazareth was a portent of an even greater rejection yet to come, viz., the repudiation of their native son and savior by the people of Israel as a whole (15:11-15).

Today's gospel pericope marks the end of Jesus' Galilean campaign and signals a new direction in the public ministry. A turning point in Mark's gospel, the rejection episode was immediately preceded by three miracle stories in which Jesus' authority, power and wisdom were manifested. Initially, the people had reacted in wonder and amazement at Jesus' works and words. But the mouths that had gaped open in admiration soon snarled in rejection when his humble beginnings at Nazareth were known. Those who had sought a wonder worker or *theios aner* (heavenly man) and thought they had found him in Jesus were filled with contempt (and envy?) at what they regarded as pretentiousness in the carpenter's son. The statement, "They found him too much for them" (v. 3), is replete with Marcan irony. Indeed, the reality of Jesus and his service as messiah was vastly different and far greater than his contemporaries' expectations. Literally translated, v. 3 ("he was too much . . .") would read, "they took offense" or "they were scandalized at him" (*skandalizomai*). In Mark's day (60s C.E.) "to find scandal in Jesus" or to regard him as a "stumbling block" (*skandalon*) had become the technical terminology for describing the obstacle which some found in Jesus, in his manner of service and in his death (Romans 9:32-33, 1 Peter 2:8, 1 Corinthians 1:23, Galatians 5:11). Evidently the evangelist has colored the scene with the difficulties and problems of his own times. By so doing he could offer encouragement and strength to those believers who found themselves rejected by family and friends because of their faith in Jesus. Similarly, the reference in v. 6 to the "lack of faith" or *apistia* became, in the decades following Jesus' death, the technical designation of Israel's disbelief and rejection of Jesus as the messiah (Romans 3:13, 11:30). Israel's repudiation stood out in sharp contrast to the acceptance of Jesus by the gentile world. The importance of faith as a requisite for the working of miracles (v. 6) is consonant with the Marcan theology as enunciated in the cures of the hemorrhaging woman and Jairus' daughter (5:34). No mere wonder worker, Jesus' cures and signs were to be understood as a response to faith, not merely an indiscriminate force or purposeless power surge.

A lesson lay herein for the Christians of the 60s and of the 1990s C.E. as well. Faith and recognition of the truth are not guaranteed by membership in the chosen people or in the institutional and orthodox organizations of the church. Faith and acceptance of Jesus require a personal and individual response on the part of all who meet him, who see his works, who hear the challenge of his words. Significantly, when he met with rejection, Jesus did not mollify or alter in any way the powerful challenge of his message. A true prophet, he did not allow "opinion polls" or popular opinion to deter his assault on evil in all its disguises. However tempting it may be to preach selectively the lighter and more palatable sections of the good news, the true disciple cannot ignore the harder and more "scandalous" parts as well, e.g., the cross, turning the other cheek, loving enemies, etc.

With regard to the family of Jesus as mentioned in today's gospel, viz., his sisters and brothers, James, Joseph, Judas, and Simon, there are a variety of views as to their actual relationship to Jesus. Many follow Helvidius in accepting the text literally and in understanding that Jesus did have full blood brothers and sisters. Others propose that those named in the gospel were Joseph's children by a former wife and therefore half-brothers and sisters to Jesus. Jerome, citing the fact that elsewhere in the gospel (15:40) James and Joseph are said to be sons of *another* Mary, regarded the brothers and sisters (of Mark 6) to be cousins of Jesus. According to the concept of the extended family in the ancient Near Eastern world (and in some areas today, e.g., Africa) cousins were regarded as, and were called, brothers and sisters. Traditional Catholic opinion supports the view that Jesus was the first born and sole child of his mother. In any case, it was their knowledge of Jesus' origins that disappointed the Jews who held the view that an aura of mystery and of the unknown would surround the emergence of the messiah (John 7:27). After all, Jesus was just the boy next door! How could anything wonderful come of that!? Surely the same reaction met the disciples of Jesus during the time of the evangelist. "I knew you when . . . and now you claim to have the good news of salvation?" Jesus' sad commentary upon the event at Nazareth, "No prophet is without honor except in his native place," was a well known proverb in the ancient world and was quoted by all the evangelists (Matthew 13:57, Luke 4:24, John 4:44). Instead of surrendering to its sad truth, modern believers are called to prove the proverb false by recognizing the powerful presence of prophecy even in the routine and familiar.

1. *Conviction, even in the face of total rejection, is possible only because of the strengths given by the Spirit (Ezekiel).*

2. *Sometimes our "thorns in the flesh" are of our own making (2 Corinthians).*

3. *Familiarity need not prejudice the believer from recognizing the truth (Mark).*

15th Sunday in Ordinary Time

God entrusted with the most important message ever delivered—the precious cargo of the good news of salvation—a man who knew how to raise sheep (Amos). To announce the arrival of the messianic era, the Lord sent forth his emissaries with no entourage and no provisions except for the power he shared with them (Mark). Does this not speak volumes about the dynamic presence of the Spirit blessing, guiding and moving God's people (Ephesians)?

Amos 7:12-15. Imagine the pique of the aristocratic Amaziah when that "country bumpkin" from the south dared open his mouth in insults and idle threats against his king. This is the background for today's first reading. Amos, the first of the so-called writing prophets, was a native of Tekoa (modern day Tequ'a), a small town approximately six miles south of Bethlehem in the southern kingdom of Judah. By trade he was a shepherd (*noqed*) who raised a rugged and hardy breed of sheep specially prized for their wool. Seasonally, he would travel from his hometown of Tekoa (ca. 1000 meters above sea level) to the lower slopes of the Judean hills where the sycamore trees grew. Unlike the sycamores of North America, those indigenous to Judah produced a small fig-like fruit of poor quality which served as nourishment for the poor. Evidently Amos was an expert in the art of dressing (v. 14) the sycamore figs. Such expertise would involve knowing how and at what point in its development to pinch or nip the fruit so that it would grow large enough to be worth eating. Some botanists think the pinching of the fruit released an injurious insect which, if left within, would impede growth and ruin the fruit. An outdoorsman and a migrant, Amos was not in any way associated with the authority of organized religion and seemed an unlikely candidate for the ministry of prophesying. Nevertheless, he became the champion of the lion of Judah (Amos 1:2).

According to the title of his book, Amos was called to bear the burden of God's word to his people during the period when Uzziah reigned in Judah (781-740 B.C.E.) and Jeroboam II was king in Israel (783-743 B.C.E.). Economically and politically, it was a period of peace and prosperity but socially and religiously it was a time of decadence and wanton disregard for the statutes of the covenant. The northern kingdom under Jeroboam II was still savoring its victory over the Aramean forces (6:13). Although the ominous threat of Assyria was looming on the horizon, it was still far enough away for the rich Israelites to enjoy their wealth and luxuries in confident security.

Today's text is an excerpt from the encounter between priest and prophet and part of an historical interlude set in the midst of a series of visions spelling out doom for Israel. With no loyalties except to Yahweh, Amos had denounced the sins of all, *even the king* (7:9), and warned of divine retribution. Infuriated, Amaziah denounced Amos, calling him a visionary (v. 12, *ro'eh, hozeh*) a term which had taken on negative connotations. Refusing that designation and the title of prophet as well, Amos denied any affiliation with those mercenary prophets who made their living by prophesying (1 Samuel 9:7f). He did not volunteer for his ministry nor was he born to it. Rather, Amos the shepherd and sycamore tender was conscripted *by God* and charged by him with his prophetic mandate. For that reason he was not tempted by a conflict of interest as was perhaps the priest and royal advisor Amaziah. After all, a pessimistic and nay-saying employee would not be kept for long on the royal payroll.

Ephesians 1:3-14. In his dissertation (1983) for the Pontifical Biblical Institute, the Japanese Jesuit Koshi Usami called Ephesians a "Christ-*agogical*" letter written by a collaborator of Paul to draw the members of the believing community into an inner understanding of the divine will on the level of Paul. By his analysis of Ephesians, Usami sought to apply an understanding of the ancient letter "to the modern Christian community in a situation . . . where Christianity is still a religion for 'foreigners' and alien to the peoples." Usami would have Christians think not in terms of "you" as distinct from "we" (Ephesians 1:11-14) but advises "the first thing that Christian communities have to do is neither seek for a *common* intellectual and *doctrinal* comprehension, not to prescribe for their members a *fixed* law for every action and moment of life, not to distinguish their communities from other groups and communities by signs and characteristics whether racial, cultural or religious." The primary requirement, suggests Usami, is "to walk in love" (Ephesians 5:2). By so doing, the host of spiritual blessings that comprise today's second reading will be poured out in abundance upon the entire community.

Because of its lack of personal references and the fact that the title of the letter was a second century C.E. addition, many believe the deutero-Pauline work now called Ephesians was intended as a circular letter to the churches of Asia Minor. A composition of prayers and paranetic preaching, Ephesians is more like a discourse than a letter. Today's reading is one of its many beautiful prayers and may have been drawn from an earlier liturgical hymn, possibly for the occasion of a baptism. Modeled on the Jewish prayer of blessing (*berakoth*), the prayer-hymn was structured concentrically as the author came full circle again and again so as to communicate his thoughts. Though later editors have added the punctuation, vv. 3-10 were originally one long sentence (the longest in the New Testament) and a veritable dangling participle of praise and blessing informed with the author's highly developed christology.

Like the Johannine evangelist, the Ephesians' author understood Christ as the summit of all creation, pre-existent and forever the means whereby all of humanity can draw near together to God. Consequently, because of the blessings God effected upon the earth, the only worthy response would be a life lived in love and unity "*in Christ.*" Repeated over 30 times in his discourse, "in Christ" was the technical term by which the author expressed the incorporation of all peoples through baptism into the mystery of Christ's resurrection and glorification. Such incorporation is possible only because of the redemption (*apolutrosis*, v. 7) wrought by Jesus Christ. *Apolutrosis* implied the setting free of one held in slavery or in someone else's power. In the Septuagint's translation of the Old Testament, God's freeing of his people from Egypt was termed *apolutrosis* or redemption (Exodus 15:13). In the Christian scriptures, Christ through his blood accomplished (v. 7) that same freedom not only for Israel but for all the people of God. Freed not merely from Egypt's tyranny but from the shackles of sin and death, those "in Christ" have arrived at the "fullness of time" (v. 10) or Christ's *kairos*.

Much more important than *chronos* or measured time whereby days and seasons are marked, *kairos* or the fullness of time is that momentous event in which God would accomplish his eternal and mysterious plan of salvation. The Johannine author called this great moment Jesus' hour (John 12:52), viz., the passion, death, resurrection, ascension and glorification. As a result of Jesus' hour or in the fullness of time, all things created will be brought into union with Christ as center and head and raison d'être. Literally, the verb (v. 10) *anakephalarosasthai* means "to place at the top of a column the sum of the figures that have been added." To put it more simply: because of the redemption, the disparate, the alienated and the divided, regardless of race, culture, politics, social status or tradition are brought together as children of one Father (v. 5: adopted sons).

Mark 6:7-13. Helmut Koester has suggested that Mark created the literary genre of the gospel as an instruction in discipleship, to sustain the life of the church and to prepare it for the inevitable experience of suffering. If that be the case, then today's pericope is an explicit example of Jesus' apostolic counsel. A sense of eschatological urgency pervades the entire text. The instruction to take nothing—not food or luggage, money or change of clothing—is more than an exhortation to simplicity and asceticism. With the belief that the messianic era was upon them, such provisions for a *long* campaign were deemed useless and unnecessary. In addition to the eschatological atmosphere of the episode, there is a message about trusting in the providence of the Father as well. When Jesus was in the desert with no bread, tempted to rely on other means of sustenance, Matthew tells us that Jesus referred the tempter to Deuteronomy (8:3), "Man does not live on bread alone but on every word that comes from the mouth of God." Jesus, disciple par excellence of the Father, found his nourishment in doing the work for which he had been sent. In sending forth his own on their missions, he challenged them to whet their *spiritual* appetites by sharing in his work. Moreover, his order, "Take no bread," can be understood as a preparation for the gifts of bread he himself would give (Mark 6:35-44 and 8:1-9), and the one loaf (Mark 8:14) which would be shared by all peoples. By carrying no bread on their apostolic mission, those sent by Jesus were freed to share an even more nourishing bread with those to whom they ministered: the bread of life, Jesus—his word, his works, his very self.

Besides their sparse traveling gear, the disciples were to make no provisions for their lodging but were to stay wherever a welcome was afforded them. By not moving from house to house they avoided the possibility of rivalry between hosts, with each trying to outdo the other in a show of hospitality. This sound, practical advice was coupled with a recommendation concerning the rejection they were bound to meet. Shaking the dust from the feet was a symbolic action performed by Jews when returning to their own land from heathen territory. Pagans and all that pertained to them were considered unclean, therefore entrance into the holy land of their fathers, Abraham, Isaac and Jacob, would require that each Israelite be purified of that uncleanness. Jesus instructed his disciples to "shake off the dust" as a sign of warning to those who rejected them, to cause them to reconsider and to lead them to repentance.

That the disciples observed this ritual is attested by the actions of Paul and Barnabas. When driven from Antioch in Pisidia, they shook the dust from their feet (Acts 13:51). Some believe the provision for sandals (v. 9) as opposed to shoes was in the interest of simplicity. Shoes required more leather and were usually worn only by the wealthy. When the prodigal returned home, his father outfitted him with a rich robe, a ring and *shoes* (Luke 15:22). Sandals, on the other hand, were a necessity, worn by even the poorest people as a protection against the stony roads and dusty pathways of Palestine.

Although some earlier form critics believed the mission episodes recounted in the synoptics (Matthew 9:35—10:1, 9-11; Luke 9:1-6, and today's gospel) were creations of the post-resurrection community, that opinion is widely rejected today. After Jesus' resurrection the preaching of those who believed consisted of the kerygma or the good news of salvation as accomplished by Jesus in his passion, death, etc. But in the missionary episode recounted today by Mark, there is no such indication. On the contrary, those sent by Jesus preached repentance, exorcised demons and healed the sick. These were precisely the actions Jesus himself had been performing as a means of *announcing* the irruption of the messianic era (1:34, 39, 43; 3:22, 23). By participating in the works of Jesus, his disciples shared in the preparation for the messianic proclamation.

Anointing with oil (v. 13) was a common practice in the ancient world. Oil was believed to have medicinal and curative qualities (Luke 10:34). Probably for this reason it became part of the Christian custom of anointing the sick and was incorporated eventually into the sacramental rite (James 5:14-15).

Finally, today's pericope is of special interest for the different light it sheds on the disciples of Jesus. Too often, their reaction to Jesus, especially as recorded by Mark, had been one of incomprehension, confusion and doubt. Their active cooperation with Jesus in his crusade against evil in all its forms should encourage all who would be his disciples. Commitment, service and a worthwhile apostolate are possible even where *perfect* faith and *complete* understanding are not present.

1. Credentials are no substitute for commitment and integrity (Amos).

2. Because of the abundance of blessings believers have inherited in Christ, hope and joy should characterize our every endeavor (Ephesians).

3. The joyful messenger of the good news needs no other equipment (Mark).

16th Sunday in Ordinary Time

When those to whom he had entrusted the care and leadership of his people failed the task (Jeremiah), the Lord involved himself intimately with human existence in the person of Jesus Christ. Reuniting the disparate and alienated segments of humanity in peace, he drew all near again to God in the paradox of his cross (Ephesians). To assure union and peace among his disciples he made each responsible in service and love for the other (Mark).

Jeremiah 23:1-6. At a time in Israel's history when it was least propitious to act as a political analyst and religious spokesperson, Jeremiah the prophet was both. Born in Anathoth (modern day Anata) about 640 B.C.E., Jeremiah grew up in the shadow of world powers struggling for domination. In the wake of the wars between the superpowers of Assyria, Egypt and Babylonia, Jeremiah prophesied to a people affected by the political upheaval that surrounded them. Assyria had conquered the northern kingdom of Israel in 721 B.C.E. and by 687 B.C.E., because of the weakness of the Judean kings, had annexed the southern kingdom as well. During that period of political dependence, the religious purity of Judah disintegrated into a cult of syncretism which tolerated the astral worship of Mesopotamia as well as the fertility rites of Canaan. In this situation Jeremiah received his prophetic call and his king Josiah instituted his religious reform (626 B.C.E. and 622 B.C.E. respectively). For the next 40 years, the voice of Jeremiah was heard, making constant interventions on behalf of Yahweh for the sake of his people.

Today's first reading is from a series of oracles (21:1-23:40) delivered by Jeremiah against the unworthy shepherds who had led his people astray. Having spoken against Jehoakaz (22:10-12), Jehoiakim (22:13-19) and Jeconiah (22:20-30), the next false shepherd in chronological order would have been king Zedekiah. But, with the text that comprises today's reading, Jeremiah turned his vision and the hopes of his people to a future time and a future shepherd-king. Because those earthly kings had proven disloyal to the covenant, to Yahweh and to their people, Yahweh himself would act as shepherd, gathering (vv. 3-4) his people to himself from where they had been scattered. If, as most believe, Jeremiah wrote these lines ca. 587 B.C.E., he had already witnessed one deportation of his people (597 B.C.E.) and knew that another even more devastating decimation was imminent.

Jeremiah's oracle, therefore, offered the hope of a return, both political and moral, a return home to Israel and a return in holiness to the one true God from whom they had wandered. Moreover, Jeremiah offered to his people the hopeful vision of an ideal king. Drawing on the promise made centuries before (2 Samuel 7), Jeremiah described the future ruler as a righteous branch or shoot of David. In Hebrew *semah tsaddiq* (righteous branch) may also be rendered legitimate heir. In either case, the meaning is clear: the future sovereign would not be a usurper or a fraud but an authentic king and therefore a true shepherd of the people. Scholars underscore this oracle of Jeremiah's as his only utterance concerning a *personal* messiah. Still, it should be noted that the prophet was probably thinking along political lines and applied his hope to a future *earthly* descendant of David. Branch (*semah*) or shoot became a classic term for the messiah (Isaiah 11:1; Zechariah 3:8, 6:12) but only with the appearance of Jesus would the branch of David bud forth in peace and salvation for Israel.

In a final criticism of Zedekiah's unworthy reign, Jeremiah named the future king and shepherd: "The Lord is our justice" (righteousness). A paranomasia (word play) on the name Zedekiah, *Yahweh Sidqenu* or "The Lord our justice" would, by his presence, effect a new era of salvation and peace for his people. That time of peace and justice was inaugurated when Jesus the good shepherd began to seek out the weak and the sinful and to draw all scattered and alienated peoples to himself.

Ephesians 2:13-18. Called the theological core of the letter to the Ephesians, today's second reading is part of a longer section (2:1-22) in which the author expounds upon the benefits made available to both gentiles ("you") and Jews ("we") in Jesus Christ. One of those benefits is the unity afforded to all—unity with one another as well as with God. Deutero-Isaiah, writing several centuries before the Christian author, had communicated to his people a similar vision of hope: "I have seen his ways and healed him; I have comforted him with true comfort; peace without measure to those who are far off, and those who are near. The Lord has said, 'I will heal them'" (Isaiah 57:18-19). It would seem that the deutero-Pauline author had this Isaian text in mind (see vv. 13-14) as he wrote to the Ephesians. In its original context "those far off" referred to the Jews exiled from their own land. But the Ephesians' author applied the phrase to the gentile converts to Christianity. In the Old Testament, the Jews drew near or were "brought near" (v. 13) to God through the blood of the sacrifice that sealed their covenant (Exodus 24:8). In the Christian Testament, all including gentiles, can be brought near to God because of the blood of Christ (v. 13) and the sacrifice of the cross (v. 16).

In contrast to the thought expressed in Romans, the Ephesian's author viewed the law as a "barrier of hostility" (v. 14) and a divisive force to be dealt with. A concrete symbol of that barrier was the stone partition that separated the outer court from the inner court of the temple, dividing the gentiles from the Jews. According to Josephus (*Antiquities*, 15:11, 5), the partition stood three cubits (4.5 ft.) high and was posted with signs forbidding (under pain of death) any foreigner (gentile) from entering. While excavating in Jerusalem in 1871, C. Clermont-Ganneau unearthed signs and inscriptions similar to those described by the Jewish historian. Evidently the segregation of Jews and gentiles was strictly enforced. Recall the violent reaction Paul encountered when he was falsely accused of bringing Trophimus, an Ephesian and a gentile, with him into the temple (Acts 21:27-40).

With Christ, however, and in his peace, all barriers, whether of stone like the temple partition or binding and constricting like the law, were obviated. The author understood Christianity or the relationship with God in Christ as a *new* creation—freed forever from its Jewish matrix. Whereas formerly, people observed the law *in order to be saved,* with Christ and because of him believers observe the moral demands of the law *because they have been saved!* Perhaps the reference to the unity of all peoples, Jews and gentiles, in one body (v. 15) can be seen as an allusion to the eucharist and the communion effected by the sacrament.

To all, both near (Jews) and far (gentiles), the message of the good news, i.e., the gospel of salvation, has been proclaimed. Because of that, all were permitted access (v. 18) to God. Access or *prosagoge* was a technical term used in oriental courts to refer to the introduction of a person into the presence of the king. Today we celebrate both the access which has been achieved and the one who has achieved it.

Mark 6:30-34. If we could compare the gospels to tapestries in which various events, teachings, sayings and discourses have been woven together to tell the good news of salvation, then today's gospel pericope would represent one of the connecting seams. Besides concluding the mission of the Twelve (6:7-13), today's text serves as an introduction to the next long section of Mark's gospel, the double version of the feeding of the multitudes (6:31-8:26). Only here (v. 30) does the evangelist confer the title "apostle" on Jesus' chosen followers. Elsewhere in the gospel, they are simply called disciples or the Twelve. Perhaps the completion of their first missionary campaign had earned for them the title "apostle," viz., one who is sent.

H. Conzelmann has pointed out that the commission is constitutive of the concept of apostle; it is given by the exalted Lord himself. Most believe the designation "apostle" became a title to specify a particular office only after the resurrection within the primitive church. It is significant that *accountability* was considered an integral part of the apostolic mission: "They *reported* to him all that they had done and what they had taught."

Their first campaign behind them, those who had been sent forth by Jesus were invited to withdraw from the crowds and the work to rest and recoup. The retreat to the deserted place may have had a secondary motivation as well . . . Herod had just executed John the Baptizer (6:27). After the miracles of Mark 5 and the death of John, there is a decided shift in emphasis in the Marcan gospel; Jesus began to focus his teaching and instruction less on the crowds and more upon the Twelve. His invitation to go off "by themselves" (*kat' idian*) is a literary signal employed by the evangelist to indicate that a special revelation or instruction will be given. In this instance, the special revelation would be the feeding of the crowds by Jesus.

In his offer of *rest* (v. 31), Jesus appears to have assumed the role of the eschatological good shepherd, the paragon of perfect care and leadership. *Rest* was always associated with the blessings which God as shepherd would bestow upon his faithful flock (Isaiah 65:10, Ezekiel 34:15, Psalm 23:2). Israel's entrance into the promised land after the 40 years' trek through the wilderness was considered as a gift of rest (Deuteronomy 3:20, 12:10, Joshua 1:13, 15). Perhaps there is a sapiential allusion in the gospel as well. Jesus Ben Sirach wrote of the disciple of wisdom finding rest with her after his labor and toil (Sirach 6:28, 51:27). Jesus of Nazareth was perceived as the incarnate wisdom of God by the early Christians and thus had the capacity to offer rest to his own after their service in his name. Ironically, because of the persistence of the crowds who pursued them, the *rest* the apostles experienced was not in the form of a respite from work. Rather, with the crowds, they were *taught* by Jesus. Later, they too would be *fed* by him. The rest Jesus afforded to his flock as their shepherd, teaching and feeding is perfectly summed up in the eucharistic liturgy.

As R. Fuller has suggested, in the liturgy of the word the messianic shepherd teaches his people; in the liturgy of the eucharist, he feeds them. Such an appreciation of the eucharistic celebration as *rest* for the disciple may encourage and revive even the weariest apostle.

Shepherdless sheep (v. 33) were a frequent motif in the Old Testament signifying the needs of the people for leadership, security, sustenance and healing. When Moses worried about a successor to assume his responsibilities he prayed to Yahweh that his people would not be left "like sheep without a shepherd" (Numbers 27:17). In today's gospel, Jesus presents himself as Moses' successor and shepherd of the people. Like Moses, he would lead and guide his people through the desert of alienation to a new relationship with God. Like Moses, he would be the mediator of God's revelation. Like Moses, he would provide manna bread (Mark 6:35-8:10) and exercise his power over the sea (Exodus 15, Mark 6:45-52).

Centuries after Moses, Ezekiel (34:1-6) had bemoaned the sad fate of his people and placed the blame for their situation upon the shoulders of those who should have been responsible for the flock of Israel, their kings. With little concern for their people, some of Israel's kings had grown fat and comfortable, taking advantage of their position, using and abusing their charges. Prophesying against them, Ezekiel warned of severe retribution from the hands of Yahweh himself. Moreover, out of concern for his scattered sheep, the Lord would "gather them together, pasture them in rich grazing ground, look for the lost, bandage the wounded, make the weak strong and show them where to *rest*" (Ezekiel 34:13-16). It was this ideal of true and good shepherding to which Jesus ascribed and with which he associated his ministry (John 10) and that of his apostles.

1. Leadership entails a dual responsibility: to one's charges and to the one from whom the authority is derived (Jeremiah).

2. Walls of separation, whether visible or not, are a scandal in the community made one by the cross of Christ (Ephesians).

3. An integral aspect of faithful discipleship is the appropriate distribution of time (Mark).

17th Sunday in Ordinary Time

When those he had filled with bread began to gather up the fragments, Jesus began to gather unto himself all the fragments of their separate lives (John). Into one body he formed them, with one hope he renewed them and with great love he shared with them the one Father and God (Ephesians). He was not a wonder-worker only once for a few (2 Kings), but a sign that would feed all of humanity for life everlasting.

2 Kings 4:42-44. Elisha, the mysterious ninth century B.C.E. inheritor of Elijah's hairy mantle and prophetic authority, was a figure so legendized in subsequent tradition that it has become virtually impossible to discern fact from fiction with regard to his accomplishments. A popular folkloric hero, Elisha was, for the most part, motivated in his deeds by a concern for the poor and faithful remnant who survived in spite of the moral decadence that surrounded them. Besides the miraculous feeding of today's first reading, the prophet was accredited with: multiplying oil to help a widow pay her debts; granting a child to an aged, barren woman and then bringing that son back to life when he died; making poisoned soup edible; healing a leper, etc. P. Ellis calls the wonders of Elisha his *fioretti* and compares them to the naïve and delightful legends told about Francis of Assisi and his band of followers. Combined with similar deeds performed by Elijah, those of Elisha served well the purpose of the Deuteronomic historian who incorporated them into his work.

Writing at a point in the history (soon after 587 B.C.E.) of his people when Jerusalem had been sacked by Babylon, the temple ruined and David's dynasty emasculated, the religious historian of Joshua-Kings helped his contemporaries to find meaning in and to make sense of the tragedy that had befallen them. By his reinterpretation of the demise of both the northern and southern kingdoms in terms of covenantal infidelity, he sought to awaken in his people their need for repentance. With stories like those that surrounded Elijah and Elisha, he attempted to renew in the hearts of the surviving remnant hope for a glorious future. Later Jewish eschatology associated the great works of Elisha (healings, feedings, resuscitations) with the era of messianic salvation.

The Baal-Shalishah of today's pericope is probably modern day Kefr Tilt, located fifteen miles north of Lydda on the coastal planes. The barley loaves offered were the sustenance of the poor, in this case the firstfruits to be offered to the Lord (Leviticus 2:12). That the faithful poor (*anawim*) were the special predilection of Yahweh is made clear in the wondrous feeding of a hundred men. Christians see in this act a prefigurement of the miraculous feedings provided by Jesus in the gospels.

For Israel, being fed with bread by the hand of God was not merely a means of satisfying a physical need. To look for bread from their maker was to exhibit that attitude of need and dependence upon his providence necessary to their survival in the Sinai desert and in the wilderness of Babylon as well. In telling the story of Elisha and the hundred hungry men, the Deuteronomic historian sought to turn the eyes of his people outward from their self-sufficiency and to whet their spiritual appetites with an eschatological hunger. Only with the appearance of Jesus, the bread of life, would that hunger be fully sated.

Ephesians 4:1-6. Because of the vocation-word or calling each has received (v. 1), each believer, taught the Ephesians' author, is challenged to assume a new way of living characterized by a virtue made possible in the Spirit. Today's pericope is from a longer section (4:1-5:21) of moral exhortations directed to all the faithful; it is part of the second half of the letter.

In examining the document addressed to the church in Ephesus, one can discern two distinct sections. Chapters 1-3 are doctrinal in nature and content. In these chapters, the deutero-Pauline author has put forth his understanding of God's great plan, viz., the creation of a new and eschatological people of God freed from social, political and religious barriers and made one by the love of God. In chapters 4-6, the author has assumed a hortatory style in an effort to help believers live according to God's plan for them as put forth in the first three chapters. Fuller has described the relationship between the two sections in terms of the indicative and the imperative. In other words, Christian living is a process of becoming what we ought (imperative) based on what we in faith have come to recognize God's plan to be (indicative). Life must reflect faith and translate the intellectual assent and psychological credence of faith into a social, emotional, *lived* commitment.

Previously, the author had described the essence of Christian vocation in terms of unity among believers established by union with the Father through Christ and in the Spirit (1:3-3:21, especially 2:18). In today's pericope, he proceeded to explain how the believer can translate that ontological unity into a moral or ethical expression. As J. Grassi has pointed out, humility in Greek literature was not necessarily a virtue; in fact it was thought of as "mean-spiritedness." But because of Christ and his altruistic and selfless service, humility (v. 2) was afforded the dignity of a virtue to be emulated by believers. Patience (v. 2) is not just a tolerance of others but the exercise of self-control wherein one is slow to retaliate when injured or offended. As the inner source and guiding force of Christian life, the Spirit makes unity, patience and humility possible.

In the sevenfold proclamation of unity with which the reading ends, the author has provided believers of all times with the reasons for a community of harmony and peace: *one* body of believers with *one* hope and *one* faith, sharing *one* baptism in *one* Lord, belonging to *one* Father in *one* Spirit. This appreciation of the unity of the transcendent God who dwelled among them was due in no small part to the influence of Judaism's strict monotheism. But while the Jews still waited for the era of the messiah and the unity he would establish, Christians in Ephesus rejoiced to have seen his day.

John 6:1-15. All four gospels relate the episode of the feeding of the multitudes by Jesus, but only the fourth evangelist called it a *sign*. Sign (*semeion*) was a term John used to refer favorably to a miracle or wondrous deed worked by Jesus. Of all the great acts of power performed by Jesus, the Johannine author selected only seven to include in his testament of good news. Each sign should be understood as a vehicle of revelation and a personal encounter with Jesus as Lord. In each sign, a challenge is issued; those who witness the sign are summoned to go beyond the sign and to believe in the one whom the sign has revealed. Today's gospel relates the fourth of the seven signs wherein Jesus is revealed as bread and bread-giver for the life of the world.

In keeping with the Johannine replacement theology, each sign has been closely associated with one of the Jewish holy feasts. By means of the theological discourses that accompany each sign, the evangelist demonstrated the fact that Jesus has replaced the meaning and significant symbols of the feast with his very self. As the author has indicated (v. 4) the feast was Passover, celebrated in the month of Nisan in conjunction with the feast of Unleavened Bread. Besides the Passover-exodus motif, the author wove eschatological and eucharistic motifs into his fourth sign. Each motif lends a richness of theological interpretation to the wondrous event of the loaves and fishes.

With regard to the Passover motif, the allusion to the season and the other elements the author included in the narrative relate Jesus' act with the event that made Israel a people. The mountain (v. 3) is reminiscent of Sinai and the questioning of Philip (v. 5) recalls the testing in the desert (Exodus 16:4, Numbers 11:13). Philip's answer to Jesus is similar to Moses' response in the wilderness (Numbers 11:22). More important, however, and more obvious is the corollary between the manna of the wilderness and the bread Jesus gave. But there is also a remarkable difference, indicating that the sign effected by Jesus is far greater than the manna of old. When the people in the desert gathered (Exodus 16:16-21) the manna, they had sufficient food for the day, but no surplus. When Jesus gave his weary and hungry followers bread, all were filled (vv. 11-13) and an abundance remained.

Their fullness and the remaining abundance introduce a messianic or eschatological motif into the narrative. Numerous messianic texts describe the era of the messiah as a time of plenty and prosperity especially for the poor who had hungered for his justice (Isaiah 55). Barley bread was the usual fare of the poorest of the poor. Significantly, Jesus' action feeds with banquet-like portions the poor ones who have come to him. Moreover, they shared in the fish as well. In later tradition the word fish (*ichthys*) was an acronym (Jesus Christ Savior, Son of God) and a symbol by which Christians made themselves known to one another. One cannot overlook the similarity between the Elisha story (2 Kings 4:42-44, today's first reading) and the loaves story in the gospel. All the New Testament evangelists drew parallels between Jesus and Elijah and Elisha because of the association those wonderworkers had come to have with the messianic age. Jesus' feeding of the crowds, therefore, signaled the start of the eschatological era of salvation. Unique to the fourth gospel, a further indication of the messianic character of the sign was the reaction of the crowd, "This is the prophet" (v. 14). But the people had misread the sign and looked upon Jesus as a political king (v. 15) who would alleviate their economic situation and fill their stomachs (v. 25). He rejected their enthusiasm until they would hunger for him as the bread of life (v. 35).

Besides looking back into Israel's tradition and remembering the manna, Jesus' sign of the loaves looked ahead to the eucharist. For reasons known only to himself, the Johannine author omitted the eucharistic institution from the last supper narrative and gathered all the eucharistic theology of his gospel into chapter six. Like the synoptics, John incorporated distinctive eucharistic language into his account, viz., "took," "gave thanks" (*eucharistesas*, v. 11). But unlike the synoptics, John alone tells us that Jesus *himself* distributed (v. 11: "passed around") the bread. Clearly this is an allusion to a last supper type of institution and the sacramental eucharist. Also unique to the fourth gospel is Jesus' directive (v. 12) to gather up (*synagein*) the fragments (*klasma*). In the Didache (9:4) both words appear: *synagein* is the word used to describe the gathering up of the eucharistic bread which, as B. Vawter points out, is a symbol of the gathering of the church. *Klasma* (fragments) is applied in the Didache to the morsels of eucharistic bread. Later in John's chapter six, when Jesus declares himself to be the bread and food for all, it becomes clear that all will be gathered (*synagein*) when he is fragmented (*klasma*) and broken upon the cross.

Finally, in the question of Philip to Jesus, "Where shall we buy bread for these people to eat?" (v. 5), there is something of the social implications inherent in the eucharistic sign. In Luke, the point is even more clear, "Why do you not give them something to eat yourselves?" (Luke 9:13). All those who eat the bread of life and truly perceive the sign in faith are gathered together by that sharing and become responsible for one another. If another is hungry, it is *we* who must buy the bread and then, when he is filled, we must break with him the greater bread of life so that he may never know hunger again.

1. Small gestures can become great wonders where there is faith (2 Kings).

2. An integration of faith and life is a process of maturation in the Spirit (Ephesians).

3. Spiritual hunger will be satisfied by Jesus, but physical hunger must be eradicated by his disciples (John).

18th Sunday in Ordinary Time

With an insatiable hunger, they pursued him—eager to see power and majesty made manifest. In answer to their ambitious desires, he offered only the gift of himself: his teaching and his life (John). Their ancestors had spurned the blessings of their desert days and had died (Exodus). But those who shared in the eternal manna became a new and wondrous creation (Ephesians).

Exodus 16:2-4, 12-15. Historical and scientific certainty about the actual route of the exodus, the location of Sinai, the number of groups trekking through the wilderness, etc., is virtually impossible. Even the various informational sources within the scriptures (J, E, P, D) contradict one another in several instances. Such discrepancies and disagreements are inevitable because the traditions regarding those events grew and developed in different locales and in different circumstances (e.g., northern kingdom, southern kingdom) shaped by different theologians with differing interests and emphases. However, there is marked unanimity of all sources with regard to the attitude of the Israelites as they made their way through the desert. The grumbling of Israel against Moses and against Yahweh is a consistent motif throughout the narratives of the wilderness tradition. More than casual griping, the murmuring incidents were an indication of a lack of faith and trust in God. Each incident was usually followed by an intercession by Moses and an intervention by God on behalf of his disgruntled people. Because of the stereotyped nature and fixed structure of the murmuring incidents (Exodus 16, 17; Numbers 20), some scholars believe the motif was repeated by the authors for homiletic purposes. Similar to the Marcan and Johannine motifs of misunderstanding, the murmuring motif enabled the writer (or preacher in the oral phase of the tradition) to point out to Israel its history of failures and to urge the people to respond anew to God's provident goodness.

In today's first reading, the complaint at the basis of the incident is a concern for food. There is little doubt that the desert conditions were harsh, but it is unlikely the people were *starving*; hence, the reference to famine (v. 3) may be an exaggeration. Probably the ease with which food (bread and meat) was readily attainable in plentiful amounts (v. 3) in Egypt was more appealing than the situation in the desert where trust in God's providence was necessary for a meaningful existence. In response to their display of faithless disregard for the wonders of the exodus (vv. 1-3), Israel's God provided not only "bread" (manna) but meat as well (quail). Both manna and quail were (and are) naturally recurring phenomena in the wilderness but, as De Vaux has pointed out, in *different parts* of the desert. Manna is the natural secretion of two species of scale insects or plant lice called the *Trebutina mannipara* and *Najacoccus serpentius*. The infestation by these insects results in the sweet secretion on the leaves of the tamarisk shrub during the months of May and June in the central Sinai. As the substance drops from the leaves to the earth, it cools in the night air and becomes firm. If allowed to remain on the ground, the substance soon melts but if gathered early (before 8:30 a.m.) before the sun parches the desert, it provides a tasty nourishing feast. Even today, the Bedouin inhabitants of the central Sinai gather and eat the phenomenon the Israelites named manna. Etymologically, the word manna is hard to trace. But the Exodus' author (16:15) has attached the popular etymology by way of explanation. When the people first saw the food, they asked, "*Man hu*? (What is this?)," hence the name.

Quail are migratory fowl that fly to Europe every spring. In the autumn they return to their regular habitat on the northwest coast of the Sinai peninsula. Exhausted from their flight over the Mediterranean, they literally drop to the earth and are easily snatched up. Because these two phenomena occur at different regions of the Sinai, it is obvious that the Exodus authors have conflated the two accounts. Regardless of the scientific explanations for the manna and the quail, Israel regarded these as gifts of God and signs of his unwavering providence.

Ephesians 4:17, 20-24. So closely did the deutero-Pauline author of Ephesians (and Colossians) associate the church with Christ (Ephesians 1:23, Colossians 1:24, etc.) that he was able to speak of the Christian life as "learning Christ" (4:20). In those letters recognized as authentically Pauline, the term "church" was usually applied to the local community of believers. But in the deutero-Pauline works, there is a decided development: "the church" came to mean the body of believers universal, inextricably united with Christ, its eternal head. Hence, the author of Ephesians spoke of "growing into him who is the head (of the church)," i.e., Christ, "unto full measure and stature" (4:12-16). For this reason, the call to holiness of today's second reading should be understood to mean: put on—not merely imitate—the *person* of Jesus Christ.

Learning Christ (becoming Christian) involved a departure, once and forever, from those values and attitudes called "pagan" by the author (v. 17). If, as is suggested, Ephesians was a circular letter or encyclical addressed to the churches in Asia Minor, those former "pagans" had grown up in a world steeped in the values of gnostic and Greek philosophy and the secular ethics derived from the principles of ethical humanism with its origin *in man*. But the *Christian* was called to a life of holiness and to a morality with its origin *in God*. Hence the Ephesian's author spoke, not of "becoming the best you can be" but of becoming an altogether new person or a new creation by baptism into Christ.

In today's reading, this pattern of renunciation and renewal, of divestiture and investiture, reflects not only baptismal theology but the baptismal liturgy as well. Once adequately prepared for the rite of initiation, the catechumens would signify their renunciation of sin and of evil by removing their outer garments. The Ephesians author referred to this divestiture as a "laying aside of the former way of life and the old self" (v. 22). Then the catechumens would plunge into the baptismal waters, thereby sacramentally illustrating their incorporation into Christ and into his body, the church, through faith. Upon emerging from the baptismal pool, the newly baptized would be clothed in white robes or garments, signs of the purity the person had achieved in baptism as well as the victory of Christ over evil in which he had begun to share.

John 6:24-35. By means of the dialogues and discourses which comprise a large bulk of the gospel material, the Johannine evangelist and redactor have succeeded in communicating the truth of Jesus' teaching while elucidating the meaning of that teaching for the benefit of the church that survived the risen Lord. For the most part, the dialogues followed a set pattern, as in today's gospel pericope. Usually a statement was made by Jesus but the revelatory truth and power of the statement went unheeded or misunderstood by those who heard it. Recall Nicodemus' "Must I enter again into my mother's womb?" when Jesus spoke of being born again (or from above; John 3:4). That misunderstanding enabled Jesus (or the evangelist) to enunciate the real truth of the statement. Once the dialogue succeeded in shifting the attention from the superficial to the real meaning of the words, it was often followed up with a monologue or discourse (by Jesus or John) which elaborated the revelatory statement more thoroughly. During the monologues or discourses, the evangelist drew out certain theological, christological, liturgical and/or sacramental aspects of Jesus' teaching as developed by the church with the light of the Holy Spirit.

Today's gospel is part of the lengthy bread of life discourse (vv. 24-59) which clarified the sign of the loaves and fishes (vv. 1-15) and drew out its messianic and eucharistic significance. The crowds who pursued Jesus had followed after him, not because they were *disciples* who believed, i.e., who had seen the sign (of the bread) with the perception of faith, but because they had been taken with the material and sensational nature of the sign. They came to be filled again with bread (a free meal) and Jesus offered to them instead the satisfying fullness of his teaching. Perhaps some had come after Jesus because they had seen in the sign of the bread an indication that the messianic age had come. Several Jewish documents (rabbinical midrashes, etc.) reflected the popular expectation that the messiah would repeat the miracle of the manna and effect a new exodus for the chosen people. Significantly, these hopes were attached to the feast of Passover, and that explains the heightened anticipation and misconception of Jesus' work by the crowds. To those who hoped for a repeat performance of the manna, Jesus spoke of non-perishable food "that remains unto life eternal" (v. 29) and of *real* heavenly bread (v. 32). The manna in the desert melted in the heat of the day, but the food of the Son of Man (v. 27) and the bread the Father gives (v. 32) would never cease to fill them with blessings. Like the Deuteronomic author who appealed to the heart of his people, "Man does not live on bread alone . . . ." (Deuteronomy 8:3), Jesus challenged those who pursued him to raise their attention from their stomachs to their hearts. He would have them spiritually hungry, thereby open to the truth of his teaching. Like Wisdom who invited all to her table to eat, believe and be filled, Jesus invited all who believed to come and eat. But whereas Wisdom's disciples grew hungry again (Sirach 24:19), Jesus' followers would never hunger or thirst (6:35). For those who ate of the real bread, every human and spiritual hunger would be sated in full communion with God in life eternal.

When told that they should *work* (6:27, 28) for the food of life, those who had come to Jesus again misunderstood. Thinking that they could attain the imperishable food by some human endeavor, they inquired what they should do. In the ensuing dialogue about work, the nature of the bread from heaven is underscored. The "work" required of them, Jesus answered, is *faith* in the one sent by God, viz., himself. R. Brown understands this dialogue as the Johannine response to the issue of faith and works that had already begun to trouble the first century church (see James, Paul). John did not counsel "faith without works" or "works without faith." Rather he understood faith *as a work* and, as R. Bultmann has explained, "Believing is not so much a work done by man as it is submission to God's work in Jesus."

In the weeks to come, the Sunday gospels will continue the discourse on the bread of life wherein it will become clear that the bread given by Jesus has a rather fluid and diverse meaning. Not only does it refer figuratively (as in today's gospel) to the bread of revelation or Jesus' teaching but also very realistically to the eucharistic and sacramental bread of Jesus himself. At times it may be difficult to discern in which sense "bread" is to be understood, but both meanings are present and intended. In the words of R. Fuller, "It would be wrong to draw a sharp line between the historical and kerygmatic and the sacramental. All are part of a single act of revelation and redemption with the historical coming of Christ as decisive and the kerygma and sacrament complementary as re-presentations of the once and for all revelatory and redemptive event."

1. True satisfaction and fulfillment are not necessarily achieved on a full stomach (Exodus).

2. Putting on Christ is a process that begins from within (Ephesians).

3. What bread do we have in mind when we pray, "Give us this day our daily bread" (John)?

19th Sunday in Ordinary Time

When by human criteria he was judged inferior and of no account, he offered to the world the precious gift of life-giving bread (John). For centuries, many had hoped and hungered to be taught and filled by him (1 Kings). All who have partaken of his bread and his word are to live in a manner worthy of his meal and his message (Ephesians).

1 Kings 19:4-8. Elijah thought his career as a prophet was at an end. He assumed that all he had labored so arduously to build (viz., the religious reform of his people) was tumbling down in shambles around him. Loyal to Yahweh alone, Elijah had bravely defied his weak king Ahab and his ambitious queen Jezebel, hurling in their faces their infidelities to the God whom they were supposed to represent as regents. A Phoenician princess and daughter of Ethbaal, king of Sidon, Jezebel brought to her marriage a dowry that included the pagan cult and rituals of her native land (modern day Lebanon). Not content to allow her religion to coexist peacefully with that of her husband, Jezebel was intent on eradicating Yahwistic religion from Israel. To that end, she banished the prophets of Yahweh and even attempted to kill them (1 Kings 18:4, 13). To replace them, she imported oracular devotees of Ba'al (400 of them!) from her own land but these were outwitted and, according to tradition, killed by Elijah, prophet of Yahweh (1 Kings 18:19ff). Because she was so evil and cunning at getting her own way, Jezebel's name became synonymous with wicked and vengeful women throughout the centuries. She regarded Elijah as her nemesis and was relentless in her efforts to exterminate him. So fierce were her threats that Elijah fled Jezebel and Israel in fear for his life. It is at this point that today's first reading picks up the saga of Elijah, man of God.

Driven to the desert by his personal and career crisis, the prophet traveled to Beersheba at the southern border of Judah. He may have feared to enter the Judean kingdom openly and expected no sympathy there because Jehoshaphat's son Jehoram was married to Athaliah, daughter of Ahab and Jezebel! Bemoaning his sad situation in the shelter of a broom tree (some translations have furze bush), Elijah considered his ministry at an end. Like Moses before him (Numbers 11:14) and Job (Job 6:9; 7:15) and Jonah (Jonah 4:3, 8) who would come after him, Elijah prayed for death as a relief from his miseries. But Elijah would learn the lesson of God's paradoxical ways. In that moment when human resources are wanting and human hopes fail, God's power can provide unimagined energies to accomplish his inconceivable plans.

Elijah's energy came to him in the form of an angel bearing food to strengthen and sustain him for the journey ahead. Angel (from the Latin *angelus*) is a transcription of the Greek *angelos* used in the Septuagint to translate *mal'ak* or messenger. Present in the earliest parts of Hebrew tradition (Genesis 16:7, 21:17; Exodus 3:2, 14:19, etc.), the angel or messenger of Yahweh was often indistinguishable from Yahweh himself. An ambassador sent by Yahweh, the angel acted as his mediary, spoke in his name and worked wonders in the manner of Yahweh himself. In early texts, the angel seemed more "a hypostatization of the divine attributes or operations" than a distinct heavenly being (J.L. McKenzie). Today, it is the general consensus that in many of the earlier passages the figure of the angel is a theological addition to the text made out of respect for the divine transcendence.

Ephesians 4:30-5:2. Some of the most interesting artifacts of the ancient world, produced as long ago as the sixth millennium B.C.E., are *seals*, the handiwork of glyptic (carving) artists. They originated as a flat stone carved with a design or logo to be pressed or stamped into soft clay. Later, in Mestopotamia (ca. 4000 B.C.E.), the cylindrical seal was developed for making impressions on clay tablets. Still later (ca. 1000 B.C.E.), the signet ring seal replaced the cylindrical seal. Throughout the centuries the seal served several purposes: (1) *Legal*—the seal served to identify objects, conclude contracts, etc. Its insignia was considered the equivalent of a signature. (2) *Artistic*—because of their beauty, seals were worn like jewelry, on the shoulder, neck, waist or wrist. (3) *Cultic*—Seals were often given as gifts to the gods; the leaving of one's seal in the god's sanctuary was considered a votive offering, representing the giver. (4) *Status symbols*—the giving of a seal represented the conferral of authority.

Given these various functions, the several scriptural references to *seals*, as in today's second reading (v. 30), may be more adequately appreciated. For example, signet rings were offered to Yahweh in the desert (Exodus 35:22, Numbers 31:50). By means of his seal, Judah was identified and bound contractually to the scheming Tamar (Genesis 38:18, 25). Pharaoh gave his signet ring to Joseph, thereby making him prime minister (Genesis 41:42). The Pseudo-Solomonic author of the Song of Songs referred to the seal as a means and sign of intimate union which would prevail even in the face of death: "Set me like a seal on your heart, like a seal on your arm. For love is strong as death and passion as relentless as Sheol" (Song 8:6).

To what, then, did the deutero-Pauline author of Ephesians refer when he spoke of Christians being *sealed* with the Holy Spirit? Certainly his thought included the confirming and sacramental seal of the Spirit. But it would be unfortunate to overlook the wealth of meanings and functions of the seal with which the author was certainly familiar. For the Christian to be sealed with the Holy Spirit of Jesus was to be *legally bound* and *contractually* committed to him. By that sealing the Christian would be *identified* as a believer and child of God. Because of the seal of the Spirit, the graced Christian would become a *worthy* gift for the Lord. "Artistically" the sealing with the Spirit rendered the believer a beautiful vessel or temple of the Lord's presence. Finally, the gift of the seal of the Spirit can be understood as a *share in the power* of Jesus himself. Thus sealed, the Christian was thereby responsible to live accordingly. To that end, the author listed several attitudes and behaviors that did not fit the sealing of the Spirit (v. 31). In addition to the avoidance of evil, the sealed believer was obligated to a life in conformity with the values made incarnate by Jesus. Mutual forgiveness (*charizomai*) required not merely the remission of debts or faults but the magnanimous forgiving and self-forgetful love which was the hallmark of Jesus' ministry. As children (5:1), believers were not to be naive and simplistic, but fresh, innovative and free of inhibitions with regard to their loving relationships to the Father. In this way, the believers would become a source of joy for the Holy Spirit (see 4:30, "Do not sadden the Holy Spirit . . . .") and, like Christ, a worthy offering.

According to the sacrificial systems of Israel and other peoples of the ancient world, the burning of the animals was thought to produce a fragrant odor, pleasing to God. Christians understood that the sacrifice of Jesus had rendered obsolete all animal sacrifices and had become the one perfect gift that obviated all others. Christians, sealed with the Holy Spirit, may participate freely and worthily in the pleasing, perfect offering of Jesus himself.

John 6:41-51. Obviously all who heard about the sign of the feeding of the crowds by Jesus did not automatically believe in him as the messiah sent by God. Even those who participated and ate their fill of bread did not necessarily come to faith. Miracles or signs in the ministry of Jesus were not guarantors of faith, nor were they scientific proofs of Jesus' identity. Rather, the signs worked by Jesus were powerful challenges, accepted by some, rejected by others, as evident in the dialogue that comprises today's gospel. Excerpted from the lengthy bread of life discourse, today's pericope reprises the scene of the wilderness wanderings wherein the people murmured against Moses and against God even after being fed with the manna and the quail (Exodus 16:2, 7, 8). In today's gospel however, the "Jews" (used pejoratively in v. 41 by the author) grumbled, not over the bread but over Jesus' claim of heavenly origin. As in the synoptic accounts, Jesus ignored their petty objections concerning his parentage and pressed them to focus on matters of greater concern, viz., their acceptance in faith or rejection of the gift of life eternal (v. 44).

A requisite for coming to Jesus, i.e., believing in him, is being *drawn* by the Father. As R. Brown has pointed out, rabbinic sources used the same expression, "to draw" or "to bring nigh (to the Torah)," to describe the process of conversion: "The natural desire of one who has love for his fellow men is to bring them nigh to the Torah for this means to make them sharers in the fuller knowledge of God" (Pirqe Aboth 1, 12). For the Johannine author, knowledge of God or "being taught by God" (v. 45) was possible when one draws near to or is converted to Jesus. As is clear in the text, faith in Jesus is not simply a human choice but a paradoxical combination of free decision and divine initiative: "No one can come to me unless the Father draws him."

In a sense the Johannine Jesus of today's gospel was intimating that those who did not freely decide to believe in him were, in fact, closing themselves to the promptings of the Father himself. In that unteachable and unreachable state, they could not appreciate or be nourished by the bread of life. In this particular section of the discourse (vv. 35- 50), bread of life can be understood in the figurative sense of Jesus' teaching or the revelation of the Father and of the truth. Only in the last verse of today's gospel (vv. 51 ff) does the sacramental or eucharistic meaning emerge of the bread of life. (See next week's gospel commentary).

Those who heard Jesus speak of himself and his teachings as life-giving bread had a rich background for understanding such a metaphor. Strack and Billerbeck's Commentary (2, 483 ff) makes the point that the rabbis equated the Torah with bread, bread which feeds, gives life, reveals God, etc. When Jesus offered himself, i.e., his teaching, as life-giving bread, he was placing his revelation above the Torah. To recognize the bread of Jesus' teaching required a deep spiritual hunger, a hunger whetted by God himself. Perhaps the Johannine author had in mind the prophecy of the eighth century B.C.E. prophet Amos: "Behold the days are coming—it is the Lord Yahweh who speaks—days when I will bring famine on the country, a famine not of bread, a drought not of water, but of hearing the word of Yahweh. They will stagger from sea to sea, wander from north to east, seeking the word of Yahweh, and failing to find it" (Amos 8:11-12).

In concluding this section of the bread of life discourse, vv. 48-50 form an inclusion with v. 35, reiterating Jesus' power to give the bread that would lead to life *eternal*. That life would be attainable only by those who had passed beyond reliance upon their physical sense into the divinely initiated experience of spiritual perception, viz., faith. Only in faith would his hearers accept the bread of his teaching as the revelation of the truth . . . and only by faith would they be able to open themselves in hungry acceptance to the eucharistic revelation that immediately follows (vv. 51-58), i.e., "the bread I will give is my flesh for the life of the world."

1. Despair has no place in the life of a disciple (1 Kings).

2. All the words and works of the believer must be consonant with and worthy of the Spirit with whom all Christians have been sealed (Ephesians).

3. Murmuring or criticism is beneficial, as long as it opens and does not close the heart and mind to the truth (John).

20th Sunday in Ordinary Time

In the journey of life there are many invitations and many solicitations (Proverbs). The ability to understand and to choose wisely is cultivated by a clear head and a determined will in the presence of the Spirit and with the support of fellow believers (Ephesians). Only one invitation will lead to life eternal; it is that bread whom we celebrate and for whom we live (John).

Proverbs 9:1-6. In his lifetime, Solomon was reputed to have uttered some 3000 proverbs (1 Kings 4:29-32) and the origins of Hebrew wisdom can be traced to his royal court but the great sage is not the sole genius behind the biblical book of Proverbs. An anthology of both early and late collections, Proverbs or *Mishle Shelomoh* (1:1) was given its final form and editing in the post-exilic period, perhaps as late as the third century B.C.E. Its predominant literary form is the proverb or *mashal*, a pithy saying based on comparison. Often the saying was expressed in a hidden manner that necessarily provoked from its reader (or hearer) a certain intellectual effort in order to penetrate its true meaning. *Mashal* also means "to rule," hence proverbs were regarded as having value for governing human behavior. The oldest of the sapiential books, Proverbs is accepted as canonical by Roman Catholics but relegated to a deutero-canonical status by both Protestants and Jews, both groups basing their decision on the Jamnia decision (ca. 100 C.E.).

Rooted in the premise that the wise person possesses not merely a knowledge of religious and philosophical truth but a measure of practical common sense as well, Proverbs exhorts the reader to seek the source of all true wisdom in God alone.

Today's first reading is an extended *mashal* on wisdom whose message and beauty become more poignant in conjunction with its antithetical counterpart, folly (vv. 13-18). Both wisdom and folly are personified as women, one a lady, the other a harlot. Each has built a house, prepared a feast and invited guests to come and partake of the fare each has provided. Ironically, both feminine personifications issue the same invitation, "Let whoever is simple turn in here . . . to him who lacks understanding I say . . . ." (vv. 4, 16). While wisdom's banquet of meat and wine is party fare and results in life for the participant (v. 6), folly's victuals of bread and water (stolen at that!) lead only to death (v. 18). Therein lay the point of the comparison and the lesson of the antithesis.

The mixing of the wines (v. 2) refers to spicing to enhance flavor. With the dressed meat, the meal was one of a truly festive character and probably reminded the faithful Israelite of the eschatological banquet (Isaiah 25:6, 55:1-5) that came to be associated with the advent of the messiah. For Christian readers, wisdom's banquet was surely reminiscent of the great wedding feast of the kingdom (Matthew 22:1-14) to which all would be invited and at which Christ himself would act as host. Wisdom's feast also provides an anticipatory and colorful background for the eucharistic feast where the wine and bread are in fact the wisdom and the teaching, the flesh and blood of the Lord himself.

Ephesians 5:15-20. Well aware that it was not sufficient to merely *wish* or to *want* to do what is right, the author of Ephesians exhorted his readers to devote themselves to *knowing* what they should do. "Like thoughtful" people (v. 15) they would do well to gear their energies into discerning God's will (v. 17). In this instance the will (*thelema*) of God does not pertain to God's plan of salvation but rather to the manner of life made normative and manifested by God in Christ's earthly existence. Such discernment of God's will, i.e., a life modeled on that of Jesus, is made possible if the believer chooses wisdom over foolishness, viz., that a God should become flesh . . . that the God-made-flesh should give himself as food . . . and ultimately that the God-made-flesh should give his very life, dying in ignominy and seeming disgrace on a cross.

An atmosphere of eschatological urgency pervades the text as the author concedes that the present age is evil . . . "these are evil days" (v. 16). But for the thoughtful believer, earnestly seeking the wisdom of the Lord's will, the evil days will be short (Romans 13:11-14) and will yield to the glory of the Lord's return. To maintain the proper state of alertness for the sudden reappearance of Jesus, the Christian cannot afford his wits to be dulled. Therefore drunkenness and debauchery were to be foregone. For the believer, the celebration of redeemed life could admit of no other intoxication save that of the Spirit. In the Orphic and mystery cults, wine was an integral part of the reveling but, for Christians, moderation was the ideal (1 Corinthians 11:21). Yet, with regard to the Spirit, they were not to be abstemious in any sense. Indeed, the author of Ephesians made a clever pun in exhorting his hearers to *be filled* (v. 18) (not with wine) with the Spirit. Recall the reaction of those who witnessed the disciples on Pentecost, filled with the Spirit of Jesus: "Unable to explain it, they asked one another, what it all meant. Some, however, laughed it off: 'They have been drinking too much new wine'" (Acts 2:12-13).

Christians, replete with the wine of the wisdom of Jesus' own Spirit, are led, not to acts of debauchery and wanton behavior but to prayer and liturgical rejoicing. Fuller cites this Ephesians text as one of the earliest references to the use of hymns in the early community. In contrast to the bawdy music of the loose-tongued imbibers, the inspired songs of believers praise God as well as edify and solidify the members of the community. Many of these wonderful hymns were quoted by the New Testament authors (Philippians 2:5-11, Colossians 1:13-20, 1 Timothy 3:16, Revelation 5:6-8, etc.). In addition to their liturgical usage, the hymns were valuable pedagogical vehicles for some of the most profound theological and christological insights in the New Testament (e.g., kenotic character of Jesus' redemptive act in Philippians 2).

John 6:51-58. Throughout the centuries, the lengthy Johannine bread of life discourse has undergone extensive analyses. Even today, a consensus has not been reached as to whether the bread of life referred to in John 6 should be interpreted in a strictly spiritual and figurative sense or in a realistic and eucharistic sense. In the early church, Clement of Alexandria, Origen and Eusebius attached a purely spiritual meaning to the bread of life, understanding that it referred solely to Jesus' revelation and to his teaching. The great fathers of the church, John Chrysostom, Gregory of Nyssa, Cyril of Jerusalem and Cyril of Alexandria accented the eucharistic and sacramental character of the bread from heaven. After the Reformation and its proponents rejected the eucharistic significance of John 6, the Council of Trent examined the issue and opted not to make a definitive statement on the issue. In modern times, a variety of solutions have been proposed, the most balanced and probably truest to the gospel being those of Feuillet, Léon-Dufour and R. Brown. These eminent scholars suggest that the *two* themes, *both* sapiential and sacramental, are interwoven throughout the discourse, with the bread of life referring, at times, to Jesus' teaching and revelation and at other times the bread of life as the eucharistic gift of Jesus himself. Feuillet and Brown concur that in vv. 35-50 the two themes appear with the emphasis on the bread as revelation. The eucharistic theme is present, though in a secondary position. However, in vv. 51-58 (today's gospel), the bread of life or living bread is to be understood exclusively in a eucharistic sense.

Many scholars believe vv. 51-58 to be the work of the Johannine redactor. Brown agrees that these verses were probably a later addition to the discourse but hypothesizes that they actually represent the Johannine narrative of the institution of the eucharist which is startlingly absent from the last supper scene. Brown claims that the evangelist himself recast the institution narrative and modeled it after the bread of life discourse of vv. 35-50. As such, the whole of chapter 6 may reflect the liturgical setting of a Christian Passover celebration which remembered the manna, rejoiced in the loaves and fish and celebrated their memory, as well as the great saving victory of Jesus, in the eucharistic feast. Today's gospel pericope is replete with the soteriological effects, not just of believing in the bread of life (6:35, 40), or accepting Jesus' revelation, but of eating (vv. 51, 54 56) the flesh of Jesus who would be lifted up and draw all to himself. The one who partakes of "the flesh, given for the life of the world will live forever" (v. 51).

The reference to Jesus' life-giving death and to the eucharistic liturgy which would forever after celebrate and sacramentalize that event is clarified by means of the Johannine technique of misunderstanding: "the Jews quarrelled among themselves . . . *How can he give us his flesh to eat?*" (v. 52). This was a valid objection. "Eating flesh" was a repulsive metaphor in the scriptures which meant "to slander" (Psalm 27:2) or "to take hostile action against someone" (Zechariah 11:9). Drinking blood was equally shocking and was forbidden by law (Genesis 9:4, Leviticus 3:17), because blood was considered the vehicle of life, sacred, reserved for God alone. Obviously the only acceptable and valid interpretation for eating flesh and drinking blood is a eucharistic one.

Although John's is the latest gospel, it is believed that the evangelist (and his redactor) preserved a more ancient and authentic tradition by referring to "flesh" rather than "body" as Paul and the synoptics have done. Flesh, in Aramaic *bisra* and in Hebrew *basar* (in the LXX *sarx*) signified the whole, living person. Moreover the word "flesh" recalled the incarnation, "The word became flesh" (John 1:14) as do the initial words of today's gospel, "bread that *came down* from heaven" (v. 51). In the eucharistic gift of his flesh-for-the-life-of-the-world, all the great moments of the Jesus-event are present, viz., the incarnation, his self-emptying kenosis, his being lifted up and his glorification. To eat of his flesh, to believe in his word, is to become a participant and beneficiary of that saving event. Significantly, whenever Ignatius of Antioch wrote about the eucharist, he used the same term, "*sarx*: flesh," as did Justin in his *Apologia*. Probably the substitution of body for flesh was a later adaptation due to the translation of the original words into Greek and a desire to put to rest the crude accusations about the cannibalistic (?!) practices of Christians! John did nothing to assuage the horror of those who objected to eating flesh, etc. Rather, he underscored the idea that eating flesh and drinking blood signified a realistic (*real* food, *real* drink: v. 55) eucharistic participation in Jesus and not merely a spiritual or intellectual encounter.

Finally, participation in the eucharistic flesh and blood of Jesus would thenceforth become the means of knowing God and of attaining eternal life: "Eternal life is this—to *know* you, the only true God, and him whom you have sent, Jesus Christ" (John 17:3). Moreover, the eucharistic experience of Jesus would result in a proleptic participation in eschatology. As the gospel states in v. 54, the one who feeds . . . and drinks . . . *has* life eternal and I *will raise him up* on the last day. That fusion of realized and final eschatology is present in every eucharistic encounter which is at once an experience of the life of Jesus, here and now, and a pledge of the eternal banquet to come.

1. It is the simple who recognize the greatness of the gift in the bread and wine (Proverbs).

2. Liturgy should be a celebration of life, not a dim reflection of it (Ephesians).

3. Those who participate eucharistically become one with the Lord who lives and who will never die (John).

21st Sunday in Ordinary Time

Life or death? The decision seems an easy one, the choice quite obvious. But the decision to choose life in the person of the bread of life is made possible only by a gift of faith from above (John). Once the challenge of faith has been met with faith, the believer is afforded the strength and support of the covenantal community (Joshua), and the loving, reverential care of Christ himself (Ephesians).

Joshua 24:1-2, 15-17, 18. Too often, the exaggerated and legendary exploits ascribed to Joshua have overshadowed and even diminished the very real importance of the covenant renewal ceremony in Joshua 24. Graphic descriptions of the crumbling walls of Jericho have been memorialized in song but only in scholarly circles has the profound significance of the ancient liturgy at Shechem been recognized. In its present position, the last chapter (24) of Joshua serves as an epilogue to all that has preceded it, viz., the Pentateuch plus Joshua, a combination some (Graf, Welhausen, Noth) have suggested should be renamed the "Hexateuch." Moreover, Joshua 24 provides an introductory covenantal orientation for all the scriptural traditions which follow it.

With great assistance from the field of archaeology, modern scholarship has ascertained that the "conquest" of Canaan was more like an *infiltration* which took place *gradually*, perhaps over a period of 125 years. This realization need not dismay the modern penchant for accuracy and attention to historical detail. Rather, the anomalies in the scriptures should cause the critic to delve into the rationale *behind* such exaggerations, simplifications and magnifications of the facts. For the authors, editors and compilers of Joshua, the guiding force behind their work was their firm conviction in the greatness of their God Yahweh and in his involvement with his people.

J. McKenzie described the value of Joshua in this way, "In Joshua and Judges we have monuments for the most primitive faith of Israel, primitive both in the sense that it is early and in the sense that it is less developed. The books should be read as the first stages in Israel's religious adventure of faith; to read them in any other way is to evaluate them by a false standard." With these facts in mind, the somewhat objectionable ideas, e.g., "holy" war, etc., can be placed in proper perspective.

Shechem (literary: shoulder) was named for its location between the "shoulders" of Mts. Gerizim and Ebal some 40 miles north of Jerusalem. An ancient shrine associated with the patriarchs Abraham (Genesis 12:6ff) and Jacob (Genesis 33:18ff), Shechem may have at one time been the shrine where the ark of the covenant was housed. In Judges (9:46) there is a reference to the temple at Shechem of El Bereth (God of the Covenant). The proceedings recorded in Joshua 24 evidence a structure probably derived from the Hittite suzerainty treaties of the second millennium B.C., e.g.: (1) preamble: the titles of the parties are declared (24:2), (2) historical prologue: a narrative of the deeds of the sovereign for the vassal (24:2-13), (3) stipulations or obligations of vassal toward sovereign (24:14, 25), (4) provision for recording, preservation and reading of treaty (24:26), (5) invocation of witnesses to confirm treaty (24:22, 26-27), (6) sanctions (blessings and/or curses) (24:20).

Today's pericope is comprised of the preamble (1-2) and the declaration of allegiance of the people to their God Yahweh (15-18). Joshua's words, "Decide today whom you will serve . . . the gods of your fathers . . . the gods of the Amorites . . .," indicate that his was not a homogeneous audience of Israelites alone. Rather, the group at Shechem was a diverse one, composed of: (1) those who had experienced the Sinai trek and infiltrations, (2) and those already living in Shechem. M. Noth has proposed that before Shechem, Israel was not a viable people at all. At Shechem, the election of Sinai that had constituted the core tribes was extended to embrace all those willing to accept the one true God.

At first evaluation, the relationship between this text from Joshua and today's gospel pericope may seem obscure. Perhaps the connection lay in the challenges issued by Jesus, "Does it shake your faith?" (John 6:67), and by his Old Testament counterpart Joshua, "Decide today whom you will serve" (Joshua 24:15). Similar examples for all believers are the responses of the disciples of the old covenant, "As for me and my household, we will serve the Lord" (Joshua 24:15), and of the new covenant as well: "Lord, to whom shall we go, you have the words of eternal life. . .we believe. . .we are convinced. . ." (John 6:69).

Ephesians 5:21-32. With these verses the author of Ephesians began what has subsequently been called the *Haustafel* or household code. A major portion of the exhortational second half of the letter which continues through Ephesians 6:9, the household code was adapted for use by Christians from similar material found in the writings of the Stoics and in Hellenistic Judaism. It should be noted that this codified advice concerning relationships was culture-bound, the product of a society that did not question the morality of slavery. Built upon the basic principle of subordination, wife to husband, child to parent, slave to master, younger to elder, the codes were changed very little when they were "baptized" for use among Christians. However, as R. Fuller has pointed out in the case of today's second reading, the process of Christianization has gone a little further. Here the Ephesians author elaborated on Christian marriage as a metaphor for understanding the relationship between Christ and the church. "Like his own body, nourishing and caring," Christ's love for the church supplies the norm for intimate conjugal union.

Drawing upon a number of traditions, the author of Ephesians applied the basic principle (v. 21, "Defer to one another out of reverence for Christ") to the marital relationship. Later in the letter, he would apply those traditions and that same principle to the other relationships that formed the matrix of his society. Citing the Genesis text about the union of the wife and her husband (Genesis 2:24), the author called this a great *mysterion* (translated "foreshadowing" in the New American Bible) referring to the relationship of Christ to the church.

In the Vulgate, Jerome translated *mysterion*, which means "hidden symbolism," as *sacramentum*. Roman Catholics anachronized later meanings (for the sacrament) into the ancient text and cited Ephesians 5:32 as scriptural support to prove Christian marriage was a sacrament. This idea finds little acceptance today even in Roman Catholic scholarly circles. Actually, the term *mysterion* is the Pauline word for a long hidden secret. In the context of today's text, the use of *mysterion* would indicate that the true meaning of the Genesis text ("For this reason. . . .") was long hidden but now manifest in the bond Christ has with the church.

In the tradition of the Levitical holiness code (Leviticus 19-26) the author described the purity of the church (5:27) as unstained and unwrinkled. In what is thought an early Christian kerygmatic formula (5:25) and a prebaptismal liturgical formula (5:26), the deutero-Pauline writer enunciated the holiness afforded the church by baptism ("bath of water") and by the sanctifying word of the gospel ("by the power of the word"). Both these metaphors were probably influenced by the ancient oriental ceremonial bathing of the bride before presenting her to her husband-to-be.

The Christian corollary to that bathing and presentation (v. 27) is of course the baptism and presentation of the newly cleansed and newly clothed catechumens to Christ. According to the Jewish customs, a certain period of time separated the contractual espousal and presentation of the bride to her husband. This lapse of time could be compared to the time between the first commitment of baptism and the eschatological presentation of the believer to Christ at the parousia. Indeed, the same verb "present" or *pariestemi* was used by Paul (2 Corinthians 4:14, Romans 14:10) to refer also to the presentation of all peoples to Christ at his second advent.

Like the Israelites in the first reading who enunciated the terms of their covenant with God by means of an already existing treaty (Hittite suzerainty), Christians can regard marriage as an analogy for understanding the bond between Christ and the church. But more importantly, the covenant between Christ and his ecclesial body should be the primary source and inspiration for all other relationships.

John 6:60-69. A popular technique at some workshops geared toward making the study of scripture more interesting is to "find oneself in the text." In other words, given a certain pericope, with whom or with what attitude do you best identify? Today's gospel would be an excellent selection for such an exercise because of the variety of attitudes toward Jesus which are depicted. Doubt, protest, revulsion, ambivalence, rejection and faithful loving acceptance are all represented in the persons of Jesus' disciples. What had Jesus said or done to provoke this gamut of emotional response?

If, as has been proposed, vv. 51-58 are exclusively eucharistic, later added to the text by the Johannine editor or redactor, then today's pericope would follow logically and sequentially the sapiential discourse (vv. 35-50). Therefore, the reactions of the disciples would have been, not to the eucharistic aspect of the bread of life but to Jesus' claim to have "come down from heaven" (v. 38) to give life (v. 40). Just as the Jews had protested Jesus' claim of divine origins (vv. 41-43), so too the disciples of Jesus took issue with that declaration (vv. 60-61). Given the sequence of the text, Jesus' statement, "What, then, if you were to see the Son of Man *ascend* to where he was before . . .?" (v. 62), appears more logical. If those who had witnessed his words and works did not believe he "came from heaven," then how could they ever accept his return to the Father in glory?!

It is significant that Jesus offered no easy remedy to the doubts and dismay of his disciples. He did not work a further sign to secure their acceptance. He did not dilute the seeming scandal of his claim. Rather, he challenged his disciples to open themselves to the gift of *faith* the Father would give: "No one can come to me unless it is granted him by the Father" (v. 65). Only in faith would they be able to hear his "words of spirit and life" (v. 63). According to Jewish thought, the words of the *law* communicated life to the people. Jesus required of his followers that same faith and confidence *in him* and *in his words* that they had formerly placed in the Torah. Only with such faith would they be able to grasp the triple mystery which he was living out in their presence, i.e., (1) the incarnation ("came down from heaven"), (2) the redemption ("my bread for the life of the world") and (3) his ascension and glorification ("the Son of Man will ascend to where he was before"). Flesh alone (v. 63) cannot grasp this triple mystery that affords life and salvation for the world. Recall the usual Johannine meaning for flesh, viz., the "natural principle in man which cannot give eternal life" (R. Brown). *Flesh* in this sense should not be confused with the *flesh of Jesus* in the eucharist and sacramental sense (vv. 51-58).

A turning point in Jesus' ministry, the declarations of chapter six and the ultimatum of faith Jesus proffered required a decision of all who were in his company. Sheer curiosity and whimsical self-interest would not sustain the type of relationship to which he called them. Like the gathered tribes of Shechem, a commitment in faith and a bond of mutual trusting love were required of Jesus' disciples. In a scene comparable to that at Caesarea Philippi (Mark 8:27-33), Peter confessed the faith of the Twelve: "You have the words of eternal life. We have come to believe . . . you are God's holy one" (vv. 68-69). Their knowledge of who he was had come by faith, and that faith was gift of the Father.

It is significant that the *same* challenges, revelations and graces of spirit and faith were offered to *all* who witnessed Jesus' words and works. But these did not automatically *assure* faith and/or commitment. Even Judas who eventually handed him over (v. 64) had been so graced but chose another route. Jesus-wisdom had invited and still continues to invite the hungry, the simple and the poor to be fed at the banquet table of his bread and of his word. To receive those great gifts, the Father's gift of faith must be met with a willing mind, a faithful heart and a committed resolve to hear the word and to eat the bread of life eternal.

1. The decision to follow the Lord is a personal one, lived out in the sheltering support of the community (Joshua).

2. Mutual respect is a moral obligation that springs from faithful commitment to Christ (Ephesians).

3. Ambivalence and rejection may not sit at the table of the bread and the word (John).

22nd Sunday in Ordinary Time

Never meant to be an end in itself, the gift of the law was intended to express and to safeguard the relationship of Israel and Yahweh (Deuteronomy). If perspectives become clouded, visions can be lost and the basic principle overshadowed by trivia (Mark). To preserve the value and mean-

ing of a gift, especially a God-given one, it is best to look beyond it to the giver himself (James).

Deuteronomy 4:1-2, 6-8. In the conviction of the Deuteronomic theologian, the Torah or law of Moses was for Israel a national treasure. Distinguishing it from all other nations, giving it an enviable and unique status, Israel's law was thought to be its claim to fame and fortune. Today, laws are regarded as a necessary and functional aspect of a viable society, safeguarding the rights of individual members and of society as a whole. But our ancestors in the faith regarded the law almost as a living entity, not created or formulated by human hands or minds but given by God as an act of divine favor and blessing. A source of wisdom and strength, the Torah was thought to bestow upon Israel not only life but even an *identity* as a people. As is indicated in today's first reading, the statutes and decrees of the law were regarded as the conditions or stipulations of Israel's covenantal relationship with God. Moreover, adherence to the law was closely related to the gift of the land, whose possession transformed the loosely united tribal amphictyony into a nation to be reckoned with. Subsequently, Israel's security and political successes as well as its pitfalls and failures were interpreted as functionally and proportionately related to the faithful observance (or not) of the law. Raised from the level of civil ordinance to religious and ethical response, the *lived Torah* was an act of faith and trust in the God whom Israel believed had enunciated it.

Excerpted from the prologue (vv. 1-14) to the promulgation of the law, today's pericope typifies the powerful exhortatory style of the Deuteronomist. The *Sh'ma, Yisrael* ("Listen, Israel," v. 1) signals the opening of a liturgical address (as in 5:1, 6:1, 9:7, etc.), indicating that the assembly of Israel was gathered to hear and to ratify the law as it would be read to them. Statutes and decrees (v. 1) or *huq* and *mishpat* were terms applied to positive decrees of law and judicial decisions made as a basis for case law.

The Deuteronomic author offered Israel several motivating factors for its faithful observance of the law: (1) *Life*, "that you may live" (v. 1). Conversely, the lawless were thought to be courting death. (2) *Land* (v. 1). (3) *Wisdom* (v. 6). *Hokmah* (wisdom) was a quality of virtue derived from the law. Perhaps in this *association* of wisdom and the law, we may find the roots of the process that eventually *identified* the law with wisdom (Proverbs 8:32-36). (4) *Nearness to God* (v. 7). Keeping the law was considered a means of intimate union with the God who was personally involved with the people of his predilection. The comparison of the nearness of the transcendent Yahweh to the gods of the other great nations (v. 7) would seem to testify to the antiquity of the text. The reference to "other gods" indicates the absence of the strict monotheism that emerged in the age of the classical prophets.

The prohibition against adding or subtracting from the law as given (v. 2) was a common feature with parallels in many documents of the ancient world (Code of Hammurabi, etc.). "Why toy with perfection?" is the attitude behind such a formulation, supported by the belief that the law as divinely initiated was sufficient unto itself as the source of life and wisdom. Perhaps this idea led to the exaggerated emphasis the Pharisees of Jesus' day placed upon the law. Those legal experts regarded the law as complete and eternally valid, thus giving it an underserved importance and absolute applicability.

James 1:17-18, 21-22, 27. Some of the cloud which has hung over the letter of James and has consequently obscured the author's contribution to the Christian scriptures can be dispelled if the reader understands the circumstances that precipitated the document. The controversy over the relationship between gospel and law remains a source of lively debate even today. Some looked to Paul's principal letters and exaggerated the apostle's stand on law by negating its value and role within the church. Law dictates behavior and has no place in the religion of freedom Jesus died to establish, said these early reactionaries. James tried to correct the misplaced emphases on Paul's thought and accentuated instead the practical and obligatory aspect of the gospel, calling it the "perfect law of freedom" (James 1:25). Unlike the misguided Pauline enthusiasts who also negated the value of works and preached of salvation by faith alone, James understood works as the "doing" aspect of a lively faith. For the next five Sundays the second reading will offer selections from the letter of James whose advice can be summarized: "Act on the word. If all you do is listen to it, you are deceiving yourselves" (v. 22).

Disputed from even the early centuries of the church, the authorship of the letter of James is still an unsolved mystery. As T. Leahy has pointed out, several factors would seem to indicate an author other than James, brother of the Lord and leader of the Jerusalem community of Christians. Written in excellent Greek (not James' language), the document is less like a letter and more like a treatise or sermon. There are no personal allusions, no indication of the Jewish-gentile conflict in which James had been so embroiled in the first decades after the resurrection. Listed by Eusebius as among the disputed books (*anitlegomena*), James was accepted as canonical only in the fourth Christian century. Because of its concern with post-Pauline antinomian developments and due to the fact that James died in 62 C.E., the document may have been written by a Hellenistic Jewish Christian and pseudonymously attributed to James. Those who accept this theory posit a late first century or early second century C.E. date.

Parenetic in style, the document was geared to avert the danger of an abstract and therefore, according to the author, unfruitful practice of Christian belief. The author's concerns were structured in a series of 12 exhortations based on the names of the 12 patriarchs (Genesis 49) and addressed to the 12 tribes of the dispersion (1:1). Greatly influenced by Jewish sapiential literature, the basic literary unity of the document has been described by K. Condon as a didactic "proverb-sequence" written in the imperative mood. Today's pericope is from the second exhortation addressed to Simeon.

Attributing all good gifts to God (v. 17), the author described the word spoken in truth as God-sent and life-giving. Some have identified this word with the Jewish law; however in the New Testament, word or logos has a more encompassing meaning. Word in the Christian context reaches back to include the law and the prophets but understands these as announcing a greater word—that of God's saving revelation spoken in the person of Jesus Christ and in the good news about him. Those who open themselves to receive this word in baptism are called to speak it forth in lives and deeds of faith. Like the Old Testament prophets before him, the author considered charitable acts toward the underprivileged (orphans, widows) as a requisite for true worship (v. 27). By believing and performing the actions of light and by relinquishing the deeds of darkness, Christians can become true children of the Father of heavenly lights (v. 17).

Mark 7:1-8, 14-15, 21-23. According to the Halakah, priests were required to wash their hands before eating as an act of ritual purification. Halakah (literally: how to walk) or the "Traditions of the Elders" as it is also called, was a compilation of unwritten legal interpretations of the law scrupulously and dutifully passed from one generation of rabbis to the next. Regarded by the Pharisees as binding and as authoritative as the written Torah, this oral law was not subject to the prohibition stated in today's first reading, "You shall not *add* to what I command you." By Jesus' day the Halakah had mushroomed into a veritable mountain of casuistry. So cumbersome had the collection of oral interpretations become that ordinary lay people were ignorant of the bulk of it and had to consult the scribes who had become specialists in the labyrinth of legal minutiae. Referred to colloquially as "fences around the law," intended to protect and to extend the law, the Halakah had become more like a *wall* that separated and alienated people from God and from true religion. Jesus criticized the misplaced attention the Halakah received and called it a "burden" (Matthew 23:4).

The validity of the Halakah was at the heart of the controversy in today's gospel. Jesus' teaching concerning the law reached further than the oral traditions of the rabbis. Indeed, he went beyond the oral law to challenge one of the basic principles of the written law, viz., the notion of clean and unclean (Leviticus 11-16). Sifting traditional ideas and categories, shaking up the status quo, questioning the value of laws that shackled instead of freed, Jesus brought to his world a new light for perceiving God and a new spirit of freedom in which to love and serve him. In that light and in that Spirit, he defended his disciples for their "untraditional" behavior.

Because the Halakah required handwashing only of priests in Jesus' day, the accusation the Pharisees and scribes leveled against Jesus' disciples may be a reflection of the Marcan church of the 60s C.E. Since contact with gentiles was inevitable, especially outside Palestine, the rules for ritual ablutions were tightened and extended to lay people. Mark's lengthy explanation of the custom (vv. 3-4) bears witness to the non-Jewish character of his intended audience. Probably at issue in the evangelist's community was the burning question: Must gentiles conform to Jewish traditions in order to become Christians?

Jesus' response to his critics and to those who found fault with his followers was based in part on the prophet Isaiah's oracle against the hypocrisy of his people, quoted here from the Septuagint (Isaiah 29:13). Because the pertinent phrase, "they teach as dogmas mere human precepts," is not in the Hebrew text, the gospel's use of the LXX would further indicate an interpolation of Jesus' basic argument by the Greek-speaking Christian community. Regardless of its origin and development, the argument is a powerful one and its message is clear. Human traditions, however ancient and dear, cannot replace or set aside the sacred precepts of God-given law. It is significant that Jesus did not negate the value of human tradition altogether but required that the system of priorities be rethought and reordered—so as to subordinate all else to the eternal reality of God.

Having dealt with the objections of the Pharisees and scribes, Jesus summoned the crowds and expanded his teaching (v. 14). His "hear me" (*shema*) is reminiscent of similar invitations in the Old Testament that called the people to attend to God's law. Earlier in his gospel, the evangelist had explained that Jesus, "moved by compassion" (6:34) taught the crowds. Perhaps that same emotion moved him in this instance; he was sympathetic to those who were overburdened by the law (oral) instead of being guided to freedom by it. Purity or holiness, taught Jesus, was not a matter of soap and water but of lived convictions based on deep faith. Nothing from without is capable of defiling the holiness that should spring from within. As W. Harrington has pointed out, there were no parallels in Judaism for this teaching of Jesus. Not only was Jesus' statement a departure from traditional thought but it set aside a large area of the Mosaic Torah as well.

The catalog of vices with which the gospel pericope concludes is a sampling of those things produced from within that pollute the human spirit. Lists of vices like this one (vv. 21-23) were regular features of Hellenistic Jewish literature adapted for use by the New Testament authors (Galatians 5:19-21, Romans 1:29-31, etc.). In the context of Jesus' teaching, the list of vices serves to illustrate the fact that the washing of hands, cups, jugs and kettles is no remedy for the corruption of envy, pride and arrogance. Only the interiorization of that washing and a heart cleansed by the truth of repentance can result in the purity that brings one near to God.

1. For Israel, the law was a source of pride and a reflection of a wise and intelligent people. Do our nation's laws evoke a similar pride (Deuteronomy)?

2. Gifts reveal the heart of the giver: God's greatest gift to us is Jesus Christ (James).

3. Even Shakespeare's Lady Macbeth understood that evil can be washed away only from within (Mark).

23rd Sunday in Ordinary Time

To those who could not see and to those who could not hear, the message of salvation was promised (Isaiah). Through the mouths of those who could not speak, the good news was proclaimed (Mark). Those who now possess the treasure of that news must share it indiscriminately and generously with all (James).

Isaiah 35:4-7. "Upon the Inferno, follows the Paradiso" was the descriptive comment of exegete Otto Procksch when he compared chapter 35 of the book of Isaiah to its preceding chapter. While these two chapters are distinctly different in tone, they are definitely related to one another and also to chapters 40-55. R.B.Y. Scott has suggested that Isaiah 34-35 are out of context in the book of the eighth century B.C.E. prophet Isaiah of Jerusalem, and may more properly by considered as an introduction to the work of Deutero-Isaiah, written by the prophet himself or by one of his sixth century B.C.E. contemporaries who shared the prophet's eschatological vision and theological insights. Like two sides of the same coin, the dark and desperate tones of chapter 34 are complemented by the lightsome and liberated quality of chapter 35. Chapter 34 is comprised of a series of judgments to be meted out in disasters of terrible and cosmic proportions, judgments that would leave Edom a ravaged waste of a land, unfit for habitation. In contrast, chapter 35 presents a wonderful vision of redemption, spelled out in health and well-being for humanity and harmony for an Eden-like earth. The same God whose judgment wrought havoc for the nations would bring vindication and bliss for Israel.

This notion of God as saving judge and bringer of peace is not unique to the book of Isaiah. Recall the book of Judges where, in episode after episode in a time of crisis, a judge (Gideon, Deborah, etc.) was raised up from among the people to act as Yahweh's regent. By the power of Yahweh's own spirit (Judges 3:10), the judge would lead the people to victory over their oppressor, after which the nation would enjoy a period of rest (Judges 3:11). In the historical context of the prophet Isaiah, the oppressor of God's people was Babylon and the time of crisis was the period of exile which God's people endured in that foreign land. While in former times a regent-judge had acted to aid God's people, the sixth century prophet envisioned *Yahweh himself* coming as vindicator and savior. Upon his appearance, the people long enslaved would be freed.

This liberation of the human spirit was depicted by the prophet in a series of dramatic physical healings. Blind, deaf and lame would be miraculously rehabilitated. Even the tongue of the dumb (*mogilalos*, v. 6) would be freed to render praise and thanks once again to their redeemer-judge. Later generations would remember this text and others similar to it (Isaiah 61:1-2) and associate these healings and this restoration with the long awaited era of messianic salvation.

James 2:1-5. Probably it never occurred to the first century author of James that his greeting "my brothers" (v. 1) and his several references to "men" (vv. 2, 3, 4) would cause him to be cited, some 20 centuries later, for discrimination—the very subject of the exhortation that comprises today's second reading! Not only James, but many of the scriptural authors exhibit their culture-bound frames of reference in which women were non-entities and, at best, subservient to male dominance. Occasionally, however, the spirit of freedom and equality, as well as the awareness of the personal worth and unique value of *every* person which Jesus brought to the world, can be perceived in the New Testament narratives (especially Luke and Acts).

James, however, in the historical context of the late first century C.E. was concerned with another form of discrimination, viz., the distinction between persons based on their economic success in life. Today's pericope from the exhortation, based on the name Judah (Genesis 49:8-12), is part of a longer section devoted to the larger subject of social discrimination. The author denounced this as entirely contradictory to and irreconcilable with faith in Jesus Christ. Today's lesson on the proper treatment of persons should be understood as illustrative of the letter's basic premise, "Be doers of the word" (1:22).

As believers of the word, Christians are called to a magnanimity of heart that would not base their concern for another on outward appearances. In the example given by the author, it seems that the persons described were not known personally by the community members but were being evaluated solely on the costliness (or not) of their attire and were being treated accordingly. Those who were well-heeled were treated with respect; those whose disadvantages showed in their appearance were not. Such behavior is unfortunately not a culture-bound tradition of first century mores but a sadly familiar scenario in any society where designer labels on the outside of the person's apparel seem to speak a louder and more impressive message than the person who wears it. To act in this manner, in any century, is to judge wrongly and corruptly by false standards (v. 4).

Because of the redemption wrought by Jesus, merely human and external norms of judgment have been rendered null and void. God's choice of the poor, the remnant or *anawim*, is a recurring theme of the Old Testament. These poor ones were the object of his special concern and were guaranteed an abundance of messianic blessing (61:1). This same emphasis on the poor appears in the literature of the Qumran community and was a basic tenet of Jesus' teaching (Matthew 5:3, Luke 6:20). With little to distract them, the poor were thought to be fully reliant on God and capable of responding wholeheartedly to the gift of faith, thereby becoming rich in the eternal treasures of the kingdom. Rather then the objects of community discrimination, then, the poor should be a source of edification, deserving of sincere respect.

Mark 7:31-37. Anyone with a map of ancient Palestine in hand will immediately perceive that Jesus' itinerary as described by Mark (v. 31) seems to be illogical and impractical. According to the text, Jesus' destination was the Sea of Galilee, which would have necessitated a southeasterly course from Tyre. Instead, Jesus headed north to Sidon and, after a circuitous journey, approached the Decapolis (Ten Cities) region near the Sea of Galilee from the east! Some have attributed this "faulty" geography to Mark's lack of knowledge of the area. But others, more correctly, have recognized in Mark's roundabout route a theological purpose. By his version of Jesus' itinerary, the evangelist has associated this section and the healing of the dumb man to the previous passage (healing of the Syro-Phoenician woman) and has provided a gentile matrix for the following pericope (feeding of the 4000 gentiles). With the series of wonders, worked in the context of the gentiles, the evangelist has succeeded in illustrating the universality of the call to salvation. As W. Harrington has observed, the healing of the man portrayed in today's gospel pericope has the added symbolic intention of showing that the gentiles, once deaf and dumb towards God, are now, because of Jesus, made capable of hearing God and paying him homage. They too have become heirs to the promise made to Israel and sharers in the freedom wrought by Jesus.

There can be no doubt that the evangelist had in mind the eschatological vision of Isaiah (first reading) as he formulated his narrative. A *hapax legomenon*, the word *mogilalos* appears only here (7:32) in all of the New Testament. It means stammerer or one with an impediment of speech. Only once does the word appear in the Old Testament, in the Isaian text (35:6) of the first reading. Not only does Mark's version of Jesus' healing echo the Isaian text but it also announces its fulfillment in the messianic activity of Jesus. With Jesus, the Jewish expectation of messianic blessings has been fulfilled in the seeing eyes of those once blind and the singing voices of those once mute.

As we have noted before, Jesus' act of taking the man off by himself (v. 31) in private (*kat'idian*) was usually a Marcan literary signal that what followed would be an epiphany or manifestation of Jesus' divine saving power. In this instance, Jesus' cure of the deaf-mute can be understood as a revelation of his messiahship and of the irruption of the age of salvation. The actions of putting his fingers in the man's ears and touching the tongue of the man with spittle were not unique to Jesus. Such actions were a common technique utilized by Jewish and Greek healers. In fact, the emperor Vespasian had been documented as having healed a person by the use of spittle.

Jesus' use of these traditional gestures was purely sacramental, i.e., they were not the *means* of the healing in themselves but merely the outward, visible signs of his messianic power. For humans whose perception is sensible, the gestures (like our sacraments) were vehicles that communicated the intangible, otherwise invisible and ineffable activity of God in Jesus Christ. By "looking up to heaven" (v. 34), Jesus exhibited his intimacy with the Father as well as the fact that his power to heal, or to cast out the "demons of deafness and stammering" (as was the contemporary belief), came not from Beelzebul but from above, from God. Opinion is varied concerning the sigh or groan (v. 34). Perhaps the sigh indicated Jesus' great sympathy for the people's need of healing and salvation. Or, perhaps, the sigh or groan was another indication of the belief of Jesus' contemporaries in demon-caused ailments. Spittle and groaning were common features, regularly used in exorcisms. In fact, if translated literally, the text describing the man's healing should read "his tongue was released" (as if from a demon).

With the word *ephphatha* (be opened), Jesus' action recalled the prophecy of Ezekiel, "On that day your mouth shall *be opened* to speak; you will learn that I am Yahweh" (24:26-27). In the action of Jesus and in the person of the dumb man, the world had received its sign and the proclamation of the good news of Yahweh's universal salvation. Recognized for their sacramental value, the use of spittle, the touching of ears, etc., and the word *ephphatha* were assimilated for use into the baptismal rite at a very early date.

Following immediately upon the wondrous opening of the man's ears and the freeing of his tongue to speak clearly, the enjoinder to strict silence seems contradictory and virtually impossible to obey. At the turn of this century (1901), W. Wrede pioneered the studies in this curious phenomenon and concluded that such commands to silence in the gospel of Mark are easier to understand as a literary device and an editorial effort on the part of the evangelist. Subsequently labeled the "messianic secret," this technique was invented by the evangelist and inserted into the gospel to explain why Jesus was not universally recognized and acclaimed as messiah during his ministry—especially after deeds as messianic as the healing of the deaf-mute.

Despite Jesus' (really Mark's) command to silence, however, his deed was proclaimed. Mark's use of the word *keryssein* for proclaim was ordinarily used to refer to the proclamation of the gospel (1:14, 13:10, 14:9). In telling of the healing of the man by Jesus, those who believe were, in effect, proclaiming the good news or gospel of salvation. The extreme amazement of the crowd underscored the significance of this event in Jesus' ministry and their "He has done all things well" served to put Jesus' work on a par with the creative action of God (Genesis 1:31). By his deeds and by his presence, Jesus had caused a new age to dawn, a new creation wherein all peoples could be freed from the darkness and silence of sin to be born anew in the life of God.

1. For a Christian to turn a deaf ear to the needs of the poor or to cast an unseeing eye on the plight of another is a contradiction in terms (Isaiah).

2. Discrimination leads to segregation. Segregation leads to alienation. Alienation leads to isolation. Isolation leads nowhere (James).

3. At times, to say nothing is to speak the clearest message of all (Mark).

24th Sunday in Ordinary Time

Shattering preconceptions, disappointing popular expectations, shocking the orthodox, he came. He brought to the cross those who loved but could not accept him, and in its shadow they began to learn the answer to his question, "Who do you say I am?" (Mark). In the mystery of innocent suffering endured for the sake of others, humanity glimpsed the loving kindness of God (Isaiah). For those so graciously and undeservedly blessed with salvation, the only worthy response is a living and a lived faith (James).

Isaiah 50:4-9. When Peter, in answer to Jesus' question, proclaimed, "You are the messiah!", he did not have *this* text of Deutero-Isaiah in mind. In fact, it is doubtful that any of his contemporaries looked to the suffering servant songs in an effort to define and formulate their messianic hopes. Composed by the prophet who was himself a victim of the exile, the four songs (42:1-4, 49:1-7, 50:4-9, 52:13—53:12) were intended as a source of hope and consolation during the time of Israel's national disgrace, to help Israel find sense and purpose in the suffering that threatened to overwhelm it. Named for their central figure, the servant songs painted for the people a portrait of one who did not in any way resemble the political, kingly and powerful warrior for whom the people had so long hoped and prayed. Rather, he appeared as even less than a man—not a leader but as one whose rights had been stripped from him. He was not hailed as king but was beaten and disgraced. He was not the subject of songs of praise but the object of jokes and scorn. In spite of his humiliation, the figure of the servant had been endowed with God's own spirit and would, by his suffering, effect peace and healing for the people. In the end, he too would be vindicated (Isaiah 42:1-2; 53:5, 10-12). But this "man of sorrows" (Isaiah 53:3) with buffeted face and plucked beard (Isaiah 50:5) was not the image that sprang to mind when Israel prayed for a deliverer.

In their original context, the songs were probably composed to help Israel see *itself* in the role of the servant. Through degradation and suffering, Israel could become for the rest of the world God's message of liberation and salvation. Some scholars have proposed that the prophet himself understood his mission in terms of the Lord's servant. Like the prophets who had preceded him, the author of the servant songs had a message to deliver which he had learned in docility from God himself: "The Lord opens my ear to hear . . . and I have not rebelled" (50:4). But his message was not merely a verbal one comprised of rhetoric and oratory, however forceful. Rather the prophet's *life* was to speak as loudly and as powerfully as his words. By enduring physical pain and abuse, by suffering human psychological and emotional persecution, he would become not only the vehicle but an integral aspect of the message itself. Through him Israel would be educated in the divine pedagogy of comfort and salvation. With the passing of Deutero-Isaiah and the end of the exile, the characteristics and vocation of the servant were associated with a *future* figure.

Significantly, Jesus did not fear to disappoint the popular messianic expectations of his contemporaries and identified himself and his mission with the sorrowful figure of humiliation and suffering, the Lord's servant. Like the servant described in today's first reading, Jesus' life was one of radical obedience and conformity to God's will. As with the servant, that obedience entailed undeserved suffering and the humiliation reserved for the most despicable criminals.

James 2:14-18. Contrary to the opinion that heated up various theological controversies, James was not refuting the Pauline doctrine of salvation by faith. Rather, the late first century author of the letter of James geared his admonitions and exhortations toward those who had misconstrued the thought of Paul, the result of which was an aberration of the truth, viz., antinomianism. Paul, like James, advocated a living and active faith which, because it had become integral to the believer's life, was manifested in ethical and moral behavior. Antinomianism sprang from a misconception of faith as a matter of the mind alone, i.e., mere intellectual assent to specified doctrinal beliefs. From this basic tenet came the implication that, since such faith was sufficient unto itself, moral response and ethical behavior were of no real account. Evidently, there were some believers in James' church whose faith had deteriorated into this shallow condition. These were those whose faith he pronounced "dead" (lifeless: v. 17).

The very heart of the letter and the precis for all of James' thought is today's second reading, especially v. 18. Dibelius thought it to be the most inscrutable text in all of the New Testament. Because of it, Martin Luther wanted the letter of James removed from the canon of Christian scriptures. Cast in the style of the Stoic diatribe, James' polemic against faith without works or without its external expression is powerfully and poignantly illustrated. To wish a needy person *well* and then to neglect the real needs of that person, the fulfillment of which would contribute to the person's *well-being*, this is like one who *says* "I believe" and then does not *live* and *act* accordingly.

James' example is not a situation found only in the first century. Many contemporary analogies spring to mind, e.g., to feel sorrow for the starving in Africa and to decry the condition of that continent's racially oppressed . . . and then to do nothing. Such a faith is lifeless. In the words of James, "What good is it?"

Although the jury is still out over the author's precise intention in v. 18, he seems to be producing a witness to further the argument he has just presented and to strengthen it. According to James, one who claims to have faith, but who does not corroborate that faith by living deeds has, in fact, no faith. And to those who accused him of an exaggerated emphasis on deeds, James countered that his works were the obedient and faith-filled implementation of God's revealed will in every aspect of life . . . and were therefore faith-in-action.

Finally, and in close alignment with the thought of Matthew's gospel, James warned that a lifeless or an unlived faith has no power to save (v. 14), i.e., from judgment. Like Matthew, James believed that, at the appearance of the Son of Man, judgment would be rendered, not on the basis of an intellectually perfect faith but on the basis of acts of faith-filled love and kindness. Those who had encountered the naked, the homeless, the hungry, the thirsty, the estranged and the imprisoned and had met their needs in faith and because of faith would receive the invitation, "Come . . . because in doing for these, you did it for me" (Matthew 25:31-46). Such an active and vital faith will lead to eternal life, whereas the faith that has remained unspoken in deeds will lay fallow and lifeless forever.

Mark 8:27-35. Integrally connected with all that preceded it as well as with all that would follow it, the episode at Caesarea Philippi was the theological turning point and literary center of Mark's gospel. Up to that point, Jesus' true identity had been shrouded in questions and confusion. Upon hearing him preach, the ordinary people knew he was exceptional and in possession of a unique authority, unlike any they had ever experienced, but they were unsure as to who Jesus really was (Mark 1:22, 27). His reputation spread throughout Galilee, but he was wrongly perceived as the mysterious figure of Elijah (Malachi 4:15) whom it was thought would herald the messiah. Others who had believed John to be messianic thought Jesus was the Baptizer revivified. Still others, recollecting the promise in Deuteronomy (18:15-18), thought Jesus to be the prophet-like-Moses. The Pharisees, scribes and Herodians (Mark 3:6) witnessed Jesus' works and heard his teaching and recognized in his radical ways a threat to their positions and prestige. In fear and resentment, these rejected him and plotted against him. Jesus' own disciples were filled with ambivalence toward him, hoping for a political messiah and confused by the image he conveyed to the people. Their lack of understanding, fear and doubt sadly punctuated the various moments of the Marcan gospel (4:13, 40-41; 6:37, 52; 7:18; 8:4; 9:6, 32; 10:35-40). Even Jesus' own relatives did not perceive his true purpose or understand his method. Thinking him to be mad, they wanted to protect him from himself (Mark 3:21). *Only* the demons and evil spirits truly recognized Jesus and identified him: "What do you want with us,

Jesus of Nazareth?" "I know who you are: *the Holy One of God*," "What do you want with me, Jesus, *Son of the Most High God?*" (Mark 1:25, 5:7).

But, at Caesarea Philippi, the confusion as to Jesus' identity was brought to a climax in the confession of Peter: "You are the messiah!" Thereafter, the evangelist devoted his gospel to the elucidation of that profound statement.

Some have downplayed the importance of Peter's declaration, citing it as a post-resurrection awareness, born of Easter faith and anachronized into the ministry by the evangelist. But others (V. Taylor, J. Klausner, etc.) recognize the confession of Peter as historical. "To deny this," claimed Klausner, "would make the whole history of Christianity incomprehensible. The story ought not to be interpreted as if no suspicion that Jesus might be the messiah had ever dawned on the minds of the disciples. Without some sense of his greatness, and a hope that in him ancient prophecies might be fulfilled, they were not likely to have forsaken all and followed him."

It must be admitted, however, that when Peter declared, "You are the messiah," his idea of what that title implied was not consonant with Jesus' conception of it. This is obvious from today's pericope which shows the apostle remonstrating with Jesus after Jesus had indicated that his messiahship was to be exercised in suffering and characterized by humiliation. Although the prediction of the passion (8:31-32) and those which would follow it (9:31, 10:33-34) were certainly reworked by the evangelist in the light of the post-resurrection faith, no doubt Jesus did bring to his messiahship an unpopular and unattractive notion. Instead of the political leader and powerful king of David's lineage for whom the people hoped, Jesus turned to the shocking, almost pitiable figure of the sixth century servant songs. To all who thought and who judged by human standards (8:33), Jesus' ideas were iconoclastic!

W. Harrington warns against exaggerating the triumphant and the confessional aspect ("You are the messiah") of the pericope to the detriment of the very difficult challenge to discipleship that is also part of the text. To do so would be to deserve the same rebuke Peter received. Jesus' "Get out of my sight" (*hypage opiso mou Satana*) was reminiscent of the temptation scene wherein the tempter and his ideas of a popular, powerful messiah were cast aside ("*hypage Satan*": Matthew 4:10). That Jesus understood his role and his mission in terms of God's standards (v. 33) is evident in v. 31 wherein he explained that the Son of Man *had to* or *must* suffer much, etc. *Dei* or "must" expressed the apologetic conviction of the first century believers and New Testament authors that all the sufferings Jesus endured—even the ignominy of the cross—were in accordance with the revealed will of God in the scriptures.

Closely linked to the revelation of Jesus as messiah and as one who would suffer is the invitation to discipleship. By summoning the crowds (v. 34), Jesus (and Mark) made it clear that the call to follow in the shadow of the cross was not reserved for the Twelve but was a challenge extended to *all* believers. In Jesus' day the self-denial required of a disciple entailed the relinquishing of preconceived messianic ideas and an acceptance of a suffering savior. In Mark's church of the 60s that self-denial included a recognition of the *whole* of christology—not only the wonder-working Jesus of the ministry and the risen Lord but also the seemingly defeated Jesus of Calvary. Today the conditions for discipleship are little changed. Renunciation of the selectively romanticized aspects of the person of Jesus, an indiscriminate, whole-hearted commitment to the contradiction of the cross, the counter-culture quality of Christian living: all are part of the believer's answer to Jesus' question, "Who do you day I am?"

1. The alleviation of suffering, especially innocent suffering, is a sacred duty (Isaiah).

2. It is far easier to talk about faith than to live it (James).

3. Part of Christian commitment is the daily evaluation and daily answering of Jesus' question: Who do you say that I am? (Mark).

25th Sunday in Ordinary Time

During his life, he received little official recognition. While he lived, the only thing ever written about him was the "criminal charge" hung above his head on the cross. Yet, his life changed the world: by his innocent suffering (Wisdom), Jesus Christ revealed to the world the mystery of God's ways of love, ways that find greatness in smallness and humble service to the poor (Mark). His way of true wisdom issued forth in peace (James).

Wisdom 2:12, 17-20. In the cosmopolitan seaport city of Alexandria, in the first century B.C.E., there was a wealth of knowledge to be had by the avid seeker of wisdom. Reputed to be the intellectual center of its day, Alexandria with its museums and many libraries attracted some of the greatest minds of the ancient world. Like its lighthouse, one of the seven wonders of the ancient world, the city stood as a beacon in the sea of academia. Founded by Alexander and named for him (ca. 322 B.C.E.), Alexandria was the capital city of the Egyptian Ptolomeic dynasty and later the site of the Roman government in Egypt. With Rome and Antioch, Alexandria was one of the ancient world's major cities and, with its 500,000 inhabitants, one of the most populous as well. In one of the city's five districts, the largest concentration of the world's Jewish population made its home. There, the Jewish scholars and philosophers (e.g., Philo) were able to exchange ideas and methodologies with their Hellenic counterparts. There can be no doubt that this intellectual interchange served as a partial impetus for the translating of the Old Testament into Greek. In addition to the Septuagint (LXX), the scholarly atmosphere of Alexandria greatly contributed to the composition of the book of Wisdom, from which comes our first reading for today's liturgy.

Written in Alexandria during the first century before Christ in fine Greek (although some believe chapters 1-10 were originally written in Hebrew), Wisdom was the Jewish answer to a Greek philosophical system that threatened to overwhelm and dilute traditional Jewish religion and culture. For its Jewish readers, the book served as an inspiration and as an encouragement to retain and preserve Judaism's monotheistic concepts and traditional values in the midst of a pagan environment. For its Greek audience, Wisdom offered—in their own language, thought patterns and literary style—a sophisticated and cultured presentation of the Jewish religion. Despite the enormous contribution Wisdom made to the Jewish world and despite its attribution to *Solomon*, the book was not included in the Jewish (or Protestant) canon of scripture.

Wisdom's first century B.C.E. date of composition precludes, of course, a Solomonic authorship. While the actual identity of the author cannot be known for certain, he (she) was probably a Greek-speaking Jew, familiar with the works of Homer, Plato, the Stoics and the Greek tragedians. Steeped in the Jewish scriptures, the author's work has been called a midrash or a midrashic homily: Meditating upon the religious and cultural-historical past of his people and reinterpreting that past in light of contemporary developments and circumstances, the author of Wisdom combined the best of Hebrew and Hellenic literary style and form.

Today's first reading is an outgrowth of the author's meditative consideration of Isaiah 52-66, wherein he shares the prophet's insights into justice and retribution. The picture of the just one portrayed in the reading seems to be based on the fourth servant song (Isaiah 52:13—53:12). A victim of resentment and unbridled antagonism, the just one is representative of all whose sincere search for God and for wisdom set them apart from the hedonists and epicureans of the ancient world. Like an external conscience, the goodness of the just one made the depravity of his contemporaries all the more poignant by comparison.

James 3:16—4:3. When Martin Luther called James "an epistle full of straw," he may also have wished that he could "huff and puff and blow it away"—or at least out of the New Testament canon! But the letter with its 108 verses of practical, moral exhortation has survived the test of time, scrutiny and continued controversy. Since the name of Jesus appears only two times (1:1, 2:1) in the entire letter, some have doubted its Christian origins. A. Meyer hypothesized that James was originally a Jewish-Hellenistic document that gave an allegorical interpretation of the names of Jacob's sons by means of a Jewish onomasticon (method used in composition whereby the first letter of each succeeding line, verse, paragraph or section corresponds to the letters in the alphabet or certain sacred names). While this artificial structure has been obscured by translation, the author of James did seem to base his work on the tribal names of ancient Israel (Genesis 49). This, however, is not sufficient reason to summarily dismiss the Christian tone and intent of the letter.

Today's pericope is a composite of two sections, drawn from different exhortations. In the first paragraph, the author has compared the fruits of true wisdom and the just deserts, as it were, of false wisdom. This section of the letter belongs to the seventh exhortation and some have proposed that Leah represents the false or earthly wisdom whereas Rachel is the counterpart of the true wisdom that comes from heaven. In the second paragraph, James has tried to discern the source of strife and discord within the community of believers. Drawn from the eighth exhortation (Gad), it is linked to the first paragraph through the proverb on the sowing and reaping of peace of v. 18. Implied through the proverb is the idea that real peace comes from true wisdom and fosters communal harmony, while discord and calamity are the result of false and empty wisdom.

Both sections are introduced by a question, with which James stated what he believed to be the issue and therefore the reason for his exhortation: "Who among you is wise and learned?" (3:13), and "Where do these conflicts and disputes originate?" (4:1). These questions reflect the problems of the late first century church. In the first case, some within the community thought themselves privy to a very special wisdom, revealed only to an elite group and withheld from others. As a result of this supposed special wisdom or knowledge (*gnosis*), this group set itself above the rest of the community. James cited this elitist group as frauds, who were not wise but proud and ambitious. True, heavenly wisdom, taught the author, would, like genuine faith, be discerned in the actions of the one who possessed it. True, interior wisdom would translate into exterior acts of generosity and compassion, marked above all by the peace it fostered.

In the second question concerning conflicts and disputes (literally *fights* and *wars*), James recognized the fact that external hostilities—whether between individuals, tribes or nations—are rooted in inordinate desires and jealousy. Such warfare exists because Christians either have not "asked" or have "asked wrongly" (vv. 3-4). In this instance, the Jerusalem Bible translation seems clearer: "Why you don't have what you want is because you don't *pray* for it; when you do *pray* and don't get it, it is because you have not *prayed* properly, you have *prayed* for something to indulge your own desires" (James 4:3-4). Similar to the exhortations to prayer in the synoptics (Matthew 7:7-11, Mark 11:24, Luke 18:1-8), the words of James reveal him as an advocate of peace and not war. His point is well made.

Mark 9:30-37. Legend has it that George Washington once enlisted the services of an artist to paint his portrait. After several sittings, the picture was completed and our first president was shocked to find that the artist had omitted from his rendering several of Washington's facial flaws, scars, etc. Immediately the chief executive ordered the artist to begin again and to paint what he saw, "warts and all!" Evidently, Mark was of the same mind as Washington because his portrayal of the disciples was often less than complimentary. Warts and all, the evangelist portrayed their lack of understanding of Jesus' person and mission. Without hesitation, he recounted their obtuseness, their fear and even their ambition. By contrast, the evangelists who wrote after Mark felt it necessary to tone down the negative and pejorative aspects of the Marcan tradition and to cast the disciples in a more favorable light. In today's gospel, with the second of the three passion predictions of Mark's gospel, the disciples' lack of comprehension may even have been exaggerated by the evangelist to serve several of his purposes.

First, as an integral part of each of the passion predictions, the disciples' confusion introduced further explanation by Jesus (and Mark) of the implications of the passion and of discipleship. In each of the predictions (8:31, 9:31, 10:33-34) the same structure appears: (1) prediction by Jesus of his betrayal, death and resurrection, (2) misunderstanding of Jesus' statement by his disciples, (3) elucidation of the implications of the cross for disciples. The fixed nature of the triple repetition seems an editorial effort on the part of the evangelist. Historically, Jesus understood his role in terms of the suffering servant (Deutero-Isaiah 42, 49, 50, 52-53) and knew the inevitable hardships such a mission would entail. Therefore, it is quite likely that he shared this fact with his followers. It is unlikely, however, that his ideas about his demise would have included *specific* references to the cross, and to scourging (9:34, 10:34).

Moreover, had the earthly Jesus made such clear statements about "rising after three days" (8:31, 9:31, 10:34), there should not have been such despair and disappointment on the part of the disciples when Jesus died. Obviously, the allusions Jesus made to his passion and death have been reworked by Mark for didactic and theological reasons. Theologically or, more accurately, *christologically,* the evangelist wished to focus not on the miracles of Jesus but on the cross as the sign and the means whereby the healing of the world of sin would be effected. There were, in Mark's day, certain false teachers who preached of Jesus as the divine and heavenly wonderworker and who wanted others to regard them as his representatives in a similar light. In order to counter this false christology and equally false idea of ministry, the evangelist utilized the triple passion prediction. With each prediction it became clearer that to walk in Jesus' footsteps was to be overshadowed by the cross and that the cost of discipleship would entail a total and unreserved commitment.

Ironically, Mark depicted the disciples on the way to Jerusalem and to the cross, arguing as to who was the greatest among them. Physically, they were with Jesus; they were following him. But spiritually and ideologically the disciples were far from him. To bring them near to Jesus' ideas and to his concept of ministry, Mark combined two sayings of Jesus (vv. 35, 37) that appear in different contexts elsewhere in the gospels. These two sayings comprise the point of the entire pericope, in this case a pronouncement story. Combined with Jesus' prophetic gesture of taking the child in his arms, the two sayings make it clear that discipleship will find its honor and greatness in service.

By means of a paranomasia (word play) the sayings (vv. 35, 37) are linked to the gesture of Jesus. *Talya* ("child" in Aramaic) can also mean "servant." To behave as a *talya* (servant) and to welcome even the least important (by worldly standards) *talya* (child), is to learn the reason for the cross and its lesson of discipleship. Moreover, to do so for the sake of Jesus is to serve not only Jesus but the Father as well. "For my sake" (v. 37) or "in my name" is a semitism for "in my power." By their service of the little ones, the disciples of Jesus would achieve, not the importance about which they had argued, but a share in the power of Jesus. If they could understand the power of the passion and the cross, they would also learn the mystery of the power of service and discipleship.

1. If the goodness of another causes us to be haunted by our own sinfulness, then the other deserves our thanks and not our scorn (Wisdom).

2. Wars are fought on battlefields but they begin in the heart. There, too, must begin the peace which puts an end to war (James).

3. Great and important positions are few and far between, but the opportunity for great service is an ever present opportunity (Mark).

26th Sunday in Ordinary Time

By the very fact of the incarnation, the mystery whereby divinity embraced all of humanity, the Spirit of God's loving and merciful goodness was unleashed upon the earth, not as the private option of one particular group or sex or nation or religious persuasion but for all peoples (Mark). Those called into the service of the Spirit are selected not by human convention but by the Lord himself (Numbers). For this reason, the poor and not the rich, the downtrodden and not their oppressors, the condemned and not their accusers will reap the harvest of eternal joy (James).

Numbers 11:25-29. To attribute Moses' collegial attitude to psychological and emotional "burn out" would be an error. In an oversimplification of the event, some have explained the appointment of the 70 elders merely as an effort to relieve Moses of the heavy burden of leadership by sharing his duties and responsibilities with those appointed. Actually, today's pericope concerning the sharing of the spirit (which God had bestowed upon Moses) with those delegated *and* with those *not* delegated is one of the earliest Old Testament attestations to the uncontrollable, free and unquantifiable nature of God's spirit. That the sharing of Moses' authority was understood as an act performed under the auspices of God is indicated by the presence of the cloud (v. 25). Today, we might speak of our awareness of God's presence in terms of conscience, inspiration, sacrament, conviction or even intuition. The Israelites described the reality of God among them in very tangible terms, viz., cloud, fiery pillar, etc. According to the Yahwist and Eloist traditions, the cloud was present outside the camp; the Priestly authors portrayed it in the center of the camp. Regardless of the precise location, the cloud or *shekinah* was conceived as a sign of God's nearness, his dwelling among his people.

Part of a longer section of the book of Numbers (10:11—20:21) that purported to describe the 38 years spent between Sinai and Kadesh, today's episode was precipitated by one of the several occasions of murmuring against Moses. In a barrage of bitter complaints, the people criticized his leadership and blamed him for the austerities of desert travel. Disenchanted with their lot they complained against the Lord whose anger was unleashed like a fire outside their camp (11:1-3). Still, they grumbled and berated even the gift of the manna, wishing instead for Egypt's onions, garlic, leeks and melons (11:4).

Nothing is known of Eldad and Medad except for this text in Numbers. Obviously their attainment of the gift of prophecy was recognized but regarded as suspect (v. 27). Because their gift of the spirit had *not* been received in conjunction with Moses, Joshua voiced the resentment and suspicions of the group and wished to censure the two "renegade" prophets. Notice Joshua's objections were against the *irregular means* whereby the spirit had been received. By sidestepping the orthodox and accepted *human* means, the gifting of Eldad and Medad illustrated the utter unconventionality and freedom of God's spirit.

James 5:1-6. "Long-range plans must replace short-term profit or our decline will be steep," says John Naisbitt in his best-seller *Megatrends*. Although Naisbitt was referring to the economic pulse of the nation and its ability to survive increasing global competition, these words could easily be imagined on the lips of James as he voiced his concerns about another economy (of salvation) and another pulse (spiritual). With an eye to the imminent parousia, the author of James encouraged his community to pour their energies into long-range plans. In other words, concern with eternal realities should replace worry over short-term profits such as material wealth, rich apparel, etc. To do otherwise, warned the first century writer, would be to entertain a sure and certain demise, Naisbitt's "steep decline."

Viewed in this perspective, against the backdrop of the impending eschatological climax, James' scathing attack on the rich is perhaps more readily understood. Consonant with his fellow scriptural authors in both the Jewish and Christian scriptures, James denounced riches and esteemed the poor. Wealth was denigrated, not because it was evil in itself but because *preoccupation* with riches tended to make the person less aware of others and their needs, less concerned with God's judgment and insensitive to the values of the gospel. Poverty, on the other hand, was not a good in itself, but seemed to foster reliance on God and a realization of responsibility for other community and society members.

In today's pericope, James' remarks against the misuse of wealth seem to be aimed particularly at employers (farm owners, landowners) who have exploited those in their employ by withholding their wages (v. 4) even after all their hard work at harvesting the fields. There is coming, admonished James, the ultimate harvest and the divine reaper will be the judge of all things living.

With several allusions to the Old Testament, James exhorted the wealthy of this world to rethink their values. "Fattened yourselves" and the "day of slaughter" (v. 5) recalled Jeremiah (12:3) who called Israel's attention to the proximity of judgment. The condemned and killed just man (v. 6) echoed the just one of the sapiential literature (Wisdom 2, 3) who was murdered by the evil in an effort to silence the accusatory voice of his goodness. Given the context of James' admonition, there may also be reference to the Wisdom of Jesus Ben Sirach: "To take away a neighbor's living is to murder him; to deprive an employee of his wage is to shed blood" (Sirach 34:22). For those who do these actions, James promised a harvest not of wealth but of decay, corrosion and fire. Those very treasures regarded as insurance against future need would be the instruments whereby the future of the evil rich would be lost.

According to W. Barclay, there were three main sources of wealth in the ancient world: (1) grain, (2) garments, (3) gold, silver. The wealth (of grain, v. 2) *has* rotted, claimed the author James. By using the perfect tense for this and the following two verbs (*has grown* moth-eaten, *have* corroded), the author indicated the *present* worthlessness of material possessions. Fine clothing and rich apparel were considered equivalent to money and traded as such in the ancient world. Garments were often given as gifts to people of high station. Recall Paul's claim that he had coveted no one's money or clothing (Acts 20:33). In the end time, indeed even now, taught James, these treasured fashions were no more than food for moths. So too, gold and silver, which do not really rust and were considered immutable by worldly standards, even these would be corroded unto nothingness (*katiasthai*). Their nothingness and valuelessness will be a testimony (v. 3) against those who have sunk all their efforts into short-term profits. In a world where high yield, short-term benefits are of paramount importance, James' words are food for long-range thinking and planning.

Mark 9:38-43, 47-48. Since illnesses and calamities of every sort were attributed to demons and evil spirits, exorcisms were commonplace in the ancient world. There were daytime demons and nighttime ones, those who attacked the head, the throat, chest, foot, etc. "Pazuzu" was thought to cause malaria; "Ashukku" brought death; "Lamashtu" was especially to be feared by pregnant women and "Gallu" was an amorphous monster feared by all. During Jesus' day, both Jewish and gentile healers effected cures by casting out the culprit demon, thus restoring to health and wholeness those whom today may have been diagnosed as epileptic, catatonic, deaf, insane, etc.

As disconcerting as it may be to modern theologians, the scriptures, especially the gospel of Mark, present Jesus as ascribing to the belief in demons held by his contemporaries. A child of his times and culture, truly immersed in the human situation by reason of the incarnation, Jesus embraced fully the beliefs and traditions of his people. Still, he brought with him the truth that *goodness* alone conquers evil; he was and is the source of goodness, the power over any demonstration of evil. This power he shared with his followers and they, in his name, i.e., in his power, cast out the "demons" that afflicted those in need.

Like Joshua in the first reading from Numbers, Jesus' disciples were threatened by and unsure of others who exhibited a similar power. Their complaint to Jesus, voiced by John (v. 38), revealed their intolerance of others and in some sense their arrogance. R. Fuller calls it "clerical arrogance" which refuses to recognize the charisms of others as valid and valuable. Jesus' attitude of tolerance and acceptance even of one outside the pale of the recognized college of apostles was a lesson, not only for his contemporaries during the ministry but also for the believers of Mark's community in the 60s.

Evidently the apostolic church faced similar problems and had to rethink its attitude toward non-Christian or anonymous Christian exorcists who claimed a relationship with Jesus and a share in his power through the works they performed (Acts 19:13-16). "Anyone who is not against us is with us" (v. 40), was Jesus' response to the activity of the strange exorcist, regardless of his visible adherence to the group. By this saying, he invited his followers to acknowledge as genuine the witness and works of all who called upon his name. Possibly, this could include not only those non-clerical or lay workers within the community but even those outside the recognized and orthodox fellowship of the visible church.

At first glance, the connection of the rest of today's gospel with the episode of the strange exorcist is not evident. Actually there is no logical subject or thematic relation among the four distinct elements of the gospel. Rather, there is a verbal linkage in the Greek text that has for the most part been lost in the translation. Appended to the exorcist episode by the catchword "in my name" (*en onomati*), the saying about the reward of the benefactors of the disciples appears in a different context in the other gospels.

The remainder of the pericope (vv. 42-43, 47-48) is comprised of a series of sayings also connected by catchwords. All are concerned with the dangers of sin and the need to avoid the occasions of sin at all costs. To cause another to sin (literally: to scandalize or to cause to stumble), especially one of the simple and poor who were the object of Jesus' predilection, was a despicable thing (v. 42). Death would be a preferable alternative to such a dastardly deed. Death by drowning was a Roman practice, abhorrent to the Jews. This fact plus the enormous size of the millstone as indicated by the evangelist, viz., the one pulled by a donkey rather than the smaller stone turned by a person, would point to the seriousness of the sin of scandal or of leading another to sin.

By means of the forceful semitic expression (vv. 43-45: cutting off of hand, foot, eye), the passage puts forth in graphic terms the necessity of avoiding even the *possibility* of being an occasion of sin for another. According to the rabbis, "The eye and the heart are two brothers of sin . . . the foot and the hand are its handmaids." While the gospel text does not, of course, suggest physical mutilation, there can be no doubt that the avoidance of leading others into sin, thereby alienating them from God and the community, was worth even the most radical self-sacrifice.

Gehenna with its unquenchable fire was actually the disreputable Valley of Hinnon, south of Jerusalem. There Ahaz had burned his sons as an offering to the god Molech (2 Chronicles 28:3). Manasseh followed suit (2 Chronicles 33:6) and the place became notorious as the scene of one of Israel's darkest periods (Jeremiah 7:31, 19:5-6, 39:35). During his reform, Josiah put an end to use of the valley for human sacrifice. He declared it unclean (2 Kings 23:10) and thereafter the Valley of Hinnon or Gehenna became a refuse dump where Jerusalem's garbage was burned. It was a loathsome place of endlessly smoldering fires and vermin. Gehenna had become a dread omen against the faithless (Isaiah 66:24), therefore the reference to it in the context of today's gospel is quite appropriate. Obviously the valley with its fires and worms lent itself as a ready metaphor to later Christian descriptions of hell as the place of eternal punishment. For believers of any age, it is far more desirable to concentrate on the cup of water to be given freely in Jesus' name in order to avoid at all costs paying the wages of sin.

1. Delegated authority is shared service, not diminished power (Numbers).

2. A long-term investment of self in fully committed service, with no eye toward earning (self-) interest, is the only commodity which will bear eternal dividends (James).

3. Even those without the appropriate lineage and acceptable credentials can speak the truth and do great works (Mark).

27th Sunday in Ordinary Time

When two individuals blend in a totally complementary relationship, that union forms the nucleus of a viable society. Blessed by God, their covenant is integral to his divine creative intent (Genesis). Called to respect and support that bond, Christians are challenged to a radical idealism and a seemingly suprahuman generosity (Mark). Strength, vision and grace are available to all in the caring love of our brother Jesus (Hebrews).

Genesis 2:18-24. Regardless of the recently renewed controversy over the matter, the scientific theories of evolution and polygenism have not been contradicted in any way by the authors of the primeval history. Nor can the scriptural authors be validly drawn into an argument to refute the scientific hypothesis of the gradual and progressive development of life and of those species that led to what we call today Homo sapiens. In keeping with their conviction in God's creation of all existing species, the Genesis authors' *theological* and *poetic* accounts of the creation of the universe and of humanity were not intended as scientific analyses of the then known world. Rather, in mysterious terms, the primeval theologians described (without the aid or knowledge of science) the manner in which humanity first appeared upon the earth.

Woman's equality with and partnership to man is spelled out in the story of her creation from a part of man, i.e., from the same substance (or species) and nature. *Sela'* or rib defies precise definition but there may be some relationship to the Sumerian where the same word designates rib and life. By this etiological explanation of the formation of the woman, the author has accented her role as helpmate and friend to the man.

Significantly, the Yahwistic theologian placed upon the lips of the man himself the acknowledgment of the value of the woman. Not legislated or revealed by God, her relationship to the man was expressed in his triple enunciation: "bone of my bone" . . . "flesh of my flesh" . . . "woman" (v. 23). Although this triple statement has been wrongly construed as an attestation to woman's inferior status with regard to man, it should be understood as the author's insistence upon the shared nature and integral union of man and woman.

Fuller has called the "therefore" (v. 24), which introduces the general principle with which the pericope concludes, the linchpin of the whole text. Given their complementary nature, their equal status and their shared humanity, the union of woman and man is presented as the fitting and fulfilling relationship of the two. Becoming one flesh means more than physical union. Flesh (in Hebrew, *nephesh*) means the whole living person in all its aspects: physical, psychological, emotional, spiritual. Regarded by the author as more binding even than the blood relationship ("a man leaves father and mother," v. 24), the bond of marriage was thought of as one ordained by God himself and as such it was indissoluable.

Hebrews 2:9-11. Solidarity is the key to understanding the second reading; it is one of the major themes of the letter to the Hebrews. By virtue of his incarnation, Jesus so united himself to the human condition that he became one with all who suffer, suffered for the sake of all and even experienced the ultimate human crisis—death. "For a little while" (v. 9, *brachu ti*, literally: "little bit"), the eternal Son became a part of time and space to effect the redemption of all peoples. By so doing, all the redeemed are free to enter by faith into solidarity with Jesus as brothers and sisters of the one Father.

Writing to Greek-speaking Christians of the Roman empire (perhaps to Rome itself), the author of Hebrews attributed the solidarity of all peoples with Christ and the mysteries of the incarnation and redemption to the gracious will or grace of God (v. 9). A few ancient manuscripts read "without" or "apart from God" rather than "through God's gracious will" (v. 9). Most scholars believe this to be the original reading that, because of its difficulty, a scribe may have changed in the interests of christology. Known to the patristic writers, the ancient manuscript's reading ("apart from God") was thought to refer to Jesus' sense of abandonment on the cross. As Dom A. Cody has explained, the variant reading, not retained in our present translation, can readily be explained "as an anti-Patripassian theological attempt to insist that it was only in his human nature, not his divine, that Christ suffered death."

By means of the innovative expression, "it was fitting" (v. 10), the Hebrews author argued that everything in the ministry and saving actions of Jesus was necessary because of God's foreordained plan of salvation. Because of the divine origin and intention of that saving plan, Christ was made perfect through suffering. *Teleioo* or "made perfect" does not imply a moral perfection achieved by overcoming personal sins and failures. Rather, the sense of Christ's being made perfect is teleological, i.e., perfect in that he has achieved a goal or fulfilled a destiny. The same verb *teleioo* appears in the Septuagint translation of the Hebrew scriptures where it refers to priestly consecration and translates the Hebrew phrase, "to fill the hands" (Exodus 29:9, 29, Leviticus 16:32). Representative of all peoples (v. 9), leader (v. 10) and consecrated priest (v. 11), Jesus Christ conducts all who journey through life's pilgrimage to heavenly rest and eternal sanctuary (4:11, 6:20).

Like its leader, the church is experiencing the "little while." For Jesus, this term referred to his earthly ministry. The "little while" his followers must traverse is the journey between the saving event of Christ and his second advent. On the way, during the little while between the two great moments of Jesus Christ, the faithful have no reason to fear or to lose hope. Our brother (v. 11), who has become a part of us (incarnation) and who has made us a part of eternity (redemption), is our priest and our leader.

Mark 10:2-16. As a recognized teacher with some following, it is not surprising Jesus was quizzed by the Pharisees on the subject of divorce. But those who questioned him were probably concerned with his opinion with regard to the Hillel-Shammai controversy over divorce. Divorce was not the only point of conflict between these two rabbis of the Pharisaic party. Hillel (50 B.C.E.—20 C.E.) was a Jewish lawyer from Babylon who settled in Palestine and founded a rabbincal school there which soon rivaled that of his contemporary Shammai. A liberal, humane and tolerant person, Hillel soon became a popular and well-liked teacher. Because he hailed from the diaspora, his interest in the temple and its cult was less emphatic than for those who saw the temple as the sacrosanct center of all. Because of Hillel's influence, Pharisaism gradually developed into a movement able to survive without the temple. Hillel's method of exegesis and interpretation fostered the detachment of the law from the realm of the cult and the incorporation of the law into everyday life. Shammai, on the other hand, was a strict and volatile aristocrat whose nationalistic attitude and austere elitist interpretation of the law did not survive the Jewish War.

On the subject of divorce, Shammai and Hillel both began from the basic text on the subject as enunciated in the Mosaic law (Deuteronomy 24:1-4). Implied in the text is the idea that a man could divorce his wife for *'erwat dabar* which means "the exposure of a thing" or "some indecency" which was interpreted by Shammai as adultery. For no other reason could a man hand his wife a writ of divorce and dismiss her from his home. Hillel gave the vague phrase a wide interpretation and permitted divorce on several grounds. A writ of divorce could be drawn up and served if a woman was a poor cook or if she spoke to strange men in public, griped about her in-laws in her husband's presence, and so on.

If this controversy was at the heart of the Pharisee's question as recorded in today's gospel, Jesus soon lifted the issue to a higher level. Rather than dispute the vagaries of the *grounds* for divorce, Jesus declared the Mosaic text to be *not law* but a dispensation from the law, a *concession* permitted by Moses because of the *sklerokardia* or hardened hearts of the people (v. 5). Rather than split hairs about nuances and loopholes in the legal code, Jesus forced the attention of his listeners: (1) first inward to their own insensitivity to God's challenge to morality, and (2) then outward to the greater principle of God's basic plan of creation (Genesis 2:24).

In typical rabbinical fashion, Jesus is portrayed by Mark as responding to the Pharisee's question (v. 2) with a counter-question (v. 4). Then in the fixed form of the rabbinic dialectic, he reduced to silence his interrogators with an ad hominem rejoinder. Calling on the only authority considered greater than Moses, viz., God himself, Jesus proceeded to show divorce as absolutely prohibited on the basis of creation. Made for one another as complementary beings, the union of man and woman resulted in a new and composite being. To breach that union was therefore a violation of God's inscrutable yet wondrous plan of creation. By this radical teaching that departed from Mosaic tradition as well as the thought of his contemporaries, Jesus was clearly attempting to restore marriage to its originally intended status as a convenantal bond between two persons. Though it may be difficult to accept, given the practice of our contemporary society, Jesus' absolute prohibition of divorce is widely attested in scripture (1 Corinthians 7:10; Matthew 19:3-9, 5:31-32; Luke 16:18).

Some have proposed that the absoluteness of Jesus' prohibition was due to the eschatological urgency of his preaching. With the parousia so imminent, the subject of divorce and its grounds paled into insignificance. Only preparedness for the kingdom and alertness to recognize it were worthwhile considerations. In time, however, the followers of Jesus became aware that the parousia was "delayed" and that their new life in Christ did not immunize them from sin and its attendant evils. This is perhaps the reason for the church's concessions to divorce already found in the late first century gospel of Matthew. Still, the original teaching of Jesus and its radical character cannot be ignored or diluted.

"Back in the house" (vv. 10-12), the private instruction of the disciples is probably a piece of Marcan editorializing in order to adapt Jesus' basic principle to the Roman matrix of his gospel. According to Jewish law, adultery always referred to the sin of a married woman against her husband. A man's infidelities against his wife were not considered adultery against her but only against the husband of the woman with whom he had consorted! But the Marcan appendix (vv. 10-12) to Jesus' basic teaching (vv. 1-9) extended the law to protect the woman's rights (as did Roman law). Therefore, the man who would marry again after dismissing his wife in divorce would be culpable of adultery.

In the second part of today's gospel pericope, also a pronouncement story, the radical quality of Jesus' behavior toward the children may pass unnoticed by those who belong to a child-oriented society. Children, like women, were usually seen and not heard, functional and necessary aspects of their society but not considered to have rights of their own. In the two sayings of Jesus that comprise the point of this story, it is clear that children are not to be hindered from coming to Jesus, who is *himself* the kingdom or the reign of God made manifest on earth. Moreover, their innocent and receptive attitude toward Jesus was to be emulated by all who would participate in the kingdom. O. Cullmann and J. Jeremias have proposed that the expression "do not hinder them" (v. 14) is a reflection of an early baptismal formula. "What is to hinder (*kolyein*) so-and-so from being baptized?" seems to have been part of the ancient ritual (Acts 8:36, 10:47, 11:17; Matthew 3:13-14).

1. Equal rights and complementarity (of the sexes) are not mutually exclusive (Genesis).

2. Because of Jesus, earth's wandering people are not aimless or alone (Hebrews).

3. Christians embrace the total gospel—both the bitter and the sweet (Mark).

28th Sunday in Ordinary Time

To reach the unreachable; to leap beyond the practical, the ordinary and the routine; to fulfill the basic requirements and then to look eagerly for more ways to be, give, care and love—to this Christ called those who would follow him (Mark). He who knows the human heart became a human word to speak to the depths of our human experience (Hebrews). He who is God's wisdom has stirred our human appetites with an insatiable hunger for eternal treasures and has endowed us with the capability for achieving them (Wisdom).

Wisdom 7:7-11. Despite his rather checkered reputation and questionable morals, Solomon had his priorities straight when he came to God in prayer. Successor to his father David, though not the qualified heir, Solomon was designated *Jedediah* ("beloved of Yahweh") by the prophet Nathan. Once he had acceded to the throne, Solomon eliminated the threat of competition by killing off most of his possible rivals. In an effort to cement his alliances with foreign powers, Solomon occasionally bowed to alien ways and customs. To accommodate his many foreign wives, Israel's third king dabbled in their religious practices, observed their feasts and courted their gods in a spirit of ecumenism above and beyond the call of duty (1 Kings 11:1-11). Nevertheless, even with his shortcomings, when Solomon stood in truth before God, he is said to have prayed, not for riches or fame or earthly power or even a long life . . . but for wisdom.

Today's first reading is rooted in the legendary figure of Solomon and is based upon the episode in his career when Yahweh promised to grant him whatever he requested (1 Kings 3:6-9). Purported by the Wisdom author to be part of the petition of Solomon, the pericope is actually an excerpt from a longer soliloquy in praise of wisdom. Identifying himself with Solomon, the sapiential author described his quest for wisdom, the treasure more valuable then any other.

To define precisely the concept of wisdom as understood by the author and his contemporaries would be a difficult task. In the Old Testament the idea appears to have had a rather fluid and diverse evolution. For example, those who fashioned the vestments for Aaron's ordination were said to possess the wisdom of their craft (Exodus 28:3). Carpenters who plied their trade with skill were thought of as having wisdom (Exodus 31:3-5, 36:1). A sailor's prowess (Psalm 107:27) at sea was said to be wise as was the skill of a professional dirge singer or mourner (Jeremiah 9:17). Not a respecter of persons, wisdom could be found in the wise advice of the sage as he served at the royal court (Jeremiah 50:35) as well as on the lips of the silver-haired old woman advising Joab on a point of military strategy (2 Samuel 20:16). In addition to these practical aspects, wisdom had an intensely moral and religious character.

Hebrews 4:12-13. If, as has been generally agreed by modern scholars, the missive entitled "to the Hebrews" was destined for an audience grown lax with regard to the gospel, today's pericope was both a powerful admonition and a challenge to renewed fervor. Most have proposed as its destination the city of Rome where one of the three largest Jewish communities of the diaspora was located. Deeply acculturated and acclimated to their Hellenistic environment, the Jewish Christians in Rome were exposed to a variety of religious persuasions, and the threat of syncretism abounded. H. Kosmala believes the letter was addressed to former Essenes who were tempted to lapse from their Christian faith into a Palestinian Judaism. Others posit the existence of apostates within the community whose presence eroded the zeal and faith of their fellow believers. Probably R. Fuller is more correct in his proposal that the addresses were an esoteric group within the church who had stagnated instead of growing to Christian maturity. In order to quicken the faith and to foster the growth of his readers, the author developed a positive and demanding Christian theology based analogously on Old Testament texts and concepts. One of the most important of these concepts, the crux of today's second reading, is that of the word of God.

Presuming all that had been revealed concerning the word of God in the Hebrew scriptures, the author described the power of God's word as a sword whose double sharpened edges have the dual capacity of (1) revealing God to the believer and (2) revealing the believer to himself. In the face of this dual revelation, there can be no stagnation or laxity because the word that reveals also judges with penetrating light and truthfulness.

As the conclusion of a longer section on heavenly rest, the two verses that comprise today's pericope are written in poetic style with the strophe complemented by its antistrophe. In the strophe (v. 12) the word of God (*dabar Yahweh*) is described as living and effective. Source of life, the word of God produces and gives life (Deuteronomy 55:32-47) to those who open themselves in faith and fervor to its power. Attested by the prophets (Isaiah 55:10-11) the efficacy of the word has been illustrated in the very history of Israel as a nation. Punctuated by the divine saving utterance, the story of God's people is a tale not merely of Israel's deeds and accomplishments but of the spoken words of the God who saves, redeems and provides for his people. In the antistrophe (v. 13) the author portrayed the power of the word to lay bare (*tetrachèlismena*) and to expose all to the light with an almost surgical swiftness and effectiveness.

Mark 10:17-30. "The man's face fell . . . he went away sad." With these two brief phrases Mark has written a telling and a touching commentary on the cost of discipleship and the challenge of following Jesus in a total and unreserved commitment. In the face of Jesus' radical invitation, the man's enthusiasm had at first virtually bubbled over in extravagant praise, then evaporated in disappointment and perhaps frustration. A pronouncement story on renunciation (vv. 17-22) and discipleship followed by the related passages, (vv. 23-27, 28-31), today's gospel pericope may best be understood as a form of catechesis on the Christian use of and attitude toward wealth.

In the first section of the gospel, the pronouncement story concerning the zealous man, there is an additional underlying theme: the inadequacy of the law to challenge the depths of the given and sincere heart. When the man approached Jesus, knelt and greeted him as "good teacher," his salutation was recognized as one that would have been appropriated for God alone. In rabbinical literature, God was often referred to as "the Good who makes good." Jesus' swift rejection of the title for himself and his referring of the man's praise to God is an indication of the fullness with which the eternal Son embraced his human condition. Later evangelists, e.g., Matthew, softened the rejection lest Jesus' denial of the title cast any doubt on his divinity.

As W. Harrington has observed, the man's question, "What must I do to share in everlasting life?", was an unusual one coming as it did from a Jew. As a faithful follower of Moses, the man would have been steeped in the tradition that the law gave life to those who kept its precepts. Implied in the man's question and in his approach to Jesus is the idea of the inadequacy of the law and perhaps a sense that even keeping the law in its entirety was somehow unfulfilling or unsatisfying.

Indeed, as the gospel illustrates, Christian discipleship was presented as an avocation that *presumed* the law as a requisite. By citing the *law* in response to the man's inquiry, Jesus drew attention to the social responsibilities inherent in the keeping of the law. Respect for life, person, family, property and truth were required of *all* who would number themselves among the covenanted people.

But the Christian covenant would make an even greater demand. Beyond the normative and the ordinary requisites of natural law, beyond the most compelling legislated responsibility to one's neighbor, the Christian disciple was called to renunciation as a means of generosity toward the poor (without judging their deservedness) and to a life of faithful adherence to the *person* of Jesus. In other words, the man was called by Jesus to surrender his traditional manner of serving God (law) and to launch out into new, uncharted and perhaps insecure waters.

Jesus' look of love (v. 19), unique to the gospel of Mark, is a clear attestation to the fact that the disciple who dared to follow Jesus would not find himself "up the creek without a paddle," as it were. With *love*, the disciple would be supported and strengthened by Jesus and by fellow disciples in the Christian community. However, the drastic nature of Jesus' challenge can be read upon the fallen countenance of the saddened man (v. 21). Unable to liberate himself from his many possessions (v. 22), the man was not free enough to respond to Jesus' love or to his invitation to go beyond the law to Christian discipleship.

Following the episode with the rich man, the gospel shifts toward a special instruction for those who have already made the leap toward discipleship. Usually such additions have been specially geared by the evangelist toward his readers as supplemental and explanatory teaching. In a series of two conversations (vv. 23-27 and 28-31) the implications of the episode with the young man have been drawn out and elucidated. The saying about the camel passing through the needle's eye and the impossible situation it presents served to underscore the radical and eschatological quality of Jesus' call to renunciation. In subsequent centuries, the extreme nature of this demand has been softened by Christian writers into a concept of a responsible stewardship of the earth and its riches.

Various possibilities have been proffered by way of explaining the camel and the needle. Some have suggested the needle may have referred to a small gate of the city (temple?) through which a camel could have passed but not without great difficulty. Others have suggested that camel (*kamelos*) was actually an error and should have read *kamilos* or cable. To thread a cable through a needle would be a Herculean task at best!

Distressed at the utter incongruence of riches and eternal life, and at Jesus' seemingly impossible call to renunciation and discipleship, the disciples, like the exuberant man ("What must I do," v. 17) inquired of Jesus, "Who can be saved?" (v. 26). In his answer Jesus (and Mark) affirmed the fact that discipleship, like salvation, is not a human achievement but a God-given gift: "For man it is impossible.... With God all things are possible" (v. 27).

In the final section of the gospel (vv. 28-31) the rewards of discipleship have been enumerated. Those who would freely divest themselves of riches for the sake of the kingdom would not be divested of everlasting treasures. Rather, disciples of Jesus who had learned to accept all as gratuitous gifts from God, and who had learned to prioritize those gifts according to the values enunciated in the gospel, would be compensated generously. Rich in the unquantifiable goods of the earth, i.e., in family, friends, fellowship, Christian disciples would be heirs to eternity as well. But, part of the inheritance of all who would follow the one who wrought salvation is the very real and harsh aspect of the cross (v. 30). Persecution, as the Christians of Mark's community had learned, was a concomitant part of discipleship and an inevitable companion for all on the way to the everlasting kingdom. In the face of persecution, those who rely solely upon their own resources will, like the man at the beginning of today's gospel, go away sad.

1. Part of wisdom is being able to recognize when a prayer has been answered (Wisdom).

2. Those who hear the good news learn of God and also of themselves (Hebrews).

3. With every call to sacrifice and service, there is also given a "look of love" and a divine caress of comfort (Mark).

29th Sunday in Ordinary Time

Jesus attracted many followers who clung to him because they saw in him the seeds of greatness. He invited those who hoped to share in that glory to follow him along the rocky road of humility and service (Mark). He challenged his disciples to an innocent love that would willingly suffer for the sake of the unjust (Isaiah). Such discipleship, love and service are possible because Jesus, who is one with his own, has led the way (Hebrews).

Isaiah 53:10-11. After Philip, the Hellenist missionary, had preached the good news of salvation to the Samaritan villages north of Jerusalem, he was inspired by God to journey southward toward Gaza and the desert that stretched between Judah and Egypt. On his way he met an Ethiopian official, the treasurer from the court of Queen Candace. A pilgrim on his way to Jerusalem, the official had been reading, though without full comprehension, the scroll of the prophet Isaiah, specifically the fourth song of the servant of the Lord (53:7-8). "About whom, pray, does the prophet speak, about himself or about someone else?" the Nubian inquired of Philip (Acts 8:34). With Philip's explanation that Jesus by his saving action has fulfilled the words written by the prophet, the Ethiopian came to faith and was incorporated through baptism into the community of believers. Indeed, as R. Fuller has observed, the fourth servant song (Isaiah 52:13—53:12), from which today's first reading is excerpted, contributed three very important features to the primitive church's perception of the crucifixion: (1) Isaiah's song aided Christians in their understanding of Christ's suffering as innocent, vicarious and redemptive; (2) the universal scope of the servant's mission ("for many") was seen as a prefiguration of cosmic dimensions of Jesus' saving work; (3) the servant's promised vindication (v. 10), when compared to the glorification of Jesus, offered the early community a means for understanding the resurrection in relation to the cross.

Prior to the Christ-event, however, a variety of solutions would have been offered to the Ethiopian official concerning the identity of the moving figure in the Isaian songs. Written during the Babylonian exile and later added to the prophet's work, the four servant songs may have been conceived as a description of the author's own vocation and mission to his people. Or, given the sad situation of Israel—bereft of honor, homeland and hope in Babylon—perhaps the author wished to offer his compatriots a means of making sense of their tragedy. By associating themselves with the figure of the servant, the exiled people of Israel may have been able to learn through their suffering and to see it as somehow having value and merit. There is evidence that some Jews in the pre-Christian era interpreted the songs messianically and applied them to a future figure who would be a savior for Israel and all the nations. Remarkably, the Qumran community did not seem to know of the tradition of the servant; and in the Targums the person of the servant was perceived as an enemy!

Although the expression, "the Lord was *pleased* to crush him in infirmity" may sound sadistic to modern readers, this was far from the author's intention. As Stuhlmueller has pointed out, the idea behind the word "pleased" is that of a strong and determined love. Rather than sadism, the reader should understand that the loving will of a caring God permitted the gift of the innocent life. Because of the sin offering (*'asam*) made in the vicarious suffering of the faithful servant, "many" (v. 11) would be justified and the servant himself would be vindicated. "Many" is a semitism for *all*, and early Christians found in this text a means for solving some of the scandal attached to Jesus' ignominious death as a criminal on the cross. Because of this and similar texts, early Christian apologists could perceive Christ, not as a victim of circumstances but as a willing and perfect gift. They understood the crucifixion not as an execution but as a freely offered sacrifice, willed by God for the salvation of all peoples. Moreover, early believers were led to see the passion and even their *own* suffering for the sake of discipleship not as the waste of human energies and the alienation of peoples but as a vital redeeming force to unite all peoples forever in God.

Hebrews 4:14-16. Although the origins of the priesthood among the Israelites are difficult to trace with absolute certainty, there is sufficient evidence to indicate that the priestly office included the following functions: (1) priests were mediators and interpreters of oracles thought to be the means whereby God communicated his will to the people (Deuteronomy 33:7-11); (2) knowledgeable in the intricacies of the law, the priests had the task to educate and instruct the people (Deuteronomy 33:10); (3) as the mediator between God and the believing community, the priest offered sacrifice in his own name and for the benefit of all the people (Deuteronomy 33:10). Little is known of the pre-exilic priesthood. What has been documented in the scriptures concerning the priestly office should be recognized as an anachronism based on later developments.

In the post-exilic period, the priesthood flourished, and the office of high priest took on great political and religious importance. As leader and guardian of the sacred cult, custodian of the historical and theological traditions of his people, president of the Sanhedrin and chief liaison between his people and the Roman occupying forces (37 B.C.E. onward), the high priest was, at the time of Jesus, the most important person in the Palestinian Jewish community. It is not at all surprising, therefore, that the author of Hebrews chose to compare Jesus and his work upon earth to that of Israel's high priest. While clarifying Jesus' superiority over his clerical counterpart, the Hebrews' author underscored the fact that, because of the appearance of Jesus and the perfect fulfillment of his priestly role, the Israelite priesthood with its system of sacrifices and so on would be defunct. For those of his community who were tempted to lapse from their Christian faith in apostasy or back into the Judaism whence they had come, the author's words were a challenge to persevere.

Like the high priests of Israel, Jesus was representative of the people but, unlike the high priests of Judaism, Jesus did not approach the throne of grace (holy of holies) alone. Because of his saving action and perfect sacrifice, humanity need no longer send one from among them to offer an *animal* in holocaust for sin or fear to approach the holy one. With Jesus' perfect sacrifice on the cross, sins have been forgiven and the walls of alienation and separation sin had built have been forever destroyed. With Jesus, *all* have been rendered capable of drawing near to the God of our faith to receive mercy, favor and help (v. 16).

In Israel's cultic practice, when the high priest would approach the altar to offer sacrifice, he had first to offer a sacrifice for the sins of his own making (Leviticus 4-5). Though plunged fully into our human condition by virtue of the incarnation, and therefore vulnerable to temptation, Jesus did not succumb to weakness. Clearly, the Hebrews' author had in mind the gospel tradition concerning the tempting of Jesus in the desert. By means of the Greek participle *pepeirasmenon* ("tempted": v. 15), used in the perfect tense, the author indicated those temptations did not occur on one occasion only but were a constant presence to be dealt with. But because Jesus did not sin, all who believe are granted access to God. With Jesus' unequivocal victory over sin and death, the throne of God that had seemed transcendently inaccessible has become a throne of grace to be approached with confidence (v. 16).

Mark 10:35-45. Peter stands out in the gospels as an example of one whose impulsiveness and cowardly denials could be transformed into vibrant faith and courageous service. Thomas also appears as a source of consolation for those who pass from periods of doubt to deeper faith. So too, the figures of James and John, the sons of thunder (Zebedee), stand as poignant illustrations of God's power to channel blind, self-serving ambition into loving Christian service. The request of the two brothers for places of honor in the kingdom reflected the common expectation of their contemporaries for a messianic kingdom of political and temporal dimensions. Integral to that expectation was a vision of Israel restored to her former greatness, with the 12 tribes once more exercising their authority with vigor. As representatives of the 12 tribes, the disciples hoped to share in Jesus' glory, and James and John evidently wished to share a little more fully than the others.

The disciples' incomprehension of Jesus' purpose and of the quality of his kingdom is blatant in this episode and has been a constant theme in Mark's gospel. Significantly, Matthew, who wrote later (80s), spared the two brothers by attributing their request for greatness to their mother (Matthew 20:20-21) while Luke omitted the story entirely. Mark, however, made great use of the disciples, their faults and foibles as symbols to illustrate to his own community the dangers and pitfalls of discipleship.

In today's reading, which concludes the central section of his gospel (8:22—10:35), Mark has focused on two of his pastoral concerns, viz., (1) the dangers of erroneous christology and eschatology, (2) the integral part *persecution* and service must play in discipleship. For those in his community who misconstrued Jesus as the *theios aner* or divine man and who in their fascination with this concept ignored the cross, Mark portrayed (through the conversation between James, John and Jesus) Jesus as one who would not only work wonders but who would also suffer and die. "Can you drink the cup I shall drink," Jesus asked them (v. 38). In the Old Testament the full cup was both a symbol of wealth (Psalm 23:5, 116:13; Jeremiah 16:7) as well as of woe (Psalm 75:9, Isaiah 51:17, Lamentations 4:21). Clearly it has been used in today's gospel as a symbol of woe, viz., Jesus' passion and death (John 18:11, Luke 22:20, Hebrews 9:15). For those who wished to taste of his glory, Jesus promised also a cup of bitter suffering that his disciples, like their master, would drink to the dregs.

"Baptism in the bath" (v. 39) does not in this case refer to sacramental baptism but rather to the experience of an almost overwhelming calamity and suffering (Psalm 42:7; 69:2; Isaiah 43:2). With surety, Jesus could promise a share in his cross for all who would be his followers, but *only* the Father could decide to reward with glory those who persevere in faith (v. 40). Here with regard to knowing the time of the coming of the eschaton (13:37), Jesus subordinated, in perfect obedience, his will to that of his Father.

Following the rather naïve request of the two brothers, Mark has appropriately included a lesson on true discipleship and its demands. Exploding their pipe dreams of self-importance and greatness, shattering their illusion of thrones, scepters and political prestige, Jesus endowed his disciples with an authority to be exercised in service. Paradoxically, those who would be *great* in the kingdom Jesus proclaimed would seem to be the last of all and the least among all. Jesus challenged his own to look at life—not from the top downward, peering over the heads of others in a pseudo-sovereignty, but from life's underside, from the seamy, less appealing aspects. They must look, not *down* but *up*, into the faces of the poor, the needy and the suffering to offer them the service they deserve as God's precious little ones.

In concluding his explanation concerning true greatness, Jesus offered himself, Son of Man, as an example of service. J. Jeremias has suggested that Jesus reserved these special instructions on discipleship and the special teaching concerning the association of the Son of Man with the suffering servant (Mark 10:45, Isaiah 53:10-11) for the 12 alone. This would explain, says Jeremias, why Jesus was not widely recognized as messianic during his ministry. Probably, it is more correct to attribute the association (Son of Man equals suffering servant) to the apologetic efforts of the early church. Nevertheless, this does not diminish the fact that Jesus himself perceived his mission in light of the Isaian figure of vicarious and innocent suffering. In that light, he gave his life in ransom for all.

Ransom or *lytron* was originally a term employed in the field of commerce. *Lytron* was the specified price paid to redeem a pledge or to recover an object that had been pawned. It was also applied to the amount of money (or goods, etc.) required to free a slave. Mark has used the term in his gospel to recall for his listeners the same term in the fourth servant song (Isaiah 53:10-11). As V. Taylor has observed, "It is wise never to forget that '*lytron*' is used *metaphorically*, but it is equally wise to remember that a metaphor is used to convey an arresting thought. Jesus died to fulfill the servant's destiny and his service is that of a vicarious and representative suffering. We are ill-advised if we seek to erect a theory based on Mark 10:45 alone, but equally so if we dismiss it as a product of later theological construction."

Jesus' death was not a prescribed payment or an act of crass commerce. Rather, by his cross and by the stripes he bore for our healing, he has snatched from the jaws of destruction those who would otherwise have perished. Perhaps a better use of time and energy would be spent in examining, not the theological difficulties inherent in the word *lytron* but in the implications of Jesus' statement, "It cannot be like that with you." Is the paradox of "greatness-and-authority-exercised-in-service" still alive in the church that professes to belong to the Lord Jesus Christ?

1. Suffering is never an appealing idea—but to suffer innocently because of another is shocking to the human sense of justice (Isaiah).

2. A basic element of effective ministry is oneness with those who are to be served (Hebrews).

3. Discipleship means leadership without domination and service without condescension (Mark).

30th Sunday in Ordinary Time

What did the blind man see that caused him to cry out to Jesus for mercy? Why did those who saw Jesus seem blind and uncomprehending? The irony of this conundrum powerfully preaches the gospel of faith and discipleship in Jesus' kingdom (Mark). In the hands of the humble and the poor will be the reins of power (Jeremiah). On the head of one who became weak and dishonored for the sake of all others will be the crown of glory (Hebrews).

Jeremiah 31:7-9. An oasis of respite and relief amid Jeremiah's otherwise pessimistic commentary on the moral turpitude of his contemporaries, today's first reading is a celebration of Yahweh's mercy and love. Excerpted from a longer section (30:1—31:40) concerning the restoration of the nation, this text is the second in a sequence of four poems that most scholars believe were circulated separately and added later to the work of the prophet. There is no general agreement concerning the exact date and circumstances of the pericope. Some have proposed an early writing and suggested the prophet was writing about the northern kingdom and its demise at the hands of the Assyrians in 721 B.C.E. Others, probably more correct, have presumed a composition later in the prophet's career; in that case, the text pertained instead to the fall of *Judah,* its exile in disgrace and finally its joyful return home. Written in the first person, with Yahweh himself as the speaker, today's pericope is a description of the returning exiles after their years of sorrow and shame. Similar to Psalm 126, Jeremiah's poem describes both the "before and after" attitudes of the people and attributes the joy that erased their tears solely to the loving deliverance of their Lord.

Jeremiah had propounded the unpopular view that the Babylonian exile was a deserved consequence of his people's infidelity to their covenantal obligations. Accordingly, the prophet looked upon the Babylonians, not as an enemy force to be hated and despised but as an instrument, albeit an unknowing one, in the hands of a loving but castigating God. Such an uncomplimentary evaluation of world events and of his nation's situation earned for the prophet the resentment and oftentimes the hostility of his fellow Jews. However, once his people had received the bitter punishment their actions had merited (i.e., the exile), the prophet transformed the blunt severity of his message into a balm of soothing comfort.

In a style similar to Deutero-Isaiah (Isaiah 40:3-5; 41:18-20; 43:1-7), Jeremiah shared with his people a vision of homecoming that paralleled in joy and triumph their first exodus from Egypt's slavery. Again the people of God would march through the desert, but in this second journey only a remnant (*anawim*) would find their way home. Constituted of the blind, the lame, pregnant and nursing mothers, the returning people would represent those who had survived the rigors of the exile and who had been miraculously rescued. The weakness and vulnerability of the group is a clear attestation to the miraculous quality of the return.

Moreover, the fact that the remnant could not have effected their own release underscored the faith of the prophet in God's providential power to save in spite of seemingly insurmountable obstacles. To that end, Jeremiah's vision of the return provided hope for his people even in the darkest days of their hopelessness and estrangement. A. Gelin's excellent book *The Poor of Yahweh* has provided modern believers with an excellent assessment of the theology of the return and of the spirituality of trust and dependence derived therefrom.

On level roads, refreshed by brooks of water (v. 9), the remnant would be led home by their shepherding, fatherly God. Both images, shepherd and father, combined with the special care given to the weak and the unprotected (blind, etc.), became synonymous with the era of messianic expectation. For this reason, the works Jesus performed, particularly the healings of the blind (as in today's gospel), the deaf, the lame, etc., were emphasized by those who proclaimed the good news. By affording healing and salvation to the poor ones of Yahweh, Jesus proclaimed by his ministry the realization of the *ultimate* return. Jeremiah's vision of Judah's return to Jerusalem was but a faint glimmer of joy compared to the victory of Jesus' returning to his Father fresh from his triumph on the cross, with all his brothers and sisters accompanying him.

Hebrews 5:1-6. A complex phenomenon that underwent evolution, the ancient Near Eastern world's system of sacrificial worship is difficult for the contemporary believer to fully appreciate. Israel's neighbors offered gifts to the gods for a variety of reasons. Basic to all the sacrifices was the particular concept of the deity the people entertained. That concept determined both the type of sacrifice and the attitude with which it was offered. For example, those who perceived their god(s) as a cruel and uncaring despot, for whom humanity was but a source of sadistic entertainment, offered gifts to appease his anger and to dissuade him from acts of aggression they attributed to him. Those who desired to share in their god's power sought to forge a union with that god and offered sacrifices in a *do-ut-des* attitude. With a motivation scarcely short of bribery, sacrifices were thought of as a payment for a blessing desired.

Among the Israelites, however, the entire system of sacrificial worship was illustrative of higher and more idealistic view of God and of life. Gifts were offered to the God who was perceived and acclaimed as *the* one, *the* holy, *the* supreme and *the* transcendent. By his offering, the giver acknowledged the infinite dominion and goodness of the one who had provided the gift in the first place. Sacrifices in Israel were ideally supposed to be sacramental in character—exterior or outward signs of an internal reality, viz., a heart full of faith, acceptance, trust and gratitude. Gifts were brought to God in praise, to express the desire for union, to give thanks and to make expiation for sins and failure.

Two of the most important Hebrew words for an offering or a sacrifice embody the rationale for all of Israel's gift giving to her God: "to bring near" (*qarob*) and "to make rise" or "to offer up fitting praise" (*'olah*). In the earliest practice, the head of the family offered sacrifice for his own, but in later times the priests of Israel were delegated to offer sacrifice for all the people. As representatives of the nation of God's chosen ones, when the occasion warranted it, they offered to God sacrifices for their own and for their people's sins. With this understanding of the Israelites' sacrificial system and of the function of the priest, the author of the letter to the Hebrews proclaimed the *superior* role of Jesus Christ as both sacrifice and priest.

Unlike the Jewish priest or levite who represented only the people of Israel, Christ—by virtue of his incarnation—has become representative of *all* of humanity. One with us in flesh and blood in pain and suffering, he has an empathy that causes him to *metriopathein* or "to deal patiently" with the erring (v. 2). A term that appears nowhere else in the scriptures, *metriopathein* may have been derived from a term in Stoic philosophy that signified the right balance between passion and a lack of feeling. As part of the "stuff" of human existence, Christ is representative par excellence of human need before the Father. While the high priest was appointed from among human beings and by them, Christ's priesthood merited a far superior status because the appointment and designation have come *from God himself* (v. 5).

Drawing upon the psalms (2:7; 110:4) to support his argument for the superiority of Christ's priesthood, the Hebrews' author joined the company of New Testament writers who saw in these particular references a basis for understanding the glorification of Jesus as part of God's foreordained plan. As R. Fuller has observed, these citations underscore the early church's understanding that Christ's priesthood flowed not only from the sacrifice of his passion and cross but also from his exaltation in glory whereby his priesthood was both divinely proclaimed and perfected. For Christians, the reality of Christ, his perfect sacrifice and superior priesthood signaled the obsolescence of offerings of animal, grain, oil, etc. With Christ and in him, all can draw near to God in confidence, because our priestly representative is one who knows us as we are and has loved us unto death and forever.

Mark 10:46-52. Up to this point in Mark's telling of the good news, only demons and evil spirits had actually recognized Jesus and proclaimed him for what he truly was. Up to this point in the first gospel, those who should have had eyes to see and hearts to believe, i.e., the disciples, had been for the most part both blind and uncomprehending of the true meaning of Jesus' messiahship and of his kingdom. But on the outskirts of Jericho, on the last leg of his journey to Jerusalem and near the climax of his career, Jesus was recognized, proclaimed and understood by the blind son of Timaeus. With this story of the cure of Bartimaeus, Mark has formed an inclusion with the story of another blind man's healing (8:22-26) earlier in his gospel. The first healing marked the beginning of that journey to Jerusalem and the second healing appears at the end of that journey. On the way, the blindness of the disciples had been a poignant theme but, in the story of the healing of Bartimaeus, the gospel has portrayed an example of a true and faithful disciple. Healed by Jesus and confirmed in his faith, Bartimaeus became a follower of Jesus on the way to Jerusalem.

Jericho, a city of Judah about 15 miles northeast of Jerusalem, was a frequent stop for travellers on their annual pilgrimages to Jerusalem for the major feasts. As such, it was a strategic spot for those in need who would plead their cause with the pilgrims in the hope that the religious spirit of the feasts would spark their generosity. Such was probably the case with Bartimaeus during that last Passover season of Jesus' life. Only Mark has provided the name of the blind man and has told his story in such vivid detail. This would suggest, perhaps, that Bartimaeus was known among the early Christian believers as one whom Jesus had restored to sight.

The contrast between Bartimaeus' request of Jesus and that of James and John in last week's gospel is striking. While the disciples who misconstrued Jesus' messiahship requested a share in his glory which they hoped to enjoy in temporal and material abundance, the blind man recognized Jesus, understood what his messiahship meant and begged for sight. He called out (literally: "he *cried* out") to Jesus, and acclaimed him as Son of David. Mark has used the same verb (cry out) in several other places in his gospel, all of which pertained to manifestations of Jesus' transcendence and messianic power (1:24; 3:11; 5:7; 9:24-26; 11:9). "Son of David" had become by Jesus' day a title rich in messianic significance. To apply it to Jesus of Nazareth indicated that *in him* the promise Yahweh had made to David through the prophet Nathan had been fulfilled (2 Samuel 7:12-16). To see in Jesus, the humble healer on his way to Jerusalem, the qualities of kingship and eternal sovereignty was truly a sign of deep insight and an act of profound faith.

Moreover, the request of the blind man for pity (v. 47) and for sight (v. 51) was a further indication of the man's accurate understanding of the nature of Jesus' reign. Opening the eyes of the blind was thought to be one of the works to be performed by the messiah (Isaiah 29:18; 32:3; 35:5). Therefore, in Jesus' action of healing, the true nature of his messiahship was illustrated and it served, as well, to proclaim his reign. In similar healings that had preceded this one, Jesus had enjoined the person to silence (1:43, 3:12, 5:19, 8:22-26). In the case of Bartimaeus, however, the *onlookers* attempted to silence Bartimaeus, yet Jesus tacitly accepted the acclaim and worked the cure expected of him as messiah, Son of David. This surprising reversal of the messianic secret motif would be repeated in the triumphal entry of Jesus into Jerusalem (11:1-11) and in the centurion's climactic act of faith at the foot of the cross (15:38).

Although no details have been provided in the gospels as to the way in which Jesus healed the man (spittle, mud, etc.), the true meaning of the event has been perfectly encapsulated in Jesus' statement: "Your faith has healed you" (v. 52). As in the story of the woman (5:34) with the hemorrhage, the healing of the person implied their salvation also. The verb *sozo* means "healed" as well as "saved." Hence, your faith has *healed*, your faith has *saved* you. Faith (*pistis*) was the necessary prerequisite for all of Jesus' acts of healing and salvation. As P. Benoit has defined it, *pistis* or faith involves a "receptivity to God's healing word, proclaimed by Jesus together with a self-abandonment to God, whose saving power was exercised in and through Jesus."

Instructed by Jesus to "be on your way," the healed Bartimaeus followed Jesus up the road. He had believed, understood, been healed and had made *his own* the way of Jesus. In early Christian circles, the *way* was another word for the life of Christian discipleship (Acts 9:2; 19:9, 23, etc.) Implied in the word is the fact that Christianity is more than a onetime profession of faith (Son of David!) and more than a unique and wondrous event (I can see!). Christianity is a way of life that must daily lead the believer from darkness to light, from blindness to sight and from fascination to faith!

1. In the hearts of the needy and the vulnerable are planted the seeds of the eternal kingdom (Jeremiah).

2. Integral to the office of priesthood is the obligation of drawing all believers near to one another and to God (Hebrews).

3. There are no seeing-eye dogs in heaven—the willfully and spiritually blind will have no one to lead them (Mark).

31st Sunday in Ordinary Time

Greatness calls unto greatness. In the face of the transcendent God who is one and has chosen to be one with his people, we can have no other response than a holy, singleminded and wholehearted love (Deuteronomy). Believers know that their professed love of God is real and true if it is matched by expressions of magnanimous love for all others (Mark). Such love finds its precedent and inspiration in the absolute, complete and unreserved gift of Jesus on the cross (Hebrews).

Deuteronomy 6:2-6. Prayed in the morning and in the evening by faithful Jews everywhere, the prayer that has come to be called the *Sh'ma Yisrael* (Hear, O Israel) or simply the *Sh'ma* (Hear!) has for centuries been both a profoundly theological expression of faith and an imperative of moral rectitude. Called by some scholars a type of credal formula, the *Sh'ma* (in its given context) embodies the religious tenets of Judaism in a few brief verses, viz., (1) the *absolute* monotheism of Yahweh ("Yahweh our God is the one Yahweh," Deuteronomy 4:6); (2) the *absolute* personal and sustained involvement of the one God with his people, Israel

("When Yahweh has brought you into the land which he promised to your fathers, Abraham, Isaac and Jacob . . . take care you do not forget Yahweh who brought you out of the land of Egypt," Deuteronomy 6:10-13); (3) and the *absolute* quality of the response owed to such a reality ("You shall love Yahweh your God with *all* your heart, with *all* your heart, with *all* your soul, with *all* your strength," Deuteronomy 6:4).

Composed at a time when Israel was already settled in the land she believed had been promised to her, Deuteronomy is a highly theological book, reflective of a society that had already experienced life on both sides of the covenantal law. A homiletic expansion of the law as an effort to adapt the law to changing needs and times, Deuteronomy was instrumental in the sweeping religious reform of Josiah in the seventh century B.C.E. Purported to be the testament of Moses delivered to Israel on the steppes of Moab before the entrance into Canaan, the work is a piece of successful summation, gathering the best and the deepest of Israel's Pentateuchal traditions. Israel learned through the prophets and especially through the Deuteronomist that Yahweh, the God of Abraham, Isaac and Jacob, the God who called them out of the land of Egypt, who was with them in the desert, who provided food and water, bread and meat, was *also* with them in Canaan. Moreover, the people of Israel gradually learned that Yahweh their God was not merely capable of exercising his power in Canaan but was *omnipotent* above *all* gods. Indeed, Israel progressively discovered through revelation that Yahweh was the one God and that there were *no other* gods. Throughout the process of sedentarization and throughout the gradual growth into radical monotheism, the Deuteronomic theologians were both auxiliary to and representative of their people's profoundest realizations. Nowhere is the inspiration more clear and the theological insight more sublime than in the *Sh'ma Yisrael* at the heart of today's first reading.

In the first portion of the pericope (vv. 2-3), the covenant and its obligations were set forth by the Deuteronomic author as stipulations necessary for the fulfillment of God's promise, viz., the acquisition and permanent possession of the land flowing with milk and honey. Centuries later, in New Testament times, these same obligations would be named as partial requirements for entrance into the eternal kingdom made present in the person and message of Jesus. In today's gospel, the further demands made by Jesus will be paired with those made by the Deuteronomic theologian.

In the second portion of today's first reading which consists of the *Sh'ma*, Yahweh the Lord is designated as the one God. At once a polemic against Canaan's baalism and the extravagant pantheon of deities other nations entertained, the statement underscored in radical terms the uniqueness of Israel's God. Not merely superior to other deities, Yahweh stood alone and supreme as *the only* God. In the face of that awareness and as an outward expression of her faith, Israel was called to a radical and total commitment of all its energies—political, spiritual, psychological and theological.

Hebrews 7:23-28. A continuation of the author's comparison of Christ's perfect priesthood to the imperfect priesthood exercised by the priests of the old covenant, today's second reading is from a longer section of Hebrews (7:11-28) that likened Jesus to the ancient Melchisedek. An ethereal figure of the Pentateuch's patriarchal sagas (Genesis 14), Melchisedek (literally: "My king is righteousness") was said to have met Abraham after his altercation with the four kings and to have given him bread, wine and his blessing. In return, Melchisedek received from Abraham a tenth of his booty, the proper portion or tithe due a priest for services rendered. Because Melchisedek's birth, death, origins and ancestry remained shrouded in mystery, rabbinic exegetes concluded he was eternal—basing themselves on the principle that what is not mentioned in the Torah does not exist.

Since the Hebrews' author ascribed to the Hellenistic notion that change and multiplicity were marks of imperfection, Melchisedek, the ideal king and eternal priest, provided an apt type or figure for describing Jesus as the eternal, kingly and unequalled priest above all priests. Like Melchisedek, Jesus was not born to his priesthood through family or tribal ties. Nor was he appointed by human persons (e.g., as was Zadok). Rather, and in line with the belief about the mysterious paragon of priestliness, Jesus was ordained for his priesthood by the foreordained will of the eternal God. For this reason, Jesus' priesthood, "in the manner of Melchisedek" or "according to the order of Melchisedek," was so far superior to that of the priests of the old covenant as to render them obsolete.

In a clear reference to the fourth of Deutero-Isaiah's songs of the suffering servant (v. 27: Isaiah 53:10), the Hebrews' author described Jesus' death as the offering of himself for sin. This "once for all" (*ephapax*) sacrifice was absolutely sufficient and put an end forever to the necessity or validity of animal offerings with which the priests of the old covenant had busied themselves. Perhaps the Jewish Christians who were among the recipients of the letter still found their traditions appealing. Having grown up immersed in a cult which expressed its thanks, sorrow, petitions and praise with the help of animal, grain and other sacrifices, they may have found it difficult to surrender these external acts to the one, great non-repeatable sacrifice of Jesus.

Such an attitude is not uncommon even today. All nostalgia, whether of the first or the 20th century, is challenged by the Hebrews' author to acknowledge the vanquisher of treasured traditions and to accept the radically new way of approaching God made available to all in the saving act of Jesus Christ.

Mark 12:28-34. For one who came to proclaim the kingdom of peace and justice, Jesus' life was fraught with controversy and conflict. Throughout his public ministry the man from Nazareth was set upon by the Pharisees, the Sadducees, the scribes, the chief priests and Herodians who, each in their turn, questioned his methods, his motives and his authority. Today's gospel relates the meeting of Jesus with one of the scribes and stands out as quite an amicable encounter amid a series of stories of more fiery controversies. As one of the last four confrontations in Jesus' public life, the scribe episode forms a group with the other three controversies and as such may represent an outline for interrogation popular among rabbis.

For example, a rabbi's opinion was often tested according to the following pattern: (1) *hokmah*, "wisdom" or a point of law (Mark 12:13-17: "Are taxes lawful?"); (2) *boruth*, "ridicule," a question asked in an effort to mock or ridicule a belief held by the one being interrogated (Mark 12:18-27: "resurrection of the dead"); (3) *derek'eres*, a query as to the fundamental principles for living a good life (Mark 12:28-34: "Love God, love neighbor"); (4) *haggadah*, a non-legal teaching, e.g., a conflict about the meaning of certain scripture texts (Mark 12:35-37: an exegetical question on Psalm 110).

Whether it was Mark or his redactor who arranged the controversies according to this pattern cannot be known for certain. However, there is no doubt that controversy was an inevitable and constant companion for Jesus and should be expected by his would-be disciples.

Not an unusual question, the scribe's "Which is the first of all the commandments?" was often posed to rabbis in an effort to find one main law upon which the others could hang and from which all others could be derived. Countless efforts had been made by each generation of rabbis and scribes to distill the many prescriptions of the law into a powerful and comprehensive concentrate.

According to W. Barclay, Sammlai had taught that Moses received the 613 precepts on Sinai—365 according to the days of the solar year and 248 according to the generations of men. David was credited with reducing the 613 to 11 in Psalm 15. Isaiah, the eighth century B.C.E. prophet, further reduced the 11 to six (Isaiah 33:15) and Micah whittled the six to three in the profoundly simple statement that embodies all of prophetic truth as well: "What does the Lord require of you—only this: to do justice, to love tenderly and to walk humbly with your God" (Micah 6:8). In the sixth century B.C.E. Deutero-Isaiah shortened Micah's three commands to two, "Keep justice and do righteousness" (Isaiah 56:1), while Habakkuk believed he had contracted all the given laws into one, "The righteous shall live by faith" (Habakkuk 2:4).

Although the scribe asked Jesus his opinion as to which law was first of all, Jesus responded with a *pair* of laws that he united and set on a par with one another. By quoting to the scribe the *Sh'ma Yisrael* (Deuteronomy 6:4), Jesus underscored the importance of the familiar prayer. Devout Jews wore this prayer in the phylacteries or prayer boxes affixed to their wrists and foreheads. The *Sh'ma* was contained in the *mezuzah* mounted on the door frame of every good Jewish home and this prayer prefaced morning and evening prayers. There could have been no quarrel with Jesus' choice of the *Sh'ma* as the greatest of all laws. All faithful Jews would have agreed to the value and necessity of wholehearted and unreserved love of the one God. Yet Jesus, as was his custom, went further than the ordinary, further than what was expected. He invited his hearers to expand their horizons and hearts to understand that the love of one's neighbor as oneself was as worthy an obligation as the love of God. Not the first to pair the two commandments (Deuteronomy 6:4 and Leviticus 19:18), Jesus' recommendation can be found in some of the intertestamental literature of about 100 B.C.E. For example, in the Testament of Isachar we find, "Love the Lord and love your neighbor" (5:2). So too in the Testament of Dan (5:3) we read, "Love the Lord through all your life, and one another with a true heart." Perhaps the unique quality of Jesus' statement is the fact that he took one law considered to be a "heavy" or great law (Deuteronomy 6:4) and another law considered to be a "light" or lesser law (Leviticus 19:18) and made them equal and interdependent. Moreover, Jesus expanded the parochial and nationalistic Israelite concept of "neighbor" to include, not just fellow countrymen (as in Leviticus 19:18) but all peoples (as in Luke 10:29-37).

In the best tradition of the prophets, the scribe replied that the keeping of Jesus' dual law was far superior to the rituals of the sacrificial cult (Hosea 6:6; Amos 5:21ff.; 1 Samuel 15:22). He had understood Jesus' summons to a love that went beyond the limitations of legalism and beyond the security of a well performed but external ritual. Because of that insight, Jesus assured him he was not far at all from the mind and heart and will of the one God made manifest in the person of Jesus. By his perception and acceptance of Jesus' words the scribe had drawn near to the eternal kingdom as it had begun to erupt upon the earth in the mission of Jesus. Modern believers with similar insight and perceptions are called by today's gospel to close the gap and be "not far" but even *one* with the kingdom or reign of God as revealed in Jesus Christ.

1. Mediocrity has no place in the commitment of faith that summons the whole heart, the whole person (Deuteronomy).

2. Ministers by their person and their work make God nearer and the path to goodness clearer for their charges (Hebrews).

3. A tithe of even 10% of all one's goods is no substitute for the 100% gift of self in love of God and neighbor (Mark).

32nd Sunday in Ordinary Time

Giving is a gentle act, best cultivated in hearts that know they have little to offer and everything to receive (Kings). Christian discipleship grows strong and vital amid a network of giving hearts (Mark) because believers have been blessed with the greatest and the finest gift of all—the love and the life of the Lord Jesus (Hebrews).

1 Kings 17:10-16. When asked about the possible permanent damage the Watergate scandal would have upon his political career, Richard Nixon replied, "History will be kind to me!" Only time will tell if Mr. Nixon was right and if modern historians will assess his political accomplishments as great enough to outweigh his moral failures when they tell the story of his administration. Such was not the case, however, with the political leaders of Israel and Judah. When the Deuteronomic historian set about the task of recording the deeds of the kings of his people, he evaluated them using a very different set of criteria. Rather than praise their diplomacy or achievements in foreign affairs, he dealt with each of Israel's and Judah's kings according to their moral rectitude and fidelity to the covenant and its laws. With the brief statement, "And he did evil before the Lord," the overwhelming majority of the kings of Israel and Judah were written off as infidels and sinners.

Drawing his information from the Acts of Solomon, as well as the chronicles of the kings of Israel and of Judah, the Deuteronomist produced this special brand of "religious history" shaped according to the following basic tenets or religious presuppositions. (1) Yahweh rewards faithfulness to the covenant relationship and punishes infidelity; the political catastrophes of God's people are due to their infidelity to the covenant. The Deuteronomist held especially responsible the kings who were to lead the people in the ways of righteousness by their own example. (2) The word of God that had guided Israel from its inception as a people would always be present. Spoken through the prophets, the word would infallibly accomplish its purpose. By way of illustration, the two books of Kings contain some 45 prophetic fulfillment stories (of which our first reading is one). (3) Regardless of events (e.g., exile, banishments and death of kings and people) that seem to militate against it, Jerusalem and its cult would remain central and the promise of the eternal Davidic dynasty (2 Samuel 7:12-15) *would* be fulfilled.

As part of the string of stories called the Elijah cycle, today's episode of Elijah with the widow of Zarephath illustrates the power of God's word, spoken through the prophet to accomplish its stated purposes. Moreover, the story serves as a polemic against the cult of the gods of Canaan who were thought to be the lords of nature, its seasons and its fertility. Elijah, by whose word the drought had come and had caused the famine that threatened the life of the woman and her son, would also have the power by his word ("The jar shall not go empty, nor the jug of oil run dry, until the day the Lord sends rain upon the earth") to alleviate both famine and drought. For the suffering exiles in Babylon, the story of the widow and her son was also a source of encouragement. Such stories, according to P. Fannon, established the existence and survival of the Israelite remnant that provided a hope for the future despite the moral bankruptcy of the kings.

Obviously, this pericope was chosen to complement today's gospel because of the character of the widow. With nothing else to rely on, she put her faith in the word of God spoken through Elijah and, because of her faith, she was blessed with life and abundance. Unlike the great kings of the Israelites, she was not swayed by power or avarice. Like the widow in the gospel whose goodness stood out in sharp contrast to that of the scribes, the widow of Zarephath teaches the powerful lesson of absolute trust and confidence in God. In the word and works of Elijah, she recognized the power of Yahweh to save, even amid the bungling of his people and their leaders.

Hebrews 9:24-28. In Jesus' day, the existing temple was that which had been begun by Herod in 19 B.C.E. and upon which the work of decoration and adornment continued until 64 C.E. Site of God's presence and home of the official cult, the earthly temple was believed to be a reflection of a heavenly model upon which it was based (Exodus 26:30; Revelation 3:12, 7:15, 11:19, 14:15, etc.). A relatively simply structure, the temple's most important area was that of the *debir* or sanctuary. "In this," said Josephus, "stood nothing whatever. Unapproachable, inviolable, invisible to all, it was called the holy of holies" (*War*, 5:219). Measuring 30 feet on a side, the cube-shaped room was empty and dark, separated from the *hekal* or holy place by a double-curtained veil. The holy of holies was entered only by the high priest and then only once a year on the Day of Atonement (Yom Kippur), the tenth day of the seventh month (Leviticus 16:1ff).

Dressed in fine linen vestments, the high priest would sacrifice two goats as an offering for sin, a ram as a holocaust for the community and a bullock as an offering for his own sin. Lots were cast for the two goats in order to discern which one would be for Yahweh and which for Azazel. The blood of the sin offering for Yahweh would be sprinkled on the sanctuary, the altar and in the holy of holies. The other goat for Azazel would be driven out to the desert after the community's sins had been confessed. Laying hands on the goat signified a symbolic burdening of the animal with the guilt of the nation, as a scapegoat. Thus, it was believed that the sins of the people and their priest were atoned in the eyes of the Lord.

When the author of the letter to the Hebrews wrote today's pericope, he certainly had at the basis of his thought the Old Testament ritual of the Day of Atonement and the holy of holies. So too his readers would have been familiar with the ancient rite. Therefore the Hebrews' author was able to refer to the temple, the priesthood and the religious observances of Israel to explain analogously the superiority of the heavenly sanctuary (over the earthly temple), of the priesthood of Jesus (over that of the earthly high priest) and of Jesus' sacrifice (over that of the animal offerings) as an atonement for sin. Unlike the high priest who entered a "manmade sanctuary" and a "mere copy of the true one" (v. 24), Jesus entered the true and lasting sanctuary, the heavenly and real presence of God. Moreover, by his entering, he opened the way for all the redeemed to enter also.

Finally, the Hebrews' author compared (v. 28) the high priest's emergence from the holy of holies after the sacrifice to that of Jesus' second appearance at the parousia. Just as the high priest's work and his yearly term of office culminated in his service on the Day of Atonement, so too, Jesus' perfect sacrifice will be crowned with all glory at his second advent. However, *all* of Christ's saving activity must be understood as eschatological: "He *has* appeared, at the end of the ages to take away sins" (v. 26). By his death on the cross Christ brought near the one God and the end time, the parousia—so near as to allow believers to begin to live here and now the joyful life of those who have been forgiven: the life of salvation.

Mark 12:38-44. A composite of two different aspects of Jesus' teaching, today's gospel is linked, albeit loosely and somewhat illogically, by the "*stichwort* principle." The same catchword *widow* appears in each unit (vv. 38-40, 41-44) and, if you will, "stitches" the units together. The homilist may wish to use the stories as foils for one another contrasting the undesirable demeanor and attitude of the scribes to that of the admirable widow. Evidently, this was the evangelist's (or his redactor's) intention in juxtaposing the units as he did.

With this harsh denunciation of the scribes (vv. 30-40), the Jerusalem controversy episodes have concluded and the scenario has been set for the impending official rejection of Jesus by the Sanhedrin (14:53-65). Having exposed the teaching of the scribes for its shallowness and inadequacy (vv. 35-37), Jesus proceeded to castigate them for their behavior. Gaffney believes the representation of the scribes as both "pompous asses and avaricious hypocrites is undoubtedly a caricature" since the faults described seem to be those of *all* religious elitists with legalistic tendencies, whether of the Jewish or Christian persuasion. Although Jesus and the scribes had their differences (2:6-7, 3:22, 7:1-13, 9:14, 11:27-33), most scholars agree that the extremely *scathing* nature of the remarks is reflective of church-synaogogue conflict of the evangelist's contemporary situation (60s C.E.).

In a society where the majority of ordinary people were not literate, the scribes were a breed apart. Educated and trained in the law, they had spent years of hard work building their reputations as experts in the law. Respected as teachers and sought after for their advice, the scribes were admired by simpler people who presumed their behavior was inspired by purely religious motives. According to Strack-Billerbeck's *Kommentar* (II, 30-33), the robe (v. 38) in which the scribes paraded around was intended for times of prayer or was to be worn when giving a judgment, performing a vow or visiting the sick. An outer garment that distinguished its wearer by its unusual (and *impractical*) length and voluminousness, the robe was evidently flaunted by the scribes in a sort of vain self-aggrandizement. Attached to the robe in compliance with the prescription in the book of Numbers (15:38) were tassels, whose purpose was to remind the Jews of their responsibilities as God's people. Obviously, Jesus (or Mark) did not condemn the actual wearing of the robe (or its tassels) because Jesus himself was known to wear one as he ministered to the sick (Mark 5:27, Matthew 9:20). Rather, it was the attitude and self-seeking with which the special garments were worn that Jesus censured.

In the synagogue, the "front seats" were located directly in front of the ark that contained the sacred scrolls of the law and the prophets. Anyone seated there would be facing the congregation, in plain view of all. At banquets, the seat of greatest honor was that to the right of the host. The next most prized seat was at the host's left, and so on, alternating down the line. All in attendance at the banquet knew the host's opinion of each guest from the position of the seats assigned. Again, the criticism here is due to the vanity with which the scribes sought honors for themselves.

This same attitude probably fostered the ostentatious practice of reciting long prayers. Such prayers, prayed *aloud*, were shaped more by human respect and pride than humility and trust in God. In the criticism concerning the scribe's abuse of widows and their savings, Jesus was not alone. Josephus the Jewish historian commented, "The Pharisees valued themselves highly upon their exact skill in the law of their fathers and made believe that they were highly favored by God . . . they inveigled certain women into their schemes and plottings."

Having thus made short shrift of the scribes who were considered among the leaders of the community, Jesus then proceeded to praise one who was considered among the least members of society in the ancient Near Eastern world, the widow. In the temple's court were some 13 trumpet-shaped receptacles, each of which was designated for a certain type of offering, e.g., incense, grain offering, oil, etc. While the wealthy people had indeed been generous in their giving, the widow went beyond the generosity and gave *all* she had. The copper coins in question were lepta, the smallest in circulation. Two lepta were equivalent to one quadrans in Roman currency and, according to Juvenal, it took at least 100 quadrans to pay for a decent meal! The fact that the woman had and gave two is significant. Though a mere pittance, she could have kept one coin for herself and her needs, but she gave all.

Mark signals the special and exemplary quality of the woman's behavior by telling his readers that "Jesus called his disciples over" (v. 43) for further instruction. Similar stories and examples were given by other rabbis to their students. In the lesson of the widow who gave her all with utter abandon to God, Jesus taught the final, formal lesson of discipleship to his followers. The ultimate lesson would be taught in the complete self-abandonment of Jesus to his Father on the cross.

Although the symbols of the illustration here are monetary ones (coins) the lesson goes far more deeply to touch on attitude and motivation. The scribes may have performed great and good deeds; but without a heart conformed to God's truth, their deeds remained just that—*a performance.* Although the widow's offering was observably insignificant, the true value of her gift was of immeasurable worth and known only to God. It was this last lesson in discipleship that would help the disciples to understand the value of the cross and the immeasurable worth of the gift of oneself.

1. Those who seem the least able to give are often the most generous (1 Kings).

2. Christ's unique sacrifice can never be repeated, only remembered—with gratitude and love and in fellowship (Hebrews).

3. A gift given for appearance's sake benefits neither giver nor recipient (Mark).

33rd Sunday in Ordinary Time

Fear of the future is not merely counterproductive; it is un-Christian. To dread the eschatological harvest of humanity's efforts is to forget the basic hope within whom all our struggles have been rooted and in whom they have ripened (Mark). He is the one who has been a part of our existence; he has known our sin and guilt, our sickness and our death and he has triumphed (Hebrews). Because of Jesus, faithful disciples can look ahead with confidence to a future of life everlasting (Daniel).

Daniel 12:1-3. As a literary genre, apocalyptic literature has acquired the onerous reputation among some Christians of being—at its best—generally misunderstood, and—at its worst—misinterpreted and grossly misrepresented. Intended by its authors as a balm and a comfort, apocalyptic has often (albeit unwittingly and through ignorance) been abused and wielded as a literary weapon to strike fear and remorse into the hearts of the naive and trusting occupant of the fundamentalist pew. Widely overlooked and sometimes even avoided by Roman Catholic homilists, apocalyptic literature is a factor to be reckoned with. Indeed, E. Kasemann has called apocalyptic the "mother of all Christian theology." Although many dispute the sweeping nature of Kasemann's claim, it is true that many of the central symbols of the New Testament (e.g., the Son of Man, the resurrection, parousia and messianism, the kingdom of God) are apocalyptic images. This fact alone makes it impossible for the serious exegete and minister of the word to avoid the challenge posed by apocalyptic literature.

A literature born of crisis, apocalyptic flourished during the period of endangered hopes, persecuted ideals and tested faith which characterized the last two centuries B.C.E. and the first two centuries C.E. In order to encourage their contemporaries to persevere in the faith, the writers of apocalyptic kept before their readers vivid images of the reality of God's kingdom and the satisfying notion of the vindication of the just. While purporting to write of the past, the apocalyptic author was actually concerned with the present situation. By means of cryptic language, numerology, visions, dreams and bizarre revelations, the author's comments enabled his readers to interpret their present realities. For example, the author of Daniel, to whom we owe our first reading for today, wrote about 167 B.C.E. to encourage his fellow Jews to remain loyal to the religion of their forefathers at a time when it was more advantageous and perhaps more alluring to ascribe to the philosophies and religious beliefs of a hostile and alien, but higher cultural system.

From the time of the Assyrian conquest of Israel (eighth century B.C.E.) and the subsequent vassalage of Judah, the reins of power in the ancient Near East were wrested from one hand by another. In successive waves, the Assyrians, Babylonians and Medes, Persians and Greeks held sway over the land promised to Abraham. At the time of his writing the author of Daniel lived in a world governed by the Greek dynasty of the Seleucids, whose leader was Antiochus Epiphanes IV. Determined to unite his vast empire, Antiochus attempted to Hellenize all its disparate elements so that one basic cultural and political system would prevail. In order to do so, the Greek ruler made Judaism a crime, forbade its practice under pain of torture and even death (1 Maccabees 1:60-64, 2 Maccabees 6-9), burned the sacred books (1 Maccabees 1:56ff) and persecuted all its adherents.

The book, named not for its author but for its protagonist (Daniel: "My judge is God"), can be divided into two parts. Chapters 1-6 are comprised of the adventures of Daniel and his friends at the royal court in Babylonia. A series of edifying vignettes, these stories aimed to strengthen their readers who were enduring similar trials at the hand of Antiochus. In the second portion of the book, the author interpreted (by means of a series of visions of four successive kingdoms) the history of the world as he knew it up to his present day.

Today's pericope is a part of that second portion of the book, an excerpt from the author's hopeful view of the future. Looking beyond history and the troubles of his present age, the apocalyptic visionary promised justice and eschatological reward. Tribulation would yield to deliverance and life everlasting for the faithful even if they had already died: "Many of those asleep in the dust of the earth shall awake" (v. 2). As one of the earliest Old Testament texts to speak of resurrection and to associate it with the eschatological climax, the importance of Daniel 12 and its influence on the New Testament cannot be denied.

Hebrews 10:11-14, 18. If the first century author of the missive to the Hebrews did not succeed in communicating his ideas through logical reasoning or by exegetical exposition or by the power of his parenetic skills, he did so by sheer dint of repetition! For the past six weeks, the second reading has concerned the basic theological premise that Christ's sacrifice and his priesthood are superior to the sacrificial system and priesthood of the Old Testament cult. In making this comparison, the author has exhausted countless illustrations and numerous examples (*and this writer!!*). In today's pericope, the seventh in the series, the comparison again brings to light the inadequacy of the daily, repeated sacrifices offered by the levitical priesthood.

According to the prescribed ritual recorded by the priestly tradition in the post-exilic book of Leviticus, there were five main types of sacrifice. (1) The holocaust consisted in the victim's being completely burnt on the altar, hence the name *'olah* (holocaust) meaning "that which rises or ascends." Holocausts were offered daily as an act of praise to the Lord on behalf of the community and also for atonement for individual sin. On the altar of holocaust it became customary to keep a perpetual fire enkindled as a sign of the uninterrupted prayer of the community. (2) Cereal or grain offerings (*minhah*) consisted of cakes baked with fine oil and incense or grains and spices to be offered by the priests on the altar. Part of the gift was burnt and the rest was considered the rightful portion of the priests and their families. (3) Peace offerings (*zebah shelamin*) were of different types: (a) the offering of an animal in *thanksgiving* to God, (b) the *votive* offering of an animal due to a vow of obligation, (c) the *free will* offering, a spontaneous gift. Not totally burned, the remainder of the offering was to be shared by the offerer and his family in the presence of the Lord. Thereby, it was believed, harmonious relations between God and his worshippers were fostered. For this reason, some (De Vaux, Cazelles) have preferred to call the peace offering a *communion* sacrifice. (4) A sin offering (*hattah*) was prescribed for the expiation of an uncleanness whether of an ethical or physical nature. For example, if the worshipper had come in contact with a corpse, contracted a disease or committed an infraction of the law, atonement was required. The fat of an animal would be burned and its blood sprinkled on the altar while the rest of the offering would be burned outside the temple. For the poor, doves could be substituted for the animal (Luke 2). (5) Guilt offerings were made in the case of more serious sin. Usually a male ram was the specified offering.

Given this very general survey of the elaborate sacrificial system of the Israelites, the point of the Hebrews' author concerning its obsolescence and inadequacy becomes more poignant. In the one unique and irrepeatable sacrifice of Jesus, perfect praise has been given to God (holocaust), absolute and intimate union has been achieved (peace offering), and sin with its guilt has been expiated (sin, guilt offerings). Because of his perfect sacrificial act, Christ is now seated in glory at the right hand of God, waiting until his enemies are placed beneath his feet (v. 14).

Mark 13:24-32. Called the "little" or the "Marcan apocalypse," chapter 13 of Mark's gospel has been considered by some as a separate entity, written by one other than Mark and added later, with little care as to its connection with the rest of the gospel. But, W. Harrington's insight is probably more correct: He views Mark 13 as the key to understanding the rest of the gospel. Entirely a Marcan construct, chapter 13 is closely associated with what has preceded it and with what would follow it. Written in the combined literary genre of the farewell discourse and apocalyptic literature, chapter 13 underscores the central position of Christ, the reality and imminence of his second coming and the necessary posture of the persecuted faithful who would be vindicated at his appearance.

Mark believed that the parousia he described would occur during his lifetime or at least during the lifetime of his generation. From his description of the last hours of Jesus on the cross (15:33ff) it is clear that the evangelist understood that the death of Jesus had ushered in the period of the end or the last age. So too, he perceived the persecution of his contemporaries as part of the great tribulation (vv. 5-23). Later, when the destruction of the Jerusalem temple did not bring down the final curtain (70 C.E.), the imminent quality of the parousia had to be reevaluated. In the later synoptics (Matthew and Luke) and in John and Paul this rethinking is evident. Although he did not expect it, the evangelist Mark was part of the same interval and shares with us the same period of waiting between the ushering in of the final age and its ultimate consummation. Therefore, the insights he offered to his contemporaries are valid even today for 20th century believers in his good news.

Mark's vision of the Son of Man "coming in the clouds with great power and glory," "dispatching his messengers and assembling his chosen" (v. 26) can be understood as the eschatological climax to all of Jesus' actions as Son of Man while on earth. As Son of Man, he had forgiven sins (2:10) and proclaimed his authority by his teaching (2:28). As Son of Man he had suffered, been rejected by the authorities and put to death (8:31, 9:31, 10:33). As Son of Man he served and had given his life for the many (10:45). By so doing he had won the conflict over evil and had defeated sin and death. For those who were still in the heat of battle, struggling to appropriate in their own lives the victory of the Son of Man (viz., Mark's persecuted contemporaries and their descendants), the vision of the glorious, powerful Son of Man was a source of strength and hope.

In the lessons of the fig tree, both the imminence of the expected Son of Man and the character of the parousia are attested. One of the most valuable trees of the ancient Near East, the fig was a symbol of abundance and peace. Regarded by the Egyptians as the tree of life, it was important as a source of food. Unlike most of the trees in Palestine which were evergreens, the fig lost its leaves and lay dormant in winter. But with the advent of spring, it would revive and become once again a wondrous spreading tree, providing both fruit and shade. The appearance of the first small green shoots on the dark limbs was regarded as a harbinger of summer and the harvest. Widely recognized as an image of the messianic era, the harvest with its activities of reaping and threshing and gathering was a sign of the judgment, separation and retribution to come. Mark would have his contemporaries understand their present sufferings and struggles in terms of the first shoots of the fig tree, i.e., a signal of the eschatological harvest begun by Jesus during his ministry and consummated by him as the glorious Son of Man.

Because of the statement concerning the Son's ignorance of the exact day or hour of the parousia (v. 32), some scholars have doubted its authenticity as a saying of Jesus. Arguing that Jesus was omniscient because he was God, these scholars have attributed the saying instead to the early church. Regardless of the origin of the saying, it would be erroneous to anachronize a fifth century Chalcedonian christology into the first century good news. However, the point of the statement (v. 32) was not to underline the fact of Jesus' limited knowledge but to point out the futility of wondering and worrying *when* the Son of Man would come. Jesus and Mark would have all believers devote themselves to preparedness and alertness for the Lord's coming rather than be swayed by anxiety and fear or misled by false announcements and imposters (Mark 13:5-6, 21, 23). To make the message of the Marcan apocalypse anything other than an exhortation to vigilance and a comfort to the suffering is an injustice, both to the living word of God and to those who try to live according to its truth.

1. When distress yields to hope and grief to joy, the glory of the resurrection has been tasted (Daniel).

2. In the liturgy that celebrates Jesus' unique sacrifice, both minister and congregation are called again to remember and renew the mysteries of forgiveness and new life (Hebrews).

3. Although nuclear weaponry has enabled humanity to simulate its own "portents in the sky," it is still beyond human power "to know the day or the hour" (Mark).

34th Sunday in Ordinary Time

There is no earthly corollary for understanding the kingship and kingdom of Jesus. Instead of a government or political entity in a temporal sense, Jesus brought among us in his words and works the very reign of God (Daniel). Campaigning, voting and maneuvering for prestigious positions are incongruent with the reign whose hallmark is service and whose signature is love (Revelation). In the person of our crowned and crucified king, the reign has begun and will never end (John).

Daniel 7:13-14. For those unfamiliar with the literary form of apocalyptic, an initial reading of the book of Daniel may seem very much like a science-fiction thriller. With its symbolic monsters and numbers, bizarre visions and otherworldly experiences, apocalyptic literature departs from the traditional and familiar to take the reader beyond the suffering and seeming inanity of time and space to a dimension of hope and peace. As noted previously, apocalyptic was a literature borne of a time of crisis and persecutions; its purpose was to encourage and support those who were struggling to survive both spiritually and politically. Writing during the second century B.C.E. the author of Daniel accomplished his purpose in sustaining the faith of his persecuted contemporaries during the tyrannical rule of the Seleucid, Antiochus Epiphanes IV. By means of his visions and dreams, Daniel was able to offer a cryptic commentary on and an interpretation of the history of his people. An excerpt from the second portion (chapters 7-12) of Daniel which contains a series of four visions, today's first reading puts before us the climax of the first of those visions.

Unfolding the great drama of his night visions, Daniel, the seer and protagonist for whom the book was named, described (7:1-8) the beasts that emerged from the Great Sea (v. 3). The sea here was not the Mediterranean, elsewhere in the scriptures referred to as the Great Sea, but rather the abyss (*tehom*), the realm of primordial chaos and evil (Genesis 1:1). The first beast, a lion with eagle's wings and a human heart, represented the Babylonian empire that had plundered Judah and taken into exile the elite of the people in the sixth century B.C.E. After the lion appeared a bear with three ribs hanging garishly from its teeth. Representative of the empire of the Medes, the bear was soon replaced by a leopard with four heads and four wings: the Persian empire. The fourth beast—fearful, terrifying and very strong—had iron teeth with which it ate, and great feet with which it trampled underfoot what remained (v. 8). So monstrous that no animal could symbolize it, the fourth beast represented the Greek empire and its ten horns were the ten kings of the Seleucid dynasty.

As the seer watched, the scene shifted to a celestial court (vv. 9-14) where one of great age (the "ancient of days") sat upon a throne in the company of tens of thousands. Having witnessed all of history, the ancient could pass judgment on all that had transpired, on the guilty and the oppressed. After the book of human actions was read and the deeds of the great beasts exposed to truth's light, the ancient one passed his sentence. Immediately the fourth beast was executed and the other beasts were stripped of their power. With this vision Daniel's contemporaries were bolstered in their hope that soon the despot Antiochus Epiphanes IV would be destroyed. Moreover, as the vision continued, Daniel and his fellow Jews were assured of a bright and happy future.

One like a "son of man" came on the clouds of heaven into the presence of the ancient one and upon him was conferred the sovereignty, glory and kingship that had been abused by the beasts. Unlike the beasts who came from the realm of evil (sea, abyss) the one like a son of man came from heaven, i.e., from God, the source of goodness. Where the monsters had abused power over *certain* groups of people for a *limited* period of time, the one like a son of man was made king over *all* peoples for *all* ages.

In Judaism, the concept of Daniel's apocalyptic son of man developed to include the notions of: (1) a heavenly man who was hidden but would appear at the end of time to judge and to save (Enoch, 2 Esdras); (2) a heavenly *ideal* man (Philo). By Jesus' day, the ideas of judge and savior had become synonymous with the son of man who was expected at the end of time. While Jesus did use the term as a self-designation, it is significant that he united to the glorious son of man concept the harsh reality of the suffering servant (Mark 8:31, 9:31, 10:33). He would indeed appear as judge and savior and receive dominion, honor, glory and kingship but not before his words and works on earth had been crowned by the saving act of the cross.

Revelation 1:5-8. In the course of human events, when a king dies, his power and title are in the act of death relinquished. Immediately the king's heir is recognized and begins to rule. How *different* from human custom and tradition is the kingship exercised by Jesus Christ. In the cruel and tragic irony of the thorny crown and on the gruesome throne of the cross, the divine heir began to rule. Precisely in the act of his dying, the true nature of his kingship was made known . . . in his passing over from death to life he began to exercise fully and forever the authority that was rightfully his. This fact has been memorialized by the author of today's second reading from the book of Revelation. By his work, the first century author sought to unveil for the eyes of his persecuted contemporaries the victory of Jesus over sin and death. He hoped to strengthen his brothers and sisters whose suffering he shared (1:9) in the hope that *soon* they too would share in Jesus' triumph, and glory in his kingship.

Although the author of Revelation identified himself as John (1:1, 4, 9; 22:8) and although very ancient tradition has ascribed the authorship to the apostle John, son of Zebedee (Justin, Irenaeus, Tertullian, Origen, Clement of Alexandria, Hippolytus of Rome), there is no clear incontrovertible evidence in this regard. Except for the fact of his name, John, and his probably Jewish origin, little else is known for certain at present of the author of Revelation.

Concerning the *time* during which John wrote, however, we can be more certain because of the number of historical allusions made in the book. Once the apocalyptic symbolism has been pierced, the beasts identified and the visions interpreted, we can say the author lived and wrote during the reign of the emperor Domitian (81-96 C.E.). Younger brother of Titus and son of Vespasian, Domitian insisted he be called *Dominus et Deus Noster*—our lord and our god. He decreed that statues of himself be erected throughout Rome and that incense be burned in worship before them. Of course, Jews, Christians and others who refused to acquiesce were persecuted mercilessly. Among those put to death for the faith was Domitian's own nephew, Flavius Clemens.

In face of the hardships and tribulations imposed upon believers by Domitian, the author of Revelation proclaimed fealty to a greater king (ruler of the kings of the earth, v. 5) and membership in a more prestigious and royal household than even that of imperial Rome. "He has made *us a royal nation of priests*" (v. 6), John reminded his fellow Christians. Part of the epistolary address of the book, today's pericope is comprised of a triple doxology (vv. 5-6), praising Jesus in his passion, resurrection and exaltation, as well as a proclamation of the parousia (v. 7) that the author believed would erupt at any moment. In a collage of Old Testament texts (Psalm 89:28, Isaiah 55:4, Zechariah 12:10, Daniel 7:13) and in heavy reliance on the concepts of the Day of the Lord and the Son of Man, John wove a saving net of hope for his contemporaries. That same tapestry of faith and courage can support all who would persevere in the Lord's way until the consummation of his kingship in eternity.

John 18:33-37. While most Christians would look upon him as an accomplice in the plot that led to Jesus' death on the cross, Pontius Pilate (and his wife) is revered as a *saint* in the Ethiopian Christian church! Because he had declared himself innocent of Jesus' blood and pronounced him without fault, the believers in Ethiopia venerate the Roman officer on June 25. The author of the fourth gospel did not similarly exonerate Pilate, nor did he cast blame upon him. Rather, he used the figure of Pilate and the interchanges between him and Jesus to make certain points very clear, viz., (1) that Jesus was indeed a king, (2) that his kingdom and his authority had a divine origin, (3) that culpability lay in the hearts of those who should have recognized these facts as truth but refused to do so.

The Johannine version of Jesus' trial before Pilate, from which today's gospel is excerpted, is a carefully styled scenario consisting of seven neat episodes (R. Brown). During the course of the trial Pilate was portrayed by the evangelist as shuttling back and forth from the outside to the inside of the praetorium. Judiciously, the Jewish authorities and the accompanying crowd who escorted Jesus to Pilate refused to enter his residence lest they become defiled and unable to participate in the Passover celebrations. With murder in their hearts, but scrupulously adhering to the letter of the law, the Jews who refused to recognize Jesus preferred the external appearance of worthiness rather than the interior reality of integrity and holiness. As the Jewish authorities presented Jesus for trial before Pilate, it was clear that they wanted to dispose of him, because only by Pilate's authority could a capital sentence be handed down. These ironies and the image of Pilate conducting his interrogation while scampering back and forth served to accent the central focus of trial—the person and the identity of Jesus.

Governor of Judea, 26-36 C.E., Pilate usually resided in Caesarea. During the festivals, or in times of political upheaval, however, he would take up residence in Jerusalem to make the authority of Rome felt, and thus to avert any possibility of rebellion. With him would come his cohort of soldiers to aid him in enforcing Rome's law and keep order among the assembled pilgrims. Those who accused Jesus and handed him over to Pilate did so on the only grounds that would have attracted the Roman's attention. As one who supposedly claimed to be "king of the Jews," Jesus was not merely a messianic pretender or even a blasphemer. To accuse him of claiming to be king, the Jews opened up before Pilate the possibility of a *political* threat to the imperial presence and to Pilate's own office as well.

In the dialogue between Jesus and Pilate, the non-political, non-partisan and non-parochial character of Jesus' kingship has been clarified. While the Johannine Jesus tacitly accepted the title of kingship, he also corrected the Roman governor's charge by reinterpreting what that kingship and kingdom truly implied. Just as the incarnate word was not "of the world" (1:10) and just as Jesus' disciples were not to be "of the world" (15:19, 17:14), so Jesus' kingdom was not "of the world." Recall the Johannine distinction between world as the created universe and world as the element hostile to the truth and light. Probably both senses of meaning were intended in Jesus' statement. Not of the world (i.e., not created), Jesus and his kingdom were divine in origin. They have come, not from human devising or ambitious political self-seeking, but from God himself.

As king, Jesus exercised a supra-political and life-giving authority over human destiny. Unlike earthly kingdoms that continue to exist even when the earthly ruler dies, *without* Jesus there would be no kingdom (*basileia*). But *with* him and in him and because of him, there is a kingship and a kingdom, whose realities are recognized and experienced by believers in the truth. Since the Stoic philosophers sometimes referred to wise men as kings, the notion of a kingdom of those who draw the inspiration of their life from the truth should not have been incomprehensible to the Roman (R. Russell). As its witness (v. 37), Jesus made present in the world from the moment of the incarnation the challenge of the truth. For those who opened themselves to the penetrating light of its judgment and responded morally and ethically to have come, not from human devising or ambitious political self-seeking, but from God himself.

As king, Jesus exercised a supra-political and life-giving authority over human destiny. Unlike earthly kingdoms that continue to exist even when the earthly ruler dies, *without* Jesus there would be no kingdom (*basileia*). But *with* him and in him and because of him, there is a kingship and a kingdom, whose realities are recognized and experienced by believers in the truth. Since the Stoic philosophers sometimes referred to wise men as kings, the notion of a kingdom of those who draw the inspiration of their life from the truth should not have been incomprehensible to the Romans (R. Russell). As its witness (v. 37), Jesus made present in the world from the moment of the incarnation the challenge of the truth. For those who opened themselves to the penetrating light of its judgment and responded morally and ethically to its demands, the truth became a way of recognizing the presence of God in the person of Jesus. That recognition and the experience of that presence are a taste of the kingdom that has begun in Jesus and that will continue forever in him.

1. Membership in the kingdom of the truth involves commitment of faith expressed in multi-lingual joy and non-partisan service (Daniel).

2. Not by formal decree or edict but by love, Christians have been freed from sin and made part of the royal and eternal household (Revelation).

3. Truly effective authority builds *from within and does not* bind *from without (John).*

Movable Feasts

For the following movable feasts, which replace the Sunday in the Roman calendar if the date of a feast falls on a Sunday, see above, Year A Movable Feasts, page 110 and following.

February 2—Lord's Presentation
June 24—Birth of John the Baptizer
June 29—Peter and Paul
August 6—Transfiguration
August 15—Assumption
September 14—Triumph of the Cross
November 1—All Saints
November 2—All Souls
November 9—Dedication of Lateran

Trinity Sunday

Creation, covenant, salvation, forgiveness are but a few of the words spoken by God to his people (Deuteronomy). Commissioned to preach and to teach, the disciples of the word made flesh go forth in every age as children of one Father to witness to their brother's loving life (Matthew). By the urging of the Spirit, the weak become powerful, the fearful become free and yet another word is spoken in the greatest love story ever told (Romans).

Deuteronomy 4:32-34, 39-48. Although the doctrine of the trinity per se cannot be found in any explicit formulation in scripture, nevertheless the roots of the doctrine are present in the existential experience of the believer in relationship to God. As R. Fuller has pointed out, the biblical experience of God is a triad one. In both the Jewish and Christian scriptures, God goes forth from himself in acts of revelation and of redemption. He creates in each receptive member of humanity a believing response to those acts or words of revelation and redemption. This triad-structured process of being and activity is the subject of our first reading today from Deuteronomy.

Deuteronomy's author and editors understood all of human history as the gradual self-revelation of God in time and space. Each event, each significant moment whereby nations were formed and destinies shaped were considered by the Deuteronomist to be words of God, speaking themselves into historical, recordable reality. Creation of the universe and of humankind was the first word of "going forth" of God (v. 32) and it is obvious that the author of today's pericope considered the exodus, the infiltration and settlement of Canaan, the covenant and gift of the law as other words in a continuous conversation of redemptive revelation. It is also clear that the Deuteronomist did not regard humanity as incapable or unthinking pawns on a sort of divine chessboard but rather, and because of God's gifts, as responsible and capable participants in the process and plan of history. Keeping the covenant and its divinely ordained statutes was the means whereby humanity could cooperate with divinity in response to his loving overtures of creation, redemption and revelation.

Today's text is from a longer theological introduction to the exposition of the covenant God had spoken among his people. By placing this recitation upon the lips of their hero, Moses, the Deuteronomist sought to restore to his people a sense of the sacred in their history and of renewed fidelity to the covenant. Because of the similarities of style and theology with Deutero-Isaiah, many believe today's pericope to have been composed during the exile. However, it is not unlikely that the text could have originated in seventh century

Judah, because it exhibits the style and theology of a levitical homily. Regardless of its exact date and setting, the text shows a certain liturgical character in which the manner of speaking of creation, the exodus (with a mighty arm and outstretched arm), etc., had become canonical or fixed . . . as would have occurred in liturgical usage. Having instilled in his hearers an awareness of God, his redemptive power and his blessings, the Deuteronomist required of his audience a response worthy of such great gifts. Ironically, at the time of his writing, a worthy response was not forthcoming from his people and the author's challenge went unanswered. Only after the suffering of the exile and its hard lessons of deprivation and shame did Israel become sensitive once again to hearing the voice of its creator-redeemer.

Israel's unique perception of history and of its various episodes or words of God paved the way for an understanding of the Christian perception of salvation. The same God who by his Spirit (*ruah*) created the world (v. 32) and shared with humanity his domination over it spoke unto the world the perfect word in his son Jesus.

Romans 8:14-17. Following immediately upon Paul's erudite exposition of the antithesis between the spirit and the flesh, today's pericope is part of a longer section in which the apostle discusses the quality and characteristics of Christian life as a result of the gift of the Holy Spirit. Because of the Spirit, Paul taught, the believer is made capable of achieving a new and eschatological status, that of being a son or a child of God (v. 14). The term "son of God" was not a novel idea, nor was it even a uniquely Christian one. Indeed, in the Jewish scriptures the term "son of God" is used in many ways and applied to a host of people. When applied to the nation of Israel, the term usually referred to the position Israel attained by reason of the covenant. Certain devout and just persons were also designated "sons of God," e.g., Moses. Like the pharaohs of ancient Egypt, the Davidic king was considered to enjoy a filial relationship with God (2 Samuel 7:14; 1 Chronicles 22:10; Psalm 2:7, 89:28). However wonderful these applications of the title "sons of God" may appear, they are only *honorific* designations and the idea of sonship should be understood only in a *metaphorical* sense.

The Christian son, or child of God, on the other hand, has become so, not merely by the conferring of a title but by reason of the action of Jesus Christ and the workings of his Spirit. In terminology borrowed from Hellenistic "legalese," Paul described the Christian as being *adopted* (*heirothesia*) into the family of God. Paul believed the gift and activity of the Spirit constituted that adoption and enabled the faithful to participate in the relationship of Jesus to the Father. Because of his eschatological status of adoption, the believer shares the same *rights* and glory as the incarnate and risen Son, Jesus. Moreover, that sharing is not a reward or recompense, as would be doled out to a slave or servant. Rather, by virtue of his/her adoption as God's child, the believer has become *heir* to all the fortunes and blessings of the divine life. Such an explanation must have been very appealing to the hundreds of thousands of slaves who existed in the Roman empire during Paul's day. For all people, both slave and free, Christianity represented a freedom and a dignity far greater than they could ever have achieved on a purely human level.

In keeping with their adoption as God's children, Paul exhorted his fellow believers to cultivate an attitude appropriate to their status and to look upon God as Father in the same way as did Jesus (Mark 14:36). "*Abba*, my Father" is a combination of Aramaic and Greek (with the Greek translating the Aramaic) and belies the close relationship Jesus shared with the Father. *Abba* is more correctly understood as an endearment one would use in the intimacy of the home in an atmosphere of warmth and love. That very intimacy and warmth are afforded each believing child of God because of the Spirit of Jesus. With confidence, the child can "cry out" (*krazo*, v. 15). This verb, *krazo*, can be used in two ways, i.e., to cry out in need, from whatever life situation or problem one finds oneself in (Psalm 3:5, 17:7, etc.) or in the sense of crying out in proclamation. Probably both senses, "crying out in need" and "crying out in creed," were intended by Paul. Although Christians were not the only group to call God "Father," it is believed that "Abba-Father" became a distinctly Christian mode of addressing God. In fact, it may be a relic of an ancient liturgical prayer or ejaculation.

In any event, it is obvious that Paul's purpose was to encourage his fellow believers by emphasizing their dignity as God's children. In the last sentence of today's reading, the reference to suffering-giving-way-to-glory would seem to indicate that Paul understood Christian hardship and persecution in terms of the passion of Jesus, the beloved Son. Therefore, the adopted children of God or the brothers and sisters of Jesus can hope to inherit a share in the same glory the Father bestowed upon Jesus.

Matthew 28:14-20. "For persecutors, let there be no hope, and the dominion of arrogance do thou speedily root out in our days; and let Christians and heretics perish in a moment. Let them be blotted out of the book of the living and let them not be written with the righteous." So went the 12th of the 18 benedictions to be recited by Jews at prayer in their synagogues. These benedictions were formulated and promulgated for general use by the academy at Jamnia under the leadership of Rabbi Johannen Ben Zakkai during the decades following the Jewish War (66-70 C.E.). With the destruction of Jerusalem as the authoritatively religious center of Judaism, Jamnia rabbis sought to strengthen their numbers by weeding out the aberrant and the heretical. Therefore, in the mid-80s C.E. by means of an edict, all Jews who attended the synagogues were required to recite the 18 benedictions. Naturally, those Jews who recognized Jesus as the messiah and had come to believe in him were unable to recite number 12 (above) and were summarily dismissed from the synagogue. At that point in time, Jewish Christians had to discover and redefine their own identity as a group distinct from their Jewish matrix but without relinquishing their Jewish roots. In response to that need and in an effort to overcome the faith-identity crisis of his fellow Jewish Christians, the author of Matthew's gospel formulated his ingenious theological synthesis. For this reason, W.D. Davies has aptly called Matthew's gospel "the Christian response to Jamnia."

Contrary to traditional thought, the author was not an eyewitness to the earthly Jesus or one of the Twelve but a second generation Jewish Christian (perhaps a former scribe) and his gospel reflects the problems and situation of the sub-apostolic church in a prosperous urban center of mixed population. Although many places have been suggested, Antioch in Syria is the most likely location for the author's community with its many gentile Christian members. The author of Matthew's gospel helped the second generation believers to understand themselves as a distinct group and to define themselves as an ecclesial entity. Indeed, Matthew's is the only gospel to employ the word church (*ekklesia*). Because of its strong emphases on order, organization and authority, Matthew's gospel was most cited by the early church fathers who assigned it the title "first gospel" without regard for its chronological position after Mark. As R.E. Brown has pointed out, Matthew's gospel provides the modern believer with an excellent view of church life in the last third of the first Christian century. From today's gospel which is comprised of the last verses of the gospel, we can gain an understanding of that church's sense of mission as well as an idea of their rites of initiation.

The scene is that of the ascending Jesus commissioning his disciples for their mission of teaching and baptizing. As in so many of the important events of Matthew's gospel, the setting is on a mountain. Like the great theophanic moments of the Old Testament, the Matthean Jesus performed his greatest tasks on the mountain (cf. Matthew 4:8, 5:1, 17:1).

Jesus' claim to full authority (v. 18) is reminiscent of Daniel's Son of Man upon whom all sovereignty had been bestowed (Daniel 7:14). Recall that the messianic title "Son of Man" had been accepted by Jesus; by it he had defined himself and his authority (Matthew 11:27, 26:64, 25:31). By virtue of that identity and that authority, the glorified and risen Jesus mandated his disciples to go forth to the *nations*. It is significant that the author has reflected in this command of Jesus the situation of his church of the 80s which had already moved beyond "Judea and Samaria" to the nations.

Again, the Jamnia experience had played a part in pushing the missionaries out of Judah and beyond the parameters of Judaism. The focus on the nations or the non-Jews is evident from the first chapters of the Matthean gospel in which the gentile Magi are portrayed as seeking the Lord of life and light.

Jesus' mandate to baptize (v. 19) using the trinitarian formula, Father, Son and Holy Spirit, probably reflects the more mature liturgical practices of the sub-apostolic community. Initially, baptism was administered only in the name of Jesus. This, however, is no reason to dismiss the doctrine of the trinity as a later and somehow less important concept. As R. Fuller explains, baptism in Jesus' name implies the confession of him as messiah, viz., as God's agent of salvation. Consequently the gift of the Spirit is a direct result of the salvation wrought by the messiah. Hence the trinity and the doctrine thereof existed in Christian experience before it was enunciated intellectually.

The final verse of the gospel contains a promise ("I am with you always") of Jesus' permanent presence with his own and constitutes the fulfillment of the Emmanuel prophecy (Matthew 1:23) at the beginning of the gospel. Unlike the earliest ideas that Christ was absent from the ascension until the parousia, the Matthean community was aware of Christ's abiding presence with them (Matthew 11:29-30, 13:41, 18:20, etc.). Today that same dynamic, permanent presence of Jesus Christ is among us, moving us onward to mission and enabling us to know the trinitarian aspects and qualities of God.

1. The only act greater than creation of humanity is the redemption of humanity (Deuteronomy).

2. All who call God "Father" are responsible for one another as members of one family (Romans).

3. The full authority Jesus received from the Father was exercised by him in suffering and in service as an example for all of his disciples (Matthew).

Corpus Christi

He offered to all a share in the cup which he alone would drink to the dregs on the cross (Mark). By that sharing and by his offering, Jesus' blood sacrifice silenced the rage and hatred of sin and spoke the words of forgiveness and reconciliation into a needful world (Hebrews). No other word is necessary—except for the Amen of all believers (Exodus).

Exodus 24:3-8. In an effort to articulate the special relationship that existed between God and humankind, Israel's religious authors borrowed from the spheres of their social, economic and political expressions. The term "covenant" (*berith* in Hebrew; *diatheke* in Greek; *testamentum* in Latin) was applied to trade agreements, to alliances between individuals and groups and to treaties among nations. When employed by the biblical writers, the word covenant referred to an agreement or pact, initiated by God with Israel, which carried specific conditions, binding terms and definitive responsibilities. Once the covenant was understood, its policies were ratified in a ceremonial act of sealing. Thereafter, the breaching of the agreement involved certain implications. Fidelity to the pact, on the other hand, was rewarded with blessings for the covenanted peoples.

Today's first reading is comprised of the Old Testament Eloist theologian's version of the ratification of the Sinai (Horeb) covenant. Because this covenant was normative for the religious, political and social life of the people, and because the Sinai pact dominated Israel's history, its ratification was of paramount importance. The act of sealing was the sign of the people's formal acceptance. That the covenant was sealed in *blood* indicated that the intention was not merely to conform to the law, which was in fact the terms of the covenant, but to enter into a sharing of life or lives. According to the Hebrew understanding, life resided in the blood (Leviticus 17:14). Hence Moses' action of sprinkling of blood on the altar, which represented Yahweh, and on the people was in effect a statement concerning the power of the covenant to bring together as one the giver of life with his living people. Although the Sinai covenant was renewed many times, the ratification in blood or the rite of blood was not repeated until the once and for all perfect sacrifice of Jesus made the covenant a new and eternal one.

In v. 5, the references to burnt offerings and to peace offerings should be understood as an anachronism, i.e., the product of a later, more developed sacrificial system than existed in Mosaic times. The *'olah* or holocaust involved the burning of the entire victim on the altar as an act of homage or adoration. The *shelem* or peace offerings were usually consumed in a festive meal for the purpose of cementing the relationships of those gathered with one another and with God. Because of the joyful nature of the peace offering sacrificial meal, it was often referred to as "eating and drinking before the Lord" (Deuteronomy 12:7, 12, 18).

When viewed in conjunction with the other two readings for today's liturgy, this text from Exodus provides us with a background for understanding Christ's redeeming blood-sacrifice (Hebrews) and its memorialization in the celebration of the eucharist (Mark). At Sinai, the Hebrew faithful signified their sharing in the life of Yahweh and were consecrated by the ritual of the blood. Because of the shedding of Christ's blood on Calvary, the Christian faithful achieve a share in the life of God. At the eucharist, those who partake of the saving cup remember Calvary and celebrate the covenant it established.

Hebrews 9:11-15. No doubt Eusebius correctly concluded that "only God knows" who wrote the rich theological treatise which has come to be known as the letter to the Hebrews. Though traditionally ascribed to Paul, internal evidence would indicate otherwise, viz., differences in vocabulary, style, structuring, use of Old Testament citations, theology, etc. Probably the most that *can* be said is that the author of Hebrews was a Hellenistic Jewish Christian acquainted with the works of Philo, the thought of Plato and the style of the Greek rhetoricians. And while the author's style and other elements may have differed from Paul's, nevertheless, the two were in accord in their efforts to show Jesus, his priesthood and his sacrifice as superior to Old Testament clergy, cult and ritual.

Today's second reading is part of a longer pericope within which the author defends the perfect priesthood and perfect liturgy of Christ. To illustrate his point, the author compared the high priest's activities on the Day of Atonement, *Yom Kippur*, with the saving action of Jesus. On Atonement Day, i.e., the tenth day of the seventh month, the high priest was to offer two goats as a sin offering and a ram as a holocaust for the community, and a bullock for himself and his sins (Leviticus 16:1ff, 23:26ff). After confessing his own sin and the sins of the people, he was to offer the sacrifices and to take their blood to the holy of holies to sprinkle the gold plate of the ark of the covenant. It was hoped that the blood which symbolized life would atone for the sins and thus God would reconcile his covenanted people to himself and to one another. A fast and the sabbatical rest were also integral to the Day of Atonement which was observed annually.

The author of Hebrews understood Jesus Christ as *the* high priest par excellence of a new covenant, and as the perfect victim whose blood sacrifice, offered not annually but once-and-for-all, accomplished perfect atonement for sin and reconciled all peoples to God. Moreover, unlike the animal blood and heifer's ashes which were thought to render one ritually pure (Numbers 19:9, 14-21), the blood of Jesus wrought a *moral* purification that cleansed the defiled and weakened conscience of the believer.

Significantly, most manuscripts have preserved v. 11's *ton mellonton agathon*, "good things to come," although two of the oldest manuscripts have *ton genomenon agathon*, "the good things which *have* come (or which came) to be." The former and more widely published reading (good things to come) may be less accurate but does emphasize the eschatological and anticipatory character of Christ's work, seeing it as a piece of the whole which will reach its final consummation at his second advent.

M. Bourke has pointed out that redemption (v. 12) should be understood in light of its usage in the Old Testament. Redemption or *lytrosis* belongs to a group of words (*lytron, lytrousthai, apolytrosis*) which convey the notion of deliverance and are used in the Jewish scriptures to refer to Israel's deliverance from the exile in Babylon (Isaiah 41:14, 44:22). In the same way *lytrosis* in Psalm 130:7-8 is used to express the deliverance of the faithful from sin. In none of these instances was there any insinuation that the "payment of a price" or a "ransom" was demanded as a condition for deliverance or redemption. There is no foundation for reading such an idea into this verse (12) despite the views of those who see the blood of Christ as the "*price*" paid (to God) for the redemption of humanity. Because of his sacrifice, Jesus has become mediator of a new and eternal covenant, not a bartering chip with a calculating God. Because of the offering of his own blood, i.e., his life, he has achieved for others at-one-ment for sin and deliverance from its guilt.

Mark 14:12-16, 22-26. Originally the feast of Passover was a pastoral one and was apparently observed prior to the exodus event. With the exodus, however, the feast was historicized and forever associated with the great deeds God had done for his people, in passing over their blood-smeared homes, in sparing their lives and in allowing them to *pass* over from Egypt's slavery to freedom (Exodus 12:1-30). After the settlement in Canaan, the Passover feast came to be associated with another feast, that of Unleavened Bread. Chronologically, the Passover feast and the ancient agricultural feast of Unleavened Bread coincided on the 14th-15th of Nisan. According to the instructions given in the book of Numbers (28:16-17), "On the fourteenth day of the first month Nisan is the Lord's passover. On the fifteenth of the month is a feast; seven days shall unleavened bread be eaten." How is it then that Mark in writing his passion narrative was unaware of the correct dates of these feasts? In Mark 14:1, the evangelist has given the impression that the sacrificing of the Passover lamb and the feast of Unleavened Bread were the same day. Actually the lambs were slaughtered on the afternoon of 14th Nisan and the feast of Unleavened Bread began at sundown, i.e., when the 15th of Nisan began. Is this discrepancy in Mark an indication that he was unfamiliar with Jewish customs, or was he more concerned with a theological setting than a chronological time frame?

In the first of the two excerpts (vv. 12-16, 22-26) from Mark's passion narrative which comprise today's gospel, Jesus' instructions concerning the preparations for the meal (vv. 12-16) accentuated his foreknowledge in a somewhat miraculous manner. Mark 14:12-16 is remarkably similar to Mark 11:1-7 wherein Jesus is cast in the light of the eschatological prophet with messianic authority and supernatural perceptions. For example, it would have been quite unusual for a man to carry a water jar. Customarily, men carried water in skins, while jars or jugs were left for women to wield. Some have suggested that the designation "the teacher" (v. 14) was sufficient identification because the owner of the house was a disciple.

Preparations for the meal per se would have included the procuring and readying of the blessed lamb, the herbs, sauces, salt water, apple and nuts, etc. None of these items appear in Mark's narrative of the supper; while the evangelist was careful to closely associate the Lord's supper with the Passover meal, his chief concern was not with the Passover lamb but with Jesus' own passover from death to life.

The institution narrative (vv. 22-26) therefore was not intended as a play-by-play description of the Passover meal. Rather, it is highly liturgical in character and probably reflects the early eucharistic tradition of the Marcan community of the 60s. From it, we can ascertain that the eucharist, both bread and cup, was celebrated near the end of the meal, unlike the earlier tradition in Paul (1 Corinthians 11) which celebrated the bread before and the cup after the meal. Seven distinct liturgical actions can also be discerned, e.g., (1) taking of bread, (2) blessing-thanking, (3) breaking bread, (4) distribution, (5) taking of cup, (6) blessing-thanking, (7) distribution. The similarity of this set pattern with the multiplication sequences (Mark 6 and Mark 8) was surely intentional; all reflect a liturgical and eucharistic understanding.

The cup with which Jesus identified and which he offered was probably the third cup of wine of the Passover meal which followed the main course, after which the Hallel psalms were sung. Jesus' interpretation of the cup, in terms of the suffering-servant (poured out for many: Isaiah 53:11-12), sheds light on the meaning and purpose of his coming passion. Although only inferior manuscripts add "new" as a modifier to covenant in v. 23, Jesus *did* by the saving sacrifice of the cross forge a *new* bond whereby God's blessings were available to all. "For many" is a semitism meaning *all*.

Just as those sprinkled with the blood at Sinai became participants in the covenant and responsible for its precepts, so, those who drink of the cup (and eat of the bread) become participants and beneficiaries of the salvation the cup (the bread) signifies. Cup and cross cannot be separated; the eucharist forms an integral part of the saving event of Calvary. This was the understanding the Marcan church reflected in its liturgical practice.

Early believers also recognized the eschatological dimension of the eucharist as v. 25 indicates. As they celebrated the Lord's supper, they remembered the covenant, commemorated the cross, and anticipated the future feasting which would accompany the definitive establishment of God's reign. In every eucharist, the believer is called upon to enter fully into this multi-dimensional experience.

1. The exterior ritual is no greater than the interior motivation which inspired it (Exodus).

2. Sacrifice is not an end in itself; the end of sacrifice is nearness to God (Hebrews).

3. The cup and the cross are both part of the same gift of love (Mark).

Year C

The Advent Season
First Sunday of Advent

They were looking to the sky for omens and portents (Luke): they were looking to the throne for a king. But he came as quietly and as surely as the new life of every spring. In the insignificant shoot of a kingdom once toppled, Israel would find justice and peace (Jeremiah). Those who wait in hope and joy for his return should remember these facts and sharpen their spiritual senses with prayer and communal love so as to recognize even his subtlest appearances (Thessalonians).

Jeremiah 33:14-16. How fitting that the liturgical year, which remembers and celebrates the seasons of our salvation, should begin in the dark, gloomy, barren time of the year. Like a cosmic audio-visual aid, the world of nature attests to the fact that the light of the *kairos* (Christ-event; Christ's hour) has pierced the waiting needful night of human *chronos* (chronological time, human history) and has changed forever the thrust of humanity's efforts and goals. It is this joy we renew in every Advent season, at the head of each new year of faith. It was precisely this hopeful spirit of joyful anticipation which the author of today's first reading wished to awaken in his contemporaries.

An almost exact reiteration of an earlier oracle (23:5-6) in the book of Jeremiah, today's pericope was probably reworked by one of Jeremiah's disciples or a redactor and uttered at a later period. The original oracle (Jeremiah 23) was, no doubt, occasioned by the destruction of Jerusalem by the Babylonians and the subsequent exile of the elite of the people (ca. 586 B.C.E.). Jeremiah attempted to bolster the hopes of his people by promising that the Davidic king toppled by Babylon would be restored by the Lord himself.

Basing his oracle on the promise made to David through the prophet Nathan (2 Samuel 7:14), the sixth century prophet reminded his contemporaries that David's was to be an *eternal* dynasty. But years passed, the exile dragged on and, with each passing year, the hopes for the restoration of a successor to David's throne grew dimmer. Because of the delay, the exiled Judahites in Babylon were tempted to give up their ancient traditions and beliefs. Many, attracted by the gods of their oppressors, began to forget the divine promises (and their fulfillments) that had punctuated their history as a people. In the face of their despair, the author of today's pericope revived the ancient oracle of his predecessor, Jeremiah, and repeated it for his contemporaries.

Semah saddiz or "just shoot" (righteous branch), also rendered "legitimate heir" (v. 15), became a classic prophetic term for the messiah or the "anointed one" of the Lord (Isaiah 11:1; Zechariah 3:8, 6:12). A shoot from David was promised; in him would righteousness and justice be done and in him would Judah flourish once more in safety and security (v. 16). Because of the just shoot, the new Jerusalem would be renamed *Yahweh Sidqenu*, "The Lord our justice" (v. 16). A paranomasia on the name of Zedekiah, Judah's last weak and vacillating king whose reign had spelled disaster for his people, *Yahweh Sidqenu* would signal the inauguration of a new era, the age of God's saving presence and activity, the age of messianism.

1 Thessalonians 3:12—4:2. Named for the wife of its founder Cassander in 315 B.C.E., Thessalonica was a major port city on the Thermaic Gulf in northern Greece. Because of its strategic location, the city became the chief naval headquarters of the Macedonian kings. After its conquest by the Romans in 168 B.C.E., Thessalonica became the capital of the Roman province of Macedonia and residence of the proconsul. Situated on the Via Egnatia, connecting Rome with its eastern provinces, the city grew in population and prestige as a center of commerce. During the second Roman civil war, Thessalonica allied its forces with Antony and Octavian, and for its loyalty was granted the status of "free city." Under this designation, the Thessalonians could elect their own assembly and magistrates who were called politarchs (Acts 17:5-6). When Paul, Silvanus and Timothy arrived in Thessalonica in (ca.) 50 C.E. during Paul's second missionary journey, they met a population comprised chiefly of Greeks. A smattering of many other nationalities were also present because the city was a trade center, and there was a sizeable Jewish colony. Toward this Jewish community the disciples directed their first efforts of evangelization. After meeting with great opposition and little success among the Jews, Paul turned his attention to the god-fearing Greeks. Eventually, Paul and companions were expelled from Thessalonica due to the hostile Jews who incited the city council against the disciples (Acts 17:1-9).

The earliest written Christian documents in the canon of the Christian scriptures, 1 and 2 Thessalonians are among the 21 books in the New Testament called *epistolai* or epistles. Until the liturgical and scholarly renewal inspired by the Second Vatican Council, the term epistle was applied to all 21 works with little regard for their distinguishing characteristics. Today, however, with more attention given to the critical study of the scriptures and to the various literary genre, a distinction has been made between letters and epistles. In this regard, the studies of A. Deissmann have proved helpful. Deissmann identified an epistle as an artistic form of literature, written in the form and style of a letter but with little resemblance to a letter in any other regard. Developed in the Greek philosophical schools of the fourth century B.C.E., the epistle was a treatise or essay written for the purpose of public instruction or as a polemical discussion of a pertinent topic. A letter, on the other hand, was a personal means of communication between two parties who were separated. Familiar in style and tone, the letter was usually written for or occasioned by a particular circumstance. According to Deissmann, only a few of Paul's works should be called epistles (Romans, Ephesians), while the rest were intended as letters. Through these letters, Paul communicated his ideas, his feelings, his theology, faith and hope. Moreover, through Paul's letters, modern believers can glimpse the life of the church in the first generation after Jesus' resurrection, and find therein support for their personal struggles in the faith. One of the most important difficulties through which Paul helped the early Christians was their dismay at the delay of Christ's second advent. Like the recipients of the oracle of Jeremiah (first reading) and like those who heard Luke's good news (gospel), the Thessalonians found themselves in the interim between a divine promise and its fulfillment. Paul's advice, like the words of Luke and Jeremiah, can be helpful to 20th century believers who share that same sense of hopeful waiting for the Lord to show himself again.

In the first letter to the Thessalonian believers, from which today's second reading is excerpted, Paul prayed that those to whom he had introduced Jesus would maintain themselves in faith and holiness until his coming. In order to be prepared for that great and glorious day, Paul exhorted his converts to remember all they had learned from him (4:1). Obviously, while among them, the apostle would have proclaimed to the Thessalonians the good news of Jesus and aided them in integrating their faith in the gospel with a life of prayer, moral uprightness and charity. From the favorable remarks Paul made in his letter, the Thessalonians must have been generous in their response to Christ: "which you are indeed doing" (4:1). Still, he called them just as Jesus did to even greater progress and deeper commitment: "So you must learn to make still greater progress."

Luke 21:25-28, 34-36. No study of Luke's gospel is complete without a consideration of the second volume of the author's work, the Acts of the Apostles. The two volumes are independent and together communicate the good news of Jesus and of the church. C. Talbert has classified Luke-Acts in the literary genre of the ancient cultic biography. The cultic biography was generally arranged in two parts: (a) the life of the divine hero was followed by (b) a narrative by his successors and selected other disciples. The two components of the biography functioned as a single work to *legitimate* the founder's successors at the time of the document's writing by showing that the line of tradition between the founder and his successors was unbroken and by showing the continuity between the founder's words and works and those of his successors.

Given Talbert's contribution, Luke-Acts presents to its readers the life and good news about the earthly Jesus (the period of Jesus), and the continuation (Acts) of Jesus' saving activity in the persons of his disciples (the period of the church). By illustrating this continuity, the author authenticated the work of Jesus' disciples among second and third generation Christians, none of whom had ever met the earthly, historical Jesus. This point is clear in the author's prologue to his gospel, "I have decided . . . to put systematically in writing for you, Theophilus, so that your excellency may realize what *assurance* you have for the instruction you have received" (1:3-4).

Assurance or *asphaleia* was one of the intended results of the author's work, i.e., to illustrate both doctrinally and didactically that God's salvation effected by Jesus continued to be proclaimed in and by his church. In this way, says J. Fitzmeyer, Luke differs from the other evangelists, because he desired to relate the story of Jesus, not only to his contemporary world and culture but also to the growth and development of the nascent Christian church.

When he approached the topic of the parousia of Jesus, the author of the third gospel also brought a different viewpoint to the issue. Perhaps the Lucan perspective on eschatology can best be summarized in the words of the two men in white at Jesus' ascension in glory, "Why are you standing here, looking up into the sky?" (Acts 1:11). Whereas Mark (whom Luke used as one of his sources) communicated to his readers in the 60s the idea of the *imminence* of Jesus' second advent (Mark 13), when Luke wrote in the 80s it had become obvious that the Marcan urgency had to be rethought. Therefore, a comparison of the Marcan apocalypse to that of Luke (of which today's gospel is an excerpt) will reveal a shift in emphasis. Mark has associated the "end" with the destruction of Jerusalem which was yet to happen; when Luke wrote, Jerusalem lay in rubble and still the "end" had not yet come.

At the time of his writing, the author of the third gospel witnessed a growing and expanding church, one which had spread far beyond Jerusalem and its Jewish roots. It was a community of many languages, many cultures, stretching throughout all of the then known world. While Mark has assumed that his generation of believers would witness the Lord's return and the consummation of all in their lifetime, Luke realized that his was a church that was here to stay. Although he certainly did not ignore the fact of Jesus' return (see vv. 25-28), Luke preferred to concentrate more on the Christian community's relation to the Lord in their present situation. In this way, the evangelist underscored the necessity of a quality moral response—one based not on the *fear* of the end but on the *values* taught by Jesus throughout his ministry.

Perhaps one might compare the difference in Mark and Luke's eschatological perspectives and the different stages of growth they represent to levels of moral growth. The first level, normally that of a young child, would be to act or to refrain from an action because of an expected and immediate reward or punishment. At the risk of oversimplification, one might compare the young, growing church of Mark's day to that young child whose actions were tempered by the imminence of the parousia and the divine judgment. At a later level of moral growth, the actions are performed because of an interiorized goal or conviction. It was this higher level of moral response to Christ to which Luke challenged his community of believers, i.e., to be *aware* of the end but not fearfully so.

Luke would not have his readers "standing, looking up to heaven" but looking at the person and challenge of Jesus in the good news as proclaimed in the lives of his disciples. To this end, he counselled believers against drunken indulgences and undue concern with worldly cares (v. 34). As a preparation for both their present and their future the evangelist continually exhorted his community to *pray* (v. 38). In that way would the quality of their lives be such that at each moment they would be in readiness to meet the Son of Man.

1. In the promised life of every new green shoot, the believer can find a sign for his belief in the coming of Jesus (Jeremiah).

2. Learning how to wait for the Lord is as important as learning how to meet him (Thessalonians).

3. Apathy, more than fear, is the enemy of the Advent spirit of joyful anticipation (Luke).

Second Sunday of Advent

Peoples and lands of the earth had been divided up like a deck of cards, held in the hands of the powerful. Tiberius, Pilate, the Herods and Lysanias, Annas and Caiphas—each enjoyed an unchallenged power in their own particular domains. Then out of the desert a voice proclaimed the day of freedom for all peoples (Luke). From that moment onward, tryrannical rulers, temporal thrones and even earthly temples had to yield to the saving power that, like the sun rising in the east (Baruch), brought life and light and a harvest of justice to all (Philippians).

Baruch 5:1-9. Historically, Baruch (whose name in Hebrew means "blessed") was a companion of the seventh century B.C.E. prophet Jeremiah. Besides supporting the prophet during the difficult period that ended in the siege of Jerusalem by the Babylonians, Baruch served as Jeremiah's amanuesis or secretary (Jeremiah 45:1). Having written out the prophet's oracles on a scroll, Baruch rewrote them when an angry Jehoiakim destroyed the scroll (Jeremiah 36:1). Believed to have been taken with Jeremiah to Egypt after the murder of Gedaliah, Baruch remained a popular figure in Jewish folklore and tradition but none of the three books that bear his name were actually written by him. In addition to the canonical book of Baruch, from which today's first reading has been selected, there are two apocryphal books: (1) Second Baruch or the Syriac Apocalypse of Baruch, and (2) Third Baruch or the Greek Apocalypse. Omitted by the Jamnia council from the Palestinian canon, Baruch does not appear in the Hebrew scriptures or in Protestant Bibles. Baruch is, however, one of the several works included in the Greek texts of the scriptures (Alexandrian canon) that have, since the Council of Trent, been considered canonical by Roman Catholics.

More of an anthology than a single work, Baruch contains a collection of various literary elements: penitential (1:15—3:8), sapiential (3:9—4:4), prophetic (4:5—5:9) and epistolary (6:1-72) all of which have been set against the purported situation of the Babylonian exile (586-538 B.C.E.). Actually, the author wrote about four centuries after the exile and was probably a Jew of the diaspora who regarded Jerusalem as his spiritual mother and true home. If the consensus of scholars is correct in the dating of the book of Baruch, then the author was probably writing for his dispersed contemporaries during the period of the Greek (Seleucid) occupation. Under Antiochus Epiphanes IV and his successors, the Jewish peoples (and others) suffered trials and hardships comparable to those of the Babylonian exile.

As. T. Maertens has observed, today's selected pericope is not an original passage, but a sort of digest of Deutero-Isaiah. Where the sixth century prophet envisioned the return of the exiles from Babylon in terms of a *new* exodus, so too the Baruch author foresaw the return home of the dispersed Jews in similar terms. Significantly, the Baruch author, like his predecessor, Deutero-Isaiah, looked beyond human capabilities and believed that God alone was the source of Israel's salvation. Beckoning Jerusalem to look to the east (v. 5), i.e., to the place where each new day is born as the sun rises, the author summoned his people to find in the word of the holy one (v. 5) the promise of their forgiveness and the dawn of their salvation. This rich imagery is deeply expressive of the spirit of messianism that flourished in the troubled centuries before Jesus and has become the vehicle for the hopes and joys of the Advent Christian.

Philippians 1:4-6, 8-11. Paul first met the Philippians (Acts 16:12-40) and preached to them the good news of their salvation on his second missionary journey, ca. 50 C.E. Philippi was the first Christian community in Europe, and its designation by Paul as a site for evangelization was due no doubt to its strategic location straddling the pass that separated Europe from Asia. A major thoroughfare for commerce, the city was also the home of a large number of Roman military veterans and their families. In addition to the Romans, a large settlement of Greeks and a small Jewish community resided in Philippi at the time of Paul's arrival. On the sabbath, Paul began his work among the Jews who met for prayer near the Crenides river outside the city. Judging from the Greek names of some of his converts and keeping in mind the efforts of the Judaizers to thwart the apostle's work among the Jews, Paul appeared to have had more success among the gentiles who came to hear him. He gained little popularity by exposing the masters of a slave girl who were abusing her "ability" to tell fortunes for the sake of a "quick denarius." Angry that Paul had exorcised the girl, the men had Paul and Silas arrested, beaten and imprisoned. Miraculously freed from prison, Paul invoked the *lex Porcia* and his status as a Roman citizen to demand an apology for the wrongful arrest and punishment without benefit of trial. Despite his stormy stay in Philippi, Paul had succeeded in bringing to Christ a good number of the people, so that the church in Philippi soon flourished and became one of the apostle's favorite communities. From the opening prayer of his letter to Philippi, which comprises today's first reading, Paul's predilection for the Philippian Christians is warmly evident.

Although the details surrounding the circumstances of the letter are still debated, the letter is one of Paul's so-called captivity letters and was either written during an Ephesus incarceration, ca. 54-56 C.E., or while the apostle was in prison in Rome ca. 62 C.E. In either case, Paul's physical bondage did not in any way hamper the freedom of spirit and enthusiastic love he communicated to the Philippians. The theme of joy (v. 4) with which Paul began his prayer would be repeated 11 times in the course of the letter and would be one of the identifying hallmarks of the doctrine included therein.

Following the traditional patterns of the Jewish thanksgiving prayer, Paul's prayer contained a blessing (vv. 3-8) and an epiclesis (vv. 9-11). With confidence, Paul was sure that the good work God had begun in the Philippians (through Paul) would be brought to completion (v. 6). Though the sense of meaning has been lost in translation, "has begun" and "will carry through to completion" were technical terms in Greek for the beginning and end of a sacrifice. As P. Wrightman has pointed out, Paul thought of the entire Christian life as a progressive sacrifice, a process through which the Christian can grow in holiness. That spirit of sacrifice and of completing the Lord's good work should sustain the believer, taught Paul, "right up to the day of Christ Jesus" (v. 6). "Day of Jesus" or "Day of the Lord" was an Old Testament term that came to signify the parousia or second coming of Jesus for Christians. For Paul, whose imprisonment could easily have ended with his own execution, the "day" must have seemed an imminent and very real possibility.

In that attitude of peaceful urgency, he prayed for the Philippians—that their love would increase (epiclesis) and that this increase of love for God and for one another result in an increased knowledge (*epignosis*) and clarity of conscience (v.10). Characteristic of Pauline theology, love was to be the basic principle of spiritual development and moral discernment. Not only should that love lead to greater knowledge of God (not fear or dread of the "Day of the Lord") but it should also hone the moral fiber of the Christian to recognize and choose the will of God in all circumstances of life.

Luke 3:1-6. As he unfolded the two volume schema of his credal proclamation of the history of salvation, the author of the third gospel gave John the Baptizer a distinct and special role, as today's gospel illustrates. John, according to the Lucan author, was the bridge between the first epoch of history or the period of Israel (law and prophets) and the second epoch (the period of Jesus). As the last of the Old Testament prophets, John summed up in his person and in his message the burden of his people's hopes and expectations. A herald of the new era, John pointed beyond himself to Jesus and prepared his contemporaries for the event that would forever change the course of their lives and the world. Because Luke wrote after Mark and Matthew and because there was a tendency in early Christianity (70s, 80s) to regard John the Baptizer as a rival of Jesus or even as a messianic figure, the Lucan author took great care to portray the Baptizer as subordinate to Jesus in all ways. Nevertheless, though secondary to Jesus', the role of John remains an important one. In the Baptizer's preaching and in his mission the old and the new have dovetailed. Like a prism, the task of John was to refract the light, to reflect it away from himself and to focus the eyes of his hearers upon the person of the Lord Jesus.

Stuhlmueller has pointed out the similarities between the Lucan portrait of the Baptizer and the sixth century B.C.E. prophet Jeremiah. Both had been called by God from the womb (Jeremiah 1:5, Luke 1:13). Both were heralds of eschatological judgment (Jeremiah 1:10, 25; Luke 3:9, 16ff) and messianic glory (Jeremiah 31; Luke 1:14, 3:15), and both men looked ahead to a new covenant relationship to be enjoyed by all, even the disadvantaged and insignificant (Jeremiah 31:31-34, Luke 7:18-23). While the practice of introducing a prophet and his mission by naming the contemporary rulers has precedents in the Hebrew scriptures (Isaiah 1:1, Jeremiah 1:3, Hosea 1:1), Luke was probably following the style set forth by the Greek authors in whom he had been well schooled. By his detailed system of dating the mission of the Baptizer, the author succeeded in synchronizing the gospel event in the context of secular (Roman) and sacred (Jewish) history and in drawing attention to the inauguration of Jesus' own ministry.

According to the Roman calendar, Tiberius reigned as emperor from August 19, 14 C.E. to 37 C.E. Therefore the 15th year of his rule would have been 28-29 C.E. But Luke, a non-Palestinian and a second or third generation Christian, probably ordered his data according to the Syrian calendar which began on October 1. Hence Tiberius' first few weeks as ruler (August 19—September 30) would have been considered as his first year, and the 15th year of his reign and the beginning of Jesus' ministry would have been in 27-28 C.E. Pontius Pilate presided as procurator of Judea, Idumea and Samaria from 26-36 C.E.; Herod Antipas, son of Herod the Great and Malthace, was tetrarch of Galilee and Perea from 4 B.C.E.—34 C.E. Lysanias' identity remains a puzzle. Some have suggested the name was a hereditary one adopted by many of Abilene's kings. A Lysanias was tetrarch of Abilene until 37 C.E. Although Annas was high priest from 6-15 C.E. and Caiphas from 18-36 C.E., the influence of Annas was so great and all pervading that Luke was able to speak of the high priesthood of Annas *and* Caiphas! Within this secular desert of needful humanity, the Baptizer was introduced as a teacher of repentance and forgiveness for the only truly just and everlasting ruler.

True to his synoptic source (Mark), Luke described John's mission in terms borrowed from Deutero-Isaiah's book of consolation (40:3ff). But, unlike his fellow synoptics (Matthew and Mark), the Lucan author with his universalist concerns extended his quoting of the prophet to include verse five: "and *all humanity* shall see the salvation of God" (3:6). In its original context the Isaian poem was spoken to the Israelites exiled in Babylon in an effort to console them: Soon they would be going home! Today's first reading from Baruch expressed similar hopes for diaspora Jews, centuries later. By the first Christian century, these texts and others like them had taken on a messianic significance. In John's day the prophet Isaiah's words gave expression to the people's hope for a savior who would draw God's people together once more. With John, we stand as believers who know that this savior has come in the first advent of Jesus; and in the spirit of the Baptizer, we await with eager anticipation and confident joy his second coming.

1. When at last all peoples come together to meet the returning Lord, theirs will be a divinely negotiated peace (Baruch).

2. If God has truly been the initiating spirit behind our good works, then his are the only criteria of success worthy of our consideration (Philippians).

3. The one who forever changed the manner of measuring time in years and seasons should be the integral center of the believer's daily routine (Luke).

Third Sunday of Advent

When at last the mighty one appeared, the work of harvesting began. The joy of his coming and the labor of the harvest were lost on those whose cares and anxieties blinded them from recognizing the truth (Philippians). However, the repentant, honest and needy were gathered unto him and these he carried home with joy to his Father (Luke). In exultant singing and dancing the celebration of reunion began, to be renewed at every eucharistic festival of forgiveness (Zephaniah).

Zephaniah 3:14-18. An oasis of relief in an otherwise unmitigated desert of nay-saying and doom, today's first reading from the prophet Zephaniah is a psalm calling Zion (Jerusalem) to rejoice in anticipation of Yahweh's sure and swift intervention. Because the positive and joyful tone of the text is so dissimilar to the rest of the prophet's utterances, some scholars believe it the work of another, added later at the editing stage of the oracles. Regardless of its authorship or date, the psalm's summons to joy and its richness of expectancy make it an appropriate one for celebrating the spirit and season of Advent.

Zephaniah had deep insight into the causes of his people's dabbling in idolatry, etc., and enumerated these as pride (1:6; 2:10, 15; 3:11), a rebellious spirit (3:1) and a lack of trust in God (1:12, 3:2). Like Amos (5:18), Zephaniah warned that the Day of the Lord would surely come for all peoples including Judah and that "day" would be a dark night of punishment and retribution for infidelities (1:7-18). When the "day" and the Lord's judgment would be visited upon his people, the prophet promised that Yahweh would "remove proud boasters from your midst and you will cease to strut on my holy mountain. In your midst I will leave a humble and lowly people . . . they will do no wrong, tell no lies . . . they will rest with no one to disturb them" (3:11-13). To these humble and lowly ones, the *anawim*, the psalm that comprises today's first reading was addressed.

Many have called this "humble and lowly people" the "remnant" of Israel, indicating that the Day of the Lord had resulted in a sort of weeding out or decimation of the people. Of course this is the sense usually derived from the text but there is another possible interpretation. Rather than decimate the people by destroying sinners, perhaps the Lord's "day" and their encounter with truth and justice could be thought of in terms of a removal—not of the sinner but of his/her sin. Then the people once puffed up with pride and arrogance would be "deflated" by the humbling process of repentance and conversion. Keeping in mind the power of God to save his people, we can then think of the humble and lowly not as *fewer* (remnant) but as *forgiven*. For that reason, the call to rejoice (v. 14) is all the more comprehensible.

The powerful and comforting image of God in the midst of his people (v. 16) recalls the God-with-us or Emmanuel prophecy of Isaiah (Isaiah 7:14) and the expected joys of the messianic era. Although the Hebrew text has "God will be silent in his love" (v. 17), the LXX amended the text to read "and renew you in his love." Actually, for forgiven sinners the silent love of an unreproachful God and the quiet understanding of a Father who desists from saying "I told you so!" would be a very appealing figure. Finally, the picture of a shouting Yahweh, singing joyfully (the JB has "dancing") over his people as on a festival day (v. 18), concludes the psalm on a note of eschatological exuberance. With the same exuberance Advent Christians celebrate the daily discovery of God in our midst. That same confident joy and dancing should characterize Advent's preparation for his ultimate manifestation.

Philippians 4:4-7. Paul's enthusiastic imperative "Rejoice!" (v. 4) has become the clarion call and hallmark of the Advent season. But actually, in its original context, the apostle's call to joy and the exhortation that followed it (our second reading for today) were initially directed toward two women. Evodia and Syntyche were recognized ministers in the more progressive Macedonian church and had evidently been associated with Paul as he worked in Philippi ("they toiled with me in the gospel"). The two had quarreled over an issue not specified by Paul in his letter and their dispute threatened the internal peace of the Christian community at Philippi. When news of the problem reached Paul in prison, he included in his letter a personal word to the two women and even recommended an arbiter to help them to come to an agreement (4:3).

"The Lord is very near" (v. 5), he reminded the Philippians. Set against the eschatological perspective of eternity, all human disputes and seemingly mountainous problems pale into insignificant molehills. If we might read between the lines of Paul's letter, he seemed to be saying, "Life is too short to spend it in needless conflict, concentrate your energies on what really matters!" To that end, the apostle recommended that the Philippians cultivate the virtue of *epiekeia*. A Greek term with no suitable (one word) English equivalent, it has been rendered: "unselfish" (v. 5) by the NAB, "moderation" by the AV, "patience" by Wycliffe, "softness" by Tyndale, "modesty" by the Rheims Bible, "forbearance" or "gentleness" by the RSV and "tolerance" by the JB. C.K. Williams added a colloquial touch and translated 4:5 as "Let all the world know you will 'meet a man half-way' "! As W. Barclay has observed, the Greeks regarded *epiekeia* as "justice, and something better than justice." Keeping in mind the personal quarrel at the basis of Paul's remarks, it would seem Christians are called to a magnanimity of heart and understanding that goes beyond the limits of strict distributive justice. By virtue of *epieikia*, the believer would not insist upon his legal and genuine rights according to the letter of the law, if such insistence would be the cause of strife and bitter discord.

Luke 3:10-18. "What ought we to do?" is a question that appears frequently in the two volume work of Luke-Acts (Luke 3:10, 12, 14; 10:25, 18:18; Acts 2:37, 16:30, 22:10). In each instance the query reflected the questioner's desire for salvation. The question functioned also as a key, opening the way to a further revelation of the good news and the challenges it offered to those who would hear it. Because of the Lucan emphasis on it and the frequency of its appearance in the gospel, T. Maertens has suggested that "What ought we to do?" was a ritual question, asked in the context of the Christian catechumenate. By asking it, the new believer indicated his readiness to be proven in the rite of initiation and to adopt a new way of life. "What ought we to do?" is a valid question that should be often upon the lips of the Advent Christian who seeks to be continually renewed in the spirit and mind of the coming Christ.

When the crowds put the question to John, his answer to them was a thorough-going, practical and positive program of conversion. For John and for Jesus, repentance was not simply a matter of feeling sorry for or regretting past sins. In the New Testament, repentance is presented as an interior conversion (i.e., a turning of the entire person—heart, mind and soul—away from evil and toward God), manifested in exterior improvement of moral behavior. Repentance, as clearly explained in today's gospel, was no longer achieved through the offering of animal or grain or oil sacrifices, but through moral reform and concern for one's fellow sinners. The joy of forgiveness was to spill over into acts of love that would share even the essential commodities of life, food and clothing: "The one with two coats should give one . . . the one with food should do the same" (v. 11).

Taxes were as dread an institution in ancient times as they are today. Tax collectors, or more correctly toll collectors (*telonai*), were Jews who had bought from the Romans the right to collect taxes from their fellow countrymen. Until the reign of Julius Caesar, wealthy Romans of the equestrian class had handled the collection of taxes in the provinces of the empire. But Julius Caesar reformed the entire system of taxation and revoked the power of the wealthy equestrians. From 44 B.C.E. onward, the direct taxes (poll, land) were collected by people directly employed by Rome. The option of collecting direct taxes or indirect ones (tolls, tariffs, customs) was auctioned off to the highest bidder. Having won the bid, the chief toll collector or *architelones* employed assistants who acted as agents to collect revenues throughout their particular districts. Because the chief toll collector was required to pay the Romans in advance the taxes to be exacted, and since he had to recoup that amount to pay his agents and make a profit as well, abuse invariably entered into the negotiations. John's answer to the toll collectors' inquiry into salvation was to be honest and fair in their dealings, to avoid greed in not "exacting anything above the fixed amount" (v. 13).

The soldiers mentioned in the gospel (v. 14) were not those of the regular imperial Roman legions or the troops of Herod Antipas, but a special force, probably hired to guard the unpopular toll takers. In that position the soldiers fell prey to the temptation to extort a toll of their own from the fearful public. Hence the evangelist's advice to these troops was not to bully or threaten, literally, "Shake no one down!" Always practical and ever the realist, Luke did not require great mysticism from the repentant—only a practical righting of personal wrongs in view of the particular temptations of their way of life.

In the second half of today's gospel (vv. 15-18), the evangelist described the preaching of John. In an atmosphere ripe with messianic expectancy he spoke his message about the coming one. Descriptively the NEB renders v. 15, "The people were on tiptoe in expectation." Indeed, for approximately two centuries before John's appearance, messianic hopes had become more pronounced. Fueled by the memories of Yahweh's promise to David (2 Samuel 7:14) and fired by the apocalyptic images of the *eschaton* (Daniel 7:13, 9:25), the people were eagerly awaiting an anointed one who would reinstate Israel and establish God's rule over all. In this spirit, many looked to the figure of John to fulfill their messianic expectations. But Luke (and later John) make it quite clear this coming one was not John but one mightier who was yet to appear. In Jewish literature the term "mighty" was often applied to the one who would lead the people in the final struggle with evil. John had baptized with water in a cleansing preparatory process but the mighty one would bring a bath of Spirit and fire. Both elements, spirit and fire, had in Jewish and Qumran scriptures come to be associated with the messianic era and with the visitation of God's eschatological judgment (Ezekiel 36:26ff; Joel 3:2; Numbers 31:23; Malachi 3:2-3; Isaiah 4:4-5, 32:15, 44:3, 49).

In the eschatological figure of the winnowing fan, borrowed from the Old Testament prophets (Isaiah 29:5-6, 41:16; Jeremiah 15:7), the evangelist described the divine harvesting of human deeds to occur at the appearance of the mighty coming one. Palestinian farmers used large, wooden, fork-like shovels to throw or fan grains into the air. As the heavier, good grain fell to the threshing floor, the empty lighter chaff would blow aside. Later the grain would be gathered and stored and the chaff would be swept up to be thrown into the fire.

For the toll collectors, the soldiers and others who heard John's preaching, the message was a powerful one. Sinful deeds and unrepentant hearts would fare no better than the burning, worthless chaff at the appearance of the mighty one. It would be far better to be gathered into the storehouse of the kingdom because of a contrite, converted heart and upright behavior. For those who await the second coming of the might one, the message is equally appropriate and no less powerful!

1. Those forgiven and renewed in God's love have reason to sing and dance—these are the joys of life our liturgy should celebrate (Zephaniah).

2. If it could be known for certain that this was the day of Christ's final appearance, how petty and insignificant most of our concerns would become (Philippians).

3. Great courage is needed to ask, "What ought we to do?" Even greater courage is needed to listen and to heed the answer to that question (Luke).

Fourth Sunday of Advent

Human standards of justice and temporal criteria for greatness were swept aside when God brought salvation to his world. In the smallest village and unto the humblest heart came the one who would make the difference for all others, for all times (Micah). His advent was first celebrated by two expectant mothers (Luke). Their joy has become the mark of every believer made holy through the saving sacrifice of Jesus Christ (Hebrews).

Micah 5:14. A contemporary of Isaiah of Jerusalem, Micah exercised his prophetic ministry in Judah during the reigns of Jotham, Ahaz and Hezekiah (ca. 742-887 B.C.E.). Like Isaiah, his better known contemporary, and like Amos and Hosea, Micah denounced the hypocrisy of a flourishing religious cult that did not translate its piety into an ethical code of social justice. Although he had lived through a series of political calamities (fall of Assyria, Samaria, invasion of Judah by Assyria), Micah regarded the enemy *within* as a greater threat than the enemy from *without*. Constantly he kept before his people's eyes through oracles and admonitions the fact that their lack of liturgical honesty and their covenantal infidelities would bring about their sure and swift demise. Sparing no one, the prophet exposed: the sins of the wealthy merchants (8:10-12), the corruption of the judicial system (3:11, 7:3), the arrogant and greedy (1:10-18, 5:56, 2:1-2, 8), the idolators (5:10-14), the so-called sacred prostitutes (1:7) and even the failures of the priests and prophets (3:5, 11). Upon all, he promised, Yahweh would pronounce judgment. But Micah's insight into Yahweh's justice did not exclude the fact of the divine mercy which he described by the covenantal term *hesed*, that sure and steady divine quality of gratuitous love in which the covenant of God and his people was rooted. This loving kindness of God would prevail even over his people's failure, and would create a future of peace and stability for the very people who had sinned so grievously. Because of his faith in Yahweh's *hesed*-love the prophet Micah could share with his embattled contemporaries a vision of the future like today's first reading.

Because the text of Micah has been so poorly preserved, riddled with the glosses and conjectures of ancient scribal and textual critics, many modern scholars would accept only the first three chapters (1-3: 12) as the genuine work of the eighth century B.C.E. prophet. The remainder of the work has been dated as post-exilic. Other scholars would credit Micah with the major work of the book and attribute the later reworking to an editor during the sixth century B.C.E. Regardless of its actual setting and precise date, the prophet's work exhibited a disillusionment with the anointed kings of Judah and looked for a future anointed one or messiah, whose rule would bring peace once again to Israel and to Judah. Not from Jerusalem's glorious height but from lowly Ephrathah would the expected one come. Although "Bethlehem" (v. 1) is thought to be an explanatory gloss and a later addition (omitted in the LXX), the fact remains that Ephrathah was sometimes used as a name for Bethlehem (Genesis 35:18, 48:7; Joshua 15:58, Ruth 4:1 1). Birthplace of Jesse, David's father, Ephrathah was the name of the clan of the tribe of Judah that had settled in Bethlehem after the infiltration of Canaan (1 Samuel 17:12). From the insignificant clan of Ephrathah, i.e., of Jesse and therefore from David's line, would come forth the future ruler of Israel. New Testament authors drew on this text and the fact of Jesus' birth in Bethlehem to substantiate their characterization of Jesus as kingly messiah and son of David.

Until the time "when she who is to give birth has borne," Israel would be "given up" (v. 2). No doubt, the text is an allusion to the Emmanuel prophecy of Isaiah 7:14 which in its original context had been applied by the prophet Isaiah to the mother of Hezekiah and wife of Ahaz. Given the insight of a few years' perspective, Micah was capable of understanding that Hezekiah and his short-lived reform had not succeeded in fulfilling the messianic expectations (of Isaiah 7:14). Therefore Micah renewed Isaiah's vision of a future messianic maternity and referred his people's hopes to some future figure. Like the young David (1 Samuel 16) and like Yahweh himself (Psalm 23), the coming one would exercise his power and majesty by shepherding his people. Those who had been scattered by the wolves of misfortune and war would be gathered and granted the peace and security of his rule that would extend to the limits of the earth (vv. 3-4). From its earliest days, Christian faith has recognized the birth of Jesus and his shepherding mission of peace (Matthew 2:8) as the fulfillment of Micah's oracle of salvation.

Hebrews 10:5-10. Like a rain on a parade, the harsh words about sacrifice and sin offerings from today's second reading may seem to dampen the joy of the Advent season in these last few days before Christmas. In truth, however, this pericope from the letter to the Hebrews, also read on the feast of the incarnation (March 25), serves as a realistic reminder of the connection between Bethlehem and Golgotha, between the cradle and the cross. Necessary to any understanding of the theological tractate called Hebrews is a grasp of the author's basic intention to lead his readers beyond the foundations of their faith to a deeper knowledge (5:11ff). To help his readers to achieve that deeper knowledge, the author pursued a course of theological argumentation based on his interpretation of select texts of scripture. Similar to the esoteric literary style of Philo of Alexandria, Hebrews was written to help the initiates in the faith toward a more profound insight into those scriptures and thereby into Christ and his saving acts.

Today's second reading is from the tractate's third selection of scriptural texts (Jeremiah 31:31-34, Exodus 25-28, Psalm 40:88) with which the author supported his theological argument for the superiority of Christ's liturgy and sacrifice over the earthly sacrificial system and of the new covenant over the old (8:1—10:18). In the verses preceding this pericope, the author had asserted his basic thesis, "Since the law had only a shadow of the good things to come, and no real image of them, it was never able to perfect the worshippers by the same sacrifices offered continually year after year" (10:1). While the law was but a shadow or a foreshadowing of salvation, only with Jesus Christ did the real image (*eikon*) of the heavenly realities become manifest. Image or *eikon* can best be understood as that form through which the essence or true nature of a thing is made manifest so that it might be readily grasped by the senses and therefore by the intellect. According to the Hebrews author, Christ by his perfect, unique and unrepeatable sacrifice made available to a saved humanity the image or true form of worship and inaugurated in his sacrificial act the second (v. 8) or the new covenant.

By placing on the lips of the Christ at the moment of his incarnation ("on coming into the world," v. 5) the words of Psalm 40:7-8, the author has asserted the importance and superiority of the Son's *obedience* over the various classes (v. 8) of sacrificial offerings (peace, cereal, holocaust, sin and guilt). These offerings had been prescribed and their liturgies ritualized by the law but their effectiveness had ceased with the appearance of Jesus. Like his ancestral prophets, the Hebrews author pronounced the Lord's preference for an *interiorized* sacrifice expressed in an obedient heart over a merely external offering. With the "body" prepared (v. 5) for him by God, i.e., by virtue of his incarnation, the Son could illustrate that perfect obedience in his entire earthly mission of hearing and doing God's will.

Luke 1:39-45. Much of the rich symbolism and tradition with which each feast of Christ's nativity is remembered and celebrated is due to the infancy narratives of Matthew and Luke. Written after the passion narratives that grew out of the earliest Christian kerygma and were later affixed to the gospels, the infancy stories have provided the reader with a type of imitative historiography. In the literary style of the classical historians (e.g., Plutarch's Fabius Maximus) who composed an infancy or early youth narrative as part of a biography of a well-known public figure, the author of the Lucan gospel prefixed to his gospel the beautiful and highly theological material of chapters one and two. Serving as a transition between the Old Testament and the gospel (that could logically begin at Luke 3:1), the narratives of Jesus' birth and early life serve also to introduce the major themes of the gospel proper. As R. Brown has observed, the Lucan infancy narrative can be delineated into seven episodes, which have been designed to illustrate the parallels between John the Baptizer and Jesus: (1) birth announcement of John, (2) birth announcement of Jesus, (3) visitation, (4) birth, circumcision and naming of John, (5) birth, circumcision and naming of Jesus, (6) presentation, (7) finding in the temple. By paralleling the relationship between the persons and missions of John and Jesus the evangelist sought to dispel doubts and to avert false suppositions among the early Christians as to whether John and Jesus were in competition or in collaboration with one another. From the outset, even before their births, it is obvious to the reader of the Lucan gospel that John and Jesus were integral agents in God's plan of salvation, with John's position as temporary and subordinate to the superior and lasting role of Jesus. The evangelist's point is clearly established even in the touching story of the meeting of the two mothers.

According to the narrative, both Elizabeth and Mary had learned of their own and of one another's pregnancies through a divine intermediary. By casting them in the same light as the longed for but expected children of the Old Testament (e.g., Sara: Isaac; Hannah: Samuel), the evangelist has underscored the unusual and God-given nature of the births. In each of the Old Testament stories, the child was miraculously given by God to perform a particular function in the divine plan for salvation history. Given that tradition, the evangelist has thus presented the conception of Jesus in an effort to point to his unique and *eschatological* role in God's saving plan. Some have attributed Mary's haste (v. 38) to her desire to maintain a certain secrecy or privacy about her unusual pregnancy. R. Brown represents the more balanced view that Mary's haste signified the obedience with which she met God's will and bowed to the divine plan in her life. Since the sixth century C.E. tradition has identified the hill town in Judah (v. 39) as Ain Karim, a small village about five miles west of Jerusulem.

Leaping (*eskirtesin*) babies in their mother's womb were a frequent reference in Biblical and extrabiblical literature thought to symbolize the destinies that would be lived out by the children. Recall Rebekah's boisterous twins, Jacob and Esau, who were said to have struggled against one another in their mother's womb—a preview of the type of relationship they would have in their adult lives (Genesis 25:22-23). In the case of Elizabeth and Mary, John's stirring was understood symbolically as his joyful recognition of the Lord whose advent he would herald in later life. That symbolic and joyful recognition was then given expression in the greeting given Mary by Elizabeth. Pronounced three times as "blessed" (vv. 42, 42, 45) by Elizabeth, Mary's greatness and honor were understood totally in relation to and because of the child she would bear. In a double clause ("blessed are you. . . blessed is the fruit": v. 42) and with the passive participle *eulogemene* (blessed), the evangelist has arranged the first two blessing of Mary in coordination. As R. Schnackenberg has noted, this structure reflected semitic style and the logic was one of subordination. In other words, Mary was praised because of Jesus. Herein we find the key to any valid and worthwhile mariology: i.e, it is rooted in and based on christology.

Some have understood the question of Elizabeth, "Who am I that the mother of my Lord should come to me?, (v. 43), as an echo of David's question concerning the ark of the covenant: "How can the ark come to me?" (2 Samuel 8:8). E. Burrows and R. Laurentin have proposed, basing themselves upon these texts, that the Lucan evangelist understood Mary as the ark of the new covenant. Others find an echo in the question to king David when the latter had come to purchase the threshing floor: "Why has my lord and king come to his servant?" (2 Samuel 24:21). By association, this similarity would seem to cast Mary in the role of queen mother. However, as J. Fitzmeyer has noted, both the ark and queen mother associations are subtle and have more substantive basis in later tradition than in the thought of the evangelist.

In her final praise of Mary (v. 45), Elizabeth is portrayed as blessing Mary for her faith. In this instance the word is not the participle "*eulogemene*" and therefore dependent on the subsequent clause, but the adjective "*makaria*," as in the beatitudes. Elizabeth's salutation will be remembered later in the ministry when a woman from the crowd would praise Jesus' mother for the physical part she played in his life, "Blessed the womb that bore you. . . ." Jesus would refer the woman's praise, not to Mary's biological role but to the greatness which is to be achieved in *faith*: "Rather. . . blessed are they who hear the word of God and keep it" (11:27-28). In this aspect of their stalwart faith, both Mary and Elizabeth can be models of true Advent spirituality. In both women, we learn that Advent is more than a season of the year—or even a season during one's life (e.g., the months of awaiting the birth of a child). Advent is a constant posture of growing faith and preparedness for the one who has come and will come again.

1. Never underestimate small towns and humble beginnings (Micah).

2. Ritual, no matter how difficult or perfectly performed, cannot substitute for an interior commitment to hear and to do God's will (Hebrews).

3. Advent's spirit of hopeful anticipation should be a contagious joy and a communal celebration (Luke).

The Christmas Season
Christmas

For the celebration of Christmas, the lectionary supplies several sets of texts (vigil, midnight, dawn, day). The ones treated here are for proclamation at the day mass.

Eternity enfleshed in time is the gift of grace we call Emmanuel, God-with-us. Infinity is made finite in a daring act of loving and giving (John). He is good news and salvation (Isaiah). He is Father and brother and Lord; he is the message of glory we celebrate today (Hebrews)!

Isaiah 52:7-10. On occasion in the ancient world, the bearer of bad news was put to death, but there would be no danger of that happening to the messenger portrayed in today's first reading. Part of a longer enthronement hymn in honor of the devastated city of Zion (Jerusalem), today's pericope envisages the joy and hope of the people on hearing of their release from exile and their imminent homecoming. Written in the sixth century B.C.E. by a prophet known arbitrarily as Deutero-Isaiah, these verses give us a glimpse of the "phoenix quality" of Israel's hope, a quality she owed entirely to Yahweh's sustaining love and provident care.

During the exile, for over a generation, Israel's beloved capital city of Jerusalem had remained in its demolished condition, the ruins a bleak witness to the political and military might of her Babylonian conquerors. For over a generation, the elite of Israel's populace had been degraded, displaced in a strange land where they had no rights of proprietorship or freedom to pray and worship as was their custom. During that time of imprisonment and curtailed freedom, a liberating enlightenment gradually took place among the exiles, due in no small part to the prophets who shared the exile. As mediator to his people of God's revealing word, the prophet helped his people to interpret all that had happened to them, both good and bad, as a part of God's message of salvation and justice. Each event in their history could be read, as it were, like a word through which God was speaking his mind, his will, his ways for his people. In joyous times, that word could be one of blessing. The darker periods, the failure and defeats, the prophets interpreted as God's word of redress and deserved punishment. In the *events* of history the prophets read for their people the creative, redeeming, purifying, loving, blessing word of God.

Hence the *event* of Israel's return from exile was truly a gospel—glad tidings, good news. Not only what God had *said* to his people, in spoken or in written words, but what he had *been* and how he had *acted* within the realm of their history enabled his people to know him as redeemer, saving God. In creation and in history God's plan is accomplished and clarified. As T. Maertens has pointed out, the *event* is central; all else, the spoken, written and prophesied words, are in service and in ministry to the event.

Today's feast celebrates the Christ-*event*. In fact, the glad tidings of the Deutero-Isaian messenger were only fully actualized, only fully heard and made comprehensible in the event of Jesus Christ. In the event of the incarnation, Yahweh truly returns and restores Jerusalem; in the event of the nativity, Yahweh draws near to comfort and console his people. In the event of Christ-made-flesh, God's message of salvation achieves its utmost clarity. What we celebrate as gospel, as good news is not mere words but persons and events.

Hebrews 1:1-6. In a sort of "before-and-after" or "then-and-now" comparison, the author of the document addressed to the Hebrews enunciated the differences between the revelation of the old and new covenants. Our reading today comprises the introduction of his work which can readily be compared to the prologue of the fourth gospel. In both texts, the image is one of Christ's divinity and equality with God.

In vv. 1 to 4, the first paragraph of our text today, the author of Hebrews speaks of the *superior* revelation which God has spoken in Jesus Christ. Unlike the piecemeal and fragmentary revelation of the Old Testament which had to be interpreted by the prophets, the revelation in Jesus is whole and entire, living and absolute. J. Moffatt has said, "Christ is God's last word to the world; revelation in him is final and homogeneous." Jesus Christ is a living being. The word of God he has spoken in the event of his ministry, death, resurrection and exaltation does not cease to be heard. The word of God in Jesus in "living and active" (4:12), ever new, ever in the process of communicating to believers the love and care of God. That living, speaking word-become-flesh is the basis for our celebration today.

Besides asserting Christ's superiority to the prophets and Old Testament revelation, Hebrews also underscores the Lord's predominance over the angels. As refulgence or reflection (v. 3, *apaugasma*) of the Father and as the exact representation (*charakter* or *eikon*) of the Father's being, Christ is placed on a par with wisdom (Wisdom 7:26). In the old dispensation, wisdom was regarded as sharing with God both a cosmological and soteriological role (Proverbs 8:22-36, Wisdom 9:9-18). This equating with wisdom in such an operative role placed Jesus Christ on a level far above the angelic hosts whom late Judaism believed were present at creation and who were granted by God a role in its government. Jewish tradition called these angelic beings "sons of God," and Alexandrian Jewish theologians called them logos, word. Because of these prevalent notions, the Hebrews' author was adamant in establishing Christ's transcendence and divinity. In New Testament times, popular Jewish belief regarded the angels as mediators of the law for humankind. In a medley of texts from the Jewish scriptures, Hebrews leaves no doubt as to Christ's superior and unequalled position. The first two texts from Psalm 2:7 and 2 Samuel 7:14 were thought messianic by late Judaism and by the Qumran community. In both quotations the unique sonship of Christ is established as well as the divinity of his messiahship. The third text (v. 6), a combination of several Old Testament citations (Deuteronomy 32:43; Psalms 97:7, 104:4). forms a compelling invitation to those angelic beings to worship the Lord Jesus Christ. With them, we the faithful join our voices in praise and honor.

John 1:1-18. John Paul Sartre in an essay on literature once wrote, "The word is a commitment, an enterprise by means of which the author embraces his age." Although unintentionally and probably inadvertently, Sartre has provided believers with an apt description of the scenario of the incarnation, the central thought of the gospel today. In the speaking into flesh of his word, in the person and event of Jesus Christ, God has committed himself to humankind and to the world in an eternal embrace.

Up until Vatican II, today's gospel text was proclaimed at the end of every Eucharist, thereby earning for itself the misnomer "last gospel." Though this practice has been discontinued, it did serve the purpose of climaxing every celebration with the compelling and beautiful truth of the incarnation. Though most situations do not warrant reading the *shortened* form of the gospel, today may be the unique instance in which the short form would be preferable for the sake of clarity. Verses 6-8 and 15 are prose comments concerning John the Baptizer which were probably inserted into the poetic prologue at a later time by the evangelist or by a disciple-redactor of the fourth gospel. To omit these comments is to allow the hymn to flow more freely with the continuity originally intended.

This hymn that introduces the gospel serves a dual function. First, it provides for the words and works of the incarnate word an eternal background or origin and proclaims as false the theories against Jesus' divinity prevalent at the turn of the first century C.E. Secondly, the prologue serves as an overture to the gospel, containing a summary of its major themes as well as a means of interpreting Jesus' message and person. Many believe the hymn to be an adaptation from a Jewish or gnostic wisdom hymn, or a preexisting Christian hymn, adapted by the evangelist for the purpose of expounding his christology. Because the hymn exhibits similarities to Semitic, Greek and gnostic ideas, a clear solution to its origins is almost impossible.

In true Semitic style, the prologue begins with a genealogy; however, unlike most Jewish genealogies, it traces Jesus' origins to the eternal divinity. "In the beginning" is, of course, a deliberate reference to Genesis 1:1 and the creation by God's word of the universe. In John 1:1 that creative word is speaking again, but no longer as subject to object, as creator to created. In John 1:1 the word who speaks a new creation has become a part of creation itself by that very utterance. That word continues to speak within human history (vv. 4, 9-10) and especially through Israel (v. 11). Those who hear and truly listen to that word can become sons and daughters with the Son. Verse 14, "the word became flesh and made his dwelling among us," draws together all the Old Testament references to God's presence with his people, in the cloud, in fire, through the prophets, in his glory, by his law (Exodus 24; Exodus 33:18; Isaiah 6:1). The same root (S-K-N) lends itself to the verbs for God's presence in nature (*shekinah*) and his dwelling among us (literally: "pitched his tent") in his word (*eskenosen*).

It is difficult to ascertain whether John wanted his readers to understand word or logos in a Greek or in a Semitic sense. To those of a *Hellenistic* background, the logos-word was regarded as an intermediary between God and the created universe. That logos gave the world its order, thus making it intelligible and comprehensible. Humankind, in turning to the logos, could find a key for unlocking the mysteries of the cosmos. Understood in this sense, Christ as logos-word would be the key to knowing about created things and about God. To the *Semitic* mind, the logos or word is a challenge which a believer can accept or reject. A word or a call from God, the logos confronts or encounters the believer and compellingly invites a response. In this sense, Christ as logos-word would be a challenger or initiator of faith, a living epiphany of a loving, saving creator. Probably, the evangelist has combined the best of both cultures in his concept of the logos or word. As T. Maertens has said, Jesus is not only bearer of the word; he is also its content.

The figure of Moses (v. 18) brings to the fore another important Semitic idea. For the Jews, Moses was *the* mediator, through whom the law or light of truth was mediated from God to his people. In the prologue, the evangelist enunciates Christ's superiority not only as mediator between God and humanity but also to the law. Rabbinical Judaism in the last centuries B.C.E. and the first centuries C.E. glorified the Torah and identified it with wisdom, source of light and life for all (Sirach 24:22-27). In his treatment of Jesus Christ-logos as superior to Old Testament wisdom and law, John's purpose is in one sense polemical. Over and against the Jewish idea of an eternal and nearly divine law, John posited Christ the word as existing from all eternity, through whom *alone* would come truth and light, life and grace.

For us who believe and who celebrate the enfleshment of the word of God as the source of life and light and truth, today is a renewal of our faith and of our commitment to the challenge of that word. Let us remember that because of the incarnation, we respond, not to a concept or an ideology or a philosophy, but to a living and loving *person*.

1. The good news of Christ proclaimed by the church in the pulpit must resound more loudly and more joyfully in the marketplace (Isaiah).

2. No longer through a glass darkly, but in the light of Christ, we behold the fullness of the Father's love (Hebrews).

3. In the word enfleshed, God speaks the language of our flesh and blood, in the pulsing of our needs and aspirations and even in the shadows of our sinful darker side (John).

Holy Family Sunday

Through the bonds of family love, God spoke his word into the world and that word, Jesus, revealed to all peoples the saving good news of his loving Father (Luke). Familial bonds that guide, protect and encourage reflect and perpetuate that divine love (Sirach). In the family of faith, believers celebrate those bonds that grow stronger in prayer and more flexible through mutual forgiveness (Colossians).

Sirach 3:2-6, 12-14. Family is the traditional word for the deepest and most treasured relationship shared by human beings. Throughout the centuries that traditional word has radically evolved in its application and significance. Where once family simply referred to the nuclear cell of society or to the clan and tribe, the term now embraces many other groupings, many of which may even be artificial and temporary. Earth has now become a global village, and "neighborhood" has earned a new definition because of the immediacy and relentlessness of the communication media. With these new definitions of family and neighborhood comes a new, frightening and perhaps overwhelming responsibility. Although his was a different world, developing at a less rapid pace than our own, Joshua Ben Sira shared similar concerns: how to discern and maintain the values of familial relationships in an evolving society.

Well-educated in the traditional values of his people and well-versed in the ways of the world in which he lived, Joshua Ben Sira treasured above all the relationship with Israel his people. Rooted in the covenant bond and flowing from it was the union of the family and therefore the clan, the tribe and the entire nation. Within the family unit, future generations were nourished physically as well as spiritually, morally and culturally to carry on the treasured faith and traditions of God's chosen people.

From the internal and indirect references in his book, it appears that Ben Sira belonged to a prosperous Jerusalem family and may even have been a member of the scribal class during the second century B.C.E. Originally written in Hebrew ca. 180 B.C.E., the book of Ben Sira was an amalgamation of the wise man's insights on the Torah, other sacred writings, wisdom and maxims for sensible living. Sirach or Ecclesiasticus (book of the church) as it has been called represents a synthesis of Ben Sira's response to revealed truth and his wise counsel concerning the application of this truth to the various circumstances of human life. Written for post-exilic Jews whose infatuation with Hellenistic culture threatened to dilute and pervert their traditional practices and beliefs, Sirach was highly valued by Judaism even though it was not accepted into the normative canon of scripture. Centuries later, Christians too looked to Sirach with high regard; in fact, except for the psalter, no other Old Testament book was used as extensively in the Christian liturgy.

Today's pericope, excerpted from a longer section of commentary on family life, offers a practical application of the fourth commandment: "Honor your father and your mother" (Exodus 20:12). Numbered among the decalog (or the stipulations for keeping the covenant), the care for one's parents was considered a sacred duty the breach of which was a breach of the covenantal relationship. Significantly, the author of Sirach did not recognize the *oral* tradition of the law through which the Pharisees multiplied the various prescriptions of the law and, with them, a maze of loopholes for avoiding the burden of the laws' restrictions. Ben Sira would have had no respect for the Pharisaic custom of *corban*, viz., consecrating property and goods to the temple, thereby avoiding the obligation of supporting one's parents. Rather than pervert, dilute or multiply the law, Ben Sira respected the sacred precepts as inmutable and God-given truth.

For that reason, Ben Sira could assert, albeit in a rhetorical manner, that the love of one's parents would atone for sin. As R. Fuller has pointed out, this statement should be understood as an *incentive* for obeying the commandment and *not* as a theological guarantee of forgiveness.

Colossians 3:12-21. Epaphras, a gentile and a native of Colossae (4:12), had heard the good news as preached by Paul and became a believer in the Lord Jesus Christ. Evidently, his faith was such that Epaphras was entrusted by Paul with the mission of bringing the gospel to his family, friends and fellow citizens at Colossae. A small city located in the Lycus River valley about 110 miles east of Ephesus, Colossae had been at its peak during the time of Xerxes (Herodotus) but thereafter had declined in importance. During Paul's day, Colossae was a center for textiles and dyed woolen materials but was overshadowed by its more prominent and prosperous neighboring cities, Laodicea and Hieropolis.

When his ministry among the Colossians and the faith growing among them became threatened by "an empty, seductive philosophy . . . based on cosmic powers rather than on Christ" (2:8), Epaphras had recourse to Paul who was then confined in a Roman prison (ca. 61-63 C.E.). Though we cannot be certain about the difficulties in Colossae since we have only Paul's response to them, most scholars agree that the questionable doctrines came from *both* pagan and Jewish sources.

With regard to the seduction from pagan philosophies, the Colossians were certainly not immune to the pervasive influence of gnosticism. In one of its several incipient forms, gnosticism threatened virtually all of the new foundations in Asia Minor. An esoteric system of acquiring secret learning through rites of initiation, combined with either a program of rigorous asceticism or libertine licentiousness, gnosticism was thought of as a "how to do it yourself" method of attaining salvation. From the Jewish sector, Colossian Christians were not forgotten by the fanatical Judaizers who resented the fact of gentile converts coming to Christ without going first through the Mosaic law, especially with regard to dietary laws, ritual observances of feasts and circumcision. Well aware of the threat to Christianity posed by gnosticism and the Judaizers, Paul in his letter to Colossae stressed the primacy of Christ, in whom "all wisdom and knowledge is hidden" (2:3). Confronting every ideal or idol or tradition that may attract the attention of the believer stands the person of Jesus. Having been *chosen, beloved* and made *holy* by Christ (v. 12) the Colossians, as all Christians, were therefore responsible for a moral integrity and uprightness whose quality was consonant with their vocation. Notice that Paul applied to gentile believers three words hitherto used to describe *Israel's* special election: "Holy," "beloved" and "chosen" had taken on a new, non-nationalistic meaning in and because of the saving act of Jesus. For that reason, peace, harmony and familial concern (v. 15) were to characterize all who found themselves together because of their faith in Jesus.

Many scholars believe that today's pericope is part of a longer baptismal catechesis (3:5—4:1) well known throughout the ancient Christian churches. Paul's exhortation (v. 14) to *"put on* love" recalled the baptismal rite of vesting the newly initiated catechumen in a white garment. As a symbol of the new life, goodness and family of faith into which they had been born, the newly baptized wore the white garment to indicate to all that they had divested themselves of their old selves (v. 5) and evil deeds and had put on the new mind, heart and spirit of Christ. White, besides being the color of purity and new life, was also indicative of victory, i.e., over sin and death. (Roman generals wore white togas in victory parades.)

In the process of their initiation, Christians were to open their hearts to the word of God (v. 18) so as to allow that word to find its home in them. T. Maertens has suggested that, besides the baptismal catechesis, the reader may also discern in today's text the basic form of the mid-first century C.E. liturgical celebration: (1) proclamation of the word (v. 18), (2) communal commentary or dialogue homily on the proclaimed word (v. 18), (3) sung responses to the word and sharing (v. 16), (4) thanksgiving to God through Jesus (vv. 15,17). That the liturgical celebration was meant to be continued and translated into every day activities is evident in the advice that follows (vv. 18-21). The *Haustafel* or "household code" (a compendium of household duties) was a common feature in the writings of the Greek philosophers. Paul "baptized" or christianized the Hellenistic form of exhortation by calling the Colossians to love, obey and refrain from nagging "in the Lord" (vv. 18-21).

Lest the modern reader be tempted to dismiss entirely Paul's remarks as chauvinistic and antiquated ("Wives, be submissive to your husbands," v. 18), it should be noted that, unlike Jewish or Greek philosophers, Paul exhorted husbands to "love your wives" (v. 18). Using the word *agape* for self-sacrificing love, Paul has really demanded of both wives and husbands a mutually selfless and giving love. During the Christmas season, as we celebrate the one who sacrificed all selflessly for the sake of love, there is ample time to renew and to restore, if need be, the quality of our familial and communal relationship *in the Lord*.

Luke 2:41-52. How easy it is to become caught up in the pathos of today's gospel narrative of the finding of the boy Jesus in the temple. A missing child, his frantic parents, the ambivalent melange of relief and reproach at their reunion, the amazement of the people at his precocious intelligence and insight, the loving goodness of a mother who did not understand, but believed in her son. . . all these details make the Lucan story a memorable and touching one. However, to dwell on these trappings, moving and poignant as they are, is to miss the real point and purpose of the evangelist's narrative. Classified as a legend by R. Bultmann and R. Fuller, today's gospel can be more correctly and properly understood as biographical apophthegm or a paradigm, i.e., a short story focused upon a central saying. As R. Brown has noted, to dismiss the classification of "legend" does not ipso facto indicate that the story should therefore be understood as historical. Indeed the story of Jesus' finding in the temple is no more or less historical than the divine voice and its setting at the baptism of Jesus. In both stories the purpose of the author was to make a christological statement. In fact the entire corpus of literature known as the Lucan infancy narrative (Luke 1 and 2) was intended as a christological affirmation. Luke has pushed back the affirmations of who Jesus was from the period when he was clearly acknowledged as messiah, Lord, savior, Son of God, etc., to the period of Jesus' childhood, birth and conception itself (Fitzmeyer).

Although they have not been accepted as canonical, there were *other* stories of Jesus' early or "hidden life," similar in purpose to that of the finding in the temple. For example, in the infancy narrative of the Gospel of Thomas, the five year old Jesus fashioned birds out of clay and blew the breath of life into them (2:3). Because he had performed this God-like feat on the sabbath, Jesus incurred the wrath of the religious authorities, just as he would later in his adult life. In another vignette, Jesus was said to have made the son of Annas wither and become sterile; again he met with opposition from the scribes, just as he would during his adult ministry. An examination of the literatures of other ancient cultures reveals similar boyhood stories of great figures. A common feature of these stories was to "make the boy the father of the man by anticipating the subject's wisdom and life work" (R. Brown). Jesus' "hidden life" stories are replete with christological significance, showing that Jesus was God's Son even as a boy (as opposed to the heresy of adoptionism), by having him work the same sort of signs he did during the ministry and by having Jesus speak in the same high christological language of the ministry. Brown is probably correct in his idea that the same instinct operative in the apocryphal gospel of Thomas (hidden life stories) was also at work in Luke 2:41-52.

Keeping in mind the author's purpose, we see the real crux of the story in Jesus' explanatory statement, "Did you not know that I had to be in my Father's house?" (v. 49).

Since this pronouncement is the key to the entire episode, all the details of time, dialogue, characterization, etc., should be seen as secondary, existing solely for the purpose of providing a story setting for Jesus' statement. For the first of *many* times in his gospel, the Lucan author used term *dei* ("I had to be," literally: "it was *necessary*"). Not only does the word (*dei*) convey a sense of necessity or urgency, but it was particular to Luke's soteriology. According to the evangelist, certain things "had to be" (*dei*) or were necessary to the saving plan of God made manifest in Jesus. "In my Father's house" (*en tois tou patros mou*) was a rather fluid expression which could also have meant: (1) "about (or involved) in my Father's affairs" (or business), (2) "among those who belong to my Father." Absolute certainty as to the precise meaning of the phrase is not possible. Nevertheless, the point of Jesus' statement is undeniable. Referring to God as his Father, Jesus asserted that his filial relationship to God transcended even the deepest bonds of human love. That awareness of his special relationship and special mission (*dei*) carried Jesus through his ministry. In the pericope of the boy Jesus found in the temple, the evangelist has foreshadowed by anticipation the reality of the man and his mission.

Throughout the narrative various reactions to Jesus were recorded: amazement (v. 47), astonishment (v. 48), lack of understanding (v. 50). All these reactions would also greet the adult Jesus during his ministry. But the response of Jesus' mother is perhaps the most noteworthy: "His mother meanwhile kept all these things in memory." Although she did not perceive with clarity the mission or mind of her son, Mary did not reject what she could not grasp. In love she kept the *rhema*, which means both words and events, in her heart, sorting them out. In faith, she grew to understand and to accept. In time, and in the perspective of post-resurrection faith, the things she had held in memory began to make sense. Later in his work, the evangelist affirmed Mary's growth in faith, naming her as one of the members of the core apostolic community (Acts 1: 14). In this aspect of her deep and persevering faith Mary has become an inspiration for all who do not fully understand but are willing to grow in faith.

1. Families grow happier in times of joy and stronger in times of sorrow (Sirach).

2. Family ties are made of blood; communal bonds are rooted in forgiveness (Colossians).

3. Those who sincerely set out to find Jesus will discover more than they ever expected (Luke).

New Year's Day

See texts for New Year's Day, Year A, page 15 above.

Epiphany

When the radiance of salvation and peace began to dispel the darkness of sin, the saving light came, not from a faraway star or from the distant horizon (Isaiah). In the word made incarnate and from within the heart of hopeful humankind, the light began to warm, enliven and transform (Matthew). Now revealed, the splendor of this saving word does not cease to speak the good news of love and forgiveness (Ephesians).

Isaiah 60:1-6. At times, the relationship between Yahweh and Israel sounded very much like a weather report. Thick clouds and darkness, glorious light and shining radiance were metaphors used to describe God's presence as well as his absence, his favor and his disfavor, etc. Today's first reading is one of many examples wherein the concrete phenomena of nature communicate deeper, intangible and transcendent realities.

Writing either near the end of the Babylonian exile (ca. 540 B.C.E.) or immediately after the exiles had returned to their beloved but devastated Jerusalem, Trito-Isaiah (chapters 60-62) painted for his people, in a series of poems, verbal portraits of what Jerusalem would and could be, once the process of reconstruction had been completed. In an effort to revive Israel's hope and to allay the pessimism that threatened to overwhelm it, the prophet portrayed a city full of light, made so by the consoling and healing presence of Yahweh. What Deutero-Isaiah had prophesied (chapter 40), Trito-Isaiah saw fulfilled (chapter 60). Once there had been darkness and thick clouds over the earth. For Israel these would have been symbols of its shame and disgrace due to its infidelity; for the pagans or gentiles the darkness and clouds would have been signs of their ignorance and lack of enlightenment concerning the true God. But Trito-Isaiah's song was one of light and glory, because within the restored city God would once more manifest himself to his people. Just as the darkness and clouds had been signals of disgrace, the light and radiance signalled for Israel the good news of salvation.

Moreover, in the spirit typical of the exilic and post-exilic prophets, Trito-Isaiah believed that Israel's good fortune, i.e., the restoration to its own land and its reinstatement in dignity as God's people, would have repercussions on the rest of humankind as well. Because of the epiphany of the Lord within it, Israel would itself become the manifestation of God's presence and goodness for the nations. Trito-Isaiah's vision of the peoples from far off lands coming to Israel bearing gifts had been prophesied by Deutero-Isaiah during the exile (48:18-22). Inhabitants of Midian, Ephah and Shebah who lived in the coastal regions (Gulf of Elam) were originally descendants of Abraham (Genesis 25:1-4). Therefore, the prophet's consoling picture of peoples from afar streaming to Israel was consonant with the promises God had made to Abraham: "All the tribes of the earth shall bless themselves by you" (Genesis 12:3).

Trito-Isaiah considered his the messianic era, the eschatological era of salvation wrought by God's hand in history through Cyrus the Persian. For his people, the prophet believed his age would be one of dominance not only in the political sphere but in the religious sphere as well. Because of Yahweh's sovereignty, Israel's sovereignty would be secure and everlasting. Because Yahweh had once again become "epiphany," because their invisible God had become visible in the events of her history, Israel had become radiant.

For those of us who live in the era of God's ultimate epiphany, we understand that Trito-Isaiah's vision was fulfilled, not only in the return of Israel to its own land and in its reconciliation with Yahweh but in the person and the event of Jesus Christ and of his church. What God did for the Israel of the old covenant, he has done for all of humankind, the new Israel, in Jesus. With Christ and through him, darkness and clouds, sin and separation have been dispelled. With Christ and with his church, light illumines and warms an alienated world, so that all peoples can walk in the freedom and healing of that light. Trito-Isaiah thought Israel reflected the epiphanic light of Yahweh. Because of Christ and his incarnation, we do not merely *reflect* the light of God but, by our incorporation into Christ, we have *become* light.

Ephesians 3:2-3, 5-6. By the time the letter to the Ephesians was written, the sharing by the gentiles in the manifestation or epiphany of God's plan of salvation had become an accepted fact. In other words, the visions of Trito-Isaiah (first reading) had begun to be realized. The author of the missive to the Ephesians firmly believed that the fullness of God's epiphany in Jesus Christ continued to be manifest in the apostles because of the work of the Holy Spirit. Although very little is known for certain about the author and destination of the document we call Ephesians, it remains nevertheless a valuable collection of prayers (1:3-3:22) and paranetic preaching (4:1-6:20) concerning the Christian life.

More in the style of a sermon or a discourse than a letter, the document's destined audience remains a mystery. Ephesians 1:1, the title of the text, is a non-canonical and non-authoritative addition, probably added to the body of the document in the second century C.E. Because of the lack of personal references and general tone of the text, some believe it was a circular letter intended for the churches in Asia Minor. Marcion, basing his claims on Colossians 4:16, entitled the letter "To the Laodiceans." If Paul wrote the letter, which many doubt, he did so around 63 C.E. during his incarceration in Rome. If he did not actually write the "letter," it may be credited to one of Paul's followers who wrote in the first decade of the second century from Asia Minor. Such disparity about authorship, date and destination does not in any way detract from the valuable lessons of theology and christology contained in Ephesians.

In the second half of the first Christian century, when the eager anticipation of an imminent parousia had been mellowed by its delay, the hearts and minds of believers needed to be refocused on their present situation. To this end the author of Ephesians propounded his ideas about the kingdom of God here and now as a foretaste and a preparation for the eternal kingdom to come. With the memorable, vivid analogies of head-body and stone-temple, the author regarded Christian living as the only appropriate response to all that God has done and given in Christ.

Today's second reading reveals the author's understanding of the kingdom as universal, comprised of both Jews and gentiles, not as strangers or enemies but as heirs of the same gift of good news, members or the one body of Christ. The three Greek words (v. 6) for "coheirs" (*sygkleronoma*), "members," (*sysoma*) and "sharers" (*symmetocha*) dismiss once and for all the ideas of the old dispensation concerning Israel's "special" or "chosen" status. The author of Ephesians teaches that in the light of Christ's manifestation or epiphany, former barriers and distinctions have melted away. In the light of Christ and by faith, all have become privileged to share in the dignity and grace of the kingdom. Race and nationality, darkness and thick clouds have no place in the kingdom of light begun in Christ Jesus.

Matthew 2:1-12. Even if Matthew had never written chapters 3-28 of his gospel, he would nevertheless have earned the title evangelist because chapters 1-2 of his work contain the burden of the good news of our salvation and the proclamation of Jesus as savior. For this reason some scholars have called the first two chapters of Matthew and Luke (the infancy narratives) a "gospel in miniature." Within the context of the wonderful stories of Jesus' birth and early days, Matthew has posited (1) the universal scope of Christian revelation, (2) an apologetic concerning Jesus' divine origin and messianic authenticity, (3) the necessity for the worldwide missiology of Jesus' church. Far from being sentimental stories of "sweet baby Jesus," the infancy narratives are a powerful, paranetic teaching tool whose implications have begun to be discovered only in this century.

As a literary form, the infancy narratives are markedly similar to Jewish legends and folk stories prevalent in the last century B.C.E. and the first century C.E. Some have compared the narratives in Matthew and Luke to Jewish midrash (from the verb *daras*, to search), a reflective interpretation of scripture. Divided into two categories, midrash contains (1) rules of conduct or guides for living (*halakah*) as well as (2) narratives (*haggadah*) or stories that declared the importance and significance of persons and events. It is obvious that the New Testament authors were aware of this Jewish literary form and accepted it as a legitimate method of scriptural interpretation. Matthew may have had this midrashic method in mind and may have used it when formulating his narratives. But chapters 1-2 of Matthew are *more* than stories and *more* than an interpretation of known scriptures. Matthew 1-2 is good news in its own right, revelation in its fullest sense and kerygmatic teaching, demanding a response in faith.

Various motifs in today's gospel were reminiscent of traditional stories known to Matthew's audience. For example, before Moses was born, his birth had been foretold; according to legend, this news filled Pharaoh with fear and dread, causing him to consult his sages to determine a course of action. Similarly, the star figured very largely in traditional folk stories about the births of great men. A star is said to have appeared when Abraham was born, striking fear into the heart of king Numrud because of its message that Abraham and his descendents would one day rule the earth. So too, a star is said to have proclaimed the birth of Nero. Popular also was the motif of a reigning monarch plotting to kill a child whom he feared would supplant him (Romulus and Remus).

Regardless of the similarities of motifs, the reader must maintain focus on Matthew's theological and christological intentions. The evangelist was concerned to portray Jesus as messiah of David's line. For this reason, he left no doubt as to Jesus' birth in Bethlehem and supported this fact with the scriptural references from both Micah 5:1 and 2 Samuel 5:2 (v. 6). Bethlehem had been David's ancestral hometown, the site of his anointing as king (1 Samuel 16:1-13; 17;12, 15;20:6, 28). It was fitting then that Jesus, as messiah and son of David, should be born there and receive the homage (v. 11, *proskynesis*) due him as everlasting king.

With regard to the star, Matthew may have had in mind the Balaam story (Numbers 24:17) wherein the greatness of Israel's ruler was witnessed by a star. Through the star or natural phenomena, the astrologers (magi) or gentiles were led to Jesus. But notice (vv. 5-6) that the natural phenomena were explained clearly and interpreted for them only by the scriptures. Herein is another of Matthew's points, an apologetic one: Gentiles who did *not* have the scriptures, but only the lesser witness of nature, were open to the truth and came to believe in Jesus. But the Jews, on the other hand, who were steeped in centuries of scriptural prophecies and attestations to the messiah did not believe in or accept Jesus. This was true not only in Jesus' day during his earthly ministry but also in Matthew's church of the 80s C.E. Just as the chief priest and scribes had rejected the earthly Jesus, the authorities in Matthew's day were ousting Jesus' followers from the synagogue. Just as the Sanhedrin delivered Jesus to Pilate, so too in Matthew's church the Christians were subjected to both Jewish and Roman persecution (Matthew 10:17-18).

In the person of the astrologers from the east, Matthew has embodied all of the gentile community and thus widened the scope of the message of salvation beyond Judaism unto its intended universal proportions. Some scholars regard the gifts presented to Jesus (v. 12) as attestations to Jesus' kingliness and divinity. Gold and frankincense were gifts usually offered to God alone (Isaiah 60:6, Jeremiah 6:20). These same scholars regard the myrrh as an omen of Jesus' passion (Matthew 15:23), a portent similar to Simeon's prediction of the piercing sword (Luke 2:35).

1. As the new Jerusalem, believers in Jesus are to radiate joy and light so that the dark clouds of doubt and alienation may be dispelled (Isaiah).

2. In the kingdom Jesus came to preach, there were no distinctions as to class or race, nor can there be in the church that preaches Jesus (Ephesians).

3. Every gift we have to offer the king he has already bestowed upon us (Matthew).

Lord's Baptism

In Baptism, the life of the Christian begins anew—a life of service and suffering, a life of conversion and growth (Acts). Once initiated into the life of grace and faith, the believer shares the mission of Jesus himself. In Jesus, the Christian is called to be light, to give sight, to dispel darkness, to work for freedom (Isaiah). Only prayer and the power of the Holy Spirit make such life possible (Luke).

Isaiah 42:1-4, 6-7. Of all the great figures in the Old Testament's cavalcade of kings, prophets, warriors and sages, the suffering servant of Deutero-Isaiah was perhaps the least likely role model for Jewish adolescents growing up in Roman-occupied Palestine. Although his mission was mandated by God himself, the servant's life was taken from him in a final act of ignominy and disgrace. Yet it was to this servant the authors of the Christian scriptures (and Jesus himself) referred in describing the mission and redemptive death of Jesus of Nazareth.

Today's text is comprised of the first of four songs or poems concerning the mysterious figure of the servant of the Lord. As one set apart or consecrated, the servant was empowered by God's own Spirit to extend to the rest of the nations the light and justice with which Israel would be blessed. By his words and works, the servant would join the destiny of the nations, i.e., of the gentiles, to that of his people Israel. Because of the similarity of style and literary quality among the four songs (Isaiah 42:1-4, 6-7; 49:1-6; 50:4-9; 52:13—53:12) and their artificial and awkward placement in the context of Deutero-Isaiah's work (Isaiah 40-55), it is thought the servant songs were an independent collection. Composed by Deutero-Isaiah or one of his disciples, they may have been inserted into the text at a later date. Indeed, if read consecutively, the songs provide a more accurate picture of the true nature of the servant. Like the rest of the prophet's work, the servant songs were intended to console and to assure the prophet's contemporaries. Probably composed during Israel's exile in Babylon, the songs were meant to offer a promising future to a people bereft of land, heritage and hope.

Exactly *who* the author had in mind as he described the servant has been a subject of many scholarly debates. Some have proposed that the prophet conceived of *his own* vocation, or that of a fellow prophet (e.g., Jeremiah?) in terms of the servant's mission. Others believe the role of the servant was intended to be assumed by the entire nation of Israel. Once redeemed by God from exile, Israel was to be a light for the nations, a covenant for the peoples and an agent of liberation for those in confinement (vv. 6-7). Other scholars, basing themselves on the idea of the remnant, have proposed that a certain group of poor and humble ones (the *anawim*) were to fulfill the mission of the servant for the rest of Israel and for all other peoples. Still others believe the servant songs referred to some future messianic, eschatological figure through whom God, would mysteriously work out his plan of salvation. In New Testament times, it is obvious from the synoptic accounts of Jesus' baptism (and passion, etc.) that Christians had began to define Jesus' mission in terms of that of the Isaian servant.

In their original context, in the sixth century B.C.E., the songs described a justice and a liberation that would be effected by the servant (vv. 4, 6-7). For Deutero-Isaiah and his contemporaries, the release from darkness was understood as their reinstatement by God in their own land and an end to the disgrace of the exile. In the light of Christian faith centuries later, given the fuller sense (*sensus plenior*) of scripture, the victory and liberation effected by the servant have been understood as freedom from sin and triumph over death's finality. But, even in its original context, the mandate of the servant was meant to be more than merely a political endeavor. Israel's political failure was perceived as symptomatic of a far more serious failing. Morally and religiously, the nation had been unfaithful and had fallen short of the standards of the covenant. Just as the prophets had interpreted the exile as the result of their immorality, so too, they coupled Israel's return home with their return to integrity and covenantal fidelity. Salvation, therefore, was not simply a political act of regaining the homeland, but also a return to and reconciliation with God.

In the scene of Jesus' baptism (gospel), Christians recognize the servant of the new covenant and eternal kingdom, and the fulfillment of Israel's hopes and prophetic expectations. In the ministry and death of Jesus, prisoners have been liberated; and in his glorious victory over death, all nations have been brought to salvation.

Acts 10:34-38. Cornelius was a Roman soldier attached to the garrison at Caesarea. By rank, he was a centurion with one hundred men in his command. A Roman historian once described the qualifications of a centurion in this way: "Centurions are desired not to be overbold and reckless so much as good leaders, of steady and prudent mind, not prone to take the offensive to start fighting wantonly, but able when overwhelmed and hard-pressed to stand fast and to die at their post."

A prayerful man, kind and generous in giving to the needy, Cornelius was a god-fearer, i.e., a devout gentile who attended synagogue, embraced Judaism's strict monotheism and observed the decalog but did not submit to circumcision or the dietary laws. The length of Cornelius' story in the Acts of the Apostles (66 verses)— longer than the Pentecost account, longer than the accounts of Paul's conversion—attests to its importance in Luke's eyes and for the early church.

The exchange between Peter and Cornelius and the latter's conversion to Christ marked a turning point in the missionary efforts of the early church. The unqualified acceptance of gentiles into the community had been precipitated by the missionary efforts of Philip and would be climaxed in the statement of James at the Jerusalem council: "From the beginning, God has taken care to draw from the pagans a people for his name" (Acts 15:14). In the Cornelius episode, Luke has made it absolutely clear that the admission of gentiles into the Christian community was part of God's plan and due to divine initiative.

Apologetically and theologically, Luke utilized the Cornelius event in an effort to put to rest two of the most thorny problems that troubled the early church: (1) Gentiles should be free to come to Christ and to receive the blessings of the messianic era without first becoming Jews. By this assertion, Luke (like Paul) affirmed the God-willed independence of Christianity from its Jewish roots and matrix. (2) Contact with gentiles does not result in ritual defilement for Jewish Christians. Though this problem may seem a minor one for modern believers, it was a major hurdle Jewish Christians had to overcome in order to make the celebration of the eucharist—*one* altar, *one* bread, *one* cup—a reality and not a lie. As J. Crowe has pointed out, the Caesarea episode and Peter's acceptance of hospitality at Cornelius' home led to a united community of Greeks and Jews in Antioch (Acts 11:19-26).

In accepting Cornelius with the declaration that "God shows no partiality; the person of any nation who fears God and acts uprightly is acceptable to him" (v. 34), Peter moved beyond the boundaries that he as a good Jew regarded as sacred and inviolable. In accepting Cornelius without reserve, Luke taught (through Peter's speech) that Christianity placed no restrictions or barriers of acceptability based on race or former beliefs. In Christ Jesus, all such limitations and exclusiveness had become obsolete and meaningless. Because of Christ's saving action, Cornelius was capable of the righteousness and uprightness previously expected and accepted only from those who had been born by blood or by faith into the Jewish heritage. In Cornelius' home, the Holy Spirit of ecumenism was at work. That same Spirit strives even today to eradicate the human barriers separating people from God and from one another.

Luke 3:15-16, 21-22. Throughout the course of the two volume work, Luke-Acts, the particular theological concerns of the evangelist-author are quite evident. In Acts, those concerns can be read in the speeches and discourses of the apostles. Comprising almost a third of the whole of Acts, those speeches are for the most part a Lucan composition and serve to explain and interpret the significance of a particular event. In the gospel, Luke's hand is most obvious in the way he has reworked his sources in an effort to spell out his own insights on christology and salvation within his evolving post-apostolic community. In today's gospel pericope on the baptism of Jesus, a number of those alterations are present.

For example, in Mark's gospel, the Baptizer was featured as the herald of the messiah promised by the prophets and long awaited by the people. As the first major character in Mark's gospel, John announced the kingdom and figured importantly in the inauguration of Jesus' ministry by baptizing Jesus. Almost a generation later, when the third evangelist wrote his gospel, some among the community clung to the belief that John the Baptizer was indeed the messiah. In an effort to clarify the roles of John and Jesus, the author of Luke's gospel portrayed John, not as the beginning figure of the gospel but as the last of the prophets of the old dispensation.

Throughout his account, Luke has depicted John as denying that he was the awaited messiah and as turning the attention of the people from himself to Jesus. In v. 16, Luke eliminated *opiso mou* ("after me"), saying merely, "there is one to come"—lest the qualification (*opiso mou*) be misunderstood and Jesus be thought of as a disciple of John. Instead, the third evangelist presented John as assuming the position of a slave and/or disciple of Jesus. To loosen the thongs of another's sandal was an act performed by a slave for a master or on some occasions by a student for his rabbinical master. So too, the baptism of John (in water) was defined as a lesser sign and a preparatory step for the greater baptism to be effected by Jesus (in the Holy Spirit and in fire). The dual character of Jesus' baptism coupled with that of John recalls the Old Testament texts in which water, Spirit and fire were combined (Isaiah 4:4-5; 32:15; 44:3; Ezekiel 36:25-26; Malachi 3:2-3) as both purifying (spirit, water) and refining (fire) force.

Rather than *feature* the moment of Jesus' baptism by John, Luke all but suppressed the event by placing it in a subordinate clause and by using the Greek genitive absolute: "and Jesus was at prayer, after likewise being baptized" (v. 21). By so shaping his narrative, the evangelist has made John's baptism of Jesus a secondary issue, a backdrop for the truly important feature of the pericope—Jesus' anointing with the Holy Spirit and the explanation of the event by the heavenly voice. C.H. Talbert has called the scene an "episode of prayer, accompanied by a vision and an audition." By separating the empowering of Jesus by the Spirit from the baptism and by connecting it explicitly with prayer, the pericope serves to underscore one of Luke's main concerns, the importance of prayer in the life of Jesus and in the lives of his disciples.

Only Luke, of all the evangelists, placed such importance on prayer. Luke specifically mentioned Jesus at prayer before or during the major events of his ministry, e.g., at the inauguration of his public ministry (3:21), before choosing his disciples (6:12), before announcing his passion (8:18), at the transfiguration (9:28), before teaching his own how to pray (11:2), at the last supper-passover (22:32), agonizing over his imminent death (22:41) and on the cross (23:48). Moreover, in Acts, the early Christians were described as placing the same emphasis and importance on prayer as the Lord in whom they believed (Acts 1:14, 2:42, 4:31, 12:12). By prayer and in prayer, the believer becomes empowered, as was Jesus, with the Holy Spirit of truth and light, to serve the Father worthily. Luke understood prayer as a *means* of discipleship, a way of integrating faith in Jesus with the life of a believer in an effort to survive persecution, apostasy and the long wait for Jesus to return.

The interpretative heavenly voice cast Jesus in the role of the servant from Deutero-Isaiah (first reading). Linguists assert that the Greek word for "son" (Luke 3:22) may be understood as the equivalent to the Hebrew for "my servant" (Isaiah 42:1). Just as the servant had pleased God, so too did God's favor rest upon Jesus at the outset of his public mission for the salvation of all peoples. Filled with God's own Spirit, empowered by the Father's favor and love, Jesus at prayer and in his baptism is a model for all would-be disciples, whose life in him is initiated in *baptism*, and constantly renewed and celebrated in *prayer*.

1. By its teaching, the church that believes in the Isaian servant must bring light and sight and freedom to all the waiting peoples of the earth (Isaiah).

2. Partiality is a human invention, unworthy of God's overwhelming gifts of love and life (Acts).

3. Prayer is the most powerful moment of our existence (Luke).

The Lenten Season
First Sunday of Lent

The normal span of life is punctuated with the question marks of temptation and the exclamation points of confessional faith (Luke). Guiding and providing through each moment of existence is the God who both creates and redeems, who has become personally involved in the human story (Deuteronomy). He is the savior of all who question, the Father of all who confess, the brother of all who exclaim, "Jesus is Lord" (Romans).

Deuteronomy 26:4-10. Each of the readings for this first Sunday of the Lenten season contains a confessional statement. In the first text, Israel confessed its faith in the action of God that brought his people out of Egypt and made them a people. The exodus from Egypt became the pivotal event in the Jewish tradition, comparable to the death and resurrection of Jesus that became the confessional statement of the New Testament kerygma, as stated in the second reading from Romans. In the gospel pericope, there is a three-fold confessional statement attributed to Jesus, presenting his firm determination to do the will of the Father despite all obstacles and temptations. In these confessional texts, the tone for the Lenten liturgy is announced. Herein, individual believers may find inspiration and encouragement to translate into their daily lives the confession of faith that binds the community together in Christ.

In its original context, the confession of faith in the Deuteronomic reading was part of a thanksgiving liturgy that accompanied the ritual offering of the first fruits. Originally an agricultural feast which predated the tribal amphyctiony, the ceremonious offering of the first fruits of the harvest to the gods was adapted by the Israelites, made to conform to Israel's strict monotheistic beliefs and historicized, i.e., associated with the historical fact of Israel's freedom from Egypt and possession of the promised land. Before Israel, other ancient people (Canaan) celebrated the first fruits with an awareness that the world in which they lived was a gift, created and governed by a greater reality. All the harmonious and mysterious workings of nature were regarded as subject to laws that were unfathomable for the finite mind. Ancient peoples saw nature as greater than themselves and the gods as greater still.

Israel brought to this concept of nature and of God the recognition that the *one* great God of nature had become personally involved with his people. Hence Israel's feast of first fruits celebrated not a nature god but the God *of nature* and the God *of history*. Israel's God was manifested not only through nature but, and more importantly, through his mighty acts of power. The recitation of those mighty deeds, performed for the sake of his people, Israel, comprises the bulk of today's first reading (vv. 5-10).

After the liturgical instructions (v. 4) concerning the rite of bringing one's offering to the Lord, the recitation or confessional statement followed. A recapitulation of Israel's salvation history, the credal formula featured three decisive events in its evolution as a people: (1) the divinely motivated demographic shift from the north and the establishment in the south of the ancestors (Abraham, Isaac, Jacob); (2) the deliverance from Egypt of the enslaved and their formation as a people by God in the desert; (3) the promise of Canaan and Israel's eventual possession of it.

Many scholars believe this credal recitation to be one of the most ancient and perhaps the most important passage of the Pentateuch. R. Fuller claims the passage (vv. 5-10) occupies a position in the Old Testament similar to that of 1 Corinthians 15:3-8 in the New Testament wherein Paul quotes the earliest formulation of Christian kerygma. What the exodus was in Jewish tradition, Christ's death and rising are in Christian tradition. Obviously, this is why the Jewish Passover that annually commemorated the exodus event became so closely associated with the death and rising of Jesus. Indeed, the two feasts have become so entertwined that the symbols of the Jewish feast —the water (Reed Sea, water from rock), unleavened bread, manna, etc.—have helped define the Christian signs and sacraments of salvation (baptism, eucharist, etc.).

Remembering the Jewish rite of the first fruits at the beginning of Lent, Christians might also recall Paul's explanation of Jesus Christ as the "first fruits of the dead" (1 Corinthians 15:20).

Romans 10:8-13. "For if you confess with your lips that Jesus is Lord and believe in your heart that God raised him from the dead, you will be saved!" This statement, in v. 9 of today's pericope, is thought to be one of the earliest formulations of Christian faith and may have been recited or sung as part of an ancient baptismal liturgy. In the context of Paul's letter, the statement serves to underscore the apostle's emphasis on justification by faith over and above justification by the law. One of the basic themes of the treatise called Romans, justification by faith was also one of the most controversial issues that separated Jewish from Christian believers. It continues to complicate relationships among Christians even today.

As one who had gown up in the heritage of Judaism, Paul understood the Jewish concept of "justification" or "making just" as the process whereby a believer was united to Yahweh by virtue of his/her obedience to the law. Keeping the law, or doing the works of the law as revealed by God through Moses, was considered a condition of the covenantal relationship between God and his people. As the nation evolved, the law was variously interpreted and applied by Judaism's official experts. When the saving acts of Jesus extended the covenantal relationship with God to include *all* peoples (gentiles), it became necessary to explain how one could become justified without the works of the law, i.e., how to become united with God (in (Christ) without having known Moses. Paul's conviction (stated here and elsewhere: e.g., Galatians) was that faith in *Jesus* could lead to justification.

By means of his midrashic explanation of certain texts from the Jewish scriptures (Deuteronomy 30:11-14, Isaiah 28: 16, Joel 3:5), Paul illustrated how Jesus as the saving word of God (v. 8) had superseded the works of the law. Paul also applied to Jesus the title Lord quoting the early creed of the Palestinian churches: "Jesus is Lord!" "Lord" was the title used by Greeks and Romans to refer to their gods and to the emperor. Moreover "Lord" (*Kyrios*) was the Septuagint's translation for the sacred tetragrammeton YHWH (Yahweh). In applying the title "Lord" to Jesus, Christians recognized in him someone greater than an emperor and more than a national god. "Lord" signified the association between Jesus' saving acts and the creative, redemptive acts of Yahweh. Therefore, "by confessing with the lips and believing with the heart in the Lord Jesus," one became heir to the creative and redeeming process of salvation. From this statement grew the lengthier doctrinal creeds (apostles' creed, creed of Nicea, etc.) and the great eucharistic prayers or canons of the liturgy. Faith in Jesus and justification by him would afford a unity to the community of believers, a unity impossible under the law, according to Paul. Where the law separated Jew from Greek, faith in Jesus would unite Jews and Greeks in one community, with one confessional statement: Jesus is Lord!

Luke 4:1-13. Traditionally the gospel for the First Sunday of Lent is the narrative of the temptation of Jesus; in year C, the Lucan account is read. Similar in structure to the Marcan and Matthean versions, nevertheless, Luke (like the other synoptics) shaped and colored his narrative according to his particular theological and pastoral concerns. Featured in the account of the third evangelist are: (1) his emphasis on the Holy Spirit and prayer; (2) the fact that Jesus was tempted as *Son* of the Father; (3) Luke's concentration on Jerusalem, indicated by the fact that he reversed the order of the *temptations* (second and third), placing Jerusalem last.

Each of the temptations is like an act in a three-act drama. In each of the acts, the author's purpose of correcting public misconceptions about Jesus' role as Son of the Father and savior becomes more and more clarified. In each act, the pronouncement of Jesus can be thought of as a confession of faith in the Father. Closely connected to the baptism scene wherein Jesus was proclaimed as Son (3:22), the temptation narrative illustrates Jesus' resolve to exercise his role as Son in perfect obedience to the Father's will. That obedience would preclude self-interest, and would eventually lead to the suffering and death on the cross.

Act I. "Full of the Spirit" (v. 1) is a Lucan theologoumenon appearing many times throughout his two volume work. In each instance, "full of the Spirit" was the evangelist's designation for the creative and dynamic presence of God. J. Fitzmeyer has pointed out that the presence of the Spirit, so pronounced in Luke-Acts, may have been the evangelist's solution to delayed eschatology.

Present as helper, consoler, guide and strength of Jesus during the ministry, the same Spirit helped, consoled, guided and strengthened his followers, until the final outpouring of the Spirit (Joel 3:1-2) at the parousia. W.F. Harrington has proposed that Luke's presentation of Jesus, full of the Spirit, meeting the power of evil head-on, is the eschatological moment.

The devil's taunt, "If you are the Son of God," introduces the interchange between good and evil. The temptation is one of distorting the divine mission for personal satisfaction. Notice that Luke has made singular the "stone into bread" (Matthew has "stones") underscoring the personal character of the temptation. Would Jesus use his position as Son for personal gain instead of for all others? Jesus' response from Deuteronomy (8:3) recalls the period of Israel's desert wandering when the people longed for the plentiful bread, onions and meat from Egypt and scorned the food divine providence showered upon them. By not seeking bread for himself *alone*, Jesus' food was to do the will of his Father (John 4:24). By his integrity and obedience, he became the eucharistic bread that feeds the world.

Act II. In this second interchange, the devil is presented as challenging Jesus to receive and exercise power in a secular, political manner. Refusing in the words of Deuteronomy (6:13), Jesus is portrayed as faithful to the authority given him by the Father. Behind the encounter is an allusion to Israel's fascination with the cults of other peoples, especially Canaan (Deuteronomy 6:10-15). Unlike Israel, Jesus could not be enticed, and his single-hearted fidelity stood as a model for the persecuted believers in Luke's first century C.E. audience.

Act III. Climaxing the encounter between good and evil in Jerusalem, Luke's third act presents the devil as goading Jesus to exercise his wondrous powers to dazzle and charm the people. Also reflected in the scene was the popular belief that, when the messiah would come, he would appear on the roof of the temple. Proving that even the devil can quote scripture, the evil one dared Jesus to test God's protection (Psalm 91:11). Without conforming to popular expectations, Jesus, in answer, alluded to Israel's weakness in the wilderness where they had tested the Lord (Deuteronomy 6:16). Unlike Israel, Jesus did not opt to test the Father to whom he was entirely obedient.

Epilogue. Luke concluded his temptation narrative, hinting that there would be a sequel: "He left him to await another opportunity." Obviously Jesus had won the battle but the war would end only on the cross. Thereon, once and for all, the power of evil fell from its pedestal, conquered by the triumphant, saving Lord.

1. The first fruits of all we are and all we have belong to the Lord, not as a tithe that is owed but as a freewill offering, lovingly given and gratefully shared (Deuteronomy).

2. Faith in the one Lord supersedes the particularities of race and culture—making the many one people and one family in God (Romans).

3. Grace gives the believer, not immunity from temptation but alertness to the strength afforded by the victory of Jesus on the cross (Luke).

Second Sunday of Lent

Integral to the life of faith is the willingness to be transformed from a lonely individual to a loving, giving member of a community (Philippians). The process of transformation requires a trust that knows not every turn in the road has been mapped out, but is still eager to embark upon the journey (Genesis). How can the believer be so optimistic and hopeful? Because the Lord Jesus has gone before us, has met with every evil, has overcome and now holds out to us the glory he has achieved (Luke).

Genesis 15:5-12, 17-18. Inextricably interwoven in a masterful narrative, the Yahwist and Eloist pentateuchal sources have produced in today's pericope about Abraham one of the most vivid and personal encounters between God and the human person. In addition to portraying the quality of Abraham's faith, the narrative also reveals the character of the covenant as unilateral and unconditional. One of several interchanges between God and Abraham, today's first reading communicates the same conviction upon which every encounter was founded, i.e., that the creator God became personally involved in human history and through that personal involvement put into motion the process of salvation which has affected all peoples.

Ancestral father of Israel, Abraham and the promise made to him by God were anticipatory of Israel's future destiny. At the heart of today's first reading were the two promises of posterity and the land. Both promises were heavy with irony. As a man with an infertile wife, Abraham had little hope of progeny. Furthermore, as an aging bedouin, it was unlikely that a great land would one day be his possession. In both instances, ordinary human means appeared hopelessly incapable of attaining the desired end. But in the face of human inadequacy the power of God can work wonders; this is the point made so clearly by the ancient writers.

In Hebrew, there are two root words which express faith. *'Aman* means to stand firm, with a strength and certainty in God's plan. *Batah* conveys the dynamism of an energetic faith and trust that admits of no passivity. Both terms have been given living expression in the life and legend of Abraham.

In the mysterious scene that followed the divine promises of progeny and land, God sealed his covenantal relationship with Abraham. "To make a covenant" (*berit karath*) in Hebrew is literally translated, "to *cut* a covenant," the terminology probably being derived from the ritual here described. According to ancient ritual, animals were killed and divided, and the contracting parties made their pact or declared their oaths to one another standing between the slaughtered animals, signifying by their act that they deserved a similar fate if they proved unfaithful to their agreement (Jeremiah 34:18). As B. Vawter has noted, similar ceremonies were performed throughout the ancient Near East: "In the text of a treaty between Ashur-nirari VI of Assyria (753-746 B.C.E.) and Matti-ilu, king of Bit-Agusi, we read: This head (of an ox) is not the head of the ox, but the head of Matti-ilu, his sons, his nobles, his people, and his country. If anyone sins against these vows, just as this head is removed, so may he be removed." Birds of prey were usually considered an evil portent and probably in this context signified the future enemies who would threaten the integrity of Israel's bond with the Lord.

Abraham's deep sleep (*tardemah*) was not so much an indication of his psychological state as a literary clue as to the special divine revelation soon to come. There were many such instances of divine communications occurring in dreams. Recall Jacob's dream, Pharaoh's nightmares and even Peter's enlightening night visions in the Acts of Apostles. Indeed, the setting sun and the enveloping darkness were also standard props signaling a theophany. Symbolized in smoke and fire (also standard for the divine presence) but breaking with the traditional mode of performing the rite, God *alone* passed through the animals. Not requiring Abraham to put his life on the line and mercifully accepting human limitations, God made with the father of our faith an *unconditional* covenant.

As the ancient authors indicated, the covenant with Abraham and the gift of divine involvement were purely gratuitous. Still, Abraham's indomitable faith, even in the face of seemingly insurmountable circumstances (his age, Sara's infertility, etc.), cannot be overlooked. In the tension between freely given, transforming grace and wholehearted faith the rhythm of salvation began. That same tension and rhythm continued throughout Israel's history until they were climaxed in the transforming and grace-filled saving act of Jesus Christ.

Philippians 3:17—4:1. First of the Christian communities established in Europe, Philippi was an extremely important link in Paul's chain of foundations, because from there he went on to preach the good news of salvation to all of Greece. Located on the Via Egnatia that connected Rome with the East and built upon the pass that separated Europe from Asia, Philippi was a cosmopolitan city, home of many peoples, philosophies and religions. Present among the diverse population were elements who proved hostile to Paul's newly formed congregation. At one extreme were the Jews who rejected those whom they believed to have perverted their ancient traditions by claiming Jesus as messiah. Also extreme were the Judaizers, Christians of a strict Jewish background who insisted that *all* Christians, gentiles included, submit to circumcision, keep Jewish feasts and observe the dietary restrictions. At the other end of the spectrum were those libertines who, ascribing to a gnostic philosophy, regarded the body as unredeemably evil and thought nothing of engaging in carnal orgies. It is difficult therefore to identify with any certainty the "enemies of the cross of Christ" about whom Paul warned the Philippians (v. 18).

Many believe Paul was referring to gnostic hedonists when he declared, "Their god is their belly!" Certainly, their immoral acts would merit his disapproval. But it could be that Paul was again criticizing the Jews and Judaizers whom he had earlier (3:2) referred to as "dogs with their mutilation." Having thus insulted the Jews for what he thought was fixation on an external sign, it may be that "their god is their belly" was a further scornful reference to the Jewish fascination with dietary practices!

To all those Christians whose faith was threatened by extreme forces from one faction or another, Paul offered himself (3:17) and his own imitation of Christ (1 Corinthians 11:1) as a normative guide and inspiration. To all who were immersed in the attractions of this world, lawful or not, Paul recalled the fact that the Christian is even here and now a citizen of heaven (v. 20). This claim was made more poignant by the fact that Philippi was a Roman military colony whose citizens enjoyed a special status (*ius italicum*) in the Roman Empire.

By virtue of baptism, Christians were united in every way to Christ in a loyalty that took precedence over every other allegiance. Paul's vision of the second coming of Jesus (v. 21) included the notion of the transformation of all believers in Christ. Not just in spirit or only in outward appearance (*schema*) but in his/her essential nature (*morphe*) each faithful follower of Christ would be glorified.

With that hope to give them strength and courage, Paul urged his beloved friends in Philippi to stand firm. He thought of them in terms of a victory crown (laurel wreath given to winners of a competition) he had won for Jesus Christ. Still, he knew that ultimate victory was yet to be enjoyed in the citizenship of heaven.

Luke 9:28-36. Together with last Sunday's gospel of the temptation of Jesus, the transfiguration episode puts before us the two aspects of Jesus' saving action. United with sinners, even to the point of being tempted (last week), Jesus' victory over sin and death has resulted in his glorification (this week). In this gospel, as in that of last week, all three levels of development are in evidence: (1) Jesus' life situation, i.e., what actually occurred during his ministry; (2) church, i.e., the event as remembered and shaped by oral tradition; (3) author, i.e., how the evangelist informed the episode with his own pastoral and theological concerns.

Though many believe the transfiguration scene to be a post-resurrectional appearance the evangelist has moved back into the ministry, others think there must be some historical basis for it within the ministry itself. V. Taylor, who supports some historical basis for the event, says that Peter's embarrassing words (Luke 9:33: "Let's build three tents") stand in the way of a post-resurrectional hypothesis. Whatever the character of the historical episode as it occurred in the ministry, the whole event has obviously been reinterpreted by the community in the light of Easter faith and reworked by the evangelist for his own congregation. As R. Fuller has observed, the 20th century homilist must now attempt a *fourth* level of understanding to bring the text to life for his community here and now.

In his version of Jesus' transfiguration in glory, Luke alone added the element of prayer (v. 29), as he did frequently throughout his gospel. This element, combined with the sleeping disciples (v. 32), has caused some commentators to compare the scene to the agony in the garden where, however, *anguish* and *not glory* was the overriding theme. Still, at the basis of both episodes, was the imminent passion of Jesus. Only Luke has related something of the conversation of Moses, Elijah and Jesus (v. 30), telling his readers that they spoke of Jesus' "passage" (Greek: *exodus*) or departure "that he was about to fulfill in Jerusalem." Jesus' "passage" obviously referred to his "passing over" or "exodus" from death to life and glory through the crucible of suffering on the cross. Using the traditional word that described the ancestral escape from Egypt (exodus), Luke has compared the imminent suffering and glorification of Jesus to a *new* passage, a *new* exodus, not just for Israel but for all people.

A variety of possibilities have been proposed to explain the presence of Moses and Elijah. A popular Jewish belief entertained the notion that those two great figures had not died in the ordinary sense and would appear once again just prior to the messianic era (Deuteronomy 18:15, 18; Malachi 3:23; Sirach 48:10). Their presence with Jesus, therefore, would seem to suggest that in him the messianic era of salvation was being inaugurated. Another possible explanation is that Moses and Elijah were representatives par excellence of the law and the prophets. As such, their presence with Jesus would have suggested to Luke's readers that the Old Testament expectations safeguarded by the law and enunciated by the prophets were being fulfilled in Jesus' "passage." Indeed, the fact that the scene of glory ended with Jesus *alone* present would underscore the fact that thenceforward Jesus and his saving "passage" rather than the law and prophets would be deserving of the believer's wholehearted faith.

Peter's offer of the three tents was probably a somewhat naive desire to prolong the moment but it could also be understood as an association with the feast of Tabernacles. An ancient harvest feast, Sukkoth or Tabernacles was one of the three major pilgrimage feasts historicized into a commemoration of the desert sojourn. From post-exilic times onward, the feast was celebrated by a reading of the law and with the people living in tents or booths for seven days. Zechariah (14:16) had foretold a worldwide celebration of the feast, with all nations coming to Jerusalem. A popular expectation based on this prophecy looked for the Lord to appear in his temple on the last day of the week-long feast. Perhaps these ideas were behind Peter's enthusiastic offer. Nevertheless, the true import of the scene was clarified not by Moses, Elijah or Peter, but by the heavenly voice (v. 35). With the pronouncement of the heavenly voice, Jesus was identified as Son and chosen one. Moreover, he was to be *listened* to!

Just prior to the transfiguration event, Jesus had told his disciples (who through Peter had acclaimed him "messiah of God") that he "must first endure many sufferings, be rejected. . . and be put to death" (Luke 9:18-22). Then Jesus had gone on to explain the ramifications of being his disciple: "Whoever wishes to be my follower, must deny his very self, take up his cross each day and follow in my steps" (Luke 9:23). In a sense, the heavenly voice, besides corroborating the disciples' faith in Jesus as messiah, was indicating that that messiahship would be explained to them by Jesus himself. If they would *listen* to him, heed his words and works, they would comprehend the fact that the glorification or transfiguration would only be achieved after the humiliation of Jesus' "passage." For Luke's readers in the 80s and for modern believers, the challenge to "listen to him" was, and is, still valid. Following the chosen one in the way of discipleship involves daily participation in the "passage" from humiliation to glory, from death to life.

1. God does not push us beyond our limitations, but challenges us to rise above them by faith (Genesis).

2. When at last we meet the Lord, it will matter little what we ate or drank or wore along the way (Philippians).

3. Christ's glorious transfiguration was an observable wonder; so too, the miraculous transforming power of grace from within the heart of the believer (Luke).

Third Sunday of Lent

Moses' encounter at the fiery bush was his first in a lifetime of experiences with the God whose name would become known as "Creator," "Liberator" and "Provider" (Exodus). As "Redeemer" he gave to his people the gifts of life and the land; he sustained them with food and with his own abiding presence (I Corinthians). As "Forgiver" and "Healer," he calls the sinful to repentance, and as "Loving Father," he holds out to the plodding the hope of a second chance (Luke).

Exodus 3:1-8, 13-15. According to ancient historians (Josephus, Philo), Moses had been privileged to receive an Egyptian education. In order to secure and maintain its authority throughout its vast empire, the Egyptian government trained select individuals in the Egyptian language and hieroglyphics as well as in the languages of the neighboring territories. Scripture tells us that Moses enjoyed a uniquely privileged (for a Semite) position in the royal court. Still, Moses hardly seemed a likely candidate for the leadership of a great nation after having angrily murdered an Egyptian and, in an act of cowardice, concealed his body in the sand. Even his fellow Semites distrusted him and Moses fled to the desert to hide. There, while tending the flocks of his father-in-law, Moses was called by God.

As in so many other instances in the course of salvation history, it was not the man's exciting and impressive resume that necessarily fit him for the task, but the extraordinary and personal intervention of God in the human story. This is precisely the point of today's narrative which reveals something of the nature and characteristics of that God.

Horeb was the Eloist's name for Sinai which later became the site of the covenant and giving of the law; Horeb may also have been a sacred place for the tribe of Midian. Many scholars believe that Moses' contact with the Midianites greatly influenced the later development of Israelite government (judges, etc.), cult (sacred meal before the Lord) and even the adoption of the name Yahweh for God. Whether these influences were validly present or not, the Exodus author has nevertheless infused the narrative with the ancient patriarchal promises and traditions, thereby gearing it toward the enslaved people, soon to be known as Israel.

In the phenomenon of the flaming bush that was not consumed by fire, the divine presence was symbolically announced. The "angel of the Lord" (v. 21 was a common Old Testament (Genesis 16:7, 13) circumlocution for the Lord himself, whose presence was further indicated by the instruction to Moses to remove his shoes and keep his distance. An ancient oriental mark of respect, the custom of removing one's shoes in a sacred place is continued today in the Eastern world. Moses' fear of looking at God was a recurrent motif in the Old Testament, based on the belief that "no one could see God and live."

All these elements added to the mystery of the encounter while emphasizing the utter transcendence and power of the one who was calling Moses. Having revealed himself as the "God of Abraham, Isaac and Jacob" (v. 6), the divine presence also renewed the promise he had made to Moses' forebears, of "a good and spacious land, a land flowing with milk and honey" (v. 8). By that promise and self-designation, the God who appeared to Moses, identified himself as the God whom the ancestors had called *El Shaddai* (God of the mountain).

Moses' request to know more of the divine presence (the name) was an understandable one. As emissary of this god, he would have been given little attention or credence without an authoritative name to refer to. Some have interpreted Moses' request as a desire to share somehow (others say "to have control over") the god's power. Ancient Near Eastern peoples identified the name with the person; to know the name was tantamount to exercising control over the one known.

The response Moses received continues to be the subject of scholarly research and dispute. Those who regarded Moses' request as a desire for a share of power or control understood the enigmatic "I am who am" (Vulgate) or "I am he who is" (LXX) as a *refusal* to be named. God, who is beyond definition either by metaphysicians or mythmakers, cannot be entirely known by humans and therefore his very infinite essence defies any finite attempt of naming. Others, more correctly, have understood the revelation of 3:14 as related to the Hebrew verb "to be" (*hayah*).

The most satisfactory explanation has been suggested by W. F. Albright: "The enigmatic formula in Exodus 3: 14, which in biblical Hebrew means 'I am what I am,' if transposed into the form in the third person required by the causative, Yahweh, can only become *Yahweh asher yihweh* (later *yihyeh*), 'He causes to be what comes into existence.'"

Therefore the God who met Moses at the fiery bush was revealed, not metaphysically but *realistically*, as the "causing one"—the creator—the God who *acts*. He would become known and knowable to Moses and his people by his deeds. It would be just as correct to interpret the sacred tetragrammeton, YHWH, as "You'll know who I am by what I shall do for you." The God who had become personally involved in human history would become better known as the human story unfolded and evolved.

1 Corinthians 10:1-6, 10-12. Paul believed in the value of history and in the lessons it had to teach. For that reason, he advised the Christians in Corinth to read into the past of their spiritual heritage so as to learn from the mistakes of their forebears in the faith. Evidently the Corinthians, like the Israelites in the desert centuries before, had begun to take God and the gifts of salvation for granted. Some among the community were guilty of a naive presumptuousness, thinking that the sacraments, especially baptism and the eucharist, were ipso facto guarantees of salvation. Perhaps this complacency and lax behavior stemmed from a perversion of Paul's own teaching about justification by faith. In an effort to clarify the nature of God's gifts and of his graces, Paul utilized the Old Testament events in a typological manner.

Recalling the passing through the Sea of Reeds and calling it a baptism into Moses, Paul interpreted Christian baptism as a new exodus. Just as the ancient exodus constituted the people of Israel as God's own in the desert and initiated the process of their salvation, so too, by baptism, believers become initiates in the saving action of Christ. By referring to the divinely given food and drink (Exodus 16:4-35, 17:5-6; Numbers 20:7-11) of the desert days of *spiritual* nourishment, Paul compared it to the eucharistic gifts with which Christians were nurtured. The reference to the rock that followed the Israelites through the desert (v. 4) was not based on scripture but on a rabbinic legend. According to the rabbis, the rock that Moses struck for water became mobile and journeyed with the people, thus providing water as needed. That rock which saved the people by providing life-giving water. . . that rock is Christ, taught Paul; in and through him, all were and are saved.

The hard lesson of the wilderness and the point of Paul's typology were that, in spite of all the saving gifts Israel received in the desert, "God was not pleased with most of them" (v. 6) and many did not survive. God's gifts of water and manna and quail did not erase the wickedness of his people. Neither, therefore, could the gifts of the new covenant (baptism, eucharist, etc.) negate the sin of a stubborn and recalcitrant people. Sacramental grace cannot substitute for the believers' cooperative efforts at good living and loving service.

Luke 13:1-9. At first glance, today's gospel pericope from Luke may sound like a "Can-you-top-that?!" contest. When those in his audience told him about the murdered Galileans, Jesus matched their story with one of his own —that of the 18 people who had died tragically in Siloam. Actually, both disasters, recorded only by Luke, were paired by the evangelist and related to the parable of the fig tree in order to underscore the urgency and importance of *repentance*. Although the incident concerning the Galileans has no parallels in biblical or extra-biblical documents, the Jewish historian Josephus chronicled similar heinous acts by Pilate. Therefore, the injustice was not totally unimaginable. In the same way, the 18 killed in Siloam by one of the great towers that guarded the aqueducts was also quite possible, even though the occurrence appears only in Luke. In both instances, a tragedy occurred, the first caused by human malice, the second the result of a freak accident. Both disasters were used by Jesus (and Luke) to correct some mistaken notions concerning sin and punishment, repentance and justice.

Rather than dwell on Pilate's culpability, Jesus focused on the popular belief that tragedy befell certain people as a *deserved* punishment for *sin* (recall John 9). Certainly, there were in Galilee greater sinners than those whom Pilate killed. And surely, the 18 who died in Siloam were no more evil than some of their neighbors in Jerusalem. By reasoning in this manner, Jesus counseled against attributing the deaths of the Galileans and Jerusalemites to their guilt. Instead, he exhorted those who heard him to regard both incidents as a somber warning to those still alive. There were some who looked upon their own escape from personal tragedy and presumed that to be divine judgment of their innocence. In an effort to challenge *all* to reform, Jesus pointed out that the light of life was as easily snuffed out for a good person as for an evil one. The absence of tragedy, therefore, should not be read as a sign of approval but as gift of God's mercy that allows more time to repent, a second chance for a new beginning. In the lesson of the fig tree, Jesus' point became unmistakably clear.

Throughout the Old Testament tradition, especially in the prophets, the fig tree was a symbol of Israel, God's chosen people (Hosea 9:10; Micah 7:1; Jeremiah 8:13, 24:1-10). In this particular Lucan context, given the references to Galilee and Siloam, it would seem that God's people were being offered another chance to recognize and receive Jesus as Lord. Usually a fig tree was expected to produce fruit after three years' time. If it had not borne any figs by that time, it was cut down and another tree would be planted in its place. In Jesus' parable, the vinedresser allowed the barren, unproductive tree yet another year. Moreover, he continued to care for it, while he waited for some positive results for his efforts. Some scholars have compared the three years of the fig tree's growth to Jesus' three-year ministry. While there may be some degree of comparison, the main point of the parable is the urgency of the situation. It was the last chance, "the eleventh hour," as it were, and the call to reform had to be heeded, else those who ignored the challenge would find themselves in the same sorry condition as the fig tree. Unlike the Galileans and Jerusalemites who had not had the advantage of a second (or third, or fourth) chance, Israel had received many invitations to growth and fruitful repentance. If Israel allowed all its opportunities to pass by, they would surely be lost.

At its second stage of development and application among the Christians of Luke's community of the 80s, the parable and the tragic incidents (of vv. 1-5) warned against inactivity and lax nonchalance while awaiting the return of the Lord. Today's text continues to speak to all who think the lifetime process of conversion can be begun tomorrow!

1. The God who is all things to all peoples has many names and faces (Exodus).

2. A sacramental encounter is not a moment of magic but it can offer grace-filled possibilities to the responsible believer (1 Corinthians).

3. Personal tragedy is no measure of guilt, nor is good fortune a proof of integrity (Luke).

Fourth Sunday of Lent

Guilt is never easy to admit, but when the guilty one knows that a loving Father with open arms waits to welcome him home, the road to repentance becomes easier and shorter (Luke). Repentance can be thought of as the only worthy response to the wondrous gift of reconciliation wrought by God in Christ (2 Corinthians). Such a gift of freedom and life should be celebrated often and joyfully (Joshua).

Joshua 5:9, 10-12. Traditionally known as Laetare Sunday, the Fourth Sunday of Lent marks the midpoint in the Lenten preparation for the resurrection feast. Appropriately, each of the three readings characterizes one of the many facets of Easter joy. In the first reading from Joshua, the people of God are portrayed as celebrating for the first time the feast of their freedom in their own land; the joy is one of promises fulfilled. In the second text from Paul, the apostle joyfully proclaims the effects of Jesus' saving act, i.e., the reconciliation of all peoples to the Father. In the gospel, the joy is that of "coming home" and rediscovering a father's forgiving and gratuitous love. Although Lent is a season of penance, it must necessarily be marked by the joyful enthusiasm and confidence today's readings communicate.

The book of Joshua purports to be an historical account of the conquest and division of Canaan among the 12 tribes under the leadership of Joshua who had been Moses' aide-de-camp. The taking of the land was regarded as the sacred fulfillment of the divine promises to Abraham; and the author(s) of Joshua accordingly presented the infiltration and conquest in quasi-cultic terms. Instead of sieges, skirmishes and armed attacks, the author describes processions, liturgical music and religious rites.

Today's first reading is from a longer section that described the period of rest at Gilgal before the siege of Jericho. While the verses of explanation were not included in today's pericope (vv. 2-8), the rest was necessary because the people had been circumcised in accordance with the law. A very ancient practice that predated the Bronze Age (3000-1200 B.C.E.), circumcision was a rite of initiation, a quasi-sacrificial offering of the person to the gods, not through the actual self-sacrifice but by the symbolic offering of the foreskin. Since the Egyptians practiced circumcision, we do not know why the Hebrews would not have been circumcised while they were slaves in Egypt. Nor do we know for certain when the rite acquired religious significance for Israel as a sign of the covenant with Yahweh (Genesis 17:8-14, Exodus 12:43-48, Leviticus 12:13).

Some have interpreted the "reproach" God removed (v. 9) as the failure of his people to be circumcised in Egypt. Others have understood the "reproach of Egypt" as a reference to the ritual uncleanness of a foreign land, but this would certainly be an anachronism. Still others (more correctly) have suggested that the "reproach" now removed was a reference to the *slavery* endured by God's people.

The remainder of the text, which shows definite signs of priestly editing, concerns the first observance of Passover, the feast that celebrated the end of the reproach of slavery in Egypt. Gilgal (literally, "circle of stones") was an important sanctuary up until the time of David. M. Noth has suggested that this story is an etiological one that explained the origin of the shrine and the feast. With the arrival of God's people in the promised land, a new way of life was initiated. Those who had been a *bedouin, pastoral* people, on the move from oasis to oasis, making their way through the wilderness, would thenceforth be a *settled* people.

This process of settling or sedentarization is signified by the ceasing of the manna. An established population could grow its own food and provide for its own needs. A new stage in Israel's development, their increased independence in Canaan was not a lessening of their need for God but an opportunity for more active cooperation with his blessings. They were no longer pilgrims and wanderers but children of their Father, at home in their own land.

In Israel's historical development, the modern believer can find an analogous understanding of the sacraments, especially the eucharist. Like the manna, the eucharistic bread of life sustains the faithful on life's journey until the ultimate passover from life through death to fuller, everlasting life.

2 Corinthians 5:17-21. "Before-and-after" pictures are a common advertising technique used by manufacturers of diet, health and beauty aids in order to boost sales for their products. So different and so much more attractive, the "after" picture is intended to provide the incentive to buy the product so as to experience a similar improvement. In a sense, Paul understood his life before and after meeting Christ in a similar way. "In Christ" (v. 17) was a typical Pauline term for explaining the *difference* between life "before" and life "after." By "in Christ," Paul meant the radical, i.e., from the roots (*radix* = root), and continuing process of transformation the life of faith entailed. But even *more* than a transformation or an evolving of the *same* being to a *better* being, Paul understood his life "in Christ" as a new creation. The passing of the old order (death, sin and darkness) and the creation of a new order (life, holiness and light) are made possible only by God who has *reconciled* humanity to himself "in Christ."

One of the most important New Testament passages on the subject of reconciliation, the present pericope is all the more poignant since it is part of Paul's personal witness as an apostle for Christ. Excerpted from a longer section (3:1—6:10) in which he described the rigors of the apostolate, it shows that Paul regarded the ministry of reconciliation as one of his foremost privileges. As a preacher of the gospel and a teacher of Christian values, and by virtue of his personal conversion, Paul had become an "ambassador" (v. 20) of God's reconciliation. His life and his mission were "sacramental," i.e., a living signification of what God had done for all peoples in Christ. Paul believed that all believers were honored to be charged with the same mission—that of being living sacraments of God's reconciliation.

Jesus had achieved the reconciliation or restoration of all peoples to God by "becoming sin." Actually, the term *hamartia,* translated "to be sin" (v. 21), would be better rendered "to be a sin-sacrifice." Although Christ did not *know* sin, that is, by way of personal experience, he embraced the contradiction and alienation of sin in order to make holy all who had been enslaved by it. For Paul, the sin-sacrifice of Jesus on the cross was the dividing point between the old and the new orders, between the "before" and "after," the starting point of the new creation.

Luke 15:1-3, 11-32. At the heart of today's gospel pericope is the joyful news of reconciliation. Where Paul had explained reconciliation in a doctrinal and theological manner, Luke conveyed a similar message in the moving and eloquent story of the father and his two sons. Because the bulk of the narrative centered on the younger son, the fact that the story was actually a *double-edged* parable has sometimes been overlooked. In the father's treatment of the younger son, the lesson of divine mercy offered reassurance to sinners. In the interchange between the older brother and the father, a stern warning was issued to the self-righteous whose resentment hardened them against the joy of God's magnanimous goodness.

In its original setting, Jesus may have told the story to defend his attitude toward sinners and toll collectors (vv. 1-3). Annoyed at what they thought to be reprehensible behavior, the Pharisees and scribes criticized Jesus because, in their estimation, the sinners and toll collectors were outcasts. That Jesus *ate* with such people and then proceeded to associate with the "righteous" was considered a personal affront by the Pharisees and scribes. By his parable, Jesus (or Luke) not only illustrated God's special and unconditional love for the wretched who repent but also the correct attitude of the community toward them.

In accordance with the law and customs in ancient Palestine, a father could dispose of his property by making a will that would be executed when he died (Numbers 36:7-9) or he could give his possessions to his children while still alive. Usually the eldest son received a double share or twice the amount that each of the other sons would receive. Since the Lucan parable mentioned only two sons, the younger son would have received a third of his father's property. Evidently he converted his share into cash and departed for a "distant land" (v. 12), probably part of the diaspora.

According to the parable, he soon squandered his money, his morals and even his Jewish religious heritage. These last losses were borne out by the fact that he had to find employment on a farm as a swineherd. Obviously, the environment was a gentile one, because pigs were unclean for Jews (Leviticus 11:7). So desperate was the son's situation that he had set aside his traditional beliefs and values.

Unable to eat the husks (literally: carob pods, v. 16), he eventually "came to his senses." Literally, this phrase (v. 17) is "he entered into himself" and was an expression in both Hebrew and Aramaic for *repentance*. In a sincere self-examination the son admitted his guilt. He no longer had any legal claim upon his father; those rights had ceased when he demanded his inheritance. Therefore the son's resolve to return home indicated that he was totally reliant on his father's mercy and goodness. How moving is the scene that follows! Apparently, the father had been waiting for the wayward son because, while he was "still far off," the father ran to meet him. Without waiting for the son's confession of wrongdoing, the father embraced him in warm welcome. Even when the son tried to admit his guilt, the father interrupted his recitation to order that a party be prepared.

The robe and ring and shoes were a sign that the son would not be received into the house as a *servant* (slaves did not wear shoes, robes or finger rings) but in his former status as *son*. A fatted calf was an indication of an extravagant feast in a land where meat was eaten rarely and only on great occasions. The father's joyful comment, "Let us eat . . . this son of mine was dead and has come back to life . . . was lost and is found," reaches out beyond the story-setting to those who heard Jesus and read Luke. The joy of the father over his returned son taught the lesson of God's love and merciful forgiveness.

Perhaps the saddest part of the story, even more pitiable than the prodigal son, was the resentful and arrogant older brother who refused to enter into the joy of the occasion. Sounding very much like the Pharisee (Luke 18) who despised the sinful publican and proudly recounted his good deeds before the Lord, the elder son catalogued his virtues before his father. But this was not the point. The father did not *compare* his sons to one another or measure one's goodness against the other. Instead, he wholeheartedly gave his love to each according to their need. By calling the older son to rejoice in his brother's return, the parable challenged those who thought themselves righteous and upright to look upon those less sure of themselves with compassion.

As T. W. Manson has observed, "The parable probes the human psyche and touches it deeply. It lays down the fundamental principle of God's relation to sinful men; that God loves the sinner *while* he is still a sinner, *before* he repents, and that somehow, it is this divine love that makes the sinner's repentance possible."

1. Celebration of gratitude to God should mark all of the special moments of life,; these are the mileposts on the journey home (Joshua).

2. As ministers of reconciliation, believers have already shared in the service they render (2 Corinthians).

3. "How very rarely does the administration of the sacrament (of reconciliation) give a real impression of introducing someone to the joy of the Father," notes T. Maertens (Luke).

Fifth Sunday of Lent

God's presence in a human life automatically creates new possibilities and choices. For Israel, the choice was one of nationhood and freedom in a covenantal relationship of limitless possibilities (Isaiah). For the accused woman, the choice was one of a new integrity created by Jesus' healing forgiveness. The Pharisees were offered the possibility of perceiving themselves and God in a new light (John). In order to choose responsibly and answer life's God-given possibilities, the believer must be daily formed by faith into the pattern of Christ's dying and rising (Phillipians).

Isaiah 43:16-21. As the founding moment of Israel's long evolution as a people, the exodus from Egypt of a band of slaves under Moses' leadership was thenceforth regarded as the *pivotal event* of Israelite history. Because of its essential importance the exodus and many of the particulars that surrounded it (the Reed Sea, Moses, desert trek, manna, water from the rock, etc.) were understood as *types* of other events that succeeded them. By definition the *typical sense* of scripture is the meaning persons, places and events possess because, according to the intention of the divine author, they foreshadow future things. Because the *types* and their *antitypes* (those they foreshadowed) appeared at two different points of time, the typical sense became apparent only when the antitype appeared. Moreover, the type is an imperfect silhouette, not a portrait of the antitype. Given this brief explanation, the modern reader can therefore look at today's text with the eyes of a Deutero-Isaiah, who saw the exodus from Egypt as a *type* of the release from exile in Babylonia. For that reason, he described the return home across the Syrian desert in terms borrowed from the pentateuchal narrative of the Exodus.

Writing during the latter half of the sixth century B.C.E. as one who shared the pain of his people's shameful detainment in Babylonia, the author of Deutero-Isaiah (Chapters 40-55) labored to lend hope and encouragement to his fellow exiles. The prophet exhorted his fellow Jews to look to the past and to remember the wondrous acts of their God all through the stages of their development as a people. But, while reminding his contemporaries of their history, he challenged them not to *dwell* in the past for its own sake, but to take *hope from* the past and look for similar divine acts of mercy and power in the *future*: "The things of long ago consider not; see I am doing something new!" (v. 18).

By this statement, Deutero-Isaiah called his people to prepare themselves, not for a *repetition* of an ancient happening (exodus), but for the *continuation* of the process of redemption initiated by that event. Rather than look upon what happened to them as merely historic occurrences, the prophet presented the facts to his people in terms of a *relationship* endangered by infidelity and alienation but in the process of being mended. By describing the return of the exiles to Israel in Eden-like images and by drawing upon exodus terminology as well, the prophet gathered all the decisive moments of Israel's relationship with their God, from the primeval creation and their birth as a nation to their reinstatement as a free people. All these realities were at the heart of the prophet's Book of Consolation and, as such, inspired today's first reading.

Philippians 3:8-14. An objective outsider, looking at Paul's life before Christ, would probably have judged him to be a rather fortunate person. Born of Jewish parents in the Hellenistic town of Tarsus, he experienced the best of both worlds. Paul enjoyed Roman citizenship and, in addition to his knowledge of the Greek language, culture and philosophies, he had also been schooled in the richness of his Jewish heritage under an eminent rabbi (Acts 22:3). He had achieved a certain status in Judaism as a recognized official and/or teacher as was evident from the authority he wielded against the Jesus movement prior to his conversion (Acts 9:1-2, 22:5, 26:12). Nevertheless, Paul looked upon all his advantages and privileges as "loss" and as "rubbish" (v. 8) compared to the wealth of blessings he had received in Christ Jesus. By this harsh evaluation of his former life and of what others would have regarded as riches indeed, Paul sought to defend Christianity against certain elements in Philippi who militated against the healthy spiritual development of community.

Chapter three of Philippians seems out of context with the rest of the letter and, as such, it is one of the most convincing proofs that the letter is a composite one, consisting of sections of two or three separate letters. In chapter three, Paul's polemical remarks were directed either at the Judaizers or at the "gnostic-enthusiasts." Both groups were extremists who thought they had attained the justice Paul knew could be achieved only by faith in Jesus Christ.

At one extreme were the Judaizers who insisted on imposing Mosaic law upon all believers, including gentiles. As Christians, the Judaizers had brought with them to the faith the Jewish ideal that being *just* consisted in being found blameless in God's sight through the perfect observance of the law. At the other extreme were the gnostic "Christian-enthusiasts" who believed themselves to be already perfected and justified by virtue of their baptism into Christ. In the middle of the two extremes stood Paul who understood that he had been justified because of Jesus and by faith in him but had not yet been perfected.

For Paul, faith in Jesus meant becoming like him, and that entailed being "formed into the pattern of his death" (v. 10). "Formed into" was a term based on the root *morphe* which indicated that such formation involved an *essential* conformity to or solidarity with the sufferings of Jesus. That conformity could not be achieved by the law or even automatically by baptism, but was a gradual process of knowing Christ expressed in continued conversion. Paul's analogy of the runner in the race is an apt illustration of the gradual nature of being "formed into" the pattern of Jesus' passion and death. Like the runner who has already begun the course, the baptized Christian has been "grasped by Christ," i.e., initiated into the process of lifelong conversion. The entire span of a believer's life—however short or long—can be likened to the race course. The goal, union with the risen Lord, is in sight, but is not yet fully achieved until the entire race has been faithfully run.

John 8:1-11. Although the story of Jesus and the accused woman was from a pre-Johannine source and did not appear in any of the earliest known manuscripts, it was nevertheless an ancient tradition and was included in the scriptural canon. As the story unfolds, Jesus is portrayed as a living expression of the divine mercy, a wise and kind judge, more concerned with forgiveness and rehabilitation than with punishment and death.

H. Riesenfeld has suggested that the early church, in its struggle to maintain strict penitential discipline, may not have been able to reconcile its practices with the *ease* with which Jesus forgave the woman. For that reason, Riesenfeld believed the story was temporarily set aside by the early church and was only later granted canonical approbation. Actually, in the interchange with the woman and her accusers, Jesus did not *laxly* ignore the woman's sin. Rather, he ordered her to *refrain* from sinning.

The real focus of the narrative should be on the attitude of the self-appointed, righteous ones whose harsh judgment of the woman clouded their consciences to their own sinfulness. Instead of saying, "Let the one among you who has no sin be the first to cast a stone at her," Jesus could just as aptly have said, "If you want to avoid judgment, stop passing judgment!" (Matthew 7:1) or "Should you not deal mercifully with your fellow servants, my heavenly Father will treat you in exactly the same way unless each of you forgives one another from the heart!" (Matthew 18:33, 35).

According to the fourth gospel, Jesus had been teaching daily in the temple precincts while spending his nights on the Mount of Olives (John 7:53-8:1). Crowds had been assembling to hear his teaching and this may have angered the Pharisees and scribes who regarded themselves Judaism's official teachers. The scribes by virtue of their legal expertise and the Pharisees because of their impeccable observance of the law's minutest prescriptions were respected but also feared by the general population. That they brought the woman to Jesus was highly irregular because such a case would ordinarily have been handled by the Sanhedrin and the Roman authorities (if the sentence were a capital one). Some have suggested that the methods and motives of those who approached Jesus were not judicial at all and that those who seized the woman were renegade zealots or religious fanatics who had taken the "law" into their own hands. In any event, the evangelist attributed their purpose to an attempt to trap Jesus so as to accuse him (v. 6).

For the woman to have been accused of adultery she would have been either married or betrothed (Deuteronomy 22:21, Leviticus 20:10). Adultery was, by law, the sin of an unfaithful *wife*. An unfaithful husband would not have been so charged unless he committed adultery with another man's wife. Then, he could have been charged, not by his own wife, but by the husband of the other woman. Besides being married or betrothed, the woman accused of adulterous behavior would have to have been seen by two people (only men were accepted as official witnesses, Deuteronomy 19:15) besides her husband. Forcing the woman to stand in open view of all (v. 3) was the position for an official legal interrogation. A comparison between this narrative and the story of Susanna (Daniel 8) will yield obvious parallels. In both cases, a woman accused was vindicated by one who took her side against an angry crowd but, unlike Susanna, the woman in the Johannine narrative was evidently guilty.

For centuries, speculation has been rife as to what Jesus actually wrote or traced on the ground (vv. 6, 8). *Katagraphen* could be translated "wrote," "traced," "recorded" or "registered." For that reason, a number of possible solutions have been offered. An ancient tradition, that probably originated with Jerome, proposed that Jesus was writing on the ground in full view of all (v. 3!) the sins of the woman's accusers. Others (T. Manson) have suggested that Jesus' action was a clever mimicry of the Roman legal practice whereby the judge would first write down the sentence and then read it aloud to the accused. R. E. Brown has researched several scriptural references that could shed light on Jesus' action. In Daniel 5:24, the mysterious writing on the wall provided a divine commentary to the situation. Was Jesus' action similar?

Or perhaps Jesus' writing was a dramatization of Jeremiah 17:13, "Those who turn away from you shall be written on the earth, for they have forsaken the Lord, the fountain of living water." Others have proposed that Jesus wrote the words of Exodus 23:1, a prohibition against offering malicious witness. There is no sure way of knowing what Jesus wrote; it may be that he merely wished to show he was unmoved by the accusations of the self-righteous. However, Jesus' *statement* (v. 7) about the first to cast a stone arrested his hearers and completely shattered the force of their argument against the accused.

Alone with the woman, Jesus exercised his authority, not as judge, but as savior (John 8:15). Without ignoring her sin ("avoid this sin," v. 11), Jesus pardoned her; he who transcended the law invited the woman to do the same. She was sent on her way contrite and resolute, not only to obey the law for the law's sake but to renew her conscience and to reform her behavior according to the loving mercy that had been shown her.

1. Life is a series of passages—from youth to old age, from small dreams to fulfilled goals, from foolhardy daring to experienced risk-taking, from failure to repentance, from death to life (Isaiah).

2. Like the avid runner who carries little with him/her so as to run the course more successfully, so the wise Christian traveller realizes the relative worth of temporal goods and goals (Philippians).

3. The finger pointed in accusation is best turned upon its owner (John).

Passion (Palm) Sunday

This Holy Week is more than a remembering of past suffering and of a painful cross. All believers are called anew this week to a discipleship that makes real in daily service the fidelity of the servant (Isaiah). He put aside his rights and privileges, accepting instead the pain and emptiness of humiliation and death (Philippians). But the servant's innocence was proclaimed by God himself who blessed with resurrection Jesus' saving work. We his disciples participate in his passion, aware that our daily crosses will lead to Easter joy (Luke).

Isaiah 50:4-7. When, in the first years after Jesus' death, the early believers in him were confronted by those who called the passion and cross a scandal, Old Testament texts like the servant songs of Deutero-Isaiah were extremely helpful. The poems' central figure was a just one whose undeserved and vicarious suffering proved in the end a miracle of God's redemptive healing for the undeserving and sinful population (Isaiah 53:5). During life, the innocent one had been attuned to God's word and will, as he daily opened himself (50:4) to the plan of salvation. His mission, according to Deutero-Isaiah, was specially mandated by God himself and the Lord had prepared his servant well for his task by breathing into him his own Spirit (42:1). Once empowered, the servant was to become *light* for the nations (49:6), to establish true *justice* among all peoples (42:1) and to bring peace and healing (53:5) to the broken and the alienated.

In their original context, the four servant songs (42:1-4, 49:1-7, 50:4-9, 52:13—53:12) were composed for a people suffering the shame of deportation and displacement from their own land. As a companion to his fellow Jews during their Babylonian exile (587—538 B.C.E.), the prophet sought to console and strengthen his contemporaries by helping them to find meaning in their sufferings. For this reason, many scholars believe the prophet intended Israel to identify with the role of the servant as portrayed in the songs. By so doing, Israel could be led to understand the exile, its humiliation and suffering, in terms of a divinely commissioned service for the sake of their own deliverance and the salvation of all peoples.

Other scholars have suggested that the prophet understood his *own* task as God's mouthpiece in terms of the servant's mission and sufferings. Certainly the prophet and others who shared his vocation (Amos, Hosea, Jeremiah) understood firsthand the rejection and degradation the servant endured. But like the innocent servant, the prophet(s) did not allow the lack of public acceptance or the ridicule of an unsympathetic audience to deter him from living out his God-given vocation.

Today's first reading is from the third of the four songs wherein the servant has been presented as specially equipped by God with the ability (well-trained tongue, v. 4) to teach and to appeal to the weary. Probably the idea here is one of parenetic preaching, i.e., an exhortatory style of speaking intended to evoke a moral change in the listener. By parenesis the servant endeavored to "rouse" the people (v. 4), i.e., to liberate them from their own indifference and hopelessness as well as to proclaim the end of the exile. The prophets in exile (Deutero-Isaiah, Ezekiel) interpreted Israel's suffering as the deserved consequences of their infidelities to God. Therefore, to "rouse" the people would also have involved causing them to sharpen their consciences toward an admission of their sin and awakening in them their need for forgiveness. Liberation was perceived then as a spiritual and religious in addition to being a political and national reality. For all his efforts, the servant was beaten and abused (vv. 5-6) by his people but nevertheless his confidence in God gave him the stamina ("face like flint," v. 7) he needed to persevere.

Philippians 2:6-11. Although Paul did not *write* a gospel per se, he did *preach* the good news of salvation and today's second reading could well be called the Pauline passion narrative. By incorporating this pre-Pauline hymn into his letter, Paul captured the essence of Jesus' passion, death and exaltation in one of the most beautiful and profound christological statements in the New Testament. Probably first composed for use at early Christian liturgies, the hymn drew together for the eucharistic assembly centuries of prophetic hopes and blended these high aspirations with the deep humiliation and degradation of Jesus' cross. From the sublime heights of divinity to the baseness of servitude, the hymn integrated into one prayer of praise the mysterious paradoxes of the saving acts of God in Jesus Christ.

As a summary of Jesus' entire mission, the hymn exhibits a parabolic rhythm (as well as a literary chiastic structure) in which the movement of Jesus, from his rightful and equal status at God's right hand (v. 6) plummets "downward" through the incarnation into the status of a slave (v. 7) and finally to the ignominy of a criminal's death on a cross (v. 8). From the baseness of the cross and *"because of this"* (v. 8) the Son was exalted and the parabolic movement continued "upward," through the glorious process of Jesus' resurrection (v. 9).

Drawn together and "upward" with Jesus toward the Father are all those who by virtue of Jesus' incarnation, passion and death have been delivered from the endless depths of sin and death. Some have chosen to call this hymn quoted in Philippians the "fifth" or the "New Testament servant song." By perfectly fulfilling the servant's vocation, Jesus received the name Lord. . . *Kyrios* (Greek) or *Adonai* (Hebrew).

In its original context as part of his letter to Philippi, Paul quoted the hymn in an appeal for harmonious community relationships. Factions, rivalry and all petty differences would fade into insignificance if each of the Philippian Christians would take for their own the "attitude of Christ" (v. 5). Like Jesus who had every right to assert himself as God, but who chose instead to empty himself (v. 7), the Philippian disciples were called to a similar selflessness. *Kenosis* or "emptying" implied a purposeful, positive and voluntary renunciation. Rather than have one's goods, talents or even one's opinions forcefully wrested from oneself by a stronger or more domineering member, Paul challenged the Philippians and all Christians to bring to their communal life the unassuming strength of total self-gift that Jesus brought to his ministry and ultimately to his passion.

Luke 22:14—23:56. Earliest believers first expressed their faith in Jesus' saving action by the simple credal formulae "Jesus is Lord!" or "Jesus lives!" Samples of the most primitive kerygmatic preaching contained little if any references to the passion and only a fleeting mention of the cross (Acts 2:23, 36;3:13-15, 17; 10:39; 13:28, etc.). Paul summed up the general attitude of both Jews and gentiles toward the fact of a suffering messiah, calling Jesus' death a scandal and a stumbling block (1 Corinthians 1:17—2:16). What prompted, then, the development of the passion tradition in which the graphic story of Jesus' suffering and saving death was set down in a fixed form?

Continuous narratives considered the *heart* of each of the four gospels, the passion accounts were the product of a faith-filled community confronted with growing apologetic, liturgical and catechetical needs. *Apologetically,* the passion traditions helped the early believers to understand and to present Jesus' suffering and death as integral to God's foreknown and foreordained plan. Drawing on the Old Testament prophecies and psalms for support, the early believers portrayed the paradox of Jesus' redemptive action as a loving work of God. *Liturgically,* the passion narratives were an outgrowth of the eucharistic assembly's remembrance and proclamation of Jesus' death until his second advent. *Catechetically,* the passion narratives presented Jesus, not as the "stumbling block" but as the cornerstone who was rejected for a time by the builders, but who survived to become cornerstone of the new and eternal kingdom (Psalm 118).

M. Dibelius in commenting on the passion stories wrote, "If what was preached was a witness of salvation, then among all the materials which were related, only the Passion was of real significance. For what it dealt with was the first act of the end of the world as then believed and hoped. Here salvation was visible, not only in the person and the word of the Lord, but also in the succession of a number of events. To set these matters in their connection corresponded to a need, and all the more, as only a description of the consequences of the Passion and of Easter resolved the paradox of the Cross. Only the organic connection of the events satisfied the need of explanation, and only the binding together of the individual happenings could settle the question of responsibility."

When each of the evangelists, with their own pastoral concerns, knit together the various motifs of Jesus' passion, each writer accented certain elements, persons, events, etc. Luke, who evidently knew of Mark and Matthew, chose not to emphasize Jesus' isolation as Son of Man (Mark) or the seeming contradiction of his royal but suffering messiahship (Matthew). Instead, Luke pictured for his community a Jesus whose *innocent martyrdom* was underscored again and again as the narrative unfolded.

Only in Luke did Pilate pass a triple verdict of *innocent* upon the falsely accused Jesus (23:4, 14-16, 22). Luke, who alone records a trial of Jesus before Herod, also depicts Herod pronouncing Jesus *innocent* (23:6). Whereas in Mark the centurion (15:39) near the cross had declared Jesus to be "the Son of God," Luke's version reads, "The centurion upon seeing what had happened, gave glory to God by saying, 'Surely this was an *innocent* man' " (23:47). Luke also includes the testimony about Jesus' *innocence* by one of the criminals crucified with him: ". . . we are only paying the price for what we've done, but this man has done nothing wrong" (23:41).

The Lucan Jesus, falsely accused and unjustly judged in a sham trial, was also wrongly executed but the evangelist used the travesty brought against Jesus to focus on his victory over every adversity. Triumphant over sin, he displayed his authoritative power in *forgiveness*. Not only did he pardon his persecutors, "Father, forgive them; they do not know what they are doing" (23:34), but he also held out the joy of reconciliation to the criminal beside him, "I assure you: This day you will be with me in paradise." Perhaps, more than in any of the other passion narratives, Luke showed Jesus to be the suffering servant of whom Deutero-Isaiah had written: one who suffered innocently and vicariously for the sake of others, who was rejected and died shamefully but in the end was vindicated by God.

According to Dufour and Fitzmeyer, the Lucan passion narrative was not formulated merely to be read objectively as a piece of inspired religious literature. The evangelist intended that those who prayed the words of Jesus' passion with him would be drawn into it and *participate* in the event of salvation. The reader is invited to become, by virtue of Jesus' passion and because of it, a *disciple*. Luke made a special point of presenting Simon the Cyrenean carrying the cross *behind* Jesus (23:26). Thereby Simon became illustrative of Jesus' teaching on discipleship, "Anyone who does not *take up his cross* and *follow me* cannot be my disciple" (Luke 14:27). In an earlier passage in the gospel, the evangelist put special stress on the necessity of taking up the cross and following Jesus *"daily"* (9:23). In the passion, Jesus is teaching what discipleship means and costs while he invites all who believe to participate with him in the saving mystery of innocent suffering, merciful forgiveness, redemptive love and service unto death.

1. Part of the challenge of discipleship is the willingness to begin again each morning (Isaiah).

2. Jesus' greatness consisted in the fact that he did not cling to the power and glory that were rightly his (Philippians).

3. Called to participate in the passion of Jesus, believers are also assured of a share in his glory (Luke).

The Easter Season
Easter Sunday

Jesus lives! The fact of his resurrection has set the world and its values upside down (1 Corinthians). Death is no longer the end but the beginning of a life that never ends (John). Life has become a multi-dimensional experience in which believers share by faith in an ancient passover, celebrate daily the many great and small passages from death to life and look ahead to the ultimate passing over from time into eternity (Acts).

Acts 10:34, 37-43. Without Easter, Good Friday would have been nothing more than a sad travesty of justice. Without the resurrection, Jesus' death would have been just one more defeat for one whose life had been characterized by gentleness, forgiveness and service. But because of the reality of Easter and the fact that Jesus lives, the cross has become a blessing and the sign of our salvation. This was the burden of the message with which the early believers in Jesus were charged. Peter's speech on the occasion of Cornelius' baptism contained precisely those same elements.

Called kerygmatic (from *kerygma*: proclamation) this discourse, as well as the other speeches of Peter and Paul in Acts, should be understood as more than homilies intended for only one specific historic occasion. While building upon the basic kerygmatic message, Luke used the several speeches in Acts as vehicles of his theological purposes to answer pastoral needs. An extremely important and effective literary tool, the speeches of Acts reached beyond their historical setting to the *reader* of Luke's work in order to convey the meaning of a particular event and/or the importance of a certain issue. Greco-Roman historians used similar techniques, placing on the lips of their characters their own historical comment and analysis of the situation. In today's discourse, as in most of the other speeches in chapters 2-13, the Lucan author has followed the same basic schema and included the same kerygmatic content, thereby providing a continuing catechesis for early believers. In addition to its catechetical and kerygmatic value, Peter's sermon was also the occasion for Luke to expand upon the importance of Cornelius' conversion.

Cornelius was a Roman soldier stationed at Caesarea, the headquarters of the Roman government in Palestine. A centurion with a company of soldiers in his command, Cornelius was known as a God-fearer, i.e., a devout gentile who was sympathetic to Judaism's strict monotheism and moral code but who did not ascribe to its dietary laws or submit to circumcision. He was a good man, noted for his charity and prayerfulness. Still, he was a pagan and Peter's acceptance of him as a believer and one upon whom the Holy Spirit had come was a landmark decision in the development of the early church.

With the baptismal initiation of Cornelius and his household, the early community took its first official and decisive step toward realizing the universal scope of Jesus' mission. Of course, the gentile mission had been begun *before* Cornelius', conversion, due to the missionary efforts of the Hellenistic Christians, e.g., Philip, Stephen, etc. But Luke's theological concerns led him to relate all significant progress and development in the early church to the auspices of the Jerusalem church. Therefore, it was Peter, leader of the Twelve, whom Luke has featured as instrumental in bringing Cornelius to the faith.

Peter's speech with its overlay of Lucan universalist theology is an excellent example of the method developed by the early disciples for proselytising gentiles. Unlike the speeches addressed to Jewish audiences, there is no indictment of the Jews for Jesus' death. Moreover, unlike the discourses intended for Jews that began with Jesus' rejection and death, the speech to Cornelius made mention of Jesus' life and ministry of good works and healing. Instead of backing his claims with scriptural references, as would have been significant for Jewish hearers and readers, Peter offers the testimony of apostolic eyewitnesses to support his statements.

With the Cornelius episode, the church officially opened itself to accept "everyone who believes in Jesus" (v. 43). That this newfound ecumenism was not entirely a human achievement was made quite clear by Luke who gave credit throughout his narrative to the Holy Spirit. Because of the Holy Spirit, Peter and his fellow Jews were able (eventually) to rise above their doubts and prejudices concerning gentile believers.

Colossians 3:1-4. When Paul wrote about the effect upon Christians of Jesus' resurrection, he encountered a special resistence among the believers at Colossae. From the internal evidence in his letter (2:1), we can deduce that the church at Colossae was not established by Paul himself but had been the work of one Epaphras, a disciple who had probably heard Paul preach the gospel in Ephesus. Evidently, shortly after its foundation, the Colossian community had fallen prey to an incipient form of gnosticism that threatened to dilute and/or distort the Christian faith.

Gnosticism (from *gnosis*: knowledge) was an esoteric philosophy whose proponents ascribed to the principle that matter was inherently evil and spirit was essentially good. Since human beings had the sad misfortune to be composites of matter and spirit, their lives were relegated to the difficult task of transcending their lesser selves (matter, body) by achieving greater and greater spiritual goals. Such goals were made accessible by *learning* the secret knowledge (*gnosis*) available only to a special elite.

Given this basic premise, two extremes of practice emerged among gnostic proponents: (1) An "ascetic extreme" that advocated a complex and rigorous asceticism in order to become free of the body. (2) A "libertine extreme" that found no value in the body and therefore sought to overcome it by "wearing it out" in orgiastic practices. Because of their rejection of matter and of the body as evil, both extremes of gnostic thought militated against a proper understanding of redeemed life.

As a result of Jesus' saving acts and by baptism into that saving mystery, Christians have, taught Paul, "been raised up in company with Christ" (3:1). As P. Wrightman in his excellent study of Colossians has pointed out, "raised" is literally rendered "co-raised," pointing to the Christians' solidarity or identification with Christ. Because of that solidarity, even *here* and *now* while *in the body*, Christians are called to greater values and to a life style consistent with their status as redeemed persons.

1 Corinthians 5:6-8. "Poppin' fresh dough" had a very different connotation among our Jewish and Christian ancestors in the faith. For the most part, leaven or yeast was regarded as an impurity and became a figurative sign for sin and corruption. According to the law (Leviticus 2:11), no offering of grain could be presented to Yahweh if it had been tainted with yeast. Plutarch, the Greek biographer, referred to leaven as the "offspring of corruption, corrupting the whole mass of dough with which it was mixed." Jesus warned his disciples to "watch out for the leaven of the Pharisees" referring to the hypocrisy of their teaching and obsequious behavior (Matthew 16:6, 11, 12; Luke 12:1). *Unleavened* bread, on the other hand, had become a metaphor for purity and holiness and the Feast of Azymes (Unleavened Bread) was from an early date associated with the Passover commemoration.

In today's pericope selected from the first of his letters to the Corinthian community, Paul employed a similar symbolism. The case in point (1 Corinthians 5:1-13) was a man who had had sexual relations with his father's wife. A matter forbidden by law (Leviticus 18:8), such immoral behavior was also abhorrent to non-Jews. Paul, however, was shocked more at the *complacency* of the Corinthians toward the man's sin than at the man's weakness. He urged the community to "sweep house," as it were, to get rid of the old yeast.

In exhorting the community to be aware of and to confront the sinner, Paul drew upon the Palestinian custom of cleaning the entire house on Passover eve to rid it of all traces of old leaven. In a sense, Paul was reminding the Christians that Passover purity had become a permanent requirement for Christians redeemed by Christ. Among Easter people, the leaven of sin had no place. Only the unleavened purity of sincerity and truth would be a worthy reflection of the grace and glory of Christ's saving sacrifice.

John 20:1-8. An empty tomb does not a *miracle* make, nor does it in any way *prove* the fact of a resurrection. Had the empty tomb been the *only* phenomenon surrounding Jesus' death, it certainly would not have become the basis for Christian faith in the resurrection. Upon discovering that the huge stone at the entrance of Jesus' tomb had been moved, Mary did not conclude that he had risen. Rather, she ran off to report what she thought to be foul play, "The Lord has been taken... we don't know where they have put him." Although the account of the empty tomb was recorded in all four gospels and was an *early* tradition, it was not included in the *earliest* testimonies to Jesus' resurrection (1 Corinthians 15:5). Christian faith in Jesus' victory over death was rooted in the *appearances* of the risen Lord to his followers. For those who came to faith in Jesus as risen by virtue of his appearances to them, the ambiguity of the empty tomb was resolved. Moreover, the narratives of the empty tomb helped to explain somehow the mysterious reality of Jesus' bodily resurrection, i.e., that the same Jesus who had walked, talked and had eaten with them, who had died and was buried, was the same Christ who was alive and who lives.

Some have suggested that the narratives of the empty tomb and resurrection appearances were concocted by the disciples, disappointed at the death of their leader. When Jesus died, however, his followers deserted him and any hopes they may have had in his messianic future were dashed. In answer to the skeptics who attributed stories of the risen Jesus to the figments of wishful imaginations, Paul stated unequivocally: "If Christ is not risen from the dead, our preaching is empty, your faith is worthless and we are the most wretched of people" (1 Corinthians 15: 19). In more contemporary language, J. L. McKenzie has restated Paul's thought: "The resurrection is a fundamental component of Christian faith which collapses without it. Faith is not a doctrine which survives its teacher; it is an experience of a reality, and that reality is the risen Christ, without whom it is an experience of nothing."

In the Johannine version of the empty tomb tradition, the Beloved Disciple functioned as did the angel messengers in the synoptic accounts, viz., to *explain* what the empty tomb and the arrangement of burial clothes meant. The Beloved Disciple had run ahead to the tomb but, upon arriving, waited to allow Peter to enter first. By means of this small detail the Johannine author has coordinated his work with the earliest tradition, "He appeared *first* to Cephas and then to the Twelve" (1 Corinthians 15:5).

Perhaps the most telling line of the entire pericope is the evangelist's editorial remark that as yet they did not understand the scripture about Jesus' rising from the dead (v. 9). As yet, it had not become clear that Jesus' resurrection was not the last act of one single life but the first moment of a new and eschatological dimension in which all people would share. The rising of Jesus from the dead has brought resurrection, life and glory to his entire body, the church, and to all who hope and believe.

1. Believers witness to their faith in the resurrection by bringing joy to those who are sad, forgiveness to the guilty and hope to the apathetic (Acts).

2a. Belonging to the company of Christ requires a daily integration of eternal idealism with temporary realism (Colossians).

2b. The "rotten apple" has been famed for its far reaching influence; but so too, the smallest good or kind word has a power which should not be underestimated (1 Corinthians).

3. Jesus' resurrection gave meaning to the paradox of the cross and makes sense of the suffering, pain and death of his followers (John).

Second Sunday of Easter

Jesus' resurrection triumph is an unending celebration that extends to his disciples the power to make the sick and broken whole (Acts). Because of Jesus' victory, those who believe can rejoice and hope even in the shadow of persecution and death (Revelation). By the power of his Spirit, the risen Lord has made forgiveness a sacrament of his presence and made peace the assurance of his love (John).

Acts 5:12-16. Without the Acts of the Apostles, a great deal of information about the nascent years of the Jesus movement would have had to be deduced secondhand and indirectly from other sources. Acts provides the modern reader with a living account of the early church's faith in the risen Lord and of its subsequent struggle to balance that faith with the trials of persecution, growing pains, inner discord and delayed eschatology.

Still, it should be understood that Acts is not merely an historical or even a strictly chronological account of the primitive community of believers; it is rather a dramatic, pictorial and highly theologized presentation. Not an eyewitness to that which he described, Luke freely rewrote certain events, telescoped others and conflated certain versions of an account with other versions. Luke wrote in the 80s for a generation of Christians who had lost their authoritative eyewitnesses to the resurrection and who needed to experience the continuous character of the faith so as to deal with a prolonged mission in this world (delayed parousia). Luke sought to teach, through Acts, how to survive, how to grow, how to flourish as a vibrant community.

Charles Talbert would have us understand Acts as belonging, with the gospel of Luke, to the ancient cultic biographical tradition. Cultic-biographies were produced by and used within religious communities or philosophical schools. Usually the biographies were in two parts: (1) career of the community's founder, retold as a norm for devotees and as an inspiration for their reverence and worship; (2) a narrative of the founder's successors and selected other disciples. The main function of this two-part work was *legitimation*. Such a biography would *legitimate* the founder's successors at the time of the document's writing by tracing the unbroken line of tradition from the founder to the disciples and by illustrating the continuities between the successors' words and works and those of their founder.

In composing his two volumes as he did, the author of Luke-Acts showed the tradition begun with Jesus was being maintained by the Twelve. This concern for "legitimation" has been reflected by the author in the gospel's preface: "so that your excellency may realize what *assurance* you have for the instruction you have received" (Luke 1:4). That assurance or "*asphaleia*" was intended to strengthen the second and third generation Christians in their fidelity to the teaching and practice of the church, confident that those teachings and practices were somehow rooted in Jesus' own ministry.

The main factor of continuity between Jesus and the church, operative in both periods, was and continues to be the Holy Spirit. The same Spirit that empowered Jesus (Luke 1:35; 3:21-22), filled him and led him to perform his mighty deeds of salvation was shown by Luke to be the force that transformed and impelled the followers of Jesus to continue the process of universal salvation (Acts 1:2, 5; 2:14-17, 33; 4:8, 31; 8:29, 39, etc.).

Today's first reading is an example of one of the Lucan literary features, called a summary. Acts contains three types of summaries (major, minor and numerical) all of which were constructed by the author as literary signals to remind and encourage the reader that the Jesus movement was indeed making sure progress.

Today's text is the third of three *major* summaries (Acts 2:42-47; 4:32-35; 5:11-16) that described, albeit idyllically and in a schematic manner, the growth of the early church. Each of the summaries featured the community as close-knit, sharing goods and talents in common, gathering around the Twelve for liturgical and catechetical nourishment and steadily increasing in number. Because of the summaries, the modern reader can appreciate the formation of those structures and institutions whereby the early believers actualized the reality of the resurrection in their daily lives. Miracles of healing and conversion were, as in Jesus' ministry, signs of the eschatological age of salvation.

Revelation 1:9-13, 17-19. While he was still among his followers, schooling them in the costly challenges of discipleship, Jesus promised that anyone who had given up all for his sake, would "receive in this present age a hundred times as many homes, brothers and sisters, mothers, children and property—*and persecution besides* —and in the age to come everlasting life" (Mark 10:30). In the book of Revelation there is bold evidence that the reality of the promised persecution had come to pass. But also present is the promise of victory and the abiding hope in life eternal.

Writing in the style called apocalyptic, the author of Revelation used the genre's mysterious symbolism, myths, numerology, visions and portents to shape his message of encouragement for those who were his companions in suffering. Rooted in a firm faith in God's goodness and in the divine plan for human history, apocalyptic literature wanted its readers to gaze beyond their present sorrows to a bright and blessed future. In the words of D. M. Stanley, "the book of Revelation is simply the apostolic kerygma transferred into the apocalyptic key in order to provide a theology of history for the Church. Its basic message is that the risen Christ, identified with Jesus of Nazareth, is Lord of this world's history."

Although the exact date of Revelation is still debated, internal evidence in the book seems to point to the period of persecution under Emperor Domitian. In their polytheistic society, the Romans forced all in the empire to acknowledge the state gods. While Judaism enjoyed a special tolerance and was recognized by Rome as a legal religion, Christians were granted no such exemption. Once Christianity was officially rejected by the Jews, its proponents were forced to obey Roman law and were liable to persecution if they did not acquiesce. Besides the veneration of the state gods, there was also a growing tendency to require that the subjects of the empire worship the emperor as divine. On both counts, Christians who refused to do so were found guilty and persecuted, in many cases until death.

Today's second reading is from the author's inaugural vision. Told in the language of the Old Testament theophanies, the experience was to equip the author to proclaim courage and victory to the seven churches of Asia Minor. Portrayed as seven lampstands, the churches were to take heart in the fact that the risen and triumphant Christ, pictured as the Son of Man (Daniel 7:10; Ezekiel 1:24-26) and belted in gold like a king (1 Maccabees 10:89, 11:58), proclaimed his sovereignty over all. Holding the keys (i.e., as master, v. 18) of life and of death, the risen Lord was present to offer to the persecuted the confidence of an eventual victory and peace: "There is nothing to fear ... once I was dead but now I live—forever and ever."

John 20:19-31. Easter's living legacy is beautifully told in today's pericope from the fourth gospel: peace and mission, a dynamic Spirit, forgiveness and faith. The traditional gospel for the second Sunday of Easter proclaimed in each year of the three-year cycle, the narrative is comprised of two resurrection appearances, one on Easter evening, the second a week later. Luke had separated the moments of the salvation event (resurrection, ascension-exaltation, gift of the Spirit) for obvious pedagogical reasons and the church's tradition has maintained that separation for liturgical and catechetical reasons. The Johannine author's coalescence of the moments into one event is a more accurate and true presentation of the fact. Therefore in the Johannine account, the resurrected Lord is presented as bestowing the Spirit and mandating his disciples on the *same* day.

Jesus' greeting of peace (*shalom*) was the conventional Jewish greeting but, in the context of the resurrection triumph, took on an added significance. Peace and joy were signals of the messianic era inaugurated by Jesus' triumph. With the gift of the Spirit, Jesus fulfilled the prophecies (Joel 3:1, Ezekiel 36:27, etc.) and his Easter legacy became one of realized eschatology. With the same Spirit of God that hovered over the primeval waters and brought forth order and life (Genesis 1), with the same Spirit that breathed into the sculpted earth and brought forth a living being (Genesis 2), with the same Spirit that had anointed kings, priests, prophets and the Lord's suffering servant, Jesus inspired, empowered and anointed his disciples.

As in all the resurrection appearances in the gospels, the Johannine author was intent upon establishing the continuity between the crucified, earthly Jesus and the risen, glorified, Spirit-giving Lord. With the wounds of his passion in evidence, the risen Jesus proclaimed the unity between the cross and his exaltation; he was one and the same Lord. In John's church of the 90s, there was a gnostic element that preferred to overlook the passion, humiliation and ignominious death of Jesus, in favor of a wonder-working, divine-man christology. This Johannine resurrection appearance with its emphasis on the scars of Jesus' suffering served as an apologia to those with a lopsided view of Christ's saving action. In addition to the concern for continuity between the earthly and risen Jesus, the resurrection appearances were also geared toward the survival of the eschatological community until Jesus' second advent. Jesus' mandating of his disciples for their mission of mercy and forgiveness assured that the ministry he had begun would continue to give life to his community. The sending forth of the disciples to forgive sins has been cited by later church theologians as a source text for understanding the sacrament of penance or reconciliation. Some have interpreted the forgiving or binding of sins (v. 23) as a reference to the church's responsibility of withholding baptism depending on the initiate's acceptance or rejection of the kerygmatic preaching. Others, drawing on the rabbinic terms *asar* and *sera'* (bind, loose) have interpreted v. 23 in the context of church discipline, i.e., the right of the church's authority to grant or to refuse membership in the community for reasons of sinfulness. Although these later ecclesiastical and juridical developments may find support in today's gospel pericope, its primary message of peace and forgiveness should not be diminished. Because of his conquest of sin the risen Lord could share that victory with all believers. Jesus' cross, the sign of contradiction, did not impart a message of impotence and failure but one of forgiveness, power and peace.

The person of Thomas has made a case for the value of doubt in the life of faith. As one who hesitated and questioned, and then moved from skeptical doubting to an even firmer, committed faith, Thomas is a source of encouragement for serious believers of all ages. Moreover the Thomas episode helped the early church come to grips with a problem that became more urgent with the deaths of the authoritative eyewitnesses to Jesus' resurrection: How could a person believe in Jesus as risen, without an appearance of the risen Lord? For a time, those who had not seen the risen Jesus relied on the eyewitness testimony of those who had. But, as is clear in the interchange between Thomas and the disciples, faith was not an automatic result of hearing eye-witness testimony ("I'll never believe it"). Nor was *seeing* firsthand a *guarantee* of faith. Even when he *saw* the Lord, Thomas still had to come to faith. In Thomas' doubts and misunderstandings, the evangelist made several apologetic and theological points: (1) Jesus' invitation to touch and examine his wounds underscored the very *real* quality of his body and put to rest the theories that the appearances were the product of apostolic wish-fulfillment or illusory phantasm. (2) Thomas was called beyond the sensational aspects of the resurrection to a committed faith. Notice, he was moved to faith not by actually touching Jesus but by the risen Lord's challenge, "Believe! (3) Thomas' "my Lord (*Kyrios*), my God (*Theos*)" united in one act of faith the church's growing awareness of the risen Jesus as equal to the eternal creator and all powerful Lord of all.

For all who share the legacy of Easter, the gift of the Spirit, the mandate of peace and forgiveness and the challenge of the risen Lord ("Believe!") are ever present realities.

1. Healing the sick and bringing peace to the troubled are the responsibilities of Easter people (Acts).

2. Visionaries help the rest of us bear with our burdens, transform the evil and look with hope beyond the banal and mundane to eternity (Revelation).

3. Faith is not the result of touching or seeing but the lifelong labor of listening and responding to God's invitations (John).

Third Sunday of Easter

Transformed by their experience of Jesus' resurrection and inspired by his Holy Spirit, the early believers found the courage to witness to Jesus even at the risk of their lives (Acts). With grace enhancing their natural talents, they shouldered new responsibilities as fishers and shepherds for the kingdom (John). Undefeated even by death, they live forever to celebrate the joyful victory with Christ for which we all hope (Revelation).

Acts 5:27-32, 40-41. During his ministry, Jesus had warned his followers that because of their association with him they would be manhandled and persecuted, summoned to synagogues and prisons, brought before kings and governors, all because of his name (Luke 21:12). But, he had also promised, "I will give you words and a wisdom which none of your adversaries can take exception to or contradict," and he had assured them: "The Holy Spirit will teach you at that moment all that should be said" (Luke 21:15; 12:12). In today's first reading, where Luke recounted the apostles' second appearance before the Sanhedrin, Jesus' warnings and reassurances were realized.

The supreme court or council of the Jewish population, the Sanhedrin (an Aramaicized version of the Greek *synedrion*) was traditionally attributed to Moses (Numbers 11: 16-25). However, the first *historical* evidence of such a governing body has been traced to the period of the Greek domination of Palestine in the second century B.C.E. (1 Maccabees 11:23, 12:6). In the first century of the Christian era, the council was comprised of three groups: (1) the elders of the chief families and clans, (2) the leaders or high priests (former high priests and elders of the high priestly families), (3) the scribes or legal experts.

Consisting of 71 members presided over by the current high priest, the Sanhedrin met in the temple complex and, even during the Roman occupation, exercised considerable authority over all matters of Jewish life, religious, political and social. With its own police force possessing the power of arrest, the Sanhedrin (according to the Talmud) was in session from the time of the morning sacrifice until the evening sacrifice. Authorized to render judgment and pass sentence in all but capital cases (upon which Rome reserved the right), the Sanhedrin was the legal voice in Israel and was recognized to a certain degree even among the dispersed Jews (Acts 9:1-2).

Given the prestige and far-reaching power enjoyed by the Sanhedrin, the boldness of the apostles as they appeared before the court is all the more remarkable. Regarded as renegades from orthodox Judaism, the apostles were prosecuted for keeping alive the story of Jesus and for professing to do great wonders in his name. In this particular instance, the apostles had been arrested for the second time (see chapter 4). Although they had been ordered to cease their teaching, they had continued and for their flagrant disregard of the Sanhedrin's censure (4:19) were put into prison to await a morning arraignment.

With exquisite tongue-in-cheek irony, Luke narrated their miraculous escape and the perplexity of the Sanhedrin who could not locate their prisoners but learned of their whereabouts from the people. Besides the fact that the apostles disobeyed an official order, the *content* of their teaching was also objectionable to the Jewish authoritative body. Casting blame for Jesus' death ("whom you put to death," v. 30) on the revered leaders and emphasizing Jesus' vindication by God ("whom God has exalted at his right hand," v. 30), the apostolic preaching seemed to call for divine retribution.

For the first time identified as "savior," Jesus was described as the reason for Israel's repentance and the bringer of forgiveness. Drawing on several implicit Old Testament references (Deuteronomy 21:23; Psalm 118: 16; Exodus 2:14), the apostolic kerygma was intended to convince the Lucan *reading* audience that the mystery of Jesus' death and resurrection was not a freak act but an essential and integral part of God's saving plan. By declaring that it was better "to obey God than men" (v. 29), the apostles set forth the principle that the individual conscience is more binding than any authority, civil or religious.

Moreover, Peter's assertion underscored the fact that the Sanhedrin was a merely human institution, steered by human motivations, e.g., "filled with jealousy" (5:17) compared to the faithful followers of Jesus who were "filled with the Holy Spirit" (4:31). According to the Jewish legal practice (Deuteronomy 19:15), two witnesses whose testimony concurred were required for evidence to be considered valid and admissible in court. In addition to the apostolic witness, Peter cited the testimony of the Holy Spirit (5:32) to support the facts about Jesus.

Omitted from the account is the favorable intercession made by Rabbi Gamaliel and the fact that the apostles were beaten the prescribed 39 lashes before they were dismissed.

Revelation 5:11-14. Intended for the edification and encouragement of the faith community in the throes of persecution and crisis, apocalyptic literature was characterized by its visions of a glorious future. For those who endured the present passing age, there would come an eternal era of light and goodness. Distinct from prophecy that described the culmination in worldly terms, apocalyptic painted verbal pictures of a *new* heaven and a *new* earth. Called by G. Von Rad "a theology of eschatological dualism," Jewish apocalyptic literature presented the understanding that "the Most High has made not one world but two" (II Esdras 7:50). A glimpse of this two epoch dualism is evident in today's second reading from the Christian apocalyptical book of Revelation.

Part of a longer pericope (chapters 4-5) that described in vivid detail an eschatological feast, the celestial liturgy was clearly modeled on the Jewish Passover ritual. In a celebration of cosmological proportions, all created beings joined to praise the Lamb who was slain. A peculiarly Christian designation for Jesus as the messiah, the title "Lamb" had a wide literary and symbolic history.

Jewish apocalyptic (Testament of Joseph 19:8) featured a conquering lamb who overcame the beasts of evil and sin by crushing them underfoot. In Deutero-Isaiah, the fourth of the servant songs (52:13—53:12) pictured the suffering one as a lamb led to slaughter by whose sacrifice the many were healed. Thirdly, there was the Passover lamb sacrificed to memorialize and celebrate the exodus event whereby Israel had passed from slavery to freedom.

All of these features, i.e., conqueror of evil, vicarious suffering, and sacramental sign of inaugural passage into new existence, were probably included in the visionary's perception of the eternal Lamb. By fulfilling his role as suffering savior and conqueror of sin and death, Jesus had become the once and forever perfect lamb by whose sacrifice believers were able to pass over with him into eternal triumph.

Present at the heavenly liturgy were angels (v. 11), who were according to the Hebrew scriptures members of the heavenly court sharing in divine decisions about the world's governance (Job 1:6-12, 2:1-6), and serving as messengers of those decisions while witnessing to humankind God's transcendent holiness (Daniel 7:9-14). Also in attendance were the four living creatures (v. 14) who according to Jewish cosmology controlled the four elements of the universe and its workings. With the elders (*presbyteroi*) all sang the same song of praise to the Lamb and to the one on the throne. In effect, according to the seer's vision the whole of creation had been drawn together in one endless act of worship because of the Lamb's salvific deeds. For those to whom the book of Revelation was addressed, the vision of the heavenly liturgy gave an added dimension to the eucharistic breaking of the bread and a new hope to those whose lives were being broken for the sake of their faith in the Lamb.

John 21:1-19. More than just a "great fish story," this resurrection appearance of Jesus taught the valuable lessons of (1) the catholicity of the apostolic ministry, (2) forgiveness and rehabilitation and (3) the ultimate cost of discipleship. An epilogue to the gospel (which clearly ended in 20:30-31) but not an afterthought, chapter 21 complements and balances the gospel's prologue and was probably composed by the same person, a Johannine disciple. As R. E. Brown has noted, the disciple-redactor "shared the same general world of thought as the evangelist and desired more to complete the gospel than to change its impact."

The pericope's first lesson, that of apostolic catholicity, is communicated through the narrative of the great catch of fish. Whereas the synoptics placed this episode within the ministry, the Johannine authors have chosen to associate the event and the transmission of power to Peter with the post-resurrection period. By so doing, they have shown that the church's missionary efforts were an extension of the risen Lord's glory, and power. After a night of catching nothing, the appearance of the risen Lord at daybreak improved matters considerably. Notice the association of Jesus with the dawn; he is shown to be the light that ends the period of darkness and brings new hope to the searching. Significant too is the fact that, in the gospels the disciples (some of whom were seasoned fishermen) never seem to catch anything without Jesus' help! But with the authorization of the risen Lord and by his power, they were successful.

In this Johannine account, their success was described in terms of the mysterious number, 153. Obviously a symbolic figure, though not explained by the author, the number 153 has been given a variety of interpretations, some with greater merit than others.

Augustine determined that 153 is the "triangular" number of 17, i.e., $1 + 2 + 3 + 4 + 5 + \ldots + 17 = 153$. Others have resorted to "gematria," i.e., the numerical value of letters, and have calculated 153 to be the sum of the letters in the Hebrew expression *qahal he labab*, church of love. Some, following Cyril of Alexandria, believe the 153 should be reduced to 100, 50, 3. The 100 should symbolize the fullness of the gentiles; the 50 would represent the remnant of Israel, and the 3 would signify the Trinity!

Probably Jerome was closer to reality when, in his commentary on Ezekiel, he mentioned that Greek zoologists had classified 153 species of fish. If this idea was intended by the gospel author, then the sense communicated would be that of the universal (catholic) scope of the apostolic mission. As disciples mandated by risen Lord, the disciples were sent to bring to salvation *all* peoples (all species) regardless of race, religion or heritage. The fact that the net resisted tearing or breaking attested to the possibility of a cohesive unity despite the plurality of different traditions, theologies, etc. All were welcome into the "net" of the kingdom (Matthew 13:47).

In the pericope's second lesson, Peter is an example of the power of divine forgiveness to rehabilitate the sinner. Earlier in the gospel, Peter had denied knowing Jesus, not just once but three times. In the risen Jesus' three-fold question to Peter, "Do you love me?," and in Peter's three-fold affirmation of his love, there is a marked correspondence with the earlier denials. With each successive protestation of his love and of Jesus' knowledge of him, Peter became the model of all who would pasture (pastor) and nourish Jesus' followers. Not a perfect leader, he was impulsive ("he jumped into the water"), dense and brash (Jesus had said to him: "Get behind me, Satan") and at times even cowardly ("I do not even know the man"). But he also had some awareness of Jesus' mission ("you are the messiah") and repented having denied him ("he went out and wept bitterly"). When graced with the power of the risen Lord, the impulsive, brash and even cowardly man was willing to accept the role of shepherd with which Jesus had himself associated (John 10). For his courageous response to love and grace, he was reissued the challenge of discipleship, "Follow me" (v. 19).

Jesus' solemn words to Peter (v. 18) contain the third lesson of the pericope. For those who would follow Jesus as fishers of salvation and shepherds of peace, the way would lead, as did Jesus', through the "valley of darkness" to the shadow of the cross. The stretching out of the hands and the carrying off against one's will (v. 18) are references to the inevitable martyrdom that was the cost of absolute commitment and faithful discipleship. Today the cost and the commitment remain unchanged, but also unchanged is the powerful presence of the risen Lord among us.

1. No human institution, political or religious, has the right to usurp the believer's conscientious decision to obey God (Acts).

2. Visions of triumph inspire; portents of doom discourage (Revelation).

3. Fishers and shepherds are sent forth to love, to feed and to suffer for the truth (John).

Fourth Sunday of Easter

Indiscriminantly, the light of salvation reaches out to all who are in darkness and in need (Acts). Jew or gentile, rich or poor, the word gathers unto life and joy all who would hear and open themselves to its power (Revelation). All that is required of those who would be saved is an open heart and the ability to recognize the loving voice of the one who calls (John).

Acts 13:14, 43-53. In his article, "On the Road and on the Sea with Paul," Jerome M. O'Connor estimated that Paul logged approximately 15,000 miles in his service of the gospel. From Paul himself, we have learned of the rigors of travel in the first Christian century and have come to a greater appreciation of his apostolic efforts: "five times I received 40 lashes less one; three times I was beaten with rods; 1 was stoned once, shipwrecked three times; I passed a day and a night on the sea. I travelled continually, endangered by floods, robbers, my own people, the gentiles; imperiled in the city, in the desert, at sea, by false brothers; enduring labor, hardship, many sleepless nights; in hunger and in thirst and frequent fastings, in cold and nakedness" (2 Corinthians 11:24-27). In today's first reading Paul's first missionary trip has been roughly outlined by Luke (13:1—14:28), a trip which according. to H. Conzelmann actually took about 13 years (see Galatians 1:21—2:1). Luke took care (Acts 13:1-3) to show that the missionary activities of the early believers were not based on the decisions of solitary individuals but were, rather, the concerted effort of the community. Deliberating together to plan the mission and inspired by the Spirit, missionaries were ordained for their task and mandated by the church.

Having been so commissioned by the Christian community in Syrian Antioch, Paul and Barnabas sailed west to Cyprus, where they preached their way westward across the island. From there, they sailed northward to modern day Turkey, gradually making their way to another Antioch in Pisidia. Founded by Seleucus Nikator, ca. 300-280 B.C.E. and named for his father, Antiochus (one of Alexander's generals), Pisidian Antioch was later made a Roman colony by Augustus. The administrative center of the southern part of the province of Galatia, this Antioch was home to a large settlement of Jews. When these had gathered to pray in the synagogue on the sabbath, Paul was invited to address them.

Having been well received, Paul and Barnabas returned to the synagogue the next week. No doubt Luke was exaggerating when he described the attendance: "almost the entire city gathered." Omitted from today's pericope, Paul's speech with its overtones of Lucan theology traced the history of Israel to the point of God's promise to David (2 Samuel 7:14). At that point, Paul explained that Jesus Christ was indeed the fulflllment of the divine promises. Our reading describes the mixed reaction of those who heard Paul's exposition. As in Jesus' ministry, many of those who heard the apostles responded enthusiastically but the leaders among the people reacted with resentment and jealousy. As the first of Paul's recorded missionary speeches, this episode seemed to set the structure for what would become the pattern of his efforts: (1) preaching first in synagogue, (2) rejection of message by Jews, openness of gentiles, (3) emergence of a new community, (4) persecution of community by Jewish authorities, (5) departure of Paul to another mission field, (6) repeat pattern.

On three occasions during his apostolic work, Paul solemnly announced that he would turn his attention away from the Jews toward the gentiles. In Asia Minor (today's text), in Greece and in Rome, Paul cited the Jews for their obtuseness: "the word has to be declared to you first of all, but since you reject it and thus convict yourselves as unworthy of eternal life, we now turn to the gentiles" (v. 46; 18:16; 28:25-27). This statement expressed both the Pauline and the Lucan theological conviction that Israel was privileged as God's chosen people to be the first to receive the message of salvation. Citing the servant song from Deutero-Isaiah, "I have made you a light to the nations, a means of salvation to the ends of the earth" (49:6), the apostles and the author underscored the fact that the universal scope (to the gentiles) of the Jesus movement was *not* caused by Jewish rejection but was part of the foreordained divine plan.

There is a note of irony in the symbolic act of repudiation with which Paul and Barnabas left Antioch for Iconium. Jews customarily shook dust from their feet when returning to Israel from a journey abroad. By removing the "pagan" dust from their feet, they were thought to be cleansed from the sin and impurity of foreign places and people. For Paul and Barnabas to perform the same act against fellow Jews was tantamount to equating them with pagans! The gesture also recalled Jesus' instruction to his disciples (Luke 9:5; 10:11).

Revelation 7:9, 14-17. For those persecuted Christians who heard the words of today's second reading, the message must have been like a soothing balm. As John the seer described huge crowds of celebrants at the heavenly feast and as he held out the promises of "no more tears, no more hunger or thirst," the real situation of his hearers was quite different. Most scholars agree that Revelation, an apocalyptic work, was written to encourage believers sometime during the reign of the Roman emperor Domitian (81-96 C.E.). Demanding to be worshipped as "Lord and God" and cruelly enforcing his demands, Domitian (also called Germanicus) extended his persecution outside Rome and throughout Asia Minor (recipients of Revelation). In Ephesus, Domitian had built a large temple where he could be worshipped. Even today parts of the statue of himself he had ordered for the temple can be seen in the museum at Ephesus. With the escalation of Domitian's persecution, Christians were for the first time forced into a direct confrontation with the imperial government. Their choice? Christ or Caesar!

Knowing firsthand the sufferings of his companions in the faith, the seer assured those who survived their present struggles of a glorious and joyful future. The enormous throng of vast ethnic diversity (v. 9) represents the catholicity or universality of the church. In the Roman empire, Christians had become unwelcome; in the empire of the Lamb, there would be no such prejudice. *All* who believed and had entered into the saving mystery of Jesus' victorious death would be present. Garments were symbols of inner attitudes and moral dispositions. Those who had believed, repented and endured could shed the scarlet robes of their sinfulness (Isaiah 1:18) and, washed in Jesus' blood, could put on the white robes of forgiveness and victory. It should be noted that the white robe and its moral signiflcance were not *consequences* of eschatological glory but *conditions* for entering into it. A symbol of baptismal initiation and the continual process of daily conversion to Christ, the white robe could be thought of figuratively as the survivor's work uniform.

For those who endured the tribulation of persecution and death, the author painted a hopeful future, rich in the Old Testament imagery. As their shelter, and provider, the Lamb would shepherd (Psalms 23, 80; Isaiah 40:11; Ezekiel 34:23) and lead them to life-giving water (Jeremiah 2:13; Psalm 35:10). Some scholars have likened this heavenly liturgy before the Lamb's throne to a celestial feast of Tabernacles. Tabernacles was a harvest feast associated with the inauguration of the new year (Leviticus 23:23). Later historicized as a commemoration of the desert trek, and as a thanksgiving for God's provident care, Tabernacles came to be associated by the prophets with the beginning of the messianic era. During the feast, lamps were lighted, palms were carried, and libations of water were poured out. In John's vision, the era of the messiah had indeed been inaugurated; for all who persevered by faith, the symbols of Tabernacles (palms, lights, life-giving water) would become a reality of unending joy.

John 10:27-30. On one of his trips to the Middle East, J. L. Porter observed shepherds in the hills of Bashan:

"The shepherds led their flocks forth from the gates of the city. Thousands of sheep and goats were there, grouped in dense, confused masses. The shepherds who had been waiting together separated, each taking a different path, each uttering a shrill peculiar call. As the sheep heard them, the masses swayed and moved as if shaken by some internal convulsion. Then points struck out in the directions taken by the shepherds; these became longer and longer until the confused masses were resolved into long, living streams, flowing after their leaders." Porter's 20th century description of the eastern pastoring style is no different from that practiced in Jesus' day. Shepherds and their flocks knew one another and could recognize one another even amid a mass of other sheep and shepherds, When Jesus claimed to have a similar relationship with those who believed in him, his hearers had existential experience of what he meant.

Part of a longer section (John 10) in which Jesus discussed the mutual responsibilities which he (and the Father) and his followers bore for one another, today's pericope is an excerpt from Jesus' reply to those who pressed him: "How long are you going to keep us in suspense? If you really are the messiah, tell us so in plain words" (10:24).

It was winter and all of Israel was celebrating the feast of the Dedication. A "late" feast, Dedication (Hebrew: *Hanukkah*; Greek: *Elkainia* = renewal) was a celebration of the Maccabean triumph over the Seleucids in 164 B.C.E. Three years earlier (167 B.C.E.) Antiochus Epiphanes IV had profaned the temple by erecting an idol (Baal Shamem) on the altar of holocausts. Daniel (9:27) and Matthew (24:15) referred to this desecration as the "abomination of desolation in the holy place." Led by Judas Maccabeus, the Israelites rebelled, routed the enemies, built a new altar and rededicated the temple (1 Maccabees 4:41-61). Thereafter, the occasion was remembered by the annual feast of Dedication.

Perhaps the nationalistic feast and its memories of revolutionary saviors (the Maccabees) had fired messianic expectations among the people. When they inquired as to whether or not Jesus had messianic aspirations, their ideas of messianism were far different from his. His hearers would readily have offered their services as rebels and guerrillas in the service of a military and kingly messiah. Like the Maccabees before them who had rid their land of foreign oppressors, the Jews who questioned Jesus longed to be free of the occupation forces of the imperial Roman empire. But Jesus had a different idea of leadership and would not encourage the nationalistic and political hopes of the people.

After offering the witness of his works (v. 25) to those who questioned him, Jesus ascribed (as he had earlier in John 10) to the figure of the shepherd. There was a definite Old Testament foundation for understanding the role of the shepherd as protector, leader, compassionate provider and king. Indeed, there was also a basis for understanding the Lord himself as shepherd of the people (Psalm 23; Ezekiel 34). In associating his work and his leadership with that of the shepherd, the Johannine Jesus was presented as *more* than a national or military leader. He was in effect equating his messiahship with the work of the Father himself: "the Father and I are one" (v. 30). For that reason, those who recognized him as shepherd would receive eternal life. For that reason also, acceptance of Jesus as messiah-shepherd would not require a national allegiance but *faith* (v. 28). R. E. Brown, citing John Chrysostom, has pointed out that if his hearers did not follow Jesus, it was not because he was not *shepherd* but because they were not *sheep!* To be a sheep, i.e., to belong to Jesus and to be an heir of eternal life, one must be "of God," (8:47) and "of the truth" (18:37). The spiritual attunement necessary for recognizing Jesus as shepherd and as messiah was cultivated only in the faith relationship to which Jesus invited his followers. Faith in Jesus, faith in the Father, made knowledge, i.e., intimate relationship and interchange, possible. That his hearers understood the implications of his statement was obvious from the verses immediately following today's gospel: "They reached for rocks to stone him" (v. 31). As they celebrated Hanukkah and remembered the past's heroic rebels, Jesus proposed to his hearers a new revolution, to leave aside their preconceived notions of temporal salvation and to accept a gentle shepherd who would lead them in truth to eternal life.

1. If the message of salvation is a non-discriminating one, so also must be the ministers of that message (Acts).

2. In a world that permits the injustices of a Poland or an Afghanistan or an Ethiopia to continue, the peaceable kingdom will never be realized (Revelation).

3. The ability to recognize God's voice is a precious gift, perfected not by intellectual acumen but by prayer (John).

Fifth Sunday of Easter

Living in the interim between Jesus' first and final advents, Christians are charged with the responsibility of remembering the past, giving meaning to the present and building the future. Responsible for a sacramental style of life that makes real in word and deed the love of Jesus (John), believers can find courage and inspiration in the early dis-

ciples for whom no effort was too great, no journey too far to undertake for the sake of the gospel (Acts). The work begun in the first century continues today during the 20th century and will reach its culmination only in the eternal kingdom (Revelation).

Acts 14:21-27. A cursory reading of the Acts of the Apostles, particularly of Paul's ministry, may leave the reader with the impression that Paul sped from one place to the next, leaving in his wake small groups of half-taught converts. Because Luke has telescoped certain incidents and condensed others into summary statements, often listing several towns or fields of mission in one sentence without any indication of a passage of time, it is difficult to assess the situation adequately. However, when Acts is read in conjunction with the Pauline letters and when extra-biblical evidence is taken into account, it can be discerned that Paul followed a general policy of remaining in one place until he had established there a firmly rooted and viable Christian community. There were, of course, instances when circumstances beyond his control forced Paul to leave a foundation before he had planned to. On such occasions, Paul sent an emissary to assess the spiritual progress of the community or sent a letter or revisited the foundation himself During a second visit, Paul (and in the case of today's first reading, Barnabas) could: (1) reinforce the basic kerygmatic preaching he had first imparted, (2) teach further with regard to principles of Christian living, and (3) deal with problems that had arisen during his absence.

In addition to the obvious foibles of human nature and the ever present danger of misinterpretation of the truth (false teaching, heresy, etc.) the major source of opposition the early foundations encountered was from the Jewish community. In most of the towns where Paul preached, he first began his work in the synagogue, among the Jewish population. Upon hearing him preach about Jesus as messiah, the Jewish leaders persecuted Paul and his proselytes because they saw Christianity not as the fulfillment of their centuries old hopes but as a threat to their own religious traditions.

Many times, even those Jews who had been converted to Jesus were among Paul's persecutors These were the Judaizers who impugned Paul's authority accusing him of watering down the gospel for the benefit of the gentiles. Paul did not see the necessity of circumcision, dietary laws, etc. for gentile Christians, but the Judaizers were fanatically opposed to what they regarded as the different or untrue gospel Paul preached to the non-Jews. With these difficulties dogging their footsteps, threatening to hinder their work, the missioners Paul and Barnabas were quick to reassure their disciples and to encourage them: "We must undergo many trials if we are to enter into the reign of God" (v. 22). With these words the missionaries promised their converts that the hostile environment within which they had to struggle would eventually yield to the joys of eternity.

Most scholars regard the installation and ordination of elders in each of the churches (v. 23) as an anachronism. Paul's first missionary journey took place ca. 48 C.E., at a time when the Christian churches had not yet adopted the institution of elders. Luke had probably attributed to the early church a development of his own community of the 80s C.E. During Paul's ministry, if Corinth can be regarded as a representative community, the ministries in the churches were mainly charismatic. R. Fuller comments: "But whether it was the charismatics of the Pauline age, the elders of Luke's time, or the threefold ministry of the second century and after, the function of all these ministries was to keep the church on the foundation laid by the original apostles." The Greek word for elder is *presbyter*, the same word from which our term priest is derived. Some have, therefore, interpreted the installation of elders as a foreshadowing of clerical ordination. It would be more accurate to forego later priestly associations with the term "elder" which probably meant one who exercised authority based on a seasoned wisdom and maturity.

Throughout Acts, Luke attributed the development and direction of the growing Jesus movement to God and especially to the Holy Spirit; the accomplishments narrated in today's pericope were no exception. Significantly, upon their return to the community of Syrian Antioch, Paul and Barnabas reported, not on their *own* accomplishments but on the work which *God* had accomplished in and through them. Their achievements, made possible through divine inspiration and motivation, were not enumerated in ledgers as so many baptisms, so many healings, so many reconciliations. What had happened along their way was not a fait accompli, but a first step, an opening of the "door of faith to the Gentiles" (v. 27).

Revelation 21:1-5. In his provocative book *New Testament Without Illusion*, J. L. McKenzie states, "Apocalypse is the cry of the helpless who are borne passively by events which they cannot influence, much less control. The cry of the helpless is often vindictive, expressing impotent rage at reality. Apocalyptic rage is a flight from reality, a plea to God that he will fulfill their wishes and prove them right and the other wrong . . . in a world which has been cruel to believers, apocalyptic believers respond as best they can—which is in desire." Following through with McKenzie's thought, the vision described by the seer John in today's second reading would represent the sublimation of apocalyptic rage at persecution and injustice into an eschatological hope.

One of the most beautiful pieces of religious literature ever composed, today's text underlines the major conviction of apocalyptic literature that however long or however arduous the struggle, *good will never be overcome by evil!* At the heart of the new heavens and earth, the key reason for the cessation of sorrow, evil, hunger, thirst and pain is the fact of God's *presence* (v. 23). Because of the *dwelling of God among his people*, i.e., because of the fact of the redemptive incarnation, all of creation has been renewed.

With images borrowed from the prophets, the new Jerusalem has been portrayed as the fulfillment of all hopes for nearness and oneness with God (Jeremiah 31:33ff; Ezekiel 37:26-28; Zechariah 2:14; 8:8). Coming from the heavens (v. 2), i.e., having a divine origin, the new relationship has been compared to a nuptial union. Reminiscent of Eden's closeness, the wilderness intimacy and the temple's sacredness, the new union would not be interrupted by the fickleness or failures of a sinful people. God's indwelling has effected an entirely new creation. Washed away with the sea were the former ways of evil and darkness. Traditionally, the sea with its mythical monsters was thought to be representative of the primeval chaos.

John 13:31-35. At that precise moment in his narrative when readers would expect to find an account of the institution of the eucharist, the Johannine author departed from his synoptic predecessors and began what has been called the last or farewell discourse. Throughout the lengthy narrative (John 13-17), it becomes increasingly evident to the reader that the one speaking is not merely the Jesus of the ministry prior to his death, but the resurrected and exalted Lord. Moreover, the message has been directed, not simply to the closest associates of Jesus Christ, but to *all* who would believe in him and be aided by his Spirit, throughout the ages of unfolding and realized eschatology.

With Judas gone (v. 31) and with the coming of his "hour," i.e., with the process of his passion-death-glorification set in motion, Jesus is presented as giving to his followers a new commandment. T. Maertens, pointing out that *entole* (commandment) was also used in reference to Jesus' *mission* (John 10:18, 12:49-50, 14:31), has described the commandment as more doctrinal than moral and less legal than institutional. Indeed, the quasi-institutional nature of Christian love is all the more evident due to its context. Where the synoptic accounts featured at this point in their narratives *the eucharist*, the Johannine author has featured the mission of love. "It is as if for him love was just as real a memorial of Christ as the Eucharist itself" (T. Maertens).

As a criterion for the quality of the love with which Christians were to minister to the world, the exalted Jesus offered *his own love*: "such as my love has been for you." *Kathos* (Greek: "such as") implies more than similarity; it involves a conformity in depth and style and expression. By so mandating his followers, the glorified Lord demanded a sacramental character of their ministry so that the activity of Christian love, like the eucharist, would communicate the visible presence of Christ: "this is how all will know you for my disciples" (v. 35). The command to love others was not peculiar to Jesus. According to the law (Leviticus 19:18) the Jews were obliged to love their neighbors as they loved themselves. But the term neighbor was limited to fellow countrymen. Jesus' command to his followers was without qualification and distinctions: *all others* were to be loved as oneself.

In addition to its universal character, the mission of charity which he left his followers was to be informed with the highest possible motivation and had for its model and cause the Lord of love and life himself. As the hour of his glorification proceeded to the cross, his followers would learn the *extent* of the love which Jesus had for them and which he required of them.

In keeping with the high christology of the fourth gospel, Jesus' first words of his last discourse speak of his glorification. Notice the fact that the verbs in vv. 31 and 32 are in the present ("now is . . . and God is . . ."), past ("has been") and future ("will glorify") tenses. Jesus' glorification and that of the Father had begun during his ministry. The signs (seven in John's gospel) he performed had been revelatory of Jesus and the Father's power over sin, suffering and death. Actually, the glorification of the Father, in the person of Jesus, had begun at the moment of the incarnation. In Jesus' hour, which according to today's pericope had already been inaugurated (12:20-29), glorification was being spelled out in the moments of Jesus' passion, death and resurrection. The future glorification would be realized in the return of the Son to the Father's right hand.

Throughout the pericope and the discourse in general, the author has made several references to time: now, not much longer, a little while, soon, etc. These references should be understood as more than the marking of chronological time. True, it would be only a short time before the moment of Calvary, but Jesus had also made such references during the ministry, when his death was not quite so imminent (7:33). "Only a little while longer" was a phrase employed by the prophets to encourage the people that they would *soon* experience the saving power of God. Isaiah had used the term to refer to the quick demise of Assyria (Isaiah 10:25), and Jeremiah consoled his hearers similarly by promising the quick end of the Babylonian oppression (Jeremiah 51:33).

In the case of the Johannine Jesus, the duration of the "little while" had already begun to evaporate with the inauguration of Jesus' hour. His moment of glorification had signaled the eschatological era of salvation. For the Johannine author, eschatology was not a matter for the end of time, but a reality realized in Jesus' hour and experienced by the faithful here and now. For that reason, the mandate of love and the seriousness with which that mandate is kept has eschatological dimensions and repercussions. Christian charity glorifies the Jesus who lived and walked in Nazareth and taught believers of the Father's love. Christian love glorifies the Jesus who lives today in his body, in his members. Finally, Christian love which anticipates and affirms the endless peace and goodness of the kingdom glorifies the future and forever Lord.

1. Ministry requires continued involvement at every level of development and interest in every matter, both great and small (Acts).

2. New kingdoms of peace and joy will not appear like magic; they must be built, stone by stone, day by day, in each and every person (Revelation).

3. If the love shared among people can be thought of as a sacrament of Christ, what then can be thought of hostile aggression, petty jealousies and ruthless ambition? (John).

Sixth Sunday of Easter

Like a massive being with clay feet and angel's wings, the church is an institution at once both human and divine. Even when the friction of opposing free wills ignites a controversy, the Spirit of God is present to bring about compromise and accord (Acts). As promised by the Lord Jesus, his gifts of peace and the paraclete will make present among his followers the possiblities of growth and unity (John), until that moment when all shall rejoice in his everlasting and glorious presence (Revelation).

Acts 15:1-2, 22-29. Theologically and structurally, the event described by Luke in Acts 15 forms the very center of his second volume. The turning point of his narrative on the church, Acts 15 marked the final appearance of Peter, and of the apostles as a body. From then onward, Paul would emerge as the primary figure in Acts. In the controversy at the heart of the chapter, the Christian church was called to resolve one of the primary sources of tension it had encountered, i.e., the relationship within the community between Jewish and gentile believers.

The first Christians, for the most part Jews who had recognized Jesus as messianic, were instilled with a centuries' old negative attitude toward those who were not Jewish. When the first Christians preached the good news of Jesus, they utilized their Jewish heritage and scriptures to present Jesus as the *fulfillment* of Jewish hopes. Their concept of Christianity as the logical sequel to Judaism raised the issue of the place of those who were outside the pale of Judaism's covenantal bonds. Consequently, there resulted among the early church communities a polarization of two distinct factions: (1) those who believed gentiles must go to Christ through Moses; these were sometimes called Judaizers and were mainly in Jerusalem but their missionary zeal sometimes impelled them to travel (as in the case of today's first reading, to Antioch, etc.); (2) those who did not understand Christianity as contingent upon its Jewish matrix and therefore did not regard its law or circumcision as relevant to belief in Jesus.

Today's first reading is an excerpted one, describing: (1) the arrival in Antioch of certain Judaizers who resented what they regarded as the libertine gospel being preached there, and (2) the conclusion to the issue as it was resolved by the authoritative community in Jerusalem. Some of the most respected Acts scholars (e.g., Haenchen) have taken the quite radical position of attributing the entire episode to Luke. Others with a more moderate stance have assigned the speeches of Peter and James to Luke while accepting an historical basis for the event. It would appear that Luke has actually conflated two different controversies and their conclusions: one presided over by Peter about the obligations of the law, and the other presided over by James concerning the legal obligations (dietary laws, feasts, etc.).

Regardless of the historical and chronological difficulties that remain unresolved, the text of the official letter sent to those Christians of gentile origin (vv. 22-29) has underscored some unquestionably valuable insights. Salvation *was not* and *is not* to be understood as a gift for a few, nor was it determined by nationality, racial or social status. *Faith in Jesus* is the sole requisite for salvation and for acceptance as an equal member in the assembly of the church. Faith in Jesus was to override centuries of heritage and hate as it brought together at the same eucharistic table those who had formerly been called "the chosen" with those who had formerly been regarded as "alien" and "unclean." That these insights were due to the work of the risen Lord among them was acknowledged in the beautiful statement, "It is the decision of the Holy Spirit, and ours too" (v. 28). Christians were accustomed to the imperial decrees from the Roman authorities that began, "It is the decision of me and my council." No doubt Luke had this in mind when he impressed upon his readers the fact that Jesus' own Holy Spirit was the counsel, inspiration and guiding force of the growing church.

Revelation 21:10-14, 22-23. H. Thoreau dreamed of Walden and A. Huxley imagined a brave new world, but neither could compare to the holy city John the Seer envisioned for his contemporaries. A city founded in and bound for heaven ("coming down out of the heaven from God," v. 10) but experienced and enjoyed already on earth, the city of John's vision stands out in bold contrast to the author's previous description of the harlot and city of Rome (chapter 17). The seer wrote at a time when the earthly city of Jerusalem and its temple had already been razed to the ground by Titus and his troops. However his vision is *not* one of *rebuilt* and *refurbished* stone edifices. On the contrary, the description of the holy city is one constructed, not by architects with stones and mortar, but by God himself with his *people*. The destroyed city and temple have been forever replaced by the assembly of the people of God, dwelling in his presence.

Drawing upon imagery from the Old Testament (Ezekiel 40-48, Isaiah 60), the seer illustrated the continuity between the chosen people of the former covenant and the church of the new and eternal covenant. Twelve gates, which opened the city in all directions, underscored the universal welcome the holy city extended to all the peoples of the earth. The number 12, besides representing Israel's 12 tribes and the 12 apostles, had cosmic significance as well. As the number of the months in the year and of the signs of the zodiac, "12" represented a harmony and synchronization with the heavenly bodies for which the ancient peoples strived. John, however, has made it quite clear that the harmonious order of the holy city and of its inhabitants would be ascribed not to astral movements or positions but to God himself.

The wall of the city with its 12 courses of stones (v. 14) was reminiscent, to John's readers, of the 12 precious stones worn by the high priest on his breastplate (Exodus 28:17ff.) In the holy city of God, these stones were enscribed with the names of the 12 apostles of the Lamb, i.e., of Jesus and the church. Clearly linking the 12 tribes with the church, the 12 foundation stones, so engraved, also signified that the holy city would be built upon the apostolic preaching and teaching.

Unlike its earthly predecessor, the new Jerusalem would have no temple, i.e., no earthly construction that might tend to limit accessibility to God. With no temple, there would be no specified priesthood, no prescribed cult or sacrificial system, no separation between sacred and profane. Because of God's abiding presence in and among his people, all activities would be permeated by holiness. The tension between church and state, between the light and dark sides of human nature, would evaporate because those who persevered through the trial and persecution and remained faithful would be illumined with the very glory of God himself. With the light of God's revelation in perpetual evidence, the holy city would have no need of created luminaries, of sun or moon.

John 14:23-28. Peace and the paraclete were the gifts Jesus wished to bequeath to his own. In the last discourse of the fourth gospel (John 13-17), the precise meaning of these gifts was explained by the earthly Jesus, but his followers would experience them only after his death. As he wrote for his contemporaries at the turn of the first Christian century, the Johannine evangelist invited them to look beyond the imminent suffering and death of Jesus, as featured in the discourse, to the glorification of the risen Lord. Moreover, he helped his community and all subsequent believers to realize that the Christian life they were experiencing was possible (and that the trials they were enduring were survivable) because of the gifts of the Lord, peace and the paraclete.

Peace-*shalom* was the traditional formula of greeting and farewell. By wishing peace to one another, faithful Jews extended to their brothers and sisters the harmony that was to characterize them as a covenanted people (Numbers 6:26). When used as the cognate verb of the noun, *shalom* "signified such things as to finish, to complete, to pay, i.e., to complete a transaction by paying a debt; thus the word may be said to signify, in general, completeness, perfection, perhaps *most precisely a condition in which nothing* is lacking" (J.L. McKenzie). A divine gift, the peace of God, once spoken, was conceived of as bringing abundance and prosperity to humankind (Psalm 85:9; Leviticus 26:3-13).

Through the work of the prophets, "peace" came to mean an eschatological and messianic era; peace with its healing governance was to be the hallmark of the awaited king and his kingdom (Zechariah 8:9-13, 9:9-10; Isaiah 2:2-4, 9:5-6, 11:1-9, 40:17-18; Ezekiel 37:24ff). That Jesus could impart this peace to his own, once his hour had come, signified that through that hour with its passion and glory, the era of salvation had finally come. Because of Jesus, the hoped for and promised peace, so idealized in the Old Testament, was to become a *reality* for all peoples. For that reason, and for the communion with God which he achieved, the author of Ephesians was correct in calling Christ "our peace" (Ephesians 2:14).

The paraclete, like the peace of Christ, would be an abiding gift for the church. Peculiar to the Johannine literature, *parakletos* was the title given by Jesus to the one who would be sent to his disciples by the Father. In today's pericope, the paraclete and Holy Spirit have been equated by means of apposition in the sentence, "the paraclete" (v. 26). As R.E. Brown has observed, "the peculiarity of the Johannine portrait of the Paraclete/Spirit centers around the resemblance of the Spirit to Jesus. Virtually everything that has been said about the Paraclete has been said elsewhere in the gospel about Jesus." Indeed, the Johannine literature even referred to "another paraclete," implying that Jesus was the first paraclete (John 14:16).

Just as Jesus was *sent* by the Father (3:17), so would the Father *send* the paraclete (14:26). In the same way that Jesus was said to be within his disciples and *remain with* them (14:20, 23, 15:4-5, 17:23, 26), so would the paraclete be *within* and *remain with* Jesus' disciples (14: 17). Whereas the earthly Jesus *guided* his own in his *truth* (14:16), so would the paraclete be their *guide* (16:13). In the same way that Jesus *taught* those who opened themselves to him (6:59, 7:14, 18, 8:20), the paraclete would also *teach* (14:26).

As R. Fuller has pointed out, following the glorification of Christ, it would be the function of the paraclete/Spirit to complete the revelation of Christ. This, of course, does not imply that the Spirit would convey ever new revelations but would, rather, unfold in an ever new *understanding* and ever new *interpretations* and *application* the once-for-all revelation of Jesus Christ, i.e., "remind you of all that I told you" (14:26). In fact, the very gospel of John, with its higher christology and more clarified identification of Jesus and his message, is a proof that the promise was being fulfilled and that the paraclete was at work among his followers. In the words of Hoskyns, "the Spirit's work is more than a reminiscence of the *ipsissima verba* of the Son of God; it is a living representation of all that he had spoken to his disciples, a creative exploitation of the gospel."

With regard to the "world" (remember the dual sense of *world* in Johannine writing), the paraclete and Jesus would receive similar responses of non-acceptance and hatred. In the same way, the faithful disciples of Jesus would be rejected and hated. But through it all, their helper, defender, advocate, witness and comforter would be the paraclete. R.E. Brown believes that the Johannine emphasis on the paraclete as the post-resurrectional presence of Jesus with his own answered two problems prominent at the time of the fourth gospel's final composition. First, there was the confusion caused by the death of the apostolic eyewitnesses and the difficulty of survival without any direct link to Jesus. Second, there was the anxiety caused by delayed eschatology, the second advent of Jesus. For both problems, the Johannine author posited the presence of the paraclete, who in a very real sense had *realized* eschatology by being the presence of Jesus among believers: peace and the paraclete, the gifts whereby they would continue to know him and live the challenge of his life.

1. Disagreements, settled in truth and justice, are an opportunity for growth and greater mutual respect (Acts).

2. Without the believing community, even the most beautiful cathedral is just another building (Revelation).

3. Peace is not the absence of war; it is the fruit of salvation (John).

Seventh Sunday of Easter

For the early believers, the witness of Stephen's faith spoke loudly and clearly of the cost of discipleship (Acts). Confident and victorious even in death, martyrs assure the persecuted and the persevering of every age that the Lord by whom they are mandated and with whom they are united in love (John) will return. For that reason our waiting must be spent in joyful anticipation and characterized by faithful service (Revelation).

Acts 7:55-60. For someone who had been appointed to the rather routine work of overseeing the daily dole for Hellenist widows and their children, Stephen had certainly gotten himself into a great deal of trouble. Obviously, one must carefully read the Acts' narratives and realize that the seven Hellenists presented by the community and approved by the apostles had performed a far greater mission for the church than the managing of a relief effort. Clearly, the seven *inaugurated* the Hellenist campaign, worked great wonders, healed the sick, preached the good news of salvation in Samaria, on the desert road to Gaza, etc. (Acts 8, Philip's work). For their efforts, the seven incurred the wrath of the Jewish authorities. Stephen, in particular, stood accused of blasphemy. Today's first reading, the account of Stephen's death, is preceded in Acts by a lengthy discourse, purported to be the martyr's defense against his accusers. Actually the "testimony" (7:1-53) was a recapitulation of Jewish history up to the time of David. In the lengthy account, no doubt a thoroughly Lucan elaboration of the Hellenist's basic ideas, Stephen (and Luke) denounced the Jews for their persecution and rejection of Moses and the prophets. Time after time they had rejected the leaders God had sent to make his way known to them. Concluding with an attack on his Jewish contemporaries for their rejection of Jesus, Stephen's didactic speech "served to advance Luke's own story of the spread of the word from Jerusalem to the end of the earth" (R. Dillon, J. Fitzmeyer.).

Without a doubt, Luke has constructed the narrative of Stephen's trial and death to parallel the trial and passion of Jesus. For example, in both cases, false witnesses gave testimony concerning the accused's proclamation of the destruction of the temple (Acts 6:13, Mark 14:56-61). Both Stephen and Jesus were brought to the Sanhedrin for trial (Acts 6:12, Mark 14:53); both referred to the coming Son of Man as an eschatological figure (Acts 7:55-56, Mark 14:62). By their statements, both Stephen and Jesus provoked the hostility of their accusers (Acts 7:57, Mark 14:63-64) and were put to death *outside* the city (Acts 7:58, Hebrews 13: 12). In addition to these parallels, the manner of death and the statements made by Stephen and Jesus were remarkably similar. Both innocent men forgave their executioners (Acts 7:60, Luke 23:46).

As T. Maertens and J. Fisque have observed, the assimilation of the martyr Stephen to Jesus becomes meaningful against the background of problems raised by the persecution of the early believers. Initially, the view taken by the early Christians was that the Jewish authorities, in their persecution of Jesus and his followers, were following the pattern of punishments they were guilty of inflicting on all envoys of the Lord (Matthew 23:29-36). But with the martyrdom and witness of Stephen, the persecution began to take on an eschatological significance so that it was regarded as an activity associated with the coming of the Son of Man. Acting as judge, separating the good from the evil, the persecution was viewed as the judgment already being experienced. Not that the *faithful* were being judged *guilty* but *their* persecutors were bringing judgment upon themselves by their own evil deeds. In the story of Stephen there is a further implication as well: that Christians had begun to realize in their own sufferings that conformity to Jesus Christ and the witnessing to his way would be a conformity to his passion and cross.

Although death by stoning was the prescribed punishment (Leviticus 24:14, Deuteronomy 17:7) for blasphemy, the legality of Stephen's execution was questionable. Besides the fact that Luke stressed the *falseness* of the testimony against him, there was no formal decision or sentencing made by the Sanhedrin; the action taken seems to have been that of a lynch mob. The vision of the Son of Man *standing* at the Father's right hand served to vindicate Stephen. Standing (rather than the usual position of sitting) at God's right hand, Jesus as advocate offered the sure defense of the truth and assured Stephen of his share in resurrected glory.

Revelation 22:12-14, 16-17, 20. "Yes, I am coming *soon*," promised the seer's vision of the glorified Jesus (v. 20). But "soon" is an ambiguous word. For a man hanging by his fingertips from a precipice, "soon" can stretch into a seemingly endless period as he shouts for help. The early Christians experienced a similar urgency as they awaited the return of the Lord and the joy of his parousia. Suffering and persecution had taken its toll; some were even becoming apathetic; "*soon*" had to be reinterpreted. Just as the climber dangling from the side of the cliff would have to deal with the time it would take for help to arrive, so did the early believers in Jesus learn to translate "soon" into productive preparation, prayerful alertness and a substantive hope. Helpful to them in their efforts were the visions of apocalyptic literature that assured the persecuted of relief and the downtrodden of victory. Ministering to his contemporaries at the end of the first century, the seer of Revelation kept before his readers the reality of the resurrected and victorious Jesus.

Today's second reading is from the epilogue of his work where the author reiterated his book's essential message. Jesus would return soon and that return would result in light and life for the upright. Throughout the pericope, it is difficult to decipher precisely *who* is speaking or at what point one speaker stops and another begins. The seer John, the Lord's angel and Jesus himself have been featured as holding out the sure promises of salvation. Nevertheless, it is clear that Jesus Christ is the one acclaimed as Lord of all, from beginning to end. Salvation has been described in terms of washing one's robes (v. 14). Elsewhere, John had identified such an activity with participation in the death (blood of the Lamb, 7:14) of Jesus that resulted in pardon for sin and purity of heart. Once reconciled through Jesus' blood, the faithful were said to have access to the tree of life, whose gates would bring one safe passage to the eternal city. The paradise once lost through sin (Genesis 3) had been gained once more though the saving action of Jesus.

"Root" and "offspring of David" were titles recalling the messianic prophecies (Isaiah 11:1, 2 Samuel 7:14) fulfilled in the person and works of Jesus (Matthew 1:1; Romans 1:3; 2 Timothy 2:8). The "morning star" was regarded in the ancient world as a symbol of power and domination. Recall the Matthean astrologers and Herod's fear at the mysterious portent (Matthew 2) associated with Jesus' birth. Probably the author of Revelation was also alluding to the text in Numbers (24:17) that in late Judaism had taken on a messianic connotation. Applied to the exalted Christ, "morning star" signalled his messianic importance as well as his universal and everlasting dominion. That the morning star had already appeared and that Jesus' messiahship and eschatological dominion are already experienced is beautifully enunciated in the ancient Easter proclamation, the *Exultet:* "May the morning star find its flame alight (Christ's candle: sign of Christian life)... that morning star which never sets... which sheds its clear light on the human race."

John 17:20-26. Each of the three readings for this Sunday's liturgy contains a futuristic element. In the first pericope from Acts, Stephen's vision of the exalted Son of Man assured the martyr of his own vindication and imminent share in that glory. In the epilogue of his book of visions (Revelation), John described the future of eternal joy for those who had emerged from life's trials still faithful to Jesus. In the selection from the fourth gospel, the Johannine author has portrayed Jesus in prayer for his *future* followers, for those who would come to faith through the work of his disciples. The third section of a longer prayer (John 17: 1-26) that has since the 16th century C.E. been called the "high-priestly prayer" (*precatio summi sacerdotis,* as per the Lutheran theologian David Chytraus, 1531-1600 C.E.), Jesus' prayer exhibits similarities to that of the Jewish priest.

On the Day of Atonement, the Jewish priest, in office for that particular year, would offer sacrifice and prayer, first for himself. Jesus' prayer for himself (vv. 1-3) is a clear parallel to the high priest's prayer but, obviously, Jesus had no need to offer sacrifice for personal sin as did his clerical counterpart. In the second section of the prayer, the priest prayed for the priests and levites; Jesus' prayer for his disciples (vv. 6-19) is a corollary to that prayer. "But," as R.E. Brown has pointed out, "if Jesus is a high priest here, it is not primarily in the sense of one about to offer sacrifice, but more along the line of the high priest described in Hebrews and in Romans (8:34), one who stands before the throne of God, making intercession for us." This vision of Jesus as the victorious Son of Man gave hope and courage to the martyr Stephen, one of those future disciples for whom the Johannine Jesus had prayed (John 17:20-26).

Set within the context of the lengthy discourse at the last supper, the prayer and the discourse in general are purported to be Jesus' last will and testament for his followers. Having come to the climax of his earthly mission, Jesus expressed to his friends with a poignant intensity his hopes and aspirations for them. Within both biblical and extra-biblical literatures we find other such farewell discourses, whose message has been made more significant by the fact of their literary genre. For example, all of the book of Deuteronomy has been assigned the historical setting of Moses' farewell address to his people, before his death and prior to Israel's infiltration of Canaan. That historical setting and orientation, although contrived (most of Deuteronomy was written in the seventh century, B.C.E.), lent importance and significance to the entire book. Indeed, Josiah made excellent use of the work as an impetus to his sweeping program of religious reform. So too, the Johannine author's use of the farewell testament literary genre has contributed to the significance of the teaching contained therein.

Throughout the fourth gospel, numerous references were made to the "hour" of Jesus, a term the evangelist employed to refer to the saving event of Jesus' passion, death, resurrection and exaltation. Most of the references stated that the "hour" had not yet come; but within the context of the farewell discourse, and with Jesus' death so imminent, his statement was a proclamation, "The hour has come!" (17:1). Once arrived, the hour represented the climax and culmination of Jesus' mission. For that reason, Jesus' consecratory prayer of himself, his disciples and future believers, provides the reader with an understanding of Jesus' hour and of his motivation in fulfilling it.

Aptly chosen for this Sunday between the Ascension and Pentecost, the gospel presents a Jesus who transcends time and space. "It is true, of course, that in the prayer of John 17, Jesus still speaks in the context of the Last Supper; but from the tone of what he says and from the tenses of the verbs, one feels that Jesus has crossed the threshhold from time to eternity and is already on the way to the Father, or at least halfway between this world and the Father's presence" (R.E. Brown).

Concerned for future believers (vv. 20-26) the Johannine Jesus prayed first for their unity and secondly for the effect their union would have upon the world. R. Fuller citing Hoskyns has pointed out that the unity for which Jesus prayed is not grounded on ecclesiastical joinery. It must not be supposed that the unity of the church is to be attained by a long history of human endeavor. Rather, the union among believers for which Jesus prayed was a share in the very life and love Jesus and the Father shared. That same union is expressed in the common sharing of the word and sacraments in which the acts of God in Christ are made ever present.

According to Jesus' prayer, the union of believers with God and with one another makes them capable of and ready for their mission to the world (vv. 21, 22). In a world that glorifies independence and autonomy, Christ's mission and his prayer for his followers would effect a life of mutual interdependence for all peoples. Christ prayed for a union based on gratuitous love, a union that could forgive the worst in others while always expecting the best of them. The realization of his prayer remains the constant challenge of his church.

1. The same visionaries who are scoffed at by myopic disbelievers give hope and courage to the faithful (Acts).

2. Authentic Christian living should engender a certain amount of eager excitement because of the believer's anticipation of the returning Lord (Revelation).

3. Union with the Lord makes the diverse and uniquely individual members of Jesus' company a powerful and loving force (John).

Pentecost Sunday

Peoples of all ages from all areas of the world and from every walk of life have been gathered together in a prayerful and powerful assembly by the Spirit of God (Acts). Where once there was an overwhelming and staggering variety of unanswered needs, now those needs can be met by the multiple gifts of the Spirit working through the unique talents of each community member (I Corinthians). Where once there was alienation and resentment, now there is the possibility of forgiveness and peace because of the ever present and ever compelling Spirit of Jesus Christ (John).

Acts 2:1-11. Pentecost (literally 50 days) is the Greek term used in the New Testament to refer to the Feast of Weeks. Originally an agrarian feast to commemorate the end of the grain harvest, Pentecost was a one-day celebration during which special sacrifices were offered (Exodus 23:16; Leviticus 23: 15-21; Deuteronomy 16:9-21). On that day, grateful farmers brought to the Lord the first fruits of their crop as a profession of their faith in the one who had provided it. Fixed at an early date on the 50th day after Passover (Deuteronomy 16:9-12), the feast was historicized, i.e., associated with the events of Israel's salvation and as such was related to the covenants made by God with Noah and then with Moses.

In second century Judaism, the feast became a commemoration of the gift of the law at Sinai. According to rabbinical tradition, Moses and the refugees from Egypt had travelled for a period of seven weeks from Egypt to Sinai. During that period, the people were morally formed by Moses and the gift of the law was regarded as God's approbation of their efforts. Similarly, Reformed Judaism today dedicates the seven week period from Passover to Pentecost to the intense religious education and spiritual formation of young people who, on the feast of Shevuoth or Pentecost, affirm as a group their willingness to live according to the principles of the law. In the Essene community of ancient Qumran, new members were admitted on the feast as they pledged to keep the Sinai law and covenant. Perhaps Luke in composing the Acts narrative of the Christian feast of the Spirit had all of these ideas in mind, viz., a harvest of thanks and faith, moral formation, the law, affirmation, new membership and the covenant.

Indeed all of these elements are included in the celebration of the Spirit-filled church. For Jewish-Christians the ancient feast of the law would become the feast of the Spirit. The feast of the gathering of grain would become the feast of the eschatological gathering of all peoples to Christ by his newly commissioned and Spirit-filled followers. The ancient feast of the covenant with its moral formation and community affirmation would become the season for all believers to become formed anew and vitalized with the very life of God in Christ. With great literary skill, the author of Luke-Acts intentionally constructed his two volume work to draw many comparisons between the life and mission of Jesus and the life and mission of those who became his church. Today's text from Acts corresponds to the birth of Jesus in the gospel. Just as Jesus' birth was an event marked by joy to be shared by all peoples and a manifestation of God's glory, so too was the spiriting of the believers in the risen Lord (Luke 2:9-11). Just as Jesus was filled by the Spirit and empowered for his ministry of healing and service, so too would be his disciples (Luke 4:18-19).

As the chief source of the *continuity* between Jesus and his church, Luke posited the presence of the Holy Spirit. When the interim between Jesus' first and second advents grew longer and as the authoritative eyewitnesses to Jesus were dying off, the Holy Spirit assured the church of the authentic and abiding presence of the risen Lord. Inextricably bound to the resurrected and glorified Lord, the gift of the Spirit should not be perceived as a unique incident, relegated to a particular time or place or group of people. Rather, the phenomenon of the Spirit was unleashed in the moment of Jesus' saving hour, in a neverending continuous gift. Therefore, the scriptural authors have described the event of the Spirit in terms of wind, breath and fire, properties that are unquantifiable. Wind and fire were standard Old Testament props, signalling a theophany. Using these symbols and drawing on the messianic prophecies (Joel 2:28-32; Isaiah 32:15), Luke's narrative of the Christian Pentecost indicated that the era of the Spirit-filled church was to be understood as the beginning of the eschatological era.

One of the initial and observable proofs of the powerful presence of the Spirit was the transformation that had occurred among the followers of Jesus. When Jesus was arrested, they had fled and remained alienated from him through the dark hours of his trial and passion. But within a few weeks, the same persons were boldly preaching about the crucified and risen Jesus to the very people whom they had feared earlier. What had caused such a radical change in these men and women? Was it, as some of the observers supposed, too liberal a dose of new wine? M. Dibelius said that even the most skeptical scholar of history would have to postulate an "x-factor" to account for the complete change of behavior of the disciples.

In his account, Luke has made it clear that the "x-factor" was the resurrected and glorified Jesus.

1 Corinthians 12:3-7, 12-13. In this, our age of synods and censures, a valuable lesson can be learned from Paul's attitude toward, and counsel to, those who claimed a monopoly on the Spirit by virtue of the gifts they had received and the ministries they exercised. The community of Corinth can be thought of as a microcosmic example of the world-wide Christian community of the 20th century. With the outpouring of the Spirit through the saving activity of Jesus, the faithful were blessed with a plenitude of gifts, varied and diverse in manifestation. Some were teachers, others counsellors; some were able to coalesce the gifts of various individuals for a common goal; others possessed an extraordinary ability to excite and motivate others. Still others were doers and achievers.

As is so often the case in human interaction, petty jealousies arose. Some in the community distrusted the gifts and ideas they did not understand. They resented those who possessed them, regarding them as too "far left" or "far right" of the norm to be authentic and/or valuable to the community. As he wrote to guide his converts in Corinth and to preserve the integrity of the gospel he had preached there, Paul did not favor one gift over another. He did not condemn the unusual or condone the commonplace. Rather, he turned the eyes of all the gifted toward the giver who was, he taught, to be the source of their unity and the reason for their existence.

In order to describe the union afforded to believers *in* and *by* Christ's Spirit, Paul drew upon a metaphor popular among Stoic philosophers, that of the body and its many complementary parts. Since Corinth was a center for Stoic thinkers, the analogy was probably a familiar one for Paul's readers. As with all the members of a living body, the unity of the Lord with the faithful and of the faithful with one another is a living entity, held together and vitalized by the Spirit. Not only does the Spirit make each member capable of authentic faith (v. 3: "no one can say 'Jesus is Lord' except in the Holy Spirit") but the Spirit is also the impetus of the graces that build up and enhance the quality of communal life. Therefore the diverse and even unique manifestations of the Spirit should be not distrusted and criticized but respected and channeled toward the common benefit of all.

As norms for discerning true manifestations of the Spirit from inauthentic ones, Paul offered the following. (1) Does the gifted one profess faith in the earthly crucified Jesus, as well as in the risen, exalted Lord? This directive would have directly applied to those gnostic Christians in Corinth and elsewhere who chose to overlook the suffering savior in favor of a divine man christology. (2) Does the gifted one enhance and edify the community by his/her gifts? This directive would have applied to those whose gifts were exercised solely for effect or *personal* fulfillment. (3) Does the Spirit manifested help to make of the distinct and many members of the community one body of Christ?

It is significant that Paul never made ordinariness or safeness or acceptability a norm in discerning spirits. Indeed, he knew the value of those whose "different" gifts could shock and awaken others to new and keener spiritual insights. As one so gifted himself, he was often the goad whose visions pushed others to a deeper and more meaningful experience of Jesus and the gospel. Paul's fearlessness and faith, his willingness to be contrary for the sake of Christ's truth cannot be forgotten by the 20th century members of the body of Christ.

John 20:19-23. In the beginning, God breathed over the waters and brought forth life and light in an ordered universe. God breathed love and peace and his own likeness into the dust of the earth and there was man and also woman. If the Johannine account of the gift of the Spirit by the risen Lord reminds the reader of the Genesis account of creation, then the evangelist has achieved his purpose. As the exalted Jesus breathed upon his disciples, they received life and peace and a bond of union with him that would sustain them until his second advent. While he was still among them and before his passion, Jesus had promised the Spirit, the paraclete, to his followers (John 14:16-17, 26). With his Spirit empowering them, they would be assured of peace and joy (John 14:27, 16:20, 22). Motivated and defended by his Spirit, they would be able to do great works, even greater than Jesus had done (John 14:12). Jesus' appearance among his own on the evening of his resurrection signaled the fulfillment of his promises to them. Moreover, along with the greeting of "peace" that Jesus extended twice to his followers, the gift of the Spirit ushered in the eschatological age. As foretold by the prophets (Joel 3:1; Ezekiel 36:27; Isaiah 11), peace and the outpouring of the Spirit upon all of humanity were to accompany the period of salvation.

Differing from the Lucan presentation of the Pentecost event, the Johannine version portrayed Jesus as giving the Spirit on the same day as his resurrection. Indeed the fourth evangelist would have us understand *all* the moments of Jesus' hour (his passion, death, resurrection, ascension and exaltation) as one event. Probably John is more theologically accurate in doing so; nevertheless, the church has, for pedagogical and liturgical reasons, followed the Lucan schematization wherein Easter and Pentecost have been presented as separated by 50 days. Intent upon showing the continuity between the earthly Jesus and the Jesus of faith, John has stressed that the risen Lord appeared with the signs of his passion in evidence. Probably aimed at a gnostic element within the Johannine community of the 90s who regarded the earthly Jesus and his passion as irrelevant, the Johannine presentation made it quite clear that the cross had been the road to glory and was not to be overlooked.

As in all the resurrection appearances, there was an obvious concern on the part of the evangelists for the believers left behind by the risen Lord. In the case of today's gospel, that concern was channelled into a mission of forgiveness and mercy. The sending forth of the disciples in the Spirit to forgive sins has been cited as a source text for the Roman church's understanding of the sacrament of reconciliation. Some have understood the forgiving (loosing) or withholding of forgiveness (binding) of sin as a reference to the power of the community to withhold baptism depending upon the candidate's acceptance or rejection of the kerygmatic message. Others, drawing on rabbinical tradition concerning binding (*asar*) and loosing (*sera*), understand v. 23 in the context of church discipline, i.e., the authority to grant or to refuse membership in the community for reasons of sinfulness. These interpretations have validity but should be understood as later theological developments and/or anachronisms.

Perhaps the primary meaning of today's gospel pericope is that the peace and forgiveness that had characterized the efforts of the earthly Jesus were being granted Jesus' disciples. By the gift of his own Spirit they would be able to continue the work Jesus had began. Because of his hour in which he had shown himself one with humanity and one with the Father and from which he had emerged victorious over sin and death, Jesus was able to share with all believers his triumph. The multi-faceted event of Easter-Ascension-Pentecost vindicated the moment of the cross and proved it to be a sign, not of failure but forgiveness.

1. Fear and confusion become manageable where there is faith in God's bold Spirit (Acts).

2. Different gifts and unusual talents are a cause for wonder and thanksgiving, not resentment and distrust (1 Corinthians).

3. Mutual forgiveness, freely given, bestows the gift of peace on the forgiven and the forgiver (John).

Ordinary Time
Second Sunday in Ordinary Time

Water was transformed into choice wine as a sign that the old order and old traditions gave way to the new. In the teachings of Jesus all believers could thenceforth slake their deep thirst for salvation (John). Through the wisdom of the cross all the redeemed are welcomed home again to their Lord and creator (Isaiah), and by the Spirit of his love the entire community has received every good gift (1 Corinthians).

Isaiah 62:1-5. Political campaign songs, written to stir up constituents and sung in an effort to inspire their trust and support for a prospective candidate and his promises for a bright future, have at times *outlived* the popularity of the politician for whom they were composed. So too, the songs sung by the prophet for his beloved city Jerusalem have outlived both the prophet and the people to whom he prophesied and have lent themselves to believers of all ages. Today's first reading is from a longer section of songs/poems composed for the political, religious and psychological edification of the people of Israel. Hoping to remind Jerusaiem of its former glory and to reassure his contemporaries that that glory would be restored, the prophet known as Trito or Third Isaiah labored among his people in the turbulent period after the Babylonian oppression (ca. 538 B.C.E.—445 B.C.E.).

Although the 66 chapters of the book called Isaiah had traditionally been attributed to one person, no serious student of the Bible today would deny the fact that several hands were at work in the lengthy prophetic composition. Begun in the eighth century B.C.E. by Isaiah of Jerusalem, the prophecies, oracles, etc., spanned a period of almost three centuries. Most scholars would separate the book into three sections: (1) chapters 1-39: Isaiah, 8th century B.C.E.; (2) chapters 40-55: Deutero-Isaiah, 6th century B.C.E. during exile; (3) chapters 56-66: Trito-Isaiah, 6th-5th century B.C.E. after the exile. In the wise words of J. L. McKenzie, Trito-Isaiah becomes intelligible as a work, precisely in the way the name indicates: "as a final collection of prophetic utterances in the spirit and thought which began with Isaiah of Jerusalem and was maintained by his editors and successors, of whom Second Isaiah was the greatest. We haven't yet fully penetrated into the mind of these prophetic scribes, or we would understand how they could collect all the sayings under one name of Isaiah, with the honest conviction that Isaiah of Jerusalem spoke through his school and his successors."

Distinct from Deutero-Isaiah (in that he placed new emphasis on the law, the temple rebuilt in 515 B.C.E. and on the cult centered there) nevertheless Trito-Isaiah shared the same ideas of universal salvation as his predecessors. In today's prophetic song, that salvation as experienced by the restored Israel has been portrayed in three beautiful images:

(1) Saved by their Lord through his anointed Cyrus (45:1), the restored Israel would be a *glorious crown* and a *royal diadem* held by their God (v. 3). Perhaps the prophetic author was making a reference to the ancient Near Eastern practice of depicting the god of a city wearing a crown patterned after the city walls. (2) Renewed in their relationship to Yahweh, reestablished in the land he had given, Israel would receive a *new name*, symbolic of the new life they had received. Those who had been scorned by the nations and mocked as "Forsaken" and "Desolate" would thenceforth be called *Hephziba* ('My Delight') and *Beulah* ("Espoused"). Both names are feminine proper names in Hebrew (2 Kings 21:1) but both are also quite appropriate as messianic titles signifying the new era of salvation for God's people.

(3) Drawing on the *nuptial imagery* popularized by Hosea, the prophet described his people's reconciliation with Yahweh in terms of the wedding of a bride (Jerusalem) and her bridegroom (Yahweh). The divine architect (builder, v. 5) of Israel's salvation would espouse himself to her once again. In that way, because of him, the protective walls of the city and all her towers would be reconstructed.

1 Corinthians 12:4-11. Undaunted by the scorn and disinterest with which the Athenians had met his eloquent preaching of the gospel, Paul traveled on to Corinth and, after 18 months there, left behind a well-established, vital Christian community. Capital of the Roman province of Achaia, Corinth was situated on the narrow isthmus between the Aegean and Ionian seas. Through Corinth passed merchants and sailors, philosophers and politicians. In addition to its cosmopolitan population, Corinth was home to a large Jewish community whose numbers had swelled due to Claudius' expulsion of the Jews from Rome. Second in importance only to Rome, Corinth was in Paul's day a strategic site for the sowing of the good news. From Corinth, the message of salvation could travel west to Rome and east to Ephesus, Troas and Antioch. Later, when Paul wrote from Ephesus to the Corinthian Christians, he addressed himself to a number of issues that had become problematic for the community, one of which was the matter of charisms or graces given by the Holy Spirit.

Some in Corinth took an inordinate pride in the gifts they had received, believing themselves to be greater or holier than others because of them. This self-presumed elite often preferred to manifest those gifts which were the *most outwardly spectacular*, e.g., the gift of tongues. Because of this, communal gatherings for prayer and fellowship turned into occasions of boastful self-aggrandisement. Upon hearing of the difficulties that threatened the liturgical integrity of the community, Paul reminded the Corinthians of the basic premise that underlies today's pericope: There are many gifts but only *one* giver; there are many gifts but only *one* goal, i.e., the common good of the whole believing community.

In naming some of the gifts of the one Spirit, Paul stressed the diversity of ways in which those gifts could be exercised for the edification of others. Wisdom in discourse is the ability to expound upon the deepest spiritual truths. Knowledge and the power to express it would make its recipient responsible for teaching how to translate those truths into the routine living of each day. By faith Paul was referring to that effective faith which could say to a mountain, "Throw yourself into the sea," and would not entertain a shadow of a doubt that it would happen! Healing and miraculous powers covered the gamut of physical, psychological and spiritual ills (exorcisms) that may have beset the members of the community. Prophecy, as in the Old Testament, was the ability to interpret God's will for one's contemporaries. Discernment of spirits enabled the believer to help others to sort out true from false prophecy and genuine prophets from frauds. Tongues were a phenomenon manifested in ecstatic but unintelligible prayer. Lest this gift be abused by false or hysterical mystics, Paul accented the importance of the gift of discerning the unintelligible for the sake of the community.

John 2:1-12. To discover the true importance of the event at Cana, we must go beyond the festivity of the wedding, look further than the choice wine and listen to more than Jesus' conversation with his mother. All of these facts do figure into the episode as secondary themes but the key to the entire text is found in v. 11, where the evangelist's comment explains: "Jesus performed this first of his signs at Cana in Galilee. Thus did he reveal his glory and his disciples believed in him." In the fourth gospel, seven signs each successively reveal more and more who Jesus was and what he was to accomplish for the world. Each of the signs, beginning with the feast at Cana and ending with Lazarus at Bethany, was intended to challenge those who witnessed them to look beyond the wonders that may have accompanied the sign, to come to faith in Jesus and thereby to glorify the Father with him.

At Cana, Jesus was being revealed as messiah and as host of the eschatological banquet of salvation. But most importantly Jesus was revealed as the one who by his teaching and his redemptive ministry was bringing to all peoples a new way of coming to God. No longer would holiness and wholeness be achieved through the religious customs of purifications and ritual ablutions of Jewish tradition. The very presence of the incarnate Lord served to render meaningless and forever obsolete all previous religious customs, feasts and institutions. In chapters 2-10 of his gospel, by a technique termed "replacement theology," the Johannine author has effectively illustrated through discourses and through actions that Jesus did indeed replace the law, the temple, its feasts and the institutions with himself.

Each of the six stone jars was filled with water for the prescribed purpose of ritual washing. Jewish law required such ablutions before and after the meal. Filled to the brim (as per Jesus' order) the jars had a capacity of about 120 gallons. That much wine at a feast was truly an embarrassment of riches, but that was precisely the evangelist's point. The wine of Jesus' teaching, the choice wine of Jesus' wisdom, was far greater than any teaching or wisdom that had gone before it.

In the synoptics, the superiority of Jesus' teaching over that of the official teachers of Judaism was illustrated in the image of the bursting old wineskin (Mark 2:19). Brown has observed that, in this light, Mary's comment, "They have no wine," becomes a poignant reflection on the barrenness of the Jewish rites of purification. Indeed, compared to the new order inaugurated by Jesus, the teaching of the Pharisees and the old order was like insipid water when compared to a fine wine! In the same way, the extravagant amount of wine called to mind the prophetic promises of an abundance of wine as a sign of the messianic era (Amos 9:13-14, Psalm 104:14, Hosea 14:7, Jeremiah 31: 12). The setting of the sign at a wedding was also richly reminiscent of the wedding banquet imagery through which Israel had traditionally enunciated its faith in the God of its salvation (see first reading, Isaiah 54:4-8, 55: 1; Proverbs 9: 1-5).

Although the role of Mary in the Cana event has at times been misconstrued and ballooned out of proportion (albeit through well intentioned piety), her place in the gospel cannot be ignored. Jesus' addressing of Mary as "woman" (v. 4), though not disrespectful, was quite unusual for a son. By using the designation "woman," the evangelist drew into the scene at Cana the "woman" of Genesis 3:15 and the "woman" of Revelation 12. In both cases, the figure of the woman was a key figure in the drama of salvation. In Genesis, the woman stood in conflict with the serpent, symbol of evil. In Revelation, the woman would engage in warfare with the dragon, also a symbol of evil. In both cases, the woman in question has been thought a symbol or a figure of the church militant, the people of God in conflict with evil.

In the Johannine gospel the evangelist has attached to the person of Mary the same ecclesial significance Appearing only at Cana and then again at the cross to receive the beloved disciple as her own, Mary is a sign of the church whose mission of conflict with evil began only after Jesus' earthly ministry had ended. This point, according to R. Brown, is made clear in the conversation between Mary and Jesus. By refusing Mary's intervention ("My hour has not yet come"), Jesus explains that his signs must reflect the Father's sovereignty and not any human or family agency. But Mary, as mother of and symbol of the church, receives her role when Jesus' hour *does* come . . . at the cross. Mother of the messiah and symbol of the church, Mary has a role in the gospel even more significant than the one pious sentiment formerly assigned her.

The narrative of the wedding celebration at Cana involves much more than Jesus' kindness at a party where the refreshments ran out. Highly theological and christological, this first of Jesus' signs spoke a revolutionary message about a new order, a new teaching and a new way of salvation. The mission of the church, founded in faith upon the one who inaugurated this new era is to continue the revolution.

1. A fresh start, a new hope, a closer relationship—all are a part of the mystery of God's merciful forgiveness (Isaiah).

2. When the common good is the common goal, the gifts of God's Spirit can be enjoyed to the fullest (1 Corinthians).

3. It was easier to change water into wine than to change the hearts and mind's of the self-righteous (John).

Third Sunday in Ordinary Time

Jesus' ministry of liberation requires that the gospel be not only preached but realized in the lives of the poor, the imprisoned, the sinful and the sick (Luke). To that end, his Holy Spirit charges those who believe in him with the task of making free—spiritually, politically and economically —every member of the worldwide community that is his body (1 Corinthians). To say Amen! Amen! to the challenge of liberation is not enough (Nehemiah). To be, to do, to live, to give, to love and to die—only then will the work of the Lord begin to be fulfilled in us.

Nehemiah 8:2-4, 5-6, 8-10. Unlike the scene at another Watergate, where an unworthy act of political ambition *eroded* the trust of a people in their government, ancient Jerusalem's Water Gate was the site of a more laudable attempt to *reconstruct* the moral and religious fiber of a foundering nation. Though the exact date of his coming to Jerusalem are still the subject of scholarly dispute, most agree that Ezra the scribe ministered to the returned exiles from Babylon in the fifth century B.C.E. Having lived in Babylon during the period of its Persian domination, Ezra was sent by the reigning Persian monarch to Jerusalem with the authority to reconstruct the religious traditions of his people.

Attributed to the Chronicler, the books of Ezra and Nehemiah have documented that reconstructive effort. Though preserved in a rather jumbled fashion and in different languages (Hebrew, Aramaic), the two works (originally one book) described the return to Jerusalem, the struggle to rebuild the temple (Ezra 9-10), Nehemiah's commission to rebuild the city walls (Nehemiah 2-6), the census and the proclamation of the law (Nehemiah 8-9), the plan to repopulate Jerusalem (Nehemiah 11) and the institution of religious reforms (Nehemiah 13).

Today's first reading is from the section on the renewal of the people in the law (Nehemiah 8-9). Armed with the law (which most believe to have been the Pentateuch or Mosaic Torah) and with the authority to enforce it, Ezra began his reform that resulted in a radical transformation of the traditions of ancient Israel. The law had once been regarded as the historical revelation of God's covenantal relationship with his people. Under Ezra and his influence, the law came to be understood as a compendium of detailed, divine legislation. This emphasis of law-over-and-above-relationship introduced into the faith of Israel that legal orientation that became so evident in the New Testament. Moreover, as J. Gaffney has pointed out, this legalism led to the increasing prestige and power of a group of scholars, like Ezra, whose expert knowledge of the scriptures was necessary in order to apply them as *legal documents* to the concrete circumstances of daily life. This post-exilic, reconstruction phase of Israel's religious history has been called the beginning of what is known today as Judaism. For that reason, Ezra has been called the father of Judaism.

Exactly how the Nehemiah reading serves to complement today's gospel is not completely clear. Perhaps the two texts should be understood as contrasting ideas: Ezra spoke of laws; Jesus proclaimed liberation. Or perhaps, the two pericopes were paired because each was set within a *liturgical* context. In fact, the scene at the Water Gate does offer a model of what synagogue worship was like in post-exilic Jerusalem. That same structure appears in the Lucan text.

1 Corinthians 12:12-30. In Corinth, near the city's northern wall, was located the temple of Asclepius, a god revered by the Greeks for his healing powers. Patients and vacationers would flock to the temple which resembled a modern day health spa or country club complete with baths, saunas, dining rooms with indoor grills, fountains, etc. Recent excavations of the Asclepion have unearthed a great number of terra cotta body parts: arms, legs, ears, etc., that represented the cures effected by the god. Some have proposed that these body parts were somehow formative in Paul's concept of the Christian community as Christ's body. If this is so, and if the terra cotta limbs functioned at all in Paul's thought processes, they were probably referred to as symbols of what Christians should *not* be: dead, divided, unloving, unloved and alienated (Murphy-O'Connor). With the Asclepion as a negative example, the apostle expounded his positive doctrine of the unifying love of the community as the body of Christ.

A continuation of his advice concerning the various charisms (last week) within the believing community, today's pericope represents Paul's pastoral concerns for the *unity* of the charismatic Christians. In language and symbolism borrowed from the gnostic factions in Corinth, Paul compared the union among Christians and between Christians and Christ to that of a body with its many members. As Fuller has observed, the gnostics used the idea of the body to express the solidarity between Christ and the baptized, just as pre-Christian gnostics used the body concept to explain the union between the revealer-redeemer and the redeemed. But, while the gnostic Corinthians understood that solidarity as an *identity* with Christ, i.e., sharing the same substance (a pneuma-substance), Paul maintained the *distinction* between Christ as head, *independent* of but united with the believers, his members.

Scholars still dispute whether Paul's idea of the body of Christ should be understood metaphorically or ontologically. Paul himself indicated his intent when he stated: "You, then, *are* the Body of Christ" (v. 27). Care must be taken however to avoid the gnostic mistake of *identifying* the substance of Christ and believer. For Paul, believers are ontologically united in sharing a common determination by the saving act of God in Christ. Instead of identification, Paul regarded believers as sharing a common dependence on the Christ event (R. Fuller).

To maintain the unity of the body in harmony and vitality, God has given each member a function that contributes cooperatively and mutually toward the well-being of the whole body. In explaining the ethical implications of each function, Paul stressed the uniqueness and indispensability of each function. Perhaps it would not be too presumptuous to add to Paul's thought that each member has importance because he/she *has* a God-given charism or function and not because he/she *is* that particular function. Notice, Paul did not place more value on one believer or another, based on their functions. Rather, all were valued as necessary in and because of Christ and the one Spirit.

Finally, the last verses of the pericope (vv. 27-30) offer a glance at the ministerial organization at Corinth. From Paul's description, and from other early New Testament references, it would appear that the apostles, prophets and teachers were preeminent in a charismatic (not yet institutional) community. As attested in Paul's letters and in the Acts of the Apostles, the charismatic ministries developed gradually into ordained and institutional ministries. It is important to remember, however, that in all the aspects of ministry the one Spirit of Jesus gives grace and unity and life to each and all of Christ's body.

Luke 1:1-4, 4: 14-21. A composite reading, comprised of the preface (1:1-4) to Luke's two volume work and Jesus' inaugural declaration (4:14-21), today's gospel pericope presents both Luke's catechetical purpose and Jesus' ministerial goals. Writing in the excellent literary style and form of the Greek classicists and historians with whom he was obviously familiar, the author of the third gospel included in his prologue six of the seven major components of a formal preface: (1) a reference to the author's literary *predecessors* ("many have undertaken . . .," v. 1); (2) the work's intended *subject* ("the events which have been fulfilled in our midst," v. 1); (3) the author's *credentials* or authoritative qualifications for writing ("transmitted to us by the original eyewitnesses and ministers of the word," v. 2); (4) the thrust of his plan or a *table of contents* ("whole sequence of events from the beginning. . .," v. 3); (5) statement of purpose for or intended *goal* ("that your excellency may see how reliable the instruction was that you received," v. 4); (6) the naming of an *addressee* or a dedication ("for you Theophilus," v. 3).

Only by omitting his own name did the gospel author differ from the classic Hellenistic format. Using formal literary language, and the balanced form of protasis (vv. 1-2) and apodosis (vv. 3-4), the author made it clear that he consciously wished to relate his work to the contemporary literature of the Greco-Roman world (Fitzmeyer). Moreover, by using the term *katechethes* (v. 4) instead of *evangelion*, the Lucan author underscored his intention that this work be received as a catechesis for those initiates in the faith, one of whom may have been Theophilus. By tracing the events of the period of Jesus from the beginning, Luke wished to offer assurance (*asphaleia*) or to illustrate the reliability (v. 4) of the catechesis catechumens were then receiving in the period of the church. For Luke, the events of which he wrote had already begun to be fulfilled (v. 1) in Jesus and were continuing to be fulfilled in the church. To emphasize that point, the evangelist employed the perfect participle, *peplerophoremenon*.

Because of his aphoristic name, "beloved of God," some (Origen, etc.) believed Theophilus to be not a real person but a symbolic name applicable to all believers. Today, most scholars believe Theophilus was a high ranking government official, as the title "Your Excellency" would indicate. It is possible he was the author's patron and, as a catechumen himself, helped to promote (economically) and to circulate the author's work.

Two of the distinctive marks (Spirit, universality) of the Lucan work evident all through the gospel and Acts are included in the transitional passage (4:14-15) that introduces the Galilean ministry. Empowered by the Holy Spirit at his baptismal anointing (3:22), all of Jesus' words and works were performed through the impetus of that same Spirit. He who had been led into the wilderness by the Spirit of God (4: 1), emerged victorious over temptation and empowered (4:14). By way of illustrating the effect of Jesus' anointing with the Spirit, the evangelist described Jesus as teaching in all the synagogues. In that first manifestation of his Spirit-filled ministry, Jesus received universal acclaim: "*all* were loud in his praise" (4:15).

Jesus' homecoming to Nazareth and his inaugural declaration there have been called by some the "magna charta of liberation theology." In a combination text from the prophecies of Isaiah (61:1ff and 58:7ff), the evangelist explained Jesus' mission as a proclamation of gladness for the poor, liberty for captives, sight for the blind, release for prisoners and a year of favor for all. Liberty (*aphesei*) and release (*aphesin*) in ordinary Christian usage came to mean forgiveness from sin and a release from all its manifestations, whether physical or spiritual. C. Talbert has observed that the Isaian references served to describe Jesus' ministry of salvation as one that liberated the *whole person*.

By his preaching and physical and spiritual healings through the power of the Spirit, Jesus effected the ultimate jubilee year (or year of favor, v. 18). First legislated in the Pentateuch (Leviticus 25:8-55) as a year of grace wherein debts would be erased, all slaves freed and all properties restored to their original owners, the jubilee year came to be a symbol of the messianic era. In the presence of Jesus, anointed with God's own spirit, the year of grace became a tangible reality for all who had become the indentured slaves of sin. By using verbs in their perfect tenses all through the text (vv. 18-21), the author indicated that the mission of liberation proclaimed by Jesus was still in the process of being achieved. Not only in the ministry of Jesus, but in his continued ministry through the church, the liberation from sin of all peoples goes on.

1. Each gathering of the community around the word of God is an occasion for renewal and rejoicing (Nehemiah).

2. The inestimable worth of each member of the community is discovered only within the context of communal sharing and support (1 Corinthians).

3. As long as injustice and oppression flourish, the Christian mission of liberation is incomplete (Luke).

Fourth Sunday in Ordinary Time

Called by God to make his word and his will known to the people (Jeremiah), the prophet's mission brings him/her suffering and rejection (Luke). But the Spirit that empowers the prophet to speak also empowers him/her to love and endure all things for the sake of the good news of salvation (1 Corinthians).

Jeremiah 1:4-5, 17-19. An excerpted reading from the initial chapter of Jeremiah, today's first reading relates the young man's call to the prophetic ministry. By setting the scene in the "days of Josiah" (v. 4), the prophet informs his readers that he was active in the service of the word during the latter half of the seventh century B.C.E. Actually, Jeremiah's tenure spanned a 40-year period of political and religious upheaval that climaxed in the fall of Judah to the Babylonians (627-587 B.C.E.).

With three very specific terms—"I *formed* you, I *knew* you, I *dedicated* you" (v. 5), the prophet explained that his appointment to discern and to interpret the divine will for his people was from Yahweh himself. The verb "to form" (*yasar*) refers to the sculpting and modelling activities performed by a potter. The same term was used by the Yahwistic author in his account of the creation of the first human (Genesis 2:7-8); hence, the term reflects the idea that God himself forms the child in the womb and that God knows humans and is their unique master from the first moment of existence (G. Couturier). The second term, "I knew you" (*yàda*), signifies more than an intellectual awareness; it also indicates an involvement of the will. "I dedicated you" (*qadash*), the third term, underscores Jeremiah's being consecrated or set apart by God for a special task.

That task of being a prophet to the nations was to be Jeremiah's life's work. As the rest of his story unfolds, the prophet will share with his readers the profound effects his call had upon him as well as the suffering which his ministry brought into his life. No other prophet has been so candid in revealing the cost of faithful commitment to the word of God.

In the second portion of today's pericope (vv. 17-19), the prophet is warned to be prepared and alert for the struggle to come. "To gird the loins" was to be in constant readiness for action, for work or even for combat. In Jeremiah's case, his prophetic ministry was, more often than not, an uphill battle to remind a disinterested and often resentful people of their covenantal commitments.

Through it all, Yahweh promised to make the prophet strong. "A fortified city" (v. 18) symbolized the stamina and courage that Jeremiah would need in order to keep the word of God's truth before his people. Though he was not promised a rose garden ("they will fight against you" v.19), nevertheless, Jeremiah had assurance that, whatever he suffered in the fray, he would not be alone. J. Gaffney has called the divine reassurance, "I am with you to deliver you," the fundamental message of the Judaeo-Christian tradition. Jesus left this same message with his followers. It still inspires those who accept the call to speak the word of God's truth and justice in this world.

1 Corinthians 12:31-13:13. A literary treasure of undisputed quality, the hymn to love, which comprises today's second reading, is regarded by some scholars as a pre-Pauline composition interpolated by the apostle into his Corinthian correspondence. Although the pericope *does* seem to be an afterthought since 14:1 flows logically from 12:31, nevertheless, it seems to be a *Pauline* afterthought. A careful study of the composition will reveal that it correlates with and serves to clarify Paul's explanation of charisms and their value (12:4-11).

Corinth was a complex community with its share of difficulties. While the believers there were enthusiastic regarding the gifts of the Spirit, some allowed their enthusiasm to deteriorate into an unbridled rivalry. There were those who, affected by the influence of a certain gnostic philosophy, thought themselves to belong to a spiritual elite, possessed of special, superior gifts. When these self-designated saints flaunted their charisma and disrupted the harmony of the community, Paul wrote to correct the error of their ways.

Besides reminding the Corinthian Christians that their gifts were not self-attained but God-given (12:11), he also underscored the fact that all gifts were to be used not for self-aggrandizement but for the edification of the community (14:26). Moreover, Paul stressed (today's text) that the motivating factor behind every charism and in the heart of every community member should be love. This is the *greater gift* to which Paul referred in 12:31.

As J. M. O'Connor has pointed out, the first three statements of the hymn share the same structure, "If I have ... but have not love ... I am ..." (13:1-3). In each statement, the conditional clause alludes to one or more of the charisms Paul mentioned in 1 Corinthians 12. For example, without love, the gift of tongues (12:10) is no better than a noisy gong or clanging cymbal! Just as in an orchestra, the gong or cymbal may make a big noise and attract attention, but of itself has little musical value. However, when added to the symphony at just the right moment as a harmonious accent, the gong or cymbal can make the overall performance more pleasing. So, too, with the gift of tongues: Harmony and the right occasion must determine when it should be exercised.

With similar references to the gifts of prophecy (12:10), knowledge (12:8) and wonder-working faith (12:9), Paul concluded that, in the absence of love, even these great gifts were *nothing*. The word Paul used meant *non-existent*! As O'Connor explained, "Those who do not love do not exist as God intended them to exist. Thus when viewed within the perspective of the divine intention for humanity (Romans 8:29), the only standard that Paul recognized, they were non-existent."

Notice that Paul did not say, "the loving person does this ..." He said, "love does" ... "love is." He personified love and challenged Christians to make it real by embodying that supreme virtue in their hearts, minds and wills. Paul understood that love would lead him to knowledge of God in this life and love would guarantee him full knowledge in the next (13:12-13).

Luke 4:21-30. Due to his commission to be God's prophet "to the nations" (Jeremiah 1:5) and because of the suffering his ministry brought upon him, Jeremiah has been called a *type* of Jesus Christ. In today's gospel, both of these aspects—the universal scope of salvation and the rigors of discipleship—are reflected in the person and mission of Jesus.

As the continuation of Jesus' inaugural appearance at the synagogue of Nazareth, this text represents the hometown reaction to one of their own. Some have said the scene could be entitled "Familiarity Breeds Contempt" because when the townspeople of Nazareth heard Jesus speak with eloquence and authority, they responded in a scornful manner. Jesus had indicated that his work was to fulfill the messianic prophecies (Luke 4:18-19 = Isaiah 61:1ff). In relating this declaration, Luke employed the perfect tense of the verb "to fulfill," *peplerotai*, thereby signifying that the reality of salvation had already begun in the person of Jesus and that the effects of his presence and of his continuing presence through the church keeps the divine word effective. (C. Stuhlmueller).

But this is more than a story about familiarity and contempt. The scorn directed at Jesus was not due to what they regarded as his familiar and humble origins. "Is this not Joseph's son?" (v. 22) was a question which reflected, rather, the expectations and demands of his townspeople. If he was indeed Joseph's son, they reasoned, why should he not be doing in *Nazareth* the great works he has done elsewhere? After all, charity begins at home ... does it not?

But Jesus declined to do in Nazareth the great acts of salvation he had worked elsewhere. Mark, in his gospel, explained it very bluntly: "He could work no miracle there apart from curing a few ... so much did their *lack of faith* distress him" (Mark 6:5-6). Luke simply referred to the prophet not gaining acceptance in his native place (v. 24). This is precisely the crux of the whole event. C. Talbert and R. Fuller refer to the story as a programmatic statement of Jesus' mission and, by implication, of the church's ministry.

Throughout his two volume work, Luke showed both Jesus and the church reaching out with the message of salvation to the chosen people, the Jews. But these, in general, chose to reject first Jesus and then his disciples. With that, the words and works of salvation were directed toward the gentiles where, in many instances, they found great welcome.

But Luke is not implying that the gentile mission was an *alternate* plan, devised because of the Jewish rejection of Jesus and/or of the church. Rather, Luke understood the universal mission of the gospel as part of God's foreordained plan of salvation. As R. C. Tannehill has observed, "It is not so much that Jesus goes elsewhere because he is rejected as that he is rejected because he announces that it is God's will and his mission to go elsewhere."

In citing the wonders worked by Elijah for the gentile widow (1 Kings 17:7-16) and of Elisha for the gentile army commander (2 Kings 5:1-19), Luke cast Jesus in the same light (but even brighter) as the revered prophets of Israel's heritage. He also drew a sharper comparison between the faith of gentiles and the lack of faith of those who had inherited the rich prophetic traditions. Later in the gospel, Luke would portray Jesus weeping for his people who had rejected him because in so doing, they rejected the messianic promises that were in him fulfilled (19:41-44).

From the outset of Jesus' ministry, the notion of rejection loomed large. This same notion was also to figure greatly in the mission of the church (Acts 13:44-50, 17:4-5), and in the lives of his disciples (Stephen: Acts 7:58; Paul: Acts 13:50). Still, that rejection—no matter how vigorously or vehemently it was expressed—would not squelch the ministry of the word.

Jesus' determination in moving through the angry mob to continue his mission is reminiscent of the prophecy of Deutero-Isaiah concerning the mission of the word: "So the word that goes from my mouth does not return to me empty, without carrying out my will and succeeding in what it was sent to do" (Isaiah 55:11). The fulfillment of this prophecy, Jesus is himself the incarnation of the word spoken by God. In all his words and works, he carried out the will of the one who sent him. Today, the mission of the church to the world should be understood and exercised in the same light and with the same fearless determination.

1. *Those who are called by God to do great things are empowered by God with great strength (Jeremiah).*

2. *Love is the greatest activity of which humans are capable; in loving, we reflect the one in whose image we are made (1 Corinthians).*

3. *Great faith is needed to recognize the miracles that happen in "our own backyard" (Luke).*

Fifth Sunday in Ordinary Time

God's call to service is a creative one; it not only summons the person to engage in a certain task but also to become all that by divine grace he/she is capable of being (Isaiah). Often the least likely candidates by worldly standards have become the greatest achievers (1 Corinthians). Perhaps this is due to the fact that the divine criterion for success is measured not in a rising line on graphs but in the raising to life of broken, sinful hearts (Luke).

Isaiah 6:1-2, 3-8. *Mysterium tremendum et fascinans*—such were the words with which Rudolf Otto, in his classic work, *Idea of the Holy,* described the encounter in truth between the infinite God and one of his finite creatures. Isaiah expressed himself differently ("Woe is me. . . . I am doomed. . . . Here I am. . . send me!") but the prophet's numinous experience was essentially the same as that detailed by Otto. A mystery at once fearful and yet attractive, the encounter between God and his prophet was a multi-dimensional experience. Besides the fact of *divine revelation* and the prophet's recognition of God as holy, Isaiah was also made painfully aware of himself as a sinner. That simultaneous double revelation of God and of himself constituted what has been called by scholars Isaiah's inaugural vision. To appreciate and comprehend this moment in the prophet's life is to understand his entire mission and message.

For the prophet, Yahweh, the God of Israel and Judah, was perceived as the "Holy One," the wholly other and transcendent one. In the Pentateuch, the term "holy" was generally applied in a *ritual* sense, indicating the cleanness or legal acceptability of a person or thing. For Isaiah, "holy" signified a *moral* condition demanded of those whose God was holiness itself. In order to express the very real but abstract concept of God's holy otherness, Isaiah utilized the very graphic, concrete Hebrew language and the traditional Old Testament props that ordinarily accompanied and signified a theophany. The shaking door, the smoke, the filling of the area with God's glory were all standard phenomena for describing the indescribable reality of God's presence.

Isaiah related his symbolic vision of the Holy One in heaven in imagery borrowed from the Jerusalem temple, where he probably had his encounter. At the basis of Isaiah's description was the popular belief that the earthly Jerusalem temple was an external expression of the heavenly temple. Seraphim, popular figures in the mythology of the ancient Near Eastern world, were spiritual beings (angels, "sons of God") who served in the heavenly courts. In Isaiah's vision, the seraphim appeared to function as a heavenly chorus whose words and actions proclaimed the profound nature of the event.

Although many have interpreted the seraphim's trisagion or triple "holy" as a prophetic reference to the Trinity, it is more correctly understood as the Hebrew superlative. Later incorporated into both Jewish and Christian liturgies, the "Holy, holy, holy" of Isaiah's vision can be thought of as both a description of God and a demanding challenge to those who would belong to him in faith. "Lord of hosts," meaning Lord of *armies,* may have "originally been part of the hallowed name given to the Ark that accompanied Israel into battle" (F. Moriarity). While the concept of God as a warrior may not appeal to modern minds, it was vitally important to Isaiah who looked to no earthly arsenal for defense and security.

In the presence of the holy one, Isaiah was struck with a sense of his own sinful unworthiness and that of his people. His "Oy Ve!" ("Woe is me!", v. 5) sprang from a conviction that, as a sinner, he could not survive an encounter with the holy one (Exodus 33:20). But the God who called and commissioned him as prophet would also equip him for the task. Purified in the symbolic action of the seraphim (v. 7), Isaiah's reticence was transformed by God's power into a firm resolve: "Here I am, send me!" (v. 8).

1 Corinthians 15:1-11. For many of the Corinthian converts to Christianity, the bodily resurrection of Jesus (and of the redeemed) was an insurmountable obstacle, defying reason and taking their faith beyond its limits. Raised in a Greek culture and schooled in Platonic and gnostic philosophies, the Corinthians were hard pressed to believe in the resurrection and exaltation of a body that they believed to be instrinsically inferior and even evil. Recent scholarship has also suggested that the Greek Christians, influenced by gnosticism, believed that through the sacraments they were already raised (i.e., living the spiritual life in Christ) and therefore did not require or even need await a further resurrection of the body. Of course, Paul had preached the good news in its entirety while laboring in Corinth but, after he departed, some exercised a certain selectivity with regard to the truths he had taught. As a result, the difficult doctrine of Jesus' bodily exaltation was rejected. In a sense, the Corinthians' error (which probably plagued other Greek churches as well) was a "happy fault" because it evoked from Paul an eloquent and theologically erudite discourse on the resurrection.

In order to bring them back to the truth, Paul reminded the Corinthian church of the tradition he had handed on to them (v. 1). That tradition had been taught to him by authoritative eyewitnesses and was, therefore, to be accepted as authentic. At a very early stage, probably as early as 35 C.E., the good news about Jesus Christ had been summarized in a succinct and fixed traditional oral formula or series of oral formulae. An outline of this credal formula is discernible in vv. 3-4: ". . . Christ died for our sins in accordance with the scriptures; that he was buried, and, in accordance with the scriptures, rose on the third day. . . ."

Paul's list of witnesses (vv. 5-8) to the risen Lord was intended to give added weight to his argument. Notice that he makes no mention of the women but only of those witnesses whose testimony would have been accepted as legal according to Jewish law (viz. *male* witnesses). Moreover, instead of the *two* witnesses required by law, the apostle mentioned several: Cephas, the Twelve, James, 500 *brothers* (male gender again) and, last of all, himself.

It is believed that the *"Twelve"* was the "early church's consecrated designation for the apostolic college" (R. Kugelman), although many dispute the actual identification of the Twelve with the specially called disciples of Jesus. Paul's mention of "all the apostles" (v. 7) probably referred to a larger, distinct group of authorized witnesses of the risen Lord, chosen from among the disciples of Jesus.

Paul's claim for himself of the designation "apostle" was based on his Damascus conversion experience. "One born out of the normal course" or *ektroma* (v. 8) is literally translated as "an aborted fetus" but can also mean, "an object of horror and disgust." This was probably the sense intended by Paul who looked upon his past persecution of the church as monstrous and horrible behavior. Like Isaiah in the first reading and Peter in the gospel, Paul attributed the fact of his calling to the favor (*charis*) or grace of God and not to any qualifications on his own part. Once called and graced for his task, however, Paul cooperated fully with the Lord as his seemingly immodest statement makes clear: "Indeed I have worked harder than all the others" (v. 10).

Luke 5:1-11. Summoned to greatness by the Lord, Isaiah, Paul and Simon Peter stand out in the scriptures not because of their excellent qualifications or suitability for their respective tasks but because of the miracle of God's grace made manifest in them. Without impressive backgrounds, they were mandated for service and became worthy in the process of bringing to others the good news of God's saving love. In his narrative of the call of Simon Peter, Luke has departed from his Marcan source on several different points. Drawing on his special sources, the third evangelist placed Jesus' calling of the first disciples, not at the very outset of his mission (as in Mark) but *later*, after having been seen preaching and healing. A later calling seems more logical and plausible because time had been allowed for Peter and the others to become interested in the teacher from Nazareth. Luke has also combined the calling of Simon Peter with the episode of the great catch of fish, an event placed after the resurrection in the fourth gospel (John 21). The debate continues as to whether Luke reflected the post-resurrectional event back to the ministry or not.

Unlike the simple Marcan account (Mark 1:16-18), Luke delved into the psychological aspects of the calling of Simon Peter. Like Isaiah, Simon felt unworthy and sinful in the face of goodness. Notice the change from "master" (v. 5) to "Lord" (v. 8), reflecting Simon Peter's awareness of the divine power Jesus had shown in causing the great catch of fish. Finally, the magnified role of Peter is obvious in the third gospel. Throughout the episode, Jesus spoke only to Peter and it was *to him* that Jesus said, "From now on, you will be catching men" (v. 10). Luke's singular attention to Peter probably reflects the preeminent position the office of Peter had attained among second and third generation believers. The importance of Peter would also be underscored by Luke in the second volume of his work, the Acts of the Apostles.

The lake (v. 1) in question was Gennesareth, the Greek name given to the Sea of Galilee. Lake Gennesareth was named for the small fertile, populous plain northwest of the lake and south of Capernaum. A pear-shaped body of water, 13 miles long and seven and a half miles wide, the lake was, for Luke, more important for theological than for geographic reasons. According to H. Conzelmann, the lake in the third gospel was the site of Jesus' manifestations of power. If this is the case, then Luke has constructed the episode to bring Simon Peter personally into the sphere of Jesus' mighty power (J. Fitzmeyer).

This idea is borne out in the miraculous catch of fish, an experience that became the basis of Jesus' prophetic commissioning: "You will catch men!" That statement literally rendered would read, "You shall be taking them alive." The implication is that, by Peter's apostolic labors in the service of the gospel, others would be saved from the death of sin and brought alive or to new life in Jesus' kingdom. Significantly, Peter had to "put into the deep and lower the nets" before he achieved success. An excellent missiological principle, Peter's action would indicate that the disciple must be willing to go to where the people are and not expect them to jump into the "net of salvation."

The impetus for Peter's labors and subsequently the source for Christian apostolate was to be the word of God (v. 1) learned from Jesus. As J. Fitzmeyer has noted, "word of God" is a particularly Lucan term used four times in the gospel, where it referred to Jesus' teaching, and 14 times in Acts to denote Christian preaching. By using the same term Luke underscored the fact that the basis for Christian preaching was the teaching of Jesus and both were ultimately rooted in the word of God himself. In the Greek, the evangelist used the subjective genitive to make it clear that he meant the word coming *from* God and not merely the word *about* God. Some of the church fathers saw in the scene of Jesus' teaching the word of God from Peter's boat a symbolic message that the real teaching of Jesus comes through the "bark" of Peter. This concept was a product of later theology and ecclesiology and probably not intended by the evangelist. Indeed, Jesus' teaching of God's word also took place in the synagogue (Luke 4), in a field (Luke 8), on a plain (Luke 8), in a Pharisee's home (Luke 7), etc.

Finally, even though he did not *feature* their calling as did Mark and Matthew, Luke included James and John in the episode at the lake. With Simon Peter, "they brought their boats to land, left everything and became his followers" (v. 11). C. Stuhlmueller contends that, with this statement and others (9:62) like it throughout his work, Luke has written the "gospel of absolute renouncement." Mark and Matthew spoke of leaving nets, boat and father (Mark 1:16-18, Matthew 4:22) but Luke understood the *absolute* demands of discipleship as costing not less than *everything*. His word *a-Kolouthein* ("they followed him": v. 11) was used elsewhere in the gospel (5:27-28; 9:23, 49, 57, 59, 61; 18:22, 28) to refer to discipleship as a commitment that severs all other bonds. This was the mandate which Peter received and of which he felt so unworthy. That same call to commitment is extended to all who would be "taken alive" by Jesus.

1. The person who would search for God's majesty will find his/her own sinfulness along the way (Isaiah).

2. Whoever said, "You can't make a silk purse out of a pig's ear," did not take into account God's grace or remember Saul (1 Corinthians).

3. Launching out into unchartered waters of the unchurched is part of the task of discipleship (Luke).

Sixth Sunday in Ordinary Time

Blest are you who will embrace the paradox of discipleship, who will be poor and hungry and hated now so as to enjoy a future fulfillment (Luke). Blest are you who have learned to rely upon God (Jeremiah), you shall experience fullness of life and a share in the glory of Christ himself (1 Corinthians).

Jeremiah 17:5-8. Today's first reading belongs to a longer collection of wisdom sayings (Jeremiah 17:5-13) whose authorship of which remains a matter of scholarly dispute. Although no real definitive arguments for or against an authentic authorship by Jeremiah have been forthcoming, many regard the sapiential motif as foreign to Jeremiah's literary style and attribute these verses to another, later author. Regardless of its origin, the blessing and curse antithesis of the prophetic text forms an excellent complement to the gospel's blessings and woes.

Historically, this pericope is difficult to place; R. Davidson has suggested that the prophet had become disillusioned with the Josianic reform because of its nationalistic emphasis. After the king's death at Megiddo in 609 B.C.E., the prophet sought to turn the attention of his people from trust in human resources to trust in God. M. McNamara, following C.H. Cornill, would associate these verses with a later time, viz., the reign of the weak puppet king Zedekiah, ca. 597 B.C.E. If this is the case, then Jeremiah would have been counseling the king against the alliance with Egypt that resulted in the Babylonian invasion of Judah.

Unsympathetic with either position, G. Couturier has argued that *all* of Jeremiah's adult life had been spent witnessing the slow but sure demise of Judah; therefore, the lesson he teaches in today's first reading is the result of a lifetime of reflection and not simply a reaction to one or another failed political reform.

A poem of two stanzas, each illustrated by an image from nature, today's text graphically describes the essence of true religion. Centuries later, Augustine would say in a similar vein, "You have made us for yourself, O God, and our hearts are restless until they rest in you!" Jeremiah expressed it in terms of trust in God by whom and for whom humanity has been created.

In Judah, where water was a scarce and precious commodity, it was common knowledge that plants could not survive if they were far from a river or stream. They withered and died; their barren branches bore silent witness to the absence of life-giving water. According to Jeremiah's comparison, so too is the person "whose heart turns away from the Lord." Alienated from God, humans have no hope for survival. However, those who turn to God, the source of all life and goodness, are like trees planted near an abundant water source; these flourish and bear fruit.

Those whose hearts are firmly rooted in the Lord can survive difficulties and remain unshaken; they can withstand the daily struggles and sufferings of life because they are centered on the one who is life. For Jeremiah's contemporaries who were suffering as a result of Judah's political upheavals, the prophet's words called them to return to the one alliance that would endure and sustain them, i.e., the covenant with Yahweh.

In our times, when self-reliance and self-sufficiency are such highly touted ideals, the prophet's words call all believers to a reflective evaluation of priorities. Trust in God as the source of life and goodness can never be replaced by technological advances or scientific achievements. Pascal echoed Jeremiah's wisdom as he compared the misery of humanity without God to the happiness of humanity with God. Kierkegaard referred to the either/or of the soul's decisive orientation with regard to God as its burden. If it is a burden, it is the burden of our freedom—freedom to rely on God and flourish or freedom to turn away from God and stagnate in emptiness.

1 Corinthians 15:12, 16-20. One of the earliest credal formulae was the simple declaration: "Jesus lives!" or "Jesus is risen!" When the Corinthian community of believers began to question this declaration and the orthodoxy of the gospel Paul had preached among them, when they began to distort that gospel by accepting certain doctrines and rejecting others, Paul responded adamantly. Today's second reading is part of his response, one of the earliest theological presentations of the doctrine of the resurrection.

Raised to worship reason and schooled in those philosophies that elevated the mind and spirit above all else, the Corinthians were reluctant, if not altogether recalcitrant, at the notion of a bodily glorification. Gnostic tendencies in the Greek culture influenced a mentality that regarded matter and, therefore, the body as intrinsically inferior, even evil. For this reason, death was regarded as the release of an immortal spirit from its confinement in a mortal prison. Moreover, some Greek Christians also believed that their participation in the sacraments already afforded them a spiritual experience of the resurrection that superseded and rendered unnecessary any future bodily rising.

Aware of the philosophical background of his Greek converts, Paul drew upon his own excellent secular education and with perfect logic argued that, if the Corinthians rejected the possibility of their own bodily resurrection, they were in effect rejecting the resurrection of Jesus. Because of the fact of the incarnation, the bodily resurrection of Christ and that of the departed believers ("the dead") are inextricably contingent upon one another.

Christ's resurrection is not just the glorious climax of his *own* life but, as Paul explained, Christ is "the firstfruits of those who have fallen asleep" (v. 20). A Jewish cultic term, *aparche* or the firstfruits was considered the promise and pledge of what would follow. Since Jesus is the firstfruits, then his resurrection is a pledge and a promise of the resurrection to life of all believers.

As R. Fuller has pointed out, Paul's argument in vv. 17-20 is not just a philosophical or theoretical one; it is solidly existential, based upon the present experience of the Christian. Those who know themselves to be forgiven sinners have been brought to this experience and awareness only through the saving activity of Christ. Because of his death and rising, Christ broke the bonds of sin and death and forged a new relationship between the Father and humanity. This relationship will continue to sustain the healed and forgiven believer in this life and will climax in an eternal union.

If this relationship ended with death, then hope is in vain, faith is an absurdity and all our efforts at virtue are an exercise in futility. But, this is not the case! Indeed, Christ's resurrection is the climactic event of our own salvation; his victory has become the victory of every sinner who experiences the forgiveness and freedom wrought by his cross. For this reason, in faith we continue to proclaim with confidence: Jesus lives; he is risen!

Luke 6:17, 20-26. Part of a longer sermon attributed to Jesus (Luke 6:20-49), today's gospel is from the Lucan version of the so-called great sermon. Whereas Matthew included a much longer sermon (Matthew 5:3-7:27) and presented it as the Magna Charta of the kingdom with Jesus as a new Moses promulgating a new law from the mountain, Luke's version is quite different. Shorter and more loosely constructed than its Matthean counterpart, the Lucan sermon of Jesus was situated on a level stretch of land where a great crowd had gathered.

Among the crowds were many of Jesus disciples and to these specifically the sermon was directed (v. 20). As R.

Fuller has noted, this means that the ethics of the great sermon were not intended for the world in general but for those who had already decided to follow Jesus. The ethical demands of the sermon presuppose grace; in other words, the challenge Jesus proffered to his disciples was achievable only because they had already entered into some sort of a relationship with him.

In deciding to follow him, however hesitantly, the disciples were already afforded the grace, i.e., the strength from the Father, to meet the demands of their commitment. Later, Paul would refer to this relationship and the grace it offered as being "in Christ." Only in the degree that a disciple "follows Christ" or is "in Christ" will he/she be capable of emulating the qualities that the beatitudes describe.

While Matthew enunciated nine statements concerning blessedness, Luke included only four and he paired each beatitude with a corresponding woe. The poor are contrasted with the rich; the hungry are compared to the full; the weeping are juxtaposed to the laughing, and the hated with those who are spoken well of. As J. Fitzmeyer has pointed out, Jesus' words touched on the concerns of daily existence of his contemporaries, viz., poverty, hunger, grief, hatred, ostracism.

These are not simply sociological designations. Rather, the series of beatitudes and woes raised those existential concerns to another dimension, and eschatological dimension. The present reality is seen in light of the future yet to be revealed. Those whose current suffering entails poverty, hunger, grief, etc., are called by Jesus to translate those sociological designations into dispositions toward God. By so doing, physical poverty could be viewed as an opportunity for learning total reliance on God and complete trust in his providence. The hunger experienced by the body could serve to whet the appetite of the spirit for God; the grief and hatred suffering brings would be understood as preparations for the profound joy the kingdom would bring.

In pronouncing as "blest" the poor, the hungry, the weeping and the hated, Luke drew upon a term, *makarios* (blessed), and a figure of speech, *macarism*, popular in Jewish as well as Egyptian and Hellenistic literatures. Paired with the woes, the beatitudes belong to a literary subform called the "ascription" (J. Fitzmeyer, T.Y. Mullins). Among the Greeks, *makarios* described the inner joy of a person, because of some good fortune they had experienced. In Hebrew thought, blessedness usually connoted the happiness of a person favored by God.

In the New Testament, however, the designation "blest" involves a paradox. It does not actually confer a blessing, rather it extols the good fortune that will come to someone for some particular reason. Therefore, the poor are not blest because they are poor but because of their ultimate outcome: "the reign of God is yours" (v. 20).

As C. Talbert has explained, "The one uttering the beatitude does so from a position within the councils of God and with an awareness of the ultimate outcome of history (as does a prophet). The content of the beatitudes may be in stark contrast with the painful reality of the present. Paradox is prominent." Nevertheless, *blessedness* is the order of the day because of what will ultimately become of the poor, the hungry, the weeping and the hated!

Sharply contrasted to the blest ones are the recipients of the four woes (vv. 24-26). Whereas the poor, etc., could look forward to ultimate joy, the rich, the full, the laughing and those who are spoken well of are already receiving their reward. Their ultimate reality, their eschatological future has been squandered away in existential gratifications.

Like the prophets of the Jewish scriptures (Amos 5:7, 18; 6:1; Isaiah 5:8, 11, 18), Jesus continues to pronounce his woes upon those who see no further than themselves or their own pleasures. In the end, they shall find themselves bankrupt of hope and divested of their dreams. While there is still time, it devolves upon all would-be disciples to accept the ethical challenge of the gospel, to live the paradox and thus to earn the designation "blest are you"!

1. Trust in God forms the network that determines and supports all our other alliances (Jeremiah).

2. Our present experience of forgiveness is a preview of the victory we shall one day enjoy with the risen Christ (1 Corinthians).

3. Blessedness is God's everlasting gift to those who embrace the temporary sufferings of discipleship (Luke).

Seventh Sunday in Ordinary Time

As the powers of this world work diligently to arm themselves against one another . . . as the peoples of the earth seek refuge in their stockpiles of nuclear destruction, the gospel calls believers to witness to another way of life. It is the way of the Father who is mercy (Luke). It is the magnanimous way of the Son (1 Samuel). It is the way of the life-giving-Spirit (1 Corinthians).

1 Samuel 26:2, 7-9, 12-13, 22-23. "The quality of mercy is not strained; it droppeth as the gentle rain from heaven upon the place beneath," wrote William Shakespeare. In today's first reading, excerpted from 1 Samuel, David epitomizes this quality of mercy and it was precisely this quality that made his behavior more befitting a king than the mean-hearted Saul. Indeed Shakespeare reflected this insight as well as he continued his soliloquy on mercy: "It is twice blest," said the 16th century bard. "It blesseth him that gives and him that takes: 'tis mightiest in the mightiest: it becomes the throned monarch better than his crown" (*Merchant of Venice* IV, 1).

A variant of the incident found in 1 Samuel 24:1-22, today's text records the events that immediately preceded Saul's demise. Jealous of the younger man, angered by his popularity among the people, Saul had determined to do away with David. After several failed attempts on his life, David fled to the desert. With a sizable following, he lived the life of a renegade, fending off the royal troops with his own brand of guerrilla warfare.

In this particular episode, Saul had pursued David into the wilderness of Ziph. While the king and his men were encamped for the night, David and some of his men crept unnoticed into their midst. In his portrayal of the sleeping soldiers, the author of 1 Samuel used the same term, *tardemah*, that described the divinely induced sleep that came over Adam and Abraham (Genesis 2:21, 15:12). The implication seems to be that God had placed Saul at the mercy of David.

According to Doughty's *Travels in Arabia Deserta*, the upright lance (v. 7) signalled the tent or headquarters of the sheik. While his men encouraged David to seize the opportunity to do away with Saul, David spared the king. There was no doubt that David had been unjustly treated. Most people would probably have excused him if he had killed Saul. But David did not regard injustice as an excuse for taking the law—which he regarded as God's will—into his own hands. Moreover, David underscored the fact that Saul, however unworthy a king, was the divine regent, anointed by God and therefore representative of God's will for the people.

An excellent prelude for today's gospel pericope, the story of David and Saul contrasts the largeness of heart (David) to which Jesus called his followers with the smallness of heart (Saul) against which he warned them. Unwilling to repay evil with evil, David in this instance is the forerunner of Jesus. In his magnanimity, he represents the love and mercy of the Father for a sinful humanity. He also reminds all believers that, just as punishment is the Lord's prerogative, so it is the Lord who will reward those who remain just and faithful (v. 23).

1 Corinthians 15:45-49. Throughout his lengthy first letter to the Christians in Corinth, Paul worked diligently at correcting a variety of abuses and misunderstandings that had occurred since his departure. Because of the apostle's sincere efforts at preserving intact the gospel as he had preached it in Corinth, Christians throughout the ages have benefited from Paul's excellent insights on an array of topics: morality, salvation, community, conscience, charisms and the eucharist.

In chapter 15, Paul addressed the subject of the resurrection—Jesus' resurrection as well as the resurrection of individual believers. Calling it the crux of the entire Christ-event, Paul declared unequivocally, "If there is no resurrection of the dead, then Christ has not been raised; if Christ has not been raised, then our preaching is in vain and your faith is in vain!" (15:13-14).

Affected by their dualistic appreciation of anthropology, the Corinthian Christians (like most Hellenistic believers) regarded the human person as a divine spark (spirit or soul) entrapped in a corruptible and worthless body. Rather than accept Paul's good news concerning the *incarnate* word of God who suffered and died and rose *in his body* for the sake of a sinful humanity, the Corinthians selectively avoided the resurrection and concentrated on what they regarded as the purely spiritual aspects of salvation.

Also influenced by the Hellenized Jewish speculations of Philo, the believers in Corinth understood that there were two Adams as presented in Genesis 1 and 2. According to Philo's exegesis, the first Adam (of Genesis 1:27) was the archetypal heavenly man, created in God's image, while the second Adam (of Genesis 2-3) was the empirical, fallen man, made of dust and destined for dust. Whereas the *first* Adam represented humanity as it was meant to be, viz., *spiritual*, the *second* Adam (according to Philo) depicted humanity as it really was, viz., corruptible. Philo had also taught about a *last* Adam who was yet to come—one who would be like the first Adam (heavenly amd spiritual) and the antithesis of the second Adam (earthly and physical).

Using Philo's ideas as a springboard, Paul also employed the two-Adam model, but he gave the Adams a different interpretation. Paul understood that the two accounts of the creation of humanity in Genesis chapters one and two both described the same Adam, a physical or natural man (v. 46); the spiritual Adam was to be found elsewhere. For Paul, the *true*, the *new* and the *last* Adam is Jesus Christ in whom and by whom all believers are saved.

Whereas the natural body links us to the first Adam, our spiritual aspect links us to Christ (v. 49) and to Christ's resurrection. His risen glory is a pledge of our own. Unlike the gnostic, dualistic philosophers who regarded salvation as a matter of *achieving* one's freedom from corporeality in order to recover a heavenly origin, Paul called the Corinthians to open themselves *body and soul* to *receive* the eschatological gifts made available to all through the death and rising of Jesus.

Luke 6:27-38. Most of us are familiar with the rather earthy saying, "I'll scratch your back; you scratch mine.." What is communicated through this graphic statement is the principle of reciprocity. Many friendships are based on this principle: one person does something for another and expects a similar return. Invitations to dinner are reciprocated, gifts are reciprocated, favors are reciprocated and even compliments are returned—kind word for kind word! At Christmas time, many people keep a ledger containing the list of cards "sent" as well as one of cards "received." When the two lists do not tally, names of delinquent correspondents are dropped from the list. When Jesus walked the earth, preaching the good news of salvation, he challenged his followers to engage in relationships that defied this pattern of reciprocity; he called those who would be his disciples to love one another and even enemies with the heart and mind of God himself. This is the subject of today's gospel.

Part of Luke's so-called sermon on the plain (in contrast to Matthew's sermon on the mount), today's pericope is comprised of four distinct units, each one concerned with elevating human relations above an "I'll-do-it-for-you-if-you-do-it-for-me" type of motivation. In his excellent study of Luke-Acts, C. Talbert has divided the units as follows: Luke 6:27-28, 29-31, 32-36, 37-38. When Jesus called his disciples to love enemies and to return good for evil (vv. 27-28), he upset what had been until then the acceptable mode of behavior.

As J. Fitzmeyer has noted, Jesus' call to love the enemy should be "understood against the background of an ancient view of enmity. One finds forms of it as early as Hesiod in the Greek world (*Opera et dies* 342), Pindar (*Pythian Odes* 2.83-84) and its best formulation in Lysias: 'I considered it established that one should do harm to one's enemies and be of service to one's friends'."

While certain Greek writers advocated changing enemies to friends through the exercise of virtue, only Jesus put his challenge to love enemies in the form of a command! Having defined enemies as those who hate, curse, maltreat and do violence (vv. 27-29), Jesus commanded his disciples not merely to give the love of warm affection (*philia*) to the enemy or even to exercise passionate dedication (*eros*) toward them. Rather, Jesus called his followers to love even enemies with the love of *agape*, viz., that love that is generated not by the attractiveness or goodness of the recipient but by the goodness of the giver. *Agape*-love does not keep an account; it loves graciously and freely without measuring the deservedness of the one loved. It is with this wondrous *agape*-love that God has loved the world and ordained to save it (John 3:16).

The second unit of today's gospel (vv. 29-31) provides ready illustrations of the manner in which love is to be expressed. Rather than repay evil with evil, Christians are to break the cycle of maliciousness by a non-violent and positive choice of goodness.

The third unit (vv. 32-36) is comprised of three questions that require Jesus' listeners to compare themselves and their actions to those of sinners. Even sinners love, do good and lend to those who do likewise. But the sinners who would be followers of Jesus are challenged to expand the scope of their care and concern, including all, excluding none. Promising a heavenly reward (verse 35), Jesus taught that the motivating factor for human relationships should no longer be the principle of reciprocity but the compassion of the Father of whom all believers are sons and daughters (v. 36).

Judging others and/or condemning them is inappropriate and unacceptable among believers. To engage in these divine prerogatives invites the judgment and condemnation of God upon ourselves. Those who would be forgiven must respond to that gift with an attitude of forgiveness toward others. As L. Morris has noted, this is not salvation by merit or works; rather, it is an open proclamation of the grace of God that changes people. A forgiving, non-judgmental, non-condemnatory spirit is evidence that the person has been forgiven and has responded to that forgiveness with commitment.

The metaphor (v. 38) that concludes today's gospel may be an adaptation of a similar rabbinical saying whose point is that generous hearts will be divinely and abundantly rewarded. Incapable of fully reciprocating the love, compassion and generosity of God, those who are the beneficiaries of such goodness must show their gratitude in love, mercy and generosity for one another.

1. Mercy showered on an enemy is more effective than any weapon (1 Samuel).

2. Body and soul, we have been redeemed; body and soul, we shall experience glory (1 Corinthians).

3. Those who call upon the same Father cannot look upon one another as enemies (Luke).

Eighth Sunday in Ordinary Time

In the scales of interpersonal relationships, duplicity, arrogance and egotism will be outweighed by integrity, humility and true mutual concern (Sirach). These qualities create disciples and build community (Luke). These qualities defeat death and prepare for immortality (1 Corinthians).

Sirach 27:4-7. When archaeologists were excavating at Qumran in 1947, they found a few fragments of the book we call Sirach. Seventeen years later, in 1964, similar excavations of the fortress-city of Masada yielded an entire copy of this work. In an ancient synagogue unearthed at Cairo, another copy of Sirach was found. All of these discoveries attest to the popularity among Jews of the wisdom of Jesus Ben Sirach even though his work was not accepted into their official canon of scripture.

Writing in Hebrew ca. 180 B.C.E., the scholarly and astute author sought to answer the needs of his people in their struggle to maintain their ancient and treasured traditions over and against the pervading influence of Greek culture. Underscoring the fact that all lovers of wisdom (philosophers) would find the source of their predilection only in Israel, Sirach extolled the law and its virtues. Wisdom will be discovered, he taught, not in abstract speculation, but in the well-lived life of one who fears the Lord.

Two generations later (ca. 130 B.C.E.) the author's grandson translated his grandfather's work into Greek to make its insights readily available to Greek-speaking Jews. Among the early Christians, this second century B.C.E. anthology of wit, wisdom and practical advice was also popular, as is evidenced by its Greek name: "Ecclesiasticus" or Book of the Church.

Today's first reading belongs to a longer section (26:19-27:21) concerning integrity and friendship and the dangers that militate against these values. Excellent advice for choosing proper companions, today's text points to a person's speech as a gauge of inner virtue. The image of the sieve and husks is borrowed from the grain harvesting process. Once the grain has been threshed, it is run through a sieve. While the grain falls through, the husks (the Greek word *kopria* means refuse) are left behind, ready to be discarded.

With this graphic image, the author of Sirach compared what happens when a person begins to speak. Whereas there may have been a doubt as to the character of persons when they are silent, all doubts are dispelled when the inner aspect of persons is revealed in open oratory. Sound advice in any age, Sirach's wisdom was repeated by the 19th century author, Mary Ann Evans Cross (better known as George Eliot) when she wrote, "Blessed is the man, who having nothing to say, abstains from giving wordy evidence of the fact."

In our times, we need only recall the temerity of some political candidates when challenged to a public debate of the issues. How many elections have been won and/or lost simply because of the power of the spoken word to reveal the integrity (or lack of it) of an individual?

An excellent preview for today's gospel, the Sirach text reminds the critical to think before they speak because what comes out of one's mouth reveals the heart.

1 Corinthians 15:54-58. In her excellent book, *Resurrection: New Testament Witness and Contemporary Reflection*, Pheme Perkins has commented on the power death can wield over those who do not believe, and of the effects that power can have on society. People, stated Perkins, cannot engage in the struggle for justice and transformation if they remain in psychological bondage to the powers of death. Only those who are neither cynical nor afraid can be counted on to persist in the quest for a truly just and human world. When Paul called the Corinthian Christians to affirm their faith in the power of Jesus over death, i.e. in the resurrection, he challenged them to affirm as well *their* freedom from death, from sin and from the law. He also challenged them to exercise their freedom "fully engaged in the work of the Lord" (v. 58).

The conclusion of Paul's discourse on the implications of Jesus' resurrection for all who believe (1 Corinthians 15), today's second reading treats of the manner in which the faithful will experience immortality. Whereas others in Corinth umderstood that an "ideal" existence could be attained by *divesting* oneself of the body and all that it entailed, Paul spoke of the *transformation* of "the corruptible frame" unto incorruptibility. By so doing and by referring to the transformation into a "*spiritual* body" (15:43), he maintained the continuity between the believer here and now and the believer in his/her future existence.

Moreover, while some Corinthian teachers and philosophers held that the attainment of the "ideal" existence or salvation from this world could be accomplished by the individual, Paul taught that the transformation to immortality has been made possible for all *only* because of Jesus Christ. His death on the cross and his rising have accomplished the victory over death. In his proclamation of this victory, Paul declared that both Hosea 13:14 and Isaiah 25:8 had been fulfilled (v. 55). Then, because he always linked death to sin and the law, Paul launched into an aside (v. 56), explaining the connection between the three entities.

Echoing the same reasoning he included in his letter to the church at Galatia, Paul explained that the law has revealed the will of God to humanity. Yet, the law did not empower humankind with the capacity for keeping it; therefore the law exacerbated human sinfulness and buried humanity deeper and deeper in the snares of death. Only Jesus Christ and his victory over death has broken this repetitive and vicious cycle, freeing those who believe from sin and the law (Romans 6:17-18, 7:7) and from death (Colossians 2:13).

In the final verses of this difficult text, Paul challenged all who enjoy the victory of Jesus over death to manifest their sincere gratitude in steadfastness and perseverance (vv. 57-

58). H. Conzelmann has pointed out that the term for steadfastness or immovability (*amentakinetos*) is a unique occurrence in the New Testament and probably reflects a spirituality influenced by Platonism.

Whereas the Platonists held that this steadfastness was attained by withdrawing from the ever-changing world of the senses, Paul taught that those who persevered in the *way of Christ* could achieve steadfastness. By this assertion, Paul underscored the idea that the Christian life is the locus in this world where the power of the resurrection is made manifest. This notion of realized eschatology would be further developed by the fourth evangelist.

Luke 6:39-45. "What you *are* speaks so loudly, I cannot hear what you are saying!" A few years ago this pithy statement was bandied about as people discussed the need for authenticity and integrity in relationships. Although it may have become trite and hackneyed from overuse, the point remains relevant; it is, in fact, the same point which is made in today's gospel.

The conclusion of Luke's version of the great sermon, today's pericope is comprised of three separate parables that were to function as object lessons for Jesus' disciples. All three parables are concerned with the principles that should govern the lives of the disciples. No doubt, the sayings as they are here arranged and in their given larger context reflect the situation of the Christian community of the 80s C.E.

Without the earthly Jesus to guide them and without the apostolic eyewitnesses (most, if not all, were dead) to give counsel, new Christians learned the gospel and the meaning of the Christian way of life from those who already walked it. With the light and presence of the Holy Spirit, Christians living together in community were responsible for one another—as teachers, guides and as disciplinarians. Not only by their words were they to witness to one another, but also by their works, behavior, etc. In this particular gospel, it is a matter of the *Christian* influence disciples should have on one another.

C. Talbert has identified the ABA structure or pattern of this pericope; the "A" texts serve to elucidate the "B" text and vice-versa. For example, the central "B" text (vv. 41-42) underscores the necessity of being self-critical and personally transformed before assuming the task of admonishing and aiding in the transformation of others. The grossly exaggerated image conjured up by the speck and plank metaphor is purposeful. L. Morris has called this a sort of burlesque humor. Imagine someone with a plank hanging out of his/her eye solicitously attempting to remove a speck from another's eye! Preposterous! But, as Morris observes, the humor of the image should not blind us to the seriousness of the lesson, whose point is: Any attempt to improve others or to correct others without a prior self-critique is absurd!

"Hypocrite," the name given in v. 42 for those who attempt to reform others without any self-involvement, is a term that has undergone quite an evolution. Initially, the word meant "one who answers." In classical Greek, hypocrite came to mean "interpreter," "expounder," "orator," and was also used to describe actors on a stage. From this latter application, it came to connote a pretender or a dissembler.

Today, as we know, hypocrite is a derogatory term for those whose actions are not consonant with their words, viz. liars, deceivers. Unfortunately, sometimes, even professed and confessing Christians earn this title for themselves. At this point, it should be noted that while the task of fraternal correction (removing specks, etc.) should not be attempted without prior self-examination, the disciple need not be completely without imperfections before the process can begin.

In the two "A" sections of today's gospel, viz., vv.39-40 and vv. 43-45, the evangelist has expanded upon the motivation for entering into the process of mutually influencing one another for the good. In the first text (vv. 39-40), the disciples are called upon to be both guides and teachers. In order to lead a blind person, one must be sighted; in order to teach, one must be knowledgeable; otherwise the blind person and the student will be lost. The sight and the knowledge here specified are the insight that comes through faith and the knowledge that comes from a faith-filled relationship with the Lord. To teach the ways of Jesus, to lead others in his way, the disciple must first embody the lessons. Only then will the process of speck and plank removal be a true witness to Christian charity.

Verses 43-45 represent the third parable and second "A" section. Herein the results of true discipleship and of authentic mutual influence are revealed. The logic of the text is simple. Good trees, like good people, produce good things; decayed trees and corrupt people give forth worthless and evil things. This section of the gospel comes full circle as it recalls the wisdom of Ben Sirach in today's first reading. Just as a person's speech (Sirach) reveals his/her mettle, so too do a person's deeds mirror the heart and mind that prompted them.

1. Better to be silent and be thought a fool than to speak and remove all doubt (Sirach).

2. Those who do not fear death's finality can bring joy and hope to this life (1 Corinthians).

3. It is easier to take reproof from a self-professed sinner than from a self-professed saint (Luke).

Ninth Sunday in Ordinary Time

How tempting it is to invent our own version of the gospel ... a comfortable and convenient interpretation that does not ruffle our pride or bend our will (Galatians). But only the authentic good news will truly witness to God's presence and attract others to the faith (1 Kings). When we cease to invent the gospel and learn to listen to its challenge, then we shall have experienced true faith. In that experience we shall recognize Jesus as Lord and Savior (Luke).

1 Kings 8:41-43. Originally considered one book and classified among the prophets in the Jewish scriptures, 1 and 2 Kings treat of four centuries of Israel's history, from the death of David to the destruction of Jerusalem. Thoroughly informed with the theological perspective of the Deuteronomic historian, 1 and 2 Kings reflect the basic ideology that Israel's successes were due to covenantal fidelity and its failures were the result of covenantal infractions. Because the author of Kings wrote at a time later than the events he chronicled (Noth says ca. 550 B.C.E.), he had the advantage of hindsight as he interpreted for his contemporaries the ebb and flow of their political accomplishments.

At the time of Kings' final editing, the temple built by Solomon had already been destroyed and with it the central system of worship that Josiah had initiated. Therefore, the words attributed to Solomon that comprise today's first reading probably stirred bittersweet emotions among the exiles. On the one hand, they grieved over glories lost and, on the other hand, they were inspired to hope as to what the future might hold. As they grieved, the Kings' author advised his fellow religionists to accept their suffering as deserved punishment for their transgressions. As they hoped, he reminded them of the faithfulness of Yahweh and of his promises concerning the continuance of the Davidic dynasty.

Part of a longer section concerning the dedication of the first temple, today's pericope is purported to be part of the actual prayer uttered by Solomon on that momentous occasion. P. Ellis has preferred to call Solomon's prayer a set of three discourses (vv. 15-21, 23-53, 56-61), each of which underscores the basic theological teachings of the exilic author. In each of the discourses, the eternity of the temple was compared to the perpetuity promised to David in 2 Samuel 7:14.

Today's text, part of the second discourse, accents the international flavor Solomon brought to his reign. The foreigner prayed for in verse 41 was not the resident alien (*ger*) whose rights were guaranteed by Israel's law (Numbers 15:14); rather, the term *nokri* (foreigner) referred to those who were drawn to acknowledge the strict monotheism and ethical integrity of Israelite religion, e.g., Naaman the Syrian (2 Kings 5) and the widow of Shunem (2 Kings 4).

An excellent complement for today's gospel wherein the centurion was drawn by faith to Jesus, this pericope from Kings reminds the believing community of its role as witness to God for a world in search of meaning. No longer drawn by the physical sign of God's presence, viz., the temple, all sincere seekers of the truth should be attracted by those who are themselves living temples testifying to the presence of a caring God for all peoples of every nation.

Galatians 1:1-2, 6-10. H. D. Betz has called Paul's letter to the Galatians "the first complete statement of Gentile Christian theology and thus its oldest self-definition, in which the new Christian religion is separated (as far as we can tell, for the first time) from Judaism." Actually addressed to a group of churches in southern (some argue for a northern locale) Asia Minor, the letter to the Galatians was written ca. 54-55 C.E. While in Ephesus, Paul had received news that his work in Galatia was being undermined and his qualifications to preach in Jesus' name were being attacked. As a cursory reading of his missionary exploits will reveal (see Acts), Paul was dogged by a certain group of overly zealous Jewish Christians who sought to undo Paul's work and/or to correct what they regarded as a misrepresented and diluted version of the good news.

When these Judaizers, following in Paul's wake, made their way through Galatia, they attempted to convince the gentile Christians that they had been somehow cheated, that Paul had given them an abbreviated type of Christianity and that they had come to preach the full message, viz., that all who would believe in Jesus and be saved must come to Jesus through Moses. In other words, the Judaizers insisted on the continued validity of the Torah, of circumcision, of dietary regulations, etc., and made these requisites for all would-be Christians.

The letter to the Galatians is Paul's apologia; it is at once vehement and firm. Over and against the Judaizers, Paul reaffirmed the good news as he had first preached it in Galatia. Faith in Jesus, claimed Paul, is the only requisite for salvation; because of Jesus' saving deeds, those who believe are thereby freed from every encumbrance. Besides the encumbrances of sin and death, Paul also regarded the law as an impediment to grace. While it once had validity, Jesus' saving words and works had made the law unnecessary. So also were the trappings of the law (circumcision, rules of clean, unclean, etc.) rendered obsolete.

P. Wrightman understands Paul's defense of the faith in Galatians as a decisive doctrinal fork in the road for the early church. At the fork, the church was given the choice of two roads to follow. One road sign read "Salvation through

Works"; and the other beckoned "Salvation through Faith." Whereas the Judaizers by their emphasis on the law were accenting works and were thereby militating against faith, Paul called for that quality of faith that would express itself in good works.

Above all else, Paul understood salvation to be the gift of a gracious loving God for a sinful humanity. His own conversion experience had taught him that Jesus was the means whereby the Father had manifested his saving will. A staunch and upright Jew who had kept the works of the law in order to be justified, Paul encountered the risen Jesus and through his conversion experience became a believer, i.e., one who by faith hopes to appropriate the undeserved and unmerited saving gifts of God.

Besides attacking the gospel he preached, the Judaizers also denigrated Paul's claim to be an apostle. This provoked Paul to redefine the concept of apostle, giving it a broader connotation than had been previously accepted. Whereas the Judaizers understood the term "apostle" to apply to the Twelve who had witnessed the ministry, death and resurrection appearances of Jesus, Paul claimed that his experience (Acts 9) of the risen Lord and the subsequent mandate he received (Acts 13:1-3) fitted him for the apostolic ministry.

If Galatians can be called Paul's quick and passionate first reaction to the faith-versus-works debate, Romans may be regarded as the apostle's later premeditated but no less passionate response to the same issue. A comparative study of the two works is its own reward.

Luke 7:1-10. Although it was probably not his primary intention, Luke has provided in this gospel pericope an excellent illustration of Paul's argument (in Galatians) concerning the faith versus law (works) issue. Included also in their gospels by John and Matthew, the narrative of the Roman centurion has been accented by Luke with certain details that distinguish it from the other versions. For example, Luke has placed this episode as the first in a series of episodes that reflect the receptivity to Jesus of various groups in Palestinian society (viz., centurion, 7:1-10; inhabitants of Naim, 7:11-17; all Judah, 7:17; disciples of John the Baptizer, 7:18-23; sinful woman, 7:36-50; etc.).

In the case of the centurion, the reception accorded Jesus was an exemplary one, made all the more remarkable by the way Luke described the Roman soldier. Only Luke lays so much emphasis on the qualities of the Roman. A gentile soldier, probably stationed in Capernaum, the centurion may have been in the service of Herod Antipas as a leader of mercenary troops; or he may have been a police or customs official (C. Talbert). In any event, he seemed to be an admirer of the Jewish religion and had acted in such a manner as to earn the respect of the elders. As S. MacLean Gilmour has pointed out, there *is* extra-biblical evidence that a Roman soldier was instrumental in the erection of a synagogue for the Jewish people. An Egyptian inscription from the second century B.C.E. tells of a pagan official who assisted in the building of a synagogue at Athribis.

Respectful of the Jewish restrictions concerning contact with gentiles, the centurion sent two delegations to meet with Jesus. First, he requested the elders to intercede for him on behalf of his fatally ill servant. When these approached Jesus, they praised the centurion, stating that because of what he had done for the Jews, he "*deserved*" (v. 5) Jesus' favor and attention. This statement reflects the Jewish attitude with regard to the law, works and salvation. By doing the good works of the law, Jews believed they would deserve and thereby merit the favor of God. But the *Christian* attitude toward the law, works and salvation is reflected in the person of the centurion.

When Jesus was not far from his home, the gentile sent word to him through his friends. Tell him, he said, "I am not worthy . . . just give an order and my servant will be cured." So humble was the gentile's declaration and so full of faith was he that Jesus was *amazed* (v. 9). Only twice in all of the New Testament do the Christian authors so describe Jesus—here and in Mark 6:6, where Jesus' amazement was provoked by the *lack* of faith of the people.

Aware that he was not worthy of favor and that he did not deserve or merit Jesus' attention, the gentile illustrates the truth that salvation is a free gift of God for an unworthy people. In the face of such an undeserved gift, the only appropriate response is humble, trusting faith. It is significant that this gentile's message to Jesus has been incorporated into the prayer of the eucharistic assembly. As each believer makes bold to share in the saving life of the Lord Jesus, we pray, "Lord, I am not worthy to receive you, but only say the word and I shall be healed."

Because of his awareness of his place before Jesus and because of his faith in Jesus' power to save, the centurion stands out in Luke's gospel as a model for gentile believers. Moreover, he prefigures a similar event in Acts 10-11 wherein another upright centurion came to faith. Notice that in Luke's gospel the centurion never spoke *directly* to Jesus; nor does Luke mention that he ever *saw* Jesus. In this he is a model for all who have not seen and yet believe. Notice also, that the Jews acted as intermediaries for the meeting between Jesus and the gentile. This was to be the special role of Israel in the economy of salvation: to bring all nations to the one God, Yahweh. Yet, as Luke has illustrated in his two volume work, this was not always the case.

Finally, the centurion's testimony to the power of Jesus' word to accomplish its purpose cast Jesus as messiah in the same light as God himself. Familiar with Jewish traditions, the centurion may have had in mind Psalm 107:20 wherein

Yahweh is praised for saving the suffering by a word of his mouth. The power to effect his purpose by a word also compared Jesus' action to God who created the universe by simply declaring that it be so: . . . "Let there be light . . . ," etc. (Genesis). No doubt Jesus' contemporaries and Luke's readers were also reminded of the prophetic text, "My word will not return to me empty without accomplishing all that it was sent to do" (Isaiah 55:11). For the centurion, the word of Jesus communicated healing and salvation. Today, for all who pray with similar humility and faith, the word will effect the same wonders!

1. The living temple of the believer reminds the world of the presence of God and calls the world to believe (Kings).

2. Those who alter the gospel to make it appealing and palatable have not understood its challenge (Galatians).

3. True faith does not dictate how God should act; true faith listens for his word (Luke).

10th Sunday in Ordinary Time

The loving giver and preserver of all life, God is unjustly accused when conceived of as a vengeful, punishing despot who wrests the breath of life from the weak and sinful (1 Kings). In the words and works of Jesus, the mind and purpose of the Father have been made known. Caretaker of the poor and help of the sinner, God restores life to the spirit as well as to the body (Luke). His mercy supersedes the law and tempers strict justice with love (Galatians).

1 Kings 17:17-24. In the first and second book of Kings the prophetic cycles of Elijah and Elisha contribute a liberal blend of legend and saga within the context of certain historical events. Each story in the two cycles portrayed the prophets as men of God and thereby established the authority of their word (over and against those who opposed that word) and validated the God for whom the prophets spoke. Illustrating the prophets' effectiveness in a series of prediction fulfillment stories, the authors of Kings asserted again and again the superiority of Yahweh over the baals of Canaan, Phoenicia, etc.

Elijah was from Tishbe in Gilead and served his people as prophet in the first half of the ninth century B.C.E., during the reigns of Ahab and Ahaziah (ca. 869-849 B.C.E.). Serious religious and political crises plagued Israel during this period. Ahab engaged his people in a series of wars against the Arameans but later allied his troops unsuccessfully with the Aramean armies when the Assyrian armies of Shalmanesar III threatened. On the religious front, Ahab was an even less effective leader. Indifferent to the religion of his forefathers, Ahab permitted his wife, the Tyrian princess Jezebel, to build a temple to her baal, Melqart, in Samaria (1 Kings 16:32). Jezebel also imported prophets from Phoenicia to convince the already interested Israelites of the benefits of her native religion.

Like a courageous warrior, Elijah faced both his king and queen, fearlessly denouncing their faults and predicting God's wrath in the form of a drought if they did not comply with the truth. For his efforts, Elijah was forced to escape into the desert where he was protected and guided by the Lord. Having taken refuge with a widow and her son in a place called Zarephath, Elijah promised the poor woman that, because of her generous hospitality to him, her food supply would not be depleted until such time as the drought would end and she could again provide for her needs (1 Kings 17:8-16). At this point in the cycle today's first reading appears.

Even though the woman recognized the prophet as a man of God, she attributed the death of her son to the fact that Elijah was a guest in her home. In a sense, she believed that Elijah's presence had the effect of calling down the judgment of a vengeful God, because of her sins: "Have you come to me to call attention to my guilt and to kill my son?" This erroneous attitude was prevalent during the Old Testament period (recall Job, Ezekiel 18: 1-32) and even survived into the Christian era (John 9:2). Like her contemporaries, the woman believed that God punished the sins of the parents in their children and vice-versa *and that physical sufferings, etc., were due to sin.* Elijah's action in restoring the woman's son to life was intended to correct the notion that God vengefully willed death as punishment for sin. Indeed, Elijah's wonderful deed underscored the loving pardon of God for the sinner whom he wished to heal and enliven.

The mysterious manner in which Elijah resuscitated the boy may have given the impression that his was a magical power like the sorcerers of Jezebel. But the ritual of stretching himself three times over the boy in the secrecy of the upper room has been shown to be an act of God, by virtue of the prayer that accompanied the prophet's actions.

Galatians 1:11-19. From the first decades of the Jesus movement, insightful believers were aware that monolithic concurrence on every aspect of theology, christology and missiology was not possible or even desirable. Paul's ideas with regard to the gentile mission and the relation of

Christianity to its Jewish matrix differed at times from those of his contemporaries in Jerusalem. So too, Stephen and Philip exercised their ministries among the Hellenist Christians in a manner distinct from their Jewish-Christian counterparts. Nevertheless, the power of the Spirit enabled the plurality of ideas and methods to merge into one viable and effective community with one purpose and one mission. At times, however, conflicts arose due to hostile elements whose misguided efforts threatened to stifle the church's growth. In Galatia, Paul encountered such a situation as is reflected in today's second reading and in the rest of his letter to the churches of Galatia.

Originally, the Galatai were an Indo-Aryan tribe related to the Celts who had settled in the central Asia Minor valley of Halys during the third century B.C.E. In 25 B.C.E., Caesar Augustus made the area a Roman province called Galatia. When Paul travelled through Galatia on his first missionary journey, he met in the various communities a mixed but predominantly gentile population. There he brought the gospel of Jesus to those who had no Jewish background and consequently his preaching did not emphasize the role of the Mosaic law or circumcision. Rather, Paul preached the good news of Jesus and taught his hearers the decisive role of *faith* in the economy of salvation.

Shortly after Paul left the Galatian province, he received news that certain agitators (Galatians 1:7) had been circulating among his new Christian converts in an effort to convince them that Paul's had not been the true gospel but a diluted version. Moreover these opponents impugned Paul's authority and tried to convince the gentile Christians that, in order to become authentic followers of Christ, they first had to adhere to the law, the ritual of circumcision, etc.

Usually the name "Judaizers" had been applied to those who attacked Paul and his work and they appeared to represent a sort of Christian Pharisaism. Upon hearing the trouble the Judaizers were fomenting, Paul reacted with surgical swiftness, eager to cut out of the gentile mission the hostile and, according to Paul, anti-Christian elements. Galatians is a polemical message, the earliest and first complete statement of gentile Christian theology. In it, Paul warned that the acceptance of the Judaizers' demand would be contrary to the gospel which insisted on freedom vis-a-vis the law. To defend himself against the accusations leveled against him Paul recalled his Damascus encounter. He explained that his gospel was not of human contrivance, but a result of divine revelation (Galatians 1:18) just as was Peter's (Matthew 16:16).

As J. Fitzmeyer has observed, Paul's conversion experience enlightened him about the essential dynamic character of the gospel, not necessarily its form. As is evident in Paul's writings, he did receive the tradition from authoritative human witnesses; this he handed on to his proselytes. By detailing (vv. 13ff) his life as a Jew and his zealous efforts *against* the church, Paul explained that the Mosaic law and its practices had hardly prepared him for his dramatic about-face and preaching of freedom from the law. These he had learned directly from Christ, whose apostle he was. Like Jeremiah and like the Isaian suffering servant, Paul claimed to have been called from the womb and commissioned to preach to the gentiles.

Differing from Luke's account in Acts, Paul claimed to have traveled to Arabia immediately after his conversion and mandate. Probably, Arabia should be understood as the Nabatean kingdom of King Aretas IV Philopatris in Transjordan, east and south of Damascus. Only casually did Paul mention his later visit to Jerusalem but the verb (*historesai:* v. 18) gives a clue to his purpose. Translated "get to know" in most translations, the verb actually means "to receive information," "to inquire." Therefore it is clear Paul *did* consult with the Jerusalem church authorities. Still, his original methods and insights were respected and helped the Jesus movement to survive the Judaizers and to recognize its essentially universal character.

Luke 7:11-17. This is one of the three occasions on which Jesus restored a dead person to life, but the restoration of the widow's son is unique to Luke's gospel. All three synoptics have recorded the raising of Jairus' daughter and only John has narrated the sign of Lazarus. Because the Nain story has been told by Luke alone, the reader should be aware of certain Lucan themes and emphases. For example, the fact that the story centers upon a woman, and a *widowed* woman at that, reflects the evangelist's penchant for showing Jesus' concern for the disadvantaged of society. Also, the whole event has been cast in such a way as to recall the same deed as performed by the prophet Elijah (see first reading). By presenting Jesus in the same light as the ninth century prophet, who had become an eschatological figure connected with the advent of the messiah, Luke underscored the actions of Jesus as having eschatological and messianic significance.

However, it is clear in the narrative that Luke did not wish to present Jesus *only* as an Elijah figure. Indeed, the evangelist has stressed the *difference* and superiority of Jesus' power by explaining that he healed *with a word*. There are none of the mysterious rituals (stretching out, breathing, etc.) in Jesus' simple actions. Moreover, whereas Elijah performed his rite over the boy *three* times and prayed to God for success, Jesus had power of himself to effect what he willed. While Luke wished his readers to *remember* Elijah, he did not want them to misconstrue Jesus' identity. While Elijah was anticipated as herald of the kingdom and of a renewed humanity, Jesus *was himself that kingdom* and the bringer of a new life to all of humankind.

Nain (modern day Nein) was a town six miles southeast of Nazareth in the valley of Jezreel. Later Jewish tradition renamed it Naim which in Hebrew means "pleasant." The funeral procession that Jesus halted was obviously accompanied by relatives and friends. Probably there were also the traditional professional mourners and dirge singers. Archaeologists in this century have discovered rock graves just east of the city; it is quite possible this was the site used by the town in antiquity. Because Luke used a rare and technical medical term in v. 15 to describe the man's action ("the dead man *sat up*"; also in Acts 9:40), some scholars have cited this text as further proof of the evangelist's medical background. "Fear" (v. 16) was the customary reaction to a manifestation of wondrous power. Followed immediately by the crowd's praising God, the response to Jesus' work indicated that his was seen as a *divine* ability.

It is significant that faith was not mentioned as a motive for Jesus' action; indeed, from the story, it would appear that compassion had moved him to act. This act, plus the nature of the miracle, underscored Jesus' work as a signal of the messianic era. Jewish tradition anticipated the age of the messiah as one in which all the suffering and the poor would be restored (Isaiah 61:1, 35:5-6). In addition, there was also a belief that, at the coming of the eschatological period, there would be a general resurrection of those Israelites who had died before the eschaton (Isaiah 26:19, 2 Maccabees 7:9-36, Daniel 12:2-3). That Luke wished his readers to see in Jesus the realization of all messianic hopes is further emphasized by his designation of Jesus as "the Lord." Used for the first time in this pericope, "the Lord" would thenceforth be repeated many times in Luke's gospel as a divine title for Jesus. *Ho kyrios* is the Greek translation for the divine name, Yahweh. Its application to Jesus in the context of a life-giving miracle is all the more appropriate.

An examination of the context of this miracle with regard to the rest of the gospel would indicate that Luke had so placed it to prepare for the answer of Jesus to John the Baptizer's disciples in 7:22. When asked if he were the one to come, Jesus replied, "Go and report to John what you have seen and heard. The blind recover their sight, cripples walk, lepers are cured, the deaf hear, *dead men are raised to life* and the poor have the good news preached to them." In answering the needs of the blind, the deaf, the poor, etc., Jesus had answered as well the questions about his identity, his power and his saving purpose.

1. By divine power, Elijah restored life to the son while God's forgiveness restored life to the widowed mother (1 Kings).

2. The call to ministry is not necessarily contingent upon qualifications, background or heredity. Freely given, vocation is a grace that must be nurtured and developed by talent (Galatians).

3. Compassion motivates the disciples of Jesus to restore life to the forgotten lonely and the poor (Luke).

11th Sunday in Ordinary Time

If salvation were a strictly juridical system of justice then no one would escape the deserved sentence of death (2 Samuel). But even the greatest sinner can hope for happiness because God has introduced the merciful loophole of loving forgiveness into an otherwise unfeeling network of legal prescriptions (Galatians). Above and beyond the law, the saving power of Jesus' death assures every believing and repentant sinner of the joy of reconciliation and redemption (Luke).

2 Samuel 12:7-10, 13. Each of the three selections for today's liturgy represents a veritable celebration of the fact of God's forgiveness. In the first reading, David's sincere repentance for his sins of murder, adultery and deceit is met by God's gracious and loving pardon.

Excerpted from one of the most masterful pieces of literature in the Bible, the pericope from 2 Samuel picks up the story of David and Bathsheba near its conclusion. Although he had inherited Saul's house and possessions, which would have included his harem (v. 8), David had become enamored of the beautiful Bathsheba, the wife of one of his lieutenants. Determined to have her for his own, David plotted against his loyal soldier Uriah and sent him into battle during Israel's second campaign against the Ammonites. His plan against Uriah successful, David took the dead man's widow for his own and soon the child of their illicit union was born.

At this point in the narrative Nathan, acting like an external conscience, confronted David with his guilt. Nathan told his king the touching story of the poor man with one ewe lamb who was the victim of a rich man's greed. Instead of killing one of the many lambs in his own flock in order to entertain a guest, the rich man took the poor man's pet lamb and slaughtered it (2 Samuel 12:1-4).

When David reacted in righteous fury at such a heartless and unjust deed ("This man deserves to die"), the prophet used the occasion to hurl the burden of his message and the point of his story at his king, "*You* are the man!" Confronted with the truth of his actions, David did not act defensively. Nor did he deny Nathan's accusation or use his power to silence the prophet.

According to the law, David's sin was punishable by the death penalty (Exodus 21:37). But, as is clear in the narrative, God's forgiveness superseded the law and David was granted the gift of continued life. Nevertheless, his sins did not go unpunished. The death of his and Bathsheba's son was interpreted according to the Jewish concept that the father's sins would be punished in his offspring. Later in the chronicles of David, his sons Amnon (2 Samuel 13:29), Absalom (2 Samuel 18:14-15) and Adonias (1 Kings 2:25) would also perish by the sword.

Traditionally Psalm 51 has been regarded as David's prayer of repentance on this occasion. In both the psalm and in today's reading, there is an acknowledgment that the injustice done against another is a sin against *God himself* (Psalm 51: "having sinned against none other than you"; 2 Samuel 12:13: "I have sinned against the Lord"). The story of David's sin and the forgiveness of God that saved him from the law's sentence of death prepare the way for the deeper understanding and experience of forgiveness made available to all sinners through the saving cross of Jesus.

Galatians 2:16, 19-21. An emotional piece of literature alternating between stern, angry condemnation and warm, affectionate pleading, the letter to the churches of Galatia is Paul's impassioned defense of his gospel and his apostleship. Today's pericope is from the first major section of the letter (1:10—2:21) in which Paul stated the thesis which he would later develop in detail in his longer letter to the Romans, viz., a person is not justified by the law but by faith in the crucified savior, Jesus.

As a Jew and as a member of the Pharisaic party, Paul could speak firsthand about his experience of the law. Strict observance, even *perfect* attention to the minutest prescription of the law, could not achieve what Jesus had achieved for all believers through the sacrifice of his saving death. Freedom from sin and death, and justification or "being in the right with God" are the gracious gifts of God. The law with its concentration on external observance is not capable of changing the heart or preventing death. Nor could the law achieve perfect reconciliation with God through the remission of sins. Only the free gifts of God's grace, made available through Jesus' death, are capable of pronouncing a person just (v. 18: *dikaioo*).

Greek verbs ending in *oo* are usually causative, producing the quality expressed by their root. Therefore, Paul's usage of *dikaioo* would seem to demand a deeper sense, not of merely being *pronounced* just (or upright) but of being *made* just. The only response appropriate to such an unmerited and gracious gift, taught Paul, is faith. Faith is the attitude that conditions the believer for receiving God's gifts. By faith, the person opens him/herself to accept God's love revealed in Jesus and to respond to that love by a life conformed to the good news.

Because of grace and faith, Paul was able to state, "Christ lives in me" (v. 20). As J. Fitzmeyer has observed, "The perfection of the Christian life is expressed here, since it is not merely an existence dominated by a new psychological motivation. Faith in Christ doesn't substitute a new norm or goal of action. Rather, it reshapes man anew internally, supplying him with a new principle of activity on the ontological level of his very being." Fitzmeyer goes on to explain that faith in Christ and the act of Christ living in the Christian result in a symbiosis of the human person with the glorified Christ. Because of the resurrection, Christ has become a "vivifying spirit" and the vital principle of all Christian activity.

In its context, Paul's argument for grace and faith over and above the law was an expansion of his criticism of Peter at Antioch (2:11-21). Paul claimed that Peter was scandalizing the Antiochene community because he had withdrawn from the practice of eating with gentile converts. As illustrated in Acts 10, Peter had made great strides in accepting gentile Christians as equals at the table of the Lord but he had later succumbed to the pressure of the Judaizers. Their insistence upon the law as a necessary factor in the process of salvation was tantamount to negating the work and saving death of Jesus. Paul regarded this as a fatal step backward and a threat to the gospel of freedom he preached. As a champion of that freedom, he remained firm in his efforts to preserve the integrity of the good news for all Christians.

Luke 7:36—8:3. Dinner scenes were a distinctly favorite context for the author of the third gospel. Some have regarded those narratives which portrayed Jesus as the invited guest at a meal as belonging to a special literary form called the symposium genre. In the course of narrating the events at the dinner, Luke adeptly drew together material from the oral tradition known to him and from his written sources. He also used these occasions to feature some unchronicled parables, unique to his gospel and especially illustrative of his major theological themes.

In the particular scene that comprises today's gospel, the evangelist has reworked his sources to create an episode, the dinner at Simon's house. During the dinner

Jesus is presented as teaching a lesson through the vehicle of a parable; the parable in turn serves to interpret and explain the episode within which it appears. The lesson of the entire narrative (parable and context) is the fact of Jesus' power to participate in the divine prerogative of forgiving sin. Forgiveness of sin, or justification as Paul chose to call it, was due to the free and grace-filled love of God. With her sins remitted, i.e., once justified by God's gracious act, the woman responded with a great and sincere outpouring of love, an example for all believing and forgiven sinners.

Simon the Pharisee had invited Jesus to his home. His rather rude and inhospitable behavior toward Jesus stands out in blatant contrast to the attitude of the forgiven woman. As one who prided himself on his strict observance of the law, Simon was appalled not only by the woman's actions but by Jesus' reaction to her. It may seem strange that the woman was able to enter the house at all. However, according to social customs of the ancient Near Eastern world, dining rooms, especially those of the rich and famous, were left open to the public. Uninvited guests and curious onlookers could pass in and out of the room at will. Those who wished could take a seat near the wall and listen to the repartee between the host and his invited guests.

Having gained entry to Simon's house in this way, the woman overstepped the bonds of social acceptability and made her way to Jesus. That Jesus permitted her extravagant show of love without condition prompted Simon to criticize, albeit silently, the authenticity of Jesus as a prophet. In excellent style, Luke has shown Jesus as the true prophet, par excellence, able to read even Simon's unspoken thoughts.

The interchange between Jesus and Simon has been called a Socratic interrogation since it follows that form of Hellenistic rhetoric used by both Jewish and Christian teachers to organize their material (C. Talbert). According to the structure of the interrogation, (1) a question is asked by the opponent ("If this man *were* a prophet, he would know," v. 39); (2) this is followed by a counter question ("Which of them was more grateful," v. 42); (3) which forces an answer from the opponent ("He I presume to whom he remitted the larger sum," v. 43); (4) and concludes with a refutation of opponent's ideas on the basis of his own forced answer ("I tell you that is why her many sins are forgiven," v. 47).

By means of his interrogation and the parable of the two debtors, Jesus led Simon to understand, at least logically and intellectually, the woman's actions and Jesus' attitude toward her. Indeed, the woman who was outside the law had been given what Simon, for all his scrupulous adherence to the law, had not been able to achieve, i.e., forgiveness and the joy of being justified or "being right" with God. As in the first and second readings, today's gospel juxtaposes the correct understanding of forgiveness or justification by God over and against the law's ineffectiveness and limitations.

Because of the ambiguity of the statement, "that is why her many sins are forgiven—because of her great love" (v. 47), it may seem that the woman's love *precipitated* God's forgiveness. Rather, it should be understood that her ability to love, and to love greatly, was due to the fact of her having been forgiven. The word *hoti* in Greek should be understood in a special causal sense which gives not the reason *why* a fact is so but *whereby* it is known to be so. The New English Bible averts the ambiguity by translating v. 47, "I tell you, her great love proves that her many sins have been forgiven; where little has been forgiven, little love is shown."

Jesus' pronouncement, "Your sins are forgiven; your faith has been your salvation" (v. 48), is a confirmation of what had occurred, i.e., the divine initiative, reaching out to bestow forgiveness or justification, meeting with the open human response of faith. This further implication was also meant to impress Simon and others who relied on the law that their refusal to respond in faith to Jesus (and therefore to God) would someday find *them* on the outside, looking in, at the great banquet of the messianic kingdom.

In the final verses of the gospel (8:1-3), Luke has reemphasized Jesus' special predilection for those who understood their need for justification and for the disadvantaged members of society. Those who had been healed physically, spiritually and psychologically, women and the poor, had a special place with Jesus in the kingdom he had come to bring upon the earth. The law that had raised objections to such people and placed barriers against them was no longer operative. Because of Jesus, the free gift of God's justification welcomed *all* believers to salvation.

1. Holiness does not consist in never having sinned but in the ability to recognize one's failures and to seek reconciliation (2 Samuel).

2. Forgiveness is not a judicial procedure dependent on the law but part of a personal relationship with a loving God (Galatians).

3. The joy of being forgiven expands the heart's capacity for greater loving (Luke).

12th Sunday in Ordinary Time

In anticipation and out of their need, Jesus' contemporaries had fashioned a variety of dreams about who the messiah would be and how he would conduct his saving campaign. Rarely, if ever, did they conceive of suffering as a battleplan or death as a strategy (Luke). That the saving grace would come through the demise of their king was an altogether new revelation (Zechariah). That they would become children of God and family to all of humankind was a blessing they had not even thought to hope for (Galatians).

Zechariah 12:10-11. As is the case with many of the biblical books, the work ascribed to the prophet Zechariah is actually a compilation of a variety of material that spanned at least two centuries, the product of two (or more) distinct hands. Chapters 1-8 have been attributed to the sixth century Zechariah, son of Berechiah, son of Iddo. A contemporary of Haggai, Zechariah worked among his people during the crucial period of reconstruction after the Babylonian exile. Chapters 9-14 reflect a later period in Israel's history, probably the early Greek period when Alexander the Great was making his power felt in Palestine.

In the two verses that comprise today's first reading, Deutero-Zechariah has put before his people a message of repentance and regeneration. As one whose thought was dominated by the final conflict between Yahweh (with his people) and evil forces opposed to God's saving plans (the nations), the prophet assured his people of an eventual eschatological victory. However, he warned that victory would be accomplished only through a process of suffering and purification.

As God's people, Israel would be brought low for a time (10:6, 13:7-9, 14:2), would suffer (12:10, 13:2) and thereby learn the value of repentance (12:10—13:1). Following its purification (13:1-6), Israel's covenant relationship with God would once again be renewed (13:9), and the eternal kingdom would be forever established. Not alone in their struggles, the people would know the compassionate guidance of their shepherd-king (11:4-18, 13:7-9) and the mysterious leadership of the suffering, transpierced one introduced in today's pericope (12:10-14).

There are obvious affinities between the suffering one, here described by Deutero-Zechariah, and the servant of the Deutero-Isaiah songs (especially Isaiah 52:13—53:12). As P. Lamarche has observed, "the figure of the Messiah who suffers for us (Isaiah 53) is completed by the figure of the shepherd who leads his flock into purifying trials (Zechariah 13:7-9). The image of the Messiah who saves us by his suffering and death is completed by the image of the shepherd who is pierced and who by his death leaves the repentant people in the position that they must look for everything from the generous mercy of God. No wonder that both Christ and the evangelists used both Deutero-Isaiah and Deutero-Zechariah to give a complete picture of the mission and passion of the Messiah."

With the death of the one who had been thrust through or pierced, there would occur an outpouring of a spirit on the people of Israel. Such an outpouring had come to be associated with the eschatological era (Ezekiel 39:29; Joel 3:1). It is particularly significant that the spirit would be one of *grace* and *petition* and, as a result of its outpouring, the people would grieve and mourn. In comparing this text to the similar "new heart" text of Ezekiel (36:16-28), it seems clear that the prophet would have us understand that it is God himself who grants to his people the interior disposition that leads them to repentance and to conversion.

T. Maertens has described today's text as a piece of very advanced theology. The prophet recognized that repentance is *in itself* a gift of God which enlightens a person to beg forgiveness and that this gift has been closely associated with the mysterious mediation of a pierced victim. Contemplation of the victim ("They shall look on him") inspired mourning "as for an only son." The New Testament authors drew upon this text in describing Jesus' status as God's only Son and therefore as the ultimate, precious gift (John 1:18, 3:16; Colossians 1:15).

"Hadad-Rimmon" was identified by Jerome as a city near Megiddo which was the site of annual ritual mourning for the two ancient Syrian gods Hadad (storm god, Baal Shamem in Ugaritic texts) and Rimmon (weather god). Megiddo was also the site of Josiah's death in battle 609 B.C.E. as recalled in the Syrian rendering of today's text. For his efforts to reform his people and thereby reconcile them with Yahweh, the slain Josiah was mourned; his life and efforts were only a shadow of the reconciliation and renewal to be achieved by the saving sacrifice of God's only Son Jesus.

Galatians 3:26-29. After 1 and 2 Thessalonians, Galatians is Paul's earliest letter and one of the first written Christian documents. Composed in Ephesus ca. 54 or 55, Galatians reflects the fact that, even in its first generation, the early Christian community faced serious issues that threatened its unity and development. One of these issues was the conflict between Jewish and gentile believers and their disagreement concerning the place of the Mosaic law in the economy of salvation. In Galatians, Paul underscored the importance of the Christian life of faith as a saving *relationship* initiated by God. By God's grace and not human merit, i.e., not through works of the law, believers have been blessed with salvation. By responding to the Father through faith in Jesus Christ, believers have been privileged to become children (sons, v. 26) of God.

By the saving work of Jesus, all have been reconciled to God, or justified as Paul chose to call it. Those who believe and are baptized into Christ share, without distinction as to race, social status or sex, in the fruits of justification, viz., the forgiveness of sins and the union with God as his beloved children: "All are one in Christ Jesus." Baptized into (*eis*) Christ expresses the incorporation of the believer into the whole process of redemption. The reference to being "clothed with Christ" (v. 27) as with a garment was a figure familiar to both Jewish and gentile Christians. In the Greek mystery religions, those who wished to be initiated into the secret cult put on the robe of the god, thereby identifying with him. But Paul no doubt had in mind the Old Testament usage of the term wherein being clothed signified the acceptance of a new moral disposition (Job 29:14, 2 Chronicles 6:41). Justified by Christ, baptized into Christ, clothed with Christ, the union of believers with God and therefore with one another supersedes all other bonds. Therefore human standards of discrimination, i.e., Jew vs. Greek, slave vs. free, male vs. female, have no validity and should not be indulged in by the believing community.

Luke 9:18-24. All the episodes in chapter nine of Luke's gospel take on added significance when seen in the light of Herod's question asked at the beginning of the chapter: "Who is this man. . . .?" (9:9). By way of response, Luke has narrated the event of the loaves (vv. 10-17), wherein Jesus is identified as the giver of life-giving bread. In the transfiguration scene (vv. 28-36), the evangelist has answered the question of Jesus' identity and mission. Greater than the Old Testament prophets, greater even than the law, Jesus was portrayed as the one through whom God would speak and work among his people. In curing the possessed boy (vv. 37-43), Jesus was revealed as the power of goodness who could control and conquer evil. In today's gospel, Peter's answer to the question of Jesus' identity sums up and clarifies every other nuance of meaning in its explicit christological statement: "You are the messiah of God" (v. 20).

From the beginning of the 20th century, the historicity of Peter's confession has been called into question. Some have attributed the statement to a resurrection experience and believe the evangelist reflected the apostle's resurrection faith back into a ministry context. Others taking a more radical position (R. Bultmann, E. Kasemann) have denied that the statement has any historical basis in Peter's life and have instead attributed the confession to the faith of the early church. In the context of the ministry, Peter's answer should not be understood as a confession (or denial!) of Jesus' divinity. In other words, by calling Jesus "messiah," Peter obviously did not recognize Jesus as the incarnate Son of God and savior of the world. Full faith in Jesus and full recognition of him as a divine agent of salvation would come to Peter and the other disciples only after and because of the resurrection. But, Peter's designation of Jesus as "messiah of God" indicated his awareness of and hope in Jesus as the anointed one (not neccesarily divine) in whom all the Old Testament expectations could become realities.

That Peter and the others present were not yet cognizant of what Jesus' messiahship would mean has been reflected in the strict enjoinder to silence (v. 21). Fresh from the wonder of the loaves event Peter no doubt shared the popular messianic expectation of his contemporaries for a kingly, political, glorious figure, who would rout the Roman occupying forces and reestablish Israel again in its own right as a powerful earthly kingdom. But these conceptions were incongruous with the purpose and methods of Jesus. The prediction of the passion and death of Jesus (v. 22) served to correct the false notions of messiahship and to cast Jesus in the light of the suffering servant (Zechariah 12:10, Isaiah 53) and the apocalyptic Son of Man (Daniel).

Because of the studied and somewhat artificial (triple prediction) character of the passion predictions, some would deny their value as authentic sayings of Jesus. While it *does* seem clear the predictions have been reworked by the early Christian community in light of Jesus' saving death this should not lead to the radical conclusion that the notion of suffering and death was not original to Jesus during his ministry. Given his continuous criticism of the Jewish authorities and the antagonism these confrontations engendered, Jesus did not naively expect to avoid conflict in his life. Indeed, the brutal death of John the Baptizer was a clear indication that those whose message was unpopular with the powers that be would eventually suffer the consequences. Characteristically, Luke has indicated by the use of the word "must" (*dei*) that the passion and death of Jesus were not merely the reaction of an angry, insulted authority to an instigator, but were an integral part of God's foreordained plan of salvation (see also 4:43; 13:33; 17:25; 22:37; 24:7, 26, 44).

Following his Marcan source, Luke closely associated the cost and conditions of discipleship with the passion prediction. Again critics have debated the authenticity of this statement as an historical utterance of Jesus. Those who support the genuineness of the challenge have claimed that Jesus' reference to the cross is to be understood as a prophetic foreshadowing of the type of death he would die. Since the cross was a familiar enough form of execution in Roman occupied Palestine, the term *could* have been used by Jesus. Others attribute the reference to the evangelist and his post-resurrection community. Unlike his Marcan source, however, Luke has inserted "*daily*" as an adverbial modifier to the taking up of one's cross. By this addition Luke "changed the focus of discussion from the unique eschatological moment of death to the day-by-day struggle of following Jesus" (Fitzmeyer). Luke reapplied Jesus' words to the new situation of a persecuted church, waiting and preparing for a delayed parousia.

C. Talbert has expressed a unique insight with regard to the taking up of one's cross each day. Says Talbert, this should not be understood only in the sense of bearing the burdens of daily life. The cross was an instrument of death, carried by the condemned to the site of execution. Therefore, to take up one's cross daily means to live daily as a condemned person, as one who has been stripped of every form of worldly security, even physical existence. For such a person there is nothing and no one to whom there can be permanent attachments except to the one who has gone before, carrying his cross.

Jesus' concept of messiahship was intrinsically bound up with his challenge to discipleship. Both would be characterized by suffering, saving love. Both would be vindicated by the triumph of eternal life and joy.

1. Suffering is never attractive or desirable but at times it is the pathway to conversion and deeper faith (Zechariah).

2. Baptism is an initiation into a relationship that supersedes all other relationships and forms their basis (Galatians).

3. In the lifelong process of answering Jesus' question, "Who do you say I am?", believers learn the costly, daily lessons of discipleship (Luke).

13th Sunday in Ordinary Time

Called to discipleship, the responding believer: is challenged to sacrifice his past for an unforeseen future (1 Kings); is blessed with a freedom that enables him/her to serve others without self-interest (Galatians); is booked in a no-frills travel plan that involves hardship but offers an eternal and glorious destination (Luke).

1 Kings 19:16, 19-21. Central to each of the three readings for this celebration is the motif of the call or vocation of the believer. In the first reading, Elijah is depicted as mediating the prophetic mandate of Yahweh to Elisha; in the second reading from Galatians, Paul's words remind all believers of their call to freedom from the law and from sin; the gospel features Jesus' sober challenge to his would-be disciples.

In order to respond to their vocations as portrayed in these three pericopes, those summoned were called to relinquish their ties with the past so as to embrace in faith an unseen future. In each instance, however, the believer was not left to his/her own resources; on the contrary, the call of God blessed the believer with the grace to respond fully and effectively.

Part of a longer narrative that related Elijah's escape to Horeb and his encounter there with God (1 Kings 19:1-21), today's first reading introduces Elisha and assures the continuity of the word of God as spoken through the prophets. Moreover, the fact that Elijah was instructed by God to appoint Elisha as his successor is an indication that the call to the prophetic service was due to *divine* initiative and not merely a *personal* career choice.

Unlike the ecstatic and often frenetic "sons of the prophets" who camped outside villages and rendered their "divination" for a fee, Elijah and Elisha (like Samuel before them) were regarded as valid emissaries of God. As such, their words, i.e., their promises to God's people, were shown to be effective. In no less than 45 prophecy-fulfillment stories, the author of 1 and 2 Kings achieved his purpose of bolstering the faith of his contemporaries in exile that the word of God would never cease to speak for them.

With 12 yoke of oxen, Elisha would have been considered quite well-to-do (v. 19); since plows were usually pulled by one or two oxen, Elisha had at least 12 plows at work in his field when Elijah came upon him. The hairy mantle or cloak that Elijah threw over Elisha was the recognized and distinctive attire of the prophet (2 Kings 1:8; Zechariah 13:4, Matthew 3:4).

Called '*addereth* in Hebrew, the garment was usually made of camel or goat hair. In the gesture of casting the cloak over another, the owner of the garment signalled either ownership and responsibility (as in Ruth 3:9) or the investiture and initiation of a successor. Later, Elisha would take up this cloak for himself when his mentor was carried away in a whirlwind (2 Kings 2:13-15); in this symbolic act, the Kings' author explained that the Spirit had come to rest on Elisha.

When Elisha requested to say goodbye to his parents, the response of Elijah seems harsh. P. Ellis has suggested that his answer might simply mean, "Go ahead. Have I done anything to stop you?" That he was wholly committed to what lay ahead is shown in Elisha's magnanimous gesture of sacrificing his oxen on a fire made of his plowing tools! Turning away completely from his former livelihood and attaching himself completely to his new vocation, Elisha prefigures that generous renunciation and total gift of self that Jesus would ask of his disciples centuries later.

Galatians 5:1, 13-18. When Paul wrote to the Galatians about freedom, he had to qualify carefully his statements lest he be misunderstood as a proponent of licentiousness. Many of the Christians in the region of Galatia were gentile converts, whose former experiences of liberty were bound up in pagan self-indulgence. When Paul reminded them of the freedom to which they had been called in Christ, he was quick to say that it was not a freedom *for* lust but a freedom *from* it. Those who enjoyed the liberty of Christ were called to exercise that liberty in loving service, i.e., by loving their neighbors as themselves (v. 14). Paul understood this as the *fulfillment of the law*.

Since he had been vehement up to this point in his criticism of the law, how are readers of Galatians to understand this last Pauline reference (v. 14)? In his commentary on Galatians, P. Wrightman has suggested that Paul's notion of the law is best understood as comprising three distinct yet interrelated movements. In its initial phase, Paul's attitude toward the law is entirely negative; he sees it as unnecessary to salvation. "When the law asserts itself," says Wrightman, "as necessary for salvation, it becomes in effect an idol" (Galatians 5:4).

In response to the Judaizers who demanded that the Mosaic Torah be included in the Christian view of salvation, Paul rejected this notion outright. The sufficiency of Jesus' saving death entirely negated such syncretism; for this reason, Paul referred to the practice of the law, circumcision, dietary regulations, etc., as a second "yoke of slavery" (v. 1).

The second aspect of Paul's view of law consists in his assertion that salvation is God's free and undeserved gift to humanity. In his death and rising, Christ availed humanity of a new relationship with God as sons and daughters. Those who by faith appropriate the gift of salvation are to live accordingly.

The final movement in the Pauline notion of law understands Christian loving service as an *outgrowth* or *overflow* of the saving relationship believers enjoy with Christ. It is in this sense that Paul's statement about fulfilling the law should be understood (v. 14). Loving service or good works are a *consequence* of the believer's relationship with Christ, not a *requisite* for it; therefore, good works do not earn or merit salvation.

Centuries after Paul and in reaction to what he believed to be an over-emphasis on works by the church, Martin Luther stressed the necessity of "faith only" for salvation. "Sin strongly," declared the reformer, "but believe more strongly still!" Today, both mainline Lutherans and Catholics have come to a fuller understanding of the Pauline theology of faith, works and salvation.

In the final verses of this pericope, Paul compared the freedom to which Christians have been called as a life in the spirit and the slavery to the law and to sin as a life in the flesh. More than bodily existence or corporeality, *flesh* for Paul encompassed the entire person who chose self-sufficiency rather than a relationship with Christ. Spirit, on the other hand, is that quality of life enjoyed by the redeemed; these have chosen Christ in faith and by that choice have been transformed. Guided by the Spirit, i.e., by the will of God, these are the truly free, the truly loving, the truly fulfilled.

Luke 9:51-62. Scholarly consensus today agrees that Luke, in writing his version of the good news, relied heavily on Mark's gospel. Writing in the 80s C.E., Luke knew the earlier work and followed its basic structure and outline, using at least 55% of the material contained in Mark. But Luke had other sources as well (*Quelle*, Luke's own access to tradition, witnesses, etc.), and his theological concerns and pastoral interests caused him to depart from his Marcan source in marked fashion. Two of the more obvious departures have been called interpolations and omissions.

Today's gospel comprises the introduction to the so-called "Greater Interpolation" of Luke 9:51 to 19:28. Also called the travel account, this third major section in the Lucan work has been called an independent gospel within a gospel. Herein the author has traced the travels of Jesus to Jerusalem and has telescoped every parable, event and teaching within this section to emphasize the importance of the journey. Names of other villages and cities have been omitted so as to mention only Jerusalem as the site where salvation would be accomplished.

Geographical and chronological accuracy have been subordinated to the author's major concern: to invite his readers to trace Jesus' steps toward the greatest event in human history. Bound together by an inclusion that sets the tone for the entire passage, the section begins with Jesus being rejected by the Samaritans (9:51) and climaxes with the ultimate rejection of Jesus in Jerusalem (19:28).

C. Talbert has suggested that the function of the travel account is largely didactic. First, the reader is invited to understand his/her own following of Jesus as being on a journey or a pilgrimage through life. In Acts, Luke would refer to Christian discipleship as being on the Way (Acts 9:2, 19:9 etc.). Secondly, the believing reader is taught in no uncertain terms that the way of life to which Jesus calls is a journey that leads to death. Still, disciples on the way may be confident because Jesus has gone ahead, has endured the struggle and even death, and has emerged victorious.

Today's introduction to the travel account consists of two sections: (1) the rejection of Jesus and his disciples by the Samaritans (vv. 51-56), and (2) the challenges of discipleship. Evidently, James and John had earned their nickname "sons of thunder" (*Boanerges*). When they were shunned by the Samaritans, they requested that Jesus behave in a manner similar to that of the legendary Elijah who had called down fire from heaven to destroy two captains and 100 men sent by king Akaziah (2 Kings 1:10-12).

But Jesus was not Elijah and, as he had taught his disciples previously, his was a mission of mercy and forgiveness (Luke 6:27-35). O. Cullmann has suggested that the zealot-like tendency illustrated in James and John's attitudes was prevalent among Jesus' contemporaries and one that he worked hard to subdue and sublimate. Having redressed their wont for violence and revenge, Jesus continued to make his way to Jerusalem.

In the second portion of today's gospel, the cost of discipleship is made radically clear. Three would-be disciples of Jesus are presented and each is shown as misunderstanding the nature of the commitment that discipleship entails. The first would-be disciple (vv. 57-58) offers, "I will be your follower wherever you go." But this person had yet to learn the lesson that to follow (*akolouthein*) Jesus did not simply mean to travel the road behind. Rather, the following of discipleship entailed a symbiotic union with Jesus so that his way of life with all its suffering and pain would also be embraced by his disciple. Warning that homelessness and insecurity were part of the commitment, Jesus was "up front" about the rigors of following him.

To another would-be disciple, Jesus invited, "Come after me" (vv. 59-60). In the seemingly harsh interchange about burying his parents, the importance of priorities in the life of the disciple is emphasized. We are *not* to understand that the person's parents were dead and that Jesus was so unfeeling as to deny Jewish filial piety (Genesis 49:28-50:3; Tobit 4:3, 6:15).

No doubt, the would-be disicple's parents were alive and he found Jesus' call inconvenient. Let me wait, he may have thought, until my parents are gone . . . then I'll be free to come. How frequently in our own lives the call to follow is inconvenient and we excuse ourselves as not ready or too weary or too over-extended. But the urgency in the invitation is clear. C. Stuhlmueller suggests that Jesus' response (v. 60) be understood as "Let the spiritually dead bury the physically dead; mine is message of life!"

In the interchange with the third would-be disciple (vv. 61-62), the importance of single-heartedness is underscored. Those who glance away from a plow will make crooked furrows; the high claim of discipleship calls for resoluteness and determination.

Significantly, Luke has preserved the anonymity of the three would-be disciples. In this way, he has enabled the readers of the good news to see themselves in the context of the journey. As professed followers of Jesus, it devolves upon us to accept his challenge to single-hearted, detached and determined discipleship.

1. Those who relinquish their past attachments to embrace discipleship will be blessed with a new sense of belonging and purpose (1 Kings).

2. Called to freedom in Christ, believers are to exercise their liberty in loving service (Galatians).

3. Those who accept to follow Jesus may experience rejection and insecurity, but will never be without the strength of his grace and blessing (Luke).

14th Sunday in Ordinary Time

As brothers and sisters to all the world, the Lord Jesus sent forth his followers. They were to live simply, they were to love fiercely and they were to be undaunted in their daily encounters with sin and suffering (Luke). In returning to Jesus, they were to bring all whom they had found who were in need of comfort, pardon, joy and peace (Isaiah). By coming home together to the Father all would be healed; on the way all would be created anew by the merciful love of the cross (Galatians).

Isaiah 66:10-14. When describing the people of Israel and their relationship with God, the prophets drew upon a wealth of picturesque metaphors. One of the most popular of these comparisons was that of the bride and bridegroom—nuptial imagery. At the beginning of its history as a people, the covenant by which Israel was related to God was likened to a marriage bond. The wilderness years when Israel was totally dependent upon Yahweh for guidance, sustenance and protection were compared to the intimacy of a honeymoon. For sins of social injustice and religious syncretism that breached the terms of the covenant, Israel was called an unfaithful and adulterous wife. The exile in Babylon, with its shame and banishment from their homeland, was regarded as a period of forced separation from Israel's beloved spouse. Consequently, the return from exile was considered as a reconciliation between the chastised bride Israel and the forgiving husband Yahweh. In today's first reading, the nuptial imagery has come to full flower in the picture of

Jerusalem as a loving mother, nourishing and comforting her children in fulfilled peace.

From the final section of the book of Isaiah (chapters 56-66), attributed to one known simply as Trito-Isaiah, today's text is part of a longer poem concerning Jerusalem's restoration. Whereas his predecessor, Deutero-Isaiah (chapters 40-55), struggled to help his people survive their exiled years in Babylon (587-538 B.C.E.), Trito-Isaiah's task was that of bolstering his people's hopes and firing them with zeal to rebuild their land, restore their religious practices and reestablish their social structures *after* the exile (ca. 530-510 B.C.E.). For that reason, the latter prophet's work was permeated with renewed emphasis on the cult, the law, observance of the sabbath, the importance of the temple, etc. Around these institutions and traditions the prophet attempted to gather the disparate and at times disconsolate returnees from Babylon. Not an easy task, Trito-Isaiah's efforts at reconstruction often took the form of visions of a glorious future that he shared with his people. His vision of mother Jerusalem is one of the most touching in all of sacred scripture. Called by one scholar the "acme of tenderness," today's pericope is one of the most cherished expressions of God's gifts of grace to humanity. Notice the almost imperceptible shift in the metaphor: At first it is Jerusalem who mothers and nurses her child; then, in v. 13, it is the Lord himself who parents and comforts his people. Loved and forgiven by the Lord, Jerusalem (which represented Israel) was to become for all other peoples the sacrament of divine love and forgiveness.

A second metaphor, that of the *river*, has also been employed by the prophet in describing Israel's glorious future. In a land where arid deserts and fierce parching winds were relieved only by short seasonal rains, rivers were regarded as treasured blessings. In the Jewish and Christian scriptures, rivers or flowing streams were symbols of salvation and/or of the Spirit of God. (Ezekiel 47:1-12, Zechariah 14:8, Revelation 22:1, John 7:38). In today's Isaian pericope, the river or torrent was applied metaphorically in the prosperity and wealth that would one day belong to Jerusalem. Prosperity (in Hebrew *shalom*) or peace was not simply the absence of war. In Hebrew, *shalom* has a religious as well as a secular meaning. From the same cognate word, meaning wholeness or completeness, *shalom* embodied all the blessings of material well-being and spiritual fulfillment. A relational concept, *shalom* was thought to exist, not ontologically or in itself, but between people, and between people and God.

Galatians 6:14-18. Letter writing was a common form of communication in the ancient world, enhanced by the existence of an organized postal system. Established during the Persian Empire, ca. sixth century B.C.E., the postal services were available only for governmental and military uses but private persons also sent letters via paid couriers, slaves and/or friends. According to J. Fitzmeyer, there were four modes of letter writing in antiquity: (1) to write oneself, (2) to dictate word for word, sometimes syllable by syllable, to another, (3) to dictate the *sense*, leaving the formulation to an amanuensis or secretary, (4) to allow a secretary or friend to write in one's name without specifying the content. The most commonly used methods were (1) and (3) and there is evidence in Paul's letters that he availed himself of the services of an amanuensis (Romans 16:22, Galatians 6:11). In those instances when the apostle *dictated* his thoughts, he authenticated them, as his own, by a few words (epilogue) in his own hand and his signature (1 Corinthians 16:21, 2 Thessalonians 2:2, 3:17). Today's second reading, part of the conclusion (6:11-18) of Paul's message to the churches of Galatia, represents his personal authentication of the letter. Besides assuring its recipients that the message had originated with Paul, the conclusion to Galatians is also a recapitulation of the major themes of the letter.

While accusing his opponents in Galatia (Judaizers) of neglecting to preach the true message of salvation (viz., the redeeming value of the cross of Christ) out of fear of persecution, Paul himself rejoiced in the fact of the crucified savior. By "cross" (v. 14), Paul referred to the *whole* process of the Christ-event whereby Jesus revealed the Father, glorified him through his words and works, suffered, died and rose to life and victory over sin and death. By "world" (v. 14), Paul meant all that stood in enmity with God, withstanding the blessings of grace, rejecting Jesus and the gifts of salvation. Included in Paul's concept of "world" were those enemies of the cross who insisted upon the law and circumcision as necessary for salvation. Because of the Christ-event Paul regarded himself as crucified to the world. Christ's death and resurrection, symbolized by the cross, were not simply events that produced benefits for the believer, but the cross is an event in which the believer himself participates. Through faith and baptism (Romans 6:3-11), the cross and the gospel are appropriated by an act of will and become relevant, through the believer, for the world. Paul understood this appropriation as becoming a "new creation" (v. 15).

Not a masochist, Paul understood his physical, emotional and psychological sufferings as having a prophetic value. With the cross, the sign of contradiction, Paul's brand marks and those of every believer should deliver a challenge to the world. Only those persons who have endured a share in the cross are capable of firing the revolution that will change the world. The tried and persecuted will constitute a purer and more faithful church wherein the kingdom of God is made evident and available to all, Jew and gentile, slave and free, male and female.

Luke 10:1-12, 17-20. In the first reading from Trito-Isaiah, Jerusalem was featured as the source of consolation and salvation wherein the "Lord's power would become known to his servants" (Isaiah 66:14). In the travel account of Luke's gospel from which today's composite pericope has been selected (9:51—10:44), Jerusalem also played an important part. It was to Jerusalem that Jesus was headed, in order to become *himself* the source of consolation and salvation for all peoples. Enroute to the city, Jesus performed many signs that revealed God's power in him. He cast out demons, overcame illness, forgave sins, warned of those dangers that militated against the kingdom and challenged his followers in the hard lessons of discipleship. Today's gospel is comprised of some of the principles of missiology and the demands of discipleship Jesus' followers would encounter.

At the beginning of the narrative, Jesus compared the work of the missionaries to the harvesting of an already ripened crop. A popular theme in the Old Testament, the harvest was a figure for the messianic era of judgment and salvation (Amos 9:13-15, Psalm 125:5-6, Joel 4:13, Jeremiah 5:17). Also an important Lucan theme, the importance of *prayer* as a necessary component of the mission has been emphasized in Jesus' advice: "Ask the harvest-master (viz., the Father) to send workers to his harvest" (v. 2). The shift in metaphor from reapers to "*lambs* among wolves" warned of the hostility the disciples would encounter on the way and also of the fact that all who were sent went forth as sheep of the one good shepherd who was Jesus himself.

Jesus' instructions concerning the manner in which his disciples would travel, the sparseness of their gear, the foregoing of even the minimal social amenities ("greet no one"), were similar to advice given to other prophetic messengers (2 Kings 4:29) and underscored the immediacy of the kingdom which Jesus would soon bring to bear in their midst. With the reign of God looming on the horizon, it would have been foolhardy and myopic to dissipate their energies on anything else. Indeed, just as every aspect in Jesus' life was subordinated to the priority of the kingdom, the same value system was to be observed by his would-be disciples. Bearing the message of "*peace*" to each welcoming home, the disciples were, in effect, bringing the message of salvation in Jesus Christ. C. Stuhlmueller has pointed out that "*peace*" in Luke's gospel is continually associated with the gift of salvation (1:79, 2:14, 29, 7:50, 8:48, 12:51, 19:38). Staying in one house, eating what was offered was an exhortation to a simple style of life (no social "gadding about") as well as an indication that the former dietary restrictions were obsolete and *every* food was considered acceptable. In the ominous statement concerning the unwelcoming towns and the ritual of shaking off the dust (v. 11), all were warned that the mere fact of nearness of the kingdom did not, ipso facto, mean it would be accepted. Indeed, there would be some who would reject the peace, the messengers and ultimately the kingdom itself. Upon these, God's judgment would lie heavily. The infamous city of Sodom (Genesis 19:24-28) had not had the opportunity for repentance which was being extended to Jerusalem et al. Therefore, the implication was that those who had had the invitation to repent and had rejected it were more culpable and would be judged more severely (v. 16).

Upon returning from their mission (v. 17), the disciples were elated at their successes. They had been able to cast out the demons of sickness, pain and ignorance. The figure of Satan falling from the sky was probably an allusion to those Jewish traditions that conceived of the "adversary" (i.e., Satan) in the throne room of Yahweh in the heavens *bartering* against the welfare of God's people (Job 2:1ff, Zechariah 3:1ff). Satan's "fall" from the sky (v. 18) can be understood as the eclipsing of the powers of evil by the emerging kingdom of truth and justice. Snakes and scorpions, familiar and feared predators of the Judean desert, were frequently used as symbols of moral evil in the Old Testament (Genesis 3:1-14; Numbers 21:6-9; 1 Kings 12:11, 14). As his emissaries, Jesus' disciples would, during his earthly ministry and during the continued ministry of the church after his resurrection, share in his power over evil and in his responsibility for goodness in the world. By way of channeling their enthusiams, Jesus reminded his disciples of the first century and all subsequent disciples that theirs is a mission not of sensationalism but of salvation. Headlines may bring instant fame for those who capitalize on flashy methods and exciting delivery but those whose names will be "written in heaven" are those whose simple, day-by-day, person-to-person efforts at conversion speak the message of peace and further the establishment of the kingdom.

1. Like a father providing for and protecting his own and like a mother comforting and caring for her child—so does our God love each of us (Isaiah).

2. The cross is a paradoxical symbol; it speaks of defeat and shame and death. But, for those who believe, it has become the hallmark of salvation and the reason for our joy (Galatians).

3. Discipleship requires little equipment, much grace and great perseverence (Luke).

15th Sunday in Ordinary Time

The ways of God are not unfathomable or beyond the grasp of human capabilities; his will is made known through the grace that moves each heart to goodness (Deuteronomy). His greatness is shown in the challenge to love that he extends to all his children. Love fully; love freely; let love break barriers, defy limits and expand the boundaries of family and neighborhood to include all persons in need (Luke). As a model of goodness and a challenge to greatness, the life of Jesus Christ calls all believers to holiness (Colossians).

Deuteronomy 30: 10-14. The last book of the Torah and traditionally ascribed to Moses, Deuteronomy was set within the fictional context of a farewell testament. With the people assembled on the east side of the Jordan river and poised to enter the promised land, Deuteronomy's author has presented Moses as delivering his last words of exhortation and instruction. Shortly thereafter (according to the fictional context), Moses died and the people proceeded to conquer the land of Canaan. In actual fact, the book of Deuteronomy is a much later work and the product of many hands. Described by W.L. Moran as a "summa theologica," Deuteronomy represents an original and bold synthesis of Israel's sacred traditions, rites and institutions. Bringing together under the same theological umbrella the patriarchal promises, Sinai's revelation, the desert trek, the Canaan infiltration, the sacred feasts, etc., the Deuteronomist distilled many of these national treasures to their purest essence and refracted others in the prism of his special concerns. Despite the fact that the work contains both ancient and late material and bears the evidences of centuries of development, the Deuteronomic theologian(s) brought all together in a profound unity. His is tridimensional theology, rooted in his present situation, a theology of reform and renewal, spawned of crisis.

Central to the Deuteronomic author's thought was the premise that the divine Torah or law was the key to human achievement and success. Inextricably bound together was the fact of Israel's fidelity to the precepts of the law and the enjoyment of God's favor. In accord with this basic premise, the Deuteronomist interpreted the events of history as God's blessings and/or chastisements, contingent upon and in proportion to Israel's responsibility to its legal, covenantal obligations.

Today's pericope is from a section of the book thought to have been composed for the edification of the community during the Babylonian exile (29:16—30:20). In accord with his concepts of law and history, the Deuteronomist had interpreted the exile as Israel's deserved punishment for the breach of the covenantal law. Consequently, Israel's only hope for rescue would depend upon conversion to the Lord and the law. Therefore, he called his people to "return to the Lord, your God, with all your heart and all your soul" (v. 11). Not an esoteric system of philosophy or a merely cerebral exercise, the statutes of the law were well known to Israel. They were the terms of the covenant of love God had forged long ago with their forebears. Therefore, the people could not excuse their failures by citing the law's mysteriousness or unattainableness (v. 12). Nor could they expect to fulfill their obligations by a mere modification of their external behavior or by empty lip service. The law had become part and parcel of Israel's very existence as a people: "It is something very near to you, already in your mouths and in your hearts" (v. 14). The law had become the gauge of loving fidelity: "You have only to carry it out" (v. 14). A principle of life, the law revealed God's will, not as a controlling or constricting force from without but as an inspiring and motivating principle from within.

Colossians 1:15-20. Although the authorship of the letter to the believers at Colossae remains a disputed issue (60% of scholars deny a Pauline authorship), there is virtually no disagreement about the exalted nature of the christology and ecclesiology the letter reflects. Colossae was located on the banks of the Lycus river about 100 miles east of Ephesus (about 10 miles east of modern day Denizli in Turkey). Not founded by Paul but by one of his converts, Epaphras (2: 1), the Colossian community was a predominantly gentile one. From the internal evidence of the letter it seems that a certain religio-philosophical system had begun to threaten the integrity of the faith, seducing the Christians to ascribe to its esoteric system of secret knowledge, a form of pre-gnosticism that claimed to be superior to Christianity.

Attacking his opponents directly, the author of Colossians asserted: (1) the primacy of Christ, over and above the angels, (2) the value and necessity of the cross and (3) the cosmic effects of salvation. The heart and high point of the letter, today's second reading is a christological hymn, whose concepts are far more advanced than any of the previous Pauline letters. A hymn of two strophes, the first section (vv. 15-17) underscored the nature of Christ and his unique role in creation. As the *eikon* or image of God, Christ made present in an active manner the invisible God. The term *eikon* (image) was reminiscent of the Jewish concept of wisdom as God's helper in creation and as the pure emanation from the almighty (Wisdom 7:25-26). *Eikon* also recalled the Greek concept of the logos, the ordering principle by which God created. As God's *eikon* or image, Jesus is not a static representation, but the *actual counterpart of God* in the visible world. As Lord of creation, Christ has power over the visible and invisible aspects of creation, i.e., over all creatures *and* over the thrones, dominations, principalities and powers. These were the four ranks of angels which, according to Hellenistic Judaism, guarded heaven's seven levels. Created beings who owed their existence to Christ, these were not to be the objects of worship. By means of the three prepositional phrases in v. 16, the author identified Christ as: the center of the created universe (in him), the cause of or agent of creation (through him), the *telos* or goal toward which all of creation must proceed (for him). Attached to this exalted understanding of Christ was an ecclesiology that conceived of the church as a cosmic reality (v. 18).

As in the high christology of the Johannine prologue, the Colossians author called his readers to expand their understanding of the historical Jesus to see the earthly Jesus as part of an *event* that transcended the beginning as well as the end of his life. As L. Keck has pointed out, the Christ-event can be grasped only when perceived in its entirety; the historical Jesus is framed by the pre-existence of God's Son and the post-existence of the resurrected one. For the ancients, pre-existence was another dimension, beyond the world of time and space. *Existence*, was perceived as real but temporal, while *pre-existence* was thought to be *really real and eternal*. In Jewish thought, certain things existed in this super-real pre-existence, before becoming temporal events, e.g., the Torah, wisdom, etc. Christians understood that the pre-existing reality known as wisdom or God's logos became historical and temporal in the person of Jesus. To Hellenistic Jewish Christianity we owe the development of incarnational theology. Instead of recognizing Jesus as Lord at his resurrection (Acts 2:36) or at his baptism (Mark 1:9-11) or even at his conception (Matthew 1-2, Luke 1-2), the author of Colossians (and John) proclaimed Jesus as Lord from all eternity and forever.

Luke 10:25-37. Three decades ago, outside a New York apartment complex, the cries for help of a certain Kitty Genovese went unanswered. Her murder attracted extensive media coverage and a shocked nation began to examine its private and corporate consciences. What factors had fostered such insouciance? How could an entire neighborhood hide behind closed doors and allow a fellow human being to die? Obviously the principle underlying this question is that "while mere neighborhood does not create love, love does create neighborliness" (T.W. Manson). When the Lucan Jesus told the story of the neighborly Samaritan, this is precisely the point he wished to make.

Recounted only by Luke and occasioned by the question of the lawyer ("What must I do to inherit everlasting life?"), the parable of the good Samaritan is part of a longer exposition in haggadic form and in reverse order of the two great commandments. Today's gospel with its provocative parable serves to explain the ramifications of loving one's neighbor as oneself, whereas next week's gospel (10:38-42: Mary and Martha) interprets the command to love God with one's whole heart, soul, mind and strength (C. Talbert). Skillfully constructed in the form of a controversy dialogue with two parallel sections, today's text is comprised of a series of questions and answers: (a) lawyer's questions (vv. 25, 29), (b) Jesus' counter-questions (vv. 26, 30-36), (c) lawyer's answer (vv. 27, 37a), (d) Jesus' commands (28, 37b). As a result of this dialogue and the parable at its heart, Luke succeeded in illustrating Christian commitment as a challenge that questions traditional values, shatters stereotypical modes of behavior as it offers the new and radical alternative of a life motivated by love.

In order to understand the full scope of the message Luke intended to convey, a certain amount of background information is necessary. As C. Talbert has pointed out, the lawyer's question concerning eternal life should be considered from his Jewish standpoint. As a Jew, he meant, what can I do to be a part of the new age (of the messiah)? . . . or what must I do to belong to God's people? Significantly, unlike his synoptic counterparts, Luke has arranged the dialogue between Jesus and the lawyer so as to have the lawyer answering both of his own questions. In the first query concerning eternal life, the command to love God and to love neighbor as oneself is actually a combination of two familiar Old Testament prescriptions (Deuteronomy 6:5, Leviticus 19:18). In the gospels, however, it is not merely the *combination* of the two commands that is significant but the *corrolating* of the two laws as having *equal importance*. Moreover, the extent to which Christians were to go to carry out the double command made the Christian demand unique and far greater than the lawyer's traditional Jewish perception of it.

The Jews interpreted *neighbor* in terms of one's fellow countrymen (Leviticus 19: 18). Moreover, in Jesus' parable the fact that the priest and the levite passed by the man who had been robbed and left for dead would not have surprised a Jewish audience. Indeed, those privileged members of Jewish society were actually *observing* the law by not defiling themselves with what they probably perceived to be a dead body (Numbers 9:11-13, 14-19; Leviticus 21:1-3, 10-11). On the other hand, the parable's intended audience harbored a deep resentment against Samaritans. Perceived by the Jews as heretics and schismatics, the Samaritans were the descendants of a mixed population resulting from the Assyrian defeat of the northern kingdom in 722 B.C.E. In defiance of the post-exilic reforms instituted by Ezra and Nehemiah and refusing to be included in the renewal, the Samaritans built their own temple on Mt. Gerizim. Jews despised Samaritans and even went miles out of their way to avoid their territory. In light of this centuries' old prejudice, the parable must have shocked the sensibilities of its audience, for it portrayed the Samaritan as the hero and the revered clerics as the villains.

Having succeeded in shattering the comfortable and inadequate traditions of his hearers, the Lucan Jesus then asked, "Which of the three was neighbor to the man?" He demanded of those who claimed to love God a radical transformation in their attitudes toward one another. "Neighbor" would thenceforth be defined not in terms of territorial proximity or of national allegiance, but in terms of benevolence and need. Overriding the laws of clean/unclean, without regard for recompense, Christian love would perceive as neighbor anyone to whom one could show compassion and care. "Neighborliness is not a quality in other people; it is simply their claim on ourselves. We have literally no time to sit down and ask ourselves whether so-and-so is our neighbor or not. We must get into action and obey; we must behave like a neighbor to him" (D. Bonhoeffer).

1. The gap between knowing what is right and doing it is closed when natural talents respond to grace (Deuteronomy).

2. Christ makes known the unknowable God, makes tangible the transcendent and makes possible every promise (Colossians).

3. Neighborhood is a place with distinct boundaries; neighborliness is a virtue that extends a caring love to all without distinction (Luke).

16th Sunday in Ordinary Time

Precious lessons can be learned in life's simplest moments. As he and Sarah hurried to prepare a meal for guests, Abraham learned the value of unhesitating faith and the certainty of God's promises (Genesis). As she wearied herself with the rituals of gracious hospitality, Martha learned that her time and efforts could be better directed (Luke). In the rejection and trials he endured for the sake of the gospel, Paul learned to appreciate and to communicate more effectively the mystery of Jesus' saving acts (Colossians).

Genesis 18:1-10. Since nothing truly comparable exists in western society, it is somewhat difficult to fully appreciate the obligation of hospitality which characterized the ancient Near Eastern world. Like a finely choreographed and intricate dance, the process of accepting outsiders into one's home and turning them from strangers to guests was governed by specific rules and principles. In today's first reading and in the gospel, oriental hospitality is the chosen context for important revelation. Mamre, probably modern day Ramet-el Khalil, was a holy place named for one of Abraham's allies in his conflict with Chedorlaomer and the four kings (Genesis 14: 13-24). The focal place of Abraham's movements in southern Palestine, Mamre was the site of many theophanies. There Abraham had built an altar (Genesis 13:18) and had purchased the nearby cave of Machpelah for a family tomb.

Today's first reading, from the Yahwist tradition (J), has preserved in beautiful anthropomorphic style one of those theophanies. In vivid detail, the Yahwist theologian describes the mysterious visitation. From the outset it is clear that the visitation was a divine one: "The Lord appeared to Abraham" (v. 1). However, due to the fact that two or three independent traditions were coalesced, it is not clear exactly *how* the Lord was manifested to Abraham. For example, in v. 2, the Yahwistic author mentioned "three men," yet Abraham addressed them as one person, "Sir." Later in the narrative, the visitors would be referred to as "two angels" (19:1). Regardless of these unresolved contradictions, the theophanic importance of the episode cannot be denied.

True to his heritage, seemingly unaware of their true identity, Abraham scurried about to offer his visitor(s) the best of his household. With Sarah busy making bread, Abraham played host in a lavish manner. Three seahs or measures of fine flour was equivalent to about four pecks—an enormous amount for so few people. So too, the offering of an entire steer underscored Abraham's prodigal generosity and attested to the paramount quality of his hospitality. Similar accounts of humans entertaining the gods and/or goddesses while unaware of their true identity were common among the mythologies of the ancient world. Usually, in these accounts, blessings were heaped upon the human host in proportion to his/her hospitality. No doubt, the Genesis author was aware of these accounts and adapted the motif to his own monotheistic style and purposes. In Abraham's case, his hospitality was rewarded with a divine revelation in the form of a birth announcement: "This time next year, Sarah will have a son" (v. 10). Immediately, and without hesitation, Abraham believed.

Unlike the polytheistic myths wherein the world and human beings were the pawns and playthings of the gods, the Abraham story bears witness to a *concerned* God, personally involved with his people, directing them and leading all to a single goal. The divine visitation to Abraham portrays a God who acts and blesses and fulfills promises. In addition to illustrating God's caring involvement, the episode at Mamre can be understood as prefiguring the ultimate visitation of God to humanity, the incarnation. Abraham's welcoming faith had been rewarded with an experience of the transcendent God. El Shaddai had become familiar and near enough to eat, converse and partake of Abraham's generous offerings. In the incarnation, the transcendent creator God became one with created flesh and blood—so near and so united with humanity as to effect its purification and redemption.

Although today's first reading concluded with the annunciation of Isaac's birth, the episode continued to recount Sarah's reaction. The ancient author stated simply, "And Sarah laughed!" (Genesis 18:12). Whether she laughed in disbelief and/or for sheer happiness at the wonder of such a marvelous event is uncertain. Nevertheless, Sarah's amusement and Abraham's unhesitating faith reflect the incredulous joy and unswerving fidelity that are part of every Christian's response to the God who draws near and visits his people in the person of Jesus Christ.

Colossians 1:24-28. If Colossians is in fact one of the antilegomena or deutero-Pauline letters, then today's pericope bears evidence of the fact that the author must have known Paul and was intimately familiar with his experiences and apostolic aspirations. Those who, on the other hand, support a Pauline authorship date the letter near the end of the apostle's life, during his Roman imprisonment (ca. 58-60 C.E.). In those few verses from his letter to Colossae, the author has summed up his (Paul's?) convictions about his work and the repercussions that work would have had upon those he served. Believing that he had been entrusted with the greatest and ultimate mystery, the mystery of Christ, the author defended his position against those proponents of a pre-gnostic Jewish philosophy who threatened Christianity in Colossae. These opponents prided themselves on being a select elite privy to a secret knowledge or *mysterion* (mystery). In the face of their proud parochialism, the Colossians' author preached the saving mystery of Christ for "*all persons*," "every person" (v. 28).

Choosing another favorite gnostic word, the author claimed the authority to teach the mystery of Christ or the gospel in its "fullness" (v. 25). No one had the monopoly on enlightenment with regard to the gospel; indeed, the full measure of God's saving word extended to all—even to the gentiles. Because he had devoted himself wholeheartedly and unstintingly to his ministry, the author had experienced for himself the hardship and suffering Jesus endured as a prelude to his glory. Because of his identification with the person and mission of Christ, he found joy in his sufferings and regarded them as a share in redemption (v. 24). Just as the very presence of Jesus (during his earthly ministry) raised challenges, provoked choices and caused division, so too, the apostolic minister would endure those same conflicts each time he/she dares to preach of Jesus (see also 2 Corinthians 1:5-7, 1 Thessalonians 2:14-16, Acts 5:40-42).

In his own flesh, the author filled up what was lacking in the sufferings of Christ. As R. Fuller has observed, this does not imply that anything was lacking in Christ's suffering and atoning death. Rather, the clue lies elsewhere in the undisputed Pauline letters. Therein (Romans 8:17-18; 2 Corinthians 1:4-5, 4:8-10), Paul described his sufferings as an *epiphaneia* or manifestation of Christ's cross. What is lacking is not the atoning power of the cross, but its manifestation in the church as a present reality. In Greek, the verb *antanaplero* (to fill up what is lacking) implies a duality that excludes the complete identification of the sufferings of the author (or Paul) with those of the whole Christ. This, according to J. Grassi, means that others have a role to play. In what sense that role will be exercised is implied in the author's assertion that his sufferings were "for the sake of his (Christ's) body, the church" (v. 24).

Until the eschatological consummation, the church will be "filling up what is lacking" in the sense that the body of believers must continue to develop both intensively and extensively. By virtue of their baptism, all Christians are called to close the gap between the actual and the potential, between what the church is and what it can and must become. This can only be accomplished by living an authentic Christianity that will inevitably include suffering. But, as with Jesus, the suffering of the cross is a sure promise of life and a prelude to resurrection glory.

Luke 10:38-42. Peculiar to Luke's gospel, today's episode with its description of Martha's "busyness" and Mary's "ease" has come down to us from medieval interpreters as an example of the superiority of the contemplative life over the active life. Such an understanding is incomplete and misleading. Besides anachronizing the monastic style of a later age into a first century Christianity, this limited interpretation neglected the author's intended purpose. W. Grundman, C. Talbert and C. Stuhlmueller agree the Mary and Martha scene exhibits a structure that connects it to the previous parable of the good Samaritan. Both pericopes served to illustrate the double commandment of love: The good Samaritan story was told as an explanation of what it means to love one's neighbor as oneself (Leviticus 19:18); the episode at Martha's home provided an exposition on what it means to love God with all one's heart, soul, mind and strength (Deuteronomy 6:5).

According to the evangelist, Jesus was a guest at Martha's home. Therefore, it was not unusual that she as hostess would have been responsible for providing the hospitality. Some have suggested that Martha's agitation was compounded by the fact that Jesus' disciples were probably also present as guests. Therefore Martha was not merely preparing a simple meal for two or three people but a large buffet for several guests. In addition to preparing and serving the people, the rules of hospitality required that the host/hostess provide for the physical comforts of each guest, e.g., water for washing feet, hands, oil for anointing head, etc. Nevertheless, Martha's expressed resentment, "Lord, are you not concerned. . . tell her to help me" (v. 40), prepared the way for the essential point of the story.

Jesus' response to Martha is full of minor textual problems. Even the ancient manuscripts have varying translations, e.g., (1) only a few things are needed, indeed only one, (2) only a few things are needed, (3) there is need of one thing (only). Some have suggested that Jesus was telling Martha that only a few things (i.e., dishes) were necessary for the meal. Even *one* dish would suffice. Others, setting the episode in an eschatological context, would interpret it as a reference to the subordinate and passing significance of material things. With the kingdom so near, few things are necessary and, *least* of all, *material* preoccupations. Some have cited the sisters' virginity (?) as a sign of the kingdom's imminence.

But the final sentence (v. 42) of the pericope has helped to clarify the textual difficulties of v. 41. "Mary has chosen the better portion and she shall not be deprived of it" elevates the episode beyond an argument between the two sisters. The "one thing required" (v. 41) was the seeking of the kingdom (Luke 12:29-31). Centuries before, the psalmist had expressed a similar prayerful hope, "One thing I ask of Yahweh, one thing I seek; to live in the house of Yahweh all the days of my life, to enjoy the sweetness of Yahweh and to consult him in his temple" (Psalm 27:4). This virtue was illustrated in Mary's undivided attention to Jesus. In Jesus' presence, the "one thing required" was to listen and to hear the word. More important than passing and mundane concerns, hearing the word (Luke 11:27-28) and listening to Jesus are what it means to love God with one's whole heart, soul, mind, strength.

Mary had positioned herself "at Jesus' feet" (v. 39). "To sit at a person's feet" was equivalent to being that person's disciple, or studying under someone. In the Acts of the Apostles, Luke described Paul's rabbinical education as his being seated at Gamaliel's feet (Acts 22:3). Mary's position and her single-hearted attention communicate the evangelist's powerful message: To love God with all one's self is to be a disciple of Jesus. The essence of discipleship begins, not in the preparation of a great banquet but in attention to the word of God who is Jesus. As J. Fitzmeyer has noted, "A diakonia (service) that bypasses the word is one that will never have lasting character; listening to Jesus' word is the lasting good that will never be taken away from the listener." At Jesus' feet, Mary is the model of the disciple who has learned that life comes not from bread alone (or earthly cares) but from every word that comes from the mouth of God (Deuteronomy 8:3).

1. In the person of uninvited or unwelcome guests, the Lord can be served with graciousness and care (Genesis).

2. Faithful service inevitably involves suffering; it is only the mediocre servant who escapes unscathed (Colossians).

3. Anxiety about mundane and trivial matters saps precious energies that should be focused on the kingdom (Luke).

17th Sunday in Ordinary Time

Prayer is a hunger, as necessary to life as food and water . . . a hunger that can be satisfied only by God. Prayer is the grateful joy that knows salvation has come in Jesus Christ (Colossians). Prayer is a friendship that does not fear to be bold in petition (Genesis). Prayer is discipleship that trusts all to the one who has given all, and looks ahead with hope to a glorious future (Luke).

Genesis 18:20-32. Sodom and Gomorrah were two cities of the ancient world whose reputations for evil have not only survived but have grown more sordid with the passing of the centuries. Infamous for certain sexual aberrations and inhospitality (Genesis 19:1-11), Sodom and Gomorrah have become synonymous with evil and depravity of every kind. Although a precise location for these cities has not been discovered, archaeological researchers of this century believe that the ruins of Sodom and Gomorrah lie beneath the shallow southern end of the Dead Sea. Featured in today's first reading from the Yahwist tradition of the Abraham cycle, Sodom and Gomorrah provide the background for a lesson on divine justice and retribution.

A continuation of the narrative of the divine visitors (Genesis 18—see last Sunday's first reading), today's pericope makes it quite clear that Abraham is conversing with the Lord himself. With an almost surprising anthropomorphic style, the Yahwist has underscored the intimacy of Abraham's relationship with God. For example, the ancient theologian spoke of the Lord "standing before Abraham" (v. 22) engaged in active dialogue with him. As the dialogue proceeds, the two sound like people at a market bartering back and forth until a satisfactory deal has been struck. Though Abraham's deep faith in God and religious reverence are never in doubt, there is none of the awesome transcendence and distance between God and humanity that characterized the later theologians (Priestly, Deuteronomic).

In relationship to today's gospel pericope on prayer, Abraham embodied and exemplified all the qualities to which Luke called his community: (1) *an intimate relationship with God*. . . Luke instructed his community, "When you pray, say 'Abba (Daddy, Papa) Father' "; (2) *perseverance* . . . just as Abraham did not relent but kept bartering, so the Christian believers were instructed to persist in asking, seeking, knocking; (3) *daring*. . . even in the seemingly hopeless case of Sodom, Abraham had hope and proceeded with confidence to bring his needs to God.

Colossians 2:12-14. Because there are no existing written documents to represent the case of the pre-gnostic faction in Colossae, the gist of the controversy must be deduced from the New Testament letter to that community. As he continued his polemic, the author of Colossians (whether it was Paul near the end of his life or a Pauline disciple who wrote at a later date) asserted the superiority of the Christian faith over and above the syncretistic beliefs and practices of his opponents. Theirs was a seductive philosophy (2:8) that posited the superiority of superhuman spiritual beings over Christ (2:18), imposed circumcision (2:11), observed the Jewish feasts, new moons, sabbaths and dietary restrictions (2:16, 21).

In today's reading, the Colossians author asserted the total sufficiency of Jesus Christ and his saving action on the cross. Because of that gift of salvation, believers were dispensed from all former practices and called to union with Christ through baptism. Those who clung to the rite of circumcision believed it to be a sign of their solidarity with one another as children of Abraham (Genesis 17:9-27) and members of the covenant community (Genesis 17:1 1). In the verse (2:11) immediately preceding today's pericope, the author called Jewish circumcision a rite "made with hands" that did not accomplish anything but a removal of a tiny particle of "flesh." *Christian circumcision* or *baptism* on the other hand stripped off the "flesh" entirely. "Flesh" here is to be understood in the Pauline sense, i.e., the carnal nature of a person, which willingly ascribes to the ways of sin and the ways of the "world."

Stressing the gratuitous nature of baptismal grace (v. 13), the author underscored the necessary role of Christ and the cross in the economy of salvation. With a "metaphor so violent as to practically rupture itself" (Moule), the author described Christ's saving death as having cancelled the bond that stood against us by snatching it up and nailing it to the cross (v. 14)! *Cheirographon* (the *bond against us*, with all its claims) is a hapax legomenon (i.e., it appears nowhere else) in the New Testament. In extra-biblical literature the term referred to a handwritten bond of debt or a promissory note. Some scholars have interpreted this bond or I.O.U. as the Jewish obligation to the law (J.A.T. Robinson). This indebtedness was, of course, cancelled by Christ's redeeming activity. But the majority of scholars have understood the bond cancelled by Christ as humanity's I.O.U. to death because of sin. Superior to all other beings, principalities and powers, Jesus Christ, by the contradiction of the cross and through the Christian circumcision that is baptism, summons evey believer in peace and forgiveness to eternal solidarity with God.

Luke 11:1-13. Jesus had resolutely taken the road for Jerusalem; he had embarked upon that journey which would climax in his death on Calvary (Luke 9:51). As he and his disciples travelled through the villages, they entered upon an intense period of their apostolic formation. Those who followed Jesus were to learn that attachment to material possessions was like a tether that hindered their growth and blinded them to the kingdom (9:57-62). They were to be instructed in the perils they would meet during their ministry (10:3). His disciples were to learn of the necessity of single-hearted service (10:6-12) and of the power over evil they would share and exercise (10:17-20) in Jesus' name. They would know that theirs was to be an undiscriminating and universal ministry that reached out to all in need (10:29-37), motivated by the dual command of love (10:25-28). They would also be formed in prayer; they would learn from the Lord himself how to pray—how to stand alone and together in truth before God. Prayer as communion with God in Jesus, prayer as a means of discipleship, prayer as a way to wait for and to prepare for Jesus' second advent—these are the subjects of today's gospel from Luke.

Beside the Lord's Prayer (vv. 1-4), Luke has included in today's gospel pericope other selected passages (v. 5-8, 11-13) on prayer and has drawn all together in the dramatic setting of Jesus *himself* at prayer. While it is obvious in the other gospels that Jesus was a man of prayer, only Luke put stress on the fact. At prayer after he had been baptized (3:21), before his choosing of the Twelve (6:12), before Peter's confession of faith and the predictions of the passion (8:18), at his transfiguration (9:28), before teaching his own to pray (11:2), at the last supper (22:32), during his agonizing night in the garden (22:41) and on the cross (23:46), Jesus taught the necessity of prayer in every aspect of the disciple's life. A sign of dependence and trust in God, it was also a mark of true faith and genuine hope.

Luke's version of the Lord's Prayer is shorter than Matthew's, the former having five petitions, the latter seven. Most scholars agree that Luke's simpler rendition may be the more original and that the Matthean "Our Father" was probably expanded during liturgical usage by the Jewish Christian community of the first century C.E. Besides presenting a more abbreviated version of the prayer, Luke has altered the wording of some of the petitions. As a result, the entire prayer has taken on a different orientation.

As C. Talbert[1] has pointed out, during Jesus' earthly ministry the prayer functioned as a means to petition God for an immediate shift of the ages (coming of God's reign). In the time of the evangelist, the prayer taught the disciples the method and content of prayer in the midst of the historical process: daily bread, forgiveness, victory over temptation, the gift of the Spirit and the ultimate victory of God. The shift in the function of the prayer arose from the lived experience of the church that continued to await the eschaton but also realized that the victorious power of Jesus' Holy Spirit was already at work among the disciples. This power was enough to sustain them until the second advent.

Abba, which has been translated Father (v. 2), was actually a more familiar term of address, like "Papa" or "Daddy." Without parallel in the Jewish prayers of that time (or even of the first Christian millennium) *Abba* signaled that special loving relationship Jesus enjoyed with his Father and in which he invited his followers to share. Both the petitions for the hallowing of God's name and the coming of the kingdom were expressed by Luke in the aorist passive form of the verbs, giving a once-for-all aspect and eschatological significance to these petitions. However, Luke has altered the sense of the third petition, changing Matthew's "this day" to "day after day" or "each day." This subtle change suggests *continuation* of giving and has allowed the eschatological interpretation to include the pressing problems of temporal life (e.g., bread for sustenance, eucharistic bread, etc.).

In place of Matthew's "debts" in the fourth petition, Luke substituted "sins." Some have suggested that this alteration would have made the sense of the petition more understandable to a gentile audience; others regard the change as an example of Luke's understanding of the Christ-event (J. Fitzmeyer). Because of Jesus, the "debt" of *sin* has been forgiven. Having been shown such great love, the Christian's only response would be to forgive others in the same loving manner. Remember Luke's narrative about the woman who loved much because she had been forgiven much (Luke 7:47). In the final petition, "subject us not to the trial," *peirasmos* was a technical term for the great tribulation that would precede the era of the messiah. This great tribulation was anticipated in the hardships and trials of faith endured by all faithful disciples.

Peculiar to Luke, the parable of the "friend at midnight" (vv. 5-8) was borrowed from Palestinian folk traditions and was rooted in the oriental's profound sense of hospitality. Like an extended rhetorical question, vv. 5-7 put forth an *absolutely* unthinkable situation. *No one* would refuse a friend, no matter how importunate the request. Although the focus of the parable has traditionally been centered on the midnight visitor, the central figure is actually the friend who inconvenienced himself and his family to answer the request made of him. At the heart of the amusing parable is the lesson: If a friend would answer another's need because of the obligation of hospitality and the friend's persistence (actual translation is shamelessness!), *how much more will your loving Father answer your prayers!*

In the final verses of the instruction on prayer (vv. 9-13), Jesus exhorted his disciples to pray with confidence. A human father knows enough to give his children what is for their good, i.e., fish and eggs rather than snakes and scorpions. But, the *heavenly* Father is the very *source* of *life* and *goodness* for all who have become his children in Jesus. Whereas Matthew said the Father would give "good gifts" to all who asked (Matthew 7:9-11), the Lucan Jesus promised the *Holy Spirit* (v. 13). As the good gift par excellence, the Holy Spirit would empower the disciples to minister as Jesus did and enable them to survive in hope and in joy until his return. In the presence of the Holy Spirit, the kingdom was already present and pressing toward that eschatological fullness when every petition of the Lord's Prayer would be forever realized.

1. Even a trace of goodness amid a sea of evil and apathy can have a redeeming effect and will not be overlooked by God (Genesis).

2. In the daily process of becoming Christian, believers learn more and more of the freedoms achieved by Christ on the cross (Colossions).

3. Prayer is the essential and first vocation of every believer (Luke).

18th Sunday in Ordinary Time

At the end of our earthly life each of us will meet God, face to face but with empty hands. When the moment arrives for us to cross death's threshold, we will do so without baggage, souvenirs or gifts (Luke). Only the meaning we have brought to the lives of others (Ecclesiastes) and the gospel values we have learned and lived will endure (Colossians). These eternal virtues will witness to our life in Christ and be our legacy in death.

Ecclesiastes 1:2, 2:21-23. In one of his often quoted poems, T.S. Eliot commented "The world ends. . . not with a bang but a whimper." Qoheleth, the ancient philosopher and author, seems to have shared Eliot's world view. As evident in today's first reading, the author was convinced that, when all is said and done, the whole of life is a heap of absurdity and ambiguity. Based on his own experience and the witness of history, he had concluded "all things are vanity!" (1:2, 11:9). Vanity or *hebel* (Hebrew), literally translated as "breath" or "vapor," appears 35 times in the text of Ecclesiastes. Elsewhere in the Old Testament (Psalm 39: 6-7, 94:11) the word referred to that which is transient, worthless and empty. By asserting "vanity of vanities," the author stated the theme of his book in the Hebrew form of the superlative. As one who had carefully examined the world in which he lived, Qoheleth reported sadly that all things (e.g., riches, labor, philosophy, pleasures, etc.) were inherently lacking. Indeed, in the end, death would snuff out even the brightest of life's moments with utter certainty and finality. Faced with this reality, Qoheleth resolved to find meaning, however fleeting and transitory, in the joys God gives to humankind during its earthly existence.

Qoheleth is the Hebrew name of the book we call Ecclesiastes. As the feminine singular participle of the qual form of *qahal* (assembly, congregation), the term probably designated someone who performed a service for the assembly, e.g., a teacher or preacher (see 12:9). Our English title Ecclesiastes, from the Greek *ekklesiastes*, referred to the one who convokes the *ekklesia* or assembly.

Actually, the text of Ecclesiastes exhibits a late form of Hebrew and was probably composed during the third or fourth century B.C.E. As R. Murphy has observed, although the author was in the mainstream of the ancient Near Eastern wisdom movement, Qoheleth was sharply critical of his fellow philosophers. Some of the earlier sages had categorized nature and human conduct, allowing themselves the unaffordable luxury of fixed positions, e.g., justice issued forth in life whereas wickedness led to death. "They had put the Lord into a straight-jacket tailored by human insights; thus had they endangered divine prerogatives" (R.E. Murphy). But Qoheleth shattered the mold of neat categories and spoke out in favor of divine sovereignty and independence.

In today's first reading the ancient author has underscored one of the many aspects of life's vanity, that of the futility of labor. After a life of endless toil in which a person has devoted the best of skills and energies, what has that person to show for all the efforts? In the end, the person dies and all the fruits will be enjoyed or squandered by others. Incensed by the injustice whereby a person never completely acquired what he/she merited by reason of just toil, Ecclesiastes concluded: "All is vanity." R. Fuller has regarded this ruthless exposure of what human life is like apart from God as a preparation for hearing the good news of the involved God in Jesus Christ. All of life in every aspect is futile if viewed apart from God.

Colossians 3:1-5, 9-11. Where Qoheleth had observed life and concluded that human existence amounted to no more than a vain and transitory emptiness, the author of Colossians understood and experienced life as a participation in glory and a sure promise of even greater joy in the future. What accounted for the difference in the outlooks of these two persons? Faith and the experience of God in the person of the incarnate Christ had caused the Christian author to recognize God's involvement in his creation, his care and provident lordship over all humanity (Colossians 2:9-15). By the grace of Christ's cross and in the man-for-others, believers had come to a new awareness of human life. No longer was the span of a person's years a mere "grin-and-bear-it" waiting period for better things; nor was life to be thought of as a *means* of salvation. Rather, in the perspective of Jesus' passion and resurrection, Christian life was to be understood as a *consequence* of salvation. In today's second reading the Colossians author was intent on explaining how the fact of salvation should be evident in the believer's daily existence.

In baptism, the faithful already have a share in the risen life of Christ; we have "been raised up in company with Christ" (v. 1). It follows then that every aspect of human existence—moral, social, intellectual, etc.—should reflect that doctrinal fact. Rather than *effecting* or *achieving* a relationship with God (with Christ), the Christian's moral response flows *from* that relationship. Solidarity with Christ was forged in the initiatory rite of baptism but this solidarity was to be maintained and deepened by continual and daily conversion to Jesus and to the values taught in the gospel. The theme of "putting aside the old self" and "putting on the new" was probably suggested by the ancient baptismal ritual. Before entering the baptismal waters, the catechumens disrobed as a sign of their willingness to abandon their former ways of sin. Elsewhere in the undisputed Pauline corpus, the "putting off of the old self" was referred to in terms of being freed from the first Adam in whom all had died and being united with Christ in whom all would come to life (1 Corinthians 15:22).

Using terms familiar to the pre-gnostic adversarial elements in Colossae, the author described baptismal life as being "hidden with Christ in God" (v. 4). Just as a dead body is "hidden" or buried in the earth after death, the Christian's participation in Christ is a "being hidden in his death" ("After all, you have died," v. 3). This being "hidden" or having "died in Christ" necessitated a death to the world of sin as well. Evil desires, idolatry, etc., were to become totally foreign to the new self hidden in Christ. In the process of becoming the person he/she was intended to be, the Christian would also grow in *knowledge* (another favorite gnostic term). Not an abstract form of intellectualism but a *relational* knowledge (in the biblical sense), this growth in knowledge would result in the renewal or re-creation of the believer.

Luke 12:13-21. In ancient Greece, peripatetic schools were a frequently observed phenomenon. Learned philosophers and academicians led their charges from place to place, imparting insights and information and drawing forth principles by which to live from their shared observations. Jesus and his entourage en route to Jerusalem could be compared to one of the ancient walking academies. As he led them on the way to the cross, Jesus educated his disciples in the costs of discipleship and the demands of the kingdom. Today's gospel pericope represents a portion of that apostolic formation specifically concerned with the appropriate attitude toward possessions and preparedness for the coming reign of God.

Comprised of a pronouncement story (vv. 13-15) and a parable (vv. 16-21), the gospel text can be better understood when seen in connection with the context that occasioned Jesus' teaching. Jesus had been approached to arbitrate between two brothers. Legislated in the Hebrew scriptures (Numbers 27:1-11, Deuteronomy 21:15ff), matters of legacy often posed thorny problems and were frequently brought before rabbis for their discernment. That the issue was presented to Jesus as a layman, and that he was addressed by the revered title "teacher" (*didaskale*), is indicative of the respected position he held in the eyes of some of his contemporaries.

Still, Jesus declined to act as arbiter, not because he did not have the authority to do so, but in order to correct the misplaced attention of the people. By refusing to become embroiled in such material matters, Jesus wished to align the attitudes of his disciples toward their true purpose and concerns in life. As his followers and as heirs of an eternal inheritance, believers in Jesus were called to reevaluate themselves and their possessions in terms of the new way of life he held out to them. The heart of the pronouncement story was Jesus' exhortation to avoid greed and to understand that possessions, even great possessions, are no guarantors of life (v. 15). In other words, Jesus could have said to his disciples: Life does not consist in material possessions; a person will be valued not for what he/she *has* but for what he/she *is* and *can become*. The covetousness or greed that motivated the request for arbitration was to be recognized as an attitude foreign to the coming of the kingdom and hostile to the freedom from "things" to which Jesus summoned his own. Jesus' coming among his people as Son of Man and his ultimate coming at the shift of the ages challenge believers to lift their focus from secular and temporal disputes to the eschatological and eternal judgment. After all, death is the threshold which will automatically resolve every temporal matter and over which only eternal values will pass.

In the subsequent parable (vv. 16-21) the point of the pronouncement story (vv. 13-15) has been poignantly and powerfully illustrated. Moreover this verbal illustration (proper to Luke's gospel) successfully dovetails the ideas of the first two readings and precisely applies them to the life of the believer. For example, since all of the material universe is as transient as a vapor or wisp of air (*hebel*: vanity, Ecclesiastes 1:2), then it stands to reason that the Christian should focus energies on those things that have lasting significance ("higher realms," Colossians 3:1). Indeed, in his myopic sense of what mattered in life, the satisfied rich man even quoted Qoheleth, "Eat heartily, drink well, enjoy yourself!" (Ecclesiastes 2:24; 3:12-13, 22; 5:17; 8:15; 9:7-8).

Fortifying himself against material needs and assuring himself of the relaxing security of a full barn, the rich man had neglected to look beyond this life to the eternal harvest. For this lack of insight and foresight, God would call him by the deserved name "fool." In the Old Testament the "fool" was one who had denied or forgotten God (Psalm 13: 1). By failing to take God into account in the practical aspects of his life, the "fool" had forgotten that his very life was but a loan which God could recall at any moment. For the fool, death would be a rude awakening. He/She would learn in death the hard lesson the Spanish proverb expresses so succinctly: "There are no pockets in a shroud!" Death would teach the insight, albeit too late, that a preacher once communicated to his radio congregation, "I never saw a hearse pulling a U-HAUL!" In a more serious manner, the author of Enoch had also exhorted, "Woe to you who acquire silver and gold, but not in righteousness, and say, 'We have become very rich and have possessions and have acquired everything we have desired. Now let us do what we have planned, for we have gathered silver and filled our storehouses!. . .' Like water your life will flow away, for riches will not stay with you!" (1 Enoch 97:8-10).

When Luke recounted this message for the Christians of the 80s C.E., he was attempting to keep before the eyes of those second and third generation believers the *urgency* of the kingdom. He reminded them (via the pronouncement story and parable) that the eschatological message of the good news concerned a future event, but that it also exercised a pressure upon present realities. For disciples-in-training of every age, today's gospel is a reminder that "the amassing of a superabundance of material possessions for the sake of 'la dolce vita' becomes the height of folly in light of the responsibility of life itself amid the assessment of it which will take place once it is over" (J. Fitzmeyer).

1. Anxiety over material profit is futile energy better spent in discovering life's many surprises and rejoicing over its immeasurable blessings (Ecclesiastes).

2. When the heart is focused on lasting realities, petty concerns fade into perspective and parochial biases disappear (Colossians).

3. A high yield C.D. may give a sense of security but the only worthwhile investments are long term commitment and discipleship (Luke).

19th Sunday in Ordinary Time

That Jesus will return to his own at the shift of the ages is an undisputed fact. That Jesus' return will spell justice is a surety. The only point of uncertainty is the precise time of his arrival (Luke). For that reason, in an effort to maintain a posture of readiness and welcome, believers are called to a daily growth in hope and a deepening of faith (Hebrews). Then, with joy and conviction, all can look forward to their climactic passing over from death to everlasting life (Wisdom).

Wisdom 18:6-9. Ancient Alexandria, a bustling and cosmopolitan metropolis on the Mediterranean sea near the rich delta of the Nile, was founded in 332 B.C.E. by Alexander the Great. Capital of Egypt and a major shipping port, Alexandria boasted a 445-foot-high lighthouse, whose beacon attracted to Egypt's shores ships from exotic places. With the ships came a vast array of precious commodities, a variety of peoples and a host of different world views, politics and ideologies. Home of a great museum, a famed university and an unparalleled library (over 400,000 volumes!), Alexandria was one of the major intellectual centers of the ancient world. The population of over a million inhabitants included a great variety of philosophers, poets, scientists, academicians and theologians (Philo, Clement, Origen, Apollos, etc.) as well as the largest Jewish community in the diaspora (in the first century C.E.). It was in Alexandria that the Septuagint or Greek translation of the Hebrew scriptures was accomplished. It was also in Alexandria that the author of today's first reading wrote.

Wisdom or the Wisdom of Solomon, written in the first century B.C.E., was attributed pseudonymously to the king who had lived some 1000 years before. Aware of the all pervasive and attractive influence of the Hellenistic culture, the Wisdom author's purpose in writing was to strengthen the faith of his coreligionists in Alexandria and to help them rediscover and maintain the richness of their heritage and traditions. Ironically, although the work served to preserve the riches of Judaism at a crucial moment in its development, Wisdom was not included in the Hebrew canon. Protestant Bibles categorize the book as deuterocanonical or apocryphal while Roman Catholics number Wisdom among the canonical books of scripture.

Today's pericope is from the second part of the book of Wisdom (11:2—19:22). An extended homily on salvation history, in particular on the exodus experience as the pivotal event in Israel's development as a people, this section of the work is thought to be a separate composition, written in the author's later years. A. Wright believes chapters 11-19 of Wisdom represent the best single example in the Bible of a midrash, i.e., a composition that explains the scriptures and attempts to make them understandable and meaningful for a later generation. Structurally, midrash may take the form of a verse by verse commentary, a homily or a rewritten version of a lengthy but excellent homily, which may originally have been a sermon for Passover. In order to understand the entire midrash it is necessary to appreciate the *summary* with which the author began his homily and the *principle* to which he would repeatedly return throughout his work.

In 11:2-4, the Wisdom author summed up Israel's survival and eventual emergence as a people in its own right: Israel enjoyed God's predilection; it was Israel alone, of all the peoples on earth, who had been chosen, liberated and cared for by God. Egypt, on the other hand, suffered a deserved punishment from the very phenomena that spelled blessings for God's people (11:5-6).

As part of the final antithetical comparison, today's first reading recalled for the author's contemporaries in Alexandria the blessings of their exodus redemption. As he had promised their fathers the patriarchs (v. 6), the Lord preserved his people, secured their freedom and assured them of progeny and land. In the experience of the exodus from Egypt, the cherished promises to Abraham became possibilities. By faithfully remembering their traditions and celebrating the Passover year after year, the Jews were called to a renewed dedication to the God to whom they owed their existence and continued survival.

Hebrews 11:1-2 8-19. Everyone has an "Isaac"—some person, attitude, place or possession without which we think we have no identity, no future and no possibility for happiness. For Abraham, his cherished son Isaac was all these things and more. In the gift of Isaac, God assured Abraham that the promises of land, prosperity and progeny were beginning to take shape. In Isaac, Abraham's hopes for continued existence took on real possibilities. In Isaac, the dreams of an old and barren couple were fulfilled. Yet, all these factors notwithstanding, Abraham's faith in God was so authentic and so intense that he was willing to let go of his Isaac and thereby to forfeit all he had hoped would come to pass because of his son. The Hebrews' author, near the end of the first Christian century, praised Abraham's honest faith and held it out as a model for his fellow believers.

Part of a longer section on faith and endurance (11:1—12:13), today's second reading was not intended as a *definition* of faith, although the theologians of the early and medieval church considered it to be one. Rather, the author of the letter to the Hebrews intended this pericope as a metaphorical *description* of faith. Existential and not essential in character, v. 1 is actually a description of the subjective attitudes of the the believer toward God. Characterized by assurance (*hypostasis*) and conviction (*elenchos*), the faith of the true believer, as perceived by the author of Hebrews, is quite similar to that eager and trusting expectation later defined as hope.

Assurance has sometimes been erroneously translated as "substance" or "essence" due to a misreading of *hypostasis* within this given context. But "assurance" or "guarantee" conveys the author's intention more accurately here. Indeed, this is the sense *hypostasis* often bears in the LXX and in the works of various Greek writers of the Christian era. In the Hellenistic world, *hypostasis* referred to actually possessed landed property. For the readers of the Hebrews missive who were probably familiar with its colloquial Hellenistic usage, *hypostasis* would have had particular significance. Faith would have been understood as the believer's *assurance* that he/she already had a title of possession in the heavenly world. As M. Bourke has pointed out, *hypostasis* or assurance concerns that which is not yet present but is confidently awaited, and *elenchos* or conviction pertains to that which, while a present reality, is not known except by faith. Martin Buber understood these two attitudes as the double aspect of faith.

A healthy balance of assurance and conviction enables believers to maintain both the existential and eschatological dimensions of faith. It was this balance of faith cooperating with grace that Søren Kierkegaard chose to call the "leap of faith." For Abraham, that "leap" involved *letting go* of Isaac so as to *let God* make of him a great nation. With assurance about the future and conviction in the present, all believers are challenged to do likewise, i.e., to *let go* of their Isaacs, of the fears, preconceived ideas, possessions or attitudes that hinder true faith. In so doing, believers can, thereby, *let God* act and become a more recognized and recognizable presence in human life.

Luke 12:32-48. A compilation of parables and sayings on judgment and vigilance, today's gospel from Luke bears evidence of all three stages of textual development (Jesus, church, evangelist). In its original context during the ministry of Jesus, the parable of the doorkeeper (vv. 35-38; see Mark 13:33-37) was directed at Jesus' contemporaries in an effort to help them to see that the master, i.e., the messiah, had come in the person of Jesus. Indeed, he was knocking at the door, calling attention to his mission of service, but some, e.g., chief priests, scribes, chose to sleep through the moment and to entertain instead their dreams of a kingly, political messiah.

At its second level of development, within the Lucan community of the 80s C.E., the parable was understood to refer to the *second* coming of Jesus. As his faithful disciples, the early Christians were to be ever watchful and in a constant state of preparedness for his return. In that way, even if he came as suddenly and unexpectedly as a night prowler (v. 39, see also 1 Thessalonians 5:2), they would not be caught unaware. When the Son of Man did at last return to find his loyal disciples alert and ready for the eschatological judgment, he would reward their eager expectation by serving them at table. This idea of the master waiting upon the servants was a reference to the messianic banquet in which all those who had remained faithful would joyfully share.

In its third stage of development the evangelist recast the original parable and informed it with a Passover motif. "Let your belts be fastened around your waists and your lamps be burning ready" (v. 35) was part of the traditional Passover legislation, to be observed when the exodus was commemorated each year (Exodus 12:11). Whereas the Wisdom author (see first reading) wove his homily around the memory of the exodus event to remind his contemporaries of the richness of their blessings and heritage, Luke pointed to the exodus as a type of the Christian Passover from death to life which Jesus had accomplished by his saving death on the cross. The early Christians entertained an eager hope that Jesus' second coming would coincide with the Passover-Easter feast.

As R. Fuller has observed, when Christ did not actually return as expected, the church celebrated the eucharist, aware that in the sacramental remembrance Jesus did come and was present, even in advance of his final coming. Therefore, the early community recognized that Jesus' promise, "He will seat them at table and proceed to wait on them," was already being fulfilled, in an anticipatory way, at each eucharistic celebration. Modern believers are also aware that each eucharistic sharing is a reminder of the ancient exodus, a celebration of Jesus' passover and a sure promise of the eternal sharing that will be initiated in the eschatological passage into glory.

Peter's question (v. 41) concerning the intended audience of the parable was not part of the original tradition (see Matthew 24:43-51) and was probably added by Luke in order to bring a new twist of interpretation to the parable. By sharpening the application of the parable, Luke drew attention to the responsibilities of the community who awaited Jesus' return. They were, indeed the "little flock" to whom the Father had been pleased to give the kingdom (v. 32) and because of that the early Christians were to act as dependable and conscientious stewards of that which they were inheriting.

In its original context during Jesus' earthly ministry, the stewards responsible for their fellow servants' welfare would have been the religious leaders of the people. Experts in the law and in the sacred traditions, they *should* have been aware and capable of alerting others to the saving action of God in the words and works of Jesus. At its secondary stage of development, during the first Christian century, the parable served as a warning to the leaders of the Jesus movement. As Jesus' disciples and as the stewards of the new Israel, the church leaders had been entrusted with a great gift. Therefore, they would be held more accountable and judged more culpable if they neglected their responsibilities.

Notice the gradation of the punishment that would be meted out by the master-Son of Man upon his return: (1) those who did not take the master's return seriously and knowingly neglected their authority and abused their charges would suffer the gravest penalty; (2) those who merely neglected their duties through a lack of preparedness would suffer severely; (3) those who were unintentionally neglectful would be the least culpable. As C. Talbert noted, this reflects Jewish thought about sins which were unconscious and therefore less guilty than those that were deliberate (Numbers 15:27-31, Deuteronomy 12-17, Psalm 19:12-13). It should be noted, however, that ignorance of the master's return, i.e., total unawareness of the eschatological judgment, does not eradicate guilt; in fact it results only in a lesser degree of punishment.

For the Christians of the first century, for whom delayed eschatology had become an issue to be reckoned with, today's gospel pericope underscored the *certainty* of Jesus' return and counselled vigilance and preparedness. Although the "delay" or interim between Jesus' first and second advents has already stretched into 20 centuries, the need for responsible stewardship has not lessened, nor can the attitude of watchfulness be relaxed.

1. Remembering the pivotal events of life constitutes the heart of meaningful liturgy (Wisdom).

2. Faith is not only what we think about God but also the willingness to let God be who he is and to let God act in our life (Hebrews).

3. Preparedness for Jesus' return cannot be left until the last minute. Since the time of advent is not known, readiness must be an integral concern of daily living (Luke).

20th Sunday in Ordinary Time

In the lifelong commitment of becoming Christian, the daily struggle is as important as the goal (Hebrews). Included in the process of transformation is the realization that ours must often be a counter-culture, and a counter-politic (Jeremiah). Committed to the contradiction of the cross and to a gospel that challenges the status quo, the believer works toward a peace that comes through division and a joy that is borne of pain (Luke).

Jeremiah 38:4-6, 8-10. Incidents similar to the one recorded in today's first reading earned for the prophet Jeremiah a lasting place in English language usage, even among those unfamiliar with the Hebrew scriptures. Jeremiad, a noun, is defined in A.S. Hornby's Oxford Advanced Dictionary of Current English as "a long, sad and complaining story of troubles, misfortunes, etc."

Today's pericope is from a longer section (37:1—38:28) in which some of the interchanges between Jeremiah and Zedekiah were recorded. Zedekiah was a weak and inconsistent leader, the last of Judah's kings. After Babylonia overpowered Assyria, Zedekiah was appointed as vassal king of Judah, subject to Babylon. Easily swayed, Zedekiah allowed himself to be persuaded by some of the Palestinian nobles to revolt against their Babylonian overlords. Jeremiah had counselled against the rebellion as foolish and suicidal. Instead, the prophet had exhorted king and people to prayer and repentance. When the Babylonian armies swiftly retaliated against the rebels in Judah, Jeremiah advised a hasty and humble surrender.

At one point in the siege, during the respite of 588 B.C.E., the king asked that Jeremiah intercede before Yahweh on behalf of the people. In answer, Jeremiah replied that Nebuchadnezzar would make short shrift of Jerusalem with nothing better than an army of wounded soldiers in his command (37:10). Infuriated at the prophet's lack of cooperation and accusing him of going over to the enemy, the Palestinian nobles had Jeremiah arrested.

Because Jeremiah did not desist in preaching his message of doom for Jerusalem, the nobles approached Zedekiah once again. At this point today's first reading picks up the narrative. While the nobles were attempting to bolster their weakened troops, they believed that Jeremiah was "demoralizing the soldiers." Literally translated, "he weakens the hands of the soldiers," the prophet's efforts at demoralization would, they thought, eventually lead to defeat. When they demanded the death penalty for the prophet, Zedekiah handed Jeremiah over to the nobles with the lame but characteristic excuse, "He is in your power" (v. 5), because in fact he had no power over them. In order to avoid the possible outcry a public execution may have caused, the nobles had the prophet lowered into a cistern and left him to die.

Over the years, especially in recent decades, many of the ancient cisterns have been excavated. These were undergound chambers used for storing water. During the rainy season, the cisterns would be filled with the runoff of rain water and would serve as safe storage places. During the dry periods between the rainy seasons, the cisterns provided the life-sustaining water necessary for survival. Because of this they were considered as priceless possessions and their locations were often kept a secret to deter foul play (e.g., theft, polluting of water supply, etc.). Since the cisterns were usually bottle-shaped and access to their contents was gained by lowering a vessel on a rope, it was virtually impossible to escape from one. But Jeremiah's escape came in the form of a rescue by an Ethiopian eunuch, a courtier of the palace. Ebed-Melech, whose name simply meant "servant of the king," interceded with the king on behalf of the prophet. Ironically, it was not one of his own countrymen but a foreigner who became the symbol of God's salvation.

Hebrews 12:1-4. Part of a longer section (11:1—12:29) on the importance of faith and the necessity of discipline, today's second reading concludes the author's long cavalcade of Old Testament heroes (see last week's second reading). Those heroes—Abraham, Isaac, the prophets, etc.—were presented by the author of Hebrews as models of faith whose qualities were to be admired and emulated by Christians. After reminding them of the wealth of their spiritual heritage, the author turned his attention toward his contemporaries and their situation, exhorting them to persevere in the faith as their ancestors had done before them. By means of an athletic metaphor, the late first century writer described Christian existence as an endurance race or a marathon, that required great dedication and perseverence.

Not alone in their struggle for victory, Christians are supported by a "cloud of witnesses" (v. 1). A term used in the Greek classics, the "cloud" of witnesses was a host of Old Testament heroes, portrayed as the spectators of the track or athletic field. Their presence was meant to encourage those presently involved in life's struggles. Because they had not only survived the "contest" of life, but had also emerged victorious through faith and by grace, the "cloud" of heroes assured their descendants of eventual triumph as well.

Athletic competitors in the ancient olympic events submitted to a rigorous, extensive training program. Part of their preparation for a particular event involved freeing themselves of every possible hindrance, *even their clothing*(!), to concentrate more intently on their pursuit of victory. Analogously, the Hebrews author advised his fellow believers to "lay aside every encumbrance of sin that clings to us" (v. 1). Just as excess weight and unnecessary baggage deter the runner, so do sin and the distractions of evil pervert the course of the Christian athlete. Athletes are coached to maintain a firm concentration on their intended goal; so too Christians are advised to "keep their eyes fixed on Jesus." Besides being the goal of all of life's efforts, Jesus is the believer's model and inspiration. As our leader or pioneer (*archegos*) Jesus has gone before us, setting the course and the pace by his passion and death on the cross. For his fidelity and endurance, he now sits in victory at God's right hand. Through baptism into the saving event of Jesus' death and rising, Christians have received the promise of a share in Christ's triumph, once life's course has been run.

In the final verse of today's pericope, the author reminded his readers that Jesus had faced great opposition during his mission. Those to whom these words were addressed were facing opposition as well in the form of persecution for their faith in Jesus. From both Jewish and Roman authorities, the Christians encountered rejection and open aggression. But, as the author stated in the verse immediately following today's text, "You have not yet resisted to the point of shedding blood" (v. 4). Therefore, he urged his readers to take heart and to maintain the daily struggle of Christian existence, remembering that it may indeed lead to martyrdom. But in the end, they would join Jesus and the cloud of witnesses in glorious victory.

Luke 12:49-53. One of the less appealing aspects of the good news, today's gospel with its hard statements about Jesus' mission may sometimes be passed over by preachers and teachers who prefer the more attractive passages on peace, love and reward. Nevertheless, the crisis of decision and divisiveness Jesus' presence brought to bear on the world is an integral part of his message. As the climax of the section, addressed specifically to his disciples (12:1-53), today's text represents a composite of three originally independent sayings (vv. 49, 50, 51-53). Each saying deals with the effect Jesus' ministry (and that of his disciples after him) would have upon the world.

W.F. Harrington has called vv. 49-50 a glimpse into Jesus' soul. By describing his mission in terms of fire and baptism, Jesus made it clear there could be no neutrality or indifference to his words and works. R. Bultmann and W. Kummel believed these sayings were later additions to the gospel, made by the early church or the evangelist. After the resurrection, looking back with the perspective of hindsight at Jesus' life and its climactic conclusion on the cross, the early believers, according to R. Bultmann et al., described Jesus' mission in terms of fire, etc. But it is quite possible, and indeed very probable, that Jesus, *during* his earthly ministry, understood that the challenging character of his preaching would meet with growing opposition and would eventually result in hostile aggession towards him.

Early in Jesus' public life, John the Baptizer described Jesus as the one who would baptize with Spirit and fire (3:16). In v. 49, Jesus is presented as longing ("How I wish") for the earth to be ablaze with his fire. A familiar scriptural symbol, fire was a frequent metaphor for God himself and for his intervention among his people. For example, fire was the phenomenon through which God chose to communicate his presence to Abraham (Genesis 15:19), to Moses (Exodus 3:2), to Israel in the desert (Exodus 13:21-22) and on Sinai (Exodus 19: 18). A symbol of God's holiness and in some instances of his protection (Zechariah 2:5), fire was also considered to be God's servant (Psalm 104:4; Hebrews 1:7). God's word had been compared to fire by the prophet Jeremiah (Jeremiah 23:29).

Because of its destructive potential and its purifying qualities, fire proved an apt symbol for the action of God among his sinful people. The Day of the Lord had long been associated with the purging fire of God's intervention (Zechariah 13:9) and the exile in Babylon was also described as a purification by fire (Isaiah 43:2, Psalm 66:12). In his desire to ignite fire upon the earth, Jesus knew he was to be the crucible wherein all humanity would be judged, purified, refined and enkindled in an eschatological conflagration.

Baptism (v. 50) in this particular context did not refer to the sacrament by which Christians would later become aflame with Christ's mission. Rather, baptism (from the Greek *baptizein*, in Hebrew *tabal*) meant to be bathed, dipped or immersed. In referring to a baptism he was yet to receive and to his own anguish, Jesus was alluding to the inevitable ordeal he would suffer at the hands of those who rejected him and his message. This image is probably derived from the psalmist (Psalm 124:4-5) who described his personal experience of tragedy in similar terms. In the parallel passage in Mark's gospel (Mark 10:38), the baptism is referred to as "a bath of pain" and clearly refers to Jesus' passion and death. C. Talbert has pointed out that Jesus' "baptism" was the precondition for the release of fire upon the earth; this corresponds to the Lucan chronology: Pentecost (tongues of fire) follows passion. Through Jesus' baptism of suffering and death, the fire of judgment and purification would be unleashed.

The igniting of the fire of eschatological crisis and challenge would bring inevitable discord and division. Because the presence of a blazing fire cannot be ignored, no one could remain neutral in the presence of the redeeming, judging Son of Man. By the radical nature of his words and works, Jesus' presence demanded a choice. Those who accepted the challenge of purification were converted; those who rejected the searing truth of his fire perished. That discord would be a characteristic effect of Jesus' mission had been announced by Luke in the infancy narratives. Simeon had proclaimed, "This child is destined to be the downfall and rise of many in Israel, a sign that will be opposed" (2:34). In other words, in Jesus' coming, each person on earth would be presented with an ultimatum (for him or against him) whose terms would be more binding than the blood ties that unite a family.

The disintegration of the family unit—father against son, son against father, etc.—reflected an apocalyptic tradition that went back to the prophets. Micah had attributed the breakdown of civil and family loyalties to the moral decadence of his people (Micah 7:1-6). "Social disruption has always been associated in the oriental mind with the reign of terror which will precede the age of salvation; in Jewish apocalyptic it figures as one of the signs of the end" (J. Jeremias). Because the shift of the ages and therefore the crisis of decision was inaugurated by Jesus' saving mission, the situation of social disintegration occurred during Jesus' ministry. The same condition existed in the post-resurrection community as a result of the preaching of the cross. As part of the contradiction of the cross and the continuing enigma of Christianity, the faith that brings union, peace and eternal life must also include division, discord and death.

1. Even if a society succeeds in silencing one of its prophets, the word of God will be heard through another (Jeremiah).

2. The daily struggle to become Christian can be compared to an athletic competition but it is certainly not a game (Hebrews).

3. The challenge of the gospel purifies and separates before it unites and brings peace (Luke).

21st Sunday in Ordinary Time

God is full of great surprises! Unlike his creatures, he does not limit his gifts of grace or the scope of his concern. Indiscriminantly he calls all peoples to himself, making no case about race, holding no grudges against the eleventh hour penitents (Isaiah). At heaven's great banquet, forgiven self-righteous image seekers will be grateful tablemates with forgiven murderers and thieves (Luke). Life here and now must be a preparation for the universal feast to come; prejudice should be disciplined by justice, and narrowness of heart by selfless love (Hebrews).

Isaiah 66:18-21. In 1892, Bernard Duhm was the first to suggest that chapters 56-66 of Isaiah constituted a third book and were in fact written by an author other than Isaiah of Jerusalem (chapters 1-39, eighth century B.C.E.; Deutero-Isaiah, chapters 40-55, sixth century B.C.E.). Attributed to one known simply as Trito-Isaiah, today's first reading is part of that third section of Isaiah and, more specifically, part of the longer poem concerning the restoration of Jerusalem. Where his predecessor Deutero-Isaiah had struggled to help his contemporaries to survive their years in exile in Babylonia (587-538 B.C.E.), Trito-Isaiah's prophetic work took place in the years after the return of the exiles to Judah.

In a thought similar to that of Ezekiel (Ezekiel 3:23, 11:22-23, 43: 1-9), Trito-Isaiah understood Israel's renewed greatness to be reflection of God's glory (v. 18). An important concept in the Old Testament, glory (*kabod*) meant "weight" or "importance" and signified an outward, brilliant manifestation of God's greatness. In today's pericope, Jerusalem has been described as the focal point of God's glory. In her restored capacity, the holy city was to serve as a beacon light, guiding all the nations of the earth to herself or, more precisely, to an experience of God within and through his people.

Precisely what the prophet meant by "sign" in v. 19 has yet to be firmly established. However, it would seem he was referring to the remnant (*anawim*) of the people, the faithful survivors of the exile whom the Lord would set forth as a signal or standard for the nations. From among the survivors the Lord would send forth missionaries to the far reaches of the earth. Others have suggested the "sign among them" to be the Jewish diaspora spread throughout the world—a visible proof of God's constant care and protection. Whatever the exact identity of the "sign," it is clear that the prophet understood the vocation of the sign to be missionary and its scope universal. Reflecting God's salvific power and glory, the sign would beckon to Jerusalem those who had never known the Lord. Their task would be catechetical (faith-sharing) and evangelical (proclaiming the good news of God's glory).

Centuries later, Trito-Isaiah's vision came to life again in the person of a faithful survivor from Nazareth. In his eschatological visions, Jesus spoke of the sign of the Son of Man who would come in power and glory and who would dispatch his angels to assemble the chosen from the four winds and the farthest bounds of the earth and sky (Mark 13:4, 26-27). Only then, when Jesus had *himself* become the sign Israel had been called to be, would the universal vision of the sixth century prophet be fulfilled.

Hebrews 12:5-7, 11-13. When the prophet Nathan mediated the everlasting covenant between God and the house of David, part of his message to David was the assurance of divine discipline: "I will be a father to him and he a son to me; if he does evil, I will punish him with the rod such as men use, with strokes such as mankind gives. Yet I will not withdraw my favor from him" (2 Samuel 7:14-15). Ten centuries later, the Christian author of the letter to the Hebrews exhorted his readers to accept the painful and harsh realities of life as an expression of God's loving discipline, not necessarily as a chastisement for wrongdoing but as a necessary part of their formation as Christians. By discipline (in Greek *paideia*), the author referred to that whole process of education and training by which young people are helped to shape themselves in those qualities of mind and body that characterize the real adult, viz., strength, soberness and the ability to cope with life (D.A. Cody).

As a loving and responsible father, the God who was personally involved with his people would have been remiss if he had not included the aspect of discipline in his dealings with his own. But God did not chastise his people via thunderbolts from the sky. Rather, as in the case of David and his descendants, God chose to let his people grow through the experience of "rods and strokes such as mankind gives." In other words, through the vicissitudes of human experience and interaction, God's people would be shaped.

From their Jewish heritage, the Jewish Christians who read the Hebrews missive would have been familiar with the methods that rabbis used with their students. Often, their corrective measures were severe but these were always meted out in a paternal manner. Rabbis called their charges "sons" and the bond that grew between teacher and students was often a lifelong one (Sirach 4:17, 23:2). The Hebrews author also recalled for his Jewish Christian readers the familiar maxim (vv. 5-6 = Proverbs

3:11-12) wherein the hardships endured by the just are understood as rigorous training from God himself.

Urging his readers to look beyond the pain of discipline, i.e., beyond their present suffering from persecution, rejection, etc., the writer of Hebrews encouraged them to see the eventual fruit of their training. For those who endured suffering and graduated, as it were, from the "Christian college of hard knocks," there would be a degree of peace and justice summa cum laude. In another reference to the book of Proverbs, the author counseled his fellow Christians toward a constant and honest moral life-style: "Make straight the paths you walk on" (Proverbs 4:26). From the athletic imagery of a race course (see last week's second reading), the Hebrews' author shifted the attention of his contemporaries to the road pilgrims traveled on their way to God. In the end, once the pilgrimage had been successfully completed and they were sharers in glory with Christ, the necessity and value of discipline would fall into its proper perspective. Until that time, they were to accept it as a means of growth and of Christian discipleship.

Luke 13:22-30. In keeping with his concern for the centrality of Jerusalem in Jesus' saving mission, Luke inserted editorial notes throughout his travel account to remind his readers that Jesus was still enroute to the holy city. Today's gospel pericope begins with one of those editorial reminders: "all the while making his way toward Jerusalem." For Luke, Jerusalem was to be the focal point of the great mystery of redemption. In Jerusalem, God would manifest the extent of his love for his people in the passion, cross and resurrection of Jesus. Unlike the other evangelists, Luke began his gospel (and Acts) in Jerusalem (1:5) and ended it there also (24:52). The lengthy travel account in Luke's gospel (9:51—18:14), sometimes called the Big Interpolation, has been colored by Lucan theology to the extent that no other place names have been mentioned. Although these omissions and the seemingly exaggerated length of the journey lend an artificial character to the account, nevertheless, Luke succeeded in focusing his readers' undivided attention on the place where their salvation would be accomplished.

As C. Talbert has observed, the travel account serves other functions as well: (1) the didactic material given in the context of the journey fits Luke's conception of life as a pilgrimage wherein the Christian faith is the only true direction or "the way" (Acts 9:2, 19:9); (2) the journey was a special period of formation for Jesus' followers; during the journey, they learned of the urgency of the kingdom and of the detachment and dedication necessary to become a part of it.

After his editorial focus on Jerusalem, Luke utilized a collection of sayings (that had different contexts in the other gospels) in order to teach four important lessons about the kingdom: (1) entry into the kingdom is not guaranteed (v. 24); (2) the arrival of the kingdom is imminent (v. 25); (3) there will be no favoritism in the kingdom (v. 25-27); (4) the standards of the kingdom contradict and obviate worldly standards (v. 28-30).

The first lesson, concerning entrance into the kingdom, was occasioned by a question: "Lord, are they few in number who are to be saved?" (v. 23). A perennial problem put before many of Israel's teachers throughout its history, the question probably grew out of the rabbinical tradition that taught that "all Israelites have a share in the world to come" (m. Sanh 10:1) and that "this age the Most High has made for many, but the age to come for a few" (4 Ezra 8:1). The usual and expected answer to the question was that *all Israelites*, great and small, would have a place in the future kingdom. These would constitute the few; but the many tax collectors, sinners and non-chosen elements of the world (gentiles) would be excluded.

Jesus' response shook the traditional and complacent belief that Israel was guaranteed salvation. In a direct blow to those whose sense of being God's chosen ones had ballooned into presumptuousness, Jesus warned of a "narrow gate." Indeed, the gate to the kingdom was as narrow as the cross. For those who could not accept Jesus and the cross as the means of his messiahship, there would be no entrance. Probably the passage also bears the influence of later developments in the post-Easter church when the breach between Christianity and its Jewish matrix widened into a gulf of separation, and when the gentiles outflanked the Jews in their receptivity to the gospel. Certainly there is no implication in the text that a specified and quantifiable number of people would be saved. Therefore, those who even today misconstrue this text and others like it (the references in Revelation to the 144,000) in order to calculate heaven's census are gravely mistaken.

Like the first lesson, the second is comprised of a warning. Because the arrival of the kingdom was imminent, and the time may prove shorter than one had planned for, it was necessary to act immediately so as not to be left knocking in vain on a *closed* door (v. 25). During Jesus' ministry, the saying was probably directed at those who refused to recognize him and his mission. In a short while, he warned, their chance would be lost. During the post-Easter-period, the saying was probably applied to the second coming. In both applications, the lesson was a challenge to decisive action.

The third lesson on favoritism (vv. 25-27) was directed at those who thought themselves privileged citizens and heirs apparent to the kingdom. Again, this lesson, like the first, was a warning for the Jewish community but there was also a powerful message for Christians. Mere lip service or an uncommitted protestation of faith ("Sir, open for us") would not gain entrance to the kingdom. Nor would the fact of familiarity with Jesus ("we ate and drank in your company... you taught us") guarantee admission. It was not enough simply to have been *around* Jesus. What was necessary for salvation was a committed faith that issued forth in a relationship of *knowing* and *being known* by the Lord. Without that faith and personal relationships, those who knocked would be told. "I do not know you... away from me, evildoers!"

In the pericope's final lesson about the kingdom, all who would become members were taught to put aside their preconceptions about membership so as to open themselves to the divine criteria. Given a verbal glimpse into the eschatological banquet hall, Luke's readers were told they will be astounded to find themselves on the outside looking in at the patriarchs and prophets enjoying the feast with *gentiles*. Trito-Isaiah's universalist vision would at last become a reality when people from east, west, north and south were gathered together in the kingdom. Today, preconceptions, though of a different type, concerning those who deserve to be saved still exist. Institutional card-carrying churchgoers may regard the so-called "unchurched" as lost. Some denominations believe themselves to have prerogatives over others. This gospel with its powerful lessons should prod the presumptuous with new ideas and rattle the complacent into action.

1. One day, there will be a worldwide liturgy celebrated in the vernacular of mutual respect and love (Isaiah).

2. As with the pruning of a tree, the fruits of discipline are not always immediately evident (Hebrews).

3. In a world that tolerates apartheid, poverty, nuclear arms, etc., there is no clear understanding of membership in Jesus' kingdom (Luke).

22nd Sunday in Ordinary Time

True self-knowledge is not acquired by lengthy psychoanalysis or self indulgent navel gazing. The person who would truly know and appreciate him/herself must first look away from self toward God (Sirach). In drawing near to God's goodness and holiness, the truth of who we are and who we can become comes to light (Hebrews). Humble awareness precludes pompous self-seeking and frees us for that altruistic love that puts all others first (Luke).

Sirach 3:17-18, 28-29. A faithful Jew of the second century B.C.E., Joshua Ben Eleazar, Ben Sira, was steeped in the traditional values of his people. An inhabitant of Jerusalem and possibly a member of the scribal class of lawyers, Joshua Ben Sira, or Sirach as he has come to be known from the Greek rendering of his name, was fortunate to have been born into prosperity and to have maintained the wealth necessary to devote his time and efforts to study and to travel. He was able to gain the practical wisdom and experience that came from these endeavors. It is believed that during his travels, Ben Sira was often a guest in foreign lands and at foreign courts where he may have served in the capacity of emissary or diplomatic representative of his native Israel.

Originally written in Hebrew ca. 180 B.C.E. and later translated into Greek by his grandson ca. 132 B.C.E., the book of Ben Sira represents an amalgamation of the wise man's keen insights on the Torah, on other sacred writings, on wisdom and maxims for sensible, successful living. Sirach or Ecclesiasticus (Book of the Church) is an excellent synthesis of Ben Sira's response to revealed truth combined with his wise counsel concerning the application of this truth to the various circumstances of daily living. Ben Sira wrote for post-exilic Jews whose infatuation with Hellenistic philosophy and culture threatened to dilute and to pervert their traditional practices and beliefs. The ancient sage's work was highly valued by his fellow countrymen even though it was not accepted into the normative canon of Hebrew scripture. Christians also regarded Ben Sira's wisdom with great respect; no other Old Testament book, with the exception of the Psalter, was used as extensively in the early Christian liturgy.

An excerpted text, joining together portions of two successive short essays, the first verses of the reading are on the subject of humility and the latter verses are concerned with pride. The context of today's reading is that of a parent counseling his child in the fine art of dealing with other people. In his exhortation regarding humility the author praised the value of a modest, gentle life, free of pretentiousness and excessive ambitiousness.

Humility is not to be perceived as a *passive* acceptance but rather, like faith, as an *active* virtue of positive trust. One of the greatest qualities of the Isaian suffering servant (Isaiah 53:7ff) was his humility—his active cooperation with the Lord's power to save his people. When the prophets spoke of the messiah's advent, humility was one of the attributes they assigned to him (Zechariah 9:9). In the psalms, the ideal virtuous person was humble, the person who put all his hope in God, regarded as the source of all greatness (Psalm 10:17, 22:26, 25:9, 34:2, 37:11 etc.). The antithesis of pride that asserted the self in a complete self-reliance, humility, according to Sirach, is especially necessary for those in a higher social stratum: "Humble yourself the more, the greater you are" (v. 18). Like the author of Proverbs, Ben Sira compared pride to foolishness and humility to true wisdom.

In the end, he counseled, the proud would have already received their reward but the humble would enjoy the favor of God (v. 18). In the gospel for today, the Lucan Jesus is presented as counseling his dinner companions toward the humility described by Ben Sira.

Hebrews 12:18-19, 22-24. In the second half of the first Christian century, ca. 80 C.E., some members of the Jesus movement were faced with a crisis of identity. Those Christians who had been Jews and had come to believe in Jesus as the messiah whom their people had long awaited, were subjected to hostile elements from within Judaism and from the Roman authorities as well. As the rift between Jews and Jewish Christians widened, the latter were forced to redefine their faith, rooted in but also distinct from its Jewish matrix. This crisis was precipitated by the fact that in the mid 80s C.E. the Jewish authorities officially ousted the Jewish Christians from the synagogues, thus severing all official ties with them. Once they were separated from Judaism as such, Christians were no longer regarded as a breed (albeit a troublesome one) of Jewish sectarians. Therefore, Christians lost their status as *religio licita* (or legal religion as Judaism was considered by Rome) and were subject to persecution by the imperial Roman authority. Because of the hostilities from Judaism and from Rome, some Christians were tempted to compromise or even abandon their faith in Jesus and to return to the safe and relatively unpersecuted haven of Judaism.

When the author of Hebrews wrote in the 80s C.E. he was fully aware of the faith crisis of his coreligionists. To that end, in his letter, he attempted to bolster their faith in Christ and in Christianity by showing that the new covenant brought by Jesus was in every way superior to the old covenant. Indeed, the Hebrews author based his theology on the premise that Judaism, its cult and its priesthood were obsolete, totally and permanently superseded by the religion based on faith in Jesus Christ. In today's pericope, the author has furthered his argument in favor of Christianity by contrasting the law of Judaism with the gospel of Jesus Christ. The law or the old covenant has been evoked in images of fear and transcendence similar to those in the Pentateuchal theophanic accounts (Exodus 19:12-14, 16-19, 20:18-21). Stressing the untouchableness of God and the awesome dread those encounters engendered in the hearts of humankind, the Hebrews author underscored the fact that the Sinai pact was lived out in an earthly, temporal environment.

The assembly of the Christian covenant, by contrast, was heavenbound. With their names enrolled in heaven, members of the gospel covenant in Jesus' name shared proleptically in the glory of the heavenly Zion. This "now" and "not yet" (or "still to come") aspect of Christian existence is due to the fact believers in Jesus are pilgrims journeying on the way to heaven. Already anticipating the good things to come, through baptism into Jesus, the eucharist, etc., Christians can share already here and now in that which they will fully enjoy in eternity. For those who were tempted for whatever reason to turn away from Christ to return to Judaism, the author's picture of the heavenly city festal gathering of the redeemed made it clear that such a choice would be a foolish step backwards.

Luke 14:1, 7-14. According to B. Malina in his entry on "Banquets" in the recently published *Harper's Bible Dictionary* (1985), people in biblical times used food and drink both as nourishment and as ways of saying something to each other. A meal to which others were invited was an important form of communication with significant social messages exchanged between the host and those who were invited as well as those who might have been invited but were not and also those who declined the invitation. Just as the media used for communication in speech is language, so the media at the festival meals in ancient times was the food and drink and their setting. The quality of food and drink chosen, their mode of preparation, method of service and the seating (or reclining) arrangements all said something about the host's assessment of those invited. Places of greatest honor were those to the right and left of the host; the further away a guest was seated bore evidence to all of his depreciated value in the eyes of the host.

Luke had a special predilection for banquet scenes and he more than any of the other evangelists has portrayed Jesus at table as teacher and nourisher of the people. In today's gospel pericope, the context of Jesus' instruction is a sabbath meal celebrated in the home of one of the Pharisees. Notice that Jesus was both carefully observed (v. 1) and careful *observer* (v. 7). Those who watched Jesus closely were probably concerned with his propriety in keeping the sabbath ritual. The meal was prepared the day before, on the Parasceve or Day of Preparation, so as to keep the sabbath's law concerning rest. After the temple or synagogue service which usually took place at the sixth hour (noon), guests would gather in the host's home to share the dinner. When they were invited to a home, Pharisees usually expected to be seated in a place of honor and, because of their scrupulous observance of the

Torah, they usually were. After witnessing their jockeying around for the coveted seats, Jesus began to teach.

Although Luke has called it a parable the content of Jesus teaching in vv. 7-14 is a group of sayings, called by some scholars a banquet discourse or symposion. Directing his attention first toward the dinner guests, Jesus' words about seeking the lowest place seem to be an echo of the Old Testament proverb: "In the presence of the king, do not give yourself airs; do not put yourself where great men are standing. Better to be invited, 'Come up here,' than be humiliated in the presence of the prince" (Proverbs 25:6). Such wisdom was really a form of etiquette, warning that embarrassment would befall the person who pushed himself forward too brashly. Much more preferable in a social context was that unpretentious behavior that allowed praise and honor to come from others.

But Jesus was not merely concerned with good manners nor should his sayings be reduced to advice about social graces. Rather, it is clear from the subsequent verses that Jesus was trying to lift the attention of his companions from etiquette to eschatology. More important than their social status in the eyes of others was their good standing in the eyes of God. Like the author of Sirach, the Lucan Jesus recommended to his companions the virtue of humility. The person who asserts his/her own importance has already been rewarded with the fleeting and dubious dignity that self-assertion brings. But the truthful person who recognizes the greatness of God as well as his/her own lowliness and need will one day share the honor of union with the Lord at the banquet that never ends.

When he turned his attention to his host, Jesus taught a further lesson about the kingdom. The Pharisee into whose home Jesus had been invited had invited others *like himself*: friends, relatives and those with wealth whose presence would reflect well on the host and his household. Moreover, all those invited would have been able, and *indeed*, would have been expected to reciprocate the favor by inviting the host to dine at their respective homes. In light of this social give-and-take, Jesus' advice must have seemed shocking and even ridiculous. To invite the beggars, crippled, blind and lame would be to entertain those from whom one could expect *no* recompense or reciprocation. Such persons would not have brought prestige to the household by their presence. In fact, the obvious possibility that such persons were unclean (disabilities, etc., were erroneously equated with sin; see John 9) would have reflected badly and brought shame upon the host.

But, Jesus challenged his companions and, with them, *all Christians* to recognize the reversal of human values integral to the good news and to the kingdom (v. 11). From the inauguration of his mission, Jesus had shown God's special love for the poor, the lame, the blind, etc. (Luke 4:18 = Isaiah 61:1-2). Those whom the world with its misguided criteria rejected would be the special guests at the banquet of the eschatological kingdom. Jesus challenged his followers to show the same altruistic love for the homeless, the downtrodden and the outcast as they would have liked to exchange with the wealthy and well-placed members of society. In so doing, they would be living the truth of the good news and their humility would be eternally rewarded (v. 14) by God himself.

1. The proud and pompous may impress and dazzle but the humble person is loved and befriended (Sirach).

2. God's drawing near to his people through the mystery of incarnation is the supreme act of humility (Hebrews).

3. When the beggars of society, the crippled, the blind and the lame become our preferred guests, then the kingdom cannot be far off (Luke).

23rd Sunday in Ordinary Time

Followers of Jesus are summoned to a determined and deliberate commitment that does not permit itself detours or distractions (Luke). Through baptism, disciples are initiated by God's own Spirit into the process of seeking and finding God's wisdom (Wisdom). Integral to that process is a singlehearted love of the Lord that supersedes all other bonds (Philemon).

Wisdom 8:13-18. Latest of all the Old Testament scriptures, the book of Wisdom was written in Alexandria about two generations before Christ ca. 60 B.C.E. Wisdom was the Jewish answer to a Greek philosophical system that threatened to overwhelm and dilute traditional Jewish religion and culture. For its Jewish readers, the book served as inspiration and encouragement to preserve Judaism's monotheistic concepts and traditional values in the midst of a Hellenized environment. For its Greek reading audience, Wisdom offered in their own language, thought patterns and literary style a sophisticated, cultured presentation of the Jewish religion. Despite the fact the work was purported to be the *Wisdom of Solomon*, the book was not included in the Jewish (or Protestant) canon of scripture.

Of course, the first century B.C.E. date of composition precludes a Solomonic authorship. While the actual identity of the author cannot be known for certain, he was probably a Greek-speaking Jew familiar with the classic works of Homer, Plato, the Stoics and the Greek tragedians. Since he lived and wrote in the cosmopolitan seaport city of Alexandria, the author was able to avail himself of a wealth of knowledge. The intellectual center of its day, it boasted a world-famous museum and a library with over 400,000 volumes in circulation. Founded by Alexander the Great and named for himself, ca. 322 B.C.E., Alexandria was the capital of Egypt's Ptolemeic dynasty and later became the seat of Rome's government in Egypt. After Rome and Antioch, Alexandria with its population of 500,000 was the third-largest city of the ancient world. Home to the largest concentration of Jews in the diaspora, Alexandria provided the environment for Jewish scholars and philosophers to exchange and debate ideas and methodologies with their Hellenistic counterparts. There can be no doubt this intellectual interchange served as a partial impetus for the translation of the Old Testament into Greek, known as the Septuagint (LXX).

Today's first reading is rooted in Judaism's legendary sage, Solomon, and is based upon the episode in his career when Yahweh promised to grant the king whatever he requested in prayer. The earliest version of Solomon's prayer has been recorded in 1 Kings 3:6-9 where the monarch asked God for understanding. A later version in 2 Chronicles 1:8-10 illustrates Solomon's desire for the wisdom necessary to govern his people well. In today's pericope the Wisdom author has expanded Solomon's prayer and deepened its theology. Enveloped by a literary inclusion (vv. 13, 17: "counsel"), the prayer reflects a first century Greek philosophy that attributed humanity's inability to know God's intentions (will, plans) to the fact that the mortal body weighs down the mind. Because this concept (v. 15) is so reminiscent of Plato's thought (*Phaedo*, 30.81c), the author of Wisdom has been falsely accused of dualism. Dualism distinguished sharply between matter and spirit, regarding matter as earth-bound and intrinsically evil. While such an idea was foreign to the Old Testament which taught that things created are good ("and God saw what he created and saw that it was good" Genesis). the dualistic influence of Plato's philosophy *did* eventually have a lasting and detrimental effect upon later theologies.

Philemon 9-10, 12-17. Slavery was an accepted, major institution in the ancient world. There were royal or crown slaves, in service to the king; there were also temple slaves who performed duties for the cult officials. Even ordinary people owned slaves who served as domestic help. Most were slaves because they had been taken as part of the booty in war: others were forced into slavery because they had defaulted on debts. But many freely sold themselves into slavery in order to earn a living, pay debts, etc. (Leviticus 25:39, Exodus 21:5-6, Deuteronomy 15:16-17, 1 Kings 9:21. Numbers 31:25-47). Regarded as the chattel or *property* of the owner, slaves were mentioned in the laws of the Torah, but these usually safeguarded the rights of the slave-owners. For example, if another person injured, stole or killed a slave, legislation demanded that restitution be made to the slave's owner because his property had been damaged or lost. It has been estimated that during the first Christian century, one third of Rome's population of 1,200,000 were slaves and that there were over 60,000,000 slaves throughout the empire. Onesimus was one of these many slaves, the subject of Paul's letter to Philemon.

A priceless literary gem, Philemon represents the only truly personal letter in the New Testament, addressed from one individual to another and occasioned by private concerns. Traditionally, it was thought that Paul wrote the letter from his Roman imprisonment but lately, i.e., for most of the 20th century, the letter's point of origin has been thought to be Ephesus. Because of the instances involved and the fact that Paul did endure an Ephesus incarceration, ca. 54-55, the Asia Minor locale seems more feasible.

Philemon was probably a prominent member of the church at Colossae; the community there met in his home for prayer and fellowship. Onesimus, the slave of Philemon, had apparently run away and may also have been guilty of stealing something of value from his master (vv. 11, 18). Onesimus had fled to Paul for refuge and during his stay with the apostle was converted to Christ. Paul referred to him as "my child whom I have begotten during my imprisonment" (v. 10). Evidently Onesimus, whose name meant "useful," had indeed become so, for Paul wished to keep him as an assistant in his work for the gospel (v. 12). Nevertheless, Paul recognized Philemon's right of proprietorship and sent the slave back to his rightful owner. While he did not attack the right of Philemon to *own* another person and thereby did not challenge the institution of slavery per se, Paul's appeal to Philemon "to accept and to know Onesimus as a beloved brother in the Lord" is quite significant. As J.M. O'Connor has expressed it, "Paul was faced with the alternative of influencing men through a violent change in a social institution or of changing men, who would then, from conviction, abolish the institution." Onesimus' new status in Christ made him an equal brother of Philemon in the Lord. That relationship was deeper and more binding than any slave contract.

By calling Philemon to accept Onesimus as a brother in Christ, Paul sought to transform the relationship from one of legality to one of love. Since we know nothing further of the developing relationship between the slave and his master, we can only assume that their reconciliation was an amicable one. But institutions are slow in renewing themselves. Not until the 18th century did the Christian conscience succeed in eradicating, at least legally, the age-old practice of slavery. Yet laws do not ipso facto create morality and slavery persists in our society and throughout the world. Paul's appeal for partnership in the Lord has yet to be fully realized.

Luke 14:25-33. Volunteer work is a demanding endeavor, requiring great generosity, time and effort. Statistics indicate that 100% of the services rendered to the Christian community are performed by a mere 13% of the congregation. But volunteerism is not necessarily discipleship. One of the benefits of being a volunteer is that there is always the option to take a break, to "sit this project out," as it were, or even to quit! "Discipleship," on the other hand, "is not periodic volunteer work, on one's own terms or at one's convenience" (R.J. Karris). As is clear in the strong statements in today's gospel, discipleship is total, unconditional, limitless commitment to Christ. Integral to the challenge of discipleship is the willingness to be converted daily to Christ in one's words and works, and to persevere in the process even at the cost of suffering and death.

Still en route to Jerusalem where he would teach the ultimate lesson of discipleship, Jesus is presented in this gospel pericope as addressing a "great crowd." From the verses immediately preceding this text, it would seem that Jesus' words were directed to those who had been invited to the messianic banquet, i.e., the poor, crippled, blind, lame, those on the highways and along the hedgerows (Luke 14:21, 23). But, they would learn, the invitation to the banquet was just the first step. Those who were invited to enjoy the messianic feast would also be called to drink deeply of the cup (Mark 10:38) of Jesus' suffering and death. Significantly, Jesus' summons to discipleship was issued not only to Peter or the Twelve or even to the seventy-two but to the multitudes. In other words, discipleship was not a *special* vocation extended to a few; it is *the* vocation of *all* who believe in the Lord Jesus.

Structurally, today's gospel selection is comprised of a catena of sayings on discipleship, followed by two parables. Like many of the semitic sayings, the forcefulness of the first saying regarding turning one's back on father, mother, etc. (v. 26) is shocking. Literally the challenge was even stronger, stating that the one who would follow Jesus should *hate* parents, etc. Hate or *misein* (Greek) is the opposite of *agapan* or love. Matthew softened the expression, stating "Whoever *loves* father or mother. . . *more than me* is not worthy of me" (Matthew 10:37). Most scholars believe, however, that Luke's severe wording was the more original. To hate one's family did not imply *animosity* but *detachment* in the strongest possible terms. Part of the cost of discipleship is the willingness to forego the joys of security of family ties so as to be bound completely to Christ. Of course, Jesus did not advocate the *renunciation* of familial responsibilities. Indeed, he castigated the Pharisees for their selfish and so-called religious custom of "korban" (Mark 7:12). Disciples of Jesus were to know that their first priorities were Jesus and the kingdom. "Hating" parents simply meant loving Jesus first and foremost, above family, even above self (vv. 26, 27).

From that love would flow the willingness and the ability to follow Jesus by taking up the cross. Because of this reference to the cross, it is clear that by the time the gospel was written, the circumstances of Jesus' death were well known. Luke has used the same word for "take up" (or carry: *bastazo*) which was used to describe Jesus' carrying his cross on the way to Calvary (John 19:16). Furthermore, in other passages in his gospel, Luke added "after me" (23:26) and the adverb "daily" (9:23) in order to stress the close association discipleship would have with Jesus' saving act on the cross.

In the two short parables with which the pericope concludes, Jesus communicated the necessity of entering into the process of discipleship with a clear head and the intention of persevering. Like the man who undertook the task of building the tower, the disciple was to determine sensibly what would be needed in order to complete his undertaking. While the tower would require certain materials (plans, money, etc.), what would the disciple require? Counting the cost was a necessary aspect of every serious project; but discipleship was not to be a calculated, measured response. Jesus' advice to his disciples,"calculate the outlay," (v. 28) was a summons to remember that the only "outlay" worthy of discipleship was the complete and entire gift of oneself. Following Jesus would cost *not less* than everything. To know that, at the outset, was the beginning of responsible discipleship. As for "materials," these would be the graces and charisms given to Jesus' followers through the Spirit.

In the second parable about the king's intent on doing battle, Jesus urged his disciples to a realistic assessment of the work at hand. Only a totally inept fool would risk the lives of his army of 10,000 men by sending them headlong into a battle against 20,000 men. By underestimating the enemy's strength, the king would have lost the battle and his men. Instead, however, the king with the fewer soldiers resorted to a strategic ploy and made peace with his more powerful enemy. The point of the parable is not in the compromise made but in the king's wise assessment of the task at hand. The same wisdom and foresight would be required of Jesus' disciples. The assurance of success, like the bonds of one's family, was a luxury the true disciple would be called upon to renounce. When they seemed unequal to the task at hand, Jesus' disciples were not to shrink from the labor but trustingly to give their all, knowing that anything less was unworthy of the one whom they followed.

1. God's wisdom and ways cannot be ascertained by intellectual gymnastics but by an openness to revelation through the Spirit (Wisdom).

2. Faith in Jesus unites as brothers and sisters those who would otherwise never have considered one another as friends (Philemon).

3. Christian discipleship is not a temporary or a voluntary option; it is rather a demanding, total, lifelong commitment (Luke).

24th Sunday in Ordinary Time

A uniquely blessed encounter, the experience of divine forgiveness is like a homecoming (Luke) because ours is not a God of our own making, an idol created by our wishful imaginings or need (Exodus). Ours is the creator God who involved himself with us in Christ and set us free from sin (1 Timothy).

Exodus 32:7-11, 13-14. Linking all three of the readings for this Sunday's liturgy is the theme of atonement or returning to God in repentance. In the first pericope from Exodus, it is the people of Israel who are reunited with the God of the covenant after their apostasy. The second reading presents Paul rejoicing over the fact of his conversion, offering his experience as an example for other sinners. Today's gospel is a veritable celebration for sinners as it dramatizes in triple parables the merciful love of God that seeks out the sinner, moves him/her to repentance and rejoices at his/her home coming!

Although most scholars believe the issue of the golden calf to be an anachronism, i.e., the transference of a later event (the installation by Jeroboam of two calves at the Dan and Bethel shrines: 1 Kings 12:28) back into the earlier wilderness period, it must be admitted that the Exodus authors and redactors had a definite purpose in placing the incident where they did and in allotting it such a degree of importance. As Brevard Childs has explained, not only does the calf-apostasy occupy a length of three chapters but it also produces an enormous literary rupture right in the middle of the divine instructions at Sinai. In spite of their recent deliverance from Egypt and the wondrous events at Sinai, Israel became apostate before Moses even descended the mountain!

Childs has said that this incident illustrates that "at the heart of sacred tradition lies Israel's disobedience and rebellion. The Old Testament understood this episode of flagrant disobedience, not as an accidental straying, but as *representative* in its character." In other words, the relationship between God and humanity can always be characterized as the divine fidelity reaching out to redeem and forgive human infidelity.

The image of the bull or calf as an object of worship was known in the ancient world since at least the 13th century B.C.E. Apis in Egypt was represented by a molten calf as was Baal in Canaan. Among the Israelites, the fabrication of the molten image was not so much a deviation to idolatry as it was a desire to have a visible representation of Yahweh.

Karl Barth called the episode a good example of how human religion could confuse the *vox populi* with the *vox Dei*. The institution can at any moment produce a "calf" on its own, in seeking to be relevant to the "people's need." But need does not create religiom. Although Aaron had ordered the making of the calf in a dubious effort to salvage the faith of his people, all that resulted was a compromise that threatened the integrity of their relationship with God.

Moses' mediation with Yahweh on behalf of his sinful people resulted in a renewal of the promises of land, posterity and prosperity that had been made to Abraham. With this incident, the theological framework of the scriptures has been defined. When his overtures of love and invitations to relationship are answered by human arrogance, God will nevertheless remain merciful and receptive to humanity. Centuries later, God would send his Son to be mediator par excellence of his relationship with his people and incarnate pledge of his merciful love.

1 Timothy 1:12-17. What Israel learned at the foot of Mt. Sinai, Paul experienced for himself on his way to Damascus, viz., the gratuitous quality of God's forgiving love. Since the 19th century, many scholars have doubted that Paul actually wrote the so-called pastoral letters (1 and 2 Timothy, Titus) but the letters are so informed with the apostle's thought that his influence (even if it be an indirect one) cannot be denied. Written *as if* Paul were the author, the pastorals contain much information about Paul's ministry and even some direct quotations. Today's second reading is an example of authentic Pauline information.

Addressing himself to Timothy, Paul's legate in Ephesus, the author of 1 and 2 Timothy intended to formulate directives and guidelines for the late first or early second century church. Among his recommendations were: (1) an exhortation to maintain intact the deposit of the faith, (2) a warning against the dangers of heresy (in this case it was a brand of Jewish gnosticism), (3) criteria for appointing qualified leaders, (4) principles governing public worship or liturgy.

In the verses immediately preceding today's pericope, the author recommended the good news of Christianity as a sound teaching and the only sure defense against every kind of sin and sinner (1:8-11). Then, using himself and his own conversion experience as a model, Paul illustrated the power of God's grace to transform and to renew. Calling himself a former blasphemer and a man of arrogance, Paul attributed his complete reversal of values and life-style solely to the grace that had been granted him in "overflowing measure" (v. 14). Paul used the specific term *hypotuposis* in describing himself as a example. *Hypotuposis* means an outline or a first-draft. As James Gaffney has commented on this text, "The outline of his (Paul's) experience is the very outline of the gospel, the good news that God's benevolence is extended through Jesus Christ to those who deserve it least, to sinful unbelievers, so that they may have faith in him and gain everlasting life."

Whereas most people would prefer to leave an unsavory past behind and to blot unpleasant memories from their minds, Paul actually seemed to glory in remembering what he had been and what he had done. On several occasions in his letters and in Acts, Paul is presented as reminding his readers of his past sin. William Barclay would have us understand Paul's desire to keep his memory fresh as (1) a safeguard against pride, (2) a sure way to remain grateful for the love that had been shown him, and (3) an impetus to even greater efforts for Christ.

Perhaps his utter humility is what has maintained Paul's appeal throughout the centuries; by opening his heart and confessing his guilt, he continues to befriend the guilty. By the same token, he shows the guilty that the source of their forgiveness and their hope for a new life is in Christ Jesus.

Luke 15:1-31. While the Lucan parable of the lost son and the forgiving father is also featured as the gospel for the Fourth Sunday of Lent (Year C), the inclusion today of the two shorter parables (lost sheep, lost coin) makes the evangelist's message even more poignant. As Luke has indicated in v. 1, the tax collectors and sinners were drawn to Jesus; they were attracted by his mercy and concern for their welfare.

But the scribes and Pharisees, who were also drawn to Jesus, albeit for different reasons, resented the fact that Jesus welcomed those whom they regarded as the pariahs of society. Religious professionals, schooled in the law and in its observance, the scribes and Pharisees thought they knew the mind and heart of God concerning sinners. Jesus, by his words and works, confronted them with the shocking and "unseemly" reality that God not only loves sinners; indeed, he seeks after them and welcomes them with joy!

All three of the lost items in the gospel were things the scribes and Pharisees would have judged not worth searching for. After all, what logical person would leave a herd of 99 sheep to search for a stray? And who would actually sweep clean a house to find one coin when they had nine others? And who would open him/herself to greater misery by seeking out a prodigal child who had disgraced the family name and disassociated himself from his sacred heritage when you had another fine and upright son at home?

This trio of parables could be regarded as Jesus' answer to the criticism of the scribes and Pharisees, viz., that those who seem worthless and irretrievably lost are actually the predilect of the kingdom! The twin parables of the lost sheep and lost coin serve to introduce the more important third parable and to increase the pathos of the narrative. By alerting the reader to the "illogical" ways of God, they challenge believers to open themselves to a similar acceptance of and care for others.

In ancient Palestine, a father could legally abdicate or dispose of his property by making a will that would be executed when he died (Numbers 36:7-9) or he could give his possessions to his children while he lived. The eldest son would receive a double share of the property and the other sons would divide the remainder. Evidently, the younger son took what would have been one third of his father's property, converted it to cash and left for a "distant land" (v. 12). Obviously, the land was in gentile territory because after he had squandered his money, the son had to find employment as a swineherd; pigs were regarded as unclean by Jews, who neither ate nor raised them (Leviticus 11:7).

Finally, the son "came to his senses." Literally translated, this phrase in v. 17 is rendered "he entered into himself" and it was an expression in both Hebrew and Aramaic for turning back to God or repentance. Although he no longer had any legal claim on his father, the son's confidence in returning home is meant to encourage every sinner. No one can rightfully make a claim upon God; all we are and all we have is God's gracious gift. Even the very notion of repentance is made possible by the prompting of divine grace.

In the touching scene that follows, it becomes clear that the father had been eagerly waiting for the son to come home. Without a word of reproval, the father ordered a party to be prepared; he called for a robe, a ring and shoes. These garments were a sign that the son was not to be received as a *servant* (slaves did not wear robes, shoes or finger-rings) but in his former status as *son*. The entire gospel is summed up in the father's proclamation: "This son of mine was dead and has come back to life. He was lost and is found." In the joy of the father over his returned son, the lesson of God's mercy and love was taught.

For the tax collectors and sinners, the parable was, no doubt, a source of hope. But the scribes and Pharisees, like the elder son in the parable, resented what they regarded as an injustice. Like the elder son, the scribes and Pharisees could enumerate their good deeds, their virtues, their generosity in tithing, etc. And like the elder son who expected something from his father, the scribes and Pharisees expected something from God. By calling the elder son to rejoice in his brother's return, the parable challenges those who think themselves righteous to look upon others with compassion and to look inward upon themselves with humility. Just as no repentant sinner is irretrievably lost, nor will we find any self-canonized saints in heaven!

1. Idols of our own making are no substitute for a true experience of God (Exodus).

2. The memory of forgiven sin should fill us with gratitude and inspire us to service (1 Timothy).

3. The joy of every sinner's reconciliation should be celebrated by the entire community (Luke).

25th Sunday in Ordinary Time

When justice and charity are relinquished to profits and progress then the business of making money has become a god and true religion is lost (Amos). But when the prudence and ingenuity of the entrepeneur are incorporated by the disciple, then religion benefits (Luke). Christians are not called to an isolated existence untouched by secular affairs but to an involvement with the world; by their very presence the lives of others are improved (1 Timothy).

Amos 8:4-7. Each of the three selections for today's liturgy pertains to the subject of stewardship. In the text from Amos, the shepherd of Judah called to be God's prophet and steward of his word confronted his fellow countrymen from the north. Amos railed against Israel for having violated the sacred trust of the covenant and its laws. In the second reading, Timothy, the faithful steward of God's people in Ephesus, was reminded that one aspect of responsible discipleship was that of prayer for all in authority, even and especially those who were the stewards of civil and secular power. The gospel text with its curious parable about the conniving manager offered a skillful lesson in stewardship for all Jesus' disciples.

Amos was the first of the so-called writing prophets (although his was probably a secretarial endeavor) who functioned actively as a prophet sometime during the 40 year span when Uzziah was king of Judah (781-743 B.C.E.). A rugged man from Tekoa (modern day Tequ'a is about six miles south of Bethlehem) in Judah, Amos made his living by shepherding (Amos 1:1) a breed of sheep especially valued for their fine wool. A migrant worker, Amos traveled from the hill country of Judah (ca. 3000 feet above sea level) where he tended sheep, to the lower slopes of the Judean hills where he was seasonally employed as a "dresser of sycamore trees" (Amos 7:14). Actually, the trees were a form of wild fig that required a skillful hand to pinch or nip the fruit. This process would release an insect that impeded the ripening of the fig and would have eventually rotted the fruit. While he was at work (Amos 7:15), Amos received his prophetic call to go from his native Judah to the northern kingdom of Israel. There, a most unlikely candidate, he was to confront the more sophisticated northerners with their faults and to convince them that, unless they repented, they would meet a disastrous end.

Socially and religiously the situation in the northern kingdom was in a state of rapid deterioration. Ignoring the equity and charity that were to characterize their covenantal fellowship, the rich lived in fine stone homes, elaborately decorated with wood and ivory inlay. While the wealthy feasted on fine foods and rich wines, the poor eked a wretched and miserable existence from a land depleted by war (2 Kings 12:24-25), drought and blight (Amos 4:7-9).

In the verses immediately preceding today's first reading (8: 1-3), Amos shared with his audience one of his several oracular visions. The prophet described his inspiration as a basket of fully ripe summer fruit just waiting to be eaten. The fruit, so ripe as to be only moments away from spoiling, was compared by Amos to Israel, so ripe in its sins as to be only moments away from God's devouring justice. In today's reading, the prophet has attacked in particular those who despoiled the people of Israel by their fraudulent business practices. Evidently, these merchants and tradespeople were so caught up in the business of making money that they were impatient when the feasts of the new moon and sabbath occurred. During the holy days, sacrifices were offered and all were to observe the prescribed rest in honor of the Lord (Numbers 28:11-15).

Not only did these predatory merchants regard the sabbath rest as a loss in profits, but their business methods were completely unscrupulous. The "diminishing of the ephah" and "the adding to the shekel" were dishonest weighing procedures similar to the butcher who keeps his thumb on the scales! Significantly, these injustices were bring perpetrated on the poor as they tried to buy wheat for bread, the very staff of life.

1 Timothy 2:1-8. In one of the many memorable scenes of the play, *Fiddler on the Roof*, the village rabbi had just taught his congregation that there is a blessing for everything. "Is there," the people inquired, "a blessing even for the *Tsar*?!" In reply, the rabbi intoned, "May God bless and keep the Tsar. . . far away from us!" Although this is probably not the style of prayer the author of 1 Timothy had in mind, nevertheless he *did* counsel his charges to pray for all, "especially for kings and those in authority." This and other counsels concerning the pastoral care and ordering of the Christian community have caused the two letters to Timothy and the one to Titus to be referred to as the pastoral letters or simply the pastorals. All three letters were instructive in nature, advising the communities in Ephesus (1 and 2 Timothy) and Crete (Titus) to: (1) remain faithful to the traditional deposit of the faith, (2) defend the faith against heretical elements, (3) appoint and obey qualified leaders among the local communities, (4) regulate and safeguard the integrity of public worship, (5) support the faithful in their efforts to live grace-filled lives in accordance with their particular vocations in life.

Since the 19th century the authorship of the letters has been in question, the main objections to a Pauline authorship being: (a) the situation of the churches and the advanced structure of the community organization seem to indicate a second century date (Paul died in the mid-60s C.E.); (b) the heresies attacked in the letter seem to be a brand of second century Jewish gnosticism; (c) the style and vocabulary of the pastorals differ greatly from the undisputed Pauline corpus; (d) the doctrinal elements featured so largely in the earlier letters (the cross, the Spirit, being "in Christ," charisms, etc.) have yielded to an emphasis on tradition, organization of the institution, etc.

While the exact authorship and date of the pastorals remain a subject for debate, most scholars agree that the author was familiar with Pauline theology; some of the passages within the letters are quotations from Paul himself.

Timothy had been converted by Paul on the apostle's first mission to Ephesus (ca. 47 C.E.). When Paul passed through a second time, Timothy joined him and worked as his companion. Later, Paul left Timothy in Ephesus to shepherd the community of believers there. At the time when 1 Timothy was written, the situation of the Christian community was a perilous one. Because they were regarded by Rome as lacking in civic virtues (they refused to worship the emperor, etc.), Christians were subject to recurrent persecutions. Probably, the advice to pray for all peoples, especially the authorities, was aimed at easing the tension between the believers and the empire. This seems clear in the author's statement: "that we may be able to lead undisturbed and tranquil lives" (v. 2). Moreover, the author underscored the universal scope of God's plan of salvation: "for he wants all to be saved and come to know the truth" (v. 4). Rome was not merely to be tolerated as a hostile environment; even Rome was to enjoy the benefits of Jesus' mediation and ransom (v. 5). Down to the present age, Christians continue to thrive within an alien and at times aggressive society. The exhortation to prayer and the reminder that salvation is *for all* remain valuable lessons.

Luke 16:1-13. Often described as a controversial and difficult parable, Luke's story of the rich man and his clever manager is more easily understood against the background of ancient Palestinian economics and usury laws. According to the parable proper (vv. 1-8a) the manager had been caught in the act of swindling his master (probably by embezzlement) and was given notice of his termination. Given the known history of the times, the rich man may have been an absentee land owner who had entrusted his business affairs to a manager. The manager (agent, steward, in other translations) was a trained and trusted employee, who had the authority to represent his master in all business transactions. In that capacity, the manager could make loans, rent or lease property, collect debts and fees, etc.

On each business transaction, the manager, like the tax collector, was to recoup his master's money in full. In the process he was free to earn for himself on each transaction a commission that took the form of interest added on to the principal. According to the law (Exodus 22:25, Leviticus 25:36, Deuteronomy 23:19ff), it was forbidden to take interest on loans to fellow Israelites. But, as W.J. Harrington points out, ways had been found of evading the law. It was argued that the law applied only to the destitute in order to protect them from exploitation. If it could be proven that the intended borrower had at least *some* of the commodity he wished to borrow and was under no compulsion, a loan could be permitted. "In this way commercial transactions were concluded by a legal fiction, without infringing on the letter of the law" (W.J. Harrington). Wheat and oil, the commodities mentioned in the parable, were especially liable to this kind of legal maneuvering because *most* people had at least the *minimum* of both materials. Therefore the manager's action of exacting interest on the wheat and oil (his own commission) and then of reducing that interest on his own volition was an accepted legal procedure.

Seeing that his employment was soon to be terminated due to his *past* dishonesty, the manager realized he could "not dig ditches" (v. 3). According to the literal translation of v. 3, the manager was "physically incapable" of such manual work. In addition to this physical limitation, he had the psychological burden of being ashamed to beg. Therefore, aware of his capacities and incapacities, the manager set about making provisions for his future so that, when he was fired, he would have friends to support him and to welcome him into their homes. To that end, he called his master's debtors and reduced their debts by 50 and 20 per cent respectively. In actual fact, he had done his master no injustice; he had *not* acted dishonestly. He had merely surrendered *his own* commission, viz., the *interest* he as manager had added to the principal owed his master. For this prudent act his master praised the manager for "being enterprising" (v. 8a).

With this understanding of the Palestinian economic situation, the parable need no longer perplex the interpreter. Consequently the point of the parable, expressed in v. 8b seems clear. Faced with a crisis, the manager (one of the worldly) acted swiftly and employed even radical means in order to deal with his situation. In its original context the parable described for its hearers their own situation, i.e., Jesus' preaching of the kingdom was the crisis to be dealt with. In response to that crisis, radical choices had to be made and swift action had to be taken lest the summons to salvation be forfeited (by the other worldly).

Attached to the parable (vv. 1-8a) and its primary meaning (v. 8b) is a string of sayings that represent other, later interpretations, added by the evangelist and the first century church. All the sayings are linked by a complex network of catchwords, the connection of which is lost in translation. In the first interpretation (v. 8), Jesus' disciples were exhorted to make good use of this world's goods so as to reap an eternal reward ("a lasting reception"). If the cunning manager could provide so well for his future by using material things, Jesus' followers should be capable of equal prudence and wisdom. Given the general Lucan attitude toward material possessions, it would seem that the evangelist was referring to the giving of alms, sharing in common, etc. By prudent use of material goods, the hardships of the poor could be lessened and the cause of the kingdom would be furthered.

In its second interpretative comment (vv. 10-12), the scene shifts from the eschatological aspect of the kingdom to the daily preparation for it. By proving themselves worthy in: (1) little things, (2) elusive wealth, and (3) someone else's money, the would-be stewards of God's people can become worthy of (1) greater trust, (2) lasting wealth, (3) his/her own reward. The third and final interpretation (v. 13) has no real connection to the parable but describes that quality of total dedication Jesus expected from his disciples. One could not serve both God and money. Money or "mammon" (from the root *'amen*: to be firm) meant "that in which one puts one's trust." Jesus' disciples were to faithfully *serve and trust in God alone* while *making wise use* of money for the sake of others. As C. Talbert has expressed it, wealth or mammon is to be used *sacramentally*, as a *means* of expressing love of God by helping others. This ideal of the wise management of wealth was reflected in the life-style of the early community (Acts 2:44-45, 4:32, 34, 6:1ff). Today's Christians are called to the same ideal of responsible and caring stewardship.

1. Dishonest dealings in the business place makes weekend worship a lie (Amos).

2. If politicians received as much prayerful support as financial backing, who knows what the impact might be (1 Timothy)?

3. Naivete with regard to worldly affairs is a detriment to true discipleship (Luke).

26th Sunday in Ordinary Time

In a world where the "haves" and the "have nots" are easily distinguished, Christianity has not yet made an impact (Amos). Generous sharing of the goods of the earth, of talents and resources is the necessary result of Christian commitment (1 Timothy). When the idle are moved to serve the burdened poor, the message of Christ is proclaimed and the universal love of the kingdom is mirrored upon the earth (Luke).

Amos 6:1, 4-7. Because they enjoyed the lion's share of the earth's riches, the wealthy upper class of Israelite society assumed that they were especially favored by God. Chosen by God, created as his people, they believed they were reaping the deserved benefits of their holy alliance with the God of their ancestors. Moreover, the wealthy entertained the idea that the Lord would come among his people at the appointed time and crown their achievements with even greater blessings. To that end, they looked forward to the "Day of the Lord" with joyful anticipation. Amos had an entirely different perception of the situation. He did not deny the special vocation of God's people or the fact there would indeed be a Day of the Lord. But Amos rightly understood Israel's special election as a call that involved responsibility and demanded accountability from those who had been so blessed. In a dramatic twist of thought, he acknowledgd Israel's special position while at the same time warning that this special position would be the cause of its downfall, e.g., "You *only* have I known of all the peoples of the earth: therefore I will punish you for all your iniquities" (Amos 3:2). In the same manner, the prophet assured Israel that the Day of the Lord in whose glory they longed to share would be for Israel "all gloom without a single ray of light" (5:20).

Structurally, Amos' message was couched in a series of oracles, words and woes, and visions. In the oracles against the nations, the prophet curried the attention of his audience by prophesying doom upon the hated enemies of Israel and Judah. Once he had gained their sympathy, the prophet concluded his series of oracles (1—2:16) with an oracle for each of the kingdoms of Israel and Judah. Here the prophet included his coreligionists among those heathens who displeased the Lord and he promised them a similar fate.

Following the oracles the prophet enumerated a list of words and woes directed at Israel. Today's first reading is from the third woe concerning self-indulgence (6: 1-14). An excellent companion text to today's gospel, the Amos pericope, contrasting the difficult situation of the poor with the extravagant lifestyle of the rich ensconced upon their ivory beds, is a vivid one. Similarly elaborate furnishings, such as beds inlaid with ivory panels, have recently been excavated at the site of Arslan Tash in northern Syria, east of Carchemish. No doubt similar pieces existed in Israel, in drastic contrast to the straw pallets upon which the poor rested.

Where the poor rarely ate meat and were fortunate occasionally to add fish to their simple diet of bread, the rich feasted on tender young lambs. In addition, they also had a penchant for calves fed only with milk and confined to their stalls lest their meat become toughened (v. 4). (Veal was as popular and controversial then as now!) Untroubled by financial worries, the rich were free to while away their leisure time making up their own songs and devising their own accompaniments Probably the reference to David (v. 5) was an ironic comparison; while the great king had made music as a prayer to God, the rich used it for their own enjoyment. Wine drunk from bowls and anointing with fine oils added to the luxuriating atmosphere of the exorbitant lifestyle.

As God's prophet, Amos viewed these extravagances as divinely intolerable. What the people perceived as evidence of political stability, Amos understood as religious complacency and imbalance. The prophet's words virtually drip with the disgust he felt at such insensitivity.

1 Timothy 6:11-16. Because of its formal structure and solemn exhortatory style, today's second reading (the conclusion of the letter) is thought by most scholars to be a liturgical formulation. E. Kasemann contends that the pericope is part of an *ordination* ceremony. Timothy, the ordained in this particular instance, has been reminded of the faith he confessed at his baptism and is called to bear witness to Christ as a loyal teacher of that faith. The charge to keep God's command (v. 14) may be the actual ordinational consecration and is reminiscent of Moses' commission to Joshua at his ordination (Numbers 27:19). According to R. Fuller, Joshua's consecration was the Old Testament type that provided both the synagogue and the early church with the model for their ordination ceremonials. Other scholars, taking a more general view of the pericope, regard the exhortation in 1 Timothy 6 as a reference to Timothy's *baptismal* commitment. In either case, the text presents an appeal to live a life in accord with the faith that has been professed. As such, it contains timely advice and inspiration for all believers.

As a model of faith the author of 1 Timothy offered the image of the accused Jesus appearing before Pontius Pilate (v. 13). Probably the reference here is to Jesus' confession, "I was born for this, I came into the world for this: to bear witness to the truth and all who are on the side of truth listen to my voice" (John 18:39). However, the author of 1 Timothy may also have had in mind Jesus' "noblest profession" of faith, proclaimed by his death on the cross.

Charged with "fighting the good fight of faith" (v. 12) and remaining loyal to his initial commitment at baptism, Timothy (and with him *all* Christians) was to prepare for Jesus' appearance at the chosen time (v. 15). "Appearance" or "*epiphaneia*" referred primarily, of course, to Jesus' coming in glory at the parousia. *Epiphaneia* was a Greek term that frequently referred to the manifestation in glory of the pagan gods and emperors who claimed divine honors. No doubt, the author used the term apologetically here and applied it to Jesus Christ, who alone was divine and deserving of every honor and glory. Significantly, the second century Christian author of 1 Timothy understood that the appearance of Jesus would occur at God's "chosen time" (v. 16). "*Kairos idios*" (proper time) was not a chronological indication but, like Jesus' "hour" (in John's gospel), referred to the moment in which God would work out his plan of salvation. The third and fourth generations of Christians had to come to grips with delayed eschatology and had learned to direct their efforts toward living dedicated and productive faith lives. For modern believers, who experience the same delay and anticipate the same appearance of the Lord, the pastoral advice to Timothy and his church is valid and timely.

Luke 16:19-31. Stories like that told in today's gospel parable have been found among ancient Egyptian folkloric tales and in the legends of the rabbis. But there is nothing legendary or folkloric about the serious message Jesus communicated. Particular to the Lucan gospel, the parable of the rich man and Lazarus was addressed primarily to an audience of Pharisees (vv. 14, 18) but the point of the parable was later reinterpreted by the early church and carries a message for all would-be disciples. A rich man (erroneously named Dives in some translations due to a mistranslation of the Vulgate) indulged in a very comfortable life in this world. His clothing of purple and linen indicates that his means and life-style were comparable to that enjoyed by kings and princes. Purple garments were usually of fine wool, dyed with murex from Tyre; the fine linen referred to elegant undergarments only the very rich were able to afford.

While the rich man "feasted splendidly every day," Lazarus experienced the hardships of life. A diseased indigent unable to defend himself even from the dogs that licked his sores, Lazarus was ritually unclean in several aspects and represented all that was abhorrent to Jesus' Pharisaic audience. Moreover, the very fact of his difficult situation led the self-righteous to presume (albeit erroneously) his sinfulness, and therefore his condition of moral uncleanness as well! The contrast between the two men is a drastic and dramatic one. Lazarus was shunned as a sinner while the rich man was honored. His wealth was looked upon as a sign of divine favor and reward for a life lived in accordance with God's law.

Enter the "grim reaper," death, and the situation of the two men was radically changed. The reversal was both a shock and a challenge to Jesus' audience. In death, Lazarus was without human consolation. With none to attend him, God's angels came to carry him to Abraham's bosom. Traditionally in Judaism, the death of a just person was described as "going to Abraham" or "being gathered unto Abraham." Both ideas were probably an outgrowth of the Old Testament passages (Genesis 15:15, 47:30) that referred to being "gathered to the fathers," i.e., to the patriarchs. Abraham's bosom was also a symbol of the eschatological banquet (Luke 5:34) where the righteous would preside in seats of honor at the right hand or near the bosom (*kolpos*) of the host.

The rich man, on the other hand, received a proper burial but then found himself in Sheol's place of torment. Most of the Old Testament texts referring to Sheol or the underworld (Hades, Tartarus) depict it as a dark, gloomy place where both the good and the evil were relegated to a nebulous, joyless existence. But, approximately two centuries B.C.E., there emerged a doctrine of resurrection and of retribution after death, due largely to the influence of Persian and Zoroastrian cults. At that time the notion of Sheol also evolved, until it was conceived of as a place with two separate compartments, one for the just who were awaiting the resurrection of the dead and the other for the evil who were already being punished.

According to Enoch 22, the two compartments were adjoining in order that the inhabitants of one area could see those in the other and vice versa. This notion is reflected in today's Lucan parable; while the poor man enjoyed the solace of Abraham's bosom, the rich man looked on from afar. The association of tortuous flames with the retribution of the evil after death is a late scriptural notion but has survived to create much of our medieval and modern imagery concerning hell.

The rich man's first request for relief ("send Lazarus to dip the tip of his finger in water") and Abraham's subsequent denial of the request illustrate the finality of death and serve to elaborate the first major point of the parable. Like so many of Jesus' teachings, the parable enunciated the fact that worldly status is no indication of divine favor. Nor does worldly status guarantee salvation. Moreover, the parable underscored the universality of the kingdom's composition; *all* were called to enter, even the unclean beggars like Lazarus.

In the rich man's second request, the second point of the parable has been clarified. Not wishing his five brothers to suffer similar consequences, the rich man asked that Lazarus be sent to warn them to mend their ways. In response, Abraham declared that the brothers had the teachings of Moses and the prophets. Knowing the obtuseness of his brothers, the rich man asked that Lazarus himself be sent with a call to repentance. Abraham answered that those who ignored the law and the prophets would not be moved even by the testimony of a messenger from the abode of the dead.

The fact that this is the *only* gospel parable in which a character has been named, *plus* the fact that the person has been named *Lazarus* ("he whom God helps"), inclines the reader to associate this figure with the Lazarus of the Johannine gospel (John 11:1-44). In both instances, even the resurrection of a person from the dead failed to convince the obdurate who refused to hear God's word. R. Bultmann has associated this parable with Deuteronomy 30:11-14 where Moses insisted that the keeping of the law is not difficult and does not need someone to go to the heavens or travel the sea to make its word known or clarify its message.

No doubt the early church related the parable to the resurrection of Jesus as well. Those who had refused the message of the *earthly* Jesus remained unconvinced even by the fact of his resurrection from the dead. The parable of the rich man and Lazarus provides a warning and a challenge to all who hear it. Awareness of God and conversion are possible only on *this* side of the grave. To refuse the chance for repentance is to refuse the invitation to live and the opportunity for everlasting happiness in the kingdom.

1. Creature comforts should be shared blessings, not status symbols that separate rich from poor (Amos).

2. The noble profession of faith by a committed Christian inspires others to similar dedication (1 Timothy).

3. Those who refuse to see the truth in the routine and ordinary circumstances of life will probably overlook it in the extraordinary and sensational moments as well (Luke).

27th Sunday in Ordinary Time

When evil flourishes and seems to overwhelm the just, the faithful are filled with questions (Habakkuk). When suffering threatens to undo the work of the gospel, and when its disciples are made to endure persecutions and hardships, the faithful are filled with questions (2 Timothy). When there seems to be no reward for work well done and when total dedication is met with a challenge to even greater service, the faithful are led to question (Luke). To all these questions, there are no pat answers or solutions, only an earnest request: Lord, increase our faith.

Habakkuk 1:2-3, 2:2-4. Virtually nothing is known for certain of Habakkuk's personal life, and what little is known of the circumstances in which he lived has been deduced from indirect sources. But, there is *no* doubt whatsoever as to the prophet's attitude toward God. With bold strokes and the brilliant execution of his literary skills, Habakkuk used the 58 verses that comprise his entire work to put before his contemporaries a perennial problem: the fact that the evil prosper and the just seemingly do not.

Although Habakkuk's argument and God's response could be appropriately applied to any age (even one's own), it seems that the source of the prophet's difficulty stemmed from the political and religious circumstances of the late seventh and early sixth century B.C.E. Some scholars attribute Habakkuk's outrage to the fact that the Assyrians were having their way with God's chosen people. Having plundered the north (721 B.C.E.), the Assyrian power had reached into Judah, controlled the king and therefore every facet of Judean public life, until their defeat by the armies of Babylonia in 612 B.C.E.

Others believe Habakkuk's anger was vented at the corrupt situation that existed in Judah after the death of Josiah. When he acceded to the throne, Jehoiakim (609-598 B.C.E.) relaxed Josiah's reform and allowed the deplorable practices from Manasseh's reign to be resumed (see Jeremiah 22:13-19). Most scholars agree Habakkuk regarded the Babylonians (named as Chaldeans in 1:6) as God's instruments, whereby he would chastise the wickedness of his people and put an end to the vicious cycle of "violence, ruin, destruction and misery" (1:2-3).

The first portion of today's pericope records part of Habakkuk's complaint (1:2-3); the second portion contains God's response (2:2-4). The prophet was instructed by God to "write down the vision clearly upon the tablets." Such writing or engraving (if tablets were stone or wooden) conveyed the quality of permanence which God's message was to have. Pertinent for Habakkuk's day and for his people, God's living word communicates a timeless message for peoples of every age.

In its literal translation the text of 2:2 reads "so that he who *runs* may read." This is a further indication of the *importance* of God's response; Habakkuk was to write it in such bold letters that even someone passing by "on the run" could see it plainly and read it at a glance. If the prophet followed his instructions "to the letter" (!) then *his* may have been the *first* billboard in the ancient world.

In answer to his people's impatience, God replied that the "vision still has its time, presses on to fulfillment and will not disappoint" (2:3). Moffat compared the vision's inevitableness to Francis Thompson's Hound of Heaven: God's words would "on swift inexorable feet" seek out their purpose and at the appointed time become a reality. On the human side, what would be required from those who long for God to speak and to act was faith (2:4). Faith (in Hebrew *'emunah*, the root from which our "amen" is derived) is that posture of the just person who trusts and hopes and relegates the power for the future to God.

2 Timothy 1:6-8, 13-14. Timothy, the Christian disciple from Lystra, converted to Jesus by Paul, understood what it meant to "live by faith" (2:4). At the turn of the second century, persecution of the church had become an integral aspect of its existence. Many had already given their lives for the sake of their faith, and those who survived experienced daily the "hardships the gospel entailed" (2 Timothy 1:8). Because the author of 2 Timothy understood the challenges of discipleship and the temptation to fall short of the gospel's demands, he exhorted Timothy and, through him, the church at Ephesus to remember the powerful graces of their baptism (and in Timothy's case, the grace of his ordination). "Stir into a flame the gift of God" (2 Timothy 1:6) referred to the grace of the sacrament that had initiated the believers into the life of Christ and into his service. However, the "gift received" could also have meant the gospel, i.e., the words and works of Jesus that believers were to make real and present by their lives of service and love.

According to R. Fuller, this passage from 2 Timothy reflects the sub-apostolic situation. At that point in the development of the community, the ministerial gifts were thought to be conveyed through ordination or the laying on of hands (v. 6), rather than by direct inspiration as in 1 Corinthians. Moreover, it seems that by the second Christian century, the apostolic message had been consolidated into a "pattern of words" or a fixed tradition. In the mind of E. Kasemann these developments can be characterized as "early catholicism," a term which for

Kasemann implies a degeneration and corruption of the freer charismatic period. But more correctly, R. Fuller, in defense of the early church, understands the fixing of tradition as a legitimate and necessary adaptation, following the disappearance of apostolic eyewitnesses and their consequent ability to exercise the kind of personal control over the charismata as Paul did in Corinth.

Timothy and all who succeeded the apostles in leading the community were, however, not merely to *preserve* tradition ("guard the rich deposit of faith," v. 14) intact and unchanged. Rather, by lives of faithful service, they were to bear *living* witness to the teaching they had received, to "unpackage it" and make it relevant for their contemporaries. But, as Timothy and his church had already experienced, tradition is not preserved and made relevant in a vacuum. Forces from within and from outside the community militated against its growth and caused the faithful to suffer. Some, like Peter and Paul and many others, were called to endure even the loss of their lives for the sake of the church's continued growth.

By way of encouragement, the author of 2 Timothy recalled for his readers the example of faith Paul had lived out in their midst. Above all, those who would safeguard the church and prompt it toward continued growth were to remember that they had been imbued with "no cowardly Spirit" (v. 6). That same Spirit "who dwells within us" (v. 14) continues to strengthen and guide the church to this day.

Luke 17:5-10. "No rest for the weary" might be an alternate title for the parable that comprises the heart of today's gospel. When the disciples of Jesus have worn themselves out serving the needs of the kingdom and its members, they should not expect reward or even recognition. After all, the parable teaches, that is no more than your duty!

Today's pericope is better understood when viewed against the background of its larger context in chapter 17. In Luke 17:1-10, the evangelist gathered together a mosaic of four sets of sayings and a parable, all loosely linked by their relationship to the various aspects of discipleship. The first two sets of sayings dealt with giving scandal to others (vv. 1-2) and the necessity of fraternal correction and constant willingness to forgive others (vv. 3-4). Upon hearing of the stringent demands which were the very *minimum* to be expected of them as followers of Jesus, the apostles were prompted to ask, "Increase our faith" (v. 5). At this point in the interchange today's gospel begins.

In both Mark's and Matthew's gospels, the request for an increase of faith has been set in different contexts. In Mark's gospel, the request occurs on an occasion when the apostles were being taught the power their prayer could have if it were supported by a firm faith (Mark 11:22-23). In Matthew's gospel, the request comes as a result of the apostles' awareness of the ineffectiveness of their powers to heal and to exorcise (Matthew 17:29). But Luke has chosen to teach a different lesson by placing the request of the apostles for faith in the context of the *moral* demands of discipleship, i.e., avoidance of scandal and the obligation of continual forgiveness.

Jesus' response to his apostles' request is typically semitic. With vivid and extreme language (similar to the saying, "If your eye is a problem, cast it out," etc.), he indicated that even a minute amount of faith can accomplish great things. The sycamore tree in question here was really a black mulberry tree with quite an extensive system of roots. Therefore, the idea of uprooting one posed a very difficult task indeed. Moreover, the idea of a tree transplanted into the sea added to the unlikeliness of the situation.

Obviously, a literal or fundamental interpretation of Jesus' saying would fall ridiculously short of its intended meaning. More important than the physical uprooting of a tree or its transplanting were the implications of Jesus' words with regard to the moral demands of discipleship. Although he compared it to a mustard seed, the quantity of faith was not as important as the *quality* of faith. In other words, a truly genuine faith can render the impossible *possible*.

As C. Talbert has observed in his commentary on this saying, faith is not magic and cannot be thought of in that manner. In the same way, M. Tolbert agreed, "Faith is not a means by which we control God. . . . We cannot use it to back God into a corner and force him to produce a sensational show which will enable us to make the headlines." Rather, genuine faith is a response to God's initiative in the context of a personal relationship; faith is willing cooperation with God's action.

Such a response to God would enable the believer to reprove and to forgive readily, to be a model and not a scandal for others. These actions should not be thought of as exceptional feats that merit reward, but the ordinary *duty* of every faithful disciple, as the parable in vv. 7-10 illustrates.

It is significant that the servant featured in the parable was performing *double* duty. He worked all day in the fields as a farm hand and then after that he served his master in the home as a domestic servant. Even with this heavy load, the servant was doing no more than what was expected of him; therefore, he should not and did not expect a reward or even the expressed gratitude of his master. For Jesus' disciples the implications were obvious. Even if their actions *never* posed a scandal for another person, even if they forgave those who wronged them on *every* occasion, they were doing no more than their duty. In fulfilling those minimum requirements they were not guaranteed salvation. No amount of service, however well performed, could merit the gift that was God's alone to give. Therefore, even perfect human actions should not give rise to boasting. Rather, the true disciple recognized him/herself as a "useless servant" (v. 10).

A difficult word, "useless" or *achreios* (in Greek) implied that nothing had been gained by "those to whom nothing is due" (J.A. Fitzmyer). As A. Plummer has noted, "That God does not need man's service is not the point. . . the point is that man can make no just claim for having done more than was due. No matter how much a person does in God's service, there is still a sense in which he/she is still an unprofitable servant," i.e., one to whom no favor is owed. For the Pharisees in Jesus' audience, the parable served to deflate their pride in their accomplishments. Even in keeping *every* precept of the law, they had not satisfied the requirements of discipleship.

For the early Christians and for all who labor for the sake of the kingdom, the parable reiterated Paul's doctrine of the ineffectiveness and insufficiency of human works, as it underscored the reality of justification by faith. For Jesus' apostles and all subsequent followers, the moral is clear: there is no point at which work for the kingdom can be halted. In the commitment that costs no less than everything, one's quota is never reached.

1. Only the person who truly believes that God hears prayer will dare to argue with him (Habakkuk).

2. Like a seed that requires proper tending in order to produce a flower, faith is a grace that must be fostered in order for it to grow and to mature (2 Timothy).

3. Faith is the fuel of true and total Christian commitment (Luke).

28th Sunday in Ordinary Time

Cures and conversions are often found together in the scriptural record of our faith because wholeness and holiness are two aspects of the spiritual integrity to which God calls his people (2 Kings). In response to the Lord's blessings, his people are called to a fidelity that never fears to speak or tires of living his word (2 Timothy). With a prayer for the deep faith that invites salvation, we remember to return thanks to the one who heals both body and spirit (Luke).

2 Kings 5:14-17. Elisha, whose name in Hebrew means "God is salvation," was active in the northern kingdom of Israel for about 50 years, during the reigns of Jehoram, Jehu, Jehoahaz and Jehoash (ca. 850-800 B.C.E.). As the mysterious inheritor of Elijah's hairy mantle and prophetic authority, Elisha became such a legendary figure in subsequent tradition that it has become virtually impossible to sift fact from fiction with regard to his accomplishments. A popular and folkloric hero, the prophet was for the most part motivated by a genuine concern for the poor and faithful remnant who survived in spite of the moral decadence that surrounded them.

Writing at a point in his people's history when Jerusalem had been pillaged by Babylon (shortly after 587 B.C.E.), when the temple had been destroyed and the future of his people seemed abysmal at best, the religious historian of Joshua-Kings helped his contemporaries to find meaning in their tragedy and to make sense of it. By reinterpreting the demise of both the northern and southern kingdoms in terms of covenant fidelity, the Deuteronomist sought to awaken in his people their need for repentance and conversion. With stories like those from the Elijah and Elisha cycles, he tried to renew in the hearts of the surviving remnant a hope for a glorious future based on God's faithfulness to his word. Later Jewish eschatology associated the great wonders of Elisha—the healings, restorations to life, miraculous feedings, etc.—with the era of messianic salvation.

Naaman was a Syrian, a commander in the army of his king, Benhadad II (2 Kings 8:7). A leper (though it is doubtful his disease could be diagnosed as Hansen's disease), Naaman learned of Elisha's reputation for working wonders from an Israelite slave girl. Well thought of by those in his command, Naaman was encouraged to seek out Elisha and request a cure. With Benhadad's permission and a personal letter for the king of Israel (probably Jehoram), Naaman departed Syria for Samaria. Though Israel was enjoying a tenuous peace with Syria, Jehoram was alarmed by the letter and suspected the Syrian king of trying to provoke a conflict.

Feeling helpless to meet the request for a healing, Israel's king was eventually rescued from his dilemma by Elisha. The prophet had heard of Naaman's visit and summoned him to his home. Without even going out to meet the Syrian commander, Elisha sent instructions that Naaman should wash in the Jordan and thereupon he would be healed. Annoyed at Elisha's lack of concern for his station and at what he deemed a simplistic remedy, Naaman had to be persuaded to follow the prophet's instructions. Eventually, he acquiesced, bathed in the Jordan and was miraculously healed.

In the act of his being cured, Naaman became aware of the superior power of Israel's God at work in Elisha and determined to worship Yahweh even upon returning to his native

Syria. To that end he took earth from Israel home with him in order to build an altar to Yahweh. No doubt, the text reflects a vestige of the ancient notion that the power of the gods was somehow limited geographically. In the story of Naaman, however, the Deuteronomist made a clear statement with regard to the *universal* scope of Yahweh's power. Naaman's action and his statement, "Now I know that there is no God *in all the earth* except in Israel," served to bear out his doctrine. In today's gospel, the same message of universal salvation is continued in the healing and coming to faith of the Samaritan leper.

2 Timothy 2:8-13. Many scholars posit a deutero-Pauline authorship and an early second century date for the pastoral letters (1 and 2 Timothy, Titus), but most agree that the letters *do* contain some authentically Pauline passages. One of those Pauline texts comprises the first half of today's second reading. Because of the tone of finality the passage reflects, vv. 8-10 may be an excerpt from Paul's farewell letter to Timothy. Imprisoned in Rome near the end of his life, the apostle was concerned that those he had brought to Christ would continue in faithful service to the gospel he had preached to them. Aware that the good news would continue to be heard despite the fact that some of its heralds were silenced ("There is no chaining the word of God"), Paul urged Timothy and all Christians to accept their suffering as an inevitable factor in the church's development.

Moreover, the letter urged believers toward an awareness that no amount of repression could successfully eradicate the fact of God's saving word. More than a merely human communication, the saving word of God's good news had become incarnate in the person of Jesus. That divine intervention into human history assured for all times that the word would be heard. It would not cease to speak to every aspect and every area of human existence. Paul understood that his responsibility and that of all would-be disciples (and pastors, as in Timothy's case) was to remember the word and assimilate it so as to be able to speak it faithfully in a life of total service to the Lord and his people.

In the second portion of the reading (vv. 13-15), the author has quoted from an early Christian hymn that celebrated the union of the Lord with those who preached his message. As G. Denzer had pointed out, "When Paul spoke of dying and rising with Christ, he had in mind not only the sacramental death and resurrection of baptism (Romans 6:3-11) but also the development of this experience in the Christian life, with special emphasis on the physical suffering and dangers of the apostolate (1 Corinthians 15:31, 2 Corinthians 4:8-11)." The final stage of the believer's union with Christ will take place at the parousia (Colossians 3:3-5, Philippians 3:10-11, 1 Corinthians 15:42-44).

"If we deny him, he will deny us" (v. 12) may seem to contradict the statement, "If we are unfaithful, he will still remain faithful" (v. 13). But this seeming inconsistency can be better understood in the light of Jesus' absolute faithfulness to his Father and to the Father's will. Never would Jesus fall short of fidelity to his mission. In a similar manner, the believer is called to a complete responsiveness to Jesus. To deny that call, i.e., to refuse to hear and proclaim the word of Jesus, is only possible because of the free will with which each person has been endowed. In the unhappy event that a person freely chooses to deny Christ, he has automatically chosen to be denied by the Lord. With these sobering thoughts, the author of 2 Timothy exhorted his readers to remember the word, to remain faithful and to persevere through every trial, knowing all the while that "if we hold out to the end, we shall also reign with him!"

Luke 17:11-19. An "umbrella term," leprosy was used in the ancient world to describe a vast variety of anomalies of the skin and/or of objects (Leviticus 13). For example, mildew and mold in fabrics or on the walls of buildings (Leviticus 13:49, 14:37) were considered "leprous" and rendered the objects unclean. Rashes, skin eruptions of every kind, acne, boils, even baldness (!) were thought to be forms of "leprosy" and required ritual purification for the one who had contracted the condition as well as for all with whom he/she came in contact.

In those instances, probably rare, when the condition was actually Hansen's disease, strict measures were taken to protect the community from contamination. Usually the afflicted persons were ostracized from their towns or villages but remained near enough on the outskirts to receive charity. If approached by others, the leprous individuals were required to warn of their condition by announcing, "Unclean! Unclean!" Often, leprosy was (as were other ailments) thought to be a deserved punishment from God for sin and therefore its victim was considered morally as well as ritually unclean (Numbers 12:10-15; 2 Kings 5:27, 15:5; 2 Chronicles 26:20-21). While there can be no certainty with regard to the *actual* disease suffered by the ten people in today's gospel, their condition clearly separated them from society and required ritual purification and the approval of the legal authorities for their social restoration.

Traditionally, the episode of the ten lepers, a story peculiar to Luke's gospel, has been regarded as a moralizing example, illustrating *gratitude* as the proper attitude toward God's blessings. Of course, the importance of appreciation is an integral aspect of the narrative, but it is not the *only* message the evangelist wished to convey to his readers. In the simple statement, "This man was a Samaritan" (v. 16), and in the series of three rhetorical questions asked by Jesus—"Were not all ten made whole? Where are the other nine? Was there no one to return and give thanks to God except this foreigner?" (vv. 17-18)—the evangelist has broadened the application of his narrative. Besides the importance of gratitude to God, Luke accented: (1) the universality of God's saving concerns: *all* were to receive the messianic blessings of healing and wholeness, even the Samaritans whom the Jews despised; (2) the contrast between the Jews' *rejection* of Jesus and his *acceptance* by those outside the so-called "chosen people"; (3) the contrast between merely being *healed* and being *saved*.

The narrative of the ten lepers has marshalled a variety of opinions from scholars of the New Testament. For example, M. Dibelius labelled the pericope as "a legend about Jesus" told by Luke to bring to light Jesus' purity, wisdom and virtue. R. Bultmann regarded the narrative as a biographical apothegm or pronouncement story with the pronouncement occurring in vv. 17-18. At first, V. Taylor agreed that the ten lepers story was a pronouncement story but later decided that it was simply a story about Jesus. Probably, it is more correct to understand the Lucan narrative as a double miracle story with several layers of development.

Obviously, the first miracle of wonder was Jesus' healing of the ten lepers. But there is a second though less obvious miracle in the coming to faith of the Samaritan. The other nine lepers had experienced the same healing as they made their way to show themselves to the priests. This act was a ritual requirement for restoration to the community. It is significant that the cure was not instantaneous but required the obedience of those afflicted by disease. Just as Naaman had to comply with Elisha's instructions to wash in the Jordan, the lepers were expected to obey Jesus' orders to go to the priests. On their way, they were cured, but only the Samaritan returned to Jesus. It was he *alone* to whom Jesus said, "Your faith has been your salvation" (v. 19).

As C. Talbert has observed, the mere experience of being healed did not save. Rather, it was by his acknowledgement of what God had done through Jesus that the Samaritan could experience a salvation *beyond* the physical cure. Healing issues forth in salvation, only when God's gracious initiative is recognized and when one's response to that initiative is faith. In the act of responding to God in faith, a relationship results and salvation is possible. "Realizing that he had been cured," or literally, *seeing* that he had been cured, the Samaritan was drawn into a deeper insight, that of faith.

Luke was often the champion of foreigners and their openness to Jesus (Luke 7:9, 10:25-32; Acts 10-11). In the figure of the foreigner, the evangelist showed that it is often the least likely person who is capable of recognizing God's hand at work and of responding appropriately. Many regard the narrative as a foreshadowing of the eventual rejection of Jesus and of the gospel by the Jews and its enthusiastic reception by the gentiles (Acts 28:26-27). For Luke's contemporaries in the 80s, the narrative also served as a missionary impetus. As Jesus' disciples, the early believers were to cast the seeds of the gospel in all directions, without discrimination or preconceived ideas about the results. In so doing, they would remain faithful to the universal intention of Jesus' mission. Disciples of the 20th century are called to the same degree of openness and availability to all who through their words and works will be brought closer to the Lord Jesus.

1. Even greater than physical healing is the power of God to bring a person to faith (2 Kings).

2. Regardless of the sufferings true discipleship entails, no follower of Jesus will ever be without his support (2 Timothy).

3. Many experience the extravagance of God's blessings but not all recognize the hand of the giver (Luke).

29th Sunday in Ordinary Time

Prayer happens in that moment when the believer stands in truth before God, aware that all he/she is or has or will ever hope to accomplish depends upon the Lord (Exodus). Guidance and inspiration in prayer can be found in the living word of God that speaks to every aspect and possibility of human existence (2 Timothy). When prayer is relentlessly persevering and full of faith, there are no limits to what can be accomplished (Luke).

Exodus 17:8-13. Rarely, if ever, has a more unusual battle plan been recorded! While Joshua and his handpicked army set out to engage the Amalekites, Moses positioned himself on a hill with arms outstretched in prayer to God. While Moses' arms remained firm, the battle went in the Hebrews' favor; when Moses' weary arms sagged, the tide of the battle turned against his people. Historically, the details of this story require great stretches of the imagination, but theologically the author's point is quite clear, viz., never underestimate the efficacy of prayer and *never*, no matter how dismal the situation, lose faith in God's power to save.

Originally the Amalekites were linked to Amalek, the son of Eliphaz, Esau's son (Genesis 36:12). A nomadic confederation of tribes, the Amalekites dwelt in territory that covered the desert regions of the Sinai, the Negeb, the Arabah and parts of Arabia (1 Samuel 15:7). Not mentioned outside the Bible, the Amalekites appear in the scriptures as Israel's constant enemy. Since the tribes of Amalek controlled the caravan routes between Arabia and Egypt, they naturally resented the intrusion of the refugees from Egypt. Consequently, the Amalekites put forth every effort to block Israel's entrance into Canaan and remained a threat to Israel's stability until their defeat by David.

The Pentateuchal authors intended to write not mere war annals, but a *religious* story that featured God's protection of his people and their interests. Thus, the elements of faith and prayer figure more importantly than soldiers, battle implements and military engagements. This fact has been dramatically communicated in the author's obsevation that the success of the battle hinged on Moses' posture at prayer. As J. Gaffney has noted, "The implications of this symbolism are deeply consistent with the theological convictions that shape the entire narrative. The Hebrews' salvation, preservation and progress are to be accounted for, not by their own valor and skill, but by the benevolent intervention of an invisible God."

In the incident at Rephidim, Moses was established as the mediator of his people, one upon whose endurance and faith the welfare of the entire nation depended. In this sense, Moses' action could be understood as typological: Moses as intercessor could be symbolic of Christ through whom and by whose perfect mediation all peoples would be saved. Perhaps there is some significance too in the fact that Moses, of himself, was unable to sustain his attitude of prayer. Only when he was supported by Aaron and Hur did he succeed in maintaining his prayerful stance before God and his people. For all believers who have known difficulty in solitary prayer, the experience of prayer in communion with others, supported by them, is a welcome joy.

As a complement to today's gospel, Moses' persistence in prayer and its resulting efficacy can be compared to the relentlessness of the widow who did not let the unjust judge rest until he had heard her case.

2 Timothy 3:14—4:2. In the first quarter of the second Christian century, the time when most modern scholars agree that the pastorals were written, the expanding body of believers in Jesus looked for norms by which to guide and define its growth. Some have called this the period of "early catholicism," that time during which the church became less charismatic and more institutionalized. With the passing of all the eyewitnesses to Jesus, as the delay of eschatology became an accepted fact of life, the body of the faithful and its leaders looked to the serious question of survival in an alien and often hostile environment. In the pastoral letters that purport to contain the advice of the dying Paul, the answer to the question of survival is clearly enunciated in terms of *structure*.

True to the apostolic heritage, but with an eye toward the inevitable sociological development of the church, new leaders emerged—presbyters, bishops and deacons. This new clergy, of which Timothy was a member, was charged with the responsibilities of caring for and ministering to the community as they channeled the talents and services of others toward the common good. Part of the role of the sub-apostolic church leaders was to safeguard the faith as they had learned it. To that end the author of the pastorals exhorted Timothy, and with him all believers, to turn to the source and wellspring of their faith: to the scriptures and to the one whom the sacred writings had foretold—to Jesus Christ.

As the pericope that comprises today's second reading states, Timothy had known the scriptures from his infancy. According to Jewish teaching, the Jewish child was to begin to learn the sacred writings at the age of five. In the case of Timothy whose father was a gentile, Timothy's teachers would have been his Jewish mother Eunice and grandmother Lois (2 Timothy 1:5). Later in life, Timothy would have been sent to the synagogue school where young boys and men continued their education in the word of God and in the traditions of their people.

No doubt the scriptures referred to in 2 Timothy would have been the Jewish scriptures or Old Testament. By this time, most of the Christian scriptures (later to become canonical) were already written but had not been compiled or organized into a body of unified material. As Christians, Timothy and his community were to look to God's promises in the Jewish scriptures and to trace their fulfillment to the person of Jesus, realizing that Christ's ministry, death and resurrection were the New Testament flowering of the Old Testament seeds of faith.

The term "inspired of God" (v. 16) was commonly used by Greek-speaking Jews (Philo, Josephus) and represents an adaptation of Old Testament ideas into Hellenistic categories, an adaptation that became more evident as the church became more widespread. The term "all scripture" (v. 16), *pasa graphe*, can mean "each passage of scripture" or "the entirety of scripture." The latter meaning is more preferable and may be a safeguard against the fundamentalist penchant for extracting one particular verse or section of scripture and interpreting it without regard for the context in which it appears.

Of course, the knowledge of the scriptures was not to be the exclusive responsibility or privilege of Timothy and/or other church leaders. For their part, the leaders of the church were to make known what they had learned, "to preach the word, to stay with the task whether convenient or inconvenient" (4:1-2). In commenting upon the relevancy the church should have for believers, Sir Edwyn Hoskyns proposed: "Whether the Church of England (or the Roman Catholic Church) can present the truth of the Christian religion to our generation will depend very largely upon the extent to which well-disposed clergy and laity can cooperate in wrestling with the truth of the Church."

Luke 18:1-8. As the heroes and heroines of his narratives, Luke often featured the least likely characters, e.g., the *Samaritan* who helped the man who was mugged, the *dishonest steward* whose business acumen was praised by Jesus and, in the case of today's gospel, the relentless *widow*. Widows were usually poor, uninfluential people in the ancient world. As members of a marginalized and often oppressed group of society, widows, along with orphans, aliens, the economically deprived and the sick, were called the "poor" in the scriptures. Defenseless before the legal, social and religious authorities of her day, the widow was a symbol of powerlessness and disgrace. Because of their plight, widows and the other "poor" of Israelite society were thought to enjoy God's special protection. Later, these "poor" or *anawim* became the symbols of all who hunger and thirst for justice and, as such, their spiritual posture of need and dependence upon God became exemplary for all believers.

In marked contrast to the widow is the other figure in today's parable, the judge. An unsympathetic and unappealing character, the judge is described as one who respected neither God nor man. Since he was not moved by human concern nor motivated by his devotion to God's law, the judge's lack of attention to the widow is not surprising. Some scholars have suggested that the widow was a plaintiff in a court action she had brought against a wealthier and probably more esteemed opponent. Perhaps the judge delayed hearing her case, or rendering a judgment in the case because he did not wish to offend the more notable defendant. There is an implication in the text ("I am going to settle in her favor," v. 5) that the woman had right on her side, but had been denied justice because of her lowly status. Others have suggested that, in keeping with the judge's corrupt nature, it would not be surprising if he had delayed his decision, in hopes that the poor widow could raise sufficient monies or goods for a bribe!

In any event, despite the judge's character and in spite of his mishandling of the case, the widow prevailed. Using the only weapon in her arsenal, her relentless persistence, she wore the judge down and won her case. The English rendering of v. 5 ("or she will end by doing me violence") is somewhat less colorful than the literal translation. In Greek, the verb *hypopiazein* means "to hit under the eye" and is a term borrowed from boxing. What the judge actually feared was getting a black eye from the angry widow. *Hypopiazein* was also used figuratively and could have meant to sully the character or reputation of another. It is doubtful that this was Luke's intended meaning because even the judge himself had admitted that he "cared little for God or man" (v. 4). Therefore, he probably attached little importance to whatever the widow might have said to others about him.

But the point of the parable, as with *all* parables, was greater than the characters (however interesting) and/or details featured in it. In this particular instance, the key to the parable's message lay in its introductory verse (v. 1) and in its "punch line" (v. 7) as well as in its context with regard to the rest of the gospel. In his editorial note (v. 1), Luke explained that the parable taught a lesson to Jesus' disciples on the necessity of persevering and confident prayer. Like the widow who did not give up even in the face of seemingly insurmountable odds, Jesus' disciples were to remain faithful in prayer.

C. Talbert has suggested that this parable and its message should be seen as part of a longer section in the gospel (17:20—18:8) in which the evangelist has treated three problems of eschatology: (1) the desire to know and to calculate when the kingdom will come (see 17:20-21); (2) an over-realized eschatology (see 17:22-37); (3) the doubt regarding an ultimate settling of accounts or final judgment by God (see 18:1-8).

Today's parable functions as an exhortation to the poor and oppressed that they should not lose heart. Moreover, the success of the widow over the corrupt judge served to encourage believers not to give up their hope that the parousia and its reward would come. If a corrupt judge, with no care for human need or God's law, would finally grant a poor widow's request just to be free of her pestering, how much *more* would God vindicate his faithful people when they pray to him. For many, that vindication would come only with the advent of the parousia but, as the parable assures, it *will* come. For those who await God's intervention, the only worthy spiritual posture is an unhesitating and confident *faith*.

As C. Talbert has also observed, the parable of the persistent widow speaks to those who were plagued with doubt. How could the disciples of Jesus in the 80s C.E. maintain their faith when their situation seemed futile and hopes for a better future seemed unattainable? How can the disciples of Jesus in the 1990s C.E. maintain a vital faith when so much both within and beyond the believing community seems to militate against it? Luke's answer? Pray! Pray actively, persistently, relentlessly and with an indomitable trust that God does and will act. There may even be some blackened eyes along the way. But, never cease to pray.

1. Praying, like most human activities, becomes easier when supported by others in community (Exodus).

2. Scripture can be a great teacher if we learn how to listen without manipulation or selectivity (2 Timothy).

3. Persevering prayer, born of confident faith, is willing to wait for God's justice (Luke).

30th Sunday in Ordinary Time

Prayer is primarily a personal relationship with an involved God who cares for each of his creatures with a unique love. When individuals come together to pray to the God in whom each of them believes, prayer becomes communal. In that experience, those with deeper faith can teach those who struggle (2 Timothy) and the poor can reveal to the rich what is of true value (Sirach). When believers pray together, the proud can learn from the humble sinner of the absolute necessity of truth and of the luxury of God's mercy (Luke).

Sirach 35:12-14, 16-18. "If Jesus, son of Sirach were alive today," wrote D. Suter in an recent article on Ecclesiasticus (*Harper's Bible Dictionary*, 1985), "he'd be a professor of public administration." Since his work reads something like a modern textbook on proper social protocol and business ethics, those under his instruction would presumably go on to pursue careers in public service, diplomacy, etc. In his own day, Jesus ben Sirach was probably a teacher of youth, their wise guide and mentor in the art of living well. He wrote in Hebrew ca. 180 B.C.E. but his work was translated into Greek by his grandson ca. 132 B.C.E. In its retranslation, it served as a worthy vehicle of Jewish thought and wisdom, struggling to survive the influences of Hellenistic culture. A valuable book, Ecclesiasticus or Sirach provides the modern reader with an excellent synopsis of the character of Judaism and Jewish society in the period prior to the Maccabean revolution (169-164 B.C.E.). In Sirach, one can observe a highly polarized social order in which rich were alienated from poor, male from female, Jew from gentile and the pious from the impious. Moreover, amid the anthology of passages on various topics that constitute the book of Sirach, one can perceive the gradual development of a way of life centered on the law.

Today's pericope has been selected from that section of the book (25:1—36:17) wherein Sirach compiled his instructions on a wide variety of topics, from the proper attitude toward wives and daughters to the appropriate etiquette at banquets. In the section devoted to sacrifice and prayer (34:18—35:20), Sirach made it clear he was in total agreement with Israel's prophetic heritage. Sacrifice to God is pleasing and acceptable only when it is offered by one who is motivated by truth and who is faithful to God's law. As a *merely external* exercise, the sacrificial cult is hypocritical and an abomination in God's eyes. After his assertion (34:18—35:12) that an evil person's sacrifice has no value Sirach introduced the theme of God's impartiality. The rich person's extravagant sacrifice does not merit more of God's attention or favor, nor does the poor person's sacrifice gain less notice.

Basic to Sirach's thought and in sharp contrast to later New Testament theology was the idea that each person receives from God what he/she deserves according to a rigid merit system. God was thought of as operating according to an inflexible and impartial method of justice wherein the standard of human merit was the Torah or divine law. While this rigid standard of legal justice excluded privileged treatment for the rich and influential, it also negated the factor of divine mercy in the form of undeserved and unmerited grace.

An excellent choice to offset today's gospel message, Sirach represented the best of Old Testament thought concerning justification by the dutiful performance of the law. Even though this work was not considered canonical by Jews, nevertheless, Sirach was popular within Judaism until as late as the 11th century. No doubt the Pharisee depicted in the Lucan parable (see gospel) had thoroughly assimilated Sirach's ideas on religion and justification when he prayed, "I give you thanks, O God, that I am not like the rest of men." But the Pharisee had not yet learned the surprising wonder of God's mercy, a lesson that would be taught in the person of Jesus and through the language of his cross.

2 Timothy 4:6-8, 16-18. In his historical annals, Eusebius was the earliest extra-biblical author to write of Paul's second imprisonment in Rome under Nero: "After defending himself, Paul was again sent on the ministry of preaching, and coming a second time to the same city, suffered martyrdom under Nero. During this imprisonment, he wrote the second epistle to Timothy, indicating at the same time that his first defense had taken place and his martyrdom was at hand." While Eusebius' testimony about Paul's death during Nero's persecution (ca. 64 C.E.) is generally accepted, most scholars today do *not* agree that Paul wrote the *entirety* of 2 Timothy. Rather, an early second century date has been proposed for the letter which is however thought to contain some genuine fragments of Paul's writings. One of those genuine fragments comprises the conclusion of 2 Timothy and our second reading for today's liturgy.

Employing the imagery popular among Greek writers of his day, Paul referred to his life as a libation being poured out (v. 6). Libations of wine and oil sometimes accompanied Jewish sacrifices (Exodus 29:40, Numbers 28:7) but the practice was especially common among Greeks and Romans. Before or during meals and at religious ceremonies, a goblet of wine was poured out upon the ground in homage to the gods. Making use of this Hellenistic custom, Paul metaphorically indicated that his life, which he fully expected to end in martyrdom, could be likened to a sacrificial libation. His blood poured out in an offering for the sake of his faith in Jesus would not be a vain waste but would have salvific value for the sake of others (2 Timothy 2:10, Philippians 2:17).

In similar style, Paul saw his imminent death as the end of a fight well fought and/or a race run successfully (v. 7). Throughout his life in Christ, Paul had been motivated by his love and commitment to the Lord. He had "kept the faith" (v. 7). It would be an injustice to Paul to understand by this statement that he had merely preserved the "deposit of the faith" intact (1 Timothy 6:14, 20). By keeping the faith, the apostle referred not only to a *doctrinal* but also to a committed *way of life,* courageously lived, in spite of all odds and in defiance of all indifference and persecution. For that reason, Paul looked forward to the crown that would be given him on that Day (i.e., the parousia) by the just judge, the Lord himself. Crowns of laurel, pine or olive were awarded to the winners of athletic contests. Paul knew that the end of his life would be a true victory because in dying he would share forever in Jesus' conquest of sin and evil.

In the second part of today's pericope, Paul referred to the "first hearing" of his case (v. 16). This would have been a preliminary session for the purpose of determining whether or not his case would be brought to trial. Evidently, at the first hearing, no one came forward in defense of Paul. Historical evidence is scanty in this regard and it is unclear as to why the Christian community in Rome did not appear in Paul's behalf. Some have suggested that the Christians in Rome were not entirely convinced of Paul's orthodoxy with regard to the gospel and therefore were not willing to risk appearing in Nero's court. In any event, in 2 Timothy, Paul made it clear that he *did* experience the strength and support of the Lord himself ("The Lord stood by my side and gave me strength," v. 17).

Luke 18:9-14. Jesus had a habit of questioning the status quo. By his teaching and through his life style, he challenged the value system of his contemporaries, causing them to rethink centuries-old traditions and cherished opinions. The parable of the prayer of the Pharisee and of the tax collector was another instance of Jesus' challenge to the society in which he lived.

The Pharisee was a respected member of Palestinian society. As a devotee of the law even to its most minute prescription, the Pharisee was an exemplar, a norm by which others gauged their own performance. While the law in post-exilic Judaism required that faithful Jews fast but one time a year (Leviticus 16: 29,31) on Yom Kippur (the Day of Atonement), the Pharisee went beyond the law. On Monday and Thursday of every week, the Pharisees abstained even from water. By way of explanation for the choice of these two days, the rabbis proposed that Moses had gone up to Sinai on Thursday and that he had descended from the mountain 40 days later on a Monday. Besides the atoning character of fasting, the practice of abstaining from food and drink was an expression of mourning (2 Samuel 12:21), penitence (1 Kings 21:27, Ezra 10:6), and supplication (Nehemiah 1:4, Daniel 9:3).

While the disciples of John the Baptizer were known to fast (Luke 5:33) as the Pharisees did, Jesus' followers were advised differently. The Didache (ca. 100 C.E.) directed Christians not to fast "with the hypocrites on the second and fifth days of the week but on the fourth day (Wednesday) and the parasceve (day of preparation for the sabbath)." In itself, fasting was not repudiated by Jesus or by Christians. Rather, the *attitude* of the Pharisee toward his accomplishments left much to be desired.

So too with the matter of tithing. Earlier in his gospel, Luke had mentioned the tithe on all they owned and on every purchase. Tithing in itself is, of course, a harmless deed that could in the end be of benefit to others if the proceeds are distributed among the needy. But the Pharisee had turned the deed of tithing as well as his fasting into occasions of self-aggrandisement before God.

Notice that his prayer was one of thanksgiving, tinged with the odiousness of comparison. "I give you *thanks,* O God, that I am not like the rest... or even like this tax collector." Similar to a prayer quoted in the fifth century B.C.E. Babylonian Talmud, the Pharisee's prayer exhibited his hauteur before God and humanity. Not only did he not truly know or understand God, the Pharisee did not even have a correct concept of himself. He presented himself before the source of all goodness and righteousness and listed a catalogue of his *own* merits and virtues. So satisfied was the Pharisee with his accomplishments of keeping the law that he did not even ask the source of life for his blessing. Granted, the Pharisee had done well in obeying God's precepts but he credited *himself* and his *own* efforts rather than the Lord who had enabled him to do all things. With an attitude similar to that expressed in the first reading from Sirach, the Pharisee believed he had *justified himself* before God.

At the other extreme of the social and religious spectrum was the tax collector. Despised for a resented occupation regarded as unclean, the tax collector was shunned by his contemporaries. Unlike the Pharisee who probably positioned himself in a prominent place at the forefront of the court of Israel, the tax collector hung back. With head bowed, he *truly* prayed, i.e., he stood in honesty and humility before God in full awareness of God's goodness and his own sinfulness. Not a catalogue of his own virtues or a thanksgiving for his unique status before others, the prayer of the tax collector was a prayer of penitence and a petition for mercy.

Jesus' commentary upon the two men at prayer ("Believe me, this man went home from the temple justified but the other did not," v. 14) must have surprised his listeners. It was taken for granted that the Pharisee was a just person. According to Jewish law, the tax collector could also have been justified *if* he made full retribution *plus one fifth* to all those he had swindled, and then took up a new and acceptable occupation. Even with all the good intentions in the world, this would have been an almost impossible feat. But Jesus' comment indicated that the old ways of thinking and of measuring goodness were being reversed. In the new era of Jesus, i.e., the age of salvation, justification would be understood as God's gift and not a human accomplishment.

Directed toward "those who believed in their own self-righteousness," Jesus' parable returned the prerogative of judgment to God. By judging himself *and* others, the Pharisee was guilty of a sort of idolatry. As J.A. Fitzmeyer had pointed out, "This saying (v. 14) about justification is important for it may reveal that the New Testament teaching on the matter is somehow rooted in Jesus' own attitude and teaching. One achieves uprightness before God not by one's own activity but by a contrite recognition of one's own sinfulness before him." Therefore the Pauline teaching (Romans, Galatians) about justification has its roots in the teaching of Jesus but these roots should be understood as generic.

What has Luke's parable to teach to a church where the categories are no longer defined as "Pharisee" and "tax collector"? For those whose prayer is truthful, the parable prompts believers to realize there are pharisaic attitudes in all of us. So, too, there are elements of sinfulness and shame. Forgiveness, reconciliation, redemption are gifts of God that only the humble will recognize and only the needy will receive.

1. Social status has no effect whatsoever on the efficacy of prayer (Sirach).

2. The struggle of the persecuted speaks an eloquent, wordless prayer to God (2 Timothy).

3. In prayer, the only norm against which the believer can truly compare him/herself is the Lord; all other comparisons are odious (Luke).

31st Sunday in Ordinary Time

The wise and loving concern with which God created the universe is the same wise and loving concern that waits patiently for sinners to repent (Wisdom). That very concern seeks out the lost and makes them welcome (Luke). One day, all who persevere in faith will experience that welcome for all eternity (2 Thessalonians).

Wisdom 11:22-12:1. Attributed to Solomon, Israel's tenth century B.C.E. king and most noted sage, the book of Wisdom was actually written less than a century before Christ (ca. 60 B.C.E.). The author is believed by most scholars to have been a Greek-speaking Jew living in Alexandria, a city famous throughout the Mediterranean area for its rich intellectual and scientific climate. Like Jesus Ben Eleazar Ben Sira who wrote before him, the author of Wisdom was concerned for the sacred traditions of his fellow Jews living in the diaspora. Although the Jewish community in Alexandria was one of the three largest in the then-known world, the influence of Greek philosophy, art and culture proved very attractive and some were abandoning the faith of their ancestors to embrace secular systems of thought. Spurred on by the growing Jewish skepticism with regard to their national heritage and the traditional solutions to age-old issues, the author of Wisdom plunged into a study of the Jewish scriptures to provide pertinent answers and challenges for his contemporaries.

The entire second half of the book (Wisdom 11-19), from which our first reading has been excerpted, represents a *midrash* on the exodus from Egypt and the plagues. *Midrash*, which in Hebrew means to search, inquire and interpret, is a specific type of biblical interpretation which assumes that the biblical text has an inexhaustible fund of meaning that is relevant to and adequate for every question and situation (P. Achtemeier). It was this wealth of meaning and relevance that the author of Wisdom wished to offer his fellow Jews. Rather than search for wisdom amid the Greek systems of philosophy, he would have them realize that the source of true wisdom is to be found only in Israel and in Israel's God!

Part of a reflection on the utter transcendence of God and on his mercy, today's first reading focuses on the love God has for all he has created. Unlike the gods of the Greek pantheon who occasionally dabbled in human affairs to satisfy their whims or curiosity, the God of Israel became personally involved with his creatures. This personal involvement is called love by the Wisdom author (11:23), viz., the love that overlooks sin and gives time for repentance. Repentance, or *metanoia* in Greek, signifies that complete reversal of attitude and life style that would turn away from the lure of pagan art and culture in order to return completely and wholeheartedly to the one God of Israel.

To explain the divine motivation for loving all souls (11:26), the author of Wisdom reminded his contemporaries that the imperishable spirit of God himself (12:1) pervades all that exists. Whether by spirit he meant wisdom as the instrument of divine immanence (1:7, 7:24, 8:1) or the spirit of God breathed into humanity at creation (Genesis 2:7) is difficult to ascertain. In either case, it is the Wisdom author's conviction that the wisdom and/or spirit in all things is from the God of Israel. Within a century, the author's thought would be revised by the Christ-event. As R. Fuller has noted, "In the New Testament the dominant conception of the Spirit is not universally immanentist but eschatological. It does not dwell in all things by creation but is a gift to those who believe in Christ Jesus."

2 Thessalonians 1:11-2:2. When Paul preached the good news of salvation in Thessalonica ca. 49 C.E., he intended that the "word of the Lord would echo forth resoundingly" (1 Thessalonians 1:8) from that city throughout all of Macedonia and Achaia. As history has revealed, Paul's intentions were realized because, from the time of the apostle's ministry to the present day, Christianity has been a vibrant factor within Thessalonica (modern day Salonika). Having survived the Roman empire and its oppressive persecution, the Christian community at Thessalonica continued to resist as each successive wave of tribal barbarians swept through Europe. Because of the city's reputation for fidelity to Christ, medieval historians referred to it as "the Orthodox city." Even today vestiges of the ancient Hippodrome can be found interspersed among the modern Turkish edifices; these ancient ruins continue to testify to the courage of the 15,000 who were massacred there during the reign of Theodosius. But compared to this late fourth century persecution, the conflict that prompted the writing of 2 Thessalonians ca. 51 C.E. had not yet grown as intense.

Many today doubt that Paul wrote the second letter to Thessalonica because it represents such a radical shift in thought concerning eschatology (as compared to 1 Thessalonians). Others propose that circumstances in the city demanded that Paul revise his thoughts so as to answer the needs of a growing struggling community. In either case, the second letter was written within a few months of the first and was intended to correct certain misunderstandings which had arisen in the community.

Evidently, someone had brought either a message or a letter (purported to be from Paul) to the believers at Thessalonica which asserted that the *Day* of the Lord, i.e., the second coming of Jesus, had already occurred. False teachers in the city, influenced by early gnostic tendencies, exacerbated the situation as well. With their perverted interpretation of the gospel, these taught that human beings were separated into categories with varyimg degrees of enlightenment and therefore importance. Some were called spiritual beings or pneumatics who enjoyed an experience of the realm of light. Others with a lesser share of enlightenment or knowledge were believed to be "of this world" with little hope of anything better. According to the false teachers, the gospel revealed to the spiritual elite their true nature; as such they already enjoyed full knowledge and immortality. They preached that the day of the Lord had already come!

Today's second reading represents a partial answer to this false teaching. Rather than agitate over a *Day* which he asserted had *not yet* arrived (2 Thessalonians 2:2), the author of 2 Thessalonians called his brothers and sisters in the faith to concentrate on their calling here and now (2 Thessalonians 1:11). By their diligent efforts to become worthy of their call, they would be preparing for the *Day* in a proper manner. Call or *klesis*, as J. Forestell has pointed out, referred to the call of the Thessalonians from paganism to Christianity; it was also the beginning of their orientation to glory. To persevere in the faith and then to arrive at glory was, according to the author of 2 Thessalonians, not a matter of human achievement (as in gnosticism) but a "gracious gift" of God (2 Thessalonians 1:12). This gracious gift came to Zacchaeus (see next reading) in the person of Jesus.

Luke 19:1-10. What *really* made Zacchaeus climb the sycamore tree? In this wonderful narrative, unique to his gospel, the Lucan author has explained that the man was short. But there has to be something beyond his physical stature that impelled Zacchaeus to climb. In his commentary on the gospels, John Calvin described Zacchaeus as being attracted by that quality of God that draws people unto himself, even while they do not know him. Then, when they have come near, God reveals himself. Rudolf Otto referred to this as the experience of the holy, "*mysterium tremendum et fascinans.*" Whatever first attracted Zacchaeus to Jesus, it becomes evident, as the narrative unfolds, that his was a true encounter with the Lord and his conversion experience resulted in his salvation. A paradigm of the process of conversion, the Zacchaeus narrative contains all the elements of salvation history in a fascinating short story.

Zacchaeus, as chief tax collector in Jericho, was probably a man of much wealth and few friends. From the time of Julius Caesar, the options for collecting Rome's taxes were auctioned off to the highest bidder in each municipality. In order to win the bid, the prospective tax collector would have had to pay to Rome in advance all the taxes due in his locale. Then, he would hire agents who would help in collecting the taxes so that he could recoup his initial investment, pay his agents and make a generous profit as well. Because the tax collectors extorted sizable amounts of interest in addition to the taxes fixed by Rome, they were despised by their own townspeople. Their careers and their methods placed them outside the pale of acceptable society. As the gospels reveal, the tax collectors were often lumped together with sinners as being unclean and outside the law. According to Zacchaeus' neighbors, he was certainly no son of Abraham!

Nevertheless, Zacchaeus was drawn to Jesus; and Jesus, the incarnation of God's love and mercy for sinners, was drawn to him. As R. Fuller has pointed out, in the Zacchaeus incident Luke dramatized the fact that it would no longer be the law that determined humanity's relationship to God. After all, Zacchaeus was considered in breach of the law. Rather, a person's relationship to God would be determined by his/her attitude toward Jesus! Zacchaeus' attitude is first shown in his climbing the tree. Then, after Jesus had come into his home, his attitude was further revealed in his willingness to correct his wrongdoings.

According to the law as recorded in the Jewish scriptures, when one who had cheated another confessed his guilt and *volunteered* to make restitution, the amount required was equal to the amount stolen plus one fifth more (Leviticus 6:5, Numbers 5:7). However, if a person were caught in the act and then *forced* to make restitution, the amount exacted would be four or fivefold the amount stolen (Exodus 22:1-4, 2 Samuel 12:6). It is significant that Zacchaeus opted for the greater penalty. Not only did he freely admit his dishonesty, he volunteered to make the ultimate restitution. Moreover, and in keeping with one of the requirements Jesus asked of his disciples, Zacchaeus volunteered to give half of what he owned to the poor. When Jesus made a similar chailenge to one of the ruling class (Luke 18:22), the wealthy man went away sad.

Jesus' declaration, "Today salvation has come to this house" (v. 9), confirmed the integrity of Zacchaeus' conversion and affirmed the quality of his faith. In the person of Jesus, Zacchaeus had met and experienced the saving power of God. He showed himself to be a true son of Abraham, viz., one who, by faith, had become an heir to all the promises God had made to the patriarch. In the Jewish tradition, those promises translated into land, posterity and prosperity; in the Christian tradition, those promises translated into an experience of the reign of God present in Jesus, i.e., salvation.

While the final verse of this gospel pericope concerning the Son of Man searching and saving the lost is thought by many to be a later addition to the story and a commentary by the post-resurrection community, it is nevertheless an apt description of Jesus' ministry. The searching of God, made tangible in Jesus, reached out to Zacchaeus and made him whole. That day, Zacchaeus became truly worthy of his name; the experience of Zacchaeus, whose name means "pure one" or "righteous one," challenges every sinful believer to do whatever is necessary to welcome salvation into his/her heart.

1. True wisdom does not judge and condemn. True wisdom understands and forgives (Wisdom).

2. If we live each day as if it were our last, then we shall prepare a worthy welcome for the Lord (2 Thessalonians).

3. If one day salvation knocked at our door, would we recognize and welcome him? (Luke).

32nd Sunday in Ordinary Time

Jesus is risen! This disarmingly simple statement and all that it implies has radically altered the course of human events. His rising has become the pledge of our own (Luke) and his strength has become our strength, his ministry our own (2 Thessalonians). Because he lives, death no longer wields the final blow; death has become the passage to fuller life (2 Maccabees).

2 Maccabees 7:1-2, 9-14. Of the four books which bear the title Maccabees, only the first two have been accepted into the scriptural canon by the Roman Catholic church. Despite the fact that this literature is a veritable testimony to Jewish courage and faith, later disputes over Hasmonean politics and disappointment at certain instances of corruption within that dynasty caused these works tb be omitted from the Jewish canon.

The Maccabee for whom the books are named was Judas Maccabeus, one of the sons of the priest Mattathias who instigated the Jewish revolt of 167 B.C.E. Maccabee is popularly believed to mean "the hammer," referring to the power of the revolutionaries as they resisted their Seleucid oppressors. But most scholars agree that the term is probably derived from the Hebrew *maqqabyahu* which means "designated by God."

Written before 1 Maccabees, 2 Maccabees was the work of an Hellenistic Jew from the diaspora (many argue for an Egyptian origin), an epitomist who based his efforts on the work of an earlier author, Jason of Cyrene. While Jason's five-volume work has never been recovered, the author of 2 Maccabees, writing ca. 100 B.C.E., has preserved much of Jason's records concerning those events that precipitated the Jewish rebellion. Second Maccabees can be divided into three distinct sections. Part one (1:1—2:18) is comprised of two letters to the Jews in Egypt, instructing them on the manner of celebrating the feasts of Tabernacles and Hanukkah. In the second section (2:19—10:19), the author summarized Jason's work up to the temple dedication in 164 B.C.E.; and the third section (10:10—15:39) traced the life of Judas from 164 B.C.E. until his victory over Nicanor in 160 B.C.E.

His purpose in writing was to edify and to encourage his Jewish contemporaries in their resistance to the process of Hellenization. Following the lead of Alexander, his successors attempted to perpetuate the Greek mind and spirit throughout all their empire. Many Jews, especially the more liberal, better educated and wealthy, welcomed Hellenization as a necessary aspect of higher civilization. It was this sort of ecumenical posture that instigated the resistance among the more traditionalist Jews and began the movement known as the Hasidim. These *Hasidim* or "pious ones" were the forerunners of the later Pharisaic party; they were fierce defenders of the law, and their spirituality inspired those who fought to preserve their ancient heritage intact.

Today's first reading illustrates some of the atrocities the Jews endured during the Seleucid persecution. In the story of the seven brothers and their mother's valiant witness to their faith, the author of 2 Maccabees wished to present his contemporaries with heroes in their cause. Although our reading is an excerpted one, each of the brothers and their mother went to their death proclaiming their unswerving faith in the God of Israel.

But the most significant aspect of the episode is the developing doctrine of a personal resurrection. As N. McEleney has pointed out, there is a progression of thought in each brother's address to the king; today's text climaxes in the proclamation that the wicked will not know resurrection but the just shall live forever. While the doctrine of an afterlife and of a personal resurrection surfaced in Judaism ca. 200 B.C.E., it was not universally accepted. As today's gospel will reveal, the issue remained a bone of contention and was the source of many theological debates among Jesus' contemporaries.

2 Thessalonians 2:16-3:5. The pair of letters written to the believers at Thessalonica are the earliest among all the New Testament writings. As such, they give modern readers a glimpse into the nascent church as it struggled to develop its own identity in the absence of the earthly Jesus. Although the letters were written within two decades of Christ's resurrection, they reflect, nevertheless, considerable development of doctrine.

J. Forestell has listed the doctrinal teachings of 1 and 2 Thessalonians as follows: (1) Jesus is proclaimed as Lord and Son of God who has been raised from the dead; (2) God gives the Holy Spirit to those who believe in the good news of Jesus; (3) Christians will experience the Day of the Lord when Christ returns as savior and judge; (4) the Christian way of life should be characterized by faith, hope and charity; (5) persecution is an integral aspect of the life of the believer.

Because Christ's second coming and the circumstances that would surround it were a burning issue for the first generation of Christians, that subject was given preeminent importance in these letters. In the first letter, Paul had instructed the Thessalonians to recall the teachings of Jesus as he had handed them on to them while in Thessalonica, viz., that the Lord would surely come and share his risen glory with the faithful, *but* that no one knew the time of his arrival. When the Thessalonians expressed true Christian concern for those who died before Jesus' advent, Paul assured them that the faithful dead would rise and be taken up into glory along with the living.

In the second letter, the shift of thought concerning the parousia had led many to attribute 2 Thessalonians to another author. The apostasy therein described and the man of lawlessness or Antichrist seem to be the problems of a later time. Nevertheless, both letters are consistent in calling all Christians to prepare worthily for their encounter with the Lord.

Today's second reading is comprised of three short prayers. In the first (2:16-17) and in the third prayers (3:5), the author prayed for the community that they would remain constant in their efforts and consoled in the fact that theirs was truly the work of the gospel. The second prayer (3:1-4) is a request that the community pray for the author and for his ministry. Aware of the pitfalls that he would encounter (confused and evil people, faithlessness), the apostle expressed the conviction of the first generation church: that intercessory prayer has efficacy. Indeed, the community united in prayer is the greatest resource of the church. That resource will cause the work of the Lord to make progress (v. 1). Today, no less than in the first century, the prayer of the believing community is a force to be reckoned with.

Luke 20:27-38. In Jesus' day, the political situation greatly affected the attitudes toward religion of the various elements of society. The two major political factors were Hellenism and the Roman empire. Whereas Hellenism could be described as the cultural penetration of Greek ways into every aspect of Jewish life, the Roman empire constituted the dominating power that controlled all lives in its jurisdiction and legislated their freedoms. In reaction to these political forces, several parties emerged, viz., the Pharisees, Sadducees, Essenes, Herodians, Zealots, etc.

While the Essenes' reaction to the political scene was to withdraw from it completely, the Zealots on the other hand favored an active resistance that eventually erupted in the Jewish war in 66 C.E. A lesser and short-lived party, the Herodians, were supporters of the rule and policies of Herod Antipas; some even promoted Herod as the messiah of Israel. But the two major parties were the Pharisees and Sadducees; these two groups and their different theologies form the basis of the dispute in today's gospel.

Less numerous than their rivals the Pharisees, the Sadducees nevertheless exerted considerable influence on their society. Believed to be the spiritual descendants of Zadok (Solomon's high-priest, 1 Kings 2:35), the Sadducees were mainly of the aristocratic and priestly classes and claimed the exclusive right to preside over temple liturgies, sacrifices, etc. Religiously conservative, the Sadducees accepted only the Pentateuch as normative; therefore, they denied the development of doctrines found in later Jewish scriptures, e.g., angels, resurrection, final judgment, afterlife, etc.

The Pharisees were the spiritual descendants of the "pious ones" or *Hassidim* who had supported the revolt led by the Maccabees against Antiochus Epiphanes IV in the second century B.C.E. Claiming Ezra as their founder, the Pharisees preferred to concentrate on the religious life of their people; they shunned the political involvements favored by the Sadducees. Although they were "legal eagles" even to an exaggerated degree, the Pharisees also believed in the development of doctrine and were open to the messages of the prophets, the writings and later theological developments, e.g., resurrection, angels, judgment, afterlife, etc.

In addition to the Torah, the Pharisees developed an oral law called the "traditions of the elders" in which they interpreted and expanded the Torah to apply to every imaginable circumstance. Theologically, Jesus favored the Pharisaic point of view; he did, however, grapple with the Pharisees on several occasions, in an attempt to call them to a true understanding of the law as a bond of love and not a burden of minutiae.

When the Sadducees approached Jesus with the problem featured in today's gospel, they knew his ideas. No doubt, it was their intention to prove Jesus in error by their argument, a true *reductio ad absurdum*. Their protracted and highly improbable example was based on the levirate law (Deuteronomy 25:5, Genesis 38:8) which provided for the marriage of a widow to her deceased husband's brother. The law was meant to assure the continuance of the family line.

But Jesus was not to be enmeshed in their petty debate over who would be married to whom. Aware that the Sadducees accepted only the Pentateuch, Jesus argued with them on their own terms. Citing their greatest authority, Moses, Jesus explained to the Sadducees that, when Yahweh appeared at the burning bush (Exodus 3), he identified himself as the God of the patriarchs, Abraham, Isaac, and Jacob. Though these had been dead for centuries, if God is truly a God of the living, they must somehow be alive, argued Jesus.

Jesus' statement implied that when God has a relationship with someone, as he did with the patriarchs, then that relationship will never be dissolved, not even by death. Paul also struggled to explain the quality of risen life and expressed this same idea in his letter to the church at Rome: "I am certain that neither death, nor life . . . nor any other creature will be able to separate us from the love of God that comes to us in Christ Jesus, our Lord" (Romans 8:38-39). Asserting his conviction concerning the resurrection, Jesus challenged the Sadducees who quoted the Mosaic law on levirate marriage to accept the same Mosaic tradition concerning immortality!

In explaining the characteristics of resurrected life, the Lucan Jesus asserted that it was not merely a continuation of this life with its traditions and institutions, as the Sadducees' argument implied. Rather, Jesus taught, resurrected life is an entirely *new* mode of existence wherein marriage would have no relevance. Luke described those risen from the dead as "angels," "sons of the resurrection" and "sons of God" (v. 36). Because of Jesus' saving death and the relationship with the living God that Jesus afforded to all of humanity, these descriptions of the risen faithful would become a reality. In the reality of the resurrection, our faith finds meaning and fulfillment.

1. For those who believe, death wields no finality (2 Maccabees).

2. The united prayer of the believing community is one of the most potent forces in the universe (2 Thessalonians).

3. Concern over how things shall be in heaven should not detract from our present commitments (Luke).

33rd Sunday in Ordinary Time

For some, the Lord's return evokes eager and joyful anticipation; for others, dread and fear (Malachi). The difference in attitude takes a lifetime to acquire, a lifetime of faithfulness spelled out in responsible service and attentive prayer (2 Thessalonians). As we share this period of preparation, it is better to turn from those whose preaching about fiery revenge and brimstone transforms Jesus' return into a thing of fear, and to turn toward the saving promise of the Lord: "I will give you words and a wisdom" and "By your patient endurance you will save your lives" (Luke).

Malachi 3:19-20. Writers usually reflect in their work the flavor and character of the times in which they live. Social developments, political upheavals, economic booms and disasters—all have a way of finding expression in an author's work, regardless of his/her chosen genre. The biblical authors too mirrored for their contemporaries (and for us) their perceptions of their world, its people, their problems and the role religion played in shaping their lives. A recurrent theme found in literature, and in the scriptures as well, is the inequity that exists in society. The "haves" and the "have-nots" often appear at either end of a social spectrum. What transpires between the two extremes has provided inspiration to fuel many an author's creative imagination. While unable to solve all the world's problems with a pen, the writer nevertheless plays an important role in calling attention to the issues and perhaps in directing the attention of the reader toward possible solutions. When the author of today's first reading wrote, he wished to raise the consciousness of his post-exilic contemporaries with regard to their social failings and to remind them of their religious responsibilities,

Writing during the fifth century B.C.E. (ca. 460-450 B.C.E.) the anonymous prophet, who was simply named Malachi by a later editor (because of the reference in 3:1 to *mal'akki,* my messenger), attempted to help his people during the turbulent period of reconstruction. Although the exile in Babylon had ended and the people had been allowed by Cyrus the Persian king to return home, they were frustrated and demoralized. With material aid from Persia and under the leadership of a foreign governor (1:8), the returnees struggled to rebuild the temple. By 515 B.C.E. the temple was completed (Ezra 6:15) but the newly constructed house of worship did not ipso facto re-create the prayerful assembly. At the time of the prophet's ministry, the liturgical and communal life of the people had greatly deteriorated.

Besides the problems of laxity among the clergy, slovenly ritual (1:6—2:9), the withholding of tithes (3:8, 10-14) and foreign influences in religious practices (2:10-16), there existed an ever growing gap between the rich and the poor. Ironically, it seemed to Malachi and his people that the godless, the very people who seemed to scorn God and his law, also appeared to enjoy the lion's share of his blessings. In sharp contrast, the poor and often the most faithful people were left without enough to subsist on. In bringing this shameful injustice to the attention of his people, the prophet warned that a day would come when the situation would be reversed.

A day of judgment, and a day of reckoning, the Day (v. 19) of the Lord had first been prophesied by the eighth century B.C.E. prophet Amos (5:18), According to popular belief, the Day of the Lord was anticipated as a time of victory and joy, a time when the Lord would exalt his people over their, enemies. Israel's recollection of God's intervention on their behalf in the past prompted a belief in an eschatological *day* par excellence when Yahweh would intervene definitively and actualize his promises to the patriarchs (G.Von Rad). But Amos and his fellow prophets shattered the naive pipedreams of their contemporaries. Rather than joy and victory, they promised that the Day of the Lord would prove to be a day of judgment for Israel (Amos 5:18-20), for the other nations (Obadiah 15) and for Judah (Joel 1:15). Indeed, it would be a day when people would try to hide themselves in the dust in terror of the destroying whirlwind of the Lord's fury (Zephaniah 1:14-18, Isaiah 2:10-11).

In post-exilic Jerusalem, the prophets reintroduced the theme of the Day of the Lord, describing it, as did Malachi, in terms of a fiery cosmic convulsion. As a result of this upheaval, the righteous would be rewarded but the evil would perish forever. The same blazing sun that would destroy the wicked (v. 19) will bring healing for those who fear the Lord (v. 20). "Sun of justice" (v. 20) is an epexegetical genitive phrase meaning the "sun *which is* justice." The phrase drew upon a very common symbol in the ancient Near Eastern world. Literally the word "rays" (v. 20) should be translated "wings." The sun god was represented in Persia and in Egypt as a *winged* solar disk whose presence provided warmth and light and, therefore, *life* to all. The scriptural authors adapted this symbolism and applied it to Yahweh, the one God of all whose presence spells life and light for the good as it sentences the evil to the destroying fire. When applied by Christian authors to Jesus, the title "Sun of justice" signified the second advent of the Son of Man as judge as well as the first coming of the incarnate Son of God, the light of the world.

2 Thessalonians 3:7-12. When Paul wrote to the Christians in Thessalonica in the middle of the first Christian century (ca. 50-51 C.E.), the city was experiencing a welfare problem. Some of the community, prompted by erroneous ideas about the parousia, had opted for a kind of premature retirement. Because of the idleness of some of its members, the rest of the community was burdened financially. In addition to the economic problem they imposed on the others, those who had religiously rationalized their indolence were a social nuisance as well. By using a clever play on words (*meden ergazomenous alla periergazomenous*) that has lost its punch in translation, Paul called them busybodies!

Most scholars attribute the problem described in today's second reading to the fact that many in Thessalonica (and elsewhere) expected the parousia to take place *imminently*. Those who support this idea believe that Paul had preached so enthusiastically about Jesus' advent that his hearers abandoned their normal means of livelihood to await the return. Others, probably more correctly, attribute the idleness in Thessalonica to an "over-realized eschatology." In other words, some of the believers may have been misled by an early form of gnosticism to believe that the Day of the Lord had already come. Since they thought that they were *already* experiencing the parousia, they assumed that the curse of having to work (Genesis 3) had been revoked. Therefore, they assumed a Qoheleth-like philosophy of "eat, drink and be merry."

In his commentary on this particular text advising homilists as to its application, R. Fuller cautions against a too simplistic, fundamentalist interpretation. In our society, says Fuller, idleness is hardly due to an over-realized eschatology. In a society whose economic injustices condemn a large segment of the population to unemployment, it is no longer true that those who do not work should not eat. Therefore it is an injustice to the word of God *and* to the unemployed to lift the words of Thessalonians out of their first century context and apply them *literally* to a 20th century problem. What is at issue here is a problem of hermeneutics: how can the preacher or teacher get the text to convey its correct meaning in an altered situation. To accomplish this, great sensitivity is needed—sensitivity to the depth of meaning in the sacred word and to those who will hear it and try to live by it.

At the basis of Paul's advice to the Thessalonian Christians was his concern for the advancement of the gospel and for that community harmony in which gospel values could flourish. His admonition was directed against those who thought the kingdom had *already* come. If they truly believed that, then their actions should have been inspired by loving altruism and not by lazy selfishness. As an example, Paul offered his own tireless service of the kingdom. With no concern for himself but only for those others who had not heard the good news, Paul worked to the point of exhaustion. For the sake of the kingdom present and yet to come, Paul's advice and example continue to be timely and relevant.

Luke 21:5-19. As the end of the liturgical year approaches, our thoughts are drawn through the selected readings to the second advent of the Son of Man. We have come full circle, from last year's Advent celebration of his first coming to an eager anticipation in the coming year of his ultimate appearance. In the unfolding of the year, we have experienced the love and the life of Jesus in every aspect of his incarnate existence. As we arrive at the end of another cycle of liturgical celebration, we are faced with the reality that the cross is still a powerful part of our experience and that full knowledge of the resurrection has yet to be ours.

For that reason, the liturgy puts before us those selections of scripture called apocalyptic. With these words, the evangelists bolstered the courage and hopes of the early Christians to persevere in patient alertness. With its emphasis on the *eschata* or last things, apocalyptic literature assures the faithful that there will be a just culmination of all their efforts. No matter how powerful evil seems to be for the present, goodness will never be overcome by evil. This is the message of the cross and the heart of apocalyptic hope.

Often called crisis or persecution literature, early Christian apocalyptic literature was not so much concerned with *prediction* as with *interpretation*. To help their contemporaries survive their *present* sufferings, apocalyptic writers enabled their readers to understand those struggles as part of the birth pangs of the "end." By their endurance and constancy in the Lord, the faithful could meet that end with confidence and not fear, with joy and not dread. At the time of Luke's writing, the Christian community of the 80s was already experiencing its share of the cross in the form of persecution from both Jewish and gentile sources.

Today's pericope, an excerpt from a longer apocalyptic discourse (Luke 21:5-30) was occasioned by an admiring remark about the temple's adornment (v. 5). The temple in this particular context would have been the so-called "third" or "Herodian" temple. In 20-19 B.C.E. Herod the Great undertook the enormous task of completely refurbishing the second temple (finished in 515 B.C.E.). According to the first century C.E. Jewish historian Josephus, Herod "erected a new foundation wall, and enlarged the surrounding area to twice its former dimensions" (*Jewish Wars*, 1.21,1, 401). Herod's work at renovation continued for decades, and was still in process during Jesus' earthly ministry and was finally completed ca. 63 C.E., just seven years before it was demolished by Titus' troops.

Here is Josephus' description: "The exterior of the structure lacked nothing that could astound either mind or eye. For, being covered on all sides with massive plates of gold, the sun was no sooner upon it than it radiated so fiery a flash that people straining to look at it were compelled to avert their eyes, as from rays of the sun. To approaching strangers, it appeared from afar like a snow-clad mountain; for, all that was not overlaid with gold was of purest white. From its summit protruded sharp golden spikes to prevent birds from settling upon and befouling the roof. Some of the white stones in the structure were forty-five cubits in length, five in height and six in breadth" (*Jewish Wars*, 5.5, 6, 222-224).

Given this description of its magnificence, it is not surpising that the temple, even though incomplete, evoked the admiration of those who saw it. Therefore, Jesus' prophetic oracle (v. 6) about its destruction was a shock to both the ethical and esthetic sensibilities of his hearers. Naturally, their first reaction to such a statement was to ask *when* it would happen and *how* would they recognize the onset of such a calamity (v. 7). As R. Fuller has pointed out, there is sufficient reason to believe that Jesus *did* actually predict the temple's destruction (Mark 14:58, 15:29; John 2:19; Acts 6:14), but with the series of crises that followed, this saying of Jesus was expanded into an apocalyptic discourse by the early church. For example, in today's gospel, the predictions of war, earthquake, pestilence and famine reflect events of the 60s and 70s C.E. that had taken place before Luke's writing in the 80s. If, therefore, these events took place in the past, what meaning can such a text have for the present?

What *is* important for modern believers to remember is that, while those particular historical crises of which Luke wrote have passed, the struggle to survive the forces of evil remains a present reality. For that reason, the Lucan Jesus' advice concerning Christian attitudes and behavior remains valuable and apropos. At the outset (v. 8) Jesus counseled those who heard him "not to be misled." The Greek verb *planan* (misled) means a departure from the truth or from fidelity. Rather, Jesus exhorted, remember that when suffering comes there will be support for the faithful. Unlike the other synoptics (Mark 13:11, Matthew 24:20) who promised that the Holy Spirit would be at hand to counsel the disciples, the Lucan Jesus pledged, "*I* will give you words and a wisdom" (v. 15).

Persecution should be perceived as an opportunity for bearing witness to the Lord: "You will be brought to give witness on account of it. . . all because of my name" (vv. 13, 12b). Literally, v. 13 could be translated, "You will be called on to act in a way that testifies to your fidelity to me or to what you really are." Like the early believers, some will pay the ultimate price (Acts 7:54-60, 12:1-12). But for *all*, the advice *was* and *remains* the same. Confident hope, joyful anticipation and patient endurance spell not merely survival but victory and salvation.

1. In the same experience of Jesus Christ some will be found guilty and others will be judged worthy of his presence (Malachi).

2. Those who day by day love the Lord and remember his words are already prepared for his coming (2 Thessalonians).

3. Many who wear themselves out seeking and predicting signs of the end may be surprised by its appearance (Luke).

34th Sunday in Ordinary Time

Our king came from humble stock; his ancestors tended sheep in the hills of Bethlehem (2 Samuel). He did not rise to power in the customary ways; he had no army, no crown or royal jewels, no throne except a cross and no one to acclaim his kingship except disbelieving passersby who mocked his authority (Luke). Yet, his is the power through which the world was created. He is the word by which humanity is redeemed. Jesus Christ is our Lord and king (Colossians).

2 Samuel 5:1-3. David, the shepherd boy who became king, was not a perfect man nor was he a perfect ruler. Indeed, his career as Israel's leader was marred by his shortcomings and by sins as serious as *murder*. Nevertheless, when the Israelites reached into the treasury of their traditions for a description of the ideal king, it was David they remembered and made a legend. As Israel's hope for a glorious future developed (a hope subsequently called "messianism"), it was rooted in David's house and developed from it. Centuries after David, when the New Testament authors tried to substantiate Jesus' position as messiah, they emphasized his Davidic lineage while they celebrated what they understood as the fulfillment (in Jesus) of the promises (2 Samuel 7:14) God had made to David.

In the Old Testament, one can distinguish two main postures with regard to kingship: the so-called "anti-" and "pro-" monarchic tendencies. Those who were anti-monarchic (1 Samuel 7:3—8:22, 10;17-27) regarded the attempt to stabilize the government by imitating the monarchies of other nations as a rejection of the Lord's theocratic rule of his people. The king was seen as a usurper of Yahweh's unique authority. Anti-monarchists were well aware that kingship (or any absolute authority) can easily deteriorate into tyranny. Ideally, Israel's kings were to *represent* the Lord and to mediate between the Lord and his people; but, in actual fact, the reality fell far short of the ideal in the majority of cases.

In the pro-monarchic texts of scripture (1 Samuel 9:1—10:16) there is no indication of divine disapproval. In fact, Samuel has been portrayed as God's prophet, seeking out and anointing Saul. Through his anointing, Saul was revered as one possessed by God's own Spirit. The king was looked upon as a sacramental expression of Yahweh's authority among his people, As R. Fuller has noted, today's first reading is an example of this pro-monarchic attitude while 1 Samuel 8 is the classical formulation of the anti-monarchic posture. Where 2 Samuel 5 stressed the humane aspects of kingship and the solidarity of *God-with-Israel* in the person of the shepherd-king, 1 Samuel 8 voiced the concerns of those who feared despotic abuse of power and monarchic excesses.

Prior to the events narrated in today's text (according to the version in 1 and 2 Samuel), Saul had died and David had become king of Judah. At that time, Judah had a separate government as a vassal state of the Philistines. After Saul's death, his son Ishbosheth, aided by Saul's general Abner, became king of Israel. Shortly thereafter, Abner deserted Ishbosheth, after the new king rebuked his general for marrying a woman from Saul's harem. An angry Abner offered David his allegiance. In the ensuing power struggle, both Abner and Ishbosheth were killed.

Colossians 1:12-20. One of the most profound christological pronouncements in the New Testament, the hymn (vv. 15-20) that comprises the bulk of today's second reading is an eloquent expression of the cosmic dimensions of Christ's leadership. E. Kasemann believes the hymn was part of an ancient baptismal ritual; as such, the hymn may represent the profession of faith in Jesus on the part of the newly baptized. The author of the letter to the Colossian Christians quoted the hymn in an effort to remind the believers of their *initial* profession of faith, a faith they seemed in danger of adulterating with false notions or of abandoning altogether. Because we have only the author's reaction to it, it is difficult to reconstruct the actual controversy at Colossae that occasioned this letter. If the author *was* Paul, then the letter was written near the end of his life (ca. 61-63 C.E.) while the apostle was imprisoned in Rome.

Not founded by Paul but by one of his converts, Epaphras (2: 1), the church at Colossae was predominantly gentile. From the internal evidence of the letter it seems that a certain religio-philosophical system had begun to seduce Christians with its claims of "secret knowledge." This esoteric system, a form of pre-gnostic thought, presented itself as superior to Christianity. Attacking his opponents head on, the Colossians' author asserted the primacy of Christ and therefore of the Christian faith over every other ideology.

In this hymn of two strophes, the first section (v. 15-17) underscored the nature of Christ and his unique role in creation. As the *eikon* or image of God, Christ made present in an active manner the invisible God. The term *eikon* was reminiscent of the Jewish concept of wisdom as God's handmaid in creation and as the pure emanation from the almighty (Wisdom 7:25-26). *Eikon* also recalled the Greek concept of the *logos*, the ordering principle by which God created the cosmos. As God's *eikon* or image, Jesus was not the *static* representation but the *actual* counterpart of the invisible God in the visible world.

As Lord or king of creation, Christ has power over the visible and invisible aspects of creation, i.e., over all creatures, even the heavenly beings, the thrones, dominations, principalities and powers. According to Hellenistic thought, these were the four ranks of angels that guarded heaven's seven levels. Created beings who owed their existence to Christ ("in him, everything in heaven and on earth was created"), these heavenly beings were *not* to be worshipped. Only Christ, the center of the created universe ("in him"), the cause or agent of creation ("through him") and the goal ("for him") toward which all of creation should proceed, is worthy of all homage and veneration.

As in the advanced or high christology of the Johannine prologue, the Colossians' author understood the historical or earthly Jesus as part of an event that transcended the beginning as well as the end of his life. The Christ event included the historical Jesus framed by his preexistence as God's Son (word, wisdom) and by his postexistence as the resurrected glorious king.

Luke 23:35-43. Up until the 13th century, the cross as the symbol of our salvation was fashioned not with a corpus but with jewels. Precious gems spoke to the faithful of the *victory* Jesus had achieved over sin and death and of his *reign* as king of heaven and earth that had been established on the unlikely throne of the gibbet. Although crucifixes have been styled more realistically since then, due to the initiative of Francis of Assisi, the notion of Jesus' triumphant kingship has not been lost. By their portrayals of Jesus' passion and crucifixion, the evangelists, especially Luke and John, underscored the fact that Jesus went to his death, not as a defeated victim but as victorious crown prince, not as the last act of a sad dramatic tragedy but as the culminating scenario of a well-planned love story.

By means of the threefold taunt or mockery that comprises the heart of the Lucan crucifixion scene and the first portion of today's gospel (vv. 35-39), Luke highlighted the saving power of Jesus on the cross. All three taunts—(1) that of the leaders, "He *saved* others; let him *save* himself if he is the messiah of God, the chosen one" (v. 35); (2) that of the soldiers, "If you are the king of the Jews, *save* yourself" (v. 36), and (3) that of one of the criminals crucified with Jesus, "Aren't you the messiah? Then *save* yourself and us"—contained the Greek verb *sozein* (to save). By an ingenious twist of irony, Luke has organized his narrative so that the enemies of Jesus are his very confessors and the theological interpreters of the saving event of his dying!

How clever of Luke, that Israel's leaders (v. 35) were made to call Jesus by the titles "messiah" and "chosen one." Messiah, which means "anointed" one, traditionally combined the notions of king and savior of Israel. By calling Jesus the "chosen one," the leaders were made to evoke for Luke's readers the triumphant scene of Jesus' transfiguration (9:35), as well as the redeeming work of the suffering but vindicated servant of Deutero-Isaiah (42: 1). C. Talbert has suggested that the threefold taunt (by leaders, soldiers, one of the criminals) combine to form a threefold *temptation* of the crucified Jesus, much like that of Luke 4:1-13. In each case the temptation or taunt served as a literary foil to highlight Jesus' innocence and power, not his weakness.

Customarily, the Romans hung the charge (charges) brought against the accused over his head on the cross. In Jesus' "crime" is an act of faith and allegiance in the Lord. In the remainder of today's gospel pericope, in the exchange between Jesus and one of the criminals, the manner and scope of Jesus' "crime" of kingship is illustrated.

Proper to Luke's gospel, the dialogue between Jesus and one of the criminals first established Jesus' innocence: "We are only paying the price for what we've done, but this man has done nothing wrong." Secondly, the dialogue underscored the "evangelistic effects" of Jesus' saving death. C. Talbert explains that Jesus' innocent dying had the effect of converting the criminal. Such a conversion was consonant with the motif (especially stressed in Luke's gospel) of Jesus as mediator of forgiveness to outcasts (5:29ff, 7:36ff, 15:1-2, 18:9-14, 19:1-10). In the criminal's request, "Remember me, when you enter upon your reign" (v. 42), there is an acknowledgment of Jesus' kingship and of his authority to grant pardon and mercy.

For all of Luke's readers, the criminal's confident request served as a reminder of the scope of Jesus' kingly power. His was not a command that mustered armies, planned battles or levied taxes; Jesus' authority reached beyond politics and beyond space and time to mediate the joys of God's love and eternal reward: Jesus' authority, as acclaimed in the criminal's request, carried with it the unique power to acquit the repentant of their guilt. J.A. Fitzmeyer says that this scene sums up the Lucan *theologia crucis*. This episode is the evangelist's way of accenting the salvific aspects of Jesus' death and the regal status he will achieve. Moreover, the scene communicates the saving effect Jesus' death had and will have on human beings, even crucified criminals.

Paradise, the experience of it on that very day, was Jesus' promise to the repentant criminal (v. 43). *Paradeisos* in Greek was adapted from an old Persian word *pairidaeza* that meant an enclosed space or garden area. In the intertestamental literature of Judaism, paradise meant the realm reserved for the righteous dead (Testament of Levi 18. 10) The Apocalypse of Abraham (21) explained that the just went straight to paradise whereas the wicked were forever relegated to the underworld. In 1 Enoch (60:18, 21; 61:12; 70:4), the author claimed that the righteous *already* dwell in the garden of life. When the word was translated into Hebrew, it usually referred to a treed park; in the Septuagint version of Genesis, paradise was used synonymously with Eden, the idyllic garden home of humanity.

In New Testament literature, paradise referred to the realm of bliss in heaven (2 Corinthians 12:4, Revelation 2:7) and, as the Lucan text indicates, this bliss was thought to begin (albeit proleptically) with the inauguration of the messianic age. That Jesus could make such a promise to the criminal was the evangelist's way of illustrating that everything that had been said of Jesus, whether in faith or in scorn, was in fact true! He can save! He is messiah! He is the chosen one and king of glory who can forgive sin, has conquered death and can grant entrance into the eternal joy of paradise. In these capacities we celebrate his kingship today.

1. Leadership is a process of moving forward together in mutual cooperation, respect and concern (2 Samuel).

2. For leadership to be truly effective, those who lead must have confidence in those who follow and vice-versa (Colossians).

3. One of the most powerful uses of authority is the willingness to pardon others (Luke).

Movable Feasts

For the following movable feasts, which replace the Sunday in the Roman calendar if the date of a feast falls on a Sunday, see above, Year A Movable Feasts, page 110 and following.

February 2—Lord's Presentation
June 24—Birth of John the Baptizer
June 29—Peter and Paul
August 6—Transfiguration
August 15—Assumption
September 14—Triumph of the Cross
November 1—All Saints
November 2—All Souls
November 9—Dedication of Lateran

Trinity Sunday

In the tri-dimensional experience of salvation, believers come to know the love of the Father, made tangible in the person of Jesus and ever present in the activity of the Spirit (John). With inscrutable wisdom, that same love miraculously ordered the universe, filling each creature with mystery and wonder (Proverbs). That same love is the reason for our hope and joy (Romans).

Proverbs 8:22-31. Attributed to Solomon, Israel's famed king reputed for his wise ways, the book of Proverbs is actually an anthology of Hebrew wisdom from several different sources. Some of the material does date back to Solomon's reign in the tenth century B.C.E. (e.g., 10:1—22:16) but most was written during later stages and the work received its final form in fifth century B.C.E. post-exilic Judah. After the fall of Jerusalem (587 B.C.E.) and during the subsequent exile, the disgraced people learned in retrospect the lessons of the prophets. There emerged a new focus on the law as the secure hope for Israel's salvation. Foremost among Israel's teachers became those scribes and sages whose lives had been dedicated to the study of the law in all its ramifications.

But post-exilic Judah was not easily restored to its former grace and fervor. In the words of J.T. Forestell, "Apathy best describes the attitude of the majority toward the messianic idealism of the past. Individualism and immorality were rampant. Self-aggrandisement led to the exploitation of the poor by the rich." Seeing the need, the wise men stepped into the breach and proposed to their contemporaries the pursuit of wisdom, an ideal that had both international and individual appeal.

Initially perceived as a sort of socio-political talent for knowing how and what to do in a given situation, wisdom was considered necessary for enjoying a happy and successful life. But "Israel's presuppositions made it inevitable that preeminent wisdom should be attributed to God and that any share of it by others should be considered not merely a product of training and experience but a blessed gift of God" (J. Gaffney). Gradually, with the influence of Greek philosophy, attention shifted from *derivative* human wisdom to God's *original* wisdom. With this shift in emphasis, wisdom as a divine quality began to be perceived as a distinct entity. Not merely in an adverbial sense (God acts *wisely*) or in an adjectival sense (God's deeds are *wise*), wisdom was regarded as a personified instrument assisting God as a helpmate and a companion (God *and* wisdom!).

Because this concept developed at a relatively late date (5th century B.C.E.) when the attractions of polytheism had waned, the biblical authors could write of an hypostatized or personified attribute of God without endangering Israel's strict monotheism. Some scholars believe that the notion of personified wisdom was catalyzed by the demise of the monarchy and the seeming hopelessness for restoration to come from the Davidic line. Indeed, lyric poems such as the one that comprises today's first reading transferred to wisdom, as an attribute of God, the faith and hope that the people had formerly placed in a Davidic messiah.

Describing wisdom as a person, firstborn of God, the Proverbs' poet identified the personalized concept as a crafter of creation and playful companion of the creator (vv. 30-31). T. Maertens and J. Frisque have observed that his poem reflects a development in the Jewish concept of time and the new meaning of life as perceived in wisdom. Like all peoples, the Israelites were anguished at time's impermanence and uncontrollable, relentless passing. Yesterday was forever gone except for its memory; soon today would be gone and no one could be sure of tomorrow. In hope, the Jews had looked toward an eschatological period, a time inaugurated by the messiah wherein eternity would be harvested and its hour would last forever. Maertens suggests that today's poem has corrected that notion: that eschatology and eternity do not depend only on a future king or belong only to the realm of the future! Rather, the gift of wisdom and the presence of wisdom inform the present with eternal joys and truths. As a seeker of wisdom, each believer must appreciate the eternal realities here and now and appropriate them through faith.

Romans 5:1-5. Although biblical scholars have a variety of opinions about the literary character of the letter to the Romans, there is unanimous accord with regard to the value and significance of Paul's work. Some have called the letter Paul's *gospel* and believe it to have been a summation of the apostle's doctrine of Christianity. Others have termed Romans a "letter-essay," sent to a specific people and concerned with certain subjects but supplemental to the author's other works. The instruction included in the letter-essay was intended to clarify, abridge and develop the author's basic ideas and theology. Still others regard Romans as Paul's last will and testament, "a summary of his most important themes, elevated above the moment of definite situations and conflicts into the sphere of the eternally and essentially valid" (M. L. Stirnewalt).

J. Fitzmeyer has argued against these suggestions and has proposed that Romans is *not* a complete sketch of Paul's doctrine *or* his last will and testament but rather a presentation of his missionary reflections on the historic possibility of salvation, offered to all peoples in the good news of Jesus Christ. When Paul wrote to Rome from Corinth sometime during the winter of 57-58 C.E., he directed his thoughts to a community of Christians beset with difficulties from within and without. In 49 C.E. Claudius had expelled all Jews from Rome; Jewish Christians were included in the expulsion. Nero rescinded Claudius' order in 54 C.E. and many returned to Rome only to find themselves at odds over several issues with the Hellenist Christians who had remained in the city. In addressing himself to the problems in Rome, Paul brought to his message the insights he had gained during his eastern mission, especially in his conflicts with the Judaizers. There, Paul had grown firm in his conviction that justification as God's free gift of salvation was extended to all, both Jews *and* Greeks, and was dependent not on the deeds of the law but on faith in Jesus Christ. That justification reconciled the Christian to God and bestowed a peace which no difficulty, however great, could threaten.

Notice that Paul used the present indicative tense stating "we are at peace" (5:1), meaning that the effects of justification are already enjoyed by believers. Alienation and enmity have yielded to reconciliation because of Jesus. "Through our Lord Jesus Christ," a term Paul used frequently, affirmed the integral part Jesus played in the Father's saving plan. In and through Jesus, believers have "access" (v. 2) to grace. Other translations render "access" as safe harbor. Instead of dwelling on their trials and afflictions (*thlipsis*), Paul called the believers in Rome to rejoice in them and to see the disputes between Roman authorities as a passage to greater endurance and firmer hope (vv. 3-4). At the basis of his assertion that salvation was assured to the believer was Paul's solid faith in God's love manifested in Jesus and continually experienced in the presence of the Holy Spirit (v. 5). Paul's description of the triadic structure of the Christian experience aided later theologians in their development of the doctrine of the trinity and continues to encourage all believers to hope and to endure.

John 16:12-15. Feasts in honor of a doctrine rather than of an event of salvation were introduced into the liturgical calendar in the late Middle Ages. As R. Fuller has observed, purists might argue that these doctrine-oriented feasts be altogether abandoned and struck from the liturgical calendar, "but the Spirit has spoken even in the medieval church!" In today's gospel pericope, the Johannine author has underscored that same fact of the Spirit's abiding presence with and continuous guidance of the believing community.

Part of the farewell discourse at the last supper, whose purpose was to prepare the disciples for their future service, today's text centered mainly on the role of the paraclete. When Jesus announced his imminent departure from them, his followers were saddened and fearful. With him, they had evolved into a community whose cohesiveness centered upon his presence and his strength. Without him, they felt lost and alienated. To encourage them, Jesus had promised he would send them another, like himself, to be their helper, advocate and guide. This helper, their paraclete, as they would come to realize, was the Spirit of Jesus himself.

The full burden of Jesus' message, his messiahship, his unorthodox behavior, his radical reinterpretations of traditional beliefs and practices, even his identity, were not completely grasped by his disciples during his earthly ministry. "I have much more to tell you, but you cannot bear it now," said the Johannine Jesus shortly before the process of his passion and death was set in motion. While some systematic theologians have interpreted this (John 16:12) as referring to the continuing nature of revelation until the death of the last apostle, others have understood it as a reference to the gradual unfolding of dogma all during the church's existence. But R. E. Brown, truer to the text and more attuned to the Johannine author's intentions, reminds modern readers of another statement of Jesus, "I revealed to you *everything* I heard from my Father" (John 15:15) and concludes that John 16:12 means that only after Jesus' resurrection and with the aid of his Spirit would the *fullness* of his revealed message be understood by his followers. The "more" Jesus had to tell would be told in terms of a deeper understanding of what had *already* been revealed, Again, Brown notes, "it is unlikely that in Johannine thought there was any concept of *further* revelation after the ministry of Jesus, for Jesus is *the* revelation of the Father."

As the Spirit of truth, the Paraclete would guide the disciples in the way of all truth. *Hodegein* (to guide on the way) is related to *hodos* (way) and reflects the former declaration of Jesus, "I am the way" (John 14:6). In other words, the paraclete as helper of the post-resurrection community would guide believers in the way(s) of Jesus. The Spirit's presence and the openness of the community to that presence would be a guarantee of authenticity and continuity that Jesus' witness to the Father and his ministry were being carried on by those who believed in him. In vv. 13-15, the verb *anangellein* (announce) has been used three times. According to R. E. Brown, the word means to say over again what has already been said. Since the prefix *ana* is used in the same way as the English prefix "re-" (again), the text would probably have been more accurately translated, "he will reannounce to you" (vv. 13-15). In apocalyptic literature the verb *anaggellein* was used to refer to the *interpretation* of visions or dreams *already* received.

Hence the evangelist was asserting the role of the Paraclete as one who would *refresh* in the hearts of Jesus' followers the good news they had already received and as one who would clarify and illuminate the revelation given in the person of Jesus. Included here as well is the notion that the Paraclete would help to interpret and reinterpret that revelation within the evolving community. For the disciples of Jesus in the first century, the presence of the Paraclete meant an unbroken bond with the risen Lord. Moreover, the Spirit of truth acted as a shield against the heresies that threatened to dilute the authentic message. In the Johannine church of the 90s, gnostic (and other) elements from within and from outside the group claimed to have a monopoly on the truth and on inspiration. In his last discourse, the Johannine author affirmed the presence of the true Spirit of Jesus *with* the church. Today that Spirit is no less active, no less forceful and true, as he refreshes in the hearts of fervent believers their responsibility to Jesus' mission and message.

1. More than just a haphazard accident of the galaxies, creation reflects the wisdom and care of a loving hand (Proverbs).

2. Hope is the conscious attitude born of authentic faith in God's gift of justification (Romans).

3. Always present with the believing community, Jesus' Spirit continually brings new light and deeper understanding to the truth of the gospel (John).

Corpus Christi

Sacramentally, the eucharist is the celebration of the body of Christ, betrayed, blessed, broken, proclaimed and remembered (1 Corinthians). His life effected the blessing of God's salvation for all the peoples of the earth (Genesis). But the sacramental eucharist is also a challenge to the body of Christ, the assembly of believers here and now, betrayed by injustice, broken by suffering. Each time the eucharist is celebrated, the challenge is reissued. . . to proclaim his death and to remember his sacrifice in each member of his body, until he comes (Luke).

Genesis 14:18-20. As early as the second Christian century, due to the thought of Clement of Alexandria Christians have traditionally looked upon the references to bread and wine in today's Genesis pericope as types relating to the eucharist. From the fourth century, Cyprian taught that the offering of Melchizedek to Abraham should be understood as a *real* sacrifice prefiguring the perfect sacrifice that Jesus would offer to the Father. In its original context, however, the tradition about Melchizedek was intended to refer to an entirely different set of circumstances.

A very ancient tradition, perhaps as early as the 14th century B.C.E., the Melchizedek episode was later added to the very unusual chapter in which it appears to explain and interpret the rest of the material. In the legendary battle of the four kings versus five other kings (Genesis 14:1-12), Lot (nephew of Abraham) was seized and his possessions were taken as booty. Upon hearing this news, Abram mustered his supporters and pursued the enemy kings and their troops. With only 318 in his command, Abram was to rescue Lot, retrieve all his possessions and return home. At this point in the narrative, Abram met Melchizedek.

One of the most difficult issues the early monarchy had to address was the problem of gathering into one viable and united kingdom a people accustomed to the relative independence and autonomy of the amphictyonic tribal federation. When he became king, David summoned all who were united in the one covenant with the one God, Yahweh, and gathered them around the one throne in Jerusalem. To secure his position of authority and to rally the tribes together, David moved the ark, which had been the palladium of the amphictyony, to Jerusalem. B. Vawter would have us understand today's first reading (as well as the reference to Melchizedek in Psalm 110) as propaganda for the same end, i.e., the legitimation of Jerusalem as capital and David as king.

As the Israelite king in Jerusalem, David was to be the rightful successor of the ancient priest-kings in Jerusalem, represented here by Melchizedek. David's claim of throne and city were supported by the facts (even though they were legendary ones) that: (1) Melchizedek was an ancestor of the Jebusites from whom David had claimed the city, and (2) Melchizedek had made an oath of allegiance with Abram who was David's ancestral father.

In addition to the purposes of propaganda and legitimation, the mysterious Melchizedek episode may have also been intended as an appeal for the acceptance of the Zadokite priesthood as the official Israelite priesthood (2 Samuel 8:17). Zadok was chosen by David as head of the Jerusalem shrine. As a member of a dynasty that was probably Jebusite in origin, Zadok could rightfully claim to be a priest "according to the order of Melchizedek" (Psalm 110: 1-4), The bread and wine offered by the ancient priest-king to Abram probably had covenantal significance. So too, the blessing offered to Abram and the assurance that God himself had led Abram to victory over the kings were a heritage David and all subsequent Israelite kings claimed for their own.

1 Corinthians 11:23-26. Excerpted from a longer section of his letter in which Paul advised the Corinthians about their appropriate behavior at religious gatherings (11:2—14:40), today's second reading contains the apostle's teaching concerning the specifically eucharistic portion of the Lord's supper. Using the technical language of rabbinical teaching, Paul claimed to be "handing on" (*paradidomi*) what he had "received" (*paralambano*). Not an exact or complete description of the proceedings of the last supper, the account recorded by Paul bears the liturgical and stylistic features of a Hellenized tradition, probably of Antiochene origin. Nevertheless, today's pericope contains the earliest extant theology concerning the institution of the eucharist.

In Corinth, as in other Christian foundations, the eucharistic memorial was originally celebrated within the context of a community meal or agape which Paul called the Lord's supper. Unfortunately, the factions that existed within the Corinthian community were carried over into the prayerful assembly. Rather than being a sign which reflected their unity, the rite became a counter-sign: a negative witness testifying against the lack of love and concern within the Corinthian church. Some who came to celebrate their common sharing were more well-to-do than others (R. Kugelman suggests these may have been the Apollos faction) and brought better and more abundant food and wine. While some sat in special seats, eating and drinking to their satisfaction, and others even overindulged, the poorer members in the assembly went hungry. Some were even so enthusiastic about the agape portion of the meal that, when the sacramental moment of the celebration arrived, they were in no condition to recognize and participate in the Lord's saving bread and wine. For these reasons, Paul insisted upon the importance of the eucharistic aspect of the gathering.

In reminding the Corinthians of their responsibility to Christ and for one another, Paul described the Lord Jesus as saying, "This is my body, which is for you." Included in this statement are the facts that Jesus died for our salvation (Romans 5:6-8, 1 Corinthians 15:3) and that his suffering and death were for our sake, i.e., he suffered and died in the place of each and every sinner. The vicarious and redemptive nature of Christ's death as summed up in this eucharistic statement are reflective of the suffering servant figure described in Deutero-Isaiah (52:13—53:12). In fact, the four servant songs of the sixth century prophet were of great help to the early Christian believers who struggled with the notion of a suffering, dying savior. The cup of the new covenant in Jesus' blood recalled for Paul's readers the Sinai covenant that had been sealed with the blood of a sacrifice (Exodus 24:8) and the new covenant to be written in believing hearts, as foretold by Jeremiah (31:31). Just as the Passover meal had celebrated the deliverance of Israel from Egypt (Exodus 12:14), the Lord's supper was to remember and celebrate the deliverance from sin and death of all peoples by Jesus Christ.

Reminding the Corinthians of the profound importance of their coming together as a community to share the Lord's supper, Paul underscored the eschatological significance of the meeting as well. As a eucharistic assembly, their united action was a proclamation (*kataggallete*) of Jesus' saving death. The Lord's supper looked back to and was rooted in the cross but was also focused on the future parousia when the sacramental presence of the Lord would be replaced by full participation in his eternal presence. Relevant for all times, Paul's advice reminds the community that the feast of Corpus Christi celebrates the *body* of Christ in the sacrament of Jesus' saving act and the *body* of Christ in the persons of those who remember and believe and continue his ministry.

Luke 9:11-17. Narrated six times within the New Testament, the account of the multiplication of the loaves is the only miracle common to all four gospels. In the Lucan gospel the episode may be understood as part of the evangelist's answer to the question raised by Herod in the text immediately preceding today's pericope: "Who is this man about whom I hear all these reports?" (9:9). By following Herod's question with the loaves story, Luke has provided an eloquent answer that describes the man Jesus in prophetic terms, in messianic-kingly terms, in eucharistic language and with eschatological overtones. Those who witnessed the event and those who later received the tradition concerning Jesus' action were no doubt reminded of the prophet Elisha who was reputed to have performed a similar wonder with 20 loaves of bread for 100 men (2 Kings 4:42-44). Elisha's action bore witness to the mighty deeds of the God for whom he spoke. Jesus' actions had a similar effect upon those who believed in the power of the Father being manifested in him. The sign of the loaves was also looked upon by early Christians as the fulfillment of the Old Testament promises concerning God's providential feeding of his people (Isaiah 25:6, 65:13-14; Psalm 78:19, 81;16-17). Probably the original interpretation of the episode was a messianic one. Jesus' feeding of the crowds was a sign of the imminent kingdom of God. Notice, Luke did mention that Jesus had been teaching the crowds about the reign of God and healing those in need (v. 11).

Both the actions of healing and providing abundant food for the hungry were looked upon as messianic portents. In v. 17, the statement that "all ate until they had enough" (literally, "were filled," *echortasthesan*) reflected the bounty associated with the messiah's reign (Psalm 37: 19; 132:15). In the Johannine gospel the messianic implications of the sign are accented even more poignantly by the fact that, immediately following the event, the people rushed at Jesus to make him king (John 6:15). Rejecting their political ambitions for him, Jesus would soon prove that his messiahship and kingship were to be exercised in a far different manner than had been popularly anticipated. While Luke did not relate the incident about the crowd's desire to make Jesus king, he did follow his narrative with a prediction of the passion and a lesson on the cost of being a disciple to a messiah like Jesus (9:18-27). By so doing, he clarified the idea that the nature of Jesus' messiahship was not merely a sensational display of royal power but a salvific process that would include suffering for the messiah-king and his would-be followers.

From the earliest times, Christian believers attached a eucharistic significance to Jesus' action and related the gestures of Jesus ("taking, raised eyes, blessed, broke, gave") to those at the last supper. In each of the loaves episodes (Mark 6:30-44, 8:1-9; Matthew 14:13-21, 15:32-38; John 6:1-13) and in the Emmaus account (Luke 24:30), the eucharistic language is recorded with the same words in the same sequence. As J. Gaffney has observed, modern Christians tend to look only to the last supper as the institution of the eucharist. But the New Testament saw two further sources for the rite: (1) the meals of the earthly Jesus with his followers, and (2) the appearance meals of the risen Lord with his own. The character of those meals should lend a greater understanding to the meaning of the eucharist. At those meals, *all* who believed were fed, were healed. Moreover the food was offered to saints and sinners, even to the pariahs of society.

After the people had eaten to their satisfaction, the fragments were collected, enough to fill 12 baskets. Fragments or *klasmata* is the technical term used in the *Didache* (9:3-4) for the broken particles of eucharistic bread. That there was so much left over was to be interpreted as a sign of God's abundance; the number 12 probably recalled the 12 tribes and also the 12 apostles who were to be the leaders of the new Israel. The eucharistic implications of the loaves event teaches a serious lesson to the 20th century eucharistic assembly. T. Maertens calls it a matter of conscience. Because of the eucharistic gift of Jesus, world hunger becomes the responsibility of the eucharistic assembly, and the persistence of hunger should be regarded as a deserved accusation of guilt. The eucharistic bread should not fill and satisfy *totally*: it is of its very nature a taste of the fullness to come and of the unity that should be. Therefore the eucharist should leave the participants hungry for greater fullness, deeper sharing and a more comprehensive unity. In a word, the liturgy of the bread is not the end of sharing but a summons to *greater* sharing.

1. The sacred gifts of bread and wine bring blessing and deeper union to all who share them (Genesis).

2. In the breaking of the bread and the sharing of the cup, the cross of Christ is proclaimed and the promise of resurrection and joy is affirmed (1 Corinthians).

3. Intrinsic to the sign of the eucharist is the fact of its abundance. . . all are welcome at the feast, all can share to their complete satisfaction, all are blessed with life (Luke).

www.ingramcontent.com/pod-product-compliance
Lightning Source LLC
Chambersburg PA
CBHW080723230426
43665CB00020B/2595